KEYS TO THE RAIN

KEYS TO THE RAIN

The Definitive
Bob Dylan Encyclopedia

OLIVER TRAGER

BILLBOARD BOOKS
An imprint of Watson-Guptill Publications/New York

"Odds and ends, odds and ends/Lost time is not found again."

—From "Odds and Ends" by Bob Dylan

Executive Editor: Bob Nirkind
Edited by Marian Appellof
Production Manager: Ellen Greene
Cover and interior design by Jay Anning, Thumb Print

First published in 2004 by Billboard Books
An imprint of Watson-Guptill Publications
A division of VNU Business Media, Inc.
770 Broadway, New York, NY 10003
www.wgpub.com

Library of Congress Cataloging-in-Publication Data
The CIP data for this title is on file with the Library of Congress.
Library of Congress Control Number: 2004112246
ISBN: 0-8230-7974-0

Manufactured in the United States of America
First printing, 2004
1 2 3 4 5 6 7 8 9 / 10 09 08 07 06 05 04

For Elaine:
"Something there is about you that strikes a match in me."

For Cole:
"May you stay forever young."

CONTENTS

ACKNOWLEDGMENTS

Books don't end up on your lap without the work, help, and dedication of many people.

My sincerest thanks go to my agent, Leona Schecter, not only for getting my manuscript into the right hands but for her support and feedback throughout the very difficult process of writing a book.

Bob Nirkind has been at the helm of Billboard Books for quite a spell and for good reason. He knows his music and how to get the best out of the people around him, a rare gift. I truly appreciate his tenacious efforts in shepherding this project.

Don't let anybody kid you; just about every writer is made more literate by an ace copyeditor, and no one could have done better than Marian Appellof, who took an ornery project under her wing and made it readable.

It would be hard to present an encyclopedia of Bob Dylan's music without dropping at least a lyric or two from his songs. Jeff Rosen has been riding shotgun at the Dylan office for years and we all owe him a very special thanks not only for his help on this book but also for all the other fine work he has done. Mentioned less frequently is his assistant, Lynn Okin, who deserves a thank-you for her work in expediting various matters pertaining to this project.

Encyclopedias are, ultimately, the work of scores of other writers, critics, and thinkers. What you hold is, in many respects, a synthesis of the vast archive of Dylanology that has amassed around my feet over the past quarter century. Dylanists already know these authors' names and works, most of which can be found in the accompanying bibliography. Nonetheless, I'd like to personally acknowledge some of those that have been especially important to my book. And if their critiques, notions, potions, or verbal gris-gris bleed through my own prose from time to time, let me take this opportunity to laud and applaud these writers while directing the earnest and intrepid reader to pursue their studies of Dylan's life and art by tracking down the thoughtful work of this stalwart crew.

Anthony Scaduto and the late Robert Shelton wrote two of the earliest and best biographies of Dylan, and their analyses helped set me on the path toward compiling this tome. But they are just two of numerous others who, though unknown by the general population and usually overlooked by the academy, have created enough copy to fill up a whole wing of some university's library. Görgen Antonsson, Paul Cable, Jonathan Cott, Aidan Day, Andy Gill, Michael Gray, John Herdman, Clinton Heylin, Patrick Humphries, C. P. Lee, Greil Marcus, William McKeen, John Nogowski, Stephen Pickering, Christopher Ricks, Stephen Scobie, Gavin Selerie, John Way, Paul Williams, and Paul Zollo are among the more devoted scribes whose writings and research struck me as particularly insightful as I absorbed the great body of their work.

The late John Bauldie remains one of the more significant figures in the world of Dylanology as publisher of *The Telegraph*, the long-gone fanzine to end all fanzines published in Great Britain. The pages of *The Telegraph* were filled with not just the writings of Mr. Bauldie, but also with the work of an amazing range of talent who brought their energies to the entire range of the subject.

On this side of the pond one can find another secret hero of Dylanology residing in Grand Junction, Colorado. Mick McCuistion has been publishing the glossy *On the Tracks* magazine and *Series of Dreams* newsletter for the better part of a decade and running a kind of Dylan clearinghouse for all types of archival material. With his wife, Laurie, and at least one of their kids, Mick has picked up where *The Telegraph* left off, exploring the never-ending, wide-ranging world of Bob Dylan and his music with the kind of verve and pluck one might associate with a certain cub reporter at the *Daily Planet.*

And then there are all the i-dotting, t-crossing, statistic-keeping, set list–ordering, Web site–maintaining, p- and q-minding, ether-writing neon madmen and women who have played an even lesser-known but no less important role in stirring the thickening roux that currently serves as the foundation of much of the most vital Dylanological gumbo. Michael Krogsgaard was the first to publish books containing detailed set lists and recording dates stretching back to the earliest part of Dylan's career, an invaluable resource for this compilation.

In my attempt to create a chorus of the voices whose writings on Dylan and other subjects relate to various musical traditions, I present excerpts from the work of many others. A number of these appear here through reprint agreements. To this end, I'd like to thank Woody Guthrie Publications, Inc., Sanga Music, Inc., Danny O'Keefe, Don Fleming of the Alan Lomax Archive, Syracuse University Press, Alfred A. Knopf publishers, *The New York Times*, *The Washington Post*, HarperCollins publishers, Henry Holt and Company, Paul Zollo, Alex Ross, John Herdman, C. P. Lee, Paul Williams, Rolling Tomes, Jeff Place, Guy Logsdon, Smithsonian Folkways Recordings, and Max Dyer.

There are numerous and excellent Web sites devoted to all things Dylan. Some of the more useful of these are Bill Pagel's links site (www.boblinks.com), Karl Erik Andersen's daily update site (www.expectingrain.com), Alan Fraser's rarities site (www.searchingfor-agem.com), Olof Björner's yearly chronicles (http://my.execpc.com/~billp61/pre1995s.html), Manfred Helfert's roots pages (www.bobdylan-roots.com), Matthew Zuckerman's influence page (www.expectingrain.com/dok/div/influences.html), Eyolf Østrem's comprehensive song site (www.dylanchords.com), Ron Lake's interview site (www.interferenza.com/bcs/interv.htm), Lesley Nelson's amazing folk music site (www.contemplator.com/folk.html), and Columbia Records' official Dylan homepage (www.bobdylan.com).

For those who like to interact on the Web, some of the more underappreciated Dylan critics can be found on Google's rec.music.Dylan. Foremost among these are Christopher Rollason, Kees de Graaf, Patricia Jungwirth, Peter Stone Brown, John Howells, and Craig Jamieson.

I love a book with images and this one has many unusual and unexpected treats. My friend Mitch Blank and Dylanist extraordinaire at Getty Images was particularly helpful in gathering graphic material. Many thanks also to Carolyn McMahan at AP/Wide World, Irwin Gooen, Jeff Friedman, Wolfgang Frank at Fantasy Records, Deanna Kolb at Praise Ministries, Sharon K. Boles, Tom Diamant of Arhoolie, Joe Gilford, Madeleine Gilford, Stephanie Smith of Smithsonian Folkways, and Kelly Kress of the Southern Folklife Collection.

I would also like to express gratitude to my friends and family for their support and patience. My parents, stepparents, brother, and sister were especially supportive this time around. On top of all lists are my dear wife, Elaine, and my son, Cole, who know firsthand how difficult it is to live with a writer. To them I owe my deepest appreciation, love, and a promise to write shorter books.

Introduction:

SOMETHING IS HAPPENING

Walking the starry dynamo of the deep postindustrial American night, you might, without warning, find yourself on the other side of the bloody tracks. Taking a left down Rue Morgue Avenue, you spot the black corpses of Hattie Carroll, Emmett Till, and Hezikiah Jones swinging from the hangin' tree. All the windows have bars instead of glass and Death Row is SRO with the likes of Hurricane Carter, George Jackson, and Joey Gallo playing the dozens. You stop in at the St. James Hotel for a beer to find Lenny Bruce and Lord Buckley sharing a bill with Skip James, Robert Johnson, and Moondog. Outside, the Fortune Telling Lady hands you the Jack of Hearts and points to Desolation Row, but you head to Montague Street where Melinda, Ramona, Angelina, Veronica, and Mavis call from the windows of the Gates of Eden, competing for your attention. You have your eyes on Johanna and, just like the night, she gets lost in the crowd near Grand Street, where you're cornered by the Jokerman and his neon madman, who tries to sell you a ticket to the next world war. Muddy Waters, he tells you, is the opening act. You beg off and ditch him near Elizabeth Street, where music from a topless joint beckons. You step down into a basement where Johanna sips martinis with Gypsy Davey and Diamond Joe. Woody Guthrie is in the corner strumming a cheap blue guitar with Leadbelly while Willie McTell, Lemon Jefferson, Ray Charles, and Gary Davis pass a jug by the woodstove and hurl darts at a "wanted" poster of Billy the Kid. The Ragman throws down his chalk and starts a rumble with Stagger Lee over a Stetson but Annie Oakley pulls out her six-shooter and splits the apple sitting atop Bill Monroe's twelve-gallon hat. You're still trying to connect with Johanna but Rosemary has you by the arm, saying she has a big brass bed she'd like to show you upstairs. You turn around to see Johanna sneak out the door. You follow her to Twelfth Street and Vine, where infinity is always going up on trial in a place called the Secret Museum of Bob Dylan. She disappears inside but is nowhere to be found in its fluorescent-lit halls. Along with a lame forgery of a winking Mona Lisa, portraits of Rimbaud, Allen Ginsberg, and Dante hang from the walls by their ankles. You get a bad case of the highway blues as you spy Einstein, Robin Hood, and Shakespeare playing slapjack in the sculpture garden while Hank Williams stirs up a fresh pot of gumbo . . . but Johanna's not here.

The Secret Museum of Bob Dylan is the Limbo in which you find yourself—a hall of mirrors that, once you're inside, is nigh impossible to escape. But since you're here, you might as well chuck some more logs on the fire, pull up a chair, and begin slowly peeling away the onionskin of Dylan's music and muse layer by tear-inducing layer. Encyclopedia, discography, songography, lexicon, abecedary . . . call it what you will, *Keys to the Rain* is a reference book with a madness to its method—an entree into the Secret Museum but not necessarily a ticket out. Here you'll find the stories behind not only Dylan's own songs, but also about the scores of songs he's performed in concert or in recordings: who wrote 'em, where they came from, where you can find 'em.

Yes, all you hard-core types will find omissions and God knows what else wrong here. Entries for songs Dylan performed before he came to New York City are not included. Neither are songs from informal recording sessions, songs written but never recorded, unreleased outtakes, or any of the unreleased mate-

rial from The Basement Tapes and their ilk (Greil Marcus has already covered that ground quite spectacularly in his book Invisible Republic, I'm sure you'll agree). A tougher cut (and one that we feel terrible about) was leaving out thumbnail biographies of the core musicians who have supported Mr. Dylan on stage all these many years, including: Joan Baez, the Band, the Grateful Dead, Tom Petty and the Heartbreakers, Mick Ronson, Scarlet Rivera, Tony Garnier, Bucky Baxter, Charlie Sexton, etc. All of these omissions were made for reasons of space and not for lack of respect to any involved in helping to create the music. Perhaps we'll stash that stuff on an Internet site near you to properly present our research in an accessible format.

HOW TO USE THIS BOOK

Keys to the Rain contains several different types of entries. The most common are for songs Dylan himself wrote, or that were composed by other artists and performed by Dylan either in concert or on a recording. Also common are entries for albums; these include releases under Dylan's own name, as well as various kinds of compilations (such as "best of" and "tribute" collections) and releases by other artists on which Dylan participated in some fashion. Still other entries are for persons, films, books, videos, and CD-ROMs. Each category is designated by a symbol that precedes the entry title. All entries are fairly self-explanatory even for those who are not intimate with Bob Dylan's recorded legacy. A quick look at the key below will familiarize the reader with the way information is presented.

Category Symbols

S song

A album

P person

F film

B book

V video

C CD-ROM

Main entry (song, album, person, film, book, etc.)

Selected artist and album on which song has appeared. List is chronological except if it appears on a Dylan album or an album by the song's composer; this information precedes subsequent chronology.

Album/CD information including record company, serial numbers for all formats, recording dates, release date, producer(s), photographer(s), and liner-note author(s). Information for non-Dylan album/CD entries is less extensively annotated.

Composer(s)

Year album/CD was released.

Year song was recorded if different from album/CD release year.

Critical analysis and/or historical background of given entry.

Musicians on album/CD.

Track list.

S "All Along the Watchtower" (Bob Dylan)
Bob Dylan, *John Wesley Harding* (1967); *Bob Dylan's Greatest Hits, Volume II*/'68 (1971); *Bob Dylan at Budokan* (1979); *Biograph* (1985); *MTV Unplugged* (1995)
Jimi Hendrix, *Electric Ladyland* (1968)

Capturing a pre-apocalyptic landscape in a dozen crystalline lines, Dylan's stark observation of humanity has stood as one of his great statements since its release as the centerpiece of *John Wesley Harding* in 1968. It's as if he's stared into the void and is eager to file a report before the final curtain drops.

A *Bringing It All Back Home*
Columbia Records LP CL-2328, CD CK-9128, CS CS-9128; Sony Music Entertainment, Inc., SACD 90326. Recorded January 14 and 15, 1965. Released March 22, 1965. Produced by Tom Wilson. Liner notes by Bob Dylan. Cover photography by Daniel Kramer
Bob Dylan—guitar, harmonica, keyboards, vocals. John Hammond Jr.—guitar. John Sebastian—bass. Kenny Rankin—guitar. Bobby Gregg—drums. John Boone—bass. Al Gorgoni—guitar. Paul Griffin—piano, keyboards. J. Bruce Langhorne—guitar. William Lee—bass. Joe Macho—bass. Frank Owens—piano.
"Subterranean Homesick Blues," "She Belongs to Me," "Maggie's Farm," "Love Minus Zero/No Limit," "Outlaw Blues," "On the Road Again," "Bob Dylan's 115th Dream," "Mr. Tambourine Man," "Gates of Eden," "It's Alright, Ma (I'm Only Bleeding)," "It's All Over Now, Baby Blue"

Staring menacingly from a chaise longue with a gray Persian on his lap and an austere woman (Sally, his manager Al Grossman's wife) reclining behind him in a decadent living-room scene littered with seemingly random but actually very carefully selected and placed cultural detritus, the Dylan we see on the cover of *Bringing It All Back Home* s...

A

A

[S] "Abandoned Love" (Bob Dylan)

Bob Dylan, *Biograph/'75* (1985)
Everly Brothers, *Born Yesterday* (1986); *Wings of a Nightingale* (1998)
Sean Keane, *All Heart No Roses* (1993)
The Beatles (performed by George Harrison), *Artifacts I—The Definitive Collection of Beatles Rarities 1969–1994* (1995)
Various Artists (performed by Chuck Prophet), *Outlaw Blues, Volume 2* (1995)
Michel Montecrossa, *Born in Time* (2000)
Barb Jungr, *Every Grain of Sand: Barb Jungr Sings Bob Dylan* (2002)

Dylan wrote the brilliant "Abandoned Love" as he was putting together his *Desire* album and organizing the Rolling Thunder Revue in the summer of 1975. His one impromptu performance of the song—probably just days after he wrote it—was at the Other End on Bleecker Street in New York City's Greenwich Village on July 3, 1975, during a Ramblin' Jack Elliott gig. It was that live version of the song that Paul Cable, in his book *Bob Dylan: His Unreleased Recordings* (New York: Schirmer Books, 1980), described as "Beautiful, eerie, easily as good as *Blonde on Blonde* lyrics and a tune that is unusual and perfect."

Recorded for *Desire* but eventually dropped from that collection in favor of "Joey," "Abandoned Love" is an up-tempo lament about the rejection of a lordly woman whose manipulative ways have haunted the narrator for way too long. It is underscored by Scarlet Rivera's mournful violin, which perfectly captures the resigned mood and theme of this exotic song filled with loss and yearning. It proved to be one of the highlights of Dylan's *Biograph* retrospective package, on which it was eventually released a decade later.

Dylan composed "Abandoned Love" as he was in the early throes of his breakup with his wife Sara. And though he would usually steer clear of ever admitting any hint of autobiography in one of his songs, it is hard not to make that connection here. Our narrator plays the fool but does not lose his cool as he comes to terms with the dissolution of a relationship. He tries to come off as if *he* is the one making the decision to split, but the tracks of his tears are easily discerned. The song is not without anger and relief as he speaks of wearing a ball and chain and refers to his ex as a queen, implying that he's sick and tired of fulfilling her (and everybody else's) wishes and expectations.

Dylan's 1975 Other End performance of "Abandoned Love" is the stuff of lore. After backing up Elliott for a couple of famous songs (Woody Guthrie's "Pretty Boy Floyd" and Leroy Carr's "How Long, How Long Blues"), he then lit into his new baby, solo. The lyrics he sang that night did differ slightly from the *Biograph* release.

[S] "Abraham, Martin and John" (Dick Holler)

Dion, *Dion* (1968)
Smokey Robinson and the Miracles, *Greatest Hits* (1968)
Marvin Gaye, *Hits of Marvin Gaye* (1972)
Harry Belafonte, *This Is Harry Belafonte* (1990)
Mahalia Jackson, *Great Mahalia Jackson* (1991)
Leonard Nimoy, *Spaced Out: The Best of Leonard Nimoy* (1997)

This homage to three assassinated leaders—Abraham Lincoln, Martin Luther King Jr., and John F. Kennedy—was written in 1968, the year that the bell tolled for Dr. King and Senator Robert F. Kennedy. Dylan's torch song arrangement was sung as a duet with Clydie King in concert in late 1980 and 1981 and served as a kind of renewed commitment to and reminder of Dylan's interest in progressive politics after the distractions of his religious turn in the late 1970s and early 1980.

"Abraham, Martin and John" was originally and most famously recorded by Dion DiMucci, formerly of Dion and the Belmonts, in 1968. Musician and folklorist Tom Glazer, in the liner notes to *Songs of Peace, Freedom & Protest*, calls the song "a most affecting rock and roll hit.... From the look of this song, it seems too simple to be of much interest, but try to listen to Dion sing it on his hit record."

Biographical information on Dick Holler, the song's composer, is virtually nonexistent. Hearsay information suggests that he wrote songs with titles such as "Bob Dylan Request No. 1," as well as "Hey There Tricky Dicky," "Cole, Cooke and Redding," and "Greater Miami Subterranean Rock."

Indeed, the poignant song of martyrdom was a hit for Dion as 1968 drew to a close. It was a turbulent year in American history with the escalation of the Vietnam War facing strong opposition and the Robert Kennedy and King assassinations fresh in people's minds. The emotional Holler song was a perfectly timed stroke of genius—a lilting, folksy ballad that barely left a dry eye as it climbed to No. 4 in the U.S. charts. Holler devotes a verse to Bobby Kennedy at the song's conclusion ("Has anybody here seen my old friend Bobby?") that depicts the spirit of the slain senator joining his brethren over a hill. This verse, on at least a couple of the tapes of Dylan performing the song, appeared to elicit a particularly warm applause from the audience, who seem to be acknowledging his return from fundamentalist Christian doctrine to the old "protest" days.

Hopelessly naïve to the harsh truths of realpolitik, "Abraham, Martin and John" tries to act as a reminder of the best its subjects had to offer. The song also comments on history's cold and fickle hand, as one day we "just looked around and they're gone."

"Absolutely Sweet Marie" (Bob Dylan)

Bob Dylan, *Blonde on Blonde* (1966)
Bob Dylan/Various Artists (performed by George Harrison), *Bob Dylan: The 30th Anniversary Concert Celebration* (1993)
Flamin' Groovies, *Jumpin' in the Night* (1979); *Groovies' Greatest Grooves* (1989)
Ola Magnell, *Gaia* (1983)
Jason and the Scorchers, *Fervor* (1983); *Midnight Roads and Stages Seen* (1998); *Wildfires & Misfits: Two Decades of Outtakes & Rarities* (2002)
Storing, *Butter, Bread and Green Tsiis* (1990)
Rich Lerner, *Performs Songs by Bob Dylan* (1990); *Napoleon in Rags* (2001)
Steve Gibbons, *The Dylan Project* (1998)
David Nelson Band, *Visions Under the Moon* (1999)
Various Artists (performed by C. J. Chenier), *Blues on Blonde on Blonde* (2003)

An elixir to those who found Dylan's mid-'60s songs a bit dour, "Absolutely Sweet Marie" is an exuberant, pure Beale Street, up-tempo skip complete with a slew of memorable lines that could be anybody's koan—most memorably, "To live outside the law you must be honest."

In addition to the one-liners, Dylan uses some intriguing stage props and characters in this tune, too: a ruined balcony, a yellow railroad, a Persian drunkard, and a riverboat captain. These either help set the scene or play roles as the narrator (an actual or figurative ex-con), bitter about the time he's done for Marie, is left empty-handed. He moves from one barely camouflaged symbolic expression of sexuality to another: from complaining of frustration ("beating on my trumpet" when "it gets so hard, you see") to boasting of potency (jumping the railroad gate, the six white horses, etc.) in the tradition of the old blues masters like Blind Lemon Jefferson. This song feels like an old Piedmont blues but with touches that are strictly Dylan (note the Persian drunkard)—even the allusion to Blind Lemon's six white horses seems to have found greener pastures. Sparked by a great organ introduction and driven by tight ensemble playing, the *Blonde on Blonde* "Sweet Marie" includes a pungent harmonica break.

During a 1991 interview published in Paul Zollo's book *Songwriters on Songwriting, Expanded Fourth Edition* (New York: Da Capo Press, 1997), Dylan placed "Sweet Marie" in poetic context, with specific, almost rabbinical, deconstruction of the line "I stand here looking at your yellow railroad/in the ruins of your balcony" that, on the surface, might first appear to be a throwaway or at best poetic mumbo-jumbo:

> [T]hat's as complete as you can be. Every single *letter* in that line. It's all true. On a literal and on an escapist level. . . . Getting back to the yellow railroad, that could be from looking someplace. Being a performer, you travel the world. You're not just looking out of the same window everyday. You're not just walking down the same old street. So you must make yourself observe whatever. But most of the time it hits you. You don't have to observe. It hits you. Like, "yellow railroad" could have been a blinding day when the sun was so bright on a railroad someplace and it stayed on my mind. . . . These aren't contrived images. These are images which are just in there and have got to come out.

The famous line about living outside the law may have been cribbed from *The Line Up*, an obscure early Eli Wallach film from 1958, directed by Don Siegel (with a great, pre-*Bullitt* car chase through the San Francisco hills), in which a curiously ambivalent drug trafficker explains the ethics of criminality thusly: "When you live outside the law, you have to eliminate dishonesty." To bring this lineage full circle, the screenwriters of 1997's *Titanic* saw

fit to insert yet another variation of the line in that film—coming from the lips of Leonardo DiCaprio, no less.

Speculation surrounding the origin of the title is pretty far-flung, with everything from a type of biscuit to a famous carnival "Fat Lady" to a popular nineteenth-century Irish song by Percy French (see "Mountains of the Mourne") thrown up for consideration.

Dylan didn't perform "Sweet Marie" live until his Never Ending Tour kicked off in 1988. It has remained in the playlist since as an intermittent, mostly early-concert inclusion.

◙ "Accidentally Like a Martyr" (Warren Zevon)
See also Warren Zevon
Warren Zevon, *Excitable Boy* (1978)

Just weeks after Warren Zevon announced that he had terminal cancer, Dylan hit the road to start his fall 2002 tour in Seattle. Dylan's memorable show that October evening included three Zevon compositions, an extraordinary, unprecedented tribute to a deserving if generally underacknowledged talent. "Accidentally Like a Martyr," an early Zevon hit dealing with the pitfalls of charisma and cults of personality, is a song that undoubtedly would have seemed all too familiar to Dylan.

◙ "Acne" (Unknown/possibly Eric von Schmidt)
aka "Senior Prom," "Teenager in Love"
Ramblin' Jack Elliott (performed with Bob Dylan and Danny Kalb), *The Ballad of Ramblin' Jack* (soundtrack) (2000)

Dylan shared the vocals with Danny Kalb and Ramblin' Jack Elliott on this hard-on-the-ear coming-of-age spoof song every teenager should take to heart. The doo-wopish satire, about the narrator going to his senior prom, was clumsily handled by Dylan and company as a small part of a twelve-hour, multiact hootenanny at Riverside Church and broadcast in late July 1961 on the long-gone and still dearly missed New York City FM radio station WRVR. Ramblin' Jack's "doowahs" in the background, while augmenting the spirit of the song quite nicely, completely drown out Dylan's vocals at certain points on the lone, surviving performance of "Acne." Folkster Eric von Schmidt is sometimes given credit as the composer of "Acne" in various Dylan discographies but it is such a scrap of a song that any attribution seems suspect at best. Probably the most amazing thing about "Acne" is that it saw commercial release nearly thirty-nine years to the day of its original recording when it was included on the soundtrack to *The Ballad of Ramblin' Jack*, a quirky documentary film about Jack Elliott, a great eccentric American troubadour who befriended Dylan early on. Dylan recorded "Acne" the following winter at the New York City apartment of radio host Cynthia Gooding, whose show he appeared on just around that time.

ⓐ *Across the Borderline*/Willie Nelson
Sony Music CD 52752, CS 52752. Released 1993. Produced by Don Was.

Willie Nelson's grand tour of contemporary song finds him showcasing the works of, among others, Paul Simon, Lyle Lovett, Willie Dixon, Bob Dylan, and himself. In working with these artists, Nelson deftly mixes his brand of country swing with English art rock and South African–flavored folk rock. Nelson duets with Dylan on "Heartland," their collaborative piece inspired by Farm Aid (the annual series of benefit concerts to aid the American farmer), and he also covers Dylan's jaded complaint from *Oh Mercy*, "What Was It You Wanted?"

Even though he made a bold move by hiring rock producer Don Was to shepherd the album, Nelson remained wise to the folkways that underlie this music, infusing each gem of a song with his sympathetic personality as he creates as austere and clear-eyed a portrait of America as anything from the pages of novelist John Dos Passos.

ⓢ *"Across the Borderline"* (Ry Cooder/John Hiatt/Jim Dickinson)
Ry Cooder, *Get Rhythm* (1987)
Flaco Jimenez, *Partners* (1992)
Willie Nelson, *Across the Borderline* (1993)
Jim Dickinson, *A Thousand Footprints in the Sand* (1997)
Miller Anderson, *Celtic Moon* (1998)

It's hard to determine where Dylan learned "Across the Borderline," a melodic if cynical piece of far-flung illegal immigrant romance with Old West and anti-Oz undertones. Written from the point of view of someone who seems to know firsthand that the streets of the U.S. are not paved with gold and that those who venture to the land of broken promises will encounter far more than they bargained for, the song was jointly penned by three great songwriters but wasn't officially released until about a year after Dylan started performing it during his 1986 tour with Tom Petty and the Heartbreakers. Maybe Willie Nelson shared it with him during a late-night woodshedding session, perhaps he saw the movie for which it was written, or maybe it merely appeared on a demo tape that came in the mail one day.

Whatever the case, "Across the Borderline" remained in Dylan's set lists as a sporadic inclusion during the Never Ending Tours of 1988 through 1992 before disappearing for a while and then popping up again in the late 1990s. In Dylan's hands, the tune always came off as almost unbearably romantic and heartbreaking, the tragic hero depicted in the song about to walk to his inevitable doom.

A

"Across the Borderline" had its beginnings in the early 1980s, when British film director Tony Richardson charged Ry Cooder with coming up with a song for the three-and-a-half-minute opening sequence for *The Border*, which starred Jack Nicholson. In the scene, a young couple attempts to cross the U.S.-Mexican border.

As related by Richard Williams in the book *Lives of the Great Songs* (Tim de Lisle, ed.; London: Penguin Books, 1995), Cooder recalled the origins of "Across the Borderline": "I thought, what can I do? Woody Guthrie already wrote the anthem of those people when he came up with 'Deportees.' Then one day I was out jogging and I thought of the words for the first verse—that yellow-brick-road thing."

[S] "Ain't Gonna Go to Hell for Anybody"

(Bob Dylan)

aka "Ain't Gonna Go to Hell," "I Ain't Gonna Go to Hell for Anybody," "I Ain't Gonna Go to Hell for Nobody"

Written, performed, and maybe recorded (but never released) during the *Saved* period in 1980, the fervently evangelistic, blues-drenched, Bible-thumpin' "Ain't Gonna Go to Hell for Anybody" functioned as a kind of onstage work in progress. The song also served as a charged gospel rave and a spot for Dylan's backup singers of the time to really shine (the versions that commence with the a cappella chorus are of special note) during the one year that particular band was together. Here Dylan asserts he "ain't gonna go to hell for anybody—not for father, not for mother, not for sister, not for brother."

[S] "Ain't No Man Righteous (No Not One)"

(Bob Dylan)

aka "Ain't No Man Righteous"

Jah Malla, *Jah Malla* (1981)

Various Artists (performed by Jah Malla), *I Shall Be Unreleased/'81* (1991)

The kind of Dylan song even a Christmas Eve Salvation Army band could have fun singing (drum, trumpet, and tambourine in hand) on a snowy, big-city street corner, "Ain't No Man Righteous" is one of the more powerful gospel compositions from Dylan's singer/songwriter/evangelist.

The title of "Ain't No Man Righteous" is drawn from the New Testament. Chapter 3, verse 10 of Paul's Epistle to the Romans summarizing the Old Testament's Psalm of David (Psalms 14:2–3) declares: "As it is written, There is none righteous, no, not one" (Romans 3:10). And a line from the song ("Put your goodness next to God's and it comes out like a filthy rag") seems a conscious reworking of Isaiah 64:6, which reads: "But we are all as an unclean thing, and all our righteousnesses are as filthy rags."

Like so many of his songs from his 1979–80 religious era, Dylan sees hypocritical sinners everywhere. Despite its danceable reggae beat, "Ain't No Man Righteous" is a dark vision of a world where everybody needs to repent and there is no escaping the Final Judgment.

Thought to be recorded for the *Slow Train Coming* sessions, Dylan performed "Ain't No Man Righteous" as a midset cautionary tract exclusively during his 1979–80 gospel tour. Regina Havis, one of Dylan's backup singers at the time, took a lead vocal on the song in at least one concert during the spring 1980 tour.

At his November 16, 1979, show in San Francisco, Dylan introduced "No Man Righteous" by saying, "We're gonna do something here we haven't done before. This is a song nobody knows—nobody in the band even knows it. That's how I can tell who really wants to stick with me and who doesn't."

A

He may have been joking—but then again, maybe not.

▣ "Ain't No More Cane" (Traditional/Huddie "Lead-belly" Ledbetter)

aka "Ain't No More Cane on the Brazos," "Ain't No More Cane on This Brazos," "Go Down Old Hammer," "Go Down Old Hannah," "No More Cane," "No More Cane on the Brazos"

Bob Dylan/The Band, *The Basement Tapes*/'67 (1975)
Leadbelly, *Leadbelly*/'35 (1976)
Various Artists (performed by Ernest Williams and James "Iron Head" Baker), *Afro-American Spirituals, Work Songs and Ballads*/'33 (1961)
Various Artists, *Negro Prison Camp Worksongs*/'47 (1951)
Odetta, *Tin Angel* (1954)
Lightnin' Hopkins, *Country Blues* (1960)
Chad Mitchell Trio, *Singin' Our Minds* (1965)
Pete Seeger, *Folk Music of the World* (1991)
Chris Smither, *An American Folk Song Anthology* (1996)

This song is named in some versions for the Brazos River, which flows through a sugar-cane- and cotton-growing region west of Houston, Texas. In antebellum days the area's rich plantations were worked by large numbers of slaves. After the Civil War, and even into the early twentieth century, the local field labor was provided by convicts (almost without exception African-American) leased from the Texas penitentiary system. A work song sung by the prisoners (and no doubt slaves before them) as they cut the heavy cane grown in the area, "Ain't No More Cane" speaks to the horrible conditions they toiled under. "Go Down Old Hannah," Leadbelly's version, which he learned while incarcerated at Texas's notorious Sugarland prison (aka the Central State Prison Farm), began as a widely circulated work holler memorializing some tragic prison history that took place on a scorching day in 1910 (more than a decade before Leadbelly arrived), when some Texas convicts died of sunstroke and others risked being shot while attempting to escape. This desperation is reflected in this harrowing take on the song, where the men were so beaten down that they pray every hammer stroke will be their last: "Go down old hammer, don't you rise no more/If you rise up in the morning make it Judgment Day." Other interpretations of the lyrics spring from its alternative title "Go Down Old Hannah," in which "Old Hannah" is the name (some say of Africa's Yoruba tradition) given to the sun. Here, their misery will cease only when the sun takes pity on them and refuses to rise on the morrow.

Archivists John A. Lomax and his son Alan (Leadbelly's liberators and greatest champions) recorded several versions of "Ain't No More Cane" during their Library of Congress field trips in the 1930s. Recorded again in 1947, it was released some years later on a Folkways album called *Negro Prison Camp Worksongs*. Dylan may have lifted the song from any of these sources or, most probably, from an Odetta LP.

Dylan was performing "Ain't No More Cane" as early as his breakthrough Gerde's Folk City gigs in the fall of 1961, and he performed it through 1962 until it faded from his repertoire. He never forgot it, though: on February 16, 1983, just over two decades later, Dylan dropped into the Lone Star Café in Greenwich Village, where he joined Levon Helm and Rick Danko onstage during their set for impromptu and raucous send-ups of some real oddities, including "Ain't No More Cane." Buyer beware: *The Basement Tapes* version of "Ain't No More Cane" does not include Dylan and is one of four songs on that collection performed only by the Band, in whose hands it feels like a radical celebration.

▣ "Alabama Getaway" (Jerry Garcia/Robert Hunter)
The Grateful Dead, single (1980); *Go to Heaven* (1980)

After his short 1987 tour with the Dead and well before Jerry Garcia's death in August 1995, Dylan incorporated a few Garcia/Hunter tunes—"Black Muddy River," "Friend of the Devil," and "West L.A. Fadeaway" (as well as Hunter's "Silvio," which he cowrote with Hunter)—into the small handful of tunes by others in his live repertoire. "Alabama Getaway" was introduced soon after Garcia's passing and remained a constant late-concert rocker through 1999. When performing it as a roadhouse plea complete with ecstatic slide guitar riffs from a sideman du jour, Dylan seemed to gesture back to his old *Blonde on Blonde* persona and relish in the song's kiss-off salvo: "The only way to please me/turn around and leave/and walk away."

"Alberta #1" (Traditional/arrangement by Bob Dylan)
aka "Alberta, Let Yo' Hair Hang Low"
Bob Dylan, *Self Portrait* (1970)
Leadbelly, *Good Morning Blues/'48* (1996)
Big Bill Broonzy, *Big Bill Broonzy Story* (1961)
Doc Watson, *Essential Doc Watson* (1986)
Eric Clapton, *Unplugged* (1992)
Jambalaya Cajun Band, *Laisse les Jeunes Jouer!* (1994)
Bob Gibson, *Joy Joy!: The Young and Wonderful Bob Gibson* (1996)
Champion Jack Dupree, *Truckin' on Down* (1998)
Roger McGuinn, *McGuinn's Folk Den, Volume 4* (2000)

A downshift blues pleading to a woman to let her long hair hang down Rapunzel-style, "Alberta #1" doesn't exactly help *Self Portrait* pick up momentum. Dylan claims credit as composer on the album release of "Alberta #1," but in the *Self Portrait* songbook he is listed as an arranger—a more accurate attribution, for he really only revised the melody of a traditional song in this version.

While some have suggested that "Alberta" is an old barrelhouse song that originated on

Fannin Street, the infamous red-light district in Shreveport, Louisiana, where the likes of Blind Lemon Jefferson and Leadbelly once roamed, the liner notes by folklorist Dr. Harry Oster for the album *Angola Prisoner's Blues* also suggest that the song accompanied the convicts' job of scraping headland, which entails using hoes and rakes to clear and spruce the strip of land running alongside a road. Additionally, a comparison of the lyrics and melody reveals it to be at least a first cousin in song to "(It Makes) A Long Time Man Feel Bad," another old blues Dylan visited early on.

Roger McGuinn also connects the song with labor. As he wrote on his "Folk Den" Web site: "['Alberta'] is a song sung by the stevedores who worked on the Ohio River. There were two types of river songs. The first was the fast 'Jump Down Turn Around' type. The other kind was slow and bluesy. That could be because when it came time to load and unload these boats, it was a pretty busy session—hence the faster songs. But there was lots of time in between to sing songs like this one."

And, of course, it is a well-known fact that the slaves would use their songs as a way of gradually lulling their drivers into a lackadaisical awareness, thereby easing the strain of their exhausting physical toils.

"Alberta #2" (Traditional/arrangement by Bob Dylan)
Bob Dylan, *Self Portrait* (1970)

A slightly better downshift blues than its *Self Portrait* counterpart "Alberta #1," "Alberta #2" (a version nevertheless marred by the infamous chorus that marked the nadir of the album) serves as a bookend to *Self Portrait*. As with "Alberta #1," Dylan claims credit as composer on the album release of "Alberta #2," but in the *Self Portrait* songbook he is more accurately listed as an arranger, as he simply revised the

A

melody of a traditional song. The release of two "Albertas" on *Self Portrait* was the first of several times that Dylan would include different arrangements of a tune on a single record. A couple of versions of "Little Sadie" may be found on *Self Portrait* as well, and alternate takes of "Forever Young" appear on 1974's *Planet Waves*.

⬛ **"All Along the Watchtower"** (Bob Dylan)
Bob Dylan, single (1968, 1974); *John Wesley Harding* (1967); *Bob Dylan's Greatest Hits, Volume II/'68* (1971); *Bob Dylan at Budokan* (1979); *Biograph* (1985); *MTV Unplugged* (1995)
Bob Dylan/The Band, *Before the Flood* (1974)
Bob Dylan/The Grateful Dead, *Dylan and the Dead* (1989)
Bob Dylan/Various Artists (performed by Neil Young), *Bob Dylan: The 30th Anniversary Concert Celebration* (1993); *Concert for the Rock and Roll Hall of Fame* (1998)
Jimi Hendrix, *Electric Ladyland* (1968); *Smash Hits* (1969); *Isle of Wight* (1971); *Kiss the Sky* (1984); *Live and Unreleased—The Radio Show* (1989); *Wild Blue Angel: Live at the Isle of Wight* (2002)
Alan Bown, *The Alan Bown* (1968)
Brewer and Shipley, *Weeds* (1969)
The Brothers & Sisters of Los Angeles, *Dylan's Gospel* (1969)
Affinity, *Affinity* (1970)
Savage Grace, *Savage Grace* (1970)
Bobby Womack, *The Facts of Life* (1973)
Barbara Keith, *Barbara Keith* (1973)
Dave Mason, *Dave Mason* (1974); *Certified Live* (1976); *Live at Sunrise* (2002)
Spirit, *Future Games (A Magical Khauana Dream)* (1977)
Golden Harvest, *Golden Harvest* (1978)
XTC, *White Music* (1978)
Mahogany Rush, *Tales of the Unexpected* (1979)
Nashville Teens, *In the Beginning* (1983)
Jan Akkerman, *From the Basement* (1984)
Michael Hedges, *Watching My Life Go By* (1985); *Strings of Steel* (1988)
Richie Havens, *Sings Beatles & Dylan* (1986)

Randy California, *Shattered Dreams* (1986)
Giant Sand, *Ballad of a Thin Line* (1986)
U2, *Rattle and Hum* (1988)
Tito Schipa Jr., *Dylaniato* (1988)
Winter Hours, *Wait Till the Morning* (1989)
Johnny Fuzzy Kruz and the Mind Explosions, *Electric Jam for Feet and Brain* (1990)
Indigo Girls, *Back on the Bus, Y'All* (1991)
Ellis Paul, *The Times They Are A-Changin* (1994)
The Golden Earring, *Love Sweat* (1995)
7 Lvvas, *Pirata* (1995)
The Grateful Dead, *Dozin' at the Knick/'90* (1996); *Postcards of the Hanging: Grateful Dead Perform the Songs of Bob Dylan* (2002)
Various Artists (performed by Michael Hedges), *May Your Song Always Be Sung* (1997)
Various Artists (performed by Larry McCray), *Tangled Up in Blues: The Songs of Bob Dylan* (1999)
Dave Mathews Band, *Listener Supported* (1999), *Everyday* (2002)
Bandits, *Bandits Soundtrack Album* (1999)
Michel Montecrossa & the Chosen Few, *Eternal Circle* (1999)
Various Artists (performed by David West), *Pickin' on Dylan* (1999)
Rolling Thunder, *The Never Ending Rehearsal* (2000)
Blacksmith Hopkins, *The Woodstock Sessions* (2000)
Various Artists (performed by Tom Landa and the Paperboys), *A Nod to Bob* (2001)
Various Artists (performed by Dames), *Duluth Does Dylan* (2001)
Various Artists (performed by the Watchtower Four), *Ali (Original Soundtrack)* (2001)
Various Artists (performed by Tolo Marton), *May Your Song Always Be Sung: The Songs of Bob Dylan, Volume 3* (2003)
Taj Mahal, *Hanapepe Dream* (2003)
Todd Rubenstein, *The String Quartet Tribute to Bob Dylan* (2003)

Capturing a pre-apocalyptic landscape in a dozen crystalline lines, Dylan's stark observation of humanity has stood as one of his great statements since its release as the centerpiece of *John Wesley Harding* in 1968. It's as if he's stared into the void and is eager to file a report before the final curtain drops.

Dylan was living with his family in the rustic environs of Woodstock, New York, when he composed *John Wesley Harding* and was, reportedly, devoting considerable time to Torah and Talmud study. Such study is reflected in the song, which many have pointed out recalls in thematic tone and imagery chapter 21 of the Book of Isaiah, foretelling the fall of Babylon. Dylan uses Isaiah as his starting point. With its menacing guitar introduction and eerily detached singing, and Dylan's ability to manipulate the mood by placing colloquial speech into the mouth of an archaic persona in a spectral setting, "All Along the Watchtower" captures the emptiness and fragility of the human condition through a minimalist's cast of characters—the joker (a traumatized fool not quite out of *King Lear*) and the thief (a cynical outlaw or perhaps that fellow who escaped crucifixion)—and their dialogue.

Yet Dylan inverts their common roles with distant irony. It is the very serious-sounding joker who despairs that scoundrels ("Businessmen they drink my wine, plowmen dig my earth") have run of the world and the casual-sounding thief who assures him ("No reason to get excited . . . there are many here among us who feel that life is but a joke"). The pair form a dyad that some have theorized represents Dylan in conflict within himself or perhaps his uneasy relation with the demands and obligations that his fame brought on him. Or perhaps Dylan's thief, who specifically mentions that "the hour is getting late," is meant to symbolize the Messiah and his return. Wasn't it in the Book of Revelation that Jesus said, "I will come on thee as a thief, and thou shalt not know what hour I will come upon thee" (Revelation 3:3)?

In the last verse of "All Along the Watchtower," however, the joker and the thief have vanished (killed? kidnapped? hiding?), replaced by the haunting, symbolic, and not altogether clear, austere narrative that ends the song just as other characters are introduced (the growling wildcats, the vigilant princes, the ladies-in-waiting, the barefoot children) and the action ("two riders were approaching") is really about to begin—another in medias res Dylan employs several times on *John Wesley Harding*.

At the safe remove of his Woodstock idyll, Dylan was more able to observe those who not only trundle in his wake, but exact their pounds of flesh as well: earth-digging plowmen (critics, fellow songwriters, sycophants, psycho fans, etc.) and wine-drinking businessmen (record company weasels, managers, and the like).

For the literary-minded, there is a dash of T. S. Eliot here, too. In "The Love Song of J. Alfred Prufrock," his first notable piece, published in 1915, Eliot famously writes, "In the room the women come and go/Talking of Michelangelo." In "All Along the Watchtower" Dylan changes the tense but keeps the spirit of the line intact, singing, "While all the women came and went/barefoot servants too." In addition, the first stanza or two of "Prufrock" flow in a manner not dissimilar to the way Dylan invokes the muse in "Mr. Tambourine Man." Another Dylan-Eliot connection: Eliot's 1925 poem "The Hollow Men" is referenced/transformed in Dylan's "Dignity." And, most famously, Eliot is part of the weird circus parade in "Desolation Row," where he is depicted fighting in a captain's tower with his colleague, and shaper of "The Waste Land," Ezra Pound.

In the liner notes of his 1985 *Biograph* album Dylan mentioned that the song came to him during a thunderstorm. Ten years later, in

A

September 1995, while discussing songwriting with arts and features editor John Dolen of the *Sun-Sentinel* of Fort Lauderdale, Florida, Dylan mentioned that the song "leaped out in a very short time."

Jimi Hendrix's deservedly lauded (but perhaps overplayed) *Electric Ladyland* voodoo version of "All Along the Watchtower" from 1968 was Hendrix's only Top 40 single, hitting No. 20 on the *Billboard* chart, and did more than anything to spread the song far and wide.

Dylan has kept "Watchtower" constantly in his regular set list since he resumed touring in 1974, and there are five very different but equally effective versions in his commercially available catalogue. The song, with its eschatological aura and musical flexibility, found a place as the third selection of nearly every concert Dylan played in the early to late 1990s and is *the* most-performed piece in his repertoire by some large measure. He did manage to lay off performing "Watchtower" for a spell in the very late 1990s but returned to it early in the third millennium with his band, which included Charlie Sexton and Larry Campbell, in a souped-up, show-closing display featuring a wave of thick, twangy guitars.

🅂 **"All I Really Want to Do"** (Bob Dylan)
Bob Dylan, *Another Side of Bob Dylan* (1964); *Bob Dylan's Greatest Hits, Volume II/'64* (1971); *Bob Dylan at Budokan* (1979); *The Bootleg Series, Volume 6: Live 1964—Concert at Philharmonic Hall* (2004)
The Byrds, *Mr. Tambourine Man* (1965); *Greatest Hits* (1967/1999); *Byrds Play Dylan* (1980); *Byrds* (1990); *Definitive Collection* (1995)
Hugues Aufray, *Chante Dylan* (1965)
Duane Eddy, *Duane Does Dylan* (1965)
The McCoys, *Hang On Sloopy* (1965)
Billy Strange, *Folk Rock Hits* (1965)
The Surfaris, *It Ain't Me Babe* (1965)

Baroque Inevitable, *Baroque Inevitable* (1966)
Sebastian Cabot, *Sebastian Cabot, Actor—Bob Dylan, Poet* (1967)
The Hollies, *Hollies Sing Dylan* (1969)
Bold, *Bold* (1970)
World Party, *Party Revolution* (1986)
The Four Seasons, *Four Seasons Sing Big Hits* (1988)
Flower Power, *Flower Power* (1990)
Various Artists (performed by Sebastian Cabot), *Golden Throats, Volume 2: More Celebrity* (1991)
Julian Coryell, *Duality* (1997)
Cher, *Bang Bang: The Early Years* (1999)
Gerard Quintana and Jordi Batiste, *Els Miralls de Dylan* (1999)

Anticipating the outrageous rhymes and wordplay that he would take to even greater extremes in the next couple of years, Dylan's wild delivery on the original release of "All I Really Want to Do" perfectly suits a simple song about a simple man who simply wants to be nothing more than what he is and to keep his relationships that way as well—though he senses that this may be simply impossible.

With what can sound like a touch of sarcasm in his voice on the *Another Side* release, Dylan runs down the list of all the things he doesn't want to do (or be) to the listener (on the surface, a woman, but probably also his audience on a deeper level), at one point saying, "I don't want you to . . . be like me" with a quick little laugh that speaks worlds about the insecurity at the root of many if not all the songs on that album. Even the very notion that someone would *want* to be like him, the laugh suggests, strikes him as ludicrous—and that he would even ask someone to be like him, downright insane. While the singer may spend the entire song claiming that he wants to be only chums, the voice and the overtones more than hint that this is an end-run seduction.

"All I Really Want to Do" has also been interpreted as a parody of the then-early feminist dialectic and how men responded to it. Given the mid-'60s context of the times in which the song was written, it was hip to criticize the testosterone-poisoned machismo that was perceived to be partially fueling the world's many divides, be they racial, sexual, or you name it. And while the singer in Dylan's song is, on the one hand, partaking in the very type of conversation that was ubiquitous in 1964 and doing so with all the humor, friendliness, wit, and rhyme he can muster on the fly, he is also making the point that power struggles have been part of all relationships whether any "ism" is attached to them or not. As with one of those classic, highbrow Mike Nichols and Elaine May comedy bits, part of the enjoyment of listening to "All I Really Want to Do" is derived from its place in the culture that engendered it. And while it may be funnier and more meaningful to those who lived through that era and survived to tell the tale, the song feels dated.

Dylan first performed "All I Really Want to Do," a rarity in his live catalogue, during his final all-acoustic tour in 1965. For his big-band renditions in 1978, he recast it à la Simon and Garfunkel's "59th Street Bridge Song" (aka "Feelin' Groovy") while having a blast with the mischievous lyrics.

[S] "All My Tomorrows" (Sammy Cahn/Jimmy Van Heusen)

aka "All My Tomorrows Belong to You"
Frank Sinatra, *All the Way* (1961)
Nancy Wilson, *Yesterday's Love Songs* (1963)
Shirley Horn, *You Won't Forget Me* (1990)
Tony Bennett, *Essence of Tony Bennett* (1993)
Mark Murphy, *Songbook* (1999)

Written by Tin Pan Alley maestro Sammy Cahn and his last important collaborator, Jimmy Van Heusen, in 1959 and introduced to the world by Frank Sinatra in the film *Hole in the Head* that same year, "All My Tomorrows" is a saccharine love song of absolute devotion that Dylan raggedly performed at a single concert during his 1986 tour with Tom Petty.

Cahn (born Samuel Cohen, June 18, 1913, New York City; died January 15, 1993, Los Angeles) rose from the mean streets of the Lower East Side as the son of Polish Jewish immigrants to become one of the most nimble American lyricists of the twentieth century. His career spanned more than half a century, from his days playing violin on the bar mitzvah circuit to the sale of his first hit in 1935 through every major phase of the mid-twentieth-century American popular entertainment landscape: burlesque, vaudeville, the Swing Era, the Broadway musical, and Hollywood. Cahn's diversity as a songwriter knew no bounds. This, after all, was the guy who could write lovesick ballads like "Only the Lonely" *and* intoxicatingly infectious schmaltz like "Let It Snow! Let It Snow! Let It Snow!"

A natural inductee into the Songwriters' Hall of Fame, Sammy Cahn also mounted a successful one-man show in the 1980s and wrote one of the more popular rhyming dictionaries used by songwriters.

Cahn will be remembered best for collaborations with Jule Styne and Jimmy Van Heusen on many of the songs that helped build and then revive Frank Sinatra's career. At its best, a Sammy Cahn/Jimmy Van Heusen song is marked by sophistication and drama: chromatic bass lines and melodies building sequentially through a succession of diminished chords that suggest a rhythm section in the background.

Van Heusen (born Edward Chester Babcock, January 26, 1913, Syracuse, New York; died February 7, 1990, Los Angeles) took his nom de plume from the famous shirt manufacturer. His

A

Lyricist Sammy Cahn (left) and composer Jimmy Van Heusen (right), 1963.

(Photo: Arnold Newman/Getty Images)

first big break came through a meeting in the 1930s with pop composer Harold Arlen, who helped the younger man sell his first songs to Harlem's storied Cotton Club revue in New York. After a stint as an elevator man, Van Heusen was hired as a staff pianist at one of the Tin Pan Alley music publishers based in the Brill Building. Establishing a partnership with Johnny Burke, another Brill Building denizen, Van Heusen made the move to Hollywood and sold "Swinging on a Star" there in 1940. That song, written for the sentimental 1944 Bing Crosby film *Going My Way* (Bing plays a priest in a tough New York neighborhood), was the first of three Van Heusen com-

positions to win an Oscar. Extraordinarily prolific, Van Heusen also wrote songs for many of those camp Crosby/Bob Hope "Road" films. Sinatra recorded seventy-six songs written by Van Heusen, a distinction he shares with no one. After establishing a music publishing company with Burke, Van Heusen began his collaboration with Cahn. "Love and Marriage," one of the better-known Sinatra versions of a Cahn/Van Heusen tune, was written for a 1955 television adaptation of Thornton Wilder's *Our Town*; "High Hopes," another famous Sinatra vehicle, was written for a 1959 film, *A Hole in the Head*; and "Call Me Irresponsible" was penned for a 1963 stinker, *Papa's Delicate Condition*.

▣ "All the Tired Horses" (Bob Dylan)
Bob Dylan, *Self Portrait* (1970)
The Sports, *Play Dylan & Donovan* (1981)

In an unsettling commencement to a cluttered album, Dylan doesn't even sing on this jingle. Instead, he delegates the dubious task to a small choir of female voices who merely repeat the title as a lullaby over and over, and then some more. "All the Tired Horses" sounds like something he made up while serenading his children to sleep, somehow thought would be cute and/or profound to include on an album, and, most outrageously of all, sell in a store— for money.

▣ "And It Stoned Me" (Van Morrison)
aka "Stoned Me"
Van Morrison, *Moondance* (1970)
Various Artists (performed by Widespread Panic), *Hempilation Volume 1—Freedom Is Norml* (1995)

Dylan first performed Van Morrison's pastoral slice of summertime rock gospel with Morrison himself as they wrapped up a 1989 concert in Greece. Dylan pulled out "And It Stoned Me" one last time when the Never Ending Tour resumed stateside less than two weeks later in a version that suffered from its stiff, martial arrangement.

Ritchie Yorke wrote in his 1975 biography *Van Morrison: Into the Music* (London: Charisma Books) that "And It Stoned Me" is "about a real experience. It's just about being stoned off nature. Remembering how it was when you were a kid and just got stoned from nature and you didn't need anything else."

[S] "Angel Flying Too Close to the Ground"

(Willie Nelson)

Bob Dylan, single (1983)
Willie Nelson, *Honeysuckle Rose* (soundtrack) (1980)
Jerry Butler, *Time & Faith* (1992)
Various Artists (performed by Kelley Deal with Kris Kristofferson), *Twisted Willie* (1996)
Fantastic Shakers, *Shakin' the Shack* (1998)

Easy-listening Bob at its best, "Angel Flying Too Close to the Ground" is an *Infidels* outtake released in 1983 as the B-side of Dylan's single "Union Sundown." Dylan seems to be having some fun on the cut. Willie Nelson's original was first heard in the 1980 film *Honeysuckle Rose* (based on the famed 1930s flick *Intermezzo* and later retitled *On the Road Again*), in which Willie starred. According to legend, the song is dedicated to a late, hard-partying, pedigreed Texan known as "Loose Bruce."

[S] "Angelina" (Bob Dylan)

Bob Dylan, *The Bootleg Series, Volumes 1–3: Rare and Unreleased, 1961–1991*/'81 (1991)
Ashley Hutchins All Stars, *The Guv'nor* (1994)
Michel Montecrossa, *Born in Time* (2000)
Gerry Murphy, *Sings Bob Dylan* (2002)

An extraordinary *Shot of Love* outtake unlike anything else in the Dylan canon, "Angelina" is part surreal film, part cubist painting, and every bit as fractured as that combination suggests. Angelina's identity might be the last of the questions raised by the song, for Dylan may be addressing one woman, any, or many. Like its 1960s namesake, "Farewell Angelina," "Angelina" collects an intriguing collage of imagery and biblical (specifically, "Sermon on the Mount") references. Dylan scholars find lyrical connections to Ezekiel 28:17, Matthew 11:12, Revelation 6:2, and 1 Kings 6:8, to name a few. Through it, Dylan's logic-defying and mysterious pastiche only makes this muse (both a friend and an enemy) more intangible.

Connections also have been made between "Angelina" and the opening chorus of Gilbert and Sullivan's *Trial by Jury*, which partly reads: "For to-day in this arena/Summoned by a stern subpoena/Edwin, sued by Angelina/ Shortly will appear." Angelina is summoned later in the opera with an echoing recitative that also sounds familiar: "Oh, Angelina! Come thou into Court!/Angelina! Angelina!" Gilbert apparently drew these characters' names from "The Hermit, or Edwin and Angelina," a ballad or epigraph found in Oliver Goldsmith's mid-1760s novel *The Vicar of Wakefield.*

All influences aside, "Angelina," like "Desolation Row," "Idiot Wind," or "Slow Train Coming," might best be heard as a Dylan "State of the Union" song. And though it is seemingly addressed to a single woman, he might as well be singing to the United States or even Mother Earth herself.

Dylan's performance on his lone studio recording of "Angelina" is striking as he combines the passion and mystique of his best work of the mid-1960s. Indeed, "Angelina" can be heard as a 1980s latter-day version of 1966's "Visions of Johanna" as he beseeches this woman (or these women) of the shadows.

◪ *Another Side of Bob Dylan*

Columbia Records LP CL-2193, CD CK-8993, CS CS-8993; Sony Music Entertainment, Inc., SACD 90327. Recorded June 9, 1964. Released August 8, 1964. Produced by Tom Wilson. Liner notes: "Some Other Kinds of Songs . . . " Poems by Bob Dylan. Cover photo by Sandy Speiser.

"All I Really Want to Do," "Black Crow Blues," "Spanish Harlem Incident," "Chimes of Freedom," "I Shall Be Free No. 10," "To Ramona," "Motorpsycho Nitemare," "My Back Pages," "I Don't Believe You," "Ballad in Plain D," "It Ain't Me, Babe"

Another Side of Bob Dylan was perhaps the earliest indication that Dylan was never going to stand still. Here, on his fourth album, he makes the first major transition of his career, transforming himself from a traditional folkie mixing an original if predictable blend of social protest and romance into an artist willing to view the world and himself with a more jaundiced eye. Songs such as "Chimes of Freedom" and "My Back Pages" clearly demonstrate that Dylan was beginning to experiment seriously with the contour of language itself while at the same time explore the deeper levels of the human experience, realizing that things were never as black-and-white as they originally might have appeared. Dylan also

Bob Dylan in his apartment, New York City, 1964.

(Photo: Ted Russell/Time Life Pictures/Getty Images)

made an enduring statement of artistic growth and personal independence with "It Ain't Me, Babe" but was not above taking a vicious swipe at his ex-girlfriend Suze Rotolo with the embittered "Ballad in Plain D." Nonetheless, there is humor and eroticism on the album too, as songs like "Motorpsycho Nitemare" and "Spanish Harlem Incident" clearly show. A marked departure from the dour social agenda permeating *The Times They Are A-Changin'*, *Another Side* was a stepping-stone between Dylan's folk and surrealist periods.

The cover of the album reflects his growth. It is a mature and considered-looking Bob Dylan who appears in a simple black-and-white photo that shows him hanging out on the street, elbow on one raised thigh and hand on his opposite hip. Just your plain old average everyday visionary checking out the scene in Midtown Manhattan.

As he did with "11 Outlined Epitaphs," which served as liner notes to *The Times They Are A-Changin'*, Dylan includes more of his own writing with *Another Side*. Adorning the LP sleeve of this album were "Some Other Kinds of Songs . . . ," a collection of clever, diminutive vignettes.

The only Dylan studio album to be cut in a single session, *Another Side of Bob Dylan* was recorded on June 9, 1964, before a small audience of friends. That rapidity reflects the manner in which the songs were written, as they were all composed during a one-week stay in Vernilya, Greece, in the late spring of 1964.

In its time, *Another Side of Bob Dylan* was moderately successful, spending five weeks on the *Billboard* charts and rising to No. 43.

A final note: Dylan hated the album's title, thinking it conveyed a negation of his past work. Though he begged producer Tom Wilson to change it, Dylan had yet to acquire the clout to call that shot.

[S] **"Answer Me, My Love"** (Carl Sigman/Gerhard Winkler/Fred Rauch)

See also "It's All in the Game"

Nat "King" Cole, single (1954); *Best of Nat King Cole* (1997)
The Impressions, *One by One* (1965)
Bing Crosby, *Radio Years, Volume 1* (1987)
Frankie Laine, *Greatest Hits* (1995)
Gene Ammons, *Gene Ammons Story: Gentle Jug* (1996)

In 1992, thirty-eight years after Nat "King" Cole scored a Top 10 hit with "Answer Me," Dylan was surprising the octogenarians in his audience with lovely and unguarded acoustic renditions of this old tearjerker of a pop ballad about a guy withering on the vine as he tries to coax his gal into telling him what he did or said wrong. He sounds like he knows he's guilty; he just can't figure out exactly of what. Dylan also performed one electric version of the song during the 1991 Never Ending Tour.

A 2003 book by Alan Clayson and Spencer Leigh about the Beatles, *The Walrus Was Ringo: 101 Beatles Myths Debunked* (New Malden, Surrey, England: Chrome Dreams), asserts that Paul McCartney "may have subconsciously borrowed the tune and lyrics to 'Yesterday' " from "Answer Me, My Love."

[S] **"Apple Suckling Tree"** (Bob Dylan)

Bob Dylan/The Band, *The Basement Tapes*/'67 (1975)

Delivered from the point of view of a vaguely threatening character who can change moods that veer from the disorderly to the augural in an eye blink, "Apple Suckling Tree" comes off as at least a sensuous come-hither come-on. But the half-written ditty, featuring some bright organ work from Garth Hudson and absolutely triumphant singing by Dylan, feels like an old folk tale or Greek myth without a story. In modern parlance, there's no "there" there—it's a nonsense song that plugs into some subter-

A

ranean source and sounds like a twisted nursery rhyme. With its chugging, hurdy-gurdy rhythm, sung with an infectiously woozy drawl that would be at home anywhere below the Mason-Dixon Line, the tune closely resembles the venerable traditional song Dylan recorded twenty-five years later, "Froggie Went A-Courtin'." And what exactly, pray tell, *is* an apple suckling tree?

"Are You Ready?" (Bob Dylan)
Bob Dylan, single (1980); *Saved* (1980)
Various Artists (performed by Fairfield Four), *Gotta Serve Somebody: The Gospel Songs of Bob Dylan* (2003)

"Are You Ready?," a rollicking bass blues that dimly (and superficially) recalls better compositions from a much earlier period in Dylan's career, such as "A Hard Rain's A-Gonna Fall," was among the first of his songs directly beseeching his audience after the exclusive introduction of gospel material during his born-again Christian phase. Both on record and in concert, Dylan sounds like an AM radio stump preacher rallying his flock as he asks them the most important of questions.

With its threatening edge of judgment and the battle of Armageddon echoing the "Be ye therefore ready also: for the Son of man cometh at an hour when ye think not" from Luke 12:40 and other similarly dire New Testament passages, "Are You Ready?" was used solely as a first encore during late-spring 1980's all-gospel shows and was trotted out once in 1981 as Dylan was beginning to turn back to more familiar musical territory. It still sounded fresh when he took it into the studio for his *Saved* LP at the conclusion of the 1980 tour.

"Around and Around" (Chuck Berry)
Chuck Berry, *Chuck Berry Is on Top* (1958)

The Rolling Stones, *12 X 5* (1964); *Love You Live* (1977)
The Grateful Dead, *Steal Your Face* (1976); *Dick's Picks Volume 1/'73* (1993)
Kingfish, *Live N' Kickin'* (1977)

Injecting little of the dynamism into this minor Chuck Berry classic as its composer did, Dylan utilized this barn-burning Lynyrd Skynyrd Southern boogie at one 1992 concert to conclude a show-opening trio of songs that seamlessly segued into one another in a manner that would have made the Grateful Dead proud.

"Around and Around" had an informal genesis as Berry recalled in *Chuck Berry: The Autobiography* (New York: Harmony Books), his 1987 memoir, saying that it "sprouted from a jam session during a rehearsal before a concert. Sometimes I didn't jam before a concert but these guys were on-the-ball musicians and we almost had a concert before the concert started that evening. For nearly two hours we jammed, playing standard sweet songs to gut-bucket rock and boogie. One of the riffs we struck upon never left my memory and I waxed in the tune with words about a dance hall that stayed open a little overtime. Rocking 'til the early morning had been used so ''til the moon went down' was the same time of day. Let it be known that at the actual experience, the police didn't knock."

"Arthur McBride" (Traditional)
aka "Arthur McBride and the Sergeant"
Bob Dylan, *Good as I Been to You* (1992)
Martin Carthy, *Prince Heathen* (1969)
Planxty, *Planxty* (1973)
Paul Brady and Andy Irvine, *Andy Irvine/Paul Brady* (1976)
Dave Swarbrick, *Swarbrick* (1976)
Richard Searles, *Emerald Castles* (1992)

A bloody tale of resistance, "Arthur McBride" tells the story of two men—"me and my

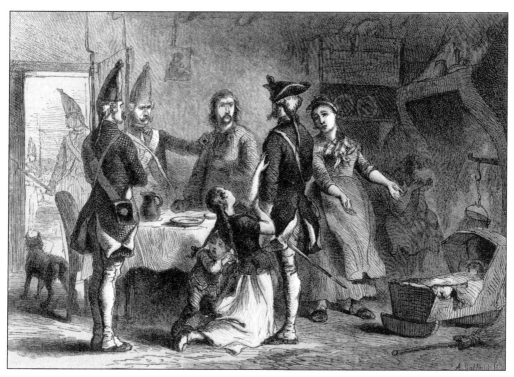

British soldiers hiring German troops for service in America.
(Library of Congress)

cousin, one Arthur McBride"—who, when walking along the beach on Christmas morning, encounter two soldiers and their drummer boy. The group begins conversing pleasantly enough, with the sergeant trying to coax Arthur and his cousin into joining the military campaign by describing the fruits of military service. When the two men balk, things turn ugly. The cousins, threatened with forced conscription, slug the tar out of their oppressors. It's all pretty grim stuff, though belied by Dylan's singing of a sweet, catchy melody. Rarely have the themes of resistance and comeuppance been so profoundly explored.

History would quite naturally produce a song like "Arthur McBride": recruiting ser-

geants were perhaps the most reviled authorities in nineteenth-century life in the British Isles. Poverty gave many men little choice but to sign on and was a dose of insult added to injury in the case of the Irish, who were not even joining their own army. And, as if to demonstrate how little things have changed, contrast the economic plight of those who prevail in "Arthur McBride" against those subjected to modern recruiting methods that, where little education and few opportunities exist, make the military appear an attractive solution. And, to be honest, it often is.

"Arthur McBride" was first collected in Limerick, Ireland, about 1840 and almost undoubtedly dates from the mid-nineteenth century.

While it possibly originated in Donegal, Ireland, "Arthur McBride" moved across the Irish Sea to Scotland around the same time and became widely known there and in England. Folklorist A. L. Lloyd said that it was his favorite song, calling it "that most good-natured, mettlesome and un-pacifistic of anti-militaristic songs" and considered that "in temper and action it is something of a model for songs of disaffection and protest."

Informed speculation suggests that Dylan learned the song when he heard the 1976 LP *Andy Irvine/Paul Brady*, which includes a classic Brady solo recording of "Arthur McBride."

The spring 1996 issue of *The Telegraph* (#54) contained this excerpt of a letter written by Paul Brady to Gavin Selerie in 1996: "As regards 'Arthur McBride,' I didn't 'hear' it in America; I found a version of it in a book (*A Heritage of Songs*, ed. Carrie B. Grover [reprint; Norwood, Penn.: Norwood Editions, 1973]). I adapted that, wrote and/or changed a line or two here and there, joined two stanzas together, melodically with a half resolve in the middle rather than a resolve after each stanza as the book does, which I found too repetitive and not allowing the power of the song to develop."

"Arthur McBride" is also notable for its insanely archaic language and diction. That Dylan handles words like "shillelagh" (a cudgel) and rowdy-dow-dow (fight) with such aplomb adds greatly to his presentation's authentic feel.

◘ "As I Went Out One Morning" (Bob Dylan)
Bob Dylan, *John Wesley Harding* (1967)
Dr. Robert, *Other Folk* (1997)
Second Floor, *Plays Dylan* (2001)

"As I Went Out One Morning" is a brooding, allegorical song about a man who rescues a woman in chains only to discover that he has been manipulated into embarking on his act of heroism and that she "meant to do [him] harm." A character identified as Tom Paine finally "command[s] her to yield" and apologizes to the rescuer for her actions in this protest song about those who took Dylan to task for having supposedly turned his back on the so-called folk movement. Interestingly, Dylan nods back to the days when he adapted folk music to create those songs that others wanted him to return to.

The folk music lexicon is chock-full of works with opening lines like this one, and "As I Went Out One Morning" has been linked to the Appalachian song "Lolly Toodum." But Dylan, as always, used this familiar form and some familiar characters to make his own point. Tom Paine, of course, is the main figure, and he appears as a symbol for freethinking in reference to the American philosopher's famous declaration that his own mind was his church. Paine was also the revolutionary writer of *Common Sense*, and Dylan's suggestion that Paine would have been disgusted to see his ideas twisted into dogma seems plain enough. So Dylan gets to comment on the collision of values in the late 1960s while executing a dual reversal of the image of the distressed damsel as an antagonist.

It is no accident that Dylan employs Tom Paine in this song, for Paine has particular meaning for Dylan beyond his advocacy for free thought. In 1963 the Emergency Civil Liberties Committee presented Bob Dylan with its prestigious Tom Paine Award. Unfortunately, at the awards ceremony a nervous and reportedly drunk Dylan delivered a speech that referenced Lee Harvey Oswald (President John F. Kennedy's alleged assassin) in a not altogether negative light; his speech proved so unpopular (if misunderstood) that he was booed and rushed from the stage. Evidently confused by the event, Dylan made various attempts to amend and/or explain the situation, and this song marks perhaps the final gesture.

Dylan's only concert performance of "As I Went Out One Morning" came in the early phase of his comeback tour with the Band in 1974.

B

"Baby Got to Go"
aka "Baby, Don't You Go"

Little is known about this song, reported to be a cover and performed just once as an encore by Dylan during his first tour with Tom Petty and the Heartbreakers on a swing through Australia in February 1986. Discographers can't seem to decide what the title is, but some think that "Baby Got to Go" may be from Smokey Robinson's quill.

"Baby, I'm in the Mood for You" (Bob Dylan)
aka "Babe, I'm in the Mood for You," "Sometimes I'm in the
    Mood for You"
Bob Dylan, *Biograph*/'62 (1985)
Odetta, *Odetta Sings Dylan* (1965)
Tears, *Tears* (1970)
City Preachers (with Inga Rumpf), *Folklore* (1982)
Dion, *Bronx Blues* (1991); *King of the New York Streets*
    (2000)

Dylan's exuberant performance of "Baby, I'm in the Mood for You" for the *Freewheelin' Bob Dylan* sessions was, according to his comments in the *Biograph* liner notes, "probably influenced by Jesse Fuller. I'd done a few of his songs, 'San Francisco Bay Blues' and some others, this was more'n likely my version of his thing."

Dylan recorded a few versions of "Baby, I'm in the Mood for You" on July 9, 1962, for, but not used on, his sophomore album, *The Free-wheelin' Bob Dylan*, with the second being the one selected for *Biograph*. He also recorded the seductive, testosterone-soaked declaration for Witmark (his music publisher at the time) later in the year. Given the obvious enjoyment he had during these sessions, it is somewhat surprising that no tapes of Dylan's performing the song live have surfaced, and there is little evidence suggesting that he ever did so.

"Baby, Let Me Follow You Down" (Traditional/Eric von Schmidt)
aka "Baby, Let Me Lay It on You," "Mama, Let Me Lay It on
    You"
Bob Dylan, *Bob Dylan* (1962); *The Bootleg Series, Volume 4:
    Bob Dylan Live 1966 (The "Royal Albert Hall" Concert)*
    (1998)
The Band (performed with Bob Dylan), *The Last Waltz* (1978)
Blind Boy Fuller, *Complete Recorded Works, Volume 2
    (1936–1937)* (1992)
Rev. Gary Davis, *Blues & Ragtime* (1993)
Dave Van Ronk, *Just Dave Van Ronk* (1964)
Mance Lipscomb, *Texas Songster* (1989)
Etta Baker, *Railroad Bill* (1999)
Robyn Hitchcock, *Robyn Sings* (2002)

A song with a past as murky as Dylan liked to pretend he had when he first recorded it, "Baby, Let Me Follow You Down" seems to date back to at least the 1930s, though Dylan specifically cited folk musician Eric von Schmidt as his source when, on his debut album, he introduced the tune with the following, fanciful rap: "I first heard this from Ric von Schmidt. He lives in Cambridge. Ric's a blues guitar player. I met him in the green pastures of Harvard University . . ." Von Schmidt, in turn, has said that he learned it from an obscure folkie named Geno Foreman, who, according to von Schmidt,

B

"had learned 'Baby, Let Me Lay It on You' off a Blind Boy Fuller 78 record and he taught me that." Confusing matters are the author's credit, given as Ric von Schmidt on *Bob Dylan* and as the Rev. Gary Davis on *The Last Waltz*—not surprising in the case of the latter, because "Baby, Let Me Follow You Down" has been traced to Davis's own "Baby, Let Me Lay It on You" and a host of other related tunes recorded in the late 1930s by the likes of Memphis Minnie, Snooks Eaglin, Big Bill Broonzy, and the aforementioned Blind Boy Fuller (aka Fulton Allen). In addition, in the liner notes to *Bob Dylan*, Dylan says he believed that Ric had gotten some elements of "Baby, Let Me Follow You Down" from an old recording by Horace Sprott, an Alabama sharecropper whom Frederic Ramsey Jr. had recorded for Folkways (probably on *Music from the South*, volumes 2–4). It has been noted as well that Dylan rewrote the song in January 1964 as a Witmark demo. A month later, he (or an associate) filed a copyright (later withdrawn) for that arrangement.

"Baby, Let Me Follow You Down" is essentially a traditional East Coast blues and, along with Rev. Gary Davis's aforementioned "Baby, Let Me Lay It on You," may be related to either "Paper of Pins" or "The Keys to Heaven," folk songs collected both in the East and in Mississippi, of which Memphis Minnie's "Can I Do It for You?" is a probable variation.

Around the same time, when Dylan was performing "Baby, Let Me Follow You Down" regularly in the early 1960s, he sang it with a striking sensuousness: a raging harmonica and three-finger guitar picking gave it a positively harplike aura. Suze Rotolo, Dylan's girlfriend at the time, is remembered by some as regarding it as "her song." Later, after putting the song away for a while, Dylan returned to "Baby, Let Me Follow You Down" in 1966 during his tours with the Hawks (later known as the Band), when they

tore through an almost unrecognizable electrified version that especially angered British "traditionalists" who saw it as perhaps Dylan's greatest turncoat gesture at the cataclysmic shows in May 1966. Dylan and the Band played it again at the 1976 Last Waltz show as a special one-off. It resurfaced during the Never Ending Tour in 1988 and 1989, when Dylan again included it in his acoustic sets and sang it like a guy who'd done many a following down and hadn't yet tired of it.

In response to the harsh response he was receiving for his electric sets during the 1966 British tour, Dylan introduced "Baby, Let Me Follow You Down" at his May 12, 1966, show in Birmingham, England, thusly: "If you want some folk music, I'll play you some folk music . . . this is a folk song my granddaddy used to sing to me . . . it goes like this . . ."

▣ **"Baby Please Don't Go"** (Traditional)
aka "Another Man Done Gone"
Big Joe Williams, *Piney Woods Blues* (1958)
Mance Lipscomb, *Texas Sharecropper and Songster* (1960)
Muddy Waters, *At Newport 1960* (1961)
Mose Allison, *Mose Alive!* (1965)
Lightnin' Hopkins, *Gold Star Sessions, Volume 1* (1991)
Big Bill Broonzy, *Baby Please Don't Go* (1994)
Mississippi Fred McDowell, *I Do Not Play No Rock 'n' Roll* (1995)

Similar in every way to the traditional "Another Man Done Gone"—a title it is sometimes given, too—"Baby Please Don't Go" is such a blues standard that it might well be regarded as "bluesbiquitous." Muddy Waters, Big Joe Williams, and numerous others may have claimed it as their own, but when Dylan performed and recorded his versions in late 1961 and early 1962, he was clearly following Big Joe's blueprint. Dylan probably learned it from the master bluesman himself, and his performances of the plea owe a clear debt to both the

Williams and Mance Lipscomb versions. Dylan recorded "Baby Please Don't Go" for his second album, *The Freewheelin' Bob Dylan*, but it did not end up being included on the disc.

"Baby Stop Crying" (Bob Dylan)
Bob Dylan, single (1978); *Street Legal* (1978)
Simien Terrance, *Jam the Jazzfest* (1998)

Helped by the saxophone mixed into the final wash, Dylan plays the role of the great consoler in this *Street Legal* song every man who ever fruitlessly tried to comfort his woman can take to heart. He performed it exclusively during his 1978 big-band tour. Though it proves he could write a breezy-sounding pop song at the drop of a hat, the song's threat of violence (the narrator requests a pistol in the opening verse) did not exactly make it easy FM radio fare. Perhaps that's why it failed to even chart. Of the content, Dylan once commented that "the man in that song has his hand out and is not afraid of getting it bit."

Indeed, "Baby Stop Crying" is sung from the point of view of a guy hopelessly entangled. Gone is the aloof, Marlon Brandoesque toughness of his earlier romantic one-sided conversations in songs such as "Queen Jane Approximately" or "You're a Big Girl Now." And if the song does have moments of humor, "Baby Stop Crying" must be considered a minor work in the Dylan catalogue.

Back Room Blood/Gerry Goffin
Genes CD 4132. Released 1996.

Dylan took a producer's credit, contributed some background musicality, and even cowrote a couple of songs ("Tragedy of the Trade" and "Masquerade") for this rarity filled with odes as downtrodden and cynical as anything from his own pen. Goffin (born February 11, 1939,

Queens, New York), who came into Dylan's world through Barry Goldberg back in the 1970s, is well known among the circle of songwriters. He was married to and musical partners with Carole King, whom he met while attending Queens College in the late 1950s. Together they wrote a sterling string of hits for the Shirelles ("Will You Love Me Tomorrow"), Bobby Vee ("Take Care of My Baby"), Little Eva ("The Loco-Motion"), and Steve Lawrence ("Go Away Little Girl"). Later he moved into work as a lyricist for the pop elite, earning an Oscar nomination for "Theme for Mahogany (Do You Know Where You're Going To?)," a No. 1 hit for Diana Ross in 1985. He was elected into the Rock and Roll Hall of Fame in 1990.

Backtrack
Directed by Dennis Hopper. Starring Dennis Hopper, Jodie Foster, Dean Stockwell. Released 1991.

This meandering, seemingly made-up-on-the-spot piece of B-grade on-the-lam neonoir features an uncharacteristically sultry Jodie Foster in the role of a conceptual neon-light artist who witnesses a mob hit, only to be pursued and wooed by professional assassin Hopper, who's out to make sure her petulant lips stay permanently sealed.

Along with Dylan, who plays a chainsaw-wielding wood sculptor, Vincent Price, Dean Stockwell, Joe Pesci, John Turturro, Charlie Sheen, Alex Cox, and Helena Kallianiotes (an old Dylan flame from the *Renaldo & Clara* days) make cameos of one stripe or another.

"Backwater Blues" (Traditional/Bessie Smith)
aka "Back Water Blues," "It Rained Five Days"
Bessie Smith, *The Bessie Smith Story, Volume 3* (1951)
James P. Johnson, *1938–1942* (1996)
Leadbelly, *In Concert* (1996)

Big Bill Broonzy, *Sings Folk Songs* (1956)
Dinah Washington, *Ultimate Dinah Washington* (1957)
Jay McShann, *Still Jumpin' the Blues* (1999)
Jimmy Witherspoon, *At the Renaissance* (1960)

A song that chronicles the sudden and often deadly risings of the Mississippi River, the ancient and venerable "Backwater Blues" is a piece Dylan probably performed with reasonable frequency early in his career, even though only one version, from his inauspicious November 1961 Carnegie Chapter Hall concert, has been preserved on tape. In that version, Dylan exhibited some powerful vocals and relatively complicated, if sometimes haphazard, guitar work and tipped his hat to his source when he introduced the work by saying, "Here's a song I guess just about everybody knows. Leadbelly used to sing this."

Leadbelly indeed recorded "Backwater Blues"; however, Bessie Smith, "Empress of the Blues," is generally credited with the song's formalization and, sometimes, even its composition. In fact, there is some wonderful history behind "Backwater Blues" and Smith's involvement with the song. The 1927 flooding of the Mississippi (a virtually annual occurrence in some parts) was particularly spectacular, covering an area the size of Scotland, forcing authorities to gather workers for the levee repairs—even, on occasion, holding them there at gunpoint. The local authorities were so desperate that they even called in blues singers to aid in the propaganda effort to engage additional flood-relief labor. In his spoken introduction to a 1950s performance of the song, Big Bill Broonzy reported that "They sent for a lot of musicians. They didn't have to send for me 'cos I was already there . . . and whoever wrote the best song got 500 dollars. So Bessie [Smith] got the 500 dollars, so we always played hers . . . 'Backwater Blues.'"

On *News & the Blues: Telling It Like It Is*, a 1991 CD compiling blues songs that reported on history in the making, Lawrence Cohn offered some sensitive insights into Smith's composition. Noting the song's popularity, Cohn says that "Rather than offering a factual account of the tragedy, Smith's recording, through the accumulation of vivid, intimate details, and told from the perspective of one of its victims, presents an emotionally charged, deeply personal account of the flood that, as do all well-crafted blues, proved greatly moving to her listeners. The power and immediacy with which she addresses the subject is surely the reason hers eclipsed all other recordings dealing with this tragedy."

Forty years after first visiting "Backwater Blues," Dylan reexplored the themes and attitude of the song in his own "High Water (for Charley Patton)."

[S] "Ball and Biscuit" (Jack White)

The White Stripes, *Elephant* (2003)

Hot off the World Wide Web: third-millennium punk bluester Jack White (born John Anthony Gillis, July 9, 1975, in Detroit) joined Dylan for an encore performance of White's "Ball and Biscuit"—a Willie Dixon/Blind Willie McTell/ Janis Joplin/Beatles–influenced boast and one of the White Stripes' sexiest songs during Dylan's Motown stopover on the small-venue tour in spring 2004.

[S] "Ballad in Plain D" (Bob Dylan)

Bob Dylan, *Another Side of Bob Dylan* (1964)
Michael Chapman, *The Man Who Hated Mornings* (1977)
Various Artists (performed by Emily Saliers), *A Tribute to Bob Dylan, Volume 3: The Times They Are A-Changin'* (2000)

With more than a dash of regret and some large measure of bile too, "Ballad in Plain D" is one of Dylan's most nakedly autobiographical, if misnamed, songs: it's actually rendered on *Another Side of Bob Dylan* in plain C. Simply composing and then calling attention to the song in the key of D calls to mind such words as death—a word that might well sum up Dylan's frame of mind at the time he wrote this. Or maybe the word was "dull." Certainly this plain song proved that if Dylan was employing poetic techniques to address major philosophical and political concerns at the time, he was not as adept at using his creative arsenal to elucidate personal matters of the heart and hearth.

Shortly before writing "Ballad in Plain D," in mid-March 1964, there was an agonizing argument with his then-girlfriend Suze Rotolo at her sister Carla's apartment on New York's Lower East Side. According to the Rotolo version of the evening's events (as reported in Bob Spitz's 1989 book *Dylan: A Biography*), Carla (apparently the song's "parasitic sister") and Dylan allegedly scuffled on the floor. The row ended Bob and Suze's relationship and the couple did not reestablish a friendship for several years. Eventually Suze understood why Bob wrote the song, but she remained embittered for some time—and who could fault her?

Undoubtedly reporting on his acrimonious breakup with Suze, Dylan spat venom at her and her entire family with this bitter diatribe in verse. Some people think that the maudlin (and pretty bad, even by Dylan's own admission) "Ballad in Plain D," composed on the heels of the fight and performed only once later in the summer (though no tape seems to circulate), was at least partially based on "Once I Had a Sweetheart" (also known as "The False Bride"), an old English folk song. "Ballad in Plain D" is one of the last works in which Dylan reveals himself, warts and all, before learning to shield himself with lies.

But a model and primary source is Child Ballad No. 10, "The Two Sisters" (also known as "Oh, the Dreadful Wind and Rain" and other titles), among the most mysterious of folk songs to spring from the British Isles. (Francis James Child, 1825–1896, was an American philologist and ballad collector; see his five-volume work *The English and Scottish Popular Ballads*.) The story in the song is filled with passion, violence, jealousy, murder, and the supernatural and has varied tremendously over the centuries, but the scenario and sentiment is essentially the same: two sisters love the same man. He gives one an engagement ring. The spurned sister becomes jealous and murders her sibling by pushing her into a river. The body is pulled downstream, where a fiddler happens upon the corpse and proceeds to make a fiddle out of her bones and hair. But the completed instrument will play only one tune: the very tune being sung telling of its own death. In some of the versions, the fiddle's song also identifies the murderer.

Despite the age of "The Two Sisters," it was certainly a current song for Dylan in 1964, as evidenced by a tape of his performing it on the May 1960 Karen Wallace recording produced in Saint Paul. In any event, the parallels between "The Two Sisters" and Dylan's own relationship with Suze Rotolo and her family are pretty obvious, and Dylan was smart enough to recognize and utilize them. And "Ballad in Plain D" wasn't the only Dylan song "The Two Sisters" found its way into: the melody and certain refrains of the old ballad can be heard in "Percy's Song."

"Ballad of a Thin Man" (Bob Dylan)
Bob Dylan, *Highway 61 Revisited* (1965); *Bob Dylan at Budokan* (1979); *Real Live* (1984); *Hard to Handle* (video) (1986); *The Bootleg Series, Volume 4: Bob Dylan Live 1966 (The "Royal Albert Hall" Concert)* (1998)

Bob Dylan/The Band, *Before the Flood* (1974)
The Sports, *Play Dylan & Donovan* (1981)
Thee Fourgiven, *Voilà* (1986)
Top Jimmy & The Rhythm Picks, *Pigus Drunkus Maximus* (1987)
Janglers, *Janglers Play Dylan* (1992)
The Grass Roots, *Where Were You When I Needed You* (1994)
Various Artists (performed by Calamity Jane), *Outlaw Blues, Volume 2* (1995)
The Golden Earring, *Love Sweat* (1995)
James Solberg, *L.A. Blues* (1998)
Various Artists (performed by James Solberg), *Tangled Up in Blues: The Songs of Bob Dylan* (1999)
The Grateful Dead, *Postcards of the Hanging: Grateful Dead Perform the Songs of Bob Dylan* (2002)
Robyn Hitchcock, *Robyn Sings* (2002)
Big Brass Bed, *A Few Dylan Songs* (2003)

One of Dylan's most menacing songs, quite unlike the sleek 1930s series of comedy mystery flicks starring William Powell and Myrna Loy from which it draws its title, "Ballad of a Thin Man" is a stinging, crawling blues directed at "Mr. Jones," a clueless poseur who just doesn't get it, a pitiless slummer who still manages to make it to church on Sunday with a smile on his face, an upright citizen who manipulates every loophole on his 1040 tax returns. But this superficial Philistine, who jumps through each hoop society has to offer, suddenly finds himself in *way* over his head when entering the dark domain of this particular ring of the Inferno. The gnawing claustrophobia facing Mr. Jones increases with every salvo—from the moment he confidently walks into the room until he is easily broken, backed into a corner surrounded by the geeks he pretends to rise above. By the time the curtain falls, he has been thoroughly eviscerated.

From its harsh opening piano chords to its dizzying finale, "Ballad of a Thin Man" plays out like a chapter from Franz Kafka's *The*

Trial, with Dylan playing the role of the Great Inquisitor, acetylene torch in hand.

Dylan freaks gave up trying to figure out who Mr. Jones was decades ago, realizing him to be a composite irritant.

In response to a query by Nora Ephron and Susan Edmiston in an oft-cited 1965 interview conducted in the New York office of Dylan's manager Albert Grossman as to Mr. Jones's true identity, Dylan quoted whole sections of "Thin Man" in *not* answering their question. "He's a pinboy. He also wears suspenders," Dylan jibed. "He's a real person. You know him, but not by that name . . . I saw him come into the room one night and he looked like a camel. He proceeded to put his eyes in his pocket. I asked this guy who he was and he said, 'That's Mr. Jones.' Then I asked this cat, 'Doesn't he do anything but put his eyes in his pocket?' And he told me, 'He puts his nose on the ground.' It's all there, it's a true story."

Jerry Garcia best articulated the song's essence in his 1981 interview with David Gans and Blair Jackson, as recounted in Gans's book *Conversations with the Dead: The Grateful Dead Interview Book* (New York: Citadel Underground, 1991). "'Ballad of a Thin Man,'" Garcia said, "tells that person who's lame that they're lame, why they're lame, which is a very satisfying thing to do. Certainly something everybody knows about."

Throughout his career Dylan has performed "Thin Man" like a guy with the world's largest chip on his shoulder. It's been remarkably consistent through each phase and shade of his ever-shifting persona. Unlike virtually everything else in his catalogue, "Thin Man" has never been dramatically rearranged—the acidic paranoia of the original is neatly preserved, waiting to be unleashed on another unsuspecting victim.

"Thin Man" has always been a concert staple for Dylan. After his fierce versions with the

B

Hawks in 1966—in which he played the song on piano (as heard on *The Bootleg Series, Volume 2* or in the 1972 film *Eat the Document*)—and in 1974 (*Before the Flood*), he created a flashy arrangement for his 1978 big-band tour (*Bob Dylan at Budokan*) before settling on a more straightforward reading that has carried him through just about each tour since 1984 (*Real Live*).

◨ "Ballad of Donald White" (Bob Dylan)
aka "The Ballad of Donald White," "Donald White"
Various Artists (performed by Bob Dylan as "Blind Boy Grunt"), *Broadside Reunion/'62* (1972); *The Best of Broadside 1962–1988* (2000)

Forty years since its composition, "Ballad of Donald White" still resonates as a first-person confessional from a man with nowhere to go but the gallows. The narrator awaits his fate as he recounts the circumstances of his life that led to this moment of reckoning, retrospection, and society's cruel retribution. And if it sounds like a selfish and cowardly cop-out to blame society for one's crimes, diagnostic songs like this one, pointing out modern civilization's inability to nurture its displaced souls, were at the forefront of the folk movement.

The song is based on a true story; Dylan probably first learned of White's case from a television program broadcast in February 1962 (his claim of having read about Donald White as early as 1959 in a Seattle newspaper being somewhat doubtful). The program—a film called *A Volcano Named White*—was about crime and capital punishment. A Seattle convict who was released from prison due to overcrowding, White found it impossible to cope in society, and he asked to be returned to prison but was refused. Finally, he killed a man in order to return to prison and was subsequently executed. In the program, White, a twenty-four-year-old black man, was sitting in his prison cell in Texas talking about his life, its oppression, his cries for help that were ignored.

Friends of Dylan recall that he was so deeply affected by the stark portrayal on the show that he immediately and intuitively churned out the song. Some of Dylan's political invectives from the era began as items clipped from newspapers, but not this one.

Bonnie Dobson's version of "Peter Amberly" is usually cited as the folk-song source for Dylan's "Ballad of Donald White." In "Peter Amberly" the narrator has been fatally injured and describes his fate as his life ebbs away.

Bootleg recordings of Dylan performing "Donald White" circa 1962 have long been in circulation, and though there is little evidence of his performing the song much on the coffeehouse circuit, presumably he did so.

◨ "Ballad of Easy Rider" (Bob Dylan/Roger McGuinn)
Roger McGuinn, *Easy Rider* (1969)
Various Artists (performed by the Byrds), *Easy Rider* (soundtrack) (1970)
The Byrds, *The Ballad of Easy Rider* (1970)
Ferrante and Teicher, *Getting Together* (1970)
Percy Faith and His Orchestra, *Leaving on a Jet Plane* (1970)

Dylan never recorded this freewheeling travelogue of a song, but he is given partial songwriting credit as the writer of its first verse, scribbled, according to lore, on a napkin. The piece was composed for *Easy Rider* (1969), the then-controversial picaresque motorcycle hippie road flick starring Peter Fonda, Dennis Hopper, and Jack Nicholson.

◨ "The Ballad of Frankie Lee and Judas Priest" (Bob Dylan)
Bob Dylan, *John Wesley Harding* (1967)

Jerry Garcia/David Grisman, *Been All Around This World* (2004)

A philosophical shaggy-dog story about temptation and those who succumb to it, Dylan's jaundiced "Frankie Lee and Judas Priest" carried a brittle warning to those who too casually put their trust in others. Staged as a one-act play, the song stars two characters who play their roles with results that are at once tragic and humorous. But beneath the song's light exterior lies a sad tale of personal betrayal and deceit leading to death. Some interpret the song as being a veiled attack on Dylan's former manager Albert Grossman, with whom he was feuding and from whom he would split in 1969.

As the longest (and maybe the dullest) *John Wesley Harding* track, "The Ballad of Frankie Lee and Judas Priest" features a parable masking as a dialectic: the straight-shooting Frankie is duped by the double-dealing Judas Priest in what can be read as an updating of the Devil's tempting of Jesus in the wilderness—except here the Devil gets his due. Perhaps not too surprisingly, Dylan seems to identify with Frankie, who eventually gives in to the temptations of the flesh. Never the materialist, Dylan rarely, if ever, exhibited the archetypal rock star's public exploits and indulgences.

In his 1998 book *Don't Think Twice, It's All Right,* Andy Gill deconstructed "The Ballad of Frankie Lee and Judas Priest" in even greater detail, writing that "The early verses, in which Frankie agonizes over Judas' offer of money, presumably echo Dylan's recent contractual negotiations, or those earlier in his career: certainly Judas' attempt to rush Frankie into a hasty decision 'before [the dollar bills] all disappear' closely reflects standard negotiating practice in the music business. As, indeed, does Judas' dangling of carnal carrots to help sway Frankie's mind, in the form of the brothel in which he eventually exhausts himself. To Frankie, such worldly delights are represented as 'Paradise,' though the devilish Judas recognizes their true price is 'Eternity'—Frankie's mortal soul."

That Frankie takes the bait and ends up dying, paradoxically enough, of thirst in the arms of his betrayer after sixteen nights of hedonism, should come as no big shock. And, as if to drive home the point that temptation and false promises lead to poor decisions and often tragic results, Dylan signs off the song with this unsettling aphorism: "And don't go mistaking Paradise/for that home across the road."

Given the nature of the song and its purported genesis, it was with some surprise that Dylan revived it for his concerts with the Grateful Dead in 1987. A poorer song choice probably couldn't have been made, for this intimate parable was lost in the large football stadium venues where the shows took place. "Frankie Lee and Judas Priest" is an elongated comic tall tale cast in the style of the frontier ballad with echoes of both Mark Twain and Robert Service—the kind of long, circuitous, and playfully obscure song Dylanists relish sinking their teeth into. But because Dylan pulls off a dozen thoughtful rural Zen-like aphorisms, it really deserves to be *listened* to and pondered—an impossibility at the Grateful Dead shows before crowds of 70,000. Fortunately, Dylan periodically resurrected it in the ensuing years for far more effective renditions with Tom Petty and the Heartbreakers and on the Never Ending Tour, when he performed the song a few times in 1988 and then again in 2000.

[S] **"Ballad of Hollis Brown"** (Bob Dylan)

aka "The Rise and Fall of Hollis Brown: A True Story"
Bob Dylan, *The Times They Are A-Changin'* (1964)

Mike Seeger (performed with Bob Dylan), *Third Annual Farewell Reunion* (1995)
Nina Simone, *Pastel Blues* (1965)
Hugues Aufray, *Chante Dylan* (1965); *Au Casino de Paris* (1996)
Nazareth, *Loud and Proud* (1974)
Leon Russell, *Stop All That Jazz* (1974)
The Stooges, *Death Trip* (1987); *Open Up and Bleed* (1988)
The Neville Brothers, *Yellow Moon* (1989)
Stephen Stills, *Stills Alone* (1991)
Old Blind Dogs, *Legacy* (1995)
The Zimmermen, *The Dungeon Tapes* (1996)
Kevin Kinney, *The Flower & the Knife* (2000)
Various Artists (performed by Hootie and the Blowfish), *A Tribute to Bob Dylan, Volume 3: The Times They Are A-Changin'* (2000)
Dudley Connell and Don Rigsby, *Another Saturday Night* (2001)
Various Artists (performed by the Neville Brothers), *Doin' Dylan 2* (2002)

A harrowing portrait of a destitute, desperate South Dakota farmer who kills himself and his family when he finally reaches the end of his rope, "Hollis Brown" remains among Dylan's most haunting songs.

Dylan casts the stark narrative of rural poverty and disaster as a folk ballad with a traditional blues verse structure and a touch of backwoods Appalachia, employing a droning guitar figure that recalls some of those sad murder ballads like "Railroad Boy" he so treasured from Harry Smith's *Anthology of American Folk Music* (Smithsonian Folkways, 1952; reissued 1997). Dylan builds a pressure-cooker story of poverty and isolation in which slow-brewing violence seems not only inevitable but predestined. The family living in a decrepit shotgun shack has endured Old Testament–style bad luck, and there appears to be no way out but death. Rats have infested their flour, the horse is dead, a drought has claimed their crops, and their well is bone dry—a scene of unrelenting disconnection that could also be playing itself out in another form in any inner-city slum. As Dylan builds his keen narrative of domestic hopelessness, a shotgun emerges much as the dagger does in Shakespeare's *Macbeth*, taking on a power of its own and seemingly forcing itself on poor Hollis Brown, who finally takes matters into his own hands. Yet juxtaposed with this wretched scene, seven new people are born in the distance. Whether this is a hopeful sign or a hint that fate is about to play out in similarly dark fashion one can only wonder. In eleven verses, Dylan shows himself to be a young man possessing a high sense of drama with sharp, cinematic eyes. If this were a film it might look something like *The Grapes of Wrath*, *In Cold Blood*, or *Badlands*.

Dylan was performing the song, originally published in *Broadside* magazine as "The Rise and Fall of Hollis Brown: A True Story," soon after writing it in the last half of 1962, and he recorded it for Columbia and as a Witmark demo. He returned to the tragedy during his 1974 comeback tour with the Band, when they delivered throbbing electric renditions. Fittingly, "Hollis Brown" was also an inspired choice to lead off Dylan's three-song Live Aid set in 1985. As Never Ending Tour fodder, "Hollis Brown" came off sounding like his stark, dramatic performances of "John Brown," another doomed hero from his canon, and was performed in a variety of ways: solo acoustic, acoustic with his band, and as an electric arrangement.

"The Ballad of Ira Hayes" (Peter LaFarge)
Bob Dylan, *Dylan* (1973)
Peter LaFarge, *Ira Hayes and Other Ballads* (1962)
Johnny Cash, *Bitter Tears* (1964)

Ira Hayes, an American Pima Indian and U.S. Marine who took part in the raising of the flag on Iwo Jima in World War II, 1955.

(Photo: Hulton Archive/Getty Images)

Patrick Sky, *Patrick Sky* (1965)
Kinky Friedman, *Lasso from El Paso* (1976)
Hazel Dickens, *By the Sweat of My Brow* (1983)
Townes Van Zandt, *Roadsongs* (1992)

Never performed in concert by Dylan but rehearsed with the Grateful Dead in 1987, "The Ballad of Ira Hayes" tells the true story of a Native American World War II hero who returns home to ignominy, anonymity, and an alcoholic's death. Dylan's turgid, piano-based spoken version of the song, clearly but poorly modeled on the famous Johnny Cash version, was vengefully released by Columbia on *Dylan*, an album that its namesake can honestly say he had nothing to do with.

The author of "Ira Hayes," Peter LaFarge (born 1931, Fountain, Colorado; died October 27, 1965, New York City), was touted as one of America's "angry young men" who sparked the folk boom of the 1950s and 1960s. In reality, LaFarge was a sensitive, poetic man and versatile writer who not only composed new folk music but also turned out articles, plays, and poetry in his short lifetime.

A descendant of Rhode Island's virtually extinct Narragansett Indian tribe, LaFarge was raised as a Tewa Indian on a Hopi reservation until he was about nine years old, when he was adopted by Oliver LaFarge, the writer and champion of Native American causes and author of *Laughing Child*, the 1930 Pulitzer Prize–winning novel sympathetically dealing with the Navajo Indians.

Through his adoptive father, Peter became interested in folk traditions as a youngster and, at age fourteen, had his own radio show on a station in Colorado Springs, which led to a meeting with Woody Guthrie's cohort Cisco Houston. Houston tutored LaFarge in the finer points of singing, guitar playing, songwriting, and, most saliently, life.

After service in the Korean War, in which he won five battle stars but suffered a serious head injury, LaFarge led the life of a roustabout—working as a rodeo hand, a bronco rider, and a sometime boxer—before finding his way to New York City, where he became a vital member of the Greenwich Village renaissance of the late 1950s and early 1960s. It was there that he began hitting the East Coast coffeehouse circuit and eventually made the scene at the Newport Folk Festival and the like. A regular contributor to the folk-music magazine *Sing Out!*, LaFarge was the author of many songs sung and recorded by others: "Coyote," "Black Stallion," "As Long as the Grass Shall Grow," and "Ira Hayes."

Of "Ira Hayes," LaFarge recalled in *Sing Out!*: "The Pima Indians, whose reservation is just outside Phoenix, Arizona, are cousins of my people—the Hopi Indians of the New Mexico Pueblos. Cisco (Houston) worked me terribly on this one, and contributed the line, 'wined and speeched and honored' after I was hung up for a week over getting that into four lines. He refused to put his name on the song; he wanted me to have it because, he said: 'I'm leaving soon.' In the heart-breaking years when protest songs were not fashionable, this one struggled for a brief glimpse of the truth."

Naturally, LaFarge crossed paths with Ramblin' Jack Elliott, Dave Van Ronk, Pete Seeger, and the young Bobby Dylan. While some may regard him as barely a footnote in the Dylan biography, LaFarge was the first politically attuned Native American to garner widespread notice. Having been acquainted with LaFarge, it is no wonder Dylan was later attracted to the likes of activist-songwriter John Trudell in the 1980s. As a Native American in the already exotic hub of Lower Manhattan, LaFarge cut an unusual figure, and his powerful songs were welcomed for their message. He is remembered as something of an unofficial guardian to Dylan and made sure that the young troubadour kept his nose clean. Dylan remembered LaFarge in the *Biograph* liner notes, calling him "one of the great unsung heroes of the day."

Though LaFarge was signed to Columbia around the same time as Dylan, his relationship with the big-time label was short-lived. He found a home at Folkways Records and recorded albums between 1962 and 1965 devoted to Native American themes. Johnny Cash came across LaFarge and his music and was inspired to cut *Bitter Tears* in 1964, an entire album devoted to the Native Americans' plight. *Bitter Tears* featured several of LaFarge's songs, including "Ira Hayes," and Cash's single release of the song reached No. 3 on the country music charts despite the ambivalence of disc jockeys uncomfortable with its overt political message.

But the success of "Ira Hayes" signaled LaFarge's descent. The conflicting factors of newfound wealth, the jealousy of some of his peers, his refusal to alter his political agenda, and his stoic monotone performance style all contributed to his swift ruin. By the time Dylan was making his first stabs at recording with a full band in 1964, LaFarge's static act had worn thin. Vietnam replaced civil rights as the cause du jour and the rise of folk-rock rendered LaFarge's bare-bones sound a stodgy, if well-intentioned, relic. His death was reported as a stroke but some have suggested it was suicide.

LaFarge's story, while sorrowful, barely approaches the subject of his most famous song. The story of Ira Hayes is one of America's most tragic. Hayes was born on January 12, 1923, on the Pima Indian Reservation in Sacaton, Arizona, and was raised there. Life was predictably tough for his poor farming family as they eked out a subsistence living in the arid conditions of the reservation—exacer-

B

bated by the U.S. government's cutting off the Pimas' water supply. When World War II broke out, Hayes joined the U.S. Marine Corps, for obvious reasons: he would be able to leave the reservation, eat regularly, and be paid. Told by his tribal chief to be an honorable warrior, Hayes did just that, fighting in three major Pacific battles against the Japanese.

The turning point of Hayes's life occurred on February 23, 1945, when he etched his name into the history books on Mount Suribachi above the island of Iwo Jima. It was there that a small group of Marines raised the American flag to claim victory over the Japanese occupancy of the island. Ira was among those rushing to help his comrades hoist the flag just as a photographer snapped what soon became among the most famous frames in history. It was Ira's outstretched hands that are seen giving the final thrust to the flag and its symbolic place in the American psyche. As if to underscore the bravery of the six men depicted in the photograph, three never made it off the island alive. Additionally, of Ira's platoon of forty-five men, only five survived.

Hayes was stunned at being hailed as a hero upon his return home. And, after accepting an invitation by President Harry S. Truman to travel the nation as part of a tour to help raise money for the war effort, he became confused and disoriented. Returning to the reservation to escape the unwanted attention did little to salve Hayes's emotional wounds. As people continued to write him or even dropped by unannounced to "see the Indian who raised the flag," Ira escaped to the bottle. After another night of drinking and still lamenting over his fallen "buddies," Ira fell down drunk in an irrigation ditch and froze to death, alone and forgotten by a country that had called him a hero. The ditch where he died was the single source of water that was provided for his people by the same

government he'd proudly served. He is buried in Arlington National Cemetery.

LaFarge's song is as good an epitaph as any for Ira Hayes. But perhaps Hayes's epitaph can be found in response to a question. After a ceremony where he was praised by President Dwight Eisenhower once again for being a hero, a reporter asked Ira, "How do you like the pomp and circumstances?" Ira just hung his head and said, "I don't."

A final note: Hayes's life was depicted in *The Outsider*, a 1961 film starring Tony Curtis.

Ⓐ*The Ballad of Ramblin' Jack*/Ramblin' Jack Elliott
Vanguard CD 79575. Released 2000.

Dylan's quirky contribution to this quirky documentary about Woody Guthrie protégé and troubadour Ramblin' Jack Elliott is pretty minimal: the infamous three-minute coming-of-hormones rock 'n' roll parody song "Acne" drawn from their July 1961 performance at New York City's Riverside Church with Danny Kalb. Though he was no innovator, Ramblin' Jack had a handle on American roots music that is undeniably his own, and the highlights of both the 2000 film of the same name and its accompanying soundtrack are his duets with its high ecclesiastical figures: Odetta, Johnny Cash, Derroll Adams, Sonny Terry, Norman Blake, and Guthrie.

Ⓢ"Band of the Hand (It's Hell Time Man!)"
(Bob Dylan)
aka "Hell Time, Man!"
Various Artists (performed by Bob Dylan), single (1986); *Band of the Hand* (soundtrack) (1986)

The title track of a truly rank *Mod Squad*–style B-film directed by Paul Michael Glaser, the fire-and-brimstone "Band of the Hand"—a shallow, formulaic social critique with apocalyptic pretensions—could be heard on Dylan's 1986 world tour with Tom Petty and the Heartbreakers. During its short life as a doom-and-gloom concert presentation worthy of a Times Square sandwich board during the Petty era, "Band of the Hand" showed that ensemble, backup singers included, at a rousing, gospel-rockin' peak.

Dylan's songs had been used in films before, but this may have been the first time he had whipped one up for a reel in which he never appears.

In a treatment characteristic of several of his mid-1980s songs, Dylan is believed to have drawn a scrap of this composition's final verse from a 1941 film noir titled *I Wake Up Screaming.* In that film, Laird Cregar gives Victor Mature this typical tough-guy rap: "One day you'll be talking in your sleep, and when you do I wanna be around." Dylan, who as a teenager spent hours in the Hibbing, Minnesota, movie house absorbing such dialogue, transformed those words into his song: "I know your story is too painful to share/One day, though, you'll be talkin' in your sleep/And when you do I wanna be there."

Ⓐ *Band of the Hand* (soundtrack)/Various Artists
LP MCA-6167; CS MCAC-6167. Released 1986.

Dylan's title song, recorded with Tom Petty and the Heartbreakers, is perhaps the best thing about this Petty-produced soundtrack album, which also includes Andy Summers, formerly of the Police.

Ⓢ "Barbara Allen" (Traditional)
aka "Barb'ra Allen," "Barb're Allen," "Barbara Ellen," "Barbie Allen," "Barbie Allan"
Nick Marlor, single (1936)
Queen Hule Hines, single (1939)

Jo Stafford, *American Folk Songs* (1950)
Various Artists (performed by Jessie Murray, Fred Jordan, Charlie Wills, May Bennell, Thomas Moran, Phil Tanner), *Classic Ballads of England and Ireland, Volume One*/1949, 1951, 1952, 1954 (2003)
Everly Brothers, *Songs Our Daddy Taught Us* (1958)
Joan Baez, *Joan Baez Volume 2* (1961)
Pete Seeger, *World of Pete Seeger* (1973)
Merle Travis, *Folk Songs of the Hills* (1996)
Doris Day, *Complete Doris Day with Les Brown* (1998)

An entry in both Dylan's earliest and latest performances in which he convincingly renders the fate of a cold wench whose denial of love to a young man has killed him and transformed her into an unrequited lover in death buried right beside him in the churchyard, "Barbara Allen" is one of the best known, excruciatingly gorgeous, and most widely sung of all traditional ballads in the English language—the veritable *Romeo and Juliet* of Anglo-American balladry. In both the Old World and in America, most variants of the song strongly resemble one another. This probably owes to its frequent publication on broadsides, in songsters, chapbooks, and penny garlands since the seventeenth century. One of those variants has a sequel that Dylan also sang: a rose rises from one of the pair's graves, a briar rises from the other, and the two climb to the top of the old church and there intertwine for eternity.

In his liner notes for *O Love Is Teasin'* in 1985, Lenny Kaye broke down "Barbara Allen" as follows:

> The story is a simple one. In "Scarlet Town," a young man named Sweet William lies on his death bed and calls for Barbara Allen. He asks for her love; she coldly informs him that he is dying. There is some discussion over who slighted whom. She leaves and is smitten by remorse when she hears "the death bell knelling." She asks her father to dig her grave.

B

This done, she "will die for him tomorrow," and buried next to Sweet William in the old churchyard, a rose that blossoms from his heart, and a briar that springs from hers, "grew and grew . . . till they twined a true love's knot."

Sung in hundreds of variants, the restraint of each stanza is a study in economy, with love's infectious malady setting a fateful trap from which neither William nor Barbara can escape.

In both Britain and America "Barbara Allen" has been among the most popular of all the traditional ballads. Samuel Pepys wrote about the "perfect pleasure" of hearing it sung by an actress in his famous diary on January 2, 1666. A century later Oliver Goldsmith declared that the "music of the finest singer is dissonance" compared to hearing his old dairy-maid sing "Barbara Allen," which brought him to tears. Versions of "Barbara Allen" (Child Ballad No. 84) have been collected in Europe from Scandinavia to Italy and in the U.S., nearly seventy from Virginia alone.

Alan Lomax researched "Barbara Allen" extensively and even attempted an able psycho-logical deconstruction of the song, writing in *The Folk Songs of North America* (Garden City, N.Y.: Doubleday, 1960):

> In 1942, a gnarled old Georgia farmer, who had been my guide through the mountains, said, "Just do me one favor now, before we say goodbye. Just sing me that old song about Bob'ry Allen one time. My old mammy used to sing it to me, and it looks like ever' time I hear it, it just makes the ha'r rise straight up on my head." This ballad, if no other, trav-elled west with every wagon. As someone remarked, they sang "Barbara Allen" in Texas "before the pale faces were thick enough to make the Indians consider a mas-sacre worth while." What, then, is the content of the story which so consistently drew tears from the English, and raised the hackles of the pioneers?

> In the normal ballad there is almost no incident. A girl refuses a man who says he is dying for her love. He expires when she turns from him; then she, too, dies of remorse. In fact the song dwells largely upon the sickbed scene and upon Willie's feeling of weakness, his pallor and his helplessness in the face of the proud and angry maid. Barbara is glad to see her Willie dying because of a small mis-understanding which would have been cleared up in a moment. Her remorselessness and Willie's extraordinary demise are not really explained, but represent an undercur-rent of powerful feelings which it is assumed the audience understands. In fact, the song is the vehicle for the aggressive fantasies of women and frustrations of men, of which both the ballad singers and their listeners are unconsciously aware. They apparently believe that men can actually die of love.

After performing somewhat tuneless ver-sions of "Barbara Allen" at his Greenwich Vil-lage coffeehouse gigs in the very early 1960s, Dylan returned to "Barbara Allen" on a visit to England in 1981, when he surprised audiences with an electric rendition. From 1988 through 1991, Dylan retained the traditional melody and arrangement for acoustic and electric interpre-tations alike; in either guise it was a fairly con-stant and always welcome turn during the Never Ending Tour's phases. As with his per-formances of songs like the traditional "Peggy-O" or his own "Boots of Spanish Leather," Dylan assumes the roles of both characters in singing "Barbara Allen," seamlessly slipping from one to the other as the tragedy and poetry of the tale unfold.

A lovely version of "Barbara Allen" can also be heard in *Scrooge*, the 1951 film version of the Charles Dickens classic *A Christmas Carol* starring Alastair Sim.

▲ *Barry Goldberg*/Barry Goldberg
Atco Records LP SD-7040, 1973. Produced by Bob Dylan and Jerry Wexler.
"Stormy Weather Cowboy," "Silver Moon," "Minstrel Show," "Big City Women," "It's Not the Spotlight," "(I've Got to Use My) Imagination"

Dylan took a coproducer credit (probably for assisting in Goldberg's one-record deal) on this now-forgotten album that one might still find in the bins of used-record stores. And Dylan can be heard playing percussion and contributing background vocals on most of the Barry Goldberg–penned tracks. "(I've Got to Use My) Imagination" saw limited release as a single. A friend of blues guitarist Michael Bloomfield's, Goldberg first met Dylan when he was tapped to play piano at the notorious 1965 Newport Festival electric performance.

Goldberg (born 1941, Chicago) was one of a handful of aspiring white musicians who frequented Chicago's blues clubs during the early 1960s. He became a fixture in the shtetl of white blues musicians that in the mid-'60s stretched from the Great Lakes to the Atlantic Ocean. It was on the South Side of the Windy City that he befriended guitarist Bloomfield and planted the seeds for what became the Goldberg-Miller Blues Band with itinerant Texan Steve Miller. Goldberg assumed leadership of the group upon his partner's departure, and the group's sole album still stands as a fine example of pop-influenced R&B. After a spell with Bloomfield's great band Electric Flag, Goldberg resumed his own career in 1968 with the Barry Goldberg Reunion. But although albums (including the humorously and aptly

titled *Two Jews Blues*) featured contributions from the likes of Bloomfield and Duane Allman, Goldberg was never able to translate his status as a sideman into a coherent, successful solo path. Even so, as an in-demand session man, songwriter, and producer, Goldberg has remained incredibly active, utilizing an arsenal of musical chops that has allowed him to work with a whole spectrum of talents that include Charlie Musselwhite, Leonard Cohen, Kenny Burrell, James Cotton, Tracey Nelson, Rod Stewart, and Percy Sledge. Goldberg reunited with Dylan in 1989 when he was brought on to play piano as a sideman for a studio recording of "People Get Ready" that was used in *Flashback* (1990), a screwball comedy starring Kiefer Sutherland and Dennis Hopper.

▲ *The Basement Tapes*
Columbia Records LP C2-33682, CD C2K-33682, CS CGT-33682. Recorded in the basement of Big Pink, West Saugerties, New York, summer 1967. Released June 26, 1975. Produced by Bob Dylan and the Band. Compiled by Robbie Robertson. Liner notes by Greil Marcus. Photography by Reid Miles.
Bob Dylan—guitar, harmonica, piano, keyboards, vocals. Robbie Robertson—guitar, drums, vocals. Rick Danko—bass, mandolin, violin, vocals. Levon Helm—mandolin, bass, drums, vocals. Garth Hudson—organ, piano, accordion, keyboards, tenor saxophone, clavinet. Richard Manuel—harmonica, piano, drums, keyboards, vocals.
"Odds and Ends," "Orange Juice Blues (Blues for Breakfast)," "Million Dollar Bash," "Yazoo Street Scandal," "Goin' to Acapulco," "Katie's Been Gone," "Lo and Behold!," "Bessie Smith," "Clothes Line Saga," "Apple Suckling Tree," "Please, Mrs. Henry," "Tears of Rage," "Too Much of Nothing," "Yea! Heavy and a Bottle of Bread," "Ain't No More Cane," "Crash on the Levee (Down in the Flood)," "Ruben Remus," "Tiny Montgomery," "You Ain't Goin' Nowhere," "Don't Ya Tell Henry," "Nothing Was Delivered," "Open the Door, Homer," "Long-Distance Operator," "This Wheel's on Fire"

A bootleg LP jacket of *The Basement Tapes*.
(Author's Collection)

Two discs (and a slew of complementary bootlegs) of random brilliance from Dylan's retreat to upstate New York in 1967 with the Hawks, *The Basement Tapes* provides the missing link between Dylan's surrealisms of the mid-'60s and the focused minimalisms that made up *John Wesley Harding* in 1967. Dylan wrote sixteen of the twenty-four tracks on the album and collaborated on two of the others: "Tears of Rage" with Richard Manuel, and "This Wheel's on Fire" with Rick Danko. While some of the songs have become well known ("The Mighty Quinn," "Too Much of Nothing," "Tears of Rage," "This Wheel's on Fire," "Crash on the Levee," and "You Ain't Goin' Nowhere"), other pieces of whimsy still come as fresh surprises ("Odds and Ends," "Yea! Heavy and a Bottle of Bread," and "Lo and Behold!"). Still other minor masterpieces found on the bootlegs of the unreleased material—such as "I'm Not There (1956)" and "Sign on the Cross"—may never see the "official" light of day. Also among

the unreleased songs are many, many covers of well-known as well as very obscure songs written during the subterranean phase.

The story behind *The Basement Tapes* is the stuff of legend and even a little bit of fact. After his motorcycle accident in the summer of 1966, Dylan retreated with his family to Woodstock, New York, for a period of recuperation and reflection in the tranquil environs of the Catskill Mountains and local forests. In the spring of 1967, he was joined by the Hawks (soon to be renamed the Band), who moved into a house in nearby West Saugerties that they dubbed Big Pink (in honor of its size and gruesome paint job) and for which they later named their debut LP in 1968. Naturally, it wasn't too long before Dylan was joining them in Big Pink's basement for the lengthy jam sessions that would produce many hours of tape. As rumors of the sessions spread, they took on mythological proportions and the reels from them grail-like status.

Tapes from the sessions mysteriously reached collectors in 1967 and 1968 after they were circulated as music publishing demos and then assembled on rock's first known bootleg album, *Great White Wonder*. (For the full story on that and the entire underground-vinyl industry, Clinton Heylin's 1995 exposé, *Bootleg*, is a must-read.) The songs gained notoriety through more traditional methods as well. B. Feldman, Dylan's English publisher, was especially successful in obtaining cover versions, scoring big hits with Manfred Mann's rendition of "The Mighty Quinn" and "This Wheel's on Fire" by Brian Auger and Trinity. Stateside, country-rock versions of "Nothing Was Delivered" and "You Ain't Goin' Nowhere" were popularized by the Byrds on their *Sweetheart of the Rodeo* LP in 1968.

Perhaps because its contents had long since reached Homeric status among Dylan fans by the time of its eventual release in the early summer of 1975, *The Basement Tapes* stayed on the charts for nine weeks, rising as high as No. 7. The album cover is a classic, perfectly capturing the essence of the music contained within: a bizarre, carnivalesque photo of Dylan and the Band with an insane cast of characters posing in a grimy basement; the whole sick crew seems to have stepped right out of the songs. Greil Marcus, who two decades later wrote *Invisible Republic* (later retitled *The Old, Weird America: The World of Bob Dylan's Basement Tapes*), a fancifully great book about the material and the historical ethos that informed it, offers some scholarly, if largely less salient liner notes for the release. Marcus's basic theory is that the historical community of American folk music is deep, fluid, perverse, and conflicted, and that *The Basement Tapes* is a kind of small village where all these elements sing together in holy cacophony. Marcus's country is not Woody Guthrie's land made for you and me but rather, in the words of Luc Sante, writing for *New York* magazine, the "playground of God, Satan, tricksters, Puritans, confidence men, illuminati, braggarts, preachers, anonymous poets of all stripes."

Recalling the creative process that produced this still intangibly atmospheric collection of songs, Robbie Robertson said to Marcus in *Invisible Republic*, "We used to get together every day at one o'clock in the basement of Big Pink. And it was just a routine. We would get there to keep one of us from going crazy, we would play music every day. And Dylan wrote a bunch of songs out of that, and we wrote a bunch of songs out of that."

In the *Biograph* liner notes, Robertson elaborated: "The songs were mostly done in humor. They were either outrageous or comical. It was a big songwriting period, and we all had lots of songs. The idea was to record some demos for

other people. They were never intended to be a record, never meant to be presented. It was somewhat annoying that the songs were bootlegged. The album was finally released in the spirit of 'well, if this is going to be documented, let's at least make it good quality.'"

For the passionate fan of the *Basement* sessions, the unreleased material put out on the so-called *Genuine Bootleg Series* can be found with a little hunting, but for a price. And for the true believer, *Marquee Mark*, the 1997 live recording by the Crust Brothers (a one-off combination of Pavement mastermind Stephen Malkmus and Pacific Northwest band Silkworm), featuring some rough and magic, one-night-only versions of some seven *Basement* cuts, is an absolute must.

Perhaps critic Robert Christgau's first words regarding *The Basement Tapes* are also the last and finest. Praising the collection as the year's best in the *Village Voice* in 1975, he suggested that "We needn't bow our heads in shame because this is the best album of 1975. It would have been the best record of 1967 too. And it's sure to sound great in 1983."

And need it be added, in 2083 as well?

◢ Before the Flood

Asylum Records LP S-201, reissue, Columbia Records LP KG-37661, CD C2K-376661, CS CGT-37661. Recorded January 30, February 13–14, 1974. Originally released June 20, 1974; Columbia reissue released August 1982. Produced by (probably an uncredited) Bob Dylan and the Band with engineering assistance by Phil Ramone and Rob Fraboni.

Bob Dylan—guitar, harmonica, piano, keyboards, vocals. Robbie Robertson—guitar, vocals. Rick Danko—bass, violin, vocals. Levon Helm—mandolin, drums, vocals. Garth Hudson—organ, piano, keyboards, saxophone, clavinet. Richard Manuel—organ, piano, drums, keyboards, vocals.

"Most Likely You Go Your Way (And I'll Go Mine)," "Lay Lady

Lay," "Rainy Day Women #12 & 35," "Knockin' on Heaven's Door," "It Ain't Me, Babe," "Ballad of a Thin Man," "Up on Cripple Creek,"* "I Shall Be Released,"* "Endless Highway,"* "The Night They Drove Old Dixie Down,"* "Stage Fright,"* "Don't Think Twice, It's All Right," "Just Like a Woman," "It's Alright, Ma (I'm Only Bleeding)," "The Shape I'm In,"* "When You Awake,"* "The Weight,"* "All Along the Watchtower," "Highway 61 Revisited," "Like a Rolling Stone," "Blowin' in the Wind"
(* performed by the Band without Dylan)

A double album memento chronicling Dylan and the Band's triumphant winter 1974 U.S. tour, *Before the Flood* features high-octane performances of many of Dylan's then and now most famous songs and a fine selection of solo work by the Band sans Bob. As such, the first officially released live album by Dylan and the Band hit No. 3 and stayed on the charts for ten weeks, earning both Dylan—his tenth—and the Band gold albums.

Before the Flood has aged fairly well over the years even if appraisals of the record-breaking tour that preceded it have not—Dylan's propensity for shouting his lyrics in the oversized stadia through which the tour swung and the blustery nature of his musical arrangements that year can get a little wearisome, as the circulating concert tapes bear out.

When Dylan hit the road with the Band in early January 1974, it had been nearly eight years since the then thirty-two-year-old performer had been on tour, though he had made a few seat-of-the-pants stage appearances, such as the 1967 Woody Guthrie memorial concert and the 1969 Isle of Wight festival. The demand for tickets was unprecedented even for the enormous arenas lined up for the run—650,000 people paid $93 million to see the forty shows staged in six whirlwind, coast-to-coast weeks.

Whereas Dylan had opened his 1966 shows with an extended acoustic set showcasing his surrealisms of the period, the 1974 concerts commenced with Dylan and the Band tearing through about a half-dozen favorites, followed by a short set by the Band. After an intermission, Dylan would perform three or four solo acoustic numbers before the Band rejoined him for a rock-solid final set and de rigueur three-song encore. Most of the concerts began and ended with "Most Likely You Go Your Way (and I'll Go Mine)," a curious and subtle in-joke bookend that could imply that Dylan was back to stay—or maybe not.

No doubt a lot of water had passed under the bridge between Dylan's last tour in 1966 (which included the cataclysmic electric sets with the Hawks) and 1974: Vietnam, the Martin Luther King Jr. and Bobby Kennedy assassinations, the victories of the civil rights movement, Watergate, Woodstock, Altamont, Attica, Charles Manson, etc. The counterculture had become, in certain respects, the culture. So Dylan on his return had the aura of the conquering hero—some even dared to whisper "prophet"—about him.

If the performances on the tour lacked subtlety or variation, they were pitched with the confidence of a performer who knew from where he had come and where he was going. Dylan displayed purpose on this tour; there was no suggestion that he was merely playacting the role of a relic from the 1960s going through the motions for nostalgia's sake. "Most Likely You Go Your Way," "Just Like a Woman," "All Along the Watchtower," "Like a Rolling Stone," "Blowin' in the Wind," and all of the others, old and new, brimmed with triumph and celebration as the Dylan myth was made flesh before the masses. And when he got to the president of the United States having to stand naked from "It's Alright Ma (I'm Only Bleeding)," he sounded as topical as ever to an audience riveted by the downfall of Richard Nixon.

He brought the house down whether in Chicago, New York City, St. Louis, Seattle, or Los Angeles. Times (or was that *things?*) had changed once again.

[S] "Belle Isle" (Traditional/arrangement by Bob Dylan)

aka "The Blooming Bright Star of Belle Isle," "The Star of Belle Isle"
Bob Dylan, *Self Portrait* (1970)
Ed Trickett, *Telling Takes Me Home* (1972)
In Transit, *In Transit* (1980)
Band of the British Grenadier, *British Grenadiers* (1987)

Dylan's intentions were admirable when he decided to cover this ancient Celtic piece of business via the rainy, misty stirrings of Newfoundland. Maybe, however, he should have tried singing in key and dropped the string arrangement when it came time to record it.

Dylan is credited as the author of the song on *Self Portrait.* But Michael Gray, in his two-part article "Back to Belle Isle," published in *The Telegraph* #29 (spring 1988) and #31 (winter 1988), makes a persuasive case that it is an old Irish folk song that came to Canada, underwent various changes, and was later skillfully rearranged by Dylan. Gray traces "Belle Isle" from "Loch Erin's Sweet Riverside," itself an offshoot of "Erin's Green Shore." Gray also presents the following entry, by Edith Fowke, for "The Blooming Bright Star of Belle Isle" in the *Encyclopedia of Music in Canada* (Toronto: University of Toronto press, 1981) to support his case: "Newfoundland adaptation of an old Irish love song, 'Loch Erin's Sweet Riverside.'. . . First published in Greenleaf and Mansfield's *Ballads and Sea Songs of Newfoundland* (Cambridge, Mass., 1933), 'The Blooming Bright Star of Belle Isle' is also included in *The Penguin Book of Canadian Folk Songs* (London, 1973) by Edith Fowke." Gray's main point is to link these songs with the heart of the peculiar Newfoundland folk-song forms, various forms of traditional song, and Dylan's own Nashville-tinged expression of and response to these oeuvres. He also suggests that Dylan may have learned the song not from an LP, but from a performance of it. A version of "Belle Isle" nearly identical to the one recorded by Dylan, however, appeared in *Reprints from* Sing Out!, volume 9, in 1966 (New York: Oak Publications).

Another dispute over "Belle Isle" concerns the location of the very place itself. Some camps insist that it is Bell Island in Conception Bay, off the eastern coast of Newfoundland near St. John, while others point to another Belle Island between New Brunswick and Newfoundland.

Whatever the answers to these questions of source and geography may be, there is no doubt that "Belle Isle" is among the most obscure songs Dylan ever chose to explore, as it describes an unearthly visitation of a muse-like nymph to a young man simply going for a walk to Loch Erin. This would seem to solve (or maybe even further confuse) the location riddle, as Loch Erin (or Lough Erne) is a lake that can be found in Northern Ireland's County Fermanagh, which contains an island called Belle Isle.

[S] "Bessie Smith" (Rick Danko/Robbie Robertson)

Bob Dylan/The Band, *The Basement Tapes/'67* (1975)
The Crust Brothers, *Marquee Mark* (1998)

Not a tribute to the late, great gutbucket blues chanteuse, as the casual observer would assume on first glance, the "Bessie Smith" of *The Basement Tapes* is a sleepy blues lament to a girlfriend. The jury is still out (but most thumbs are firmly pointed down) as to whether or not Dylan performs on the officially released version of this tune sung by Rick Danko.

B

[S] **"Big Joe, Dylan and Victoria"** (Big Joe Williams)
Victoria Spivey, *Three Kings and a Queen, Volume Two*/'62 (1972)

While some have credited Dylan for the composition of this instrumental celebrating a one-time collaboration of Dylan with Victoria Spivey and Big Joe Williams, the album's label clearly denotes it as a Williams tune. Dylan does, however, contribute harmonica licks on the track.

Williams (born Joseph Williams, October 16, 1903, Clarksdale, Mississippi; died December 17, 1982, Macon, Georgia) was a blues guitarist and singer. After working as an itinerant musician as a teenager, he gravitated to Chicago, where his successful early recordings for Bluebird have long since become collectors' items. Along with studs like Muddy Waters, Big Joe Williams was both a traditionalist and an inventor, an uncompromising figure who helped consolidate the blues into a distinct form. With a howling, frightening voice that seemed to echo the haunted visage of Charley Patton, and tricky guitar work (often played on a unique nine-string instrument) that could have been acquired at the same crossroads Robert Johnson was said to frequent back in the Delta, Williams played an important part in shaping the blues of postwar Chicago, but his role has diminished. The recordings he made with harmonica man Sonny Boy Williamson (II) of standards like "Baby, Please Don't Go" and "Someday Baby," as well as his own "Highway 49," actually made him some money that, along with his reemergence during the folk revival of the early 1960s, allowed him to retire in relative comfort.

[A] ***The Big Lebowski*** (soundtrack)/Various Artists
Mercury Records CD 536903, CS 536903. Released 1998.

True to Joel and Ethan Coen's rep as America's highest-profile quirky filmmakers, *The Big Lebowski*, a comically idiosyncratic glimpse into the subterrain of contemporary society (a mistaken-identity caper with Raymond Chandleresque overtones starring Jeff Bridges, John Goodman, Ben Gazzara, John Turturro, and Steve Buscemi), features a soundtrack that is a delightfully odd blend of just about every genre one can name: folk, blues, opera, jazz, pop, rock, and world music exotica. But, like much of the Coens' generally overrated fare, neither the film nor its accompanying musical mélange really adds up to a compelling unified whole. Along with Dylan's "The Man in Me" from his 1970 LP *New Morning*, the audio gumbo includes Elvis Costello ("My Mood Swings"), Townes Van Zandt (a cover of the Rolling Stones' "Dead Flowers"), Nina Simone (her cover of the Duke Ellington/Paul Francis Webster classic "I Got It Bad and That Ain't Good"), Yma Sumac ("Ataypura"), Captain Beefheart ("Her Eyes a Blue Million Miles"), and Henry Mancini ("Lujon").

[S] **"Big River"** (Johnny Cash)
Johnny Cash, *I Walk the Line* (1964)
The Grateful Dead, *Steal Your Face* (1976)
Roseanne Cash, *Right or Wrong* (1979)
Bill Monroe, *Bluegrass 1959–1969* (1991)
Ian and Sylvia, *Long Long Time* (1994)

A footloose chronicle of a Cupid-struck picaro's unsuccessful chase for his evasive lover as he ventures down the Mississippi River from St. Paul to Baton Rouge in pursuit of her, "Big River" recalls the wide-open spirit of Mark Twain's riverboat Americana. Johnny Cash wrote and first recorded the song when he was signed with Sun Records and conspiring with label mates Jerry Lee Lewis, Carl Perkins, and Elvis Presley in the mid- and late 1950s.

Dylan recorded "Big River" with the Hawks during the *Basement Tapes* sessions in 1967, with Cash himself during their *Nashville Skyline*–era experiments in 1969, and with Eric Clapton and Ron Wood at a 1976 party in Malibu. Dylan rehearsed (but did not perform) "Big River" in anticipation of his 1981 tour, though he did pull it out for one rockabilly encore in 1988 and gave it another go in 2000 in a version that sounded as if the band had just walked out of a studio at Sun Records and onto the stage. The Grateful Dead tore this song apart, and it was under the cloak of their arrangement that Dylan performed "Big River" with the Dead during their Summer Getaway tour mini-collaborations.

"Big Yellow Taxi" (Joni Mitchell)
Bob Dylan, *Dylan* (1973)
Joni Mitchell, *Ladies of the Canyon* (1970)
Sugar Beats, *Really Cool Songs* (1973)
Monty Alexander, *Jamboree: Ivory and Steel* (1988)
Amy Grant, *House of Love* (1994)
Pinhead Gunpowder, *Jump Salty* (1994)

Dylan covered a lot of other people's material in his recording sessions of the early 1970s, little of it with any success. A lamer, more out-of-touch rendition than Dylan's of a good, fun song like Joni Mitchell's "Big Yellow Taxi" would be hard to find. Fortunately, Dylan had nothing to do with the release of his version (recorded with slightly altered lyrics, a ghoulish organ, and a frightful chorus just after Mitchell's release of the song). The blame can be placed on Columbia Records for including it on *Dylan*, an album released specifically to humiliate its former (and future) star, who had temporarily jumped ship to David Geffen's newly formed Asylum Records.

According to Mitchell, in a discussion with journalist Alan McDougall in the early 1970s,

"Big Yellow Taxi" was inspired by a trip to Hawaii. "Living in Los Angeles, smog-choked L.A., is bad enough," she said, "but the last straw came when I visited Hawaii for the first time. It was night time when we got there, so I didn't get my first view of the scenery until I got up the next morning. The hotel room was quite high up, so in the distance I could see the blue Pacific Ocean. I walked over to the balcony and there was the picture-book scenery, palm tree swaying in the breeze and all. Then I looked down and there was this ugly concrete car park in the hotel grounds. I thought, 'They paved paradise and put up a parking lot,' and that's how the song 'Big Yellow Taxi' was born."

"Billy 1" (Bob Dylan)
Bob Dylan, *Pat Garrett and Billy the Kid* (1973)
Naked Prey, *Naked Prey* (1984)
Triffids, *Stockholm* (1990)
Two Approaching Riders, *One More Cup of Coffee* (1997)
Rolling Thunder, *The Never Ending Rehearsal* (2000)
Gillian Welch, *Revelator* (2002)
Various Artists (performed by Billy Goodman), *May Your Song Always Be Sung: The Songs of Bob Dylan, Volume 3* (2003)

With a clear, *New Morning*–like voice, Dylan sings the first and best of three Billy the Kid ballads on a soundtrack album (his first) not known for its diverse material. Dylan's cycle of "Billy" songs perfectly captures the desperado, on-the-lam, life-is-cheap sensibility at the core of Sam Peckinpah's film *Pat Garrett and Billy the Kid*, for which it was composed, and Marty Robbins's *Gunfighter Ballads*, which may have inspired it.

"Billy 4" (Bob Dylan)
Bob Dylan, *Pat Garrett and Billy the Kid* (1973)

Dylan's Billy the Kid ballads continued on the soundtrack album with predictable, if compelling, results. With their sparse, Spanish guitar-tinged arrangements, all the "Billy" songs evoke visions of dusty hills, the smells of corn tortillas and refried beans, the taste of flat beer, the prospect of finding a good woman before nightfall—or doom.

[S] "Billy 7" (Bob Dylan)

Bob Dylan, *Pat Garrett and Billy the Kid* (1973)

The last of three versions of the same song on an album (something Dylan has done neither before nor since) sounds more like it has Kris Kristofferson, one of the film's costars, singing than it does the composer. This particular tune seems not to have been included in the film's final cut.

[S] "Billy's Surrender" (Bob Dylan)

aka "Billy Surrenders"
Bob Dylan, *Pat Garrett and Billy the Kid* (1973)

A mournful instrumental closed Peckinpah's film and Dylan's soundtrack LP. While the song ended up being called "Billy's Surrender," Dylan's working title for it was "Speedball," perhaps in reference to a heroin-and-cocaine cocktail with which the musicians were rumored to be fueling themselves during the marathon recording session that produced the collection.

The *Pat Garrett* soundtrack was notable for Dylan's run-ins with Jerry Fielding, a renowned and outspoken film composer signed on to assist with the music. Fielding, to put it politely, thought that Dylan's approach to the project and his musical results were lacking, a sentiment reportedly not lost on Dylan. "Billy's Surrender," with its overwhelming static and repetitive phrase played ad nauseum, has no development or variation and was probably one of the tunes that drove Fielding up the wall. The song does, however, perfectly fit the scene with which it was combined, occurring when Billy is portrayed in a Christ-on-the-crucifix image as Pat and his posse approach.

[A] *Biograph*/Bob Dylan

Columbia Records LP C5X-38830, CD C3K-38830, CS CXT-38830. Released October 28, 1985. Compiled and supervised by Jeff Rosen. Liner notes by Cameron Crowe.

"Lay Lady Lay," "Baby, Let Me Follow You Down," "If Not for You," "I'll Be Your Baby Tonight," "I'll Keep It with Mine,"* "The Times They Are A-Changin'," "Blowin' in the Wind," "Masters of War," "The Lonesome Death of Hattie Carroll," "Percy's Song,"* "Mixed-Up Confusion,"* "Tombstone Blues," "Groom's Still Waiting at the Altar,"* "Most Likely You Go Your Way (and I'll Go Mine)," "Like a Rolling Stone," "Lay Down Your Weary Tune,"* "Subterranean Homesick Blues," "I Don't Believe You (She Acts Like We Never Have Met),"* "Visions of Johanna,"* "Every Grain of Sand," "Quinn the Eskimo," "Mr. Tambourine Man," "Dear Landlord," "It Ain't Me, Babe," "You Angel You," "Million Dollar Bash," "To Ramona," "You're a Big Girl Now,"* "Abandoned Love,"* "Tangled Up in Blue," "It's All Over Now, Baby Blue,"* "Can You Please Crawl Out Your Window?,"* "Positively 4th Street," "Isis,"* "Jet Pilot,"* "Caribbean Wind,"* "Up to Me,"* "Baby, I'm in the Mood for You,"* "I Wanna Be Your Lover,"* "I Want You," "Heart of Mine," "On a Night Like This," "Just Like a Woman," "Romance in Durango,"* "Señor (Tales of Yankee Power)," "Gotta Serve Somebody," "I Believe in You," "Time Passes Slowly," "I Shall Be Released," "Knockin' on Heaven's Door," "All Along the Watchtower," "Solid Rock," "Forever Young*"

(* song or version previously unreleased or rarely circulated)

When these five vinyl platters looking back at Dylan's first two decades of music hit the stores, fans got on their knees in supplication of the Lord. As such, *Biograph* virtually invented the commodity of the "box set" to celebrate an artist's career with hits, rarities, and (in Dylan's case especially) some of the treasure trove of unreleased songs and live recordings that had been leaking out and circulating unofficially since the 1960s.

Hitting the stores just in time for the 1985 Christmas rush, *Biograph* made it to No. 33 during a brief two-week chart stint, earned Dylan his fifteenth gold record, became only the second such five-record set to break the Top 50, impressed fans, gained new ones, regained old ones, charmed critics, and sent music-industry execs running to their vaults.

In addition to the undeniable excellence of the collection itself, another reason for celebrating *Biograph* was the extensive and incisive liner notes accompanying the music. Dylan got together with writer Cameron Crowe to produce not only a booklet that gave perspective on a lengthy and broad-ranging career that was just hitting the quarter-century mark, but also an annotated, song-by-song analysis that afforded some insight into Dylan's creative process.

Part of the reason *Biograph* remains unique is the presentation of the material. Producer Jeff Rosen was smart in not simply releasing an overview that tackled the material in dry, chronological order. Rather, he grouped the songs by tone and theme, thereby plunging the listener into atmospheres and auras of mood rather than into some academic exercise in Bob Dylan Appreciation 101.

For the hard-core Dylan cognoscenti, the previously unreleased and, in some cases, unheard, tracks was the raison d'être for ensuring that *Biograph* had a secure place by the hearth. More than a dozen cuts fit that bill—including "Up to Me," "Abandoned Love," and the live "Visions of Johanna" from 1966 and "Isis" from 1975—but even some of the less obvious choices for inclusion here ("You Angel You," "On a Night Like This," "Groom's Still Waiting at the Altar") created new impressions of Bob Dylan even for those who thought they knew everything.

The album's success not only created the box-set phenomenon in general but also paved the way for the release of the even more resounding *Bootleg Series, Volumes 1–3* six years later.

Biograph, it should be noted, was also the name of perhaps the foremost old-time blues record label.

▣ "Black Cross" (Joseph S. Newman/Richard M. "Lord" Buckley)
aka "Hezikiah Jones," "Hezikiah"
Lord Buckley, *Way Out Humor* (1959); *Lord Buckley in Concert*/'59 (1964/1985); *Dig Infinity!: The Life & Art of Lord Buckley* (book with CD)/'59 (2002)
Perth County Conspiracy, *Alive* (1971)

Before Cool (B.C.) there was Lord Buckley (born Richard Myrle Buckley, April 5, 1906, Tuolumne, California; died November 12, 1960, New York City)—the original viper, the hall-of-fame hipster, the baddest beatnik, the first flower child, the premier rapper. Though Buckley was best known for his "hipsemantic" retellings of Bible stories, Shakespeare soliloquies, and modern poetry in the 1950s, his career as an entertainer stretched back to his humble, turn-of-the-century roots in a tough mining and lumber town in the foothills of the Sierra Nevada, where he busked on the street corners to earn small change from assorted roughnecks.

Warp speed to the 1930s, '40s, and beyond: Buckley eked out a scattershot career that carried him from the Depression's dance marathons and Capone's murkiest Windy City dives to Swing Era tours with Woody Herman and Gene Krupa, appearances with Ed Sullivan's U.S.O. troupe, and forays onto bebop's first stages and vaudeville's last. Somewhere along the way, Buckley (in the tradition of American musical royalty that includes Duke

B

Ellington, Count Basie, King Oliver, and Prince) became a lord, creating a kingdom in miniature complete with his own peculiar sense of protocol and a lifestyle that might conservatively be described as libertine. In keeping with his title, Buckley assumed the manner of an English nobleman, fashioning himself, as he would have it in one of his album titles, "a most immaculately hip aristocrat"—his massive frame cloaked in a tuxedo, a fresh carnation attached smartly to the lapel, and a mischievous twinkle in his eyes as he twirled his Daliesque mustache and gracefully drew on his omnipresent Lucky Strike.

By 1950 he had fully developed the style that he had been honing for twenty years, effortlessly inhabiting the persona of "His Lordship" wherever he swung. The campy bits in his act were deemphasized, and in their place were the classic Lord Buckley raps recasting incidents from history and mythology into set pieces that combined scat singing, black jive talk, Brooklynese, and the King's English. This odd alchemy often yielded spectacular results, as in "The Nazz" (short for Nazarene), a cool gospel of Christ and his disciples that revealed Buckley's gifts and power in all their raging glory.

In addition to "The Nazz," Buckley employed his distinctive brogue and compelling storytelling gifts to celebrate Mahatma Gandhi ("The Hip Gahn"), the Old Testament ("Jonah and the Whale"), William Shakespeare ("Willie the Shake"), ancient Rome ("Nero"), and Abraham Lincoln ("Gettysburg Address").

Buckley's choice to translate the classics was more than a mere gimmick. By taking tales with which his audience was already familiar, he showed how the spirit of the old heroes and heels contained contemporary meaning and importance. He infused his tales with visionary qualities and definite, if sometimes subtle, points of view.

His Lordship's death came in the midst of a scandal involving the New York City Police Department's confiscation of his cabaret card, an antiquated statute that prevented not only performers but all nightclub employees from working if they had a police record, however minor. Though the official cause was reported as a stroke, there are many other theories and conflicting versions of Buckley's last days. Maybe, as one friend put it, "Lord Buckley was so heavy, Jake, he just *fell* off the planet."

Buckley made several recordings in the 1950s, mostly on small labels, but all worth tracking down. The hidden gem on his 1959 *Way Out Humor* LP is a rendering of poet Joseph S. Newman's "Black Cross," a haunting invective against racism from the latter's book *It Could Be Verse!* How Buckley came upon Newman's work is open to question, but it is significant that Newman was virtually the only artist whose oeuvre Buckley performed straight and unhipped. The decidedly serious "Black Cross" was one of Lord Buckley's favorite pieces, a disturbing portrait he often performed late in his career just as the civil rights movement was gaining a full head of steam. "Black Cross" is an attempt to grasp the blind hatred of the lynch mob. Its hero is Hezikiah Jones, a man "black as the soil he was hoeing." As Buckley tells Hezikiah's story, he slowly, eloquently paints a picture of a dignified, self-educated man with noble principles who, when accused of not believing in anything from "the white man's preacher," answers with the honesty that proves to be his doom.

The man who created Hezikiah Jones, Joseph S. Newman, never made much money from his poems. But poets have seldom been judged by stock portfolios, and Newman should be no different. *It Could Be Verse!*, published in 1948 when its author was fifty-seven, was a deceivingly thin and cheap ($2.75!) vol-

Richard M. "Lord" Buckley, American humorist, Chicago, 1960.

(Photo: Ed Dephoure. Author's Collection. Courtesy of Dick "Prince Owl Head" Zalud)

ume of light verse packed with more humor and insight than many books of greater worth and girth. In the space of 180 pages, Newman elegantly expostulated on an eclectic collection of subjects, including anthropology, biology, comparative religion, and the history of the world. From four-line bits of doggerel to epic rewrites of *The Odyssey* and other classics, Joe Newman's poetic waxings knew no bounds.

Best remembered as a curmudgeonly newspaper columnist for the *Cleveland Press*, Newman was the uncle of the actor Paul Newman. Newman continued to churn out his columns and an occasional book until the day he died, at age sixty-eight, on November 10, 1960, coincidentally just two days short of Buckley's passing.

Dylanologists all agree that Lord Buckley helped fuel the singer-songwriter's inspiration and early aesthetic. Although the two never met, Buckley was important in Dylan's development. In the Dylan catalogue, credit for the song is more often than not given to Lord Buckley, and this warrants correction, as the author-

ship has been indisputably established with Joseph S. Newman, not Buckley.

Though Dylan reportedly performed "Black Cross" regularly over a period of about a year very early in his career, there are but two extant recordings of his interpretation of "Black Cross"—the first from the December 22, 1961, set known affectionately as the Minnesota Hotel Tape and the second from an autumn 1962 gig at the Gaslight Café in Greenwich Village. These sometimes appear in Dylan discographies and on various bootleg releases as "Hezikiah Jones" or simply "Hezikiah." Both versions are exceptional conjurings of the grizzled character of Hezikiah Jones and the bigoted deacon. Buckley was well into his fifties when he first performed the poem, while Dylan was barely twenty, so hearing his voice break as he narrated how "they hung Hezikiah . . . high as a pigeon" provides an astonishingly dramatic moment.

In this fashion, Dylan tailored "Black Cross" into one of his finger-pointing protest songs

B

similar to the originals he was beginning to perform, such as "John Brown" and "Ballad of Hollis Brown"—sympathetic compositions that focused on the violent fate of its primary characters.

Lord Buckley's influence seems to have informed some of Dylan's later work. "Highway 61 Revisited," for instance, takes Buckley's method of hipsemantic translation of familiar story and legend to new levels. A close look at the soft-focus, saturated cover photograph of Dylan's 1965 album *Bringing It All Back Home* reveals another album, *The Best of Lord Buckley*, prominently displayed on the mantelpiece in the background amid the funky but carefully chosen cultural detritus littering the portrait. Additionally, Dylan references Buckley in his obscure 1963 poem "Blowin' in the Wind" (not the famous song) and in his novel *Tarantula*, which he worked on sporadically through the mid- to late 1960s and which was ultimately published in 1971.

For more on Lord Buckley and Joe Newman, visit www.lordbuckley.com or read my book *Dig Infinity!: The Life and Art of Lord Buckley* (Welcome Rain Publishers, 2002) or "Black Cross," an article cowritten with Cleveland radio journalist David C. Barnett in *On the Tracks* magazine #15 (January 15, 1999).

"Black Crow Blues" (Bob Dylan)
Bob Dylan, *Another Side of Bob Dylan* (1964)

A funky little piano blues that Dylan plays in his wonderfully untutored style (his first on a commercial release and one that in some odd way alternately recalls the lilting calypsos of Harry Belafonte and piano boogie-woogies of Meade "Lux" Lewis), "Black Crow Blues" is a slight, if humorous piece of off-the-wall/off-the-cuff surreal stand-up. It proves again Dylan's strong grasp of the idiom—a hitchhikin', on-

the-road deal where the narrator sounds as if he's talking to himself about having left his woman a few towns back. His shifting moods are viewed dispassionately by a flock of black crows in a meadow near the highway down which he trundles. Maybe not the stuff of Poe's "The Raven," but an effective bête noire nonetheless.

"Black Diamond Bay" (Bob Dylan/Jacques Levy)
Bob Dylan, *Desire* (1976)
Various Artists (performed by Ronald Born), *May Your Song Always Be Sung: The Songs of Bob Dylan, Volume 3* (2003)

Combining the cinematic elements of "Lily, Rosemary and the Jack of Hearts" with the sheer comic-book looniness and narrative framing of "Bob Dylan's 115th Dream," "Black Diamond Bay" weaves a circuitous, virtually indecipherable, yet totally engaging shaggy-dog story involving, in no particular order, a woman, a Panama hat, a Greek man, a ring, a soldier, an earthquake, Walter Cronkite, and true love. The song also works as a kind of shady allegory, even if its true subject (or even what is being allegorized) is not immediately evident.

"Black Diamond Bay" is one of those relatively obscure Dylan songs that his adherents love deconstructing. They often point to the 1915 Joseph Conrad novel *Victory*, in which there is a "black diamond bay," a coal port and depot on an island in the Far East. Elements of the novel (the hotel, a volcano, an enigmatic woman) appear in the song, encouraging interpreters to see it as an updated, if very hallucinatory, retelling of the novel and perhaps a dash of some other Conrad as well. Close and repeated listenings to "Black Diamond Bay" also raise questions of viewpoint, for the narrator of the last verse may well not be the same individual who has described the action up until that point. And the black diamond bay itself? Perhaps it is a metaphor for a place that's being destroyed while its inhabitants go about living their meaningless lives even though it is obvious the place is doomed.

Regardless of the song's meaning, Dylan's skills as a storyteller (and cowriter Jacques Levy's) are at a peak in "Black Diamond Bay" as all the characters' lives are woven together, showing the development and transformation of each in a manner that would make the Bard himself proud. And let's not overlook the sharp use of irony as the song ends with the narrator watching the scene on TV, merely dismissing it as "another hard luck story that you're gonna hear."

Great story song or not, "Black Diamond Bay" flows musically in its mysterious evocation of suspicious, *Casablanca*-like doings at an unnamed Caribbean-type island resort. Dylan also manages to stuff it full of his more audacious rhyming schemes, evidenced by the last verse as Dylan and Levy keep all the narrative plates spinning in the air as if they were performing on *The Ed Sullivan Show*.

And for those who heard the song as Dylan's Pilate-like explanation for removing himself from the fray of leftist politics, Robert Shelton offered this comment in *No Direction Home*, his 1986 Dylan biography:

More whimsy surfaces in the "Black Diamond Bay" scenario, where life is again reflected in a card game. Dylan has always loved the shaggy-dog story and the confrontations of the poker game. (Baudelaire, in "Spleen," locked the Jack of Hearts and Queen of Spades in dialogue.) All the bizarre things that happen in "Black Diamond Bay" suddenly appear through a different lens when the perspective shifts in the last verse. The

song's minutely observed action is instantly reduced to a news item the narrator glimpses as he idly watches TV in L.A. Are we all global village idiots whom television has reduced to voyeurism, or has television so deadened us to catastrophe that we can't tell a real crisis from a fictional one?

For those obsessed with Dylan minutiae, *11 X 14*, the best-known film by experimental auteur James Benning, features not one but two single-shot scenes during which the entire song "Black Diamond Bay" plays in the background.

"Blackjack Davey" (Traditional)

aka "Black Jack Davey," "Blackjack Davy," "Black Jack Davy," "Black Jack David," "The Black-Guarded Gypsies," "Gypsy Davy," "Gypsy Laddie," "Gyps of David," "Seven Yellow Gypsies," "Wraggle-Taggle Gypsies"
Bob Dylan, *Good as I Been to You* (1992)
Various Artists (performed by Harry Cox, Jeannie Robertson, Paddy Dorran), *Classic Ballads of Britain and Ireland, Volume 2*/1953, 1960, 1952 (2000)
Jean Ritchie, *British Traditional Folk Songs & Ballads* (1961)
Milt Okun, *Adirondack Folk Songs & Ballads* (1963)
Taj Mahal, *Mo' Roots* (1974)
Bryan Bowers, *View from Home* (1977)
Buell Kazee, *Buell Kazee* (1978)
Cliff Carlisle, *Blues Yodeler and Steel Guitar Wizard/'30s* (1996)
Rebecca Pidgeon, *Four Marys* (1998)
Woody Guthrie, *Woody Guthrie—This Land Is Your Land: Asch Recordings, Volume 1* (1999)

Dylan has written at least a few great songs about the themes of adultery and stolen love ("Lily, Rosemary and the Jack of Hearts" and "Man in the Long Black Coat," to name two), so it is not surprising that he would be attracted to a traditional, minor-chord ballad of a rogue who makes off with a woman (jailbait in some versions, married with children in others) and

B

the devastation that follows—and one that references some high-heeled shoes made of "Spanish leather" at that. That Dylan sang "Blackjack Davey" both early and late in his career says much about where he was going and from whence he had come.

Traditionally, "Blackjack Davey" is a playlet with five speakers: Blackjack Davey, the woman he woos, her husband, a servant, and a narrator. Each gets at least a bit of stage time as the action moves from the woman's home, where Blackjack Davey first seduces her, and through the woods where the husband discovers them "wrapped up" together by the riverbank. It is there that the husband makes one final plea to his young wife to return home with him, promising that all will be forgiven. The last stanza, relayed from the woman's point of the view, shows just how beguiled she is by the spell cast by her demon lover when she sings, "Last night I slept in a feather bed/Between my husband and baby/Tonight I lay on the river banks/In the arms of Blackjack Davey/Love my Blackjack Davey."

Dylan's 1992 acoustic version of this mysterious tale of illicit love and tragedy as released on *Good as I Been to You* (and subsequently performed during his acoustic band sets in 1993) is his definitive one, but the song was in his repertoire in early 1961. In all his renderings, Dylan's fluid movements between the characters' shifting narrative and point of view wring the full drama of this famous song of romance, wanderlust, abandonment, score-settling, and their consequences. He probably learned "Blackjack Davey" from Woody Guthrie's well-known recording of "Gypsy Davy," but it is an old song—actually an American rendition of Child Ballad No. 200—and is also often called "Wraggle-Taggle Gypsies" or "Seven Yellow Gypsies." "Blackjack Davey" is another American spin on the same

story. The piece was not only on Dylan's set lists, either: it was a source of material, with "shoes of Spanish leather" furnishing the focal point of a Dylan song of an almost identical name; and let's not forget, one Gypsy Davy makes a cameo appearance in his "Tombstone Blues."

According to the ballad hunter Francis Child (who published, between 1882 and 1898, a five-volume work titled *The English and Scottish Popular Ballads*), printed versions of "Gypsy Davy" probably date to at least 1720. The first documented printing was in *Tea Table Miscellany* (1740), and "Lady Cassilles Lilt" (aka "Johnny Faa, the Gypsie Laddie") can be found in the so-called Skene Manuscripts, one of the most important Scottish genealogical collections, which contain documents (including music) from the seventeenth century. Variants and alternate titles include "Johnny Faa," "Davy Faw," "The Egyptian Laddie," "The Gypsy Davy," and "Lord Garrick."

The actual history behind "Blackjack Davey" has been traced back to 1624 and the execution, by Scottish officials, of Johnny (or Johnnë) Faa, a Gypsy chieftain. The Gypsies were expelled from Scotland first in 1541 and then again in 1609. But they just couldn't stay away. In 1624 a Johnny Faa (the name was common among the Romany) and seven other men were sentenced to hang, and Helen Faa and ten women were sentenced to be drowned (the women's execution was stayed). Sometime around 1788 this ballad became associated with John, the sixth earl of Cassilis, and his first wife, Lady Jean Hamilton. Before her marriage Lady Jean had been in love with "Johnny Faa, of Dunbar." Years later, after Lady Jean had borne two children, Johnny Faa returned and persuaded her to elope. The couple was caught, however; Johnny Faa and seven Gypsies were hanged, and Lady Jean was banished and confined for life in a tower built for her imprisonment. After the hanging, eight heads, effigies of the Gypsies, were said to have been carved in stone in the tower.

Although Woody Guthrie's recording of "Gypsy Davy" likely introduced Dylan to "Blackjack Davey," there is no doubt that Dylan had heard, learned, and adapted other versions before attempting his own. He probably had come across Cliff Carlisle's recording from the 1930s, for example, which is shorter and less complex than his own. In contrast, Dylan's "Blackjack Davey" is practically identical to that of Mike Seeger's in the 1980s. Seeger's version, in turn, derives from that sung by Almeda Riddle.

[S] **"Black Muddy River"** (Jerry Garcia/Robert Hunter)

The Grateful Dead, *In the Dark* (1987)
Various Artists (performed by Israel Vibration), *Fire on the Mountain, Volume 2* (1996)
Norma Waterson, *Norma Waterson* (1996)

"Black Muddy River" is a Grateful Dead gospel dirge stuffed with biblical and literary allusions. The line "I can't tell my pillow from a stone," for example, recalls the story of Jacob in Genesis, chapter 28 (". . . he took of the stones of that place, and put them for his pillows, and lay down in that place to sleep); the lyric "When I can't hear the song for the singer" echoes a line from Irish poet W. B. Yeats's work "Among School Children" ("How can we know the dancer from the dance?"); and there is an implicit parallel to the river Styx. "Black Muddy River" finds lyricist Robert Hunter with the taste of mortality in his mouth. Deeper rootsologists might note that the song's opening phrase, "When the last rose of summer pricks my finger," references "'Tis the Last Rose of Summer," British poet Thomas Moore's nineteenth-century song that shares a similar elegiac tone with Hunter's in "Black Muddy River." Others might point out that a hint of the Osborne Brothers of bluegrass fame figure in here somewhere too—their song "Roll River Roll" from the 1960s starts with the words "Roll muddy river, roll on," a refrain Hunter utilizes in the chorus of "Black Muddy River." And there may even be a scent of Stephen Foster's "Oh, Susanna" sprinkled in "Black Muddy River" as well.

As Hunter told David Gans (musician, journalist, and host of radio's syndicated *Grateful Dead Hour*) in 1988, "Black Muddy River" was "just an examination of what it's like to be forty-five years old. It's just a good look into the deep dark well, and the heart resonances in that area. And a statement of individual freedom, that no matter what happens, I have this black muddy river to walk by."

Dylan performed "Black Muddy River" at three 1992 shows as a brooding, early-concert dirge, handling the song's tricky melody with the ease of a Deadhead singing the song in the shower, which is to say, not very well. Still, he gives the impression that something meaningful is being imparted.

[S] **"Blessed Be the Name"** (Traditional/William H. Clark/Ralph E. Hudson/William James Kirkpatrick)

aka "Blessed Be Thy Name," "Blessed Is the Name," "Blessed Is the Name of the Lord"
Mississippi John Hurt, *Avalon Blues: The Complete 1928 Okeh Recordings* (1996)
Soul Stirrers, *Shine on Me* (1950)
Pilgrim Travelers, *Best of the Pilgrim Travelers, Volume 1* (1970)
James Hall, *King of Glory* (1995)
Benny Hinn, *Healing* (1998)

Dylan's sole performances of "Blessed Be the Name" transpired during the "born-again" gospel shows of late 1979 and early 1980. The titular phrase first appears in the Bible in Job 1:21, and the hymn itself is a predictable and fairly pedestrian combination of elements from both Testaments.

While some hymnologists regard this piece as a traditional song whose authorship is lost to time and myriad interpreters associate it primarily with the gospel blues, others attribute the lyrics to William H. Clark and the music, added later, to Ralph E. Hudson and William James Kirkpatrick. Biographical information on Clark is hard to come by, but information on the musical composers is not.

Hudson (born July 9, 1843, Napoleon, Ohio; died June 14, 1901, Cleveland), like Walt Whitman, served the Union as a nurse in the American Civil War. He went on to teach music at Mount Vernon College in Alliance, Ohio, and served as a Methodist Episcopal minister in northern Ohio until his death. His most fruitful period transpired in the 1880s with the publication of a series of original sacred song collections: *Salvation* and *Echoes* (1882), *Gems of Gospel Songs* (1884), *Songs of Peace, Love and Joy* (1885), *The Temperance Songster* (1886), and *Songs of the Ransomed* (1887).

Kirkpatrick (born February 27, 1838, Duncannon, Pennsylvania; died September 20, 1921, Germantown, Pennsylvania) grew up in a musical family. In 1854 he went to Philadelphia to study music and learn carpentry, which would be his trade. But music interested him more than mechanics, and soon all his spare time was devoted to its study. At first he aspired to becoming a concert violinist, but when he joined Philadelphia's Wharton Street Methodist Episcopal Church in 1855, sacred music became his exclusive pursuit. As there were few church organs in that day, his violin and cello were in constant demand for choir rehearsals, singing societies, and church programs. During the 1850s he began writing

hymns and anthems and began studying vocal music under a Professor T. Bishop, then a well-known singer of oratorios and ballads. Kirkpatrick's first published composition was "When the Spark of Life Is Waning," which appeared around 1858 in the *Musical Pioneer* in New York. He went on to publish about fifty hymn collections, many in collaboration with John Robson Sweeney. His seriousness in music led Kirkpatrick to join the Harmonia and Handel and Haydn Sacred Music Societies, where the greatest singers of the day performed. This firsthand experience allowed him to become familiar with the principal choral works of the great composers, an exposure that enhanced the depth of his own aesthetic.

■ "Blind Willie McTell" (Bob Dylan)

Bob Dylan, *The Bootleg Series, Volumes 1–3: Rare and Unreleased, 1961–1991/'83* (1991)
Various Artists (performed by Dream Syndicate), *I Shall Be Unreleased/'88* (1991)
The Band (with Champion Jack Dupree), *Jericho* (1993)
Barrence Whitfield, *Hillbilly Voodoo* (1993)
Rick Danko, *In Concert* (1997)
Marty Ehrlich, *Sojourn* (1999)
Bones, *Another Man Done Gone* (2000)
Ian Mathews and Elliott Murphy, *La Terre Commune* (2001)
Various Artists (performed by Black Cat Bone with Mick Taylor), *May Your Song Always Be Sung: The Songs of Bob Dylan, Volume 3* (2003)

An *Infidels* outtake greater than anything on that fine comeback album (and arguably anything else Dylan has *ever* recorded), "Blind Willie McTell" stands as one of Dylan's mid-period masterpieces—an homage to the blues cipher and a personal vision of slavery's dark legacy in American history with more than a nod to "Strange Fruit," Abe Myerpole's song of lynching made famous by Billie Holiday. Featuring Mark Knopfler on guitar with Dylan, the song was first a rumored gem and then a choice piece of bootleg tape filler. But it didn't surface for official public consumption until *The Bootleg Series, Volumes 1–3* was released in 1991. An unreleased electric version recorded during the *Infidels* sessions is also said to be in circulation.

Why the song was left off *Infidels* in the first place is a matter of some speculation. Dylan has said at least twice that he was dissatisfied with the final result, but that explanation seems a bit thin when one considers that excluding "Blind Willie McTell" from *Infidels* in favor of the far lesser fare that did make the cut weakened and forever marred the album for what it woulda, coulda, and shoulda been.

As he has in so many of his notable works, Dylan drew from biblical and American folk-music sources to compose "Blind Willie McTell." Bert Cartwright's article "The Bible in the Lyrics of Bob Dylan: 1985–1990" in *The Telegraph* #38 (spring 1991), for example, points out lyrical and thematic allusions to 2 Kings 24:10–16, 2 Peter 2:6, and 1 Peter 2:3. From the American folk idiom Dylan borrows the St. James Hotel (a brothel or a morgue also known in song as the St. James Infirmary, depending on the source) in name and tune, further coloring the thematic sensibility of enslavement. While he may also be alluding to a real St. James Hotel in Minneapolis (there's another in Red Wing, Minnesota), the "St. James Infirmary" appears in a number of jazz, blues, folk, and cowboy songs—if not in the very title, then as a location, nearly always representing a Last Chance Café—the bottom of the heap. In any case, these many related songs seem to derive from "The Unfortunate Rake," a British ballad, and a 1960 Folkways LP by that title, produced by Kenneth S. Goldstein, documents the folk process for these song variations.

Blind Willie McTell playing 12-string guitar, ca. 1925.
(Photo: Frank Driggs Collection/Getty Images)

The first lines of "Blind Willie McTell" ("Seen the arrow on the doorpost/Saying 'This land is condemned/All the way from New Orleans/To Jerusalem'") introduce the song's interwoven thematic and inspirational cores, the Bible and slavery, as they recall the Old Testament's Exodus and stations on the Underground Railroad, which had arrows painted on their doorposts as a secret code to runaway slaves—explicitly and unconsciously making the connection with the blood of lambs on the Israelites' doors on the first Passover. Dylan implies that both lands—the biblical Egypt and the slaveholding South—were damned.

The song goes on to metaphorically paint a kaleidoscopic, profoundly impressionistic portrait of the black experience in America in a series of vivid, somber images—a veritable Hieronymus Bosch of a country-gospel folk blues, with everything from slavery to minstrelsy to revivalism and prophecy rearranged into a vision as important as anything in Dylan's canon. "Chain gangs," "charcoal gypsy maidens," "barren trees," "big plantations burning," "cracking whips," "ghosts of slavery ships," "tribes a-moaning," "the undertaker's bell"—these are mind-breaths that can, and should, take the listener to some difficult places.

After four verses of such imagery, Dylan's paraphrase of 1 Peter finishes the song in more concrete surroundings, from a vantage point "gazing out the window/Of the St. James Hotel"—we all want Heaven, "but power and greed and corruptible seed/Seem to be all that there is"; he pulls images from the black experience, from the South, and into each of our presents. Yet still, despite what our individual hardships may be, Dylan reminds us at the end of each verse—and at the end of the song— that "nobody can sing the blues/Like Blind Willie McTell."

Perhaps more than anything else, "Blind Willie McTell" and Dylan's covers of McTell's "Broke Down Engine" and "Delia" on *World Gone Wrong* were responsible for reviving recent interest in McTell's legacy. McTell (born May 5, 1901, Thompson, Georgia; died August 19, 1959, Almon, Georgia) is the grand poohbah of the Atlanta blues school of the 1920s and 1930s, and his astonishing fluidity on twelve-string guitar helped to define the ragtime-influenced Southeast and Piedmont guitar styles of the era. The twelve-string was popular among Atlanta musicians, but particularly useful to McTell for the extra volume it provided when he plied his trade singing on the streets. His exploitation of his instrument's res-

onance and percussive qualities on his dance tunes was even more notable, considering his remarkably delicate touch on slow blues. His distinctive thin, nasal voice gave his music a ghostly quality, a potent ingredient when combined with his demonic abilities on the guitar.

McTell recorded prolifically and cut grooves for many labels under a variety pseudonyms from 1927 to 1956. The blues, of course, are what McTell is remembered for, but he recorded rags, ballads, pop tunes, and folk numbers as well; he also recorded sacred and secular duets with his wife, Kate, in 1935. Though he was never a commercial success, his influence on Atlanta locals and both black and white musicians from points beyond the horizon was important. The Allman Brothers Band, for example, recorded and still open many of their shows with searing versions of McTell's signature song, "Statesboro Blues."

As with many sightless bluesmen, McTell's blindness is the cause for some debate among bluestorians. Some claim he was born sightless, while other sources insist that he lost his vision as a teenager. Regardless, it is well established that McTell had been blind for a number of years when he began recording, and that he had attended several schools for the blind, where he learned to read Braille. He learned how to play guitar from his mother, and when she died he joined up with the traveling medicine shows popular at the time on the carnival circuits. As time passed, though, Atlanta's storied Decatur Street was where he could usually be found, busking for tips and spare change with his old running buddy Curly Weaver. Around Atlanta, he developed his performance style at house parties and fish fries, where he sharpened the dramatic guitar stylings evident on his first records for Victor and Columbia in 1927 and 1928.

McTell recorded regularly until 1932 but

sporadically (and some say less effectively) after that, skirting contractual obligations by adopting various monikers—such as Blind Sammie and Georgia Bill—for studio sessions. Under his own name, there was a memorable Chicago date for Decca in 1935 and an important recording for John Lomax's Folk Song Archive of the Library of Congress five years later, both of which feature him discussing his life and his music and playing a variety of material. These records offer priceless insight into the art of one of the true blues greats.

With the end of World War II came another committed stab at commercial viability for Atlantic and Regal Records, but McTell failed to attract much attention and returned to the street corners for his sustenance. He made his final recordings in 1956 at a session arranged by a record-shop manager. Perhaps the roustabout life led to a more introspective vision of himself, as his recordings of the 1940s and early 1950s found him moving in the direction of spirituals. But McTell proved to be as commanding as ever even in his later work, some of which ranks among his best. The Blues Foundation inducted him into its Hall of Fame in 1981.

The Band began covering "Blind Willie McTell" as a stinging electric blues in the early 1990s, but Dylan didn't touch it in performance until the summer of 1997. Rendered as a rapturous electric psychedelic blues, it was an instant concert highlight. In an artful irony, Dylan originally recorded (coincidentally or not) "Blind Willie McTell" on what would have been its subject's eighty-second birthday.

Ⓐ *Blonde on Blonde*

Columbia Records LP C2L-41, CD CK-841, CS CS2-841; Sony Music Entertainment, Inc., SACD 90325. Recorded October 20, November 30, and December 1, 1965; January 21, 24, 25; February 14–17; and March 8–9, 1966. Released May 16, 1966. Produced by Bob Johnston. Album photography by Jerry Schatzberg.

Bob Dylan—guitar, harmonica, piano, keyboards, vocals. Al Kooper—organ, guitar, horn, keyboards. Robbie Robertson—guitar, vocals. Joe South—guitar. Rick Danko—bass, violin, vocals. Bill Atkins—keyboards. Wayne Butler—trombone. Kenny Buttrey—drums. Paul Griffin—piano. Garth Hudson—keyboards, saxophone. Jerry Kennedy—guitar. Sandy Konikoff—drums. Richard Manuel—drums, keyboards, vocals. Wayne Moss—guitar, vocals. Hargus "Pig" Robbins—piano, keyboards. Henry Strzelecki—bass. Charlie McCoy—bass, guitar, harmonica, trumpet.

"Rainy Day Women #12 & 35," "Pledging My Time," "Visions of Johanna," "One of Us Must Know (Sooner or Later)," "I Want You," "Stuck Inside of Mobile (with the Memphis Blues Again)," "Leopard-Skin Pill-Box Hat," "Just Like a Woman," "Most Likely You Go Your Way (and I'll Go Mine)," "Temporary Like Achilles," "Absolutely Sweet Marie," "4th Time Around," "Obviously Five Believers," "Sad-Eyed Lady of the Lowlands"

"The closest I ever got to the sound I hear in my mind was on individual bands in the *Blonde on Blonde* album. It's that thin, that wild mercury sound. It's metallic and bright gold, with whatever that conjures up. That's my particular sound."

That oft-quoted statement made by Dylan to Ron Rosenbloom of *Playboy* magazine in 1978 is as good an introduction as any to one of Dylan's true masterpieces. *Blonde on Blonde* is a monument to the Dylan muse and everything a great work of art, rock 'n' roll, or otherwise, should be: profound, poetic, irreverent, funny, expressive, and diverse . . . the list could go on forever. If Dylan had never recorded another note, this would have turned him into a myth instead of merely an icon—and still might yet. It is a collection for the ages: rare is the person, be they musician, poet, Wall Street arbitrageur,

B

postdebutante, or grease monkey, who comes away unaffected by *Blonde on Blonde.*

The two-disc release (rock's first double album) closed Dylan's mid-1960s rock 'n' roll trilogy, which began with *Bringing It All Back Home,* accelerated to light speed with *Highway 61 Revisited,* and imploded in the black hole of *Blonde on Blonde.* From the outset, *Blonde on Blonde* is unique. Its title is, at least, a riff on Bertolt Brecht's *Brecht on Brecht,* a rather literary touch for rock 'n' roll at the time. And let's not forget that the first letter of each word in the title form an anagram that spells the word "Bob." But that is not readily apparent, as the cover carries neither the artist's name nor the album's title, but has its blurry, brownish photo of a wild-haired Dylan printed sideways, such that the album could be opened for a body-length portrait of the artist as a chaos-embracing young man. Something was definitely going on here, but what?

Investigation of that question is well paid by listening to what is within. Painting portraits in word and sound that range from the kiss-off ("One of Us Must Know [Sooner or Later]") to tortured love ("Just Like a Woman"), from "I sing the body electric" Walt Whitman–style visionary introspection ("Visions of Johanna") to sly parody ("4th Time Around"), from wild blues-rock ("Leopard-Skin Pill-Box Hat") to Beat Generation–style storytelling ("Memphis Blues Again"), from still-weirdly-murky-even-after-all-these-years ("Sad-Eyed Lady of the Lowlands") to farcical existentialist polka ("Rainy Day Women #12 & 35"), Dylan crafted a humid masterpiece that simply gets better with the passage of time. Savor it like a vintage wine. On *Blonde on Blonde,* the bitterness evident on much of the previous two albums was transmuted into humor, absurdity, and even hints of compassion. *Blonde on Blonde* is a gush of Dylan wordplay, endlessly

inventive and overflowing with razor-sharp wit and an overwhelming world-weariness.

Adding to the mythic aura of *Blonde on Blonde* is the mostly on-the-fly nature of its creation. With the exception of a tune or two, Dylan reportedly wrote most of the album in his Nashville hotel room or on site at the studio while the musicians played cards.

If *Highway 61 Revisited* reinvented garage rock, *Blonde on Blonde* threw that sound into a cauldron of neon saltwater taffy that blends blues, country, rock, and folk into a careening and dense sound. That sound can be traced to Robbie Robertson and his intense, weaving guitar, and the crack session musicians who fill in the myriad nuances that make this a set of songs that could have a whole wing of the Louvre devoted to them. An album of enormous depth and jest, providing infinite lyrical and musical revelations on each play, *Blonde on Blonde* presents a musical and poetic theater of the absurd laced with biting guitar riffs, translucent organ figures, sharp pianos, and even woozy brass bands. It's the jewel in the crown of Dylan's early electric rock 'n' roll period.

Though it was the first of four consecutive albums Dylan recorded in Nashville, *Blonde on Blonde* is nearly free of any country twang. As critic Dave Marsh once wrote, the album was "rock 'n' roll at the farthest edge imaginable, [with] instrumentalists and singer all peering into a deeper abyss than anyone had previously imagined existed."

ⓢ "Blood in My Eyes" (Traditional/Lonnie Chatmon)
See also "World Gone Wrong"
aka "I've Got Blood in My Eyes for You"
Bob Dylan, *World Gone Wrong* (1993)
Mississippi Sheiks, *Complete Recorded Works, Volume 3* (1991)

Dylan pays homage to the Mississippi Sheiks with his dark reading of "Blood in My Eyes,"

American blues guitarist Bo Carter (right) and members of his band the Mississippi Sheiks, ca. 1920s.

(Photo: Frank Driggs Collection/Getty Images)

about a take-no-prisoners visit to a prostitute. The Sheiks cut the tune at an October 25, 1931, field recording by Columbia as "I've Got Blood in My Eyes for You." It is thought that Dylan probably learned "Blood in My Eyes" shortly before he recorded it in the early 1990s, as the song had been out of print for many years.

The Mississippi Sheiks (the name taken from Rudolph Valentino's 1921 movie *The Sheik* and correctly pronounced "shakes") were a standard-setting string band popular from the mid-1920s and mid-1930s. Led by fiddler Lonnie Chatmon and his brothers Armenter (aka "Bo" Carter) and Sam along with a floating amalgam of musicians, the Sheiks mixed country music with the blues fiddle in a stylistic repertoire that sometimes skirted on the salacious, with deliciously suggestive titles like "Banana in Your Fruit Basket," "Pin in Your Cushion," and "Your Biscuits Are Big Enough for Me." The Chatmons, by the way, were the nephews of Charley Patton. "Sitting on Top of the World" was their big hit, selling in the millions to both blacks and whites.

Maybe Muddy Waters eulogized the Sheiks best when he remembered, "I knowed the Mississippi Sheiks. Yessir. Walked ten miles to see them play. They was high-time . . . makin' them good records, man."

Dylan's only performances of "Blood in My Eyes" came at two of the four November 1993 Supper Club shows in New York City and, marked by sideman Bucky Baxter's thick Dobro playing, were true to his dire treatment of the song on *World Gone Wrong.* Also, Eurythmics frontman Dave Stewart directed a video of the song featuring Dylan, garbed as a top-hatted dandy, strolling through London's Chelsea neighborhood.

ⓐ *Blood on the Tracks*

Columbia Records LP PC-33235, CD CK-33235, CS JCT-33235; Sony Music Entertainment, Inc., SACD 90323. Recorded September 16–25, 1974, in New York City, and December 27–30, 1974, in Minneapolis. Released January 17, 1975. Produced by Bob Dylan (uncredited). Engineered by Phil Ramone. Album notes by Pete Hamill. Album photography by Paul Till. Album art by David Oppenheim.

Bob Dylan—guitar, harmonica, keyboards, vocals. Tony Brown—bass. Buddy Cage—steel guitar. Paul Griffin—organ. Eric Weissberg—banjo, guitar. Charlie Brown—guitar. Bill Berg—drums. Barry Kornfeld—guitar. Richard Crooks—guitar. Gregg Inhofer—keyboards. Tom McFaul—keyboards. Ken Odegard—guitar. Bill Peterson—bass. Chris Weber—guitar. Billy Preston—bass.

"Tangled Up in Blue," "Simple Twist of Fate," "You're a Big Girl Now," "Idiot Wind," "You're Gonna Make Me Lonesome When You Go," "Meet Me in the Morning," "Lily, Rosemary and the Jack of Hearts," "If You See Her, Say Hello," "Shelter from the Storm," "Buckets of Rain"

A Bob Dylan masterpiece, *Blood on the Tracks* is a great, tormented, bittersweet collection of songs that are arranged with such care and sung with such devotion that a psycho-spiritual folk gestalt is created.

Whether wistfully putting the pieces of a life back together ("Tangled Up in Blue"), singing the blues ("Meet Me in the Morning"), looking upward ("You're Gonna Make Me Lonesome When You Go"), ruing karma ("Simple Twist of Fate"), vengefully pointing a finger ("Idiot Wind"), or simply telling a mighty fine yarn ("Lily, Rosemary and the Jack of Hearts"), Dylan lays his life as bare as he ever has or will—no matter what he says publicly.

Generally regarded as a desperate plea to his wife, Sara, Dylan has slowly obscured the circumstances behind these remarkable songs, once even claiming that his conception and execution of the album was influenced more by a newfound interest in painting than by marital discord. Painting might certainly have played a role; songs, particularly "Tangled Up in Blue," are rife with splashes of imagery and eschew conventional narrative.

Still, it nevertheless seems that Dylan was in such extreme distress that reaching out through his music was his only way of keeping himself together. But the jagged, emotional turmoil that runs throughout the record is always near the surface. As he admitted to Mary Travers in a 1975 radio show: "A lot of people tell me they enjoy that album. It's hard for me to relate to that. I mean, people enjoying that kind of pain."

The circumstances behind the recording of *Blood on the Tracks* is legendary. Dylan cut the album in the early autumn of 1974 in New York City with a band composed mostly of Eric Weissberg and Deliverance. As the album went into production and was primed for release that winter, Dylan began to have some serious second thoughts as he celebrated the holidays with his family in Minnesota. A few phone calls later, he found himself in a Minneapolis recording studio with a pickup band he had never laid eyes on ready to rerecord the album. The results of those sessions were peppier versions of the songs recorded in New York. Some of these later recordings were combined with material from the earlier session to produce the final gestalt. While some believe that the New York material is superior (a few of the alternate tracks and outtakes have officially surfaced over the years on *Biograph* and *The Bootleg Series, Volumes 1–3*), it is hard to imagine *Blood on the Tracks* in any other configuration than the one with which the world has long become accustomed.

Despite, or maybe because of, the naked pain and its brilliant, crystalline expression, *Blood on the Tracks* became, with *Planet Waves*, Dylan's second No. 1 album in two years. It remained numero uno for two weeks running and on the charts for fourteen weeks in all, eventually earning Dylan his fifth platinum record in 1989. It will always be cited as one of his finest works and one of the best albums ever made, even if it didn't achieve the widespread influence of his earlier work.

The front-cover art, with its red-wine-colored ambiance, appears to be a pointillist portrait of the recording artist in profile, in keeping with Dylan's interest in painting. His classes at New York City's Art Students League have been viewed by some as a window into his crafting of the *Blood on the Tracks* songs. Yet further inspection of the album credits the image as a photo taken by Paul Till. Early pressings included equally impressionistic liner notes by Pete Hamill, which won the New York journalist and novelist a Grammy Award. Later editions replaced the liner notes with an abstract painting by David Oppenheim on the back cover; still later editions carry both.

Blood on the Tracks remains a stunning, mature statement in which Dylan fuses the conflicting elements and uncertainties of life with the virtues of kindness and generosity. In offering some of the most intense music of his career, the album would be a standard, if not *the* standard, against which all his subsequent work would be measured.

Final notes: *Blood on the Tracks* excited such interest that *Rolling Stone*, in an unprecedented move, devoted its entire review section to the release. Also, *A Simple Twist of Fate*, a 2004 book by Andy Gill and Keith Odegard (guitarist from the Minneapolis sessions), tells a complete story of the album's making.

▣ "Blowin' in the Wind" (Bob Dylan)
aka "Blowing in the Wind"
Bob Dylan, single (1963); *The Freewheelin' Bob Dylan* (1963); *Bob Dylan's Greatest Hits* (1967); *Before the*

Flood (1974); *Bob Dylan at Budokan* (1979); *Biograph* (1985); *The Bootleg Series, Volume 5: Live 1975—The Rolling Thunder Revue* (2002)

Various Artists (performed by Bob Dylan), *Evening Concerts at Newport, Volume 1/'63* (1964); *The Concert for Bangladesh* (1971); *God Bless America* (2001)

Bob Dylan/Various Artists (performed by Stevie Wonder), *Bob Dylan: The 30th Anniversary Concert Celebration* (1993)

Various Artists (performed by the New World Singers), *Broadside Ballads, Volume 1* (1962); *The Best of Broadside 1962–1988* (2000)

Peter, Paul & Mary, *In the Wind* (1963); *In Concert* (1964); *Ten Years Together* (1970); *Holiday Celebration* (1988); *Around the Campfire* (1998)

Bobby Darin, *Golden Folk Hits* (1963); *As Long as I'm Singing: The Bobby Darin Collection* (1995)

Stan Getz, *Reflections* (1963)

Chad Mitchell, *Blowin' in the Wind* (1963); *Chad Mitchell Trio Collection* (1997)

Ray Bryant, *Live at Basin Street* (1964)

Sam Cooke, *Sam Cooke at the Copa* (1964); *Man Who Invented Soul* (1968)

Glen Campbell, *Astounding 12-String Guitar* (1964)

Marianne Faithfull, *Come My Way* (1965); *Music for the Millions* (1985)

Dick Dale, *Live at Ciro's* (1965)

Trini Lopez, *Folk Album* (1965)

Walter Jackson, *Welcome Home* (1965)

Dannie Richmond, *In Jazz for the Culture Set* (1965)

The Silkie, *You've Got to Hide Your Love Away* (1965)

Pete Seeger, *Little Boxes & Other Broadsides* (1965)

King Curtis, *Live at Smalls Paradise* (1966)

New Christy Minstrels, *New Kick* (1966); *Very Best of the New Christy Minstrels* (1996)

Lou Donaldson, *Blowing in the Wind* (1966)

Earl Scruggs, *Changin' Times* (1969)

Joan Baez, *From Every Stage* (1976); *European Tour* (1981); *Rare, Live & Classic* (1993); *The Essential Joan Baez: From the Heart—Live* (2001)

Stevie Wonder, *Anthology* (1977); *Greatest Hits, Volume 1* (1979)

B

The Hollies, *Other Side of the Hollies* (1978); *Long Cool Woman* (1979)

Ray Conniff, *Always in My Heart* (1978)

Chet Atkins, *Solid Gold Guitar* (1982)

Leontyne Price, *God Bless America* (1982)

Golden Throats, *Golden Throats: The Great Celebrity Sing Off* (1988)

Kingston Trio, *Tom Dooley* (1989)

Mormon Tabernacle Choir, *Songs from America's Heartland* (1991)

The Searchers, *30th Anniversary Collection* (1992)

Richard Dworsky, *Back to the Garden* (1992)

Tyson Moses Jr., *I Made Up My Mind* (1992)

Lorie Line, *Beyond a Dream* (1992)

Apple, *Neither Victims nor Executioners* (1994)

Judy Collins, *Live at Newport* (1994); *Both Sides Now* (1998)

Gospel Hummingbirds, *Taking Flight* (1995)

Johnny Rivers, *Rocks the Folks* (1996)

Lester Flatt and Earl Scruggs, *1964–1969, Plus* (1996)

Elvis Presley, *Platinum (A Life in Music)* (1997); *Touch of Platinum* (1998)

The Brothers Four, *Greenfields and Other Gold* (1997)

Steve Alaimo, *Anthology* (1997)

Edwin Hawkins, *Very Best of the Edwin Hawkins Singers* (1998)

Ted Hawkins, *Love You Most of All* (1998)

Duane Eddy, *Duane Does Dylan* (1998)

Various Artists (performed by Low), *Duluth Does Dylan* (2001)

Todd Rubenstein, *The String Quartet Tribute to Bob Dylan* (2003)

Various Artists (performed by the Abyssinians), *Blowin' in the Wind: A Reggae Tribute to Bob Dylan* (2003)

It's hard to name a song that was more vital to Dylan's career than "Blowin' in the Wind." Thanks in large part to this one song, it is now virtually axiomatic that Dylan changed the face of popular music. To put it plainly, "Blowin' in the Wind" put Bob Dylan and America's youth culture on the map with a statement that easily stands at the pinnacle of the modern protest song.

With a simple melody and subtle, questioning lyrics, "Blowin' in the Wind" struck chords deep within both the civil rights and nascent antiwar movements of the early 1960s, giving widespread voice to sentiments that until then had rarely before been explicitly articulated in popular music. Even now, more than forty years since the song's composition and after millions of renditions by innumerable singers around the world, the queries Dylan raises in it don't appear as if they are going to be answered anytime soon. Each verse includes three rhetorical questions that cut to the marrow of injustice and ends with a Taoist koan presenting the clarity of the only true answer. Perhaps they can never be answered properly—and therein lies their brilliance and the secret of the song's effectiveness.

Dylan's first comments on the song were found in the *Freewheelin'* liner notes. "The first way to answer these questions in the song," he suggests, "is by asking them. But lots of people have to first find the wind."

In the October–November 1962 issue of *Sing Out!*, he went a few steps further: "There ain't too much I can say about this song except that the answer is blowing in the wind. It ain't in no book or movie or TV show or discussion group. Man, it's in the wind—and it's blowing in the wind. Too many of these hip people are telling me where the answer is, but oh, I won't believe that. I still say it's in the wind and just like a restless piece of paper, it's got to come down some time . . . I still say that some of the biggest criminals are those that turn their heads away when they see wrong and know it's wrong. I'm only 21 years old and I know that there's been too many wars . . . You people over 21 should know better . . . 'cause after all, you're older and smarter."

Even with Dylan's trademark stamp, this song for the ages could have been spoken by the ancient sages—it seems to have been around at least that long. The song caught some early flak from the political left for asking but not answering questions, but Dylan was more troubled by the accusation, eventually refuted, that he hadn't even written the song.

"Blowin' in the Wind" was not only a popular success, but Dylan's first major commercial success as well. By the time Dylan's own version of the song was released, it had already been a major hit for Peter, Paul & Mary.

The melodic roots of "Blowin' in the Wind" can be found in another song Dylan was performing at the time he wrote it, a traditional plaint from the slavery era entitled "No More Auction Block," which was recorded by, among others, Paul Robeson and Odetta, the latter from whom Dylan most likely learned it. A Dylan performance of this piece can be heard on *The Bootleg Series, Volumes 1–3.*

"Blowin' in the Wind" has been a constant in Dylan's set lists throughout his career, though arrangements have varied tremendously. The song was probably incubating in Dylan's mind before he first performed it at a Monday-night hootenanny at Gerde's Folk City in April 1962, in a debut notable for the newly penned lyrics, which were taped to the mic, the ink evidently still drying. In the early and mid-1960s, it appeared as an earnest crowd-pleasing solo acoustic performance. When he returned to the stage in 1974 with the Band, "Blowin' in the Wind" was reinvented as an electrified howl. Two years later, on the Rolling Thunder Revue, he was performing clipped acoustic duets of the song with Joan Baez. In the 1980s it was presented as either a majestic electric display or as an acoustic whisper. By the late 1990s and early aughts, Dylan had shed "Blowin' in the Wind" of all its folky contours and transformed it into a weary elegy short of self-righteousness—a sort of bluegrass song that might

work in either a sacred-harp church choir, sporting a new three-part harmony chorus, or even in a barroom as a drunken lament, with guitars a-chimin'.

"Blue Bonnet Girl" (Glenn Spencer)
Sons of the Pioneers, *Tumbling Tumbleweeds* (1997)

Dylan's only performance of "Blue Bonnet Girl," a song sung by a guy pining for a kiss under the Texas moon, came at a Never Ending Tour stop in Bloomington, Indiana, the night after Halloween 2000 as a sort of after-the-fact trick-or-treat surprise. Here his band sounded like a barbershop quartet in an arrangement of the song that would have fit in just fine on *"Love and Theft."* Glenn Spencer wrote the song in 1936 for the Sons of the Pioneers, of which his brother, Tim, was a member. Years before, during his *Basement Tapes* phase with the Hawks in 1967, Dylan covered "Cool Water," another famous piece of business written by Bob Nolan, one of the Sons of the Pioneers' founding fathers.

"Blue Moon" (Lorenz Hart/Richard Rodgers)
Bob Dylan, *Self Portrait* (1970)
Dizzy Gillespie and Roy Eldridge, *Roy and Diz* (1954)
Clifford Brown, *Brownie: The Complete EmArcy Recordings* (1954)
Elvis Presley, *Elvis Presley* (1956)
Ella Fitzgerald, *Sings the Rodgers and Hart Songbook* (1956)
Sha Na Na, *Sha Na Na* (1971)
Stéphane Grappelli, *Vintage 1981* (1981)
Frank Sinatra, *Concepts* (1992)

In some kind of warped neo–Rudy Vallee bit (or auditioning for the part of the world's premier Elvis impersonator), Dylan turns crooner for *Self Portrait*'s "Blue Moon," an exercise made no easier by the inclusion of a female chorus. Though never performed by Dylan in

Richard Rodgers seated at the piano with Lorenz Hart at right, 1936.

(Photo: *New York World-Telegram and Sun* Collection/Library of Congress)

concert, the song had been in his consciousness many years before the *Self Portrait* sessions: a fragment of "Blue Moon" (presumably learned from an Elvis record and sung by Robert Zimmerman into an old wire recorder in Hibbing, Minnesota, circa late 1950s) was one of four songs preserved from a home teenage session with his friend John Bucklen and that appeared in a BBC musical and sociocultural documentary about Highway 61—the actual road, not the Dylan song or album of the same name.

The tune that became "Blue Moon" was composed by the team of Richard Rodgers and Lorenz Hart in 1933. With different lyrics, it was called "Make Me a Film Star" (some sources say "Prayer") and was to have been sung by Jean Harlow in the film *Hollywood Revue of 1933.* That project was scrapped, and Hart changed the lyrics and retitled the song "The Bad in Every Man" for Shirley Ross for the 1934 film *Manhattan Melodrama.*

Hart changed the lyrics a third and final time, producing "Blue Moon." It hit paydirt— the only Rodgers and Hart hit not specifically associated with a stage production or film. When Hollywood got around to making *Words and Music,* the 1948 Rodgers and Hart biopic, Mel Tormé sang "Blue Moon" in a cameo turn.

Elvis recorded "Blue Moon" in July 1954 at Sun Studios, and his 1956 single enjoyed a seventeen-week stay on *Billboard*'s Top 100 chart, peaking at No. 55. *Viva Las Vegas,* the King's 1964 film costarring Ann-Margret, included a short instrumental version of the song. Other films in which it appeared: *At the Circus* (1939), with Harpo Marx playing it, appropriately, on the harp, and *An American Werewolf in London* (1981), in which Bobby Vinton's version was used as the opening theme.

Richard Rodgers (born June 28, 1902, Arverne, New York; died December 30, 1979, New York City), perhaps the most crucial figure in twentieth-century American popular music, was responsible for more than a few of the most well-loved songs in the canon. With lyricists Lorenz Hart and, later, Oscar Hammerstein II, his two best-known collaborators, he created such perennial favorites as *Pal Joey*, *Oklahoma!*, *South Pacific*, *The Sound of Music*, *Carousel*, and *The King and I*—perhaps the six most popular American musicals ever.

When he was but sixteen he met the twenty-three-year-old Lorenz Hart (born May 2, 1895, New York City; died November 22, 1943, New York City) and began a collaboration with a single, focused mission: to reinvent popular music by supplying songs with poetic lyrics replacing the banality they felt had taken over the art form. That their partnership lasted nearly a quarter of a century is some kind of testament to the success of their vision.

An ace librettist, Hart created lyrics notable for their shimmering utilization of inner and multisyllabic rhymes and a misanthropic edge disguised by a veneer of lighthearted superficiality. He seems to have cast a pretty cold eye on life—and it on him: his alcoholism led to mental illness, and he died of double pneumonia.

As for Rodgers: who says there are no second acts in America? Rodgers and Hart was a successful team, but Rodgers and Hammerstein was a keeper. If Rodgers and Hart modeled their songs on the limited vocal and emotional range of Tin Pan Alley, Rodgers and Hammerstein expanded the song form beyond the symmetry of four phrases in thirty-two bars. With Oscar Hammerstein II (born July 12, 1895, New York City; died August 23, 1960, Doylestown, Pennsylvania), the shows and hits continued to flow, flower, and flourish. *Oklahoma!*, for example, has been called the first American vernacular opera, won the Pulitzer Prize for drama, enjoyed more than 2,200 Broadway performances, and changed American musicals forever.

Not only do many of its songs remain in the popular lexicon, its merging of song, dance, and drama reconfigured the contour of the art form. Additionally, Agnes de Mille modeled the show's choreography on American square dance and replaced the hackneyed chorus girls and production numbers of musical comedy that had become so entrenched.

Hammerstein died in 1960 and Rodgers began a slow physical and artistic decline. Recent scholarship, specifically *Somewhere for Me* (New York: Alfred A. Knopf, 2001), a warts-and-all biography of Rodgers written by his daughter Meryle Secrest, runs contrary to the bon vivant of his public image. Despite thirty-nine musicals and some nine hundred songs under his belt, Rodgers was never a happy man. Rather, he was a horrendously depressed alcoholic whose retreat to the bottle runs counter to the jubilant emotion of his work.

As for "blue moon": the term is generally used to denote "a very long time" and its origin has come under some recent scrutiny. As popularly understood, a blue moon is the second full moon in a calendar month. In most years, there are twelve full moons, one in each month. But when there are thirteen full moons in a year, one month gets the "blue" one. It doesn't happen all that often, and it isn't actually blue in color, though it's possible that dust particles in the atmosphere can make it appear so, just as with any other moon. We could as accurately call it "another white moon" but, musically speaking, we'd be the poorer for it.

However, according to *Sky and Telescope* magazine, there's been a terrible misunderstanding due to an overly simplified definition of blue moons that appeared in a 1946 issue. The magazine's editors, firm adherents of the better-late-than-never approach, ran a correction in the May 1999 issue. In fact, what that long-ago definition *should* have said was that a blue moon is the third full moon of a season in which four appear, if thirteen full moons appear in a twelve-month period. Got that, astronomers?

B

[S] **"Blue Moon of Kentucky"** (Bill Monroe)

Bill Monroe, *Essential Bill Monroe (1945–1949)* (1992)
Elvis Presley, *The Sun Sessions/'54* (1976)
George Jones, *Blue Moon of Kentucky* (1966)
Patsy Cline, *Last Sessions* (1985)
Paul McCartney, *Unplugged (The Official Bootleg)* (1991)
Hot Tuna, *Live at Sweetwater 2* (1993)

That high, lonesome sound. You can hear it in that voice a-callin' in the pines. It's that Orange Blossom Special comin' round the bend. That pitched honeydew whine whistling from the hickory-flavored moonshine still under the blue moon of Kentucky there in the indigo heavens as God's lanterns flicker into view. The hound dog bayin' in the magnolia fields. The hoofs of a Derby champ churning turf on the backstretch at Churchill Downs. The copper kettle boiling on another frigid eighth of January. You can hear it, can't you? Oh, just listen. There's the thump of a bass fiddle, there's the strum of a cheap blue guitar, and the bright, happy twang of a banjo. Something's missing, though; oh, there it is: the thin, wild mercury of an F-style Martin mandolin popping wheelies and darting like a cosmic firefly through the layers of sound. Where did it come from? Was it the Blue Hill Mountains, Scotland, or Venus? No one seems to be quite sure. But they all agree that without Bill Monroe, it would sound a whole lot different. Bill Monroe? You know him, don'tcha? The Homer of Bluegrass? The Einstein of the mandolin? Well, if the name doesn't exactly ring a bell, you've probably come across his musical progeny. Johnny Cash, Garth Brooks—heck, even the good ol' Grateful Dead owe more

Bill Monroe, American bluegrass innovator, ca. 1960s.

(From the John Edwards Memorial Collection #30003, Southern Folklife Collection, Wilson Library, University of North Carolina at Chapel Hill)

than a little something to that austere man under a white Stetson hat, the miles on his face etched like a road map to his soul.

"Blue Moon of Kentucky" is a song that works on a deep spiritual level as the singer invokes the orb's power to guide a departed lover back into his arms. The song was written in the 1940s and had its widest national exposure when it appeared on the B-side of Elvis's first hit single, "That's Alright, Mama," in 1954.

According to the Monroe legend, "Blue Moon of Kentucky" was written when he was on tour. Driving back from Florida, he saw a large full moon rising above the highway. Reminded of the moons he had seen back home in Kentucky, Monroe was inspired to write about it, using music's best poetic device: put a gal in the song. In this wistful waltz with lyrics full of sad resignation, the singer calls on the moon to shine upon his false lover. He wishes, of course, that he could have a second chance with her.

A spectacular singer, mandolin virtuoso, and author of more than five hundred songs, Bill Monroe (born William Smith Monroe, September 13, 1911, Rosine, Kentucky; died September 9, 1996, Springfield, Tennessee) helped lay the foundation of modern country music and is the universally recognized grand-pappy of bluegrass music. Dylan once described Monroe's music by saying, "That's what America is all about."

For those who think that a white mandolin player from Kentucky can't wax just as mystical as a mojo-minded black bluesman from the Mississippi Delta, check out Bill Monroe's idea of the creative process: "I never wrote a tune in my life. All that music's in the air around you all the time. I was just the first one to reach up and pull it out."

Bob Dylan's only performances of "Blue Moon of Kentucky" came as encore duets with Paul Simon during their summer 1999 tour.

The Blues Project/Various Artists
Elektra Records LP EKL/EKS 7264. Released 1964.

Credited as Bob Landy (that's "Dylan" spelled inside out), Dylan contributed some piano licks on "Downtown Blues," a track from this early anthology of the Greenwich Village folk-blues scene. The disc includes appearances from the likes of Dave Van Ronk, Eric von Schmidt, Geoff Muldaur, John Sebastian, Mark Spoelstra, and David Blue, among others, but should not be confused with the loose musical amalgam of the same name spearheaded a few years later by Danny Kalb, who also appears on this album.

"Blue Suede Shoes" (Carl Perkins)
See also "Champaign, Illinois," "Matchbox"
Carl Perkins, *Up Through the Years, 1954–1957* (1986)
Elvis Presley, *Elvis Presley* (1956)
Charlie Rich, *That's Rich* (1965)
John Lennon, *Live Peace in Toronto 1969* (1969)
Jerry Lee Lewis, *Killer Collection* (1969)
Albert King, *Blues for Elvis: Albert King Does the King* (1970)
Jimi Hendrix, *Hendrix in the West* (1972)

Written by the late rockabilly maestro Carl Perkins, "Blue Suede Shoes" was one of the catalysts behind the rock 'n' roll revolution of the mid-1950s.

There are two versions of how Perkins found his inspiration for this tune. Perkins himself claimed that while playing at a high school dance in Jackson, Tennessee, in December 1955, he saw a young boy who, while dancing with his gorgeous date, warned her, "Don't step on my suedes," after she had scuffed one of his prized pieces of footwear. Perkins said he stayed up all night after the show, writing on a brown potato sack the lyrics for a song with a boogie-woogie beat.

Johnny Cash has told a different version of

B

the song's roots, saying that it was inspired on an evening in 1955 when he was sharing a bill with Perkins and Elvis Presley in Amory, Mississippi. Cash said he told Perkins about a black sergeant he'd served under in the U.S. Air Force by the name of C. V. White. Sergeant White got into the habit of stopping by Cash's room to ask him how he (White) looked and, before departing, would say, "Just don't step on my blue suede shoes!"—even though White was wearing regulation military shoes. Perkins thought the story was good enough for a song, and while Elvis performed onstage, he wrote "Blue Suede Shoes."

On December 19, 1955, Perkins recorded "Blue Suede Shoes" in two takes and included a cyclonic guitar solo, about which he later remarked, "I had never played what I played in the studio that day. I know God said, 'I've held it back, but this is it. Now you get down and get it.'"

"Blue Suede Shoes" hit No. 2 on the *Billboard* Hot 100 singles chart, stopping just under Elvis's "Heartbreak Hotel." Presley released an EP with his own version of "Blue Suede Shoes" in 1956, holding back on a single release until Perkins's record had slipped from the charts so as not to cause unwelcome competition for his buddy. Elvis later sang "Blue Suede Shoes" in his 1960 movie *G.I. Blues.* Kurt Russell performed it (with a Ronnie McDowell overdub) in the 1979 biopic *Elvis.*

Dylan's only performance of "Blue Suede Shoes," a minimal supporting background vocal for Van Morrison and his band at a January 1998 shared-bill show in Boston, was made in homage to Perkins, who had passed away just days before.

◪ Bob Dylan
Columbia Records LP CL-1779/PC-8579, CD CK-8579, CS PC-

8579. Recorded November 20 and 22, 1961, in New York City. Released March 19, 1962. Produced by John Hammond. Liner notes by Robert Shelton (under the pseudonym "Stacey Williams"); jacket also carries a reprint of Shelton's September 29, 1961, *New York Times* review of a Dylan performance. Cover photo by Don Hunstein.

"You're No Good," "Talkin' New York," "In My Time of Dyin'," "Man of Constant Sorrow," "Fixin' to Die," "Pretty Peggy-O," "Highway 51 Blues," "Gospel Plow," "Baby, Let Me Follow You Down," "House of the Risin' Sun," "Freight Train Blues," "Song to Woody," "See That My Grave Is Kept Clean"

Dylan's eponymous debut album unveiled a sensitive, if not quite yet influential, interpreter of country folk and blues songs. Typical of the era, there are but a couple of original songs here and they barely steal the show on this exuberant collection, which is a pretty fair reflection (as surviving tapes reveal) of what the folkie waif was performing on the coffeehouse stages of Greenwich Village at the time.

The Animals are said to have found "House of the Risin' Sun" on this album, while Led Zeppelin cribbed "In My Time of Dyin'." But the most striking track is the Dylan original "Song to Woody," his tribute to Woody Guthrie, that left no doubt about its author's intention to reignite and carry the ailing folkster's dimming torch. "Talkin' New York," Dylan's sardonic commentary on his reception in the Big Apple, is the only other original song here, but it hardly matters, as they both sound oh-so derivative from the rest of the batch.

Recorded in November 1961 over the course of but two days at the cost of a mere $402 and overseen by the legendary producer and Columbia A&R man John Hammond, *Bob Dylan* was the first of three Dylan studio albums that never made the *Billboard* charts (the other two being *Knocked Out Loaded* [1986] and *Down in the Groove* [1988]). No won-

Bob Dylan at Gerde's
Folk City, New York
City, 1961.

(Photo: Irwin Gooen. Courtesy of
Irwin Gooen)

der that when the album tanked, critics openly laughed and called Dylan by the name that had already been whispered in Columbia hallways for months: "Hammond's folly."

With his hands wrapped around his guitar neck, a baby-faced twenty-year-old Bob Dylan posed for the album's cover wearing a fur suede jacket and then-trademark corduroy sailor's cap. Who would have thunk that this rube would be defining "cool" four years hence?

Musically, *Bob Dylan* breaks little ground. It did and does provide much insight into both Dylan's influences and later artistic sojourns: all those incessant country and folk clichés that fill his early acoustic albums (ironically or otherwise) become understandable, as a song like

B

"Highway 51 Blues" was certainly the inspiration, or at least a touchstone, for "Highway 61 Revisited." Even the melody of "It's Alright Ma" can be heard as having its stripped-down roots on songs from this debut.

And what great taste the former Bobby Zimmerman showed with his selection of material. Amid the dour "House of the Risin' Sun," Ric von Schmidt's sensuous "Baby, Let Me Follow You Down," a bitingly humorous "Hard Times in New York Town," an angry hit of the ancient folk dirge "Pretty Peggy-O," a squealing "She's No Good," and a creepy death-song cycle ("Man of Constant Sorrow," "In My Time of Dyin'," and "See That My Grave Is Kept Clean"), this young North Country Jew takes the listener on a Southern journey *way* off the beaten path. Ironically, by the time *Bob Dylan* was released nigh on half a year after it was in the can, Dylan had begun moving on to more serious fare and regarded its appearance in record bins with some embarrassment, feeling he had grown considerably since his brief foray into the studio.

Yet so much of the Dylan we've come to know four decades down the highway is already here in embryo: the gravelly voice, the wailing speech-song, the cross-fertilization of folk and blues stylings, the mocking put-downs and teasing wordplay, the mysterious but evocative imagery, the apocalyptic pseudo-prophecy, the obsession with death, the air of mythos.

◪ *Bob Dylan at Budokan*

Columbia Records LP PC2-36067, CD G2K-36067, CS CGT-36067. Recorded at Nippon Budokan, Tokyo, February 28 and March 1, 1978. Released April 23, 1979. Produced by Don DeVito. Album notes by Bob Dylan.

Bob Dylan—guitar, harmonica, vocals. Billy Cross—guitar. Ian Wallace—drums. Alan Pasqua—keyboards. Rob Stoner—bass, vocals. Steven Soles—guitar, vocals. David Mansfield—pedal steel guitar, violin, mandolin, guitar, Dobro. Steve Douglas—saxophone, flute, recorder. Bobbye Hall—percussion. Helena Springs—vocals. Jo Ann Harris—vocals. Debbie Dye—vocals.

"Mr. Tambourine Man," "Shelter from the Storm," "Love Minus Zero/No Limit," "Ballad of a Thin Man," "Don't Think Twice, It's All Right," "Maggie's Farm," "One More Cup of Coffee (Valley Below)," "Like a Rolling Stone," "I Shall Be Released," "Is Your Love in Vain?," "Going, Going, Gone," "Blowin' in the Wind," "Just Like a Woman," "Oh, Sister," "Simple Twist of Fate," "All Along the Watchtower," "I Want You," "All I Really Want to Do," "Knockin' on Heaven's Door," "It's Alright, Ma (I'm Only Bleeding)," "Forever Young," "The Times They Are A-Changin'"

A two-disc keepsake of Dylan's 1978 world tour, *Bob Dylan at Budokan* was, unfortunately, recorded during an early stop on the road—well before Dylan and his versatile band caught lightning in a bottle later in the year. Columbia would have been much wiser to release material from the European leg of the year-long globe trot, for by that point the ensemble and their leader's performance were at a peak.

At Budokan has Dylan performing what are, in some cases, radically rearranged interpretations of many familiar songs. Many found the style overdone but few could deny the passion and intensity if they were lucky enough to catch this crack band on a good night. Perhaps because of the glitzy, late-period Elvis Presley–style big-band production, and the fact that it was Dylan's third live album in five years, *At Budokan* didn't do the greatest business. Still, it hit No. 13 during its seven-week stay on the charts.

Although *At Budokan* includes material from *Blood on the Tracks* ("Shelter from the Storm," "Simple Twist of Fate"), *Desire* ("Oh, Sister," "One More Cup of Coffee"), and even a tune from the new *Street Legal* ("Is Your Love in Vain?"), Dylan focuses on the older material in his repertoire for this collection, drawing twelve of the twenty-two cuts from the pre-1967 era. No matter where you turn, though, all of the material differs extravagantly from the original recorded versions. And that is the main thing that distinguishes this album, band, and tour in Dylan's career: the arrangements. Backed by a seasoned combo that included the core from the Rolling Thunder Revues of 1975 and 1976 (Rob Stoner, David Mansfield, and Steve Soles) and a three-woman choir (Helena Springs, Jo Ann Harris, and Debbie Dye), Dylan took a jazzier, almost Nelson Riddle–like approach to some of his most hallowed songs. It may not be up to Herb Alpert and the Tijuana Brass standards, but is unique to this period of Dylan nonetheless. Some have suggested that the entire enterprise was inspired by the death of Elvis Presley, who left the building only half a year before the tour took off. Elvis, of course, presented his music in a similar context in his last few years. That Dylan sported a white, sequined leisure suit at some of the shows (as depicted on the album's back cover) is further indication that he was paying some kind of homage to the King.

A couple of other things (besides the music) set *At Budokan* apart. Dylan included a short, poignant message to the people of Japan as a bit of album-note filler, for one, and incidentally, this album—the artist's twenty-third—was Dylan's first to include lyrics to the songs in the packaging. These unique features are there for a reason: Columbia, and probably Dylan himself, had not originally intended *At Budokan* for release in the U.S., only consenting to that after demand could not be quelled. Therefore, the harsh criticism the album garnered in America seems unwarranted, given that the decision to release it at home may not have been Dylan's. The critics' main beef was the perception that the material was rearranged for the sake of rearranging it—not to explore the songs' nuances to reveal new meanings. Yet the same probably could have been said about the bulk of *Before the Flood* in 1974 or *Hard Rain* in 1976—but Dylan was not exactly riding high when the LP was released. It was much easier to kick a man when he was down.

[S] **"Bob Dylan's Blues"** (Bob Dylan)

Bob Dylan, *The Freewheelin' Bob Dylan* (1963)

"Unlike most of the songs nowadays that are being written uptown in Tin Pan Alley, that's where most of the folk songs come from nowadays, this one, this isn't written up there, this one is written somewhere down in the United States."

With that caustic introduction to "Bob Dylan's Blues" on *The Freewheelin' Bob Dylan*, Dylan delivers arguably his first experiment in musical subversion, mixing conceits, traditions, and icons into a new and, in this case, humorous form—which would be further twisted into the beautifully grotesque in songs ranging from "Bob Dylan's 115th Dream" and "Desolation Row" a few years hence.

But "Bob Dylan's Blues" is pure, pleasurable nonsense as it moves from a tall tale involving the Lone Ranger and Tonto to more personal, if frivolous, fare. All in all, it's a nice antidote to some of the more serious material found by its side on *The Freewheelin' Bob Dylan.* Musically the song is barely a blues, but Dylan's harmonica work peppering his vocal delivery is not to be missed.

Nat Hentoff's liner notes to the *Freewheelin'* album include excerpts from his interview with Dylan, who said that he composed this piece spontaneously, that it was an example of one of his "'really off-the-cuff songs. I start with an idea, and then I feel what follows. Best way I can describe this one is that it's sort of like walking by a side street. You gaze in and walk on.'"

Dylan also cut "Bob Dylan's Blues" as a Witmark demo, but, along with a performance of it on Skip Weshner's radio show on WBAI-FM in New York, only a 1963 nightclub recording of the song from the Bear in Chicago seems to have survived.

[S] "Bob Dylan's Dream" (Bob Dylan)

Bob Dylan, *The Freewheelin' Bob Dylan* (1963)
The Silkie, *You've Got to Hide Your Love Away* (1965)
Peter, Paul & Mary, *Album 1700* (1967)
Judy Collins, *Judy Sings Dylan . . . Just Like a Woman* (1993)
Phil Carmen, *Bob Dylan's Dream* (1996)
Michel Montecrossa and the Chosen Few, *Eternal Circle* (1999)
Various Artists (performed by Eric Taylor), *A Tribute to Bob Dylan, Volume 3: The Times They Are A-Changin'* (2000)

Hinting at songs like "Tangled Up in Blue" or "Something There Is About You" he would write more than a decade later, Dylan composed and performed this ode to lost youth and fractured community when he was still just a footloose young lad himself. The song was probably accidentally left off the first pressings of *The Freewheelin' Bob Dylan*, but it replaced "Rambling, Gambling Willie" on all subsequent releases of that sophomore effort. Performed exclusively in 1963, it resurfaced in Dylan's acoustic sets more than forty times in 1991, when he had literally aged into the song.

While not widely recognized as an important work outside Dylan's circle of fans and scholars, "Bob Dylan's Dream" is a burnished jewel full of wanderlust and quiet ceremony—a sister song to the equally reflective and better-known "Girl of the North Country."

Thrust into the maelstrom of New York City and his quick rise, Dylan, in this song, looks back to Hibbing, Minnesota, with nostalgia and a touch of world-weariness as his life had become more complicated.

As for the influences informing "Bob Dylan's Dream," Dylan credited "Lord Franklin," a song that British folkster Martin Carthy showed him. Inspection of "Lord Franklin" reveals both the melody and a few lyrical seeds as well, particularly in the last two lines. "They sailéd east and they sailéd west/To find their passage they knew not best/Ten thousand pounds would I freely give/If I only knew if my husband lived," goes the older song. Compare that to the lines in "Bob Dylan's Dream": "Ten thousand dollars at the drop of a hat/I'd give it all gladly if our lives could be like that."

According to the *Freewheelin'* liner notes, "Bob Dylan's Dream" is another song Dylan carried for a time in his mind before writing it down. It was initially inspired, he claimed then, by an all-night conversation he had with folklorist Oscar Brown Jr. in Greenwich Village. "Oscar is a groovy guy and the idea of this came from what we were talking about," Dylan revealed in the sleeve notes. "Bob Dylan's Dream" languished for a while though, for want of music, until he encountered "Lord Franklin." Dylan then adapted that old melody for his fond and wistful look back at the easy camaraderie and idealism of the young when they are young—a sorrowful requiem for the friendships that evaporate as the road of life unfurls.

[A] *Bob Dylan's Greatest Hits*

Columbia Records LP KCL-2663, CD CK-9463, CS KCS-9463. Released March 27, 1967. Produced by Tom Wilson, Bob Johnston, John Hammond. Photography by Roland Scherman.
"Rainy Day Women #12 & 35," "Blowin' in the Wind," "The Times They Are A-Changin'," "It Ain't Me, Babe," "Like a Rolling Stone," "Mr. Tambourine Man," "Subterranean

Homesick Blues," "I Want You," "Positively 4th Street," "Just Like a Woman"

Columbia Records compiled this ten-song retrospective of Dylan's work while the artist was recuperating from the infamous motorcycle accident he suffered during the summer of 1966. *Greatest Hits* combines Dylan's folk-protest standards ("Blowin' in the Wind" and "The Times They Are A-Changin'"), poetic flights and fights ("Mr. Tambourine Man" and "Subterranean Homesick Blues"), and epic rock radio hits ("Like a Rolling Stone" and "Rainy Day Women #12 & 35"). "Positively 4th Street," previously available only as a single, was included as a bonus track.

While it is unclear whether his seclusion after the accident contributed to the Dylan mystique, the public's appetite for his music was still very much at a high—as evidenced by the business this nice repackaging did. *Greatest Hits* hit No. 10 and stayed on the album charts for twenty-one months on the way to being Dylan's first album to go platinum. No doubt it achieved Columbia's goals: make money, keep Dylan's name in the marketplace, and spur interest in his next release, which would be *John Wesley Harding* in 1968.

Early editions of *Bob Dylan's Greatest Hits* included the famous poster of Dylan by graphic designer Milton Glaser—the one of Bob's head in black silhouette springing a Medusa-like burst of colorful hair. Some of us may still gaze on it now and then as it hangs on our office wall beside the iMac.

Ⓐ *Bob Dylan's Greatest Hits, Volume II*

Columbia Records LP KG-31120, CD C2K-31120, CS CGT-31120. Released November 17, 1971. Compiled by Bob Dylan (uncredited). Produced by Bob Johnston, Tom Wilson, John Hammond, Leon Russell. Photography by Barry Feinstein.

"Watching the River Flow," "Don't Think Twice, It's All Right," "Lay Lady Lay," "Stuck Inside of Mobile with the Memphis Blues Again," "I'll Be Your Baby Tonight," "All I Really Want to Do," "My Back Pages," "Maggie's Farm," "Tonight I'll Be Staying Here with You," "She Belongs to Me," "All Along the Watchtower," "The Mighty Quinn (Quinn, the Eskimo)," "Just Like Tom Thumb's Blues," "A Hard Rain's A-Gonna Fall," "If Not for You," "It's All Over Now, Baby Blue," "Tomorrow Is a Long Time," "When I Paint My Masterpiece," "I Shall Be Released," "You Ain't Goin' Nowhere," "Down in the Flood"

This grab bag of material, some dating back to 1963, and not necessarily full of what could be described as "greatest hits," was released as a sprawling two-disc set and is notable for its rarities—especially the 1971 single "Watching the River Flow" and the previously unavailable 1963 live performance of "Tomorrow Is a Long Time."

The album did great business, hitting No. 14 and staying on the charts for seventeen weeks on the way to becoming Dylan's third platinum success. *Greatest Hits, Volume II* was, unlike his first greatest-hits release, put out with Dylan's involvement. The cover art follows the same murky blue theme as the first greatest-hits package, this time with photos of Dylan performing in August 1971 at George Harrison's benefit concert for Bangladesh.

The term "greatest hits" only loosely describes this collection. Yeah, some genuine chart-makers such as "Lay Lady Lay" and "Tonight I'll Be Staying Here with You" are included. But by and large, *Greatest Hits, Volume II* consists of songs that in many cases became known, even classics, through cover versions by others. There are a number of rarities found throughout, including the aforementioned "Tomorrow Is a Long Time," the live Isle of Wight take of "The Mighty Quinn (Quinn, the Eskimo)," and Big Pink songs ("I Shall Be

Released," "Down in the Flood," and "You Ain't Goin' Nowhere"—not in their *Basement Tapes* versions but as recorded in 1971 with Happy Traum), making this album something a Dylan devotee would cherish and a Dylan neophyte could use as an excellent primer.

Ⓐ *Bob Dylan's Greatest Hits, Volume 3*

Columbia Records CD CK-66783. Released November 15, 1994. Produced by Gordon Carroll.

"Tangled Up in Blue," "Changing of the Guards," "The Groom's Still Waiting at the Altar," "Hurricane," "Forever Young," "Jokerman," "Dignity," "Silvio," "Ring Them Bells," "Gotta Serve Somebody," "Series of Dreams," "Brownsville Girl," "Under the Red Sky," "Knockin' on Heaven's Door"

Twenty-three years after Dylan's last greatest-hits album was released, in 1971, came his third—a respectable, if ultimately disappointing, compilation of the better-known songs Dylan produced over the period. Standard, predictable choices like "Knockin' on Heaven's Door," "Forever Young," "Tangled Up in Blue," and "Hurricane" are present, but so are some of Dylan's overlooked fare like "The Groom's Still Waiting at the Altar" and "Brownsville Girl." But there are some real clinkers here, too ("Under the Red Sky," "Silvio," "Changing of the Guards"), and four cuts that had already been rereleased, repackaged, and otherwise overexposed by way of *Biograph*. The only reason just about any of the faithful took the plunge was due to the inclusion of a fine, never-before-released track entitled "Dignity," a medium-major newish song in the big-picture "Hard Rain's A-Gonna Fall" tradition.

Ⓐ *Bob Dylan—Limited Edition Hybrid SACD Set*

Sony Legacy CD 90615. Released September 16, 2003.

The Freewheelin' Bob Dylan, Another Side of Bob Dylan, Bringing It All Back Home, Highway 61 Revisited, Blonde on Blonde, John Wesley Harding, Nashville Skyline, Planet Waves, Blood on the Tracks, Desire, Street Legal, Slow Train Coming, Infidels, Oh Mercy, "Love and Theft"

In a merging of technology, cultural history, artistic will, and a corporate strong-arm shove or two, fifteen Dylan albums were remastered by Sony/Legacy Records reconciling modern scientific attempts with dissimilar and degenerating master tapes, some recorded more than forty years before. The new technology, Super Audio CD (SACD), provides greater sound dynamics through higher sampling rates.

Legacy's series of Dylan reissues was one of the more recent undertakings by any major record label, representing the most significant marriages of emerging technological breakthroughs with recordings of such historical, social, and artistic significance. In its renovation of one of the culture's most significant catalogues, the label created hybrid CDs. All fifteen remastered titles have two layers of stereo, but six have a third layer that contains a discrete 5.1 multichannel Surround Sound mix—a feature that requires a corresponding SACD player, amplifier, and speakers—providing listeners with a dynamic, "live-in-the-studio" experience.

According to Steve Berkowitz, Sony/Legacy senior vice president for artists and repertoire, the decision to coalesce Dylan's catalogue in SACD was simple. "Our goal was to change them," he told the *Wall Street Journal*. "Our goal was to represent, in a more [audio] vérité way, what the musicians actually did. You can make them sound better, but they've gotta feel the same."

Purchased separately or in the streamlined box set listed here, the hybrid discs (spanning every era of Dylan's career) can be played on both standard-issue CD players and the all-new SACD machines. Bottom line: the music does sound fresh and more immediate. Will the remixes provide some new revelatory insight or cosmic epiphany not afforded from a scratchy LP? Not sure whether Sony's suits and bean counters considered that possibility in their decision to go to market.

[S] **"Bob Dylan's New Orleans Rag"** (Bob Dylan)

aka "New Orleans Rag"

Sessionographers are still debating whether this humorous tall tale about a serendipitous and regretful visit to a Crescent City brothel was recorded during the 1964 *Another Side of Bob Dylan* sessions or *The Times They Are A-Changin'* sessions a year earlier. Meanwhile, Dylan was performing the tune like a rascally Bourbon Street songster during his concerts of that era and planned to include his "New Orleans Rag" rarity on the never-released *Bob Dylan in Concert* LP. If Marcel Duchamp had sat down to rewrite "House of the Risin' Sun," this is the song he might have come up with.

[S] **"Bob Dylan's 115th Dream"** (Bob Dylan)

Bob Dylan, *Bringing It All Back Home* (1965)

Recounting a cockeyed trip on the *Mayflower*, Dylan's rambling knee-slapper of a surrealist tall tale and shaggy-dog story wrapped up into one phantasm is marked on *Bringing It All Back Home* by a false start that features artist and producer Tom Wilson cracking up. The contagious laughter is so natural that Dylan and Wilson decided to leave it in.

It had been 113 dreams between his first dream song (1963's "Bob Dylan's Dream") and this one; nowhere to be found (in name anyway) are the others. This slippery, witty, seemingly off-the-cuff song satirizes the New World as it follows the Captain Ahab–captained *Mayflower* breaking off its hunt for his metaphorical Moby-Dick to make a stop in a farcical modern America. Using cinematic, choppy jump cuts plucked straight out of a Keystone Kops film, the tune's cascading lyrical froth and tempo keep this frontal-lobe flick flying at Mach One. Dylan's dreams would soon turn more darkly grotesque, but this vision is decidedly funny, the kind of dream one awakes from laughing.

On the recording Dylan reveled in the sheer joy of the absurdist wordplay, but when he performed his "115th Dream" at a string of 1988 Never Ending Tour shows, it was uncharacteristically humorless.

[A] ***Bob Dylan: The 30th Anniversary Concert Celebration***

Columbia Records CD C2K-53230, CS C2TK-53230, LP C3-53230. Produced by Jeff Rosen and Don DeVito. Recorded October 18, 1992, at Madison Square Garden, New York City. Released August 24, 1993. Liner notes by David Wild.

Bob Dylan—guitar, vocals. Johnny Cash—vocals. Roseanne Carter Cash—guitar, vocals. Kris Kristofferson—guitar, vocals. Willie Nelson—guitar, vocals. Richie Havens—guitar, vocals. Tracy Chapman—guitar, vocals. Shawn Colvin—guitar, vocals. Steve Cropper—guitar. George Harrison—guitar, vocals. Al Kooper—organ. Roger McGuinn—guitar, vocals. Tom Petty—guitar, vocals. Lou Reed—guitar, vocals. Johnny Winter—guitar, vocals. Ron Wood—guitar, vocals. Neil Young—guitar, vocals. Lisa Germano—violin. Sue Medley—backing vocals. Rick Danko—guitar, vocals. Mike Campbell—guitar. Dennis Collins—backing vocals, choir, chorus. Jim Keltner—drums. Sheryl Crow—background vocals, choir, chorus. Liam Clancy—guitar, vocals. Tommy Makem—banjo, vocals. Mickey Raphael—harmonica. Kenny Aronoff—drums. Jerry Barnes—choir, chorus. Katreese Barnes—choir, chorus. Richard Bell—accordion. Mary Chapin Car-

B

penter—guitar, vocals. John Cascella—accordion, keyboards. June Carter Cash—vocals. Randy Ciarlante—drums, vocals. Cissy Houston—choir, chorus. Bobby Clancy—percussion, vocals. Paddy Clancy—harmonica, vocals. Eric Clapton—guitar, vocals. Donald "Duck" Dunn—bass. Howie Epstein—bass. Ron Fair—piano. Anton Fig—percussion, drums. David Grissom—guitar. Levon Helm—mandolin, vocals. Garth Hudson—accordion. Chrissie Hynde—guitar, vocals. Booker T. Jones—organ. Brenda King—backing vocals, choir, chorus. Curtis King—background vocals, choir, chorus. Eddie Levert Sr.—vocals. Mike McCready—guitar. John Cougar Mellencamp—vocals. Robbie O'Connell—guitar, vocals. Christine Ohlman—background vocals, choir, chorus. Pat Peterson—background percussion, vocals. G. E. Smith—guitar, mandolin. Benmont Tench—organ. Eddie Vedder—vocals. Mike Wanchic—guitar. Don Was—bass. Jim Weider—guitar, vocals. Walter Williams—vocals. Stevie Wonder—harmonica, piano, vocals. Reggie Young—guitar. Kerry Marx—guitar. Leotis Clyburn—choir, chorus. Sam Strain—vocals.

"Like a Rolling Stone" (performed by John Mellencamp), "Leopard-Skin Pill-Box Hat" (performed by John Mellencamp), "Blowin' in the Wind" (performed by Stevie Wonder), "Foot of Pride" (performed by Lou Reed), "Masters of War" (performed by Eddie Vedder), "The Times They Are A-Changin'" (performed by Tracy Chapman), "It Ain't Me, Babe" (performed by Johnny Cash and June Carter Cash), "What Was It You Wanted?" (performed by Willie Nelson), "I'll Be Your Baby Tonight" (performed by Kris Kristofferson), "Highway 61 Revisited" (performed by Johnny Winter), "Seven Days" (performed by Ron Wood), "Just Like a Woman" (performed by Richie Havens), "When the Ship Comes In" (performed by the Clancy Brothers and Robbie O'Connell with special guest Tommy Makem), "You Ain't Goin' Nowhere" (performed by Mary-Chapin Carpenter/Roseanne Cash/Shawn Colvin), "Just Like Tom Thumb's Blues" (performed by Neil Young), "All Along the Watchtower" (performed by Neil Young), "I Shall Be Released" (performed by Chrissie Hynde), "Don't Think Twice, It's All Right" (performed by Eric Clapton),

"Emotionally Yours" (performed by the O'Jays), "When I Paint My Masterpiece" (performed by the Band), "Absolutely Sweet Marie" (performed by George Harrison), "License to Kill" (performed by Tom Petty and the Heartbreakers), "Rainy Day Women #12 & 35" (performed by Tom Petty and the Heartbreakers), "Mr. Tambourine Man" (performed by Roger McGuinn), "It's Alright Ma (I'm Only Bleeding)" (performed by Bob Dylan), "My Back Pages" (performed by Bob Dylan), "Knockin' on Heaven's Door" (performed by Bob Dylan and ensemble), "Girl of the North Country" (performed by Bob Dylan)

In the autumn of 1992, Columbia Records brought it all back home when the company organized a concert at New York's Madison Square Garden to celebrate the thirtieth anniversary of the release of Dylan's first album. The concert and inevitable souvenir album commemorating it were, however, more than a mere showcase of talent pushed onstage for the benefit of record-company weasels. Rather, it was an extraordinary and genuine display of musical superstardom at its egoless and camaraderie-filled best, exquisitely teaming song with artist and style. Seeing and hearing more than two dozen A-list acts interpreting a whole spectrum of Dylan's compositions stood (and still stands) as a strong testament to Dylan's exalted status in the American music pantheon. From the old to the new, from the familiar to the obscure, from John Mellencamp's concert-commencing "Like a Rolling Stone" to Lou Reed's menacing "Foot of Pride," from Johnny Cash and June Carter Cash's Nashvillized "It Ain't Me, Babe" to Eddie Vedder's dire "Masters of War," from Stevie Wonder's soulful "Blowin' in the Wind" to Johnny Winter's raging bottleneck blues "Highway 61 Revisited," and on through Eric Clapton, Neil Young, George Harrison, and finally to Dylan himself, the concert was a wild commercial and artistic success.

These types of all-star get-togethers can be severely hit-or-miss, and if there was a bit of melancholy associated with the evening (a nagging sense that Dylan's best days were behind him), hope sprang eternal with the new life breathed into great songs. Much of that came from the artists featured, of course, but much also owes to the crack backing band: keeping things grounded while gracefully shifting styles from performer to performer were Booker T and the MG's, who served as the house band for the evening, guitarist and Never Ending Tour alum G. E. Smith, who acted as the event's musical director, and Al Kooper, who sat in on organ. They proved as flexible as the material was malleable.

Fittingly, the night was not without its controversy, however. Irish rock chanteuse Sinéad O'Connor was met with boos as she approached the microphone to sing "I Believe in You," perhaps Dylan's most shameless religious song from the deeply Christian *Slow Train Coming* album. O'Connor was in the national spotlight at the time following her recent appearance on television's *Saturday Night Live*, during which she tore up a picture of Pope John Paul II and sang Bob Marley's "War." The irony was thick. Her defenders pointed out that not only was she slated to sing a song of profound religious commitment, but also that she was being scapegoated in much the same manner that Dylan himself had been when he was (unsuccessfully) hung out to dry upon "going electric" at the Newport Folk Festival in 1965. Sinéad, unable to even begin singing "I Believe in You," quickly ended her appearance by delivering a line from the same Marley song before being escorted, visibly shaken, off the stage by Kris Kristofferson. Nothing of her appearance was preserved for the audio release.

The double CD hit the *Billboard* charts at No. 40, which turned out to be its high-water mark. Still, it spent eleven weeks in all on *Billboard*'s charts and earned Dylan his eighteenth gold album. Neither the album cover, with its predictable collage of photographs depicting the pantheon of performers, nor the liner notes (a lot of drooling from the pen of David Wild) are particularly noteworthy. Thank goodness the night, and the music, were both.

The show was originally broadcast on pay-per-view television and later released on video. It's also shown on television occasionally during PBS pledge drives.

For the award obsessed, Neil Young's performance of "All Along the Watchtower" received a 1994 Grammy Award nomination for best solo rock vocal, and the Bob Dylan, Roger McGuinn, Tom Petty, Neil Young, Epic Clapton, and George Harrison performance of "My Back Pages" was nominated for a '94 Grammy as best rock performance by a duo or group with vocal.

▣ Bob Dylan Versus A. J. Weberman
Folkways Records FB 5322 (Broadside No. 12). Released 1977.

In what may well rank as the oddest and, at one point, at least temporarily legal Dylan releases, *Bob Dylan Versus A. J. Weberman* consists of a couple of January 1971 telephone calls between Dylan and Alan Jules Weberman—the galaxy's premier Dylanologist. A. J. was a scruffy East Village yippie who developed an elaborate unified-field theory of Dylan that not only posited his subject as a major radical poet but also created an elaborate concordance dissecting nearly every word in every Dylan song as being of profound, near-kabbalistic significance. And yes, A. J. was the guy who sniffed around Dylan's garbage outside the latter's house on 94

MacDougal Street for clues to prove his points, prompting an ugly confrontation between the two on the sidewalks of New York.

Somewhere along the way, Weberman wangled an interview with Dylan as part of an article he was writing about the elusive songwriter and his art. The recordings on this album appear to be a follow-up to the initial interview and after Weberman allowed Dylan to vet the article. Dylan comes off as a pretty ordinary guy, fiercely protecting his privacy while rudely correcting Weberman's article. The conversation alternates between the hostile and the humorously strained, with Dylan saying at one point, "I've got a good song about you. It's called 'Pig'," and Weberman countering that Dylan was little more than a profiteer capitalizing on the counterculture who hadn't written a meaningful, consequential song in years. Back and forth the dialogue goes, and why Dylan doesn't hang up on the guy is hard to figure—it's as if he's morbidly fascinated by this obsessive character dancing on the fringes of his stage. Eventually, the conversation peters out with little solved or gained.

Rounding out the album is East Village agit-prop rocker and friend of John Lennon David ("Have a Marijuana") Peel and his band with a tribute song appropriately titled "A. J. Weberman."

The rarity of *Bob Dylan Versus A. J. Weberman* is due to its extremely limited release. Folkways Records slipped the disc into stores, but quick legal action prompted Folkways guru Moe Asch to discontinue distribution.

For all the controversy surrounding Weberman and his tactics, he was an engaging and, in some respects, important writer. His still consequential book *Coup d'État in America* was one of the first to analyze the 1963 assassination of John F. Kennedy. And his self-explanatory 1980 book *My Life in Garbology* is a must for admirers of the Collyer brothers.

"Boogie Woogie Country Girl" (Doc Pomus/Reginald Ashby)

See also *Till the Night Is Gone*
Various Artists (performed by Bob Dylan), *Till the Night Is Gone* (1995)
Sleepy Labeef, *Rockin' Decade* (1978)
Paula Lockheart, *Incomplete* (1980)
Big Joe Turner, *Big Bad & Blue: The Big Joe Turner Anthology* (1994)
Excello Legends, *Excello Legends* (1998)

Dylan actually sounds like he's having a good time with this curtsey to songwriting legend Doc Pomus, cut specifically for *Till the Night Is Gone*, the Pomus tribute album listed above. Dylan's high-octane highway sound torques up "Boogie Woogie Country Girl," Doc's paean to a hard-rockin' Daisy Mae written by Pomus and sometime collaborator Reginald Ashby, with Big Joe Turner's gale-force vocal majesty in mind. Rumor has it that Dylan and his band recorded upwards of an album's worth of unspecified material at the sessions that produced "Boogie Woogie Country Girl."

"Boom Boom Mancini" (Warren Zevon)

See also Warren Zevon
Warren Zevon, *Sentimental Hygiene* (1987)

Dylan's fall 2002 tour was marked by his performance of several Warren Zevon songs as a kind of living memorial to man who had just announced that he was dying. And Dylan's choice of material here is notable. After writing his own songs about martyred boxers, one of whom died in the ring (1963's "Who Killed Davey Moore") and another who ran afoul of the law (1975's "Hurricane"), Dylan chose a flinty song, indulging in Zevon's usual obsessions with machismo, about a man who had slain another between the ropes.

The Ray "Boom Boom" Mancini story is,

however, one of the brighter to emerge from the galaxy of pugilism. During the early 1980s, Mancini was, after Sugar Ray Leonard, one of the era's finest practitioners of the sweet science. Ray Mancini (born March 4, 1961, Youngstown, Ohio) inherited the skills and his nickname from his father, Lenny, himself a top-class fighter in the 1940s. Barely twenty-one years old, the younger Mancini took the WBA lightweight crown from Antonio Frias in a one-round KO. Over the next three years, Mancini defended his crown against Orlando Romero, Doo Koo Kim (the South Korean fighter who died as a result of injuries sustained in their fight), and Bobby Chacon (the other boxer who figures in the lyrics to Zevon's song). When Mancini finally hung up his gloves in 1993, he had compiled an impressive 29–4 record that included twenty-three knockouts. He has sustained a seemingly successful post-ring career as a bit Hollywood actor and small-time film producer, playing characters with names like Zeto, Chico, Aldo, Mr. Black, and Boom Boom, appearing in movies with titles like *Mutants in Paradise*, *Timebomb*, and *The Search for One-Eyed Jimmy*.

◪ The Bootleg Series, Volumes 1–3: Rare and Unreleased, 1961–1991

Columbia Records CD C3T-47382, CS C3K-47832. Released March 20, 1991. Supervised and compiled by Jeff Rosen. Liner notes by John Bauldie.
"Hard Times in New York Town," "He Was a Friend of Mine," "Man on the Street," "No More Auction Block," "House Carpenter," "Talkin' Bear Mountain Picnic Massacre Blues," "Let Me Die in My Footsteps," "Rambling, Gambling Willie," "Talkin' Hava Negeilah Blues," "Quit Your Low Down Ways," "Worried Blues," "Kingsport Town," "Walkin' Down the Line," "Walls of Red Wing," "Paths of Victory," "Talkin' John Birch Paranoid Blues," "Who Killed Davey Moore?," "Only a Hobo," "Moonshiner," "When

the Ship Comes In," "The Times They Are A-Changin'," "Last Thoughts on Woody Guthrie," "Seven Curses," "Eternal Circle," "Suze (The Cough Song)," "Mama, You Been on My Mind," "Farewell, Angelina," "Subterranean Homesick Blues," "If You Gotta Go, Go Now (Or Else You Got to Stay All Night)," "Sitting on a Barbed Wire Fence," "Like a Rolling Stone," "It Takes a Lot to Laugh, It Takes a Train to Cry," "I'll Keep It with Mine," "She's Your Lover Now," "I Shall Be Released," "Santa-Fe," "If Not for You," "Wallflower," "Nobody 'Cept You," "Tangled Up in Blue," "Call Letter Blues," "Idiot Wind," "If You See Her, Say Hello," "Golden Loom," "Catfish," "Seven Days," "Ye Shall Be Changed," "Every Grain of Sand," "You Changed My Life," "Need a Woman," "Angelina," "Someone's Got a Hold of My Heart," "Tell Me," "Lord Protect My Child," "Foot of Pride," "Blind Willie McTell," "When the Night Comes Falling from the Sky," "Series of Dreams"

Opening the archival floodgates with the release of this fifty-eight-song, three-disc collection of outtakes and unreleased tunes spanning his entire career, Dylan (or, more appropriately, album producer Jeff Rosen) finally offered a compendium that demonstrated what the choir had been preaching all along: that Dylan throwaways were quite often better than everybody else's keepers. *The Bootleg Series, Volumes 1–3* proved once and for all that, even while turning out the defining albums of his time, Dylan was holding back songs of often better quality.

Dylan is not only among the most widely bootlegged twentieth-century performers, but was also one of the first. It is no secret that his legions of fans have long and rabidly traded recordings of live shows, outtakes, demos, and other rare material, and that much has been and still is available via bootleg-CD shops. In fact, *Great White Wonder*, containing Dylan's Witmark demos and other material, was the infamous 1968 boot that turned the enterprise from a collector's fetishist pastime into an industry. *The Bootleg Series*, though, even if it only hints at the vast musical treasures still collecting dust in vaults, succeeds at beating the bootleggers at their own game by supplying the definitive collection of what had been heard only on bootlegs—plus some entirely new material. *The Bootleg Series, Volumes 1–3* was regarded by many as a revelation.

Highlights include "He Was a Friend of Mine," "House Carpenter," "Paths of Victory," *Highway 61 Revisited* outtakes from the 1960s; scrapped tracks from the sublime *Blood on the Tracks* in the 1970s; and, most powerfully surprising: Dylan's often overlooked material from the 1980s—especially the eerie masterpiece "Blind Willie McTell," which had long been a collector's grail. It should go without saying that the *Bootleg Series* is a must for any serious Dylan fan.

Unlike *Biograph*, which arranged its material thematically, *The Bootleg Series* is presented chronologically. This allows the listener to check out the sweep of Dylan's career, from a hotel room in Minnesota in 1961, before he cut his first album, to an *Oh Mercy* outtake nearly three decades later. In between, one can chart a journey through the artist's muses and musics and experience a career as layered and labyrinthine as any Old Master oil on canvas: from hayseed folkie to gnarled rock sage, with every hopscotch stop along the way. The late John Bauldie's liner notes, produced in a sharp, sixty-eight-page booklet that accompanies the set with an array of photographs, are as enlightening as the notes packaged with *Biograph*.

For all his meshuga about looking back to archival material, Dylan finally gave his fans and admirers what they had been pining for with this "bootleg" smorgasbord. But if he was really smart, he'd follow the Grateful Dead's lead and release material from the vaults on a

more regular basis, say one or two a year. As it was, Dylanists had to wait more than eight years before being graced with another "official bootleg" release from his golden stash.

The Bootleg Series, Volumes 1–3 sold very well for a box set, hitting No. 33 during its short two-week stint on the charts.

The Bootleg Series, Volume 4: Live 1966 (The "Royal Albert Hall" Concert)

Columbia Records CD C2K-65759. Recorded May 17, 1966, Free Trade Hall, Manchester, England. Released October 13, 1998. Produced by Jeff Rosen. Photography by Dan Hunstein, David Gahr, Art Kane. Liner notes by Tony Glover.

Bob Dylan—guitar, harmonica, piano, vocals. Robbie Robertson—guitar. Rick Danko—bass, backing vocals. Garth Hudson—organ. Richard Manuel—piano. Mickey Jones—drums.

"She Belongs to Me," "Fourth Time Around," "Visions of Johanna," "It's All Over Now, Baby Blue," "Desolation Row," "Just Like a Woman," "Mr. Tambourine Man," "Tell Me, Momma," "I Don't Believe You (She Acts Like We Never Have Met)," "Baby, Let Me Follow You Down," "Just Like Tom Thumb's Blues," "Leopard-Skin Pill-Box Hat," "One Too Many Mornings," "Ballad of a Thin Man," "Like a Rolling Stone"

"If I thought this record was any good, it would have been released a long time ago."

That quote from the artist himself is one reason Dylan's fans regard his self-criticism with a touch of skepticism. The so-called Royal Albert Hall concert (actually from Free Trade Hall in Manchester, England) is so good that it may be *the* defining musical and historical moment in a career that has had many of them.

This concert was not just another stop on Dylan's May 1966 British tour with the Hawks. Rather, coming as it did at the height of Dylan's move toward highly surreal, poetic folk and electric music, circumstances that evening turned it into a bellwether point in the history

Dylan plugs in at the Olympia in Paris, France, 1966.

(Photo: RDA/Getty Images)

of Dylan, folk-rock, rock, and, some say, culture itself.

Perhaps the Hawks' guitarist Robbie Robertson best articulated the moment when, in the mid-1980s, he remembered, "That tour was a very strange process. You can hear the violence, and the dynamics in the music. We'd go from town to town, from country to country and it was like a job. We set up, we played, they booed and threw things at us. Then we went to the next town, played, they booed, threw things at us, and we left again. I remember thinking, 'This is a strange way to make a buck.'"

Yes, Dylan had been recording and releasing electric rock 'n' roll for over a year when he walked onstage for his appearances with an electrified ensemble. But that didn't soften the tremendous controversy and even hostility generated by the old-guard folkies in the audience who had once formed Dylan's original constituency and who now viewed him as something worse than a sellout. Even dividing his sets between acoustic and rock formats did not seem to quell the outrage, which has been compared to that which met Stravinsky during the initial performances of *The Rite of Spring*.

The acoustic half of the Manchester show finds Dylan at a rarely matched peak as he explores the best of his then-recent compositions with a stony grace and lonely genius. Even nearly forty years down the pike, the acoustic sets from this tour sound as if they have been delivered down from on high. Steeped in hallucinatory wordplay and sung with whispered vapors, "She Belongs to Me," "Fourth Time Around," "Desolation Row," and, especially and as always, "Visions of Johanna," set a standard against which many a Dylanist has compared every subsequent performance.

The electric half of the show is another matter entirely, as Dylan walked out with the Hawks and tore into eight tunes with fierce clarity and raw, almost angry energy. Leading off sledgehammer-style with a take-no-prisoners rendition of "Tell Me, Momma," Dylan and his band proceeded to shower their audience with droplets of wild mercury. By the time the group reached "Like a Rolling Stone" at concert's end, the tension and energy filling the performers and audience is palpable.

During the second set, the stoned cosmic-folkie tranquility that had marked set one is replaced by an agitated din, as the protesters on hand continually heckle and berate the performers and battle with the more open-minded attendees in this postmodern hootenanny from Limbo. Dylan comes across as aloof as he and Robbie Robertson trade electric guitar runs like

gunslingers at the O.K. Coral. But there is true drama here—all leading to the climactic moment when someone in the crowd clearly shouts "Judas!" Dylan responds by first heckling back—"I don't believe you ... you're a liar!"—and then by telling his bandmates to "Play fucking loud!" The band charges into a stormy version of "Like a Rolling Stone" that holds nothing in reserve.

For the ultimate dissertation on the Manchester event, interested readers should seek out C. P. Lee's monumental last word on the matter, *Like the Night*, published by Helter Skelter in 1998.

The Bootleg Series, Volume 5: Live 1975—The Rolling Thunder Revue

Columbia Records/Sony Music Entertainment LP CK-87047-1-Q. CD C2K-87047. Recorded November 19, 1975, Memorial Auditorium, Worcester, Massachusetts; November 20, 1975, Harvard Square Theatre, Cambridge, Massachusetts; November 21, 1975, Boston Music Hall, Boston; December 4, 1975, Forum de Montréal, Montreal, Canada. Released November 26, 2002. Produced by Jeff Rosen. Photography by Ken Regan/Camera 5. Liner notes by Larry "Ratso" Sloman.

Bob Dylan—guitar, vocals. Bobby Neuwirth—guitar, vocals. Scarlet Rivera—violin. T-Bone J. Henry Burnett—guitar. Steven Soles—guitar, vocals. Joan Baez—guitar, vocals. Roger McGuinn—guitar, vocals. Mick Ronson—guitar. David Mansfield—steel guitar, mandolin, violin, Dobro. Rob Stoner—bass. Howie Wyeth—piano, drums. Luther Rix—drums, percussion, congas. Ronee Blakely—vocals.

"Tonight I'll Be Staying Here with You," "It Ain't Me Babe," "A Hard Rain's A-Gonna Fall," "The Lonesome Death of Hattie Carroll," "Romance in Durango," "Isis," "Mr. Tambourine Man," "Simple Twist of Fate," "Blowin' in the Wind," "Mama, You Been on My Mind," "I Shall Be Released," "It's All Over Now, Baby Blue," "Love Minus Zero/No Limit," "Tangled Up in Blue," "The Water Is Wide," "It Takes a Lot to Laugh, It Takes a Train to Cry," "Oh, Sister,"

"Hurricane," "One More Cup of Coffee (Valley Below)," "Sara," "Just Like a Woman," "Knockin' on Heaven's Door"

Throughout Dylan's career there have been certain periods—even certain months or weeks—when his art shone with a golden luster. Late November and early December of 1975 was such a period. Rarely has his music been better or the man hipper. This was a month into the fabled Rolling Thunder Revue, Dylan's ersatz cosmic postmodern Dada "medicine show" caravan that not only featured a large, ornery, and very tight backup band, but served as a kind of gathering of the tribes, a reassessment of agendas artistic and social as it toured the Northeast on the cusp of the country's bicentennial in surprise, small-venue whistle-stop fashion. By the time the circus was hitting towns like Worcester, Massachusetts, and Boston, Dylan and his crew were in high mercurial mode, dashing through his back pages, showcasing selections from *Blood on the Tracks*, and previewing songs from its soon-to-be-released follow-up, *Desire*.

Coming on the heels of his blindingly overhyped return to the concert stage with the Band the year before, Rolling Thunder was conceived as an antidote to that frenzied, hockey-rink cross-country jaunt. And while everyone seemed to have made scads of moolah, Dylan seemed quick to realize that this was not a direction he wished to pursue with any immediate regularity. So, after cutting *Blood on the Tracks* in late 1974, he encamped in Greenwich Village in mid-'75, developing and recording new songs and surrounding himself with a coterie of old and new friends.

Not wanting to leave all this unbridled creativity in the studio, Dylan and company decided to take to the road and spread their gospel in some kind of alchemy that combined the footloose bohemianism of Jack Kerouac, the Beats, and the pranksterish activism of guerilla theater with rock 'n' roll. And what company Dylan was savvy enough to hire! With Mick Ronson, Steven Soles, T-Bone Burnett, and Dylan himself forming the guitar bedrock, David Mansfield providing support on a bevy of stringed instruments, the ever-mysterious Scarlet Rivera playing a white-hot electric violin, and a revolving cast of core and surprise guests (Joan Baez, Bob Neuwirth, Allen Ginsberg, Roger McGuinn, Ramblin' Jack Elliott, Ronee Blakely, and Joni Mitchell among them), the Revue was an anarchist force to be harnessed and reckoned with on a night-to-night basis.

And if things weren't confusing enough, Dylan had hired a film crew and encouraged his troupe to enact an ongoing Bertolt Brecht-meets-Julian Beck psychodrama onstage and off that eventually resulted in *Renaldo & Clara*, his fantastic mess of a film vérité released some years later.

No one recording could adequately represent the gonzo spirit of those vital autumn nights in '75 that stretched on for hours, but *The Bootleg Series, Volume 5* does encapsulate Dylan's sets in magnificent fashion. From a raucous send-up of the relatively rare "Tonight I'll Be Staying Here with You" ("get ready!" yells Dylan in mid-song), commencing the proceedings in inviting fashion, the troupe flies through a few old favorites that includes an acid-rock arrangement of "It Ain't Me, Babe," a revamped, rocked-out, and uncharacteristically optimistic "A Hard Rain's A-Gonna Fall," and an indignant, funereal "Lonesome Death of Hattie Carroll."

For many, the highlight of the collection might be the killer acoustic set that concludes the first disc and begins the second as Dylan teams up with Baez a decade after their first

B

blush of art and romance to show that, if anything, they'd improved over time, with renditions of "Blowin' in the Wind," "Mama, You Been on My Mind," "I Shall Be Released," and "The Water Is Wide," the last a traditional song popularized by Baez. Sandwiched in and around there's a quintet of exceptional Dylan performances alone with his steel-stringed Martin guitar tearing though nimble renditions of "Mr. Tambourine Man," "Simple Twist of Fate," "It's All Over Now, Baby Blue," "Love Minus Zero/No Limit," and "Tangled Up in Blue," with Dylan's darting, reedy vocals carrying the affair.

The Rolling Thunder shows were the first live renditions of the *Blood on the Tracks* songs, and the crowd can be heard reacting with enthusiasm to their new old favorites. But Dylan also used the tour as an opportunity to launch *Desire*, unveiling five songs from the album: the neo-western "Romance in Durango," the mystical vision-quest "Isis," the elegiac "Oh, Sister," the controversial "Hurricane," and the intangible "One More Cup of Coffee (Valley Below)." "Hurricane" was, of course, the centerpiece of the new harvest, if not the Revue shows themselves. But if some of the gleam and consequence has faded from the song (Dylan has not performed it since phase one of that tour ended at the ill-fated and poorly attended "Night of the Hurricane" benefit concert at the Houston Astrodome in late January 1976), at least it set a tone of activism so sorely missing from popular music in the midst of the self-indulgent mid-'70s glit/glam-rock fetishism.

Which is not to say that the Revue was lacking in any theatricality. Wearing a wide-brimmed fedora bedecked with flowers, palm leaves, and feathers and his face smeared in white makeup, Dylan, along with his Revue cohorts, strutted their stuff like a band of ragamuffin gypsies who pulled their wagons into a lot on the outskirts of town with as hip-swivel-

ing and visually dramatic a show as any Dylan has ever produced.

A glimpse of this can be enjoyed on the two-song DVD included in this *Bootleg Series* package. Snatched from *Renaldo & Clara* is an image of Dylan's face flickering mysteriously in and out of the shadows cast by his chapeau during a solo acoustic rendition of "Tangled Up in Blue." And during a seismic presentation of "Isis," he comes off as some bizarre cross of an Old Testament seer and psychedelic minstrel enveloped in the canopy of sound and movement emanating from the musicians surrounding him.

Yes, there may be a few omissions here: the Revue's stellar version of "When I Paint My Masterpiece" that opened most of the concerts was left off the collection. Also M.I.A. are the Dylan/Baez performances of "I Dreamed I Saw St. Augustine" and their covers of Merle Travis's "Dark as a Dungeon," the traditional "Wild Mountain Thyme," the semi-obscure torch song "Never Let Me Go," and Dylan's solo acoustic rendition of his own "I Don't Believe You (She Acts Like We Never Have Met)." And finally, the show-ending rave-ups of Woody Guthrie's "This Land Is Your Land" that featured different musicians improvising on the lyric might have been a nice inclusion. Hair-splitting, completist quibbles aside, *Volume 5* of this all-too-infrequent blow-the-dust-off-the-tape-boxes archival series may be the best of the lot.

Finally, Larry Sloman's lengthy neojournalist liner notes, excerpted from his one-of-a-kind travelogue *On the Road with Bob Dylan*, and the accompanying photographs add even more body to an already weighty package.

The Bootleg Series, Volume 6: Live 1964—Concert at Philharmonic Hall
Columbia Records/Sony Entertainment CD 86882. Recorded

October 31, 1964, at Philharmonic Hall, New York City. Released March 30, 2004. Produced by Jeff Rosen. Photography by Daniel Kramer, Hank Parker, Sandy Speiser. Liner notes by Sean Wilentz.
Bob Dylan—guitar, vocals. Joan Baez—guitar, vocals.
"The Times They Are A-Changin'," "Spanish Harlem Incident," "Talkin' John Birch Paranoid Blues," "To Ramona," "Who Killed Davey Moore?," "Gates of Eden," "If You Gotta Go, Go Now (Or Else You Got to Stay All Night)," "It's Alright Ma (I'm Only Bleeding)," "I Don't Believe You (She Acts Like We Never Have Met)," "Mr. Tambourine Man," "A Hard Rain's A-Gonna Fall," "Talkin' World War III Blues," "Don't Think Twice, It's Alright," "The Lonesome Death of Hattie Carroll," "Mama, You Been on My Mind,"* "Silver Dagger,"* "With God on Our Side,"* "It Ain't Me, Babe,"* "All I Really Want to Do"
(* performed with Joan Baez)

The beginning of the end of the beginning: Bob Dylan pre-plugged. No, Halloween night 1964 was not the final all-acoustic solo guitar Dylan concert ever, but it is a high-water mark for the later period of his early career. A mere two years removed from pass-the-hat-style gigs at dumps like the Gaslight Café in Greenwich Village and two years from the motorcycle wreck that would keep him out of public commission until 1974, Dylan plays with both the charm of a masquerading young man who nurtured his audiences at those funky little bistros and with the fire of a seer all too eager to step onto a larger public stage.

The stage that particular evening was one of the nation's most renowned: Philharmonic Hall (now called Avery Fisher Hall) in New York City's then newly opened Lincoln Center performance facility. And Dylan rises to the occasion, changing before our eyes from the folkie waif of yore into a sharp-tongued weaver of thought dream, mind-breathy visionary poems. For along with the familiar, progressive, finger-pointing cold commentaries on the state of the nation's soul ("The Times They Are A-Changin'," "Talkin' John Birch Paranoid Blues," "A Hard Rain's A-Gonna Fall," "The Lonesome Death of Hattie Carroll," "Talkin' World War III Blues"), Dylan introduces his inner surrealist with longer, hypnotic songs of paradise lost ("Gates of Eden"), found ("Mr. Tambourine Man"), or misplaced ("It's Alright, Ma"). And he's certainly at ease in presenting the many shades of encounters with the opposite sex, from songs of wooing ("Spanish Harlem Incident"), romance ("Mama, You Been on My Mind"), complicated relationships ("To Ramona" and "All I Really Want to Do"), sly, put-up-or-shut-up sexuality ("If You Gotta Go, Go Now"), commitment or the lack thereof ("It Ain't Me, Babe"), alienation ("I Don't Believe You"), and breakup ("Don't Think Twice").

Dylan's stage persona and humor can't be ignored either. Seductive and fresh, it reveals only the smallest of hints that the chip on his shoulder would grow boulder-sized by the time he hit Britain for the tour that produced *Don't Look Back* the following spring. You just want to put your arms around the guy, cradle him like a lost, little puppy, and give him a cup of warm milk with honey.

If it's context you want, the show took place only days before President Lyndon Johnson trounced conservative Republican Senator Barry Goldwater in the presidential election, a few weeks after Nikita Khrushchev was ousted as leader of the Soviet Union, and China detonated its first nuke, a few months after civil rights workers James Chaney, Andrew Goodman, and Michael Schwerner were murdered in Mississippi, a half-year since the Beatles hit the stage of *The Ed Sullivan Show*, and eleven months removed from the assassination of President Kennedy. And let's not forget that any show set for All Hallows' Eve is bound to stir a ghost or two.

B

Yet this is no nostalgia trip. If Dylan were to perform this same set of songs tonight, he might well be praised (or accused) of saliently commenting on these very fluid times.

As a little bonus, Joan Baez joins Bob for a few songs near the show's finale, and for a few minutes anyway, the king and queen of folk music reign supreme.

[S] "Boots of Spanish Leather" (Bob Dylan)

Bob Dylan, *The Times They Are A-Changin'* (1964)
Linda Mason, *How Many Seas Must a White Dove Sail* (1964)
Joan Baez, *Any Day Now* (1968); *Vanguard Sessions: Baez Sings Dylan* (1998)
Golden Gate Strings, *Bob Dylan Songbook* (1965)
Richie Havens, *Electric Haven* (1966)
Sebastian Cabot, *Sebastian Cabot, Actor—Bob Dylan, Poet* (1967)
Dan McCafferty, *Dan McCafferty* (1975)
Nanci Griffith, *Other Voices, Other Rooms* (1993); *Winter Marquee* (2002)
Dubliners, *30 Years A-Greying* (1994)
Seldom Scene, *Scene It All* (2000)
Michel Montecrossa, *Born in Time* (2000)
Michael Moore, *Jewels and Binoculars* (2000)
Various Artists (performed by Ida), *A Tribute to Bob Dylan, Volume 3: The Times They Are A-Changin'* (2000)
Various Artists (performed by Martin Simpson), *A Nod to Bob* (2001)
Robert Deeble, single (2001)
Gerry Murphy, *Gerry Murphy Sings Bob Dylan* (2002)
Various Artists (performed by Robert Deeble), *May Your Song Always Be Sung: The Songs of Bob Dylan, Volume 3* (2003)

A restless, forlorn ballad for the ages and sages—a classic Dylan tale of two lovers, a crossroads, and the open sea—"Boots of Spanish Leather" was written to and about Suze Rotolo, Dylan's early '60s New York City girlfriend who in 1964 had finally left him and traveled to Italy to get away from it all. "Boots of Spanish Leather" is cast as a dialogue between parting lovers excruciatingly breaking free of each other. Though the song is quite personal, Dylan's use of antique vocabulary, song structure, and pronunciation to summon scenes of another century's armadas afloat on tempest-tossed seas journeying to far-flung lands thereby broadens the song and casts it deeper in the folk idiom.

With austere charisma, raw emotion, and brutal honesty, Dylan casts himself as a romantic poet witnessing his own love affair in its death throes in "Boots of Spanish Leather." As the conversation between the lovers ebbs and flows to its final, if predestined, conclusion, the singer appears to identify with the young lover being left behind, who slowly begins to connect the dots that the end of their affair is nigh. Part of the song's brilliance is Dylan's ability to obscure the genders of the speakers while somehow making it clear that the woman is flying the coop and leaving the man on the city docks to watch as her ship disappears over the horizon. As the discussion heats up, the woman attempts to placate the man by offering to send him some token "to remember me by." But the man is not interested in material goods, poetically insisting that "If I had the stars of the darkest night/And the diamonds from the deepest oceans/I'd forsake them all for your sweet kiss/For that's all I'm a-wishin' to be owning." But the psychic tug-of-war between the two heightens as she tries to wash her hands of any guilt and (in evident denial of the relationship's end) by continuing to adamantly coax a request for some kind of gift to assuage the intensity of the moment. But he's having none of it. Sometime after, he gets a letter from her on a lonesome day informing him that not only is the date of her return uncertain, it is dependent on how she's feeling. Stung but not too surprised, the man responds with a request that serves as the final nails being driven into the relationship's coffin: "So take heed, take heed of the western wind/Take heed of the stormy weather/And yes, there's something you can send back to me/Spanish boots of Spanish leather."

Dylan's performances of "Boots of Spanish Leather" have been universally excellent, consistently ruminative, hung over with mourning. It was first recorded as a Witmark demo in 1963, given a few nonconcert displays in 1963, and included on a British television broadcast recorded when Dylan began his 1965 swing through Great Britain. Though "Boots of Spanish Leather" is as classic a Dylan song as can be found, it is rather notable that he didn't start performing it with any regularity until the Never Ending Tour commenced in 1988. Since then, he has kept it in moderate rotation as a vital centerpiece of his acoustic sets, reminding one and all why Dylan alone at the mic (still thinking of Suze?) can make a sold-out theater weak at the knees.

"Born in Time" (Bob Dylan)
Bob Dylan, *Under the Red Sky* (1990); *Live 1961–2000—Thirty-nine Years of Great Concert Performances/'98* (2001)
Eric Clapton, *Pilgrim* (1998)

Waxing mystically poetic, if a little sappy, about natural law and destiny in meeting up with an amour (lonely nights connected in black-and-white dreams on shaky streets hearing each other's hearts, and so on), Dylan performed this unusual, wondrous song on piano in its official release and on guitar starting in 1993 during the Never Ending Tour.

"The Boxer" (Paul Simon)
Bob Dylan, *Self Portrait* (1970)
Simon and Garfunkel, *Bridge over Troubled Water* (1970)
Paul Simon, *Paul Simon's Concert in Central Park* (1991)
Paul Butterfield, *Live* (1971)
Emmylou Harris, *Roses in the Snow* (1980)
Joan Baez, *European Tour* (1981)
Waylon Jennings, *Right for the Time* (1996)

"The Boxer"—Paul Simon's autobiographical allegory with a nod to Rod Serling's *Requiem for a Heavyweight* about a loner living on society's fringes—is an oddity even for Dylan's odd *Self Portrait*. In fact, the selection in context is nothing short of bizarre: not only is it limply performed, but Dylan somehow also saw it fit to overdub his vocals, thereby creating a watery duet effect.

Simon began writing "The Boxer" in the summer of 1968 and finished it that December. Simon's description of composing one of his greatest songs can be found in Victoria Kingston's *Simon & Garfunkel: The Definitive Biography* (London: Sidgwick & Jackson, 1996): "'The words to the first verse . . . came with the melody line; they had a flow to them that made them easy to sing. Consequently, I found I had started a song about a poor boy who had squandered his resistance for a pocketful of mumbles. I just tried to make the rest of the lyrics follow as naturally as possible.'"

The narrative ballad tells the story of a vulnerable young man who leaves home to seek his fortune and encounters hardships and loneliness. Discovering the city's street people, he finds among them unexpected nobility, and gains the courage to face up to his mistakes and come to terms with reality.

According to Kingston, "Rumours suggested that it was written about Bob Dylan's life and, admittedly, there could be some parallels. But then, when viewed on a superficial level, it could be about anyone. Clearly it is in fact a very personal song, written from the inside. Paul commented: 'I would say it's autobiographical, although it sure surprised me. When we recorded it, someone said to me, "Hey, that's a song about you." And I said, "No, it's not about me; it's about this guy who..." and as I'm saying it, I thought, "Hey, what am I saying? This song is about me and I'm not even admitting it." One thing is certain, I've never written anything about Dylan; and I don't know of his personal life.'"

When released by Simon and Garfunkel in 1968, "The Boxer" hit *Billboard*'s Top 10.

Dylan handled a couple of other Simon songs with greater success. He rehearsed Simon's "Boy in the Bubble" with the Grateful Dead in preparation for their 1987 tour and covered "Homeward Bound" in 1991. Handling harmonica duties, Dylan finally did perform "The Boxer" with Paul Simon during their shared mini-set while on tour in mid-1999.

Bringing It All Back Home

Columbia Records LP CL-2328, CD CK-9128, CS CS-9128; Sony Music Entertainment, Inc., SACD 90326. Recorded January 14 and 15, 1965. Released March 22, 1965. Produced by Tom Wilson. Liner notes by Bob Dylan. Cover photography by Daniel Kramer.
Bob Dylan—guitar, harmonica, keyboards, vocals. John Hammond Jr.—guitar. John Sebastian—bass. Kenny Rankin—guitar. Bobby Gregg—drums. John Boone—bass. Al Gorgoni—guitar. Paul Griffin—piano, keyboards. J. Bruce Langhorne—guitar. William Lee—bass. Joe Macho—bass. Frank Owens—piano.
"Subterranean Homesick Blues," "She Belongs to Me," "Maggie's Farm," "Love Minus Zero/No Limit," "Outlaw Blues," "On the Road Again," "Bob Dylan's 115th Dream," "Mr. Tambourine Man," "Gates of Eden," "It's Alright, Ma (I'm Only Bleeding)," "It's All Over Now, Baby Blue"

Staring menacingly from a chaise longue with a gray Persian on his lap and an austere woman (Sally, his manager Al Grossman's wife) reclining behind him in a decadent living-room scene littered with seemingly random but actually very carefully selected and placed cultural detritus, the Dylan we see on the cover of *Bringing It All Back Home* seems like the kind of cat you might be wise to keep your distance from.

The image hints at what's inside: Dylan taking a leap into a brave new world—a stranger in a strange land. It's almost as if in the cover shot he's daring his audience to buy the album and accept the music and his decidedly non-folkie image and content—he is challenging from the outset. Part rock 'n' roll, part acoustic, all intense, *Bringing It All Back Home* was a gutsy move for the twenty-four-year-old singer-songwriter, for it is here that he began turning his back on the ardent folk community that had nurtured him and elevated him to a kind of savior—and whom he could have milked for years. With this album, Dylan established himself as the guy to catch, strides ahead of his peers, critics, and audience—and his engine was just getting primed.

It was around this time that Dylan commented that "Chaos is a close friend of mine.... Truth is chaos. Maybe beauty is chaos." On *Bringing It All Back Home*, Dylan sings of the chaos and the absurdities of a changing world, the lack of communion between the genders and generations as he ridicules the dullness, inadequacies, and pointlessness of the straight world and its system. At the same time, though, he chides those of his own generation who seemed content to settle for the comfortable, protected world of the middle class, from whence they could let others make decisions for them while they themselves sought status and security at the expense of losing their curiosity and sense of adventure. Much of this is not exactly new to Dylan or the folkie genre, but

Bob Dylan at the 1965
Newport Folk Festival.

(Photo: Diana Davies. Courtesy of the
Center for Folklife and Cultural Heritage, Smithsonian Institution)

what was new was the language—dark, surre-alistic images, biting sarcasm, and prickly humor—and form that Dylan employed. Those who felt that he was eschewing protest music got it all wrong. Rather than shining a light on the Hattie Carrolls or Emmett Tills of the world, Dylan was now railing against just about everything in sight.

Though shaped by traditional structures, Dylan's new lyrics throughout the record are catalogues of wide-ranging reference full of cutting-edge Zen hipsterisms. From its hot-wired Dantesque "abandon all hope ye who enter" commencement with "Subterranean Homesick Blues," Dylan draws a line in the sand for his listeners. He follows this impudent start on the first side of the LP with an anti-love song ("She Belongs to Me"), a universal plaint ("Maggie's Farm"), a true love song ("Love Minus Zero/No Limit"), and a triumvi-

B

rate of semisurrealistic subversions and diversions ("Outlaw Blues," "On the Road Again," and "Bob Dylan's 115th Dream"). But these songs serve as scarce preparation for side two's four-song poetic flights, each of which ranks among Dylan's most durable classics: his call to a muse ("Mr. Tambourine Man"), his call to the netherworld ("Gates of Eden"), his call to his mother ("It's Alright, Ma [I'm Only Bleeding]"), and his call to his past ("It's All Over Now, Baby Blue").

Pushing the envelope in other directions, Dylan broke the pop convention that the album track should be limited to the length of a three-minute single and inaugurated what was known by the late 1960s as the "heavy" album track—in this case, "It's Alright, Ma (I'm Only Bleeding)."

Dylan's jittery, Beat-style liner notes echo his songs' wordplay and lyricism, calling to mind the literary fancies he toyed with in *Tarantula*, the novel he had begun working on at the time.

Bringing It All Back Home did quite well in the marketplace. Dylan's best-selling LP to that time, it climbed to No. 6 on the charts, and it stayed on the charts for thirty-two weeks in all. It earned gold album distinction (500,000 copies) in the summer of 1967. Commercially and artistically, Dylan's gambit succeeded. In 2002, *Billboard* magazine reported that the album had finally gone platinum (more than one million units sold), some thirty-six years after its initial release.

◪ *Broadside Ballads, Volume 1*/Various Artists
Folkways Records LP FH-5301. Released 1963.

Under the cover of his "Blind Boy Grunt" moniker for contractual reasons (he was signed with Columbia Records at the time), Dylan performs a few early rarities: "John Brown" (listed

as "Jon Brown"), "Only a Hobo," and "Talkin' Devil." Pete Seeger, Peter LaFarge, Phil Ochs, and Happy Traum (who performs Dylan's "I Will Not Go Down Under the Ground," aka "Let Me Die in My Footsteps") fill out this still-evocative period piece from the days of folkie yore.

◪ *Broadside Reunion*/Various Artists
Folkways Records LP FR-5315, CS 5315. Released 1972.

Again hiding Dylan behind the "Blind Boy Grunt" handle for old times' sake as much as to dodge Columbia Records' lawyers, Folkways released a quartet of Dylan performances dating from the early 1960s ("Train A-Travelin'," "I'd Hate to Be You on That Dreadful Day," "The Death of Emmett Till," "Ballad of Donald White") on this archival sampler.

◧ *"Broke Down Engine"* (Traditional/Blind Willie McTell)
See also "Blind Willie McTell"
aka "Broke Down Engine Blues," "Broke Down Engine #2"
Bob Dylan, *World Gone Wrong* (1993)
Various Artists (performed by Lonnie Clark), *Down in the Black Bottom: Lowdown Barrelhouse Piano*/'29 (2000)
Blind Willie McTell, *Definitive Blind Willie McTell* (1994)
Martin Simpson, *Special Agent* (1981)
Paul Geremia, *My Kinda Place* (1986)
Buddy Moss, *Complete Recordings, Volume 2: 1933–1934* (1992)
John Cephas and Phil Wiggins, *Bluesmen* (1993)

Dylan dances with the devil on the hardest-rockin' song on his all-acoustic, all-cover-song *World Gone Wrong* collection—especially when he raps on his guitar to simulate the song's narrator banging at the door of the woman (or maybe the Gates of Hell) he's just got to see.

In his liner notes accompanying *World Gone Wrong*, Dylan says that "Broke Down Engine" is "a Blind Willie McTell masterpiece," continuing, "it's about revival, getting a new lease on life, not just posing there—paint chipped & flaked, mattress bare, single bulb swinging above the bed."

The lyrics, in time-honored fashion, employ the railroad locomotive as its primary metaphor—paradoxically both religious and sexual. Dylan took the line "she can do the Georgia crawl" from "Broke Down Engine" and put it in his own "Gonna Change My Way of Thinking" from the *Slow Train Coming* LP back in 1970. Blind Willie McTell recorded this driving blues at least four times, the first time being in his hometown of Atlanta on October 23, 1931, and the last about two decades later when he was coaxed out of obscurity by Ahmet Ertegun, who, along with his brother, founded Atlantic Records.

The origins of "Broke Down Engine" are themselves obscure. An earlier version by Lonnie Clark, recorded in 1929 in Indiana, ranks among the better known by hard-core bluesologists. But given his avowed admiration of McTell, Dylan no doubt learned the song from one of Blind Willie's recordings.

[S] **"Brownsville Girl"** (Bob Dylan/Sam Shepard)

Bob Dylan, *Knocked Out Loaded* (1986); *Bob Dylan's Greatest Hits Volume 3* (1994)

Justifiably or not, just about every Bob Dylan composition longer than five minutes is usually saddled with the "masterpiece" label pretty soon, if not immediately, upon its release, and this sage dust-rolling epic penned with playwright and actor Sam Shepard is no exception. The only reason to go near the dreadful *Knocked Out Loaded*, "Brownsville Girl" is a humorous, hard-to-decipher, eleven-minute yarn involving a Gregory Peck movie—never named but reckoned to be *The Gunfighter*, from 1950—and the singer's identification with Peck's character.

Gregory Peck in a still from *The Gunfighter*, 1950.

(Photo: 20th Century Fox/Getty Images)

B

Dylan does tell a marvelously picaresque story here that, despite the laid-back, "aw shucks" drawl infusing his yarn, is full of nefarious situations, double-crosses, derring-do, reunion, and heroism. The story begins with the narrator recalling standing in line to screen the Peck film. This, in turn, prompts a memory of a pan-Texas trip of undisclosed reason with the woman to whom he sings and titles "Brownsville Girl" in honor of. After driving all night to San Antonio, where they sleep near the Alamo (a symbolic locale pregnant with disaster and death), she leaves for Mexico to find a doctor but never comes back. Perhaps she is seeking an abortion, but if someone is injured, the narrator doesn't let on. Somehow he has continued his trip with another woman, crossing the Texas panhandle toward Amarillo, where they decide to pay a visit to a guy named Henry Porter. He's not home but his woman, Ruby, invites the narrator in for a chat, but nothing is revealed except that she is jaded and ready to leave the area. The narrator then begins musing about *The Gunfighter* again, implying that he played a part in the Peck film while at the same time merging the real-time paranoia of the song's narrative. Suddenly he's a pompadour-topped fugitive being pursued by a gun-toting mob. The action moves swiftly: after his picture is plastered on the front pages, there appears to have been an off-screen arrest and trial, during which the Brownsville Girl miraculously reappears for a dramatic courtroom appearance (perhaps filled with phony testimony) that seems to have guaranteed our man's acquittal. When all is said and done, he's still standing in line waiting to screen the film and musing about the meaning of it all as the curtain drops on the story/song.

"Brownsville Girl" began life in a rough composition called "New Danville Girl" in reference to the original "Danville Girl," a classic lonesome hobo song also known as "The Gambler" and recorded by Woody Guthrie, among others. Some believe that "Brownsville Girl" may also have been a response to Lou Reed's "Doin' the Things That We Want To," a song that references *Fool for Love*, Sam Shepard's respected play.

Sam Shepard had been in Dylan's orbit long before they collaborated on "Brownsville Girl." Dylan first commissioned him during the 1975 leg of the Rolling Thunder Revue to write a screenplay for the film that turned into *Renaldo & Clara*. But the script, such as it was, was abandoned in favor of a more improvisationally impressionistic approach. (Shepard did contribute his ideas to the film and can be seen in it as well.) Shepard's *Rolling Thunder Logbook* (New York: Viking, 1977) is an arty, intriguing take on the famous tour. Years after working with Dylan on "New Danville Girl" and "Brownsville Girl," he "interviewed" Dylan for an entertaining though typically unrevealing feature article published in the June 1987 issue of *Esquire*.

Shepard (born November 5, 1943, Fort Sheridan, Illinois) grew up as an Army brat; his itinerant early childhood suited him well in allowing him to observe rural Middle America and plumb its darker depths in his later, groundbreaking theater work. Shepard set off to New York City as a teenager and it was there, by age twenty, that his first two plays were staged. Over the next fifteen years, Shepard's prodigious theatrical explorations and subversions resulted in ten Obies and one Pulitzer Prize for *Buried Child* in 1979. *Curse of the Starving Class* (1977), an unblinking portrait of a farming family teetering on the emotional and financial brink, and *True West* (1983), a brutal portrait of two brothers, are probably his most appreciated and best-known endeavors as a playwright.

If Shepard had ceased working in 1980, he'd

be regarded as the late twentieth century's answer to Eugene O'Neill. But Shepard, ever the maverick, branched out into more dangerous ground. As an actor, screenwriter, and director, he has worked in just about every imaginable genre. His thespian turn as the wealthy landowner in *Days of Heaven*, Terrence Malick's 1977 dreamy Depression-era elegy, made him a subterranean heartthrob, and his rugged portrayal of test pilot Chuck Yeager in *The Right Stuff* in 1983 garnered him a Best Supporting Actor Oscar nomination. His other acting credits include *Raggedy Man* (1981), *Frances* (1982), *Crimes of the Heart* (1986), *Steel Magnolias* (1989), and *The Pelican Brief* (1993). As a screenwriter, Shepard penned *Paris, Texas* (1984), *Far North* (1988), and *Silent Tongue* (1992). *Far North* was his debut as a director, a film he reportedly wrote for his longtime partner, the actress Jessica Lange. Just about all of his work is populated with his trademark drifters, grifters, and eccentrics adding a sociopathic edge to his no-holds-barred diagnosis of the pathologies that drive contemporary society.

Much has been made about the Gregory Peck film referenced in "Brownsville Girl." Most agree that it is *The Gunfighter*, an unusual bad-guy-becomes-good-guy, one-against-the-odds *High Noon*–style western. An overlooked gem of the entire genre, William Bowers's script received an Oscar nomination for best original screenplay.

Dylan's choice of *The Gunfighter* and Peck could be a clue to a partial understanding of the song. Perhaps, like the character in the film, Dylan felt as though he had done his bit to protect the town from anarchy—that he could walk away from it all if not for the unruly doings of man, his own conscience, and those damn muses calling him back into the fray. As for Peck, his on- and off-screen stature in show business as an articulate, passionate, and outspoken (if low-key) advocate for the left could not have been lost on Dylan.

Considering the length and breadth of the song, Dylan's sole 1986 performance of "Brownsville Girl," during his first tour with Tom Petty and the Heartbreakers, should forever stand in the anything-is-possible realm—even if it is merely an elongated, mesmerizing repetition of the refrain aided by the soaring voices of his backup singers du jour and not the epic retelling of his sunbaked, dust-in-the-mouth odyssey.

"Brown Sugar" (Mick Jagger/Keith Richards)
Rolling Stones, *Sticky Fingers* (1971)
Little Richard, *King of Rock 'N' Roll* (1971)
Innovations, *Play the Rolling Stones* (1998)

Maybe it was just a coincidence, but Dylan's choice to cover one of the more down-and-dirty Rolling Stones songs (and that's saying a lot) came just as the Stones were embarking on their 2002 tour, a journey marked by heavy media scrutiny and praise for the band's validity and power despite its members' ages. That the song describes the pleasures of black women, a delight Dylan has evidently sampled, made this pick from the Stones' catalogue all the more, shall we say, cocky. Dylan's note-perfect, crowd-pleasing rendition, complete with his Never Ending Tour backup band (and usually the audience too) supplying the "yeah, yeah, yeah, whooooos," was just as dynamic as any laid down by the Stones, so much so that one might have sworn that Keith Richards himself had sneaked onstage to remit a guitar lick or two.

In its day, the lustful "Brown Sugar" was a major hit for the Rolling Stones when it was released in 1971, soaring to No. 1 on the U.S. charts.

"Brown Sugar" had its genesis in the Australian outback in the summer of 1969. During

B

some downtime from his disastrous star turn in the shooting of *Ned Kelly*, a Tony Richardson–directed, paint-by-numbers bioflick about that country's most infamous outlaw spiced with some original folk songs by Shel Silverstein (see "A Coupla More Years"), Jagger was playing an electric guitar through a small amp as the chords to the song materialized out of thin air. He soon scratched out some lyrics, playing off both the street name of a potent form of unrefined heroin from Southeast Asia and the enticements of sepia beauties. Later that year he recorded the song with the Stones at the famed Muscle Shoals, Alabama, studio that produced some of the era's great platters and, a decade hence, Dylan's *Slow Train Coming* album. As Stephen Davis wrote in his book *Old Gods Almost Dead: The 40-Year Odyssey of the Rolling Stones* (New York: Broadway Books, 2001), "Brown Sugar" represented what the group had come to Alabama for: "a furious and alive record of a coked-up band rocking out the Deep South."

ⓢ "Buckets of Rain" (Bob Dylan)

Bob Dylan, *Blood on the Tracks* (1975)

Various Artists (performed by Bob Dylan), *Wonder Boys Soundtrack* (2000)

Bette Midler (performed with Bob Dylan), *Songs for the New Depression* (1976)

Happy Traum, *American Stranger* (1978); *Bucket of Songs* (1983)

Wendy Bucklew, *The Times They Are A-Changin'* (1992)

Jimmy LaFave, *Road Novel* (1998)

Steve Howe, *Portraits of Bob Dylan* (1999)

Mary Lee's Corvette, *Blood on the Tracks* (2002)

Wendy Bucklew, *After You* (2002)

Various Artists (performed by Bette Midler), *Doin' Dylan 2* (2002)

Various Artists (performed by Wendy Bucklew), *May Your Song Always Be Sung: The Songs of Bob Dylan, Volume 3* (2003)

Closing an otherwise desperate album with a light reappraisal of commitment, "Buckets of Rain" is a final, Sinatra-like tip of the hat sung with the playfulness of an old Piedmont songster. Though Dylan seems to liken the relationship he describes here with the ferocity of a deluge, he plaintively sings to his love, describing in light, sensual brushstrokes why he still finds her special. The song took on a warmer, even more intimate glow when he recorded "Buckets of Rain" with Bette Midler for her 1976 LP, *Songs for the New Depression*.

Those looking for Dylan's influences in "Buckets of Rain" must stretch far and wide. In his book *Song & Dance Man III: The Art of Bob Dylan* (London and New York: Continuum International Publishing Group, 2000), Michael Gray suspects that Dylan's dignified lyric "All ya can do is do what you must/You do what you must do and ya do it well" is a rewrite of a blues couplet ("Whenever you're doing whatever you should/Just do your best to do it good") from "Do It Right," an obscure 1929 Kid Wesley Wilson and Harry McDaniels song. Later in his tome, Gray untangles the "little red wagon" referenced in the fourth verse, charting its course from its possible origins in everything from the children's nursery rhyme "Skip to M'Lou" to its use as an uncommon blues phrase denoting anal sex, its appearance as part of a title of a 1939 Western swing song, and as the title of a Woody Guthrie song, which is probably how Dylan first happened upon it.

"Buckets of Rain" was performed only once, when it was a surprising opener for Dylan's final 1990 concert in Detroit. Rumor has it that Doc Watson was performing this one in the late 1990s.

ⓢ "Bunkhouse Theme" (Bob Dylan)

Bob Dylan, *Pat Garrett and Billy the Kid* (1973)

A pleasant if forgettable acoustic instrumental that sounds like the soundtrack music it was meant to be.

[S] "Bye and Bye" (Bob Dylan)

Bob Dylan, *"Love and Theft"* (2001)

On the surface this easygoing, lilting ballad is something one would expect from Leon Redbone or, from an earlier era, Bing Crosby. Some Dylanists have traced the musical source for "Bye and Bye" to "Having Myself a Time," a song popularized by Billie Holiday and written by Leo Robin and Ralph Rainger. But Dylan's Tin Pan Alley pleaser slowly gives way to the sentiments of a scary stalker.

As Richard Harrington wrote in his September 16, 2001, *Washington Post* review of *"Love and Theft"*: "In 'Bye and Bye,' Dylan sings 'The future for me is already past/You were my first love, you will be my last.' Take him literally and it's about obsessional desire for a particular woman. But it's also about American roots music and Dylan's abiding appreciation for it, and inspiration from it, over the course of half a century."

In early 2002, Dylan began airing the lounge-geared "Bye and Bye" in performance venues as wide ranging as small theaters to hockey rinks, where it sounded like it could be an assessment of risk taking: "I'm walking on briars; I'm not even acquainted with my old desires."

C

[S] "Call Letter Blues" (Bob Dylan)

Bob Dylan, *The Bootleg Series, Volumes 1–3: Rare and Unreleased, 1961–1991/'74* (1991)
Jeff Lang, *Cedar Grove* (1999)

Along with "Up to Me," "Call Letter Blues" was one of two outtakes from the September 1974 New York sessions that produced *Blood on the Tracks* and was eventually released many years later. In this case it is presumed that because it is a structural and thematic doppelgänger for "Meet Me in the Morning," another bluesy *Blood on the Tracks* song about a busted romance on an album already filled with much of the same, "Call Letter Blues" was regarded as redundant and relegated to the scrap heap.

Despite Dylan's insistence to the contrary, the confessional nature of this song and, indeed, of many of the songs from *Blood on the Tracks*, would lead one to conclude that he was addressing his failing marriage in this surge of inspired, though tortured, creativity. True to form, the narrator here is found wandering alone on the city's streets tormented by the toning church bells that seem to follow him around every corner. Approached by the night's call girls, he appears to rebuff their advances, so bedeviled is he by the abandonment of his true love. At home, his alienation is even more evident: he is tongue-tied when visitors ask of his departed wife and by his children's questions regarding the whereabouts of their mother. All the while, he is unable to escape his thoughts of her with another man. Call letters are those used by radio stations to identify themselves, so perhaps the singer hopes his woman will hear this plea over the airwaves in somebody else's room.

[S] "Canadee-I-O" (Traditional)

Bob Dylan, *Good as I Been to You* (1992)
Patrick Galvin, *Irish Love Songs* (1958)
Ed McCurdy, *Ballad Record* (1961)
Nic Jones, *Penguin Eggs* (1980)

The story of a young woman disguising herself as a man to follow her sweetheart to war or sea is a common one in folk ballads, but often the outcome is tragic. Dylan gives this one, about a woman who stows away on ship to follow her sailor boy, a happy ending with a twist: rather than being thrown overboard by the crew after her ruse is discovered, or even escaping with her man, she instead marries the captain, who saves her from the other sailors.

"Canadee-I-O" is not to be confused with "Canaday-I-O," one of many lumberjack songs about conditions in the Canadian and American lumber camps of the mid-nineteenth century thought to have originated when shanty boys from Maine were recruited to work in winter camps along the St. Lawrence River. One of the earliest documented versions of the "Canadee-I-O" performed by Dylan can be found in *English Peasant Songs*, a significant 1929 compilation collected by Frank and Ethel Kidson.

Dylan could well have learned "Canadee-I-O" from the Nic Jones version on *Penguin Eggs*, Jones's outstanding 1980 album—his last before a terrible car crash put an end to his career, though not his life. However, though he uses the same words and tune as Jones, Dylan adapts the song to his comfort zone. He did catch some flak for allegedly not throwing arranger's credit (or royalties) to Jones.

Dylan has never performed "Canadee-I-O" in concert, but did include this dusky jewel for his first album of folk and blues cover songs, *Good as I Been to You.*

[S] **"Candyman"** (Traditional)

aka "Candy Man," "Candy Man Blues"
Richard "Rabbit" Brown, *The Greatest Songsters: Complete Works (1927–1929)* (1990)
Rev. Gary Davis, *Pure Religion!* (1957)
Ramblin' Jack Elliott, *Hard Travelin'* (1961)
Dave Van Ronk, *Just Dave Van Ronk* (1964)
Mississippi John Hurt, *Today!* (1966)
Sammy Davis Jr., *Greatest Hits, Volume 1* (1978)
Jorma Kaukonen, *Magic* (1985)
Taj Mahal, *Giant Step* (1996)
Stefan Grossman, *Shake That Thing: Fingerpicking Country* (1998)

Dylan's penchant for reinterpreting chestnuts from the folk and blues traditions was never more evident than at the outset of his career. His versions of "Candyman" from the early 1960s—they can be found on a number of unauthorized recordings in circulation—draw on both the sexual and violent nature of this title character so celebrated in early Southern blues. Many of these original rural versions have their roots in a pre-blues number entitled "Salty Dog" and are considerably more salacious than Dylan's or others recorded by folkies from the '50s, '60s, and beyond. Lines like "He's got a stick of candy nine inches long," and so forth, did not always sit well on the coffeehouse circuit and would easily raise the hackles of President George W. Bush's attorney general, John Ashcroft, and his ilk. Though Dylan's versions were not without their charming raunch, he seems to rely more on the model set forth by Rev. Gary Davis's 1957 recording or Jack Elliott's 1961 derivation than on the earlier, bluer renditions made infamous by "Rabbit" Brown and the like.

Though somewhat bowdlerized, Dylan's "Candyman" is much like his predecessors in that he is liable to return to town, woo the women, win the craps games, and settle old scores before returning to the dark vacuum from whence he came.

[S] **"Can't Help Falling in Love"** (George Weiss/ Hugo Peretti/Luigi Creatore)

Bob Dylan, *Dylan* (1973)
Elvis Presley, *Blue Hawaii* (1961)
Luka Bloom, *Acoustic Motorbike* (1992)

James Galway, *Wind of Change* (1994)
Stray Cats, *Runaway Boys* (1997)
Doris Day, *Move Over Darling* (1997)
Neil Diamond, *As Time Goes By—Movie Album* (1998)
The Jordanaires, *Sing the King* (1998)
Julio Iglesias, *Mia Vida* (1998)

With a solemn organ, harmonica, and tuneless singing, "Can't Help Falling in Love" must be taken as Exhibit A in any case arguing that Columbia Records was out to humiliate their former and future blue-chip artist with the release of *Dylan* without its namesake's input or authorization, following his jump to David Geffen's Asylum Records in 1973. The version appearing on *Dylan* was recorded by Dylan during his *Self Portrait* rehearsals in New York City in August 1970.

Written for Elvis Presley's movie *Blue Hawaii*, "Can't Help Falling in Love" was based on the classical French composition "Plaisir d'Amour" by Giovanni Martini (1741–1816). Elvis first recorded the song in 1961 and had an instant hit that reached No. 2 during a fourteen-week stay on *Billboard*'s Hot 100 chart.

George David Weiss (born April 9, 1921, New York City) was a Juilliard School of Music alum whose songs have found their way into the popular culture via Elvis, films, and late Tin Pan Alley. An accomplished musician, he played violin and reeds in late Swing Era dance bands before going on to a career as a songwriter and producer, working with an array of talent that included everyone from Elvis to Kathie Lee Gifford and jazz percussionist Mtume. Weiss composed some songs for short animations, cowrote the scores for a couple of Broadway shows (*Mr. Wonderful* and *First Impressions*), and was, for a time, president of the Songwriters Guild of America.

The other two cocomposers of "Can't Help Falling in Love," Hugo Peretti (born December 6, 1916, Italy; died May 1, 1986, Englewood, New Jersey) and Luigi Creatore (born December 21, 1920, Italy), were best known as a team whose careers moved from the ghetto slums of New York City's tough Little Italy and Hell's Kitchen neighborhoods to the borscht belt, Tin Pan Alley, and the heights of the record biz as both songwriters and producers. And this from a couple of guys whose first joint project was a children's record. Check out the résumé of those whose careers they shepherded as producers: Sarah Vaughan ("Make Yourself Comfortable," "How Important Can It Be," "Whatever Lola Wants," "Mr. Wonderful"), Georgia Gibbs ("Tweedle Dum" and "Dance with Me Henry"), R&B guy Jimmie Rodgers ("Honeycomb" and "Kisses Sweeter Than Wine"), Sam Cooke ("Chain Gang," "Twisting the Night Away," "Another Saturday Night," and more), the Isley Brothers ("Shout"), and the Tokens ("The Lion Sleeps Tonight"). They released a couple of popular 1959 albums of their own: *The Cascading Voices of the Hugo and Luigi Chorus* and *Let's Fall in Love*.

Finally, the team of Weiss, Peretti, and Creatore composed two other songs for Elvis: "Ku-u-i-po" and "Wild in the Country."

◙ "Cantina Theme" (Bob Dylan)

aka "Workin' for the Law"
Bob Dylan, *Pat Garrett and Billy the Kid* (1973)

Melodically similar to "Knockin' on Heaven's Door" in its sleepy evocation of the Southwest and plucked from the same sessions that produced that famous cut, "Cantina Theme" is a light *Pat Garrett* instrumental featuring background choral moaning, bongos, and acoustic guitars—in other words, the atmospheric soundtrack music it was composed to be.

[S] **"Can't Wait"** (Bob Dylan)
Bob Dylan, *Time out of Mind* (1997)

Regularly featured in the latest stages of the Never Ending Tour, "Can't Wait" finds a man at the end of his rope and Dylan using his nasty rasp to undercut the song's romantic blandishments. He can't live without the love of his object of affection, but is too restless to let another second pass before allowing her to decide whether to return to him or not. As Dylan sings this song, one can practically see him watching each grain of sand plummet from the top of the hourglass and into its bottom as he restlessly awaits her choice.

Ever impatient in this bluesy plea with some subtle religious undercurrents, Dylan casts a cold eye on familiar territory: emotional and romantic abandonment. Ever the outsider, Dylan is "strolling through the lonely graveyard" of his mind as he attempts to shake himself back to life. He views the world around him with detachment. Observing that some people are on their way up and others are headed south, Dylan seems to be wondering which escalator he is on.

Distinguishing this song from most other live performances of the *Time out of Mind* material, Dylan infused "Can't Wait" with a funky, sometimes jazzy, sometimes Latin beat that gave it an onstage charge.

[S] **"Can You Please Crawl Out Your Window?"** (Bob Dylan)
aka "Please Crawl Out Your Window"
Bob Dylan, single (1965); *Biograph/'65* (1985); *Masterpieces* (1978)
Jimi Hendrix, *Anthology* (1994); *BBC Sessions* (1998)
Patricia Paay, *Beam of Light* (1975)
Wilko Johnson, *Ice on the Motorway* (1981)
Transvision Vamp, *Little Magnets vs. The Bubble* (1991)
The Original Sins, *Outlaw Blues* (1992)
Michel Montecrossa, *Born in Time* (2000)
Carla Olson, *Ring of Truth* (2002)

Dylan cut at least a few biting versions of this absurdist put-down song—one of his most cynical digs at a member of the opposite sex—in 1965: two with Michael Bloomfield and Al Kooper during the *Highway 61 Revisited* sessions and three during his first studio powwow with the Hawks. The early Bloomfield version was mistakenly and briefly released as a single when an engineer confused it with the similarly toned "Positively 4th Street." When released on a legit A-side single in November 1965, "Can You Please Crawl Out Your Window?" climbed to No. 58 on the *Billboard* charts. The later cut with the Hawks was made commercially available on *Masterpieces* and *Biograph*.

While some Dylanists appear to have a negative impression of this cold-eyed song (and let's face it: it's no "Positively 4th Street"), "Can You Crawl Out Your Window?" is laced with wonderfully snappy internal rhyme schemes and sharp imagery. Those first lines ("He sits in your room, his tomb, with a fistful of tacks/Preoccupied with his vengeance/Cursing the dead that can't answer him back/I'm sure he has no intentions/Of looking your way, unless it's to say/That he needs you to test his inventions") set the tone for Dylan's diatribe and, when combined with the blithe, hurdy-gurdy garage-band rock score accompanying the words, fit perfectly with the meaning. Although the song's theme is a bit limited (Bob disses the domineering, off-screen boyfriend while coaxing some damaged goods out for the night, simultaneously reminding her, "You can go back to him any time you want to"), the manner in which the message is delivered is at once original, tangy, and sympathetic. The catalogue of brilliant slurs he levels at the girl's boy toy are worthy of a hepster playing the dozens on a Harlem stoop circa 1962, among them: "He looks so truthful, is this how he feels?/Trying to peel the moon and expose it/With his businesslike anger and his bloodhounds that kneel/If he needs a third eye he just grows it." Or consider these angry, sarcastic put-downs: "He just needs you to talk or to hand him his chalk/Or pick it up after he throws it." And if one is still on the fence about paying the price of admission to this fun-house mirror of a song, how about these lines: "Why does he look so righteous while your face is so changed/Are you frightened of the box you keep him in." Ending with a pungent salvo about faith's ironic blindness with a touch of a looming doomsday ("While his genocide fools and his friends rearrange/Their religion of the little ten women/That backs up their views but your face is so bruised/Come on out the dark is beginning"), the narrator makes his final plea to Little Miss Lonely leaning on her sill.

C. P. Lee's critique of the Dylan/Hawks version of "Can You Please Crawl Out Your Window?" in his book *Like the Night: Bob Dylan and the Road to the Manchester Free Trade Hall* (London: Helter Skelter Publishing, 1998) is one of the few detailed appraisals of this generally overlooked composition. Lee contextualizes the song in terms of Dylan's going electric and the reaction he knew he was going to elicit:

> For a group who hadn't been playing together for even a month, the recording of "Can You Please Crawl Out Your Window" is quite remarkable and demonstrates the power and range that they'd later find together on stage. "...Window" is basically hatred you can dance to. But, bizarrely, hatred with a glockenspiel! Like a child's musical box with grinding electric guitar played like only [Robbie] Robertson could, smeared over the top. With

its rinky-dink cowbell percussion and words of spewed resentment—What the Hell was Dylan up to with this song?

With its direct reference to a male protagonist it has been the perceived wisdom to deconstruct this song along lover/jealousy lines. Perhaps as a plea to Sara Lownds, who[m] he [Dylan] was to marry on November 22, a month after the song was finished, perhaps as a put-down to one of his old Greenwich Village buddies? Or perhaps it's a commentary on the audiences that The Hawks had been encountering on their travels?

If the female in the song is Dylan's muse, or even his sensibility, then it makes unusual sense to regard the masculine aspect of it as Dylan's vision of a nemesis in the form of the archetypal Traditionalist; scowling, righteous and preoccupied with his vengeance for what is perceived as Dylan's selling out Folk music. Dylan snarls, "He looks so truthful, is this how he feels?" in reference to the implied purity of the Traditionalist. Dylan talks of how the male's "Genocide fools and his friends rearrange their religion of the little ten women...."

Whatever the meaning of the "little ten women," it appears that they back up the views of the male even though the face of the female is "so bruised." Although it is not clear what she was bruised from. From the arguments over "selling out," commerciality, purism?

Part of the lore surrounding "Window" concerns its place as a final nail in the coffin of Dylan's relationship with folkie/activist Phil Ochs, who, after offering a less than flattering critique of the song to Dylan en route to a New York City disco, was ordered out of the limo as Dylan slapped him with the ultimate salvo: "You're just a journalist."

C

There is some evidence that Dylan performed "Can You Please Crawl Out Your Window?" at at least one 1965 concert—the October 1 affair held at Carnegie Hall in New York City during the generally unheralded fall tour from that very transitional year.

⬛ "Car Car" (Woody Guthrie)
aka "Car Song," "Riding in My Car," "Take Me Riding in My Car"
Woody Guthrie, *Woody Guthrie: This Land Is Your Land—The Asch Recordings, Volumes 1–4* (1999)
Odetta, *Tin Angel* (1954)
Pete Seeger, *Children's Concert at Town Hall* (1963)
Peter, Paul & Mary, *In Concert* (1964)
Donovan, *Catch the Wind* (1965)
Baby Sitters, *Best of the Baby Sitters* (1991)
Various Artists (performed by Bruce Springsteen), *'Til We Outnumber 'Em* (2000)

An early entry into Dylan's performance catalogue (there are a trio of versions from 1961 in circulation), "Car Car" was part of Woody Guthrie's song cycle for children from the 1940s.

Guthrie, forever the unrepentant and irascible man-boy, had a wonderful, non-condescending, and easy ability to cast himself as a child in creating his songs for young people. He had written songs for his children from a marriage in the 1930s, but the cycle for which he was famous was made for his children with Marjorie Guthrie in 1946 and 1947, earning plaudits from the Parents-Teachers Association and the National Education Association. Some, like "Car Car," are pure whimsy, but others, such as "Don't You Push Me Down," can legitimately be utilized by parents as object lessons in how to stand up for oneself—a message not foreign to those familiar with Guthrie's decidedly serious protest fare.

⬛ "Caribbean Wind" (Bob Dylan)
Bob Dylan, *Biograph/'81* (1985)
The Revelators, *Amazing Stories* (1991)
Various Artists (performed by the Revelators), *Life in the Folk Lane, Volume 2* (1995)
The Zimmermen, *The Dungeon Tapes* (1996)
Black Sorrows, *Very Best Of (Johnny Gumbo's Nude Lounge)* (1998)

A beguiling and compelling song left off a satisfying yet overlooked platter, "Caribbean Wind" is a *Shot of Love* outtake that saw a small breath of life as a concert powerhouse in its sole live outing at San Francisco's Warfield Theater in November 1980. It's one of those brilliant Dylan songs full of passionate wanderlust and mythic drama—as long as you don't try to explain what it's about or attempt to sing along. Unfortunately, by the time Dylan recorded it, several months after performing it, "Caribbean Wind" had gone through several rewrites, each more watered-down than the last, rendering its completed studio take a dying ember in comparison to its previously incendiary concert display.

In the *Biograph* liner notes Dylan said that he started writing "Caribbean Wind" upon waking from "a strange dream in the hot sun. There was a bunch of women working a tobacco field on a high rolling hill. A lot of them were smoking pipes. I was thinking about living with somebody for all the wrong reasons." In those notes, Dylan also describes the frustration of having an initial flash of inspiration, only to let it evaporate by fiddling with it too much or not trusting its power: "The inspiration's gone and you can't remember why you started it in the first place."

Written on this side of his intense gospel phase, "Caribbean Wind" was perhaps Dylan's way of looking back at the events and feelings leading up to his conversion. When, in the song, he sings, "I was playing a show in Miami, in the theater of divine comedy," he may be referring to his December 16, 1978, concert at the Sportatorium near Miami, his last show before attending Bible school in the early months of 1979. And while he was already in the midst of his "born-again" flash (he played the new, religious "Do Right to Me Baby" that same night), the reference to Dante's monumental *Divine Comedy* trilogy, which deals so urgently, excruciatingly, and sublimely with man's relationship to God and himself, would seem to be Dylan saying (with perfect 20/20 hindsight) that it was at the concert, or at least during that period in late 1978, when he grasped what the future held for him. If the seething "dark heat" of *Street Legal* represented a journey into the *Inferno* (a brusque, contorted place of perversion and anguish where love hides in deceit's shadows), and *Slow Train Coming* and *Saved* (with their songs of warning, admonishment, asceticism, and a covenant renewed) were analogous to *Purgatory* and a rise to *Paradise*, then "Caribbean Wind" represents a reembrace of the real, less-defined world with all its many masks. Adhering to the fairly widespread agreement that *Shot of Love* and *Infidels* are secular albums steeped with religious reference, "Caribbean Wind" contains elements of all three levels of Dante's vision: temptation ("It certainly was possible as the gay night wore on" and "the hoax of free speech"), the cautionary, moral tones ("the furnace of desire . . . bringing everything that was dear to me nearer to the fire"), and the pot of gold at the end of the rainbow when the narrator escapes from the trap of all *isms* to rekindle the embers of his artistic inspiration. Unfinished? No doubt. Crammed with all kinds of unfocused, filler lyrics that don't exactly lend themselves to narrative interpretation? Agreed. Regardless, "Caribbean Wind" brings Dylan's *Shot of Love* vision into sharper relief. With these refractory, cubist images and nonnarrative, impressionistic points of view, this song brings to mind "Tangled Up in Blue" as a first cousin. Maybe vagueness was exactly what Dylan had in mind.

◪ *Carolyn Hester*
Columbia Records LP CL-1796, CS CS-8596. Released 1962.

One of Dylan's first big professional breaks came when he played some harmonica at a recording session for Carolyn Hester, a transplanted Texas folkie who was making a name for herself on the East Coast. Dylan appeared on three songs included on Hester's eponymous Columbia debut album: "I'll Fly Away," "Swing and Turn Jubilee," and "Come Back, Baby."

Hester (born 1937, Waco, Texas) came to New York City in the mid-1950s. Seeking fame and fortune as a folk singer and actress, she already had an LP on Coral Records (on which she had been helped by Buddy Holly) under her belt. By 1960 she was playing regularly in Greenwich Village at such haunts as One Sheridan Square. She met the writer and folkster Richard Fariña at the White Horse Tavern, and after a courtship of less than two weeks, they married and soon afterward moved to Boston, with its bustling folk music community.

Singing songs from her native Southwest as well as standard folk tunes, Hester was a folk-scene mainstay in the 1960s. *Carolyn Hester* garnered rave reviews, but she herself fell into relative obscurity for a long stretch when the folk music renaissance of the early 1960s began to peter out. She tried her hand at folk-rock, even cutting two ill-advised psychedelic-influenced discs. After straying from the music business for most of the 1970s and 1980s, she mentored Nanci Griffith and resumed performing, making rare appearances on the folk circuit with a graduated, contemporary folk presentation. She duetted with her pupil on Dylan's "Boots of Spanish Leather" on Griffith's *Other Voices, Other Rooms* album and, fittingly, duplicated the feat at Dylan's 30th Anniversary concert at New York's Madison Square Garden in 1992.

[S] "Carrying a Torch" (Van Morrison)

Van Morrison, *Hymns to the Silence* (1991)
Tom Jones, *Carrying a Torch* (1991)
Evangeline, *Evangeline* (1992)

Dylan, ever the Van Morrison celebrant, was known for a long time to slip an odd homage or two to the world's preeminent Celtic rocker into his sets by the time he performed "Carrying a Torch," Morrison's aching cry for an unrequited love, in the late 2002 Never Ending Tour. That unusual tour also regularly featured songs from a variety of popdom's big voices of the late twentieth century: the Rolling Stones, Warren Zevon, and Don Henley.

"Carrying a Torch," like most of the songs drawn from Morrison's *Hymns to the Silence*, is another Van the Man trip into both the mystic and the all too real, casually hanging out in the spiritual world as he sings these hymns with a combination of the flourishes that marked his best albums: R&B, folk, pop, Celtic, rock, and gospel.

[P] Johnny Cash

Born J. R. Cash, February 26, 1932, Kingsland, Arkansas; died September 12, 2003, Nashville

Johnny Cash, "the Man in Black," was a supernova of American music. His genius and complex, sometimes enigmatic personality, manifested in both his songwriting and performances, made him an icon in the American pantheon.

A chip off the same unrepentantly righteous block and a graduate of the school of hard knocks that produced Woody Guthrie, Cash had an impoverished, hardscrabble youth that gave him more material for song than most people get in a lifetime. After nearly dying of starvation as an infant, Cash took his first steps across the dirt-floor sharecropper's shack he shared with his sprawling, cotton-picking family. Despite the death of two children, floods, and backbreaking labor, the proud Cash clan persevered through the Great Depression with dignity, adhering to a spiritual faith instilled by a determined, Pentecostalist mother.

It was during those years that J. R. (as he was named by his parents) first began absorbing the plainspoken stories and down-home music of the sharecroppers—stories and sounds he would one day smelt into his own unique ore. Johnny finally broke away from his kin, however, working at an auto-body plant in Pontiac, Michigan, before enlisting in the U.S. Air Force when he was twenty-two. While stationed in Germany he served as a radio operator and, more importantly, took up the guitar and made his first, meager stabs at writing songs. One of them, "Hey Porter," later wound up as the A-side of his first single.

After his discharge, Cash took up residency in Memphis and became a door-to-door appliance salesman. Determined to start a career in music, he enrolled in a radio announcing course. But it was when he joined forces with guitarist Luther Perkins and bassist Marshall Grant, a couple of guitar-playing grease monkeys he met through his brother Ray, that things began to gel. Rehearsing at night, they billed themselves as Johnny Cash and the Tennessee Two (or simply the Tennessee Three) for a series of semiformal appearances at church socials and country fairs in preparation for an

C

audition with Sun Records, where they impressed Sam Phillips, the fledgling label's patriarch, and won a contract. Almost instantly they scored a big country hit with "Cry, Cry, Cry" (Sun's first country hit) and a crossover pop-chart-topper with "I Walk the Line," a stern avowal of sexual fidelity marked by Cash's husky and cavernous baritone and a song that would later become his signature tune.

Fed up with Phillips's already evangelistic autocracy, Cash signed with Columbia and was teamed with Don Law, the legendary producer who helped put Nashville on the map. The men shared a traditional, down-home approach to making music and crafted a Spartan sound that retained the best of Cash's premier Sun work.

But hit singles were not Johnny Cash's road to glory. Rather, the revolution that his music engendered came via his albums, arguably the first "concept" or thematic albums found in the folk or country idioms. These thoughtful Cash collections began in 1960 with *Ride This Train*, an American travelogue, and continued in 1963 with his homage to the American laborer in *Blood, Sweat and Tears*. A 1964 release, *Bitter Tears*, was a collection of Indian protest songs revealing a deeper glimpse of the recording artist's advancing aesthetic.

This important period occurred when Cash began to exert what resulted in his incalculable influence on the tapestry of American music, for, as Rich Kienzle observed in *Country Music* magazine, he "strengthened the bonds between folk and country music so that both sides saw their similarities as well as their difference. He helped to liberalize Nashville so that it could accept the unconventional and the controversial."

Constantly touring for most of the '60s, Cash built a solid reputation as a topflight act,

Johnny Cash walks inside the gates of California's Folsom Prison, preparing to perform there, 1964.
(Photo: Hulton Archive/Getty Images)

which earned him featured spots not only on both country-and-western and major network television variety shows, but in films as well. Folk-music audiences also admired him greatly and he headlined the big-time festivals and performed in clubs across the country. But beyond the simple, chugging rhythm of his tunes, the booming baritone's songs won the hearts and minds of his admirers with their authority and simple, everyday Hemingwayesque poetry.

By this point in his career, the rigors of life on the road and his own depressive tendencies had left Cash a shell of a man, his body and soul wracked by a dependency on amphetamines and barbiturates. Missed engagements and wild binges cost him not only his reputation but also his wife, who filed for divorce. When he was found close to death by a policeman after a serious 1967 pill-popping binge in a tiny Georgia village, things hit as rock-bottom as they ever would again.

The change in his life can be traced to the day he met June Carter, daughter of Mother Maybelle Carter of the Carter Family, among country music's most beloved and enduring clans. The two would eventually marry in 1968 after June helped him dry out, undergo treatment for his self-abuse, and rediscover his Christian faith.

In short order, the name Cash carried worldwide cachet. Between the release of *Johnny Cash at Folsom Prison*, his guest appearance on Bob Dylan's 1969 *Nashville Skyline* album (on which they performed a keening duet on Bob's "Girl of the North Country"), and his recording of Shel Silverstein's comedic "A Boy Named Sue," Cash was becoming a household name.

But Cash retained an outlaw edge that the Nashville elite never fully embraced. The quality of his work, though, was never questioned, and on its strength he was offered a prime-time television show in 1969. Undoubtedly the highwater mark of *The Johnny Cash Show* was Dylan's 1969 appearance, when the two reprised their "Girl of the North Country" duet, and Dylan performed "I Threw It All Away" and "Living the Blues."

Cash and Dylan had first crossed paths at the 1964 Newport Folk Festival, and the two were filmed backstage at one of Dylan's British concerts in May 1966. A snippet of them duetting appeared in the scrambled cinéma vérité commemoration of that tour, *Eat the Document*. But the apex of their musical collaboration— the dozen or so songs left on the cutting-room floor when Cash visited Dylan at Nashville's Music Row Studio in February 1969 while the latter was recording *Nashville Skyline*—is unknown to the casual fan of either artist. Only one of these songs, "Girl of the North Country," made it onto *Nashville Skyline*; however, the balance of the session may be found in pristine fidelity on the pirate disc *The Dylan/Cash Session*, as well as on other bootleg recordings. Cash might even steal the show in this loose, informal meeting of two giants as he seems to take charge leading the combo (which includes Carl Perkins on electric guitar) through breezy, rockabilly-flavored renditions of five Cash songs ("Big River," "I Walk the Line," "I Still Miss Someone," "Ring of Fire," "Guess Things Happen That Way"), a couple of Dylan songs ("Girl of the North Country" and "One Too Many Mornings"), a couple of oldies but goodies ("That's All Right, Mama" and "Matchbox"), and a dash or two of country gospel and folk. Incidentally, it was around this time that Dylan presented Johnny with "Wanted Man," an on-the-lam desperado song that had Cash's style written all over it.

Like Dylan, Cash was a relentless self-reinventor. And while he never shed and gained quite as many skins as his protégé, his willingness to experiment with his music and persona made him impossible to pigeonhole. Whether turning toward religion in the 1970s, forming the Highwaymen with Kris Kristofferson, Willie Nelson, and Waylon Jennings, or gravitating to the younger songwriters of the day for material and inspiration, Cash cast a restless, brooding presence over his music.

By the time of his appearance at the 1992 Bob Dylan thirtieth-anniversary celebration at Madison Square Garden and a stand at Carnegie Hall, Cash had long since secured himself a deserved place in the pantheon of twentieth-century American music even as he won over new, younger fans. Dylan had already paid tribute to the Man in Black by performing or recording at least five Cash favorites: "Belshazzar," "Big River," "Folsom Prison Blues," "Give My Love to Rose," and "I Walk the Line."

In retrospect, it is no surprise that Cash should have attached himself to producer Rick Rubin (best known for his work in heavy metal and rap) for the release of *American Recordings*, the first of several bare-bones albums with Rubin in which he applied his fatalistic stamp to songs by not only Bruce Springsteen, Leonard Cohen, Tom Waits, and Loudon Wainwright III, but also by neo-headbangers Nine Inch Nails and others whose parents were kids when he first knocked on the front door of Sun Records. The inspired Cash-Rubin partnership culminated with the solemn, spooky, heavily lauded 2003 video of his cover of Nine Inch Nails' "Hurt," in which snapshots and footage of a youthful Cash contrast starkly with images of his senescence.

The last years of Johnny Cash were painful. Stricken by a degenerative nerve disease, he withered away before our eyes, eased only by his will to continue creating, even after the death of June in the spring of 2003. It was only fitting that he followed her into the void at summer's end.

Country music historian Paul Hemphill may have best eulogized the Man in Black when, describing a characteristic Johnny Cash performance, wrote, "Cash, wearing all black, Cash with human suffering in his deep eyes and on his tortured face, Cash, insolent and lashing out from the stage, Cash, in a black swallowtail coat and striped morning pants like an elegant undertaker, Cash swinging his guitar, pointing it at his listeners as though it were a tommy gun, all of these things captured the whole world."

And Dylan's public statement following Cash's death cut to the heart:

I was asked to give a statement on Johnny's passing and thought about writing a piece instead called "Cash Is King," because that is the way I really feel. In plain terms, Johnny was and is the North Star; you could guide your ship by him—the greatest of the greats then and now. I first met him in '62 or '63 and saw him a lot in those years. Not so much recently, but in some kind of way he was with me more than people I see every day.

There wasn't much music media in the early '60s, and *Sing Out!* was the magazine covering all things folk in character. The editors had published a letter chastising me for the direction my music was going. Johnny wrote the magazine back an open letter telling the editors to shut up and let me sing, that I knew what I was doing. This was before I had ever met him, and the letter meant the world to me. I've kept the magazine to this day....

Truly he is what the land and country is all about, the heart and soul of it personified and what it means to be here; and he said it all in plain English. I think we can have recollections of him, but we can't define him any more than we can define a fountain of truth, light, and beauty. If we want to know what it means to be mortal, we need look no further than the Man in Black. Blessed with a profound imagination, he used the gift to express all the various lost causes of the human soul. This is a miraculous and humbling thing. Listen to him, and he always brings you to your senses. He rises high above all, and he'll never die or be forgotten, even by persons not born yet—especially those persons—and that is forever.

Or perhaps Cash summed things up even better when he said in 1994, "I'm obsessed with living. The battle against the dark one and the clinging to the right one is what my life is about."

C

◨ "Catfish" (Bob Dylan/Jacques Levy)
Bob Dylan, *The Bootleg Series, Volumes 1–3: Rare and Unreleased, 1961–1991*/'75 (1991)
Various Artists (performed by Bob Dylan), *Diamond Cuts*/'75 (1997)
Joe Cocker, *Stingray* (1976)
Kinky Friedman, *Lasso from El Paso* (1976)

An outtake from *Desire*, "Catfish" (cowritten, as were most of the songs from that album, with Jacques Levy) is a straightforward hero tale about Jim "Catfish" Hunter, the star baseball pitcher of North Carolina heritage who made his mark with the Oakland A's and New York Yankees during both teams' 1970s glory days.

The 1975 *Desire* recording sessions, in New York, were notoriously chaotic, with as many as two dozen musicians milling around, contributing to and/or sabotaging the proceedings. But most of them seem to have retired to a local watering hole by the time Dylan laid down the prowling version of "Catfish" eventually released on *The Bootleg Series, Volumes 1–3*. With its slow, bluesy, and brooding arrangement, the song has more than a touch of a late-night, red-eyed feel. Regardless, Dylan put together a far rockier arrangement of "Catfish" with bass player Rob Stoner for the Rolling Thunder Revue in 1975, which, though apparently never performed at a Revue show, was eventually included in part on the *Renaldo & Clara* soundtrack.

Lost in the shuffle when considering "Catfish" is that it stands as Dylan's sole but nonetheless noteworthy contribution to the rich artistic and cultural legacy of baseball, a canon that includes music (player J. R. Blodgett's 1858 "Baseball Polka"; Jack Norworth and Albert Von Tilzer's 1908 "Take Me Out to the Ball Game"; Bob Chester and Orchestra's 1941 "Joltin' Joe DiMaggio"; Buddy Johnson's "Did

You See Jackie Robinson Hit That Ball?"; and John Fogerty's 1985 hit "Centerfield"), literature (Ernest Lawrence Thayer's 1888 poem "Casey at the Bat"; Ring Lardner's 1916 novel *You Know Me Al*; John Updike's loving 1960 account of Ted Williams, "Hub Fans Bid Kid Adieu"; Roger Kahn's 1972 memoir of the Brooklyn Dodgers, *The Boys of Summer*; W. P. Kinsella's 1982 novel *Shoeless Joe*; Eric Rolfe Greenberg's 1983 novel *The Celebrant*, about the turn-of-the-century New York Giants; and just about any reportage from the quill of Roger Angell), the Broadway musical (*Damn Yankees!*), movies (*Pride of the Yankees*; *Fear Strikes Out*; *Bang the Drum Slowly*; *The Natural*; and *Bull Durham*), comedy (Bud Abbott and Lou Costello's "Who's on First" routine), painting (Norman Rockwell's tableaux are a good place to start), and food (hot dogs).

Though Levy has been suggested as the song's compositional catalyst, Catfish Hunter's talent, unassuming personality, and small-town folksy charm had probably not escaped Dylan's notice. When Catfish stood up to maverick Oakland A's owner Charles O. Finley in a contractual dispute, Dylan and Levy saw the stuff of song. Supposedly Hunter expressed annoyance when informed of their work, saying something along the lines of, "Who is this guy Dylan to write a song about me?" In any event, although Beat poet Anne Waldman wrote a poem about Curt Flood, the sacrificial lamb of baseball's notorious reserve clause, "Catfish" is the only known song about baseball free agency.

James Augustus Hunter was born on April 9, 1946, near Hertford, North Carolina. There, "my three brothers taught me to throw strikes," he said when inducted into the Baseball Hall of Fame in 1987. "And thanks to them I gave up 379 home runs in the big leagues." Such was

Catfish Hunter's self-deprecating humor. While he overstated the case that day (he surrendered only 374 big-league homers), he also neglected to mention that he developed his pinpoint control by throwing baseballs at a hole in the barn door in a trial-by-fire Hunter family ritual: the last brother to hit the hole had to do the chores.

The nickname "Catfish" was bestowed by Finley to embellish the (Finley-concocted) tall tale that Hunter had once run away from home and come back with two catfish as a peace offering. This story upset Hunter's mother, who didn't want people believing that her little boy had run off when he hadn't. The nickname never stuck in those parts, anyway; around Hertford, he was always known as Jimmy.

Hunter was one of those rare players who never knew the minor leagues: he went straight to the majors from high school in 1965 as a nineteen-year-old bonus baby with Finley's cellar-bound Kansas City Athletics.

In 1968 Charley Finley moved the A's to Oakland, California, and it had an immediate effect on Hunter. Just a month into the new season, he threw the first regular-season perfect game in the American League since 1922, retiring all twenty-seven Minnesota Twins who ventured to home plate that fateful night of May 8. The A's, meanwhile, were steadily building into a powerhouse that would win three consecutive World Series from 1972 to 1974 with a larger-than-life cast of characters that included Reggie Jackson, Vida Blue, Bert Campanaris, and Rollie Fingers.

Although the A's were an immensely talented team that knew how to win, all was not happy with the players; they were not a harmonious bunch in the clubhouse, but they got along even less well with owner Finley. The latter, a shameless publicity hound and miser, gave his players myriad reasons to want to

Jim "Catfish" Hunter pitching in the World Series against the Cincinnati Reds, Riverfront Stadium, Cincinnati, October 17, 1976.
(AP/Wide World Photos)

leave. So, after winning the 1974 American League Cy Young Award, Hunter charged that Finley had violated his contract. At issue was a stipulation that the A's send half of Hunter's $100,000 annual salary to a North Carolina bank as payment on an annuity. Because Finley had not complied, star pitcher Hunter won his grievance and thus became a free agent.

Hunter was venturing into the unknown. In 1970 Curt Flood of the St. Louis Cardinals unsuccessfully challenged baseball's reserve clause (essentially a version of indentured servitude that bound a player to his franchise even when his contract expired); not for another year would L.A. Dodger Andy Messersmith and Montreal Expo Dave McNally win free agency, thereby establishing the players' union's power and spurring a tremendous escalation in athletes' salaries. With his case, Jim Hunter was the first to demonstrate what baseball players' services were worth in the open market.

At that time, ballplayers in organized baseball—the major and minor leagues of the United States and much of Canada—were bound to a team, under contract or not, for life, much like serfs. They could leave their team only if traded to another team or were released from their contractual commitments. There was no competitive labor market for the services of players, so as a result, salaries were artificially depressed. That changed when the arbitrator decided in favor of Jim Hunter.

The unprecedented bidding war that followed Hunter's declaration of free agency was won by the New York Yankees, who signed him on New Year's Eve in 1974 to a five-year contract worth $3.35 million.

Hunter won twenty-three games for the Yanks in 1975, and in 1976 went 17–15. The Bronx Bombers made it to the World Series that year but were swept by Cincinnati's Big Red Machine. Injuries curtailed Hunter's appearances in 1977 and 1978, the years when the Yanks returned to prominence in World Series winnings.

The Yankees of the mid- to late 1970s made the swingin' A's of just a few years earlier look like choirboys. This was the "Bronx Zoo" era, when owner George Steinbrenner competed with his riotous band of brawling pinstripers for ink on the back page of the city's tabloids. With a rogues' gallery that included not only Hunter and Reggie Jackson, but also Thurman Munson, Lou Piniella, Graig Nettles, Rich "Goose" Gossage, and Bucky Dent, these Yanks had a take-no-prisoners, us-against-the-world siege mentality that captured the city's imagination during a particularly dire phase of its social and economic history.

After retiring from baseball at the end of the 1979 season with a lifetime 224–166 record complemented by a slick 3.26 ERA, Hunter continued to do what he had done before baseball and during his off seasons in the sport: farmed cotton and peanuts in Hertford.

The right arm that took Hunter to the Hall Fame stopped working around November 1998. After tests, he was diagnosed with amyotrophic lateral sclerosis, the progressive and incurable neuromuscular illness known as Lou Gehrig's disease—named, ironically, after the "Iron Horse," the Yankees' Hall of Fame first baseman of the 1920s and 1930s, who was stricken with it in 1939 and died two years later. Hunter passed away on September 9, 1999, at his home in Hertford.

Perhaps Hunter's words after a disappointing 1977 World Series outing sum up both his philosophy and his sport's redemptive qualities: "The sun don't shine on the same dog all the time."

"Cat's in the Well" (Bob Dylan)
Bob Dylan, *Under the Red Sky* (1990)
Rich Lerner, *Napoleon in Rags* (2001)

Once again prophesying an apocalypse he seems sure is just around the next corner, Dylan employed the talents of guitarists David Lindley and brothers Stevie Ray and Jimmie Vaughan to crystallize his hypnotic end-time vision of the moment for release on *Under the Red Sky*.

At first glance this looks like a simple song, one of many *Under the Red Sky* postmodern folk nursery rhymes following in the wake of the barnyard apocalypse found in Willie Dixon's "Tail Dragger," "Little Red Rooster" (both covered in threatening and ribald fashion by Howlin' Wolf), and the like. Closer inspection, however, reveals a jewel in the rough, a song so steeped in liturgical reference it could make an Old Testament seer say "I told ya so": a Brothers Grimm menagerie marches in a parade of doom in this eschatological drama occurring just before the curtain drops and the final battle is fought.

Dylan casts "Cat's in the Well" as a blues in the key of myth and biblical legend in his personification of the animal kingdom in a manner similar to his infamous "Man Gave Names to All the Animals" from *Slow Train Coming* more than a decade previously. Here he has a cat, a wolf, a horse, and dogs all playing bit parts in his allegorical one-act. A certain suspense is laid out from the start: a cat is stuck in a well with no escape in sight; if it goes deeper, it drowns. But in typical lose-lose fashion, that hungry wolf stalking the turf topside is sweeping its bushy tail across the ground just waiting to gobble that feline up should it stick its furry little head over the edge.

The barnyard is a familiar setting for many nursery rhymes, and while Dylan draws on a few of them here ("Jemmy Jed," "The Bull's in the Barn," "Old Mother Hubbard"), the primary source for "Cat's in the Well" is pretty well thought to be "Ding Dong Bell, Pussy's in the Well."

On his Never Ending Tour, Dylan performed some pretty ace versions of "Cat's in the Well" after its release and has kept it in the performance rotation since then. But its appearance on the autumn leg of the 2001 national tour gave one pause in the face of global unease, specifically the violence unfolding in Central Asia and the Middle East (and again two years later on his European swing as the casualties mounted in Iraq) as Dylan sang with genuine outrage, "The world's being slaughtered and it's such a bloody disgrace."

"Champaign, Illinois" (Bob Dylan/Carl Perkins)
See also "Blue Suede Shoes," "Matchbox"
Carl Perkins, *On Top* (1969); *Brown-Eyed Handsome Man* (1972); *Back on Top* (2000)

While some Dylan scholars date the composition of this song as early as 1962, others more accurately point to either Dylan's February 1969 studio session with Johnny Cash or his appearance on television's *Johnny Cash Show* of May 1969 as the likely dates of its genesis. This was partially cleared up in Carl Perkins's obituary in the January 28, 1998, issue of the *New York Times*, which reported that "During one of Mr. Cash's television specials, Mr. Perkins met Mr. Dylan and they collaborated on a song called 'Champaign, Illinois,' which Mr. Perkins recorded in 1969."

As a song, "Champaign, Illinois" ain't much. Try this profound line from the chorus on for size: "Champaign, Illinois, Champaign, Illinois/I certainly do enjoy Champaign, Illinois." Not exactly the wild mercury stuff of *Blonde on Blonde*.

Carl Perkins played guitar at the Dylan/ Cash session and on the Cash television show, and although there is no Dylan recording of "Champaign, Illinois," the music and words were published under his name in *Country Song Hall of Fame: Bob Dylan*, #16 in this songbook series (London: Southern Music Publishing Company).

C

[S] "Changing of the Guards" (Bob Dylan)

Bob Dylan, single (1978); *Street Legal* (1978); *Bob Dylan's Greatest Hits, Volume 3* (1994)
Frank Black, single (1988)
Rich Lerner & the Groove, *Cover Down* (2000)

With some brass and reeds lending a distinct mariachi flavor and the backup singers adding a fervent, gospelized punch, "Changing of the Guards" opens *Street Legal* in magisterial fashion as Dylan handles the Lewis Carroll–like lyrics as if he were the White Rabbit on his way to Limbo. It's a song of alienation, but Dylan is not specific about the estrangement he describes. He once commented, "It means something different every time I sing it. 'Changing of the Guards' is a thousand years old."

As an A-side single release, "Changing of the Guards" did not reach the *Billboard* Top 100, and it was trotted onto the concert stage during the 1978 world tour.

While "Changing of the Guards" has been criticized as a song in which Dylan unsuccessfully and cynically parodies his anthemic self in haunting fashion, a little poking around indicates that he did have something pretty deep in mind here. He begins with the autobiographical observations that for sixteen years (that would jibe, more or less, with the amount of time between his arrival in New York City in 1961 and the composition of this song) he has shopped his wares in a marketplace full of every manner of backstabber and thief. He (the song's "good shepherd"—a central allegorical image plucked safe and sound from the New Testament) grieves over a field where desperate men and women are divided against one another. Whether or not the narrator's idea of himself as a peaceful Jesus mourning over humanity's seemingly infinite strife is on the mark, his vision is clear: the fight for station and control of a world ruled by power and death is a sad state of affairs indeed. As the song winds down, Dylan presents a wrathful Christ not unlike the one displayed in Pier Paolo Pasolini's *Il Vangelo secondo Matteo* (*The Gospel According to St. Matthew*), the 1964 three-reeler by that insane genius of an Italian filmmaker. By the song's end, Christ has been transformed from a man with a grieving heart into one of vengeance who will overturn those false idols quick as you can say "Messiah."

[S] "Chimes of Freedom" (Bob Dylan)

Bob Dylan, *Another Side of Bob Dylan* (1964)
The Byrds, *Mr. Tambourine Man* (1965); *Greatest Hits* (1967); *Byrds Play Dylan* (1980); *Definitive Collection* (1998); *Full Flyte (1965–1970)* (1998)
Dino, Desi and Billy, *I'm a Fool* (1965)
West Coast Pop Art Experimental Band, *Volume One* (1966)
Julie Felix, *Flowers* (1967)
The Brothers & Sisters of Los Angeles, *Dylan's Gospel* (1969)
Barracudas, *Los Angeles & Vicinity* (1982); *Live in Madrid* (1986)
Mike Wilhelm, *Mean Ol' Frisco* (1985)
Bruce Springsteen, *Spare Parts* (1988)
Various Artists (performed by Bruce Springsteen), *Chimes of Freedom* (1988)
Youssou N'Dour, *The Guide (Wommat)* (1994)
Phil Carmen, *Bob Dylan's Dream* (1996)
The Zimmermen, *After the Ambulances Go* (1998)
Various Artists (performed by Joan Osborne), *The Sixties—TV Soundtrack* (1998)
Enzo Pietropali, *Stolen Songs* (1999)
Eliza Gilkyson, *Misfits* (2000)
Rocky Erickson, *Hide Behind the Sun* (2000)

"Chimes of Freedom" is a jewel in Dylan's poetic crown. Employing all the pigments available on his ample poetic palette, Dylan utilizes a triple-whammy of the alliterative inscape of Gerard Manley Hopkins, the organic vision of William Blake, and Shakespeare's violent sense of drama in his creation of this powerfully compassionate paean to the downtrodden with a romantic sweep of language and universality. In his mixed-sensorial suggestion that freedom's chimes flash, Dylan dangles the notion that humanity has yet to grasp the promises of liberty floating just out of reach, like a feather caught by the wind.

Similar to "A Hard Rain's A-Gonna Fall," with its rapid-fire sequence of snapshot images, "Chimes of Freedom" depicts a world where the bells are tolling amid great changes and upheaval across the globe, evocative of Native America's vision of "A Great Cleansing." The beginning of "Chimes of Freedom," set against a looming, middle-of-the-night tempest, seems to find Dylan foreshadowing a period of *Twilight Zone*–style darkness with his words and mood. But the sun slowly rises over the course of the song and his hope here is nothing short of all the world's people rising as one to proclaim their survival (as in the finale of Beethoven's Sixth Symphony, *Pastorale*) after another tough night on history's dangerous road; as the sounds of chiming church bells fill the air, the storm clears and dawn breaks.

Even before Dylan wrote "Chimes," its composition was anticipated by the late 1963–early 1964 "11 Epitaphs," which constituted the liner notes to *The Times They Are A-Changin'*. Whatever its genesis, Dylan began getting it on paper about a week into a cross-country car trip with Victor Maimudes, Pete Karman, and Paul Clayton that began in New York on February 3, 1964. Dylan debuted the song in mid-February in Denver and featured it in his concerts through 1964. It was shelved until the 1987 concerts with the Dead and others with Tom Petty and the Heartbreakers, only to fade away again. On January 17, 1993, it made a surprise, barely comprehensible appearance when Dylan joined the festivities surrounding Bill Clinton's presidential inauguration at the Lincoln Memorial in Washington, D.C. Finally, Dylan briefly dusted off "Chimes" for a revival in the fall 2000 Never Ending Tour of the Mid-Atlantic states.

In the 1980s "Chimes of Freedom" became the de facto theme song for the Amnesty International benefit tour led by Sting.

Chronicles/Booker T. and Priscilla Jones
Atlantic Records LP SD-7040. Released 1973.

Dylan has shown up at some unlikely sessions, but his appearance on *Chronicles* ranks among the weirdest as he snuck his harmonica onto Donna Weiss's "Crippled Crow," a track on this soul record from one of the guys who helped define the Stax sound.

Booker T. and the MGs formed in Memphis in 1962, spinning off from the Mar-Keys. Composed of organist Booker T. Jones, guitarist Steve Cropper, bassist Lewis Steinberg, and drummer Al Jackson Jr., the MGs scored their first hit with "Green Onions," a gutbucket instrumental piece that evolved out of a hazy blues riff improvised while killing time in the studio. With its simple, smoky atmospherics punctuated by Cropper's cutting guitar, the MGs' pared-to-the-bone sparseness produced a string of funky tunes with rich titles like "Jellybread," "Chinese Checkers," and "Soul Dressing." When Donald "Duck" Dunn replaced Steinberg on bass, the band's intuitive interplay became the foundation of just about everything coming out of the Stax label for years, most notably Wilson Pickett's "In the Midnight Hour," Sam and Dave's "Hold On, I'm Comin'," and Rufus Thomas's "Walkin' the Dog," on which Booker T. blew some sax as well as attending to his organ duties. And as a racially integrated band of medium profile, they broke some social ground in their display of music's powerful ability to unite.

C

The MGs' last big singles charted in the early 1970s when Jones, after earning a B.A. in music at Indiana University, moved to California and began recording with his wife, Priscilla. The remaining MGs stayed in Memphis and have reconvened sporadically, most famously as the house band at Columbia's thirtieth-anniversary Bob Dylan celebration in 1992 and, as a result of that gig, as Neil Young's backing group for a tour in the mid-1990s.

"City of Gold" (Bob Dylan)
Bob Dylan/Various Artists (performed by Dixie Hummingbirds), *Masked and Anonymous* (soundtrack) (2003)
Dixie Hummingbirds, *Diamond Jubilation: 75th Anniversary Celebration* (2003)

A lost gem from Dylan's gospel phase and a highlight of his November and December 1980 concerts, "City of Gold" has the grace and simplicity of a traditional spiritual as it features him singing in an unusual a cappella–style arrangement complete with wonderful, swooping backup harmonies from his chorus. Here Dylan sings of an Oz-like citadel "far from the rat-race with the bars that hold" and pleads to whomever might be listening from on high to "throw down a rope."

But this vision of a nonsectarian Jerusalem (never mentioned in the song but implied through inference and reference) is an ecumenical one, drawing on the sensibility of the Rev. Gary Davis's "Twelve Gates to the City" and maybe even Hank Williams's plaint against King Midas, "House of Gold." As encore material, the song acted as a kind of farewell benediction to his flock. While Dylan may have attempted a recording of "City of Gold" at the 1981 *Shot of Love* sessions, the song in any event landed on the scrap heap of long-gone but dearly missed Bobscura.

The only official release of "City of Gold" was a fairly recent affair by the Dixie Hummingbirds and includes Dr. John on piano, Levon Helm on drums, and members of Dylan's then-current touring band: bassist Tony Garnier, percussionist George Recile, and guitarist Larry Campbell.

"Clean-Cut Kid" (Bob Dylan)
Bob Dylan, *Empire Burlesque* (1985)
The Textones, *Midnight Mission* (1984)
Carla Olson, *Wave of the Hand: The Best of Carla Olson* (1995)

Ruthless and clever but charmless, "Clean-Cut Kid" has been interpreted as everything from a cynical lament about a Vietnam vet on the verge of committing suicide when he can't adjust to civilian life to a wiseass portrayal of celebrity and the American nightmare. Imagine "The Ballad of Ira Hayes" recast as a bouncy semisurrealist revision set against the backdrop of a Vietnam War hero returning to an unfamiliar land, and some idea of the feeling of "Clean-Cut Kid" can be gleaned. Another cultural signpost with which Dylan was perhaps familiar is *Born on the Fourth of July*, Ron Kovik's anti–Vietnam War memoir about his experiences in that embattled country and coming back crippled or, as Dylan sings it here, "They took a clean-cut kid/And they made a killer out of him,/That's what they did." And finally, perhaps it is a Daliesque update of his own early '60s antiwar song, "John Brown." On a completely different track, the song can be heard as a kind of autobiographical lament of Dylan's state of mind and/or artistic/personal sense of self at the time. That is to say, perhaps he felt that his own spirit had soured since entering public life nearly a quarter-century before, that he had pursued folk music as a clean-cut kid, been swept up into the vortex of the American pop cult celebrity machine, and been summarily spit out the other side with a loss of focus and identity.

If "Clean-Cut Kid" is specifically about Vietnam vets, Dylan's point here is that above and beyond the "napalm health spa" environments they had to endure as grunts on the killing ground, these vets had to confront the attitudes of the American left, which at the extreme, hurled "Baby Killer!" insults at them upon being thrown "back into the rat race without any brakes." With his portrayal of the American Dream gone bust, Dylan created a song that was as cutting as Bruce Springsteen's "Born in the U.S.A.," released around the same time. But with its herky-jerky tempo and unfocused point of view, "Clean-Cut Kid" was never destined for Top 40 land.

"Clean-Cut Kid" was given a snappy concert workout during the 1986 and 1987 tours with Tom Petty and the Heartbreakers, and a gnarlier rave-up by the first incarnations of the Never Ending Tour in 1988 and 1990.

◪ Clinch Mountain Country/Ralph Stanley & Friends
Rebel Records CD 5001. Released 1998.

Clinch Mountain Country is a double CD set on which national treasure Ralph Stanley performs duets with a few dozen country and bluegrass stars, including Dwight Yoakam, Patty Loveless, Vince Gill, George Jones, BR5-49, and Junior Brown. Dylan is there as well, singing lead on a memorably doleful version of "The Lonesome River," a song Stanley wrote with his older brother, Carter. According to Rebel Records, Dylan initiated the recording before the rest of the album was planned and called singing with Ralph Stanley "the highlight of my career." Ralph Stanley, for his part, commenting on the duet with Dylan in the May 20, 1998, issue of the *New York Times*, said,

"That was the first time I ever met him. I'd heard of him."

Along with Bill Monroe and his Blue Grass Boys, the Stanley Brothers were key in the genesis of bluegrass. The vocal and instrumental duo of Ralph (born February 25, 1927, Big Spraddle Creek, Virginia) and Carter Stanley (born August 27, 1925, McClure, Virginia) hailed from Virginia's storied Clinch Mountains, the spawning ground of so many folk and country music luminaries. With the likes of the Carter and Stoneman families haunting the nearby valleys, there was no shortage of musical tradition lacing the hills like the morning mists. But it was the boys' mother, a locally admired singer and banjoist, who had them singing harmony and stuck instruments in their hands when they were barely out of diapers. So Ralph began picking the banjo while Carter strummed a guitar, and if their talents and tastes would carry them far from home, they never left behind the "lined-out" hymns of the local Baptist church—those raw, emotional harmonies that are the very essence of bluegrass.

"White Dove," and especially "Rank Strangers to Me," are two songs heavily associated with the Stanley Brothers that Dylan has shown a fondness for in performance.

◪ "Clothes Line Saga" (Bob Dylan)
aka "Answer to Ode," "Clothesline," "Clothes Line," "Talkin' Clothes Lines Blues"
Bob Dylan/The Band, *The Basement Tapes*/'67 (1975)
Various Artists (performed by Suzzy and Maggie Roche), *A Nod to Bob* (2001)

A sly response to "Ode to Billy Joe," Bobbie Gentry's murder ballad pop hit of the day, and maybe with even a nod to holy trickster fool jazz pianist Fats Waller (his classic "Clothes Line Ballet" is a must for all fans of jazz

"A Monday Washing,"
New York City, ca.
1900.

(Photo: Detroit Photographic
Co./Library of Congress)

bizarro), "Clothes Line Saga" shows how Dylan could write a darkly subversive song with a vanilla veneer about nothing more than hanging clothes out to dry while gossiping with neighbors over the backyard fence—and have it be *so* much more than that. While not exactly on the level of Boccaccio's *Decameron* as a response to Dante's *Divine Comedy*, this moody vignette, a stylistic anomaly in the Dylan catalogue, is laced with understated, "dumb-hick" humor and characters fit for a Chekhov play. Yet it makes a strong statement about the power and importance of simple conversation, as if to point out that interchange such as that portrayed in "Clothes Line Saga" does more to keep a community intact than grand, superficial gestures.

But "Clothes Line Saga" may also be a veiled commentary at the U.S. resumption of attacks on North Vietnam during the end of January 1966, when President Lyndon Johnson ordered air raids after a cease-fire at the end of 1965. That respite from hostilities gave hope to many as expressed by the Byrds, who may have been referring to such possibilities of peace in Vietnam in their folk-rock spin on Ecclesiastes, "Turn! Turn! Turn!", released at the end of 1965, with the last line "A time for peace I swear it's not too late." The country was severely divided in 1966 as to what route to take in Southeast Asia. Vice President Hubert Humphrey (like Dylan, a Minnesotan), never the strongest hawk, came out in support of Johnson's renewed offensive on January 31, 1966, saying, in part, that the raids were necessary "to restore military pressure on North Vietnam," blaming Hanoi's rejection of all U.S. peace overtures. Dylan's lyrics firmly place the action of "Clothes Line" on "January the thirtieth" and put part of the focus of the discussion between the characters on the news that "The Vice-President's gone mad!" Not that Humphrey's waffling on the big issues when it counted was news. The same guy who had been such a champion of the civil rights movement as early as the late 1940s also barred the integrated Minnesota delegation from being seated to placate delegations from other states and prevent a walkout at the 1964 Democratic National Convention, this after having failed to buy off voting-rights firebrand Fannie Lou Hamer with a political deal earlier in the year. The Humphrey connection might have cut even closer to home: as senator, he addressed the Hibbing, Minnesota, Chamber of Commerce in 1956, an event Dylan's dad, Abe Zimmerman, a respected local merchant, must have attended.

As heard on *The Basement Tapes*, the music is so barely nonexistent and Dylan's singing voice no more than a drawl that only Garth Hudson's organ manages to act as the glue keeping the ensemble together. Quintessential ore from *The Basement Tapes*, "Clothes Line Saga" was written and recorded in 1967 in Woodstock, New York, at the outset of Dylan's convalescence from his summer 1966 motorbike crash and long hiatus from performing. There is even some scuttlebutt that he wrote "Clothes Line" under the influence of a prescribed asthmatic inhaler that he and Rick Danko (the Band's bass player and fellow *Basement* denizen) enjoyed fooling around with.

Some have compared "Clothes Line" favorably with Dylan's "Highlands" from thirty years later on *Time out of Mind*, contrary to those who place the latter song as a kind of bookend to "Sad-Eyed Lady of the Lowlands" in pointing to both the length of the two songs and, of course, the verbal highlands/lowlands antonymy. In both "Clothes Line" and "Highlands," however, Dylan's brushstrokes conjure a persuasive painting in sound and words, capturing the tedious ennui of day-to-day existence. Dylan's ability to portray banality in both songs (contrast the con-

versations in the two) shows an artist on top of his game doing no more than smelting artistic significance from ordinary experience.

C

◙ "Cocaine Blues" (Traditional/Luke Jordan)
  aka "Cocaine," "Cocaine Habit Blues," "Cocaine Bill and Morphine Sue," "Take a Whiff on Me," "Honey, Take a Whiff on Me"
  Dick Fariña and Eric von Schmidt (with Dylan performing as "Blind Boy Grunt"), *Dick Fariña & Eric von Schmidt* (1962)
  Luke Jordan, *The Roots of Rap/'27* (1996)
  Memphis Jug Band, *Memphis Jug Band—Double Album/'30* (1990)
  Ramblin' Jack Elliott, *Jack Takes the Floor* (1958)
  Dave Van Ronk, *Inside Dave Van Ronk* (1969)
  Mother McCree's Uptown Jug Champions, *Mother McCree's Uptown Jug Champions/'64* (1999)
  The Byrds, *Untitled* (1970)
  Rev. Gary Davis, *From Blues to Gospel* (1971)

When Huddie "Leadbelly" Ledbetter recorded the most popular early version of this song under its better-known name, "Take a Whiff on Me," he captured the loose attitude toward cocaine shared by many black musicians in the 1920s and '30s. Dylan was undoubtedly familiar with Leadbelly's rendition, but his readings from performances both very early and very late in his career far more strongly resembled Luke Jordan's "rapped" delivery, a style Jordan developed on the medicine-show circuit in the early 1900s. The song is enough to make one wonder exactly what ingredients the medicine show's snake-oil salesmen were sprinkling into their mysterious cure-all elixirs.

Fariña and von Schmidt are said to have learned the song, included on their dual eponymous album (on which Dylan appeared), from Rev. Gary Davis at the 1961 Indian Neck Folk Festival in Connecticut. To bring the lineage full circle, Davis told Richard Noblett in 1966 that he "learned ["Cocaine"] from a carnival show," though he developed the guitar accompaniment himself.

According to John A. Lomax and Alan Lomax in their book *American Ballads and Folk Songs* (New York: Macmillan, 1934), "Cocaine" (and its related songs of various configurations) has an obscure history. "The origin of this cheerful ditty of the dope-heads is doubtful," they write. "At any rate," they continue, "the Southern barrelhouse Negroes sing it and have made it their own.... Most of the stanzas, as we heard them in prisons, are unprintable."

Dylan's early use of "Cocaine" in performance seems not to have stretched much beyond late 1961 to fall 1962. From 1997 through 1999 he included it somewhat regularly in acoustic sets in a rendition that was at once giddy and harrowing as the singer desperately calls out for help ("this old cocaine is makin' me sick") while at the same time managing to sound happily stoned. But because it does not exactly damn the relative evils of the white powder in its conveyance of the sniffer's woozy, if diseased, bliss, "Cocaine" is not the kind of "Just Say No" tract that could sneak past the notice of any parental advisory board.

🅂 "Cold Irons Bound" (Bob Dylan)

Bob Dylan, *Time out of Mind* (1997); *Live 1961–2000—Thirty-nine Years of Great Concert Performances/'97* (2001)
Bob Dylan/Various Artists (performed by Bob Dylan), *Masked and Anonymous* (soundtrack) (2003)
Druhá Tráva & Peter Rowan, *New Freedom Bell* (1999)
Jing Chi, *Jing Chi Live* (2003)

In biting, ricocheting guitar licks, rockabilly drums, distorted organ, and voice floating in a blimp of its own echo, one can still hear, to paraphrase "Visions of Johanna," the ghost of electricity howling from the bones of Dylan's

face in "Cold Irons Bound." The narrator hears voices, but there's no one around ... no one who can lend a helping hand, anyway. One thing for certain is that our antihero is going up the river in chains for unnamed Kafkaesque crimes if the universe doesn't swallow him whole first. Reality, he now sees, has too many heads, so why deal with it? Best to just hit the road, Jack, and melt back into the night.

But despite its funky, on-the-lam sensibility, "Cold Irons Bound" is a bitter song of adieu as our guy comes to terms with the loss of his woman. The aural torment is palpable as he moves from a Sunday morning church service to the mists of the countryside to the winds of Chicago in a futile escape.

Like many a Dylan song, "Cold Irons Bound" has been scrutinized for many possible meanings. Some interpreters have surmised that rather than referring to prison shackles or perhaps the railroad tracks leading out of town, the "cold irons" to which the narrator is bound is the name of a town or city.

If Dylan modeled "Cold Irons Bound" on a film, then he may have had a 1968 classic, *Cool Hand Luke*, in mind. In that movie Paul Newman (playing the title role of Luke) is sometimes an escaped convict shuffling along in leg shackles, alternately free and imprisoned; Luke may have been able to flee his captors temporarily but he is still in captivity, manacled like a wild animal, haunted and eternally burdened like Charles Dickens's Jacob Marley in *A Christmas Carol*. Dylan's narrator may have dumped his lover girl but he is still an inmate in her psychic cell block.

Dylan has kept "Cold Irons Bound," a standout Never Ending Tour choice and one of the best tunes on *Time out of Mind*, as common performance fodder since its debut. Without a doubt it has the most accomplished and unusual instrumental introduction of any song Dylan has ever performed. Sung with his dusty death-rattle, "Cold Irons Bound" was a scary journey into some outer ring of Dylan's icy Inferno.

[S] "Come Back, Baby" (Traditional/Walter Davis)

aka "Can't We Talk It Over," "Let's Talk It Over," "One More Time"

Carolyn Hester (with Dylan as "Blind Boy Grunt"), *Carolyn Hester* (1962, 1994)
Walter Davis, *Complete Recorded Works, Volume 4 (1938–1939)* (1995)
Mance Lipscomb, *Texas Songster, Volume 2* (1964)
Dave Van Ronk, *Inside Dave Van Ronk* (1969)
Tom Rush, *Tom Rush* (1972)

Carolyn Hester remembers Dylan suggesting "Come Back, Baby" as a recording possibility and teaching it to her at Suze Rotolo's apartment in 1962 as they prepared for the studio session that eventually resulted in Hester's Columbia Records debut. Though Dylan almost assuredly learned it from Dave Van Ronk, "Come Back, Baby" is an old song of murky, probably Southern origin, one of many unrelated or semirelated songs sharing the same title. Walter Davis recorded the earliest known version of this particular variation in the late 1930s, but bluesologists believe that Davis's recording is a personal interpretation of a traditional song.

Progressing with the style of a lazy blues, Dylan appears to have utilized the chord progression for his own "Pledging My Time" for *Blonde on Blonde* some five years after recording the song with Hester. A previously unreleased version of "Come Back, Baby" with Dylan from the sessions that produced *Carolyn Hester* was included on the 1994 CD reissue of that historic album.

Walter Davis (born March 1, 1912, Grenada, Mississippi; died October 22, 1963, St. Louis) never made superstar status or even latter-day blues sainthood. Nevertheless, with his two-fisted approach to the piano style and funereal vocals, Davis was among the most prolific blues performers to emerge from prewar St. Louis. His pedestrian work no doubt kept his career in check as he watched both his livelier peers and acolytes—Leroy Carr and Roosevelt Sykes—go on to bigger things. He did live long enough to work with everybody from blues singer Big Joe Williams to jazz drummer Art Blakey. A stroke led him to the ministry during the early 1950s, a path he followed to his grave.

[S] "Coming from the Heart (The Road Is Long)" (Bob Dylan/Helena Springs)

The Searchers, *The Searchers* (1980)
Various Artists (performed by the Searchers), *Doin' Dylan 2* (2002)

A tape of Dylan rehearsing "Coming from the Heart" with his band in April 1978 suggests that he wrote or was writing it with backup singer Helena Springs (confirmed by her listing as coauthor when the lyrics were published in his book *Lyrics, 1962–1985*) around that time. After that, "Coming from the Heart" seems to have been performed at only one show, at a rare concert in Dylan's home state of Minnesota, on Halloween 1978. The tune for the song is, at least, nearly an exact copy of "Never Let Me Go," the Joe Scott ballad Dylan was performing as a duet with Joan Baez during the 1975 Rolling Thunder Revue. Itself a conciliatory ballad sung by a more experienced man of the world to his lover in the midst of her personal turmoil, "Coming from the Heart" pledges undying devotion in the plush language of an old-time troubadour romancing his amour by the light of a full moon under her balcony with lines like this: "Make me up a bed of roses/And hang them down from the vine/Of all my loves you've been the closest/That's ever been on my mind."

◪ **Com'n Back for More**/David Blue
Asylum Records LP 7E-1043. Released 1975.

Because Dylan hooked up with many of his old New York City friends in the mid-1970s, it was no surprise that he should show up, harmonica firmly planted in the back pocket of his dungarees, to lend his talents on one track ("Who's Love") from David Blue's jazz-rock endeavor. The record also featured Joni Mitchell and members of her jazzy band du jour, the Los Angeles Express.

David Blue (born Stuart David Cohen, February 18, 1941, Providence; died December 2, 1982, New York City) was a Greenwich Village folkie who became a close friend of Dylan's in the early 1960s. In those days he was an unabashed Dylan imitator. Even so, Blue's career as a performer and recording artist need not be forgotten. His eponymous debut album, *heavily* influenced by Dylan's *Highway 61 Revisited* and *Blonde on Blonde*, features "Grand Hotel," his one truly remarkable song. His 1973 release *Nice Baby and the Angel*, his most fully realized Dylanesque work, included an all-star California cast: Dave Mason, Graham Nash, David Lindley, and Glenn Frey.

Blue's fascination with Dylan had dwindled by the time the cameras rolled for Dylan's film *Renaldo & Clara* on the Rolling Thunder Revue in the fall of 1975, but his hilarious, Greek-chorus-like recounting of their early 1960s days, delivered while playing pinball, should forever enshrine him in the pantheon of hipsters. But if not, pop-cultural mythology declares Blue to be the inspiration for the Joni Mitchell song "Blue," and similar conjecture associates him with Dylan's "It's All Over Now, Baby Blue." Both attributions, it should go without saying, are rather suspect. David Blue's image lives on, and in association with Dylan: wearing a trench coat and bowler hat and sitting cross-legged on the floor next to Rick Danko, he appears on the cover of *The Basement Tapes.*

Blue died in 1982, when he suffered a heart attack while jogging around Washington Square Park in the heart of Greenwich Village.

◪ **The Concert for Bangladesh**/Various Artists
Apple Records LP STCX-3385. Released 1971.

Rock 'n' roll's first major benefit concert—for famine crisis in newly formed Bangladesh in the summer of 1971—was the crowning glory of George Harrison's public life and set the standard for all rock benefits that followed. The concert was a huge deal at the time in other respects as well, as it marked one of Dylan's precious few public performances in the five years since his motorcycle accident in the summer of 1966. His surprise appearance at the show and on the triple album memorializing the event was easily the concert highlight, and the entire album side devoted to his set still stands up as one of the most moving of his career. "A Hard Rain's A-Gonna Fall," "It Takes a Lot to Laugh (It Takes a Train to Cry)," "Blowin' in the Wind," "Mr. Tambourine Man," and "Just Like a Woman" mixed the political, sacred, and romantic in bringing down the house.

The other material on the album, though somewhat dated, still sounds pretty good too. Fans of this period and type of rock revel in the record, as it showcases Harrison near his best, with ex-Beatle mate Ringo Starr, Eric Clapton, Leon Russell, Billy Preston, and Ravi Shankar all in good form and along for the ride.

◧ **"Confidential"** (Dorinda Morgan)
aka "Confidential to Me"
Various Artists (performed by Sonny Knight), History of Dot
    Records, Volume 1 *(1996)*
Fleetwoods, Best of the Fleetwoods *(1990)*

While Dylan and the Hawks may have given "Confidential" a tentative reading when they recorded it during the *Basement* sessions of 1967, this secret disguised as a song came back strong when Dylan performed it like a man finally taking off a mask at a costumed ball during the early incarnation of the Never Ending Tour.

The song was a hit in 1956 for Sonny Knight, a rock 'n' roll singer from Los Angeles who is now better known under his real name, Joseph C. Smith, and as the author of *The Day the Music Died*, a 1981 novel about racism and the beginnings of rock. Dorinda Morgan, the song's author, is best known as the producer of two Beach Boys retrospective releases.

Dylan first performed "Confidential" in 1989 at the famous Toad's Place gig in New Haven, Connecticut. Thereafter it appeared—always as a romantic crooning "from-me-to-you" rarity—in both acoustic and electric guises through 1995.

[S] "Congratulations" (Bob Dylan/Traveling Wilburys)

Traveling Wilburys, *Traveling Wilburys, Volume 1* (1988)

At first glance, "Congratulations" comes off as one of the Wilburys' bleaker songs—until the humor is heard, that is. A repeated listen or two reveals a composition in which the narrator seems to be actually telling the person he's congratulating to screw off.

The Traveling Wilburys' songbook, which was published to accompany the release of the Wilburys' debut album, indicates that the copyright for "Congratulations" is held by Dylan's music publishing concern, Special Rider Music, suggesting that Dylan was the primary contributor to (if not the sole composer of) the song. That his lead vocals dominate the track should leave little doubt of his hand as, at least, the song's primary shaper.

This was one Wilburys song that Dylan actually took onstage during the Never Ending Tours of 1989 and 1990.

[S] "Cool Dry Place" (Traveling Wilburys)

Traveling Wilburys, *Traveling Wilburys, Volume 3* (1990)

On the Wilburys' debut album, Dylan practically stole the show with a hilarious yet suspenseful "Tweeter and the Monkey Man," which perfectly imitated Bruce Springsteen's songs of the *Nebraska* period. Here, with "Cool Dry Place," Tom Petty turns the tables on Dylan by pulling off a number that would have been at home on any classic Bob Dylan LP.

[S] "Copper Kettle" (Traditional/Albert Frank Beddoe)

aka "Get You a Copper Kettle," "The Pale Moonlight"
Bob Dylan, single (1970); *Self Portrait* (1970)
Oscar Brand, *American Drinking Songs* (1956)
Joan Baez, *In Concert, Part One* (1962)
Chet Atkins, *This Is Chet Atkins* (1971)
Country Gentlemen, *Live in Japan* (1972)

With "Copper Kettle," Dylan takes a pretty interesting traditional-sounding song, puts strings behind it, and sings out of tune as part of his one-man self-wrecking crew, *Self Portrait*. Yet Dylan manages to breathe life into this slice of neo-Appalachia with this quaint, atmospheric rendition of an old song, evoking the spirit of the era from which it emerged. One can almost smell the fire of the backwoods still as Dylan leads his Carter Family–style ensemble through this archaic backhills number.

Though "Copper Kettle" is a new song (it was written or at least recodified by Albert Frank Beddoe from an older song for a 1953 folk opera, *Go Lightly, Stranger*), the subject of moonshining has by no means been neglected in folklore or song. More than a few songs have taken on the subject of the "copper kettle," its

C

Night view of men gathered around a still in the woods.

(Sketch by A. W. Thompson, *Harper's Weekly*, 1867/Library of Congress)

products, and resultant entanglement with the law. The original "Copper Kettle" came from Kentucky, but underwent numerous alterations before Dylan committed it to tape.

The Joan Baez Songbook (New York: Ryerson Music Publishers, 1964) has this to say about "Copper Kettle": "Here, in song, are a moonshiner's recipe and instructions for making whiskey. It was written by Albert Frank Beddoe and included by him in a little-known collection of ballads from Bexar County, Texas. Its present popularity places it first on the moonshiner's hit parade."

"Corrina, Corrina" (Traditional/adapted and arranged by Bob Dylan)
aka "Alberta, Alberta," "Corrina Corrine," "Corrina Blues," "Corrine, Corrina," "Roberta, Roberta"
Bob Dylan, single (1962); *The Freewheelin' Bob Dylan* (1962)
Blind Lemon Jefferson, *King of the Country Blues/'26* (1985)
Bo Carter, *Bo Carter, Volume 1 (1928–1931)* (1996)
Lightnin' Hopkins, *Lightnin' Hopkins, 1946–1960* (1960)
Mississippi John Hurt, *Today* (1966)
Steppenwolf, *Early Steppenwolf* (1969)
Doc Watson, *Then and Now* (1973)
Bob Wills & the Texas Playboys, *Tiffany Transcriptions, Volume 2* (1986)

Marianne Faithfull, *Rich Kid Blues* (1988)
Tampa Red, *Complete Recorded Works, Volume 3* (1991)
Art Tatum, *1940–1944* (1995)
Bill Monroe, *Bluegrass 1970–79* (1995)
Mance Lipscomb, *Mama Don't Allow* (1996)
Muddy Waters, *Hoochie Coochie Man Live!* (1996)
Jimmy Witherspoon, *Tougher Than Tough* (1997)
Dean Martin, *Country Dino* (1998)

Dylan, in a rare, early turn with a backup band, released a lilting, folk-rock version of this much-transmuted and transfigured plaint on his sophomore effort as well as a slightly different recording on a B-side single released at the same time. Covered in hundreds of versions and styles by the widest and most unlikely array of the best-known and obscure recording artists, "Corrina, Corrina" had its greatest popular success with one Ray Petersen (remembered for "Tell Laura I Love Her," his rendition of the morbid teenage car crash epic). In Petersen's R&B hands and using a new Mitchell Parish lyric, the song hit No. 9 on the *Billboard* charts in 1960.

The earliest popularity of this nugget of old Deep South blues is attributed to a 1928 single by Mississippi Sheik Armenter "Bo" Chatmon (aka Bo Carter, born March 21, 1893, Bolton, Mississippi; died September 9, 1964, Memphis), though Blind Lemon Jefferson may have had the first recorded version as "Roberta, Roberta" (aka "Corinna Blues") a couple of years earlier. Thereafter, it practically became a standard in the 1930s and was covered by dozens of singers in all genres ranging from Western swing to pop, R&B, and jazz before becoming a necessary rite of passage for apprentice folksingers of the 1960s. Blues scholars place "Corinna" in a general family of songs that derive from the familiar "C. C. Rider." Between Blind Lemon and Dylan stood scores of "Corrinas" recorded by everybody from Big Joe Turner to Dean Martin, but none mixed tenderness and jealousy as deftly as Dylan.

As such, Dylan's version is more than just an "arrangement" with melody and mood. Rather, he abandons the happy-go-lucky jugband feel of many interpretations and instead crafts "Corrina, Corrina" into a yearning memory of a woman whose shade he invokes by the singing of the song. Dylan's amalgam has some interesting features: the "bird that whistles" line is drawn from Robert Johnson's "Stones in My Passway," and the falsetto jump in his singing of the line "Baby, ple-ease come home" was a common device used by Dylan at the time (it may also be heard on songs such as "Quit Your Low Down Ways"). Given the many versions of the song and the interpretation Dylan renders, it is difficult to pin down Dylan's antecedent, though he did mention Lonnie Johnston's influence in the *Biograph* liner notes. The task is made even more difficult by the *Freewheelin'* liner notes, in which he writes, "I'm not one of those guys who goes around changing songs for the sake of changing them. But I'd never heard 'Corrina, Corrina' exactly the way it first was, so that this version is the way it came out of me."

Dylan's focus on "Corrina" appears to have been limited to a very short burst of performances and recordings in the spring and summer of 1962 leading up to its release on *Freewheelin'*, never to be visited again. Only one live version (a May rendition from Gerde's Folk City) has survived and remains in circulation.

An often overlooked detail on the *Freewheelin'* release of "Corrina, Corrina" and "Don't Think Twice" is the subtle backup band—staffed by Bruce Langhorne on guitar, George Barnes on bass guitar, Gene Ramey on bass, pianist Dick Wellstood, and drummer Herb Lovelle—providing light accompaniment.

An essay by Christopher A. Waterman, "Race Music: Bo Chatmon, 'Corrine Corrina,' and the Excluded Middle" in *Music and the Racial Imagination* (Ronald M. Padano and Philip V. Bohlman, eds.; University of Chicago Press, 2000), is an extensive meditation on Chatmon's original. Waterman traces the historical, social, and cultural genesis of the song and makes a strong case that "Corrina, Corrina" is among the most archetypal and influential compositions in the American folk canon. Intercepting the song's complex seventy-year trajectory from several angles, Waterman locates Chatmon's "Corrina" within a broader musical and social terrain while attempting to account for the marginal status to which both the song and the musicians who first performed and recorded it (Chatmon and the Sheiks foremost among them) have been relegated in subsequent journalistic and academic writing about American music. He goes on to highlight the song's layered and shifting relationship to evolving discourses of racial difference, identity, and commensurability. Waterman's basic argument is that "Corrina," Chatmon, the Mississippi Sheiks, and the music they created, recorded, and performed have been neglected due to a what he suggests is a perverse and misguided reverse racism by the primarily white ethnomusicological academic elite because they drew on a mixture of traditions and styles that did not accord with the raw, primal, and theoretically unfiltered sounds of fellow Mississippian Robert Johnson and his cadre. Perhaps the academy never knew that Muddy Waters, himself a disciple of Johnson's, once walked ten miles to see the Sheiks perform.

▣ "Country Pie" (Bob Dylan)
Bob Dylan, single (1969); *Nashville Skyline* (1969); *Live 1961–2000—Thirty-nine Years of Great Concert Performances/'00* (2001)
The Nice, *Five Bridges Suite* (1970)
Various Artists (performed by American Hip), *Duluth Does Dylan* (2001)

Dylan has some rollicking, crazy fun on this piece of what critic Dave Marsh called "mere babble." *Nashville Skyline* throwaway fluff that has Dylan sounding like he's salivating in anticipation of his literal and/or figurative (artistic? sexual? pharmacological?) dessert, "Country Pie" makes one wonder between laughs: is this the same guy who wrote "Subterranean Homesick Blues" a mere four years before? It was in that earlier song that Dylan used a similar, tricky syntax to cram his phrases with catalogues of cosmic woes. But here, he employs similar techniques to list pie fillings without even telling us which he prefers!

Calling the song "a declaration of independence," Hubert Saal wrote in the April 4, 1969, issue of *Newsweek*, "[W]hen Dylan talks of eating pies, all kinds, he means writing songs, all kinds. And when he goes on in the song to say 'Ain't runnin' any race,' he seems to be rejecting the musical direction his many admirers have chosen for him in the past or would choose for him in the future."

In what has to rate as one of the more creatively whacked-out interpretations of a line from a Dylan song, it was suggested that the reference to a "big white goose" was a symbol for heroin.

Somehow "Country Pie" seemed right at home when Dylan began performing it in the late winter of 2000 in perversely electric, Charlie Daniels–fast, grab-your-partner-and-dance versions.

▣ "A Coupla More Years" (Shel Silverstein/Dennis Locorriere)
aka "A Couple More Years"

Dr. Hook, *Little Bit More* (1976)
Waylon Jennings, *Are You Ready for the Country* (1976)
The Statler Brothers, *Country America Loves* (1977)
Waylon Jennings and Willie Nelson, *Waylon & Willie* (1978)
Lou Rawls, *When the Night Comes* (1983)
Willie Nelson, *Night Life* (1992)

"Shel Silverstein writes great songs. Really. Like he's one of my favorite songwriters."—Bob Dylan, 1964.

Shel who? Well, if you have to ask, you probably never read *Where the Sidewalk Ends* to a five-year-old's infectious squeals.

Silverstein (born September 25, 1932, Chicago; died May 10, 1999, Key West, Florida) edged into a career in the arts as a result of an awkward adolescence. "When I was a kid—12 to 14, around there—I would much rather have been a good baseball player or a hit with the girls," he reported to *Publishers Weekly*. "But I couldn't play ball. I couldn't dance. Luckily, the girls didn't want me. Not much I could do about that. So I started to draw and to write. By the time I got to where I was attracting girls, I was already into work, and it was more important to me."

While serving with the United States military in Japan and Korea, Silverstein began drawing cartoons for *Stars and Stripes*, the American armed-forces publication, and he originally gained fame as a cartoonist and satirist for *Playboy* magazine in its infancy. Satirical songs such as "A Boy Named Sue" (recorded by Johnny Cash), "One's on the Way" (recorded by Loretta Lynn), and host of others interpreted by Doctor Hook first gained his writing a national audience, but Silverstein's own recordings created a deserved cult following. It is his children's books, however, full of snatches of loopy, cosmic poetic whimsy and cockeyed pen-and-ink drawings, that may well secure him his everlasting fame.

Silverstein's career as an author for children seeking life beyond Disney began in 1963 with the publication of *Uncle Shelby's Story of Lafcadio, the Lion Who Shot Back*, a yarn about a lion who acquired a hunter's gun and practiced until he became good enough to join the circus. Silverstein developed mass following in 1964 after the publication of *The Giving Tree*, a story about a tree that surrenders its shade, fruit, branches, and, finally, its trunk to a boy in order to make him happy.

Silverstein's combination of silliness and sophisticated wordplay is well illustrated in "Eggs Rated," a poem from his 1996 collection *Falling Up*, in which he wittily replaces the syllable "ex" with "egg," as in "Eggstra fluffy/Eggstremely tasty/Cooked eggsactly right," on his way to determining that the eggs are "much more eggspensive than I eggspected." The humor comes with a decidedly ghoulish sensibility, too, as reflected by "Safe," another poem from *Falling Up*, in which a child very carefully prepares to cross a street. He looks both ways before confidently proceeding—oblivious to a steel safe hurtling down from the heavens.

Silverstein's goofy, gross, macabre, and yet always enchanting poetry for children sold more than fourteen million books and is probably his most cherished legacy. *Where the Sidewalk Ends: The Poems and Drawings of Shel Silverstein* and *A Light in the Attic*, two collections of children's poetry, both enjoyed long runs on the best-seller lists. *Attic* spent 182 weeks on the *New York Times* list and *Sidewalk* was No. 11 on *Publishers Weekly*'s all-time list of hardcover best sellers.

With his shiny bald head, thick beard, and penetrating eyes, Silverstein was an easily recognizable figure around Greenwich Village through the 1960s and '70s, spreading his talents in many, sometimes virtually opposite, directions. As a contributing cartoonist to *Play-*

C

boy magazine, his work was known to a certain demographic the world over. As a songwriter he could turn out compositions of rare beauty, insight, and novel goofiness by the Stetson-full for the country-music community. As a recording artist he created about a dozen solo (mostly small-label) albums. He was also the author of nine plays.

Dennis Locorriere (born June 13, 1949, Union City, New Jersey), cocomposer of "A Coupla More Years," was a founding member of the unique country-rock band Dr. Hook and the Medicine Show. After forming in New Jersey in 1968 and on the strength of Silverstein's songs and their loony stage show, Dr. Hook established their high-water mark with the 1972 megahit "The Cover of the Rolling Stone."

Dylan included his cover of "A Coupla More Years," a warm portrait of a May–December romance, in his late 1980 concerts during his return to secular music after the brief but intense all-gospel, all-the-time performances of late 1979 and early 1980. He can also be caught singing it during his truly dreadful barnyard "seduction" scene with the actress Fiona in the 1987 straight-to-video megabomb *Hearts of Fire.*

▣ "Covenant Woman" (Bob Dylan)
Bob Dylan, single (1980); *Saved* (1980)
Rich Lerner and the Groove, *Cover Down* (2000)

Before Dylan's conversion to born-again Christianity, he was fond of writing love songs with a spiritual undercurrent. During his gospel phase, however, Dylan flipped that and leaned more toward religious songs with hints of romance. Perhaps songs like "Covenant Woman" were supposed to be addressed to the Virgin Mother or the woman who stood by him during his period of Bible-thumping—or both. Yet there is a scent of his earlier love-on-the-lam songs lingering around the fringes of

"Covenant Woman," mixed with a hefty biblical reference or two just to keep us honest.

Old Testament buffs can make links between the lyric "You know that we are strangers in a land we're passing through" to similar and related lines strewn throughout the Torah that deal with the Jews' trek to the domain of milk and honey. Exodus 22:21 ("Thou shalt neither vex a stranger, nor oppress him: for ye were strangers in the land of Egypt") and a slew of others all utilize the "stranger in a strange land" motif to get the point across quite well. Dylan was certainly hip to Woody Guthrie's appropriation of the idea in "Pretty Boy Floyd": "Others tell you of a stranger that come to beg a meal/And underneath a napkin left a thousand-dollar bill."

Hairsplitting scholar-believers can find relief in the lines from "Covenant Woman" ("I've been broken, shattered like an empty cup/I'm just waiting on the Lord to rebuild and fill me up") that dovetail with Isaiah 40:31 ("But they that wait upon the Lord shall renew their strength").

The version of "Covenant Woman" on *Saved* is pretty stale, but when Dylan was performing it in 1979 and 1980, the song could be an extraordinarily affecting, no-holds-barred showstopper. And his harmonica runs on just about all renditions are things of slippery beauty.

▣ "Cover Down" (Bob Dylan)
aka "Cover Down/Break Through"

A standout composition that never saw official release, "Cover Down" is a blues-rock gospel sermon with a great soul riff and devoid of the confrontational nature of other *Slow Train Coming*–era material. It could be in the repertoire of any Christian heavy-metal band. Dylan performed around two dozen stump-preacher versions of this eschatological, frenetic song in

April and May of 1980. As these were his last all-gospel shows, "Cover Down" was among the final devotional songs Dylan penned during this furious period of his life.

[S] "Crash on the Levee (Down in the Flood)"

See "Down in the Flood (Crash on the Levee)"

[S] "Cross the Green Mountain" (Bob Dylan)

Various Artists (performed by Bob Dylan), *Gods and Generals* (2002)

Dylan wrote "Cross the Green Mountain" and recorded it with his band for *Gods and Generals*, an epic but generally turgid Civil War film that told the story of Confederate army general Stonewall Jackson (played by Robert Duvall) released in late 2002. A haunting, moving ballad, reminiscent of his earliest works with the added insights of a lifetime, "Cross the Green Mountain" clocks in at around seven minutes in length and was heard over the closing credits of the film.

In typical kiss-ass but not altogether ingenuous Hollywood P.R. fashion, Ron Maxwell, the director of *Gods and Generals*, said, "In this song, Dylan has in a sense returned to his roots as a folk-country balladeer—the same roots that nourished the mountain men of western Virginia, the home of Thomas Jonathan Jackson, and countless others who fought for both the Blue and the Gray. It isn't easy for a single song to evoke the feelings of an entire war. But Dylan's new song, written expressly for our film, achieves this elusive goal. It is at once specific to our characters and story, and universal in its statement on the tragedy of war and the poignancy of the lives swept up in it. The poetry of the lyrics, the driving rhythms, the melodic line—it's classic Dylan."

In a separate interview, Maxwell elaborated on Dylan's involvement with the project, telling *Entertainment Weekly* that "[Stonewall] Jackson grew up in what is now West Virginia. We thought, what artist best embodies the spirit of this man? Folk music comes out of Appalachia. It's what [Civil War] people were listening to. 'Cross the Green Mountain' includes twelve meandering verses that imply the story of Stonewall Jackson, but it's also about the whole Civil War, and it's about more universal themes. People will hear an echo of an earlier Dylan."

[A] *Cruzados: Unreleased Early Recordings*/Cruzados

Released 2000. Produced by the Cruzados.

The Cruzados, formerly the Plugz, was a Los Angeles–based rock band with a Latin twist that was ever so briefly but famously associated with Dylan when the group backed him up for his mercurial appearance on *Late Night with David Letterman* in March 1984. Somewhere in there the band managed to coax Bob into the studio to contribute harmonica licks to "Rising Sun," a minor rocker that seems to be playing off both Dylan's flirtation with the sacred (born-again Christianity) and the profane (as in "House of the Rising Sun," a song about the perils of the brothel). While not a bootleg, this collection of songs was privately produced by the Cruzados and obtainable, in 2000, through the group's official home page on the Web. "Rising Sun" became more widely available when released in 2003 on a "various artists" tribute album titled *May Your Song Always Be Sung: The Songs of Bob Dylan, Volume 3.*

[S] "Cry a While" (Bob Dylan)

Bob Dylan, *"Love and Theft"* (2001)

A straight, late Bob Dylan blues that would have been quite at home on his previous doom-

and-gloom-laden album *Time out of Mind*, "Cry a While" is a rhythm-shifting pile driver harking back to classic acoustic country music, borrowing its menacing bass line from Tommy Johnson's late-1920s Delta standard "Big Road Blues." At the same time the song references Dylan's own guitar-playing past with the turn-around lick employed on "Leopard-Skin Pill-Box Hat" and his longevity when he sings, "I don't carry dead weight, I'm no flash in the pan." And for all his intellectualism, Dylan shows he can be as ribald as they come in "Cry a While," snorting lines that could have fallen off a Redd Foxx party record: "Don Pasquale makin' a 2 a.m. booty call."

Dylan began performing "Cry a While" almost immediately after its *"Love and Theft"* release during the fall 2001 Never Ending Tour that first showcased songs from the album. Finally, it was the *"L & T"* song he chose to perform at the 2002 Grammy Awards ceremonies, a rendition praised by Bonnie Raitt as "perhaps the funkiest performance by a white guy that I have ever seen. He's at the top of his game."

[S] "The Cuckoo Is a Pretty Bird" (Traditional)

aka "The Coo Coo Bird," "The Cuckoo Bird," "The Dove"
Various Artists (performed by Clarence Ashley), *The Anthology of American Folk Music/'29* (1952/1997)
Jean Ritchie, *Singing Family of the Cumberlands* (1955)
New Lost City Ramblers, *New Lost City Ramblers* (1962)
Carolyn Hester, *The Life I'm Living* (1963)
Holy Modal Rounders, *Holy Modal Rounders* (1964)
Peter, Paul & Mary, *Song Will Rise* (1965)
Doc and Merle Watson, *Ballads from Deep Gap* (1971)
Ramblin' Jack Elliott, *Hard Travelin'* (1977)
Everly Brothers, *Home Again* (1985)
Rory Gallagher, *The Bullfrog Interlude* (1992)
Various Artists, *Black Banjo Songsters of North Carolina and Virginia* (1997)
Dry Branch Fire Squad, *Dry Branch Fire Squad* (2001)

A fragmentary song that could serve as the eternal soundtrack in Limbo, "The Cuckoo Is a Pretty Bird" has been one of the most influential and oft-recorded pieces since at least Clarence Ashley's 1929 eerie vocal and banjo recording from Tennessee appeared on Harry Smith's 1952 *Anthology of American Folk Music* (Smithsonian Folkways Recordings). Whether interpreted as a song about a guy who's lost all his money in poker or is a stalker of young women, or cast in folk, country, bluegrass, old-timey, or rock arrangements, this composition never seems to leave the subconscious mind once it has fluttered in. Dylan is known to have performed it just once—an autumn 1962 gig at the Gaslight Café in New York City's Greenwich Village was the only one captured for posterity—but a couple of other Dylan renditions of it around that time are also at least rumored to have transpired.

The version Dylan sang may be a cousin to at least one other familiar to Dylanists ("The Roving Gambler") and a couple that might not be ("Rye Whisky" and "Down the Old Plank Road")—all dissimilar to one another except that they share some common verses. This is not to say that the Dylan rendition and its likely model (by Clarence Ashley) make any sense. One verse is about a bird, another about building a cabin, yet another about wooing a gal. However, a majority of the older renditions, especially those collected from England, tell a story or at least purport to. But most versions are mere expressions of mood and little more, as the lyrics have reconfigured themselves through the centuries. The song is generally concerned with love, especially love betrayed or denied, and a repertory of such verses provides a handy kit for making countless songs almost at will. As folklorist A. L. Lloyd wrote of "The Cuckoo" in his 1967 book *Folk Song in England* (London: Lawrence & Wishart): "few of these floating lyrics are datable. They are the product of some sentimental flowering of the spirit, but whether they were all produced at the same period or represent the accretion of centuries would be hard to say."

Greil Marcus devoted considerable ink to "The Cuckoo" in *Invisible Republic*, his 1997 book about Dylan and *The Basement Tapes*—an album on which "The Cuckoo," with all its spooky nonsense, would have been most at home. Observing that many of those singing on the first side of Harry Smith's Folkways *Anthology of American Folk Music* "sound as if they're already dead," Marcus posits that it is "as if they're lining out an unspoken premise of the old Southern religion: only the dead can be born again."

"No performance captures this sensation more completely than the first number on this magical side," Marcus writes of "The Cuckoo." "There is no more commonplace song in Appalachia; the song has been sung for so long, by so many different communities, as to seem to some folklorists virtually automatic, a musicological version of the instinctive act, like breathing—and therefore meaningless."

Writing that "Ashley's performance made one thing clear: however old the singer was, he wasn't as old as the song," Marcus delved even further into how a composition like "The Cuckoo" percolates through time and space. Discussing it as an archetypal "folk-lyric" song, Marcus writes that it is "made up of verbal fragments that had no direct or logical relationship to each other, but were drawn from a floating pool of thousands of disconnected verses, couplets, one-liners, pieces of eight. Harry Smith guessed the folk-lyric form came together some time between 1850 and 1875. Whenever it happened, it wasn't until enough fragments were abroad in the land to reach a kind of critical mass—until there were enough

fragments, passing back and forth between blacks and whites as common coin, to generate more fragments, to sustain within the matrix of a single musical language an almost infinite repertory of performances, to sustain the sense that out of the anonymity of the tradition a singer was presenting a distinct and separate account of a unique life. It is this quality—the insistence that the singer is singing of his or her life, as an event, taking place as you listen, its outcome uncertain—that separates the song, from which the singer emerges, from the ballad, into which the singer disappears."

"Dancing in the Dark" (Bruce Springsteen)
Bruce Springsteen, *Born in the U.S.A.* (1984)

Dylan's only performance of "Dancing in the Dark," Bruce Springsteen's winsome torch song, came during the legendary January 1990 surprise rehearsal gig at Toad's Place, a club in New Haven, Connecticut. Dylan manhandled the song with rough clumsiness, spending the entire performance finding his range and all but losing that lonely-guy-on-the-prowl-licking-his-wounds portrait Springsteen so nimbly captured.

Despite its central position in the Springsteen recorded and performance canon, "Dancing in the Dark" has never been held in high esteem by certain purist elements of the Boss's following, condemning it on two main grounds: (1) its pop sound makes it difficult to plumb the depths of its rather dark and complex core, and (2) as the song depicted in the first big-time Boss video at the dawn of MTV, it smacked of the kind of commercialism and overexposure that his fans had always eschewed. The popu-

D

larity of the video also brought many newer fans to Springsteen that his old faithful resented for jumping on a bandwagon and spoiling a scene that they had long cultivated. Still, "Dancing in the Dark" anticipated the material on *Tunnel of Love*, his less successful follow-up album a few years later.

"Dancing in the Dark" was written, according to Dave Marsh's Springsteen bio, *Glory Days*, under pressure from manager Jon Landau to fill out the *Born in the U.S.A.* album. Rather than being mere filler, though, "Dancing in the Dark" turned out to be a strong statement by the artist. "This is a protest song worth keeping," wrote Marsh, "a marching song against boredom, a battle cry against loneliness, and an accounting of the price the loner pays. And on top of that, it's also the moan of an extremely physical person who can't wait to hit the road again."

"Dark as a Dungeon" (Merle Travis)

Merle Travis, *Best of Merle Travis* (1990)
The Maddox Brothers and Rose, *America's Most Colorful Hillbilly Band* (1961)
Glen Campbell, *Big Bluegrass Special* (1962)
Chad Mitchell, *Himself* (1966)
Johnny Cash, *Johnny Cash at Folsom Prison* (1968)
Cisco Houston, *Folkways Years, 1944–1961* (1994)
David Grisman and Daniel Kobialka, *Common Chord* (1995)
Ramblin' Jack Elliott, *Friends of Mine* (1998)
Jerry Garcia/David Grisman, *Been All Around This World* (2004)

"It's as dark as a dungeon way down in the mines" is the grim warning posed by Merle Travis's "Dark as a Dungeon." He elaborated on those sentiments in a spoken introduction to the song on one of his albums (*Folk Songs of the Hills*): "I never will forget one time when I was on a little visit down home in Ebenezer, Kentucky. I was a-talkin' to an old man that

had known me ever since the day I was born, and an old friend of the family. He says, 'Son, you don't know how lucky you are to have a nice job like you've got and don't have to dig out a livin' from under these old hills and hollers like me and your pappy used to.' When I asked him why he never had left and tried some other kind of work, he says, 'Nawsir, you just won't do that. If ever you get this old coal dust in your blood, you're just gonna be a plain old coal miner as long as you live.' He went on to say, 'It's a habit, sorta like chewin' tobaccer.'"

This plaint by Merle Travis (born November 17, 1917, Rosewood, Kentucky; died October 20, 1983, Tahlequah, Oklahoma) was hard-earned. The son of a sometimes impoverished, hardworking Kentucky coal miner, Travis may best be remembered as the author of "Sixteen Tons," but his lesser-appreciated "Dark as a Dungeon" could just as well have been his epitaph. Although he himself never toiled in the mines, the hardships and struggle of the miner's life were burned into his consciousness, and he never forgot them.

Among the coal miners he knew was Ike Everly (father of the Everly Brothers), who showed young Merle the basics of fingerpicking (called "thumbpicking" in Kentucky) on the banjo, his first instrument. The style Travis developed from those lessons—now called Travis picking—popularized fingerpicking and, when transferred to the guitar, expanded the guitar's range as a solo instrument by incorporating bass and melody lines into one pattern. His influence on Chet Atkins and Doc Watson is apparent in their music, and rather obvious when one considers that they both named their firstborn children Merle in his honor.

A brief stint in the Marines left Travis with a touch of wanderlust, and he relocated to Los Angeles in 1944, where he hooked up with the

"It's dark as a dungeon way down in the mine" (Merle Travis).

(Library of Congress)

B-western movie circuit and played in local bands. With advice and string-pulling from country-western mover and shaker Tex Ritter, he wrote "No Vacancy" in 1946, a topical song dealing with the displacement of returning veterans. Sided with "Cincinnati Lou" as a single, it scored big on the charts. That success (coupled with the commercial and cultural mark Burl Ives was making with his folk-song albums) inspired Travis's concept album *Folk Songs of the Hills* in 1947. But the set of four 78-rpm discs was a commercial failure even if it yielded several classics, including "Sixteen Tons," "Over by Number Nine," "Nine Pound Hammer," and "Dark as a Dungeon." The album is now, of course, a collector's item, a beautiful all-acoustic solo guitar performance by a master virtuoso.

That early stumble did little to derail the Travis express. Along with million-selling hit "Smoke! Smoke! Smoke!," Travis scored a half dozen Top 10 records, including "Divorce Me C.O.D.," "So Round, So Firm, So Fully Packed," and "Three Times Seven."

Travis had many talents. He coinvented the solid-body electric guitar and originated the style of headstock that places the tuning machine heads all on one side—ideas taken up by Leo Fender and now a trademark of Fender guitars. Merle also acted in the movie *From Here to Eternity* (in which he sang "Re-Enlistment Blues"), worked as a script writer for Johnny Cash's TV show, and was a good cartoonist.

But he was a known wild man whose arrests for drunken driving, narcotics possession, and domestic abuse kept his career in check despite scoring with a passel of hit country singles in the 1940s and 1950s. Recording dates with Hank Thompson and Chet Atkins kept him out of hock through the 1960s and 1970s, and, just as he mellowed in the 1980s, when full recognition for his contributions to American music finally began coming his way, he died of a massive heart attack.

"Dark as a Dungeon," ironically enough, was written far from the dank and dangerous black pit it takes as its subject. According to Travis, "The saddest songs are written when a person is happy. I was driving home after a date with a beautiful girl in Redondo Beach, California. I had a recording session to do the next morning and needed some material. I parked my car under a street light and wrote the verse to 'Dark as a Dungeon.'"

For an extensive scholarly treatise on "Dark as a Dungeon" and other Travis coal-mining songs, check out the chapters "Two by Travis" and "Nine Pound Hammer" from Archie Green's 1972 book *Only a Miner: Studies in Recorded Coal-Mining Songs*.

Whether sung by its creator or bitterly interpreted by sons of mining towns such as Hibbing, Minnesota, "Dark as a Dungeon" manages to express the peculiar isolation of the miner's lot. No other song portrays so well the loneliness, the constant danger and doom, and the strange attraction that keeps a man working "way down in the mines." Dylan made it a high point of his 1975 Rolling Thunder Revue acoustic sets but only rarely thereafter during the Never Ending Tour—always making the damp chill of the coal caverns fade into a glowing warmth as he sang it like a black-lung survivor sitting by a woodstove.

[S] **"Dark Eyes"** (Bob Dylan)

Bob Dylan, *Empire Burlesque* (1985)
Judy Collins, *Judy Sings Dylan . . . Just Like a Woman* (1993)
Jan Preston, *Accomplices* (1995)
Two Approaching Riders, *One More Cup of Coffee* (1997)
Steve Gibbons, *The Dylan Project* (1998)
Susan McKeown, *Mighty Rain* (1998)
Michel Montecrossa, *Born in Time* (2000)
Michael Moore, *Jewels and Binoculars* (2000)
Rolling Thunder, *The Never Ending Rehearsal* (2000)
Various Artists (performed by Two Approaching Riders), *May Your Song Always Be Sung: The Songs of Bob Dylan, Volume 3* (2003)

"Dark Eyes" is an overlooked late Dylan bauble—a stately folk ballad appraising and defending the artistic life and vision against the sour games of the wine-drinking businessmen and earth-digging plowmen he thought he had long ago dispatched in "All Along the Watchtower." There is also a sense that the poet questions whether or not his words have any meaningful penetration when he sings in the chorus, "A million faces at my feet but all I see are dark eyes."

Like one of those midnight Edgar Allen Poe love poems, "Dark Eyes" is filled with grace notes that sound like cries for help and images of fleeting beauty that turn into signs of prophecy.

Dylan once mentioned in an interview that this rumination on a disjointed world came to him all at once in a dream. At another point he said, "That particular song just sort of came, I won't say easy, but all in one piece like that."

"Dark Eyes" begins with a discussion of gentlemen (well-schooled, successful types) talking and walking while drinking under the midnight moon as Dylan distances himself from their sophisticated, cosmopolitan manners. We can practically hear their idle chatter, which they may well believe is intelligent and salient. The artist/narrator appears to feel otherwise ("I live in another world where life and death are memorized"), slipping off either physically or emotionally from their bombast and into that time-out-of-mind space where eternity can be fleetingly glimpsed. The sensuality and emotion he feels there give the world an invisible structure and fill him with a deep, if alienated, sense of self that raises him above the petty travails discussed in his company. He knows that the world is a pretty materialistic place "where the earth is strung with lover's pearls," but he prances in the nether realms of the soul where the only thing that can be glimpsed are dark eyes.

In verse two, the narrator is drawn deeper into his phantasm of intuitive vision. The tangible sound of a faraway rooster presents imagined images of a praying soldier (is he about to enter mortal combat?) and a lost child (selling himself on Rue Morgue Avenue?). Another sound is then introduced, that of a beating drum summoning the dead from their graves that scares even "nature's beast"—a Book of Revelation–style monster looming over the scene ready to snatch both the pious and the pitiable. Our artist, however, is not moved to flight by this cheap George Romero remake: all he sees are dark eyes.

But his reveries are not strong enough to pull him away from the world of the gentry, for in verse three, their pragmatic, dignified airs belie their darker motives. To them, revenge is always sweet. Dylan hears them but intimates that he will never truly comprehend their cold, emotionless logic. Because they are too busy playing their lame games, they will never recognize true beauty or know what it feels like to be engulfed in the fire of creation.

The two worlds collide when, in the last verse, Dylan sings of "the French girl" (symbolic of romance, the artistic life, and a gesture to Dylan's shrouded world, as well as a reference to a modern folk song written and made famous by Ian and Sylvia back in the early 1960s) and a "drunken man" at the wheel (symbolic of the greedy, materialistic world evidently out of control with a lust for power without consideration of a payback). Dylan

seems genuinely anguished as he sings these last lines, almost as if he is realizing that the artist's own quest may be just as bankrupt, self-centered, and impotent as those he lifted his nose at earlier in the song. The dark eyes engulfing him over the footlights on the lip of the stage almost mock him in an unfortunate but venerable epiphany: the historical dance between the sacred and the profane, between romance and classicism, between reason and sensuality, are ancient and, perhaps, interdependent.

Dylan performed "Dark Eyes" only once during his 1986 tour with Tom Petty and the Heartbreakers, but returned to it nearly a decade later when it was displayed at a number of concerts as a heartbreaking acoustic duet with Patti Smith during their memorable 1995 tour.

In *High Tide*, a 1987 Australian film directed by Gillian Armstrong (who also directed the Dylan/Petty video *Hard to Handle*) and starring Judy Davis, there is a scene where Davis is falling down drunk in a washroom of a campground/trailer park and sings a pretty good portion of "Dark Eyes," then raves, "What a great fuckin' song."

◪ *David Bromberg*
Columbia Records LP 331104. Released 1971.

Dylan blew harp on the painfully sensitive "Sammy's Song" on David Bromberg's debut LP, which featured contributions from a great assortment of top-notch, if generally unheralded, talent that included David Amram, Will Scarlett, Norman Blake, and Jody Stecher.

Guitarist Bromberg (born September 19, 1945, Philadelphia) may be the ultimate sideman, a true musician's musician whose impact on contemporary folk both as an interpreter and contributor has been indelible. His first recording dates came with Tom Paxton and Jerry Jeff Walker in the mid-1960s, and he has been an in-demand session man since. But he has been releasing albums himself for three decades now with a mélange of styles that place him more in the David Grisman school of American acoustic eclectica than as a folkie troubadour. As a band-leader, his popularity peaked as a concert attraction in the 1970s when an evening with David Bromberg at your friendly neighborhood venue was an egalitarian and educational revue that mixed blues, folk, country-western, rock 'n' roll, and jazz. A taste of that musical gumbo can still be sampled as Bromberg continues to record and perform to this day.

Dylan reunited with Bromberg for a 1992 recording session in Chicago that produced, among other cuts, a version of "Catskill Sere-nade." Written by Bromberg and sung by Dylan, the song is an exotic, archaic-sounding retelling of Washington Irving's venerable tale "Rip Van Winkle."

"Day of the Locusts" (Bob Dylan)
Bob Dylan, *New Morning* (1970)

Drawing on the vision of celebrity gone mad as portrayed in Nathanael West's 1939 novel *Day of the Locust*, and the Old Testament's wrath of pestilence in his assessment in song of receiv-ing an honorary doctorate from Princeton Uni-versity in 1970, "Day of the Locusts" may be Dylan's most concentrated statement of institu-tional mistrust. Surely it is one of the strongest examples that literary history affords us of looking a gift horse in the mouth, saying, in effect, that the knowledge you can get at an Ivy League school does not necessarily lead to a richer life and can lead to the absolute death of the spirit. Dylan's reference to the "judges" in the song has been taken to mean the professors in their academic robes, whose degrees are

really death sentences. Whatever the case, Dylan makes no bones in the song about want-ing to flee this scene as quickly as possible.

David Crosby accompanied Bob and Sara Dylan to Princeton on that fateful day and is, according to him, the person Dylan refers to when he says, "The man standing next to me, his head was exploding." Crosby recalled the day to Raymond Foye in a conversation reprinted in *The Telegraph* #45 (summer 1993): "I got Dylan incredibly high on some killer weed. I was visiting him and Sara in the Vil-lage . . . Sara was trying to get Bob to go to Princeton University, where he was being pre-sented with an Honorary Doctorate. Bob didn't want to go. I said, 'C'mon, Bob, it's an honor!' Sara and I both worked on him for a long time. Finally, he agreed. I had a car outside—a big limousine. That was the first thing he didn't like. We smoked another joint on the way and I noticed Dylan getting really quite paranoid behind it. When we arrived at Princeton, they took us to a little room and Bob was asked to wear a cap and gown. He refused outright. They said, 'We won't give you the degree if you don't wear this.' Dylan said, 'Fine. I didn't ask for it in the first place.' I said, 'C'mon, Bob, these people have gone to a lot of trouble . . .' Finally we convinced him to wear the cap and gown. I was standing next to him during the ceremony . . . just like the song says. When it was over, we made a quick exit."

Tim Dunn gave some background on the history of honorary degrees in his article "Feats of Pride" in *On the Tracks* #14 (Septem-ber 15, 1998), writing:

> Princeton University has bestowed honorary diplomas since its first commencement in 1748. Until 1895 honorees simply were informed by letter but since then the recipi-ents' attendance has been required. Since

Dylan with Coretta Scott King after they were each given honorary degrees
from Princeton University, June 1970.
(Photo: William Sauro/New York Times Co./Getty Images)

1905, as part of the ceremony, a formal citation has been read upon the presentation of
each individual's diploma . . .

College dropout Bob Dylan received his
Doctor of Music at Princeton's commencement on a hot 9 June 1970, having been
selected by undergraduates on the nominating
committee. Attending the late morning event
with him were wife Sara, aide Ben Saltzman,
and David Crosby. . . . Described as "nervous"
and "uncommunicative," Dylan nearly
departed before the ceremony but, upon seeing the gathering crowd, changed his mind.
Joining the majority of graduates, he chose
not to wear a mortarboard and only reluc-
tantly donned the black robe. He also wore an

armband adorned with the peace symbol.

No speech was required and Dylan barely
smiled as university president Robert F.
Goheen read from the parchment scroll. The
formal citation honored Dylan for "brilliantly
distinguishing himself in good works" and
proclaimed him "deservedly worthy of the
highest public honors." A second informal
citation also was read which noted that,
despite nearing age 30, "his music remains
the authentic expression of the disturbed and
concerned conscience of young America."

. . . The underground press expressed
unhappiness about his association with
"Amerika"; probably "serious scholars" har-
bored resentment or reservations.

◙ **"Days of '49"** (Traditional/F. Warner/J. A. Lomax/
A. Lomax/arrangement by Bob Dylan)
aka "The Days of Forty-Nine"
Bob Dylan, *Self Portrait* (1970)
Milt Okun, *Adirondack Folk Songs & Ballads* (1963)
Sandy and Jeanie Darlington, *Sandy & Jeanie Darlington*
(1966)
Jim Kweskin, *Lives Again* (1977)
Fred Holstein, *Chicago & Other Ports* (1977)
Jeff Davis and Jeff Warner, *Days of '49* (1977)
Ed McCurdy, *Cowboy Songs* (1996)

Song, story, and film have long glamorized the great gold rush of 1849, and while Hollywood may have gotten the story wrong, this song did not. The discovery of gold at Sutter's Mill in California came at crucial point in American history. The Mexican War, which many denounced as unjust and imperialist, had recently ended and unemployment and poverty followed in its wake. To thousands of poverty-stricken, landless Americans, the discovery of "easy riches" in the Sierra Nevada seemed the logical solution. So off they went—families, teenagers, single men, single women, and grandparents of all nationalities and all religions from across the globe. A few found not-so-easy wealth, but most found a new poverty.

In a great number of cases, fathers had gone without their families, hoping to send for them after they had struck it rich. Naturally, many "bachelor" communities sprang up, and in the process of movement and dislocation, a new kind of democracy grew—a comradeship and kinship born of common suffering and search. "Days of '49," which came out some years after 1849, depicts both the democratic comradeship and the venal manipulations of the gold-mining camp in sepia tones.

Jeff Davis determined the source of "Days of '49" in the liner notes to *Days of '49*, a folk album he recorded with Jeff Warner in 1977; he

wrote that the song "came originally from *Old Put's Golden Songster*, put together by Old Put himself in Gold Rush Days. He found that, while there was no money in the mines, there were plenty of miners willing to pay for any kind of music or entertainment, this being a scarce commodity. The real money in the gold field was made by the grocers, dry-goods salesmen, saloon keepers, and, I guess, musicians. Put probably intended the song to be comic, but people have since found sad truth in it."

For all the criticism *Self Portrait* has caught over the years, the collection did reinforce what a powerful interpretive singer Dylan can be. The rough-and-ready "Days of '49" (chronicling the ornery exploits of some rum prospectors seeking to stake a claim) stands among the LP's legit jewels as Dylan breathes new life into this antique curio.

◙ **"Dead Man, Dead Man"** (Bob Dylan)
Bob Dylan, *Shot of Love* (1981); single/'81-live (1989); *Live 1961–2000—Thirty-nine Years of Great Concert Performances*/'81 (2001)
Steven Keene, *Keene on Dylan* (1990)

A fire-and-brimstone sneer, a song to Christ or a departed friend, a song of mourning and resurrection, whatever one wishes to call it, "Dead Man, Dead Man" was more than just the tongue-in-cheek, self-referential inclusion in the 1987 Dylan/Grateful Dead concerts that the title might imply. It may also be Dylan's most fully realized reggae song—or better yet, an "apocalypso."

One of the last eschatological songs in Dylan's catalogue, "Dead Man, Dead Man" is unrelenting, steeped in such rich imagery that Dylan snaps off at a fevered clip with a "Positively 4th Street" vehemence, highlighting the emotional and spiritual blindness of the person to whom he's singing (who may be himself).

Lines like "there's a bird's nest in your hair" would seem to indicate this person can't (or just won't) see the truth or place any faith in anything, be it God or Satan. Whether the bird's nest is a symbol of evil thoughts, dark ideas, wicked plans, or simply selfishness is really beside the point. Dylan's concern for the deadened soul he addresses would seem paramount.

Dylan recorded "Dead Man" in April 1981 for his sharp *Shot of Love* LP and began performing it couple of months later. Always a concert powerhouse—especially when staged with his backup vocalists in the early and mid-1980s—"Dead Man" was performed throughout the generally unheralded year of 1981. It was shelved for the next half decade before making a welcome return for the Grateful Dead tour in the summer of '87, and stayed in the rotation when Dylan rejoined Tom Petty and the Heartbreakers for a European and Middle Eastern tour later in the year. Thereafter, it was resurrected only for a few Never Ending Tour 1989 concerts and one in 1990.

[S] **"Dear Landlord"** (Bob Dylan)

Bob Dylan, *John Wesley Harding* (1967); *Biograph* (1985)
Joan Baez, *Any Day Now* (1968); *Baez Sings Dylan* (1998)
Joe Cocker, *Joe Cocker!* (1969); *Live in L.A.* (1976); *Long Voyage Home* (1995)
Crocket, *Gathering at the Depot* (1970)
Hamilton Camp, *Paul Sills' Story Theatre* (1970)
The Original Marauders, *Now Your Mouth Cries Wolf* (1977)
Janis Joplin, *Janis* (1993)
Ashley Hutchings, *The Guv'nor* (1994)
Michael Moore, *Jewels and Binoculars* (2000)

Dylan's first piano song since "Ballad of a Thin Man," "Dear Landlord" is a minor-key plea and perhaps the most confessional song on *John Wesley Harding*, thought to address his manager Albert Grossman, or show business, and/or his audience and their expectations with its imploring request: "Please don't put a price on my soul."

While some have linked the song's catalogue of sins to the immigrant in Proverbs 6 (*see* "I Pity the Poor Immigrant"), others see Dylan's tenant as more personal and literal: Dylan was living in a cottage owned by Grossman in Woodstock, New York, when the song was written in 1967, early in what would be Dylan's eight-year hiatus from touring. This made his manager his actual landlord. Additionally, Dylan had not delivered on projects he promised to the recording, publishing, and television industries, so one could say he was behind on his rent. And perhaps his fans, with their rising calls for a return to the public fray, needed this reality check in song. With "Dear Landlord," Dylan seems to be asking all parties to just leave him alone and forgive his debts, no matter what the contract says. In fact, maybe the contract could be disposed of altogether.

All references aside, Jon Landau nailed the spirit of "Dear Landlord" in "John Wesley Harding," his review of the titular album in the May 1968 issue (#15) of *Crawdaddy*, writing that the song is:

> . . . given a recognizable layer of meaning which is in turn obscured somewhat by incongruent images. And again, more striking than the words in and of themselves is Dylan's interpretative power as a vocalist. While the landlord has been thought to represent all manner of authority—everyone from his manager to the government—that type of speculation is unimportant. What is important is Dylan's attitude toward the subject. He is not out for blood, yet at the same times he isn't willing to give in. He is empathetic but realistic. "If you don't underestimate me I won't underestimate you." I will recognize you but you are going to have to deal with me.

D

This is a truly incredible transformation in attitude when seen in contrast with "Ballad of a Thin Man." The role of the vocal is totally complementary to the verbal level meaning. What I particularly dig is the firmness in Dylan's voice. No reliance on exaggerated mannerisms but a simple and direct statement. Also, the melodic structure of the song is one of the most sophisticated Dylan has ever devised and his piano playing is quite incisive and competent.

After years of neglecting "Dear Landlord," Dylan performed the song for a brief period during his fall 1992 Never Ending Tour and revived it even more briefly in 2003.

"Dear Mrs. Roosevelt" (Woody Guthrie)
Various Artists (performed by Bob Dylan), *A Tribute to Woody Guthrie, Part One/*'68 (1971)
Various Artists (performed by Woody Guthrie), *We Ain't Down Yet!* (1994)
Joel Rafael, *Woodeye: Songs of Woody Guthrie* (2003)

Thousands of young people wrote to First Lady Eleanor Roosevelt for help during the Great Depression, asking for clothing, money, and other forms of assistance. With that knowledge and in that spirit, Woody Guthrie wrote this World War II protest song in the form of a letter to Mrs. Roosevelt in the 1940s.

Dylan's sincere, one-night-only reading of "Dear Mrs. Roosevelt" was performed with the Hawks (soon to be the Band) as part of their special set at the 1968 Woody Guthrie memorial concert in New York City's Carnegie Hall. Given that his performance took place at the height of the Vietnam War, some took Dylan's letter in cover song as addressed to the White House—certified mail, return receipt requested.

After Guthrie died on October 3, 1967, tribute concerts to him were organized at Carnegie

Hall in New York in January 1968, and at the Hollywood Bowl in Los Angeles in September 1970. Dylan's appearance with the Hawks for a short workout at the New York show was his first public appearance since his motorcycle accident in the summer of 1966.

"Death Is Not the End" (Bob Dylan)
Bob Dylan, *Down in the Groove* (1988)
Gavin Friday, *Each Man Kills the Thing He Loves* (1990)
Nick Cave, *Murder Ballads* (1996)
The Waterboys, *Live Adventures of the Waterboys* (1998)
Peter Bellamy, *Wake the Vaulted Echoes* (1999)

Dylan's born-again Christian phase supposedly ended years before he subjected his record-buying audience to "Death Is Not the End," a turgid piece of apocalyptic portent ensuring an afterlife in a manner that calls to mind dirt roads and pickup-truck radios. With images of burning cities and garlanded eternity, the song sounds like something Dante and Hieronymus Bosch might have written for the Statler Brothers while under the influence of too much Bud Lite.

"Death Is Not the End" was recorded during the *Infidels* sessions in 1983 and didn't languish in the can long enough. The best that can be said here is how much like one of the many cover songs on *Down in the Groove* it sounds—as if Dylan were deliberately writing a song to sound like somebody else.

Death of a Ladies' Man/Leonard Cohen
Warner Bros. LP BS-3125, CS CK 44286, CD 44286. Released 1977.
See also "Hallelujah"

Dylan contributed backing vocals to "Don't Go Home with Your Hard-On" on *Death of a Ladies' Man*, one of Leonard Cohen's most idiosyncratic and least successful albums. Here he turned from the Spartan settings that mark most of his work and embraced producer Phil Spector's trademark Wall of Sound that does to Cohen's songs what the whale did to poor Jonah. The songs are just fine, especially "True Love Leaves No Traces" and "Paper Thin Hotel," but this was an artist/producer match made in hell.

"The Death of Emmett Till" (Bob Dylan)
aka "The Ballad of Emmett Till," "Emmett Till"
Bob Dylan, *Broadside Reunion/'62* (1972)
Joan Baez, *Joan Baez in Concert, Part 2* (1963)
Coulson, Dean, McGuinness, Flint, *Lo & Behold* (1972)
Bettina Jonic, *The Bitter Mirror* (1975)

A mawkish *Freewheelin' Bob Dylan* outtake and brief performance pick from the era, "The Death of Emmett Till" is based on the true story of the death of a black teenager from Chicago murdered for a thrill in 1955 by white men in Mississippi who were tried and acquitted by a jury that, according to Dylan's song, included participants in the crime.

"The Death of Emmett Till" was written in or around February 1962 by a twenty-year-old Bob Dylan, numbering it among the first handful of songs that he ever wrote. Though not classic Dylan, the song is a straightforward, emotionally charged narrative account of both the brutal slaying of the fourteen-year-old Emmett Till and of the scandalous failure of American justice to punish his killers. Even with a self-righteous exhortation clumsily tacked on at the end, the song stands as a stark reminder of a truly dark page in then-recent American history—the youth's "fateful tragedy," as the song's opening verse reminds everyone, happened "not so long ago."

One reason the Till story may have made such a huge impression on Dylan is that he and Till were born just months apart. News of the incident must have reached Hibbing, Minnesota, and it's impossible to think that the fourteen-year-old Bobby Zimmerman didn't make a connection.

"Emmett Till" is an obvious precursor to a couple of his much more sophisticated compositions: "The Lonesome Death of Hattie Carroll"

Emmett Till and his mother, Mamie Bradley, ca. 1950.
(NAACP Records/Library of Congress)

from 1963 and 1975's "Hurricane." One can argue that these two songs might not have been written had it not been for such rougher proto-types as "Emmett Till." Years later, Dylan spoke of the song with little pride, saying, "I used to write songs like I'd say, Yeah, what's bad? Pick out something bad, like segregation. OK, here we go! And I'd pick one of the thousand million little points I can pick and explode it. I wrote a song about Emmett Till which in all honesty was a bullshit song. I realize now that my rea-sons and motives behind it were phony."

Whatever his "reasons and motives," Dylan performed "The Death of Emmett Till" with gusto in his folk-club sets in 1962, used it as a showcase vehicle on several radio programs, and recorded it in July 1962 for *The Free-wheelin' Bob Dylan*—where it ended up on the trash heap.

Dylan is said to have composed "Emmett Till" specifically for his February 23, 1962, appearance at a benefit concert for the Con-gress of Racial Equality. He was clearly proud of the song when he performed it on the WBAI *Broadside* radio show in March 1962 (recorded and later released on the *Broadside Reunion* LP) for delighted hosts Izzy Young and Sis Cun-ningham. When he performed "Emmett Till" on Cynthia Gooding's WBAI *Folksinger's Choice* radio show that same month he intro-duced the song by saying it had been written "just last week" with a melody "stolen from Len Chandler." He then proceeded to perform the song at a relatively jaunty pace, wrapping his voice creatively around the notes and favorite phrases—"blood red rain" and "ghost-robed Ku Klux Klan."

Emmett Till's true story was well known to every self-respecting, card-carrying, civil-rights-marching, desegregation-demonstrating Greenwich Village folkie in the early 1960s. But because it has been more than four decades

since Dylan wrote this song, and nearly five since the events that inspired him, it is only nat-ural that "The Death of Emmett Till" has until recently lost some of its time- and place-spe-cific topicality and been eclipsed by other tales of racial and social injustice and outrage.

A resident of Chicago's South Side, Till traveled South with his cousin Curtis Jones to visit relatives in Money, Mississippi. While Chicago had more than its share of racism and segregation, nothing could have prepared him for what he witnessed in Mississippi even after having journeyed there in the Jim Crow, "blacks only" train carriages that carried him to Money.

Emmett and Curtis stayed with Curtis's grandfather, Mose Wright. But soon after arriv-ing, an innocent gag turned deadly. Emmett joined a group of teenagers, seven boys and one girl, to go to Bryant's Grocery and Meat Market for refreshments to cool off after a long day of picking cotton in the hot sun. Bryant's Grocery, owned by a white couple, Roy and Car-olyn Bryant, sold supplies and candy to a pri-marily black clientele of sharecroppers and their children. Emmett went into the store to buy bubblegum. Some of the kids outside the store would later say they heard Emmett whis-tle at Carolyn Bryant.

Till was marked. When store owner Roy Bryant heard about what happened, he drove out to Wright's cabin with his half-brother J. W. Milam "to get the boy who done the talkin'."

Wright tried to intervene, explaining to the men that Emmett was just a naïve kid from Chicago who had yet to learn how he was sup-posed to act with white folks in the South. But the men were hearing nothing of it: they dragged Emmett screaming from the cabin, shoved him into the backseat of their truck, and warned Mose not to call the police. That was the last time Mose Wright ever saw Emmett Till alive.

Though the men later claimed that they had merely wanted to give the teenager the fright of his life, the precise circumstances of the crime still remain uncertain. It is known that Bryant and Milam drove to the Tallahatchie River, that they made Emmett carry a seventy-five-pound cotton-gin fan to the river from the back of the truck, and that they ordered him to strip and beg for mercy. When Till refused, he was shot in the back of the head. Milam, who reportedly did the shooting, later told a journalist that when Till continued to be feisty and arrogant, they had no choice but to kill him.

But they didn't merely kill Emmett Till, as Dylan surmised: "They rolled his body down a gulf amidst a bloody red rain/And they threw him in the waters wide to cease his screaming pain/The reason that they killed him there, and I'm sure it ain't no lie/Was just for the fun of killin' him and to watch him slowly die."

Mose Wright was true to his word. Terrified by a situation he had lived with from the day he was born, he never did notify the police. Curtis Jones, however, called the sheriff's office the following morning to tell them that Emmett had been abducted. Milam and Bryant were quickly arrested and charged with kidnapping Emmett Till, but it wasn't until three days later that Till's body was discovered in the Tallahatchie River. The heavy fan was still tied around his neck with barbed wire; his forehead was crushed on one side, an eye was gouged out, and his skull bore a bullet hole. His face so badly mangled by the beating that Mose Wright could identify it only by the initialed ring Emmett wore.

Ignoring the sheriff's instruction to bury the badly decomposed body quickly, Emmett's mother demanded that her son's corpse be sent back to Chicago, where thousands filed passed the open coffin in the days prior to Emmett's September 3, 1955, funeral, attended by 2,000 people. When the popular African-American magazine *Jet* published a photo of the gruesome contents of the casket, the whole world got a chance to see what white Mississippi could do to a young black. The black community was galvanized as all eyes, black and white, turned toward Mississippi and civil libertarians began their campaign to establish equal rights and justice for all.

When Milam and Bryant were indicted on a murder charge, there was much lip service paid to the notion that justice should, and would, be done.

The trial commenced in September 1955 under extreme tension. Curtis Jones, prevented from giving evidence by his mother, who feared he might suffer a fate similar to that of his cousin, was not present. But Mose Wright was. In an act of supreme bravery he stood before a white judge, an all-white jury, white armed guards, and a white gallery (save the few black journalists reporting on the trial) and, when asked if he could recognize Emmett's abductors, pointed at the accused.

As Mose remembered later, he could "feel the blood boil in hundreds of white people as they sat glaring in the courtroom. It was the first time in my life I had the courage to accuse a white man of a crime, let alone something as terrible as killing a boy. I wasn't exactly brave and I wasn't scared. I just wanted to see justice done." (From *Eyes on the Prize: America's Civil Rights Years, 1954–1965*, by Juan Williams; New York: Viking, 1987.)

Despite Mose Wright's statement and equally damning testimony by another African American local, the defense never called Milam or Bryant, choosing instead to parade a few character witnesses before the jury. When the prosecution and defense had completed their cases, the all-white, all-male jury was treated to this extraordinarily succinct summation from

John C. Whitten, one of the five defense attorneys: "Your fathers will turn over in their graves if these men are found guilty. I'm sure that every last Anglo-Saxon one of you has the courage to free these men." (From *Eyes on the Prize*, cited above.)

It took the jury less than an hour to return a verdict of not guilty; its members claimed that they had not been convinced that the grotesquely disfigured body recovered from the Tallahatchie River had been satisfactorily identified.

The bitter outrage following the verdict was widespread, but rallies in several cities and condemnation in the editorial pages of major newspapers were of little consequence. Even the kidnap charges brought against Milam and Bryant were dismissed and the two walked away as free men. In a final insult, the two men admitted their guilt in a 1956 *Look* magazine interview, but because of the strictures involving retrial for absolved crimes, they were never brought back to court.

Interest in the Till case was revived in 2003 with the airing of *The Murder of Emmett Till*, a documentary by Stanley Nelson given wide release on PBS television's *American Experience*, and with the 2003 passing of Till's mother, Mamie Till Mobley, who never stopped fighting for justice regarding her son's brutal demise. (See also Keith Beauchamp's documentary *The Untold Story of Emmett Louis Till.*) For an extensive inquiry into this event, *A Death in the Delta: The Story of Emmett Till* by Stephen J. Whitfield (New York: Free Press, 1988) is recommended.

Lady Justice may be blind, but now and then her blindfold seems to slip off her impassive face. Spurred partly by revelations contained in the films and the renewed interest in the Till travesty, the U.S. Justice Department announced on May 10, 2004, that it was opening a criminal investigation into the case in light of new evidence. Though Bryant and Milam are long dead, the films suggest that there were other people involved in Till's murder besides the two original suspects.

So, when listening to "Emmett Till," disregard Dylan's disavowal of the composition and its intent but think of a young black man and the times that, some say, have yet to change.

[S] "Deep Elem Blues" (Traditional)

aka "Deep Elm Blues," "Deep Ellem Blues," "Deep Ellum Blues"

Singles: Ida May Mack (1928), Texas Bill Day (1929), The Lone Star Cowboys (1933), The Shelton Brothers (1935), Dallas Jamboree Jug Band (1935)

Les Paul, *Complete Decca Trios/'36* (1991)

Jerry Lee Lewis, *Ole Tyme Country Music* (1970)

Johnny Cash, *Country Comeback* (1970)

The Good Old Boys, *Pistol Packin' Mama* (1975)

The Grateful Dead, *Reckoning* (1981)

Charlie Daniels, *Blues Hat* (1997)

Charlie Feathers, *Get with It: The Essential Recordings* (1998)

Elm Street was the hub of the notorious red-light district in Dallas, Texas, from the late 1800s until the 1930s. During that period, the byway's name came to signify the entire neighborhood surrounding it and the word Elm morphed into "Elem" (or "Ellem") and then into "Deep Elem." Leadbelly and Blind Lemon Jefferson were the more famous songsters and rounders who performed and debauched there, sharing the sidewalks and saloons with a familiar assortment of pimps, prostitutes, grifters, sportin' men, flim-flamming politicians, and, no doubt a straying or crusading preacher or two. It was natural for the neighborhood to be romanticized in song, and "Deep Elem Blues," describing the temptations, pleasures, and dangers lurking in the shadows, is easily the best known.

The Deep Elem neighborhood once again sprang to life in the 1980s and became Dallas's trendy destination, spawning many nightspots and groups like Edie Brickell and New Bohemians.

"Deep Elem Blues" showed up at a couple of Dylan's 1962 New York City engagements—a spring gig at Gerde's Folk City and a session at the home of his friends the Whitakers. Dylan claimed that Big Joe Williams himself taught him the song, but informed speculation suggests Dylan simply swiped the famous Jerry Lee Lewis version.

"Delia" (Traditional/Blind Willie McTell)

See also "Blind Willie McTell"

aka "All My Friends Are Gone," "Little Delia," "One More Rounder Gone"

Bob Dylan, *World Gone Wrong* (1993)
Blind Willie McTell, *Atlanta Twelve String* (1992)
Paul Clayton, *Bloody Ballads* (1956)
Bob Gibson, *Offbeat Folksongs* (1956)
Roy Book Binder, *Travelin' Man* (1970)
Harry Belafonte, *This Is Harry Belafonte* (1990)
Stefan Grossman, *Shake That Thing: Fingerpicking Country* (1998)
David Johansen and the Harry Smiths, *David Johansen and the Harry Smiths* (2000)
Various Artists (performed by Spider John Koerner), *A Nod to Bob* (2001)
Eric Taylor, *Scuffletown* (2001)

Devastating. "Delia," a low-key black murder ballad, is as haunting and diabolical as anything Bob Dylan ever sang. After murdering Delia, a gambling girl who simply does not care for him, the killer (and song's partial narrator), Curtis, goes on the lam, is eventually captured, tried, and sentenced to, as the judge in the song says, "ninety-nine." Alone in his cell, Curtis drinks from an old tin cup and finishes the song to Delia, whose ghost seems to linger close by. As he sings, Curtis finally begins to

sense the truth in the song's short chorus, "all the friends I ever had are gone."

Dylan did some character study on Delia and Curtis in his *World Gone Wrong* liner notes. Pointing out that the song is about "counterfeit loyalty," Dylan wrote: "Delia herself, no Queen Gertrude, Elizabeth I or even Evita Peron . . . the guy in the courthouse sounds like a pimp in primary colors. He's not interested in mosques on the temple mount, armageddon or World War III . . ."

Originally an American prison song that transmuted into a honky-tonk number, "Delia" has a broad, circuitous, and confusing history. Dylan himself acknowledged in the *World Gone Wrong* liner notes that his "Delia" is "two or more versions mixed into one."

There are dozens of versions of "Delia" floating around but Blind Willie McTell probably has a lock on the song in the folk consciousness, even though none of his recordings of "Delia" saw daylight until 1972. He first recorded the song—which he called "Little Delia"—on November 5, 1940, in Atlanta for one of John A. Lomax's field recording expeditions for the Library of Congress. His definitively plaintive rendering of the song, the one that makes it his, came from his 1949 session in Atlanta, which also produced "Broke Down Engine," another *World Gone Wrong* track. In McTell's hands "Delia" took on unearthly qualities worthy of a Shakespearean tragedy performed on an opening night at the Globe Theater. And so is Dylan's compassionate, lucent version. His "Delia" achieves a depth of feeling hardly equaled in his entire career and is more or less a mixture of McTell's and a North Carolina variant called "All My Friends Are Gone." Interestingly, both McTell and Dylan recorded "Delia" when they were about a half century old.

But the other versions, histories, and arrangements of "Delia" no doubt seeped into

D

Dylan's vision of the song as well. He was probably aware of "Delia's Gone" (aka "One More Round") popularized by Bahamian blues singer Blind Blake, a kitschy version of Joseph Spence (who is not to be confused with the great Chicago bluesman and songster of the same name). A true American hybrid in whatever version is unearthed and too old to have a definitive version anyway, "Delia" is an extension of the traditional late nineteenth-century ballads well known to both black and white performers.

Less attention, somewhat surprisingly, has been paid to the historical roots of "Delia." A Georgian by the name of John Garst did some poking around in the local Savannah archives in 2000 and discovered that a fourteen-year-old girl named Delia Green was shot by Moses "Coony" Houston, approximately fifteen years of age, in Savannah's poor, black, and violent Yamacraw neighborhood shortly before midnight on Christmas Eve, 1900. Delia died in the afternoon of Christmas Day in her bed at home. Newspapers and court papers reveal somewhat conflicting evidence as to the circumstances surrounding the shooting. The basic story appears to be that Delia was living at the home (perhaps a brothel) of a family named West. She and Coony had been, according to the newspapers, "more or less intimate" for several months prior to the shooting. But they had a row on Christmas Eve that resulted in the contents of West's pistol being discharged into Delia's gut. Whether this was an accident or not (Coony claimed he was merely clowning around with the gun when it went off) or whether the gathering at the West domicile involved the consumption of alcohol are a couple of the points of contention that came out in the trial. In the end, Coony was sentenced to life in prison but paroled after twelve and a half years.

An old recording circulates of Dylan performing a version of "Delia" very early in his career from a May 1960 party in Minneapolis. He returned to "Delia" as a powerful statement when he included the tragic tale on his *World Gone Wrong* collection and performed a few dagger-in-the-heart versions around the time of the release in 1993 in both acoustic band and electric arrangements. Dylan shelved the song for a decade but revisited "Delia" at four 2000 shows, again as an acoustic offering.

In his December 1993 *Mojo* magazine review of *World Gone Wrong*, Bill Flanagan diagnosed the song and Dylan's relationship with it, writing, "When Dylan sings, in this version of 'Delia,' 'All the friends I ever had are gone,' it breaks your heart. His world-worn voice reveals the cracks behind his stoicism in a way that this most unsentimental of singers would ever allow in his lyrics. The weight of nobility and loss are as appropriate to this older Dylan's singing as anger and hunger were to the snarl of his youth."

"Deportees (Plane Wreck at Los Gatos)"
(Woody Guthrie/Martin Hoffman)
aka "Deportee," "Plane Wreck at Los Gatos (Deportees)"
Woody Guthrie, *We Ain't Down Yet!* (1994)
Pete Seeger, *Pete Seeger Sings Woody Guthrie* (1962)
Cisco Houston, *Cisco Houston Sings Woody Guthrie* (1963)
Joan Baez, *Blessed Are . . .* (1971)
Rich Lerner, *Trails and Bridges* (1996)
Nanci Griffith, *Other Voices Too (A Trip Back . . .)* (1998)

Woody Guthrie was inspired to write "Deportees," one of his true, still-topical masterworks, after reading a newspaper account of a plane crash near Los Gatos, California, in 1949. The plane was flying home a large group of Mexican workers (pejoratively referred to as "wetbacks") who had entered the United States illegally, induced by promises of well-paying jobs from unscrupulous agents of the large fruit orchards in California. The newspaper didn't bother listing the names of those killed. Like surplus crops, they were just expendable.

Some suggest that "Deportees" was Woody's last great song. Interestingly, though, according to Joe Klein's book *Woody Guthrie: A Life* (New York: Alfred A. Knopf, 1980), this memorial to the nameless migrants "all scattered like dry leaves" in Los Gatos Canyon wasn't exactly a song in its original incarnation. As Guthrie wrote it, says Klein, "Deportees" was virtually without music: "Woody chanted the words—and [the composition] wasn't performed publicly until a decade later when a schoolteacher named Martin Hoffman added a beautiful melody and Pete Seeger began singing it in concerts."

Dylan's throwaway disaster of a performance of "Deportees" at the May 1974 "Friends of Chile" concert in New York should be avoided at all costs, but his renditions with Joan Baez from the 1976 leg of the Rolling Thunder Revue (as seen on the still unreleased 1976 national television broadcast of *Hard Rain*) were urgent and transcendent—the dreams stuff are made of.

◪ *Desire*

Columbia Records, LP PC-33893, CD CK-33893, CS JCT-33893; Sony Music Entertainment, Inc., SACD 90318. Recorded July 28–31 and October 24, 1975, New York City. Released January 16, 1976. Produced by Don DeVito and Bob Dylan. Album notes by Bob Dylan. Liner notes by Allen Ginsberg. Photography by Ken Regan.

Bob Dylan—guitar, harmonica, piano, keyboards, vocals. Emmylou Harris—vocals. Scarlet Rivera—violin. Rob Stoner—bass, vocals. Vincent Bell—bass. Ronee Blakley—vocals. Dom Cortese—mandolin, accordion. Steven Soles—guitar, vocals. Eric Clapton—guitar. Luther Rix—percussion, conductor. Howie Wyeth—piano, drums.

Mexican migrant onion picker in a field near Tracy, California, 1935.

(Photo: Dorothea Lange/Library of Congress)

"Hurricane," "Isis," "Mozambique," "One More Cup of Coffee (Valley Below)," "Oh, Sister," "Joey," "Romance in Durango," "Black Diamond Bay," "Sara"

Note: All songs except "One More Cup of Coffee (Valley Below)" and "Sara" written with Jacques Levy.

Cut with a band Dylan was assembling for the Rolling Thunder Revue, *Desire* is an exotic, endearingly messy mélange that remains Dylan's most commercially successful release. With a nod to his protest songs of the past ("Hurricane"), dime-store novellas in song ("Romance in Durango" and "Black Diamond Bay"), a dusky, allegorical epic ("Isis"), a celebration of an American pariah ("Joey"), a spiritual dirge ("Oh, Sister"), and a final melancholy plea to his estranged wife ("Sara"), *Desire* doesn't quite stand up as the unified whole of its predecessor, *Blood on the Tracks*, but it is still fine as fine can be.

With *Blood on the Tracks*, *The Basement Tapes*, and his high-profile tours with the Band and the Rolling Thunder Revue, Dylan was in the limelight in the mid-'70s, and all certainly contributed to *Desire*'s seventeen-week stay on the charts, during which it actually hit No. 1 for a short period. The album cover, which for a time was ubiquitous in college dorms across America, captures the seat-of-the-pants, whirlwind spirit of Rolling Thunder, as it depicts Dylan playing the gypsy, under a cowboy hat—an overlarge fur coat over his shoulders and a scarf around his neck whipping in the wind. The back cover carries a collage of photos featuring Dylan, various band members, and one of his wife Sara—the only time her image was included on one of his albums. That she appears here is both odd and appropriate: the marriage was falling apart, yet *Desire* also includes a song for and about her. Along with the pictures on the back, Dylan offers some short, impressionistic album notes that were joined by a longer Allen Ginsberg contribution on an insert.

The *Desire* recording sessions were notoriously chaotic, even for Dylan. What is most notable about the record was Dylan's unusual collaboration with playwright/psychologist Jacques Levy, who was probably best known in musical circles up to that point for his work on the risqué Broadway production *Oh! Calcutta*.

Every song on *Desire* except "Sara" and "One More Cup of Coffee" was written with Levy. Still, they all seem like Dylan songs, not collaborations. The album's sound, though, is clearly a collaboration that benefits from the intense, almost frenzied musical interplay that would characterize the first leg of the Rolling Thunder Revue. Nothing evidenced this more,

and helped the record more, than Scarlet Rivera's eerie violin; the lilting, luscious, and enchanting music contained here is aided immeasurably by her contribution. Though Dylan doesn't go nose-to-nose, toe-to-toe, or belly-to-belly with his inner demons as he did on *Blood on the Tracks*, he does create a picaresque vision for his audience to behold.

▣ "Desolation Row" (Bob Dylan)
Bob Dylan, *Highway 61 Revisited* (1965); *MTV Unplugged* (1995); *The Bootleg Series, Volume 4: Bob Dylan Live 1966—The "Royal Albert Hall" Concert* (1998)
Dan Tillberg, *Karlek Minus Noll* (1982)
The Rockridge Synthesizer Orchestra, *Plays Classic Dylan Tracks* (1997)
Manfred Maurenbrecher, *Manfred Maurenbrecher* (2001)
The Grateful Dead, *Postcards of the Hanging: Grateful Dead Perform the Songs of Bob Dylan* (2002)
Robyn Hitchcock, *Robyn Sings* (2002)
Chris Smither, *Train Home* (2003)

As apocalyptically portentous as W. B. Yeats's "Lapus Lazuli," Allen Ginsberg's "Howl," a Bosch triptych, or any song about the abyss of personal loneliness, "Desolation Row" is perhaps the most nightmarish vision in Dylan's canon. Robin Hood, Einstein, Romeo, Cinderella, the Good Samaritan, the Hunchback of Notre Dame, Bette Davis, Ezra Pound, T. S. Eliot, and the songwriter himself are just a few of those who make cameos in this carnival of the grotesque as Dylan transforms cultural legend into a barren dream of despair.

There is no escape from this science fiction noir where mythology and history's heroes and heels lurk in the shadows of every alleyway on this queerest of streets. By the time he committed his dark dream to vinyl, Dylan had long become adept at writing songs that took society to task. And while at least some of those songs contained an element of hope or the possibility of redemption, he doesn't even pretend to try to find it here. Against this canvas of doom—be it universal or personal—Dylan introduces us to some pretty shady characters whose veiled motives make the visitor to this particular ring of fire quickly begin to search for a way out— even if it means boarding the *Titanic* at daybreak with a nonrefundable one-way ticket. Turn left and you're in the cyanide hole. Turn right and somebody is looking to attach you to a heart attack machine. In this surreal, existentialist byway of the ludicrous there is no exit or even a dead end. Dylan may rearrange the faces and give all his actors new names, but it is clear that in his remaking of *Modern Times* into *Metropolis*, he is, despite his gallows humor, adopting a scorched-earth policy for this Möbius strip paved with toxic quicksand.

Some of the power in the eleven-minute vortex in entropy—an inverted State of the Union Address if ever there was one—no doubt derives from Dylan's absurdist pairings on the crowded stage of his song. With so many characters in so many unexpected, unfulfilling, symbiotic clinches appearing in his edgy Purgatory (the sex-phobic Ophelia with the libertine Dr. Filth, the sightless commissioner tied to the tightrope walker, Einstein and the jealous monk locked in the fixed "science vs. religion" debate, Pound and Eliot with their hairsplitting quibbles over poetics, prurient Romeo and the easygoing Cinderella erasing all desire with her casual manipulations), Dylan's ruthless combination of fear and frustration makes listeners wonder when (not if) they will see themselves stumbling along with the diseased parade.

A great irony of "Desolation Row" is that its release came on the heels of accusations that Dylan had abandoned so-called protest songs. Yeah, right. Here is a song that would appear to protest just about everything, and Dylan clearly cherished it from its inception. When asked by

critic/journalist Nat Hentoff during their farcical 1966 interview published in *Playboy* magazine what he would do if elected president, Dylan answered that he would "immediately rewrite 'The Star-Spangled Banner,' and little schoolchildren, instead of memorizing 'America the Beautiful,' would have to memorize 'Desolation Row.'"

Some have traced Dylan's original spark of musical inspiration to "The Clown's Baby," a song collected by John A. Lomax in *Songs of the Cattle Trail and Cow Camp* (New York: Macmillan, 1919). Probably American in origin, the tune is credited to one Margaret Vandergrift, although she may be only the person from whom Lomax collected the song. Whatever the source, "Desolation Row" stands apart from the balance of *Highway 61 Revisited* as Dylan eschewed a larger ensemble for the stately, Spanish-tinged sound of just two guitars. As keyboardist Al Kooper recalled, "I just think Bob wanted to set it apart in some way, shape, or form, and instrumentation was just the way he chose."

Jack Kerouac's 1965 novel *Desolation Angels*, with its title and its phrases "perfect image of a priest" and "her sin is her lifelessness," may also have been appropriated by Dylan here.

For those seeking autobiographical traces in "Desolation Row," look no further than its first half a dozen words: "They're selling postcards of the hanging." On June 15, 1920, in Duluth, Minnesota, a mere twenty-one years before Dylan was born in that city, a mob of thousands there dragged three black men, Elias Clayton, Elmer Jackson, and Isaac McGhie, who'd come to town with the John Robinson Show Circus, from a jail and hanged them from a lamppost at the intersection First Street and Second Avenue East. The event grew out of a dubious accusation by a white teenager that

A postcard of the hanging: the lynching of Elias Clayton, Isaac McGhie, and Elmer Jackson, Duluth, Minnesota, June 15, 1920.
(NAACP Records/Library of Congress)

the men had raped his female companion and forced him to watch. Eventually it came out that the boy had made up the story, but the three roustabouts were arrested and jailed on June 14, along with three others from the circus who survived the inquisition. As was common practice for decades, the memory of the tragedy was kept alive by postcards; these were sold in Duluth for some time after the event and easily could have been seen by Dylan as a youngster growing up in northern Minnesota. After much soul searching and a local committee with the blinders off and a bit in its teeth, a 53-by-70 foot sculpture atoning for the lynching was unveiled in Duluth in September 2003.

The famous *Highway 61 Revisited* cut with Nashville session guitarist Charlie McCoy is also worthy of note. Dylan had told McCoy to play whatever he felt like and the guitarist responded with inventive and spectacular acoustic filigrees. But that rendition serves only as a blueprint for what Dylan has done with the song in concert.

Perhaps because of its length and naked, surreal lyrical angularity that may make it difficult to remember, Dylan has had an on-again, off-again relationship with "Desolation Row" as a performance vehicle. Almost always performed acoustically, the song was a regular feature of his monumental concerts in 1965 and 1966. It remained in Dylan's set lists when he returned to performing in 1974 with the Band. After that, "Desolation Row" was shelved for the next decade, until Dylan brought it back for some passable renditions on his 1984 tour. Two years later, he proceeded to butcher it in a duet with Bob Weir of the Grateful Dead when he joined the Dead onstage during that summer's Dylan/Tom Petty–Grateful Dead tour. In 1987, though, he worked up an effective electric arrangement for his fall tour with Petty and company, and it made its debut as a Never Ending Tour highlight in 1990. These latter-day arrangements have retained the elusive, talismanic qualities that made "Desolation Row" famous long ago, despite being departures from the original. Dylan's second official release of "Desolation Row" on his *Unplugged* album in 1995, for example, is markedly different from that on *Highway 61 Revisited*. In 1965 he performed the epic with a sneer and in 1974 he toyed with alternating dynamics in the phraseology to create an off-kilter tension. But his quiet, conspiratorial voice two and three decades later makes the corrosive song even more paranoid, if possible, than before. In a neat vocal sleight-of-hand, Dylan took to gradually raising the octave range from verse to verse, so that by the end of the song, his pitched delivery accurately portrays a man desperately trying to share what he has witnessed under the streetlights of the abyss with anybody brave enough to listen.

For something completely different, check out *The Superhuman Crew* (J. Paul Getty Museum Publications, 1999), a book that features artist James Ensor's painting *Christ's Entry into Brussels in 1889* and the lyrics to "Desolation Row," packaged with a CD of Dylan's recording of the song from *Highway 61 Revisited*. Look at Ensor's art while listening to Dylan's—each enhances the other.

Finally, iTunes, the online pay-for-music digital jukebox introduced by Apple in 2003 to reinvent the Napster model legally, red-flagged "Desolation Row" with a hard-to-figure "explicit lyrics" warning. Guess that's what you get for thinking different.

🎵 "Detroit City (I Wanna Go Home)" (Danny Dill/Mel Tillis)

See also "Long Black Veil"
Bobby Bare, single (1962); *All-American Boy* (1994)
Kai Winding, *Modern Country* (1964)
Tom Jones, *Green, Green Grass of Home* (1967)
Johnny Cash, *Johnny Cash Show* (1970)
Arthur Alexander, *Greatest Hits* (1989)
Solomon Burke, *Home in Your Heart* (1992)
Dean Martin, *Great Dean Martin, Volume 2* (1995)
Lester Flatt and Earl Scruggs, *1964–1969, Plus* (1996)

In typical regionally sensitive fashion, Dylan kicked off a 1990 Never Ending Tour show in Michigan with "Detroit City," a song about displaced Southerners ("homesick hillbillies," they call themselves) looking for a better life (but not necessarily finding it), written by a couple of cats who grew up nowhere near Motown—Mel Tillis and Danny Dill.

Dill spoke of the song's inspiration in 1973, telling Dorothy Horstman for her book *Sing Your Heart Out, Country Boy* (New York: E. P. Dutton, 1975): "About three years before we wrote this, I played a little old club in Detroit . . . and I saw these people that are in this song. They did go north. When I was a kid, they'd say, 'Where's John now?' 'Well, he's gone off up to Detroit.' I sat there and talked to these people. They were from Alabama, west Tennessee, Kentucky, and they'd go to Detroit and work in the car factories. Now, they had more cash money in their pockets than they'd ever seen in their lives, but they were homesick. And to keep from being so lonely, they'd go sit in a bar and drink. And when they did get home, they'd get home with no money. They wasted, literally, ten or fifteen years of their lives, and they wanted to go home all the time. They'd think they were rich, but they'd spend it. Then, eventually, they'd dovetail and catch that southbound freight and ride back home where they'd come from."

"Detroit City" is associated primarily with Mel Tillis (born August 8, 1932, Tampa, Florida), a formidable presence in country music—a renowned songwriter and beloved performer whose career stretches back to the mid-1950s. Tillis grew up in rural Florida, where he contracted malaria when only three years old. This left him with a permanent stutter, which he turned into an endearing trademark as he embarked on a country-music journey, developing a signature sound fusing honky-tonk with the accepted Nashville trends of the 1950s and 1960s.

Tillis's first break came in 1956 when he was employed picking strawberries. He had learned to play guitar as a teenager, and, in response to the backbreaking work, he wrote a song called "I'm Tired." The tune found its way into the hands of country singer Webb Pierce ("More and More"), who had a big hit with it—enabling Tillis to trade his blue collar for one with sequins.

Finding that he never stuttered when he sang, Tillis moved to Nashville to pursue a career in music. Quickly making a name for himself as a performer and songwriter, Tillis won a deal with Columbia in 1958, peeling off a string of hits for others including Pierce ("Tupelo County Jail" and "I Ain't Never"), Ray Price ("Heart over Mind") and Carl Smith ("Ten Thousand Drums"). When Bobby Bare hit the country and pop charts with "Detroit City," in 1963, Tillis's rep as a hit maker was sealed.

The Tillis road show was a force to contend with: with his band, the Statesiders (named after his 1966 hit "Stateside"), Tillis averaged two hundred fifty concerts annually and was also much in demand for appearances on network television shows.

Since the 1960s, Tillis has been successful in a number of areas. A robust character who has appeared in several films, including Burt Reynolds's *Smokey and the Bandit II*, he became a very successful businessman, and at one time owned several music-publishing companies.

He's got a sense of humor too: a typical Tillis performance would begin with Mel taking the stage and telling his audience, "I'm here to d-d-dispel those rumors going round that M-M-Mel T-Tillis has quit st-st-st-stuttering. That's not true. I'm still st-st-stuttering and making a pretty good living at it t-t-too."

"The Devil's Been Busy" (Traveling Wilburys)
Traveling Wilburys, *Traveling Wilburys, Volume 3* (1990)

This Wilburys message song concerning environmental apocalypse features Tom Petty on vocals and is not without its lighter aspects—not the least of which is that its narrator is standing in the middle of a golf course as he tells us exactly how man has managed to so thoroughly despoil the planet.

"Diamond Joe" (Traditional)
Bob Dylan, *Good as I Been to You* (1992)
Bob Dylan/Various Artists (performed by Bob Dylan), *Masked & Anonymous* (2003)
Ramblin' Jack Elliott (performed with Bob Dylan, credited as "Tedham Porterhouse"), *Jack Elliott* (1964)
Various Artists (performed by Charlie Butler), *Afro-American Blues and Game Songs/'34* (1942/1999)
Cisco Houston, *Cowboy Ballads* (1961)
Tom Rush, *Got a Mind to Ramble* (1963)
Jerry Garcia Acoustic Band, *Almost Acoustic* (1990)
Don Edwards, *Songs of the Trail* (1992)

Though Dylan included this much-traveled cowboy song, about the cruelty of a lying, conniving cattle boss, on *Good as I Been to You* (the first of his two all-acoustic albums of traditional folk and blues tunes, released in the early 1990s), he apparently never performed it in concert. Though the tune may be Irish in origin, "Diamond Joe" was adapted in the folk tradition to tell many a tale about a cattle-driving scoundrel who mistreats the narrator on the American frontier.

Dylan's first recorded performance of "Diamond Joe" came in a brief and pseudonymous appearance on *Jack Elliott*. According to John Way in *The Telegraph* #44 (winter 1992), Ramblin' Jack picked up "Diamond Joe" from Cisco Houston, whose own recording of the song appeared on *Cowboy Ballads* in 1961. Houston worked as a cowboy in the 1930s and may have learned the song during that stint. Earlier versions of "Diamond Joe" are hard to find on vinyl and make Dylan's source—especially for the tune—difficult to pinpoint. It may be a simple case of Dylan's grafting the version released by the Jerry Garcia Acoustic Band on *Almost Acoustic*. Dylan's *Good as I Been to You* performance of "Diamond Joe" is immaculate, as he handles the guitar parts with nimbleness and the vocals with evil delight.

In any case, recorded evidence of the song goes back to at least the 1920s: a couple of black singers were recorded singing different versions of "Diamond Joe" in the Darien, Georgia, penitentiary at different times in 1926, during the first spell of John A. Lomax's Library of Congress field recordings, but neither of these have been released. John Lomax and his son Alan wrote in *Cowboy Songs* that some form of "Diamond Joe" could be traced to the 1880s. Additionally, the Georgia Crackers recorded a hillbilly blues version of the song in the 1920s.

ⓐ Dick Fariña & Eric von Schmidt
Folklore Records LP LEUT-7. Released 1967.

Recorded during Dylan's January 1963 winter sojourn to London, occasioned by his performance in the BBC production of *The Mad-*

Album cover illustration for *Dick Fariña & Eric von Schmidt*, 1964.

(Blank Archives/Getty Images)

house on Castle Street, this vinyl rarity was released only in Great Britain. Dylan, famously and pseudonymously credited as "Blind Boy Grunt" in an attempt to stay below Columbia Records' radar, plays harmonica and contributes backing vocals on a real grab bag of material that includes "Glory, Glory," "Overseas Stomp," "You Can Always Tell," "Xmas Island," "Cocaine," and "London Waltz." Also lending support is Ethan Singer, best known for his work as a member of the Original Charles River Valley Boys.

Although Dylan's involvement is pretty low-key on this collector's item, he couldn't have picked two more overlooked and intriguing fellows to jam with. Fariña (born March 8, 1937, Brooklyn, New York; died April 30, 1966, Carmel, California) came to folk music by way of a childhood spent in Cuba, Ireland, Brooklyn, and, most importantly, Cornell University, where, during his 1950s undergraduate days,

D

he had buddied around with Thomas Pynchon (who dedicated his 1973 masterpiece novel *Gravity's Rainbow* to Fariña). Eventually Fariña's interests and talents as a songwriter, novelist, and political activist drew him to the East Coast folk music community. Certainly his trip to Cuba in the midst of its revolution earned him a subpoena to testify before the House Un-American Activities Committee, an experience he memorialized in "House Un-American Blues Activity Dream," a song that casts a cold eye on HUAC and the civil rights crimes committed on U.S. soil that that hallowed group found all too easy to ignore. Yet it is also rumored that Fariña was associated with the Irish Republican Army around the same time. With his dark good looks, obvious talent, and air of mystery, he may be the archetypal worldly wise and engaged bohemian.

Settling in New York City in 1960 and working in, of all places, an advertising agency as a copywriter, Fariña met folksinger Carolyn Hester, with whom Dylan recorded in 1961. Up until that point Fariña had concentrated on fiction and poetry, but Hester inspired an interest in playing and performing music. Fariña and Hester wed and moved to London but the marriage fell apart. While living there he began writing *Been Down So Long It Looks Like Up to Me*, the novel about his days at Cornell for which he is still best remembered.

Fariña returned stateside in 1963. That year, he met, began performing with, and married Mimi, the younger sister of folksinger Joan Baez. The couple were signed to Vanguard Records and released two excellent albums in 1965. *Celebrations for a Grey Day*, the first of these, included the classic Fariña song "Pack Up Your Sorrows." With their wholesome, Appalachian-tinged compositions featuring Fariña's fine dulcimer playing, Richard and Mimi were a popular duo on the circuit. Their experi-

ments with electric instruments anticipated folk rock, and Fariña's songs, at their best, can still send a Dylanesque chill up the spine.

In a profoundly cosmic twist of fate, Fariña was killed in a motorcycle crash on April 30, 1966, in Carmel, California, on his way to the party celebrating the publication of *Been Down So Long*. His death robbed a generation of an excellent writer and gifted musician. Joan Baez's "Sweet Sir Galahad" should stand as his epitaph in song. Considering that Dylan nearly bought the farm himself only months later when he cracked up his Triumph motorcycle on the backroads of Woodstock, New York, Fariña's death would, in retrospect, seem even more haunting. Author David Hajdu explored Fariña's life and how it intertwined with others in his book *Positively 4th Street: The Lives and Times of Joan Baez, Bob Dylan, Mimi Baez Fariña, and Richard Fariña* (New York: Farrar, Straus and Giroux, 2001).

When Bob Dylan first met him, Eric von Schmidt (born May 29, 1930, Westport, Connecticut) was a singing/songwriting practitioner of folk/blues whose Harvard Square apartment had become something of a musical salon, making him a galvanizing force in the Cambridge, Massachusetts, version of the early 1960s folk music renaissance. This was a scene von Schmidt later documented well and nostalgically with Jim Rooney in their 1979 book *Baby, Let Me Follow You Down* (Garden City, N.Y.: Anchor Books).

Eric grew up in an artistic family as the son of Harold von Schmidt, a renowned illustrator whose western-flavored paintings in the tradition of Frederick Remington or Winslow Homer graced many a cover of the *Saturday Evening Post*. When all is said and done, the younger von Schmidt may also be best remembered for his artwork, with its "Appalachian Gothic" style splashed with a dash of Bosch, a touch of Brueghel, and maybe even a sprinkle or two of Ben Shahn that found its way onto the covers of Vanguard albums by Rev. Gary Davis, Woody Guthrie, Joan Baez, Pete Seeger, Dave Van Ronk, and Cisco Houston. And the quirky children's books von Schmidt illustrated for Sid Fleischman (*Chancy and the Grand Rascal*, *By the Great Horn Spoon!*, and *Mr. Mysterious & Company*) should not be ignored either when considering the breadth of von Schmidt's total body of work.

Exposed to the music of Burl Ives, Hoagy Carmichael, Andrés Segovia, and Duke Ellington by his mother, von Schmidt experienced his first major folk music epiphany in the late 1940s, when he came under the spell of Leadbelly after hearing him perform "Goodnight Irene" live on the radio. Soon he was teaching himself how to play guitar and riding the Penn Central line down to New York to jam in the city's folk dens. It was there that he befriended Jack Elliott, Tom Paley, and Oscar Brand, on whose WNYC radio program he performed a banjo version of "Pretty Polly." After high school, von Schmidt did a stint in the army; he was stationed in Washington, D.C., a blessing for the young folkie: being there allowed him to continue his studies in the University of Leadbelly, scouring the massive song and music archives of the Library of Congress's famed folklore department. Two more years studying art in Italy on a Fulbright scholarship still wasn't enough to steer him from his passion for music, and when he finally returned to New England in the late 1950s, it was to Harvard Square that he gravitated and Tulla's Coffee Grinder, the local folk music nexus and spawning ground, where he set up shop.

Those very early years on the folk scene were informal and casual. But when Joan Baez made her debut appearances in 1958, things changed fast. Riding the wave of the "folk music craze," new venues like Club 47 in Harvard Square and the Unicorn in Boston opened, and the young practitioners, von Schmidt included, began to be recorded.

Von Schmidt met Dylan in 1961 when the younger folkster stopped in town for a gig. It was during that trip that von Schmidt taught Dylan "Baby, Let Me Follow You Down" (Dylan mentions him as the source of the song in his introduction to it on his debut album) and probably "He Was a Friend of Mine" and "Acne" as well. His connection with Dylan continued on after that, though. Von Schmidt's album *Folk Blues* is among the cultural detritus littering the cover photograph of Dylan's 1965 album, *Bringing It All Back Home*. And Dylan is among the many to cover "Joshua Gone Barbados," von Schmidt's most famous song, which deals with the exile of Bahamian leader Gilles Joshua from his country. Dylan's recording of the song transpired in 1967 with the Hawks during the *Basement Tapes* era and is one of the better unreleased jewels from those sessions.

A fixture on the thriving Cambridge folk scene through the 1960s, von Schmidt relocated to Florida in 1970 after a failed marriage. Throughout the 1970s he continued to release albums. Rededicating himself to art in the 1980s, von Schmidt moved to New Hampshire with his second wife and began performing and recording again in the 1990s.

"Dignity" (Bob Dylan)
Bob Dylan, *Bob Dylan's Greatest Hits, Volume 3* (1994); *MTV Unplugged* (1995); *Live 1961–2000—Thirty-nine Years of Great Concert Performances/'94* (2001)
Various Artists (performed by Bob Dylan), *Touched By an Angel: TV Show Soundtrack* (1998)
Joe Cocker, *Organic* (1996)
Nana Mouskouri, *Return to Love* (1997)
Two Approaching Riders, *One More Cup of Coffee* (1997)

Carl Edwards, *Coffeehouse Cowboy* (1998)
Solas, *Edge of Silence* (2002)
Robyn Hitchcock, *Robyn Sings* (2002)
Various Artists (performed by Elliott Murphy), *May Your Song
    Always Be Sung: The Songs of Bob Dylan, Volume 3* (2003)

A trunk song (that is, a stashed-away and for-gotten leftover) Dylan had written some years before he unveiled it on *Greatest Hits Volume 3* and included on his *MTV Unplugged* appear-ance (and recording) just a few months later, "Dignity" struck some Dylanists as little more than overhyped, glorified filler at best and crass exploitation at worst, though Dylan did perform the song at a few 1995 European shows. Because it was the first "new" Dylan composition many had heard in years, and because it trod, albeit in a mature way, on the familiar ground of his latest diagnosis of the world gone wrong, it's not hard to see why it received a 1996 Grammy nomination for best rock song. Here Dylan personifies the concept of dignity as an intangible and slippery, shad-owy phantom character who skirts around the background scenery in a way not dissimilar to the titled playing card in his own song "Lily, Rosemary and the Jack of Hearts." Of course, this literary conceit is nothing new. John Bun-yan's *Pilgrim's Progress* (which in some ways "Dignity" mirrors), for example, is steeped in personifications of such human concepts as ignorance and mercy. Even with these and other high-minded artistic allusions and biting subtexts, "Blind Willie McTell" or even "Foot of Pride," the critics contend, this is not quite.

Defenders of "Dignity" place it more accu-rately in the lineage of the big Dylan songs of his latter career. This is an arc that probably began with "Jokerman," took a left turn with "Brownsville Girl," stopped for a smoke with "Angelina," picked up steam with "Dignity," and crested with "Things Have Changed." If a

greater number of these statements were avail-able in abundance on just about any Dylan album from the 1960s, even the casual Dylan watcher has to be satisfied when they do emerge. Hey, nobody seems to complain when Martin Scorsese takes a few years between films.

Structurally and thematically, "Dignity" owes itself a debt to at least a couple of Dylan's earliest great works, "A Hard Rain's A-Gonna Fall" and "Desolation Row." As in both of those songs, here the narrator is on a quest—adrift in a landscape of uncertainty and corruption described as a "valley of dry bone dreams." He meets a series of characters whose (sometimes self-referential) relation to both himself and "Dignity" is unsettling. For instance, when he begins the song by describing a "fat man lookin' in a blade of steel" and a "thin man lookin' at his last meal," he suggests an uneasy relationship between the two. Is the fat man about to drop the guillotine blade on the neck of the thin man, or is he merely going to wield a carving knife as a mortal weapon? Even drop-ping the name of the thin man appears to be a self-referential nod to the clueless dupe of his famous ballad and a hint that Mr. Jones is finally about to meet his maker. Or perhaps, on a completely different track, this is a veiled ref-erence to the cat-and-mouse game played by Sydney Greenstreet and Humphrey Bogart in *The Maltese Falcon*, surmised to be a Dylan film favorite, which he drew on for some of the lyrics in the *Empire Burlesque* songs. And the hollow man would seem a direct reference to "The Hollow Men," T. S. Eliot's diagnostic poem of the post–World War I Western world. Such is the power (and fun!) of Dylan's great songs: they allow for so many varied interpre-tations and source hunting.

From there, the narrator takes the listener on a guided tour of a neo-Desolation Row spe-cially face-lifted for the millennium by some unscrupulous real estate developer. Through this shifty terrain worthy of a dime-store mystery novel, we follow him on his search for dignity, an elusive trait that seems to have bypassed humanity and has gladly sold its soul for some loose change or a half-empty bottle of Tokay. Whether engaging in a surreptitious meeting with Mary-lou at her own wedding, visiting the land where the vultures feed, hanging out in a watering hole populated by vampires, encountering Prince Phillip (or his calypso double?) at the home of the blues, trying to read a note on a jerking boat (the *Titanic*?), or venturing into a dozen other weird scenes inside the gold mine, with their promises and inevitable dead ends, our wandering searcher (Moses disguised as Sam Spade) seems only to come up with his hands as empty as when he set out on his journey. This postcard of the hanging has been returned (postage due) "address unknown."

Age has treated "Dignity" well: Dylan's spring 2003 concerts featured a stripped-down, nearly bubbly arrangement highlighted by his razor-edge vocals taking the listener on a tour of a world that seemed to have lost any sense of the titular word.

◪ "Dink's Song" (Traditional)

"Fare Thee Well," "Fare Thee Well, O Honey," "Noah's Dove," "Nora's Dove"
Charles Seeger, single (1936)
Josh White, *Volume 5—In Chronological Order/'44* (1998)
Cisco Houston, *Hard Travelin'* (1958)
Barbara Dane, *Folk Festival at Newport, Volume II* (1959)
Pete Seeger, *American Folk Favorites Volume III* (1960)
Dave Van Ronk, *Dave Van Ronk Sings* (1961)
Carolyn Hester, *Carolyn Hester* (1962)
Roger McGuinn (performed with Pete Seeger and Josh White Jr.), *Treasures from the Folk Den* (2001)
Jeff Buckley, *Live at Sin-é* (2003)

A beloved curiosity from Dylan's unreleased early trove, "Dink's Song" was originally collected by the American folk and blues archivists John A. Lomax and his son Alan. While Dylan boldly fibbed that he learned it from "some lady named Dink," he—in the true folk tradition—drew freely from Cisco Houston, Dave Van Ronk, and Pete Seeger, and perhaps threw in an original line or two in the invention of his own version of the song.

In 1934 the Lomaxes wrote of the origins of "Dink's Song" in *American Ballads and Folk Songs*: "A levee was being built along the Brazos River in Texas. The contractor had brought his mules and his mule-skinners with him from the Mississippi River. But he had neglected to provide one thing—women; and the men were raising Hell all over the bottom, with their midnight creeping, their fighting, and their razor play. It was a distinct hindrance to the progress of work on the levee. So it was that the contractor went to Memphis, hired a boatload of women, brought them down to the levee-camp, and turned them loose. It was not long before every man had a woman in his tent to wash his clothes, cook, draw water, cut firewood, and warm his bed. Dink was one of these women, and twenty-five years ago, after she had downed nearly a quart of gin, she sang these blues. The tune is lost."

In his 1947 autobiography, *Adventures of a Ballad Hunter* (New York: Macmillan), John A. Lomax elaborated on his find:

> While Dink sang this song in the Brazos bottom of Texas, as she washed her temporary man's clothes, her little two-year-old nameless son played in the sand at her feet. "He ain't got no daddy, an' I ain't had no time to hunt up a name for him," she explained.
>
> "Do you love this new man of yours, Dink?" She scrubbed a garment vigorously on the

wooden washboard as she answered: "Some o' dese days I'm a goin' to take all dat man's clothes an' put em' in dis washtub an' get 'em good an' soakin' wet. Den I'm goin to roll up dese wet clothes in a gob an' cover de pile up right nice in the de middle o' de bed—smooth down de covers, an' stick 'em all in 'round de edges. Den I'm goin' on off up de river . . ."

A few months ago I inquired about Dink at Yazoo City, Mississippi, her home, she had told me. "Done planted up there," said a Negro woman, pointing to a nearby tree-clad hill. I could see a few slabs of marble shining through the low green foliage. Dink had sung me a spiritual about a lonesome graveyard, with the refrain: "I wouldn't mind dyin' if dyin' was all!"

The original words referred to "Noah's dove," a bird sent out by Noah in search of dry land as the Great Flood receded. Over time and through the oral tradition "Noah" became "Nora."

Considering he was a white male and all of twenty-one years old when he first sang the song, Dylan shows a profound empathy with Dink in his rendition. His performances of "Dink's Song" can be found on a couple of his earliest recordings and was evidently a favorite of his in those long ago days. Its appearance on *Great White Wonder*, the world's first Dylan bootleg, made it among the first unreleased works by Dylan most of the world ever heard. He briefly revived "Dink's Song" during the Rolling Thunder Revue in 1976.

🖪 "Dirge" (Bob Dylan)
Bob Dylan, *Planet Waves* (1974)

Dylan plays piano on this frightening, conversational piece that, coupled with his venomous delivery of the lyrics, was reminiscent of the

"Positively 4th Street" anger his audience vicariously dug back in the day. Accordingly, "Dirge" is sometimes interpreted as another farewell to the 1960s and his old, "voice of a generation" self, as it features Dylan embracing solitude and dismissing all of the things that he used to need as now inconsequential. In so doing he thematically echoes songs like "My Back Pages." But, beginning with the line "I hate myself for loving you" and saying that "in this age of fiberglass I'm looking for a gem," it's hard—at first blush, anyway—not to hear "Dirge" as directed at Sara Dylan, his wife at the time—venting after seven years of marriage in a catharsis of scorching resentment. But coming on an album full of songs of joy and devoid of hints of marital discord save "Dirge," this theory can go only so far as the singer recounts a soulless visit to Lower Broadway. Others hear a confession of heroin use or even a homosexual infatuation in its self-flagellation. And maybe there's a hint in the rumored working title, "Dirge for Martha." This would seem to point to a romantic affair of which the narrator is ashamed but relieved to end when the "final curtain fell."

🖪 "Dirt Road Blues" (Bob Dylan)
Bob Dylan, *Time out of Mind* (1997)

With its rockabilly hook and titular allusion to Charley Patton's and a half dozen similarly titled blues songs describing the archetypal ramblin'-man sensibility, "Dirt Road Blues" would have been a perfect choice for inclusion during the Never Ending Tour—no wonder Dylan chose not to perform it. In the song's *Time out of Mind* incarnation, Dylan's vocals are so submerged he sounds like one of those echoey voices heard on an old 78 rpm "race" record—like the kind Patton himself was first heard on. As a de rigueur Dylan blues (there's one on just about every album), "Dirt Road Blues" is pretty lightweight, missing the edge of tunes like "New Pony" or "Meet Me in the Morning."

"Dirty World" (Traveling Wilburys)
Traveling Wilburys, *Traveling Wilburys, Volume 1* (1988)

A down-and-dirty song dealing with sexual desire, subservience, and rejection, "Dirty World," from the momentous and fruitful collaboration of the hip novelty confederation known as the Traveling Wilburys (of which Dylan was a member), portrays a desperate narrator coming to grips with the fact that his eye candy has left him for another man.

The songbook published to accompany the release of the Wilburys' debut album indicates that the copyright for "Dirty World" is held by Special Rider Music, Dylan's publishing company, suggesting that he was the primary contributor to the song. Dylan is the lead vocalist on the track and no doubt plays guitar on it as well.

George Harrison discussed "Dirty World" in a 1988 interview with Great Britain's *Radio One*:

Bob's very funny—I mean, a lot of people take him seriously and yet if you know Dylan and his songs, he's such a joker really. And Jeff [Lynne] just sat down and said, "Ok, what are we gonna do?" And Bob said "Let's do one just like Prince! Hahaha!" And he just started banging away—"Love your sexy body! Oooh-oooh-oooh-oooh bay-bee." And it just turned into that tune. Nothing like Prince! Nothing like him!

I don't know how other people write songs, but I picked up a bunch of magazines and gave everybody a magazine—Roy Orbison had *Vogue*! I had some copies of *Autosport* which I gave to Bob Dylan, and then we just started reading out little things like "five-speed gearbox" and stuff like that,

and wrote down a big list of things, and then we reduced it to about twelve that sounded interesting, and had the list on the microphone—and then we just did the take. And whoever sang first, sang the first one on the list and we sang round the group until we'd gone and done 'em all.

Disconnected: The Dial-a-Poem Poets/
Various Artists
Giorno Poetry Systems LP GPS-003. Released 1974.

New York poet John Giorno came up with "Dial-a-Poem" (a New York City phone number that, if dialed, would play a new poem every week) in the early 1970s and persuaded his friends and peers to contribute to his unique public service. Allen Ginsberg evidently gave him "Jimmy Berman Rag," which had been recorded with Dylan in November 1971. After being available over the telephone for a week or so, the cut disappeared until Giorno brought it out on this rare and unique compilation sampler.

"Disease of Conceit" (Bob Dylan)
Bob Dylan, *Oh Mercy* (1989)

Perhaps revisiting the terrain of "Shot of Love," with its dichotomy between spirit and flesh, or "Saved," with its well-intentioned if stale sermonizing, "Disease of Conceit" reminds us that the realm of the senses is constantly and unsettlingly full of danger and uncertainty. And if the song comes off at times as a bit heavy-handed, with its catalogue of symptoms that can read like a schoolmarm's list of dos and don'ts, the narrator's sense of empathy and implied shared experience as a sufferer of the malaise turns the song into the spoonful of sugar that helps the medicine go down. The *Oxford Concise Dictionary* defines conceit as "personal vanity," and it is an anthro-

D

pocentric view of the world that Dylan attacks as the ultimate vanity here. Although his strident vocal delivery, full of stagy preachiness, has led some to suggest that "Disease of Conceit" is *Oh Mercy*'s flimsiest, the song does establish some power as it rolls on, and this, along with its stirring, striking, and dissonant chord changes, made it a surprise performance sleeper when Dylan (playing piano) first displayed it live in 1989. It has made sporadic public appearances in the years since, with Dylan on guitar.

◪ *Divine Secrets of the Ya-Ya Sisterhood*
(soundtrack)/Various Artists
Sony CD 86534. Released 2002.

Following his *O Brother, Where Art Thou?* music production success, hopes were high for T-Bone Burnett's work for the *Ya-Ya Sisterhood*, a feel-good chick flick with a New Age spiritual spin starring Sandra Bullock and Ellen Burstyn as a battling daughter and mother. But if this mix of roots music melding vintage sounds with new recordings of semi-standards and of traditionally styled songs doesn't quite come off as the integrated vision presented in *O Brother*, there is still some great music to cook gumbo to here. So, you get Jimmy Reed ("Found Love"), Mahalia Jackson ("Walk in Jerusalem"), and Ray Charles ("Lonely Avenue") thrown in with Macy Gray's take on Billie Holiday's "I Want to Be Your Mother's Son-in-Law" and Taj Mahal's Fats Waller homage "Keepin' Out of Mischief Now."

Dylan's Cajun waltz contribution, "Waitin' for You," is styled like an old field recording and fits in well with the rest of the collection.

◪ **"Dixie"** (Daniel Decatur Emmett)
aka "I Wish I Was in Dixie," "I Wish I Was in Dixie's Land"

Bob Dylan/Various Artists (performed by Bob Dylan), *Masked and Anonymous* (soundtrack) (2003)
Duane Eddy, *Shazam* (1960)
Elvis Presley, *Aloha from Hawaii* (1973)
Bryan Bowers, *Home Home on the Road* (1982)
Mormon Tabernacle Choir, *Songs of the Civil War and Stephen Foster* (1992)
Boxcar Willie, *Truck Drivin' Son of a Gun* (1999)

More than a century before a young wannabe folkie wastrel hailing from central Minnesota named Zimmerman was loving and thieving, cutting and pasting the songs and sounds he admired into a song of his own, another man hailing from the fringes of the Midwest by the name of Daniel Decatur Emmett was doing his share of cribbing and cobbling the sense and sensibilities of American roots music into a form that could be consumed by the emerging popular culture of a divided country.

Dan Emmett wrote "Dixie" on April 3, 1859, for Bryant's Minstrels, who introduced it the following night at their show at New York City's Mechanic's Hall, when it was performed by the entire cast as the "plantation song and dance" concluding the revue. "Dixie" was first performed in the South in Charleston, South Carolina, in December 1860 by the Rumsey and Newcomb minstrel troupe.

Despite its origin in Northern "blackface" minstrelsy, "Dixie" was unhesitatingly adopted by the Confederacy in the Civil War era, and it became the South's rallying song and anthem. Meanwhile, and paradoxically, it retained its popularity in the North, both in its original form and in numerous parodies. President Abraham Lincoln counted it among his favorites and, upon hearing the news of Confederate General Robert E. Lee's surrender on April 9, 1865, requested that the song be played by the Union band.

Emmett (born October 29, 1815, Mount Vernon, Ohio; died June 28, 1904, Mount Vernon,

Ohio), a self-taught fiddler, composer, and minstrel performer with little formal education, was, along with Stephen Foster (*see* "Hard Times"), a central figure in this maligned mid-nineteenth-century American folk form. After a hitch in the U.S. Army from 1834 to 1835, during which he became an expert drummer and fifer, he joined a circus in Cincinnati, and it was there that he wrote the words of his first "black" song to the tune of "Gumbo Chaff," a popular number at the time. By the early 1840s he was touring with the noted Angevine circus, performing in blackface as a banjoist and singer.

Emmett teamed up with blackface dancer and singer Frank Brower (1823–1874), said to be the first black impersonator to play the bones, forming a novel fiddle and bones duo in New York. By February 1843 the two were performing at the Bowery Amphitheater as the Virginia Minstrels, with a combo that included a banjoist and tambourine man. "Entirely exempt from the vulgarities and other objectionable features which have characterized negro extravaganzas," as their own advertisements put it, an evening with the Virginia Minstrels consisted of their version of the black arts: music, dancing, anecdotes, and oratory. After a flush of initial success that brought them to a failed tour of England, Emmett and Brower split in 1844.

By then the minstrel craze had caught on and Emmett began countering the competition by giving his troupes florid, respectable-sounding titles such as "Operatic Brothers and Sisters" while inserting so-called wench numbers in the shows, in which the male dancers in his troupe would impersonate females as a titillating bonus. He turned to writing musical farces he termed "Ethiopian Burlettas," which launched "machine poetry," in which his semiliterate black characters parodied the Industrial Age; this genre anticipated twentieth-century black

Cover of an American minstrel show songbook, published by Belmont Music Company, Chicago, 1938.
(Hulton Archive/Getty Images)

sitcoms such as "Amos 'n' Andy," "Sanford and Son," and "The Fresh Prince of Bel Air."

After assuming part ownership of Charles T. White's Minstrels, who performed on New York City's Bowery in Lower Manhattan between 1853 and 1854, Emmett took his entrepreneurial instincts to an even higher level when he opened Chicago's first minstrel hall and, over the course of the next few years, took his show as far north as St. Paul and as far south as Selma, Alabama.

When the troupe disbanded in late 1858, he returned to New York City and joined the Dan

Bryant Minstrels, performing with and writing for the group through 1862. His primary contribution to the Bryant show were the tunes and words for its finales, known as walk-arounds—secular imitations of the black "shout" drawn from the spirituals and other music sung by plantation slaves—but he also played banjo and other instruments, acted in comic skits, and sang parodies to earn his keep. "Dixie" was easily Emmett's most successful walk-around. In this 32-measure song in two equal sections of verse and refrain, Emmett imitated the black call-and-response pattern; the chorus answers the soloist in the verse with "Look away" and in the refrain with "Hooray."

Emmett's move to Chicago in the late 1860s began his slow career decline, hastened when he lost his voice after hooking up with Haverly's Minstrels. He was then relegated to fiddling in local saloons. His rough-hewn black tunes and lyrics, lacking the sentimental appeal of Stephen Foster's best minstrel songs, were unappealing to genteel society, and he gradually slipped into poverty and semi-obscurity by 1880. Rescued by a couple of benefits staged by younger minstrels and employment as a fiddler in Leavitt's Gigantean Minstrels, which eventually and successfully toured the South riding on the coattails of the still-popular "Dixie," Emmett finally returned to Mount Vernon, where he retired in pride.

Dylan alternated an instrumental version of "Dixie" with another unlikely instrumental choice, "Marine's Hymn (From the Halls of Montezuma)," to open a short string of 1990 concerts at the height of the Persian Gulf conflict—a pairing vaguely reminiscent of Elvis Presley's concert merging of "Dixie" with "Battle Hymn of the Republic" as the civil rights movement peaked. Dylan & Co. included a seductively languid version of the American classic in the 2003 film *Masked and Anonymous* that laced perfectly into the backdrop of a civil war looming over that movie's "plot."

[S] **"Dolly Dagger"** (Jimi Hendrix)

Jimi Hendrix Experience, *Rainbow Bridge* (1971)
James Byrd Group, *Apocalypse Chime* (1996)

One of Dylan's weirder cover-song choices, Hendrix's "Dolly Dagger" is a simple riff-rocker dedicated to Hendrix's girlfriend Devon Wilson. Hendrix, of course, loved Bob Dylan and covered a few of his songs ("All Along the Watchtower," "Like a Rolling Stone," "Can You Please Crawl Out Your Window," and "Drifter's Escape" among them), so perhaps this was Dylan's way of paying yet another tribute to the saint of the Stratocaster.

Dylan attempted a version of "Dolly Dagger" during the January 17, 1992, rehearsal for David Letterman's tenth-anniversary show at New York City's Radio City Music Hall. (What a piece of television history *that* would have been had he performed it!) He debuted a rendition when the Never Ending Tour hit Australia two months later. While Hendrix's original is a rather busy blues affair that requires some concentration to play and listen to, Dylan seemed divorced from his backing band as they knocked out their Jimi licks in a style unsympathetic to their leader's singing in a watered-down arrangement. Still, Dylan seemed to be having fun, especially with the lyric "she drinks her blood from a jagged edge."

[S] **"Don't Fall Apart on Me Tonight"** (Bob Dylan)

Bob Dylan, *Infidels* (1983)
Aaron Neville, *Grand Tour* (1993)

"Don't Fall Apart on Me Tonight" will probably

always catch flak for its apparent male chauvinism. Some revisionists, however, have suggested that it should be regarded as a plea or confession of self-doubt to the woman who symbolizes the narrator's connection to some bedrock of reality as he battles the tempests of creativity. Still, whichever side one takes, there can be little argument that *Infidels* would have been better received with "Blind Willie McTell" as its final song instead of this one, fit for a letch trying to pick up an underage girl while ordering a highball in a trendy Southern California bar.

"Don't Let Your Deal Go Down" (Traditional)
aka "Never Let Your Deal Go Down"
New Lost City Ramblers, *Early Years (1958–1962)* (1991)
Lester Flatt and Earl Scruggs, *Lester Flatt & Earl Scruggs* (1959)
Merle Travis, *Merle Travis and Joe Maphis* (1964)
Ramblin' Jack Elliott, *Bull Durham Sacks and Railroad Tracks* (1970)
John Jackson, *Don't Let Your Deal Go Down* (1970)
Bill Keith, *Beating Around the Bush* (1992)
Charlie Poole, *Old-Time Songs* (1994)

"Don't You Let Your Deal Go Down" is but one example of an age-old line of card-game songs containing more than a wee hint of violence. Others include the old traditional "Last Bad Deal Gone Down" (or sometimes "Last Fair Deal Gone Down"), famously interpreted by Robert Johnson, Merle Travis's show-off titular instrumental, and the Grateful Dead's "Deal," which was inspired by its predecessors.

Dylan's cover version of "Don't Let Your Deal Go Down" is, in fact, most often mixed up with the Dead's "Deal," but they are two separate songs. Matters were probably confused because both compositions contain the line "don't let your deal go down." Dylan probably

first heard the song in question from the New Lost City Ramblers, the folk-revival group popular in the early 1960s and whom he credits for a few *World Gone Wrong* songs. According to the liner notes to *The Early Years: 1958–1962*, an album by the Ramblers released by Smithsonian Folkways, that group's version of "Don't Let Your Deal Go Down" was first performed as a blues tune prior to 1911. Charlie Poole and the North Carolina Ramblers later recorded and popularized it as a bluegrass/country song in 1925.

Dylan opened a couple of European shows with the song in 1992, rendering it as a bluesy ode to double-dealing rounders everywhere.

Don't Look Back
Leacock-Pennebaker Films. Released 1967. Produced by Albert Grossman and John Court. Directed by D. A. Pennebaker.

The definitive portrait of the artist as a young asshole, *Don't Look Back* is a scathingly honest (and often hilariously funny) cinéma vérité document of Dylan's spring 1965 visit to Great Britain. The no-budget, black-and-white glimpse into the noirish underbelly of Bob Dylan, "star," was shot and crafted by New York filmmaker D. A. Pennebaker, who was invited to tag along on the tour.

Pennebaker catches Dylan at a key juncture in his subject's career—the moment when he was first encountering a frightening brand of mass-hysterical, Beatlemania-like celebrity. Watching from a perspective so many years later, one can see harbingers of the fractured electrified psychedelia to come, as Dylan's boredom with performing "The Times They Are A-Changin'" and other so-called protest songs couldn't be more plain. That the film begins with the famous "cue-card" short of "Subterranean Homesick Blues" (featuring

Dylan in London, 1965.

(Photo: Evening Standard/Getty Images)

Dylan standing in an alley with cards containing key words from the song, tossing them away as the song progresses as if he's in some dreamscape version of a Charlie Chaplin film) was an immediate indication that Dylan was in the throes of violently and dramatically shedding his artistic skin.

Don't Look Back works precisely because memorable set pieces like the cue-card short mingled with recurring characters and themes to give the sense that a story is being told: the endless parade and charade of press conferences (the first public indications of Dylan's ability to turn a normally perfunctory event into a mind-tripping, psychodramatic joust pitting good against evil), the verbal skewering of the "science student" in one particularly and infamously uncomfortable backstage scene, the on-camera disintegration of his relationship with Joan Baez augmented by the shameless flirtation of female reporters and assorted groupies, the matter-of-fact absorption and cool disposal of sycophants, manager Albert Grossman's poker-faced, Mephistophelian machinations to cut his client deals with rock 'n' roll snake-oil salesmen of every stripe, Donovan's emergence on the pop scene and his meeting with Dylan at a party, and the high comedy of Dylan's encounter with the patronizing "Sheriff's High Lady" and her brood all add up to something much more than a standard documentary.

Don't Look Back gained stature as a groundbreaking documentary, but Dylan (probably because he came off as a bit of a schmuck, albeit an immensely talented and interesting one) has never exactly bubbled when discussing the film. In 1969 he said, "You know this movie, *Don't Look Back*. Well that splashed my face all over the world, that movie *Don't Look Back*. I didn't get a *penny* from that movie, you know." When asked by Jann Wenner of

Rolling Stone if he liked the film, he responded, "I'd like it a lot more if I got paid for it."

In 1978 Dylan was more analytical, perhaps more honest about his feelings when he said, "*Don't Look Back* was . . . somebody else's movie. It was a deal worked out with a film company, but I didn't really play any part in it. When I saw it in a moviehouse, I was shocked what had been done. I didn't find out until later that the camera had been on me all the time. That movie was done by a man who took it all out of context. It was documented from his personal point of view. The movie was dishonest, it was a propaganda movie. I don't think it was accurate at all in terms of showing my formative years. It showed only one side. He made it seem like I wasn't doing anything but living in hotel rooms, playing the typewriter and holding press conferences for journalists."

As can be inferred, those expecting a Dylan concert film will be disappointed. There are some healthy doses of the singer-songwriter onstage (a heartrending version of "The Lonesome Death of Hattie Carroll" is particularly memorable), but Dylan's musical presentation here is portrayed in fragmentary quick-cuts, edited in a way that more properly represents the choppy, turbulent life of a touring artist. Those expecting a Dylan "performance" film will, however, be endlessly fascinated.

The *Don't Look Back* DVD release in 2000 included five original, uncut audio performances; commentary from Pennebaker and from a close friend of Dylan's at the time, Bobby Neuwirth; a never-before-seen version of the famous "Subterranean Homesick Blues" cue-card scene; and the original theatrical trailer. On the DVD Pennebaker describes the "Homesick Blues" scene this way: "We just went out one morning and shot it, first in the little garden behind the hotel. They were having an art show or something. Almost at the end a cop came up and wanted me to stop, so we decided we'd go someplace else where there were no cops and we went in the alley. It was never supposed to be part of the film. It wasn't until later that I thought it was a good introduction. So I stuck it at the beginning of the film. You don't know who the hell he is. You need to find out why you should be watching this film. I don't know why we even did it, except Albert [Grossman, Dylan's manager] thought it could be some kind of promotional thing."

Admirers of the quick-witted, acid-tongued, and cherubic/demonic style of the mid-'60s Dylan displayed in *Don't Look Back* should track down his hour-long December 3, 1965, press conference at the studios of San Francisco's KQED, which has been preserved on both audio and video.

An endnote: Tim Robbins's wickedly sardonic 1992 film *Bob Roberts* is a smart takeoff on *Don't Look Back*, updated and cast through the prism of a modern-day American presidential campaign.

[S] "Don't Pity Me" (Sid Jacobson/Lou Stallman)

Dion and the Belmonts, *Teenager in Love/'59* (1992)

Dylan treated a Joliette, Quebec, audience to a sketchy, one-off exhibition of this pop song in 1989. "Don't Pity Me" is attributed to a pair of Tin Pan Alley denizens, Sid Jacobson and Lou Stallman (also cofounders of the tiny Shell Records label in New York City). It was a big hit for Dion and the Belmonts in 1959, when it peaked at No. 40 on the *Billboard* charts. Some suggest that the song Dylan performed that summer night was the identically titled composition written by producer and R&B composer Van McCoy (born January 6, 1944, Washington, D.C.; died July 6, 1979, Englewood, New Jersey).

[S] "Don't Think Twice, It's All Right" (Bob Dylan)

aka "Don't Think Twice, It's Alright"

Bob Dylan, single (1963); *The Freewheelin' Bob Dylan* (1963); *Bob Dylan's Greatest Hits, Volume II* (1971); *Bob Dylan at Budokan* (1979); *The Bootleg Series, Volume 6: Live 1964—Concert at Philharmonic Hall* (2004)
Bob Dylan/The Band, *Before the Flood* (1974)
Bob Dylan/Various Artists (performed by Eric Clapton), *Bob Dylan: The 30th Anniversary Concert Celebration* (1993)
Joan Baez, *Joan Baez in Concert, Part 2* (1963); *First Ten Years* (1970); *Golden Hour* (1972); *Joan Baez in Concert* (1976); *Ring Them Bells* (1995); *Live at Newport* (1996); *Baez Sings Dylan* (1998)
Peter, Paul & Mary, *In the Wind* (1963); *Ten Years Together* (1970)
New World Singers, *New World Singers* (1963)
Bobby Darin, *Golden Folk Hits* (1963); *Darin 1936–1973* (1974)
José Feliciano, *Voice & Guitar of José Feliciano* (1964)
The Brothers Four, *More Big Folk Hits* (1964)
Julie Felix, *Julie Felix* (1964)
Linda Mason, *How Many Seas Must a White Dove Sail?* (1964)
Joey Powers, *Midnight Mary* (1964)
Odetta, *Odetta Sings Dylan* (1965)
Johnny Cash, *Orange Blossom Special* (1965)
Cher, *All I Really Want to Do* (1965); *You Better Sit Down Kids* (1996); *Original Hits* (1998)
Jackie DeShannon, *In the Wind* (1965)
Chad & Jeremy, *I Don't Want to Lose You* (1965)
Trini Lopez, *The Folk Album* (1965)
Eddie Albert, *The Eddie Albert Album* (1965)
Waylon Jennings, *Don't Think Twice* (1965); *Waylon Jennings with Phase One: The Early Years* (2002)
Hugues Aufray, *À l'Olympia* (1965)
The Seekers, *A World of Our Own* (1965)
Triffids, *Triffids Are Really Folk* (1965)
Bobby Goldsboro, *It's Too Late* (1966)
Bob Dorough, *Just About Everything* (1966)
Duane Eddy, *Duane Does Bob Dylan* (1966)
The T-Bones, *No Matter What Shape* (1966)

Sebastian Cabot, *Sebastian Cabot, Actor—Bob Dylan, Poet* (1967)
Lester Flatt and Earl Scruggs, *Changin' Times* (1968); *1964–1969, Plus* (1996)
Burl Ives, *Times They Are A-Changing* (1968)
John Martyn, *London Conversation* (1968)
Magnolia Jazz Group '65, *It's All Dixie Now* (1968)
Mike Blatt, *Tomorrow* (1969)
Lenny Breau, *Guitar Sounds of Lenny Breau* (1969); *Lenny Breau Trio* (1985)
Ramblin' Jack Elliott, *Bull Durham Sacks and Railroad Tracks* (1970); *Essential Ramblin' Jack Elliott* (1970); *Me & Bobby McGee* (1995); *Kerouac's Last Dream* (1997)
Brook Benton, *Home Style* (1970)
The Ventures, *10th Anniversary Album* (1970)
Lawrence Welk, *Wonderful, Wonderful* (1971)
Stone the Crows, *Teenage Licks* (1971)
JSD, *Country of the Blind* (1971)
Booker T. and Priscilla Jones, *Home Grown* (1972)
Judy Nash, *The Night They Drove Old Dixie Down* (1972)
Sonoma, *Sonoma* (1973)
Melanie, *As I See It Now* (1975)
Elvis Presley, *Elvis* (1973); *Walk a Mile in My Shoes* (1995)
Arlo Guthrie and Pete Seeger, *Together in Concert* (1975)
Doc Watson, *Look Away* (1978)
Steve Young, *No Place to Fall* (1977); *Solo/Live* (1991)
John Anderson, *I Just Came Home to Count the Memories* (1981)
Jerry Jeff Walker, *Cow Jazz* (1982)
Four Seasons, *25th Anniversary Collection* (1987); *Anthology* (1988)
Rice Brothers, *Rice Brothers* (1989)
Bobby Bare, *The Songs of Bob Dylan* (1989)
Janglers, *Janglers Play Dylan* (1992)
Al Hunter, *The Singer* (1992)
Allan Taylor, *So Long* (1993)
Clarence "Gatemouth" Brown, *Long Way Home* (1996)
Phil Carmen, *Bob Dylan's Dream* (1996)
Billy Strange, *Strange Country* (1996)
Euro Grass, *Made in Europe* (1996)
Brothers Four, *Greenfields & Other Gold* (1997)
Waylon Jennings, *Burning Memories* (1997)

Nick Drake, *Tanworth in Arden 1967–1968* (1999)
Gerard Quintana and Jordi Batiste, *Els Miralls de Dylan* (1999)
Mike Ness, *Cheating at Solitaire* (1999)
Steve Howe, *Portraits of Bob Dylan* (1999)
Various Artists (performed by David West), *Pickin' on Dylan* (1999)
Andy Hill, *It Takes a Lot to Laugh* (2000)
Michel Montecrossa, *Born in Time* (2000)
Second Floor, *Plays Dylan* (2001)
Various Artists (performed by Ramblin' Jack Elliott), *A Nod to Bob* (2001)
Various Artists (performed by Gild), *Duluth Does Dylan* (2001)
Barb Jungr, *Every Grain of Sand: Barb Jungr Sings Bob Dylan* (2002)
Bryan Ferry, *Frantic* (2002)
Susan Tedeschi, *Wait for Me* (2002)
Big Brass Bed, *A Few Dylan Songs* (2003)
Various Artists (performed by the Reggae Rockers), *Blowin' in the Wind: A Reggae Tribute to Bob Dylan* (2003)
Matt Munisteri, *Love Story* (2004)
Various Artists, *John Wesley Harding, John Brown and Some Wicked Messengers Play Bob Dylan* (2004)

Dylan wrote "Don't Think Twice," a subtle but devastating kiss-off classic and his earliest-released antilove song, about Suze Rotolo, his first true New York love, after she had traveled to Italy for a time in early 1963. Suze is the woman clutching his arm on the cover of *The Freewheelin' Bob Dylan*, the sophomore album on which "Don't Think Twice, It's All Right" originally appeared. The tempestuous, on-and-off-again nature of their relationship evidently inspired Dylan to pen this wry exercise in simmering catharsis.

"Don't Think Twice" was considered quite modern for a folk song when it was released, due to its deft balance of tenderness and anger, hurt and aloofness. By the last verse the singer lets the dam burst: he not only accuses his former lover of being immature and wanting his soul when she should have been satisfied with the heart he offered, but also charges her with committing the most grievous of crimes— wasting his "precious time."

Reportedly, Suze was initially flattered that a song about her had become so popular. But when Dylan began to publicly introduce "Don't Think Twice" as a composition about "a love affair that went on too long," she got the message and stayed away from him. So did many of his friends, who sensed that they might become the next victims of his spiteful quill.

"Don't Think Twice" was one of Dylan's first commercial hits and is among his most widely recorded songs. The majority of the covers, however, forgo Dylan's sardonic edge and interpret the composition in a gentle tone that ignores Dylan's veiled acidity. Even so, Dylan hasn't deprived the song of its edge. In 1978, when he transformed it into a funky reggae affair with his big band, the tune's bitter wistfulness remained intact. And in the mid-1990s, when Dylan retooled "Don't Think Twice" into a love-weary acoustic vehicle for the Never Ending Tour, it retained its sharpness, even if it may have become something that now suits a younger singer.

In composing "Don't Think Twice," Dylan adapted the melody from colleague Paul Clayton's interpretation of "Scarlet Ribbons for Her Hair." Johnny Cash's "Understand Your Man" is also sometimes suggested as an influence on "Don't Think Twice," but because that song was also based on "Scarlet Ribbons for Her Hair," the similarities are unavoidable. Dylan's notes for the 1963 Newport Folk Festival program (entitled "For Dave Glover") provide another possible source for the tune, as he wrote, "Without no 'Lone Green Valley' there'd be no 'Don't Think Twice.'"

Commenting on the way others performed the song (and performance in general) in the *Freewheelin'* liner notes, Dylan said, "A lot of people make it sort of a love song—slow and easy-going. But it isn't a love song. It's a statement that maybe you can say to make yourself feel better. It's as if you were talking to yourself. It's a hard song to sing. I can sing it sometimes, but I ain't that good yet."

A final note: contrary to the *Freewheelin'* liner notes, Dylan does not perform "Don't Think Twice" on that album with a backup band.

▣ "Don't Ya Tell Henry" (Bob Dylan)
Bob Dylan/The Band, *The Basement Tapes*/'67 (1975)
Coulson, Dean, McGuinness, Flint, *Lo & Behold* (1972)
The Band, *Across the Great Divide* (1994); *Live at Watkins Glen*/'73 (1995); (performed with Bob Dylan), *Rock of Ages (Deluxe Edition)* (2001)

A raucous highlight of the *Basement Tapes* sessions, "Don't Ya Tell Henry" is a Dylan composition performed by the Band featuring vocals by Levon Helm, who takes a nice mandolin turn as well. Robbie Robertson's guitar solo also adds much to this spirited tune (which sounds so much like a loose drunken romp that it's a wonder no one fell over), and Garth Hudson's brief trombone turn adds a touch of wooziness to the song that would fit right in on almost any Band album. This children's hopscotch rhyme is stocked with a menagerie of barnyard animals that could rival the venerable "Froggie Went A-Courtin'" for its strange, *Through the Looking-Glass* setting, and is full of the rural high jinks that mark the best of the *Basement Tapes* with allusions to a tryst the eponymous (and clueless) Henry is not party to.

Dylan did perform "Don't Ya Tell Henry" with the Band when he showed up to play with them at the encore of their New Year's Eve 1971/'72 show at the Academy of Music in New York City. That version finally became available on the deluxe rerelease of the Band's live *Rock of Ages* album.

🅂 "Do Right to Me Baby (Do Unto Others)"
(Bob Dylan)

Bob Dylan, single (1979); *Slow Train Coming* (1979)
Tim O'Brien and Mollie, *Remember Me* (1993)

A basic gospel/pop-song reworking of the Golden Rule and perhaps even his own "All I Really Want to Do," the languid, reggae-style "Do Right to Me Baby" may have been the first composition Dylan wrote of his conversion to Christianity, as it was performed at his last show in December 1978—a good year before the others in the *Slow Train* batch. Like "All I Really Want to Do" (a 1964 song he was performing on his 1978 world tour), Dylan's "Do Right to Me Baby" defines his conditional goals in the relationship he sings of here by negation: it's all about what he "don't want" and an essential quid pro quo. He'll do right by her (or God) *if* she (He) does right by him. Obviously, despite his acceptance of Jesus, Dylan was still very much a guy more bound up with the Old Testament's books of Leviticus and Deuteronomy than those found in the New Testament. And critics of the admittedly simplistic song suggest that it sounds like a parody of John Lennon's "I Don't Want to Be a Soldier" or, even more damning, like the *National Lampoon* imitating Dylan as a Christian songwriter.

"Do Right to Me Baby" stayed in heavy performance rotation during the fall 1979 gospel tour, and Dylan regularly uncorked it at the early 1980 concerts, even as his born-again crusade began to peter out.

🅐 *Doug Sahm and Band*
Atlantic LP SD-7254. Released 1972.

Dylan's duet with Sahm on "Wallflower" from *Doug Sahm and Band* is well known, but his backing vocal contributions to two other Sahm tunes on this record, "Blues Stay Away from Me" and "(Is Anybody Going to) San Antone?," are worth a listen too. The latter was released as a single in 1972. Doug Sahm and Band is not their only contact: Sahm also wrote a rather cryptic song about Dylan called "Dylan Come Lately," which appeared on the 1994 Sir Douglas Quintet album, *Daydreaming at Midnight*. Dylan later covered Sahm's famed "She's a Mover."

Along with disc jockey Casey Kasem, Doug Sahm (born November 6, 1941, San Antonio; died November 18, 1999, Taos, New Mexico) is undoubtedly high on the list of Lebanese-Americans with the most impact on popular music. Sahm was a patriarch of Texas rock and country musicians, a highly knowledgeable and superbly competent performer of every Lone Star State musical style: blues, country, rock 'n' roll, western swing, Cajun, even polka. As the leader of the Sir Douglas Quintet, he created songs and arrangements that transferred the pumping accordion chords of Tex-Mex to electric organ and helped reshape American garage rock.

🅂 "Down Along the Cove" (Bob Dylan)
Bob Dylan, *John Wesley Harding* (1968)
The Band, *Across the Great Divide* (1994); *Live at Watkins Glen/'73* (1995); (performed with Bob Dylan), *Rock of Ages (Deluxe Edition)* (2001)
West, *Bridges* (1968)
Georgie Fame, single (1969)
Johnny Jenkins, *Ton-Ton Macoute* (1970)
Larry McNeely, *Larry McNeely* (1971)
Duane Allman, *Anthology* (1972)
Coulson, Dean, McGuinness, Flint, *Lo & Behold* (1972)
Bill Lyerly, *Railroad Station Blues* (1998)
Steve Gibbons, *The Dylan Project* (1998)
Hudson River Rats, *Get It While You Can* (2000)
Jesse Ballard's Paradise Island Band, *Like a Rolling Thunder '98* (2001)
Various Artists (performed by Cliff Auniger), *It Ain't Me Babe— Zimmerman Framed: The Songs of Bob Dylan* (2001)

Various Artists (performed by Georgie Fame), *Doin' Dylan 2* (2002)

Dylan's jazzy little bit of piano-propelled R&B, highlighted by Pete Drake's steel-guitar licks, is one of only a couple of real love songs found on *John Wesley Harding*—even if the love described is of the betrayed variety. After all, the woman to whom the narrator sings was seen walking down along the cove holding another man's hand. What's hard to believe is that "Down Along the Cove" was written by the same guy who penned "Visions of Johanna" just over two years before. Still, the lightly swinging shuffle is full of the kind of wild, vivid passion found in van Gogh's painting "Starry Night," containing a conspiratorial edge consistent with a crepuscular tryst. Paired with "I'll Be Your Baby Tonight" as the final songs on *John Wesley Harding*, "Down Along the Cove" seems almost a response to "The Wicked

Messenger" and provides a sensuous counterpoint to the balance of that otherwise dark, messianic collection of brooding songs, pointing to the Dixie vistas of *Nashville Skyline*.

Dylan performed "Down Along the Cove," a concert natural, only a handful of times from 1999 through 2001, reviving it briefly as a show opener in late 2003, when it acquired a sleek yet simultaneously raunchy treatment with a possible new lyric or two that brought out the song's bluesier layers.

"Down in the Flood (Crash on the Levee)"
(Bob Dylan)
aka "Crash on the Levee (Down in the Flood)"
Bob Dylan (with Happy Traum), *Bob Dylan's Greatest Hits, Volume II* (1971)
Bob Dylan/The Band, *The Basement Tapes/'67* (1975)
Bob Dylan/Various Artists (performed by Bob Dylan), *Masked & Anonymous* (2003)

Crash on a Mississippi River levee above Cabin Teele crevasse, Louisiana, 1927.

(Library of Congress)

The Band (performed with Bob Dylan), *Rock of Ages (Deluxe Edition)* (2001)

Sandy Denny, *North Star Grassman and the Ravens* (1971)

Roger Tillison, *Roger Tillison's Album* (1971)

Blood, Sweat & Tears, *New Blood* (1972)

Chris Smither, *Don't Drag It On* (1972); *Another Way to Find You* (1991)

Christine Ohlman and Rebel Monte, *Radio Queen* (1996); *Hard Way* (1996)

Lester Flatt and Earl Scruggs, *1964–1969, Plus* (1996)

Ritchie Blackmore, *Take It: Sessions '63–'68* (1998)

Jimmy LaFave, *Trail* (1999)

Leon Russell, *Face in the Crowd* (1999)

Fairport Convention, *The Best of Fairport 1972–1984* (1999)

Various Artists (performed by Blood, Sweat & Tears), *Doin' Dylan 2* (2002)

Dylan and the Hawks first recorded a couple of versions of "Crash on the Levee," one of their more familiar tunes, during the fertile *Basement Tapes* period in 1967. The unofficially released track is off-kilter and strident, but not panicked in the way such a disaster described in the song might suggest—as if the narrator has seen it all too many times before.

Later retitled "Down in the Flood" when published in Dylan's official *Lyrics 1962–1985*, the song simmers with the firsthand vitality of a deluge survivor—a theme he would reexplore nearly thirty-five years later in "High Water (for Charley Patton)." And like "High Water Everywhere," the Patton tune on which Dylan modeled "Highwater," "Down in the Flood" sounds like it is being sung by some jaded Noah of Mississippi's floodplain auguring imminent, near-apocalyptic disaster with a casualness that contradicts his predicament.

Some of the more antique-sounding lyrics from "Crash on the Levee" are drawn from "James Alley Blues," a song about one of New Orleans's more notorious turn-of-the-century byways. "James Alley Blues" is associated

with Richard "Rabbit" Brown on Harry Smith's *Anthology of American Folk Music*. Born in New Orleans in 1880, Brown died there in 1937; he seems to have recorded "James Alley Blues" in the late 1920s. A street singer in his early years, he could be found on the sidewalks of Storyville, but he frequently worked as a singing boatman on Lake Pontchartrain. His recorded legacy is very slim. Still, records of his work apparently have been passed down. When Dylan sings "Well, it's sugar for sugar, and salt for salt/If you go down in the flood, it's gonna be your own fault," he is giving a clear tip o' the hat to Brown's lines, "I been giving sugar for sugar, let you get salt for salt/And if you can't get along with me, well, it's your own fault." Other lines from "James Alley Blues" seem to have interested Dylan as well. "Sometimes I think that you're too sweet to die/Then other times I think you oughta be buried alive" by Brown, for example, is echoed in Dylan's "Black Crow Blues," and "I done seen better days, but I'm puttin' up with these" might have been the origin of "I see better days and I do better things" from Dylan's "I Shall Be Free."

And then there is the refrain that ends each verse—"But oh mama, ain't you gonna miss your best friend now?/You're gonna have to find yourself/Another best friend, somehow." The best friend business is a fairly common lyric device found in many a blues, perhaps most notably in the music of Lightnin' Hopkins, Mississippi Fred McDowell, and the like. Always the line serves as a stark reminder that best friends are not easy to come by and should be valued lest they be swept away by literal or figurative floods.

Dylan rerecorded "Down in the Flood" with Happy Traum for his *Greatest Hits, Volume II* release in 1971, but that version is far less evocative than the stuff made in the basement.

As a performance vehicle "Down in the Flood" remained on the shelf until 1995, when it was ominously rearranged and used as portentous kickoff to many a Dylan show, complete with backup vocals and a foreboding harmonica break as if to suggest that next time around, Genesis 6–7 would seem like a picnic. Dylan kept the song in heavy performance rotation in 1997, shelved it for a couple of years, and returned to it again in 2000 and '01 for a healthy smattering of displays.

◪ *Down in the Groove*

Columbia Records LP OC-40957, CD CK-40957, CS OCT-40957. Recorded April–May, 1987. Released May 31, 1988. Produced by Bob Dylan (uncredited).

Bob Dylan—guitar, harmonica, keyboards, vocals. Jerry Garcia—vocals. Steve Jones—guitar. Bobby King—background vocals. Bob Weir—vocals. Ron Wood—bass. Full Force—background vocals. Clydie King—background vocals. Peggi Blu—background vocals. Michael Baird—drums. Alexandra Brown—background vocals. Eric Clapton—guitar. Carolyn Dennis—background vocals. Sly Dunbar—drums. Nathan East—bass. Mitchell Froom—keyboards. Beau Hill—keyboards. Larry Klein—bass. Mark Knopfler—guitar. Brent Mydland—vocals. Madelyn Quebec—keyboards, vocals. Robbie Shakespeare—bass. Paul Simonon—bass. Henry Spinetti—drums. Kip Winger—bass. Randy Jackson—bass. Willie Green—vocals. Stephen Shelton—drums, keyboards. Danny Kortchmar—guitar. Alan Clarke—keyboards. Stephen Jordan—drums. Myron Grombacher—drums. Kevin Savigar—keyboards.

"Let's Stick Together," "When Did You Leave Heaven?" "Sally Sue Brown," "Death Is Not the End," "Had a Dream About You, Baby," "Ugliest Girl in the World," "Silvio," "Ninety Miles an Hour (Down a Dead End Street)," "Shenandoah," "Rank Strangers to Me"

A justifiably scorned hodgepodge, *Down in the Groove,* critics suggested, was proof positive that Dylan was suffering from a full-blown case of writer's block. There are but two legitimate originals to be found here ("Death Is Not the End" and "Had a Dream About You, Baby") on this slim, thirty-two-minute offering—coincidentally Dylan's thirty-second album. Really, though, *Down in the Groove* seems to be more of an extension of his *Knocked Out Loaded* approach to conceiving and producing an album—which is to say, no concept or approach at all. Like that pale collection of mostly half-baked originals and limp covers, *Down in the Groove* failed to make the charts.

Dylan's defense of *Down in the Groove* went something like this: "There's no rule that claims that anyone must write their own songs. You could take another song somebody else has written and you can make it yours. I'm not saying I made a definitive version of anything with this last record, but I like the songs. Every so often you've gotta sing songs that're out there. You just have to, just to keep yourself straight."

With its use of a variety of bands from a variety of sessions, *Down in the Groove* came off as a disappointing—some say even uninspired, haphazard, shoddy, or phoned-in—effort from someone who couldn't seem less interested in the idea of making records. It marks the low ebb in Dylan's later recording career.

That said, as a Bob Dylan album, the document is not without its interestingly weird strengths. Dylan's covers of the old folk chestnut "Shenandoah" (electrified here, with a Bo Diddley beat) and the Stanley Brothers' haunting "Rank Strangers to Me" stand with Dylan's best interpretive work. And the inclusion of two songs ("Silvio" and "Ugliest Girl in the World") Dylan wrote with Grateful Dead lyricist Robert Hunter adds to the album's quirkiness.

It may or may not be Dylan's worst record, but if there's any extra fun at all to be found here, it's in playing spot-the-names in the credits: Paul Simonon of the Clash and Steve Jones of the Sex Pistols on one track; Eric Clapton and Ron Wood on another; yet a third track includes reggae's rhythm masters Sly Dunbar and Robbie Shakespeare, Dire Straits lead man Mark Knopfler, and Full Force. But despite the star power, this album is pretty damn dull. Dylan seems barely interested, his monotone at its most detached, his arrangements of his chosen songs almost completely random.

Critics came out with their knives sharpened on this one and did their dirty work in broad daylight. They called songs like "Ugliest Girl in the World" insipid, declared *Down in the Groove* the nadir of his career, and prophetically stated in no uncertain terms that Dylan was going to have to climb real high to get out from the hole he'd dug for himself. "*Down in the Dumps* is more like it" was the common critique.

[S] "Down the Highway" (Bob Dylan)

Bob Dylan, *The Freewheelin' Bob Dylan* (1963)

A deep, dark 12-bar blues evoking the hardened spirits of Son House, Robert Johnson, Skip James, and all the ciphers of the Mississippi Delta, the listener-unfriendly "Down the Highway" features a breathtaking, mournful guitar figure and a cathartic vocal—Dylan's clear nod to the departure of his then-girlfriend Suze Rotolo (referenced in the fifth verse when Dylan says his baby took his heart in her suitcase all the way to Italy). Dylan was shellshocked when Suze left him and the tightly wound "Down the Highway" is a window into his churning soul as it blows down the roadside, going nowhere special except perhaps an empty room.

Dylan commented on "Down the Highway" in the *Freewheelin'* liner notes as synthesis of his early blues instincts: "The blues is more than something to sit home and arrange. What made the real blues singers so great is that they were able to state all the problems they had; but at the same time, they were standing outside of them and could look at them."

With all the desperate gloominess of a landless farmer, "Down the Highway" is unified by Dylan's astounding guitar pattern, which can still elicit a shiver in the vulnerable listener, as it probably did when he performed it at but one 1964 British show in apparent response to the audience's demand to get a taste of his older, *Freewheelin'* material.

[S] "Downtown Blues" (Geoff Muldaur)

The Blues Project (with Bob Dylan), *The Blues Project* (1964)

Dylan (credited as Bob Landy on the album) contributed some piano licks to this Geoff Muldaur song from a session that saw release later in the year on *The Blues Project*, a sampler of New York City folk music.

[B] *Drawn Blank* (Bob Dylan)

New York: Random House, 1994.

Beyond music, Dylan's special interest in the painted word took on an air of seriousness when he published *Drawn Blank* in 1994. He had long maintained an artist's studio behind his Malibu house and showed off his character sketches to interested guests with the nervous excitement of a proud parent.

A collection of sixty van Goghesque drawings and sketches (of hotel scenes, landscapes, nudes, portraits, and so forth), the arresting images in *Drawn Blank* are rendered in crayon, pencil, pen and ink, and charcoal. Those looking for autobiographical insight might seek out Howard Sounes's observations in his book *Down the Highway: The Life of Bob Dylan* (New York: Grove Press, 2001): "Mostly Bob seemed to be alone in empty rooms. He often drew the view from his balcony, a view of empty streets, parking lots, and bleak city skylines."

Rough-hewn yet inviting, what is perhaps most intriguing and revealing about the one hundred twenty-odd renderings is that they speak of a life lived on the less traveled road. Dylan's journeys have taken him all over the planet, yet here he takes us with him into the more private nooks of a reluctant public life.

Discussing the project with *Newsweek*'s Malcolm Jones Jr. in 1995, Dylan was appropriately humble. "My favorite artists are people like Donatello or Caravaggio or Titian, all those overwhelming guys," he said. "I wouldn't even know where to begin to approach that kind of mastery. The purpose of my drawing is very undefined. They're very personal drawings, I guess like someone would knit a sweater, y'know? I don't concoct drawings out of my head. It's all out there somewhere and that's the only way I can work or get any satisfaction out of doing it. These drawings, they kind of go with my primitive style of music. It's almost like meditating. I feel like I'm renewed after I make a drawing."

Jones seems to have agreed with Dylan's assessment of the work, for as he politely noted, "A lot of Dylan's art, his portraits particularly, resemble the drawings high-school kids do for fun on the covers of their notebooks. The difference is that while most people grow up and shy away from art, Dylan persists. Like his music, where professional polish has never been the point, his drawings epitomize the amateur's creed, that homemade, hand-hewn stuff is always the best."

🖬 **"A Dream"** (William Blake/Allen Ginsberg)
Allen Ginsberg, *Holy Soul Jelly Roll*/'71 (1995)

William Blake wrote the original "A Dream" (it appears in *Songs of Innocence*), but Allen Ginsberg (perhaps with Dylan's help) was probably the first to arrange it musically. Not only was the piece recorded, but it was broadcast on the New York public-television program *Freetime* as "Allen Ginsberg & Friends" with Dylan as guest guitarist in 1971.

In the liner notes to his monumental retrospective *Holy Soul Jelly Roll*, Ginsberg discussed recording "A Dream": "We went into these Record Plant sessions without tunes or words, to improvise. I had definite melodies only for the Blake songs. I wish Dylan had taken over even more as session leader. I was overeager to get him to play Blake and some mantras; he balked at the mantras, maybe he thought they were a mind-trap."

🖬 **"Drifter's Escape"** (Bob Dylan)
Bob Dylan, single (1969); *John Wesley Harding* (1968)
Joan Baez, *Any Day Now* (1968); *Vanguard Sessions: Baez Sings Dylan* (1998)
Wolfgang Ambros, *Live* (1979)
Jimi Hendrix, *Stone Free* (1981); *South Saturn Delta* (1997)
Vole, *A Tribute to Bob Dylan* (1992)
The Zimmermen, *After the Ambulances Go* (1998)

If Akira Kurosawa directed a film based on a Franz Kafka novel and cast Clint Eastwood in the starring role it might look the way "Drifter's Escape" sounds. Dylan's mysterious, allegorical (and perhaps autobiographical) song involves a man being dragged into court and accused of some unnamed crime, only to escape via divine intervention. Is the drifter a false prophet? Were the forces that helped set him free dark ones? Dylan never reveals this, preferring instead to let his antihero roam the Goyaesque landscape of his song like a phantom trickster.

"Drifter's Escape" is a tale in which the victimized outsider is threatened but not defeated by society. On *John Wesley Harding*, Dylan sings the song with the anguished desperation of a man on the lam as he merges a taste of Old West frontier justice with the Old Testament's xenophobic elements. Recalling Luke the

Drifter (Hank Williams's alter ego), this forlorn incantation has a similar tone of warning. In a scene out of Kafka, the drifter is brought before a judge and jury not exactly composed of peers to be tried *Alice in Wonderland*–pack-of-cards style for offenses unstated and unknown. God enters stage left with a bolt of lightning, making the persecutors kneel to pray, while the drifter, in true B-western style, takes advantage of the distraction to flee. In Dylan's personal history, the lightning might symbolize the Triumph chopper that he totaled the year before he wrote this song. Following this logic, *John Wesley Harding* (and its acoustic and elegiac mood) can be viewed as Dylan's backdoor escape from the constraints of popular culture.

Dylan didn't start performing "Drifter's Escape" in concert until 1992, when he displayed two arrangements of the song: the original *John Wesley Harding* style and one more akin to Jimi Hendrix's interpretation. After that, it wasn't touched until 1995, when it served as a cautionary, if tune-free, show opener for a long stretch of the Never Ending Tour. By 2001, Dylan had refined "Drifter's Escape" into a fireball of electric energy and one of his more incendiary live performances of the era in a sharp arrangement that featured the guitar playing of Charlie Sexton and his own paranoia-inflected vocals, wheezing like a guy with a head cold trying to clear his throat with an ice scraper as he narrated the escape of the featured antihero with a gusto that betrayed Dylan's allegiance to the drifter.

▣ "Driftin' Too Far from Shore" (Bob Dylan)
Bob Dylan, *Knocked Out Loaded* (1986)

Not to be confused with the country bluegrass number of practically the same title ("Drifting Too Far from the Shore") performed by the likes of Hank Williams, Bill Monroe, and Old & in the Way, Dylan composed and recorded his own "Driftin' Too Far from Shore" for *Empire Burlesque* in the summer of 1984. It failed to make the cut for that release, however, and was salvaged for the *Knocked Out Loaded* travesty. A raving, gospel-influenced wannabe, "Driftin' Too Far" might have had some potential if Dylan had only followed his instincts and handled the final mix himself.

As with several songs from his mid-1980s output, Dylan appears to have drawn on cinema and snatches of its dialogue for cut-and-paste inspiration in "Driftin' Too Far from Shore." The opening verse ("I didn't know that you'd be leavin'/Or who you thought you were talkin' to/I figure maybe we're even/Or maybe I'm one up on you") seems appropriated from *Bend of the River*, a 1952 western in which someone says to James Stewart, "I figure we're even. Maybe I'm one up on ya." Another phrase in the song ("No gentleman likes makin' love to his servant/Specially when he's in his father's house") is a twist on a line from *Sabrina*, the suave 1954 Billy Wilder film starring Humphrey Bogart and Audrey Hepburn.

Dylan performed "Driftin' Too Far from Shore" about a half dozen times during the early phases of the Never Ending Tour.

▣ "Duncan and Brady" (Traditional)
aka "Brady and Duncan," "Brady"
Leadbelly, *Where Did You Sleep Last Night?*/1940s (1996)
Dave Van Ronk, *Dave Van Ronk Sings Ballads, Blues & Spirituals* (1959)
John Koerner, Dave Ray, Tony Glover, *Lots More Blues Rags & Hollers* (1964)
New Riders of the Purple Sage, *Powerglide* (1972)
Gordon Bok, *Rogue's Gallery of Songs for 12 String* (1983)

Though it might sound like an old cowboy song with its slower, western-style ambiance worthy of a Sam Peckinpah shoot 'em up, "Duncan and Brady" is a folk blues in the murder ballad tradition. The story told in the song is pretty vague, beginning with a reference to the children's nursery rhyme "Twinkle, Twinkle Little Star" and ending with the reasons why Duncan blows Brady away. Brady, evidently a ladies' man, drives into town in his electric car and interrupts a card game at the local saloon. A jealous Duncan (apparently a cop moonlighting as a bartender) empties his .45 into Brady's heart after trying to arrest his foe for unspecified crimes. That Brady's funeral is attended by a gaggle of grieving women leads one to believe that his transgressions involved matters of the heart—and loins.

"Duncan and Brady" became popular in Texas about a century ago. Correspondence from Mrs. Tom Bartlett (of Marlin, Texas) to folk song collector John Lomax in the 1920s details some of the era's attitudes toward African Americans, but also describes the lengths a song catcher like herself might go to in securing the lore of the folk: "The 'Duncan and Brady' song is a gem, and I will not rest in peace till I get it all for you. It is a genuine ballad in that it celebrates the final adventures of a 'bad Nigger' who shot up the town. No other place than Waco was the scene of the fray, and that probably accounts for its great popularity in this region. . . . I am exerting myself greatly to get this song, having offered various Negroes of my acquaintance bribes in the way of Mr. Bartlett's old hats and shoes; and if you know their weakness for these two objects of apparel, you may feel confident of my success."

Dylan began performing "Duncan and Brady" only in 1999, but he'd probably known it from early in his folk music studies at the University of Leadbelly, though Jerry Garcia, Dave Van Ronk, Tom Rush, and David Bromberg have been suggested as sources for Dylan's latter interest in the song. Also, some sources suggest that Dylan recorded the song

at a 1992 Chicago session with Bromberg and/or for *Good as I Been to You* that same year, but did not include it on that fine album of acoustically rendered folk songs.

"Dust My Broom" (Traditional/Robert Johnson/Elmore James)
aka "I Believe I'll Dust My Broom"
See also "It Hurts Me Too"
Robert Johnson, *The Complete Recordings* (1990)
Elmore James, *Dust My Broom* (1991)
Homesick James, *Home Sweet Homesick James* (1976)
Johnny Shines, *Dust My Broom* (1980)
Etta James, *Live* (1994)

Dylan's only performance of this sexually suggestive blues special was a good one, coming during an early Never Ending Tour stop in Motown in the fall of 1991 and sounding like it blew in on the cusp of a dark Windy City breeze. On that occasion his band showed its mettle, pulling out every urban blues lick known to man in a version that could have raised the ghost of Elmore James himself. Robert Johnson recorded the first known version of the song on November 23, 1936, in a San Antonio hotel room, but the song became James's signature piece in the 1950s.

Some imagine rather sexually explicit meanings for this title phrase along the lines of getting one's "ashes hauled." Some bluesologists also deconstruct it further outside the general blues liturgy, saying that it could suggest an actual magic practice of riddance. To be sure, the broom is connected with many folk beliefs and superstitions. But according to other blues linguists, "dust my broom" may have a more conservative definition, perhaps something as simple as breaking up with a woman, being synonymous with "shaking her off." Big Joe Williams, a devout believer in magic who may have known Johnson and recorded with Dylan in 1962, shrugged the phrase off, saying it simply meant "leaving for good—I'm putting you down. I won't be back no more."

▣ "Dusty Old Fairgrounds" (Bob Dylan)
Blue Ash, *No More, No Less* (1973); *The Songs of Bob Dylan*/'73 (1989); *I Shall Be Unreleased*/'73 (1991)

A great, if very raw, early song from Dylan recalling the days he allegedly (or wished he had) spent as a carny. With the cascade of lyrics in "Dusty Old Fairgrounds," he colorfully evokes the roustabouts, hustlers, and dancing girls of a traveling road show coming to life and setting up their tents to the rambling strains of folk guitar. With a husky Minnesota burr, Dylan conveys a convincing "been there, done that" tone in the song, making sure to remind us that he spends his time "with the fortune-telling kind"—as if we couldn't have guessed. Dylan performed and recorded the energetic reel (which owes a debt to Guthrie's oft-covered "Dusty Old Dust") at his April 1963 Town Hall concert in Midtown Manhattan, which was to provide material for the never-released *Bob Dylan in Concert* LP.

Discussing "Dusty Old Fairgrounds" from

Frank Bergen's World of Mirth Carnival midway, 1948.
(Photo: Cornell Capa/Time Life Pictures/Getty Images)

that night's set list, Paul Cable wrote in *Bob Dylan: His Unreleased Recordings* (New York: Schirmer Books, 1980): "... one of them is a song with, to my mind, a title that is attractive in itself—'Dusty Old Fairgrounds.' Unfortunately, the song is really not up to much; one of the disappointing things is that it really is about dusty old fairgrounds—a whole list of them. Dylan introduces it as a route song and that is just what it is—an itinerary set to music. The tune sounds as though it is either going to evolve into something better or it is already a basically good tune that Dylan happens to be doing one of his leave-out-the-subtleties jobs on."

ⓐ *Dylan*

Columbia Records LP PC-32747, CS PCT-32747. Recorded May 1969; February, March, May, June, August 1970. Released November 16, 1973. Produced by Bob Johnston. Photography by Al Clayton.

"Lily of the West," "Can't Help Falling in Love," "Sarah Jane," "The Ballad of Ira Hayes," "Mr. Bojangles," "Mary Ann," "Big Yellow Taxi," "A Fool Such as I," "Spanish Is the Loving Tongue"

Columbia Records wreaked revenge on Dylan for signing with David Geffen's Asylum Records in 1973 by releasing *Dylan*, a lamentable collection of outtakes and warm-ups from the sessions that produced *Self Portrait* and *New Morning*. The album jacket, a pop-art silver serigraph of Dylan in close profile made from an Al Clayton photograph, was probably a good tip-off that the master's hand was in little evidence here. All things considered, *Dylan* did fairly good business, rising to No. 17 during its seven-week stay on the charts and earning its "author" his eighth gold album. *Dylan* is for the hard-core, must-have-everything fanatic collector only—or perhaps just your plain old, dyed-in-the-chainmail masochist.

Maybe the album is not as bad as people make it out to be. Still, there are no original Dylan tunes here, merely a wide assortment of covers that are all over the map musically. His nod to his peers is most evident in the unusual versions of Joni Mitchell's "Big Yellow Taxi," Pete LaFarge's Native American folk classic "Ballad of Ira Hayes," and Jerry Jeff Walker's evergreen "Mr. Bojangles." Dylan's early rock 'n' roll fetish is out front too in his distinctive cover of "Can't Help Falling in Love," Elvis's romantic hit.

"They were not to be used," Dylan said of the tapes used for *Dylan* while pointing an angry finger in the direction of Columbia Records. "I thought it well understood. They were just not to be used. I thought it was well understood. They were just to warm up for a tune. I didn't think it was that bad, really!"

ⓐ *Dylan & The Dead*

Columbia Records LP OC-45056, CD CK-45056, CD OCT-45056. Recorded July 1987. Released February 6, 1989. Produced by Jerry Garcia and John Cutler. Artwork by Rick Griffin.

"Slow Train," "I Want You," "Gotta Serve Somebody," "Queen Jane Approximately," "Joey," "All Along the Watchtower," "Knockin' on Heaven's Door"

Fans may have had fond memories of the six 1987 concerts that brought Dylan together with the Grateful Dead, but the tapes don't lie: the shows were pretty flat. Sure there were moments when the long-anticipated pairing caught lightning in a bottle; however, despite their common roots and proven ability to adopt, interpret, and reinvent all their influences, Dylan and the Dead did not exactly create the freshest musical vision onstage. Even those with more than half a century of combined musical expression behind them need to rehearse, and the seat-of-the-pants shamanistic approach to football stadium

Dylan performing with the Grateful Dead (left to right: guitarist Bob Weir, drummers Mickey Hart and Bill Kreutzmann, and guitarist Jerry Garcia), Giants Stadium, East Rutherford, New Jersey, July 12, 1987.

(Photo: Angel Franco/New York Times Co./Getty Images)

blowouts did not exactly provide transcendence. Only "All Along the Watchtower" sprouts wings and soars amid an ill-chosen track list. Still, despite dry readings of some of the numbers, such as "Joey," the Dead's ability to turn any tune into a jam-friendly, lyrical boogie is at least suggested on every song.

The officially released results were limp. But, no doubt spurred by the Dead's massive surge in popularity at the time and Dylan's customary market share, *Dylan & The Dead* did brisk business, going to No. 37 during its three-week stop on the charts. It was Dylan's fifth live record in fifteen years and earned him his first gold album since *Infidels*.

There were no liner notes on the album, which was graced instead with a nice pen-and-ink illustration by Rick Griffin (famed San Francisco acid rock poster artist) depicting an old-time locomotive engine flanked by visual cameos of Dylan (1966 era) and the Dead's skull-and-roses icon in Dylan's sunglasses.

Dylan's association with the Grateful Dead was an important one despite the flimsy excuse for the souvenir album produced by the summer 1987 concerts. Dylan cited the union as the beginning of a kind of awakening that changed his purpose and commitment, a moment when he realized that what was important was not his legend but how he stood by his work and that playing music on a regular basis was to be a central theme for the next phase of his life.

E

ⓐ *Earl Scruggs Performing with His Family and Friends*

Columbia Records LP KC-30584. Released 1971.

Dylan's first appearance on somebody else's album in many a moon was something of a secret, though it is consistent with his turn to country music at the time. Here he plays acoustic guitar on one of his new tunes ("Nashville Skyline Rag") and one associated with Scruggs ("East Virginia Blues"). The album was released in conjunction with a Scruggs television special of the same title.

ⓢ "Early Morning Rain" (Gordon Lightfoot)

Bob Dylan, *Self Portrait* (1970)
Gordon Lightfoot, *Lightfoot* (1966)
Peter, Paul & Mary, single (1965)
George Hamilton IV, single (1965), *Country Boy* (1996)
Judy Collins, *5th Album* (1965)
Ian and Sylvia, *Early Morning Rain* (1965)
Elvis Presley, *Elvis Now* (1972)
Tony Rice, *Sings Gordon Lightfoot* (1996)

Gordon Lightfoot's wistful "so long" to a departing lover, "Early Morning Rain" was first recorded by Peter, Paul & Mary in 1965; their rendition hit No. 91 on the *Billboard* Top 100 chart and No. 13 on the easy-listening chart. A year later, George Hamilton's version climbed to No. 9 on the country chart.

With his gentle burr of a voice, curly hair, sparkle in his eyes, and handsome good looks that make him appear as if he'd just stepped out of the forest primeval, singer-songwriter Gordon Lightfoot (born November 17, 1938, Orillia, Ontario) first came to public notice when he appeared at Toronto's famed Massey Hall as a mere thirteen-year-old and won a

singing competition. After pursuing an interest in barbershop quartets and singing as a member of a duo, Lightfoot struck out on his own in the early 1960s, writing dozens of songs, steeping himself in the country and folk revivals of the era, and taking lethal doses of Dylan. Lightfoot's combination of sensitivity, inventiveness, and beautiful voice resulted in a singular songwriting and vocal style that added up to early success.

Lightfoot still checks out as an insightful observer of the human condition. He takes his troubadour role seriously, and his music—be it a love song, a song of lost love, or a historical ballad (which he can knock off like few others)—leaves lasting, fluid impressions with new layers of meaning always threatening to reveal themselves.

Like Dylan, Lightfoot continues to write his own legacy. Thirty-five years down the pike and with more than two hundred songs under his belt, he remains a road warrior with a tour band nearly as hot as Dylan's. And if it's awards that impress you, Lightfoot's mantelpiece is full: he has garnered five Grammy nominations and seventeen Juno Awards (the Canadian Grammy), was a Canadian Music Hall of Fame inductee in 1986 (Dylan did the presentation), a 1970 recipient of the prestigious Order of Canada, 1997 recipient of the Governor General's award (the highest official Canadian honor), and a 2001 inductee into the Canadian Country Music Hall of Fame.

After his own adequate recording and 1970 release of "Early Morning Rain" on the grab-bag LP *Self Portrait*, Dylan worked up a glorious garage band arrangement of the song for five 1989–1991 concerts, often during his visits to Canada. Even by this late date, Dylan had let the song lose little of its sweetness and added a short but sublime guitar solo augmented by his own bittersweet turn on harmonica. In the late 1990s Dylan also began performing Lightfoot's "I'm Not Supposed to Care."

Some wonderfully casual photographs of Dylan and Lightfoot hanging out at Toronto's Mariposa Folk Festival in late July 1972 (a wispy-bearded Dylan looking particularly cool with a dark bandanna tied around his forehead) have been preserved.

◫ "East Virginia" (Traditional)

aka "Born in East Virginia," "Dark Hollow," "East Virginia Blues," "Old Virginia," "When I Left East Virginia"

Earl Scruggs (with Bob Dylan), *Earl Scruggs Performs with His Family and Friends* (1971)

Buell Kazee, *Anthology of American Folk Music/'29* (1952/'97)

Pete Seeger, *World of Pete Seeger* (1973)

Ramblin' Jack Elliott, *Hard Travelin'* (1989)

Jean Ritchie and Doc Watson, *Jean Ritchie & Doc Watson at Folk City* (1990)

Long John Baldry, *Right to Sing the Blues* (1996)

Carter Family, *Longing for Old Virginia* (1998)

In December 1970 Dylan recorded "East Virginia" as a duet with Earl Scruggs at the Carmel, New York, home of Thomas B. Allen for a documentary on Scruggs entitled *Earl Scruggs Performs with His Family and Friends*. It aired on television's NBC network a month later.

Typical of the many wild banjo pieces sung in the mountains of Kentucky, Tennessee, and West Virginia (in which one can hear as much Calvinism as the black folk tradition), "East Virginia" is sung to a familiar tune alternately known as "Greenback Dollar" or "I Don't Want Your Millions, Mister." Dylan's brooding version embellishes the song's death theme and is reminiscent of his treatment of such material from his eponymous debut LP a decade earlier.

◫ "Easy Lovin'" (Freddie Hart)

Freddie Hart, *Country U.S.A.* (1971)

Jim Ed Brown, *She's Leavin'* (1972)

Kelly Hogan and the Pine Valley Cosmonauts, *Beneath the Country Underdog* (2000)

John Hammond Jr., *Ready for Love* (2003)

Dylan opened his spring 2003 tour with a show in Dallas that included a one-time-only cover of Freddie Hart's 1971 country hit "Easy Lovin'," which, in its day, peaked at No. 1 on the *Billboard* chart and was named Song of the Year in both 1971 and 1972 by the Country Music Association. Considering its popularity, though, the song remains surprisingly undercovered.

Hart (born Fred Segrest, December 21, 1926, Loachapoka, Alabama) came by his success the hard way. His early life reads like something out of a Steinbeck novel. He grew up in a huge sharecropping family as one of fifteen children, played an instrument cobbled out of a cigar box and wire from a Model T Ford, left school as a twelve-year-old to join his parents in the fields, ran away from home, worked in the Civilian Conservation Corps camp (state-run manual labor units organized during the Depression), and lied about his age to join the U.S. Marines as a teenager to fight in World War II, where he saw fire at Iwo Jima and other South Pacific battles.

After the war he landed a gig as a roadie for Hank Williams, picked up some pointers in the fine art of songwriting, and toured with Lefty Frizzell. But he slowly soured on the notion of ever making it in music, turning to the martial arts as a black-belt karate teacher.

But he didn't cut all his music ties, penning, in 1955, "Loose Talk," which, when recorded by Carl Smith, became a hit and led to Hart's signing with Columbia. Two notable hits later ("The Wall" and "Chain Gang"), he found himself on

E

the stage of the Grand Ole Opry in 1961. After several fallow years Hart formed a band, the Heartbeats, released a couple of singles in 1965 ("Togetherness" and "Born a Fool"), hit the skids again, then signed with Capitol Records in 1970, where his song "The Whole World Holding Hands" piggybacked on the feel-good aspects of the '60s. This paved the way for the success of "Easy Lovin'" the following year, which turned out to be his high-water mark. A slow slide into relative oblivion followed over the next decade, though Hart did score the occasional hit. After some label hopping in the 1980s and a final hit, "Best Love I Never Had," he has settled into a low-key career as a touring musician. Maybe his real genius is as an investor: his wealth stems from plum farms, a trucking company, and two hundred breeding bulls. And, as if to show that he takes his name seriously, his compassion for those less fortunate has resulted in the ownership of a school for handicapped children in Southern California.

▣ *Eat the Document*

Leacock-Pennebaker Films, 1971. Filmed and directed by D. A. Pennebaker. Edited by Bob Dylan, Howard Alk, and Robbie Robertson.

A revered artifact of underground art-house cinema from the mid-1960s, *Eat the Document* picked up where *Don't Look Back* left off as it journeys into an even deeper, darker realm of Dylan's cold Inferno.

The project came together when Dylan and his manager, Albert Grossman, were invited to submit a piece to *Stage 67*, ABC TV's almost-anything-goes, one-season-only anthology program that included performances, documentaries, and plays. That the show's producers dared offer Dylan a shot in the first place is a testament to their own openness to risk and that of the cool medium in that era.

Dylan must have felt that things had worked well with documentary filmmaker D. A. Pennebaker during the making of *Don't Look Back* in 1965, and so engaged Pennebaker for what the latter viewed as an extension of their first effort. Dylan and company, however (anticipating *Renaldo & Clara* by ten years), viewed the project as an even more experimental pastiche that would include improvisations from Dylan's sideshow troupe of musicians, handlers, hangers-on, and whomever else they might encounter. Though there is the sense that the project started out as two separate endeavors (Pennebaker's concert film and Dylan's edgy, off-kilter piece of visionary celluloid), the two concepts were combined to maximize and focus the talents of all concerned.

Like *Don't Look Back*, *Eat the Document* commenced with Dylan's arrival in Great Britain for what turned out to be his cataclysmic 1966 acoustic/electric tour of the Continent. Unlike the year before, when Dylan's (unasked-for) position at the vanguard of the folk-protest movement made him a less-than-willing darling of younger fans and won a warm reception, his 1966 concerts (featuring raging electric rock 'n' roll sets with the Hawks) sharply divided his audiences and incited hostility. Pennebaker captured the conflict with an immediacy that is still riveting.

The contrasting reaction to the then *very* new Bob Dylan is sharply captured in footage of the concertgoers shot by Howard Alk outside several venues where Dylan performed. One has to remember that *Blonde on Blonde* had not yet been released and that Dylan was filling two lengthy sets (one acoustic and one electric) with material from that landmark recording as well as from his equally controversial *Highway 61 Revisited* and *Bringing It All Back Home* releases—albums that represented a significant shift for Dylan and with which much of his audience during the 1966 tour was still relatively unfamiliar. Many of the kids caught on film probably came to the shows expecting Dylan to come and out and sing "Blowin' in the Wind" exactly the way they knew and cherished it from the vinyl. Instead, they were hit with the one-two punch of his long acoustic surrealisms of set one and the sledgehammer wave of sound unleashed by Dylan and the Hawks in set two. Some of the impassioned postconcert debate captured in *Eat the Document* may seem a wee bit quaint now, but at the time, the perception that Dylan was disavowing folk/protest music and selling out to become a pop star was taken very seriously and is caught here in all its drama.

Eat the Document is still the best visual portrait of Dylan's electric stage show at this crucial period of his career—indeed, in this critical moment for pop music. His reptilian physicalizations, reportedly fueled by grass and amphetamines as much as by the adrenaline charge that accompanied unveiling his new artistic persona, are grotesquely bared. His performances of "Tell Me, Momma," "Just Like Tom Thumb's Blues," and "Ballad of a Thin Man" are as riveting as they are repugnant. Merely the way Dylan brings the harmonica to his lips and blows on songs like "Ballad of a Thin Man" looks like an image pasted from the corner of one of the darker daydreams portrayed on the canvases of Edvard Munch, Francis Bacon, or James Ensor.

Although *Eat the Document* is a bottomless source of voyeuristic fascination, some of the shtick, already familiar from *Don't Look Back*, is tiresome—especially Dylan's dadaist duels with the still-clueless press corps. The Dylan-directed improvisatory set pieces, however, are another matter entirely. A couple of these scenes come off as juvenile and clichéd at best (see the segment involving people emerging from a closet like circus clowns magically appearing from a small car). Others, though, are still uncomfortable and disturbing, such as when Dylan becomes nauseated during a car ride with John Lennon, and when Dylan and Richard Manuel attempt to barter for a teenage girl.

Pennebaker took a dim view of such proceedings. "Making home movies," he commented twenty years later, "simply doesn't interest me very much. I'm not sure how to . . . make other people's movies for them" (from "Eye to Eye: A Conversation with D. A. Pennebaker," by John Bauldie, in *The Telegraph* #26, spring 1987).

Following the tour, Pennebaker and Bobby Neuwirth (Dylan's road manager and running buddy) began editing the footage, but Dylan's motorcycle accident in the summer of 1966 suspended activity. Later that year and in 1967 Dylan, Neuwirth, and Robbie Robertson took whacks at editing it so that, in Dylan's words, as recounted in William McKeen's *Bob Dylan: A Bio-Bibliography* (Westport, Connecticut: Greenwood Press, 1993), it would be "fast on the eye" and resemble the pharmaceutically induced, speedy mood of the tour. For better or worse, *Eat the Document* anticipated by nearly twenty years the quick-cut style that defines MTV and the like.

Not surprisingly, ABC gave *Eat the Document* a resounding thumbs down, deciding that its viewers would find it "too rough, too bleak and lurid." With that, the film began its life as a venerated object in the hipster shadows. It was screened at some film festivals in the early 1970s and broadcast on WNET, New York City's public television station, in 1979, and its tantalizing reputation (similar to that of *Cocksucker Blues*, Robert Frank's raw vision of the Rolling Stones circa 1972) has no doubt grown because of its limited distribution. Dylan presumably holds the rights to at least some of the

E

film and seems to regard the endeavor as a failure, once commenting, "That film was a project we did to rescue a bunch of garbage footage."

🅂 **"Eileen Aroon"** (Traditional/Gerald O'Daly/Clancy Brothers)
Mary O'Hara, *Songs of Erin* (1958)
Jean Redpath, *Frae My Ain Country* (1973)
Northeast Winds, *Ireland by Sail* (1987)
David and Ginger Hildebrand, *Out on a Limb* (1988)
Rich Lerner, *Trails and Bridges* (1996)
Maireid Sullivan, *For Love's Caress—A Celtic Journey* (1998)
Clancy Brothers, *Jug of Punch* (1999)

"Eileen Aroon" is, according to the sleeve notes of Mary O'Hara's *Songs of Erin* album, "considered one of the finest examples of love songs in Gaelic. Tradition tells us it was composed by Gerald O'Daly, a famous harper who lived in the sixteenth century. The title means 'Eileen My Darling.'" Other sources indicate that the composer/harpist's name was Carrol O'Daly, who lived in the fourteenth century; that his version was translated from the Irish by Gerald Griffin (1803–1840); and that the tune with which we are now familiar was known as "Robin Adair," written by Lady Caroline Keppel in the eighteenth century.

Pinning down the original source of virtually any folk song as apparently old as "Eileen Aroon" is always difficult. According to www.contemplator.com, an amazingly comprehensive folk music Web site, a tune titled "Ellen a Roon" first appeared in a 1729 ballad opera by Charles Coffey. Around 1740 a song called "Aileen Aroon," with a melody that differs from Coffey's, appeared in Burke Thumoth's book *Twelve Scotch and Twelve Irish Airs with Variations*. The song's original Gaelic title was given as "Eilionóir a Rúin." The Thumoth version may be found in the collection of folklorist Edward Bunting, who began to transcribe

tunes after attending the Belfast Harp Festival in 1792. While "Eileen Aroon" or some variation thereof has been the title of a number of songs, it can be safely stated that the familiar version of the tune probably dates to the late 1700s.

Dylan included thrilling, unrepentantly romantic renditions of "Eileen Aroon" (apparently styled after a Clancy Brothers arrangement of the song) in the traditional slot for about a dozen acoustic sets or encores during the 1988 and 1989 legs of the Never Ending Tour in an arrangement that could have tumbled from the pages of Geoffrey Chaucer's *Canterbury Tales*. As with many of the ancient songs from the British Isles Dylan chose to cover, the singer pours out his heart, praising the charms of his beloved, who lives deep in the valley. In singing, he considers the consequences of what would happen if his lover were no longer true to him—"like a fixed star."

🅂 **"El Paso"** (Marty Robbins)
Marty Robbins, *Gunfighter Ballads and Trail Songs* (1959)
Pat Boone, *Great! Great! Great!* (1960)
Ray Barretto, *Carnaval* (1962)
Mills Brothers, *Country Music's Greatest Hits* (1968)
The Grateful Dead, *Dick's Picks, Volume 11/'72* (1998)

"Marty Robbins was a singing cowboy born just a few years too late." Those words are as true today as they were when country-music historian Bill C. Malone wrote them decades ago in his 1968 book *Country Music U.S.A.* (Austin: University of Texas Press). As it was, Robbins (born Martin David Robinson, September 26, 1925, Glendale, Arizona; died December 8, 1982, Nashville) was one of country and western music's greatest songwriters and success stories, churning out hit after hit for a quarter century and charting songs every year between 1958 and his death in 1982.

Robbins became a star when the Mexican-flavored "El Paso" was released in 1959. It became one of country music's biggest hits following the trend in story-songs, which were at their peak at the time of its waxing. The narrator of "El Paso" sings, as in a great *corrido* of old Mexico, about a tale that relates the events leading to his own death in the arms of the woman he loves.

Playing out like a great melodramatic B-western, "El Paso" was Robbins's first international hit, rocketing to No. 1 on the country charts, where it stayed on and off for half a year. The story told here is a great one: a roughneck hangs out at Rose's Cantina, an El Paso watering hole, admiring the beautiful, black-eyed Felina, a Mexican girl with whom he has fallen in love. An unwelcome stranger challenges the narrator for her love but is shot down by our boy, who hightails it out the backdoor and into the desert night. Soon finding out that he can't live without Felina's love, out there alone with the sand and the scorpions, he betrays his better instincts and returns to town, only to be filled with hot lead and stagger to his death in his beloved's arms.

Robbins, as quoted in *Marty Robbins: Fast Cars and Country Music*, by Barbara S. Pruett (Metuchen, New Jersey: Scarecrow Press, 1990), once recalled the origins of "El Paso": "I always wanted to write a song about El Paso, because traditionally this is where the West begins. Western stories that I read and stories my grandfather told me inspired me to write it. I went through El Paso three times before I ever wrote the song. I wrote it on Christmas vacation on my way to Phoenix. Had I been born a little sooner, the cowboy life is the kind of life I'd like to have led."

The success of "El Paso" reaffirmed and confirmed Robbins's place on the American musical landscape as a troubadour not only of the Southwest, but as an avatar of several styles simultaneously: cowboy songs, Hawaiian music, rockabilly, folk music, country pop, and mainstream pop. In the two decades following the release and success of "El Paso," Robbins scored eighteen No. 1 recordings, wrote more than five hundred songs, was a Grand Ole Opry perennial, appeared as an actor in several westerns and television shows, and published at least one novel. A veritable devil of a cardsharp, Robbins was also a not-so-renowned if high-profile stock-car racer who competed in the sport's premier events. Robbins's later musical activity was slowed by the heart ailments that eventually took his life.

Fittingly, Dylan opened and closed a 1989 New Mexico show in unusual fashion with instrumental versions of "El Paso," no doubt as a regionally specific one-off homage to Robbins.

"Emotionally Yours" (Bob Dylan)

Bob Dylan, single (1985); *Empire Burlesque* (1985)
Bob Dylan/Various Artists (performed by the O'Jays), *Bob Dylan: The 30th Anniversary Concert Celebration* (1993)
The O'Jays, *Emotionally Yours* (1991); *In Bed with the O'Jays: Greatest Love Songs* (1996); *Best of the O'Jays: 1976–91* (1999)
Hanne Boel, *Misty Parade* (1994)
Andy Hill, *It Takes a Lot to Laugh* (2001)
Michel Montecrossa, *4th Time Around* (2001)
Robyn Hitchcock, *Robyn Sings* (2002)

Rumor has it that Dylan wrote "Emotionally Yours" with Elizabeth Taylor in mind—he was photographed escorting the movie star at a celebrity do around the time the song was recorded. One of the weaker *Empire Burlesque* tracks, this moody, stiff, and cliché weeper was a surprise hit for the O'Jays a few years later. Go figure. Dylan's recording suffers from Richard Scher's synth horns, a string section, and his own stale, saccharine vocals. A black-and-white video depicting Dylan playing his guitar in a darkened room did not exactly help move units at the peak of mid-1980s, Madonna-obsessed America. More to the point, the lyrics are pale, lacking the heart and depth of the pseudo-pop he was writing twenty years before. Compare its superficiality with, say, "Spanish Harlem Incident"—a song in a similar from-me-to-you vein from 1963—and see how far Dylan misses the mark as he hit middle age. That the word "baby" is used no less than eleven times in this single is some clue that Dylan left his rhyming dictionary in the glove compartment of his car.

Dylan's Bing Crosby–style performances of "Emotionally Yours" were first displayed on his 1986 and 1987 tours with Tom Petty and the Heartbreakers, where it packed some punch—but not much. In 1993 Dylan inserted the song into a trio of Never Ending Tour set lists with somewhat more interesting, down-to-earth results.

Ⓐ *Empire Burlesque*

Columbia Records LP FC 40110, CD CK-40110, CS FCT-40110. Recorded July–August, 1984, New York City; November 1984–January 1985, Los Angeles; February–March 1985, New York City. Released May 27, 1985. No producer credited (Arthur Baker is credited with remixing the album).

Bob Dylan—guitar, harmonica, keyboards, vocals. Al Kooper—guitars, horn, keyboards. Mick Taylor—guitar. Ron Wood—guitar. Mike Campbell—guitar, vocals. Jim Keltner—drums. Bashiri Johnson—percussion. Benmont Tench—piano, keyboards. Peggi Blu—background vocals. Debra Byrd—vocals, background vocals. Alan Clark—synthesizer, keyboards. Carolyn Dennis—background vocals. Queen Esther Morrow—background vocals. Madelyn Quebec—vocals. Sly Dunbar—percussion, drums. Howie Epstein—bass, vocals. Anton Fig—drums. Bob Glaub—bass. Don Heffington—drums. Ira Ingber—guitar. Stuart Kimball—guitars. Syd McGuinness—guitar. Vince Melamed—synthesizer. John Paris—bass. Ted Perlman—guitar. Richard Scher—synthesizer. Robbie Shakespeare—bass. Urban Blight Horns—horns. David Watson—saxophone.

"Tight Connection to My Heart (Has Anybody Seen My Love?)," "Seeing the Real You at Last," "I'll Remember You," "Clean-Cut Kid," "Never Gonna Be the Same Again," "Trust Yourself," "Emotionally Yours," "When the Night Comes Falling from the Sky," "Something's Burning, Baby," "Dark Eyes"

Using Tom Petty, the Heartbreakers, and an all-star cast of studio cats to stoke the embers of his slow-burning pop rock, Dylan visits his electric roots and earlier soul influences in this powerful, much-overlooked, and usually disparaged offering. With stinging guitars, a rousing female gospel-style chorus that enhances rather than drowns Dylan's trademark vocals, and a solid collection of songs, *Empire Burlesque* tried to pick up where *Infidels*, his previous effort, left off. Even to the casual ear, though, the album suffers from a glitzy remix by dance-music poo-bah Arthur Baker. Perhaps because the remixing obscures the strength of the songs, the album tanked, making it only as high as No. 33 on the charts, where it stayed for a mere six weeks.

The problem with *Empire Burlesque* is indeed that some very good songs are masked and marred by high-tech recording flash; quite possibly, state-of-the-art studio techniques do not work at all for an artist whose oeuvre never has or will lend itself to such an approach. Or maybe Dylan's haphazard bicoastal recording schedule and musician-shuffling indecisiveness marred the affair—certainly a harbinger of mediocre albums to come over the next few years. Whatever the reason, it's a shame that some of these songs are forgotten in discussions

E

Humphrey Bogart as Sam Spade holding the Maltese Falcon, 1941.
(Photo: Warner Brothers/Courtesy of Getty Images)

of Dylan's best work of the 1980s. From the stately, solo acoustic ("Dark Eyes"), to gospel rave ("Tight Connection to My Heart"), to rock reckoning ("Seeing the Real You at Last"), to torch song ("I'll Remember You"), lone wolf on the prowl ("Something's Burning, Baby"), and one semi-epic ("When the Night Comes Falling from the Sky"), *Empire Burlesque* contained not only some genuine standouts, but also songs that had their sometimes sustained glory days in the concert sun. But there were enough truly dreadful clinkers to raise the hackles of any sane critic. Fillers like "Trust Yourself," "Never

Gonna Be the Same Again," and throwaway rock like "Clean-Cut Kid" sounded stilted in 1985 and have not aged well, to say the least.

One of the more bizarre, yet surprisingly cogent, interpretations regarding *Empire Burlesque* was put forth by John Lindley in his article "Movies Inside His Head: *Empire Burlesque* and *The Maltese Falcon*," published in *The Telegraph* #23 (spring 1986). Lindley makes a serious (and humorous) case for about ten lines from various songs on the album being lifted from films as varied as Bogart's *The Maltese Falcon* and *Key Largo* to Clint Eastwood's *Bronco Billy*.

[S] "The End of the Innocence" (Don Henley/Bruce Hornsby)

Don Henley, *End of the Innocence* (1989)
John Tesh, *Sax by the Fire* (1994)
Livingston Taylor, *Ink* (1997)

As the winds of war again blew between the U.S. and Iraq in the early fall of 2002, it seemed only fitting that Dylan (laying down the riffs on the eighty-eights) should begin dispensing a version of the postnostalgic Don Henley/Bruce Hornsby ode to the dysfunction of the Reagan era, perhaps as a parable of his feelings about the Bush administration. The song includes lyrics like "O beautiful for spacious skies/But now those skies are threatening/They're beating plowshares into swords/For the tired old man we elected king." For many this song of disillusionment was a well-timed choice, given the anxious geopolitics of the moment.

Steeped in the metaphor implied in the title, "The End of the Innocence" captures a moment when the micro and macro collide, signaling a personal and generational turning of a page. On a first listen, the song—perhaps heard on the radio while you're driving down an interstate highway—is singable yet forgettable, the very definition of middle-of-the-road classic rock. Whatever profundity the composition strives for vanishes before the next tune on the FM dial hits its chorus.

But leave it to Dylan to perform the song as if he'd written it himself. In a 2002 concert in Philadelphia, he invested more nuance and passion in his delivery than a casual listener might think was possible within the folds of the song. In Dylan's hands, "The End of the Innocence" became an anthem of woe and compromise, a badge of bitterness won by years of experience. Hammering away at the piano, he coaxed out every ounce of pathos he knew the song could offer.

[S] "End of the Line" (Traveling Wilburys)

Traveling Wilburys, single (1988); *Traveling Wilburys, Volume 1* (1988)

Dylan's involvement with this sanguine song of impending mortality seems to be pretty minimal. He contributes backing vocal and perhaps a little guitar to "End of the Line," which peaked at No. 63 as a single on the *Billboard* charts. A passable video was produced for MTV and similar media outlets.

Sadly, the song's title and catchphrase worked as a dark prophecy: it was the last song Roy Orbison released during his lifetime.

[S] "Enough Is Enough" (Bob Dylan)

One of those strange Dylan songs that appear for a tour—in this case for nine shows on the '84 European tromp as a midconcert electric plaint—and go as quickly as they came. An ornery Chicago blues in the "get out of my life, woman" mode, "Enough Is Enough" steals the "nickel is a nickel, dime is a dime" line from any one of a number of rough-and-ready 12-bar constructs composed from the time Wall Street laid an egg. The song was, apparently, never copyrighted by Dylan.

[A] *The Essential Bob Dylan*

Columbia CD 85168; CS 85168. Released October 31, 2000. Photography by David Gahr, Ken Regan, Jerry Schatzberg.
"Blowin' in the Wind," "Don't Think Twice, It's All Right," "The Times They Are A-Changin'," "It Ain't Me Babe," "Maggie's Farm," "It's All Over Now, Baby Blue," "Mr. Tambourine Man," "Subterranean Homesick Blues," "Like a Rolling Stone," "Positively 4th Street," "Just Like a Woman," "Rainy Day Women #12 & 35," "All Along the Watchtower," "The Mighty Quinn (Quinn, the Eskimo)," "I'll Be Your Baby Tonight," "Lay Lady Lay," "If Not for You," "I Shall Be Released," "You Ain't Goin' Nowhere," "Knockin' on Heaven's Door," "Forever Young," "Tangled Up in

Blue," "Shelter from the Storm," "Hurricane," "Gotta Serve Somebody," "Jokerman," "Silvio," "Everything Is Broken," "Not Dark Yet," "Things Have Changed"

This two-disc set, released with holiday season sales in mind, is a solid collection for the casual Dylan fan—the kind of set one might put together for one's parents to give them an idea of what the fuss is all about without scaring them off too quickly. There are no tracks for collectors, and no inner sanctum Dylan songs made the cut, but for those looking for most of the classics in one neat place, *The Essential Bob Dylan* is a good first stop.

ⒶThe Essential Steve Goodman
Buddha Records LP BDS-5665-7. Released 1974.

Using the tongue-in-cheek moniker of Robert Milkwood Thomas for contractual purposes (think Dylan Thomas's *Under Milk Wood*), Dylan plays piano and sings on Goodman's "Election Year Rag," which Buddha Records also released as a seven-inch single.

Steve Goodman (born July 25, 1948, Chicago; died September 20, 1984, Seattle) was a Windy City–based singer-songwriter who recorded some top-notch albums for Buddha, Asylum, and his own Red Pajamas Records. These, as well as his most famous song, "The City of New Orleans" (a hit for Arlo Guthrie and recorded by many others, including Willie Nelson), have lived on after his premature death from leukemia.

After some early notoriety on the Chicago folk scene, this engaging artist was first spotted by Kris Kristofferson, who secured him a deal with Buddha through, of all people, Paul Anka, the schmaltzy '60s lounge king. In turn, Goodman set the wheels in motion for his friend John Prine to get a deal with Atlantic. But while Prine's career took off, Goodman remained a

cult figure, better known for his songs and influence than his commercial success.

Somebody Else's Troubles was Goodman's sophomore Buddha release and included contributions from David Bromberg, Bob Dylan, and members of the Rascals. The album did not chart, but in a new contract with Asylum, Goodman retained the right to produce his next two albums, *Jessie's Jig and Other Favorites* (1975) and *Words We Can Dance To* (1976). Low-profile outings continued, but the leukemia—from which Goodman had been suffering since the early 1970s—began to catch up with him. Nevertheless, he formed his Red Pajamas label and released *Artistic Hair*, a live collection covering ten years of his performances. In the image on the album sleeve, Goodman is almost bald from the chemotherapy he was receiving.

Steve Goodman finally succumbed to kidney and liver failure following a bone marrow transplant. His beloved Chicago Cubs were about to clinch the National League East title (and lose it in dramatic, typically buffoonish and heartbreaking fashion to the San Diego Padres in the playoffs), and his posthumously released musical epitaph, "A Dying Cub Fan's Last Request," symbolizes the bittersweet heart and soul of its composer, a neglected American original.

⒮"Eternal Circle" (Bob Dylan)
Bob Dylan, *The Bootleg Series, Volumes 1–3: Rare and Unreleased, 1961–1991/*'63 (1991)
Coulson, Dean, McGuinness, Flint, *Lo & Behold* (1972)
Michel Montecrossa and the Chosen Few, *Eternal Circle* (1999)
Various Artists (performed by Coulson, Dean, McGuinness, Flint), *Doin' Dylan 2* (2002)

As the title implies, "Eternal Circle" is a somewhat repetitive, *A Thousand and One Arabian Nights*–style Chinese box of a song. An outtake

E

from *The Times They Are A-Changin'*, it was later released on *The Bootleg Series, Volumes 1–3*. Dylan wrote "Eternal Circle" in the spring of 1963, recorded it at a couple of formal and informal studio sessions between then and October of that year, and performed it during his spring 1964 tour. In 1989 it was one of dozens of numbers rehearsed (but never performed) by the Never Ending Tour band.

Purporting to be a remembrance of a singer becoming aware of what he believes to be an enthralled young female audience member ("Through a bullet of light/Her face was reflectin'") during the gratingly long performance of a song, "Eternal Circle" is deceptively clever. As the singer continues, he convinces himself that the girl's intrigue is with him and not the song. Dylan neatly twists the tale at the song's conclusion when the singer looks up to see that the girl has disappeared. This deft artistic sleight of hand causes the entire episode to be reexperienced through the singing of the song, which has, over the course of the performance, become "Eternal Circle," a new song about the old song.

Ⓐ *Evening Concerts at Newport, Volume 1*/Various Artists
Vanguard Recording Society LP VRS-9148/VSD-79148. Released 1964; rereleased 1991.

Dylan performs "Blowin' in the Wind," then his most famous song, on this sampler from the 1963 Newport Folk Festival. In addition to Dylan, the album features a choice array of the era's best: Mississippi John Hurt ("See See Rider," "Stagolee," "Spike Driver Blues," and "Coffee Blues"), Ramblin' Jack Elliott ("Diamond Joe"), the Rooftop Singers ("Walk Right In"), Ian and Sylvia ("Un Canadien Errant"), and Joan Baez ("Oh, Freedom," "Te Ador," and

"Wagoner's Lad"). Dylan also joins the event's main attractions for the de rigueur finale, "We Shall Overcome."

⒮ "Everybody's Movin'" (Glen Glenn)
Glen Glenn, *Glen Glenn Story* (1982)
Brian Setzer, *Stray Cat Strut* (1997)

Dylan broke out this obscure slice of rockabilly five times as an encore in the early phases of the Never Ending Tours of 1988, 1989, and 1990.

Glen Glenn (born Glen Troutman, October 24, 1934, Joplin, Missouri) was one of the many talented singers of the 1950s who did not attain the success for which he seemed destined. After his family relocated to San Dimas, California, in 1947, Glenn started playing guitar and met Gary Lambert, another hot local guitar hero, in high school. Country music fans, they started jamming and, by 1952, were taking their first fitful stabs at making it in the music business.

Billing themselves as "Glen and Gary—The Missouri Mountain Boys," they enjoyed their first success in country music in 1952 when they won a talent spot on a radio program called the *Squeakin' Deacon Show*, began to make the Southern California bar circuit, and, in 1956, toured Missouri and the other states around the Ozarks with Glenn's cousin Porter Wagoner (who one day would become a great country star). This very successful swing won them spots on such TV shows as *Ozark Jubilee* and *Circle 7 Jamboree*. Back home again in California later in the year, Glenn joined the Maddox Brothers. But as the new rockabilly craze swept the country, Glenn was intrigued by its possibilities when mixed with his style; he cut a couple of demos and eventually landed a record deal with ERA Records in 1958. "Everybody's Moving" was his first release and he followed up its minor success with "Laurie Ann" and his biggest hit, "One Cup of Coffee." But Glenn was drafted just as he gained success and was never able to match it upon his discharge. In 1964 he released his last single and, tired with touring, quit music to take a day job with General Dynamics and raise a family. Since the late 1980s, when his work became repopularized in Europe, Glenn has enjoyed a modest renaissance. Along with Dylan, "Everybody's Movin'" has been performed by Bruce Springsteen, Neil Young, and Tom Petty.

▣ "Every Grain of Sand" (Bob Dylan)

Bob Dylan, *Shot of Love* (1981); *Biograph/*'81 (1985); *The Bootleg Series, Volumes 1–3: Rare and Unreleased, 1961–1991/*'80 (1991)
Various Artists (performed by Bob Dylan), *Another Day in Paradise* (soundtrack) (1996)
Nana Mouskouri, *Song for Liberty* (1982)
Giant Sand, *Swerve* (1990)
Willie Hona, *Keep an Open Heart* (1991)
Emmylou Harris, *Wrecking Ball* (1995)
Various Artists (performed by Magnapop), *Outlaw Blues, Volume 2* (1995)
Rich Lerner and the Groove, *Cover Down* (2000)
Barb Jungr, *Every Grain of Sand: Barb Jungr Sings Bob Dylan* (2002)
Barbara Sfraga, *Under the Moon* (2003)

A portrait of isolation, desolation, and failure—a spiritual confession in "the hour of my deepest need"—"Every Grain of Sand" is one of Dylan's most moving and impassioned testaments. Given this spirituality and depth, it is interesting that many saw in "Every Grain of Sand" a hint that Dylan's religious period was ending rather than its probable place as a reflection of the artist's inner soul journey: a retreat from evangelism. Offering himself consolation in the song's biblical reassurance that "every hair is numbered" and sensing "a perfect, finished plan," the narrator of this monumental classic concluding the *Shot of Love* album convinces himself that such knowledge is reward enough for the pains of mortal existence.

A publishing demo recorded with Dylan on piano and Jennifer Warnes on shared vocals, complete with Dylan's dog barking in the room, was included on *The Bootleg Series, Volumes 1–3.*

William Blake's poem "Auguries of Innocence," with its simple perception of God's existence in all things, has been cited as an influence for "Every Grain of Sand," with scholars pointing to the song's lines, "I can see the master's hand/in every of grain of sand." Blake is also invoked in the doubts encountered on life's journey when Dylan sings that he hears the "ancient footsteps" betraying the presence of God—or his own demons, for "other times it's only me." A statement of assured faith this is not.

Dylan wastes no time in getting to the heart of his hymn to himself and, by extension, man's eternal dilemma. Clearly, Dylan is a broken man as the curtain rises at a most humbling moment. He has confessed "in the hour of my deepest need," his feet soaked in the tears he has shed for all the sins of his impure soul and misdeeds. The big epiphany has hit him and hit hard: "Like Cain, I now behold this chain of events that I must break." And he finally recognizes that the evil lurking in the shadows of the self are just waiting to rise up and snare even the earnest and introspective would-be saints. As in much of the balance of Dylan's gospel songs, the author engages in the awkward, forever irreconcilable waltz with the angels and demons within.

E

E

Verse two finds the singer trapped in an overgrown garden of the damaged soul. Sure, he had his good times long ago and far away, indulged in the fruits that life offered. But now the bloom is off the rose, the scent of the one-night stands and fine wine long faded from memory. As the weeds of symbol and reality that surround and threaten to choke him mock his decay, he appears to recount his conversion: "The sun beat down upon the steps of time to light the way." But first he must pass "the door-way of temptation's angry flame" knowing full well that he is his own worst enemy despite always hearing his own name emanating from the fiery furnace. Yet he perseveres "onward in his journey," grasping in some small way his part in the mosaic of creation: "that every hair is numbered like every grain of sand."

Dylan pulls it together in the third and final verse, obliquely ruminating on the swift sweep of unlikely events that have taken him not just from "rags to riches" but to this very important moment. Now, coming out the other end, he is primed to receive the grand revelation that may or may not arrive. He hears "the ancient foot-steps like the motion of the sea" all right, but when he attempts to catch a glimpse, however fleeting, of that thief in the night, nothing is revealed: "Sometimes I turn, there's someone there, other times it's only me." The face of God is M.I.A. but his fingerprint may not be. We're left, Dylan included, as it always seems to have been: "hanging in the balance of the reality of man"—or, as rendered in the version on *The Bootleg Series, Volumes 1–3,* "in the balance of a perfect finished plan."

Dylan has performed stellar, always soul-rending versions of "Every Grain of Sand" on a nearly annual but usually rare basis since 1981.

A final note: Sheryl Crow sang "Every Grain of Sand" at Johnny Cash's funeral.

◨ "Everything Is Broken" (Bob Dylan)

Bob Dylan, single (1989); *Oh Mercy* (1989)
Tim O'Brien, *Red on Blonde* (1996)
Kenny Wayne Shepherd, *Trouble Is* (1998)
Various Artists (performed by R. L. Burnside), *Tangled Up in Blues: The Songs of Bob Dylan* (1999)
Various Artists (performed by R. L. Burnside), *Big Bad Love* (soundtrack) (1999)

"Everything Is Broken," an insistent litany of dislocation denouncing the corruption of the secular world—a rollicking catalogue of psychic chaos—is the kind of apocalyptic shuffle Dylan could write in a cab ride. And who knows, maybe he did. He sings the song, with its brooding air of solemnity punctuated by a slashing harmonica call at the end of each verse, like a sentinel at the gates of civilization.

For biblical roots, Dylan may have been drawing on Isaiah 24:19, which reads, "The earth is utterly broken down, the earth is clean dissolved, the earth is moved exceedingly." Or maybe he just cut himself shaving the day he came up with the lyric.

In "Tangled Up in Jews," his article published in *On the Tracks* #22 (February 15, 2002), Martin Grossman offered a distinctly Old Testament interpretation of "Everything Is Broken" with the following observation: "In 'Everything Is Broken' he seems to be speaking of a world of shattered vessels in need of repair that echoes the Lurianic *Kabbalah* (the Kabbalah is the 'received tradition of Jewish mysticism'—the Lurianic Kabbalah, which includes a theology of the broken vessels of creation, refers to the teachings of sixteenth-century Rabbi Isaac Luria who lived in the ancient mystical center of Safad in Israel)."

In what has to rate as one of the more bizarre inclusions of a Dylan song in a film, a snippet of "Everything Is Broken" appeared in *Country Bears,* the 2002 reel (think the Blues

Brothers with Bears for eight-year-olds). Though not included on the soundtrack album, the song is played during the scene when the bad guy (Christopher Walken) smashes a model of "Country Bear Hall"—a Disneyfied notion of the Grand Ole Opry.

Dylan began performing this spunky end-days invective soon after its release in 1989, kept it in heavy rotation in the early 1990s, and let it air out for a while before returning it for the odd outing as the millennia switched and every year or so thereafter.

F

■ **"Farewell"** (Bob Dylan)
aka "Fare Thee Well"
Various Artists (performed by Pete Seeger), *Broadside Ballads, Volume 2: Songs from* Broadside *Magazine* (1963); *We Shall Overcome: The Complete Carnegie Hall Concert* (1989)
Judy Collins, *Judy Collins #3* (1963); *Recollections* (1969)
Anita Carter, *Anita Carter of the Carter Family* (1963)
The Limelighters, *Leave It to the Limelighters* (1964)
Linda Mason, *How Many Seas Must a White Dove Sail?* (1964)
Martin Yarborough, *Mixed Moods* (1964)
Dorinda Duncan, *The Songs of Bob Dylan Through the Heart of a Girl* (1965)
The Golden Gate Strings, *The Bob Dylan Songbook* (1965)
Joe and Eddie, *Joe and Eddie "Live" in Hollywood* (1965)
The Kingston Trio, *The Kingston Trio: Nick—Bob—John* (1965)
The Modern Folk Quartet, *Changes* (1965)
The Saxons, *Love Minus Zero* (1966)
Christine Smith, *Master* (1966)
Dion with The Wanderers, *Wonder Where I'm Bound* (1968); *I Shall Be Unreleased/'68* (1991)
Julie Felix, *The World Goes Round and Round* (1968)
The Hillmen, *The Hillmen* (1970)
Nana Mouskouri, *Turn on the Sun* (1974)

Liam Clancy, *The Dutchman* (1982)
Tony Rice, *Cold on the Shoulder* (1984)
Michel Montecrossa, *Jet Pilot* (2000)
Various Artists (performed by Lonnie Donegan), *I Shall Be Unreleased: The Songs of Bob Dylan* (1991)

Despite claims to the contrary, Dylan does have an inner nostalgia merchant to which he has, periodically, fallen victim. He proves it with "Farewell," a tale of love lost to wanderlust that is an outtake from *The Times They Are A-Changin'*. The song began life in early 1963 as a poem entitled "Fare Thee Well" or "Fare-The-Well (My Own True Love)" and was copyrighted through a Witmark demo (Witmark was Dylan's publishing company at the time), its publication in *Broadside* magazine #24 (April 1963), and in the October/November 1963 issue of *Sing Out!* magazine. "Leaving Liverpool," an English folk song recorded by Judy Collins as well as by the Clancy Brothers, may have been an influence in both tune and theme; the first line of "Leaving Liverpool" also showed up as the first line of Dylan's "Boots of Spanish Leather." Because of the song's similarity to "Leaving Liverpool," many considered Dylan's "Farewell" more an adaptation than an original composition.

Dylan has never released "Farewell" officially on any records, and his performance of the song, broadcast in April 1963 on Studs Terkel's *Wax Museum* radio show on Chicago's WFMT, would appear to be the closest thing we are likely to get of a public display via recording.

■ **"Farewell, Angelina"** (Bob Dylan)
Bob Dylan, *The Bootleg Series, Volumes 1–3: Rare and Unreleased, 1961–1991/'65* (1991)
Joan Baez, *Farewell, Angelina* (1965); *The First 10 Years* (1970)
Jack's Angels, *Believe in a Word* (1966)

Nana Mouskouri, *The Most Beautiful Songs* (1967)
Judy Nash, *The Night They Drove Old Dixie Down* (1972)
New Riders of the Purple Sage, *Oh, What a Mighty Time* (1975); *I Shall Be Unreleased/'75* (1991)
The Original Marauders, *Now Your Mouth Cries Wolf: A Tribute to Bob Dylan* (1977)
Steve Keene, *Keene on Dylan* (1990)
Various Artists (performed by Jeff Buckley/Gary Lucas: Gods and Monsters), *They Came, They Played, They Blocked the Driveway: Live Music from the Studios of WFMU* (1993)
Tim O'Brien, *Red on Blonde* (1996)
John Mellencamp, *Rough Harvest* (1999)
Ulf Lundell, *Sweethearts* (2000)

"Farewell, Angelina" eluded even the most fervent Dylan tape collectors to the point that for years it was assumed that he never did sing it while the reel-to-reels were rolling. He did, however, and Dylan's own version of this wistful 1965 ballad finally surfaced with the release of *The Bootleg Series, Volumes 1–3* in 1991.

Marking another step in the transition from "finger-pointing" songs to the surreal, symbolic lyrics that would characterize the moody, atmospheric compositions from this vital period of his career, "Farewell, Angelina" is a key work in Dylan's catalogue—a kind of missing link that hints at the slowly fomenting future. Seemingly random visual images pepper this beautiful song full of sadness and resignation as Dylan moves away from literal storytelling and into a more abstract realm. Like "It's Alright, Ma" and "Hard Rain," it uses incremental repetition to establish a motif while key verb changes in the final lines of verses paint a picture of urgency. Dylan once referred to this technique as "a chain of flashing images," as recounted in Robert Shelton's book *No Direction Home: The Life and Music of Bob Dylan* (New York: Beech Tree Books/William Morrow, 1986). "Chimes of Freedom"

and "Mr. Tambourine Man" are other early examples of this poetic exploration inspired by his study of the French symbolist poet Arthur Rimbaud's *Illuminations*. With his later "It's All Over Now, Baby Blue" (a cousin to "Farewell, Angelina") and "Desolation Row" (in which the cross-eyed pirates, King Kong, and time-bomb-nailing fiends from "Farewell, Angelina" would feel most comfortable), Dylan would pursue this muse to breathtaking extremes. Even phrases like "Just a table standing empty by the edge of the sea," or suggestions that the sun could be ashamed or the sky embarrassed, stand out as just a few of the series of dream-word pictures Dylan was later so facilely and farcically able to string together for whole albums like *Blonde on Blonde*.

Still, while the song's lyrics act as a kind of signpost to Dylan's future artifice, the melody is firmly rooted in the past. Indeed, it's pretty much the unaltered tune to "The Wagoner's Lad," a song Joan Baez was regularly singing at the time and that Dylan would later include as an occasional offering during his Never Ending Tour acoustic sets.

"Farewell, Angelina" was the first of two Angelina songs Dylan composed. He returned to this mysterious muse with a prayer song, "Angelina," in the 1980s.

The sole, chilling version of Dylan singing the song contains the addition of a previously unknown verse. That Dylan dropped his pick on the recording, forcing him to strum the final bars, has led some to speculate that this flaw was the reason the song wasn't released initially.

▣ "Farewell to the Gold" (Paul Metsers)
Paul Metsers, *Caution to the Wind* (1981)
Nic Jones, *Penguin Eggs* (1980)
Gordon Bok, *All Shall Be Well* (1983)

Schooner Fare, *Signs of Home* (1990)
Black Family, *Time for Touching Home* (1990)

At one memorable 1992 concert in Youngstown, Ohio—a town snuggled, appropriately enough, in the heart of the working-class Rust Belt, Dylan took a gallant stab at "Farewell to the Gold," a modern miner's lament that sounds like an old traditional song, which he sang from the point of view of a New Zealand miner who realizes his stake has been bled dry. Though his band didn't do too much with the tune, Dylan's forceful vocal performance carried the day.

A sister in song to Merle Travis's "Dark as a Dungeon," another miner's moan that has been in and out of Dylan's set lists since the 1975 Rolling Thunder Revue, "Farewell to the Gold" was penned by Paul Metsers (not Metzers, as listed in some discographies), a New Zealand folk musician (he plays guitar and dulcimer) and composer of some cult renown. Metsers's work often espouses the causes of the Green Party, the leftist, environmentally slanted, antiglobalization political movement. A move to Great Britain saw Metsers singing full-time on the English folk circuit through the 1980s, but more recently he has settled in Great Britain's Lake District, where he is in business as a maker of finely crafted traditional wooden board games. Dylan almost assuredly gained exposure to the song through the Nic Jones rendition on the 1980 album *Penguin Eggs*.

In a summer 2003 e-mail I received from Metsers, he told me this:

> I did know about Dylan doing "Farewell to the Gold," in fact, I was sent a cassette recording of it which was very interesting. Judging by his version I would say he heard the song on Nic Jones's album *Penguin Eggs* but credits neither Nic nor me during the performance. This doesn't bother me but I would no doubt feel differently if he had recorded the song. I was born in Noordwijk, Netherlands, on 27 November, 1945. My mother and stepfather emigrated to New Zealand in '52 and so I grew up there. I've lived in England since 1980 and worked as a professional musician (singer-songwriter) until 1989, recording 5 LPs during that time. They are: *Caution to the Wind, Momentum, In the Hurricane's Eye, Pacific Pilgrim,* and *Fifth Quarter.*
>
> "Farewell" . . . is about a genuine event—a flash flood which claimed the lives of scores of goldminers on the Shotover River in the province of Otago, New Zealand, in July of 1863. The characters are inventions of mine.

[S] "Father of Night" (Bob Dylan)

Bob Dylan, *New Morning* (1970)
Julie Felix, *Lightning* (1974)
Manfred Mann, *Solar Fire* (1974)
Tim O'Brien, *Red on Blonde* (1996)
Various Artists (performed by First Ladies), *Duluth Does Dylan* (2001)

A piano song with serious overtones of Christianity written and recorded well before Dylan's so-called born-again phase, "Father of Night" might have given its composer a preview of how others would receive this type of material.

The song was inspired, indirectly, by Archibald MacLeish's musical play *Scratch*, based on Stephen Vincent Benét's popular 1937 short story "The Devil and Daniel Webster." A theater producer roped Dylan into the project and he began to write some songs based on the play, including "New Morning," "Time Passes Slowly," and "Father of Night." But things did not go smoothly when Dylan met with MacLeish, songs in hand. As described in the *Biograph* liner notes, Dylan reported that he played the songs to MacLeish "and he liked them all. He thought they would fit perfectly until we got to 'Father of Night.' We didn't see eye to eye on that so I backed out of the production. . . . It was nothing really, kind of like a misunderstanding I suppose. Anyway, I took those songs and some others and recorded *New Morning*."

Regardless of its history, "Father of Night" remains a mysterious Dylan hymn as he reaches toward both the first member of the Holy Trinity and the dark unknown within that may sometimes relinquish a truth or two after the sun sets. Dylan's God here is an intuitive one, however—something quite apart from the logical, sometimes wrathful presence that would hover over *Slow Train Coming* and the like during Dylan's religious period.

⊠ *Feeling Minnesota* (soundtrack)/Various Artists
Atlantic CD 82865, CS 82865. Released 1996.

Dylan's spin on the once-you've-heard-it-you-can-never-get-it-out-of-your-head Johnny Cash classic "Ring of Fire" is one of the few items to recommend either this soundtrack album, with the eclectic likes of the Temptations, Helmet, Nancy Sinatra, Wilco, Son Volt, and Los Lobos on board (marketed to those who fancy themselves hip Gen X-ers), or the film for which it was recorded. The latter is a barely decipherable, dying-to-be-edgy, wannabe black-comedy slapstick caper directed by Steven Baigelman and starring Keanu Reeves and Cameron Diaz, with a host of cameos from Courtney Love, Tuesday Weld, Dan Aykroyd, and others.

⊠ "Female Rambling Sailor" (Traditional)
Ian Robb, *Rose & Crown* (1985)
Rude Girls, *Rude Awakening* (1992)
Rich Lerner, *Trails and Bridges* (1996)
Dave & Toni Arthur, *Morning Stands* (1998)

In the tradition of "Jack-A-Roe," "Canadee-I-O," or *Mulan*, "Female Rambling Sailor" concerns a young woman whose husband is pressed into naval service and dies in a foreign sea. She then dons men's clothing in order to join the military.

As happens in many of these songs, which were extremely common in the great age of sailing, the woman, after an act of heroism, dies in battle or from an accident on shipboard, whereupon her true identity is discovered. The phenomenon was so widespread in early eighteenth-century England that it is conjectured that the number of women dressed as men in the British army could have been sufficient to have formed their own battalions. That the high seas were similarly infiltrated is undeniable. Two such women, Mary Read of England and Anne Bonny of Ireland, became famous in 1720 when they were arrested with Calico Jack Rackam's pirates and put on trial in Jamaica. While the men were hanged, these two won clemency due to pregnancy and were jailed instead. It turned out that Read had disguised herself as a man to enlist in the British Navy when she was fifteen, gone to sea in a man-o'-war, and battled the French in Flanders as a member of the cavalry and infantry. These types of stories certainly passed into the lore and soon into songs like "Female Rambling Sailor."

Given that Dylan began singing the obscure British ballad "Female Rambling Sailor" onstage around the same time he released his *Good as I Been to You* album of traditional cover songs, it's surprising that he chose instead to record "Canadee-I-O," which has a similar theme.

Dylan has performed "Female Rambling Sailor" in concert only twice, at consecutive Australian dates in 1992.

⧉ *Festival*
Directed by Murray Lerner. Released 1967.

Short hair and cigarettes, horn-rims and chinos, clean-cut beatniks and older hipsters on the cusp of Flower Power. The sixties before *The Sixties*. The times might have been changing but Bob Dylan morphs from the fresh-scrubbed kid from his early album covers to an impish electric trickster before your very eyes.

This is the scene filmmaker Murray Lerner captured in 1963. An avid folk fan, Lerner thought he'd do a little shooting at the Newport Folk Festival during an early visit, but as he came back over the next couple of years, and the filming became more and more serious, he realized that he'd compiled a priceless record of the heyday of a unique American movement and caught for celluloid posterity some performances that had already become legendary: Peter, Paul & Mary ("Blowin' in the Wind," "The Times They Are A-Changin'"), Buffy Sainte-Marie ("Codeine"), Judy Collins ("Turn, Turn, Turn"), Mississippi John Hurt ("Candy Man"), Johnny Cash ("I Walk the Line"), Donovan ("Vietnam, Your Latest Game," which had been banned by the BBC), and an in-transition Dylan ("All I Really Want to Do" and "Mr. Tambourine Man" from 1964 and the electrified 1965 "Maggie's Farm"). Baez, Pete Seeger, Theo Bikel, Odetta, and Howlin' Wolf also make cameos in Lerner's Oscar-nominated film, which (along with Bert Stern's 1959 *Jazz on a Summer's Day* film of the 1958 Newport Jazz Festival) proved to be the great-granddaddy of all cinema vérité concert movies. Yet while it paved the way for *Monterey Pop*, *Don't Look Back*, and *Woodstock*, *Festival* (drawn exclusively from Lerner's 1964 and '65 sprocketed stash) itself got lost in the rock mania of the late 1960s, and received only a very small release. It is unfortunate, for as the *Hollywood Reporter* raved at the time: "*Festival* is one of the best documentary films in years and one of the best American films of the year. Deceptively simple in its presentation, but edited with an unfaltering eye and ear for commentary, it says more about American youth and shifting attitudes than a mountain of teenage-oriented exploitation films."

Don't look for it at Blockbuster.

⧉ "Final Theme" (Bob Dylan)
Bob Dylan, *Pat Garrett and Billy the Kid* (1973)

Brimming with an epic grandeur reminiscent of Dylan's best electric work, "Final Theme" is an instrumental recasting of "Knockin' on Heaven's Door," complete with harmonium, cellos, recorder, and flute. It is a good example of why one reviewer called the *Pat Garrett and Billy the Kid* soundtrack album "Dylan's mantra," presumably because of the music's sweet, repetitive lull. Critic Paul Nelson labeled the composition "Instrumental music so mythic that it's perfectly suitable for both weddings and funerals, births and rebirths, or whatever the essences are."

⧉ *First Blues*/Allen Ginsberg
John Hammond Records LP W2X-37673. Released 1983.

Recorded during the November 1971 Record Plant sessions in New York City, Beat poet Allen Ginsberg's *First Blues* features Dylan playing guitar and/or organ on "Vomit Express," "September on Jessore Road," and "Going to San Diego."

⧉ "Fixin' to Die" (Bukka White)
aka "Fixin' to Die Blues"
Bob Dylan, *Bob Dylan* (1962)
Bukka White, *The Complete Bukka White* (1994)

Dave Van Ronk, *Inside Dave Van Ronk* (1969)
John Koerner, Dave Ray, Tony Glover, *Lots More Blues, Rags & Hollers* (1964)
Buffy Sainte-Marie, *Many a Mile* (1965)
Col. Bruce Hampton, *Strange Voices* (1994)

Though he may also have been inspired by Dave Van Ronk, who was performing and recording "Fixin' to Die" when Dylan recorded it himself, Dylan probably learned this Bukka White special from one of White's albums. Yet while White's 1940 Okeh recording is almost hymnlike, Dylan jacked up the tempo and sang it with a growl that must have made him the best little twenty-year-old white blues imitator that side of Bleecker Street.

Even as a young man, Bukka White (born Booker T. Washington White, November 12, 1906, Houston, Mississippi [some sources claim 1909 in either Houston, Texas, or Aberdeen, Mississippi]; died February 26, 1977, Memphis) had a singular musical voice and guitar stylings that made him a favorite house-party musician. According to blues legend, White gave his young cousin, the future B. B. King, his first guitar. Between 1937 and 1940, White waxed his most memorable work on the Vocalian and Okeh labels: down-home country blues complete with the kind of harrowing, from-the-soul vocals and percussive guitar work that sounds like the kind of music a Zulu shaman might have been playing on a giant thumb piano six hundred years ago. Summoning deep mojo from his G-tuned National steel guitar, White combined beguiling, moody rhythms and chanted, hypnotic talking blues that might even be able to tame Robert Johnson's notorious hell hounds. He invites you into his life with firsthand reportage of the very bumpy road over which he traveled, be they rail-riding hobo travelogues or notes from Mississippi's infamous Parchman Farm, where he resided after he shot a man in the thigh in 1937.

Despite the "abandon all hope" reality of Parchman, White emerged from the sting of its whip unbowed. And if the recordings he made for Alan Lomax and the Library of Congress and the few meager stabs he made at returning to the stage when sprung from the prison's brick-oven-hot cell blocks failed to reignite his career, White was determined to walk the straight and narrow.

The recordings did circulate, though, and their power was not lost on people like Dylan and Buffy Sainte-Marie, whose recordings of "Fixin' to Die" inspired two students from the University of California, Berkeley (folk-blues guitarist John Fahey and blues aficionado Ed Dawson), to write to White in 1963. Addressing their letter to "Bukka White, blues singer, Aberdeen, Mississippi," they were, needless to say, stunned to receive White's written reply some weeks later. They were even more surprised when they actually met him. This was no weathered wisp ravaged by the physical and psychological cruelty of his environment they saw, but a robust man in his mid-fifties who had never stopped playing music.

There began "Bukka White, Act II," a career rejuvenation that took White to college campuses across the United States and to concert halls in Europe, as well as into the recording studio, where he cut several records of varying quality. By White's death he had, at least, enjoyed a deserved renaissance.

Joe MacDonald of Country Joe and the Fish picked up on the title of White's most famous song for the most famous "Fixin'-to-Die Rag," a snorting anti–Vietnam War rant.

Dylan's roiling "Fixin' to Die'" is flat-picked in an open D-modal tuning and commences with a bass slide or smear heard in many an ancient rough acoustic blues and later adopted by electric guitarists. Because "Fixin' to Die" appears on Dylan's debut LP and a few tapes from his first year or so in New York City (Carnegie Chapter Hall, November 4, 1961; First McKenzies' Tape, November/December 1961; *Folksinger's Choice* radio program, winter 1962), it is a pretty fair assumption that he was performing the song regularly during his early East Coast coffeehouse days, though no live performance recordings have surfaced.

⒜ *Flashback* (soundtrack)/Various Artists
WTG Records LP 46042, CD NK-46042. Released 1989.

Dylan contributed a new recording of Curtis Mayfield's "People Get Ready" (a song he had long toyed with) to *Flashback*, a screwball comedy starring Dennis Hopper and Kiefer Sutherland. In the film, Hopper plays a recently captured '60s-era, Abbie Hoffman–like political fugitive who has spent two decades underground, wanted for the crime of disrupting a Spiro Agnew rally. It's an Abbie Hoffman story–meets–*It's a Mad, Mad, Mad, Mad World* kind of thing.

⒮ "Floater (Too Much to Ask)" (Bob Dylan)
Bob Dylan, *"Love and Theft"* (2001)

With its charming banjo and fiddle lilt evoking vaudeville sentimentality and the Jazz Age, "Floater" comes off as a Hoagy Carmichael-esque swing-shuffle blues ballad that spotlights Dylan in pop crooner mode. Yet this veneer masks a darker tale of taboo, arson, strife, and escape. The narrator describes the summer idyll of fishing and goes on to allude to the evils lurking on the fringes of the small Southern town Carson McCullers–style. He's in love with his second cousin, the local muscle is out to intimidate him, he suggests that those burning trees over the hill were lit by his

match, and that his little raft will float him away to some kind of safety.

Despite the looming dangers, however, there are ample doses of wicked humor and sage wisdom laced throughout "Floater." One-linerish stuff about sitting near the teacher at school if one hopes to learn a thing or two and the narrator's take on *Romeo and Juliet* are delivered by Dylan in a manner that would make any Vegas comic proud.

And, speaking of the narrator, exactly who is this feral character ducking in and out of the song's shadows? Sometimes he sounds like Huck Finn or a wild adolescent black kid (like Jack Kerouac's Pic, the title character of his short novel published posthumously in 1971) playing hooky from a Memphis public school circa 1916. At other times he comes off like a juiced-up rounder staggering home after last call.

If the tune of "Floater" sounds familiar, it may be because Dylan seems to have lifted it hook, line, and sinker from "Snuggled on Your Shoulders," an early 1930s Guy Lombardo song recorded by everyone from Bing Crosby and Red Norvo to Tina Louise ("Ginger" from the 1960s TV series *Gilligan's Island*).

And if some of the lyrics of "Floater" seem familiar, it was one of the songs into which Dylan is said to have stuck phrases from an English translation of Dr. Junichi Saga's book *Confessions of a Yakuza: A Life in Japan's Underworld.* Dylan reshaped Saga's "My old man would sit there like a feudal lord" into "My old man, he's like some feudal lord/Got more lives than a cat." *Yakuza's* "'If it bothers you so much,' she'd say, 'why don't you just shove off?'" becomes "Juliet said back to Romeo, 'Why don't you just shove off if it bothers you so much.'" Saga's "I'm not as cool or forgiving as I might have sounded" becomes "I'm not quite as cool or forgiving as I sound/I've seen enough

F

heartache and strife" in Dylan's hands. And *Yakuza*'s "Tears or not, though, that was too much to ask" is remade into "Sometimes somebody wants you to give something up/And tears or not, it's too much to ask." There are several other instances of Dylan's loving and thieving from *Yakuza*, now not so obscure due to his crafty pillage.

Singing it with an insouciant glue-and-gravel old-time country drawl, Dylan introduced "Floater" as a mostly successful midset display during the fall 2001 Never Ending Tour in which he debuted the *"Love and Theft"* material, and there it stayed—marked by Frankie Koella's fiddle turn—through 2004, by which time Dylan's comfort zone with its loopy, interior rhyme schemes and layered story lines had improved markedly.

Ⓐ *Folk Duets*/Various Artists
Vanguard CD 795112. Released 1998.

Yet a new way to repackage the vintage, *Folk Duets* includes material from the 1963 Newport Folk Festival, including Dylan and Joan Baez ("It Ain't Me, Babe"), Dylan and Pete Seeger ("Ye Playboys and Playgirls"), Ian & Sylvia ("Four Strong Winds"), Mimi and Richard Fariña ("The Falcon"), Baez and Donovan ("Colours"), Baez and her sister Mimi Fariña ("Catch the Wind"), Geoff and Maria Muldaur ("Chevrolet"), Doc and Merle Watson ("San Antonio Rose"), Bob Gibson and Hamilton Camp ("Well, Well, Well"), Lester Flatt and Earl Scruggs ("Salty Dog Blues"), and Judy Collins and Theo Bikel ("The Greenland Whale Fisheries").

Ⓐ *Folk Hits*/Various Artists
Vanguard CD 79510. Released 1998.

Dylan and Baez shine on their oft-pressed "It Ain't Me, Babe" duet from the 1963 Newport Folk Festival. The usual suspects can be found here too: Ian & Sylvia ("Early Morning Rain," "The Circle Game," and more), Phil Ochs ("There but for Fortune"), Buffy Sainte-Marie ("The Universal Soldier"), Mimi and Richard Fariña ("Pack Up Your Sorrows"), Doc and Merle Watson ("Roll in My Sweet Baby's Arms"), Odetta ("He's Got the Whole World in His Hands"), and Ramblin' Jack Elliott (with Dylan's backup mouth harp on "Will the Circle Be Unbroken").

Ⓐ *Folkways: A Vision Shared—A Tribute to Woody Guthrie and Leadbelly*/Various Artists
Columbia Records LP OC-44034, CD CK-44034. Released 1988.

Dylan's solo acoustic guitar and vocal rendition of Woody Guthrie's "Pretty Boy Floyd" is just one of many highlights found on this tribute to Guthrie and Leadbelly. Really, there isn't a weak track here. Bruce Springsteen delivers a hard-bitten version of Guthrie's "I Ain't Got No Home," and U2 a spirited, gospel-inflected rendition of his "Jesus Christ"; Taj Mahal has his usual fun with Leadbelly's "Bourgeois Blues," while Little Richard does the same—as only he can—on "Rock Island Line." There is a lot to love about this record, and we haven't even mentioned the contributions made by Emmylou Harris ("Hobo's Lullaby"), Willie Nelson ("Philadelphia Lawyer"), John Mellencamp ("Do-Re-Mi"), Brian Wilson ("Goodnight Irene"), or Arlo Guthrie ("East Texas Red"). This is music that will never age.

The recording was a joint venture of the Smithsonian Institution and Columbia Records, and it marked the first time that contemporary musicians contributed their art to the national museum of the United States. Proceeds went to help in the purchase of historic recorded musical and archival treasures: the Folkways and Woody Guthrie Archives.

[S] "Folsom Prison Blues" (Johnny Cash)

Johnny Cash, *Johnny Cash at Folsom Prison* (1968)
Jerry Lee Lewis, *Killer Country* (1981)
Waylon Jennings, *Black on Black* (1982)
Gram Parsons, *Cosmic American Music* (1995)
Lester Flatt and Earl Scruggs, *1964–1969, Plus* (1996)

Written in 1954 and first recorded in 1956, Johnny Cash's "Folsom Prison Blues" is one of the Man in Black's signature songs. It was covered by Dylan and the Hawks (but unreleased) during the *Basement Tapes* sessions in 1967 and by Dylan during the May 1969 Nashville sessions that produced *Self Portrait*. Dylan also performed it during the Never Ending Tour from 1991 to 1993 and then again in 1999 in an arrangement that varied from the ho-hum to the percolating essence of Sun Records during its late '50s prime.

David Segal cut to the core of the song in his September 13, 2003, *Washington Post* article following Cash's death, writing that "Folsom Prison Blues" is "a song written in the mid-'50s about a killer and the senseless murder that has landed him behind bars. ('I shot a man in Reno, just to watch him die.') The unflinching violence sets up a fugue of melancholic regret. Cash's narrator knows, as he puts it, 'I had it coming, I know I can't be free.' He listens to a passing train, imagines the laughing swells in the dining car, and is tortured by his confinement. Like many of Cash's antiheroes, this one is a regular and redeemable man who failed catastrophically and must confront the consequences."

Cash was inspired to write the song after seeing a movie entitled *Inside the Walls of Folsom Prison* in 1953. Its popularity, he felt, came about "because most of us are living in one little kind of prison or another, and whether we know it or not the words of a song about someone who is actually in a prison speak for a lot of us who might appear not to be, but really are" (as quoted in Dorothy Horstman's *Sing Your Heart Out, Country Boy*; New York: E. P. Dutton, 1975).

Built of native stone in the late 1870s in central California, the all-too-real Folsom Prison was designed to be escape-proof. Indeed, very few convicts have transgressed its walls until their sentences were finished.

Dylan's deliveries of "Folsom Prison Blues" make you believe that he can actually make it over the wall. Perhaps his passion is a testament to his feelings about the song's composer: after a July 16, 1991, performance in Pittsburgh, Dylan proclaimed (as recorded on a concert tape of that event), "if [Cash] is not in the Rock and Roll Hall of Fame, there shouldn't be a Rock and Roll Hall of Fame."

[S] "A Fool Such as I" (Bill Trader)

aka "(Now and Then There's) A Fool Such as I"
Bob Dylan, single (1974); *Dylan* (1973)
Elvis Presley, *Elvis Aron Presley* (1961)
Jim Reeves, *Gentleman Jim* (1963)
Bobby Vinton, *Timeless* (1989)
Lou Rawls, *Love Songs* (1992)
Hank Snow, *Essential Hank Snow* (1997)

One of the more tolerable tracks on his otherwise dreadful *Dylan* album, "A Fool Such as I" is a song of fouled romance that epitomizes Obi-Wan Kenobi's *Star Wars* (1977) credo: "Who is more foolish? The fool or the fool who follows the fool?"

When Dylan first ran through the song with the Hawks during the *Basement Tapes* sessions in 1967, it was with more compelling results. The chorus on the official release is a bring-down and Dylan's singing style—a strange combination of Elvis Presley, cornpone, Vegas lounge lizard, and country-and-western hack—is distracting.

Though some sources suggest one "B. Abner" as the song's composer (an attribution included on www.bobdylan.com), most agree "A Fool Such as I" was written by Bill Trader in 1952 and recorded by Hank Snow later that year. Snow's recording rose to No. 4 on *Billboard*'s country chart. In early 1953 Jo Stafford, Tommy Edwards, and the Robins had their own versions of the song. Only Stafford's charted, hitting No. 20 on *Billboard*'s chart. Elvis recorded "A Fool Such as I" in June 1958 at RCA's Nashville studios while on leave from the army. His release peaked at No. 2 on *Billboard*'s Hot 10, all told spending fifteen weeks on the chart. On the R&B chart, the song hit No. 16, and it was No. 1 for five weeks in England and sold more than a million copies worldwide.

On the unreleased track from the sessions that produced *The Basement Tapes*, Dylan and the Hawks (later and more famously known as the Band) combine Hank Snow's casual style with Presley's spoken-word interlude to create a mischievous character who could either be testifying in church or making a pass at a floozy in some nickel-beer dive; Dylan's perfect timing transcends all uncertainty, leaving no doubt that whoever is being sung to will pick up the tab—at the very least.

F

[S] "Foot of Pride" (Bob Dylan)

Bob Dylan, *The Bootleg Series, Volumes 1–3: Rare and Unreleased, 1961–1991/'83* (1991)
Bob Dylan/Various Artists (performed by Lou Reed), *Bob Dylan: The 30th Anniversary Concert Celebration* (1993)
Michel Montecrossa, *Bob Dylan and Michel Fest* (2003)

A layered, enigmatic dirge originally intended for release on *Infidels*, "Foot of Pride" was one of a handful of exceptional pieces Dylan composed during a particularly fertile period in the early 1980s. Not only is it lyrically dense, but it also allows Dylan to show off what a deceptively good singer he is as he deftly handles the song's odd meter with casual ease.

A song that runneth over with biblical allusions, "Foot of Pride" is, as Terry Gans described it in his article "It Was Like a Revelation—Bob Dylan's 'Foot of Pride'" in *The Telegraph* #21 (summer 1983), one of those Dylan songs in which "the wicked are gonna get it; propaganda all is phony; and those who allow themselves to be manipulated by those who manipulate deserve what they get." Indeed, it's as if Dylan is combining the gray, conspiratorial "they" populating his mid-'60s work with the unrepentant vitriol of his gospel muse into an even more threatening vision of the world.

Few have attempted to decipher the complexities layering this song (Michael Gray did surgeon's work breaking it down in his book *Song and Dance Man III: The Art of Bob Dylan* (London and New York: Continuum International Publishing Group, 2000), but the primary warning here would seem to concern the perils of vanity. In issuing the warning, Dylan presents a dizzying series of nightmarish images that could have poured off the pages of Dante or the Bible (the Book of Daniel, Deuteronomy, Psalms), or been drawn from everyday clichés in its condemnation of charlatans who toy with what little faith humanity may still possess, philistines who abuse trust, prostitutes of the spirit and flesh who think little of manipulating the naïve in their quest for base power and riches, and bunco artists in bootleg Armani suits who profit from sin and spill their spare change on building "big universities to study in" as if to justify their avarice. Though the evil ones may seem as if they're prospering in the short run, the song insists that a price *will* be paid when "the hot iron blows" because, in true Book of Revelation style, "when the foot of pride comes down, there ain't no going back."

As for the many literary, biblical, and pop-culture references crammed into this bluesy six-stanza fugue, a brief glance at the song's first few lines alone should suffice to demonstrate how deeply Dylan can tangle up a lyric. The title itself delivers one right from Psalms 36:11 ("Let not the foot of pride come against me, and let not the hand of the wicked remove me") and then immediately goes to the Bible's story of Daniel in the lion's den for the song's initial ten words ("Like the lion tears the flesh off of a man"), recalling the Old Testament's battle royal between man and beast, and the beast within. Then, as if to emphasize the black humor here, Dylan's lyric mentions the singing of "Danny Boy" at somebody's (man's?) funeral—another backward glance at the Book of Daniel and a nod to the famous Irish drinking song. Musing on the deceased's passing ("It's like the earth just opened and swallowed him up"), Dylan keeps the Bible in the foreground with this line's references to Numbers 16:29–32 and Deuteronomy 11:6.

Dylan sings "Foot of Pride" like a one-eyed undertaker blowing a futile horn on a return trip to Desolation Row. Or maybe that was Hamlet contemplating the inevitability of death as he considered the Jester's grinning skull. But this time around the narrator appears a bit wiser and more cautious. When he introduces us to Red (a nickname and color that itself begs comparison with Satan), the crazed, drunken businessman who, instead of putting some bleachers out in the sun to promote the apocalypse (as he might have in "Highway 61 Revisited"), is now merely selling tickets to a plane crash, Dylan comes off as if he's met ten thousand "cash only" scoundrels just like him. As for messing with Red's girl for hire, Miss Delilah (a name obviously pointing to the corrupted princess who played Samson for a fool), Dylan implies that it's okay to look; just be sure not to touch. And, as in "Desolation Row" and other songs from his work of the mid-1960s, Dylan can't resist populating the irregularly rhyming death march with at least one icon from popular mythology, Errol Flynn, whose shady legacy (his weakness for underage girls and Nazis is well documented enough) fits in perfectly with this chilling shadow song.

The music, or lack thereof, for "Foot of Pride" is well chosen too: monotonously trundling forward and increasing in tempo like a horse-drawn funeral carriage traveling a country road as a thunderstorm quickly approaches from the west, with each lengthy verse punctuated at its gnawing conclusion with a clarion-sounding harmonica bleat. Additionally, and quite unusually, Dylan starts singing almost as soon as the song begins, underlining his sense of cocksure urgency as he raves. And did anyone ever sing the words "Oh yeah!", as Dylan does twice at the song's end, with such conviction? The "sky is falling" cry Chicken Little utters while running around the village square, "Foot of Pride" is most assuredly not.

Perhaps Dylan's angriest portrait of a present-day Babylon, "Foot of Pride" is scathing in its cold-eyed depiction of depravity. It is as if Dylan, back in 1983, just wanted to remind everyone that he still possessed the old prophetic visionary power that could hatch a song like this as easily as he could take a drag on a cheap cigar and blow its thick blue smoke in the Devil's face just for a laugh.

"Forever Young" (Bob Dylan)

Bob Dylan, *Planet Waves* (two versions) (1974); *Bob Dylan at Budokan* (1979); *Biograph/'73* (1985); *Bob Dylan's Greatest Hits, Volume 3* (1994)

Bob Dylan/The Band, *Before the Flood* (1974)

The Band (with Bob Dylan), *The Last Waltz* (1978); *High on the Hog* (1996)

Kitty Wells, *Forever Young* (1974)

Judy Nash, *Hommage à Bob Dylan* (1974)

Joan Baez, *From Every Stage* (1976); *Best of Joan Baez* (1977); *Rare, Live & Classic* (1993); *Greatest Hits* (1996); *The Essential Joan Baez: From the Heart (Live)* (2001)

Bonnie Bramlett, *Lady's Choice* (1976)

Peter, Paul & Mary, *Reunion* (1978)

Tony Wilson, *Catch One* (1979)

Dave Browning, *Forever Young* (1982)

Diana Ross, *Voice of Love* (1983)

Harry Belafonte, *Loving You Is Where I Belong* (1989)

Hothouse Flowers, single (1993)

The Pretenders, *Last of the Independents* (1994)

Red Hot + Country, *Red Hot + Country* (1994)

Trevor Lucas, *The Attick Tracks 1972–1984* (1995)

Tim O'Brien, *Red on Blonde* (1996)

Friend 'N Fellow, *Purple Rose* (1996)

Saving Grace, *Saving Grace* (1998)

Jimmy LaFave, *Trail* (1999)

Various Artists (performed by David West), *Pickin' on Dylan* (1999)

Rich Lerner & The Groove, *Cover Down* (2000)

Michel Montecrossa, *Born in Time* (2000)

Barb Jungr, *Every Grain of Sand: Barb Jungr Sings Bob Dylan* (2002)

Gerry Murphy, *Gerry Murphy Sings Bob Dylan* (2002)

Various Artists (performed by Bradley Brown), *Blowin' in the Wind: A Reggae Tribute to Bob Dylan* (2003)

"Forever Young" is Dylan's most famous and best loved lullaby—a rare, sentimental curio any parent would be happy to sing to an infant on the nod. The song is also something of an oddity in Bob Dylan's officially released output: one of a couple of compositions included *twice* on an album—in this case his 1974 LP *Planet Waves*. The first, better-known version is the one that rounds out the first side of the album, while the side-two version leads off with an energy and vitality that acts as an antidote for its predecessor. It is almost as if

Dylan was expressing two conflicting realities of parenthood. The speedier version contains all the unleashed affirmation a parent wishes for a child, blessing the attributes of the body and heart. The slower version, however, comes off as being sung by someone who not only knows that parental expectations can often exceed a child's abilities and are ultimately fruitless—that to give life means, paradoxically, also to give death. A third, officially released version of "Forever Young," on *Biograph*, is notable for its rawness; it was recorded into a cheap tape recorder at the office of Dylan's music publisher.

Dylan claims to have conceived "Forever Young" in Tucson, Arizona, and he confirmed its inspiration in the *Biograph* liner notes: "I wrote it thinking about one of my boys and not wanting to be too sentimental," he remembered. "The lines came to me, they were done in a minute. I don't know. Sometimes that's what you're given. You're given something like that."

"Forever Young" was a favorite during Dylan's 1974 tour with the Band, and Dylan returned to it at his former backup band's farewell concert in 1976, an event memorialized by Martin Scorsese's *The Last Waltz* and the accompanying CD. Dylan gave it the big-band treatment in 1978, and stripped it down for near-nightly outings in 1981, 1984, and 1985, and his 1987 tour with Tom Petty. On the Never Ending Tour, "Forever Young" has served as a staple throughout. And, for what it's worth, "Forever Young" was one of three songs Dylan performed in a special 1997 concert for Pope John Paul II.

In 1998 the Gap clothing company began using a reggae version of "Forever Young" as background music in an American TV advertisement for its Gap Kids line of children's apparel. Finally, the similarities between Dylan's "Forever Young" and Rod Stewart's song of the same title are more than uncanny: some versions of Stewart's single cite Dylan's publishing company, Special Rider Music, as copublisher.

▲ *For Our Children*/Various Artists
Disney CD 60616-2. Released 1991.

Dylan contributed "This Old Man," one of his weird but totally album-appropriate cover songs, to the collection of music benefiting a most worthy cause: pediatric AIDS. Because nearly all of the tracks were recorded especially for the album, *For Our Children* became a curio collector's item for the fans of the wildly diverse group of artists who participated in the project. While this does not necessarily result in a crisp presentation, it does work as music to end a child's day, as it moves from energetic to more soothing material. Other notable performances include those by Sting ("Cushie Butterfield"), Paul McCartney ("Mary Had a Little Lamb"), Little Richard ("Itsy Bitsy Spider"), Bruce Springsteen ("Chicken Lips and Lizard Hips"), Bette Midler ("Blueberry Pie"), Elton John ("The Pacifier"), James Taylor ("Getting to Know You"), Meryl Streep ("Gartan Mother's Lullaby"), and Barbra Streisand ("A Child Is Born").

▣ *"4th Time Around"* (Bob Dylan)
aka "Fourth Time Around"
Bob Dylan, *Blonde on Blonde* (1966); *The Bootleg Series, Volume 4: Bob Dylan Live 1966—The "Royal Albert Hall" Concert* (1998)
Terry Melcher, *Terry Melcher* (1974)
The Sports, *Play Dylan & Donovan* (1981)
Pete Williams, *The Times They Are A-Changin'* (1992)
Steve Gibbons, *The Dylan Project* (1998)
Chris Whitley, *Perfect Day* (2000)
Michael Moore, *Jewels and Binoculars* (2000)

Michel Montecrossa, *4th Time Around* (2001)
Various Artists (performed by the Dylan Project), *May Your Song Always Be Sung: The Songs of Bob Dylan, Volume 3* (2003)

Mixing the desultory and the surreal into a quirky breeze of a song describing a terminal, codependent (three-way?) relationship in its death throes, "4th Time Around" meanders with the lack of commitment all parties involved in the playful playlet appear to hold for one another. As poetry it does meander, Dylan rhyming whatever falls onto the page ("How come" and "Jamaican rum" being but one obvious example) in his circuitous, image-rich narrative. In a nifty lyrical sleight of hand, Dylan even manages to make clear that the woman he is singing to and the woman he singing about are acquainted (he glimpses a photograph of one woman in the other's abode). The runaway fantasy lyrics to "4th Time Around" sharply contrast with the rippling Tex-Mex folk-pop musical flow accompanying them.

Dylan was reportedly inspired by "Norwegian Wood (This Bird Has Flown)," the Beatles' romantic yet sexless jape, in composing "4th Time Around," a darker and more convoluted yarn of infidelity and a request for forgiveness. He wrote the song a mere two months after the release of "Norwegian Wood," setting John Lennon's distinctive melody to an asymmetrical love story that was even more impenetrable than the original. Though later he described "4th Time Around" as "great," Lennon once also commented that he "was very paranoid" about the song, perhaps in reference to the speed and incisiveness of Dylan's reply. Was it a playful compliment or an ironic insult? Certainly Dylan's closing lines—"I never asked for your crutch, now don't ask for mine"—could be taken either way.

F

Dylan performed "4th Time Around" regularly during his cataclysmic 1966 world tour with the Hawks. He played it just once in 1974 and 1978, respectively, before returning to it in the spring of 1999 and again in 2002 with acoustic-band renditions that caught even his most stalwart fans off guard.

F

[S] "Frankie and Albert" (Traditional)

aka "Frankie," "Frankie and Johnny," "Frankie Dean," "Frankie's Man, Johnny," "Frankie Was a Good Girl," "He Done Me Wrong," "Leaving Home"
Bob Dylan, *Good as I Been to You* (1992)
Various Artists (performed by Mississippi John Hurt), *Anthology of American Folk Music*/'28 (1952/'97)
Charley Patton, *Complete Recorded Works, Volume 2*/'29 (1990)
King Oliver, *New York Sessions (1929–1930)* (1989)
Ethel Waters, *Ethel Waters*/'30s (1998)
Leadbelly, *Midnight Special*/'40s (1991)
Thelonious Monk, *Thelonious Monk and Joe Turner in Paris* (1952)
Sidney Bechet, *Jazz Festival Concert Paris* (1952)
Anita O'Day, *Evening with Anita O'Day* (1954)
Louis Armstrong, *Great Chicago Concert 1956* (1956)
Elvis Presley, *Frankie and Johnny* (1966)
Michael Bloomfield, *Best of Michael Bloomfield* (1978)
Harvey Fierstein, *This Is Not Going to Be Pretty* (1995)
Al Hirt, *Brassman's Holiday* (1996)
Mae West, *I'm No Angel* (1996)
Doc Watson/David Grisman, *Doc & Dawg* (1997)

Dylan put his stamp all over this age-old jump blues, a sawdust-on-the-floor fable about infidelity and its sometimes murderous consequences, when he released "Frankie and Albert" as the leadoff track on the first of his two albums of blues and folk covers, *Good as I Been to You*, in 1992.

Popularized in every musical idiom, "Frankie and Albert" is an American perennial. In *The Folk Songs of North America* (Garden City, New York: Doubleday, 1960), folklorist and collector Alan Lomax suggested that the song's endurance sprung from its cathartic power. "Frankie had her greatest vogue during the suffragette period," Lomax wrote. He continues:

> She also took direct action—she cut down the predatory male with her smoking .44. Feminine listeners revenged themselves through little Frankie on a predominantly patriarchal society which treated them as second-class citizens and disapproved of their erotic life. Men sang this song to women in a spirit of guilt, anxious to prove that they were not, like Albert, vain, promiscuous, and unappreciative. Middle-class performers had the thrill of vicarious participation in the sexually uninhibited and violent life of the demimonde.
>
> For the Negro folk audience, however, the song touched upon even more painful social problems. After Reconstruction and until World War II, Negro men were, by and large, surplus labor in America. Last hired and first fired, they were forced to roam from town to town and job to job. Meanwhile, Negro women could usually get some sort of work as domestics. Temporary liaisons and casual divorce by desertion became common at a certain social level. This is what the blues tells us about. Men of charm and talent could always find a hard-working woman to keep them. As a natural consequence, the ladies protected their honor with razors, pistols, and poison.

While there is some disagreement regarding the exact historical origins of "Frankie," there is little doubt that this is a very old song. In their book *Elvis: His Life from A to Z* (Chicago: Contemporary Books, 1988), Fred L. Worth and Steve D. Tamerius suggest that composition could be traced from the War of 1812, when

U.S. infantrymen from Tennessee and Kentucky who fought under Andrew Jackson at the battle of New Orleans heard it in the Crescent City under the title "Françoise et Jean." Worth and Tamerius also posit the song's genesis to 1888 St. Louis, when, on a hot summer night, Frankie drew a derringer from her garter and gunned down her boyfriend, Johnny, who had "done her wrong."

Though the song may have been born at watering holes with a Mississippi River view, the specifics of its origin remain speculative at best. However, Lomax again was probably closest to the mark when he traced "Frankie" to North Carolina of the 1830s, noting its similarity in style and content to elements of European balladry and songs like "Barbara Allen." But unlike the doomed subject of "Barbara Allen," who unwittingly broke a heart or two, in "Frankie and Albert" the offending lover, Albert, is literally caught with his pants down, prompting his scorned woman, Frankie, to take the ultimate revenge.

Frankie is the single constant through all the versions of the song, even if her historical identity remains up for grabs. Lomax suggests that her name was Frankie Silvers, a woman who dismembered her husband with an axe on December 22, 1831, at Toe River in the Blue Ridge Mountains of western North Carolina. She was convicted and hanged in Morgantown, North Carolina, on July 12, 1833, and her legend, name, and deed have morphed through the ages so that she now shares that vague space in the folk imagination with the likes of "Pretty Polly," "Stagger Lee," and "Delia."

Dylan's *Good as I Been to You* rendition of "Frankie and Albert" reminds us just what a good guitar player he could be. Perhaps those years of playing with G. E. Smith in his early Never Ending Tour band brought back the vengeful guitar-pickin' demon evidenced here.

▲ *The Freewheelin' Bob Dylan*

Columbia Records LP 1986, CD CK-8786, CS CS-8786; Sony Music Entertainment, Inc., SACD 90321. Recorded April 25; July 9; October 26, 27; November 13–15; December 6, 1962, in New York City. Released May 27, 1963. Produced by John Hammond. Liner notes by Nat Hentoff. Photography by Don Hunstein.

Bob Dylan—guitar, harmonica, keyboards, vocals. George Barnes—bass. Leonard Gaskin—bass. Dick Wellstood—piano. Gene Ramey—bass. Howard Collins—guitar. J. Bruce Langhorne—guitar. Herb Lovell—drums.

"Blowin' in the Wind," "Girl of the North Country," "Masters of War," "Down the Highway," "Bob Dylan's Blues," "A Hard Rain's A-Gonna Fall," "Don't Think Twice, It's All Right," "Bob Dylan's Dream," "Oxford Town," "Talking World War III Blues," "Corrina, Corrina," "Honey, Just Allow Me One More Chance," "I Shall Be Free"

Still a landmark album, *The Freewheelin' Bob Dylan* put its young author on the map after the commercial disappointment of his debut LP from the previous year. On *Freewheelin'*, Dylan came of age as a songwriter, presenting a collection of almost all original material. Even today, the album still sounds fresh and is one of the sixties' vital collections of original songs in its deft synthesis of protest ("Masters of War"), civil rights commentary ("Oxford Town"), visionary hopefulness ("Blowin' in the Wind"), romance ("Girl of the North Country"), the sly kiss-off ("Don't Think Twice, It's All Right"), apocalyptic surrealism ("A Hard Rain's A-Gonna Fall"), and even a humorous end-days talking blues ("Talkin' World War III Blues"). That virtually every song on the album is now considered a classic is testimony to its importance.

Picturing Dylan walking arm in arm with Suze Rotolo, his girlfriend at the time, down a snowy West Village street, the cover of *The Freewheelin' Bob Dylan* encapsulates the folksy-yet-hip aura of the album. It is also a

F

Dylan, ca. 1963.

(Photo: American Stock/Getty Images)

F

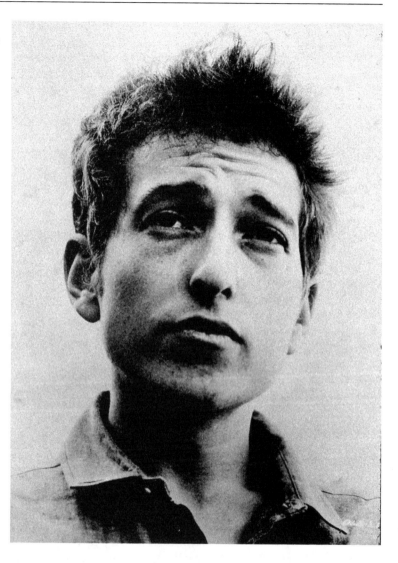

last glimpse of Bob Dylan leading the life of a relatively ordinary young man, but ironically played an integral part in the making of Bob Dylan, Cultural Icon. The famous photo was snapped late one afternoon in February 1963 by Dan Hunstein, then a staff photographer for Columbia Records, when he arrived at the couple's West Fourth Street apartment and brought them outside to the snowy street for a shoot. According to Hunstein's account as reported in the October 12, 1997, edition of the *New York Times*: "I can't tell you why I did it, but I said, 'Just walk up and down the street.' There wasn't very much thought to it."

Freewheelin' was the first Dylan album to appear on *Billboard*'s charts. It maxed out at

No. 22 on its fourteen-week run. The album went gold in 1970.

A final note: Columbia sent out promotional copies of the LP to radio stations and released about three hundred copies to the general public with four songs ("John Birch Society Paranoid Blues," "Rambling Gambling Willie," "Rocks and Gravel," and "Let Me Die in My Footsteps") that were later replaced with an alternate quartet ("Bob Dylan's Dream," "Masters of War," "Girl of the North Country," and "Talkin' World War III Blues"). One of the reasons for the change was Columbia's uneasiness with "John Birch Society Paranoid Blues," a sardonic number poking fun at the fringe yet still hysterical remnants of McCarthyism in 1963 America. Although three of the outtakes were eventually released nearly three decades later on *The Bootleg Series, Volumes 1–3*, the promotional release, which is quite rare, is considered a valuable collector's item.

"Freight Train Blues" (Traditional/John Lair)

Bob Dylan, *Bob Dylan* (1962)
Frank Warner, *Come All You Good People* (1976)
Ella Jenkins, *Seasons for Singing* (1979)
Roy Acuff, *King of Country Music* (1982)
Doc Watson and Merle Watson, *Pickin' the Blues* (1985)
Webb Pierce, *Unavailable Sides (1950–51)* (1994)
Doc Watson, *Watson Country* (1996)
Ramblin' Jack Elliott, *Kerouac's Last Dream* (1997)

"Freight Train Blues," one of Dylan's funniest early covers appearing in both his early performances and on his debut LP, is taken at runaway-train speed and includes his longest recorded sung note, clocked in at over twenty-five seconds. The authorship of "Freight Train Blues" may be lost to time, thus garnering the "traditional" label, but Michael Krogsgaard, the preeminent Dylan discographer, contends that the composer is one John Lair, who was inspired to write the song by his childhood memories of train whistles cracking the rural midnight. Lair himself said as much in a 1972 interview with Dorothy Horstman, published in her book *Sing Your Heart Out, Country Boy* (New York: E. P. Dutton, 1975): "I just remembered down there in the mountains where I came from that freight train whistle at night is an awfully lonesome sound," he said. "In a quiet country where you don't hear many sounds, if you've ever heard a few trains go through these mountain passes, you never forget them. I wrote this song especially for Red Foley."

Whatever the case, Dylan's lyrics differ from those commonly known. He told Robert Shelton, as quoted in *No Direction Home: The Life and Music of Bob Dylan* (New York: Beech Tree Books/William Morrow, 1986), that he learned the up-tempo hillbilly raillery off a Roy Acuff disc, though Shelton suspected he copped it from Ramblin' Jack Elliott.

Lair (born July 1, 1894, Livingston, Kentucky; died November 11, 1985, Renfro Valley, Kentucky) was among Kentucky's most important folklorists and rural impresarios, a vital link between the old ways and days of nineteenth-century America and the radio age. The author of more than five hundred songs and a World War I veteran, Lair had a love for the people and traditions of Renfro Valley that inspired him to build a barn capable of staging a weekly hoedown that was broadcast first on Chicago's WLS and eventually on CBS television. And Lair had a keen eye for talent. Among those who got their first wide exposure through his *Renfro Valley Barndance* radio show were Merle Travis, Red Foley, and Homer and Jethro. As a historian, collector, and writer, he built a musical library of old-time country and pioneer music that was among the world's most extensive, and he was the author of four books on the history and traditions of rural

F

Kentucky life, the most famous of which was *Songs Lincoln Loved* (New York: Duell, Sloan, and Pearce, 1954).

▣ "Friend of the Devil" (Jerry Garcia/Robert Hunter/John Dawson)
The Grateful Dead, *American Beauty* (1970)
Various Artists (performed by Bob Dylan), *Stolen Roses* (2000)
Jerry Garcia and David Grisman, *Jerry Garcia/David Grisman* (1991)
Robert Hunter, *Jack O'Roses* (1979)
Lyle Lovett, *Deadicated* (1991)

A Grateful Dead hallmark, "Friend of the Devil" describes a man on the lam from the Devil, with whom he has made a Faustian pact, and from a woman who claims he is the father of her child and a sheriff for unnamed crimes.

Dylan began performing perky, desperado bluegrass versions of "Friend of the Devil" in his acoustic sets in 1993 as if he were making up the words while going along just one step ahead of Johnny Law. He continued the practice in apparent homage to Jerry Garcia following the latter's passing in 1995, and even worked up an electric arrangement in 1996 that included a sweet Larry Campbell fiddle turn, which remained in play through 2003.

▣ "Froggie Went A-Courtin'" (Traditional)
aka "A Frog He Went A-Courting," "Froggy," "Froggy Went A-Wooin'," "King Kong Kitchie Kitchie Ki-Me-O," "Mr. Froggie Went A-Courtin'"
Bob Dylan, *Good as I Been to You* (1992)
Various Artists (performed by Chubby Parker), *Anthology of American Folk Music*/'28 (1952/1997)
Woody Guthrie, *Woody Guthrie—Buffalo Skinners: The Asch Recordings, Volume 4*/'44 (1999)
Oscar Brand, *Oscar Brand's Children's Concert* (1961)
Pete Seeger, *American Favorite Ballads* (1963)
Odetta, *Odetta Sings of Many Things* (1964)

Sam Hinton, *Whoever Shall Have Some Good Peanuts* (1964)
John Jacob Niles, *John Jacob Niles Collection* (1966)
Spider John Koerner, *Nobody Knows the Trouble I've Been* (1970)
Peggy & Mike Seeger, *American Folk Songs for Children* (1977)
Almeda Riddle, *Granny Riddle's Songs & Ballads* (1977)

One of the most famous and legitimately bizarre songs in the world folk canon, "Froggie Went A-Courtin'" concerns a wedding of cousins in the animal kingdom. Dylan sings it with good-natured spunk, shying away from the odious traps of playing it as either corn-pone or with historical gravity. In his very human reading, every oddball character and scenario is given an almost cinematic or painterly rendering. The result is a somewhat unsettling *Through the Looking-Glass* or *Wind in the Willows* tale any child could enjoy—or fear.

"A most strange wedding of the frogge and the mouse" was first advertised and licensed for performance in 1580, and though Dylan probably initially came across Chubby Parker's 1928 version on Harry Smith's *Anthology of American Folk Music*, he treats the curio like the well-known children's song it has become. It may be the oldest song Dylan has ever recorded: the courtship between a Mr. Frog and Miss Mouse first appeared on a Scottish broadside in 1549 as "The Frog Cam to the Myl Dur" (mill door). Fast forward nearly four hundred years: a 1935 game played by African-American children in Georgia incorporated the song, as revealed by a Library of Congress field recording.

Some scholars assert that the remarkable wedding is the theme of "The Frog Cam to the Myl Dur," which was sung by shepherds, according to Robert Wedderburn's *Complaynt of Scotland* (published ca. 1549), licensed for publication in 1580, and later reprinted with a tune in

Frog and Mouse dinner party, undated.

(*Hey Diddle Diddle Picture Book*/Library of Congress)

F

Thomas Ravenscroft's *Melismata* (published 1611). In Thomas D'Urfey's 1707–1720 *Wit and Mirth: or, Pills to Purge Melancholy*, there is an early political parody called "A ditty on a high Amour to St. James's." A common characteristic of these songs as well as "Froggie" is the strong accent on the first note of their refrains. This suggests an accompanying energetic gesture, or kick, as does the song's lilt and rhythm.

According to the Guy Logsdon and Jeff Place–penned liner notes for *Woody Guthrie—Buffalo Skinners: The Asch Recordings, Volume 4*: "This song has many, many variants and titles; it is usually classified as a children's song. However, its history indicates that it was a sixteenth-century English satirist's barb nursery. Queen Elizabeth I often gave different animal nicknames to those around her. She had her frog, her lap dog, and many more; the 'frog' in her court was reported to be a man intent on marrying her. It seems that the satirical song-writers had a field day with her characters, and 'Froggie Went A-Courtin'' emerged as a favorite in English-speaking countries. Its original satirical intent has long been lost, while it remains a popular children's song."

"From a Buick 6" (Bob Dylan)

Bob Dylan, single (1965); *Highway 61 Revisited* (1965)
Alex Taylor, *Dinnertime* (1972)
Gary U.S. Bonds, *Dedication* (1981)
Mick Wilhelm, *Mean Ol' Frisco* (1985)
Treat Her Right, *What's Good for You* (1991)
Johnny Winter, *Still Alive and Well* (1994)
Cypress Grove, *Buick 6* (1998)
Big Brass Bed, *A Few Dylan Songs* (2003)

A silvery, metallic bluesy rock 'n' rant that celebrates an ornery earth mother (or was that gangster moll?) as the narrator unloads his head speeding on some nefarious byway of the American soul in search of freedom and escape, "From a Buick 6" is a somewhat overlooked and sadly underperformed sneer from Dylan's mid-sixties venom-filled pen. But wherever this subterranean traveler has roamed, no matter what he's seen, what he's done, or what he calls her ("graveyard woman," "junkyard angel," "steam shovel mama," and "dump truck mama," among them), his woman is always there, "bound to put a blanket on my bed." It's yet another surrealist road blues that looks alienation and death squarely in the eye and scoffs at it. And like those old dusty blues songs mixing misogyny and need, Dylan sings "From a Buick 6" with the kind of swagger that would make Big Bill Broonzy proud.

The song is a simple rock-blues with great, nutty lyrics; some say it was influenced by a 1964 recording, "She's Mean," by Joey Gee and the Come On. Others more acutely point out that Dylan took the tune and rhythmic groove from the 1930 Sleepy John Estes recording of "Milk Cow Blues." Estes uses the phrase "keep it hid" in the first verse of his song: a similar phrase ("keeps my kid") is tucked into Dylan's song. And the Kinks' menacing variant of "Milk Cow" (as heard on their 1965 LP *Kinks Kontroversy*) is suggested as a catalyst for Dylan. A completely different take with a harmonica intro was released on the Japanese version of *Highway 61 Revisited* but was withdrawn from early stereo editions and is now a rare collector's item. When Dylan was working up his studio take for *Highway 61 Revisited* in the summer of 1965, he used "Lunatic Princess" as a working title. "Buick 6" was staged at but two documented Dylan shows in 1965 during his early electric sets with the Hawks: the

August 28th concert at Forest Hills Tennis Stadium in Queens, New York, and his September 3rd appearance at the Hollywood Bowl.

"Fur Slippers" (Bob Dylan/Tim Drummond)
See also "Saved"
Various Artists (performed by B. B. King), *Shake Rattle & Roll* (1999)

Dylan's previously unreleased 1982 song "Fur Slippers," a smoking blues written with his former gospel tours–era bass player Tim Drummond and performed by B. B. King, could be heard in *Shake Rattle & Roll*, a true borefest of a made-for-TV movie "dramatizing" the genre's early rush of popularity through very loosely mixed fact, fancy, and urban legend. The movie chronicled the rise and fall of a fictional band and also included original songs by the likes of Carole King and remakes of hits from the 1950s.

G

"Gates of Eden" (Bob Dylan)
Bob Dylan, single (1965); *Bringing It All Back Home* (1965); *The Bootleg Series, Volume 6: Live 1964—Concert at Philharmonic Hall* (2004)
Julie Felix, *Flowers* (1967)
Arlo Guthrie, *The Last of the Brooklyn Cowboys* (1973)
Steven Keene, *Keene on Dylan* (2000)
Various Artists (performed by Arlo Guthrie), *Doin' Dylan 2* (2002)
Marc Carroll, *Crashpad Number* (2003)

Dylan once introduced this song as "a sacrilegious lullaby in D minor," and that's about as apt a description as any of "Gates of Eden." An epic with Blakean overtones (the visionary poet and artist's sequential painting *The Gates of Paradise* is pointed to as one influence) and discomforting William Burroughseseque spleen, "Gates of Eden" concerns itself with salvation (or what salvation is not) and, ultimately, the universal promise and lies of dreams of Heaven and Hell.

A vision of a vision postponed—man's expulsion from Paradise—"Gates of Eden" still stands as a powerful example of Dylan as a reluctant prophet in his sad-eyed peak at the highlands. The musical accompaniment is spare, embellished with a sour harmonica flourish at the end of each verse as if to emphasize the distaste for what he has to say. In "Gates of Eden" Dylan declares that blind belief in a forgiving afterlife is the ultimate lie because it creates complacency in this one. This compendium of harsh imagery flows brittle and surreal from the blue-eyed son who was caught in a hard rain on Rue Morgue Avenue and came back with a cosmic weather report. No kings, no sins, no trials *inside* the Gates of Eden; no laughs, no truths *outside* the Gates. Oblivion is the only logical destination for all mortal souls, so get used to it, Dylan suggests upon his return from the portal the ancients claimed provided poetic wisdom. And that horrifying revelation is no less than a glimpse of the hell we may already partially occupy.

But Dylan isn't the only one searching for the truth on this barren, threatening landscape of entropy: a cloud-riding cowboy angel uses a black wax candle to ferret out the sun; babies wail in a vacuum; a savage soldier makes like an ostrich with his head in the sand, oblivious to the baying hound dogs and freedom-seeking ships; Utopian hermit monks ride the Golden Calf side-saddle and, with Aladdin (his dormant lamp close by), promise paradise; the narrator tries to sing with a lonesome sparrow in a world with no leaders, as a motorcycling black Madonna and her phantom henchman torment a gray-flanneled, bread-crumb-sinning dwarf

and the local vultures spy their prey. At the song's end, the narrator is awakened by his lover, who tells him of her dreams. But he knows that the words he has to describe his night visions are the only truthful ones.

A nice portrayal of Dylan performing "Gates of Eden" from his May 9, 1965, concert in London can be seen in the film *Don't Look Back*. While not a common song in Dylan's onstage repertoire, "Gates of Eden" has, nonetheless, appeared with a certain degree of regularity since its debut in 1964. While Dylan's previous concert presentations of "Gates of Eden" came in the form of a solo acoustic display, his early Never Ending Tour renditions had a martial, heavy metal edge worthy of Guns 'N' Roses. Dylan returned to an acoustic-band adaptation of the song by the mid-1990s, when he delivered some stunning, Django Reinhardt–style performances of this dark fever dream.

"George Jackson" (Bob Dylan)
Bob Dylan, single (1971); *Masterpieces* (1978)
Fasia, *Portrait* (1975)

Dylan's first blatant, in-your-face protest song in years, "George Jackson" is a plain and simple, if fuzzy-minded, tune about the title character—a civil rights activist and cause célèbre imprisoned and then shot down in 1971.

Dylan's well-intentioned tableau, however, barely hints at the larger story of the infamous San Quentin massacre—the 1971 prison riot that serves as a snapshot of the United States during the political upheavals of the era—and the event's two protagonists: George Jackson, Black Panther field marshal and author of the prison memoir *Soledad Brother*, and his radical lawyer, Stephen Bingham. On August 21, 1971, Jackson, armed with a 9-millimeter pistol, launched an escape attempt that incited a riot, which ultimately resulted in his own death and those of five others.

Along with a small-combo version of "George Jackson," Dylan also recorded a big-band arrangement of the song for the single, which was later included on the *Masterpieces* import. In a rare example of instant product from Dylan, the "George Jackson" single hit record stores a mere eight days after Dylan recorded the two versions on the release. The song caught many off guard, as it was common wisdom that Dylan had given up composing tunes with overt political agendas. By the same token, some criticized Dylan for writing a song they found a sop to the political left—as if he were merely trying to get them off his back. While trying to fill its own coffers, Columbia fed both cynics and idealists alike by pushing the single with this glib Madison Avenue tag: "Dylan's New Single Is a Political Act."

■ "Get Out of Denver" (Bob Seger)
Bob Seger, *Seven* (1974)
Dave Edmunds, *Get It* (1977)
Blues Traveler, *Things to Do in Denver When You're Dead* (1995)
Swinging Steaks, *Kicksnarehat* (2000)

This just in: Dylan tips his hat to nice-guy rocker Bob Seger (born May 6, 1945, Dearborn, Michigan) for a smokin' encore one-off performance of "Get Out of Denver," a sardonic slice of on-the-lam Americana, in the Motor City during a small theater swing across the U.S. in the spring of '04. No doubt Dylan was aware that local hero Seger was being inducted into the Rock and Roll of Fame that very night.

■ "Get Your Rocks Off!" (Bob Dylan)
Coulson, Dean, McGuinness, Flint, *Lo & Behold* (1972)
Manfred Mann, *Messin'* (1973)

Aviator, *Turbulence* (1980)
Pat Thomas, *Get Your Rocks Off* (1995)

At once menacing and ribald, "Get Your Rocks Off!" as performed by Dylan and the Hawks picks up where every old-maid-theme limerick leaves off and takes a stroll down every back lane in Appalachia before stopping for some ale at a burlesque house featuring a Brothers Grimm playlet.

Perhaps because the *Basement Tapes* version of "Get Your Rocks Off!" has remained unreleased, few writers have paid much attention to this bawdy slice of 1967 high jinks from Dylan's upstate New York idyll. Tim Riley, in his book *Hard Rain: A Dylan Commentary* (New York: Alfred A. Knopf, 1992), did offer this brief critique: "And the lanky, weak-kneed 'Get Your Rocks Off!,' a hilarious outtake from these outtakes, sounds like a postlude to an exhausting orgy ('Get 'em off me!,' Dylan sings). ('Rocks Off!' can't be easily summarized: with a nod to Fats Domino's 'Blueberry Hill,' the song brushes up against the same ironic double entendres as 'Rainy Day Women #12 & 35,' and the final verse alludes to the Mississippi Freedom Rides: 'Well, you know, we was cruisin' down the highway in a Greyhound bus/All kinds-a children in the side road, they was hollerin' at us, sayin':/'Get your rocks off! . . .')"

■ "Girl from the North Country" (Bob Dylan)
aka "Girl of the North Country"
Bob Dylan, *The Freewheelin' Bob Dylan* (1963); *Nashville Skyline* (performed with Johnny Cash) (1969); *Real Live* (1984)
Bob Dylan/Various Artists (performed by Bob Dylan), *Bob Dylan: The 30th Anniversary Concert Celebration* (1993)
Oscar Brand/Various Artists (performed by Bob Dylan), *The World of Folk Music: Starring Oscar Brand* (1963)
Johnny Cash (performed with Bob Dylan), *Man in Black—His Greatest Hits* (1999)

Hamilton Camp, *Paths of Victory* (1964)
The Turtles, *It Ain't Me Babe* (1965)
Silkie, *You've Got to Hide Your Love Away* (1965)
Boz Scaggs, *Boz* (1965)
Link Wray, single (1965; *Mr. Guitar* (1995)
Ramblin' Jack Elliott, *Bull Durham Sacks and Railroad Tracks* (1970)
Lester Flatt and Earl Scruggs, *Final Fling* (1970); *1964–1969, Plus* (1996)
Joe Cocker, *Mad Dogs and Englishmen* (1970)
Dennis Stoner, *Dennis Stoner* (1971)
Larry Groce, *The Wheat Lies Low* (1971)
James Last, *Goodtimes* (1971)
Howard Tate, *Howard Tate* (1972)
Clancy Brothers, *Save the Land* (1972)
Roy Harper, *Valentine* (1974)
Didier, *Hommage à Bob Dylan* (1974)
Rod Stewart, *Smiler* (1975); *Maggie May* (1981); *You Wear It Well* (1996)
Mylon LeFevre, *Weak at the Knees* (1977)
Dave Browning, *Forever Young* (1982)
Björn Afzelius, *Danska Natter* (1982)
Tito Schipa Jr., *Dylanito* (1988)
Walter Trout, *Prisoner of a Dream* (1990)
Jimmy LaFave, *Austin Skyline* (1992)
Janglers, *Janglers Play Dylan* (1992)
Tony Rice, *Tony Rice Plays & Sings Bluegrass* (1993)
Robert James Waller, *Ballads of Madison County* (1993)
Hugues Aufray, *Aufray Chante Dylan* (1994)
Fairport Convention, *25th Anniversary* (1994)
The Zimmermen, *The Dungeon Tapes* (1996)
Phil Carmen, *Bob Dylan's Dream* (1996)
Two Approaching Riders, *One More Cup of Coffee* (1997)
Carl Edwards, *Coffeehouse Cowboy* (1998)
Gove Scrivenor (with John Prine), *Shine On* (1998)
Country Gentlemen, *Early Rebel Recordings 1962–1971* (1998)
David Menefee, *Brighter Side of Blue* (1998)
Gerard Quintana and Jordi Batiste, *Els Miralls de Dylan* (1999)
Altan, *Another Sky* (2000)
Various Artists (performed by John Gorka), *A Nod to Bob* (2001)
Various Artists (performed by Father Hennepin), *Duluth Does Dylan* (2001)

Gerry Murphy, *Gerry Murphy Sings Bob Dylan* (2002)

Supposedly (and probably) written for Bonnie Beecher (a liaison from his brief university days in Minneapolis circa 1960) and/or Echo Helstrom (Dylan's first serious girlfriend back in Hibbing, Minnesota), the wistful, courtly "Girl from the North Country" is Dylan's first original love song on record. It's convincingly and affectionately delivered on *Freewheelin'* as well as at other junctures in Dylan's career. Dylan also rerecorded the song at a slower pace with Johnny Cash on wonderful duet leading off *Nashville Skyline*; this rendition is notable for some minor changes in the lyric, most memorably at the end of the song where they improvise vocally to create a kind of dappled call-and-response effect. The two performed the song in a similar fashion during Dylan's appearance on television's *Johnny Cash Show* in April 1969. Much later, Dylan included a romantic solo acoustic rendition from his 1984 tour on *Real Live*. In 1992 he closed the 30th Anniversary Concert Celebration with another solo acoustic reading of "Girl from the North Country" and continued to fuss over it through the 1990s and early '00s, giving it a variety of arrangements and treatments sometimes to the point of making the song nearly unrecognizable.

A love lyric of delicacy and longing, "Girl from the North Country" bears a well-known connection to the English folk song "Scarborough Fair." Seldom noted is the source of that traditional tune: British singer and folklorist Martin Carthy. Dylan mentions Carthy and his influence in the *Freewheelin'* sleeve notes and, in an interview some ten years later, went out of his way to credit Carthy, saying that he based "Girl" on a song he'd learned from the latter.

Carthy liked what Dylan did with "Scarborough Fair." He told Dave Brazier in 1991 for *The Telegraph* #42 (summer 1992) that he first met Dylan during the latter's initial European sojourn in late 1962 and early 1963. Dylan was there to perform in *The Madhouse on Castle Street*, a BBC television play. As Carthy remembered, Dylan finished his filming, "went away for a while," and then returned to film his part again. Carthy recalled:

> And when he came back, he'd written "Girl from the North Country"; he came down to the Troubadour and said, "Hey, here's 'Scarborough Fair' and he started playing this thing. And he kept getting the giggles, all the time he was doing it. It was very funny. I think he sang about three or four verses and then he went, "Ah, man, ah," and he burst out laughing and sang something else. So yeah, I knew what he was doing. It was delightful, lovely, 'cause I mean he . . . he made a new song.
>
> I don't know whether it is a folk tradition or not, but I took it as an enormous compliment, to the song and, if you like, to me. You know, I thought he was a tremendously honorable bloke. Still do. It was a great thing to have done.

Bonnie-Jean Beecher was the other purportedly "real" "Girl from the North Country." She first met Dylan in 1959, and the two were close throughout his days in Minneapolis. They stayed in regular contact even after he left for New York in December 1960 and throughout Dylan's rise to fame. She later married comedian Hugh Romney, who transformed himself into Wavy Gravy, still the Holy Fool and Jester King of the hippies.

According to *The Freewheelin' Bob Dylan* liner notes, Dylan first conceived "Girl from the North Country" about three years before he finally wrote it down in December 1962. "That often happens," he said. "I carry a song in my head for a long time and then it comes bursting *out*."

With its moody fusion of yearning, poignancy, and simple appreciation for a beautiful girl, the song finds Dylan illuminating all corners of his vision while simultaneously retaining his bristling sense of self—too proud to go begging for anything from anybody.

Stripped down to just his guitar and harmonica, Dylan's career-spanning performances of "Girl from the North Country" have been eternally heartfelt—whether he was twenty-two or pushing sixty-something.

▣ "The Girl I Left Behind Me" (Traditional)

aka "The Rich Old Farmer," "The Gal I Left Behind Me," "That Pretty Little Gal"

Various Artists (performed by Spencer Moore and Everett Blevins), *Southern Journey, Volume 5: Ballads and Breakdowns/*'59 (1997)

Red Clay Ramblers, *Twisted Laurel* (1977)

Albion Band, *Larkrise to Candleford* (1980)

Jim and Jesse, *The Jim & Jesse Story* (1980)

Bryan Bowers, *By Heart* (1982)

Richard Hayman, *Irish Rhapsody* (1990)

A ballad popular among Irish, Scottish, English, and American migrants as early as the eighteenth century, "The Girl I Left Behind Me" has been sung to many different melodies. While the traveling man finds a new sweetheart and leaves the old one behind in the British version, the faithful man is betrayed by the fickle girl he has left behind in most American renditions. John A. and Alan Lomax collected a couple of versions that they called "a popular soldier song."

Folklore has long surrounded "The Girl I Left Behind Me," with some sources suggesting that it was a favorite as far back as Elizabeth I's reign in the mid- to late sixteenth century—played whenever a regiment left town or a man-of-war set sail. Others contend that the tune was known in America as early as 1650 and believe it was a traditional fife tune imported from England called "Brighten Camp." Whatever the case, it is known for sure that "The Girl I Left Behind Me" became generally popular during the American Revolution. The tune was known in Ireland as "The Rambling Laborer" and "The Spailpin Fanach" and, as such, was first published in Dublin in 1791.

When Dylan performed his only collected version of "The Girl I Left Behind Me" during an October 1961 radio appearance, he insisted to host Oscar Brand that he learned his unique rendition firsthand from a farmer named Wilbur.

His likely source, however, was Alan Lomax's 1960 book *Folk Songs of North America*, which included Clarence Ashley's "Maggie Walker Blues," a variant of the original. That Ashley tune and its lyrics are thought to be the likely source for Dylan's own "Long Time Gone" as well.

▣ "Girl on the Greenbriar Shore" (Traditional)
aka "Girl on the Green Briar Shore," "The Green Brier Shore"
Carter Family, *Last Sessions: Their Complete Victor Recordings/'30s* (1998)
Tom Paley, *Folk Songs from the South Appalachian Mountains* (1959)
Greenbriar Boys, *Greenbriar Boys* (1962)
Hotmud Family, *Buckeyes in the Briar Patch* (1975)
Rich Lerner, *Trails and Bridges* (1996)

Dylan sang this old song, an American Piedmont ballad with English roots, as a cautionary tale from a mother to her young and reckless son to "never trust the girl on the greenbriar shore," whom Mother suspects will surely let him down. Predictably, the son ignores the advice, marries the girl, and is abandoned by her. In other versions of the song, the girl's parents hire an army to defend her virtue. But their armaments are no match for the sailor boy, who regains his own true love over their dead and wounded bodies on the greenbriar shore.

Dylan exhibited "Greenbriar Shore" on acoustic guitar at a couple of 1992 European shows. Some suggest that Tom Paley's version was Dylan's source. Also, the Greenbriar Boys are said to have taken their name from this song.

▣ "Give My Love to Rose" (Johnny Cash)
See also Johnny Cash
Johnny Cash, *Complete Sun Singles* (1995)
Johnny Cash/Jerry Lee Lewis/Carl Perkins, *Sun Kings* (1998)
David Allen Coe, *Original Outlaw* (1995)

Dylan covered Cash's 1957 faded death ballad as a semiacoustic encore for a short while during the Never Ending Tours of 1988 and 1989. This is one of those Dylan covers of a contemporary's song that is anything but an interesting novelty, as he brings as much nuance to "Give My Love to Rose" as the Man in Black himself.

In its day, "Give My Love to Rose" hit No. 13 on the country chart, but numbers mean little here, as the song communicated pain far more profound than most country songs, which generally sniff about little more than broken barroom romances. Similar in tone to Merle Haggard's "Sing Me Back Home," it is sung by a narrator who tells the story of encountering a dying man by the side of the railroad tracks. The dying man has just been sprung from prison after ten years and is on his way home to reunite with his wife, Rose, and a son he's never seen back in Louisiana. Obviously he doesn't make it. As he dies, he hands the singer what little money he has left, telling him to tell her to buy a nice dress.

▣ "Glory, Glory" (Traditional)
aka "When I Lay My Burden Down"
Dick Fariña & Eric von Schmidt (with Dylan as "Blind Boy Grunt"), *Dick Fariña & Eric von Schmidt* (1963)
Odetta, *Odetta Sings Ballads & Blues* (1956)

Cat-Iron, *Cat-Iron Sings Blues and Hymns* (1958)
Maddox Brothers and Rose, *America's Most Colorful Hillbilly Band* (1961)
Mississippi Fred McDowell, *Mississippi Delta Blues* (1964)
Don Nix, *Hobos, Heroes & Street Corner Clowns* (1974)
Blind Roosevelt Graves, *Blind Roosevelt Graves (1929–36)* (1981)
Joseph Spence, *Glory* (1991)
Rev. Ernest Franklin, *South Central Mass Choir* (1996)

Dylan contributed backup harmonica and vocals to Richard Fariña and Eric von Schmidt's recording of "Glory, Glory" at their January 1963 session in Dobbell's Jazz Record Shop in England.

According to the liner notes to Fariña and von Schmidt's eponymous 1963 LP, "Glory, Glory" is a "traditional Negro hymn, the tune relating closely to the Southern white hymn, 'Will the Circle Be Unbroken?'" Dylan may also have known the song from Cat-Iron's 1958 Folkways LP, which Bonnie Beecher remembers him listening to in Minneapolis circa 1961, suggesting that it was Dylan's idea to record the song.

"God Knows" (Bob Dylan)
Bob Dylan, *Under the Red Sky* (1990)

Take a little religion, throw in a pinch of Stevie Ray Vaughan playing guitar, sprinkle in a teaspoon of impassioned Dylan vocals, put it in the studio mixer, let bake for half a year, and you come out with this stale piece of bluesy gospel rock—one that developed modestly onstage in the coming Never Ending Tour years. Jimmie Vaughan, Jackson Browne, and David Lindley on slide guitar can also be heard on the *Under the Red Sky* rendition.

Ultimately "God Knows" is less a song than a harangue—a catalogue-filled rant in the style of the more successful "Everything Is Broken" from the same era.

As for the song's sources, Dylan may have drawn on *Catch-22* author Joseph Heller's 1984 novel *God Knows* for his title, and he seems to have laced in lines from "How Many Miles to Babylon"—the well-known nursery-rhyme stanza (the "million miles by candlelight"), Psalms 44:21 ("God ... knoweth the secrets of the heart"), and Paul's second epistle to the Thessalonians, which discusses "the fire next time" as the period between the Creation and Judgment Day. But even with all the portent, "God Knows" is little more than knock-off apocalyptic Dylan at best and album-filler at worst.

"Go Down, Moses" (Traditional)
aka "Let My People Go"
Paul Robeson, *The Peace Arch Concerts/'53* (1998)
Jimmy Witherspoon, *Feelin' the Spirit* (1959)
Grant Green, *Feelin' the Spirit* (1962)
Archie Shepp, *Goin' Back Home* (1977)
John Tchicai, *Ball at Louisiana Museum of Modern Art* (1981)
Charlie Haden, *Steal Away* (1994)
Mavis Staples, *Spirituals & Gospel: Dedicated to Mahalia Jackson* (1996)
Clarence Williams, *Clarence Williams 1937–1941* (1997)

Given their shared predicament of indentured servitude, it was only natural that the black slave should identify with the Old Testament Israelites and invoke the great biblical prophets. In leading the children of Israel out of bondage and toward the Promised Land, Moses was a natural and powerful model for the oppressed. Moses and the other prophets were also mighty emblems who could stand in for things and personages much more immediate, and thereby allow slaves to communicate in a sort of code under the nose of their masters. Harriet Tubman, for example, may very well have been the true subject of "Moses": as a tireless conductor on the Underground Railroad, she made scores of journeys into the

"Egypt Land" of slavery, returning north each time with a group of runaway slaves.

Alan Lomax succinctly explores the slave spirituals and "Go Down, Moses" specifically in *The Folk Songs of North America* (Garden City, N.Y.: Doubleday, 1960):

> Some of the noblest songs of freedom were composed by Negro slaves. In their spirituals they naturally chose for their heroes little David who slew the mighty Goliath; Daniel, whom the Lord delivered from the lions, and Joshua, who made the walls come tumbling down. In the trials and tribulations of the children of Israel they saw the pattern of their own bondage. Thus they could do full justice to one of the great Bible stories of liberation: the story of Moses who stood up to Pharaoh and said: "Let my people go!"
>
> In the years before the Civil War many slaves were guided along the Underground Railroad by an escaped slave called Harriet Tubman. She was called the Moses of her people because she led them out of bondage, and it is said that the Negroes made this song in her honor. Later it was sung by Negro regiments in the Civil War.

Young Robert Zimmerman probably first canted some version of "Go Down, Moses" from the *Haggadah* at the Passover table as a young mensch in Hibbing, Minnesota. As Dylan, he performed the venerable spiritual as the encore of his first-ever concert in Israel, in September 1987, and again during the High Holy Days six weeks later to close out his tours with Tom Petty and the Heartbreakers.

"Dayanu!"

Gods and Generals (soundtrack)/Various Artists
Sony Classical CD 87891. Released February 4, 2003.

This soundtrack album to the overwrought 2003 Civil War film featured mostly the elegiac score written by Randy Edelman and John Frizell, which mixed orchestral, Celtic, jazz, and bluegrass styles into a fairly unique musical vision. In fact, the only non-Edelman/Frizell track on the CD was Dylan's ghostly, rustic "Cross the Green Mountain," an eight-minute song written especially for the project.

"God Uses Ordinary People" (Bob Dylan)

Mona Lisa Young, one of Dylan's backup singers in 1979 and 1980, performed this song alone at the 1979 gospel shows. Still, not singing the song himself didn't stop Dylan from using it as a stump from which to spread the Word, as illustrated by his introduction of it at a November 1979 Santa Monica show: "You know God uses ordinary people all the time. All those guys in the Old Testament—Joshua, Moses, Abraham, Gideon—they were all ordinary people. They weren't any super heroes at all."

"Going, Going, Gone" (Bob Dylan)
Bob Dylan, *Planet Waves* (1974); *Bob Dylan at Budokan* (1979)
Richard Hell, *Destiny Street* (1982); *R.I.P.: The ROIR Sessions* (1984)
Bill Frisell, *Rubáiyát* (1990)
Steve Howe, *Portraits of Bob Dylan* (1999)

Invoking baseball's favorite home-run call as delivered by a menacing backwoods auctioneer to describe a moment of truthful personal torment, Dylan revealed that his family-oriented lifestyle in the early 1970s may not have been all he'd been making it out to be in the songs on *New Morning* and the like. Robbie Robertson's baroque guitar work and Garth Hudson's ghostly organ help create the murky landscapes for the song's soul-searching tone and cinematic images.

G

"Going, Going, Gone" is one of those unheralded Dylan songs mixing his rural and urban sensibilities, and during its short life as a performance vehicle on the 1976 Rolling Thunder tour, it proved to be a real sleeper. In 1978 he reworked the lyrics Robert Johnson–style with amazing results, only to sabotage the effort with a lousy arrangement in which he added an almost unlistenable chorus and a cockeyed blues vamp.

G

[S] **"Going to San Diego"** (Allen Ginsberg/arrangement by Bob Dylan)

aka "See You in San Diego"
Allen Ginsberg, *First Blues*/'71 (1983)

According to the insert of Ginsberg's 1982 album *First Blues*, Dylan arranged this Ginsberg poem and added guitar, piano, and vocals to the recording. It was originally intended for release on *Holy Soul & Jelly Roll*, a Ginsberg album conceived but never released for the Beatles' Apple Records in 1972.

[S] **"Goin' to Acapulco"** (Bob Dylan)

Bob Dylan/The Band, *The Basement Tapes*/'67 (1975)
The Crust Brothers, *Marquee Mark* (1998)

Describing a vexed trip south of the border, "Goin' to Acapulco" works as a piece of jaded standup, which Dylan delivers as if the older and not-much-wiser narrator of "Just Like Tom Thumb's Blues" were returning for a second go-round. Instead of visiting Sweet Melinda, he visits Rose Marie, the hooker with the heart of gold who will trade her favors for a song. As bad as that may be, it beats the loneliness of masturbation as implied in the final verse, when the singer equates his dwindling sex drive with a broken-down well. A drunken, half-awake mood permeates this song, as if the singer is not quite sure whether he's dreaming or not.

Recorded in the late summer or early fall of 1967, "Goin' to Acapulco" was published with an alternate set of words in Dylan's book *Lyrics: 1962–1982*.

[S] **"Golden Loom"** (Bob Dylan)

Bob Dylan, *The Bootleg Series, Volumes 1–3: Rare and Unreleased, 1961–1991*/'75 (1991)
Roger McGuinn, *Thunderbyrd* (1977); *I Shall Be Unreleased*/'77 (1991)
Roger McGuinn/Chris Hillman/Gene Clark, *3 Byrds Land in London* (1998)

A *Desire* outtake recorded in July 1975, "Golden Loom" is infused with vaguely mystical allusions and mythological symbolism. The song's title and central archetype recall Homer's *Odyssey*. Penelope, Odysseus's wife, uses such a device to weave a burial shroud that she knows she will never complete, cleverly buying her husband time to return from his journey and keep her from having to choose among the boorish suitors encamped at her home in Ithaca. There's also the suggestion of more than a passing influence from Jacques Levy, a clinical psychologist turned playwright turned lyricist, with whom Dylan collaborated on most of the material found on *Desire*. The notion of narcotized, sensual entrapment might extend here as well to a metaphorical commentary on Dylan's marriage, seriously on the rocks at the time of the song's composition.

Dreamlike, the fleeting images in "Golden Loom" (the fisherman's daughter, the eucalyptus trees, the ritualistic washing of the feet, the lotus, the trembling lion, and so on) attempt to nudge the listener into a state of shared spiritual awareness with the singer. The harmonies, instrumentation (spun around Scarlet Rivera's hypnotic violin), and a hint of melody that is naggingly familiar but just out of reach—like the "smell of perfume and your golden loom"—only add to the song's mythic mystery.

While Dylan never performed "Golden Loom" in concert, his bassist Rob Stoner displayed a rock version of the song during the fall 1975 Rolling Thunder tour with some regularity.

[S] "The Golden Vanity" (Traditional)

aka "The Golden Vallady," "The Golden Victory," "The Golden Willow Tree," "Lowland Low," "The Merry Golden Tree," "Silver Family," "The Sweet Trinity," "The Turkey Shivaree," "Turkish Revelee," "The Turkish Roberee"
Various Artists (performed by Dodie Chalmers), *Classic Ballads of Britain and Ireland, Volume Two*/1953 (2000)
Ronnie Gilbert, *Folk Songs and Minstrelsy* (1962)
Pete Seeger, *Together in Concert* (1975)
Peter, Paul & Mary, *Flowers & Stones* (1990)
Doug Wallin, *Family Songs and Stories from the North* (1995)
Almanac Singers, *Complete General Recordings* (1996)
Spider John Koerner, *Stargeezer* (1996)
Burl Ives, *Sings His Favourites* (1996)

This famous sea ballad (No. 286 in the Francis Child list) exists in many forms—with almost as many names for the ship in the song's title. Along with "The Golden Vanity," there is "The Weeping Willow Tree," "The Golden Willow Tree," and "Silver Family," all telling a similar tale aboard a similar ship. In the seventeenth century the noted obsessive diarist and literary groundbreaker Samuel Pepys collected one version called "The Sweet Trinity" in 1682, and a ship by that name is supposed to have been built by Sir Walter Raleigh in the Netherlands. English variants have the ship attacked by Spanish, Dutch, or French galleys, suggesting that the ballad was sung throughout the sixteenth, seventeenth, and eighteenth centuries, when England fought all three countries for control of the high seas. In American versions, the enemy ship encountered is the "Turkish Robberee" or "Turkish Revelee"—an indication that these versions may date from the late eighteenth or early nineteenth century, when Yankee seamen battled the Barbary pirates in the Mediterranean.

According to the liner notes written by Alan Lomax and Peter Kennedy for volume two of *Classic Ballads of Britain and Ireland: Folk Songs of England, Ireland, Scotland & Wales* (Rounder Records, 2000):

> This is the ballad par excellence of the underdog. The oldest version, which appears among the ballads collected by Samuel Pepys in 1682, names Sir Walter Raleigh as the treacherous captain. Perhaps it was originally composed as an attack on that gallant and ill-starred gentleman. At any rate, it became the darling of folksingers on land and sea in Great Britain and the colonies, and is still popular in schools and with modern singers of folk songs. . . .
>
> British and American versions show one important plot difference. For the most part, British singers end the story toughly and tragically with the boy left alone to drown. American singers tend to sentimentalize the end—or do their versions reflect changed attitudes between adults and children and upper and lower classes? Perhaps here sentiment and democratic folkways go hand in hand.

The periodical *Sing Out!* discussed the song in 1964: "The popular American version . . . (learned from the singing of the Carter Family) enacts its drama as a piece of high tragedy. In various other versions, shipmates rescue the cabin boy (or seaman) or the captain gives the gold and fee but holds back the daughter, etc. One theme remains constant in all versions of the ballad, however: the perfidy of the ship's captain in reneging on his promise. Perhaps this is one reason why the folk, with a great wealth of experience to confirm the untrust-

G

worthiness of nobility, gentry and the like, have kept the song alive."

Legend holds that in October 1961, a young man walked into the Ten O'Clock Scholar, a Minneapolis coffeehouse, announced that he was a folksinger, and asked if he could play there. When asked his name, "Bob Dillon" was his answer. Amid a repertoire that included "St. James Infirmary," "Sinner Man," and the odd Carter Family song, the still baby-faced son of a hardware-store owner displayed "The Golden Vanity." Almost exactly three decades later, Dylan introduced magnetic versions of the song into the acoustic sets on the Never Ending Tour.

"Gonna Change My Way of Thinking" (Bob Dylan)

Bob Dylan, *Slow Train Coming* (1979)
Various Artists (performed by Bob Dylan and Mavis Staples), *Gotta Serve Somebody: The Gospel Songs of Bob Dylan* (2003)

High on his preaching stump, Dylan delivers a severe polemic about the "authority from on high" with the kind of believability and assurance that either makes one fret about one's own spiritual doubt or miss the days when he sang about living "by no man's code," as he did on "I Am a Lonesome Hobo" from *John Wesley Harding* just ten years before. Even so, nobody made getting born again seem as hip as Dylan does with "Gonna Change My Way of Thinking."

A straight, ascending 12-bar rock blues, "Gonna Change My Way of Thinking" is quite naturally packed with biblical allusion. The centerpiece here may be the lyric "Jesus said 'be ready/For you know not the hour in which I come'/He said 'who's not for me is against me'/Just so's you all know where He's coming from." Here, in laying down these drops of blood on the tracks, Dylan cribs quotes that appear in the gospels of Matthew and Luke:

Matthew, 24:42, "Watch therefore: for ye know not what hour your Lord doth come"; Matthew 12:30 and Luke 11:23, in slightly different versions, "He that is not with me is against me; and he that gathereth not with me scattereth abroad." The song may not be as uncompromising as it initially seems, as Dylan implies that the secular life and the spiritual one are not necessarily mutually exclusive when he speaks of his woman who follows the Lord and can still do the "Georgia crawl"—a phrase cribbed from numerous skanky blues songs.

Dylan's performances of "Gonna Change My Way of Thinking" are exclusive to his 1979 and 1980 born-again tours, when he confronted his audiences with songs that held a mirror up to society's inner life and outer behavior. His return to this composition via the recording for *Gotta Serve Somebody: The Gospel Songs of Bob Dylan* with Mavis Staples in 2003 (almost assuredly based on a Jimmie Rodgers–Carter Family skit) is as notable for its dose of hokum as it is for its brimstone and fire.

Good as I Been to You

Columbia Records CD CK-53200, CS CT-53200. Production supervised by Debbie Gold. Released November 2, 1992. Photography by Jimmy Wachtel.
Bob Dylan—vocals, guitar, harmonica.
"Frankie and Albert," "Jim Jones," "Blackjack Davey," "Canadee-I-O," "Sittin' on Top of the World," "Little Maggie," "Hard Times," "Step It Up and Go," "Tomorrow Night," "Arthur McBride," "You're Gonna Quit Me," "Diamond Joe," "Froggie Went A-Courtin'"

If the 1980s represented a scattered decade's worth of albums ranging from terrific to terrible and back again, Bob Dylan's third release of the 1990s (after *Under the Red Sky* and *The Bootleg Series, Volumes 1–3*) marked a return to the acoustic folk and country blues that established his career. *Good as I Been to You* is a connoisseur's collection of classic, if at times archaic, folk music reinterpreted by a man who knows how good they could be with some long-unflexed guitar-picking chops thrown in. It was as if Dylan was bringing it all back home—poignantly returning to the musical roots that first fueled his creative engine, revitalizing a recording career that had hit the skids—or maybe he just had writer's block. Perhaps he is contemplating the matter in the cover photo, in which a weathered, unshaven Dylan, sporting a black T-shirt under a striped shirt and leather jacket, squints into the distance over the photographer's shoulder as if he is looking back into the past for these very songs.

Good as I Been to You was Dylan's first all-acoustic release since *The Times They Are A-Changin'* nearly three decades before, and it hit a respectable No. 51 during a two-month stay on the charts. The album may have been Dylan's cheapest to produce: it was recorded at his home studio in Malibu, California.

But this album is not about image or commerce. Rather, it may have been Dylan's most convincing and dramatic portrayal of humanity in years and years—a feat only to be topped by *World Gone Wrong*, his 1993 acoustic, all-cover-song follow-up to this collection. And his range of historical interest and musical styles is impressive for a person of any age or vocation. Whether visiting the back streets of St. Louis for a murder ballad ("Frankie and Albert"), the shores of Australia for a prisoner song of revenge ("Jim Jones"), the high seas for a derring-do tale of hidden identity ("Canadee-I-O"), mountain country for an ornery gun-totin' chestnut ("Little Maggie"), the impoverished underbelly of nineteenth-century America ("Hard Times"), or the British Isles for a trio of arcane and semi-arcane relics ("Arthur McBride," "Blackjack Davey," and "Froggie

Went A-Courtin'"), Dylan's road map of the soul gives perfect directions.

Dylan himself told Italian journalists in 1993 that *Good as I Been to You* came about by accident. "I taped those songs very quickly because they didn't need much arranging," he said. "All those songs are important for me—they've been following me around for years. I didn't treat them like covers, just like songs."

Amazingly, *Good as I Been to You* was Dylan's thirty-seventh album, but (with the exception of *Dylan*, which Columbia Records released without his sanction two decades before) was the first release for which he did not write a single song. Nevertheless, he sounds incredibly free while making ancient, relatively obscure material all his own.

Good Rockin' Tonight: The Legacy of Sun Records/Various Artists
Sire Records, CD 31165; CS 31165. Released 2001.

If Paul McCartney doing "That's All Right Mama," Jeff Beck and Chrissie Hynde getting together for a smoking version of "Mystery Train," Elton John taking a page out of Jerry Lee Lewis's book with a flamboyant "Whole Lotta Shakin' Going On," Live's haunting rendition of "I Walk the Line" (which turns the emotional heart of the Johnny Cash classic inside out), Van Morrison crooning with Carl Perkins on "Sitting on Top of the World," and Bob Dylan revisiting "Red Cadillac and a Black Moustache" is your idea of things to include on a Sun Records tribute album, then *Good Rockin' Tonight* deserves a place near the hearth.

Along with these choice cuts, the album captures the toe-tapping, hip-shaking, head-bobbing Sun sound in all its twistin' glory and effectively passes the Sun legacy on to the next generation with contributions from Sheryl Crow ("Who Will the Next Fool Be?") and the

G

Howling Diablos and Kid Rock ("Drinkin' Wine Spo-Dee-O-Dee").

Sam Phillips (born January 5, 1923, Florence, Alabama; died July 30, 2003, Memphis) was the mastermind behind the Sun sound when he launched his record company in 1952 by converting an old radiator shop into a recording studio. Naming the label Sun Records as a sign of optimism, Phillips provided a musical hothouse that invited spontaneity and creativity. And in this nursery sprouted a vision that still has an impact on popular music. *Good Rockin' Tonight* was released in conjunction with a documentary film of the same title aired on PBS in the U.S. in the fall of 2001.

Located at 706 Union Avenue in Memphis, Sun Studio is where some of the most important rock 'n' roll, rockabilly, blues, and R&B artists of the 1950s recorded. It was where Presley recorded "That's All Right" and Carl Perkins recorded "Blue Suede Shoes." B. B. King, Roy Orbison, Johnny Cash, and Jerry Lee Lewis also sang there.

On July 22, 2003, Sun Studio received historic landmark designation from Secretary of the Interior Gale Norton. The signing ceremony at the U.S. Capitol made the Memphis site the first recording studio in America to achieve this status. The landmark designation is "more for Phillips than some of the stars who recorded there," National Park Service historian Patty Henry told Memphis's *Commercial Appeal* newspaper. "Even if Elvis had never recorded there," she continued, "[Phillips] was very influential in pioneering the rock and roll sound."

"Gospel Plow" (Traditional/arrangement by Bob Dylan)
aka "Hold On," "Keep Your Eyes on the Prize," "Keep Your Hand on the Plow"
Bob Dylan, *Bob Dylan* (1962)
Odetta, *Odetta at Carnegie Hall* (1960)

Pete Seeger, *Pete Seeger at the Village Gate Volume 2* (1963)
Nashville Bluegrass Band, *To Be His Child* (1987)
Mahalia Jackson, *Gospels, Spirituals and Hymns* (1991)
Duke Ellington (with Mahalia Jackson), *Live at Newport 1958* (1994)

Dylan featured his soulful and growling up-tempo rearrangement of "Hold On," a venerated and venerable spiritual, in performance during the 1961 and 1962 seasons and included it, complete with some scorching harmonica work, on his eponymous debut LP. He also accompanied folk revivalist Len Chandler on "Hold On" from the steps of the Lincoln Memorial at the same August 28, 1963, Washington, D.C., civil rights march where Martin Luther King Jr. made his monumental "I Had a Dream" speech.

Often reckoned to be a black spiritual, "Hold On" was a hymn also sung in the white fundamentalist "Holiness Churches," chiefly Methodist in origin, that sprang up after the Civil War. What marked these gatherings was the freedom with which the congregation sang—some reports indicating an expression of religious fervor that matched the rural African-American churches. The Holiness Church was also noted for its emphasis on music and even dancing at its lively services, which had a great attraction for peoples of the isolated mountain communities. Folklorist Cecil Sharp heard "Gospel Plow" sung by whites in Kentucky in 1917 and thought it had been influenced by the black church.

In 1963, Dylan brashly commented in *Scene*, a British performing-arts magazine, that in "Gospel Plow" he was "consciously trying to recapture the rude beauty of a Southern farmhand musing in melody on his porch." Truly he seems barely able to control himself from taking off into the stratosphere as he sings the song on its various recordings—licit or not.

The key phrase in the song ("Hold on, keep your hand on the plow, hold on") was a folk saying from the heartland that is meant to convey strong resolve. Yet Dylan, with his yelping, yodeling whoop of voice and guitar work bustling all over his performances of "Gospel Plow," expresses the opposite, giving the impression of a man about to break down in the scorched fields.

[S] "Got My Mind Made Up" (Bob Dylan/Tom Petty)

aka "I've Got My Mind Made Up"
Bob Dylan, *Knocked Out Loaded* (1986)

One of the better songs from a throwaway album, this shrill rave is still fairly humdrum, sounding as if it was written during a coffee break in the studio just before it was recorded; a finer example of Dylan's collaborative efforts with Tom Petty during the mid-1980s would be "Jammin' Me." Here the narrator has made up his mind to ditch his woman once and for all, telling her straight out that he'd rather go hang out with a buddy on a Libyan oil refinery than be with her. "Got My Mind Made Up" received only one concert outing during the 1986 tour with the Heartbreakers, just after its release on *Knocked Out Loaded*.

[S] "Gotta Serve Somebody" (Bob Dylan)

aka "Serve Somebody," "You Gotta Serve Somebody"
Bob Dylan, single (1979); *Slow Train Coming* (1979); *Biograph* (1985); *Bob Dylan's Greatest Hits, Volume 3* (1994)
Bob Dylan/The Grateful Dead, *Dylan & the Dead* (1989)
Various Artists (performed by Bob Dylan), *The Sopranos: Music from the HBO Original Series* (2000)
Bob Dylan/Various Artists (performed by Shirley Caesar), *Masked and Anonymous* (2003)
David Allan Coe, *Castles in the Sand* (1983)
Luther Ingram, *Luther Ingram* (1986)
Dead Ringers, *Dead Ringers* (1993)
Casino Steel, *Casino Steel* (1993)
Mesa, *Mesa* (1993)
Judy Collins, *Judy Sings Dylan . . . Just Like a Woman* (1993)
Pops Staples, *Father Father* (1994)
Booker T. and the MGs, *That's the Way It Should Be* (1994); *Time Is Tight* (1998)
Johnny Q. Public, *Extra-Ordinary* (1995)
Gary Hoey, *Bug Alley* (1996)
Phil Driscoll, *Live with Friends* (1998)
Insol, *Insol* (1998)
Natalie Cole, *Snowfall on the Sahara* (1999)
Various Artists (performed by Mavis Staples), *Tangled Up in Blues: The Songs of Bob Dylan* (1999)
Devo, *Recombo DNA* (2000)
Scott Holt, *Dark of the Night* (2000)
Nona Hendryx, *Rhythm & Spirit: Love Can Build a Bridge* (2000)
Etta James, *Matriarch of the Blues* (2000)
Marva Wright, *Let Them Talk* (2000)
Rolling Thunder, *The Never Ending Rehearsal* (2000)
Rich Lerner, *Napoleon in Rags* (2001)
Aaron Neville, *Believe* (2003)
Jools Holland, *Jools Holland & His Rhythm & Blues Orchestra: Small World Big Band Volume 2, More Friends* (performed with Marianne Faithfull) (2003)
Various Artists (performed by Shirley Caesar), *Gotta Serve Somebody: The Gospel Songs of Bob Dylan* (2003)

Right-angle turns have marked Bob Dylan's trajectory so often, his career could almost be described as circular. But few had such bombshell effects as his embrace of Jesus Christ as his savior and active pursuit, recording, and performance of gospel rock as unveiled on his 1979 album *Slow Train Coming*.

Dylan lore is typically steeped in the events leading up to this most dramatic of transformations. Claiming he was visited by Jesus in a Phoenix hotel room near the end of his grueling world tour in 1978, Dylan took off the first few months of 1979 and went to Bible school.

G

G

He returned to the studio in May with a production team that included the legendary Jerry Wexler and a fresh, very different attitude toward music and life.

As the first song on Dylan's first gospel album, "Gotta Serve Somebody" publicly inaugurated Dylan's "born-again" period. The song essentially falls into a Ginsbergian catalogue, listing everybody from ambassadors to boxing champs to thieves to doctors who, despite what earthly influence they possess and exert, must nevertheless be subject to a higher power: "It may be the devil or it may be the Lord/But you're gonna have to serve somebody." He also playfully includes himself in this wanting crowd through a variety of aliases (Bobby, Zimmy, Timmy, R. J., and Ray) and mentions the domed mansion he was then building for himself in Malibu. The album was not exactly welcomed with open arms by critics and many fans alike, all of whom seemed to forget that Dylan's work had always contained a strong element of religious symbolism and imagery.

Ironically, "Gotta Serve Somebody," Dylan's best-known song from this phase, was not originally planned for inclusion on *Slow Train*. As Wexler began putting together sequences for the album, "Gotta Serve Somebody" did not appear. And, according to Dylan, "I had to fight to get it on the album, it was ridiculous."

Dylan's instincts served him well, for "Serve Somebody" won him a Grammy Award for best male rock vocal. As a single, the song peaked at No. 24 on the *Billboard* chart. But such material goals were clearly not what he had in mind when he set out on this particular musical path.

Dylan and his jubilee troupe debuted "Serve Somebody" on *Saturday Night Live* in November 1979 and performed a sensational version complete with an unusual harmonica turn at the 1980 Grammys, where he won his award.

Naturally, he displayed it front and center during his gospel phase, where it was a frequent opening for the evangelical concerts of late 1979 and early 1980, and it remained in rotation through the mid- and late 1980s. Somewhat surprisingly, given the Grateful Dead's eschewal of religious proselytization (excepting the occasional folk spiritual they performed in the early 1970s), "Gotta Serve Somebody" and "Slow Train Coming" popped up on the 1987 Dylan/Dead set lists. Dylan returned to "Gotta Serve Somebody" now and again during the Never Ending Tour, where it served as a handy fallback set opener through 1999 and was given the odd outing through 2001, when it received a new, slower arrangement. In any event, "Gotta Serve Somebody" is probably Dylan's most lyrically fluid song, as he has constantly altered the words, even, to the casual eye, spontaneously combusting them onstage in true stand-up stump preacher mode.

"Gotta Serve Somebody" may have been partially inspired by Woody Guthrie's performance of "Little Black Train," which appears on the album *Woody Guthrie with Cisco Houston and Sonny Terry, Volume 1*. Along with similarity in the structures of both songs, Dylan's line about living in a mansion not absolving someone from a relationship with his maker echoes the statement in "Little Black Train" that "Your million dollar fortune/your mansion glittering white/you can't take it with you/when the train rolls in tonight." Further parallels appear with regard to who has the last word: "Get ready for your savior/and fix your business right/you've gotta ride that little black train/to make your last ride," says "Little Black Train"; Dylan echoes this by saying that when all is said and done, everybody must "serve somebody." And while the train imagery of Guthrie's song does not appear in Dylan's song, don't forget that "Gotta Serve Somebody" appears on an album called *Slow Train Coming*, which serves the same metaphorical purpose.

John Lennon cut a funny parody in reply to "Gotta Serve Somebody" entitled "Serve Yourself." Also, in 1983, Fine Arts Films, Inc., produced a five-minute animated film of the song. Directed by John Wilson, the short was eventually made available on videocassette and was included on the commercial release *Top of the Pops* in the late 1980s. And just to twist the irony a bit further, in 2002 HBO quoted a lyric from the song in a commercial for its police drama series *The Wire*.

Gotta Serve Somebody: The Gospel Songs of Bob Dylan

Columbia Records CD 89015. Released March 2003. Executive production by Jeffrey Gaskill. Produced by Joel Moss. "Gonna Change My Way of Thinking" a Jack Frost production.

"Gotta Serve Somebody" (Shirley Caesar), "When You Gonna Wake Up" (Lee Williams & the Spiritual QC's), "I Believe in You" (Dottie Peoples), "Are You Ready" (Fairfield Four), "Solid Rock" (Sounds of Blackness), "Saving Grace" (Aaron Neville), "What Can I Do for You?" (Helen Baylor), "Pressing On" (Chicago Mass Choir), "Saved" (Mighty Clouds of Joy), "When He Returns" (Rance Allen), "Gonna Change My Way of Thinking" (Bob Dylan and Mavis Staples)

It may have taken nearly a quarter century, but Dylan's songs of conversion praising the glory of the Lord finally received proper vindication and acceptance with the release of this choice slice of "Gospel Bob," done up with just the right touches of Sunday morning sanctity and backwoods gris-gris. Finally, this important and fertile period of his career could be considered on its own merits without the baggage and gravitas that initially weighed it down.

Every cut here is a keeper, but special nods should go to Shirley Caesar's gritty cover of the title track, Aaron Neville's distinctive, light quaver of "Saving Grace," the Fairfield Four's

smooth-but-not-too-slick a cappella reading of "Are You Ready," a driving "Solid Rock" from the Sounds of Blackness (a band that includes Dylan gospel-phase musicians guitarist Fred Tackett and drummer Jim Keltner), and a soaring vocal Holy Rolling "Saved" from the Mighty Clouds of Joy.

Rounding out the collection is a special appearance by an extremely craggy-voiced Dylan, duetting with Mavis Staples on a revamped, funky, fuzz-toned guitar romp through "Gonna Change My Way of Thinking," complete with a scripted on-the-spot dialogue so full of nearly embarrassing hokum that it sounds like it slid off the black vinyl grooves of a 1940s Jazz Gillum record.

A final note: *Gotta Serve Somebody* was nominated for (but did not win) a Grammy for best gospel album of 2003.

"Gotta Travel On" (Traditional/Paul Clayton/Larry Ehrlich/David Lazar/Tom Six)

"Done Laid Around"
Bob Dylan, *Self Portrait* (1970)
The Weavers, *Greatest Hits* (1957)
Rex Allen, *Rex Allen Sings 16 Favorites* (1961)
The Springfields, *Silver Threads & Golden Needles* (1962)
Ray Bryant, *Alone at Montreux* (1972)
Bill Monroe, *Bluegrass 1950–58* (1990)
Osborne Brothers, *Bluegrass 1956–68* (1995)

This rousing, kick-the-dust-off-your-boots farewell, based on a nineteenth-century English folk song, was a natural group sing-along encore for a steady stream of Rolling Thunder shows in 1976—upwards of a half dozen members of the troupe would take a shot at on-the-spot lyric creation in the true rough-and-ready spirit of the tour.

Dylan was onto this song as early as 1960, as evidenced by its appearance on one of the earliest extant Dylan recordings, the so-called St.

Paul Tape, purportedly from May 1960. On its official *Self Portrait* release, Dylan included a twangy, tepid version of "Gotta Travel On" with conga drums and passionless vocals. Some think Dylan may have first heard the tune at a 1959 Buddy Holly concert in the Duluth Armory: Holly was then in the practice of using "Gotta Travel On" as an encore sign-off.

Spontaneous lyric combustion seems to have been integral to the song's development, as shown by Pete Seeger's account (included in a volume of *Reprints from* Sing Out!, *The Folk Song Magazine*) of how it came to him: "The following song I first learned from Larry Ehrlich of Chicago, who learned it from Paul Clayton, who learned it from Arthur Kyle Davis of the University of Virginia, who got it from a booklet, published by a now deceased French professor. His original sources, Negro folksingers of Virginia, were not listed. There may have been other verses, but Paul Clayton did not know 'em. Larry Ehrlich and others in Chicago therefore made up a couple more. And the Weavers added a few."

Clayton (born March 3, 1933, New Bedford, Massachusetts; died March 30, 1967, New York City), is arguably the best known of the authors credited for "Gotta Travel On." Known not only as a fine singer, guitarist, and dulcimer player, Clayton was also a respected music collector. Befitting a descendant of New England fishing families, Clayton helped preserve the heritage and lore of the whaling songs and sea chanteys of his region. But his extensive discography reveals a range of interests that stretched from the ballads of his native New England to folk songs of every style and locale. He gathered much of his material on collecting expeditions in the nether reaches of the United States and Canada.

Receiving early encouragement from his musically inclined parents (his dad plucked the banjo and his mom tickled the ivories), Clayton began playing the guitar when he was eleven. As a teenager, he was doing some deep listening to a growing record collection. By the time he was fifteen, he was producing and performing on his own weekly folk music program on a New Bedford radio station. At the University of Virginia he pursued his passion for folk music under the tutelage of the distinguished folklorist and archivist Professor Arthur Kyle Davis Jr. as well as on forays into the local hill country to record new material.

Setting out upon graduation to make a career in folk music, Clayton rapidly earned critical attention for his concert and festival performances. In 1954 he turned out the first of hundreds of recordings and through the 1960s was represented on all of the major folk labels. A fixture on the folk circuit, Clayton enjoyed a certain international popularity that allowed him to continue his music collecting. Many of the fruits of his travels were donated to the Archive of American Folk Song and the Helen Hartness Flanders Ballad Collection in Middlebury, Vermont.

Dylan seems to have shared a somewhat wrenching relationship with Clayton. After an early period of collaboration, which included Dylan's making a guest appearance at a Clayton concert at the Showboat Lounge in Washington, D.C., in September 1961, things seem to have soured. Some say the dissolution was brought on by tensions involving Clayton's barely closeted homosexuality, unrequited sexual longing for the folkie waif, a nerve-fraying 1964 cross-country car trip that included Dylan and a couple of others, and, perhaps most of all, by Dylan's alleged appropriation of at least one of Clayton's tunes for his own use (*see* "Don't Think Twice, It's All Right"). It is also theorized that Dylan's "It's All Over Now, Baby Blue" was composed as an attack on Clayton at the end of their friendship, though Dylan denied this. Clayton died in 1967 (a likely suicide—some sources say he jumped from a window, others that he was electrocuted in his bathtub), culminating a slow decline, fueled by amphetamines and, reportedly, a bum acid trip. Time seems to have eased Dylan's memory of Clayton, whom he lauded in the *Biograph* notes when he said, "Paul was an incredible songwriter and singer. He must have known a thousand songs. I learned 'Pay Day at Coal Creek' and a bunch of other songs from him."

Another accredited author of "Gotta Travel On" with a biography almost as great as the song is David Lazar (born 1929, Chicago; died May 19, 2002, Arlington, Virginia), a career diplomat. Foreign service minister, counselor, and Latin American specialist, Lazar was a senior adviser to the National Security Council and helped negotiate the 1977 Panama Canal Treaty, and was also U.S. representative to the Development Assistance Committee of the Organization for Economic Cooperation and Development from 1984 to 1988.

🔲 "Go 'Way Little Boy" (Bob Dylan)
aka "Go Away Little Boy"
Lone Justice, *This World Is Not My Home* (1999)
Various Artists (performed by Lone Justice), *Doin' Dylan 2* (2002)

Dylan wrote and recorded this dire song for *Empire Burlesque*, but ended up giving it to Maria McKee of Lone Justice. According to McKee, it was through Carole Childs, a Dylan intimate, that "Go 'Way Little Boy" was presented to her band. McKee says that Dylan and Ron Wood assisted in the recording session, playing (evidently uncredited) on the album and coaching her until she "sang the song *exactly like him*." Some think Dylan may play guitar and/or harmonica as well on the Lone Justice release.

🔲 "Grand Coulee Dam" (Woody Guthrie)
aka "Big Grand Coulee Dam," "Ballad of the Great Grand Coulee"
Bob Dylan, *Live 1961–2000—Thirty-nine Years of Great Concert Performances*/'68 (2001)
Various Artists (performed by Bob Dylan), *A Tribute to Woody Guthrie, Part One*/'68 (1971)
Woody Guthrie, *Columbia River Collection* (1988); *Woody Guthrie—This Land Is Your Land: Asch Recordings, Volumes 1–4* (1999)
Cisco Houston, *Cisco Houston Sings of Woody Guthrie* (1963)
Norman Blake and Nancy, *Blind Dog* (1988)
Jack Elliott, *Hard Traveling* (1989)

The best of the three one-night-only songs Dylan performed with the Hawks as part of their set at the January 1968 Woody Guthrie tribute concert at New York City's Carnegie Hall, "Grand Coulee Dam" was done up rockabilly style, complete with some scorching, no-holds-barred licks from the guitar of Robbie Robertson just to shake up the old folkies in the house.

Woody wrote "Grand Coulee Dam" after being hired by the Bonneville Power Administration (a federal entity similar to the Tennessee Valley Authority) in 1941 to celebrate and memorialize the building of the first of a series of dams across the Columbia River in Oregon and Washington. The songs were meant to be utilized as a soundtrack for a film about the projects. But, due to the lack of government funds as the U.S. was drawn into World War II, the film was never made. By the time that decision was made, however, Guthrie had spent the most productive month of his life touring the Pacific Northwest on the Bonneville Power Administration's dime, connecting with his muse as he never had before or would again.

As a result of his involvement with the mammoth public works project, Guthrie became a kind of poet ambassador in a role similar to that of the Social Realism artists of the 1930s, whose work can still be seen adorning the surviving government buildings of that era. These images often depict the brawny, vital Everyman (and Everywoman) in striking, near-mythic tributes to human progress, and Woody's Columbia River songs serve as almost an aural companion to that aesthetic even if it, ironically enough, contributed to the building blocks of the military-industrial complex. Truly, if a Diego Rivera mural could sing, it would probably sound like one of Guthrie's Bonneville songs.

Grand Coulee Dam, 1942.

(Photo: F. B. Pomeroy/Library of Congress)

While "Roll On Columbia" and "Pastures of Plenty" are two of the most famous songs to emerge from Woody's odyssey, "Grand Coulee Dam" should not be overlooked. Of the songs Guthrie composed during his Columbia River project, Joe Klein observed in his biography *Woody Guthrie: A Life* (New York: Alfred A. Knopf, 1980):

> The anthems were particularly fine, filled with lush, dense poetic imagery. "Roll On, Columbia" was a stately and elegant waltz (to the tune of Leadbelly's "Irene") that evolved the majesty of the lower river as it flowed into the sea. By contrast, "The Grand Coulee Dam" was wild and powerful like the river upstream, where the dam—still under construction when Woody visited it—was located. It was written to the "The Wabash Cannonball," and contained spectacular, detailed images and unsuspected rhymes. . . . His songs were beginning to sound like Walt Whitman's poetry, drunk with details. In "Roll On, Columbia," he felt the need to list all the river's tributaries. "The Grand Coulee Dam" included one verse devoted to the different types of factories along the river, and another stuffed with place names: Umatilla Rapids, the Priest, Cascades, Shelillo Falls. He wrote the Almanacs [the Almanac Singers, with whom he frequently collaborated], advising them to include more details in their songs: if they ever expected to reach the workers, they'd have to mention the "wheels, whistles, steam boilers, shafts, cranks, operators, tuggers, pulleys, engines, and all of the well-known gadgets that make up a modern factory."

As a final little aside, Dylan mentions the Grand Coulee Dam in his embittered cathartic diatribe from *Blood on the Tracks*, "Idiot Wind."

[S] "The Groom's Still Waiting at the Altar"

(Bob Dylan)

aka "Groom's Still Waiting at the Altar"

Bob Dylan, single (1981); *Shot of Love* (reissue) (1981); *Biograph/'81* (1985); *Bob Dylan's Greatest Hits, Volume 3* (1994)

Various Artists (performed by Andy Coburn), *Tribute to Bob Dylan, Volume 1* (1994)

Rod Stewart, single (1995)

Hammond Gamble, *Plugged In and Blue* (1995)

Michel Montecrossa, *Born in Time* (2000)

A *Shot of Love* outtake that eventually appeared on the CD release of that great LP (it was mysteriously included on some promotional vinyl releases at the time of its premier issue) and that garnered significant radio airplay in 1981, "The Groom's Still Waiting at the Altar" is a stinging electric rhythm and blues aptly hailed as a tasteful throwback to Dylan's mid-1960s work. At the same time, however, "Groom" was also representative of Dylan's new, harder-edged sound captured on *Shot of Love* and in his concerts of late 1980 and 1981.

Though in the process of emerging from his born-again Christian phase, Dylan was still using overtly New Testament and religious material when he composed "Groom." And though Bert Cartwright, in his article "The Bible in the Lyrics of Bob Dylan: 1985–1990," published in *The Telegraph* #38 (spring 1991), suggests Matthew 9:15, Ephesians 5:25, and Hosea 2:19–20 (dealing variously with spiritual commitment and naïveté) as possible sources of inspiration, Michael Gray's *Song & Dance Man III: The Art of Bob Dylan* (London and New York: Continuum International, 2000) suggests that the entire context for the song can be boiled down to John 3:28–29 and may be even more acute: ". . . I am not the Christ, but that I am sent before him. He that hath the bride is the bridegroom: but the friend of the bridegroom, which standeth and heareth him, rejoiceth greatly. . . . Gray sees this allusion as a metaphor in which the bridegroom is Christ and the Church, while the Christian faithful is the bride.

Wailing with the lobster-eyed possession of a tongue-speaking, backwoods Pentecostalist snake handler, Dylan manages to fit a mouthful of words into single lines on this barn burner, which paradoxically deals with his disenchantment with religion and a certain woman by the name of Claudette, who perhaps herself is a stand-in for Christ. Some suggest that the song was inspired by an actual incident, based on the rumor that Dylan was set to remarry but that at the last moment, things didn't exactly work out as planned.

If the song doesn't amount to much more than a series of highly stylish verses, with Dylan spewing out lines like "Put your hand on my head baby, do I have a temperature?/I see people who are supposed to know better standin' around like furniture" or "What can I say about Claudette?/Ain't seen her since January/She could be respectably married/Or running a whorehouse in Buenos Aires," it is at least a bumpy ferry ride "west of the Jordan, east of the Rock of Gibraltar"—or across the River Styx.

Careful study reveals "Groom" to be much more than that, easily one of Dylan's big songs of the 1980s ("Caribbean Wind," "Angelina," and "Blind Willie McTell") that were not released until many years after their initial recording. Yes, there's Dylan's uncompromising apocalyptic prophecy stuck at the end of each chaotic verse, but it is his ability to mix cosmic omens with mundane observation that makes the song so compelling, dizzying, and, yes, ambiguous.

[S] "Guess I'm Doin' Fine" (Bob Dylan)

aka "Guess I'm Doing Fine"

Hamilton Camp, *Paths of Victory* (1964)

Dylan recorded "Guess I'm Doin' Fine" as a Witmark demo in January 1964 for copyright and publishing purposes. Somewhere along the line, Hamilton Camp got hip to this been-down-so-long-it-looks-like-up-to-me Guthrieesque folk blues and released it on his Dylan tribute LP, *Paths of Victory*. Here, the narrator has lost his childhood, he's broke, and trouble finds him at every turn. Yet he figures he's doing okay just as long as he can walk the street with a smile on his face.

Woody Guthrie

Born Woodrow Wilson Guthrie, July 14, 1912, Okemah, Oklahoma; died October 3, 1967, New York City

"Woody is just Woody. Thousands of people do not know he has any other name. He is just a voice and a guitar. He sings the songs of a people and I suspect that he is, in a way, that people. Harsh-voiced and nasal, his guitar banging like a tire iron on a rusty rim, there is nothing sweet about Woody, and there is nothing sweet about the songs he sings. But there is something more important for those who will listen. There is the will of the people to endure and fight against oppression."

As much as anything or anyone could, those famous words of American novelist John Steinbeck, from his foreword to Alan Lomax's book *Hard Hitting Songs for Hard-Hit People* (New York: Oak Publications, 1967), crystallize the great legend and real hardscrabble life of arguably *the* most important figure in American folk music: Woody Guthrie.

He wrote songs of the America he knew and loved, songs of and for people, folk songs, patriotic songs, work songs, children's songs—and he brought a new activism to folk music. His legacy lives on, not only through his direct influence on the young Bob Dylan in the late 1950s and early 1960s, but also through his

contemporary torchbearers: Ani DiFranco, Billy Bragg, and Woody's own son Arlo.

Woody's childhood was marked by a slow decline in his family's stake, symbolized most dramatically by the fire that burned down the family house and killed his sister Clara. The Guthries' fortunes had long been characterized by cycles of boom and bust, and when his father's real estate business failed, the family moved to Pampa, Texas. There, Woody began to come into his own as a musician. He had inherited from his piano-playing mother the knack of being able to make up songs on the spot, but as a teenager in Pampa, music became a passion. With his friends Cluster Baker and Matt Jennings he formed a group called the Corncob Trio. (Woody would later marry Matt's sister, Mary.) The Corncob Trio played anywhere they could, and through performance, Woody developed his trademark sardonic, occasionally cutting, sense of humor. But at a time when he and his bandmates could easily have sung about their own misery, the Trio instead opted to sing lighthearted fare.

Woody could have easily given in to his own misery, for it was substantial. Of most concern was his mother's development of a puzzling, mind-crippling disease. He later learned it was called Huntington's chorea, a degenerative and invariably fatal nerve disorder, but no one knew that at the time. Misdiagnosed, she was declared insane and spent her last years in a mental institution. Then, in 1935 when the dust storms hit Pampa, Woody and Mary (whom he had married in 1933) headed to California along with the tens of thousands of people from Texas, Oklahoma, and Arkansas—the Dust Bowl Refugees—who had lost just about everything to the raging whirlwinds. For a taste of that dusty old dust, take a listen to Woody's great song "So Long, It's Been Good to Know Ya."

Woody Guthrie, 1943.

(Photo: Al Almuller/*New York World-Telegram and Sun* Collection/Library of Congress)

Woody's experience on the road west may have been the most profound of his life, for on that ribbon of highway, he saw hundreds of people who had been completely dispossessed. Seeing the hollow face of human desperation laid so bare aroused a sense of indignation and anger in him that he never lost, and when he saw these same people exploited and humiliated further by landowners and powerful growers after arriving in what they thought would be the "promised land" of California, his songwriting took on a blend of cynical humor, rage, and grief over their fate.

Landing a job on radio station KFVD in Los Angeles, Woody became a regular attraction on the airwaves. When he befriended singer Cisco Houston and actor Will Geer (who gained later acclaim as "Grandpa" on television's *The Waltons*), Guthrie began establishing his left-wing credentials with appearances at union meetings and migrant labor camps. Already a prolific songwriter who could churn out an original piece on demand, Woody was able to give quick expression to his reactions to the poverty he witnessed and find wide dissemination via the radio or in the many meetings he attended. Woody's political awakening and emergence as an earthy force on the American landscape coincided with a vast polarization between the rich and the poor. And if Woody's avowed allegiance to any political "ism" was always a little fuzzy, his commitment to the downtrodden was anything but. "I ain't a communist necessarily," he once said, "but I been in the red all my life."

Woody was an enthusiastic proponent of President Franklin D. Roosevelt's New Deal, and his most famous songs ("Pastures of Plenty," "Dust Bowl Refugee," "Grand Coulee Dam," and "Roll On Columbia" among them) reflect the ethos of Depression-era America. "This Land Is Your Land," for example, has come to be regarded by many as an "alternative" national anthem. What makes the best of Woody's songs so affecting and enduring is the manner in which he tempered his righteous indignation with a deep love for the desperate people and beautiful country he celebrated. As he wrote in the early 1940s (as quoted in Alan Lomax's *Hard Hitting Songs*): "For the last eight years I've been a rambling man from Oklahoma to California and back three times by freight train, highway, and thumb; and I've been stranded and disbanded, busted and disgusted. I've been with people of all sorts, sizes, shapes and calibres—folks that wandered over the country looking for work, down and out and hungry half the time. I've slept with their feet in my face and my feet in theirs; in greasy rotten shacks and tents with Okies and Arkies that are grazing today over the states of California and Arizona like a herd of lost buffalo."

Gradually, as he become more politically active and outspoken, Guthrie moved from singing about the plight of workers to advocating their banding together to do something about it. Such a message resounded with America's Communists, with whom Guthrie did associate from time to time, but his relationship with the party was always tenuous—he maintained that he was not a member of any "earthly organization."

Meanwhile, unable to deal with her husband's wanderlust, Mary Guthrie returned to Los Angeles with the couple's three children to raise the family in as stable an environment as she could provide. Still, even separated from Woody, the Guthrie family's tragic legacy dogged them nonetheless: two of Woody and Mary's children succumbed to Huntington's disease later in life, and the other died in a car accident.

Guthrie met Pete Seeger in 1940, and with that began a new phase in his life. With Lee Hayes and Millard Lampell, Seeger and Guthrie formed the Almanac Singers, a group dedicated to left-wing politics in the extreme. Pulling up stakes and moving to New York City's Greenwich Village, Woody cofounded with his bandmates Almanac House, a cooperative progressive cell, and he also immediately found himself at the epicenter of the East Coast folk movement. The move east also brought him into contact with the great Leadbelly, not to mention Sonny Terry and Brownie McGhee, all of whom he would collaborate with extensively.

But he also met, and eventually married, Marjorie Mazia, a dancer in the Martha Graham troupe, in 1941, after divorcing Mary. The couple's first child, Cathy, led to a certain element of stability in Woody's life. And while he wrote a much-acclaimed cycle of children's songs for Cathy and her siblings that followed, the publication of his loosely autobiographical

G

Bound for Glory in 1943 was his crowning achievement from this era. "Someday people are going to wake up to the fact that Woody Guthrie and the ten thousand songs that leap and tumble off the strings of his music box are a national possession, like Yellowstone and Yosemite, and part of the best stuff this country has to show the world," declared *The New Yorker*'s review of the book.

A key chapter in Woody's life was his acceptance of an offer from Washington's Bonneville Power Authority in the spring of 1941 to write music for a documentary film about the Grand Coulee Dam and the Columbia River. Woody's travels in the region and his prodigious output during his month-long visit—he reportedly wrote thirty songs in thirty days—put yet another part of the country in his blood. In an era when technology was still unequivocally celebrated and ecological concerns of secondary or no importance, Woody was greatly impressed and heartened by the dam and what it represented for the region's laborers: jobs for the jobless and cheap electricity for people who up until then could not afford it.

After three merchant marine tours with Cisco Houston during World War II (for an account, see Jim Longhi's 1997 book *Woody, Cisco, & Me*), tragedy again struck the Guthries when an electrical fire killed Cathy. Though Woody and Marjorie had two more children, Nora and Arlo, Cathy's death dealt Woody a crushing blow.

Musically, after the war and Cathy's death, Guthrie picked up where he had left off: recording a series of exemplary songs for the newly founded Folkways label, renewing his commitment to the union movement through columns for the *Daily Worker* and *People's World*, and resuming his prolific output by conscientiously composing every day. He continued this practice unabated until the end of the 1940s, when the symptoms of Huntington's disease (still undiagnosed) began to surface and take a toll. He divorced Marjorie in 1952, though she and the children would remain in the foreground of his life through his final years.

A final lust for adventure drew Guthrie away from his family and sent him on a trip with protégé Ramblin' Jack Elliott to California, where he met a much younger woman, Anneke Marshall. The two married in 1953 and subsequently had a daughter together.

But Guthrie's behavior became increasingly erratic. He returned to New York where, upon reuniting with Marjorie in 1954, he was diagnosed with Huntington's disease.

Hospitalized in 1954 and gradually immobilized by this wasting illness until he could barely talk or recognize friends and visitors, Woody endured a decline that was long, slow, and painful. It was fate's cruel trick that he was able to watch, but not participate, in America's folk music renaissance—a phenomenon that probably could never have happened without him and over which his presence indelibly hovered. Thanks to the passion and talents of Ramblin' Jack Elliott, Woody's music was kept alive as the folk boom spread throughout the United States.

Woody's environment took a turn for the better in 1959 when a New Jersey electrician, Bob Gleason, and his wife, Sidsel, heard a radio program devoted to Woody and his music. Longtime Guthrie fans, they first began visiting him at the nearby Greystone Park Hospital and, after several months, secured permission to bring him to their home on weekends. Word quickly spread through the New York City folk community that Woody was receiving visitors on Sundays in East Orange, New Jersey—a mere twenty-minute bus ride from Times Square. Marjorie and the kids, Pete Seeger, and Alan Lomax were the usual suspects to be

G

found there, but so were a handful of the younger folkie enthusiasts, including John Cohen and Peter LaFarge.

One of those who made the pilgrimage to sit at Guthrie's feet was a twenty-year-old Bob Dylan. On January 29, 1961, just five days after landing in New York, Dylan made his first visit to Woody; he may well have met Cisco Houston and Jack Elliott as well. After some easily understood shyness on Dylan's part, he did sing a song, prompting Woody to remark, as legend has it, "He's a talented boy. Gonna go far."

Dylan moved in with the Gleasons for a period around then, made some well-known early tapes at their place, and shared further Sunday afternoons with Guthrie. In his fantastic 1980 biography *Woody Guthrie: A Life,* Joe Klein (yes, "Anonymous" Joe Klein of later *Primary Colors* infamy), wrote: "A real rapport seemed to develop between Woody and Dylan, with Woody often asking the Gleasons if 'the boy' was going to be there on Sunday. 'That boy's got a voice,' he told them, 'maybe he won't make it with his writing, but he can sing it. He can really sing it.'"

Dylan had been turned on to Woody Guthrie during his brief stay in college at the University of Minnesota. "I first heard Woody Guthrie over at a house party," he told the BBC in a 1985 interview. During that interview Dylan expressed his awe of the man:

> He had a sound . . . [and] something that needed to be said. . . . I was completely taken over by him. By his spirit, or whatever. You could listen to his songs and actually learn how to live, or how to feel. . . . Woody Guthrie was who he was because he came along in the time he came along in. For me he was like a link in a chain. Like I am for other people, and we all are for somebody.

A final testament to Woody Guthrie's importance in the development of Dylan's early aesthetic is not only the sheer number of Guthrie songs in the younger man's repertoire, but in the first original composition he released, "Song to Woody." But Dylan's rambling, Beat-style poem "Last Thoughts on Woody Guthrie," performed just once at the end of his April 12, 1963, Town Hall concert in New York City, is his "so long, it's been good to know ya" adieu to the folk master.

Has any artist suffered a crueler fate than Woody Guthrie? He went from footloose poet and, as he put it, "one-cylinder guitar picker," to relatively young victim of a degenerative disease that left him crippled, voiceless, and entombed in his own body.

These words from Woody Guthrie, from a script opening a radio broadcast on New York City's WNEW, December 3, 1944, are a little long to fit on a tombstone, but they promise to come with the dust and go with the wind for at least another eon:

> I hate a song that makes you think that you are not any good. I hate a song that makes you think that you are just born to lose. Bound to lose. No good to nobody. No good for nothing. Because you are too old or too young or too fat or too slim or too ugly or too this or too that. Songs that run you down or poke fun at you on account of your bad luck or hard traveling.
>
> I am out to fight those songs to my very last breath of air and my last drop of blood. I am out to sing songs that will prove to you that this is your world and that if it has hit you pretty hard and knocked you for a dozen loops, no matter what color, what size you are, how you are built, I am out to sing the songs that make you take pride in yourself and in your work. And the songs that I sing are made up for the most part by all sorts of folks just about like you.

H

[S] "Had a Dream About You, Baby" (Bob Dylan)

Various Artists (performed by Bob Dylan), *Hearts of Fire* (1987)
Bob Dylan, *Down in the Groove* (1988)

A blues shuffle from here to eternity that sounds like it was written in a bumper car on the way to the studio, "Had a Dream About You, Baby" is very light R&B fare about another highway mama who enchants our narrator (late last night she came rollin' across his mind) until he is tongue-tied. Dylan recorded and released a couple of versions of the song, the better mix appearing on the *Hearts of Fire* soundtrack, where he sings it with real gusto. Dylan also briefly performed the song during the 1988 phase of the Never Ending Tour.

[S] "Hallelujah" (Leonard Cohen)

Leonard Cohen, *Various Positions* (1985)
Various Artists (performed by John Cale), *I'm Your Fan (The Songs of Leonard Cohen by . . .)* (1991)
Jeff Buckley, *Grace* (1994)
Various Artists (performed by Bono), *Tower of Song: The Songs of Leonard Cohen* (1995)
Patricia O'Callaghan, *Slow Fox* (1999)

Dylan's one-off concert performance of this Leonard Cohen classic transpired in its composer's hometown of Montreal during an early Never Ending Tour stop in 1988; Dylan had previously recorded the song at a 1981 rehearsal session. That sole 1988 rendition is itself worthy of note, Dylan handling the confessional with dynamic vocals, expertise, and vehement passion, mixing the sacred and profane in an ode that could be addressed to God, goddess, or woman.

As recorded by Cohen, "Hallelujah" presents itself with a refreshingly light, fragile spirituality that stands in stark contrast to his dark artistic legacy, which may explain why Dylan was first attracted to it at the tail end of his gospel period.

The 1985 album from which Cohen's "Hallelujah" was drawn, *Various Positions*, proved to be a transitional one for him, as it comes halfway between the classic balladic style of *Recent Songs* (1979) and the cool electronic inflections of *I'm Your Man* (1988). *Various Positions* was Cohen's sleekest production to date at that time, though it seems Spartan compared to later efforts.

The Mel Tormé of the terminally downbeat, Leonard Cohen (born September 21, 1934, Montreal, Quebec) was an underground hero during the 1960s and 1970s and is a poet and songwriter whose work should be regarded as highly as Bob Dylan's but isn't. While the timeless quality of his albums almost ensures that his work will not age, his gloomy poetry set to music and delivered in monotone is, admittedly, hard to take in large doses.

When all is said and done, Cohen may go down as Canada's true poet laureate. The son of an engineer who ended up in the *schmata* business and died when his son was nine, Cohen entered McGill University in the early 1950s. While there he formed the Buckskin Boys, a country-western trio, got serious about poetry, and filtered into the local bohemian scene so subterranean that it did not exactly strike fear into the city's political, social, or intellectual establishments.

Let Us Compare Mythologies, his first collection of poems, was published in 1956 while he was still at McGill. *The Spice Box of Earth*, his second book of poems, published in 1961, garnered international recognition.

Upon obtaining a grant, he traversed Europe but was especially fond of Hydra, the

Leonard Cohen in recording studio, 1979.
(Photo: Ian Cook/Time Life Pictures/Getty Images)

Greek island where he spent much of the next seven years. While writing another book of poems in 1964 (the controversial *Flowers for Hitler*), he also managed to turn out a novel, making his mark with *The Favourite Game* in 1963 and then again with *Beautiful Losers* in 1966. While *The Favourite Game* was his bildungsroman, portraying the artist growing up as a young Montreal Jew, *Beautiful Losers* offered a mixture of the sexual and spiritual longing, despair, and black humor that would later characterize his lyrics. The *Boston Globe* hailed the epic with the following accolade: "James Joyce is not dead. He is living in Montreal under the name of Cohen."

Cohen performed at the Newport Folk Festival in 1967 and was snared by Columbia Records. *The Songs of Leonard Cohen*, his impressive debut LP, portrayed a world of weary loneliness enhanced by the barest of musical accompaniment. The literate, if often bleak, subject matter won him widespread acclaim and endeared him to both critics and a generation of closet singer-songwriters. Songs like "Suzanne," "Hey That's No Way to Say Goodbye," "So Long, Marianne," and "Sisters of Mercy" redefined what a confessional could be. Film director Robert Altman realized their potential and used some Cohen songs as the soundtrack for what many consider his best film, *McCabe and Mrs. Miller*—a rough-edged vision of California's prospecting legacy starring Warren Beatty and Julie Christie. None of this, however, made Cohen the hottest ticket in town.

Cohen continued to stretch the boundaries of the pop-song landscape and reinvent himself and his work with a brilliant series of albums in the late 1960s and early 1970s: *Songs from a Room* (1969) reinforced his stature as a sentry of solitude; *Live Songs* (1973) showcased "Please Don't Pass Me By," a stunning fourteen-minute improvisation; and *New Skin for the Old Ceremony* (1974) surprised his fans with its comparatively lush orchestrations.

After taking a sabbatical from the art wars in the mid-1970s, he returned with what may be his most idiosyncratic effort, *Death of a Ladies' Man*, which began as a collaboration with Phil Spector and ended with Cohen's being strong-armed out of the final mix. Dylan and Allen Ginsberg, by the way, contributed backing vocals on one of the *Death of a Ladies' Man* tunes: "Don't Go Home with Your Hard-On."

The full flowering of his religious concerns was exhibited in 1985 on *Various Positions*. The album's tracks appear born of an arduous spiritual odyssey, and many a hard-core Cohen admirer view them as psalms for the new age.

Cohen's popular high-water mark came in 1988 with *I'm Your Man*, a superbly crafted album of tracks that became instant Cohen classics: "First We Take Manhattan," "Tower of Song," and "Ain't No Cure for Love." It is no wonder that the album went to No. 1 in several European countries. In 1992 came *The Future*, a cutting, deeply cynical diagnosis that cast a pretty cold eye on all human behavior from the bedroom to the boardroom.

After a concert tour to promote *The Future*, Cohen was drawn to a Zen retreat atop Mount Baldy in Southern California, where he would eventually spend much of the next part of his life meditating, writing koans, and cooking for Sasaki Roshi, his sensei. After almost five years, Cohen, now an ordained Zen monk with the dharma name of Jikan (Silent One),

emerged from Mount Baldy's slopes with hundreds of new poems and song lyrics. With Sharon Robinson, a former backup singer and collaborator, he crafted *Ten New Songs*, an understated, austere vision released in 2001. Still, to admirers of Cohen the album represented nothing less than Moses returning with his stone tablets from Mount Sinai's peaks.

Cohen may have been joking when he once said that he only "aspired to be a minor poet" back in the 1950s. Ironically and despite himself, this documentarian of the human condition became a cultural elder.

Dylan and Cohen have reportedly maintained a friendship dating back to the late 1960s. A nice account of an encounter between the two during the Rolling Thunder Revue can be found in Larry "Ratso" Sloman's book *On the Road with Bob Dylan*. It is not unlikely that Cohen was in attendance at the Montreal Forum in 1988 when Dylan performed "Hallelujah."

"Hallelujah! I'm Ready" (Traditional)
aka "Hallelujah! I'm Ready (to Go)," "I'm Ready"
Stanley Brothers, *Early Years 1958–61* (1994); *Bluegrass Salvation: I'm Ready to Go* (1998)
Ricky Skaggs, *Family and Friends* (1982)
Hilltop News, *I Can Make It Through* (1991)
Southern Rail, *Glory Train* (1995)

In the summer of 1999, Dylan began performing acoustic renditions of this piece of gospel bluegrass about Christ leading a sinner to salvation on the highway of the damned. He continued employing "Hallelujah, I'm Ready" onstage through his early 2002 concerts, mostly as a show opener. Made famous by the Stanley Brothers, the song has developed a certain following in bluegrass circles and is one of several country gospel tunes Dylan embraced as cover material late in his career, suggesting a renewed interest in songs of the spirit.

[S] **"Handle with Care"** (Traveling Wilburys)

Traveling Wilburys, single (1988); *Traveling Wilburys, Volume 1* (1988)

The genuine article from the Traveling Wilburys' debut smash is a wistful, Beatles-like meditation on celebrity and its price. Though primarily a vehicle for George Harrison and Roy Orbison's lead vocals, casual listening reveals Dylan and Tom Petty's gruff background harmonizing in the chorus.

In a 1988 interview with Great Britain's Radio One, Harrison recalled that he and his mates had a small case of writer's block when it came to finally sitting down, rolling up their sleeves, and getting the words down. Sitting around Dylan's garage in Malibu, California, while listening to a rough cut they had recorded, these great lyricists (perhaps a bit intimidated to be in each other's company and vexed at the task at hand) began scratching their heads. Harrison said that he looked "behind his garage door and there was this big cardboard box that said 'HANDLE WITH CARE' on it. I said, 'It's called "Handle with Care." And he [Dylan] said, 'Oh that's good. I like that!' And that was it. Once we'd got the title it just went off. I thought, 'Been beat up and battered around,' and then the lyrics just went flying around. I mean, we could have had twenty-nine verses to that tune. It was brilliant."

As a single, "Handle with Care" hit No. 45 on the *Billboard* charts. An extended version with an alternate, longer mix was released in Europe. A serviceable video of the ensemble lip-synching the song was released and helped propel the song, album, and band into the national spotlight for a spell.

[S] **"Handsome Molly"** (Traditional)

aka "Farewell, Nancy," "Lovely Molly"

Bob Dylan, *Live 1961–2000—Thirty-nine Years of Great Concert Performances/'61* (2001)

Various Artists (performed by G. B. Grayson and Henry Whitter), *Music from the Lost Provinces: 1927–1931* (1999)

Glen Neaves, *Traditional Music from Grayson and Carroll Counties* (1962)

Frank Proffitt, *Frank Proffitt of Reece, North Carolina* (1962)

Martin Simpson, *Grinning in Your Face* (1983)

Deighton Family, *Acoustic Music to Suit Most Occasions* (1988)

Michel Montecrossa, *Jet Pilot* (2000)

Only a couple of versions of Dylan singing this traditional English folk song still circulate; both are from the 1961–1962 period. Because they were recorded more than a year apart, though, it is a good bet that "Handsome Molly" was a regular inclusion in Dylan's early sets. His summer 1961 Riverside Church performance of the song is particularly noteworthy for its subtle power and musical inventiveness. (Another highlight from that tape is his endearingly hapless stand-up act—he spends literally minutes trying to jury-rig his harmonica holder between songs, all the while dropping sardonic Guthrielike quips.)

In "Handsome Molly," the narrator notices his gal's wandering eye while the two attend church, of all places. She once promised him her hand but ultimately dumps him for another, leaving him to wander to the river and dream of escape to a far-off land.

"Handsome Molly"—but one common title for essentially the same song also known as, for example, "Farewell, Nancy," as collected by Helen Creighton in her book *Maritime Folk Songs* (1962), or "Farewell, Charming Nancy," as it appears in G. Malcolm Laws's *American Balladry from British Broadsides* (1957)—follows in the tradition of the "spurned lover" family of compositions. As "Farewell, Nancy" it appeared in Patrick Weston Joyce's *Ancient Irish Music*, published in 1873 and 1888. Some research suggests it was printed as a broadside as early as 1855.

[S] "Handy Dandy" (Bob Dylan)

Bob Dylan, *Under the Red Sky* (1990)

An inviting piece of cheese marked by Al Kooper's familiar organ hooks from *Under the Red Sky*, Dylan's children's record in disguise, "Handy Dandy" may have been inspired by a poem that appears in Iona and Peter Opie's compilation of works for children in *The Oxford Nursery Rhyme Book*, published in 1955. That famed nursery rhyme collection contains a piece titled "Handy Dandy" that, in turn, uses the line "cat's in the well," which ended up as the title for another *Under the Red Sky* song.

What a fabulous character this Handy Dandy is—a charming rogue who could have walked off the pages of a Damon Runyon story or be found sipping absinthe in an after-hours Storyville bucket-of-blood a century ago. Dylan sings with exuberant vitality and uses the song's quirky structure to enhance its dynamic effect by beginning each verse with a casual, slow-paced description of one of his subject's charismatic attributes, following that with an acrobatic and spitfire, damning-with-a-faint-praise plume of verbiage, and finishing with a slow drawl. Technical wizardry or not, "Handy Dandy" portrays a guy not to be messed with. He visits the wrong women, hangs with the wrong friends, plays with guns, drinks too much, and leaves an ever-ballooning bar tab. Love him or hate him, he demands to be dealt with.

Though "Handy Dandy" has never been performed live, the *Under the Red Sky* release contains some of the finest guitar work (courtesy of Waddy Wachtel and Jimmie Vaughn) on any Dylan collection this side of *Blonde on Blonde*.

[S] "The Harder They Come" (Jimmy Cliff)

Jimmy Cliff, *The Harder They Come* (1972)
Merl Saunders and Jerry Garcia, *Live at Keystone* (1973)
Groove Yard, *Groove Yard* (1989)
Wayne Kramer, *Dodge Main* (1996)

More than any other single song, "The Harder They Come," with its incessant hook and righteously vengeful lyrics, put Jamaican pop music on the map to stay. Assisted by the classic B movie of the same title starring its composer, Jimmy Cliff, this may well be the most famous tune to come from Jamaica.

Before Bob Marley and after Lord Kitchener, Jimmy Cliff (born James Chambers, April 1, 1948, Saint Catherine, Jamaica) stands on high as a popularizer of Jamaican culture and at the head of reggae music's vanguard, blazing a trail into popular music and global acclaim that Marley later turned into a super ganja-landscaped highway.

Cliff was raised by his father in rural Jamaica and, like Ivan, the character he played in the movie *The Harder They Come*, moved to Jamaica's capital city of Kingston in 1962, dreaming of a musical career. He released a passel of early singles to little notice, but his career took off when "Hurricane Hattie," a song he wrote describing the meteorological disaster that ravaged the Caribbean in 1961, became a local hit. He was still only fourteen years old.

Cliff parlayed that success into a gig as a ska singer for producer Leslie Kong and soon won a place on a tour promoted by Jamaican politician Edward Seaga, aiming to export reggae music. It was on that sojourn that Cliff crossed paths with Island Records' founder and boss, Chris Blackwell; Cliff then moved to London in 1968, where he was groomed as a solo star for the underground rock market. Hooking up with local talent as diverse as the Incredible String Band and Ian Hunter (later of Mott the Hoople), Cliff eased from the conventional reggae audience into a more mainstream milieu with covers of such songs as Procul Harum's "Whiter Shade of Pale."

A 1968 appearance at the International Song Festival in Brazil earned Cliff a following in South America and inspired the popular but overproduced single "Wonderful World, Beautiful People." Following that, he had a modest hit with "Vietnam" in 1969—and caught some influential ears. Bob Dylan described the song as not only the best about the war, but the finest protest composition he had heard. Paul Simon heard the song and made a beeline to Kingston, booked Cliff's rhythm section, studio, and engineer, and recorded "Mother and Child Reunion"—arguably the first reggae tune to gain widespread exposure in the United States.

The big Jimmy Cliff breakthrough came in 1973 with his next move as the over-the-top, gun-totin', reefer-smokin', reggae-singing star of *The Harder They Come*, which became the country's most notorious homegrown film, an international cult hit with a soundtrack that was one of the biggest-selling reggae records of all time. Virtually overnight Jimmy Cliff became Jamaica's most marketable property.

The international superstardom for which Cliff seemed destined, however, never happened. After his relationship with Island soured, record deals with EMI, Reprise, and CBS failed to push him to the top. And when Bob Marley and the Wailers signed to Island and emerged as *the* force in reggae music, Cliff's star was seriously on the wane. Even though his music was stoked with rebellion, fierce songwriting, and hipness—gold to record-company marketers—Marley was the one who emerged as The Man. But Cliff's star still burns bright in Africa and South America, whose samba rhythms inform and enrich his latter-day material.

Dylan performed punchy, jangly versions of "The Harder They Come" at a quartet of Never Ending Tour shows in the summer of 1989.

⌷ *Hard Rain*

Columbia Records LP PC-34349, CD CK-34349, CS PCT-34349. Produced by Don DeVito and Bob Dylan. Recorded May 16, 1976, Fort Worth, Texas, and May 23, 1976, Fort Collins, Colorado. Released September 10, 1976.

Bob Dylan—guitar, vocals. Mick Ronson—guitar. David Mansfield—guitar. Steven Soles—guitar, background vocals. T-Bone Burnett—guitar, piano. Scarlet Rivera—strings. Howard Wyeth—piano, drums. Rob Stoner—bass, background vocals. Gary Burke—drums.

"Maggie's Farm," "One Too Many Mornings," "Stuck Inside of Mobile with the Memphis Blues Again," "Oh, Sister," "Lay, Lady, Lay," "Shelter from the Storm," "You're a Big Girl Now," "I Threw It All Away," "Idiot Wind"

Dylan's Rolling Thunder Tour of autumn 1975 (*see The Bootleg Series, Volume 5*) remains the stuff of legend. With its gypsy caravan sensibility, Rolling Thunder swept across New England with a casual, "October in the Railroad Earth" whistle-stop ease that would have made Jack Kerouac proud. Dylan spearheaded this gathering of the tribes, which included his core *Desire* band and a revolving cast of colorfully bizarre, fringe, and mainstream characters. The superb shows themselves lasted for hours and still rank among Dylan's greatest—full of passion, spontaneity, and pixie dust.

Rolling Thunder continued in the spring of 1976 with a relatively pared-down presentation that toured the South, Midwest, and Southwest. By the time the band hit the stage in late May, their sound had become comparatively stale and bloated, lacking the mercurial spark that had marked the autumn run.

Why, then, didn't Dylan release an album of material drawn from the 1975 leg of the tour at the time? *Hard Rain* was conceived as a companion to the TV special by the same name taped in May 1976 and broadcast the following September. While a better glimpse of the Revue at their best can be afforded by nearly any tape of their 1975 incarnation, this album is notable for the hard metallic recastings of "Maggie's Farm" (done up start-and-stop style), "Lay, Lady, Lay" (delivered as a shrill and chilly command), and "I Threw It All Away" (presented as a funereal dirge). But it is Dylan's venomous singing on "Idiot Wind" and "Shelter from the Storm" that still cuts right to the bone.

A brooding black-and-white close-up photo of Dylan in the white pancake stage makeup and eyeliner he wore on the Revue adorned the cover of *Hard Rain*, which rose to No. 17 during its brief five-week stint on the charts.

By the time Dylan recorded *Hard Rain*, his marriage to Sara had well nigh fallen apart, and this perhaps accounts somewhat for his appearance in the TV special from which some of the album was drawn—like a man possessed and on the edge. The album is strident, for sure, but as a farewell letter to his wife and a passionate evocation of his performance muse, the material has, if anything, grown stronger with age.

Hard Rain may never be called the greatest live Bob Dylan album ever, but it is great. Chaotic and raucous, it has been dubbed by some as his "punk" record, suggesting a comparison to Neil Young's *Time Fades Away* as a wrongfully overlooked live production by a major artist.

▣ "A Hard Rain's A-Gonna Fall" (Bob Dylan)
aka "A Hard Rain Is A-Gonna Fall," "A Hard Rain Is Gonna Fall," "Hard Rain's A-Gonna Fall," "Hard Rain"
Bob Dylan, *The Freewheelin' Bob Dylan* (1963); *Bob Dylan's Greatest Hits, Volume II/'63* (1971); *Hard Rain* (film) (1976); *Masterpieces* (1978); *The Bootleg Series, Volume 5: Live 1975—The Rolling Thunder Revue* (2002); *The Bootleg Series, Volume 6: Live 1964—Concert at Philharmonic Hall* (2004)
George Harrison/Various Artists (performed by Bob Dylan), *The Concert for Bangladesh* (1971)
Pete Seeger, *We Shall Overcome* (1963); *World of Pete Seeger* (1973); *We Shall Overcome: Complete Carnegie Hall Concert* (1989)
Linda Mason, *How Many Seas Must a White Dove Sail?* (1964)
Joan Baez, *Farewell Angelina* (1965); *First 10 Years* (1970); *Live Europe '83: Children of the Eighties* (1983); *Rare, Live & Classic* (1993)
Rod MacKinnon, *Folk Concert Down Under* (1965)
Per Dich, *Surt og Soødt* (1966)
Leon Russell, *The Shelter People* (1971); *Retrospective* (1997)
Bob Gibson, *Bob Gibson* (1971)
John Schroder, *Dylan's Vibrations* (1971)
The Tribes, *Bangla Desh* (1972)
Bryan Ferry, *These Foolish Things* (1973); *Street Life* (1986); *More Than This: The Best of Bryan Ferry* (1999)
The Staple Singers, *Use What You Got* (1973)
Nana Mouskouri, *À Paris* (1979)
Roxy Music, *Street Life: 20 Greatest Hits* (1986)
The Texas Instruments, *The Texas Instruments* (1987)
Ball, *Bird* (1988)
Various Artists (performed by Edie Brickell and New Bohemians), *Born on the Fourth of July* (soundtrack) (1989)
Barbara Dickson, *Don't Think Twice, It's Alright* (1992)
Vole, *A Tribute to Bob Dylan* (1992)
Melanie, *Silence Is King* (1993)
Various Artists (performed by Leon Russell), *The Songs of Bob Dylan* (1993)
Hanne Bol, *Misty Parade* (1994)
Gerard Quintana and Jordi Batiste, *Els Miralls de Dylan* (1999)
Andy Hill, *It Takes a Lot to Laugh* (2000)
Various Artists (performed by Pete Seeger), *The Best of Broadside 1962–1988* (2000)
Various Artists (performed by Both), *Duluth Does Dylan* (2001)

As stark a piece of apocalyptic visionary prophesy as anything ever committed to paper, vinyl, magnetic tape, encoded disc, canvas, memory, Memorex, or technologies not yet developed, "A Hard Rain's A-Gonna Fall" was unlike anything Dylan had written up to that point of his young career. As such it represents the first of a cycle of songs that include the likes of "Gates of Eden," "Desolation Row," "Foot of Pride," and "Dignity," in which a young-old narrator/seeker describes a journey to a symbol-steeped netherworld and returns with the news. In his 1986 book *No Direction Home: The Life and Music of Bob Dylan*, Robert Shelton uses the words "flashing chains of images" to describe "Hard Rain"; Dylan himself comments, in *The Freewheelin' Bob Dylan* liner notes, that it "is a desperate kind of song. Every line in it is actually the start of a whole song. But when I wrote it, I thought I wouldn't have enough time alive to write all those songs so I put all I could into this one."

Legend perpetuated by the *Freewheelin'* notes has it that Dylan wrote "Hard Rain" during the Cuban missile crisis of October 1962, when nuclear war with Russia seemed, for a few days, a distinct possibility. Evidence, however, shows that the song was well in development by the very early fall. "Cuban Missile Crisis," another, more pointed and far less successful unreleased Dylan song dealing with President Kennedy's Mexican standoff with the Cuban and Russian brass was written and recorded during this period as well but never performed.

"I wrote that in the basement of the Village Gate," Dylan said of "Hard Rain" in a talk with Bernard Kleinman of the radio network Westwood One in 1984. Dylan continued: "All of it, at Chip Monck's, he used to have a place down there in the boiler room, an apartment that he slept in . . . next to the Greenwich Hotel. And I wrote 'A Hard Rain's A-Gonna Fall' down there. I'd write songs at people's houses, people's apartments, wherever I was."

Tom Paxton told a different story to Terry Kelly in 1995 for *The Telegraph* #55 (summer 1996). "Bob and I were sharing a little room above the Gaslight," Paxton recalled. "You could hardly call it a changing room, because no one ever changed! It was just a little room where we played poker and hung out. One day I walked in and there was Bob with this portable typewriter. He was pounding away and I asked him what it was. He said it was 'just a poem.' I said, 'Why don't you sing it?' And that's when he decided to put music to it. You know, 'A Hard Rain's A-Gonna Fall' is a pretty long song, and as I've heard it in the years since, I've often wondered if I gave him the right advice!"

Dylan clearly based the song on "Lord Randal" (or "Lord Randall," Child Ballad No. 12), a traditional preserved through time in its nursery rhyme incarnation and that Dylan learned from British folkster Martin Carthy. The dialogue of the original—"Oh, where ha' you been, Lord Randal my son? And where ha' you been, my handsome young man?/I ha' been at the greenwood, mother, make my bed soon/For I'm wearied wi' hunting, and fain was lie down"—is easily seen in Dylan's repeated "Oh, where have you been, my blue-eyed son?" and "Hard Rain's" many other verses.

Many versions of "Lord Randal" exist, but all follow the same basic question-and-answer structure. The reply Dylan provides the "blue-eyed son" comes in a surrealistic flood of images that owes as much to Allen Ginsberg's "Howl" or "Kaddish" than to anything in popular song and evokes images of Picasso's *Guernica* and Goya's pacifist sketches, as well as the tortured poetry of the two great French symbolists Arthur Rimbaud (1854–1891) and Charles Baudelaire (1821–1867). Baudelaire's line "L'âme d'un vieux poète erre dans la gouttière" ("The soul of an old poet wanders in the gutter"), from stanza LXXV of his poem "Spleen et Idéal," would seem to be fairly clearly echoed in Dylan's "Hard Rain" when he sings: "I heard the song of a poet who died in the gutter." Likewise, Dylan's repeating questions answered with blue-eyed innocence and clarity offering fleeting glimpses of an Edenic vision parallels one of Rimbaud's first major works, "Le Bâteau ivre" ("The Drunken Boat").

Whatever his sources, influence, and inspiration were for "Hard Rain," Dylan's use of symbolism, imagery, and dark and light is truly extraordinary in this song. Here he mixes pictures of innocence with those of devastation that supersede the cold war crisis generally informing the weeks of its composition. A palpable sense of vulnerability is evoked as the blue-eyed son tells his father that his difficult journey has taken him only to places of lingering death: crooked highways, sad forests, dead oceans, the mouth of a graveyard. Dylan's brilliance here is most fiercely felt in his contrasting of images of life and death. When the narrator's father asks him whom he met, the "darlin' young one" describes the young girl and the dead pony, the white man walking a black dog, the young woman whose body was aflame, and the young girl who presented him with a rainbow. When the narrator is asked what he's seen, his answer's images are no less difficult to view: a newborn baby surrounded by wild wolves and children carrying weapons. And Dylan's poetic flirtations with surrealisms (the empty, diamond-studded highway and the white ladder surrounded by water) further his portrayal of a hopeless cosmos. There is some brightness here, however. Images such as the rainbow-sharing girl and, in fact, the entire final stanza, when the man-child narrator asserts that he will share his vision at any cost ("I'll tell it and speak it and breathe it/And reflect from the mountains so all souls can see it"), are suggestions of hope—glimmers of light in a shrouded world. The heaping on of images compounded

with the singing of each verse and Dylan's repetitive, incantatory vocal, poetic, and musical rhythms all contribute to create a near-trancelike effect in transporting the listener to and from this very harsh place.

Dylan has kept "Hard Rain" a fairly constant inclusion in his sets ever since its debut in the fall of 1962; he even led off many 1978 concerts with an instrumental big-band version of the song. While the original take on *Freewheelin'* can sound a little sterile some four decades down the pike, Dylan's performances of "Hard Rain" have grown in passion and scope in the ensuing decades. Renditions from the mid-'60s, mid-'70s, mid-'90s, and now mid-'00s have continually displayed the song at new peaks (lately with a bizarre staccato, harlequin-like vocal finale) with the reminder that a "hard rain"—biblically torrential or merely irradiated—can fall at any time.

"Hard Times" (Stephen C. Foster)
aka "Hard Times Come Again No More"
Bob Dylan, *Good as I Been to You* (1992)
Jennifer Warnes, *Shot Through the Heart* (1979)
Syd Straw, *Surprise* (1989)
Thomas Hampson, *American Dreamer: The Songs of Stephen Foster* (1992)
Emmylou Harris and the Nash Ramblers, *At the Ryman* (1992)
Noel McLoughlin, *Contemporary & Traditional Irish Music* (1998)
Nanci Griffith, *Other Voices, Too* (1998)

In *Good as I Been to You*'s heartfelt treatment of this Stephen Foster ode to destitution with dignity, Dylan sounds especially in the spirit as he asks, "Is a song the last sigh of the weary?" The way he sings it, you can bet it is. Cracked and tired, Dylan's raspy voice seems entirely suited to the material. Dylan may have been turned on to the song by Jennifer Warnes: his version is almost identical to hers on her 1979

Stephen Collins Foster, American composer, ca. 1850.
(Hulton Archive/Getty Images)

album *Shot Through the Heart*—on which
Warnes also covered Dylan's "Sign on the Window." Perhaps Dylan received a complimentary
copy of her album, but maybe he learned it
from her directly, as she sang on a couple of
Dylan tracks—notably the *Bootleg Series, Volumes 1–3* version of "Every Grain of Sand"—
in the early 1980s.

Regardless of Dylan's source, "Hard Times"
has had a small resurgence in popularity since
Studs Terkel used the title in his wonderful
1970 book of reminiscences and reflections on
the Depression years. It is not to be confused
with other songs of the same title, however,
particularly the version Woody Guthrie picked

up in his travels and recorded for the Library of
Congress in 1940.

Stephen Foster wrote "Hard Times" in the
mid-nineteenth century. It is a strikingly different composition from the minstrel songs and
sentimental ballads that made him a household
name. Foster's name might not be so familiar
today, but surely, according to composer Virgil
Thomson (1896–1989), his music is "part of
every American's culture." Few American composers have created songs as lastingly popular
as "Beautiful Dreamer," "Oh! Susanna," "Jeanie
with the Light Brown Hair," "Old Folks at
Home" (more commonly known as "Swanee
River"), "Camptown Races," and "My Old Kentucky Home, Good Night!" Yet even so, Foster's
melodies have suffered continually at the hands
of revisers and arrangers to the point that often
what we hear today is a mere corruption of
what the man actually composed.

Over the course of his lifetime, Foster composed nearly two hundred published songs and
a handful of instrumental pieces. Of the songs,
a half-dozen rank with the world's all-time
great ballads, and at least twenty-five are
regarded as American popular folk classics. He
also composed many sentimental songs,
largely in the style of the English music-hall
ballad. The works he wrote for small amounts
of money late in his career included Civil War
songs, topical songs, Sunday School hymns,
and light comedy fare.

In "Hard Times," a compassionate tribute to
the poor and oppressed, Foster refrains from
nostalgia and heavy sentimentality: he is meditating on a real and present concern. The lyric
itself is somewhat clumsy ("While we all sorrow with the poor" and "They are frail from
fainting at the door" are two particularly
unfortunate constructions) but has a sincerity
that borders on real pathos, illustrated especially in the chorus. In one striking moment,

the singer changes from observer to participant and pleads, "Many days you have lingered around my cabin door/Oh! Hard Times, come again no more."

Morrison Foster (1823–1904), Stephen's brother, provided some insight on the origins of "Hard Times" in *Biography, Songs, and Musical Compositions of Stephen C. Foster*, his c. 1896 biography of the composer. Interestingly, Morrison's is also one of the few firsthand accounts of Stephen's experience with authentic African-American music. "When Stephen was a child," he wrote, "my father had a mulatto bound girl named Olivia Pise, the illegitimate daughter of a West Indian Frenchman, who taught dancing to the upper circles of Pittsburgh society in the early [nineteenth] century. 'Lieve,' as she was called, was a devout Christian and a member of a church of shouting coloured people. The little boy was fond of their singing and boisterous devotions. She was permitted to often take Stephen to church with her. . . . A number of strains heard there, and which, he said to me, were too good to be lost, have been preserved by him, short scraps of which were incorporated in two of his songs, 'Hard Times Come Again No More' and 'Oh, Boys, Carry Me 'Long.'"

Stephen Collins Foster (born July 4, 1826, Lawrenceville, Pennsylvania [now part of Pittsburgh]; died January 13, 1864, New York City) was the youngest of ten children in a prominent family active in western Pennsylvania politics and commerce.

Stephen was different from his siblings, a dreamer who loved music. After becoming proficient on the violin and flute, he taught himself to pick out tunes on the piano. He was discouraged from his musical pursuits by his family, who deemed them unworthy and strange for a man in a pioneer world—and America, despite his family's station, was still very much a pioneer country in the mid-nineteenth century.

Still, despite becoming a bookkeeper, he continued to pursue music. His first big break came with "Oh! Susanna," popularized by the Forty-niners of the California gold rush, who made it their unofficial theme song. It garnered Stephen the fame necessary to establish himself as a songwriter. When two music publishers offered him two cents for every copy of his songs they sold, he returned home with proof that he could earn a living by this means.

His marriage in 1850 to Jane McDowell produced a daughter, Marion, but it was a paradoxical, strained relationship marked by cycles of estrangement and reconciliation. For although the union seems to have caused all concerned a degree of emotional pain, it was also the period during which Foster composed his finest songs: "Old Folks at Home" in 1851, "Massa's in de Cold Ground" in 1852, "My Old Kentucky Home, Good Night!" and "Old Dog Tray" in 1853, "Jeanie with the Light Brown Hair" in 1854, "Come Where My Love Lies Dreaming" in 1855, and "Gentle Annie" in 1856.

No doubt some of the marital difficulties concerned money. While Stephen's songs initially earned a decent wage by the standards of mid-nineteenth-century America, he was plunging into debt through overextension, mismanagement, and gradual dissipation.

After renegotiating his publishing contracts in 1860, Foster moved to New York City to be closer to the minstrel shows that were the primary outlets and popularizers for his songs. Because this was, after all, an era before phonographs or radio, minstrelsy and print were the media that most effectively and popularly disseminated a composition. Foster's skills as a songwriter, however, were quickly eroding. "Old Black Joe" made a bit of a splash, but soon he was relying on other lyricists to collaborate on compositions that once had come so easily to him. Foster turned out more than a hundred songs in his last four years, but their quality diminished as he sought ever more unscrupulous publishing venues. Such outlets were happy to have any song by Stephen Foster to put in their catalogues, no matter what the quality, as long as they didn't have to pay too high a price for his work.

Foster spent money as soon as he got it anyway. Some of it was for food and shelter, but ever-larger portions went to quench his incurable alcoholism. He sank into lower and lower depths, eventually settling in a Bowery lodging house. There, he suffered a fall in which he hit his head on the edge of a sink that landed him in the even then infamous Bellevue Hospital, where he died the next day at age thirty-seven.

A journalist friend of Foster, George Birdseye, wrote two widely reprinted articles of memories about Foster for the *New York Musical Gazette* of 1869. One passage about "Hard Times" could easily serve as Foster's epitaph: "On more than one occasion, in a grocery barroom, I have heard Stephen Foster sing that good old song of his, with a pathos that a state of semi-inebriation often lends the voice; while his pockets were in the peculiarly appropriate condition of emptiness not unusual to them, and the forlorn habitués joined dismally in the chorus."

Despite the popularity of Foster's songs during his lifetime, most of them have not aged particularly well at all in the celebration of the Southern values that upheld the ideas of slavery even as the Civil War was raging. In one of several ironies, Foster was a Northerner and his work was popular on both sides of the Mason-Dixon Line. In another twist, his hand in the rise in popularity of minstrelsy, a form of musical theater that parodied African-American stereotypes, may ultimately have helped legitimize the talents of black Americans and pave the way for their acceptance not only on the stage but in other walks of life as well.

After releasing a three-hanky version of "Hard Times" on *Good as I Been to You,* Dylan led off a string of 1993 Never Ending Tour shows with moving acoustic renditions of the Foster plaint that conjure visions of backwoods shotgun shacks, parched crops, dusty cupboards, dry wells, and empty stomachs.

"Hard Times in New York Town" (Bob Dylan)
Bob Dylan, *The Bootleg Series, Volumes 1–3: Rare and Unreleased, 1961–1991/'61* (1991)

Tuesday, January 24, 1961, is the most commonly accepted date of Bob Dylan's arrival in New York City after hitchhiking Beat Generation–style from Minnesota. On a quest to meet his idol Woody Guthrie, Dylan also had his eyes on the folk-music stages of Greenwich Village, where he hoped to make a mark, if not find fame and fortune. "I knew I had to get to New York," he recalled in 1985 in his *Biograph* liner notes. "I'd been dreaming about that for a long time."

While the friends he left behind in the North Country felt his ambition was a bit misplaced (they recall a functionally unimpressive musician and a singer of questionable merit), Dylan had effectively absorbed the Guthrie catalogue and legacy by the time he hit the Big Apple.

Less than three months later, having taken the Village coffeehouse circuit by storm with professional gigs that included opening for the great John Lee Hooker at Gerde's Folk City, Dylan made a return trip to Minneapolis. Like Robert Johnson, who, according to hoodoo legend, made a visit to the crossroads and there made a pact with the Devil that transformed his allegedly mediocre talent into unparalleled blues power, Dylan awed his friends with his newfound abilities and persona. According to Jon Pankake, an early friend of Dylan's and editor of the local *Little Sandy Review* folk magazine, as reported by Robert Shelton in *No*

Direction Home: The Life and Music of Bob Dylan (New York: Beech Tree Books/William Morrow, 1986): "The change in Bob was, to say the least, incredible. In a mere half year he had learned to churn up exciting, bluesy, hard-driving harmonica-and-guitar music."

Written in November 1961, "Hard Times in New York Town" can legitimately be attributed as a Bob Dylan composition, despite having some roots in "Down on Penny's Farm," a folk song popular with poor white Southern farmers in variations captured on recordings stretching back to the 1920s. Dylan appropriates the tune, various lyrics, and general structure, shifting the song's setting from the farm to the streets in telling the familiar tale of a newcomer weathering Gotham.

v *Hard to Handle* (video)

"In the Garden," "Just Like a Woman," "Like a Rolling Stone," "It's Alright, Ma (I'm Only Bleeding)," "Girl from the North Country," "Lenny Bruce," "When the Night Comes Falling from the Sky," "Ballad of a Thin Man," "I'll Remember You"

It's too bad that this slick though leaden video is the only officially released document of Dylan's 1986–1987 tenure with Tom Petty and the Heartbreakers, as this particularly vital period produced some excellent music. *Hard to Handle*, shot in Australia early in the first Dylan-Petty tour and directed by Aussie filmmaker Gillian Armstrong (known for such movies as *My Brilliant Career*, *High Tide*, and *Little Women*), is a real curio in Dylan's catalogue: a straight, no-nonsense concert film. Armstrong's unusual camera angles try to bring out the best in Dylan's performances, which are alternately ardent, impish, and fierce as he tears through a greatest-hits-oriented set list with a surprise or two thrown in for novelty's sake.

s "Hard Travelin'" (Woody Guthrie)

Woody Guthrie, *Columbia River Collection*/'41 (1949/'87)
John Greenway, *Big Rock Candy Man* (1957)
Cisco Houston, *Folkways Years 1944–61* (1994)
The Kingston Trio, *Best of the Best of the Kingston Trio* (1986)
Jack Elliott, *Hard Travelin'* (1989)

Woody Guthrie's credentials as a hard traveler are long established. As a boy he sold newspapers, danced street jigs, and sang for pennies. He shined shoes and cleaned spittoons. Virtually from his late teens until he was incapacitated by Huntington's disease, he traveled back and forth across the continent in old jalopies, farm workers' trucks, and freight cars. He knew the Dust Bowl, the displaced farmer, the migrant worker firsthand. He was a laborer, a sailor, a saint, a sinner, and a wanderer, and he saw the world's poverty, misery, cruelty, and injustice. And with his voice, his guitar, and this song, he dedicated his poetic genius to telling the story of "hard travelers" everywhere.

Guthrie wrote "Hard Travelin'" in 1940 and modified the lyrics for his Columbia River commission in 1941 (*see* "Grand Coulee Dam"). "'Hard Traveling' is the kind of a song you would sing after you had been booted off your little place and had lost out, lost everything, hocked everything down at the pawnshop, and had bummed a lot of steams asking for work," Guthrie said of the song in Alan Lomax's 1960 book *The Folk Songs of North America*. "It is a song about the hard traveling of the working people, not the moonstruck traveling of the professional vacationers. It tells about a man who has ridden the flat wheels, kicked up cinders, dumped the red-hot slag, hit the hard-rock tunneling, the hard harvesting, the hard-rock jail."

When Dylan was in his walking Woody Guthrie–jukebox phase in the very early 1960s, "Hard Travelin'" made an occasional appearance in his sets. Dylan not only sang the song with his husky, Midwestern burr laced with whoops and hollers, but also used the title as a lyric in "Song to Woody," his own homage to Guthrie.

[S] "Has Anybody Seen My Love"

See "Tight Connection to My Heart"

[S] "Hazel" (Bob Dylan)

Bob Dylan, *Planet Waves* (1974)
The Band (performed with Bob Dylan), *The Last Waltz* (boxed set)/'76 (2002)

H

A soft devotional ballad of unfulfilled yearning with hints of a memory for Echo Helstrom and all his old girlfriends on the wrong side of the Hibbing tracks, "Hazel" was written for *Planet Waves*, Dylan's reunion LP with the Band, produced in preparation for their 1974 tour—Dylan's heralded return to the concert stage. Dylan and the Band did not perform the song until the 1976 *Last Waltz* concert, where it was filmed and left on the cutting-room floor by Martin Scorsese. Since then Dylan soundchecked "Hazel" before a September 1978 show and pulled out a still-unreleased version during the November 17, 1994, taping of his *MTV Unplugged* appearance. (It was not included on Dylan's *MTV Unplugged* album.)

With its evocation of an idealized rural Arcadia, "Hazel" complements a couple of other songs from *Planet Waves* ("Something There Is About You" and "Never Say Goodbye") quite nicely, while contrasting with some of the other themes of discord (marital or otherwise) present on the album.

[S] "A Hazy Shade of Winter" (Paul Simon)

Simon and Garfunkel, *Bookends* (1968)
The Bangles, *Greatest Hits* (1990)
Snuff, *Flibbiddydibbiddydob* (1996)

Who knows what led Dylan to perform this early Paul Simon sleeper, a ubiquitous inclusion on "Golden Oldies" AM radio fare, a couple of times in the summer of 1992? Maybe it was the weather, or something like that. A lovely lyric and melody about parting lovers and the passage of time set against a bleak landscape, "Hazy Shade of Winter" was written and recorded in 1966, hitting the Top 20 for Simon and Garfunkel when released on *Bookends* in 1968. The Bangles had a Top 10 single with the song in the late 1980s.

[S] "Heading for the Light" (Traveling Wilburys)

Traveling Wilburys, *Traveling Wilburys, Volume 1* (1988)

Dylan's contribution to this light and breezy Wilburys tune driven by Jeff Lynne and George Harrison seems to be pretty minimal—probably some backing vocals and guitar.

[S] "Heartland" (Bob Dylan/Willie Nelson)

Willie Nelson (performed with Bob Dylan), *Across the Borderline* (1993); *Revolutions of Time* (1995)
Hugues Aufray, *Aufray Trans Dylan* (1995)

Bob Dylan and Willie Nelson spent some good ol' times together, so it was only natural that at least one collaborative effort should spring from their friendship, musical and otherwise. Their cowritten and -recorded "Heartland," a song overflowing with images of foreclosed farms and shattered dreams, is a dark vision for sure, but one that needs looking at. The song was no doubt inspired by Farm Aid, the multiyear series of concerts benefiting the U.S. family farmer, spearheaded by Nelson and inspired by Dylan's suggestion at the 1985 Live Aid concert benefiting famine relief in Africa.

The song came together in an interesting manner, over a rather long time frame. Dylan and Nelson first met as far back as 1973 when

Dylan was filming *Pat Garrett and Billy the Kid*. Nelson playfully challenged Dylan to write something with him pen-pal style, and the two sent material back and forth until a song was born. Twenty years later a tape showed up in Nelson's mail. As Nelson related the story about it to Mark Cooper for an article that appeared in *The Telegraph* #48 (summer 1994), that tape consisted of "Bob Dylan singing 'Hmmm hmm hmmm hmm hmmm hmmm hmmm hmmm Heartland . . .' *Heartland* was the only word in there. And he said, 'Write me some lyrics to that.' So I wrote some lyrics. I'd never written a farm song, but "Heartland" had to be a farm song. I didn't ask him but I was almost sure that that was what he was thinking and what he was wanting me to do."

Despite many years of his devotion to farmers' problems, most notably as a steward of the Farm Aid benefit concerts of the late 1980s and 1990, Nelson had never written a song about them until "Heartland." Until the Dylan tape appeared at his doorstep, Nelson had been concerned that any efforts to write a song about farmers' plights would be taken as a phony, publicity-mongering gesture despite its good intentions. Inspired by his friend's gift tune, Nelson sat down and wrote the lyrics. "Heartland" was finally recorded by the two in New York City shortly after the October 1994 Dylan all-star tribute concert. As Nelson told Cooper for the *Telegraph* article, Dylan "came into the studio and he'd never seen the lyrics, but he sat down and sang the song. I'm sure he liked it or else he wouldn't have left the studio with his voice on there!"

"Heartland" was released in 1993 on Nelson's *Across the Borderline* CD.

In his journey to where he stands today, holding a beat-up (but sweet-sounding) guitar, singing with a reedy, sun-beaten voice, and with his silver mane tied in braids around a grizzled face that appears to have seen it all, Willie Nelson (born Willie Hugh Nelson, April 30, 1933, Abbott, Texas) has cut one of the more independent artistic paths of the twentieth century. Reared in a tiny central Texas farming community, Nelson was surrounded by a world impregnated with music: the gospel songs of the grandparents who raised him, the blues and Mexican work songs that eased the labor of the cotton fields, the country and western swing hits filling the airwaves from Nashville and Fort Worth—and the music that percolated up ceaselessly inside him. Melodies have always come easily to Nelson, and, true to his reputation as a kind of mystic cowboy, he claims he can just pluck them out of the air because the air, he says, is full of music.

Since waxing his first single in 1957, Nelson has harvested (from the heavens or otherwise) concept albums, gospel albums, jazz albums, movie soundtracks, myriad duet projects, Christmas albums, live albums, and an album of pop standards. In the process, he has cribbed from traditional pop, Western swing, jazz, traditional country, cowboy songs, honky tonk, rock 'n' roll, folk, and the blues, in creating a distinctive, elastic hybrid.

Although now he's considered a patriarch and is celebrated for his strongly independent—if perhaps sometimes contrarian—sensibilities, Nelson was not always warmly accepted by his musical peers. Back in the day, his bowed-but-not-beaten, blues-flavored vocals set the Nashville musical establishment on its ear. His spare-sounding breakthrough album, 1975's *Red Headed Stranger*, was such a departure from the grooves then emanating from Nashville that some of the suits up at Columbia Records thought the final mix was a demo. Yet who could have predicted that a concept album featuring brief yet dense story-poems, set to the most minimal musical backing, about a preacher on the lam after killing his unfaithful wife and her lover, would turn into the block-buster that it did?

His visionary merger of traditional country with hippie audiences in the mid-'70s helped create (with the likes of Johnny Cash, Waylon Jennings, and Kris Kristofferson) a new country music genre: "Outlaw." And above and beyond everything else, Nelson's guitar playing—a peculiar blend of Django Reinhardt and the sound of Bob Wills and the Texas Playboys—is enough to warrant his stature at the top of the musical heap.

Elected to the Country Music Hall of Fame in 1993, Nelson is a true outlaw and probably the greatest institution in country music since Hank Williams.

"Heart of Mine" (Bob Dylan)
Bob Dylan, single (1981); *Shot of Love* (1981); *Biograph* (1985)
Ulf Lundell, *Sweethearts* (1983)
Peter Malick & Norah Jones, *New York City* (2003)

"Heart of Mine," a ragged, beguiling self-rebuke from Dylan's *Shot of Love* album, is filled with wise advice and cold realities of romantic attraction as Dylan goes one-on-one with his ticker, offering such cliché lines as "You can play with fire but you'll get the bill" that only he can pull off with a straight face. With its relaxed air, mixing a Latin/Caribbean groove with the doo-wop sensibility worthy of the Drifters or a cadre of Brooklyn stoop singers circa 1956, "Heart of Mine" offers Dylan's own ebulliently sung and faithfully observed battle of the oldest war—the one between the mind and the heart: "Heart of mine so malicious and so full of guile/Give you an inch and you'll take a mile."

The official release of the song sounds like a first take, with Bob plunking the piano keys, a barely audible Ron Wood helping out on guitar, and drummer Ringo Starr sharing percussion duties with studio legend Jim Keltner.

Dylan performed gutsy versions of "Heart of Mine" with some frequency shortly after its 1981 release but has done so only intermittently since. It appeared again on the *Real Live* tour in 1984, in '86 with Tom Petty and the Heartbreakers, in '87 with the Grateful Dead, and in '89 and '92 on the Never Ending Tour.

Hearts of Fire
Lorimar Motion Pictures, 1987. Starring Bob Dylan, Fiona, Rupert Everett. Produced and directed by Richard Marquand. Written by Scott Richardson and Joe Eszterhas.

A movie so bad it's good, *Hearts of Fire* is a clichéd genre *Star Is Born* that would even embarrass Ed (*Plan 9 from Outer Space*) Wood.

Dylan, in an amazing stretch of the imagination, plays Billy Parker, a semiretired and reclusive rock star who falls for aspiring rocker Molly McGuire, played by Fiona (where is she now?). Parker takes her under his wing on his tour of England, but when she is "discovered" by lecherous music promoter James Colt (Rupert Everett), Billy flies back to his stateside chicken farm while Molly makes music magic. Billy and Molly are eventually reunited when she returns for a triumphant tour of the United States.

In the believe-it-or-not category, here's a taste of the promotional material accompanying the video release of this tripe: "For as long as she can remember, Molly McGuire has picked guitar. Written songs. And dreamed about the day opportunity would knock. But opportunity never knocked. Instead, it kicked the door down, grabbed her by the guitar strap and thrust her into a world far different from her sleepy small town. . . . *Hearts of Fire*, marking entertainment legend Bob Dylan's return to movies, burns with passion, hope and music."

Dylan's disengagement from and inability to connect with this project were apparent at the press conference announcing the movie at London's National Film Theatre in August 1986. When asked why he decided to "commit" to the film, Dylan responded, "Oh, it's just the right time, right place, right words." Asked why he was playing a retired star instead of a star, Dylan nonchalantly suggested, "Well, it's just a movie. . ." To a question about whether he knew a great deal about the film yet, Dylan answered, "I know enough about the movie. I didn't write the movie, though. A lot of the questions you maybe want to ask the writer."

The flat, tepid, insipid, and uninspiring *Hearts of Fire* was released only in the United Kingdom and was the last feature film directed by Richard Marquand, who died shortly after completing the movie. Among Marquand's other credits is the third segment in the Star Wars series, *Return of the Jedi* (1983).

ⒶHearts of Fire (soundtrack)/Various Artists
Columbia Records LP SC-40870, CD CBSCK-40870, CS CBSSCT-40870. Released 1987.

Given the choice between enduring a screening of *Hearts of Fire* or listening to the soundtrack album, the masochist would choose the celluloid. Dylan's three contributions ("The Usual," "Night After Night," and "Had a Dream About You, Baby") only slightly redeem this grating collection, which also includes performances by his film costars Fiona and Rupert Everett.

⒮"The Heart That You Own" (Dwight Yoakam)
Dwight Yoakam, *If There Was a Way* (1990)
White Sands, *White Sands* (1992)
Various Artists (performed by Jim Matt), *Songs of Dwight Yoakam: Will Sing for Money* (1998)

Exploring the catalogue of the idiosyncratic

country star Dwight Yoakam, Dylan must have taken a fancy to this sage declaration when he performed "The Heart That You Own" for a very brief spell on the fall 1999 leg of the Never Ending Tour.

Dwight Yoakam has enjoyed a remarkable career as the only California-based country artist to rise to sustained national prominence since the heydays of Buck Owens and Merle Haggard. With more than eight million records sold, two Grammy Awards (and a total of fifteen Grammy nominations), not to mention stacks of accolades for his work as an actor—in films like the Academy Award–winning *Sling Blade*, where his psycho bad-guy turn is not to be missed—he has not only remained in top form for a solid decade, but seems to be improving with age.

Yoakam (born October 23, 1956, Pikeville, Kentucky) grew up idolizing Hank Williams and the stripped-down honky-tonk Bakersfield, California, sounds of Owens and Haggard. He was playing guitar by the age of six, cribbing licks off his mother's extensive record collection, and joined a variety of bands during high school, trying his hand at everything from country to rock 'n' roll. Then, after a brief matriculation at Ohio State University, he moved to Nashville in the late 1970s with hopes of cutting a record. Disappointed with the era's *Urban Cowboy* fetish, he moved to Los Angeles, where, in addition to performances in country-music venues, he shared bills on stages with a motley but vibrantly distinctive and diverse pool of talent that no doubt broadened his cultural eclecticism: the Dead Kennedys, Los Lobos, the Blasters, and the Butthole Surfers, among others. Yoakam honed a bare-bones style—a radical revivalism that even garnered its own name: "cowpunk."

Never a Nashville insider, Yoakam took a back-to-basics approach that helped return country to its roots. It may, however, have been at the expense of his career, for he has never dominated the charts like, say, Garth Brooks. In many respects, Yoakam's albums don't even really sound like country music. Rather, he manipulates the form to bring out blues and folk nuances and adds more than a little dash of rock 'n' roll.

"Help Me Make It Through the Night" (Kris Kristofferson/Fred Foster)

See also "They Killed Him"
Kris Kristofferson, *Kristofferson* (1970)
Glen Campbell, *Last Time I Saw Her* (1971)
Elvis Presley, *Elvis Now* (1972)
Willie Nelson, *Sings Kris Kristofferson* (1979)
Jerry Lee Lewis, *Live* (1995)
Sammi Smith, *The Best of Sammi Smith* (1996)

Dylan's only performance of this oft-covered Kris Kristofferson plea came during his famous, surprise fifty-song show at Toad's Place in New Haven, Connecticut, in the winter of 1990.

"Help Me Make It Through the Night," which Kristofferson wrote with Fred Foster, was first recorded by Sammi Smith in early 1971. Her recording became a No. 1 country hit, a million-seller, and Grammy winner. It also served as the theme song for *Fat City*, John Huston's 1972 boxing film starring Jeff Bridges and Stacy Keach.

"Hero Blues" (Bob Dylan)

"This is for all the boys who know girls who want 'em to go out and get themselves to kill." With those words, Bob Dylan introduced "Hero Blues" during his first legit solo Town Hall concert in New York City on April 12, 1963. The darkly humorous lyrics tell of a young man (perhaps even a folksinger) whose girlfriend

begs him to fight so she can go back and "tell all her friends." Dylan succinctly deals with this somewhat unreasonable request in the final verse when he declares, "No more good times will I crave/You can stand and shout hero/All over my lonesome grave."

The message here is pretty simple: the absolute pointlessness of dying for someone else. Permanent confinement to a lonesome grave just so someone else can become famous as the friend of a dead hero would seem a rather grim legacy, and in this context it takes on some extra meaning, given that "Hero Blues" debuted around the same time as U.S. military involvement was escalating in Vietnam.

The final verses of "Hero Blues" recall "Give Me a 32-20," Arthur "Big Boy" Crudup's 78 rpm single released during World War II. But while that might point toward one of Dylan's influences for this hillbilly blues, there is considerable debate among Dylan scholars regarding the composition of and recording dates for "Hero Blues." Disagreement roils around whether it was an outtake from Dylan's second, third, or even fourth album—or if it was an outtake at all. Dylanist Clinton Heylin posits that a version was taped as early the December 6, 1962, recording session for *The Freewheelin' Bob Dylan*, a conjecture supported by a tape from the alleged session on which the song appeared. The more heated controversy centers around whether "Hero Blues" was left off either *The Times They Are A-Changin'* or *Another Side of Bob Dylan*. Still other sources aver that the song was recorded as a demo for Witmark and was never considered for official release by Dylan. Perhaps as a personal observation of the moment, a not-too-veiled swipe at Vietnam, or a comment on cults of personality, Dylan commenced his 1974 comeback tour with the Band by leading off his first couple of shows with a rewritten and rearranged, lone-wolf-on-the-prowl desperado version of "Hero Blues."

🔊 "He Was a Friend of Mine" (Traditional/Bob Dylan)
aka "Shorty George"
Bob Dylan, *The Bootleg Series, Volumes 1–3: Rare and Unreleased, 1961–1991/*'61 (1992)
Various Artists (performed by James "Iron Head" Baker), *The Ballad Hunter Volume 5/*'43 (1982)
Leadbelly, *Where Did You Sleep Last Night?/*'44 (1996)
Dave Van Ronk, *Dave Van Ronk, Folksinger* (1962)
Eric von Schmidt, *The Folk Blues of Eric von Schmidt* (1963)
The Byrds, *Turn! Turn! Turn!* (1966); *The Nashville Session* (1990)
Smith Casey, *Afro-American Blues and Game Songs/*'39 (1978)
The Washington Squares, *The Washington Squares* (1987)
Jerry Jeff Walker, *Scamp* (1996)
Various Artists (performed by Peg Leg Will), *Kerrville Folk Festival: Early Years* (1998)
Ramblin' Jack Elliott, *Friends of Mine* (1997)
Mance Lipscomb, *Captain, Captain: The Texas Songster* (1998)

Dylan recorded "He Was a Friend of Mine," a sentimental paean to a blood brother, for his eponymous debut album, but it stayed in the can until its official surfacing on *The Bootleg Series, Volumes 1–3* some three decades down the pike.

When he was interviewed by Robert Shelton for the liner notes to *Bob Dylan,* Dylan mentioned that his "He Was a Friend of Mine" was adapted from a song he'd learned from a Chicago street singer named Blind Arvella Gray (born January 28, 1906, Somerville, Texas; died September 7, 1980, Chicago) during a brief stay in the Windy City in 1960. Supporting this claim is the original copyright Dylan filed, which indicates his song is a traditional composition with supplemental lyrics—thus allowing Dylan to take composer/arranger credit. Additionally, Cary Baker reported in his "Chicago News" column in the Swedish *Jefferson Blues* magazine in 1974, "Blind Arvella Gray went to visit a student, who since his encounters with Gray over ten years ago, has become *the* star of the counterculture—Bob Dylan. Gray remembers Dylan from streetside meetings in the early '60s; similarly, and more spectacularly, Dylan remembers him."

Gray, however, made few recordings before his death in 1980, and his only album, *The Singing Drifter,* cut in 1972, provides few, if any, connections to Dylan. It has been suggested that Dylan might have misremembered which song he learned from the street-corner maestro, as Gray did record versions of "Corrina, Corrina" (a song Dylan recorded and performed in the early 1960s) in 1960 and 1964.

Another source for "He Was a Friend of Mine" may be a traditional Southern prison song entitled "Shorty George," famously recorded by Leadbelly in 1935 and by some Texas penitentiary singers for the Library of Congress in the 1930s. In Leadbelly's hands, "Shorty George" is about a "short train" that ran out of the Sugarland prison farm to Houston. On Sundays, it brought wives, families, and lovers to the men at the prison. "Well, Shorty George ain't no friend of mine," sang Leadbelly. "Shorty George ain't no friend of mine/He keeps a takin' all the women/Keep all the men behind."

John A. and Alan Lomax provided some insight into the power of "Shorty George" in their book *American Ballads and Folk Songs* (New York: Macmillan, 1934), writing:

> Along by the Central State Prison near Sugarland, Texas, runs a narrow-gauge track, and down that track about sunset comes whistling a little gasoline motor car. It is on this train that the women who have come out for a Sun-

day with their men-folk leave the prison. "Cause it's such a runty li'l train," the convicted have named it Shorty George, but they sing about it as if it were one of those favored men, like John Henry, who can get a woman by a crook of the finger.

Iron Head, in prison for life and not subject to reprieve or pardon, since he is classed as an "habitual criminal," broke down and cried while he sang "Shorty George." "My woman, she's sca'd to come to see me; she might as well be dead. So I gets res'less, an' I wan to run away f'um dis place. I jes' cain' hardly stan' to sing dat song."

Eric von Schmidt taught himself the tune from Leadbelly's recording from the Library of Congress release. Von Schmidt, an early influence on and colleague of Dylan's, claimed credit for teaching the song to Dylan, as reported by Anthony Scaduto in his book *Bob Dylan: An Intimate Biography*.

Despite the fact that "He Was a Friend of Mine" didn't make it onto Dylan's first album, he did perform it often in Greenwich Village folk clubs. His version was adopted as a standard by other local folkies, including Dave Van Ronk, who offered his own recasting on his 1963 LP. Von Schmidt also recorded the song, and his album on which it appeared in 1963, *The Folk Blues of Eric von Schmidt,* can be seen among the cultural detritus surrounding Dylan on the cover photo for the latter's 1965 album, *Bringing It All Back Home*.

Roger McGuinn probably drew on all of these sources when he rewrote the song for the Byrds in 1966 as a tribute to the late President John F. Kennedy. The Grateful Dead also performed a ragged but sweet version of the song in the late 1960s.

Dylan performed "He Was a Friend of Mine" often in 1961 and 1962 but only once thereafter. That occurred, appropriately, when he made a surprise appearance at a February 1992 memorial tribute concert to Roy Orbison at the Universal Amphitheater in Los Angeles and joined three of the original Byrds (David Crosby, Roger McGuinn, and Chris Hillman) on a version of the song.

[S] **"Hey, Good Lookin'"** (Hank Williams)

See also Hank Williams
Hank Williams, *Complete Hank Williams* (1998)
Mose Allison, *Mose Allison Trilogy: High Jinks!* (1959)
Ray Charles, *Modern Sounds in Country & Western Music* (1961)
Faron Young, *Classic Years 1952–62* (1992)
Buckwheat Zydeco, *Menagerie: The Essential Zydeco Collection* (1993)
Dean Martin, *Country Dino* (1998)

Never to be confused with Cole Porter's 1943 song of the same title, Hank Williams's sleepy come-on sold a million copies in 1951. This version was used to overdub George Hamilton, who played Hank in the 1965 Williams biopic *Your Cheatin' Heart*. First recorded at a magical March 16, 1951, Nashville session that produced several of Williams's most famous songs, "Hey, Good Lookin'" was a huge success. Later in the year, Hank performed it on television's nationally broadcast *Perry Como Show* after doing a sketch and hawking Chesterfield cigarettes with the host.

"Hey, Good Lookin'," according to Colin Escott's *Hank Williams: The Biography* (Boston: Little, Brown, 1994): "has lyrics that seem to demand . . . insouciant treatment, peppered as they are with references to hot rods, dancing sprees, goin' steady, soda pop, and much else that prefigured the lyrical content of rock 'n' roll. Strangely, though, the rhythm plods along with a steppity-step piano, and Hank is almost dour in comparison with his performances" of other songs.

Dylan opened up one fall 1990 Never Ending Tour show in Tuscaloosa, Alabama (deep Williams country), with a mediocre version of this Hank special.

"Hey Joe" (Traditional/Billy Roberts)
The Leaves, *Hey Joe* (1966)
Jimi Hendrix, *Are You Experienced?* (1967)
Tim Rose, *Musician* (1975)
Nick Cave, *Kicking Against the Pricks* (1986)
Black Uhuru, *Now Dub* (1990)
Jerry Douglas, *Slide Rule* (1992)
Cher, *Bang Bang: The Early Years* (1999)

"Hey Joe," a violent song about a gun-toting cheated lover seeking retribution wherever he can find it, has a convoluted history and, as the song chosen for the A-side of Jimi Hendrix's first single, a special place in pop trivia. California folk singer Billy Roberts has been given credit for formalizing the song that experts on the subject deem a traditional of unknown origin. Anyway, Roberts, in need of a quick buck, sold it to Dino Valenti, later lead singer of the Quicksilver Messenger Service. After filing a copyright for "Hey Joe" under the pen name Chet Powers, Valenti taught the song to David Crosby, whom he had recently met in Greenwich Village. Crosby brought "Hey Joe" to the Byrds, and with them began performing a frantic version of the song in 1965. Later that year, the Leaves and the Surfaris (the latter group famous for "Wipe Out"), bands hailing from Los Angeles, were the first to record the song. Folkie Tim Rose, however, concocted the slow, bluesy arrangement that Hendrix learned in 1966. On October 23, 1966, aided by the backing vocals of the Breakaways, a long-gone group of session singers, "Hey Joe" became the first song the Jimi Hendrix Experience ever recorded. Amazingly, some four hundred versions have been recorded by garage bands the planet over.

Unlike most classic rock songs, "Hey Joe" feels more like it was plucked from the folk blues tradition. With its grinding chord progression, violent subject matter, and unusual Q&A format, this premeditated-murder ballad sounds different no matter whose mouth its macho "gonna kill my lady" lyrics tumbles out of.

For reasons unknown, Dylan kicked off a 1992 French show in grand fashion with his one and only performance of "Hey Joe." Maybe he caught his gal messing around with another man and just wanted to vent.

"Hey La La" (Ray Price/Leonard McRight)
aka "(Hey) La La," "My La La," "My True La La"
Ernest Tubb, *Let's Say Goodbye Like We Said Hello*/'51 (1991)
Country Gentlemen, *Classic Country Gents Reunion* (1989)
Ray Price, *Honky Tonk Years (1950–1966)* (1996)

Popularized by Ernest "E.T." Tubbs, "Hey La La" reached No. 6 on the country charts way back when. Perhaps inspired by the Country Gentlemen's rerelease of the song in 1989, Dylan performed unconvincing versions of "Hey La La"—which he arranged to sound like a Swiss folk song or a polka heard on the jukebox in a desultory Iron Range watering hole frequented by miners out with their gals on a cold Saturday night circa 1956—leading off three summer 1989 Never Ending Tour shows.

"Hey La La" was written by the well-known Ray Price (born January 12, 1926, Perryville, Texas) and the obscure Leonard McRight. Price's long career in country music stretches from his days as a Hank Williams–style honky-tonk singer to that of an affected crooner during Nashville's pop-schlock 1960s peak.

"Hiding Too Long" (Bob Dylan)
aka "You've Been Hiding Too Long"

In his 1996 book *Bob Dylan: A Life in Stolen Moments*, Clinton Heylin called this talking blues, performed just once by Dylan at his April 1963 New York City Town Hall concert, "curiously misguided." A scan of the lyrics to "Hiding Too Long" (a song musically related to "Oxford Town") demonstrates a rather heavy-handed and obvious condemnation of bigots who invoke the names of Washington and Jefferson to hypocritically hide themselves behind the cloak of patriotism and claim moral superiority even while imprisoning African-Americans—or worse.

H

[S] "Highlands" (Bob Dylan)

Bob Dylan, *Time out of Mind* (1997)

Dylan once wrote a song in which he visited a mysterious, sad-eyed lady inhabiting a low-lying murky emotional and physical landscape. In that composition, "Sad-Eyed Lady of the Lowlands," Dylan sings a devotional song to a woman under whose spell he seems to have fallen permanently. Three decades later, in "Highlands," he takes a gentler path to call upon a less complicated female in a light-hearted yet still ruminative—and very long—song, which works as a kind of portrait of the artist pushing sixty.

Yet, as a lyric that is more spoken than sung, "Highlands" is a piece that takes Dylan directly back to his coffeehouse days in the Greenwich Village of 1961 and 1962, when he would routinely employ a self-styled, half-talking blues on numbers like Lord Buckley's "Black Cross," his covers of Woody Guthrie material, or his own songs, such as "Talkin' New York" or, later, "Meet Me in the Morning." It was a vocal tool that he later utilized for the radio swami starring in "Sign on the Cross" from the *Basement Tapes* in 1967 and in his 1979 evangelical shows as he testified to his audiences through song, and that would characterize an element of his performing style as the Never Ending Tour hit stride in the 1990s.

Rumored to have been written during a Minnesota blizzard, "Highlands" has to be regarded as one of Dylan's more idiosyncratic works. "Sad-Eyed Lady," "Brownsville Girl," and perhaps "Isis" or even "Things Have Changed" are a few other songs that quickly spring to mind when putting "Highlands" in some context with the rest of his oeuvre. The song unfurls slowly, taking its own sweet time to tell the story of a lonely man waking up, considering his life, taking a walk, talking to a waitress in an empty restaurant, splitting when things get a little too involved, and resuming his stroll through the streets as he speaks his final revelations of the day. In its own sage way, "Highlands" is a summing-up of the major themes laced through *Time out of Mind*: alienation, lost youth, decrepitude, encroaching mortality, societal degradation, and the artist's need to respond to his situation.

But "Highlands" is not without its humor; it's rife with some inverted, paradoxical Dylan one-liners that manage to cut a few ways at once.

The centerpiece of "Highlands" (and where the lyric's metrical pulse take an extreme left-hand turn) is the sly, flirtatious conversation between the song's narrator and a smart-ass waitress in a Boston greasy spoon. Her insistent queries and demands parry with his coy (and uproariously funny) responses in a deceivingly rapid give-and-take that creates a loose allegory of his relationship with an ever-demanding, always too discriminating, and never-satisfied audience. It is a rare piece of interior and exterior Dylan travelogue and gives one the sense of taking a solitary walk inside Dylan's head and looking out through his peepers as he observes and engages the world. Or perhaps it is a song about an urban hermit who, as the maestro Duke Ellington once admitted, doesn't "get around much anymore."

Having ditched the waitress and all her nudginess, the narrator is back on the streets, far from the destination of his heart, still "talking to myself in a monologue" by the song's end. But things aren't much better out there, for even though he's got new eyes, "everything looks far away."

Some critics have pointed to a 1790 poem by Scottish poet Robert Burns (1759–1796), "My Heart's in the Highlands," which in itself was drawn from folk sources, as a root of Dylan's own "Highlands." But where Burns's poem is a yearning for an Edenic past that has escaped his soul, Dylan's song reverses the theme by striding into the future, however daunting, with an optimism (simultaneously jaded and jaunty) that he will once again find his muse in the imagined highlands of his mind.

"Highlands" is not a song one would think lends itself to performance, but Dylan, in fact, did display it with some regularity and astonishing effectiveness beginning in 1999.

▣ "High Water (for Charley Patton)" (Bob Dylan)
Bob Dylan, "Love and Theft" (2001)
Barb Jungr, Waterloo Sunset (2003)

As postapocalyptic a piece of postmodern hill-billy music as has ever been committed to recorded medium, "High Water (for Charley Patton)" was the centerpiece of Dylan's first album of the third millennium and may still be standing as its undisputed masterwork when the fourth dawns. The song's desperation, masked somewhat by Dylan's ingrained coolness, is clearly modeled on (or at the very least inspired by) "High Water Everywhere," the frenzied blues by Charley Patton, to whom Dylan dedi-

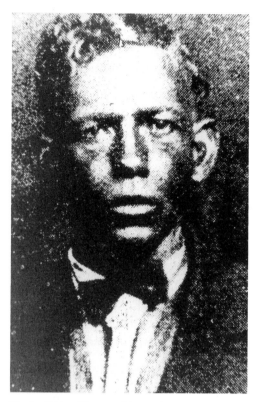

Charley Patton, blues musician and composer, ca. 1930s.

(From the John Edwards Memorial Collection #30003, Southern Folklife Collection, Wilson Library, University of North Carolina at Chapel Hill)

cated his own original. Not the Delta blues suggested by its title and levee-spilling setting, Dylan's song is a banjo-driven, well-populated mountain narrative that includes cameos from both blues shouter Big Joe Turner (who shows up just in time for the deluge depicted) and evolutionist philosopher and scientist Charles Darwin (who is being hunted down on Highway 5 by a creationist judge who wants him "dead or alive/either one, I don't care").

"High Water" is one of those songs steeped in a torrent of cultural references and literary/musical asides that so fascinate the Dylanologists—it's almost as if Dylan was toying with their obsessiveness. The ominous Jim Crow lyric ("You're dancing with whom they tell you to, or you don't dance at all") seems drawn from an 1843 minstrel show song by Daniel Decatur Emmett (*see* "Dixie"), "I Lost My Gal at the Boatman's Ball," which contains the line "Now when you go to de boatman's ball, you dance with your wife or not at all." Along with the name dropping, Dylan evokes the elemental blues of Robert Johnson ("Believe I'll dust my broom/Keeping away from the women, I'm giving them lots of room") and ancient murder ballads from Appalachian folk ("Well, the coo-coo is a pretty bird, she warbles when she flies/I'm preachin' the word of God, I'm putting out your eyes") in painting this bleak landscape, which, first heard in the days after the World Trade Center destruction, seemed like the direst piece of prophecy.

Discussing *"Love and Theft"* with some European journalists in July 2001, as recorded on a pirate CD, Dylan remarked, "Maybe you noticed that most of my songs are traditionally rooted. I don't do that on purpose. Charley Patton's '30s blues has made a deep impression on me and 'High Water (for Charley Patton)' is, in my opinion, the best song of this record."

With Larry Campbell on banjo sounding like an ancient picker from the Clinch Mountains and Dylan's words like the voice of Genesis itself, "High Water" was performed with deadly intelligence and precise, ominous delivery commencing the autumn 2001 Never Ending Tour in support of *"Love and Theft."* A year later, with Dylan plunking the ivories, "High Water" had been reinvented as a blues stomp that could have slid off the grooves of *Shot of Love.*

The hard rain has fallen and now the Flood begins.

[S] **"Highway 51"** (Curtis Jones/Tommy McClennan/C. White/Bob Dylan)
aka "Highway 51 Blues" "New Highway No. 51"
See also "Lonesome Bedroom"
Bob Dylan, *Bob Dylan* (1962)
Curtis Jones, *Curtis Jones, Volume 1 (1937–38)* (1995)
Tommy McClennan, *Travelin' Highway Man*/'39 (1994)
Memphis Slim, *Alone with My Friends* (1961)

"For the migrant Negro . . . the long ribbons of the 'odd' numbered highways have a magnetic fascination. . . . He sings of Highway 49. . . . Often he sings of Highway 61 . . . or of its fellow, Highway 51, on whose hard causeway countless thousands of flapping soles and bare black feet have made no indentation. . . . These are the best-known routes to the Southern Negroes."

Those words from blues expert Paul Oliver's 1963 book *The Meaning of the Blues* (originally published as *Blues Fell This Morning: The Meaning of the Blues*; London: Cassell, 1960) cut right to the chase. American folk and blues songs are steeped in images of travel, and Dylan (inspired by songs like Robert Johnson's "Terraplane Blues," Woody Guthrie's "66 Highway Blues," and no doubt dozens of others) was particularly taken with this theme early in his career when he was at his most footloose. "Highway 51," a deep Delta blues, was a wonderful vehicle for the wastrel persona he adopted when he first hit New York City. It is a song sodden in freedom and change as the narrator vows not to walk down the road where the woman who spurned him dwells, as if the ribbon of highway that runs by her front door is cursed.

But old songs are full of mystery and this is an early example of a Dylan song with roots that are tangled in the blues at best. To simplify, Dylan seems to have drawn on Curtis Jones's original melody from a 1938 recording,

Tommy McClennan's lyrics from a 1939 recording, and a recurring guitar figure from the Everly Brothers' 1957 hit "Wake Up Little Susie." Dylan's full-throttle, diesel-engine-tempo guitar work comes on like a full one-man-band orchestra worthy of Jesse Fuller, and his strong vocal delivery builds to some powerful peaks during the nearly three-minute workout. Death may permeate the lyrics, but Dylan fills the song with life.

Although Curtis Jones is given credit for this song on Dylan's debut album, some blues experts insist this is not his work. Rather, they bypass Jones's 1938 composition and attribute verses to Tommy McClennan, who recorded the same tune as "New Highway No. 51," and to Dylan himself. Confusing matters even further is the author attribution to one C. White that's cited on www.bobdylan.com, Columbia Records/Sony Music's Dylan Web site.

Curtis Jones (born August 18, 1906, Naples, Texas; died September 11, 1971, Munich, Germany) grew up in a sharecropping community. He was one of seven siblings and his early childhood was much the same as that of other black children of the day: as soon as he was able, he found himself working in the fields, and by the time he reached his teens, he had suffered sufficiently from the sharecropping regime.

Highly representative of the extremely influential bluesmen who are largely forgotten today, Jones was described by Paul Oliver as "the bluesman's blues singer." A blues pianist, he moved to Chicago in 1936 and began his recording career in 1937 with his most famous song, "Lonesome Bedroom Blues" (performed by Dylan on the Japanese leg of his 1978 big-band tour). This tune, inspired by Jones's failed marriage, remained in Columbia's catalogue until the demise of the 78 rpm record. Between 1937 and 1941, Jones recorded for all of the

major jazz and blues labels: Vocalion, Bluebird, and Okeh. He slowly fell into obscurity after World War II, however, where he remained until he was rediscovered in 1958, when blues enthusiast Bob Koester located him living in rundown conditions in Chicago. In the 1960s, Jones recorded albums for Bluesville, Decca, Blue Horizon, and Koester's own Delmark label. Finding an appreciative audience in Europe, he eventually moved to the Continent, where he toured extensively. Nevertheless, he died in penury and was buried in a German grave that was sold in 1979 because no one had paid for its upkeep.

Tommy McClennan (born April 8, 1908, Yazoo City, Mississippi; died c. 1962?, Chicago) was a sandpaper-throated blues growler from the Mississippi Delta backcountry who, along with Jones, was part of the final wave of rustic blues guitarists to cut major-label records in Chicago. His 1939–1942 Bluebird recordings were no-frills, no-nonsense journeys into the depths of the blues. His potent repertoire included "Bottle It Up and Go" (later covered as "Step It Up and Go" by Dylan on *Good as I Been to You*), "Cross Cut Saw Blues," and "Deep Blue Sea Blues" (aka "Catfish Blues"). His Bluebird sessions with Robert Petway in 1941 and '42 were his last and are his mostly highly regarded. McClennan died in destitution in Chicago, but bluesologists have never determined the precise date or circumstances of his death.

After waxing "Highway 51" for his eponymous debut album in late 1961, Dylan seems to have left just a couple of other versions behind. One is on an informal home recording, also from 1961, for his early New York City patrons and friends Mac and Eve McKenzie; another comes from a Carnegie Hall hoot nearly a year later. The time in between the recordings suggests that "Highway 51" may have been at least a semiregular inclusion during his coffeehouse gigs of the era. Dylan would later reprise the melody for this fast blues on "It's Alright, Ma."

Highway 61 Interactive
Produced by Graphix Zone. Released 1995.

Back in the old days before the Internet became available to the masses and CD-ROMs were all the rage, Dylan was the subject of this wonderful interactive package. The disc was a boon for collectors, most notably for the inclusion of an electric version of "House of the Rising Sun" purportedly recorded in 1962. And that's just the tip of the iceberg.

The primary screen on *Highway 61 Interactive* opens with a collage crammed with evocative Dylan memorabilia and iconography. A click of the mouse on any one of the images initiates a sequence that covers each phase of Dylan's life and career with some depth. Details include lyrics to all of Dylan's songs released up to that point, a list of every musician of renown who has covered a Dylan song, photographs of Dylan, and film clips. Most impressive is the Greenwich Village street scene, from which users can venture into a digitized recording studio, coffeehouse, club, and more. There are also ten full Dylan songs and 110 excerpts, including eight takes of "Like a Rolling Stone," that chart the studio development of that most famous tune. And throughout the disc are all kinds of little surprises that add color to and augment understanding of Dylan's legacy. For the truly intrepid, there's even a little game: visit enough of the environments and gain entry to Dylan's 1993 New York City Supper Club concert in the form of a few video clips from that famous, intimate show.

Commenting on the project to Malcolm Jones Jr. in the March 20, 1995, issue of *Newsweek,* Dylan was typically aloof in his assessment of the wonders of technology. "I'm just rooted back there in the fifties. . . . I know people who've got that online thing and games and things, but I find it too inhibiting to sit in front of a screen. On any level—I don't even like to sit and watch TV too much. I feel I'm being manipulated."

Given such sentiments, it is surprising, then, that Dylan himself reportedly suggested including the word "interactive" in the title of the release.

Highway 61 Revisited
Columbia Records LP CL-2389, CD CK-9189, CS CS-9189; Sony Music Entertainment, Inc., SACD 90324. Recorded in New York City, June 15–16, July 29–30, August 2–4, 1965. Released August 30, 1965. Produced by Bob Johnston. "Like a Rolling Stone" produced by Tom Wilson. Liner notes by Bob Dylan. Cover photography by Daniel Kramer.
Bob Dylan—guitar, harmonica, piano, keyboards, vocals. Michael Bloomfield—guitar. Al Kooper—organ, guitar, piano, horn, keyboards. Sam Lay—drums. Bobby Gregg—drums. Harvey Brooks—bass. Harvey Goldstein—bass. Paul Griffin—organ, piano, keyboards. Frank Owens—piano. Russ Savakus—bass. Charlie McCoy—guitar, harmonica.
"Like a Rolling Stone," "Tombstone Blues," "It Takes a Lot to Laugh, It Takes a Train to Cry," "From a Buick 6," "Ballad of a Thin Man," "Queen Jane Approximately," "Highway 61 Revisited," "Just Like Tom Thumb's Blues," "Desolation Row"

Upping the ante for all "serious" pop music with a scathing, crystalline depiction of a modern-age nightmare, *Highway 61 Revisited* stands as one of Bob Dylan's major achievements. Dylan made exquisite use of a crack backup band—which included Al Kooper and Michael Bloomfield—to play articulate, poetic, and incredibly bitter songs on an album overflowing with genius—yes, *genius.*

Along with *Blonde on Blonde* and *Blood on*

the Tracks, Highway 61 Revisited remains at or near the top of the heap of Dylan's oeuvre, packed with at least a half dozen certified classics, themselves populated by a bizarre cast of characters—drawn from the pages of history and the leaves of his own imagination—who make strange yet oddly appropriate cameos over the course of nine great songs.

Highway 61 Revisited commences in grand fashion with the epic "Like a Rolling Stone" and never lets up, reflecting the artist's new mask as the jaded, been-round-the-block-and-back snot-nosed visionary hipster saint. By the time the listener hits the off-ramp of this grim ribbon of black tar, Dylan's embroidery of surreal blues ("Tombstone Blues"), folk-bop apocalypse ("Desolation Row"), south-of-the-border noir ("Just Like Tom Thumb's Blues"), good ol' cubist garage rock ("From a Buick 6"), diabolical put-down ("Ballad of a Thin Man"), and faded romance ("Queen Jane Approximately") can still be fleetingly glimpsed in the rearview mirror.

Highway 61 Revisited was Dylan's first wall-to-wall electric album, and it sparked intense debate in the popular- and folk-music communities. The hard-core folkies had already bidden Dylan adieu, but it mattered not, as rock had become *the* medium through which the singer could now best express his vision, and in so doing, he redefined pop music. Wrapped in a raw, driving sound enhanced by the sidemen's free-spirited accompaniment, Dylan's poems— part Beat, part symbolist, part concrete, part Sun Studio—made clear that contemporaries could no longer be content with traditional pop forms if they expected to keep up, an influence immediately apparent on recordings by the Beatles and the Rolling Stones.

Not only was *Highway 61 Revisited* groundbreaking, the album did good business too, as it rose to No. 3 on the *Billboard* charts and earned Dylan his second consecutive gold record. It

Highway 61, New Madrid, Missouri, 1990.
(Photo: Michael L. Abramson/Time Life Pictures/Getty Images)

stayed on the charts for twenty-four weeks, buoyed by the success of the single release of "Like a Rolling Stone."

Dylan's humorously slippery liner notes followed in the same vein as those found on *Bringing It All Back Home* and reflect the nature of his lyrics of the period and the style found in his novel then in progress, *Tarantula.*

Dylan has made a career habit of denigrating or disavowing his own work but did no such thing when appraising *Highway 61 Revisited* in the *Biograph* liner notes: "I'm not going to be able to make a record better than that one. *Highway 61* is just too good. There's a lot of stuff on that record I would listen to."

[S] "Highway 61 Revisited" (Bob Dylan)

Bob Dylan, single (1965); *Highway 61 Revisited* (1965); *Real Live* (1984)
Bob Dylan/The Band, *Before the Flood* (1974)
Bob Dylan/Various Artists (performed by Johnny Winter), *Bob Dylan: The 30th Anniversary Concert Celebration* (1993)
The Leaves, *The Leaves* (1966)
Johnny Winter, *Second Winter* (1969); *Captured Live!* (1976); *The Johnny Winter Collection* (1988)
Terry Reid, *Move Over for Terry Reid* (1969)
Larry Raspberry, *In the Pink* (1975)
Dr. Feelgood, *Classic* (1990)
P. J. Harvey, *Rid of Me* (1993)
Various Artists (performed by P. J. Harvey), *Outlaw Blues, Volume 2* (1995)
Bugs Henderson, *Four Tens Strike Again* (1996)
Steve Gibbons, *The Dylan Project* (1998)
The Zimmermen, *After the Ambulances Go* (1998)
Michael Moore, *Jewels and Binoculars* (2000)
X, *See How We Are* (2002)
Various Artists (performed by Martin Simpson), *May Your Song Always Be Sung: The Songs of Bob Dylan, Volume 3* (2003)
Various Artists, *John Wesley Harding, John Brown and Some Wicked Messengers Play Bob Dylan* (2004)

Highway 61 was (and, to some extent, still is) the link Southern blacks took to the northern cities of the Midwest. It is also the road that figuratively led the rest of the planet to the muddy roots of the deepest, darkest blues. It brought impoverished rural families to urban opportunity and the country blues to the industrial North. A ribbon of highway that extends north from the Gulf of Mexico through the Mississippi Delta and Memphis to Duluth, Minnesota, Highway 61 also served Dylan as a vital poetic symbol, a vision of America.

In its original pressing, the ringing blues shuffle of "Highway 61 Revisited" is kicked off by a slide whistle ("police car" played by Dylan, according to the album credits). The studio band races to keep up, paced by the drumming and flavored with Mike Bloomfield's stinging bottleneck guitar.

The lyrics are informed by a range of traditions that include everything from the hoodoo-voodoo of the blues liturgy to Lord Buckley (*see* "Black Cross"), the comedian/storyteller best remembered for his updating of stories from literature, myth, and legend, such as "The Nazz," his hipster's take on three miracles in the life of Christ; in this, his mark can be seen specifically in Dylan's recasting of the Old Testament's Abraham and Isaac tale into a modern setting and vernacular in "Highway 61 Revisited."

Referring to Dylan's father, Abraham Zimmerman, Robert Shelton wrote in his 1986 Dylan biography, *No Direction Home: The Life and Music of Bob Dylan*: "If God were chatting with Abe close to the northern end of the highway, the son would be Dylan himself. The 'killing' would have struck him down just as he was setting off on the road. The song's ludicrousness grows with mention of Georgia Sam, poor Howard (a folk figure), Mack the Finger, Louie the King, and the bluesy mumbo jumbo of mystical magic about seventh sons. Finally, a jab at a concert promoter who, when asked to sell another world war, says he'll try. There's a disturbing undercurrent of probability."

"Highway 61 Revisited" has been a relative constant in Dylan's concert repertoire throughout his career. It was first performed live by Dylan and the Band at the famous 1969 Isle of Wight concert in England and was delivered with a howling bluster when they toured again in 1974. It sounded like a Rolling Stones' knock-off when he trotted the song out with a pickup touring band that included ex-Stone Mick Taylor on lead guitar in 1984, and has been a somewhat static inclusion in Dylan's concerts since then. Most notably and with mixed success, Dylan and company gave the song a ZZ

Top–style arrangement during the Never Ending Tour of the late 1990s, and he was still singing it with that scratchy, helium-laced croak you either come to love (or not) well into the '00s.

⬛ "Hiram Hubbard" (Traditional)
Jean Ritchie and Doc Watson, *Live at Folk City* (1963)
Charlie Brown, *Teton Tea Party* (1967)
Sweeny's Men, *Sweeny's Men* (1968)
Joe Hickerson, *Drive Dull Care Away* (1988)

A bit of folk obscurity Dylan toyed with in 1962 (most notably at his July appearance that summer at Montreal's Fin Jan club), "Hiram Hubbard" takes up the familiar folkie cause of martyrdom. The singer says that he's heard that Hiram Hubbard wasn't guilty of the crime for which he was eventually put to death, but was forty miles away when it transpired.

"Hiram Hubbard" fits right in with that group of songs (such as "Poor Lazarus") about falsely condemned men destroyed not so much for any specific crime, but for the general crime of rebelling against authority. What makes the song particularly brutal is the sense that Hubbard was also the victim of mob law—dragged out of jail, chained to a tree, and drilled in the head at point blank range. The structure of "Hiram Hubbard" is simple and compelling, with each chorus seeming to reaffirm that a horrible wrong has been done and there's nothing anyone can do about it except to repeat "Hiram Hubbard wasn't guilty" over and over.

Hiram Hubbard seems to have been a real person whose alleged crimes (and ethnicity) are, at least at the moment, lost to history. "'Hiram Hubbard' (we pronounce it H'arm) is a true tale about a local happening," says musician and folklorist Jean Ritchie of Kentucky's Cumberland Mountains, in her book *Singing Family of the Cumberlands* (New York: Oxford University Press, 1955). "The killing took place a few miles from home and the song travelled abroad and was popular for many years. To this day, some believe that 'H'arm Hubbard was not guilty,' though others say he was. It might be that he was. Songs have a way taking up for bad men. I heard the song from Dad Ritchie, who told me he gathered it up from three or four people who remembered bits of it, and then he put it back together. Within my lifetime, I have not heard anyone else sing it but him, Balis Ritchie."

⬛ "Homeward Bound" (Paul Simon)
Simon and Garfunkel, *Parsley, Sage, Rosemary and Thyme* (1966)
Mel Tormé, *Right Now!* (1966)
Glen Campbell, *By the Time I Get to Phoenix* (1967)
Paul Simon, *Live Rhymin'* (1974)
Cher, *Sunny* (1999)

According to Paul Simon legend, "Homeward Bound," a song of sweet longing and weary return, was written at the Widnes railway station in northern England. That, however, seems to be a slight, romanticized exaggeration. Simon did embark upon a tour of one-nighters at various venues in northern England in 1965. While working at several clubs in the Widnes area, he stayed with a fellow named Geoff Speed. When it was time for Simon to move on, Geoff drove Paul to the Widnes station and, as he told Simon biographer Victoria Kingston (see *Simon and Garfunkel: The Definitive Biography,* 1996): "'I think we got there just as the train was arriving and so I saw him get onto the train. He was going to Hull, I think to play at the Waterson's club. Since then, it has been said that "Homeward Bound" was written at Widnes Station, but it's not really true. I think it's a bit of poetic license. . . . Paul was certainly working on a song at my house,' said Speed. 'It had been evolving and was going round in his head. I think he had already written some of the words, but the tune was giving him problems.'"

Whatever the truth, the people of Widnes take the myth seriously. In the early '90s the town unveiled a plaque that now adorns the station, stating that "Homeward Bound" was written there.

For a guy who seems to dig Paul Simon and his songs (Dylan has performed and/or recorded several, including "The Boxer," and toured with Simon in 1999), Dylan has done a good job of botching them, and "Homeward Bound" was no exception. Dylan worked up an appealing, if flimsy, country swing arrangement of the song, which he performed with breathy vocals a couple of times in the summer of 1991 while on tour in Europe.

s "Honest with Me" (Bob Dylan)
Bob Dylan, *"Love and Theft"* (2001)
Various Artists (performed by Bob Dylan), *Grammy Nominees 2002* (2002)

A confrontational, me-to-you song in the spirit of mid-'60s excess, "Honest with Me" features some Mike Bloomfield–style guitar pyrotechnics courtesy of Dylan's right- and left-hand guitar men from the latest editions of the Never Ending Tour, most notably Charlie Sexton and Larry Campbell, who did wonders with "Honest with Me" when Dylan began performing it as an encore at his fall 2001 concerts in support of *"Love and Theft."*

In that slot, "Honest with Me" was the up-tempo highlight of the show's finale segment and featured passionate slide work by Campbell and the fury of a man in an ugly world. "Well, I'm stranded in the city that never sleeps," Dylan snarls; "Some of these women they just give me the creeps."

As with some of the songs in his back pocket, Dylan draws on the notion of memory to highlight "Honest with Me." In "Mr. Tambourine Man," he wanted "all memory and fate driven deep beneath the waves" so he could "forget about today until tomorrow." More recently, on "Million Miles," he was "drifting in and out of dreamless sleep, throwing all my memories in a ditch so deep." And still, the past brings nothing but pain. "These memories I got they can strangle a man," he sings on "Honest with Me," because "some things are too terrible to be true."

On an album dripping with the Deep South, Dylan then defiantly quotes the traditional Civil War song "I'm a Good Old Rebel": "I'm not sorry for nothing I've done," he spits out; "I'm glad I fought, I only wish we'd won."

And he hasn't given up the fight. "I'm here to create a new imperial empire," he proclaims. "I'm gonna do whatever circumstances require."

He'll even try a sly seduction. "You say my eyes are pretty and my smile is nice," he offers. "Well, I'll sell it to ya at a reduced price."

Poking deeper for reference, fans of Dr. Junichi Saga's book *Confessions of a Yakuza* might recognize how the original's "I won't come anymore if it bothers you" becomes, in Dylan's song, "Some things are too terrible to be true/I won't come here no more if it bothers you."

A final note: the version of "Honest with Me" released on *Grammy Nominees 2002* was recorded by Dylan and his band at the rehearsal for the show.

s "Honey, Just Allow Me One More Chance" (Traditional/Henry Thomas/Bob Dylan)
aka "Honey, Won't You Allow Me Once More Chance?," "Honey, 'Low Me One More Chance"

Bob Dylan, single (1965); *The Freewheelin' Bob Dylan* (1963)

Henry Thomas, *Texas Worried Blues: Complete Recorded Works 1927–1929* (1989)

Lester Flatt and Earl Scruggs, *Final Fling* (1970); *1964–1969, Plus* (1996)

Dylan's rendition of this fast and humorous ancient little ditty on *The Freewheelin' Bob Dylan* includes a laugh-out-loud-funny war whoop from the singer right in the middle. Clocking in at just over a minute, it is one of Dylan's shortest songs on record and provides nice comic relief on an album desperately in need of some. Dylan also performed the song for about a year between the springs of 1962 and 1963.

Dylan, according to Nat Hentoff's *Freewheelin'* liner notes, took this song from "a recording by a now-dead Texas blues singer," remembering only "that his first name was Henry." Undoubtedly Dylan was referring to Lone Star State songster Henry "Ragtime Texas" Thomas, who recorded the first known version of the song in 1928 when he was fifty-four years old, just two years before his death.

Songsters and Saints, Paul Oliver's wonderful 1984 study of American roots music, asserts that "Honey, Just Allow Me One More Chance" was first collected in the field by Mrs. Tom Bartlett of Marlin, Texas, for folklorist Dorothy Scarborough. Because that version corresponds so closely with Thomas's, it is suspected that Mrs. Bartlett collected the song from Thomas himself.

Dylan probably first got hip to Thomas through Harry Smith's *Anthology of American Folk Music* (Smithsonian Folkways, 1952; reissued 1997), which included Thomas's best-known song, "Fishing Blues" (aka "I'm a-Goin' Fishin'"), as its final cut. Dylan then must have discovered "Honey, Just Allow Me One More

Chance" on *Henry Thomas Sings the Texas Blues,* released on the Origin Jazz Library label in 1961. Some years hence, Dylan fooled around with both "Fishing Blues" and "Honey, Just Allow Me One More Chance" during the May 1, 1970, recording session for *Self Portrait,* so Thomas was still on his mind at least as late as then.

Thomas (born 1874 near Big Sandy, Texas; died 1930s–1950s) was the son of former slaves who became sharecroppers. He taught himself the guitar and panpipes (a homemade reed instrument that emits a high-pitched, whistling sound that was central to the region's fife-and-drum bands), leaving home as a teenager to work on the Texas-Pacific Railroad. There are legends that report him hopping freight trains and entertaining pedestrians on street corners, in parks, and at train stations, but little is actually known about him. Blind Lemon Jefferson may have been the first true star of Texas blues, but he most likely learned his guitar stylings by listening to traveling minstrels like Henry Thomas.

Though it is thought that Thomas spent most of his life in East Texas, he is rumored to have ventured to Chicago's Columbian Exposition in 1893 and to the 1904 St. Louis World's Fair. It is well established that he made it as far as Chicago, as that's where all his recordings were made.

He began recording in 1927 and cut about two dozen sides over the next two years—recordings that have been compiled on several anthologies. Something of a one-man band, he left a body of work that reveals much about the songster tradition, a repertoire that, out of necessity for the survival of a street-corner busker looking to score another Indian-head penny or two, included black folk songs, jump-ups, rags, dance tunes, novelty tunes, and early blues.

Thomas's importance as a link in the vast American musical chain is simply a product of his age. Here was someone who could actually remember the years in the late 1800s when the blues was in gestation. Thus, his recordings give a certain insight into what the music sounded like in its earliest expressions. Although he was not among the first blues singers to record, he is among the oldest "professionals" to have been captured on vinyl.

In his own version of "Honey, Just Allow Me One More Chance," Dylan modified the tune and draws upon Thomas's song as well as a host of other influences. Although the song is credited jointly to Thomas and Dylan on *Freewheelin'*, almost all the words are Dylan's. He borrows "I'm walkin' down the road with my hat in my hand/I'm lookin' for a woman needs a worried man," for instance, from Woody Guthrie's version of Leadbelly's "Take a Whiff on Me," and "Just like a-huntin' for a needle in a bed of sand,/Tryin' to find a woman hasn't got a man" from Papa Charlie Jackson's "Salty Dog Blues" of 1924 and/or "Coffee Pot Blues" of 1925—both of which use the line. Dylan's adaptation of these lyrics are as follows: in his first stanza, "Well, I'm a-walkin' down the road/With my head in my hand,/I'm lookin' for a woman/Needs a worried man," and in the last stanza, "Well, lookin' for a woman/That ain't got no man,/Is just lookin' for a needle/That is lost in the sand." Actually, while there can be little doubt that Dylan was familiar with Guthrie's work, it is quite possible that his source for the Jackson songs might be later recordings by others or some other single entirely, as the lines are stock in the country blues. The burlesqued sadness in Dylan's inconsequential and lighthearted performance also owes something to Jesse Fuller, the one-man-band folkster whose music has long fascinated Dylan.

[S] "Honky Tonk Blues" (Hank Williams)

See also Hank Williams
Hank Williams, *Complete Hank Williams* (1998)
Richard Thompson, *Small Town Romance* (1984)
Lonesome Pine Fiddlers, *Windy Mountain* (1992)
Roy Clark and Joe Pass, *Roy Clark & Joe Pass Play Hank Williams* (1995)

Despite Dylan's long-avowed love for the music of Hank Williams, it always seems like a surprise when one of Hank's tunes appears in a Dylan concert. It was no different in the winter of 1999, when Williams's "Honky Tonk Blues," a classic paean to roadhouse juke joints everywhere, was displayed as an electric romp for a string of Never Ending Tour shows.

Williams spent five years trying to record a decent a version of "Honky Tonk Blues," starting in 1946 and finally succeeding in December 1951. Unlike the positive attitude expressed in Williams's "Honky Tonkin'," the viewpoint here swings one hundred eighty degrees away and depicts the nightlife as a wearisome, purposeless treadmill.

[S] "Hoochie Coochie Man" (Willie Dixon)

aka "I'm Your Hoochie Coochie Man"
See also "I'm Ready"
Muddy Waters, *Muddy Waters* (1954)
Alexis Korner, *R&B from the Marquee* (1962)
Chuck Berry, *Live at the Fillmore Auditorium* (1967)
Allman Brothers, *Idlewild South* (1970)
John Mayall, *Primal Solos* (1977)
B. B. King, *Original Blues Masters* (1997)

Dylan has always enjoyed struttin' out a little pre-postindustrial age mojo now and again, so what better way to do it as the millennium drew nigh than with this most classic of swaggering, mystic Chicago blues linking the Delta to rock 'n' roll?

The song, its subject, and its expressions

have deep roots in the Delta blues, yet from its earliest 1952 recording, represented a stylistic break from the southern end of Highway 61. Willie Dixon, the great Chicago blues songwriter, bassist, and Chess Records arranger, pulled the many versions into one, which he copyrighted and gave to Muddy Waters, for whom it became a trademark as he sang of his birthright like it was a matter of life and death.

Before "Hoochie Coochie Man" came along, nearly all electric blues were little more than amplified versions of familiar acoustic numbers. But with "Hoochie Coochie Man," Waters got to unleash his famous, staggered stop-and-start rhythm in dramatic fashion. The stomp pattern employed in the song proved so popular with audiences and performers alike that Dixon and Waters recycled it for other songs, like "Mannish Boy," itself pilfered by Bo Diddley for his own "I'm a Man."

Despite its modernism, "Hoochie Coochie Man" is an idiomatic grab bag of Deep South gris-gris listing a mess of necessary hoodoo items and numerology to cast a spell on even the most ardent agnostic and/or hard-to-woo female: the black cat bone, John the Conqueror root, the ever-mysterious mojo, and liberal use of the number seven (derived from the Hebrew word *sheva*, meaning sated or full) with its biblical significance as the symbol of divine perfection and the prebiblical legend of the luck of the seventh son.

All music genealogies aside, "Hoochie Coochie Man" is one erotic song marked in its initial incarnation by Little Walter Jacobs's molten harmonica licks, Otis Spann's rolling staccato piano figures, Dixon's solid groove bass lines, and Muddy's sensuous, self-mythologizing delivery—a braggadocio that has continued through rock and hip-hop.

In his 1989 autobiography, *I Am the Blues*, Dixon discussed the song's sources and appeal in remembering the fortune-telling gypsy women who periodically passed through his town when he was a boy and told their "customers" what they wanted to hear: "All through the history of mankind, there have been people who were supposed to be able to tell the future before it came to pass. People always felt it would be great to be one of these people: 'This guy is a hoodoo man, this lady is a witch, this other guy's a hoochie coochie man, she's some kind of voodoo person.'"

Singing like the seventh son of a seventh son on the seventh hour of the seventh day of the seventh month, Dylan came off like an old, phlegmy bluesman in his talismanic invocation of "Hoochie Coochie Man" at a couple of Never Ending Tour shows during a 1999 swing through the northeastern U.S. and a final rendition in March 2000 in California.

[S] "House Carpenter" (Traditional)

aka "The Daemon Lover," "The Demon Lover," "The House Carpenter's Wife," "James Harris," "The Ship Carpenter," "A Warning for Married Women," "Well Met, Well Met"

Bob Dylan, *The Bootleg Series, Volumes 1–3: Rare and Unreleased, 1961–1991*/'62 (1991)

Various Artists (performed by Clarence Ashley), *Anthology of American Folk Music*/'30 (1952/1997)

Texas Gladden, *Anglo American Ballads* (1956)

Pete Steel, *Banjo Tunes & Songs* (1958)

Joan Baez, *Joan Baez in Concert, Part 1* (1962)

Dave Van Ronk, *Inside Dave Van Ronk* (1962)

Doc Watson, *The Doc Watson Family* (1963)

Bradley Kincaid, *Mountain Ballads & Old Time Songs* (1963)

Buffy Sainte-Marie, *Little Wheel Spin & Spin* (1966)

Sarah Ogan Gunning, *Silver Dagger* (1976)

Pete Seeger, *Folk Music of the World* (1991)

Doug Wallin, *Family Songs and Stories from the North* (1995)

Various Artists (performed by Almeda Riddle), *Southern Journey, Volume 6: Sheep, Sheep Don'tcha Know the Road* (1997)

"House Carpenter" is one of those folk songs

H

folksingers seem to absorb by osmosis. Dylan may have picked it up from Joan Baez and Bob Gibson, who—among others—were regularly singing it in Greenwich Village in the early 1960s. But he also could have learned the Clarence Ashley version from the *Anthology of American Folk Music*, one of Dylan's main sources of material at the time. "House Carpenter" is, along with "Barbara Allen," one of the best known of the Child ballads (No. 243), and is one of the oldest songs ever performed and/or recorded by Dylan.

The ballad tells the story of a woman abandoning her husband and newborn baby in order to run away with her lover. In the end, both the heroine and her lover are drowned, apparently as punishment for their crimes. Known in the United States and in England by a multitude of titles, various versions of the song were collected from traditional singers in both countries and appear in virtually any folksong collection available. It was known in England as a broadside sheet by the early seventeenth century and it may well be even older than that. Child gave six versions of the ballad (all of them Scottish) from oral tradition and two broadside printings, one of which is very similar to the American texts. The early versions portray the suitor as having almost supernatural qualities that are all but absent in most American versions. Dylan's rendition contains the demonic character traits of the suitor in the dramatic closing verses.

In his 1960 book *The Folk Songs of North America* Alan Lomax analyzed "House Carpenter" and its meanings with the acuity of a $100-an-hour Park Avenue psychiatrist. After pointing out that, left to their own devices (and company), women are more attracted to ballads linked with home and hearth while men are liable to gravitate to "humorous or bawdy songs that satirized love or [were] composed about work or deeds of violence," Lomax observed that if "the men sang the old ballads, this was in the presence of women and was a recognition of feminine interests."

Still, Lomax was intrigued by the predilection so many backwoods women showed in singing murder ballads. And he interpreted that interest as a kind of escape tool, a socially acceptable and creative means of dealing with the hardships, anxiety, and entrapment of frontier life.

Lomax then launches into a fascinatingly detailed analysis of "House Carpenter":

The present ballad, one of the favorite folk songs of early America, but an especial favorite in the South, characterizes man as a tempting demon and romantic love as temptation that destroys women. In the British original the returned lover, James Harris, is actually a demon from Hell (in some versions the Devil himself).

The Devil disappeared from most American versions, but the man stands out, as all the more demonic, as Death himself. The woman, believing her first lover is dead, marries and has a secure home with children. The old lover returns and offers her an escape. In the first moments of her romantic adventure, she is splendid—"she glittered and glistened and proudly she walked"—till she is "taken to be some queen." But this escape from domestic sordidness lasts scarcely a month. She begins to weep—not for her house or her husband, whom she despises, but for her children. Then, as a punishment for guilt, she and her lover sink in the sea "to rise no more."

This song was sung by women who had come with their men to Pennsylvania and the lowlands—by their daughters who lived and died hard in mountain log cabins—in turn, by their daughters sinking deeper in the squalor of backwoods life. For them, the easiest path out of a bad marriage was to run off with another man. Yet that way, the road of adventure, they would lose what they had and die in guilt, far from their children.

The "House Carpenter" ballad, in this view, represents the longings of pioneer women for love or for an escape from their log cabin life—both sinful wishes to the Calvinist. The ballad heroine has one moment of romantic splendor. Then she is hardly punished. No fantasy could have been better calculated to reinforce the Calvinist sexual morality of ancestors. It counseled them to stick to what they had. Indeed, no women have ever been more long-suffering, or more hard-working helpmates, yet they did enjoy songs about women who rebelled, especially if the rebels were punished in the last stanza.

For the ultimate obsessive, Clinton Heylin's book *Dylan's Daemon Lover: The Tangled Tale of a 450-Year-Old Pop Ballad* (London: Helter Skelter Publishing, 1999) is devoted entirely to the history and multitude of configurations of "House Carpenter." Heylin's basic thesis is that the versions of "House Carpenter" that Dylan would have been first exposed to in the early 1960s are variations on those performed by Irish immigrants who, in turn, were merely extending an evolution of a ballad initially recorded in Elizabethan chronicles, thus making it four hundred fifty years old, one of the earliest known English pop songs.

Dylan first recorded "House Carpenter" in March 1962 for his debut LP, *Bob Dylan*, but the song was left off that album and not released until *The Bootleg Series, Volumes 1–3* came out thirty years later. He also recorded the song on March 4, 1970, during the sessions that eventually provided material for *Self Portrait*, although this rendition was left stashed in the vaults.

[S] "A House of Gold" (Hank Williams)

See also Hank Williams
aka "House of Gold"
Hank Williams, *Complete Hank Williams* (1998)
Milton Estes, single (1950)
Bill Monroe, *I Saw the Light* (1959)
E. C. Ball, *E. C. Ball* (1973)
D. L. Menard, *Cajun Saturday Night* (1985)
Moe Bandy, *Gospel Favorites* (1995)
George Jones, *Vintage Collection Series* (1996)
McPeak Brothers, *Pathway to Heaven* (1996)

A troubling and deeply personal song taking aim at the moneygrubbing Hank Williams saw all too much of, "A House of Gold" (said to be written for Nashville friend Milton Estes—*see* "20/20 Vision") was a clearly a variant of Williams's own "Lost Highway" with a Cajun spin. Williams first recorded the song in late 1949 or early 1950 as a demo, and it was released in April 1951 with overdubs. Dylan performed the song a couple of times during his June 1989 swing through Europe and points in the Far East with a more uplifting arrangement than the one made famous by Williams, as if he had risen above all the trappings and temptations life dangled in front of his nose. Dylan's own unreleased late-gospel-period song, "City of Gold," may owe a little something to this Williams original.

[S] "House of the Risin' Sun" (Traditional)

aka "House in New Orleans," "House of the Rising Sun," "In New Orleans," "New Orleans," "The Rising Sun Blues,"
Bob Dylan, *Bob Dylan* (1962); *Highway 61 Interactive* (CD-ROM)/'62 (1994)
Leadbelly, *Where Did You Sleep Last Night?*/'40s (1996)
Josh White, *Complete Recorded Works, Volume 6*/'40s (1998)
Nina Simone, *Nina Simone at the Village Gate* (1961)
Woody Guthrie, *Woody Guthrie* (1962)
The Animals, *Animals* (1964)

Sporting house, New Orleans, 1940.

(Photo: David E. Scherman/Time Life Pictures/Getty Images)

H

Dave Van Ronk, *Just Dave Van Ronk* (1964)
Marianne Faithfull, *Come My Way* (1965)
Ramblin' Jack Elliott, *The Essential Ramblin' Jack Elliott* (1970)
Joan Baez, *Joan Baez Ballad Book* (1972)
The Weavers, *Wasn't That a Time* (1987)
Peter, Paul & Mary, *Lifelines* (1995)
Pete Seeger, *Sing Out* (1996)
Doc Watson, *Third Generation Blues* (1999)

No one is quite sure of the exact origin of this lament from the lips and soul of a New Orleans woman driven into prostitution by poverty, though it is one of the most famous songs in the American folk-blues lexicon. Alan Lomax reported that many jazz musicians were familiar with it before World War I, and Rising Sun, as the name for a brothel, occurs in a number of unprintable compositions of English origin. In this particular song, the forsaken woman is returning back to the house of the Rising Sun, a notorious establishment in New Orleans that was distinguished from other houses by a banner bearing an emblem of its namesake.

According to Lomax in his 1960 book *The Folk Songs of North America*, "The 'Rising Sun' occurs as the name of a bawdy house in two other traditional songs, both British in origin. The symbol is, indeed, an appropriate one. The melody can be linked with one setting of 'Little Musgrave and Lady Barnard' (Child Ballad No. 81) and with other old traditional British tunes. Yet this song is, as far as I know, unique. I took it down in 1937 from the singing of a thin, pretty, yellow-headed miner's daughter in Middlesborough, Kentucky, subsequently adapting it to the form that was popularized by [folkster] Josh White. The story, which concerns the sordid path that poverty has forced many poor country girls to follow, may date back to pre–Civil War days, when New Orleans was the true capital of the South and many country boys and girls landed there, after rafting all the way down the Ohio and Mississippi rivers."

"Little Musgrave and Lady Barnard" (aka "Little Matty Groves"), a source song for "Rising Sun" that Lomax mentions, is, according to his liner notes for *Classic Ballads of Britain and Ireland, Volume One* (Rounder Records, 2000), "entered in the Stationers Registers to Francis Coules in 1630 and was quoted in Beaumont and Fletcher's *The Knight of the Burning Pestle* and other plays in the 1630s. . . . Child includes 15 texts, [literary scholar Bertrand Harris] Bronson has 75, with tunes . . . but mostly of North American provenance. Those from New England seem closest to the Scottish, using the major-key tune most often associated with the song 'Drumdelgie.'"

If the Animals' later smash hit of the song is often said to have helped lure Dylan into rock 'n' roll, Dave Van Ronk was probably Dylan's inspiration for performing "Rising Sun." "I'd always known 'Risin' Sun' but never really knew I knew it until I heard Dave sing it," Dylan says in the liner notes for *Bob Dylan*. Dylan was performing this song at least as early as 1960, and was displaying it when he hit Greenwich Village in 1961. He included an impassioned, hysteria-edged version on his first album, having devilish fun with the tune as he takes on the persona of a woman, which he said in a March 1985 interview with Bill Flanagan (for the latter's 1986 book *Written in My Soul*) "is a quite common thing to do."

Dylan recorded an electric version of "House of the Rising Sun" in 1962 (some sources claim 1964) that was eventually released on the CD-ROM *Highway 61 Interactive*. He recorded another less-than-successful, never released rendition during the *New Morning* sessions in 1973. In 1975, the *Renaldo & Clara* film crew captured Dylan and others singing the song in a Quebec hotel room, and in 1986–1987, Dylan performed biting electric versions with Tom Petty and the Heartbreakers.

[S] "Humming Bird" (Johnnie Wright/Jim Anglin/Jack Anglin)

aka "Hummingbird"

See also "Searching for a Soldier's Grave," "This World Can't Stand Alone"

Johnnie and Jack, *All the Best of Johnnie and Jack* (1970)

Dylan introduced this sentimental train song about a guy yearning for the return of his true love just after the death of John Lee Hooker in the summer of 2001, leading to speculation that the performance was made in honor of the blues legend, with whom Dylan had shared an early bill almost exactly forty years before. After playing only one somewhat unintelligible version of the song, Dylan reintroduced "Humming Bird" as a sharp show opener with some regularity in the late summer, again on the fall 2001 Never Ending Tour in support of *"Love and Theft,"* and then again on the spring 2002 European swing.

There are dozens of songs that feature the hummingbird as a central motif, but for pure novelty and extraordinary musical execution, the 1951 Johnnie Wright and Jack Anglin recording of their original song would be hard to top in its impeccable recreation of the train journey described in the lyrics. In this rendition they capture (using merely a lap steel guitar, a fiddle, and some wonderful cooing vocals) the sound of the steaming L&N (Louisville and Nashville) line locomotive that ran between Cincinnati and New Orleans from 1946 to 1969 and the image of the title's little bird darting nearby.

Jim Anglin (born March 23, 1913, Franklin, Tennessee; died January 21, 1987) was, with his brothers Red and Jack, one of the members of the Anglin Brothers, a notable and influential country music combo that made its biggest mark in the 1930s and 1940s. Born in Tennessee but growing up in Athens, Alabama, the youngsters befriended the Delmore Brothers and were influenced by their style. The Anglin family moved to Nashville in 1930, and in 1933 the trio landed their first unpaid radio gigs, which led to a paying job on WAPI out of Birmingham, Alabama. Their growing popularity earned them the nickname "The South's Favorite Trio" and a 1937 American Record Corporation recording session that produced their first regional hit, "They Are All Going Home but One."

The Anglins bounced around the South for the next few years, proving once again that a rolling stone gathers no green stuff. Stops in Memphis, Atlanta, New Orleans, Columbia, and Charlotte failed to garner them the acclaim they had enjoyed in Birmingham. And though they did record for Vocalion, some under the artist credit of Anglin Twins or Anglin Twins and Red, much of what they cut was never released. World War II finally broke up the act when Red became one of the first draftees in 1940. Red was later involved in the Allied invasion of France, and the injuries he suffered there put an end to his musical career.

Jim Anglin served his country in the Pacific theater during World War II, and when he returned stateside, stayed in music. But this time he did it as a writer. Before the war he had sold a couple of pretty good songs ("Beneath That Lonely Mound of Clay" and "Stuck Up Blues") to Roy Acuff, and afterward he resumed the practice en route to becoming one of country music's best songwriters of the 1940s and '50s. "One by One," "Ashes of Love," and "Let Your Conscience Be Your Guide" are but three of Jim Anglin's most beloved songs from that era.

But Jack Anglin never turned his back on performing or recording. Before the war, he teamed up with his brother-in-law Johnnie Wright, who had previously made a name for himself as coleader of the Tennessee Mountain Boys. And because so many of their recordings were enhanced by the talents of the popular vocalist Kitty Wells, the group could bank on a steady stream of gigs and recording dates. Billing themselves as Johnnie and Jack, the duo had a string of hits on RCA Victor in the early '50s and remained a vital act until Jack's death in a car crash in 1963 on his way to attend Patsy Cline's funeral. During their distinctive run, Johnnie and Jack were notable for having brought a new rhythmic consciousness to country music; their use of Latin beats and the smooth force of their combo stretched the boundaries of their sound, as did their incorporation of other musical forms into their fluid mélange: bluegrass, sacred music, and, most amazingly, fabulous covers of R&B tunes. Yet whatever they touched had their fingerprints all over it.

"Hurricane" (Bob Dylan/Jacques Levy)
Bob Dylan, single (1975); *Desire* (1975); *Bob Dylan's Greatest Hits, Volume 3* (1994); *The Bootleg Series, Volume 5: Live 1975—The Rolling Thunder Revue* (2002)

Various Artists (performed by Bob Dylan, Mos Def, et al.), *The Hurricane* (soundtrack to the 1999 movie) (2000)
Milltown Brothers, single (1993)
Ani DiFranco, *Swing Set* (2000)
Various Artists (performed by A Film by Bill Wilder), *A Tribute to Bob Dylan, Volume 3: The Times They Are A-Changin'* (2000)
Todd Rubenstein, *The String Quartet Tribute to Bob Dylan* (2003)

In the early morning hours of June 17, 1966, Paterson, New Jersey, was shaken by the most notorious, still-controversial crime in its history. Two people had been brutally shot to death and two others gravely wounded in the shabby Lafayette Bar and Grill on East 18th Street. Two black men driving in another part of town were apprehended and taken to the scene of the crime, where they were confronted by an angry mob of whites. One of those men was prizefighter Rubin "Hurricane" Carter, a Paterson native and contender for boxing's middleweight crown.

So setting the scene, Carter commenced *The Sixteenth Round* (New York: Viking Press, 1974), the autobiography he wrote in prison to call attention to his plight, which he claimed was the result of a less-than-blind judicial system. After reading the book, Dylan was not only inspired to write "Hurricane" but to mount a (some say misguided) high-profile campaign to get Carter a new and fair trial.

As with virtually all of Dylan's songs of social protest, dating to his earliest compositions ("The Lonesome Death of Hattie Carroll," "Death of Emmett Till," and "Only a Pawn in Their Game"), there is a long story accompanying "Hurricane"—namely, the arrest, imprisonment, release, and semivindication of Rubin Carter, who, in Dylan's song, "coulda been the champion of the world."

Featuring Dylan singing in a voice without restraint, "Hurricane" is a fantastic conga- and lyric-driven diatribe, spiked by Scarlet Rivera's

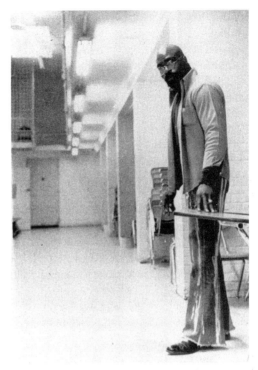

Rubin "Hurricane" Carter, Trenton State Prison, New Jersey, 1974.
(AP/Wide World Photos)

violin, that may still stand as his single moment of immediate consequential glory as he cried out for justice in a song filled with hip vernacular, vivid imagery, and impassioned, urgent performances.

Before his incarceration, Carter was one of the most exciting pugilists of the 1960s—a dynamic, Sonny Liston–style fighter with a Muhammad Ali–like flair behind his Fu Manchu mustache and under his clean-shaven scalp. "Rubin could take a man out with just one punch," Dylan sang in the song, and he was not exaggerating. At five feet eight inches tall and 155 pounds, Carter was stocky and rock solid. Twenty-one of his twenty-seven victories

H

in his thirty-nine-fight career were won by knockout. The high-water mark of his professional career probably came in 1963, on the night when he knocked out welterweight champ Emile Griffith in a nontitle bout. And in all honesty, his career was, based on his last half-dozen ring appearances, probably on the wane when he and trouble found each other once again in 1966.

Not known as an athlete who left his hostility between the ropes, Carter's on-the-edge life included every plot point worthy of a rags-to-riches-to-rags story: an impoverished childhood, reform school, hoodlum gangs, petty crime, an army stint, police entanglements, a rise to fame, and a severe crash-landing. Like many with few professional or social skills and even fewer options, Carter chose a path familiar to those barely treading water at society's lower rungs: the fight game. But, unlike so many other palookas who wind up having the word "ten" shouted by a ref over their shut eyes and supine body in the first round, Carter channeled his rage into skills of brute and cunning that would be the envy of any practitioner of the "sweet science," as boxing poet laureate A. J. Liebling dubbed the sport. Within fairly short order, Carter was cruising Paterson in a monogrammed black Eldorado.

Along the way, Carter developed an acute racial consciousness and began speaking out articulately on racial and social issues, a rarity among athletes of any stripe and virtually scandalous in the era. As a result, some say Carter became a marked man in the eyes of the New Jersey justice machine, especially after telling a newspaper reporter during the 1964 Harlem fruit riots that blacks should protect their communities from police brutality and intimidation by any means necessary. After that, Carter alleged in *The Sixteenth Round*, he became the target of systematic harassment that led

directly to the front door of the Lafayette Bar and Grill on a hot New Jersey night.

Inside that venue lay the bullet-riddled corpses of bartender James Oliver and Fred Nauyaks. Two other victims, Hazel Tanis and William Marins, had miraculously survived the attack. Living above the bar was a woman named Patricia Valentine, who, jarred awake by the gunfire, looked out her window to witness two black men jump into a white car with out-of-state license plates and drive off.

Two other supporting players in this layered, truth-for-hire saga were Alfred Bello and Arthur Dexter Bradley, who, after unsuccessfully attempting to burglarize a nearby sheet-metal factory warehouse, turned their attention to the Lafayette Bar's cash register, left untended in the wake of the bloody mayhem. Because Bello was seen with his hands in the till by Valentine, he decided to stay on the scene lest he be implicated in the shooting.

Things got progressively complicated from this point on and boil down to a thorny, deceptive picture of the facts and events, depending on who is doing the telling. This involves what kind of car was seen making its getaway, what type of taillights it had, the character of the witnesses and the accused, the discovery of spent arms casings in Carter's car, questions as to why Carter was in a leased auto and not his El Dorado, the lack of evidentiary murder weapons, the results of lie-detector tests, shaky alibis, even shakier witness testimony and recanted testimony, the poisoning $12,500 reward incentive, probably backroom deals, a state judicial system lacking credibility, hazy political motives, and the excruciatingly high stakes for everybody concerned.

Caught in the middle of all this was John Artis, the twenty-three-year-old codefendant, who was either a heartless accomplice or a guy profoundly in the wrong place at the wrong time.

After the death of Hazel Tanis a month after the incident, Carter and Artis were, over the course of the next year, arrested, indicted for triple murder, tried, found guilty, and sentenced to multiple life terms.

Carter's prison story is that of a textbook tough guy. He drew a line in the sand from day one in his refusal to don jailhouse stripes or eat the food. His harder time, spent in the hole, still wearing the sharkskin suit he walked into jail wearing, became the stuff of lore throughout the netherworld of inmate culture. He reinvented himself first as a convict lawyer and then, as a rabble-rousing author, became a national figure as he bared his predicament for the world to read, presenting his version of a conspiracy perverting the course of justice.

Dylan read Carter's book *The Sixteenth Round* during his trip to France in the spring of 1975 and visited Carter in New Jersey's state prison in Rahway when he returned. Dylan, as quoted in Larry "Ratso" Sloman's book *On the Road with Bob Dylan* (Bantam Books, 1978), said, "'. . . after meeting him I realized that the man's philosophy and my philosophy were running on the same road, and you don't meet too many people like that . . . I took notes because I wasn't aware of all the facts, and I thought that maybe sometime I could condense it all down and put it into a song.'"

Carter's story was one of the ideas Dylan brought to Jacques Levy when they began to collaborate on the material that would become the songs included on *Desire*. Following the style Dylan set forth in "Lily, Rosemary and the Jack of Hearts," in which he told a story in a form that resembled a screenplay as much as it did an old western yarn, the two came up with "Hurricane."

In its final form, "Hurricane" does come off with a harsh, in-your-face narrative of Rubin Carter's saga, softened only by the music's undercurrent of sadness. That bluntness is at the fore in the song's first line ("Pistol shots ring out in the barroom night") and remains throughout the narrative as we are taken deep into the underbelly of Paterson's criminal milieu, police modus operandi, Jersey's judicial and penal systems, and entrenched racial hostility. We are reminded that profiling is nothing new: "In Paterson that's just the way things go./If you're black you might as well not show up on the street/'Less you wanna draw the heat." Through all the flash-cuts, Dylan and Levy present a lurid, tactile spectacle taking us from the night of the killing, through the state's efforts to build a case against Rubin Carter and John Artis, to the "pig-circus" sham of a trial, as Dylan and Levy describe it, and the crushing finality of years behind bars. The flashing red lights of the police car blind, the smell of the hospital nauseates, the sound of the prison door cell slamming shut deafens, the feel of the cold bars deaden. And if Carter was not exactly a saint himself, Dylan makes no bones about whom he regards as the real bad guys: "Now all the criminals in their coats and their ties/Are free to drink martinis and watch the sun rise."

Dylan recorded a demo of the song on July 30, 1975, with Emmylou Harris during the chaotic *Desire* recording sessions, and debuted a blistering version with a small ensemble on the September TV tribute to John Hammond later that year. When Columbia Records' lawyers decided that the song was potentially libelous after noticing that the lyrics were factually flawed (placing individuals in the wrong places, for one thing), Dylan was forced to rerecord the track in late October for official release. Patty Valentine did, in fact, unsuccessfully sue Dylan and Levy for libel.

The Columbia release of this single, its heavy radio airplay, and Dylan's featuring of the song as a centerpiece of shows on the first

H

leg of the Rolling Thunder Revue in the fall of 1975 all contributed to enormous publicity for the Carter case. It all culminated on December 8, 1975, at the "Night of the Hurricane" benefit held at New York's Madison Square Garden. At one point during the show, Carter's voice was relayed from jail via telephone. A second "Night of the Hurricane," held on January 25, 1976, in the Houston Astrodome, was a financial and public relations debacle that served neither Dylan nor Carter particularly well.

On March 17, 1976, Rubin Carter and John Artis were released on bail pending a retrial after the New Jersey Supreme Court unanimously overturned their convictions, ruling that the prosecution withheld evidence favorable to the defense. Their second trial commenced in December 1976, but unlike what occurred in the first trial, the prosecution was permitted to argue that the murders were motivated by racial revenge. The two men were reconvicted and sent back to prison, with the same life sentences imposed.

The next five years were particularly rough on John Artis. He developed Berger's disease, contracted in jail, a condition that cuts off circulation to the extremities—in particular, to fingers and toes—which in his case necessitated multiple amputations. After fifteen years in prison he was finally paroled on December 22, 1981. To ease the pain of the disease Artis turned to cocaine, and ran into trouble again. He was arrested and sentenced to six years in jail in 1987, a decision influenced by his previous conviction for murder.

Carter, meanwhile, continued his legal battle. An appeal for a third trial was denied in August 1982 by New Jersey's Supreme Court in a 4-to-3 decision. Still persevering, he waited more than three years for another breakthrough: in 1985, the case was removed from the jurisdiction of the State of New Jersey and

given federal review. Judge H. Lee Sarokin at the federal district court in Newark, New Jersey, overturned the convictions of the second trial after finding that the prosecution committed "grave constitutional violations," determining that the convictions had been based upon "racism rather than reason, and concealment rather than disclosure." Finally, Sarokin advised the state against seeking a third trial "in the interests of justice and compassion."

Carter was finally retried, found not guilty, and his order of dismissal was signed on February 26, 1988. Hurricane was free at last.

As a double-sided single, "Hurricane" rose to No. 33 on the *Billboard* chart. "Hurricane" is also a feature of Dylan's film *Renaldo & Clara* in a prolonged but revealing scene filmed in the shadow of the Apollo Theater on 125th Street in Harlem as black passersby are asked about his case, with very few even seeming aware of who Carter was. This scene, by the way, would seem directly inspired by Melvin Van Peebles's 1971 no-budget blaxploitation tour-de-force, *Sweet Sweetback's Badass Song*. For the more literal-minded there is *The Hurricane*, an instructive 1999 film, based on the James Hirsch book, starring Denzel Washington (for which the latter received an Academy Award Best Actor nomination) in the title role. It must finally be mentioned that there are those who are still very much convinced of Carter's guilt, claiming the crime was one of passion committed in response to the killing of a young black man at the hands of whites just before the slayings in the Lafayette Bar and Grill.

Dylan's only performances of "Hurricane," during the first phase of the Rolling Thunder Revue in the fall of 1975 and early winter of 1976, were thoroughly invigorating affairs as Dylan and company pulled out all the stops on the centerpiece of those marathon concert happenings.

I

[S] "I Ain't Got No Home" (Woody Guthrie)

aka "Can't Feel at Home," "I Ain't Got No Home in This World Anymore," "I Can't Feel at Home," "This World Is Not My Home"
Various Artists (performed by Bob Dylan), *A Tribute to Woody Guthrie, Part One*/'68 (1972)
Woody Guthrie, *Woody Guthrie—Hard Travelin': The Asch Recordings, Volume 3* (1999)
Cisco Houston, *Folkways Years 1944–61* (1994)
Various Artists (performed by Bruce Springsteen), *A Vision Shared—A Tribute to Woody Guthrie and Leadbelly* (1988)
Jack Elliott, *Hard Travelin'* (1989)
Lone Justice, *BBC Live* (1994)
Johnny Hoy, *You Gonna Lose Your Head* (1996)

A terribly lonely self-portrait of a man turned out in the cruel world of the 1930s Depression-era Dust Bowl, Woody Guthrie's "I Ain't Got No Home" is usually approached as a spare country moan. Dylan performed the song early in his career as a typical forlorn lament, but he and the Hawks (as the Band were calling themselves at the time) gave it an up-tempo spin in their rendering at the famous Guthrie tribute show in 1968. Some say Dylan's choice of the song that night was made to emphasize the outsider ethos that had fueled his rock-star stature.

No matter how you slice it, "I Ain't Got No Home" is the rawest and most biting of Guthrie's songs. He cuts right to the chase in pointing to those he feels are responsible for the loss of his children, his wife's death, and the abject misery of his existence: bankers, police, and the "gambling man." But, at least in the earliest incarnations of the song, he realizes that his hardship is hardly unique, but happening to "a hundred thousand others and a hundred thousand more"—all victimized by the more fortunate elite. What a courageous and articulate conclusion to not only one of Guthrie's better songs, but one of the twentieth century's great folk songs.

Guthrie meant the song as a message, too—an angry response to the bouncy, jolly Baptist hymn "This World Is Not My Home" made popular by the Carter Family. Woody recorded at least four different versions of "I Ain't Got No Home" (all with his trademark ironic glee), and on one of the manuscript copies in the Asch/Folkways Collection, he wrote: "This old song to start out with was a religious piece. . . . But I seen there was another side to the picture. Reason why you can't feel at home in this world any more is mostly because you ain't got no home to feel at."

Dylan performed this song just once: with the Hawks at the January 20, 1968, Woody Guthrie Memorial Concert at New York City's Carnegie Hall.

[S] "I Am a Lonesome Hobo" (Bob Dylan)

Bob Dylan, *John Wesley Harding* (1967)
Triffids, *Treeless Pain* (1983); *Stockholm Live* (1990)
Steve Gibbons, *The Dylan Project* (1998)
Julie Driscoll, *Jools & Brian* (2001)

Dylan's simple morality tale about a man who lost his wealth when he lost his faith in his fellow man has never been performed live by its author. On its official *John Wesley Harding* release, "I Am a Lonesome Hobo" features some of Dylan's most controlled singing and a fine mouth-harp solo. Dylan gives us another view of alienation here, especially with the final, heavily moralizing lines that impart what every mother has been telling her child since pre-K: suppress jealousy, be your own person, be circumspect with your judgments to yourself—and *never* beg. Some have linked the character of the lonesome hobo with the drifter from "Drifter's Escape," suggesting that it is as if the antihero from that Kafkaesque song from *John Wesley Harding* is now hightailing it down the road (banished from society for having turned on his brother) and considering his deeds. He's spent time in the penitentiary for just about any crime you can name and has a gold tooth, as if to prove his nefarious credentials. But as he trundles down the road feeling bad, we know there is no redemption for this rounder.

I

[S] **"I Am the Man, Thomas"** (Ralph Stanley/Larry Sparks)

See also *Clinch Mountain Country*
Bill Grant, *Rollin'* (1992)
Dirk Powell, *If I Go Ten Thousand Miles* (1996)
The Stanley Gospel Tradition, *Songs About Our Savior* (1998)

A bluegrass take on the biblical "Doubting Thomas" story, "I Am the Man, Thomas" was an interesting choice for a concert opener for Dylan as the end of millennium drew nigh—and performed as a three-part harmony no less. Then again, it wasn't as if he hadn't copped to a messianic complex in the past. Along with Dallas Holms's "Rise Again," "I Am the Man, Thomas" is one of at least two songs of a religious nature that Dylan performed written in the first person of Jesus Christ.

The coauthor of "I Am the Man, Thomas" is Larry Sparks (born September 15, 1947, Lebanon, Ohio), a heralded bluegrass crooner. Sparks learned to play guitar as a child and was performing bluegrass, country, and rock as a teen. His big break came as the result of bad news when he was hired by Ralph Stanley to fill the musical shoes of Carter Stanley in the Stanley Brothers' outfit, the Clinch Mountain Boys, after Carter's death in 1966. That commenced a three-year recording and performing gig with the Clinch Mountain Boys that produced five albums. Sparks formed the Lonesome Ramblers in 1969, a group that led the vanguard of contemporary bluegrass (or "newgrass," as its adherents called it) well into the mid-1980s. Though he eventually moved to Richmond, Indiana, he maintained a presence on the bluegrass circuit as a staunch Stanley Brothers preservationist.

[S] **"I and I"** (Bob Dylan)

aka "I & I"
Bob Dylan, *Infidels* (1983); *Real Live* (1984)
The Zimmermen, *The Dungeon Tapes* (1996)
Michel Montecrossa, *Born in Time* (2000)
Various Artists (performed by Steven Keene), *May Your Song Always Be Sung: The Songs of Bob Dylan, Volume 3* (2003)

Mixing elements of kabbalah, Rastafarianism, the Old and New Testaments, and aesthetic self-appraisal, "I and I" is an extraordinarily revealing glimpse into Dylan's creative and personal life. The song takes place in the middle of a restless night as the narrator, unable to sleep beside a new lover ("a strange woman," as he sings it), goes out for a walk in search of himself and his muse.

Tim Riley, in his book *Hard Rain: A Dylan Commentary* (New York: Alfred A. Knopf, 1992), calls "I and I" the "standout" track on *Infidels*. It "updates the Dylan mythos," he says. Riley continues:

> Even though it substitutes self-pity for the other songs' [on *Infidels*] pessimism, you can't ignore it as a Dylan spyglass: "Someone else is speakin' with my mouth, but I'm listening only to my heart/I've made shoes for everyone, even you, while I still go barefoot."
>
> Dylan's relationship with himself has always been at the heart of his best work—

Dylan wearing a Jewish prayer shawl, yarmulke, and tefillin at his son's bar mitzvah ceremony at the Western Wall, Jerusalem, September 20, 1983.

(AP/Wide World Photos/Zavi Cohen)

the way the man who was born Robert Zimmerman communes with the songs, odyssey, and mystique of Bob Dylan. But "I and I" is perhaps the only song to take this subject on as an artistic issue. That he comes up a shade self-pitying (he still goes barefoot) is reconciled only by the fact that he's made the subject songworthy this late in his career. In other words, without giving up very much of his true self, he conveys the distance he feels between his inner identity and the public face he wears.

Dylan was deep into a personal reexploration of his Jewish roots when *Infidels* was released in 1983. The album was full of Old Testament references and included a sleeve photograph of Dylan touching the soil on the Mount of Olives, near Jerusalem's Old City. All of this was quite the surprise for fans who were still reeling from his late 1970s to very early '80s obsession with a particularly fervent brand of born-again Christianity. But, as he told *Washington Jewish Week* that year, the two foci of his recent obsessions were not mutually exclusive: "People who believe in the coming of the Messiah live their lives right now as if He was here. That's my idea of it anyway. . . . Roots, man—we're talking Jewish roots, you want to know more? Check on Elijah the prophet. He could make rain. Isaiah the prophet, even Jeremiah, see if their brethren didn't want to bust their brain for telling it right like it is, yeah—these are my roots, I suppose. Am I looking for them? . . . I ain't looking for them in synagogues with six-pointed Egyptian stars shining down from every window, I can tell you that much."

Other liturgical traces of the Old Testament laced through the song can be readily observed.

The tranquility of Psalms is specifically referenced in one line, and Ecclesiastes 9:11 ("I returned, and saw under the sun, that the race is not to the swift, nor the battle to the strong, neither yet bread to the wise, nor yet riches to men of understanding, nor yet favour to men of skill; but time and chance happeneth to them all") is rerendered by Dylan when he sings, "Took an untrodden path, where the swift don't win the race/It goes to the worthy, who can divide the word of truth."

Dylan has mentioned that the song was written on a Caribbean sojourn. That would at least explain both the subtle reggae beat and use of the Rastafarian term "I and I" as the song's title and lyric hook. Loosely interpreted, "I and I" is a commonly used Rasta expression meaning "the Lord and I"; it reminds the believer that he never walks alone, that the Lord is always with him.

No doubt Dylan picked up more than a tagline and a beat from Rastafarianism by way of reggae music, but it is not the only faith evident in "I and I." Rastafarianism draws heavily on the Old Testament, which could not have been lost on Dylan. However, at this juncture of his career, Dylan also seemed to be "returning" to Judaism and becoming involved with the Orthodox strain of the faith, the influence of which may or may not be seen in the chorus of "I and I." "I and I/One says to the other, no man sees my face and lives," runs half the chorus, rather transparently paraphrasing the Lord's admonition to Moses in Exodus 33:20, "Thou canst not see my face: for there shall no man see me, and live." In "I and I," then, the narrator knows that the Lord is with him—but he struggles with the knowledge that that side of himself can never be seen or perhaps truly understood. The Rasta expression contrasted with the Old Testament command provides Dylan with an interesting and succinct way to articulate the dichotomy.

Whether or not it was a renewed interest in Judaism that prompted Dylan to use the "no man sees my face and lives" line, much was made of his dabblings in Judaism (Orthodox and otherwise) around the time *Infidels* was released. Along with the photos that showed him visiting Israel, Dylan was reported to have been studying with the ultra-Orthodox Hasidic Jews of Brooklyn's Lubavitch community in Crown Heights, taking instruction from Talmudic scholars and listening to talks by Lubavitcher Rebbe Menachem Schneerson, whom many Lubavitchers regarded as the "mesach," or Messiah. For a period in the mid-1980s it was apparently not unusual to see Dylan walking along President Street to *shabbes* (Sabbath) services at Congregation B'nai Shlomo Zalman, known locally as Frankel's Shul, where he chanted prayers in Hebrew while wearing a yarmulke.

Fortunately, Dylan realized early on that "I and I" was a great song and has included it in concert since 1984. Its slinky reggae beat lends itself well to the stage, and it is full of ironic twists that make it a prime vehicle for some of Dylan's most impassioned late-career singing.

A final note: Dylan once claimed to Leonard Cohen that he wrote "I and I" in fifteen minutes.

[S] **"I Believe in You"** (Bob Dylan)

Bob Dylan, *Slow Train Coming* (1979); *Biograph/'79* (1985)
Phoebe Snow, *Rock Away* (1981)
Jacob's Trouble, *Knock, Breathe, Shine* (1990)
Various Artists (performed by Sinéad O'Connor), *A Very Special Christmas 2* (1992)
Judy Collins, *Judy Sings Dylan . . . Just Like a Woman* (1993)
Sinéad O'Connor, *Faces on Babylon* (four-song single) (1994)
Shade of Blue, *Shades of Blue* (1994)
The Five Blind Boys of Alabama, *Deep River* (1995)
B-Band, *Immortal Emotion* (1996)
Tom Jones, *From the Vaults* (1998)
Insol, *Insol* (1998)

Anne Murray, *What a Wonderful World: 26 Inspirational Classics* (1999)

Various Artists (performed by Dottie Peoples), *Gotta Serve Somebody: The Gospel Songs of Bob Dylan* (2003)

If anyone doubted that Dylan's heart was truly in his born-again material, one need only listen to this profound, spine-tingling confessional. Dylan's vocals may strain a bit on the official release, but his soul remains intact. A bold and unabashed ode to religious commitment, "I Believe in You" is one of Dylan's most intimate and powerful vocal performances. Despite the religious nature of the album on which the song is found, *Slow Train Coming*, Dylan almost sounds as if he could be singing to a woman or perhaps a child in his vulnerable lyrics. Whatever the case, his eloquent expression and representation of himself as a vigilant new believer alienated from old friends and battling with himself—no backslider he—remains a powerful one.

In his 1982 book *Voice Without Restraint: A Study of Bob Dylan's Lyrics and Their Background*, John Herdman discussed some of the gray areas lying dormant in "I Believe in You," writing that it "starts out from an emotion which he has always felt intensely—self-pity, in this case because his friends are deserting him, turning him away because of his beliefs (listen to the passionate dramatization of the first 'I' in the words 'And I, I walk out on my own . . .'). But the strength of the feeling rapidly transcends, and indeed consumes, the claims of the ego. The attitude of submission, the stripping away of pride, is something quite new for Dylan, and even without the moving intensity of his singing there is no mistaking the genuineness in the words."

Pronouns have always played a fluid role in Dylan's songwriting and the batches in *Slow Train Coming* and *Saved* are no different. Yet, for all the fuss and noise made over his conversion to born-again Christianity, it is interesting to note how infrequently the songs hatched from the experience directly address the divine. Certainly "Precious Angel," "Covenant Woman," and "Do Right to Me Baby" are sung to a woman, and "Slow Train," "When You Gonna Wake Up?" and "Gotta Serve Somebody" are offered as a challenge to a secular audience. Further, "Man Gave Names to All the Animals" and "When He Returns" come off as watered-down Genesis and Revelation. And where Dylan used to show no shyness about squarely pointing his pen at those he held in low esteem—be they the backstabbing former friend in "Positively 4th Street" or the military-industrial complex as represented in "Masters of War"—his denunciations on *Slow Train Coming* are couched at a third-person remove, as when he sings about the "masters of the bluff and masters of the proposition" in "Slow Train" or "the gangsters in power and lawbreakers making rules" in "When You Gonna Wake Up?" Only in "I Believe in You" and "What Can I Do for You?" does he figuratively get down on his hands and knees and strip himself spiritually bare before God. Still, despite the voice-cracking passion and sincerity with which he sings these songs, there is a shade of ambiguity, a sense that these words are meant for someone, not something. Certainly, Dylan's 1992 comment to *Los Angeles Times* critic Robert Hilburn that "I Believe in You" is "just about overcoming hardship" didn't exactly clear up any questions about to whom or what he was offering his soul.

Dylan first performed "I Believe in You" on his October 1979 *Saturday Night Live* appearance and went on to firmly slot it as the second song of each 1979–1980 gospel show. Thereafter it was revived with nearly annual and, at times, abundant regularity during the length of the Never Ending Tour.

[S] "I Can't Be Satisfied" (Muddy Waters)

aka "I Be's Troubled"
Muddy Waters, *Complete Recordings: 1941–1948* (2000)
Rolling Stones, *More Hot Rocks* (1972)
Bill Frisell, *Have a Little Faith* (1992)
John Hammond Jr., *You Can't Judge a Book by the Cover* (1993)
Hot Tuna, *In a Can* (1996)
Gwyn Ashton, *Wanted Man* (1997)

Before the Rolling Stones' "(I Can't Get No) Satisfaction" there was Muddy Waters's "I Can't Be Satisfied"—a history-making, man-on-the-prowl Delta-style single the blues master recorded many times over the course of his long career, which stretched from the Mississippi outback to the grand halls of Europe.

If the rock revolution can be said to have begun in any one place or time, April 1948 in Chicago may be on top of the list. It was on a Saturday morning that 45-rpm singles bearing the titles "I Can't Be Satisfied" and "I Feel Like Going Home," released on the small Aristocrat label, began emanating from wherever records were sold on the city's fabled South Side, be they five-and-dimes, beauty salons, barbershops, or even some bona fide record shops. In the custom of the day, many of these establishments were equipped with little record turntables attached to a speaker hung outside the front door. One could tell right away whether a record was going to catch on or not, judging by the number of people who walked in the door. And as the sonorous, commanding voice of Muddy Waters and the driving, urgent beat of his barrel-chested blues began knocking the lobes off passersby, the single began to fly off the racks.

Despite the amplification, the traditional-sounding tune struck a familiar chord with the neighborhood's displaced black population, most of whom, like Waters, hailed from the other end of Highway 61. And the risqué, subdued violence of the lyrics ("I know somebody/Sure been talking to you/I don't need no telling girl/I can watch the way you do") spoke to the passions of a neighborhood that was seeing its share of hard knocks.

By mid-afternoon copies of Aristocrat 1305 were already running scarce. Stores began limiting sales to one per customer in an attempt to prevent Pullman porters from buying bulk and reselling them at a markup on trains and stations points south.

In those days singles generally sold for seventy-nine cents apiece, but by nightfall, "I Can't Be Satisfied" was going for twice the price, and Muddy, then a truck driver delivering Venetian blinds, still didn't have a copy to call his own. He paid $1.10 for one the next morning, then stalked off in anger, yelling, "But I'm the one who made it!" when the shopkeeper refused to sell him another. Waters had to send his wife to buy him an additional copy, and it is said that it was a good thing the shop owner didn't recognize her.

"I Can't Be Satisfied" has long been the stuff of blues lore. The song had been in Muddy's back pocket since at least the time he first recorded a solo acoustic version for Alan Lomax and the Library of Congress in 1941 under the title "I Be's Troubled." And he harked back to his youth when recalling the origins of "I Can't Be Satisfied" during his Lomax session: "I made it up my own self. That's a song I made up. The reason I came to make that record up once, I was just walking along the road, I heard a church song, kind of mind of that. I just dashed off a little song from that. And I started playing it."

Virtually without melody, the electrified 1948 arrangement is carried by its stabbing rhythm and twangy guitar, which Waters makes sound like the Jew's harp he plucked as a kid sitting on his porch in Clarkdale, Mississippi. Alternating between his bottleneck slide and picked single-string approach, Waters engages in a sharp, aggressive musical repartee with Big Crawford slapping the bass fiddle as if his life was on the line. Perhaps Francis Davis captured the spirit of the song best in his book *The History of the Blues: The Roots, the Music, the People from Charley Patton to Robert Cray* (New York: Hyperion, 1995), writing, "What sells the song is Muddy's jolting bottleneck and slight vocal shake in the turnarounds, which make it seem as though first Muddy and then the song have been stung by a bee and swollen to twice their normal sizes. There's nothing else quite like it."

Like a guy doing it just for the fun of it at a rent party, Dylan showcased "I Can't Be Satisfied" as an effective, down-home set opener during a brief spell of the 1992 Never Ending Tour.

"I Can't Get You Off of My Mind" (Hank Williams)

See also Hank Williams
Various Artists (performed by Bob Dylan), *Timeless* (2001)
Hank Williams, *Complete Hank Williams* (1998)
The The, *Hanky Panky* (1995)
Claire Lynch, *Out in the Country* (2001)

Another response to a flighty, two-timing breaker of men's hearts, Dylan chose Hank Williams's "I Can't Get You Off of My Mind" (originally recorded by Hank in December 1948) for a well-received if uneven Williams tribute CD. Dylan's performance of this bouncy blues shuffle brims with vitality and is done up with an expressive snarl that more than hints at Williams's influence on his own songs, like "Don't Think Twice, It's All Right" and "It Ain't Me, Babe."

"(I'd Be) A Legend in My Time" (Don Gibson)

aka "Legend in My Time"
Don Gibson, *Legend in My Time* (1988)
Rick Nelson, *Sings for You* (1963)
Paul Anka, *Strictly Nashville* (1966)
Everly Brothers, *The Hit Sound of the Everly Brothers* (1967)
Bob Neuwirth, *Bob Neuwirth* (1974)
Ronnie Milsap, *Legend in My Time* (1975)

Often incorrectly described as an old country standard, "(I'd Be) A Legend in My Time" is actually from the pen and guitar strings of Don Gibson. It would seem by its title to be a case of ironic, tongue-in-cheek ego-mongering by the artist who chooses to perform it, and inspection of the lyrics reveals it to be just that.

Don Gibson, the song's author, had such an idea in mind when he wrote it in 1960, telling Dorothy Horstman in 1973 for her 1975 book *Sing Your Heart Out, Country Boy*, "This song was written on the road to Knoxville, Tennessee, in a car with Mel Foree. I was reading an article in a magazine I had picked up about an entertainer. He was talking about show business and his career and how he would like to be a legend in his time. I told Mel that that would be a good title for a song, so I started humming."

Ronnie Milsap had the greatest commercial success with "Legend in My Own Time," taking it to No. 1 on the country charts in 1974.

If the despair and loneliness in Don Gibson's compositions about romantic dissolution have broken the hearts of his many admirers listening to his sad songs, it also brought him wide acclaim. Gibson (born April 3, 1928, Shelby, North Carolina; died November 17, 2003, Nashville) grew up in a poor sharecropping family, dropping out of school in the second grade. "The only thing I was any good at was music," he said in a 1997 interview.

"Sweet Dreams," the first single Gibson waxed for MGM, hit the Top 10 in 1956, rose to

No. 2 when covered by Faron Young later in the year, and was eventually recorded by scores of others, most notably Patsy Cline in 1963.

In June 1957 he wrote two of country music's most famous songs, "I Can't Stop Loving You" and "Oh Lonesome Me." For those who remain unconvinced that hard times often inspire great works, at the time Gibson composed these tunes he was living alone in a trailer and a repo man had just fetched his vacuum cleaner and television set. "When I wrote those two songs, I couldn't have been any closer to the bottom," he recounted years later, as reported by Irwin Stambler and Grelun Landon in their *Encyclopedia of Folk, Country and Western Music* (New York: St. Martin's Press, 1969).

An impressed Chet Atkins brought Gibson to RCA in 1957 and signed on as his producer through 1964, during which time the two would help craft the slick sound synonymous with Nashville. "Oh Lonesome Me," Gibson's premier RCA single, was a huge hit when released in 1958. It spent eight weeks at the top of the country charts and crossed over into the pop Top 10. That success inspired Gibson and Atkins to develop a pop style incorporating flashes of rock 'n' roll. From 1958 to 1961, Gibson scored eleven self-pitying Top 10 singles mostly notable for their tear-jerking powers. Substance abuse issues kept Gibson out of commission for a period in the 1960s, but he returned with "Woman (Sensuous Woman)," a No. 1 hit in 1972. And though he did score a couple of times after that, a long-term return to the Hit Parade was not meant to be. He continued to perform (as a Grand Ole Opry regular) and record to nearly the day of his death.

Dylan performed "I'd Be a Legend" as a curio at a few 1989 concerts. The song has a line that could stand next to any other penned by Gibson: "If loneliness meant world acclaim/Everybody would know my name ..."

▣ "I'd Hate to Be You on That Dreadful Day" (Bob Dylan)
aka "Dreadful Day"
Various Artists (performed by Bob Dylan), *Broadside Reunion/'62* (1972)
Bettina Jonic, *The Bitter Mirror* (1975)

Dylan sang "I'd Hate to Be You on That Dreadful Day," positively reminiscent of "Positively 4th Street" but predating it by a few years, over a swinging boogie-rock piano accompaniment. According to the introduction to the songbook *Bob Dylan the Original* (New York: Warner Brothers, 1968), "Dylan's debt to Jimmy Yancey and the great boogie pianists of the '20s and '30s is acknowledged" in this song. Dylan first recorded "Dreadful Day" in the fall of 1962 at the offices of *Broadside* magazine in New York City. For contractual reasons, he recorded under the pseudonym Blind Boy Grunt, one of several such handles he used at the time. Dylan recut it in the late winter of 1963 for an extremely rare demo LP for Witmark.

Some see more depth than Jimmy Yancey in "Dreadful Day." As Daniel J. Evearitt, in commenting on the song, asked in his article "Bob Dylan: Still Blowin' in the Wind?" published in the December 3, 1976, issue of *Christianity Today*: "Is man ultimately responsible for sin? Is man really free? Yes, man is free to choose to obey or disobey divine directives, but he is responsible and will be judged."

And with lines like "You're gonna yell and scream/'Don't anybody care?'/You're gonna hear out a voice say,/'Shoulda listened when you heard the word down there.'/Hey, hey!/I'd sure hate to be you/On that dreadful day," the day of Judgment looms much as it did nearly two decades later in songs like "When He Returns" from Dylan's short-lived but intense gospel period.

Cover of the album *Broadside Reunion.*
(Blank Archives/Getty Images)

[S] **"I'd Have You Anytime"** (Bob Dylan/George Harrison)
George Harrison, *All Things Must Pass* (1970)

Dylan and Harrison penned (and very roughly recorded) "I'd Have You Anytime" in November 1968 (some insist May 1970) at Dylan's Woodstock, New York, idyll, and Harrison saw fit to include a rerecorded version of this harmonically rich love song on his first solo album (still one of his best), the generous three-disc offering *All Things Must Pass*, a couple of years later. "Nowhere to Go" (aka "Everytime Somebody Comes to Town"), a Harrison-penned song from the session, also survives. The May '70 attribution does make sense in a couple of regards. Harrison mentioned in his autobiography *I, Me, Mine* (New York: Simon and Schuster, 1980) that his visit dovetailed with Dylan's completion of *Nashville Skyline* in the spring of that year. In addition, George participated in the May 1, 1970, New York City Dylan recording sessions (the first for *New Morning*), which degenerated into a flat jam session featuring such choice tunes as Dylan's "Just Like Tom Thumb's Blues," "Song to Woody," "One Too Many Mornings," "Gates of Eden," and "Don't Think Twice, It's All Right," Lennon-McCartney's "Yesterday," and some oddball covers like "Fishin' Blues," "Ghost Riders in the Sky," and "Da Doo Run Run." Finally, Elliott Landy's photographs of the two taken in Woodstock do little to solve the debate about when the song was written and recorded.

I

▣ "Idiot Wind" (Bob Dylan)

Bob Dylan, *Blood on the Tracks* (1975); *Hard Rain* (1976);
  Masterpieces (1978); *The Bootleg Series, Volumes 1–3:*
  Rare and Unreleased, 1961–1991/'74 (1991)
Gerard Quintana and Jordi Batiste, *Els Miralls de Dylan* (1999)
Lemmings Travel to the Sea, *Lemmings Travel to the Sea* (2001)
Mary Lee's Corvette, *Blood on the Tracks* (2002)

Revealing Dylan at his greatest and angriest, "Idiot Wind" presents a breaking heart laid bare. Chiseling his language like a sculptor obsessing on an unruly chunk of marble, Dylan portrays a relationship and a nation decaying before his very eyes in a way that plays out like a shimmering piece of impressionist celluloid flickering on the screen of the Theater of the Divine Comedy.

This is an easy song to lose oneself in. Steeped in symbolism and dramatic, smoky imagery, "Idiot Wind" is powered with one of Dylan's most fervent vocal performances, creating a disquieting atmosphere that brings his vision of societal dislocation and personal acrimony all back home. Is the idiot wind the fetid air blowing from the lips of politicians as the republic crumbles, and/or is it carried in the storm between the narrator and his lover as their union dissolves?

Harrowing and scathing, "Idiot Wind" is part of the cycle of songs, including "Ballad of a Thin Man," "Positively 4th Street," and "Like a Rolling Stone," that unmercifully skewers its object with a vengeful vehemence that leaves little room for reconciliation. He lashes out in a multitude of directions, firing salvo after salvo in attacking a woman—here, a thinly disguised Sara Dylan. Okay, he makes an effort to create a fiction in the song's opening lines as he justifies his wealth, notoriety, and fear of rumor mongers ("Someone's got it in for me, they're planting stories in the press/ . . . They say I shot a man named Gray and took his wife to Italy,/She inherited a million bucks and when she died it came to me./I can't help it if I'm lucky"). But his fame is an albatross, he complains: people, full of distorted facts about him, "can't remember how to act" in his presence. Even the woman to whom he sings has seemingly lost her ability or even interest in getting close to him, prompting this rather direct and withering kiss-off: "You're an idiot, babe./It's a wonder that you still know how to breathe." Over the course of the next six, unmercifully bitter verses that flow like long banners whipping in the song's stupid breeze, Dylan widens his net to include the whole of human existence while never forgetting the person who has plunged his head, heart, and soul into such a miserable space of self-loathing and disgust as he tops off this black state of the disunion with one last, personal invective: "We're idiots, babe./It's a wonder we can even feed ourselves."

As might be expected of a song with such deep emotion, "Idiot Wind" underwent many significant changes in lyrics and mood as it evolved from the original September 1974 New York recordings (one of which features an acoustic guitar with a bass accompaniment and a closing harmonica solo; another is propelled by an ominous organ line that is distinctly more foreboding than angry) and through the ranting, recrimination-stoked December 1974 Minneapolis cut used on the album into the version performed during the second half of the Rolling Thunder Revue in 1976. This last version took the vengeance, hostility, and disgusted bitterness expressed on *Blood on the Tracks* to over-the-top extremes. The acoustic New York version was eventually released on *The Bootleg Series, Volumes 1–3*, and its quiet, tender reading makes the inherent disquiet of the song all the more disturbing, with Dylan's wounded delivery adding new levels of genuine sadness.

At the time he was writing for *Blood on the Tracks*, Dylan was also taking art classes and studying painting, trying to incorporate some of what he learned into his songs. The seemingly timeless flashes of imagery in "Tangled Up in Blue" and "Idiot Wind" reflect this. Concurrently, he used his artistic pursuits to distance himself from the song and the album.

"Idiot Wind" might be personal or not, but with it Dylan also addresses the dysfunctional soul of America in a peak moment of the song, in the penultimate chorus when he sings of the idiot wind blowing from the Grand Coulee Dam (celebrated in song by Woody Guthrie) to the Capitol. Dylan sings this big song with Old Testament fury, raging like Allen Ginsberg reading "Howl" on a good night. Robert Shelton notes this in his analysis of "Idiot Wind" in his 1986 Dylan biography *No Direction Home*, writing, "It has the sting of 'Rolling Stone' . . . It could be a ranting truth attack, an expression of the narrator's personal disorder, ruefulness, and suspicion in an equally disturbed society in which people's spoken words are in apposition to their real emotions. This is also catharsis, a venting of personal anguish as well as a portrayal of a milieu where gossiping and backstabbing have replaced caring and believing. The ultimate horror is that the wheels have stopped; the air is fetid, paralyzing the body, mind, and spirit. A man, or a couple, undergo harassment and collapse while Nixon and his family are under siege, in the denouement of the Watergate scandal."

For literary roots in "Idiot Wind," John Bauldie, in his liner notes to *The Bootleg Series, Volumes 1–3*, pointed to Shakespeare's *Macbeth*, whose desperate meditation on the meaninglessness of life is rendered in that play as "a tale/Told by an idiot, full of sound and fury/Signifying nothing" (act 5, scene 5).

Another source of the title phrase may have been Norman Raeben, with whom Dylan studied art in 1974. In a conversation with Dylan scholar Bert Cartwright, as reported in the latter's article "Dylan's Mystery Man Called Norman" in *The Telegraph #23* (spring 1986), Victoria Raeben, Norman Raeben's widow, confirmed that "idiot" was one of her husband's favorite words, and that according to his view, there is an idiot wind blowing and blinding all human existence.

A diatribe filled with invective and venom, "Idiot Wind" was performed regularly in the spring of 1976 during the second phase of the Rolling Thunder tour in a rendition so angry that it makes "Positively 4th Street" seem like a Hallmark greeting card. An example can be heard on the *Hard Rain* album and in the television special of the same title, drawn from Dylan's May 23, 1976, concert in Fort Collins, Colorado. Mocking, haughty, cathartic, chiding, hurt, and hurtful, these first performances of "Idiot Wind" create an anthem to pain and closed a turbulent phase in his life and career. Dylan returned to the song with effervescent zeal for about forty 1992 shows in versions that featured some raging harmonica work.

"I Don't Believe You (She Acts Like We Never Have Met)" (Bob Dylan)

Bob Dylan, *Another Side of Bob Dylan* (1964); *Biograph/'66* (1985); *The Bootleg Series, Volume 4: Bob Dylan Live 1966—The "Royal Albert Hall" Concert* (1998); *Live 1961–2000—Thirty-nine Years of Great Concert Performances/'66* (2001); *The Bootleg Series, Volume 6: Live 1964—Concert at Philharmonic Hall* (2004)

The Band (performed with Bob Dylan), *The Last Waltz* (1978)

Ian & Sylvia, *Lovin' Sounds* (1965)

Bows & Arrows, single (1965)

Glen Campbell, *Hey Little One* (1968)

Waylon Jennings, *Don't Think Twice* (1969)

Al Stewart, *Orange* (1972)
Vole, *A Tribute to Bob Dylan* (1992)
Steve Howe, *Portraits of Bob Dylan* (1999)
Robyn Hitchcock, *Robyn Sings* (2002)

Chiding a former lover who thinks she is doing a pretty good job of snubbing him, Dylan metes out his revenge in this song, yet another entry on his long list of kiss-off compositions.

At his October 31, 1964, concert in New York's Philharmonic Hall, Dylan innocuously introduced "I Don't Believe You" as a song "about all the people that say they've never seen you . . . I'm sure everybody has met somebody that swears they've never seen them." He blunts any edge those words might have carried by then greeting an audience member and saying, "See? I never saw him," and going on to apparently forget (in grand, Chaplinesque fashion) how the song begins.

Two years later, during his angrier appearances in 1966, Dylan was wont to introduce the song with lines like "This song used to go like that . . . now it sounds like this."

Stereotypically, a man walks away from a romantic encounter more easily than does a woman—to use the song title, she is the one saying, "I don't believe you," he "acts like we never have met." Dylan, however, turns it around and describes the intoxication of a night of passion (the way he sings of her watery and wet mouth is easily one of Dylan's most sensuous moments as a writer and performer) followed by the searing heartache of emotional dislocation when his female companion walks away. Singing of love's illusions and how it contrasts and clashes with reality, the song has a deceptively jaunty melody that counters the sardonic words.

"I Don't Believe You" went through a variety of concert arrangements, ranging from the bitter, "later for you" put-downs of the mid-1960s

to the coy renditions of the Rolling Thunder Revue a decade later to an appealing, Byrds-like version in the late 1990s. A good taste of Dylan performing the song at a peak can be found in the film *Eat the Document*, shot in Great Britain during the cataclysmic 1966 tour. "I Don't Believe You" is also included on the album (but not the film from) *The Last Waltz*, the Band's 1976 farewell concert. Thereafter, it received spot duty during the 1978 big-band tour, and was a 1981 one-off. On the Never Ending Tour, it made for irregular, semiacoustic set fodder. By 2003 Dylan had retooled the song into a riff-heavy electric polka.

A final note: when first released on *Another Side of Bob Dylan*, "I Don't Believe You" was listed on the jacket and on the label without its parenthetical subtitle. The release of the great 1966 live version on *Biograph* included the subtitle, as do the Dylan books *Lyrics, 1962–1985*, 2nd ed. (New York: Alfred A. Knopf, 1985) and *Writings and Drawings* (New York: Alfred A. Knopf, 1973).

"I Don't Want to Do It" (Bob Dylan)
George Harrison/Dave Edmunds, single (1985)
Various Artists (performed by George Harrison), *Porky's Revenge! Original Motion Picture Soundtrack* (1985)

Dylan may have written this yearning-for-lost-youth-and-love rarity as early as 1968 or 1969 and shown it to George Harrison during the session that produced "I'd Have You Anytime." There are several Harrison renditions in circulation—all handled by George with a distinct Liverpudlian air—dating as far back as 1970. But the one he recorded in 1985 some fifteen years after first encountering it was used in *Porky's Revenge!*, the final installment in the raunchy, sophomoric movie series. A 1976 Ringo Starr version of the song is also rumored to have been recorded. Dylan never committed the song to tape.

[S] "I Dreamed I Saw St. Augustine" (Bob Dylan)

Bob Dylan, *John Wesley Harding* (1967)
Joan Baez, *Any Day Now* (1968); *Vanguard Sessions: Baez Sings Dylan* (1998)
Incredible Broadside Brass Bed Band, *The Great Grizzly Bear Hunt* (1971)
Julie Felix, *Lightning* (1974)

Drawing on labor history and Catholic history, Dylan's allegorical song about messianic prophecy may be a tongue-in-cheek commentary on his role in contemporary society. But then again, he just may be taking his dreams way too seriously.

Dylan's first two lines in "St. Augustine" ("I dreamed I saw St. Augustine alive as you or me") paraphrase "Joe Hill," the Earl Robinson–Alfred Hayes union hymn to the singing Wobbly organizer/martyr. Here Dylan's holy stand-in can be seen as gently deriding (or exalting) both. The subtext is that ideologies are stale anachronisms as the singer thirsts for salvation and for answers, not mere dogma. In so saying, Dylan sounds isolated, bereft of a comforting faith. But if Augustine could be martyred and die a bishop and a revered religious icon, then Dylan can too. For the Gnosticly inclined, Augustine's visionary memoirs of his early profligate life, ensuing rebirth, and quest for grace, *Confessions* and *City of God*, are a must.

Literary types have had a field day with "I Dreamed I Saw St. Augustine." Perhaps Dylan glimpsed himself being transformed into a kind of pop saint and wrote this song in response to that distasteful predicament, realizing that without full understanding of life, the self-sacrifice involved with the attainment of true sainthood is futile. In this examination of sinner-turned-saint, Dylan's interest in the mass psychology of martyrdom (those who become martyrs and those who worship them) couldn't be more plain. Yet, in true Dylanesque fashion, he waxes mysterious in specific regard to his reference to "the glass" mentioned in the lyrics. Window, mirror, or even a barrier, it appears to aid in Dylan's idea of spiritual transformation, be the objects leftist hoboes or Catholic deities.

A 1754 engraving by Pierre-Jean Mariette after a painting by Jean-Baptiste Corneille depicting St. Augustine of Hippo.
(Hulton Archive/Getty Images)

The song's title subject, St. Augustine, is considered one of the Roman Catholic Church's early fathers. Born in A.D. 354 in Carthage, he spent his early years as a carouser, even fathering an illegitimate son. After hearing St. Ambrose, bishop of Milan, however, Augustine decided to convert to Christianity and was baptized on Easter in 387. From that point he used his considerable intelligence to explore his own faith and the nature of Christianity—to enormously influential effect, perhaps second only to that of St. Paul.

On the other side of the coin, the song's opening couplet is a direct paraphrase of "Joe Hill," the personification in body and in song of American radical politics. Born Joel Hägglund (later to be known as Joe Hillström) on October 7, 1879, in Gävle, Sweden, Joe Hill immigrated to the United States, played piano in a saloon on New York's Bowery, was a manual laborer on the West Coast, and in 1910 joined the Industrial Workers of the World—the IWW, most commonly known as the Wobblies. Over the next few years he campaigned for working-class causes, becoming a popular songwriter with a gift for capturing the meaning of these causes in song. His most famous titles include "The Preacher and the Slave," "Casey Jones," "The Union Scab," "Scissor Bill," "Mr. Block," and "The Tramp."

Hill's songs gained currency among workers, as they were sung at rallies and on picket lines and were eventually published by the International Workers of the World in 1913 in *The Little Red Song Book*. Though Hill's colloquial, class-conscious compositions are uncomplicated and metrically simple (he often merely refitted popular songs and hymns with new lyrics), he was one of the premier leaders of the early, pre–Woody Guthrie, twentieth-century political folksong movement in America.

In 1914, during bitter struggles over labor organizing and free speech in Utah, Hill was arrested and convicted for allegedly murdering a prominent Salt Lake City man—a charge that, given the political climate of the era, especially with regard to unions, appears to have been a frame-up. Despite appeals from President Woodrow Wilson and the Swedish government, he was executed by a firing squad in Salt Lake City on November 19, 1915. His body was taken to Chicago, where more than 30,000 people attended his funeral procession and eulogies were read in nine languages. The following May Day his ashes were scattered in every state (except Utah) and numerous countries abroad. His description of his approach to songwriting, as recorded in *The Little Red Song Book*, could just as well be chiseled on his tombstone: "If a person can put a few cold, commonsense facts into a song and dress them up in a cloak of humor to take the dryness out of them, he will succeed in reaching a great number of workers who are too unintelligent or too indifferent to read a pamphlet or an editorial on economic science."

Dylan's performances of "I Dreamed I Saw St. Augustine" are pretty uncommon. After recording it for *John Wesley Harding* and performing the song at the famous 1969 Isle of Wight show with the Band, Dylan joined Joan Baez for memorable duet renditions during both phases of the Rolling Thunder Revue in 1975 and '76. Dylan returned to the song with Tom Petty and crew in 1986 and 1987 and included it in shows in the early years of the Never Ending Tour through 1992 as a special rarity.

"If Dogs Run Free" (Bob Dylan)
Bob Dylan, *New Morning* (1970)
Al Kooper (with Bob Dylan), *Al's Big Deal (Unclaimed Freight)* (1975)

A bluesy scat song, this stylistic rarity recorded with Maeretha Stewart for *New Morning* conjures visions of the duo performing in a smoky cocktail lounge as part of Tony Clifton's opening act (Clifton was an alter ego of comedian Andy Kaufman). There's a touch of parodied detachment in the delivery, echoing a poet reading his latest ditty in a beat coffeehouse.

When Al Kooper covered "If Dogs Run Free" for his *Big Deal* LP in 1975, Dylan was there in the studio playing backup guitar on the track. You can look it up.

Singing like a combination of Billie Holiday and Louis Armstrong, and with his band sounding like the classic John Coltrane quartet, Dylan introduced "If Dogs Run Free" in concert in the fall of 2000 and kept it as a fairly solid inclusion in his sets through 2001.

"If I Don't Be There by Morning" (Bob Dylan/Helena Springs)
Eric Clapton, *Backless* (1978); *Just One Night* (1980); *Time-pieces Volume II: Live in the Seventies* (1983); *Crossroads* (1988)
The Hoodoo Kings, *The Hoodoo Kings* (2001)

Eric Clapton has recorded numerous Bob Dylan songs over the years, "If I Don't Be There by Morning" (an on-the-lam lyric involving a man returning—or not—to his lover) being one of the more obscure. His source for this song was a demo tape made by Dylan and Helena Springs in 1978 in and around the spring recording of *Street Legal* and the globe-trotting big-band jaunt that lasted throughout the year.

Springs, a Dylan backup singer at the time, was quoted in *The Telegraph #34* (winter 1989) as saying that Dylan had offered to work on some songs with her during a mid-March stop in Brisbane, Australia, on the 1978 tour, dating the start of the short but productive collaboration to early March.

Considering that she composed with Dylan many more songs (most of which remain unreleased) than any mortal, living or dead, precious little is known about Helena Springs. Her date and place of birth, her upbringing, and how she first came to be included in Dylan's entourage remain sketchy. This is not aided by her apparent lack of involvement in the music business as

such. Other than her work with Dylan, in whose group and on whose albums (*Street Legal, At Budokan, Slow Train Coming*) she sang from 1978 through the end of the '79 gospel tour, her activities seem pretty limited to work as backup singer on albums by artists of lesser profile: Ménage à Trois (*Ménage à Trois*, 1980), Matt Bianco (*Matt Bianco*, 1986), Tommy Shaw (*Ambition*, 1987), Spandau Ballet (*Through the Barricades*, 1989), Bobby Lyle (*Ivory Dreams*, 1989), and those masters of modern British irony, the Pet Shop Boys (*It's a Sin*, 1987; *I Wouldn't Normally Do This Kind of Thing*, 1994; *Alternative*, 1995; *Actually*, 2001; *Please*, 2001).

Of the songs Springs composed with Dylan, only a few have seen some kind of official release ("If I Don't Be There by Morning," "Stepchild," "The Wandering Kind") or life as Dylan performance rarities ("Coming from the Heart," "I Must Love You Too Much"); still others may or may not have been demoed ("Baby Give It Up," "Brown Skinned Girl," "Her Memory," "More Than Flesh and Blood," "Responsibility," "Someone Else's Arms," "Stop Now," "Take It or Leave It," "Tell Me the Truth One Time," "What's the Matter?," "Without You," "Your Rocking Chair").

"(If I Had to Do It All over Again, I'd Do It) All over You" (Bob Dylan)
aka "All Over You," "If I Could Do It All Over, I'd Do It All Over You," "If I Had to Do It Again (All Over You)," "If I Had to Do It All Over Again"
Dave Van Ronk, *In the Tradition* (1963)
The McCoys, *Human Ball* (1969)
Stefan Grossman, *Hot Dogs* (1972)
Paul Revere and the Raiders, single (1973); *The Legend of Paul Revere* (1990)
Rick Derringer and the McCoys, *Outside Stuff* (1974)
Various Artists (performed by Paul Revere and the Raiders), *I Shall Be Unreleased: The Songs of Bob Dylan* (1991)

Dylan appears to be paying a tribute to the spicy hokum of Tampa Red and Jazz Gillum with "All Over You," a song of obscure and humorous origin. He may have picked up on the title phrase in Ian Fleming's James Bond thriller *Goldfinger*, which contains the following passage: "Miss [Pussy] Galore was determined to have the last word. She said sweetly, 'Know what, Jacko? I could go for a he-man like you. Matter of fact, I wrote a song about you the other day. Care to hear its title? It's called 'If I Had to Do It All Over Again, I'd Do It All Over You.'" Coincidence? You be the judge.

In his book *Bob Dylan: His Unreleased Recordings* (New York: Schirmer Books, 1980), Paul Cable, an early Dylan bootleg discographer, described "All Over You" as "the nearest thing to a rugby song that has yet come out of America."

Dylan's interest in the song appears to have been fleeting, since he performed it only briefly and just rarely after its composition in early 1963.

[S] "If Not for You" (Bob Dylan)

Bob Dylan, *New Morning* (1970); *Bob Dylan's Greatest Hits, Volume II*/'70 (1971); *Masterpieces* (1978); *Biograph*/'70 (1985); *The Bootleg Series, Volumes 1–3: Rare and Unreleased, 1961–1991*/'70 (1991)
George Harrison, *All Things Must Pass* (1970)
Olivia Newton-John, *Olivia Newton-John* (1971); *Let Me Be There* (1973); *First Impressions* (1974); *Crystal Lady* (1974); *48 Original Tracks* (1994)
Jay Fallen, *Heart of the Country* (1971)
John Schroder, *Dylan Vibrations* (1971)
Anita Kerr Singers, *Daytime, Nighttime* (1972); *Favorites* (1994)
Suzanne, *Sunshine Through a Prism: The Best of Suzanne* (1972)
Glen Campbell, *I Knew Jesus (Before He Was a Star)* (1973)
Richie Havens, *The End of the Beginning* (1976); *Sings Beatles and Dylan* (1990)
Janglers, *Janglers Play Dylan* (1992)
The Paragons, *Sing the Beatles and Bob Dylan* (1998)
Susan McKeown, *Mighty Rain* (1998)
Jimmy LaFave, *Trail* (1999)
Barb Jungr, *Every Grain of Sand: Barb Jungr Sings Bob Dylan* (2002)
Robert Crenshaw, *Dog Dreams* (2003)

A most infectious Dylan love song—complete with a passionate harmonica solo and a loping, syrupy pedal-steel-guitar riff—"If Not for You" opens *New Morning* in welcoming fashion.

If Dylan, as he claimed, had Sara in mind in writing "If Not for You," the song is a nice note to her. In *Hard Rain: A Dylan Commentary* (New York: Alfred A. Knopf, 1992), Tim Riley describes "If Not for You" as a song that "seeks out a strain of sentimental affection that doesn't grate." With it, Riley says, Dylan "gives you the sense that to try to read this song ironically—as a lover trying to convince himself of his feelings, like the overbearing groom in 'Wedding Song'—is to miss out on the unforced sincerity he hits here. The track glides on feelings that aren't articulated—only a very complex and abiding love could inspire this kind of unaffected flattery, levied with such rich shades of experience. Dylan's funneled delivery enriches these deliberately uncomplicated lyrics ('anyway it just wouldn't ring true . . .')."

"If Not for You" is apparently a product of a studio date shared by Dylan and George Harrison. As *Rolling Stone* reported in June 1970, Dylan and Harrison had spent a day together in a New York studio laying tracks for possible inclusion on a future Dylan album.

While that official type of collaboration didn't occur until the Traveling Wilburys' projects of the late 1980s and early 1990s, "If Not for You" emerged from that May 1, 1970, session. Both Dylan and Harrison rerecorded the song separately for their own projects. Dylan rehearsed, but did not perform, the song for Harrison's 1971 Bangladesh benefit show as well as for his 1978 world tour. He likewise rehearsed it with the Grateful Dead in spring 1987 for their tour that summer, but it was again left on the scrap heap. The pattern repeated in 1989 during his Never Ending Tour band with rehearsals. Finally, in 1992, Dylan began performing the song, aided by Bucky Baxter's appropriate pedal-steel licks mimicking the original release, and it became a common repertoire item through the end of the decade and beyond.

[S] "I Forgot More Than You'll Ever Know"

(Cecil A. Null)
Bob Dylan, *Self Portrait* (1970)
Skeeter Davis, *Essential Skeeter Davis*/'53 (1996)
Johnny Cash, *Man in Black 1959–62*/'60 (1991)
Wanda Jackson, *Greatest Hits* (1979)
Jackson Browne, *Tell Me Why* (1990)
Dolly Parton/Tammy Wynette/Loretta Lynn, *Honky Tonk Angels* (1993)

Dylan was fooling around with Cecil Null's "I Forgot More Than You'll Ever Know" as early as his 1965 British tour, as evidenced by its appearance on the edited, but nevertheless bootlegged, footage from the film *Don't Look Back*. The song is a faded and jaded boast to a former lover's new beau—at once a grim warning and wistful romantic memory.

Null (born April 26, 1927, War, West Virginia; died August 26, 2001, Bristol, Virginia) wrote "I Forgot More Than You'll Ever Know" in 1947 but couldn't get it recorded until 1953. The song, he told Dorothy Horstman during a 1973 interview as published in her 1975 book *Sing Your Heart Out, Country Boy* (New York: E. P. Dutton) "stems from the old saying. So many times I've heard people say, 'I forgot more than you'll ever know about this job or this thing or whatever.' I thought it would be a good idea for a song because everybody was already familiar with the title. The song was not written from true life. If every songwriter wrote true things about himself, most wives would have left long ago."

In the hands of Skeeter Davis, "I Forgot More Than You'll Ever Know" became a No. 1 hit in 1953. Nearly two decades later it still had legs when Jeanne Pruett hit the Top 60 with her rendition in 1972. In all, it has been recorded more than thirty times.

Along with Carter Family cofounder Mother Maybelle Carter, Cecil Null is regarded as one of the great popularizers of the autoharp, even crafting a variant of the instrument, the Musaharp, carved from birds-eye maple. As an autoharp teacher and innovator, Null, who had the ability to play the instrument like a guitar, no doubt heightened interest in and sales of the instrument. And his book *Pickin' Style Auto-Harp*, demonstrating his highly melodic, plucked approach, remains a classic. His understanding of the instrument became so well regarded that he was hired by Mother Maybelle to service her autoharp. Their relationship would result in his 1964 homage "Mother Maybelle."

Null was a creative soul from early on—a poet at age nine and a guitar player by his midteens. Later, during a hitch with the U.S. Navy in World War II, he discovered that he had a knack for songwriting while drumming up some entertainment for his shipmates. Upon his discharge from military service, he began an earnest study of American folk music.

Joining a group calling themselves the Pioneer Pals, Null got his first widespread public exposure over the radio airwaves of WOPI in Bristol, Tennessee. He maintained a steady career as a performer in medium-profile Tennessee country-western bands through 1964, when he teamed with his wife, Annette, as Cecil

Null and Annette. As country music's answer to Ian & Sylvia, the duo performed widely and recorded on a variety of labels through the early 1970s.

Dylan's decent reading of this cool piece of country music dozens-playing was one of the true redeeming elements of *Self Portrait.* An even better rendition was performed when "I Forgot More Than You'll Ever Know" was effectively revived (embellished with Howie Epstein's beautiful turn on mandolin, evoking the style and sentiments of Null's best recordings) for memorable vocal duets with Tom Petty during Dylan's Temples in Flames tour with the Heartbreakers in 1986.

I

[S] "If You Belonged to Me" (Traveling Wilburys)

Traveling Wilburys, *Traveling Wilburys, Volume 3* (1990)

Dylan updates 1965's "She Belongs to Me," his earlier, diabolically snide assessment of a relationship, with this song pledging true commitment. Not only does he take a wonderful turn on lead vocal, but he also blows a nice harmonica solo for good measure.

[S] "If You Gotta Go, Go Now (Or Else You Got to Stay All Night)" (Bob Dylan)

aka "If You Gotta Go"
Bob Dylan, single (1965); *The Bootleg Series, Volumes 1–3: Rare and Unreleased, 1961–1991*/'65 (1991); *The Bootleg Series, Volume 6: Live 1964—Concert at Philharmonic Hall* (2004)
Manfred Mann, single (1965); *Semi Detached Suburban* (1979); *The Best of Manfred Mann* (1980)
The Lions, *Many Sides of Lions* (1965)
Mae West, single (1966)
Fairport Convention, *Unhalfbricking* (1969)
The Flying Burrito Brothers, *Burrito Deluxe* (1970); *Close Up the Honky Tonks* (1974); *The Songs of Bob Dylan* (1989)
Rick Nelson, *Rick Nelson in Concert* (1970)
Larry McNeely, *Glenn Campbell Presents Larry McNeely* (1971)
Stoneground, *Family Album* (1971); *1969–1976* (1995)
Eric Andersen, *Party!* (1983)
Pontiac Brothers, *Big Black River* (1985)
Eric Ambel, *Roscoe's Gang* (1989)
Various Artists (performed by Manfred Mann), *I Shall Be Unreleased: The Songs of Bob Dylan*/'65 (1991)
Janglers, *Janglers Play Dylan* (1992)
Sue Foley, *Big City Blues* (1995)
Hugues Aufray, *Aufray Trans Dylan* (1995)
Hillcats, *Mild* (1996)
Lloyd Cole, single (1999)
Cowboy Junkies, *Rarities, B-Sides and Slow, Sad Waltzes* (1999)
Various Artists (performed by Cowboy Junkies), *May Your Song Always Be Sung Again* (2001)
Various Artists (performed by Accidental Porn), *Duluth Does Dylan* (2001)

Dylan began performing "If You Gotta Go, Go Now"—which could well be described as "Let's Spend the Night Together" with one-liners—in the fall of 1964, regularly inserting it as some much-needed light relief between two otherwise "heavy" songs ("Gates of Eden" and "It's Alright, Ma") in concert through his tour of England the following spring, his last as a solo acoustic performer. It is a sly song that plays with seduction and commitment, the singer essentially pressing the issue as if to say, "If we're going to do it, let's do it already, or stop playing with my head and wasting my time." Either way, he promises to still respect her in the morning.

The speedy, electric band version released on *The Bootleg Series, Volumes 1–3* was originally recorded for *Bringing It All Back Home* and released with "To Ramona" as a single in 1967.

A final note: Mae West's impossible-to-find, haughty and bawdy, barrelhouse 1966 single version of "If You Gotta Go" should be scouted out at all costs.

5 **"If You See Her, Say Hello"** (Bob Dylan)

Bob Dylan, single (1975); *Blood on the Tracks* (1975); *The Bootleg Series, Volumes 1–3: Rare and Unreleased, 1961–1991/'74* (1991); *Masterpieces* (1978)

Bob Dylan/Various Artists (performed by Francesco De Gregori), *Masked and Anonymous* (2003)

Annie McLoone, *Fast Annie* (1976)

Sean McGuiness, *The New Look Back Basement Tape* (1987)

Ethel Mertz Experience, *The Times They Are A-Changin'* (1992)

Klaudia and Rico/Flying Helmets, *At the Same Place Twice in Life* (1996)

The Zimmermen, *After the Ambulances Go* (1998)

Ross Wilson, *The Woodstock Sessions: Songs of Bob Dylan* (2000)

Rich Lerner and the Groove, *Cover Down* (2000)

Mary Lee's Corvette, *Blood on the Tracks* (2002)

Jeff Buckley, *Live at Sin-é* (2003)

In what may be the most painful song on *Blood on the Tracks*, Dylan sings "If You See Her, Say Hello" with a cool that only hints at how close to the edge he really is. We're talking closing time at the Last Chance Café here as Dylan looks deep into the bottom of his empty glass and begins filling it with tears. He can't escape his memories of the woman he still loves, and he sings of her with a pathos and intimacy that would be the envy of Sinatra. The inviting mandolin, bed of organ sounds, hi-hat cymbals, and Ranchero-style acoustic guitars in this recording of the song help him sound nonchalant, even if it is obvious that his insides are being torn asunder by doing so. So when he, crushed and embittered, sings, "We had a falling out like lovers often will/And to think of how she left that night/It still brings me a chill," he is still picking away at those scabs. The emotions are very close to the surface and his feelings keep sneaking out—his attempts to be casual despite his internal typhoon only give the lyric the sad veneer of a Chaplinesque tramp at his lowest. His fantasies of her whereabouts ("... she might be in Tangier/She left here last early spring/Is living there I hear") and respectful inquiries of her frame of mind only serve to underscore his state of wallowing self-pity and remorse: "I always have respected her for busting out and gettin' free" and "Though the bitter taste still lingers on from the night I tried to make her stay." Instead of offering consolation, though, the memories only provoke deeper feelings of bitterness and blame, culminating in the subtle but rancorous payoff line: "Tell her she can look me up if she's got the time."

"If You See Her, Say Hello" was one of the *Blood on the Tracks* songs Dylan rerecorded in December 1974 after being dissatisfied with the first pressings of the album. The first version, cut in New York on September 12, 1974, appears on *Biograph*. While few live presentations could ever hope to match the uncharacteristically openhearted delivery found on *Blood on the Tracks*, Dylan has done justice to this touching, bitter farewell when he's pulled it out through the years. When he began to perform the song as a solo acoustic offering on the second leg of the Rolling Thunder Revue in the spring of 1976, a mere year and a half after first recording "If You See Her," it was a totally revamped version that he displayed, showing shades of both "I Forgot More Than You'll Ever Know" and his own "Dirge." This time around, Dylan rewrote some of the lyrics and performed the song so that the man is haunted by the woman, shackled by her power and hating himself for granting her an upper hand. Singing to the woman's new lover, he starts out acting relieved that she's gone but winds up admitting that he doubts his will to reject her when she returns to him, an eventuality for which he has no doubt. Dylan did not return to the song until the Never Ending Tour of the 1990s, when he revived a healthy chunk of the *Blood on the Tracks* folio.

[S] **"(I Heard That) Lonesome Whistle"** (Hank Williams/Jimmie Davis)
See also Hank Williams
aka "Lonesome Whistle," "Lonesome Whistle Blues"
Hank Williams, *Complete Hank Williams* (1998)
Johnny Cash, *Sings Hank Williams* (1971)
Gene Vincent, *I'm Back and I'm Proud* (1970)
Charlie McCoy, *Harpin' the Blues* (1975)
Don Gibson, *Sings Hank Williams Sr.* (1992)
Townes Van Zandt, *Highway Kind* (1997)

Dylan may have been performing this Hank Williams plaint around the time he recorded it during the *Freewheelin'* sessions (his January 1962 recording for Cynthia Gooding's WBAI *Folksinger's Choice* radio program suggests a wider public display). But the surprise here is that he returned to the chestnut for a pair of consecutive shows in 1990. He also referenced the title in the lyrics of his own "Tonight I'll Be Staying Here with You" in 1969.

Dylan could have learned the song from the 1951 Hank Williams original or from Johnny Cash's Sun Records version—it is likely that he was familiar with both. "Lonesome Whistle" was one of only three songs from Williams's July 25, 1951, session that were deemed ready to issue, and it was perhaps the most unusual of them all due to its subject matter. The title was truncated from "(I Heard That) Lonesome Whistle Blow" to "Lonesome Whistle" so that it could fit on jukebox cards, and writing credit was shared by Williams and Jimmie Davis, the renowned country music maestro, musically best known as the composer of "You Are My Sunshine." Though some regard it as a trite and cliché-ridden prison song, Williams supposedly wrote the lyrics after riding on a train with a convict under armed guard—even though this was past the time when Williams rode trains. With the form and content of a folk song, "Lonesome Whistle" gained its impact from the way Williams grafted the sound of a train whistle onto the word "lonesome."

Where Hank's work ends and Davis's begins on "Lonesome Whistle" is a little tough to say. But one thing is certain: Jimmie Davis (born September 11, 1899, Beech Springs, Louisiana; died November 5, 2000, Baton Rouge, Louisiana) had one of the more unusual travels across the cultural and political landscape of

Governor Jimmie Davis of Louisiana leading the crowd in singing "You Are My Sunshine" at his inaugural ball, Baton Rouge, 1960.
(AP/Wide World Photos)

the U.S. in his embrace of everything from hokum to off-color country blues to gospel music to hit songwriting while being elected governor of Louisiana twice along the way.

Raised in an impoverished sharecropping family, Davis rose to earn both bachelor's and master's degrees and began teaching history at a small Shreveport college in 1928. An invitation to sing old-time songs on the local radio station led to performing engagements and, promptly, a Victor Records recording contract. Adopting the style of his musical hero Jimmie Rodgers, Davis enjoyed his first phase of popularity from the late 1920s to the mid-1930s (during which he recorded some seventy sides), presenting a mix of sentimental cornpone and bluesy selections as he edged into hokum—a genre of song steeped in the sly double entendre best exemplified in "Tom Cat and Pussy Blues." On some of these songs he was accompanied by black country blues guitarists. He scored his first major hit, "Nobody's Darling but Mine," after moving to the Decca label and switching his persona to capitalize on the Gene Autry "singing cowboy" model. This phase culminated in the composition of "You Are My Sunshine," easily his greatest hit and one of America's most beloved songs.

In the 1930s, Davis gave up teaching and moved into civil service, first as a clerk at the Shreveport Criminal Court, then as police chief in 1938 before being elected Louisiana's commissioner of public service in 1942. All the while, he continued recording and even wedged in appearances in three westerns. This ability to merge the lines between show business and politics came to a peak in 1944 when Davis was elected to his first four-year term as the governor of Louisiana. During his first term, he placed five singles in the Top 5, including a No. 1 hit in 1945, "There's a New Moon Over My Shoulder." In 1947 Davis starred in *Louisiana*, a

thinly disguised autobiographical film sketching his rise to prominence. Imagine if former Minnesota governor Jesse Ventura had been champion of the World Wide Wrestling Federation during the past several years and you can glean some idea of Davis's place in his era's political-cultural fabric. His career as an entertainer continued when his first term expired in 1948; he moved to Capitol Records and developed an increasing interest in and association with gospel music. But he also stayed connected to politics and was, incredibly, elected to a second term as the state's chief executive in 1960 on a segregationist platform. Davis moderated that stance during his term to quell civil unrest in Louisiana during the following, difficult years in the history of the American South. Not surprisingly, his high-profile position allowed him to score a Top 20 hit, "Where the Old Red River Flows," his first since the 1940s. He moved back into gospel music after his second term and maintained a steady recording and performing schedule well into his eighties, when poor health finally began to slow him down. Still, he gave the occasional performance until his death at the age of 101!

▣ "I'll Be Your Baby Tonight" (Bob Dylan)

Bob Dylan, *John Wesley Harding* (1967); *Bob Dylan's Greatest Hits, Volume II/'68* (1971) *Biograph/'68* (1985); *Masterpieces* (1978)

Bob Dylan/Various Artists (performed by Kris Kristofferson), *Bob Dylan: The 30th Anniversary Concert Celebration* (1993)

Burl Ives, *Times They Are A-Changin'* (1968)

The Hollies, *Hollies Sing Dylan* (1969)

Emmylou Harris, *Gliding Bird* (1969)

The Brothers Four, *Let's Get Together* (1969)

Ray Stevens, *Have a Little Talk with Myself* (1969)

José Feliciano, *Souled* (1969)

Engelbert Humperdinck, *Sweetheart* (1969); *Greatest Songs*

(1995); *Classic Engelbert Humperdinck* (1998)
Casey Anderson, single (1969)
Georgie Fame, single (1969)
Linda Ronstadt, *Hand Sown . . . Home Grown* (1969); *Different Drum* (1974); *Retrospective* (1977)
Jim Kweskin, *American Avatar* (1969)
Leapy Lee, *Little Arrows* (1969)
The Brothers & Sisters of Los Angeles, *Dylan's Gospel* (1969)
Noel Harrison, *The Great Electric Experiment* (1969)
Underground All-Stars, *Extremely Heavy* (1969)
Ramblin' Jack Elliott, *Bull Durham Sacks and Railroad Tracks* (1970); *Me & Bobby McGee* (1996)
Lester Flatt and Earl Scruggs, *Nashville Airplane* (1970); *1964–1969, Plus* (1996)
Gary and Randy Scruggs, *All the Way Home* (1970)
Anne Murray, *This Is My Way* (1970)
White Lightning, *Fresh Air* (1970)
George Baker Selection, *Little Green Bag* (1971)
Rita Coolidge, *This Lady's Not for Sale* (1972)
Goldie Hawn, *Goldie* (1972)
The Statler Brothers, *Sing Country Symphonies in E Major* (1972)
Uncle Dog, *Old Hat* (1973)
Hank Williams Jr., *Living Proof: The MGM Recordings* (1974)
Tracy Nelson, *Sweet Soul Music* (1975)
Louisiana Jazz Band, *Louisiana Jazz Band* (1975)
Peters and Lee, *Favorites* (1975)
Ray Price, *Reunited* (1977)
Graham Bonnet, *No Bad Habits* (1978)
Marianne Faithfull, *Faithless* (1978); *Rich Kid Blues* (1985)
Maureen Tucker, *Playing Possum* (1981)
Geoff Muldaur, *Pottery Pie* (1987)
Sinners, *From the Heart Down* (1987)
Robert Palmer, *Don't Explain* (1990); *Very Best of Robert Palmer* (1995)
Michelle Malone, *The Times They Are A-Changin'* (1992)
Janglers, *Janglers Play Dylan* (1992)
Bobby Darin, *As Long As I'm Singing* (1993)
Woodford and Company, *Very Best of the Nineties, Volume 5* (1994)
Sonya Hunter, *Finders, Keepers* (1995)
The Ka'au Crater Boys, *Valley Style* (1995)
Totte Bergstrom, *Totte Bergstrom* (1996)
The Walker Brothers, *Collection* (1996)
Bernadette Peters, *I'll Be Your Baby Tonight* (1996)
The Bellamy Brothers, *Reggae Cowboys* (1998)
Jimmy LaFave, *Trail* (1999)
Various Artists (performed by John Hammond Jr.), *Tangled Up in Blues: The Songs of Bob Dylan* (1999)
Rolling Thunder, *The Never Ending Rehearsal* (2000)
The Blues Doctor, *Backs Bobby Dylan* (2001)
Gail Davies, *Gail Davies & Friends Live and Unplugged at the Station Inn* (2001)
Barb Jungr, *Every Grain of Sand: Barb Jungr Sings Bob Dylan* (2002)
Norah Jones, *Come Away with Me* (bonus CD) (2003)
Various Artists (performed by Norah Jones), *Now Love 5* (2003)

Invoking the muse of Hank Williams, Dylan plays with cliché in "I'll Be Your Baby Tonight," an amiable, self-contained song devoid of philosophical layering or symbolic mumbo jumbo that encourages the enjoyment of life's simple pleasures. In closing *John Wesley Harding*, an otherwise ominous album stuffed with austere parables, this sweet song acts as a healing balm and points to *Nashville Skyline*.

After Dylan debuted the song at the 1969 Isle of Wight concert in England, "I'll Be Your Baby Tonight" has barely missed a tour. By 2002, the Never Ending Tour band performances of the song were marked by multi-instrumentalist Larry Campbell's swelling pedal steel guitar.

[S] "I'll Fly Away" (Albert E. Brumley)

See also "Rank Strangers"
Carolyn Hester (with Bob Dylan), *Carolyn Hester* (1962)
Sy Oliver, *Oliver's Twist & Easy Walker* (1960)
Johnny Cash/Jerry Lee Lewis/Carl Perkins, *Survivors* (1982)
B. J. Thomas, *Peace in the Valley* (1982)
Faron Young, *Classic Years 1952–62* (1992)

Various Artists (performed by Alison Krauss and Gillian Welch),
O Brother, Where Art Thou (soundtrack) (2001)
Andy Griffith, *Bigger Than You and I* (1996)
Albert E. Brumley Jr., *I'll Fly Away* (2004)

Dylan was a harmonica-playing sideman when he contributed to "I'll Fly Away" at Carolyn Hester's September 29, 1961, recording session. It was at that session, incidentally, that he met Columbia A&R legend John Hammond, who would soon sign him to his own contract, thus paving the way for what turned out to be an interesting career. Along with Dylan, the Hester recording of "I'll Fly Away" includes Bruce Langhorne on guitar and fiddle and William E. Lee (filmmaker Spike's dad) on bass. It was recorded in two takes.

Albert E. Brumley wrote "I'll Fly Away" in 1929, a few years before its 1932 copyright. He described its origins in a 1973 letter he wrote to Dorothy Horstman that she excerpted in her 1975 book, *Sing Your Heart Out, Country Boy*: "I was picking cotton on my father's farm and was humming the old ballad that went like this: 'If I had the wings of an angel, over these prison walls I would fly' and suddenly it dawned on me that I could use this plot for a gospel-type song. About three years later, I finally developed the plot, titled it 'I'll Fly Away,' and it was published in 1932. Those familiar with the song will note that I paraphrased one line of the old ballad to read 'Like a bird from prison bars have [has] flown.' When I wrote it, I had no idea that it would become so universally popular."

Brumley (born October 29, 1905, Spiro, Oklahoma; died November 15, 1977, Powell, Missouri) was one of the great figures in Southern music who helped bridge the gap between its place in the church and its possibility in the marketplace. Brumley may have been raised on a cotton farm but songs were his true perennial

Albert E. Brumley, composer of "I'll Fly Away" and "Rank Strangers."

(Property of Albert E. Brumley & Sons, Inc. Used by permission)

crop. He studied at the old Hartford Musical Institute in Hartford, Arkansas, under some of the country's most distinguished practitioners of sacred music, including Virgil O. Stamps, E. M. Bartlett, Thomas Benton, and Homer Rodeheaver, to name just a few. While there he became a member of the Hartford Quartet singing group. As a singing teacher, he moved around the Ozarks teaching his art and craft in the region's schools. It was during this seminomadic period as an educator that he met Goldie Edith Schell in Powell, Missouri. And it was in Powell that they married in 1931, raised their six children, and remained for the rest of their lives.

Even as a young man, Brumley was one of those guys who always seemed to have a new, original song in his heart. But it wasn't until Goldie prodded him to send "I'll Fly Away" to the Hartford Music Company that he even seemed to have considered making any money from it. To his surprise the Hartford Music Company published the song in a religious book entitled *The Wonderful Message*, and as the song gained national recognition, it began to be published in church hymnals. Impressed with Brumley's talents and commercial prospects, Hartford hired him as a staff songwriter. The new job was a gamble to be sure, but one that paid off with a career that left him near the top of the heap of America's most prolific writers of sacred songs (or what he called "memory songs") and more than eight hundred compositions to his credit. Nevertheless, "I'll Fly Away" was Brumley's most often recorded song, with five hundred plus renditions by others estimated to have been recorded. An astute businessman, in the mid-1960s he founded his own music publishing company, Albert E. Brumley & Sons, which became so successful that he was soon able to buy out his former employer, the Hartford Music Company.

With its spare, rural settings and simple spiritual messages, Brumley's music still reflects the austere philosophy of the heartland. Maybe that's one reason the Smithsonian Institution, in its study of gospel music, dubbed Brumley "the greatest white gospel songwriter before World War II."

His legacy is kept aflame not only by the millions of people who sing his songs in churches across the globe every week, but also by the Annual Albert E. Brumley Sundown to Sunup Sing, among the world's largest outdoor gospel sing-alongs.

Dylan would later record Albert Brumley's haunting "Rank Strangers" for *Down in the Groove* and cover it during the early phases of the Never Ending Tour.

[S] "I'll Keep It with Mine" (Bob Dylan)

aka "Alcatraz to the 9th Power," "Bank Account Blues"

Bob Dylan, *Biograph*/'65 (1985); *The Bootleg Series, Volumes 1–3, Rare and Unreleased*/'66 (1991)
Judy Collins, single (1965)
Nico, *Chelsea Girl* (1967)
Fairport Convention, *What We Did on Our Holidays* (1969); *Meet on the Ledge: The Classic Years* (1999)
Mike Harrison, *Rainbow Rider* (1975)
Richard Thompson, *Doom and Gloom from the Tomb* (1985)
Marianne Faithfull, *Strange Weather* (1987)
Various Artists (performed by Bettie Serveert), *I Shot Andy Warhol* (soundtrack) (1996)
Greg Trooper, *Popular Demons* (1998)
Various Artists (performed by Greg Trooper), *A Tribute to Bob Dylan, Volume 3: The Times They Are A-Changin'* (2000)

Dylan probably wrote this elusive, mysterious song in the spring of 1964 and gave it to the equally elusive and mysterious vamp Nico, after meeting (and some say romancing) her in Paris. Nico later recorded "I'll Keep It with Mine" for her debut album, *Chelsea Girl*. Dylan first recorded "I'll Keep It with Mine" as a Witmark demo in June 1964. A later, murky solo-piano version recorded during the *Bringing It All Back Home* sessions in January 1965 was eventually released on *Biograph* in 1985, and his 1966 stab at it in the studio with some backing musicians appeared on *The Bootleg Series, Volumes 1–3*; both are well worth seeking out. On this latter rendition, producer Bob Johnston coaxes the song into existence. From the fumbling chaos of the piano, ghostly organ, bass, and Dylan's world-weary voice, the haunting "I'll Keep It with Mine" emerges with a delicate coherence that provides a glimpse of how Dylan's wild, mercury sound sprang to life.

Still, none of this explains exactly what the song is about; it sounds like Dylan talking a lover down from off a ledge. Somewhat reminiscent and maybe even a precursor of "It

Takes a Lot to Laugh (It Takes a Train to Cry)," "I'll Keep It with Mine" is steeped in spectral wordplay as the singer soothes and humors his woman with surreptitious and hazy promise. The "it" that he's going to keep with his? The "mine" he's going to stash the "it" with? A token of her love? A secret? Whatever, Nico took it to her grave and you can bet Dylan's lips are sealed even if it all sounds like it means more than it actually does.

[S] "I'll Not Be a Stranger" (Traditional/James B. Singleton/arrangement by Mo Fenton/R. & L. Williams/J. Watson/K. Maul)

Stanley Brothers, *For the Good People* (1960); *Early Years 1958–61* (1994)
Robin & Linda Williams, *Good News* (1995)
Traditional Grass, *I Believe in the Old-Time Way* (1997)

Dylan played this rare traditional associated with the Stanley Brothers at a couple of shows on the northern rim of bluegrass country during the fall of 1997. There is some confusion and debate regarding the song's authorship. For though it may be traditional in origin, "I'll Not Be a Stranger" was copyrighted in 1956 by James B. Singleton, Stamps Quartet Music Co., Inc. To this day, the song can still be found in many a Southern hymnal. Additionally, several people are given arranger's credit in various discographies. Similar in theme to another song performed by the Stanley Brothers, "Gathering Flowers for the Master's Bouquet," "I'll Not Be a Stranger" is sung from the point of view of a man so confident of his goodness in God's eyes that he knows that when he dies and goes to heaven, he will return to the good company he has known his entire life. On a more basic level, the song is about a good-hearted country bumpkin venturing to the big city in search of work and community.

[S] "I'll Remember You" (Bob Dylan)

Bob Dylan, *Empire Burlesque* (1985); *Hard to Handle* (video) (1986)
Various Artists (performed by Grayson Hugh), *Fried Green Tomatoes* (soundtrack) (1992)
Michel Montecrossa, *4th Time Around* (2001)

Call it a confessional Tin Pan Alley–style ballad or call it embarrassingly maudlin, "I'll Remember You" was one of those *Empire Burlesque* songs that came off a little forced on the official release—Dylan's duet with Madelyn Quebec is seriously hit-and-miss—but has absolutely *ruled* as a performance vehicle since its 1986 concert debut. Live, Dylan brings his conversational, willow-weepy, from-the-heart, remembrances-of-embraces-past voice to wring the august most out of his stylish adieu that rewrites some dialogue from *The Big Sleep*—the impenetrably wonderful 1946 Humphrey Bogart–Lauren Bacall noir classic with a screenplay coauthored by William Faulkner. Even if the lyrics can seem, at their empty worst, an embarrassment to any self-respecting high school poet, Dylan always pulls this one off in deeply emotional fashion.

The specific *Big Sleep* reference comes from a mumbled Bogart line ("There's some people you don't forget, even if you've only seen them once") that Dylan turns into "There's some people that/You don't forget/Even though you've only seen 'em/One time or two."

[S] "I'm a Steady Rolling Man" (Robert Johnson)

Robert Johnson, *The Complete Recordings* (1990)
Robert Lockwood Jr., *Plays Robert and Robert* (1982)
George Thorogood, *Baddest of George Thorogood* (1992)

Dylan jump-started one of his 1978 big-band shows with a rock-solid rendition of this Delta blues classic. It's a funny song coming from Robert Johnson, as a steady rolling man he was anything but.

I

[S] "I'm Glad I Got to See You Once Again"
(Hank Snow)

See also "I'm Movin' On"

Hank Snow, *Travelin' Blues* (1966); *The Singing Ranger, Volume 2* (1990)

A song of adieu about a guy who will still be around when his ex gets the heave-ho from her current amour, Hank Snow's "I'm Glad I Got to See You Once Again" has the strange distinction of being the most misidentified tune in Dylan's live cover-song catalogue. Performed just once at an August 1988 Los Angeles concert, it has been labeled in most discographies as a work in progress or as "I'll Be Around"—a smoldering torch song from the idiosyncratic but important Alec Wilder that was made famous by his greatest champion, Frank Sinatra, who recorded it for his 1954 album *In the Wee Small Hours*, regarded among Sinatraphiles as his *Blood on the Tracks*.

Snow had been off the charts when he recorded "I'm Glad I Got to See You Once Again" for *Travelin' Blues*, a 1966 album of personal favorites and originals.

[S] "I'm in the Mood for Love" (Dorothy Fields/Jimmy McHugh)

Erroll Garner, *Body & Soul* (1951)
Sarah Vaughan, *Complete Sarah Vaughan on Mercury* (1954)
Spike Jones, *Best of Spike Jones, Volume 2* (1977)
Charlie Parker, *Bird—Complete on Verve* (1991)
King Pleasure, *Moody's Mood for Love* (1992)
Jackie Gleason, *Best of Jackie Gleason* (1993)
Frank Sinatra, *My Shining Hour* (1994)
Tina Louise, *It's Time for Tina* (1998)

A rare and goofy Never Ending Tour encore (mostly acoustic performances at a few shows in 1988 and 1989), "I'm in the Mood for Love" was written in 1935 and introduced to the public in the motion-picture musical *Every Night at Eight*. There, it was performed by Frances Langford, who also sang it over the credits. It was also featured in the 1938 film *Palm Springs* and in the 1946 film *People Are Funny*. Gloria DeHaven sang it in the 1944 film *Between Two Women* and Dean Martin sang it in *That's My Boy*, a 1951 film. Enormously popular, the song has been recorded more than three hundred times and has sold sheet-music copies in the millions.

The song's primary and best-known author was Dorothy Fields (born July 15, 1905, Allenhurst, New Jersey; died March 28, 1974, New York City). Fields was not only an accomplished librettist and lyricist, but was also one of the few, and probably the best and most successful, female writers of standard popular songs back in the days when good music was popular and popular music was good. The first woman to be elected to the Songwriters Hall of Fame, Fields collaborated with such distinguished talents as Jerome Kern, J. Fred Coots, Harold Arlen, Oscar Levant, Cy Coleman, and of course the wonderful Jimmy McHugh, with whom she composed "I'm in the Mood for Love."

Fields grew up in showbiz: her father, Lew, was part of Weber and Fields, a famous vaudevillian comedy team, and her two brothers made names for themselves on Broadway. Lew Fields became a Broadway producer after his daughter's birth, and, thanks to his show-business connections, a fifteen-year-old Dorothy took the lead in *You'd Be Surprised*, one of the earliest Rodgers and Hart musicals, which played for one night at the Grand Ballroom in New York City's Plaza Hotel.

Shortly after her high school graduation, Fields was introduced to the composer Jimmy McHugh of Mills Brothers Music, the outfit that struck it rich representing Duke Ellington. McHugh (born July 10, 1894, Boston; died May 23, 1969, Beverly Hills, California) was a prolific pop composer who got his start in the biz at the

Boston Opera House as an office boy and later as a Tin Pan Alley song plugger in New York City. After a slow rise through the ranks of success with his own tunes, he formed a partnership with Fields that catapulted him to Broadway's A-list composers. Along with "I'm in the Mood for Love," the two penned dozens of songs, including the beloved "I Can't Give You Anything but Love" (1928) and "On the Sunny Side of the Street" (1930). After his collaborations with Fields, McHugh wrote songs for movies through the 1950s, working with a string of renowned Hollywood songwriters: Harold Adamson, Johnny Mercer, and Frank Loesser.

At any rate, the early Fields-McHugh collaborations included sundry novelty songs and some numbers for Cotton Club revues. They made their Broadway debut with the complete score for *Blackbirds of 1928* starring Bill "Bojangles" Robinson. The show ran for more than five hundred performances and included a number of songs that became standards, most famously, "I Can't Give You Anything but Love."

McHugh and Fields moved to Hollywood in the early 1930s, and proceeded to write songs for films, but ended their exclusive partnership in 1935, when Fields and Jerome Kern collaborated on the score for *Roberta*. She and Kern continued to work as a team through the remainder of the 1930s and were slated to reunite in 1945, but Kern died. Fields then teamed up with Irving Berlin for one of the most famous Broadway shows ever: *Annie Get Your Gun*, a musical loosely based on the life of sharpshooter Annie Oakley. It ran for 1,147 performances at the time and enjoyed a successful Broadway revival in the late 1990s and early 2000s with a string of high-profile actresses and celebrities (Bernadette Peters and Reba McEntire foremost among them) taking the leading role. Fields's work in the theater and film continued unabated for the next quarter century, making her a veritable institution on the Great White Way. *Seesaw* was her Broadway swan song and included "It's Not Where You Start (It's Where You Finish)"—a showstopper for Tommy Tune—and could well have served as Dorothy Fields's epitaph, as for nearly fifty years she had done just that: finish on top.

"I'm Movin' On" (Hank Snow)

Hank Snow, *Singing Ranger, Volume 3* (1994)
Ray Charles, *The Genius Hits the Road* (1960)
King Curtis, *Blow Man, Blow* (1962)
Elvis Presley, *From in Memphis* (1969)
Charlie Feathers, *That Rockabilly Cat* (1979)

Dylan covered Hank Snow's rolling, fiddle-heavy song of hitting the road after another failed love during a slew of 1986 shows with Tom Petty and the Heartbreakers. Following that, it was soundchecked in 1988 and performed at a trio of 1993 Never Ending Tour shows.

"I'm Movin' On" was an important composition to Snow, as he recounted in his 1994 autobiography, *The Hank Snow Story* (written with Jack Ownbey and Bob Burris; Urbana: University of Illinois Press, in association with the Canadian Country Music Hall of Fame): "I did have one special song I'd been working on for over a year," he wrote. "It was as good as anything I'd ever written, and I wanted to record it most of all. I had sung it to many people, in many places, who said it would be a hit record. The song was 'I'm Movin' On.' 'I'm Movin' On' has been my signature song since I recorded it in 1950, and it's still my most requested number forty-five years later.... When I was in the most desperate need of a hit, the Good Lord also guided me to record it."

And at another point, Snow recalled, "'I'm Movin' On' was written about four years before it was ever recorded. On my first session, which was held by RCA in Chicago in 1949, the song was turned down flat by Steve Sholes, recording director. Later on, in the spring of 1950, in Nashville, Mr. Sholes had not remembered the song, so I recorded it. The song, by the way, has been recorded by between fifty and sixty artists around the world."

The Hank Snow story is a tribute to the talent, hard work, and tenacious perseverance of a self-made artist. Overcoming many obstacles, Snow first achieved stardom as Canada's foremost country-music artist. Later, he achieved similar acclaim in the United States, along the way becoming a respected member of the Grand Ole Opry in Nashville, the very heart of country music.

Even the untrained ear can hear the influence of Jimmie Rodgers and Hank Williams suffusing the sound of Snow's entire catalogue. As it was for those two deities of the genre, the guitar for Snow was no mere accessory to accompany his voice. He was an accomplished instrumental soloist in his own right, having played lead guitar on a number of his own recordings and cut several albums alongside the incomparable Chet Atkins. Similarities between Snow and Atkins ranged from the intensity and vibrant feeling each put into his music to their mutual fondness for railroad songs.

Snow (born Clarence Eugene Snow, May 9, 1914, Brooklyn, Nova Scotia; died December 20, 1999, Madison, Tennessee) grew up in a small fishing village on the southwestern coast of Nova Scotia near the town of Liverpool, where life's cold, hard realities profoundly affected the family. Poverty and divorce set in motion a vicious cycle that had Snow and his two sisters bouncing from one abusive situation to another. Snow would later immortalize the experience in songs such as "The Drunkard's Boy."

At the age of twelve Snow struck out on his own, shipping off to sea as a cabin boy on a fishing schooner. It was here that the most important events in the young man's life took place.

During one such sea trek, a crewman pulled out an old guitar and suggested that the cabin boy sing. He did, and at that moment the die was cast. Snow quickly taught himself to play the guitar, and whenever duties on board allowed, he sang his heart out. When he ran out of the songs he knew the words to, he improvised some of his own. In 1930, after barely escaping death by shipwreck, he gave up the sea to become a lumberjack back in Canada. While lumbering, Snow (evidently inspired by Jimmie Rodgers) began his musical career as "The Yodeling Ranger" on a radio station in Halifax.

Snow made his first recording for RCA Victor in Canada in 1936 and became Canada's number-one best-selling recording artist a couple of years later. Yet while Hank Snow was moving forward, becoming successful in his homeland, he was unable to establish himself across the border in the United States, despite changing his moniker to the "Singing Ranger" in 1944. Twice he journeyed to Hollywood and after each time returned to Canada, disappointed and financially broke but not spiritually broken. In 1948 he decided to give the States a final try, traveling to Dallas, where he did a live show over radio station KGVL and appeared at the Roundup Club.

After that trip, RCA Victor released some of his Canadian recordings in the U.S. When the records sold well in Texas and then spread to the east Tennessee area, Snow's star began to rise. It was a small start, but still it looked encouraging. Then, in the fall of 1949, Snow appeared as a supporting act in a show headed by another future country music legend, Ernest Tubb. Tubb, impressed by what he saw, succeeded in getting Snow a slot on the Grand Ole Opry in 1950. Hank's first major international hit, "I'm Movin' On," soon followed.

A sharp businessman, Snow met Colonel Tom Parker, who later managed Elvis Presley, and formed a booking company with him. Just as Tubb had done for him, Snow convinced the Grand Ole Opry to book Presley in 1954. Returning the favor, Presley later recorded songs by Snow.

Snow spent most of the 1950s and '60s cutting a singular path through country music, fusing Hawaiian sounds, Latin music, rockabilly, and boogie without ever betraying his roots. However, when Nashville began slicking up its sound with heavy production effects and the addition of strings in the 1970s, Snow began to falter. RCA unceremoniously dropped him in 1981 after he had recorded for the label for nearly fifty years. Despite his anger at the treatment, Snow remained unbowed. He continued performing to almost the end of his life.

Interestingly enough, for a man who sang, in his deep baritone, songs of savored freedom, life on the road, and soured love affairs, Snow walked the straight and narrow, enjoying a sixty-three-year marriage to Minnie Aalders, a woman he met way back in Halifax during his days on the radio. Perhaps his greatest legacy was not his music but the foundation he established, in the late 1970s, to prevent child abuse and thus provide youngsters with the aid he never received as an abused youth himself.

"I'm Not Supposed to Care" (Gordon Lightfoot)
See also "Early Morning Rain"
Gordon Lightfoot, *Summertime Dream* (1976)

Perhaps because he was considering taking it to the concert stage as a brooding, heartbreaking Texas swing ballad, Dylan recorded this Lightfoot number (a semiconvincing rewrite of Lightfoot's own classic, "Early Morning Rain") in both 1989 and 1994, but didn't start performing it until four years hence, when it popped up at but three Never Ending Tour shows in both acoustic and electric guises.

"I'm Ready" (Willie Dixon)
See also "Hoochie Coochie Man"
Willie Dixon, *The Chess Box* (1989)
Muddy Waters, single (1954); *The Best of Muddy Waters* (1958)
Otis Spann, *Blues Never Die* (1969)
Junior Wells, *Sings Live at the Golden Bear* (1969)
The Band, *Moondog Matinee* (1973)
Albert King, *Albert* (1976)
Kenny Neal, *Blues Fallin' Down Like Rain* (1998)

Willie Dixon was a man who wore many hats: composer, bandleader, and arranger. But one talent may reside on high: his ability to turn out a great lyric. Of all the A-list songwriters to emerge in the years immediately following World War II, Dixon, along with Hank Williams in country music and Chuck Berry in rock 'n' roll, stands on the top of the heap as the preeminent poet of his idiom. And with a frontman like the indomitable Muddy Waters uttering his verse with force and power, words like "I got an axe handle pistol/On a graveyard frame/That shoots tombstone bullets/Wearing balls and chain/I'm drinkin' TNT/Smokin' dynamite/I hope some screwball/Start a fight," as he does in "I'm Ready," could make any new-millennium hip-hopper shit his pants for pure, believable malevolence.

Waters made the first recording of "I'm Ready" in 1954 in a jump-jive arrangement that swings like the Basie band in its prime. That is to say, like many a Dixon composition, it is a modernist, jazzy production that eschews any acoustic Delta roots while bushwhacking a trail to rock 'n' roll. But Waters's crack band—Otis Spann on piano, Jimmy Rodgers on guitar, Fred Below on drums, and, most sensationally, Little Walter Jacobs as the featured soloist making a case for being the Charlie Parker of the mouth harp, with menacing, beehive-buzzing chords that, under

Willie Dixon, American blues musician and composer, playing double bass during a concert, ca. 1960s.

(Photo: Express Newspapers/Getty Images)

Muddy's vocals, must rate as one of music's great instrumental runs—puts a halo around the entire proceeding.

The song has a funny history. As reported by J. J. Perry of the Bloomington, Indiana, *Herald-Times* in an article that appeared in that paper June 11, 1999, Muddy Waters had asked legendary sideman and harmonicist Willie Foster to join him for a weekend gig in Canada in 1953. The plan was to meet in Chicago on a Saturday morning, but Foster arrived instead on Friday evening. Perry's article continues with a quote from Foster: "I knocked on the door, and he [Muddy Waters] was shaving. He said, 'You here? I told you to come tomorrow.' I said, 'Yeah, but I'm here today.'" Foster, as quoted by Perry, goes on: "[Waters] said, 'I mean you ready!' And I said, 'Ready as anybody can be!' He popped his finger and turned to Willie Dixon and said, 'Are you thinking what I'm thinking? That's a record, man!'"

At that, according to Perry, Muddy Waters invited Foster in, and the three of them (Waters, Dixon, and Foster) spent the night writing "I'm Ready" while drinking gin—as mentioned in the song.

I Am the Blues, shouted the title of Willie Dixon's autobiography, and he was right. Whether he wore the aforementioned chapeau of a composer, producer, arranger, bass player, recording artist, session musician, talent scout, or Chess Records bandleader in the 1950s and early 1960s, Dixon (born July 1, 1915, Vicksburg, Mississippi; died January 29, 1992, Burbank, California) was always *the* quintessential master blues modernist. Along with Waters, Dixon was the single most influential figure in shaping the postwar Chicago blues sound. "Hoochie Coochie Man," "I Just Want to Make Love to You," "Evil," "Spoonful," "I Ain't Superstitious," "Little Red Rooster," "Back Door Man," "Bring It On Home," and "My Babe" are just a few of the scores of genre-defining compositions Dixon penned.

Of major significance were the bridges Dixon helped build between the blues and rock 'n' roll. Dixon regularly cut sides with Chuck Berry in the late 1950s as an arranger and bassist, then later saw his classic songs covered by the great English and American bands of the 1960s and 1970s, including Cream, Led Zeppelin, the Rolling Stones, the Doors, and, most notably, the Grateful Dead, who included eight Dixon songs in their voluminous performance repertoire.

Dixon gave back to the music and the people who made it by becoming the ambassador of the blues. In 1982 he created the Blues Heaven Foundation with royalty money from his song catalogue; the goal of the nonprofit organization (which continues to operate despite Dixon's passing) is to secure the blues its rightful respect, protection, and recognition and to educate present and future generations about what he liked to call "the facts of life"—the blues. Blues Heaven also gives financial aid to destitute blues artists.

Much of Dixon's last work concerned itself with social consciousness and bespoke a dedication to world peace and improving the human condition. Appropriately, his last credit, "Eternity," a composition coauthored with the Dead's Bob Weir, is Zen-like in its simple musing on the biggest of questions.

"I'm Ready," Dixon's declaration of many possibilities, was presented in about thirty 1978 concerts as Dylan's lead-off blues vocal—a little treat for that year, and that year only.

[S] **"I'm So Restless"** (Roger McGuinn/Jacques Levy)

Roger McGuinn, *Roger McGuinn* (1972)

Dylan showed up, harmonica in hand, at Wally Heider's Los Angeles studio in the fall of 1972 to contribute to this piece written by McGuinn and Jacques Levy, a cat with whom Dylan would cowrite most of the material on *Desire* a few years hence.

[S] **"I Must Love You Too Much"** (Bob Dylan/Helena Springs)

aka "Love You Too Much"
See also "If I Don't Be There by Morning"
Greg Lake, *Greg Lake* (1981)
The Band, *High on the Hog* (1996)

It is thought that Dylan and backup singer Helena Springs wrote this song in late 1978; it was copyrighted January 2, 1979. Just a few renditions of Dylan performing the rocking "I Must Love You Too Much" survive from his big-band tour of autumn 1978. More than just a little misogynistic (full of embittered accusation and shame), the song was written at the peak of Dylan's divorce proceedings and reflects personal turmoil and anger.

Emerson, Lake and Palmer guitarist Greg Lake is sometimes credited as one of the three cocomposers of "I Must Love You Too Much." Lake and Dylan probably never actually sat down together (or even met) for the composition of the song. Rather, Lake rewrote part of it, changed the words, added several new verses, gave the song a new title ("Love You Too Much"), and later claimed a credit for it. Dylan must have liked what he did with it, though, as Lake's rewrite is included in Dylan's *Lyrics, 1962–1985* (2nd ed.; New York: Alfred A. Knopf, 1985). To confuse matters, the Band's cover is of Dylan and Springs's initial version.

[A] ***Infidels***

Columbia Records LP QC-38819, CD CK-38819, CS PCT-38819; Sony Music Entertainment, Inc., SACD 90317. Recorded April 11–May 8, 1983, at Power Station Studios, New York City. Released November 1, 1983. Produced by Bob Dylan and Mark Knopfler.

Bob Dylan—guitar, harmonica, keyboards, vocals. Mark Knopfler—guitar. Mick Taylor—guitar. Alan Clarke—keyboards. Robbie Shakespeare—bass. Sly Dunbar—drums, percussion. Clydie King—background vocals.

"Jokerman," "Sweetheart Like You," "License to Kill," "Neighborhood Bully," "Man of Peace," "Union Sundown," "I and I," "Don't Fall Apart On Me Tonight"

After three gospel-infused albums in as many years, Dylan's zealous embrace of Christianity began to wane. When he returned to the studio in 1983, he seemed intent on making a first-rate record and, working with Mark Knopfler of Dire Straits—who had also produced *Slow Train Coming*—Dylan did just that. In addition, Columbia Records got behind the new album, *Infidels*, as they hadn't for any other Dylan effort in years, hoping to signify a comeback for the singer-songwriter, whose reputation had suffered on account of his religious preoccupation and focus of the last few years. The combination of Dylan's "return" to secular music and Columbia's new commitment made for a considerable commercial comeback and artistic breakthrough. *Infidels* was advertised as a nonreligious album, and it worked—it went to No. 20 during a ten-week chart stint, and it earned Dylan his fourteenth gold album. The change of direction is indicated from the outset, even before the music comes on: the album cover features a tight color close-up of an unsmiling Dylan wrapped in his customary Ray-Bans looking very much like the cool, snaggle-haired hipster-trickster of '60s yore. *Infidels'* back-cover charcoal drawing of a man nuzzling a woman was probably drawn by Dylan—it sure looks like his raw visual style.

With the songs on *Infidels*, Dylan put aside his obsession with Christianity as his sense of moral outrage rekindled. Whether he was commenting on the Middle East ("Neighborhood Bully"), meditating on the failures of the labor movement ("Union Sundown"), slyly condemning the Reagan era ("Man of Peace"), struggling with his spiritual muse ("I and I"), or looking at the big picture while ranting like a hopped-up street-corner preacher in Bughouse Square ("Jokerman"), the collection was a solid, unified, and aware piece despite some even better material left in the can.

He wasn't done with religion, however. *Infidels* seemed to herald Dylan's move toward Orthodox Judaism. A photograph on the album sleeve shows Dylan touching soil on the Mount of Olives overlooking Jerusalem; that and "Neighborhood Bully," mention of the Old Testament's Leviticus and Deuteronomy in "Jokerman," and the kabbalistic elements laced through "I and I" excited, naturally, speculation that he was reexploring his Jewish roots. Even calling the album *Infidels* suggested that Dylan was declaring that he was now no longer a Christian.

In fact, Dylan had spent considerable time in 1983 at Chabad Lubavitch, the Brooklyn, New York-based Jewish Hasidic sect that incorporates music as a central aspect of its rituals and group life (*see* "I and I"). Around the same time, he was photographed wearing a yarmulke and prayer shawl at the bar mitzvah of his son Jesse at the Western Wall in Jerusalem's Old City.

Dylan, as always, downplayed his interest in any singular system or ideology. Whatever his true stance, he went on record by saying in the *Biograph* liner notes that "all these political and religious labels are irrelevant" and calling the born-again phase "part of my experience. When I get involved in something," he explained, "I get totally involved. I don't just play around."

Regardless of debates on Dylan's spiritual outlook at the time, most agreed that with *Infidels* he once again proved himself a perceptive social diagnostician of America's failing spiritual health. Released at a particularly tense moment during the cold war (this when the Soviet Union was the "Evil Empire" and had just shot down South Korean passenger jet KAL 007 over alleged airspace violations), the album was hailed by the *New York Times*, which said that its "incendiary political rants, quasi-Biblical tirades and surreal love songs capture the apocalyptic mood of the moment with shuddering immediacy."

At least eight original songs and a slew of covers were recorded but not used on the LP—much to its lasting detriment. Along with "Blind Willie McTell," "Foot of Pride," and some others that eventually appeared on *The Bootleg Series, Volumes 1–3*, only Dylan's rendition of Willie Nelson's "Angel Flying Too Close to the Ground" and "Death Is Not the End" saw light of day, the former as a B side for the "Union Sundown" single and the latter on *Down in the Groove*.

Breaking free from born-again Christian doctrine, Dylan delivered a fine album. He was aided immeasurably by a stellar backup combo that included guitarists Mick Taylor and Mark Knopfler and the ace reggae rhythm ensemble Sly & Robbie. With crystalline songs sung with a voice that hadn't sounded so bitterly sweet in nearly a decade, *Infidels* renewed the faith among those of Dylan's fans whose interest had maybe begun to wane a little with all the God-squad stuff of the later 1970s and early 1980s.

[S] "In My Time of Dyin'" (Traditional/Blind Willie Johnson/Bob Dylan)

aka "In My Dying Room," "Jesus Goin' to Make Up My Dying Bed," "Jesus Gonna Make Up My Dying Bed," "Jesus Is Making Up My Dying Bed," "Jesus Is a Dying-Bed Maker," "Well, Well"

Bob Dylan, *Bob Dylan* (1962)
Blind Willie Johnson, *The Complete Blind Willie Johnson*/'27 (1993)
Various Artists (performed by the Thankful Quartet), *Atlanta, Ga. Gospel 1923–1941*/'27 (2000)
Charley Patton, *King of the Delta Blues*/'29 (1991)
Various Artists, *Norfolk Jazz & Jubilee Quartets, Volume 6: 1937–1940* (1995)
Various Artists (performed by Dock Reed), *Negro Folk Music of Alabama: Religious Music* (1951)
Josh White, *Josh at Midnight* (1955)
Mississippi Fred McDowell, *My Home Is in the Delta* (1964)
Led Zeppelin, *Physical Graffiti* (1975)
Lydia Lunch, *Shotgun Wedding* (1991)

In the liner notes to *Bob Dylan*, even future Dylan biographer Robert Shelton (under the pseudonym Stacey Williams) comments that it is unclear where Dylan picked up this ancient bit of gospel blues, though Josh White's versions have been cited as a likely source. As Shelton (aka Williams) reported in the notes, "Dylan had never sung 'In My Time of Dyin'' prior to this recording session. He does not recall where he first heard it."

Josh White, Shelton further points out, sang a considerably sweeter version of "In My Time of Dyin'" on his *Josh at Midnight* album of the mid-1950s; he had also recorded it in 1933 under the pseudonym "the Singing Christian." Dock Reed's disconsolate version from a 1951 Folkways release may also have come across Dylan's turntable, as Reed's unaccompanied rendition has the ragged edge evidenced in Dylan's outing. But to these ears, Dylan's rendition probably comes closest to sounding like the version by the mysterious Blind Willie Johnson, whose recording of "John the Revelator" Dylan most certainly had encountered on Harry Smith's *Anthology of American Folk Music* (Smithsonian Folkways, 1952; reissued 1997). Whatever the case, when Shelton played Dylan's version for Josh White, the older man smiled approvingly and said, "That boy really knows what he's doing!"

Reflecting his study of Robert Johnson and Richard "Rabbit" Brown (the latter a Southern songster who gained fame in the first few decades of the twentieth century in New Orleans), Dylan's excellent, highly inventive interpretation of "In My Time of Dyin'" uses an old modal tuning and some skillful slide work (using a lipstick cover he borrowed from his girlfriend at the time, Suze Rotolo) to establish a totally new texture, different from Josh White's and Dock Reed's, by creating a stark, antique flavor. Dylan's voice, too, is an urgent vehicle for the song's emotion: his identification with the composition's death-haunted narrator is amazing for such a young singer.

Dylan never did perform "In My Time of Dyin'" in any known concert, but the version on his debut album stands as one of his finest recorded outings. While Dylan does not receive any credit for an arrangement on the album, his configuration and direction of the song, though left unpublished, was copyrighted by Duchess Music in 1962 and by Leeds Music in 1978.

[S] **"In Search of Little Sadie"** (Traditional/Bob Dylan)

aka "Little Sadie," "Sadie," "Transfusion Blues"
See also "Little Sadie"
Bob Dylan, *Self Portrait* (1970)
Johnny Cash, *Now, There Was a Song!* (1960)
Clarence Ashley and Doc Watson, *Old Time Music at Clarence Ashley's, Volume 2* (1963)
Ian Calford, *Strapped for Cash* (2000)

"In Search of Little Sadie" is one of the most embarrassing cuts Dylan ever released: there is no tune, his singing is all over the place, and his mind seems to be in the next galaxy. Dylan claims composer credit for this traditional folk song on *Self Portrait*, but the *Self Portrait* music book lists him as arranger. To confuse matters further, www.bobdylan.com (a Columbia Records Web site) gives him full composer's credit. As poorly as his rendition of the song comes off on record, Dylan somehow saw fit to release another arrangement of it on the same album but under the slightly different title "Little Sadie."

Both versions of the murder ballad are based on an older song and part of the family of country folk songs that include "Delia," which Dylan recorded some two decades later on *World Gone Wrong*. "In Search of Little Sadie" tells the violent story of a man who shoots a woman late in the night and is so cool about his deed that he is able to go back home and get some sleep while the "forty-four Colt smokes under my head." He is inevitably pursued, arrested, tried, and convicted but hardly seems to wince when sentenced to forty-one years "to wear the ball and stripes."

[S] **"Inside Out"** (Traveling Wilburys)

Traveling Wilburys, *Traveling Wilburys, Volume 3* (1990)

On the Wilburys' sophomore effort, Dylan and George Harrison harmonize while Tom Petty takes the chorus for this song describing a topsy-turvy world.

[S] **"In the Evening (When the Sun Goes Down)"** (Leroy Carr)

aka "When the Sun Goes Down"
Leroy Carr, *Complete Recorded Works, Volume 6: 1934–1935*/'35 (1996)
Leadbelly, *Where Did You Sleep Last Night?*/'43 (1996)
Lou Rawls, *Stormy Monday* (1962)
Ella Fitzgerald, *These Are the Blues* (1963)
Big Joe Turner, *Big, Bad & Blue: The Big Joe Turner Anthology* (1994)
Charles Brown, *Complete Aladdin Recordings of Charles Brown* (1995)
Pete Seeger, *Kisses Sweeter Than Wine* (1996)

The only surviving recording of Dylan performing this sleepy old Leroy Carr blues dealing with secret nocturnal romance was made during a visit back to his home state of Minnesota around the holidays in 1961.

Leroy Carr (born March 27, 1905, Nashville; died April 29, 1935, Indianapolis) grew up in Indianapolis and died there at the mere age of thirty. In his short life, however, he became probably the top blues star of his day, composing and recording two hundred sides that include such well-known and influential pieces as "How Long Blues," "Prison Bound Blues," and "Blues Before Sunrise."

The self-taught Carr had little time for formal schooling and a thirst for the road; he did a stint in the circus, and a hitch in the army, spent some time as a bootlegger, and was a house-party institution. His recording career commenced when he met guitarist Scrapper Blackwell in 1928 and the pair cut "How Long Blues" for the Vocalion label. An instant best seller, the song led to an improbable seven-year ride in which Carr and Blackwell recorded such hits as "Midnight Hour Blue," "Blues Before Sunrise," and "Shady Lane Blues." "How Long Blues" was one of the first million-selling blues records—Carr and Blackwell, in fact, had to record the song four different times in less than a year because the master copy—from which the records were pressed—kept wearing out.

Heavy drinking and carousing can lead to bad endings for those who pursue them unabated, and Carr's fate was no different. A known bootlegger with a fondness for his product led to a death from acute alcoholism. Still, he left behind a vast catalogue of blues that influenced many pianists who followed him in the pre-World War II period.

◙ "In the Garden" (Bob Dylan)
Bob Dylan, *Saved* (1980); *Hard to Handle* (video) (1986)
Rich Lerner, *Performs Songs by Bob Dylan* (1990); *Napoleon in Rags* (2001)

"Well now, it's about that time of the evening when we have to bid each other adieu . . . but before I get out of here I've got to sing you all just this one song . . . a song about my hero . . . everybody's got a hero, right? To lots of people Muhammad Ali's a hero . . . yeah . . . and Albert Einstein, ya know he sure was a hero. I guess you could say even Clark Gable was a hero . . . Michael Jackson . . . Bruce Springsteen . . . I don't care nothing about them people, though . . . none of those people are my heroes . . . they don't mean nothing to me . . . I'm sorry but this is the truth . . . I'm gonna sing you a song about my hero now . . ."

With those words, recorded on the 1986 video *Hard to Handle*, Dylan affectionately introduced "In the Garden" during a February 1986 Australian concert with Tom Petty and the Heartbreakers. As "In the Garden" hails from the born-again period—it appears on *Saved*—it is not difficult to figure out that the "hero" of whom Dylan speaks is Jesus Christ. The garden is the garden of Gethsemane, where Jesus was captured by the Romans before his crucifixion.

"In the Garden" may be Dylan's best gospel song. It is passionate, it is faithful, it is musically complex and dramatic, and it carries an edge as well. Writing in *Isis* #25 (July 1989), J. R. Stokes, in his incisive comparison of "In the Garden" with "Hero Blues," suggests that the edge might stem from the weakness Dylan perceived in himself in contrast to his "hero": "Now you may call it propaganda or you may call it truth but there is a building of ancient architectural interest near to where I live that is seldom visited but is fronted by a hoarding

Tree of Agony, Gethsemane, Jerusalem, ca. late 1800s.

(Photo: P. Bergheim/Library of Congress)

which declares 'Jesus died to save you.' If you believe that then you probably also believe Dylan's words that your saviour 'rose from the dead.' If these affirmations are true, then Dylan's own special hero was everything that Dylan himself wasn't. Firstly Dylan's hero was quite prepared to, and ultimately did, die for others and secondly he was able to defeat death so that no grave could hold him. Dylan as a hero on the other hand wasn't prepared to die for anyone and, once dead, could only envisage eternity in a lonesome grave."

In his book *Song & Dance Man III: The Art of Bob Dylan*, Michael Gray probably did the best job of putting the song into its correct biblical context when he wrote, "'In the Garden' (the phrase itself is from John 19:41) actually centres upon two gardens, and two compelling sections of Christ's story: the part in which Judas betrays him to the armed gang of high priests and elders and their henchmen in the garden of Gethsemane and he is arrested (lead-

ing to his crucifixion); and the part in which, when he rises again from the sepulchre 'in the garden' at Calvary, Mary Magdalene and then the eleven remaining disciples meet him one more time in Galilee. Like the title phrase 'in the garden,' Nicodemus, the named character in the song's second verse, serves to link the stories either side of the crucifixion, since he is there beforehand, asking Christ why a man must be born again (John 3:1–7) and he is there again afterwards, helping Joseph of Arimathaea to place Christ's body in the garden sepulchre (John 19:39). Dylan's first verse deals with his arrest, in the course of which Peter slices off a high priest servant's ear and is all for further swashbuckling resistance. (He is over-keen to prove his ardour because Jesus has just told him he'll deny him three times before the rooster crows at the break of dawn.) Jesus now tells him to put his sword away: 'Put up again thy sword into his place: for all they that take the sword shall perish with the sword' (Matthew

26:52) or 'Peter, put up thy sword into the sheath: the cup which my Father hath given me, shall I not drink it?' (from John 18:11). Dylan's next two verses follow and fuse texts from Mark 2:9 and John 5:1–30 and from Luke 19:37–38 and John 6:15. His last verse quotes from Christ's last words to the disciples after his resurrection: 'All power is given unto me in heaven and in earth. Go ye therefore, and teach all nations, baptizing them in the name of the Father, and of the Son, and of the Holy Ghost: Teaching them to observe all things whatsoever I have commanded you: and, lo, I am with you always, even unto the end of the world. Amen.' (Matthew 28:18–20)."

In context and theme, "In the Garden" also vaguely echoes Woody Guthrie's "Jesus Christ." Both songs focus not so much on the glory of Christ and the Resurrection as on the wrongs done the Savior. But whereas Woody Guthrie emphasized Christ's humility ("Jesus Christ" was a man . . . a carpenter true and brave"), his betrayal by Judas and death ("They laid Jesus Christ in his grave"), Dylan addresses the refusal of the masses to see Christ as the Savior, even when presented with the evidence. "When they came for him in the Garden did they know?" Dylan asks. "When He healed the blind and crippled, did they see? When he rose from the dead, did they believe?" Guthrie's song was about Jesus. Dylan's is about a man.

Other influences on Dylan's composition of "In the Garden" may include an old hymn by the same title as well as a tune also called "In the Garden" that Elvis released on his 1967 gospel record, *How Great Thou Art.*

"In the Garden" has been one of Dylan's favorite concert choices since its earliest performances in the fall of 1979. Interestingly, during the 1980s, Dylan would perform "In the Garden" more than any other tune save "Like a Rolling Stone." In fact, it was the only song from *Saved* to find a long life after the initial performances of that material during Dylan's gospel tours of 1979 and '80; it still occasionally pops up on the Never Ending Tour.

The chords may have just come to Dylan when he composed the song on piano or they may have been knocking around the back of his mind: "I think I invented the chord changes to 'In the Garden' while trick or treating with Dylan in 1978," the poet Allen Ginsberg once told interviewer Peter Jones. If so, in Alex Ross's opinion, Ginsberg might have provided Dylan a musical key to properly reflect the nature of Dylan's lyrics. Writing in the May 10, 1999, *New Yorker*, Ross says, "The disturbing gospel number 'In the Garden' shows the agony of Jesus in Gethsemane by wandering through ten different chords, each one like a betrayal."

[S] **"In the Pines"** (Traditional/Huddie "Leadbelly" Ledbetter)

aka "Black Girl," "Rolling Mill Blues," "Where Did You Sleep Last Night?"
Leadbelly, *Where Did You Sleep Last Night/'44* (1996)
Pete Seeger, *American Favorite Ballads* (1958)
Bill Monroe, *The Music of Bill Monroe 1936–1994* (1994)
Kentucky Colonels, *Long Journey Home* (1964)
Clifford Jordan, *Clifford Jordan* (1965)
Joan Baez, *Very Early Joan* (1983)
Sandy Rothman, *Bluegrass Guitar Duets* (1994)
Nirvana, *MTV Unplugged in New York* (1994)

One of the more widely known and still popular country blues, this spooky song is often attributed to Leadbelly, and indeed Dylan's versions most closely resemble his. But Dylan's early renditions stand apart from just about all known versions of the song in their incoherence. Perhaps he just didn't remember the song correctly.

Although Leadbelly usually gets writer's credit, "In the Pines" dates back to at least the

I

1870s, and its appearance in such a wide variety of repertoires only hints at its diverse, essentially unknowable history. With scores of versions having been recorded in arrangements ranging the gamut of any American musical idiom one can name, the reasons a song like "In the Pines" lingers in the collective unconscious of the folk mind can be more properly addressed by a Jungian analyst than an ethnomusicologist. But then, when wasn't the human soul more attracted to subject matter with obsidian at its core than a sentimental bromide? And stories of forbidden romance with violent retribution have long been the stuff of popular memory.

With probable origins in the Southern Appalachians, "In the Pines," as Dolly Parton pointed out in the liner notes to her 1994 album *Heartsongs*, was still very much part of the oral tradition when she was growing up in Tennessee: "The song has been handed down through many generations of my family. I don't ever remember not hearing it and not singing it. Any time there were more than three or four songs to be sung, 'In the Pines' was one of them. It's easy to play, easy to sing, great harmonies and very emotional. The perfect song for simple people."

Indeed, the very slippery nature of the lyrics, plot, and characters to be found in any version of the song support its uncanny ability to continually morph and enchant. And its fairly unique question-and-answer format leaves plenty of elbow room for armchair dissection. Is the person being asked the questions a "little girl," a "black girl," or "my girl"? Is the person asking the questions her father, mother, sister, brother, husband, or spurned (or unrequited) lover? Does the reference to shivering have a sexual, meteorological, or religious connotation? What of the subplot involving the captain and his watch, the reference to the "longest train," or the apparent murder by decapitation ("His head was found 'neath the driving wheel/And his body ain't never been found") mentioned in the lyrics of so many renditions, including Dylan's? Or was the grisly death merely a tragic accident?

All experts seem to agree that "In the Pines" must be a fractured amalgam of songs, local histories, and shared taboo, where the dark woods—"where the sun never shines"—can represent a near-mystical place of escape, teenage initiation, or even death.

Given its many ingredients, scattered references, versions, and interpretations, "In the Pines" is no easy song to make complete sense of. "This unique, moody, blues-style song from the Southern mountain country is like a bottomless treasure box of folk-song elements. The deeper you dig, the more you find," wrote James Leisy in his 1966 book *The Folk Song Abecedary* (New York: Hawthorn Books).

Dylan was performing "In the Pines" at least as early as 1961, including it regularly in his Greenwich Village sets. He returned to the song in July 1969 when, under the alias of Elmer Johnson, he joined the Band as a surprise guest during an extended encore at their Edwardsville, Illinois, concert. Dylan did a semi-metal version of the song (reminiscent of his own arrangements of "Gates of Eden" at the time) at a July 1989 Never Ending Tour concert in Milwaukee, and a plaintive "In the Pines" was one of eighteen cover songs he performed at the January 1990 guerrilla show at Toad's Place in New Haven, Connecticut. The song also shows up on numerous rehearsal tapes from throughout Dylan's career.

[S] "In the Summertime" (Bob Dylan)

Bob Dylan, *Shot of Love* (1981)

While some may point to "In the Summertime" as the hands-down clinker on *Shot of Love*, this truly enigmatic song can perhaps best be heard as a strange combination of twisted, balladic Gershwin and all kinds of biblical references (Proverbs, Corinthians, Romans, Revelation, Matthew, Leviticus, Daniel, and Mark)—a deft mix of the romantic and spiritual with a hint of cataclysm narrowly averted and revelation attained. Despite sounding like a first take, complete with some of Dylan's most grating harmonica work, "In the Summertime" contains rousing elements of Old Testament–style salvation. Yet, at its best, "In the Summertime" is a nostalgic from-me-to-you remembrance of things past, "when you were with me."

In tone and temperament, "In the Summertime" feels very much like a sister song to "I'll Remember You," released on *Empire Burlesque* a few years later. Both songs even share a sense of dislocated time in the lyrics. Where "I'll Remember You" says "some people that/You don't forget,/Even though you've only seen 'em/One time or two," "In the Summertime" begins with the words "I was in your presence for an hour or so/Or was it a day? I truly don't know."

Dylan did showcase "In the Summertime" with similar results at about a dozen 1981 shows during the underrated tour in support of the underrated *Shot of Love* album. And then, in his amazing fall 2002 Never Ending Tour, when he unveiled so many oddball cover songs and rarely performed original material, he reinstated the song as an early concert choice in an arrangement that reduced it to its folk roots, with Dylan singing with slurred, jazzy aplomb while plunking the piano keys, Charlie Sexton's mean guitar, and sideman Larry Campbell's mandolin filigrees.

◪ "I Pity the Poor Immigrant" (Bob Dylan)

Bob Dylan, *John Wesley Harding* (1967); *Hard Rain* (video) (1976)

Joan Baez, *Any Day Now* (1968); *Hits/Greatest and Others* (1973); *Vanguard Sessions: Baez Sings Dylan* (1998)
Judy Collins, *Who Knows Where the Time Goes* (1968); *Both Sides Now* (1971)
Richie Havens, *Richard P. Havens* (1969)
Planxty, *Words and Music* (1983)
Jimmy Riley, *20 Classic Hits* (1993)
Gene Clark, *Flying High* (1998)
Michael Moore, *Jewels and Binoculars* (2000)

Thematically related to "I Am a Lonesome Hobo" and "Drifter's Escape" (other songs on *John Wesley Harding* depicting reviled outsiders), "I Pity the Poor Immigrant" may be heard as an archetypal American story portraying the detestable state of the chronic and tortured user who paradoxically detests life yet fears death.

Italian immigrant family at Ellis Island, ca. 1910.
(Library of Congress)

The roots of "I Pity the Poor Immigrant" in tune, sensibility, and especially in Dylan's singing of the song on the album, can possibly be traced to "Come All Ye Tramps and Hawkers," a traditional Scottish ballad. It is one of the most beautiful melodies in Anglo-Scots tradition and Dylan uses it well, perhaps emulating Bonnie Dobson's singing of the Canadian song "Peter Amberley," which borrows from "Come All Ye Tramps and Hawkers." Some have pointed out a similarity between the tune for "Immigrant" and that of Ewan MacColl's "Come, Me Little Son." Dylan's singing is in top form, in any case, and his contrast of the immigrant's desperate actions against his soft delivery diminishes the harshness of the deeds—aided too by a hint of redemption in the final line, "When his gladness comes to pass."

But there is a healthy dose of the Old Testament here too. *John Wesley Harding* has been called rock's first biblical album and many references to the good book can be found sprinkled throughout most, if not all, of its songs. According to Dylan legend, a copy of the Bible lay open in his Woodstock, New York, study throughout this period. In specific regard to "Immigrant," Dylan's passages of choice seem to be drawn from Leviticus (26:19, 20, 26, 33, 38) and Deuteronomy (28:23, 28, 36)—books that Dylan would later, interestingly enough, reference in "Jokerman." The essence of these references is that God punishes those who do not obey the Ten Commandments by turning them into immigrants and casting them into a threatening environment. The passages from Leviticus ("and I will make your heaven as iron, and your earth as brass: And your strength shall be spent in vain . . . and ye shall eat, and not be satisfied") could have been practically cut and pasted from the Bible's pages and into Dylan's song.

Showing sympathy to the character while the song itself is ominous in tone, "Immigrant" finds Dylan playing with the conflicting instincts driving his song's title character: the desire to create a new, positive reality in a strange land is at odds with the materialistic elements of human nature. And it is the baser human qualities that characterize Dylan's immigrant—a gluttonous, duplicitous, and harsh man clearly out of control. Dylan wrote "I Pity the Poor Immigrant" in 1967 in Woodstock after his self-imposed recuperative exile following his motorcycle crash a year before. Perhaps the song was his way of sending a message from the wilderness of his upstate idyll of how ill the city and, by extension, American society (both defined by and composed of immigrants) seemed to him. It has also been suggested that the song's theme relates to his father, Abraham Zimmerman, and/or Dylan's manager, Albert Grossman—both sons of Jewish immigrants from Eastern Europe.

While the studio release of "I Pity the Poor Immigrant" was an understated, slightly downcast western ballad (as if Dylan was running on musical fumes), his performances of it with Joan Baez during the 1976 leg of the Rolling Thunder Revue (an example of which may be seen on the *Hard Rain* video) were lively to say the least—full of vibrant gypsy swagger, and an underrated highlight of the second edition of the Revue.

[S] "I Shall Be Free" (Bob Dylan)

Bob Dylan, *The Freewheelin' Bob Dylan* (1963)
Paul James, *Acoustic Blues* (1989)
Various Artists (performed by Paul James), *May Your Song Always Be Sung: The Songs of Bob Dylan, Volume 3* (2003)

This singin' and talkin' surrealistic ditty allows Dylan to showcase his humor (in adult nursery-rhyme style) as he rambles in circles and covers such wide-ranging subjects as women, racism, President Kennedy, Yul Brynner, Little Bo Peep,

Mr. Clean, Willie Mays, and Liz Taylor. This pastiche is one of the earliest examples of Dylan's use of pop culture iconography in a song that fantasizes about what fame and fortune could bring for a young holy fool such as he.

The roots of this composition can be found in "We Shall Be Free," a song performed by Woody Guthrie, Leadbelly, Cisco Houston, and Sonny Terry, and the traditional "You Shall Be Free," with more than a pinch of Guthrie added. Guthrie's recording of the latter was probably Dylan's main inspiration for "I Shall Be Free." Leadbelly's 1944 "We Shall Be Free," with Guthrie on guitar, may also have been on Dylan's radar screen. Folklorist Howard Odum collected "We Shall Be Free" from black singers early in the twentieth century, and he stated in 1911, as reported by Paul Oliver in his book *Screening the Blues: Aspects of the Blues Tradition* (London: Cassell, 1968), that it was "originally adapted from a religious song, 'Mourner, You Shall Be Free.'" This would seem to confirm John H. Cowley's conjecture in his essay "Don't Leave Me Here: Non-commercial Blues: The Field Trips, 1924–60," included in Lawrence Cohn's book *Nothing but the Blues: The Music and the Musicians* (New York: Abbeville Press, 1993), that stanzas of "We Shall Be Free" can be traced to the mid-nineteenth century.

In its utter silliness, "I Shall Be Free" provides anticlimactic levity to an otherwise serious album, as if Dylan were determined to counter his portrayal in the public as a voice for the young generation with some blithe nonsense. It is curious that on this album, which contains at least a half dozen blockbusters, two of its tamest tunes—"Honey, Just Allow Me One More Chance" and "I Shall Be Free"—are snuck in at the end of the LP like a conscious decision on Dylan's part to, as the old showbiz axiom goes, leave 'em laughing.

Dylan never performed "I Shall Be Free" in concert, and unreleased, informal versions recorded around the time of *Freewheelin'* are an uncommon find.

"I Shall Be Free No. 10" (Bob Dylan)
Bob Dylan, *Another Side of Bob Dylan* (1964)

Dylan's final talking blues, "I Shall Be Free No. 10" returns to the clever, hillbilly intellectual nonsense of his earlier "I Shall Be Free" that closed out *The Freewheelin' Bob Dylan* in 1963. Its Woody Guthrie–style comic relief is Dylan at his effortless best, parodying both the fancy footwork and motormouth of boxer Cassius Clay (later Muhammad Ali), whom he satirizes in verse two, and using derision rather than condemnation and declaration to get his politically progressive points across regarding the insanity of the cold war and the emergence of rightwing senator Barry Goldwater as a force to be reckoned with. Dylan's interest in the nursery rhyme, specifically children's counting songs, is apparent in the second verse as well. This is a folk form Dylan would never stray too far away from and would return to with gusto in *Under the Red Sky* a quarter century down the road.

Dylan never performed "I Shall Be Free No. 10" in concert; on its album release the song comes off as a plunge into whimsy and dadaist nonsense. Some have heard it as humor with a dramatic purpose as Dylan utilizes it in its recorded context as Shakespeare used the Fool in *King Lear*: to leaven the sense of suffering and global disorder that marked his most famous early- to mid-1960s songs.

"I Shall Be Released" (Bob Dylan)
Bob Dylan (with Happy Traum), *Bob Dylan's Greatest Hits, Volume II* (1971); *Masterpieces* (1978); *Bob Dylan at Budokan* (1979); *Biograph/'71* (1985); *The Bootleg*

Series, Volumes 1–3: Rare and Unreleased,
1961–1991/'67 (1991); *The Bootleg Series, Volume 5:
Live 1975—The Rolling Thunder Revue* (2002)
Bob Dylan/The Band, *Before the Flood* (1974)
Bob Dylan/Various Artists (performed by Chrissie Hynde), *Bob
Dylan: The 30th Anniversary Concert Celebration* (1993)
Nina Simone, *Blues* (1967); *Essential Nina Simone* (1967);
To Love Somebody (1969); *Here Comes the Sun* (1971);
Artistry of Nina Simone (1982); *Best of Nina Simone*
(1989); *Best of Nina Simone* (1992); *Nina Simone*
(1997); *Very Best of Nina Simone, 1967–1972: Sugar in
My Bowl* (1998)
The Shepherds, *Something New* (1967)
Hugues Aufray, *Au Casino de Paris* (1968); *Aufray Trans Dylan*
(1995)
The Band, *Music from Big Pink* (1968); *The Last Waltz*
(1978); *Anthology* (1978); *To Kingdom Come* (1989);
Across the Great Divide (1994); *Live at Watkins Glen/'73*
(1995)
Joan Baez, *Any Day Now* (1968); *Carry It On* (1971); *From
Every Stage* (1976); *Vanguard Sessions: Baez Sings Dylan*
(1998); *The Essential Joan Baez: From the Heart—Live*
(2001)
Peter, Paul & Mary, *Late Again* (1968); *Flowers and Stones*
(1990)
Big Mama Thornton, *Stronger Than Dirt* (1968)
Joe Cocker, *With a Little Help from My Friends* (1969); *Long
Voyage Home* (1995); *Connoisseur's Cocker* (1997)
Hamilton Camp, *Welcome to Hamilton Camp* (1969)
Marc Ellington, *Marc Ellington* (1969)
Marmalade, *There's a Lot to Talk About* (1969)
Black Velvet, *Love City* (1969)
The Brothers & Sisters of Los Angeles, *Dylan's Gospel* (1969)
The Free, *The Funky Free* (1969)
The Box Tops, single (1969)
Pearls Before Swine, *These Things Too* (1969)
Rick Nelson, *In Concert* (1970); *Rick Nelson: 1969–1976*
(1995)
Bill Haynes, *I Shall Be Released* (1970)
Rabbi Abraham Feinberg, *I Was So Much Older Then* (1970)
Peter Isaacson, *Sings the Songs of Dylan, Donovan* (1971)
Punch, *Punch* (1971)

Marjoe Gortner, *Bad But Not Evil* (1972)
Telly Savalas, *Telly* (1972)
Youngbloods, *Night on a Ridge Top* (1972)
The Rivals, *I Shall Be Released* (1972)
Bette Midler, *Bette Midler* (1973); *Divine Madness* (1980)
Morgan Brothers, *Mixing It Up Good* (1974)
Bridge, *Bridge* (1975)
Ishan People, *Roots* (1976)
Marjo Snyder, *Let the Sun Shine* (1976)
Happy Traum, *Bright Morning Star* (1980)
Srangen Dren, single (1986)
The Flying Burrito Brothers, *Farther Along: Best of the Flying
Burrito Brothers* (1988); *Out of the Blues* (1996)
Box Tops, *Ultimate Box Tops* (1989); *Best of the Box Tops:
Soul Deep* (1996)
Jerry Garcia Band, *Jerry Garcia Band* (1991)
Miriam Makeba (with Nina Simone), *Eyes on Tomorrow* (1991)
Judy Mowatt, *Rock Me* (1993)
Terrance Simien, *There's Room for Us* (1993)
Mahotella Queens, *Women of the World* (1993)
Heptones, *Sea of Love* (1995)
Elvis Presley, *Walk a Mile in My Shoes* (1995)
Hollow Reed, *Hollow Reed* (1997)
The Tremeloes, *Very Best of the Tremeloes* (1997)
Jimmy D. Lane, *Long Gone* (1997)
Two Approaching Riders, *One More Cup of Coffee* (1997)
Moti, *Evolution* (1997)
Earl Scruggs, *Rockin' Thru the Country* (1974); *Live at Austin
City Limits* (1977); *Artist's Choice: The Best Tracks* (1998)
The Paragons, *Sing the Beatles and Bob Dylan* (1998)
The Hollies, *Hollies Sing Dylan* (1999)
Various Artists (performed by Mike Mullins and David West),
Pickin' on Dylan (1999)
Kevin Kinney, *The Flower and the Knife* (2000)
Michel Montecrossa, *Jet Pilot* (2000)
2 of Us, *From Zimmermann to Genghis Khan* (2001)
Dylanesque, *Basement Fakes* (2001)
Pearls Before Swine, *Jewels Were the Stars* (2003)
Jeff Buckley, *Live at Sin-é* (2003)
Todd Rubenstein, *The String Quartet Tribute to Bob Dylan*
(2003)
Paul Weller, *Fly on the Wall* (2003)

Various Artists (performed by Mighty Diamonds), *Blowin' in the Wind: A Reggae Tribute to Bob Dylan* (2003)

One of Dylan's most enduring songs, "I Shall Be Released" works as high allegory with its prisoner/hero dreaming of release—be it by parole, pardon, or escape. As always, Dylan's own versions vary: while the 1967 *Basement Tapes* rendition (released on *The Bootleg Series: Volumes 1–3* in 1991) is made all the more poignant by the haunting falsetto harmony sung by the late Richard Manuel, Dylan's spare, homey version with Happy Traum recorded for and released on *Bob Dylan's Greatest Hits, Volume II* sounds like the two are nipping at a flask next to a woodstove on a snowy night.

Dylan has kept the song in pretty constant performance rotation since its debut in 1975 during the nightly acoustic duet slot he shared with Joan Baez on the Rolling Thunder Revue in 1975 and 1976. By 1978, however, the delicacy and longing that had made "Released" such a winner on *The Basement Tapes* was dropped in lieu of a version in which Dylan talked through the poetry like some wasted hepster—one of the reasons *Bob Dylan at Budokan* was so thoroughly trashed, though variants from later on that tour find Dylan's performances of "Released" were powerful indeed. After 1978, Dylan didn't perform the song again until his 1984 tour of Europe, when it appeared as an encore at a couple of shows. When he performed it at the January 20, 1986, Martin Luther King Jr. birthday celebration in Washington, D.C., it was with substantially rewritten, civil rights–specific lyrics. And, beginning with his last Tom Petty tour in the fall of 1987 through the present day, Dylan has kept the song close at hand, perhaps as a reminder to himself and everyone else who listens that the Big House wall, whether of reality or the mind, is never far away.

"Isis" (Bob Dylan/Jacques Levy)

Bob Dylan, single (1975); *Desire* (1975); *4 Songs from Renaldo & Clara* (EP)/'75 (1978); *Biograph*/'75 (1985); *The Bootleg Series, Volume 5: Live 1975—The Rolling Thunder Revue* (2002)

Steve Keene, *Keene on Dylan* (1990)

The Poster Children, *Outlaw Blues* (1992)

Popa Chubby, *Hit the High Hard One* (1996)

Various Artists (performed by Maryanne), *A Tribute to Bob Dylan, Volume 3: The Times They Are A-Changin'* (2000)

Wall carving of Isis, Egyptian goddess of fertility, wearing a headdress with a solar disk between cow horns.

(Hulton Archive/Getty Images)

Doug Hoekstra, *Around the Margins* (2001)
Todd Rubenstein, *The String Quartet Tribute to Bob Dylan*
   (2003)

"This is a song about marriage" was how Dylan occasionally introduced "Isis," a most mysterious and symbolic carol that he performed live only during the Rolling Thunder Revue tours of 1975 and 1976. Amid all the hoopla surrounding the Revue, the fact that Dylan was inaugurating some great new songs and vivid performances often went unheralded. "Isis" was among the best of this crop and a true highlight of the shows as Dylan unleashed one of his most intangibly stark and maniacally talismanic testaments onstage night after night in arrangements that fused reggae, funk, metal, and waltz. Those frenetic displays were in sharp contrast to the version of the song as released on *Desire*, where it was rendered as a brooding and dreamy, piano- and violin-driven dirgelike travelogue.

Patti Smith supposedly advised Dylan not to play an instrument during the Rolling Thunder outings of "Isis." When Dylan told her he didn't know what to do with his hands, she told him to make a fist. Dylan evidently followed her recommendation and the bare vision of Dylan performing the song in *Renaldo & Clara* (and as heard on *The Bootleg Series, Volume 5*) is nothing less than overwhelming.

An allegorical epic about a man who leaves his woman to join a mysterious stranger who lures him into a grave-robbing expedition that goes awry, "Isis" explores the notions of commitment and false allegiance. That the woman casually accepts him back at the end of the song belies the hero's journey from which he has just returned.

Dylan discussed working with Jacques Levy and composing "Isis" in his 1991 interview with Paul Zollo and published in Zollo's book

Songwriters on Songwriting, Expanded 4th Edition: "['Isis'] was a story that meant something to him . . . It just seemed to take on a life of its own, [*laughs*] . . . there are so many views that don't get told. Of history, anyway. That wasn't one of them. Ancient history, but history nonetheless." He continued:

> With this "Isis" thing, it was "Isis" . . . you know, the name sort of rang a bell but not in any kind of vigorous way. So, therefore, it was name-that-tune time. It was anything. The name was familiar. Most people would think they knew it from somewhere. But it seemed like just about any way it wanted to go would have been okay, just as long as it didn't get too close. [*Laughs*] . . . Too close to me *or* him.

Though Dylan's song is not exactly about her, the ancient Egyptian goddess Isis is surely the song's patron—the presence that pervades its twists and turns. Isis figures prominently in Egyptian mythology as the moon goddess, a healer, a magician, and an exemplary wife and mother—indeed, she was the goddess of marriage. During the age of the Roman Empire, the cult of Isis gained immense popularity not only in Egypt but also throughout the Mediterranean world. According to myth, Isis raised her husband, Osiris, from the dead, protected her son, Horus, from a variety of certain deaths, and knew the secrets of immortality. She was faithful, intelligent, strong, and beautiful. Like Osiris, Isis was associated with vegetation and the cycles of the seasons and the Nile River. Ancient beliefs attributed the annual rainfall, which sustained the people of the Nile Valley, to the tears Isis shed for Osiris.

Dylan biographer Robert Shelton takes the mythological connection a few steps further. Pointing out that in one of his incarnations Osiris marries a woman named Sarah (the

Bob Dylan performing "Isis," Madison Square Garden, New York City, December 8, 1975.

(Photo: Allen Bank. Jeff Friedman Collection)

name of Dylan's wife at the time of the song's composition), Shelton suggests that Dylan was commenting on the dynamic in his own household, specifically the way the songs might imply that his wife was regarding him as a stranger.

Jonathan Cott offered this succinct deconstruction of "Isis" in his 1984 study, *Dylan* (Garden City, New York: Doubleday): "Isis . . . in Dylan's song, [is] the estranged wife whom the mortal hero has to win back in a quest of endurance. Traveling east and north to a land filled with pyramids of ice (though it feels like the Mexico of Coronado) with a fortune hunter (who may be only another aspect or 'double' of the hero himself), the hero fails to find the precious jewels but turns to try to win back his goddess wife."

And let's not fail to note that the nasty vixen in "She Belongs to Me," Dylan's antilove song penned around the time he was first getting together with Sara, wore an Egyptian ring, or that Dylan places the date of the marriage of the narrator and Isis in this song as the fifth of

May, or Cinco de Mayo, a day of great importance in Mexico as it marks the victory of that country's army over the French in the 1862 Battle of Puebla, which came to represent a Mexican symbol of unity and patriotism. That date adds another layer of allusion and confusion to the song's intangibility in that both Egyptian and Mexican histories involve pyramids, which figure prominently in Dylan's song. But is this Isis (this "mystical child" who drives the singer "insane") merely another in the long line of witchy women that alternately manipulate and/or shelter him, or the final prefiguring of Dylan's move to Christ? On a different tack, the songs on *Desire* that deal with women ("Sara," "Oh, Sister," "Romance in Durango," "Mozambique") are all of a conciliatory nature, and "Isis" fits comfortably into this matrix, sharply contrasting with the tortured nature of the songs on his previous album, *Blood on the Tracks*, that describe relationships as anything but serene.

Woody Guthrie's "Trail of the Buffalo" (a song with which Dylan was familiar, about a misbegotten adventure with unscrupulous characters) can easily be heard as a model for his own "Isis."

When asked by Derek Barker, editor of the Dylan fanzine *Isis*, if the song had anything to do with the Egyptian goddess, Levy responded: "No, no, no. It has nothing to do with that at all. If you can picture, we are sitting at a piano together and we are writing these verses in an old Western ballad kind of style. You know the kind of thing that he spent a couple of years doing with the Band in the Basement. Well, this is a similar kind of thing, and just as the Band wrote 'pulled into Nazareth,' you know, well, 'Isis' has about as much to do with Egypt as Fanny has to do with Nazareth. The only thing it has to do with the Egyptian goddess is that we threw in the pyramids, which were a substitute for the hills of Wyoming." (Isis #90, May 2001.)

"Is Your Love in Vain?" (Bob Dylan)
Bob Dylan, *Street Legal* (1978); *Bob Dylan at Budokan* (1979)
Soyka and Yanina, *Neopositive* (1992)
Show of Hands, *Covers* (2000)
Barb Jungr, *Every Grain of Sand: Barb Jungr Sings Bob Dylan* (2002)

Cleverly rewriting Elvis Presley's "Can't Help Falling in Love" while echoing Robert Johnson's blues plaint "Love in Vain," Dylan's torch song is stuffed with pretentious self-pity as he asks a new amour some plain, pressing, egotistical questions, again, as Michael Gray wrote in *Song & Dance Man III: The Art of Bob Dylan*, "evoking the struggler, the man unable to stop yearning for an earthly salvation," despite his low regard for earthly pleasures. Yet "Is Your Love in Vain?" still came off as a pretty good, if somewhat plodding, song both as released on *Street Legal* and as performed exclusively on the 1978 big-band tour (saved for posterity on *Bob Dylan at Budokan*).

"I Still Miss Someone" (Johnny Cash/Ray Cash Jr.)
See also Johnny Cash
Johnny Cash, *Man in Black 1963–69* (1996)
Gram Parsons, *Safe at Home* (1967)
Linda Ronstadt, *Linda Ronstadt* (1971)
Emmylou Harris, *Bluebird* (1988)
Leo Kottke, *Great Big Boy* (1991)
Lester Flatt and Earl Scruggs, *1964–1969, Plus* (1996)
Clark Terry, *Lucky* (1999)

One of the highlights of the film *Eat the Document* is the backstage meeting between Dylan and Johnny Cash and their duet on this Cash classic, with Dylan on piano. Dylan and Cash also recorded an unreleased version of "I Still Miss Someone," a forlorn ballad about a man still pining for the woman who dumped him, during the 1969 *Nashville Skyline* sessions. Remarkably, Dylan returned to "I Still Miss Someone" as a surprise choice at one of his 1986 shows with Tom Petty and the Heartbreakers.

A straight-from-the-heart tale of lost love Cash cowrote with his cousin Roy and first recorded in August 1958, "I Still Miss Someone" is an early example of a direct narrative story translated into a readily accessible form. Here the singer pines (or maybe even mourns) for a blue-eyed lover. Other couples stroll by his door amid the romance of autumn's brilliance, but he can't muster himself to move on.

"It Ain't Me, Babe" (Bob Dylan)
Bob Dylan, *Another Side of Bob Dylan* (1964); *Bob Dylan's Greatest Hits* (1967); *4 Songs from Renaldo & Clara* (EP)/'75 (1978); *Masterpieces* (1978); *Real Live* (1984); *Biograph*/'64 (1985); *Live 1961–2000—Thirty-nine Years of Great Concert Performances*/'75 (2001); *The Bootleg Series, Volume 5: Live 1975—The Rolling Thunder Revue* (2002); *The Bootleg Series, Volume 6: Live 1964—Concert at Philharmonic Hall* (2004)
Various Artists (performed by Bob Dylan and Joan Baez), *Folk Duets*/'63 (1998)

Bob Dylan/The Band, *Before the Flood* (1974)

Bob Dylan/Various Artists (performed by Johnny Cash and June Carter), *Bob Dylan: The 30th Anniversary Concert Celebration* (1993)

Joan Baez, *Five* (1964); *Hits/Greatest and Others* (1973); *Vanguard Sessions: Baez Sings Dylan* (1998)

Johnny Cash, *Orange Blossom Special* (1965); *The Essential Johnny Cash* (2002)

Johnny Cash and June Carter, *Carryin' On* (1967)

Dino, Desi and Billy, *I'm a Fool* (1965)

Duane Eddy, *Duane Does Dylan* (1965)

Fleetwoods, *Folk Rock* (1965)

Jan and Dean, *Folk 'n' Roll* (1965)

The Turtles, *It Ain't Me Babe* (1965); *Turtles' Greatest Hits* (1982); *Best of the Turtles* (1987); *Golden Hits* (1998)

Spokesmen, *The Dawn of Correction* (1965)

The Surfaris, *It Ain't Me Babe* (1965)

Joe and Eddie, *Walkin' Down the Line* (1965)

Davy Jones, single (1965)

The Silkie, *You've Got to Hide Your Love Away* (1965)

Nancy Sinatra, *These Boots Are Made for Walking* (1966)

Sebastian Cabot, *Sebastian Cabot, Actor—Bob Dylan, Poet* (1967)

Earl Scruggs, *Changin' Times* (1969)

Mike Blatt, *Tomorrow* (1969)

Margaret and Michael, single (1971)

John Schroeder, *Dylan Vibrations* (1971)

Brian Ferry, *Another Time Another Place* (1974)

The Mike Curb Congregation, *The Mike Curb Congregation* (1977)

Moonjacks, *Pop Corn* (1978)

Johnny Thunders, *So Alone* (1983); *Hurt Me* (1984)

The Muskrats, *Rock Is Dead* (1986)

Healers, *Secret Show* (1990)

Spirea-X, *Outlaw Blues* (1992)

Kristen Hall, *The Times They Are A-Changin'* (1992)

Various Artists (performed by Davy Jones), *The Songs of Bob Dylan* (1993)

Lester Flatt and Earl Scruggs, *1964–1969, Plus* (1996)

Gonn, *Frenzology 1966–1967* (1996)

The Sound Factory, *Unplugged Rock & Pop Classics II* (1996)

Gerard Quintana & Jordi Batiste, *Els Miralls de Dylan* (1999)

Tess McKenna, *The Woodstock Sessions: Songs of Bob Dylan* (2000)

Gail Davies, *Gail Davies & Friends Live and Unplugged at the Station Inn* (2001)

2 of Us, *From Zimmermann to Genghis Khan* (2001)

Various Artists (performed by Lucy Kaplansky), *A Nod to Bob* (2001)

Various Artists (performed by Mayfly), *Duluth Does Dylan* (2001)

Various Artists (performed by Margaret and Michael), *It Ain't Me, Babe—Zimmerman Framed: The Songs of Bob Dylan* (2001)

Various Artists (performed by Hederos & Hellberg), *May Your Song Always Be Sung: The Songs of Bob Dylan, Volume 3* (2003)

A famous and durable Dylan composition inspired by his breakup with Suze Rotolo, "It Ain't Me, Babe" is a bitter adieu not without its sense of ironic humor, as the poet salvages his wounded pride by spending the entire song trying to convince his lover of his unworthiness—only to make himself more desirable. Dylan has commonly used the conceit of the love song to metaphorically address relationships, and here he rejects not only the romanticized ideology of true love, but the conditions and projections of his audience as well. If you're looking for protection, healing, loyalty, chivalry, or anything else with which society has burdened the male gallant, the singer says, "leave at your own chosen speed"—a bitingly cynical send-off to a needy lover. Even admitting that he "will only let her down" should she attempt a reconciliation seems an honest admission of his inability to live up to the culture's artificial standard. As the final track on *Another Side of Bob Dylan*, the song leaves the listener with a powerful statement of personal and artistic independence for a guy determined not to be held by anyone.

In the *Biograph* liner notes Dylan spoke of writing "It Ain't Me, Babe" in Italy during his visit there in early 1963 as part of the harvest of songs that included "Girl from the North Country" and "Boots of Spanish Leather." While he may have begun some outline of the song during that sojourn, his memory doesn't really jibe with the chronology of the release and performance of those songs, which transpired over the span of about a year and a half.

A mention about the roots of the song's opening line ("Go 'way from my window") is in order here. Dylan probably cribbed this from two sources: the Sleepy John Estes plaint "Drop Down Mama" (which commences with "Go 'way from my window/quit scratchin' on my screen") and "Go 'Way from My Window," a traditional song from the British Isles collected by folklorist John Jacob Niles that Dylan recorded at an informal get-together in May 1960 in St. Paul.

The earliest performances of "It Ain't Me, Babe" in 1964 and 1965 (sometimes as a duet with Joan Baez) were slow and almost march-like, their gloom creating an atmosphere that trapped the listener. By late 1965, Dylan had transformed it into a herky-jerky, stop-start electric arrangement during his underrated fall tour with the Hawks. Later, with the Band in 1974, Dylan refashioned the song from a confident declaration of personal independence into a haughty challenge, an interpretation he ran with in *very* electric versions with the Rolling Thunder Revue, complete with Grateful Dead-style jams and a *killer* harmonica run bursting out of the finale of Mick Ronson and Steve Soles's twin guitar solos. As different from the stripped-down original as any Dylan composition may have gotten, these Rolling Thunder renditions stand as the peak of the song's performance life (and side by side with any Dylan performance) as he toyed with phrasing as daring and nimble as a man teetering on a netless trapeze, lingering over phrases ("Ssssssstep lightly on the ledge") that added an opaque drama to this minimalist screed. Even so, Dylan returned the song to its original hushed-whisper sense and sensibility in acoustic outings in the 1980s, 1990s, and 2000s, embellished by Freddie Koella's melancholy fiddle playing in 2003. That same year, "It Ain't Me, Babe" changed again, this time into an electric, near-orchestral country arrangement with Dylan on keyboards while blowing his mouth harp—touching the melody like a light breeze on a candle flame that refuses to be extinguished.

[S] "I Threw It All Away" (Bob Dylan)

Bob Dylan, single (1969); *Nashville Skyline* (1969); *Hard Rain* (1976)
Cher, *3614 Jackson Highway* (1969)
Peter Isaacson, *Sings the Songs of Dylan, Donovan* (1971)
John Schroder, *Dylan Vibrations* (1971)
Yo La Tengo, *President Yo La Tengo* (1989)
George Fox, *With All My Might* (1990)
Elvis Costello, *Kojak Variety* (1995)
Various Artists (performed by Nick Cave), *To Have and to Hold* (soundtrack) (1997)
Ramblin' Jack Elliott, *Kerouac's Last Dream/'81* (1997)
Insol, *Insol* (1998)
Jimmy LaFave, *Trail* (1999)
Pat Nevins, *Shakey Zimmerman* (2003)

Dylan covers a common, ironic theme with this beautiful love song: a man rues the loss of something he never knew he had in the first place. If you tried to drink this song, it would taste like a sawdust-and-vinegar cocktail served neat, so toxic is its sentiment.

Thought to be the first song Dylan wrote for *Nashville Skyline*, the album version of "I Threw It All Away" is the best example of his showcasing the new croon he developed for that release. But "I Threw It All Away" is regarded as a classic not because of the manner in which he sings it. It is his audacious ability as a songwriter that shines here. Who else would have the gall to follow a profound, bountiful image reflecting absolute contentment ("Once I had mountains in the palm of my hand/And rivers that ran through every day") with throwaway clichés that say virtually nothing ("Love is all there is, it makes the world go round") and still make it work?

"I Threw It All Away" is also significant in that Dylan (or at least his alter ego in song) takes responsibility for the failure of the relationship of which he sings. In songs as different from one another as "Don't Think Twice, It's All Right," "It Ain't Me, Babe," and "One of Us Must Know," he had shifted the blame to the woman as he acrimoniously sifted through the events or offered emotional autopsies that resulted in a breakup. But here he not only takes the rap, he takes it up as a burden as if to remind himself of his loss.

After releasing "I Threw It All Away" on *Nashville Skyline* and displaying it on *The Johnny Cash Show* in 1969, Dylan performed biting versions with the Rolling Thunder Revue in 1976. His strident vocals dominate those renditions and make it a different but not necessarily better song. Dylan brought "I Threw It All Away" back in 1978 during the big-band tour, but didn't touch the song again until the 1998 incarnation of the Never Ending Tour. Reexploring it once again in 2002, Dylan transformed the song into an acoustic, early set inclusion.

[S] "It Hurts Me Too" (Tampa Red)

aka "When Things Go Wrong"
See also "Dust My Broom," "Love Her with a Feeling"
Bob Dylan, *Self Portrait* (1970)
Tampa Red, *Complete Recorded Works, Volume 11: 1939–1940*/'41 (1993)
Elmore James, *The Sky Is Crying*/'50s (1993)
Otis Spann, *Complete Candid Recordings* (1960)
Paul Butterfield, *Original Lost Elektra Sessions* (1964)
John Mayall, *Looking Back* (1969)
Hound Dog Taylor, *Hound Dog Taylor and the Houserockers* (1971)
The Grateful Dead, *Europe '72* (1972)

"It Hurts Me Too," a famous, oft-recorded piece of empathic blues, is attributed to Tampa Red and most closely associated with Elmore James, but Dylan could have been familiar with almost anyone's version when he inexplicably (and poorly) rewrote the lyrics for *Self Portrait.* The common versions of "It Hurts Me Too" is sung by a suitor pleading with a woman to leave the man who mistreats her. In suggesting that his boudoir door is still wide open, he also offers solace and forgiveness. Dylan removes that third, misogynistic character from the plot and thus waters down the impact in his restrained rendition.

James didn't cut his first record until 1952, when he was thirty-four years old, but he is regarded as the first great electric-blues slide guitarist whose approach and style influenced virtually *everyone* who followed him.

[S] "(It Makes) A Long Time Man Feel Bad"

(Traditional)
aka "Makes a Long Time Man Feel Bad," "A Long Time Man," "Long Time Man"
See also "Alberta"
Various Artists (performed by prison groups), *Prison Blues of the South: Live at the Mississippi & Louisiana State Penitentiaries*/'30s (1994); *Negro Prison Blues and Songs* (1998)
Harry Belafonte, *Midnight Special* (1962)
Ian and Sylvia, *Ian and Sylvia* (1962)

Only a couple of 1961 and '62-era recordings of Dylan performing this obscure piece of prisoner folk blues are in unofficial circulation. The "long time" in the title quite naturally refers to the length of the inmate's sentence.

Three sources stand out as places where Dylan may have learned the song (closely related to "Alberta," as heard on *Self Portrait* et al.): Ian and Sylvia's eponymous 1962 LP, which also included a couple of other Dylan favorites of the time ("Rocks and Gravel" and "Handsome Molly"); the Harry Belafonte 1961 *Midnight Special* recording session, at which he was a probable harmonica sideman; or a Lomax field recording no doubt stumbled upon in the living room of a friend.

I

▣ "It's All in the Game" (Carl Sigman/Charles Gates Dawes)

See also "Answer Me, My Love"
Tommy Edwards, single (1958); *It's All in the Game* (1990)
Rick Nelson, *Best of Rick Nelson, Volume 2/'59* (1991)
Rahsaan Roland Kirk, *Complete Recordings of Roland Kirk* (1961)
Sammy Davis Jr., *What Kind of Fool Am I* (1962)
Van Morrison, *Into the Mystic* (1979)
Lawrence Welk, *Reminiscing* (1986)
Andy Williams, *Unchained Melody* (1990)
Robert Goulet, *In Love* (1995)

Dylan shared lead vocals with backup singer Clydie King for covers of this composition at a string of 1981 concerts. The game mentioned in the title is, of course, the game of love; the song is sung to a woman in the midst of a rocky romance as consolation (and unspoken but implicit design) by an interested third party. Lyrics and music come from two very different people and time periods: in 1951 Tin Pan Alley pop meister Carl Sigman wrote the lyrics to accompany "A Melody in A Major," an instrumental composed by General Charles Gates Dawes in 1912. The result was "It's All in the Game," a song that for six weeks in 1958

Charles Gates Dawes, ca. 1921.
(Press Illustrating Service/Library of Congress)

topped the charts as a Tommy Edwards hit.

Dawes, as his title may indicate, was not a musician by trade but a public servant who became vice president of the United States under Calvin Coolidge. (One might wonder if he was channeling Bob Dylan when the muse for "Melody" spoke to him.)

A Republican statesman whose family could rightfully boast a role in the American Revolution (an ancestor of his had ridden with Paul Revere), Dawes (born August 27, 1865, Marietta, Ohio; died April 23, 1951, Evanston, Illinois) was the Alan Greenspan of his day, pursuing careers in business, finance, politics, and, evidently, music. From 1897 to 1901 he was America's currency comptroller, and in 1902 was an organizer and official for trust companies and banks. Dawes became a major in the U.S. Army in 1917 and, a little over two years later, was discharged as a brigadier general. He was on the military board of allied supply in 1918 and 1919 and subsequently served as the U.S. Bureau of the Budget's first director in 1921 and 1922. Dawes's tenure as vice president ran from 1925 through 1929. From 1929 to 1932 he was ambassador to Britain, and in 1932 he became president of the Reconstruction Finance Corporation to aid the Depression-struck U.S., serving in that capacity until 1935. Most famously, he shared the 1925 Nobel Peace Prize with British statesman Sir Joseph Austen Chamberlain for their work in helping to rebuild Europe after World War I.

Though Sigman's accomplishments were not on the same grand scale as Dawes's, he is remembered as the songsmith who inspired generations to hum. Sigman (born September 24, 1909, Brooklyn, New York; died September 26, 2000, Manhasset, New York) grew up in the same Crown Heights neighborhood Dylan is reported to have visited to study Torah with the Lubavitch sect of Judaism in the mid-1980s. The son of a shoe-store owner, Sigman eschewed his law school education to pursue his true love: music. Through his mentor Johnny Mercer (*see* "Moon River"), this classically trained pianist evolved into a sleek lyricist whose greatest, most succulent creations have embedded themselves into the fabric of Americana ("Ebb Tide," "Enjoy Yourself," "Crazy, He Calls Me," "Robin Hood," and "Pennsylvania 6-5000") and have been recorded and performed by artists as diverse as Duke Ellington, Guy Lombardo, the Tijuana Brass, Sonny and Cher, Mitch Ryder, Vic Damone, Tony Bennett, Billie Holiday, the Platters, the Righteous Brothers, Deep Purple, Natalie Cole, and Frank Sinatra. His last big hit was "Where Do I Begin?," the theme for *Love Story*, the 1970 tearjerker star-

ring Ali McGraw and Ryan O'Neill.

A Brill Building fixture, Sigman was one of Tin Pan Alley's last heroes until rock's emergence rendered the refined popster of his ilk obsolete. But his music was never forgotten. Even at his passing, a Mercedes-Benz television commercial using "Enjoy Yourself" was being regularly broadcast during the Sydney, Australia, Summer Olympics. A final bit of the Sigman legacy remains: a phone number. His 1938 song "Pennsylvania 6-5000" was written as an homage to the Hotel Pennsylvania, the site of many a big-band-era concert. If you dial (212) PE6-5000 in New York City right now, the hotel operator is sure to answer.

"It's All Over Now, Baby Blue" (Bob Dylan)

Bob Dylan, *Bringing It All Back Home* (1965); *Don't Look Back* (film) (1967); *Bob Dylan's Greatest Hits, Volume II/'65* (1971); *Biograph/'66* (1985); *The Bootleg Series, Volume 4: Bob Dylan Live 1966—The "Royal Albert Hall" Concert* (1998); *The Bootleg Series, Volume 5: Live 1975—The Rolling Thunder Revue* (2002)

Bob Dylan/Various Artists (performed by the Grateful Dead), *Masked and Anonymous* (2003)

Various Artists (performed by Bob Dylan), *The Music Never Stopped: The Roots of the Grateful Dead/'65* (1995)

Joan Baez, *Farewell, Angelina* (1965); *Golden Hour* (1972); *Greatest Hits* (1973); *Live at Newport* (1996); *Vanguard Sessions: Baez Sings Dylan* (1998)

The Byrds, *Turn! Turn! Turn!* (1965); *Ballad of Easy Rider* (1969); *Byrds Play Dylan* (1980); *The Byrds* (1990)

Barry McGuire, *Eve of Destruction* (1965)

Cops & Robbers, single (1965)

The Grateful Dead, *Vintage Dead/'66* (1970); *Dick's Picks, Volume 9/'90* (1998); *Postcards of the Hanging: Grateful Dead Perform the Songs of Bob Dylan* (2002)

Them, *Them Again* (1966); *Basquiat: Original Soundtrack/'66* (1994)

The Chocolate Watch Band, *The Inner Mystique* (1967)

Druids of Stonehenge, *Creation* (1967)

Thirteenth Floor Elevators, *Easter Everywhere* (1968)

Dion, *Wonder Where I'm Bound* (1969); *The Road I'm On: Retrospective* (1997)

Danny Cox, *Birth Announcement* (1969)

Bold, *Bold* (1970)

Leon Russell, *Leon Russell and the Shelter People* (1971); *Leon Live* (1973)

Turley Richards, *Expressions* (1971)

Judy Nash, *The Night They Drove Old Dixie Down* (1972)

Manfred Mann, *Glorified Magnified* (1972)

Animals, *Before We Were So Rudely Interrupted* (1976)

Little Bob Story, *High Time* (1976)

Graham Bonnet, *Graham Bonnet* (1977)

Link Wray, *Bullshot* (1979)

Flash, *My Generation* (1983)

Ap Daalmeijer, *Studio* (1983)

Marianne Faithfull, *Rich Kid Blues* (1985)

Falco, *Falco 3* (1986)

Shadowland, *Shadowland* (1989)

Richie Havens, *Sings Beatles and Dylan* (1990)

Steven Keene, *Keene on Dylan* (1990)

Energy Orchard, *Stop the Machine* (1992)

The Famous Charisma Box, *Famous Charisma Box* (1993)

Van Morrison, *Best of Van Morrison, Volume 2* (1993)

Tom Constanten, *Morning Dew* (1993)

Various Artists (performed by Cops & Robbers), *The Songs of Bob Dylan* (1993)

Judy Collins, *Judy Sings Dylan . . . Just Like a Woman* (1993)

Phil Carmen, *Bob Dylan's Dream* (1996)

Roger Chapman, *Kiss My Soul* (1996)

West Coast Pop Art Experimental Band, *Volume One* (1997)

Country Gentlemen, *Early Rebel Recordings 1962–1971* (1998)

Hole, *Celebrity Skin* (1998)

Jimmy LaFave, *Trail* (1999)

Steve Howe, *Portraits of Bob Dylan* (1999)

Hole, *The Crow* (2000)

Andy Hill, *It Takes a Lot to Laugh* (2000)

Rolling Thunder, *The Never Ending Rehearsal* (2000)

Stephen Cummings, *The Woodstock Sessions: Songs of Bob Dylan* (2000)

Various Artists (performed by Kelly Hogan), *A Tribute to Bob Dylan, Volume 3: The Times They Are A-Changin'* (2000)

The Blues Doctor, *Backs Bobby Dylan* (2001)

2 of Us, *From Zimmermann to Genghis Khan* (2001)

Various Artists (performed by Cops & Robbers), *It Ain't Me Babe—Zimmerman Framed: The Songs of Bob Dylan* (2001)

Michel Montecrossa, *Jet Pilot* (2000)

Barb Jungr, *Every Grain of Sand: Barb Jungr Sings Bob Dylan* (2002)

Bryan Ferry, *Frantic* (2002)

Robyn Hitchcock, *Robyn Sings* (2002)

Joni Mitchell, *The Word* (2003)

Bidding adieu to a woman, old friend, former friend, the political left, and/or his own innocence, Dylan smelted artistic gold with "It's All Over Now, Baby Blue." The song (is it a lullaby, or a wake-up call?) depicts a cold world in which nothing is certain. Yet it still brims with a kind of dark hope as Dylan vocalizes his pain, capturing brutal emotions and taming them into a fragile surrender.

Dylan is said to regard Gene Vincent (who wrote a "Baby Blue" song of his own) as one of his early rock 'n' roll influences, but "It's All Over Now, Baby Blue" is the very antithesis of Vincent's saccharine original.

"It's All Over Now, Baby Blue" came at the critical moment when Dylan was moving from the "finger-pointing" songs of his early years into a more surreal, solipsistic realm. Perhaps conversing with himself, Dylan looks back one more time before forging ahead. And though the title speaks of endings, the composition is about fresh beginnings. When Dylan sings "Forget the dead you've left, they will not follow you," for example, he does not mean it as an epitaph, for he immediately beseeches the listener to "Strike another match, go start anew." In verse two ("Take what you have gathered from coincidence"), his lyrics dovetail with the sensibility of Swiss psychiatrist Carl Jung's theory of synchronicity—a philosophy or observational technique that might be described as the art of meaningful serendipity. In his 1949 foreword to Richard Wilhelm's German translation of *The I Ching*, the ancient Chinese book of divination that began to find new audiences in the 1960s, Jung wrote that synchronicity "takes the coincidence of events in space and time as meaning something more than mere chance, namely a peculiar interdependence of objective events among themselves as well as with the subjective (psychic) states of the observer." (Note: the English-language version from which this material is quoted is from a translation by Cary F. Baynes, originally published in 1950 by Princeton University Press, Bollingen Series volume 19.) Similarly, Dylan seems to be telling his audience to make connections for themselves and not be spoon-fed someone else's idea of reality.

But along with these generalized philosophical worldviews, Dylan floats some pretty potent symbols and the characters that embody them. Consider, for instance, "your orphan with his gun," "your seasick sailors," "your lover who has just walked out the door," the "empty-handed painter from your street." All of these appear to threaten the person to whom he sings, a person who appears as divorced from reality as the subject of "Ballad of a Thin Man" or as paranoid as the woman in "To Ramona." Like them, Baby Blue had best pay attention, as the very ground he/she stands on may not be as safe as it seems, with Dylan carefully pointing out that "the carpet, too, is moving under you."

Some have suggested that the "Baby Blue" in the song may be Paul Clayton, a blue-eyed New York friend of Dylan's in the early 1960s. Clayton (*see* "Gotta Travel On") was a folksinger and field collector of folk songs who is said to have played for Dylan "Scarlet Ribbons for Her Hair," a song that later provided the melody for "Don't Think Twice." Clayton, who became a little too devoted to Dylan for the latter's comfort, was along for the fabled February '64 road trip from New York to San Francisco and committed suicide shortly afterward. Others suggest David Blue, a singer/songwriting New York City colleague of Dylan's from the early 1960s who can be seen on the cover of *The Basement Tapes* and acting as the hipster pinball wizard chorus in Dylan's 1978 film *Renaldo & Clara*.

Dylan probably wrote "It's All Over Now, Baby Blue" in early January 1965; he made a mono studio recording of it on January 13, 1965, and another in Columbia Studio A two days later. Dylan's earliest public performance of "Baby Blue" was on television's *Les Crane Show* on February 17, 1965. It quickly became the standard closing number for concerts of the era. Dylan delivered a resonant, powerful rendition of the song during his historic appearance at the 1965 Newport Folk Festival, and an unearthly live version from his 1966 European tour is included on *Biograph* and *The Bootleg Series, Volume 4*. When he returned to the stage with the Band in 1974, the song took on a more blustery feel—which he muted considerably for the Rolling Thunder Revue in 1975 (as heard on *The Bootleg Series, Volume 5*) and 1976. By 1978, Dylan had effectively dressed up "Baby Blue" with a teetering rock 'n' roll arrangement that brought forth a general tone of heretofore buried optimism. He brought "Baby Blue" back to earth thereafter, establishing it as an acoustic-set regular on nearly every tour from 1980 onward. The versions Dylan performed in the 1990s and '00s were positively clipped. By 2003, with Dylan punctuating the accents on keyboards, a sweet orchestral arrangement of the song was introduced, unearthing yet new subtleties to a beloved standby.

▣ "It's Alright, Ma (I'm Only Bleeding)" (Bob Dylan)

Bob Dylan, *Bringing It All Back Home* (1965); *Don't Look Back* (film) (1966); *Bob Dylan at Budokan* (1979); *The Bootleg Series, Volume 6: Live 1964—Concert at Philharmonic Hall* (2004)

Bob Dylan/The Band, *Before the Flood* (1974)

Bob Dylan/Various Artists (performed by Bob Dylan), *Bob Dylan: The 30th Anniversary Concert Celebration* (1993)

Various Artists (performed by Roger McGuinn), *Easy Rider* (soundtrack) (1970)

Nannie Porres, *I Thought About You* (1971)

Billy Preston, *Everybody Likes Some Kind of Music* (1973)

Bettina Jonic, *The Bitter Mirror* (1975)

Hugo Race, *Second Revelator* (1993)

Singin' Mike Singer, *Singing Mike Singer Sings Good Ol' Folk Songs* (1997)

7 Lwas, *Nu* (1998)

Various Artists (performed by Eric Andersen), *May Your Song Always Be Sung: The Songs of Bob Dylan, Volume 3* (2003)

"It's Alright, Ma (I'm Only Bleeding)" is a monumental achievement: Dylan catches lightning in a bottle with an ominous guitar figure and a to-the-bone delivery of his caustic and prophetic poetry, casting the coldest of eyes on a bankrupt society in fifteen kaleidoscopic verses topped off with four slightly different, cautionary choruses. This absolute protest epic (the title itself would seem to be a hepcat's recasting of the old cowboy's last dying words: "It only hurts when I laugh") has at least a dozen unforgettable hip koans, all of which became indelible proverbs—especially if one learned them before turning eighteen. "Darkness at the break of noon," "he not busy being born/Is busy dying," "money doesn't talk, it swears," "Propaganda, all is phony," "Advertising signs that con you/Into thinking you're the one," and, most famously, "even the president of the United States/Sometimes must have/To stand naked" are just a few that are doubtless being uttered about something somewhere on the planet even as your eyes pass across this page.

Rock critic Andy Gill sees "It's Alright, Ma" taking the themes in "Gates of Eden" a step further. "Though more direct in its imagery, 'It's Alright, Ma' shares the same sense of entropy as 'Gates of Eden,'" he writes in *Don't Think Twice, It's All Right: Bob Dylan, The Early Years* (New York: Thunder's Mouth Press, 1998). "But rather than disguise his critique behind clouds of allusion, here Dylan unsheathes his verbal dagger and plunges it squarely into the breast of contemporary American culture, in lines requiring little or no deciphering. The title itself is a sly multiple pun, recalling both Dylan's own 'Don't Think Twice, It's All Right' and 'That's All Right, Mama,' the Arthur Crudup song which provided Elvis Presley with his breakthrough first single." Gill continues:

> The opening image of "Darkness at the break of noon" echoes the title of Arthur Koestler's anti-Communist novel *Darkness at Noon*, suggesting that the human spirit can be cast into shade just as much by the rampant consumerism of a capitalist society in which manufacturers can make "everything from toy guns that spark/To flesh-colored Christs that glow in the dark," as by the dead hand of consumerism. The machinations of corporate America and its Madison Avenue advertising industry thought-police, the song claims, are just as effective as communist brainwashing and show-trials in determining people's attitudes and mapping out their psyches . . .
>
> The stripped-bare backing offers little distraction (or protection) from the words, which cut through the parade of hypocrisy and deceit like a machine-gun. Following the

descending chord-sequence as it spirals abjectly away down the plughole, Dylan's deadpan declamatory delivery here is surely one of the most potent precursors of rap, though the occasional tug of nihilism glimpsed in lines like "There is no sense in trying" and "I got nothing, Ma, to live up to" is nowhere near as hopelessly final as the nihilism of Nineties hip-hop culture.

Robert Shelton, in his 1986 biography *No Direction Home: The Life and Music of Bob Dylan*, calls "It's Alright, Ma" a sad song and focuses on its commentary and the power with which it is delivered: "'It's Alright, Ma' disputes that Dylan had become socially unconscious. He moved his protest here to a higher level, to polemize the human condition. In a remarkable verse, Dylan previews the sexual revolution that didn't erupt until years later. He lashes out at the 'Old lady judges' he knew so well in Hibbing. The fierce defense of security, he knows, is no insurance against death. His targets have widened to include advertising, propaganda, obscenity, false gods, and goals. Despite his anger, he accepts lies and malaise as part of life, tempering an outraged snort into sadness. Implicitly, he sees that the flaws of life are beyond good and evil. This is almost a spoken poem, like Ginsberg's 'Howl.' In fact, an excellent melodic, rhythmic base provides hammer strokes for nailing down a steel spike. Repetition of certain phrases heightens dramatic impact, builds tension."

In *Song & Dance Man III: The Art of Bob Dylan*, Michael Gray traces the roots of the "money doesn't talk, it swears" line back to a 1903 Victor catalogue of "Darky ditties," one of which is entitled "If Money Talks, It Ain't on Speaking Terms with Me" that later merged into some early blues songs. Gray also points out that Dylan may have plumed his own song

"Let Me Die in My Footsteps" with the line "'Stead of learning to live they are learning to die" for the famous "he not busy being born/Is busy dying" of "It's Alright, Ma."

"It's Alright, Ma" has long held an urgent presence in Dylan's set lists. It was one of four *Bringing It All Back Home* songs Dylan performed on his 1965 tour, but it never sounded more prescient than it did on his '74 tour with the Band, when audiences responded vigorously to the line regarding the president of the United States having "to stand naked"—the country then embroiled in the Watergate scandal, which ultimately forced President Richard Nixon's resignation later that year. (The line got a pretty good response almost a quarter century later, too, during the Clinton-Lewinsky imbroglio, but even more so as Bush II prepared for Gulf War II.) "It's Alright, Ma" was briefly included in Rolling Thunder Revue sets, and, during Dylan's globetrotting big-band tour in 1978, he effectively used his large ensemble to add sonic exclamation points to this poetry of torture. Dylan has pretty consistently kept "It's Alright, Ma" in rotation, performing it throughout the 1980s and as a driving South Side Chicago blues dirge during the odd Never Ending Tour show in the 1990s. The song appeared in Dylan's concerts somewhat more regularly in the early 2000s. In these later outings Dylan spat out the lyrics like rifle shots using an arrangement that bore more than a passing resemblance to Sonny Boy Williamson's "Help Me" and with a vehemence of a prophet sick of being ignored—the words "You follow, find yourself at war" taking on even greater significance as events in Iraq unfolded in 2003 and 2004.

A final note: after its release on *Bringing It All Back Home*, Dylan's version of "It's Alright, Ma" was requested by producer Peter Fonda for use at a key juncture in *Easy Rider*, the famous 1969 druggie biker flick starring Fonda, Dennis Hopper, and Jack Nicholson. When Dylan refused to let his version be used for the soundtrack album, Roger McGuinn cut a rendition for the release.

"It's Dangerous" (Victoria Spivey)

Victoria Spivey (performed with Bob Dylan and Big Joe Williams), *Three Kings and the Queen, Volume 2/'62* (1972)

Dylan blows some mouth harp and plays guitar on this rare blues track recorded with Victoria Spivey and Big Joe Williams in March 1962 for Spivey's compositional contribution to her self-produced LP, *Three Kings and the Queen*. (The "three kings" were singer Williams, pianist Roosevelt Sykes, and guitarist Lonnie Johnson.)

"It's Hard to Be Blind" (Traditional/Rev. Gary Davis/Bob Dylan)

aka "It's Hard to Be Poor," "Lord, I Wish I Could See," "There Was a Time When I Was Blind," "There Was a Time I Went Blind"

Rev. Gary Davis, *From Blues to Gospel/'56* (1971/'92); (with Pink Anderson) *Gospel Blues and Silent Songs/'50* (1991)

Hard-core blues enthusiasts have discovered that Dylan adapted his own version of "It's Hard to Be Blind" from the traditional "It's Hard to Be Poor" and Blind Reverend Gary Davis's "There Was a Time When I Was Blind"—both Job-like moans to the Creator for inflicting sightlessness upon the singer. Dylan set the record straight with comments to the latter of his two extant 1961 recordings, neither of which is available on official release: "I wrote my own new song to it, it's called 'It's Hard to Be Poor,' but I'll sing it Gary's [way]."

"It's Too Late" (Chuck Willis)

Chuck Willis, single (1956); *Stroll On—The Chuck Willis Collection* (1994)

Otis Redding, *The Great Otis Redding Sings Soul Ballads* (1965)

Derek and the Dominos, *Layla and Other Assorted Love Songs* (1970)

Jerry Garcia and Merl Saunders, *Keystone Encores, Volume 1/'73* (1989)

Roy Orbison, *The Sun Years* (1989)

Link Wray, *Missing Links, Volume 4: Streets of Chicago* (1997)

Dylan's only performance of "It's Too Late," Chuck Willis's languid, self-pitying ballad of busted love, transpired in the summer of 1991 during a rare tour of South America.

Willis (born Harold Willis, January 31, 1928, Atlanta; died April 10, 1958, Atlanta) was an R&B songwriter and vocal stylist who hit it big as both, and is one of those seminal figures from the early 1950s who have been all but forgotten as history chugs along. Willis rose to prominence first as a local Atlanta sensation and then as a national splash when he placed nine sides in the R&B top ten, including "Goin' to the River," "C.C. Rider" (which popularized a fad dance known as the Stroll and featured a tenor sax solo courtesy of Daddy Gene Barge that would make even King Curtis wilt), "I Feel So Bad," "What Am I Living For," "Juanita," and his most enduring composition, "It's Too Late." A mournful, dramatic lament sung by someone coming to terms with the fact that a lover has left for good, "It's Too Late" was first recorded with a female vocal group known as the Cookies and hit No. 3 in 1956.

As a stage performer, Willis is best remembered as a turban-wearing blues shouter and vulnerable blues balladeer. His death from peritonitis (abdominal ulcers that he ignored and refused to treat because an operation would have removed most of his stomach) robbed a generation of a talent that, while not quite at the level of, say, an Otis Redding, should be more widely remembered. He had two ironically titled posthumous hits: "What Am I Living For" and "Hang Up My Rock 'n' Roll Shoes." Despite his brief life and career, Willis was influential in the development of rhythm & blues, as evidenced by those who have covered his material: Derek and the Dominos, the Animals, Buddy Holly, Jerry Lee Lewis, the Band, and Otis Redding.

[S] "It Takes a Lot to Laugh (It Takes a Train to Cry)" (Bob Dylan)

aka "Phantom Engineer"

Bob Dylan, *Highway 61 Revisited* (1965); *The Bootleg Series, Volumes 1–3: Rare and Unreleased/*'65 (1991); *The Bootleg Series, Volume 5: Live 1975—The Rolling Thunder Revue* (2002)
Various Artists (performed by Bob Dylan), *The Concert for Bangladesh* (1971)
Michael Bloomfield/Al Kooper/Stephen Stills, *Supersession* (1968)
Phluph, *Phluph* (1968)
Blue Cheer, *New! Improved!* (1969)
Martha Velez, *Friends and Angels* (1969)
Jim Kweskin, *American Aviator* (1969)
American Avatar, *Love Comes Rolling Down* (1969)
Leon Russell, *Leon Russell and the Shelter People* (1971)
Stoneground, *Family Album* (1972)
Dinger Bell, *Southern Country Folk* (1972)
Clean Living, *Clean Living* (1972)
Jerry Garcia and Merl Saunders, *Live at the Keystone* (1973)
The Earl Scruggs Revue, *The Earl Scruggs Revue* (1973); *Family Portrait* (1976)
Tracy Nelson, *Tracy Nelson* (1974)
L.A. Jets, *L.A. Jets* (1976)
Chris Gartner, *The First* (1980)
Bad News Reunion, *Two Steps Forward* (1981); *Last Orders Please* (1983)
Chris Farlowe, *14 Things to Think About* (1982)
Marianne Faithfull, *Rich Kid Blues* (1985)
The Heart of Gold Band, *Double Dose* (1989)
Steve Keene, *Keene on Dylan* (1990)
Aquablue, *Carousel of Dreams* (1997)
David Garfield, *Tribute to Jeff Porcaro* (1997)
Phoebe Snow, *I Can't Complain* (1998)
Steve Gibbons, *The Dylan Project* (1998)
Richard Hunter, *The Second Act of Free Being* (1998)
Kingfish, *Sundown on the Forest* (1999)
Various Artists (performed by Taj Mahal), *Tangled Up in Blues: The Songs of Bob Dylan* (1999)
Little Feat, *Chinese Work Songs* (2000)
Andy Hill, *It Takes a Lot to Laugh* (2000)
Grateful Dead, *Postcards of the Hanging: Grateful Dead Perform the Songs of Bob Dylan* (2002)

Dylan began working on this bluesy song (mixing the age-old idea of the railroad as a symbol of masculine virility with the cliché of the emotionally vulnerable poet) in June 1965, completed it within a month, and included it on his epochal LP *Highway 61 Revisited*, released later that year. But unlike the balance of the songs on that album in which Dylan's sneering bark castigated so much that was happening around him, "It Takes a Lot to Laugh" finds his voice full-throated, warm, and even inviting as he sings, however obliquely, through the smoldering barrelhouse plaint.

Discussing the evolution of "It Takes a Lot to Laugh" (originally titled "Phantom Engineer"), keyboardist Al Kooper said in the *Biograph* liner notes that the songs on *Highway 61* "changed all the time" in the studio. "We would try different tempos, he would try other words. Most of the songs had different titles. It was a long time, for example, before I realized that 'It Takes a Lot to Laugh, It Takes a Train to Cry' was not called 'Phantom Engineer.'" Many early studio renderings of the song, on unofficial releases, are much more up-tempo than that on *Highway 61*.

Like many of the tunes on *Highway 61 Revisited*, the song is a moody, shuffling blues expressing feelings of frustration and loneliness through a string of barely connected images obliquely hinting at a relationship, with even more buried allusions to a Christ-like death "on top of the hill." While nobody on record has ever had the gall to ask Dylan just what the title means, the song, in its final *Highway 61* mix, echoes the loping blues that spilled from Midwest cities like Kansas City or St. Louis in the 1940s. Even many of the lines in the song are stock blues lines. "Don't the moon look good shining through the trees" and "Don't my gal look fine when she's comin' after me," for instance, can be found in Charley Patton's "Poor Me," Kokomo Arnold's "Milkcow Blues," and the traditional "Rocks and Gravel"—all tunes with which Dylan was undoubtedly familiar.

"It Takes a Lot to Laugh (It Takes a Train to Cry)" is a Dylan concert perennial. Since performing it in his notorious electric set at the Newport Folk Festival in July 1965, Dylan has hardly let it miss a tour (or reinterpretation) right up to, including, and beyond his triumphant 1994 Chicago blues-style delivery at Woodstock II. By late 2003, Dylan had grafted a drunken harmonica solo onto the song's front end.

[S] "I've Been All Around This World" (Traditional)

aka "Been All Around This World," "Hang Me, Oh Hang Me"
Sam Hinton, *Sam Hinton Sings the Song of Man* (1961)
Dave Van Ronk, *Inside Dave Van Ronk* (1962)
Grateful Dead, *History of the Grateful Dead, Volume 1 (Bear's Choice)* (1973)
Hot Rize, *Red Knuckles and Hot Rize: Live* (1982)
Jerry Garcia Acoustic Band, *Almost Acoustic* (1988)
Joe Val, *Diamond Joe* (1995)
Jerry Garcia/David Grisman, *Been All Around This World* (2004)

This dire, obscure old-time amalgam of a badman ballad folk song in which the narrator returns to town to settle some old scores was probably first recorded by Justus Begley, a singing banjo player from Hazard, Kentucky, for the Library of Congress's Archive of Folk Song in October 1937. Another original source may have been Grandpa Jones, last of the Uncle Dave Macon school of bizarro banjo pickers and a master of cornpone entertainment who some claim opened for Dylan at a 1963 New York City concert. But the roots of the song run into the arcane. The "Hang Me" verse itself may derive from "My Father Was a Gambler," a song from the Ozarks said to be about a murderer who was hanged for his crime in 1870 and recorded nearly sixty years later. Another possible antique source for "All Around This World" is "Dixon and Johnson" (aka "The Three Butchers"), first collected in the British Isles in the 1890s but not introduced to the U.S. until a later date. *The Hobo's Handbook*, a 1930 song collection gathered by George Milburn, reportedly includes a composition entitled "I've Been All Around This World," but it is not known whether this version bears any similarity to the song Dylan performed. At the very least, the renditions sung by Dylan, the Grateful Dead, and Dave Van Ronk seem to be truncated versions of a much longer song with a more coherent story line. To bring the issue full circle, Dylan (in true T. S. Eliot fashion) laced the title into his own *Time out of Mind* song "Tryin' to Get to Heaven" when he wrote/sang, "I was riding in a buggy with Miss Mary-Jane/Miss Mary-Jane got a house in Baltimore/I been all around the world, boys/Now I'm trying to get to heaven before they close the door."

Dylan first performed "I've Been All Around This World" in December 1962 as part of a BBC television play entitled *Madhouse on Cas-*

tle Street, in which he was cast (surprise!) as a folksinger. He returned to the song some twenty-seven years later when he began occasionally including it in both acoustic and electric versions during the Never Ending Tour in 1990 and 1992.

[S] "I Walk the Line" (Johnny Cash)

See also Johnny Cash
Johnny Cash, *At Folsom Prison and San Quentin* (1976)
Kai Winding, *Modern Country* (1964)
Jerry Lee Lewis, *Whole Lotta Shakin' Goin' On* (1974)
Waylon Jennings, *I've Always Been Crazy* (1978)
Dean Martin, *Country Dino* (1998)

"I Walk the Line" was the first record Johnny Cash landed on the charts after he became a singer and writer for Sun Records in 1956. The tune later served as the title song of the 1970 film starring Gregory Peck and Tuesday Weld. A paean to fidelity and life on the straight and narrow, the popular Cash song was No. 1 on the country charts and No. 17 overall back at the time of its release.

David Segal summed up "I Walk the Line" nicely in a commemorative *Washington Post* article, published September 13, 2003, following Cash's death:

> One of his first hits, "I Walk the Line" is a declaration of undying love, with a twist. The song opens with Cash humming to steady himself into the right key—it changes on nearly every verse—and then opens with this startling line: "I keep a close watch on this heart of mine." Cash isn't worried about his girlfriend cheating—the subject never even comes up—he's sweating the very real possibility that *he* will screw the whole thing up.
>
> This turned into Cash's great and recurring subject: the fight between good and evil that churns on internally. His narrators are forever fretting about a civil war in their hearts, unsure of which side they will take when the shooting starts. "I Walk the Line" is really about the nagging sense that temptation will defeat better judgment, a pledge by a guy who is under no illusions about his own capacity to self-destruct.

Cash wrote "I Walk the Line" after a conversation with Carl Perkins while the two were sitting backstage in the dressing room before a concert in Gladwater, Texas. Cash said he wanted to write a song with real consequence and meaning, so Perkins suggested a title. As reported in *Man in Black: His Own Story in His Own Words* (Grand Rapids, Michigan: Zondervan, 1975), Cash recalled that "The lyrics came as fast as I could write. In 20 minutes, I had it finished."

Dylan may have captured the essence of the song best himself. After Cash's death he wrote, in a brief remembrance distributed nationally via www.bobdylan.com, the following: "Of course, I knew of him before he ever heard of me. In '55 or '56, 'I Walk the Line' played all summer on the radio, and it was different than anything else you had ever heard. The record sounded like a voice from the middle of the earth. It was so powerful and moving. It was profound, and so was the tone of it, every line; deep and rich, awesome and mysterious all at once. 'I Walk the Line' had a monumental presence and a certain type of majesty that was humbling. Even a simple line like 'I find it very, very easy to be true' can take your measure. We can remember that and see how far we fall short of it."

Dylan's only performances of the classic came with Paul Simon during the short encore duet sets the two shared on their 1999 summer tour, though he did record the song with Cash during his 1969 visit to Nashville to cut *Nashville Skyline*.

[S] "I Wanna Be Your Lover" (Bob Dylan)

Bob Dylan, *Biograph/'65* (1985)
Coulson, Dean, McGuinness, Flint, single (1972); *Lo & Behold* (1996)
Wilko Johnson, *Call It What You Want* (1983)
The New Salem Witch Hunters, single (1986)
The Blue Aeroplanes, *Friendloverplane* (1988)

This New York studio throwaway would have fit right in on *Blonde on Blonde*, the album Dylan was recording when he cut "I Wanna Be Your Lover." A surrealistic blues romp recorded with the Hawks in the fall of 1965, "I Wanna Be Your Lover" became a bootleg favorite and is generally regarded as Dylan's good-natured bow to Lennon and McCartney's "I Want to Be Your Man"—the only song recorded by both the Beatles and the Rolling Stones. The chorus is a direct rip-off of the Beatles tune, but Dylan casts the whole affair as some kind of Daliesque garden party with Rasputin and Phaedra making cameos as the narrator yearns for the woman he can't seem to convince to leave with him, even rhyming the words "hers" and "yours" in remarkable fashion. Dylan also mentions a "Jumpin' Judy" in reference to the immortal character found in a whole family of prison blues songs collected by the likes of John and Alan Lomax in the mid-1930s. The raucous studio workout (at least three versions were recorded) eventually released on *Biograph* was thought to be a failed attempt at recording a single. Said Dylan in the *Biograph* liner notes, "I always thought it was a good song but it just never made it onto an album."

[S] "I Want You" (Bob Dylan)

Bob Dylan, single (1966); *Blonde on Blonde* (1966); *Bob Dylan's Greatest Hits* (1967); *Hard Rain* (video) (1976); *Bob Dylan at Budokan* (1979)
Bob Dylan/The Grateful Dead, *Dylan & the Dead* (1989)
Cher, *Cher* (1967)
Gary Burton, *Tennessee Firebird* (1967)
The Hollies, *Hollies Sing Dylan* (1969)
John Braden, *John Braden* (1969)
John Schroder, *Dylan Vibrations* (1971)
Didier, *Hommage à Bob Dylan* (1974)
Valerie Le Grange, *Valerie Le Grange* (1980)
Ralph McTell, *Water of Dreams* (1983)
Steve Keene, *Keene on Dylan* (1990)
Sophie B. Hawkins, *Tongues and Tails* (1992)
Janglers, *The Janglers Play Dylan* (1992)
Arjen Lucassen, *Strange Hobby* (1996)
Peter Keane, *Walkin' Around* (1996)
Steve Gibbons, *The Dylan Project* (1998)
Various Artists (performed by Cliff Eberhardt), *A Nod to Bob* (2001)
Various Artists (performed by Gary Burton), *May Your Song Always Be Sung Again* (2001)
The Blues Hunter, *Backs Bobby Dylan* (2001)
Barb Jungr, *Every Grain of Sand: Barb Jungr Sings Bob Dylan* (2002)
Various Artists (performed by Sophie B. Hawkins), *Doin' Dylan 2* (2002)
Various Artists (performed by Cyril Neville), *Blues on Blonde on Blonde* (2003)

Dylan's most traditional pop song deftly balances some of his most romantic if muddled images and his most personal plea. The last song cut for Dylan's perennially resonant *Blonde on Blonde* album, "I Want You" was finished in the Nashville hotel room where Dylan stayed while making the record. Dylan had taught Al Kooper the piano part, and Kooper played it over and over while the author worked out the final lyric. As an A-side single, "I Want You" hit No. 20 on the *Billboard* chart—not bad for a bit of chaotic pop surrealism portraying the happy, intoxicating infatuation of newfound love and including a cast of characters that could have jumped right off a Dalí canvas: a guilty undertaker, a weeping mother, the Queen of Spades, a chambermaid, a dancing child with his Chinese suit, a lonesome organ grinder, and a drunken politician. The song was once rumored to be the title cut for the album that became *Blonde on Blonde.*

In its original release, "I Want You" has an exuberant, irresistible melody, a searing harmonica solo, and an intriguing guitar filigree by Nashville session man Wayne Moss. The song captures the unbound feeling of a new romance, with Dylan sounding fresh and vibrant. From his teeming tangle of characters and images, Dylan emerges from each chorus with a simple, straightforward testament declaring the most basic of desires. While some critics consider "I Want You" to be lightweight pop, others see Dylan toying with the myth of true love in his metaphorical implementation of his characters, their situation, and the implied, as yet unrequited, longing of the singer. "I Want You," they say, is about wanting but never getting.

Dylan first performed "I Want You" with an impromptu unit that included members of the Band and Neil Young in March 1973 at the benefit concert for SNACK (Students Need Athletic and Cultural Kicks) at San Francisco's long-gone home of the football '49ers, Kezar Stadium. It became a painful dirge on the 1976 leg of the Rolling Thunder Revue; then, in 1978, Dylan drastically altered the song, daringly transforming it into a wistful torch ballad for his 1978 Elvis-style World Tour, creating an effective, haunting version that had his beautiful singing backed up Steve Douglas on recorder. The infectious, up-tempo version of "I Want You" returned in 1981, but Dylan didn't touch the song again until the Tom Petty and Grateful Dead tours of 1986 and 1987, respectively. Thereafter, Dylan has periodically visited "I Want You" during the Never Ending Tour. And as late as 2003 it was featured with a chunky though vital power chord arrangement.

A final note: the 2003 film *Identity*, starring Amanda Peet and John Cusack, makes unusual use of the song.

[S] "I Was Young When I Left Home" (Bob Dylan)

Bob Dylan, *"Love and Theft"* (Deluxe Edition)/'61 (2001)

On its sole surviving December 1961 Minneapolis recording, Dylan sings like an escaped convict riding the rails out of town. "I Was Young When I Left Home" is one of his earliest compositions and an important stepping-stone evidencing his ability to transform elements of old blues and folk songs into something he could begin to call his own. The song has hints of the traditional "900 Miles," Robert Johnson's "Walkin' Blues" (and a score of other prewar blues songs), and Bobby Bare's "Detroit City."

[S] "I Will Love Him" (Bob Dylan)

Dylan performed the devotional "I Will Love Him" only at two Canadian shows while in the midst of his spring 1980 all-gospel tour. This spare, sacred ballad predicting that the Second Coming is just around the corner seems to have been written on the fly during the harvest that produced the songs for *Saved.* And though he appears to have focused on it with a fair degree of intensity during that week north of the border (one Montreal rehearsal shows he and his band put the song through six takes), "I Will Love Him" was left on the scrap heap when the tour chugged into the lower forty-eight.

[S] "I Will Sing" (Max Dyer)

Alleluia! Another spring 1980 gospel-tour one-off from an Akron concert, this song has Dylan sounding as if he is about to lead a Salvation Army platoon over the hill to reclaim Paradise.

"I Will Sing" is a modern hymn written by Max Dyer (born June 27, 1951, Billings, Montana), now a respected improvising folk/jazz cellist who holds a master's degree from Rice University's Shepherd School of Music and has led music residencies at Oxford and Cambridge Universities. Today he is a producer for Nightwatch Recording and is the artistic director of the New World Renaissance Band. Dyer has worked in the studio with, among others, Jack Gladstone (a Blackfeet Indian singer-songwriter), the Galactic Cowboys (a speed-metal rock band), and contemporary gospel singers Kim Hill and Michael W. Smith.

During the 1970s Dyer performed and toured with a Christian folk group, and it was then that he came to compose "I Will Sing." But how Dylan came upon the still apparently unreleased song remains in question.

In an e-mail he sent me dated August 28, 2003, Max Dyer wrote, "I am still amazed by the fact that Bob Dylan used my song in his concert! This was brought to my attention by Scott Marshall a couple years ago when he was working on his book *Restless Pilgrim* [Scott Marshall with Marcia Ford, *Restless Pilgrim: The Spiritual Journey of Bob Dylan.* Lake Mary, Florida: Relevant Books, 2002.] What follows may be more than you care to know about my little song!" Dyer continued:

> The song came into being in 1972 or 1973 when I was a member of Church of the Redeemer, Houston—a charismatic Episcopal Church with about 40 communal households that was on the forefront of the Charismatic Renewal of the time. The church was featured as *Guideposts* magazine's "Church of the Year" and was also the focus of a CBS documentary "Following the Spirit." Central to my involvement in the church was the Way Inn Coffeehouse ministry, which was a popu-

lar watering hole for young Christians. Most of us in that ministry lived together communally. We spent all day Saturdays planning and rehearsing for the evening ministry. It was always a really creative and fun time.

> As I remember, I was changing my clothes before supper up in my bedroom—the 20 or so others in the ministry were in various places in the house or downstairs fixing spaghetti. There was a fresh spirit of anticipation among us—hearts were lifted. Alone in the bedroom which I shared with several others, I began to sing and sort of dance around in a spontaneous way. "I will sing, I will sing a song unto the Lord," a rollicking little tune popped out: I was just caught up in the joy of the moment. Still humming to myself I headed downstairs to join the others now sitting around in the big living room eating. I gravitated to Ed Baggett, one of the leaders of the ministry, and I shyly mentioned that I had a new song in my mind. I remember his receptivity and gentle encouragement. As I began singing quietly, close to his ear, Ed immediately began to hum along with me. That made me feel better, safer. Others near us joined in and in no time this little tune spread throughout the room and we were all singing together with one voice. New verses were contributed spontaneously and we went on singing for some time. This little song was no longer only mine, it immediately became part of us—a fresh gift from God that gave us a new way to worship Him together.

> In later years, as the ministry of the Church of the Redeemer extended to Great Britain through the invitation of the bishop of Coventry, the ministry of the Way Inn became christened "the Fisherfolk" and had a worldwide impact. "I Will Sing" became a popular worship song in many countries and languages. I loved to sing it in Swedish!

I was very gratified to learn that this song was useful in bridging racial bounds in the apartheid-stricken South Africa of the '70s and was equally owned by blacks and whites worshipping together at the first large racially mixed gatherings.

I remember the closing service of the once-a-decade Anglican Lambeth Conference in Canterbury Cathedral. We, the Fisherfolk, had been chosen to lead the worship at the culmination of this august and glorious event. I remember a bright and vivid pause after the final hymn, and without hesitating to consider the consequences, I began to sing in a loud voice, "I will sing I will sing!" Spontaneous celebration broke out in the great cathedral! I remember the singing going on and on. The light seemed so bright! A score of red-clad Anglican bishops wound their way in a long chain through the church, finally encircling the high altar, the cathedral saturated with the praise of God. "I will sing! I will sing a song unto the Lord!"

I am humbled that God has chosen to use my little song in such unexpected ways.

J

[S] "Jack-A-Roe" (Traditional)

aka "Jackaro," "Jack Munro," "Jack the Farmer," "Jack the Sailor," "Jack's Gone A-Sailing," "Jack Went A-Sailing"
Bob Dylan, *World Gone Wrong* (1993)
Tom Paley, *Folk Songs from the Southern Appalachians* (1953)
Jean Ritchie, *Songs from Kentucky* (1956)
Peggy Seeger and Ewan MacColl, *Two-Way Trip* (1961)
Joan Baez, *Joan Baez in Concert, Part 2* (1963)
Grateful Dead, *Reckoning* (1980); *Fallout from the Phil Zone/'77* (1997)

The legend of a woman who cloaks herself in man's garb in order to perform an act of heroism is among the most venerable in the folk tradition. Mulan, the heroine of a Chinese poem written sometime during the fifth to sixth century A.D. and subject of Disney's 1998 animated feature by that name, and Éowyn, a character who bravely slays orcs on the Gondorian battlefields of Middle Earth in J. R. R. Tolkien's beloved 1954–1956 Lord of the Rings trilogy (since memorialized in Peter Jackson's 2001–2003 film series), are but two manifestations of this archetype. "Jack-A-Roe" is among the more enduring of songs telling such a story of cross-dressing derring-do.

Historians have traced "maiden warrior" legends to ancient Greece and beyond. By comparison, the song we know as "Jack-A-Roe" derives from the broadsides of the British Isles and is about three centuries old at most. Some folklorists suggest that "Jack-A-Roe" originated during the Marlborough Campaign of 1702, when Europe tore itself apart once again in the War of the Spanish Succession, but there were many actual cases of disguised women serving on board ship in the seventeenth and eighteenth centuries. The theme is extremely common in folk songs originating in the British Isles—though not all of these songs have the happy ending that "Jack-A-Roe" does.

As with "Barbara Allen" and "In the Pines," variations of "Jack-A-Roe" can be found in the folk traditions of the Ozarks and Appalachians, in Missouri, Kentucky, North Carolina, and Virginia. Known also as "Jack the Sailor," "Jack's Gone A-Sailing," "Jack Munro," "Jackaro," and even "Jack the Farmer," the American versions generally share similar plot lines and language as the British "originals," though there are regional differences and adaptations of the story. As is customary in the oral tradition, versions were often localized to make them more appealing to specific audiences. Melodically, the modern versions of "Jack-A-

Roe" combine elements of medieval, baroque, and old-time hillbilly music.

Dylan's arrangement of "Jack-A-Roe" on *World Gone Wrong* is basically a composite of two versions of "Jack Went A-Sailing," a title collected by songcatcher Cecil Sharp in Kentucky in August 1908, and Georgia in 1910.

In addition to the versions collected by Sharp, folklorist Gavin Greig has found several variants that, despite their Scottish origin, base the story in England, in Chatham, Chester, or London. In some of them Jack-A-Roe is named Pretty Polly (a girl who shows up often in the folk lexicon).

Though Dylan's offering stays fairly close to the early-twentieth-century versions of the song, he may not have done the work of adapting them: his "Jack-A-Roe" is a craggy variation of the well-known Joan Baez renditions. In these versions, the daughter of a wealthy London merchant is in love with "Jack the Sailor" despite having many other worthy suitors. When Jack ships off to an unnamed war in a distant unnamed land, the daughter attempts to join him, enlisting by donning herself in manly attire. Though she is met by doubt at the recruiting office, she gives her name as "Jack A Roe" and, after claiming "it would not make me tremble to see ten thousand fall," is signed up. Arriving at the tumult after a grisly battle, she miraculously happens upon her wounded beau and finds a doctor to heal his wounds. By song's end the couple is married, and the storyteller casually proposes matrimony to a presumably enchanted listener.

In North America, the practice of women donning men's garb to defend the flag occurred at least as late as the Civil War. In *They Fought Like Demons: Women Soldiers in the American Civil War*, a 2002 book by DeAnne Blanton and Lauren M. Cook, the lives and experiences of some two hundred and fifty women on both sides of the conflict who went to war disguised as men are documented, though the authors believe there are more who remain undetected. One of the more intriguing aspects of their research was that male soldiers usually accepted their female comrades once they were unmasked. As the Civil War dragged on, even the rigid social conventions of the time ebbed away. This was especially true on the Confederate side, where manpower was short and officers were desperate to keep the ranks filled. By 1864 many of the Confederate female soldiers had ceased pretending, growing their hair long again and showing their figures.

There is some mystery regarding the meaning of "A Roe" in the song's title and the girl's name. The title may also be a corruption of Jack Munroe (or Munro), one of the previously mentioned names by which this song may be found in America as well as in the British Isles. It has also been suggested that the "A" is simply a middle initial.

When Joan Baez performed the rendition of "Jack A Roe" that appeared on *In Concert, Part 2*, Dylan may well have been stageside, but on *World Gone Wrong* he credited Tom Paley for turning him on to the song. Paley's version, in any case, is virtually the same as the one sung by Baez.

In his inimitable, elliptical fashion, Dylan gave some impressions of "Jack-A-Roe" in the liner notes to *World Gone Wrong*: "the song cannot be categorized—is worlds away from reality but 'gets inside' reality anyway & strips it of its steel and concrete. inverted symmetry, legally stateless, travelling under a false passport. 'before you get on board, sir . . .' are you any good at what you do? submerge your personality."

As mentioned, Dylan included a wary, upbeat recording of "Jack-A-Roe" on *World Gone Wrong*, his 1993 collection of folk and blues covers, and he briefly performed the song in concert around that time.

ⓐ Jack Elliott
Vanguard Recording Society LP VSD-79151. Released 1964.

"Tedham Porterhouse" was probably the funniest moniker Dylan chose to hide behind for contractual purposes. Here, on this early offering from Ramblin' Jack Elliott, Tedham plays harmonica on "Will the Circle Be Unbroken."

ⓢ "Jack O' Diamonds" (Bob Dylan/Ben Carruthers)
Ben Carruthers, single (1965)
Fairport Convention, *Fairport Convention* (1970)
The Muskrats, *Rock Is Dead* (1986)

Originally appearing in *Some Other Kinds of Songs . . .*, the collection of verse printed on the sleeve of *Another Side of Bob Dylan*, this minor Dylan poem was set to music in 1965 by Ben Carruthers for *Man Without Papers*, a television program on Great Britain's BBC. Fairport Convention also took a swipe at setting the poem to music. All these permutations are at least loosely connected with the original "Jack O'Diamonds" credited to Mance Lipscomb, with whom the prison song (about a magical playing card that may deliver freedom) is most closely associated, though there are a passel of other variations with related titles going back to the mid-1920s and recorded by everybody from Blind Lemon Jefferson to Sippie Wallace, James "Iron Head" Baker, and Odetta.

ⓢ "Jammin' Me" (Bob Dylan/Tom Petty/Mike Campbell)
Tom Petty and the Heartbreakers, single (1987); *Let Me Up (I've Had Enough)* (1987); *Playback* (1995); *Anthology: Through the Years* (2000)

Written during the *Knocked Out Loaded* period in May 1986 when Dylan was renting way too much studio time in Van Nuys, California, for an album that should have been left in the can, "Jammin' Me" might well be described as a slightly dated, free-associative, catalogue-style, politically pretentious rock rant that manages to mention Eddie Murphy, Vanessa Redgrave, and El Salvador. While Tom Petty mentioned in a 1987 interview on VH1 that "we wrote eight or nine verses," the printed lyrics accompanying *Let Me Up*—the loose and rowdy Heartbreakers album on which it appeared—include only six. Petty and company also cut a video version of the song.

Petty discussed writing "Jammin' Me" in somewhat greater detail in the liner notes to the Heartbreakers' 1995 boxed set *Playback*: "Bob Dylan and I wrote that. I was living in an apartment at the Sunset Marquis and Bob came around and wanted to write a few songs for an album he was doing. He took that song 'Got My Mind Made Up' and rewrote the words, the same day we wrote 'Jammin' Me.' It was mostly written while he was reading the entertainment section. That's where Eddie Murphy and Vanessa Redgrave and all those people came into it. Those were Bob lines [for] which I've taken shit for years. It was a good song about the overload of information, how frightening satellites and those things were to us at the time. We both felt overloaded. We wrote it to a slightly different chord progression, then [guitarist] Michael [Campbell] came up with this great progression, that great riff, and I took it without really asking Bob and put it to this different music. Later on I played it back to him and he said, 'Yeah, it works.'"

ⓢ "Jesus Is the One" (Bob Dylan)

Among Dylan's last hard-core gospel compositions, "Jesus Is the One" was written on the road in Oslo, Norway, during his 1981 *Shot of*

J

Love tour and proclaimed at about ten concerts during that swing—paradoxically enough, just as Dylan was slowly returning to secular music.

[S] "Jet Pilot" (Bob Dylan)

Bob Dylan, *Biograph/'65* (1985)
Michel Montecrossa, *Jet Pilot* (2000)

"Jet Pilot" is supposedly the original, shorthand version of what some say would become "Tombstone Blues" (though there seems to be little lyrical or melodic connection between the two songs—"From a Buick 6" seems a more likely possibility). The song offered a rare and humorous peek (complete with a surprise ending involving the true gender of the one being sung about) at the historic 1965 *Highway 61 Revisited* recording sessions when it was released on *Biograph* two decades later. Other interpreters, however, posit that this piece of New York rough trade was recorded at the pre–*Blonde on Blonde* sessions in October 1965, postdating the composition of either one of the two *Highway 61* suggestions. The clearest heads would be wise to just place this minimalist he/she curiosity in a class by itself. At a mere fifty-one seconds, "Jet Pilot" is the shortest song Dylan has ever released.

[S] "Jim Jones" (Traditional/Mick Slocum)

aka "Jim Jones at Botany Bay"
Bob Dylan, *Good as I Been to You* (1992)
Martyn Wyndham-Read, *Undiscovered Australia* (1970)
A. L. Lloyd, *The Great Australian Legend* (1971)
The Bushwackers, *The Shearer's Dream* (1974)
John Kirkpatrick, *Among the Many Attractions at the Show Will Be a Really High Class Band* (1976)
Martin Carthy, *Signs of Life* (1998)

Narrated by a man condemned to the wretched British penal colony at Australia's Botany Bay, "Jim Jones" describes the harsh fate of convicts. "Don't get too gay in Botany Bay," warns the sentencing judge, "or else you'll surely hang." That is unlikely to be a problem, though, as the narrator at one point declares, "I'd rather have drowned in misery/Than gone to New South Wales." Naturally, he dreams of escape—and revenge: "by and by I'll slip my chains . . . /And some dark night . . . /I'll shoot the tyrants one and all." Despite the violence, "Jim Jones" is poignant as well; perhaps that is why Robert Hughes quotes it in brilliantly telling the ghastly story of the penal colonies in *The Fatal Shore*, his late-1980s seminal history of Australia's founding.

There's nothing like a song about tyranny and revenge, and Dylan handles this one with verve. A man faces a judge and is sentenced to work making big rocks into little rocks in New South Wales with the threat of execution by hanging if he does not cooperate. Along the way, his ship encounters pirates and storms, and he declares that he would rather join the pirates or take a one-way trip to Davey Jones's locker than face the brutal conditions awaiting him in port. When he finds himself in the penal colony, he promises to break his chains, join a gang of escapees in the bush, and wreak mortal retribution upon his captors. The way Dylan sings it, there is little doubt that he will.

Sometimes known as "Jim Jones at Botany Bay," the song was printed under that title in Charles MacAlister's *Old Pioneering Days in the Sunny South* in 1907. John Way suggests in *The Telegraph* #44 (winter 1992) that judging from the lyrics, "Jim Jones" was composed between 1828 (when convicted highwayman Bold Jack Donahue, mentioned in the last verse and himself the subject of at least one bad-man ballad, emerged as a "bushranger" escapee) and 1830 (when Donahue was killed). The song, in fact, is of a type called a transportation ballad, specifi-

Illustration of a Hobart Town chain gang in Botany Bay, Australia, 1831.
(Mansell/Time Life Pictures/Getty Images)

cally about convicts being sent to Australia. It is, however, somewhat unique, as A. L. Lloyd points out in his 1967 book *Folk Song in England*: "Most of the transportation ballades are passive enough in outlook; self-pity if not repentance is the mood. None of the surviving songs of the penal settlements shows the smouldering sense of vengefulness that characterises the excellent 'Jim Jones at Botany Bay.'" Lloyd goes on to state that "Jim Jones stands out from the ruck of transportation songs by reason of its strong bloodshot defiance" and asks, "Why has such a well-made mettlesome piece failed to keep its hold on the interest of the singer and audience when flabbier creations on the same theme have ostentatiously survived into our own time?"

Even though the *Good as I Been to You* track listing indicates that Dylan arranged the song or came up with the tune on his own, it has been established that Dylan's arrangement came from Mick Slocum, one of the original three members of the Original Bushwackers and Bullockies Band, later simply the Bushwackers. Based in Melbourne, they became Australia's premier performers of so-called bush music, a variant of Australian folk music closely related to traditional Irish music. After doing for the Australian folk idiom what Fairport Convention did for English folk music, Slocum moved to a new band, the Sundowners.

Dylan's few performances of "Jim Jones" in the early 1990s were extraordinary, as he pitched the song in octave-raising desperation to simulate the flight and revenge of the imprisoned antihero with cinematic and sympathetic depth.

"Jimmy Berman Rag (Gay Lib Rag)" (Allen Ginsberg/Bob Dylan)
aka "Jimmy Berman Newsboy Gay Lib Rag"
Various Artists (performed by Bob Dylan, Allen Ginsberg, et al.), *Disconnected/'71* (1974)
Allen Ginsberg (performed with Bob Dylan, et al.), *First Blues/'71* (1983)

Some sources credit Dylan as assisting on the arrangement of this piece of Ginsberg agitprop. More concretely, it is established that Dylan contributed backing vocals, guitar, organ, and/or piano on this obscure track, which first appeared on poet John Giorno's *Disconnected* compilation collected from the best (and most marketable) of the long-gone but not quite forgotten Dial-a-Poem public-service series available in New York City during the 1970s and early 1980s.

"Joey" (Bob Dylan/Jacques Levy)
Bob Dylan, *Desire* (1975)
Bob Dylan/The Grateful Dead, *Dylan & the Dead* (1987)
Johnny Thunders, *So Alone* (1983)

"Joey" is a remarkable epic noted for its cinematic clarity and operatic grandeur—just try to ignore Dylan's twisted moralizing. Here Dylan paints a picture of a life and death so vivid and precise that every frame can be easily seen and experienced as if the listener were witnessing it on the screen at the neighborhood art-house cinema. Even more striking is Dylan's vernacular-laced rhyme scheme and meter, which make the immediacy of the imagery particularly vital.

"Joey" puzzled Dylan's flock when first released on the popular 1975 *Desire* album, and its revival by Dylan when he hooked up with the Grateful Dead twelve years later was greeted with even greater wonderment. After all, this is a song about Joseph "Crazy Joe" Gallo, a ruthless, yet (to Dylan) romantic New York City mobster who was gunned down while he celebrated his birthday at Umberto's Clam House on the streets of Little Italy in the spring of 1972. Even his critics admit, though, that Dylan pulls off this dusky jewel of a song with sly, black humorous mastery, expressing it as if he were an aging local urchin, with a colloquial eyewitness intimacy that makes it sound like a monologue delivered on a Mulberry Street stoop.

Joey Gallo (born April 6, 1929, Brooklyn, New York; died April 7, 1972, New York City) grew up on the tough Red Hook end of President Street in Brooklyn. He is one of the most maligned and intriguing Mafia leaders of the modern era. Though many rival Mafia men considered him a flaky liability (a reputation that Gallo himself nurtured), his connections with New York's arty high rollers set such a lifestyle standard that future bosses like John Gotti would attempt to emulate him with little success.

In his way, Gallo was a visionary: he saw that as the racial composition of inner-city ghetto America changed, the nature of organized crime had to change as well. He realized that nothing in crime is carved in stone—that

Joseph (Joey) Gallo in the corridor of Brooklyn Courthouse, 1961.

(Photo: Lee Lockwood/Time Life Pictures/Getty Images)

situations and power structures change. Since more and more "street action" would be taken over by blacks and Hispanics, because of sheer mathematics, the mob men who acted first and fast to exploit this would grow in power, compared to those old-line Italian and Jewish gangsters who continued to sneer at the young hoods of color moving in on the action.

Crazy Joe's epiphany crystallized when he befriended black criminals during a trip to prison for extortion in the 1960s. Before the visit to the hoosegow, Gallo was regarded as merely a violent enforcer. But during his stay, he broke down convict color lines by having a black barber cut his hair; he also became buddies with Leroy "Nicky" Barnes, tutoring him on taking over control of the drug racket in New York's Harlem and elsewhere. More significantly, he sent released black prisoners to work in crime operations controlled by his family.

Gallo used his prison time well. An omnivorous reader, he could fluently discourse on Camus, Flaubert, Kafka, Balzac, Sartre, and Céline upon his release in 1971.

Back on the street, it was back to "business as usual." But Gallo began moving in different circles, becoming quite a unique celebrity, a sort of "house mobster" in the homes of various show-business people. It was a great cover for a guy who was muscling in on the turf of his rival crime lords.

In 1972, Gallo was in the Copacabana nightclub celebrating his forty-third birthday at a party. About 4:00 A.M. the party broke up, and Gallo, his bodyguard, and four female friends and relatives adjourned to the Chinatown–Little Italy area in search of food. They ended up at Umberto's Clam House, where Gallo and his bodyguard sat at a table with their backs to the door, feeling secure that the Mafia code barring any rubouts in Little Italy would protect them. This proved to be a fatal error.

The bosses made an exception in Crazy Joe's case. A man walked in with a .38-caliber pistol in his hand. Women screamed and customers fell to the floor as the gunman opened up on Gallo and his bodyguard. Gallo fled to the front door but his attacker followed him outside. There he pumped more hot lead into Gallo, who staggered across the sidewalk to a few feet from his Cadillac, where he collapsed and died.

Dylan's epitaph is as good as any Red Hook tombstone peddler's: "Joey, Joey/King of the streets, child of clay/Joey, Joey/What made them want to come and blow you away?"

In the summer of 1975, Dylan began working on the songs that would make up his album *Desire* with Jacques Levy, a theatrical master of all trades. "Joey" was written in mid-July after a dinner at the New York apartment of actor Jerry Orbach and his wife, Marty, both of whom had been close friends with Gallo. After an evening of stories about the gangster (including tales about Gallo's wedding in the very apartment in which they were sitting), Dylan and Levy returned to the theater rat's flat and wrote "Joey."

Initial reaction to "Joey" was not positive. Many felt that, along with potentially cheapening the message in "Hurricane," *Desire*'s other biographical song, protesting the plight of then-imprisoned former prizefighter Rubin Carter, Dylan was glorifying the Mafia. Fortunately, literary heads have cooled over time with the acceptance that Dylan's fascination with the social pariah is long-standing.

As recorded on a promotional disc released by CBS in 1981, Dylan discussed the place of "Joey" in his oeuvre with New York City DJ Dave Herman: "I think what I intended to do is just show the individualism of that certain type of breed, or certain type of person that must do that. But there is some type of standard I have for whoever I'm writing about. I mean, it amazes me that I wrote a song about Joey Gallo."

As Dylan told Paul Zollo in 1991 for Zollo's book *Songwriters on Songwriting, Expanded 4th Edition*: "['Joey' is] a tremendous song. And you'd only know that singing it night after night. You know who got me singing that song? [Jerry] Garcia. Yeah. He got me singing that song again. He said that's one of the best songs ever written. Coming from *him*, it was hard to know which way to take that [*laughs*]. He got me singing that song again with them [the Grateful Dead]. . . . It was amazing how, right from the get-go, it had a life of its own, it just ran out of the gate and it just kept on getting better and better and better and it keeps on getting better. It's in its infant stages as a performance thing. Of course, it's a long song. But, to me, not to blow my own horn, but to me the song is a Homer ballad. More so than 'A Hard Rain,' which is a long song, too. But, to me, 'Joey' has a Homeric quality to it that you don't hear everyday."

Some Dylanists still cringe when he begins singing "Joey" in concert, but it has improved remarkably with age, aided by Dylan's wise decision not to sing about half of the lyrics as originally rendered and recorded. Dylan had never performed "Joey" in concert until 1987 shows with the Dead, and although it didn't translate particularly well at the stadium venues where it was first delivered, the song's revival evidently intrigued Dylan, as he has kept performing it occasionally in his post-Dead incarnations. It has blossomed into a slick and powerful concert sledgehammer, lately with a never-say-die mouth harp solo that vied with the guitars for center stage.

For more info on Joey Gallo, find a copy of Donald Goddard's book *Joey* (New York: Harper & Row, 1974).

◪ "John Brown" (Bob Dylan)

aka "Jon Brown"

Various Artists (performed by Bob Dylan as "Blind Boy Grunt"), *Broadside Ballads, Volume 1* (1963); *The Best of Broadside 1962–1988* (2000)

Bob Dylan, *MTV Unplugged* (1995)

The Staple Singers, *Pray On* (1967); *I Shall Be Unreleased/'67* (1991)

Rabbit McKay, *Passing Through* (1969)

Heron, *Twice as Nice and Half the Price* (1971)

Jim Dickinson, *Dixie Fried* (1972); *Free Beer Tomorrow* (2002)

Bettina Jonic, *The Bitter Mirror* (1975)

"John Brown," a biting screed demolishing Hollywood conceptions of war heroes, was written in 1963 during the early days of the U.S. military involvement in Vietnam and at the height of the cold war. Sharing the tone and subject matter of *Johnny Got His Gun* (Dalton Trumbo's World War–I era novel, published in 1938), "John Brown" is a story about a boy who leaves home to fight in an unnamed war on unnamed foreign soil for a never explicated cause. His mother expresses her pride at his decision and brags of his feats to "everyone in the neighborhood." Such euphoria is sobered, however, when the mother goes down to meet her son at the train station upon his return— only to find him crippled, blind, and maimed. When she asks him how he came to be this way, he tells her in an angry, unrecognizable voice that when he went to battle, he realized he was merely a "puppet in a play," that he could only "kill someone or else die trying," and saw that his enemy's face "looked just like mine." He then coldly drops his worthless medals into her hand and hobbles off to a life of despair. An event like this may be impersonally reported on the news, but Dylan brings home all of its horrifying consequences in his embittered, cinematic composition.

The roots of the song may lie in the lyrics of "Mrs. McGrath," thought to be a traditional ballad, and sung to the tune of "900 Miles" with a free adaptation of that traditional melody. "Mrs. McGrath," according to William Cole's *Folk Songs of England, Ireland, Scotland, and Wales* (Garden City, New York: Doubleday, 1961), hails from the late eighteenth or early nineteenth century, when many poor Irish boys, in search of food and shelter, were joining British forces going to war against Napoleon. "Mrs. McGrath" (Cole notes that it's pronounced "McGrah") is a "bitter and ruefully witty commentary on that unfortunate situation, much as is the well-known 'Johnny, We Hardly Knew Ye.'" The similarity between "Mrs. McGrath" and "John Brown" may be seen clearly when Mrs. McGrath goes to meet her son on his return: "Well, up comes Ted without any legs/And in their place he's got two wooden pegs/She kissed him a dozen times or two/Saying, 'Holy Moses, it isn't you!'"

After writing and initially performing "John Brown" in the autumn of 1962, Dylan first formally recorded the song in January 1963 at the New York City offices of *Broadside* magazine in a version released later that year as "Jon Brown" on *Broadside Ballads, Volume 1*. A second, rarer version was cut in August 1963 for a Witmark demo LP, and a live version was recorded on April 12, 1963, at New York's Town Hall for the never-released *Bob Dylan in Concert* LP. *Broadside* published "John Brown" in issue #22 (March 1963) and there indicated a 1962 copyright for the song. Dylan did not perform the song again until his sets with the Dead. Thereafter he intermittently worked it into his repertoire during his acoustic sets in the 1990s, and somewhat surprisingly played it at his *MTV Unplugged* session in 1994. By 2001, as U.S. bombs were falling on Kabul, "John Brown" was the showstopper of his fall

A one-legged man waits to cross a road in Vienna, Austria, 1947.

(Photo: Ernst Haas/Getty Images)

tour. Occupying center stage and lit by a single spotlight, accompanied by the barest of instrumentation from his band in an arrangement that returned the song to its Appalachian, banjo-flavored, snaggle-toothed roots, Dylan, singing in a bronchial rasp that might frighten even the Marlboro Man into a tar-free life, unflinchingly told the story of the doomed boy leaving home once again to fight "a good old-fashioned war."

◪ *John Wesley Harding*

Columbia Records LP CL-2804, CD CK-9604, CS CS-9604; Sony Music Entertainment, Inc., SACD 90320. Recorded October 17, November 6, and November 29, 1967.

Released December 27, 1967. Produced by Bob Johnston. Liner notes by Bob Dylan. Cover photo by John Berg.

Bob Dylan—guitar, harmonica, piano, keyboards, vocals. Pete Drake—guitar. Kenny A. Buttrey—drums. Charlie McCoy—bass.

"John Wesley Harding," "As I Went Out One Morning," "All Along the Watchtower," "I Dreamed I Saw St. Augustine," "The Ballad of Frankie Lee and Judas Priest," "Drifter's Escape," "Dear Landlord," "I Am a Lonesome Hobo," "I Pity the Poor Immigrant," "The Wicked Messenger," "Down Along the Cove," "I'll Be Your Baby Tonight"

John Wesley Harding was a shock to the music industry and Dylan's fans alike when it was released amid intense anticipation in very late 1967. Not only was it his first official album of new work to be released since his much-discussed motorcycle accident in Woodstock, New York, a year and a half before, but was also a total about-face from the humid, psychedelic, electrified rock 'n' roll impressionism that had marked his previous three efforts: *Bringing It All Back Home, Highway 61 Revisited*, and *Blonde on Blonde*. As provocative as Dylan's electrification had been when he plugged in to perform rock 'n' roll at the Newport Folk Festival in 1965 a mere two and a half years earlier, the pensive acoustic strains heard on *John Wesley Harding* spun almost as many heads. The record did excellent business. It rose to No. 2 on the charts, lasting there a month for its twenty-one-week total run. It earned Dylan his fifth straight gold album. There were no singles released from the LP and no known outtakes.

Reflecting on his recent biblical study and informed by the rustic sound of rural America and flush with its myths, Dylan mixed apocalyptic vision ("All Along the Watchtower"), religious parable ("I Dreamed I Saw St. Augustine" and "The Wicked Messenger"), personal conflict ("Dear Landlord"), the tall tale ("The Ballad of Frankie Lee and Judas Priest"), forbidden

love ("Down Along the Cove"), and social diagnosis ("Drifter's Escape"), all of which continue to reveal layers of meaning and appreciation. Each song but one ("Frankie Lee and Judas Priest") stuck to a strict three-verse structure, as if Dylan were intentionally challenging himself to present a portrait of unified simplicity as far from the psychedelic vortical watercolor of *Blonde on Blonde* and the like as he could. It was as if Jackson Pollock had suddenly decided to paint like Grandma Moses or William Faulkner to write a haiku, and is a remarkable testament to Dylan's talent that he could shift poetic styles so fluently or dramatically.

Despite its subtleties and demands, *John Wesley Harding* managed to be highly influential on account of the superb quality of the writing as well as for the way it broke ground for and anticipated the many major changes that were about to transpire in popular music—particularly the rise and success of such acoustically based singer-songwriters as Joni Mitchell, Jackson Browne, and Crosby, Stills, Nash, and Young. Even the theretofore hopelessly psychedelic Grateful Dead were bitten by the bug, as evidenced by acoustic concert sets and the release of *Workingman's Dead* and *American Beauty* in 1970.

The quiet, on-the-surface-simple *John Wesley Harding* comprised open-ended yarns that were as much parables as songs—the best-known of which has turned out to be "All Along the Watchtower," thanks to Jimi Hendrix.

Still, had the world been more aware of *The Basement Tapes*—Dylan's work at Big Pink with the Hawks in the period between *Blonde on Blonde* and *John Wesley Harding*—the shift would not have seemed quite so seismic.

Part of the reason *John Wesley Harding* came as such a shock to so many owes to the pop-music milieu into which it was released. In 1967, pop music was anything but austere.

J

Lush, heavily produced albums like the Beatles' *Sgt. Pepper's Lonely Hearts Club Band* and the Rolling Stones' *Their Satanic Majesties Request* were the era's standard setters, so an album as minimalist and retro as *John Wesley Harding* seemed like it blew in from another century.

It was no accident that *John Wesley Harding* sounded the way it did. In fact, as Dylan told Anthony Scaduto in the latter's *Bob Dylan: An Intimate Biography* (New York: Grosset & Dunlap, 1971), "I would have liked a good sound, more musical, more steel guitar, more piano. More *music.* . . . At that time," Dylan commented, "so many people were into electronics, and I didn't know anything about that. I didn't even know anybody who knew it. I didn't sit down and plan that sound. It wasn't a question of this is what I'm doing and come over here."

In 1985, Dylan said in the *Biograph* liner notes that "We recorded that album, and I didn't know what to make of it. . . . You've got to know or you don't know and I really didn't known about that album at all. So I figured the best thing to do would be to put it out as quickly as possible, call it *John Wesley Harding* because that was one song that I had an idea what it was about, why it was even on the album. I figured I'd call the album that, call attention to it, make it something special . . . the spelling on that album, I just thought that was the way he spelled his name. . . . People have made a lot out of it, as if it was some sort of ink blot test or something. But it never was intended to be anything else but just a bunch of songs, really, maybe it was better'n I thought."

In addition to containing some of Dylan's most intriguing songs, *John Wesley Harding* also boasts one of his most curious album covers. Front and center is a very rural-looking Dylan wearing what appears to be his *Blonde on Blonde* jacket and *Nashville Skyline* hat. He is flanked by two exotic-looking men wearing unusual outfits—Bengali Bauls, it turned out—with a more conventionally dressed man who appears to be a local farmer, behind. The Baul culture of Bengal and India is distinguished for its music, and the Bauls on *John Wesley Harding* were houseguests of Dylan's manager, Albert Grossman, at the time the picture was taken, as they were giving concerts in New York then. The Bauls, incidentally, once mentioned that they rehearsed with Dylan and that the session was recorded. The other man in the photo is sometimes reported to be a fellow by the name of Charlie Joy, supposedly a local Woodstock carpenter. Some have suggested that Dylan's choice to populate the cover of this album with individuals representing an Indian music tradition was a swipe at the Beatles, who were in the midst of their very high-profile visit to the subcontinent in pursuit of instant karma with the Maharishi Mahesh Yogi. Also, George Harrison's embrace of Ravi Shankar–flavored Hinduism was not at all on the same page as the Bauls, an iconoclastic religious sect whose philosophy might be described conservatively as libertine. Some people claim to see the faces of the Beatles hidden in the tree in the background of the *John Wesley Harding* cover picture. It was almost as if Dylan was stripping down the Beatles' *Sgt. Pepper's Lonely Hearts Club Band* (music and album cover included) to its bare essentials.

Dylanists have had a field day interpreting and reinterpreting *John Wesley Harding*'s meaning. The more arcane speculation involves Dylan's embrace of kabbalah, an intense form of Jewish mysticism, as the theme of the album. These scholars suggest that while adopting the persona of a nineteenth-century American visionary troubadour on the order of a Walt Whitman or a Henry David Thoreau, Dylan was also imbuing the album with more

J

than a touch of Old Testament philosophy. They specifically point to the album title's initials (JWH), consisting of three-quarters of the tetragrammaton JHWH, a transliteration of the four Hebrew letters that form a biblical proper name of God (Yahweh). According to strict Jewish law, one should never say or write God's name out completely lest his mighty wrath be provoked. This is a theme Dylan would touch on later in his 1983 song "I and I."

Perhaps this is why Dylan remarked, in an interview with Jonathan Cott published in the November 16, 1978, issue of *Rolling Stone*, that "*John Wesley Harding* was a fearful album—just dealing with fear, but dealing with the devil in a fearful way, almost. All I wanted to do was get the words right."

Anthony Scaduto led the pack of *John Wesley Harding* decoders by making a cogent case in his 1971 Dylan biography (referred to on the preceding page) that the album represents a complex system of interconnected symbolism as detailed as anything this side of a Tibetan mandala sand painting.

Dylan's liner notes (also titled "John Wesley Harding") capture the ironic, sometimes dark, yet humorously optimistic tone of the album in their elliptical New Testament parody.

Even more than three decades down the pike, *John Wesley Harding* still stands as a landmark album marking a huge change in Dylan's writing style. No longer does he seem a man intent on changing the world as he looks forward to the crooning vistas of *Nashville Skyline*.

[S] "John Wesley Harding" (Bob Dylan)

Bob Dylan, *John Wesley Harding* (1967)
McKendree Spring, *McKendree Spring* (1969)
Winny and Amy, *Hommage à Bob Dylan* (1974)
Wesley Willis, *Black Light Diner* (1997)
Second Floor, *Plays Dylan* (2001)

Setting the tone for the eponymous album it leads off, "John Wesley Harding" is a spare, three-verse, chorusless parable about a traveling man who "carried a gun in every hand" but "was never known to hurt an honest man."

Dylan's character is more or less named after but is not necessarily based on history's John Wesley Hardin, the infamous Lone Star State desperado. But rather than tell the John Wesley Hardin story, Dylan, in scholar and critic Bill King's phrase (in his unpublished 1975 dissertation, "The Artist in the Marketplace"), "condenses into poetic form the mythic outline of the outlaw hero." Dylan's song is a bad-man ballad about a decent man.

As cast by Dylan, "John Wesley Harding" works as a fable in miniature; Dylan consciously employs a rough folk voice to aid in creating his musical daguerreotype (it gives the song "an open-range roll, the feel of caked mud on the boots," says Dylan biographer Robert Shelton in his 1986 book *No Direction Home: The Life and Music of Bob Dylan*). Keeping the story brief, Dylan has Harding disappear, just as he has from most of the history books. The image of this Clint Eastwood–like protagonist who holds guns in both paws must have freaked out the era's whole youth culture, reeling as its members were from Vietnam and its domestic consequences.

[S] "Jokerman" (Bob Dylan)

Bob Dylan, single (1983); *Infidels* (1983); *Bob Dylan's Greatest Hits, Volume 3* (1994)
Caetano Veloso, *Circulado Ao Vivo* (1997)

Juxtaposing images, lyrical references, literary sources, and wide-ranging concepts and relating them with the mysterious wisdom of an oracle or the randomness of some kind of cockeyed seer, Dylan presents one of his most dramatic, beguiling visions in song in "Jokerman."

Whether he is talking about himself, his muse, Jesus Christ, Native America's coyote of ancient legend, some trickster saint drawn from the fog of mythohistory, an archetypal superhero of his own concoction and composite, or the drifter he met in a West L.A. hash house will probably never be known. More than likely, he seems to be explaining his turn away from hard-core, take-no-prisoners Christian fundamentalism to a more ecumenical though still spiritually potent form of expression, all the while warning of the hazards of the modern world in a manner similar to that employed in a couple of other exemplary compositions from this era: "Every Grain of Sand" and "Groom's Still Waiting at the Altar."

Reggae's rhythm masters Sly Dunbar and Robbie Shakespeare appear on *Infidels* and their mark on "Jokerman" is evident. Dylan's keen interest in the music and culture of the Caribbean (especially Bob Marley's unique Rastafarian amalgam of Judaism, Christianity, paganism, and politics) had to have been a factor in his concept and execution of "Jokerman." And he may well have been aware of "Joker Man Blues," a semi-obscure song from the semi-obscure Piedmont bluesman Buddy Moss.

With its brooding lyricism, "Jokerman" surfs along the crest of the major issues and stories in Judeo-Christianity and dives right into a chiseled synthesis of riffs from the Old and New Testaments in the very first line of the song: "Standing on the water casting your bread." Here we are pointed toward both Christ's stroll on the Dead Sea and the venerable Old Testament proverb from Ecclesiastes 11:1 ("Cast thy bread upon the waters: for thou shalt find it after many days") that serves as a dictate to mankind. The latter is also the textual foundation for the Passover rite when Jews cast bread crumbs into a river as a symbol of the casting out of sins—an image and theme

Dylan was dealing with as early as "Gates of Eden" nearly twenty years before he wrote "Jokerman."

As is the case with many Dylan epics, the depth and intensity of the lyrics to "Jokerman" are sustained over an extraordinary number of verses—yet more evidence of an artist overflowing with the abundance of creation. We are taken on yet another journey through Dylan's Night Town, which includes stops at pagan idols, classical allusion, the Bible, medieval mysticism, romantic poetry, movies, and the blues. Wasn't it Greek mythology's Hercules who was born with a snake in both fists? Dylan throws much of the Old Testament in here: the books of Leviticus and Deuteronomy detail Hebraic law, and the references to the wicked cities Sodom and Gomorrah seem a clear destination of where Dylan thinks humanity is headed. And surely Dylan is aware of the early-nineteenth-century British poet John Keats, who, like Dylan, employed the image of the nightingale to haunting effect. Dylan, as we know, loves cinema, and his mention of the rifleman and the preacher, two of the more archetypal characters found in his favored B-western film genre, help paint his portrait of an uncertain world filled with unsavory desperadoes. All these elements contribute to the kind of paranoia familiar to those who have strolled down Desolation Row as night comes stepping in. Dylan's mention of those "nightsticks, water cannons, tear gas, padlocks, Molotov cocktails and rocks behind every curtain" is delivered with the vehemence of someone quite certain that another pogrom is inevitable.

And Dylan comes off as sensitive to the role and risk of the artist shaman (i.e., himself) quite accustomed to displaying the big picture to an audience of any size. Whether seen as a Messiah or false prophet, such a figure is always going to be in at least a little bit over his head, as revealed in lines like "You're a man of the mountains, you can walk on the clouds/Manipulator of crowds, you're a dream twister."

Through it all, a kind of salvation is offered as at least a possibility: "Freedom just around the corner from you."

But what does it all mean? Dylan seems to be searching for some ultimate answer to the grand sweep of the universal mystery as he beseeches the Jokerman for a little insight. Predictably, the illusory Jokerman does not respond. Again, Dylan is leaving his listeners to their own devices in constructing an answer.

Typical of Dylan, he claimed not to have been satisfied with the final cut. As he told Paul Zollo in 1991 and as it appeared in Zollo's *Songwriters on Songwriting, Expanded 4th Edition*, "That's ['Jokerman'] a song that got away from me. Lots of songs on that album [*Infidels*] got away from me. They just did. . . . They hung around too long. They were better before they were tampered with. Of course, it was me tampering with them. [*Laughs*] Yeah. That could have been a good song. It could've been. . . . It probably didn't hold up for me because in my mind it had been written and rewritten and written again. One of those kind of things."

Dylan teamed up with Madison Avenue adman George Lois to make a then-unusual video for "Jokerman." Utilizing imagery from classic art, mythology, history, and Dylan's career combined with the lyrics floating by subtitle-style, the video creates a kind of cinematic sand painting.

Mark Knopfler contributed some crystalline guitar work on the *Infidels* release of "Jokerman." It did not chart as a single. Nonetheless, Dylan performed the song heavily during his 1984 tour but then put it aside until the Never Ending Tour of 1994 and 1995, when he opened many shows with blazing renditions of this piece of rock kabbalah. After a 1998 one-off, Dylan revived "Jokerman" for a few shows at the butt end of his 2003 European tour and sang, reportedly, with the aid of a lyric sheet.

"Just a Little Bit" (Del Gordon/Rosco Gordon)

Rosco Gordon, *Just a Little Bit* (1993)
Etta James, *Tell Mama* (1968)
Jimi Hendrix, *In the Beginning* (1972)
Delbert McClinton, *Keeper of the Flame* (1979)
Joe Louis Walker, *Live at Slim's, Volume 2* (1992)
Elvis Presley, *Walk a Mile in My Shoes* (1995)
Them, *Story of Them Featuring Van Morrison* (1997)
Robert Lockwood Jr., *Complete Trix Recordings* (1999)

Dylan only performed the 1960 hit "Just a Little Bit" at one 1981 concert, in an apparent response to an audience request. Rosco Gordon, another secret hero of Western Hemisphere music, certainly brought the song to national attention and is sometimes credited with its composition, though his brother Del is also sometimes cited, as is the team of Ralph Bass, John Thornton, and Fats Washington.

Gordon (born April 10, 1934, Memphis; died July 11, 2002, Queens, New York) was a rhythm-and-blues singer and piano player whose influence on reggae was even more profound than the mark he left on rock 'n' roll. Beginning in the 1950s, he had a string of hits that included a signature shuffling beat that first came to be known as "Rosco's rhythm." In the late 1950s he toured widely, reaching South America and the Caribbean, where his off-kilter rhythmic approach helped shape the sound of early ska, a direct precursor of reggae. Gordon's songs, like "Booted," "No More Doggin'," "Do the Chicken," and "Just a Little Bit," easily filtered into the burgeoning rock scene of the late 1950s and early 1960s, but for years he earned no royalties. Paid a mere $250 for "Just a Little Bit," which became one of the most popular rock and R&B standards of the 1960s, selling more than four million copies in cover versions by the likes of Elvis and the Beatles, Gordon enjoyed no financial bonanza through his talents. "When I found I had lost the rights to over three hundred songs," he once said, "it felt like someone was choking me when I tried to sing."

Becoming so heartsick with the music biz, he quit in the early 1960s, moved to New York, and bought a stake in a dry-cleaning business after winning a poker game with a pair of deuces. By the end of the decade he began edging back into music, founding the Bab-Roc label, which he operated out of his home. It wasn't until 1981 that he took the concert stage again and resumed touring a few years later. A vital performer and recording artist, Gordon released his last album, *Memphis, Tennessee*, in 2000. A great sketch of an elderly but spry Gordon can be seen in the third installment of the PBS Martin Scorsese–produced series *The Blues* ("The Road to Memphis"), directed by Richard Pearce. The program mentioned that, true blues road warrior that Gordon was, his bags were packed for a gig in Milwaukee when he died.

"Justine" (Don Harris/Dewey Terry)

Don & Dewey, *Jungle Hop* (1991)
The Righteous Brothers, *Moonglow Years* (1991)
Sunrays, *For Collectors Only: Vintage Rays* (1996)
Johnny Legend, *Rockabilly Bastard: Best of Johnny Legend* (1997)

During his first tour with Tom Petty and the Heartbreakers in the winter of 1986, Dylan opened a series of Pacific Rim concerts with Don and Dewey's 1957 high, frantic hit "Justine," about a no-nonsense party girl who leaves her man desperate for a good night's sleep: "She a mama's, papa's, sister's, brother's, uncle's crazy child/Wow!"

A rock 'n' roll Hydra sounding like an adrenalized Ray Charles in duplicate, Don Harris (born June 18, 1938, Pasadena, California; died December 1, 1999, Los Angeles) and Dewey Terry (born July 17, 1937, Los Angeles) cut a string of high-octane novelty rockers for Specialty Records in the late 1950s and early 1960s, only to watch other acts ride their gimmick to greater acclaim and paydirt. Like that multiheaded mythological beast, Don and Dewey seemed linked at the literal and figurative hip from birth. Raised in Southern California, they met as eleven-year-olds in typically serendipitous showbiz fashion: Dewey was walking down the street and heard Don practicing. He liked what he heard, walked to the front door, and knocked like opportunity personified. Ascending from high school auditorium gigs to the Squires (a local Southern California doo-wop outfit) to Billy Berg's (the famed Hollywood boîte where Charlie Parker and Dizzy Gillespie had introduced bebop to the West Coast a decade before), the duo landed at the Las Palmas on Sunset Boulevard, where they were scouted by Art Rupe, the unsavory weasel who headed Specialty Records. Anxious to replace Little Richard, who, after seeing the Soviet spacecraft *Sputnik* arc over the Australian stadium where he was performing, found religion and quit rock 'n' roll, Rupe courted and signed the duo. Billed by Specialty as the "Twin Little Richards," Don & Dewey set off on a Chitlin' Circuit that included the likes of Screamin' Jay Hawkins, Big Maybelle, Redd Foxx, and Moms Mabley, with a stop or two at Harlem's Temple of Soul: the Apollo Theater. Though their star dimmed through the mid-'60s, they stayed active, performing on hundreds of bandstands across the land, participating in the secular second coming of Little Richard and an annual stint at the Dunes in Las Vegas.

Describing their act in his October 21, 1999, *L.A. Weekly* article, Jonny Whiteside wrote:

> Melding the gospel passion of Sister Rosetta Tharpe, the soul grit of James Brown, the tortured blues of Guitar Slim and the lusty carnival rock & roll of Little Richard, they jammed it all into a reckless beat grinder, twisted the crank and delivered the final product with a howling force that could only have come from the streets of Los Angeles.
>
> The Don & Dewey mix of heat, jive and unadulterated talent was a shock in its day. Not yet 21 when they started on Specialty, these cats were upstarts, hardcore; they not only wrote, played and produced all their songs, they both flat-out Screamed Into The Microphone. When they weren't hollering, they spoke in wildly poetic, almost indecipherable tongues (*langga langga oli-oki changa-chang*). They did the jungle hop with the beeb-a-lee bop, mammer-jammered at the hootenanner and got clean for their mama's papa's sister's brother's uncle's crazy child—the one with the champagne eyes. They did it all, leaping from slam to simmer on perfectly vocalized close-harmony ballads that anticipated the glories of mid-'60s soul with blueprint accuracy. Hell, when Dewey went into a recitation, Don even urged him to "Go on, *rap!*"

Harris eventually traded his guitar for a violin in the 1960s and, billed as "Sugarcane" Harris (a nickname reportedly given to him many years before by Johnny Otis, on account of Harris's reputation as a ladies' man), sawed his rocked-out fiddle for the likes of John Mayall and Frank Zappa. There are a thousand Sugarcane Harris stories to go along with his extravagant personality. Like the only time he ever arrived exactly on time at rehearsal, violin in hand, announcing he was ready. According to the same *L.A. Weekly* article referenced above, the bandleader's jaw dropped and Don said, "You said two o'clock sharp, right?" to which the leader replied, "Yeah but the rehearsal was two weeks ago!"

Don and Dewey reunited in the 1990s for U.S. and European gigs. After Sugarcane's death at decade's end, Terry continued a low-key performing and recording career and is still based in Southern California.

[S] "Just Like a Woman" (Bob Dylan)

Bob Dylan, single (1966); *Blonde on Blonde* (1966), *Bob Dylan's Greatest Hits* (1967); *Bob Dylan at Budokan* (1979); *Biograph/'66* (1985); *Hard to Handle* (video) (1986); *The Bootleg Series, Volume 4: Bob Dylan Live 1966—The "Royal Albert Hall" Concert* (1998); *Masterpieces* (1978); *The Bootleg Series, Volume 5: Live 1975—The Rolling Thunder Revue* (2002)
Bob Dylan/The Band, *Before the Flood* (1974)
Various Artists (performed by Bob Dylan), *The Concert for Bangladesh* (1971)
Bob Dylan/Various Artists (performed by Richie Havens), *Bob Dylan: The 30th Anniversary Concert Celebration* (1993)
Jonathan King, *Or Then Again* (1966)
Richie Havens, *Mixed Bag* (1967); *On Stage* (1972); *Sings Beatles & Dylan* (1990); *Resume: The Best of Richie Havens* (1993)
Gary Burton, *Tennessee Firebird* (1967)
David Newman, *House of David* (1967)
The Hollies, *Hollies Sing Dylan* (1969); *Long Cool Woman* (1979)
Area Code 615, *Area Code Six One Five* (1969)
Joe Cocker, *With a Little Help from My Friends* (1969); *Long Voyage Home* (1995); *Anthology* (1999)
Danny Cox, *Birth Announcement* (1969)
Kentucky Express, *Kentucky Express* (1969)
Nina Simone, *Here Comes the Sun* (1971); *Sings Songs of the Poets* (1976); *Let It Be Me* (1987); *Classics* (1995); *Nina Simone* (1997)

Rick Nelson, *Rudy the Fifth* (1971); *Rick Nelson and the Stone Canyon Band, Volume 2* (1997)
Bob Gibson, *Bob Gibson* (1971)
John Lee Hooker, *Coast to Coast* (1971)
Mike Batt Orchestra, *Portrait of Bob Dylan* (1972)
Roberta Flack, *Chapter Two* (1972)
New Edition, *Sunshine Saturday* (1976)
Marie Cain, *Living Alone* (1976)
Joe Bourne, *It All Comes Back* (1977)
Manfred Mann, *Semi Detached Suburban* (1979); *Chapter Two: The Best of the Fontana Years* (1994)
Rod Stewart, *Tonight I'm Yours* (1981)
Larry Norman, *Barking at the Ants* (1981); *Ruff Mix III* (1991)
Doug Sahm, *Return of the Formerly Brothers* (1989)
The Byrds, *The Byrds* (1990)
Bill Frisell, *Have a Little Faith* (1992)
Judy Collins, *Judy Sings Dylan . . . Just Like a Woman* (1993)
Stevie Nicks (performed with Bob Dylan, harmonica), *Street Angel* (1994)
The Philosopher Kings, *The Philosopher Kings* (1994)
Phil Carmen, *Bob Dylan's Dream* (1996)
Bugs Henderson and the Shuffle Kings, *Four Tens Strike Again* (1996)
John Waite, *When You Were Mine* (1997)
Insol, *Insol* (1998)
Steve Howe, *Portraits of Bob Dylan* (1999)
Andy Hill, *It Takes a Lot to Laugh* (2000)
Various Artists (performed by Eric Bibb), *Blues on Blonde on Blonde* (2003)
Jeff Buckley, *Live at Sin-é* (2003)
Various Artists (performed by Lehbanchuleh), *Blowin' in the Wind: A Reggae Tribute to Bob Dylan* (2003)

Purportedly inspired by socialite/artiste Edie Sedgwick, an archetypal rich girl gone bad, but probably also alluding to Joan Baez and any one of a number of femmes fatales spinning in his orbit, "Just Like a Woman" is not only one of Dylan's most popular songs but also one of his most controversial. Yet whether interpreted as a misogynistic rant or a darkly affectionate testa-ment to eternal misunderstanding between the sexes, "Just Like a Woman" remains most appealing as a lilting confessional of a faded and perhaps clandestine romance.

This is one of Dylan's most expertly crafted pop songs, and its radio-friendliness not only translated into significant airplay at the time of its release but has kept it in at least light rotation on those classic rock and (gulp!) golden-oldies FM radio bandwidths. Could such a literal, sharp, and singular song crack the Top 40 today as "Just Like a Woman" did in 1966? The answer to that question would probably speak to both Dylan's talents and popular culture's decay over the course of the past four decades. When released as an A-side single, "Just Like a Woman" hit No. 33 on the *Billboard* chart.

At least as early as the beginning of the 1970s, charges of misogyny were hurled Dylan's way as reported and described in Robert Shelton's 1986 Dylan biography *No Direction Home*. Feminist critic Marion Meade wrote in the *New York Times* of March 14, 1971, that "there's no more complete catalogue of sex-ist slurs" than "Just Like a Woman," and goes on to point out that Dylan "defines women's nat-ural traits as greed, hypocrisy, whining and hysteria." But while the song's title, a dismissive male platitude, might easily and justifiably anger women, serving as even more grist for Meade's arguments, Dylan (a master of irony if ever there was one) was most likely merely toy-ing with that platitude. After all, doesn't the narrator give at least a vague accounting of his actions and sensitivities in the song's bridge (always a good place to get to the heart of the matter) when he sings, "It was raining from the first/And I was dying there of thirst/So I came in here/And your long-time curse hurts/But what's worse/Is this pain in here/I can't stay in here/Ain't it clear that—/I just can't fit/Yes, I believe it's time for us to quit")? And if he doesn't exactly clear things up with surrealisms like "Tonight as I stand inside the rain" or "With her fog, her amphetamines and her pearls" while at the same time shifting the point of view of this state-of-the-sexual-disunion address from the third person to the second person and back again, Dylan does succeed in portraying a defensive but maturing guy genuinely sorry, but not solely guilty, for the way things have turned out. Ultimately, Dylan's poem on the failure of human relationships can be seen as criticizing sexist men as much as the woman, or women, who let them down. Would a man who supposedly disrespects women so much ever inspect the shades of a romantic relationship with the nuanced scrutiny our singer applies to his subject here?

"I think I was on the road," Dylan recalled of writing "Just Like a Woman" in the 1985 *Biograph* liner notes. "I think I wrote it in Kansas City or something, on Thanksgiving, yeah I'm pretty sure I did . . . I was invited over to somebody's house for Thanksgiving dinner but I didn't go, didn't feel like doing anything. I wasn't hungry, I stayed in my hotel room and wrote this."

Though Dylan has not performed "Just Like a Woman" as frequently as some of the other classics in his catalogue, the song has barely missed a tour. A certain highlight of his acoustic sets in 1966 and 1974, "Just Like a Woman" has remained a constant confessional in both semiacoustic and electric arrangements through just about all of Dylan's incarnations. As Never Ending Tour fodder, "Just Like a Woman" became a minor-key honky-tonk tune with the words slurred into nearly incomprehensible gusts: "But she breaks, uh, jusslikealilgirllll."

Edie Sedgwick (born April 30, 1943, Santa Barbara, California; died November 15, 1971, Santa Barbara) was allegedly a subject of "Just Like a Woman." The lyrics concerning the fog,

amphetamines, and pearls are seen as directly linked to her. Raised in a wealthy California family with roots in New England's early history, Sedgwick attached herself to Andy Warhol's Factory, the artist's creative sanctuary described by Warhol's biographer Victor Bockris as "a perpetual happening—a cultural center, part atelier, part film studio, part experimental theater, part literary workshop, and Salvation Army for all artists and would-be artists who couldn't find shelter elsewhere." At the Factory, Sedgwick became one of Warhol's first postmodern "it" girls—his urban vamp of the moment.

In *Edie: An American Biography* (New York: Alfred A. Knopf), an excellent 1982 oral history of the underground celebrity, author/editor Jean Stein indicates that Edie was having some sort of intimate relationship with Bob Dylan even as he was marrying Sara Lownds. Stein also suggests that much of *Blonde on Blonde* was written for her. Perhaps she is right: songs like "Leopard-Skin Pill-Box Hat," "Just Like a Woman," "One of Us Must Know," and "Most Likely You Go Your Way" all dwell on breakup rather than union. After the breakup, Sedgwick had a major affair with Dylan's crony Bob Neuwirth, also described in Stein's book.

And, of course, there is the special Patti Smith poem "Village '65 Revisited" about Sedgwick from the *Village Voice*, July 27, 1982: "I don't know how she did it. Fire. She was shaking all over. It took her hours to put her makeup on. But she did it. Even the false eyelashes. She ordered gin with triple limes. Then a limousine. Everyone knew she was the real heroine of 'Blonde on Blonde.'"

⬛ **"Just Like Tom Thumb's Blues"** (Bob Dylan)
Bob Dylan, single (live) (1966); *Highway 61 Revisited* (1965); *Eat the Document* (film)/'66 (1971); *Bob Dylan's Greatest Hits, Volume II*/'65 (1971);

Masterpieces/'66 (1978); *The Bootleg Series, Volume 4: Live 1966—The "Royal Albert Hall" Concert* (1998)

Various Artists (performed by Neil Young), *Bob Dylan: The 30th Anniversary Concert Celebration* (1993)

Gordon Lightfoot, single (1965)

Barry McGuire, *This Precious Time* (1966); *Anthology* (1993)

Nina Simone, *Essential Nina Simone* (1967); *To Love Somebody* (1971); *Nina Simone* (1997); *Very Best of Nina Simone* (1998); *Masters* (1998)

Judy Collins, *In My Life* (1967); *Both Sides Now* (1971); *Living* (1972)

Jennifer Warnes, single (1968)

Steve Marcus, *Lord's Prayer* (1970)

Jamie Brockett, *Jamie Brockett 2* (1970)

Frankie Miller, *Once in a Blue Moon* (1973)

Sir Douglas Quintet, *Live Texas Tornado* (1983)

The Bluebirds, *Outlaw Blues* (1992)

Various Artists (performed by Henry Kaiser), *Outlaw Blues Volume Two: A Tribute to Bob Dylan* (1993)

Medicine Head, *New Bottles & Medicine . . . Plus* (1995)

Linda Ronstadt, *We Ran* (1998)

Jimmy LaFave, *Trail* (1999)

The Grateful Dead, *View from the Vault* (video) (2000); *Postcards of the Hanging: Grateful Dead Perform the Songs of Bob Dylan* (2002)

Bill Kirchen, *Tied to the Wheel* (2001)

Robyn Hitchcock, *Robyn Sings* (2002)

Big Brass Bed, *A Few Dylan Songs* (2003)

An unburnished tableau of a dissipated night in a Mexican border town, "Just Like Tom Thumb's Blues" portrays the sad, desperate emptiness of a man at the end of his rope. With a nod to *A Touch of Evil*, Orson Welles's menacing 1958 border-town film noir, and maybe Malcolm Lowry's amazing 1947 novel *Under the Volcano*, about the last day in the life of a hopelessly alcoholic diplomat, "Just Like Tom Thumb's Blues" is a gloomy, cloudy song studded with classic lyrics as Dylan plays the role of tour guide on this visit to the underworld.

Lost in the rain on Easter and inebriated by Burgundy wine and "the harder stuff," the alienated narrator slums in Juarez's seamy skid row, yet he keenly observes society's dregs (Saint Annie, Sweet Melinda, "all the authorities," the sergeant-at-arms, etc.) just down the street from Poe's Rue Morgue or under Lowry's volcano. The imagery recalls Goya's dark period—it's as if one of those works has suddenly moved out of its frame on the museum wall to slink across the cold marble floor before making a getaway to warmer climes. Dylan's mournful music helps paint the harsh, bereft scene; the jangly honky-tonk piano only adds to the bleakness. By the song's end, he's ready to pack it in, tail between his legs, admitting that "the joke was on me/There was nobody even there to call my bluff . . ."

Meanwhile, Dylan biographer Robert Shelton may have figured out what Tom Thumb—never mentioned in the song—has to do with the whole thing. Shelton points to the French Symbolist poet Arthur Rimbaud, whose work captivated Dylan. In "Ma Bohème" (aka "My Bohemian Life" or "Wandering"), Rimbaud writes, "I went off, my fists in my torn pockets; . . . My only pair of trousers had a big hole. Tom Thumb in a daze, I sowed rhymes as I went along. My inn was at the Big Dipper. . . . rhyming in the midst of fantastic shadows, like lyres I plucked the elastics of my wounded shoes, one foot near my heart!" (From *Rimbaud: Complete Works, Selected Letters*, translated by Wallace Fowlie. Chicago: University of Chicago Press, 1966.)

Tom Thumb in a daze, sowing rhymes: Dylan's narrator is indeed just like Rimbaud's character. Rimbaud was not Dylan's only influence, of course; among others was Jack Kerouac. "Housing Project Hill" comes from the beat writer's then-new *Desolation Angels*, a title Dylan references for his own "Desolation Row"

Ciudad Juárez, México, ca. 1902
(Photo: Detroit Publishing Co./Library of Congress)

found on the same LP as "Tom Thumb": *Highway 61 Revisited.*

Predictably, Dylan's many versions of "Just Like Tom Thumb's Blues" have varied tremendously over the years. The first concert performances of the song are laments rather faithful to the *Highway 61 Revisited* version, presenting a south-of-the-border miasma that dimly recalls the Coasters. It didn't take long for Dylan and the Hawks to put it in their pressure cooker and turn the song into a steamroller, bursting with frustrations and energy rather than dragging with apathy and lethargy. Through it all—from

the woozy studio take to his soul-baring live outings with the Hawks in 1965 and 1966 (check out Dylan's semi-self-suppressed film vérité *Eat the Document* for a skin-crawling rendition) through a jaunty rearrangement in 1978 and beyond—"Just Like Tom Thumb's Blues" retained a biting theatrical edge.

The titular character has roots in both history and fable. "Tom Thumb" was the title of a Brothers Grimm tale and General Tom Thumb an attraction for P. T. Barnum. Ah, the fairy tale and the circus—two subjects near and dear to Mr. Bob Dylan.

K

 "Kansas City" (Jerry Leiber/Mike Stoller)
See also "Let's Stick Together"
Little Willie Littlefield (single) (1952)
Wilbert Harrison, *Cruisin' 1959* (1959)
Little Richard, *The Fabulous Little Richard* (1959)
J. T. Adams and Shirley Griffith (single) (1961)
James Brown, *Live at the Apollo* (1963)
Fats Domino, *Getaway with Fats Domino* (1965)
The Beatles, *Live at the BBC* (1994)
Various Artists, *The Best of Kansas City* (1994)

Dylan has performed "Kansas City" only once, at a 1986 Kansas show with Tom Petty and the Heartbreakers. But it is a song with a history steeped in controversy and a hint of thievery. Jerry Leiber and Mike Stoller, the great rock 'n' roll hit songwriting team, usually get credited with authorship (and the royalty checks), but soul singer Little Willie Littlefield has also laid claim to the song, saying he recorded a tune called "K.C. Loving" and sold the rights to Leiber and Stoller. The latter, after grafting some equally simplistic lyrics over Littlefield's composition, went on to reap the benefits of an easy day's work from the many recordings of the renamed "Kansas City." Whatever the original authorship, "Kansas City" knocked around for a few years after the Littlefield–Leiber and Stoller deal before finally hitting pay dirt with Wilbert Harrison's recording in 1959, which hit No. 1 and spent twelve weeks in the Top 40.

Anybody questioning the notion that "irony rules" would be wise to investigate the success of Leiber (born April 25, 1933, Baltimore) and Stoller (born May 13, 1933, Belle Harbor, New York). Wonderstruck by black music, these two white boys still rank among the 1950s' and '60s' most inventive R&B and rock 'n' roll songwriters and producers. Their songs have been

covered by everyone from Elvis Presley to the Coasters, the Drifters, and the Grateful Dead. Showered with awards from every musical hall of fame imaginable during the late 1980s, Leiber and Stoller will be remembered as the ones who took R&B from the ghetto into the mainstream, creating pop classics that transcended musical and racial categories. "Smokey Joe's Café," a revue of their greatest hits, had a successful Broadway run in 1995.

Summing up their success, in a piece published in the *New York Times* on March 18, 1995, Mr. Leiber said: "I don't know why, but we really didn't believe that there was any longevity to rock-and-roll. Cole Porter and Irving Berlin, they wrote standards. We might write some hits, but they weren't going to be standards."

"Key to the Highway" (Traditional/Charles
Segar/Big Bill Broonzy)
Big Bill Broonzy, *Bill Broonzy Story* (1961)
Jazz Gillum, *Key to the Highway, 1935–1942* (1996)
Count Basie, *Just the Blues* (1960)
John Lee Hooker, *Burning Hell* (1964)
Derek and the Dominos, *Layla & Other Assorted Love Songs* (1970)
Muddy Waters, *London Sessions* (1971)
Little Walter, *Essential* (1993)

A standard-key, classic blues capturing the romance and desperation of love on the run and the comfort of dangerous places, "Key to the Highway" was performed by Dylan exactly once—at a public rehearsal gig in Florida before the Never Ending Tour of 1998.

"Key to the Highway" was written, or at least formalized from the folk tradition, by Big Bill Broonzy and the lesser-known, still somewhat mysterious Charles Seger (either the misidentified folklorist, musicologist, and patriarch of the Seeger clan that produced a

Big Bill Broonzy, American blues musician and composer.

type of labor that would be the envy of anybody wishing to really sing the blues: farmer, redcap, preacher, and tavern owner. After serving in the army in World War I, he moved to Chicago in the early 1920s and switched to guitar, becoming a leading figure in a burgeoning Chicago blues scene—first at house and rent parties and then the bars and clubs, where he was a fixture in the 1920s on through the 1940s. One of the best-selling blues artists during the late 1930s, Broonzy appeared at John Hammond's groundbreaking "Spirituals to Swing" concerts of 1938 and '39. This rich phase of Broonzy's career found him befriending and playing with the era's blues giants, including Memphis Minnie, Tampa Red, Memphis Slim, and John Lee "Sonny Boy" Williamson (Sonny Boy Williamson I, not harmonica whiz Rice Miller, who was known as Sonny Boy Williamson II). And his gregarious, charismatic personality also suited him well as a mentor to the young blues performers who migrated to Chicago.

In his blues compositions, Broonzy's themes run that gamut of the African-American experience, ranging from mischief to respect. Contrast, for example, "Key to the Highway," a song about escape from sexual and romantic entanglement ("I'm gonna leave her running, 'cause walkin' is most too slow"), with "When Do I Get to Be Called a Man," a song about African-American dignity in a world where a black man was always a "boy," and some idea of Big Bill's range of concerns can be gleaned.

After World War II, edgier, more electric blues and rhythm-and-blues styles supplanted Broonzy's older urban style. In 1951 Broonzy began touring Europe and introduced traditional blues and African-American folk songs and spirituals to audiences there. In 1955 *Big Bill Blues*, his autobiography as told to Danish writer Yannick Bruynoghe, was published

son Pete, or a really obscure Chicago blues pianist). Broonzy, one of the most popular blues recording artists in the 1930s and 1940s, is a critical link between the coarse rural blues and its more polished urban sibling. That Eric Clapton is credited with reviving the song during his rightly acclaimed Derek and the Dominos period is a testament to both the staying power of Broonzy and "Key to the Highway."

Broonzy (born William Lee Conley Broonzy, June 26, 1893, Scott, Mississippi; died August 15, 1958, Chicago) moved to Arkansas as a young boy and, by the age of ten, had learned to play the fiddle—a skill he quickly used to work for tips at country dances and picnics as well as in churches. As with so many bluesmen, his day-job résumé is sprinkled with the

(London: Cassell). An active performer until the very end, he died of cancer.

[S] "Kindhearted Woman Blues" (Traditional/Robert Johnson)

Robert Johnson, *The Complete Recordings* (1990)
Muddy Waters, *They Call Me Muddy Waters* (1971)
Johnny Winter, *Texas Blues* (1998)
Robert Lockwood Jr., *I Got to Find Me a Woman* (1998)

As John Way suggests in *The Telegraph* #44 (winter 1992), Dylan's reading of Robert Johnson's Delta blues classic, heard on a number of unofficial recordings circa 1962, includes fragments of Johnson's "32-20 Blues"; an old blues scrap lyric ("ought to be buried alive," which Dylan may have picked up from Richard "Rabbit" Brown's "James Alley Blues"); and a line from the traditional "Corrina, Corrina."

The first song Johnson ever recorded, at a legendary three-day November 1936 session in a San Antonio hotel room, "Kindhearted Woman Blues" is filled with hints of the hoodoo that marked so much of the Delta Blues King's best work. The phrase "She studies evil all the time," for example, is one such speculative target as the suggestion of secret plotting and even sorcery is raised. But some bluesologists read *evil* here as a once-common African-American colloquialism for spitefulness. In most traditional blues usage, the word, when applied to women, relates more to contrariness or unwillingness to comply and can usually be read in a lighter, less malevolent vein. As for the word *studies,* it is also a common blues usage and is synonymous with "thinks about," as in "I ain't studying about you."

[A] *Kindred Spirits: A Tribute to the Songs of Johnny Cash*/Various Artists

Sony CD-86310. Released 2002.

With "Train of Love," his Sun Records–modeled arrangement about a poor schmo left loveless at the station platform, Dylan all but walks off with this fairly pedestrian Bruce Springsteen–produced homage to The Man in Black. Other notable appearances on the album include Dwight Yoakam ("Understand Your Man"), Roseanne Cash ("I Still Miss Someone"), Little Richard ("Get Rhythm"), Keb' Mo' ("Folsom Prison Blues"), and the Boss ("Give My Love to Rose"). Dylan's cut was drawn from his April 1999 involvement with a Cash tribute concert in New York City, to which Dylan contributed via videotape due to previous commitments.

[A] *Kingdom Blow*/Kurtis Blow

Mercury Records LP 830-215-1. Released 1986.

If the argument can be made that Dylan (with "Subterranean Homesick Blues," "It's Alright, Ma," and his dabblings with talking-blues forms) is a forefather of rap music, then things came full circle when he lent some backing vocals and a mid-1980s-style rap to "Street Rock," a cut from Kurtis Blow's *Kingdom Blow.* Unfortunately, even Dylan's involvement couldn't save this Blow record. With its mixture of autobiographical songs ("The Bronx"), B-boy narratives ("I'm Chillin'"), and novelty tracks ("Magilla Gorilla"), Blow's sixth Mercury album didn't click commercially or artistically.

Blow (born Kurtis Walker, August 9, 1959, New York City) was one of rap's first mainstream stars, emerging in the early 1980s with a brand of syncopated, talking vocalese that combined social protest and Afrocentrism with rap's traditional boasting and posturing when it was still considered fresh. "The Breaks," from 1980, was his landmark recording—remarkable at the time of its release for a pace and verbal dexterity that would make Homer, Jeremiah, or Fats Waller proud.

ᔆ **"Kingsport Town"** (Traditional/Bob Dylan)
Bob Dylan, *The Bootleg Series, Volumes 1–3: Rare and Unreleased, 1961–1991/'62* (1991)
Cat Power, *The Covers Record* (2000)
Eleni Mandell, *Country for True Lovers* (2003)
Michel Montecrossa, *Country Heroes* (2003)

Dylan recorded "Kingsport Town" on November 14, 1962, at one of a string of on-the-fly New York City studio dates as he and producer John Hammond scrambled to put *The Freewheelin' Bob Dylan* in the can. In this mostly rote song of lovers forced to part as the long arm of the law closes in on the singer, Dylan begins to point to new artistic vistas with lines like "Who's gonna kiss your Memphis mouth when I'm out in the wind." Dylan's semi-original is clearly an adult update on Woody Guthrie's juvenile if romantic version of the traditional "Who's Going to Shoe Your Pretty Little Feet?", a song that had been in Dylan's back pocket since he began talking his way onto the small coffeehouse stages back in Dinkytown—the Bohemian quarter adjacent to the University of Minnesota—in 1960. "Who's Going to Shoe Your Pretty Little Feet?" itself has roots in an early eighteenth-century ballad entitled "Lord Gregory," also known as "The Lass of Roch Royal," et. al. (Child Ballad No. 76). Eventually released on *The Bootleg Series, Volumes 1–3*, "Kingsport Town" is marked both by Dylan's thick, put-on Okie twang and by the alliterative poetry that he seems to be making up on the spot. He seems not to have performed the song in concert.

ᴀ **Knocked Out Loaded**
Columbia Records LP OC-40439, CD CK-40439, CS OCT-40439. Recorded July 1984–May 1986. Released July 14, 1986. No producer credited. Album art by Charles Sappington.
Bob Dylan—guitar, vocals, keyboards. T-Bone Burnett, Ira Ingber, Al Perkins, Jack Sherman, Dave Stewart, Ron Wood—guitars. Larry Meyers—mandolin. Steve Douglas—saxophone. Steve Madaio—trumpet. Al Kooper, Vince Melamed, Patrick Seymour—keyboards. James Jamerson Jr., John McKenzie, John Paris, Vito San Filippo, Carl Sealove—bass. Clem Burke, Anton Fig, Don Heffington, Raymond Lee Pounds—drums. Philip Lyn Jones—conga. Mike Berment, Milton Gabriel, Brian Parris—steel drums. The Children's Choir (Majason Bracy, Lara Firestone, Keysha Gwin, April Hendrix-Haberlin, Dewey B. Jones II, Larry Mahand, Angel Newell, Herbert Newell, Crystal Pounds, Daina Smith, Maia Smith, Medena Smith, Damien Turnbough, Chyna Wright, Elisecia Wright, Tiffany Wright), Peggi Blu, Carol Dennis, Muffy Hendrix, Queen Esther Marrow, Madelyn Quebec, Annette May Thomas—background vocals. Tom Petty and the Heartbreakers (Tom Petty, Mike Campbell—guitars. Benmont Tench—keyboards. Howie Epstein—bass. Stan Lynch—drums).
"You Wanna Ramble," "They Killed Him," "Driftin' Too Far from Shore," "Precious Memories," "Maybe Someday," "Brownsville Girl," "Got My Mind Made Up," "Under Your Spell"

A marginal jumble and a mostly dispensable hodgepodge of tracks recorded in the mid-1980s, *Knocked Out Loaded* is redeemed only by the rambling, hallucinatory opus "Brownsville Girl," cowritten with playwright Sam Shepard. That many of the songs are covers and originals with an outtake flavor drawn from other sessions has not helped the album's standing among Dylan's fans. It was as if Dylan, in a froth to deliver Columbia a record he owed them, scoured through a pile of recently recorded material and played eeny-meeny-miney-moe. Naturally—and justifiably—the record sold poorly and was the first Dylan record since *The Times They Are A-Changin'* that failed to chart.

Knocked Out Loaded does feature one of Dylan's weirdest album covers. Front and back carry a Charles Sappington painting resembling a dime-store pulp-fiction novel from the

1930s, depicting two men (one looking vaguely like Dylan if he were to have starred in a *Treasure of Sierra Madre* remake) locked in mortal combat as a sarong-wrapped woman stands behind, ready to smash a huge ceramic vase over them. The sarong, the sombrero worn by one of the men, and a thatched roof in the background gives the scene a vaguely exotic or tropical aura.

The album title may have been drawn from "Junko Partner"—a song recorded by, among others, the Holy Modal Rounders on *Holy Modal Rounders, Volume 2* and by the Clash on *Sandinista!* (where it's titled "Junco Partner")—which contains the following stanza: "Down the road came a Junco Partner/For he was loaded as can be/He was knocked out, knocked out loaded."

As for the album and its songs, Dylan told Mikal Gilmore of *Rolling Stone* for the issue published July 31, 1986, "It's all sorts of stuff. It doesn't really have a theme or a purpose." Most listeners agreed.

More sympathetic ears may discern deeper levels in the collection, pointing out that the artist's spiritual, universal, activist, reclusive, folkie, and rock 'n' roll natures and concerns are expressed, albeit haphazardly, through the diverse song selections: the thousand faces of Bob merging into a complete whole, however strange, conflicting, and mysterious that might be.

Still, no matter how you slice it, *Knocked Out Loaded* is a piecemeal work patched together from a variety of sessions with different groups of musicians. Dylan touches upon juke-joint R&B ("You Wanna Ramble"), reeling Stones-style blues-rock ("Got My Mind Made Up," cowritten by his touring partner at the time, Tom Petty, and featuring Petty's band the Heartbreakers), and a gospel arrangement of a topical Kris Kristofferson tune depicting the violent political events of the era ("They Killed Him"). But it all adds up to too much of nothing.

Of course, the main excuse for *Knocked Out Loaded* would seem to be "Brownsville Girl," the eleven-minute picaresque opus cowritten with playwright Sam Shepard. This is vintage Dylan, with the singer struggling to encompass an entire worldview in the context of a midtempo, brassy, Tex-Mex blues travelogue. It is a multileveled, rough-edged dusty diamond that stands among the most unique pieces in Dylan's entire catalogue and is delivered so effortlessly that it reminded everyone that he was still at least in touch with the better part of his muse.

[S] **"Knockin' on Heaven's Door"** (Bob Dylan)

Bob Dylan, single (1973, 1979); *Pat Garrett and Billy the Kid* (1973); *Masterpieces* (1978); *Bob Dylan at Budokan* (1979); *Biograph*/'73 (1985); *Hard to Handle* (video) (1986); *Bob Dylan's Greatest Hits, Volume 3* (1994); *MTV Unplugged* (1995); *Live 1961–2000—Thirty-nine Years of Great Concert Performances*/'74 (2001); *The Bootleg Series, Volume 5: Live 1975—The Rolling Thunder Revue* (2002)
Bob Dylan/The Band, *Before the Flood* (1974)
Bob Dylan/The Grateful Dead, *Dylan & the Dead* (1989)
Bob Dylan/Various Artists (performed by "Everyone"), *Bob Dylan: The 30th Anniversary Concert Celebration* (1993)
Sandy Denny, *Who Knows Where the Time Goes* (1974)
G. T. Moore, *G. T. Moore and the Reggae Guitars* (1974)
Eric Clapton, single (1975); *There's One in Every Crowd* (1975); *Just One Night* (1980); *Time Pieces: Best of Eric Clapton* (1982); *Time Pieces, Volume II: Live in the Seventies* (1983); *After Midnight* (1984); *Backtrackin'* (1984); *The Cream of Eric Clapton* (1987); *Crossroads* (1988); *Crossroads 2: Live in the Seventies* (1996)
Roger McGuinn, *Roger McGuinn & Band* (1975)
Arthur Louis (with Eric Clapton), *Knockin' on Heaven's Door* (1976)
Kevin Coyne, *In Living Black and White* (1977)
Booker T. Jones, *Try and Love Again* (1978)

Pete Carr, *Multiple Flash* (1978)

Joe Sun, *Living on Honky Tonk Time* (1980)

Cold Chisel, *Swingshift* (1981)

Jerry Garcia Band, *Run for the Roses* (1982); *Don't Let Go/'76* (2001)

Danny & Dusty, *The Lost Weekend* (1985)

The Alarm, *Spirit of '76* (1986)

Ladysmith Black Mambazo, *Heavenly* (1987)

Randy Crawford, *Rich and Poor* (1989); *Best of Randy Crawford* (1996)

The Heart of Gold Band, *Double Dose* (1989)

Sisters of Mercy, *Doctor Jeep* (1990); *Heaven's Door* (1991)

Guns N' Roses, *Use Your Illusion II* (1991); *The Live Era: 1987–1993* (1999)

Dead Ringers, *Dead Ringers* (1993)

Leningrad Cowboys, *Happy Together* (1994)

Royal Philharmonic Orchestra, *Rock Dreams: Knockin' on Heaven's Door* (1996)

Rat Dog, *Furthur* (1996)

Beau Jocque and Zydeco Hi Roller, *Gonna Take You Down* (1996)

Gregg Smith, *I Wanna Rock Ya* (1997)

Ricki Erik, *My Heart Will Go On* (1998)

The Paragons, *Sings the Beatles and Dylan* (1998)

Minority Militia, *Criminal Network* (1999)

Michel Montecrossa and the Chosen Few, *Eternal Circle* (1999)

Various Artists (performed by Al DiMarco and David West), *Pickin' on Dylan* (1999)

The Grateful Dead, *View from the Vault* (video) (2000)

Jerry Garcia/David Grisman/Tony Rice, *The Pizza Tapes* (2000)

Various Artists (performed by Crazy Betty), *Duluth Does Dylan* (2001)

Roger Waters, *Flickering Flames: The Solo Years, Volume One* (2002)

Wyclef Jean, *Masquerade* (2002)

Warren Zevon, *The Wind* (2003)

Todd Rubenstein, *The String Quartet Tribute to Bob Dylan* (2003)

Scott Mateo Davies, *Caravana Flamenco* (2003)

Various Artists (performed by Judy Mowatt), *Blowin' in the Wind: A Reggae Tribute to Bob Dylan* (2003)

It was something of a surprise when "Knockin' on Heaven's Door," a song Dylan composed for *Pat Garrett and Billy the Kid*, Sam Peckinpah's 1973 rough jewel of a western, emerged as a hit. The elegy in song was all over the radio during the summer of the film's release. Who would have guessed that it would turn into one of his biggest-selling singles ever?

Dylan said that he wrote the song as a mood piece specifically for the stark, powerful scene in which the town sheriff (Slim Pickens) dies in the arms of his wife (Katy Jurado). But it is hard not see both song and film as an allegorical meditation on the mindlessness of Vietnam. It does fit well, both lyrically and musically, as Alex Ross points out in the May 10, 1999, *New Yorker*: "More often, the chords are mesmerizingly simple. In 'Knockin' on Heaven's Door,' there are just four of them, but they occur in an unresolved, drooping sequence—a picture of the 'long black cloud' that comes down."

Dylan first began performing "Heaven's Door" during his whirlwind tour with the Band in 1974, when its elegiac qualities were brought forth particularly well thanks to some choice vocal harmonies supplied by Rick Danko and Richard Manuel. As a show-closing encore during the 1975–76 Rolling Thunder Revues, "Knockin' on Heaven's Door" offered Dylan and his scruffy ensemble the opportunity for some unique, improvised verse-swapping among the charmingly ragtag headliners. In 1978 Dylan worked up a moderately surprising reggae version for his big-band world tour. By the 1980s, when it became a natural encore selection, Dylan all but performed "Knockin' on Heaven's Door" to death as it endured a few too many by-the-numbers outings—although it could often be profoundly moving on a good night, such as Dylan's 1997 command performance for Pope John Paul II.

After Elton John's "Candle in the Wind,"

Tina Turner's "Simply the Best," and Frank Sinatra's "My Way," "Knockin' on Heaven's Door" was, for a spell, the most-requested non-traditional song at funerals in Great Britain. By the time Dylan's *MTV Unplugged* rendition received a 1996 Grammy nomination for best male rock vocal performance, "Knockin' on Heaven's Door" had become anthemic to the point of cliché.

L

■ **"Lady Came from Baltimore"** (Tim Hardin)
Tim Hardin, *Live in Concert* (1968)
Joan Baez, *Joan* (1967)
Ronnie Hawkins, *Hawk* (1971)
Johnny Cash, *John R. Cash* (1974)
Bobby Darin, *As Long as I'm Singing: The Bobby Darin Story* (1995)

Along with some 1994 acoustic performances of Tim Hardin's traditional-sounding original, done up as a light country amble colored by sideman Bucky Baxter's mandolin and Dylan's own harmonica, Dylan refers to "Lady Came from Baltimore" in "Trying to Get to Heaven" off his 1997 album *Time out of Mind*. Like one of those dastardly Child Ballads of yore, "Lady Came from Baltimore" concerns itself with a man who woos a woman with the sole intention of robbing her. Instead, he is the one played for the fool and winds up having his love stolen by his ill-chosen victim.

Tim Hardin (born December 23, 1941, Eugene, Oregon; died December 29, 1980, Hollywood, California) was a master singer of his own delicate, heart-on-the-sleeve songs fusing blues, jazz, and folk into a memorable canon. Despite a lack of breakthrough popularity, Hardin, for an all-too-fleeting moment, filled the vacuum left by an absent Dylan at the decade's end.

Unrelated to the outlaw John Wesley Hardin (see *John Wesley Harding* and "John Wesley Harding"), Hardin was the son of music-loving parents. He dropped out of high school without graduating at the age of eighteen and joined the Marines—a move that would seem a bit out of character for a kid who dug drama class.

After his military posting in Southeast Asia (where many believe his heroin addiction became full-blown), Hardin moved to New York in 1961 and enrolled in the American Academy of Dramatic Arts there. While in New York he gravitated toward the Greenwich Village folk-music scene.

His 1965 move to Los Angeles proved a paradoxical key professionally, artistically, and personally. While his romance, marriage, and generally tortured life with Susan Morss provided the material for many of the songs that he would write in the coming years, their relationship proved to be spiritually fatal.

If Hardin's debut album, *Tim Hardin 1*, was marred by an ill-advised string section, *Tim Hardin 2* stands with the era's best confessional folk-rock. He made it to the main stage at Woodstock in 1969, but his songs are best known through the recordings of others: Rod Stewart, Nico, and Fred Neil all recorded a Hardin tune with varying commercial success. But it was Bobby Darin's 1966 recording of Hardin's most famous song, "If I Were a Carpenter," that made the Top 40 and found its way into the repertoire and recordings of others, including Johnny Cash, Bob Seger, and Leon Russell.

During the 1970s, Hardin's heroin habit overwhelmed him and his performances reached ever new plateaus of the embarrassingly psychotic. His commercial prospects dimmed, his personal life unraveled, and his albums became more miss than hit, a slow, painful descent wore on, eventually ending in a heroin/morphine overdose just a week north of his thirty-ninth birthday.

▣ "Lady of Carlisle" (Traditional)

aka "Bold Lieutenant," "The Distressed Lady," "In Castyle There Was a Lady," "The Lady's Fan," "Lion's Den"

Various Artists (performed by Basil May), *The Music of Kentucky: Early American Rural Classics 1927–1937, Volume 2* (1995), *Anglo-American Ballads, Volume 1/'30s* (1999)

Various Artists (performed by Pete Seeger), *American Ballads* (1957)

Ian and Sylvia, *Four Strong Winds* (1963)

Various Artists (performed by Mrs. Maguire), *Folk Songs of Britain, Volume 7: Fair Game and Fowl* (1963)

Martin Henderson, *Cameo* (1977)

Rich Lerner, *Trails and Bridges* (1996)

Dylan's only Southern mountain-style performance of this old traditional song (variants of which may be found in both the British Isles and the southeastern United States) came out of the blue as the exuberant final encore of a 1992 show in Australia. The fable of courtly love in which an aspiring knight performs ritual feats of heroism to win his lady's hand here concerns a brave lieutenant who sets off to perform valiant deeds for his maiden.

The Basil May interpretation of "Lady of Carlisle" (Sharp Ballad No. 66) lays out the simple story for the ages quite plainly: two men, a brave soldier and a courageous seaman, approach a fair lady. The lady can't choose between the two, so she tests them by leading them to a lion's den into which she throws her fan, saying, "Which of you to gain a lady will return her fan or die." In modern vernacular, the soldier basically replies, "Get real!" and splits. But the sailor does venture into the beast's domain to prove his love. Whether he

safely returns or not is the question pondered by folk nerds the planet over.

The oldest known versions of the song are titled "The Distressed Lady" or "Trial of True Love," printed in Thomas Percy's *Reliques of Ancient English Poetry, Volume 1* (1765).

According to Mike Seeger's notes in the *Old-Time String Band Songbook*, "This ballad has a history based in classical European poetry (Friedrich Schiller & Robert Browning) and it entered into the folk tradition via the street ballads and broadsides."

The point of all this is, of course, to indicate that we are talking about a very old song here. Dylan's model would seem to be Ian and Sylvia's spirited arrangement as they performed it on their 1963 album *Four Strong Winds*.

In the mid-1970s, Robert Hunter dramatically recast the tale and Jerry Garcia added an Elizabethan-style score to create part of the Grateful Dead's "Terrapin Station" (aka "Lady with a Fan") song suite.

▣ "The Lakes of Pontchartrain" (Traditional)

aka "Creole Girl"

E. G. Huntington, *Our Singing Heritage* (1956)

The Louisiana Honeydrippers, *Bayou Bluegrass* (1961)

Planxty, *Cold Blow and the Rainy Night* (1974)

Mike Waterson, *Mike Waterson* (1977)

Paul Brady, *Welcome Here Kind Stranger* (1978)

Christy Moore, *The Time Has Come* (1983)

Martin Simpson, *Grinning in Your Face* (1994)

Deanta, *Ready for the Storm* (1994)

Dylan may have first heard "The Lakes of Pontchartrain," one of his greatest cover songs—the "Shelter from the Storm"-like tale of a destitute soldier who is saved and salved by a Creole girl in a shotgun shack on the shores of the titular lake—during his early coffeehouse days, or perhaps even much later from Paul

L

Brady's late-1970s album *Welcome Here Kind Stranger*, itself titled after a line in the song. Brady, who appears to have shown Dylan the song in 1984, discusses his experience with the song, along with some of its history, in the liner notes to *Welcome Here Kind Stranger*: "I learnt this song from Christy Moore, whose version comes from Mike Waterson. Someone came up to me after a concert in New York and said it had a parallel in an old historical novel about an Irish deserter from the Confederate Army at the end of the American Civil War who was trying to make his way to Cuba . . . and it was to this same story that the song referred. The railroad fits that period and perhaps 'foreign money' refers to worthless Confederate dollars? As for the Irishman, well, another version of the song turns up in *Songs of the People* (No. 619), which helps to lend credence to that theory. I'd love to know more about it."

As summarized by Gavin Selerie in "Tricks and Training: Some Dylan Sources and Analogues" (Part Two) in *The Telegraph* #51 (spring 1995), the version of the song Brady speaks of, published in *Sam Henry's Songs of the People* (Athens: University of Georgia Press, 1990), is an Ulster text collected in 1935 from a singer in Ireland's County Antrim who heard it from another Antrim man, Frank McAllister, around 1905. McAllister, in turn, said that he learned the song from "a woodsman in America," according to Henry. Planxty's *Cold Blow* liner notes argue that the song may date from as far back as the eighteenth century when British and French soldiers were fighting each other and Americans in Louisiana. According to *The Christy Moore Songbook* (self-published in 1984), however, "The Lakes of Pontchartrain" is "reputed to be an American Civil War song about a soldier who found himself on the wrong side of the line after the truce and was helped out of his predicament by a woman."

But speculation regarding the origins of "The Lakes of Pontchartrain" hardly ends there. According to the *Golden Encyclopedia of Folk Music* (Hasbrouck Heights, New Jersey: Lewis Music Publishing, 1985; distributed by Hal Leonard Publishing), it began as an "English street ballad about 100 years ago," while the liner notes to Deanta's *Ready for the Storm* assert that it is a "traditional Creole love song, which is commonly mistaken as being of Irish origin." Still others trace "Pontchartrain" to "The Lass of Mohee," another variant in the "Shenandoah" family of folk songs with even more obscure roots.

Whatever the song's origins, it first appeared in print in 1922, published by Louise Pound in *American Ballads and Songs,* and by A. H. Tolman and N. O. Eddy in *The Journal of American Folklore*. Pound credits Ival McPeak as her source, while Tolman and Eddy give credit for their version to a Mr. M. Peak. Thus, it is thought that these figures are the same— perhaps linked to the McPeake family of Belfast, Northern Ireland, a renowned source for folk-song material.

Many of the older versions of the song— variants of which can be found in the traditions of Michigan, Iowa, Wisconsin, Kentucky, Missouri, Vermont, and Nova Scotia, as well as Louisiana—mention railway ties or lines and crossings, suggesting that the familiar version of "The Lakes of Pontchartrain" dates from the 1850s or later. A railroad did run from New Orleans to Jackson, Mississippi, at the time of the Civil War, so the reference to the town of Jackson in the common variant of the song performed by Dylan must postdate 1821, when the town was named after Major General Andrew Jackson—the man who defeated the British in the moot Battle of New Orleans in January 1815 and who later became U.S. president. This does not preclude the notion of an earlier version of "Pontchartrain," in which the basic man-woman relationship is recounted.

The Telegraph #54 (spring 1996) contained this excerpt of a letter written by Paul Brady to Gavin Selerie in 1996: "'The Lakes of Pontchartrain' continues to defy us in determining its origins. The latest thing I heard was that it came from the Spanish American (Cuba) war and that the soldier was from the St. Patrick's brigade, who were American Irish Catholics who sided with Cuba and many of whom were executed in the USA even though they were American citizens. Me I don't care where it's from or what it's about. I just like singing it."

"Pontchartrain" was also covered by Planxty, a Celtic folk-rock band spearheaded by Christy Moore. The sleeve notes to their album reported that: "In the eighteenth century, British and French soldiers were fighting Americans in Louisiana and Canada. It seems likely that some returning solider brought 'The Lakes of Pontchartrain' back with him." Planxty, by the way, supposedly learned the song from Mike Waterson.

Dylan primarily performed the song acoustically during the Never Ending Tour in 1988. When it popped up for the odd turn thereafter, it remained one of his most fully realized performances of a cover tune as he threw himself into the role of the homeless wayfarer with the vigor of an Actor's Studio veteran.

For the geographically challenged or curious, Louisiana's Lake Pontchartrain is five miles north of New Orleans. It is a constant flood menace in New Orleans, its waters having to be kept at bay by great earthen dikes, or levees. Thanks to the lake and the fact that most of New Orleans is actually below sea level, the land in the city and surrounding area is so waterlogged that no cellar can be built and all tombs are above ground. In blues history, Roosevelt Sykes and his wife used to fish on the

thirteen-mile-wide Lake Pontchartrain, and years before, the enigmatic Rabbit Brown was once employed there as a singing boatman.

Language Barrier/Sly Dunbar and Robbie Shakespeare Island Records LP 90286. Released 1985.

Perhaps as a partial payback for their contributions to his *Infidels* and *Empire Burlesque* releases of the mid-1980s, Dylan contributed a harmonica part to "No Name on the Bullet" from the master reggae rhythmsmiths' *Language Barrier* release. Other guests on the album include Herbie Hancock, Afrika Bambaataa, and Manu DiBango.

Drummer Sly Dunbar and bassist Robbie Shakespeare will go down as reggae's cornerstone rhythm battery. Among Jamaican music's most influential forces and trailblazers, Sly and Robbie first performed together when they backed Peter Tosh in 1975. A year later, they formed the Revolutionaries, one of the era's leading dub bands.

As the founding fathers of Taxi Productions in 1978, they produced an impressive roster of reggae's influential artists: Black Uhuru, Gregory Isaacs, Prince Far-I, Dennis Brown, and Max Romeo, not to mention up-and-comers, including Jimmy Riley, the Wailing Souls, and the Tamlins. Their success earned them a worldwide distribution deal with Island Records, which resulted in a series of compilations of the Taxi material, production gigs for reggae legends such as Jimmy Cliff, and invitations to record with Dylan, Mick Jagger, Joe Cocker, Grace Jones, and Robert Palmer.

"Last Night" (Traveling Wilburys)
Traveling Wilburys, *Traveling Wilburys, Volume 1* (1988)

Dylan's involvement with this Tom Petty–driven Wilbury piece of roadhouse rock 'n' comedy about life on the road seems to be limited to backing vocals and guitar.

[S] "Last Thoughts on Woody Guthrie" (Bob Dylan)

Bob Dylan, *The Bootleg Series, Volumes 1–3: Rare and Unreleased, 1961–1991/'63* (1991)
Chris Copping, *Last Thoughts on Woody* (2001)

Dylan's ultimate homage to one of his first great influences came as the finale of his watershed April 12, 1963, concert at New York City's Town Hall. Woody Guthrie was still alive but not well, slowly withering away from Huntington's disease just miles from the Town Hall stage where Dylan chose to honor him before moving on.

Benediction, valediction, and folkster's bar mitzvah rolled into one, this is the moment when the ragamuffin waif who had blown into New York City just over two years before claimed the mantle as a singular creator. After showcasing new material like "Masters of War," "With God on Our Side," and "Bob Dylan's Dream," the exciting concert ends with a one-time-only exclamation point: Dylan returning to the stage to read this stunning poem.

With singsong rhythms trotting along at Allen Ginsberg–style "mind breath" intervals, singing like Walt Whitman's Body Electric, and recalling Guthrie's own 1944 prose-poem "Talking About Songs" or even Jack Kerouac's "October in the Railroad Earth," Dylan's elongated phraseology does poetic loop-the-loops around just about anything from his pen you can name while portraying the human drama as something heroic, glistening, and (most importantly) accessible. You can feel Dylan's excitement as the performance unfolds. It seems that he cannot read the gushing, free-flowing language fast enough, leaving him breathless as he tries to unleash his torrent of words at the pace and cadence with which he hears them in his mind.

"Last Thoughts on Woody Guthrie" was to be included on *Bob Dylan in Concert*, a never-released live album that was scratched as it became artistically obsolete in the face of Dylan's lyrical flights in 1964.

[F] *The Last Waltz*

Directed by Martin Scorsese. Produced by Robbie Robertson and Jonathan Taplin & United Artists. Released 1978.

Perhaps the best concert film ever made, Martin Scorsese's documentary of the Band's final performance at Winterland (San Francisco's old rock 'n' roll barn) on November 25, 1976—Thanksgiving—is both a monumental musical revue featuring many of the generation's greatest performers and a bittersweet love letter to an era fast fading from sight. Interweaving stellar, timeless performances with revealing, "road warrior" interview segments, Scorsese guides the viewer into the music and lives of these relatively young men wise and wizened long beyond their years.

The Band and all their guests, representing a wide range of the American musical experience, were in splendid form for this show. Muddy Waters, Neil Diamond, Joni Mitchell, Neil Young, Van Morrison, and Dylan were just a few of the headliners pulling out every conceivable stop along the way and then some. Dylan displays brilliant cockiness with "Baby, Let Me Follow You Down," and his rendition of "Forever Young" may be the highlight in a film full of highlights.

[A] *The Last Waltz*/The Band, Various Artists

Warner Bros. Records LP 3WS-3146, CS 3W5-3146, CD 3146-2. Released 1978.

A great record from a defining and legendary event: the Band's 1976 Thanksgiving night

L

farewell concert at San Francisco's Winterland Arena. The Band performed an ample chunk of their own repertoire, and luminaries from every period of their career participated to throw in their two or three cents' worth: Ronnie Hawkins ("Who Do You Love?"), Neil Young ("Helpless"), Muddy Waters ("Mannish Boy"), Van Morrison ("Caravan"), Eric Clapton ("Dry Your Eyes"), Joni Mitchell ("Coyote"), and Paul Butterfield ("Mystery Train"). But Dylan's appearance at the gig's end is perhaps the highlight of highlights of both film and LP, as he displays his best chops on a quartet of wonderful offerings. Reprising the technique he used with the Band during their 1974 concert tour, Dylan opened and closed their set with the same song ("Baby, Let Me Follow You Down"), sandwiching in "I Don't Believe You" and an effervescent "Forever Young" before joining the all-star cast in the show's finale, "I Shall Be Released." The four-hour concert was a keeper for the ages.

[S] "Lawyers, Guns and Money" (Warren Zevon)

See also *Sentimental Hygiene*
Warren Zevon, *Excitable Boy* (1978)
Hank Williams Jr., *Five-O-Five* (1985)
Rick Derringer, *Required Rocking* (1996)

Typical of the kinds of lyrics Warren Zevon wrote so well, this composition describes a lethal combination of ingredients and includes some sly geopolitical subtext. The song is about a kid (or was that a world power?) who gets in a little over his head by playing footsie with the wrong people and needs to be bailed out. Dylan chose to cover this song briefly as he started his 2002 world tour—just weeks after Zevon's announcement that he was suffering from terminal cancer, and a few weeks before the U.S. edged closer to the abyss in Iraq.

[S] "Lay Down Your Weary Tune" (Bob Dylan)

Bob Dylan, *Biograph/'63* (1985)
Bill Henderson, *When My Dreamboat Comes Home* (1965)
The Byrds, *Turn! Turn! Turn!* (1966); *Byrds Play Dylan* (1980)
Jim and Jean, *Changes* (1966)
Coulson, Dean, McGuinness, Flint, *Lo & Behold* (1972)
Martin and Finley, *Dazzle 'Em with Footwork* (1974)
Ashley Hutchings, *The Guv'nor, Volume 1* (1994); *The Guv'nor, Volume 2* (1996)
Fairport Convention, *A Chronicle of Sorts 1967–1969* (1995)
Tim O'Brien, *Red on Blonde* (1996)
13th Floor Elevators, *The Interpreter* (1996)

A naturalistic lyric sung to a romantic melody, "Lay Down Your Weary Tune" can be heard as an impressionist lullaby that finds Dylan moving to the kind of visionary poetry found in slightly later, more famous songs such as "Chimes of Freedom" and "Mr. Tambourine Man." Often considered a polite goodbye to so-called protest songs and an embrace of his deepest muse, the song, as Dylan mentioned in the *Biograph* liner notes, was based on a Scottish ballad he had heard on an old 78 record and that had totally possessed him.

Dylanologist Michael Gray, who calls "Lay Down Your Weary Tune" "one of the very greatest and most haunting creations in our language," related the song to a broad range of sources, including, but not limited to, Ralph Waldo Emerson's 1839 poem "Each and All," J. R. R. Tolkien's Lord of the Rings trilogy, the Rev. J. M. Gates's "Oh Death, Where Is Thy Sting," pillaged from the *Anthology of American Folk Music*, and possibly an LSD experience. In his distillation, Dylan, in Gray's eyes, created his ultimate pantheistic canvas in song, "a vision of the world, that is, in which nature appears not as a manifestation of God but as containing God within its every aspect."

In *Song & Dance Man III: The Art of Bob*

Dylan, Gray devotes an entire chapter to "Lay Down Your Weary Tune" by way of heralding this generally overlooked diamond in the rough. Gray describes the melody as one that "seems to wrap itself around us, in allegiance to the associations of 'wove,' 'strands,' 'waves,' 'unwound,' 'unbound,' and 'winding strum' in the lyrics. And by its very impingement it urges the felicity of Dylan's analogies between nature's effects and the sounds of musical instruments. As it flows through each line, with a graceful and liquid precision, the melody nurtures and sustains us in an awareness of how involving and creative such analogies are made to be. The tune, in fact, offers itself as an embodiment of 'the river's mirror'; its water smooth does indeed run like a hymn."

Dylan wrote the sublime "Lay Down Your Weary Tune" at Joan Baez's house in Carmel, California, in the early autumn of 1963 and recorded a stunning one-take version (eventually released on *Biograph*) of the hymn to the mysteries of the soul at the October 24, 1963, recording session for *The Times They Are A-Changin'* before its only known concert performance at a Carnegie Hall show two nights later. That recording, which remains unreleased, was to have been included on the shelved *Bob Dylan in Concert* LP. *Sing Out!* magazine published the song, bearing a 1963 copyright, in its February/March 1964 issue.

▣ "Lay, Lady, Lay" (Bob Dylan)

Bob Dylan, single (1969); *Nashville Skyline* (1969); *Bob Dylan's Greatest Hits, Volume II/'69* (1971); *Hard Rain* (1977); *Biograph/'69* (1985)

Bob Dylan/The Band, *Before the Flood* (1974)

The Byrds, *Dr. Byrds and Mr. Hyde* (1969); *Original Singles, Volume 2* (1982); *The Byrds* (1990); *Definitive Collection* (1995)

Cher, *3614 Jackson Highway* (1969)

The Brothers & Sisters of Los Angeles, *Dylan's Gospel* (1969)

Keith Jarrett, single (1969)

Sandie Shaw, *Reviewing the Situation* (1969)

Ramblin' Jack Elliott, *Bull Durham Sacks & Railroad Tracks* (1970); *Me & Bobby McGee* (1995)

Ben E. King, *Rough Edges* (1970)

Tony Mottola, *Guitar Factory* (1970)

Jackie DeShannon, *Songs* (1971)

Nicky Thomas, *Tell It Like It Is* (1971)

The Isley Brothers, *Giving It Back* (1971); *Isleys Live* (1972); *Timeless* (1979); *Beautiful Ballads* (1994)

Melanie, *Garden in the City* (1971); *Four Sides of Melanie* (1972); *Melanie Magic* (1999)

Claude Denjean, *Moog* (1971)

José Feliciano, *Memphis Menu* (1972)

Mike Batt Orchestra, *Portrait of Dylan* (1972)

James Last, *Music from Across the Way* (1972)

Music from Free Creek, *Music from Free Creek* (1973)

The Harry Roche Constellation, *Spiral* (1973)

The Mystic Moods Orchestra, *Love the One You're With* (1975)

Hoyt Axton, *Fearless* (1976)

Roger Young, *Roger Young and the Reason Why* (1978)

Kevin Ayers, *Diamond Jack and the Queen of Pain* (1983)

Everly Brothers, *EB84* (1984); *Wings of a Nightingale* (1998)

Richie Havens, *Sings Beatles and Dylan* (1990)

Albert Lee, *Black Claw and Country Fever* (1991)

Either/Orchestra, *Brunt* (1993)

Duran Duran, *Thank You* (1995)

Ministry, *Filth Pig* (1995)

Booker T. and the MGs, *Time Is Tight* (1998)

Insol, *Insol* (1998)

The Paragons, *Sing the Beatles and Bob Dylan* (1998)

Various Artists (performed by David West), *Pickin' on Dylan* (1998)

Various Artists (performed by Isaac Hayes), *Tangled Up in Blues: The Songs of Bob Dylan* (1999)

Steve Howe, *Portraits of Bob Dylan* (1999)

Dave Cloud, *Dave Cloud Present: Songs I Will Always Sing* (2000)

Second Floor, *Plays Dylan* (2001)

Dylanesque, *Basement Fakes* (2001)

Todd Rubenstein, *The String Quartet Tribute to Bob Dylan* (2003)

L

Cassandra Wilson, *Glamoured* (2003)
Big Brass Bed, *A Few Dylan Songs* (2003)
Various Artists (performed by Chalice), *Blowin' in the Wind: A Reggae Tribute to Bob Dylan* (2003)

A famous Dylan love song, "Lay, Lady, Lay" was recorded in 1969 after a studio hiatus of nearly a year. Rising to No. 7 on the singles charts and going on to become Dylan's biggest-selling single, the song enjoyed a success that almost never happened, as Dylan recounted in the *Biograph* liner notes. "Clive Davis (then president of Columbia Records) heard the song and wanted to release it as a single," Dylan said. "I begged and pleaded with him not to. I never felt too close to the song, or thought it was representative of anything I do . . . he thought it was a hit single, and he was right."

Dylan had composed the song for *Midnight Cowboy*, the great 1969 film exploring the hustling underbelly of New York City starring Dustin Hoffman and Jon Voight, but submitted it too late for inclusion. Fred Neil's "Everybody's Talkin'" was used instead, became the song du jour, and probably served the movie better anyway.

"Lay, Lady, Lay," and indeed the album on which it appeared, *Nashville Skyline*, signaled a shift in Dylan's creative process modus operandi. Whereas earlier in his career he had written the lyrics first and then composed the music to fit the words, he began consciously developing solid melodies. As recounted in the *Biograph* liner notes, Dylan crafted an inviting four-chord progression and cast some "la-la-la" dummy lyrics against them, which rapidly changed into the familiar lyrics. Those lyrics, and Dylan's crooning delivery of them, are straightforward yet romantic and create a near-perfect erotic overture. Yes, the sexual demand stated in the title and repeated throughout the song is blunt to say the least, while lines like "And you're the best

thing that he's ever seen" are clichéd and sterile. But Dylan manages to cast himself as a sexy protagonist with Elvis Presley's sensuality and desirability—his seductive croon sweeping over Pete Drake's luscious pedal steel guitar licks and Ken Buttery's light percussion.

Hints of root sources for "Lay, Lady, Lay" are few and far between. The line "lay across my big brass bed" does appear on "Rough Alley Blues," a rare 1931 blues tune sung by the obscure Ruth Willis and including one of Dylan's heroes, Blind Willie McTell, on guitar.

One unsubstantiated rumor about "Lay, Lady, Lay" involves the song's being offered to the Everly Brothers and being refused because they misunderstood the lyrics as "across my big breasts" instead of "across my big brass bed." When the confusion was cleared up, the Everlys did eventually record "Lay, Lady, Lay."

Dylan performed "Lay, Lady, Lay" with the Band in 1974 as the second song of every one of those shows in a version that was the biting yang to the countrified keening yin of his *Nashville Skyline* hit, sounding more like a harsh proposition at a brothel in a Gold Rush boomtown. He further succeeded in erasing any memories people might have had of the lilting 1969 smash hit with his raucous Rolling Thunder arrangement, in which he yelled rather than sang. Furthermore, he presented himself as a surly rather than sexy suitor and toyed with the lyrics at that point to reflect a certain raw sexual emotion, transforming "you can have your cake and eat it too" into "you can have your cake but just try to eat it," making it devoid of the playful nuance evidenced on *Nashville Skyline*. Dylan performed "Lay, Lady, Lay" just once in 1984 but revived it in 1986 during the Tom Petty tour and has delivered about one hundred mostly electric versions during the Never Ending Tour, where, by the early '00s, it had been transformed into a lap steel guitar song with devilish overtones and a creepy rap.

◫ "Legionnaire's Disease" (Bob Dylan)
The Delta Cross Band, *Up Front* (1981)

A Dylan song full of dark humor written in 1978 and used in soundchecks at the time, "Legionnaire's Disease" dealt with the mysterious strain of pneumonia that killed thirty-four conventioneers who had attended an American Legion gathering in Philadelphia in 1976. Hysteria ran so high in the weeks following the outbreak that family members turned on one another, though it has since been discovered that the disease cannot be spread person to person but by certain types of air conditioners that can circulate a deadly organism if not properly cleaned.

For Dylan, the song not only worked as an allegory commenting on sick times, but took its place in the lineage of an overlooked and bizarre folk idiom: compositions named after an illness or disease. These include "Meningitis Blues" (Memphis Minnie), "Pneumonia Blues" (Blind Lemon Jefferson), "High Fever Blues" (Bukka White), Leadbelly's tuberculosis songs, and Woody Guthrie's venereal-disease songs, to name just a few, and the scores of songs about AIDS.

Billy Cross, a member of Dylan's band in 1978, brought the song to the Delta Cross Band, which recorded "Legionnaire's Disease" for the album *Up Front*.

◫ "Lenny Bruce" (Bob Dylan)
Bob Dylan, *Shot of Love* (1981); *Hard to Handle* (video) (1986)
The Zimmermen, *The Dungeon Tapes* (1996)

> "I am not a comedian. I am Lenny Bruce."
> —LENNY BRUCE.

For reasons primarily related to their iconoclasm and use of language, Dylan and Lenny Bruce were linked at the literal, figurative, and cultural hip from early on. Still, Dylan's courtly paean to this giant of twentieth-century stand-up, which cemented their association for all time, turns out to be a strange, damning-with-faint-praise homage that doesn't quite ring true. Saying Lenny Bruce shouldn't have been martyred because he "never cut off any babies' heads" is missing the point of America's most significant stand-up social diagnostician and does minimal service to the performance artist's legacy.

Leonard Alfred Schneider (born October 13, 1925, Wantagh, New York; died August 3, 1966, Hollywood, California) grew up near Jones Beach on Long Island. A product of a broken home, Lenny Bruce emerged neurotic, starved for affection, and dazed by the social boundaries of the adult world.

Increasingly drawn under the spell of his mother, Sally Marr, a sometime stand-up comic and entertainer who occasionally took him to burlesque shows, Bruce began performing as a young man. His first break came when he found himself a winner on *Arthur Godfrey's Talent Scouts*, a 1949 radio amateur contest.

Bruce began his career doing shtick, impressions, and emcee work in strip clubs. On this circuit he met and married Harriet Jolliff in 1953, a hot, redheaded stripper known professionally as Honey Michel and Honey Harlowe. In 1955 their daughter, Kitty, was born, but by the end of the decade, the family was shattered by divorce and drug abuse.

During these years Bruce's comedy was in flux, turning hipper and (according to the critics) "sicker" as he twisted and vamped on many old standards, breaking taboos and pushing the boundaries of propriety. While critics did a slow burn, Lenny became incendiary. A portion of the humor was in the so-called sick genre, but much of its overall power lay in Bruce's charismatic ability to create vividly etched satiric characters.

L

American comedian Lenny Bruce performing onstage with exotic dancer
Windee Gayle and a jazz band at the Orchid Room, Waikiki, Hawaii, in the 1950s.
(Hulton Archive/Getty Images)

Audiences encouraged Bruce toward more free-form comedy, to follow his instincts rather than rely on set bits and one-liners, to do more observational material, drawing, like a jazz musician, from the feeling and emotion of the moment. When some of his sexual or religious work garnered negative reviews, he was challenged only to push the envelope even more.

Lenny Bruce had his heyday during the late 1950s and early '60s. He was comedy's reckless visionary, the one who defied conventions, the law and the system. But like most visionaries, he was taken down by it all in the end.

As Bruce moved farther and farther afield of the era's comedic mainstream, the forces against him were strong and getting stronger. The First Amendment protected Bruce from the censors with regard to his religious and political material, but when it came to his use of "dirty words," the law was clearly on the state's side. "If anyone believes that God made his body, and that body is dirty, the fault lies with the manufacturer," Bruce would joke. But it was no joke to those whom he genuinely offended. He was busted several times for obscenity, and in his struggle to clear himself of the charges, he became entangled in a legal quagmire that drained away first his money and then his strength. In the long run, however, his doggedness permanently changed attitudes and laws on obscenity.

Bruce's drug use was widely known throughout the entertainment business, and after his acquittal on obscenity charges in Britain in 1963, he was deported from the United Kingdom, barred from performing in Australia, and busted for either narcotics possession or obscenity in Los Angeles, Chicago, Hollywood, New York, and San Francisco.

Still he struggled on, his performances increasingly marked by an obsession with law and language, trying to make sense of the nonsense. His audiences weren't buying it: as a reflection of his declining popularity and drawing power, *Variety* reported that he made $108,000 in 1960 and only $6,000 in 1964. By 1965 he was belly-up financially and, a year later, dead of a still somewhat suspicious morphine overdose in Los Angeles (Phil Spector dubbed it an "overdose of police"). One sure thing: Lenny Bruce has remained just as controversial and every bit the polarizing figure in death as he was in life.

This was borne out in late 2003 when New York governor George Pataki officially pardoned Bruce for cursing in public forty years before, after a campaign led by celebrities, actors, writers, and First Amendment lawyers alike. The debate raged again—was Lenny rolling over in his grave, or having the last laugh between sets at an after-hours haunt in Hades?

Lenny Bruce changed the playing field: no longer would comics have to come out in a cute little suit and tell cute little mother-in-law jokes or feel as if they were "working dirty" if they talked openly about sex and other taboo subjects. Clearly he was an enormously talented and insightful individual who would have absorbed whatever around him he found necessary to forge his particular vision and challenge the social boundaries that he deemed restrictive—which, to his eyes, just so hap-

pened to be practically all of them. Those lucky enough to have caught Bruce in performance on an inspired night said that it was like a roller-coaster ride, as free-associative ramblings streamed forth in a virtual torrent of ideas, jumping from '50s jazz hipster slang to a liberal dosage of Yiddish vernacular that sounded like code to the uninitiated. And Bruce, even to the end, had an impish little-boy charm that always gave the impression that he was letting his audience in on a big, dark secret.

In the years since Lenny Bruce's passing, other comedians have utilized elements of his style and teachings, but with almost universally mediocre results. Only Dick Gregory, Richard Pryor, Robin Williams, George Carlin, Jonathan Winters, Chris Rock, and a very small handful of others have artistically high-stepped through the gates Bruce opened and radically furthered the nature of stand-up. Of course, *Lenny* (the 1974 biopic starring Dustin Hoffman and directed by Bob Fosse) and *Lenny Bruce: Swear to Tell the Truth* (a riveting 1998 documentary directed by Robert Weide) are required viewing for all born and unborn Bruce freaks. Even more recently is a book titled *The Trials of Lenny Bruce: The Fall and Rise of an American Icon* (Naperville, Illinois: Sourcebooks MediaFusion, 2002) by Ronald K. L. Collins and David M. Skover.

Long before Dylan composed "Lenny Bruce," he referenced the comedian in "Blowin' in the Wind," a poem (not the famous song) published in the December 1963 edition of *Hootenanny* magazine. Perhaps he was inspired by seeing Bruce in concert, as Clinton Heylin, in his book *Bob Dylan: A Life in Stolen Moments* (New York: Schirmer Books, 1996), reports he did on November 30, 1963, at the Village Theater, later known as the Fillmore East.

Of the composition and intent of "Lenny Bruce," Dylan told New York disc jockey Dave

Herman in 1981 (in a promo distributed by Columbia Records): "I wrote that song in five minutes! It is true, I rode with him once in a taxicab. I found it was a little strange after he died, that people made such a hero out of him. When he was alive he couldn't even get a break. And certainly now, comedy is rank, dirty and vulgar and very unfunny and stupid, wishy-washy and the whole thing. . . . I guess it has to do with where I grew up, admiring those type of heroes, Robin Hood, Jesse James. . . . You know, the person who always kicked against the oppression and . . . had high moral standards. I don't know if the people I write about have high moral standards, I don't know if Robin Hood did, but you always assumed that they did."

He also discussed "Lenny Bruce" with music journalist Neil Spencer for the August 15, 1981, issue of *New Musical Express*. "'That was a really quick song for me to write,' Dylan said. 'I wrote that in about five minutes . . . I didn't even know why I was writing it, it just naturally came out. I wasn't, you know, meditating on Lenny Bruce before I wrote it.'"

Dylan has performed "Lenny Bruce" with loose regularity since touring in support of *Shot of Love* in 1981. Onstage it has developed into the grand homage its studio release only hinted at, and when Dylan performs it, at least for one more night, hipsters the world over can chant the sacred mantra: "Lenny lives!"

[S] "Leopard-Skin Pill-Box Hat" (Bob Dylan)

Bob Dylan, single (1966); *Blonde on Blonde* (1966); *The Bootleg Series, Volume 4: Live 1966—The "Royal Albert Hall" Concert)* (1998)
Bob Dylan/Various Artists (performed by John Mellencamp), *Bob Dylan: The 30th Anniversary Concert Celebration* (1993)
Woody Herman, *Woody Herman Presents a Great American Evening, Volume 3* (1983)
Jimmy LaFave, *Austin Skyline* (1992)
Various Artists (performed by Vole), *A Tribute to Bob Dylan* (1992)
Robyn Hitchcock, *Robyn Sings* (2002)
Various Artists (performed by Walter Trout), *Blues on Blonde on Blonde* (2003)

A minor, sloppy blues, "Leopard-Skin Pill-Box Hat" is probably the most infectious *Blonde on Blonde* tune—full of cunning, comic insult—and one to which Dylan has sporadically returned in performance over the years. The version on *Blonde on Blonde* was unique in Dylan's oeuvre, containing, according the album liner note info, Dylan's only credited guitar solo on record (at least until then), though this would seem to reference the song's instrumental introduction and not the longer, more legit solo midway through that is undoubtedly Robbie Robertson's. "Leopard-Skin Pill-Box Hat" is not on the same plateau of emotion as the best of the *Blonde on Blonde* batch, but it is still pure Dylan: like taking a stroll through Andy Warhol's Factory.

Others see "Leopard-Skin Pill-Box Hat" as a Dylan meditation on the void of materialism as he satirizes the superficiality of fashion, with the inane millinery (and the woman who lives under it) being the object of the author's ridicule. With a caustic sneer, Dylan seems to easily dispatch the whims of faddism (and the society of disposability that produces them) with layers of put-downs that cut a fine line of nettled mirth. Still, he can't help but marvel at the object itself as it "balances on your head/Just like a mattress balances/On a bottle of wine."

For those source hunters in attendance, the melody, lyrics, and poetic scansion of "Leopard-Skin Pill-Box Hat" compare well with Lightnin' Hopkins's "Automobile (Blues)": "I saw you riding 'round in your brand new automobile/Yes, I saw you ridin' around, babe, in your brand-new automobile/Yes, you was sitting there happy with your handsome driver at the wheel/In your brand new automobile."

As for the inspirational source of the hat in question, Dylan once said, "Mighta seen a picture of one in a department store window. There's really no more to it than that."

"Leopard-Skin Pill-Box Hat" was released as a single in 1966 and rose to No. 81 on the *Billboard* chart. After displaying "Leopard-Skin Pill-Box Hat" in the middle of his electric sets during his historic 1966 concerts, Dylan has trotted the song out for the odd airing through the years, singing it with the passion of an old (if a bit daft) bluesman. For a period in the late 1990s, Dylan even led off a number of Never Ending Tour shows with the song.

French singer and songwriter Gilbert Bécaud, 1967. (Photo: Keystone/Getty Images)

[S] **"Let It Be Me"** (Mann Curtis/Pierre Delanoë/Gilbert Bécaud)
aka "Je t'appartiens"
Bob Dylan, *Self Portrait* (1970)
Gilbert Bécaud, *Bécaud Olympia* (1975)
Jill Corey, single (1957)
The Everly Brothers, *The Fabulous Style of the Everly Brothers* (1960)
Elvis Presley, *Walk a Mile in My Shoes* (1995)
Billy Vera and Judy Clay, *Storybook Children* (1995)

"Let It Be Me" was written by Pierre Delanoë and Gilbert Bécaud in 1955 under the French title "Je t'appartiens" and was first recorded that year by Bécaud. Mann Curtis wrote English lyrics to the tune and Jill Corey introduced it in an episode of the 1950s TV series *Climax!* Her recording peaked at No. 57 on *Billboard*'s Top 100 chart. But it wasn't until the Everly Brothers recorded "Let It Be Me" that it became a megahit, reaching No. 7 for them in 1960.

Dylan, a not-so-secret Everlys fan, included a pure, if respectful, pop redrafting of "Let It Be Me" on his *Self Portrait* collection, staying true to their wistful pop vision. In 1981 Dylan released another recording of the song as a single in Europe on which he shared the vocals with backup singer Clydie King. He performed the song at a pair of consecutive shows that year as well.

The best known of the composers of "Let It Be Me" was Bécaud (born François Gilbert Silly, October 24, 1927, Toulon, France; died December 18, 2001, Paris), a popular French crooner and prolific songsmith. Raised in the south of France, he exploited his talents as a pianist after a move to Paris after World War II by accompanying nightclub singer Jacques Pills on his gigs around and about the City of Lights.

Pills's marriage to Édith Piaf gave Bécaud's singing career a boost due to his close connection to France's most beloved chanteuse. As Bécaud's star rose, his magnanimous stage presence earned him a great nickname: "Monsieur 100,000 Volts." At the opening of Paris's famed Olympia theater in 1954, his energetic style whipped the audience into such a frenzy that they tore up the venue's newly installed seats. His look became a sort of trademark: he always appeared onstage in a navy blue suit, white shirt, and polka-dot tie.

As his popularity and influence grew, Bécaud became associated with a group of French singers identified with a movement known as "la chanson française" (literally, "French song"). Chanson française is best characterized by its poetic lyrics, but Bécaud was admired even more by his colleagues for his melodies. And while Piaf, Yves Montand, Charles Trenet, and Charles Aznavour (*see* "The Times We Have Known") may have received greater international fame, Bécaud got his share of wide acclaim. Certainly many of his songs enjoyed success in their English versions.

Along with "Let It Be Me," "Et maintenant" ("What Now My Love"), "Le jour où la pluie viendra" ("The Day the Rains Came"), and "Seul sur son étoile" ("It Must Be Him") were a few of his more than four hundred-odd compositions that enjoyed global notice, with covers by everyone from Sonny and Cher to Roberta Flack. While he toured extensively and even appeared for three weeks on Broadway in 1966, his fellow countrymen were always his most loyal fans. And he traversed the River Styx in romantic fashion: aboard his houseboat on the River Seine.

[S] **"Let Me Die in My Footsteps"** (Bob Dylan)

aka "Don't Let Me Die in My Footsteps," "I Will Not Go Down Under the Ground"

Bob Dylan, *The Bootleg Series, Volumes 1–3: Rare and Unreleased, 1961–1991/'62* (1991)
Various Artists (performed by Bob Dylan with the New World Singers), *Broadside Ballads, Volume 1* (1963)
Coulson, Dean, McGuinness, Flint, *Lo & Behold* (1972)
Various Artists (performed by Happy Traum), *The Best of Broadside 1962–1988* (2000)
Second Floor, *Plays Dylan* (2001)
Various Artists (performed by Alastair Moock), *May Your Song Always Be Sung: The Songs of Bob Dylan, Volume 3* (2003)

A refusal to join the lemminglike, lockstep race to fallout shelters—an upsetting fad popularized during the 1950s and that lasted well past the Cuban missile crisis of 1962—Dylan's "Let Me Die in My Footsteps" is a proud declaration to stand and fight the threats of war. Bomb shelters, he says in essence, teach us to die, not to live.

Regarded as Dylan's first so-called anthem and sung as a statement against death by nuclear holocaust, "Let Me Die in My Footsteps" is thought to have been written in late February 1962. In his diary, Izzy Young (the proprietor of the Folklore Center, a hallowed Greenwich Village cultural nexus at the time) noted that on February 22, 1962, Dylan had stopped by and played him the song. But even at this early date, Dylan was drawing on the Bible with the same aplomb with which he drew on Woody Guthrie. The lines that begin the second verse ("There's been rumors of war and wars that have been/The meaning of life has been lost in the wind") are clearly cribbed from the words Christ spoke as reported in Matthew 24:6 and Mark 13:7.

"Let Me Die in My Footsteps" was performed frequently throughout 1962 and was one of four songs recorded for and originally included on early test pressings of, but ulti-

Prefabricated fallout shelter, fully equipped, 1961.

(Photo: Dmitri Kessel/Time Life Pictures/Getty Images)

mately dropped from, *The Freewheelin' Bob Dylan* in favor of the even more portentous "A Hard Rain's A-Gonna Fall" (some sources say "Masters of War"). Dylan had prepared the liner notes for its inclusion, which also never saw the light of day until both the song (with one verse cut) and notes were released on *The Bootleg Series, Volumes 1–3* some three decades later. Dylan wrote:

> This song has been on my mind for about two years. I was in Kansas, Phillipsburg or Marysville I think. I was going through some town out there and they were making this bomb shelter right outside of town, one of these sort of Coliseum-type things, and there were construction workers and everything. I was there for about an hour, just looking at them build, and I guess I just wrote the song in my head back then, but I carried it with me for two years until I finally wrote it down.

> As I watched them building, it struck me sort of funny that they would concentrate so much on digging a hole underground when there were so many other things they should do in life. If nothing else, they could look at the sky and walk around and live a little bit instead of doing this immoral thing. I guess that it's just that you can lead a lot of people by the hand. They don't even really know what they're scared of.

> I'd like to say that here is one song that I am really glad I made a record of. I don't consider anything that I write political, but even if I couldn't hardly sing a note, or even if I couldn't stand on my feet, this is one song that people won't have to look at me or even listen to closely or even like me, to understand.

Dylan evidently tired of performing "Let Me Die in My Footsteps"—perhaps because his other material dealing with similar subject matter was so much stronger. During a recording demo of the song for copyright purposes at the offices of the music publisher M. Witmark and Sons in New York in December 1962, he cut off midway (as heard on available bootleg tapes of the session), complaining that singing the song again was "a drag—I've sung it so many times."

Around the same time (and under the famous pseudonym Blind Boy Grunt) Dylan took another crack at performing "Let Me Die in My Footsteps" for a *Broadside* magazine recording (*Broadside Ballads, Volume 1*) released in September 1963. On this version (which is titled "I Will Not Go Down Under the Ground"), Happy Traum takes the lead vocal and Dylan harmonizes on the chorus and provides accompanying guitar. At Dylan's early gigs, the audience liked to join in for a moving group harmonization of the chorus.

"Let's Begin" (Jim Webb)
Leah Kunkel, *I Run with Trouble* (1980)

Dylan's concerts of the very early 1980s were notable for featuring a surprising number of oddball cover songs such as "Let's Begin," on which he shared the vocal with Clydie King at a handful of 1981 shows. They gave the song, about old lovers commencing to renew their romance, a catchy, original reading, introducing a playful intimacy.

Although almost every Dylan discography cites the great songsmith Jimmy Webb (born August 15, 1946, Elk City, Oklahoma) as the author of the song, its mention on any Webb discography is nonexistent. Fred Tackett, Dylan's ace lead guitarist of the time, had been a featured sideman at many a Webb session date, so it is presumed that if the song is in fact a Webb composition, Tackett was responsible for bringing it to Dylan.

"Let's Keep It Between Us" (Bob Dylan)
aka "Can We Keep It Between Us?"
Bonnie Raitt, *Green Light* (1982)
Various Artists (performed by Bonnie Raitt), *The Songs of Bob Dylan* (1989)

Written when he was putting *Shot of Love* together, the R&B-heavy "Let's Keep It Between Us" can viewed as one of those confidential, promise-not-to-kiss-and-tell torch rockers Bill Clinton might have been advised to teach his spring flings, or perhaps as a testament to maintaining a romance.

"Let's Keep It Between Us," a piano song performed exclusively during Dylan's shows of November and early December 1980, was one of several new works displayed during that period that signaled a turn away from the heavy born-again Christian compositions of the past year. At the time, it was evidently still a work in progress; at his December 3, 1980, show in Portland, Oregon, Dylan introduced the tune thusly: "This is a new song—I don't know how old it is—anyway, it's called 'Can We Keep It Between Us?'" and proceeded to perform the song with that lyric.

In his book *Bob Dylan, Performing Artist: The Middle Years, 1974–1986* (Novato, Calif.: Underwood-Miller, 1992), Paul Williams observed:

> Dylan's voice takes on a different character as he accompanies himself on piano; it has a resonance which, although the tonal space it occupies is actually quite limited, seems to expand to fill the listener's universe in every direction. Intensity and intimacy. This performance, built around Dylan's voice and piano, with explosive accompaniment from Willie Smith on organ and Tim Drummond and Jim Keltner on bass and drums, always strikes me as a sort of masterpiece in black and white, so stark, so focused, so penetrating . . .

The song may also be heard as having spiritual connotations. One's private relationship with the divine can be harmed or destroyed by the attention of the public or of well-meaning friends—the analysis and judgments and opinions and gossip and for-your-own-good interference of the world at large. "Let's Keep It Between Us," though unheard since 1980, has the potential to be an enduring Bob Dylan theme song (like "It Ain't Me, Babe"). I wish he'd get out his piano and sing it more often.

[S] "Let's Learn to Live and Love Again"

(Jimmy Rule/David Briggs)

Jack Scott, *Scott on Groove* (1989)

Dylan's only two performances of this tearjerking plea for romantic reconciliation (associated with rocker turned country-pop star Jack Scott) came during the summer 1990 segment of the Never Ending Tour.

Guitarist and keyboardist David Briggs (born January 26, 1951, Melbourne, Australia), the better known of the song's cowriters, has worked with an amazing collection of A-list entertainers, including Joan Baez, the Monkees, Neil Young, Jerry Jeff Walker, Ian and Sylvia, Alice Cooper, Elvis Presley, Eric Andersen, Kris Kristofferson, Leon Russell, Bob Seger, Earl Scruggs, and John Prine. Briggs played piano and organ at eight of Elvis's recording sessions as well as at some of the King's live concerts (at $3,000 a week). He later became a member of the country-rock band Area Code 615, which also featured Charlie McCoy, a notable mid-'60s Dylan sideman.

[S] "Let's Stick Together" (Wilbert Harrison)

aka "Let's Work Together"

See also "Kansas City"

Bob Dylan, *Down in the Groove* (1988)

Wilbert Harrison, *Let's Work Together* (1969); *Kansas City* (1994)

John Mayall, *Sense of Place* (1990)

Dwight Yoakam, *If There Was a Way* (1990)

George Thorogood, *Let's Work Together Live* (1995)

Dylan laconically laid into this heartwarming bit of early soul on *Down in the Groove* but never performed it in concert.

"Let's Stick Together" comes to *Down in the Groove* courtesy of Wilbert Harrison, who was more than merely a two-hit wonder known for "Kansas City" in 1957 and "Let's Work Together" twelve years later. As a singer, drummer, pianist, mouth harpist, and guitarist, Harrison left a varied, idiom-crossing musical legacy that ranged from calypso to soul to R&B to rock 'n' roll to Jesse Fuller–style eccentric folk blues.

Harrison (born January 5, 1929, Charlotte, North Carolina; died October 26, 1994, Spencer, North Carolina) casually absorbed the region's country and gospel sounds but didn't get serious about his talent or showbiz until leaving the navy in the early 1950s, when he discovered a passion for Caribbean music. A first-prize award at a Miami, Florida, amateur contest in 1953 led to a record deal with the Rockin' label, on which he released his debut single, "This Woman of Mine."

A move to Newark, New Jersey, in 1957 led to steady work in the city's clubs and deals with first Savoy and then Fury Records, which caused all kinds of complicated legal wrangling when his waxing of "Kansas City" rose to No. 1. Both companies cried foul and began suing each other in a process that dragged on for years and stymied Harrison's career.

Harrison rebounded in 1969 with "Let's Work Together," an infectious two-part single later covered and popularized by Canned Heat and Bryan Ferry, the latter of whom retitled the song "Let's Stick Together." By that point, Harrison was working and recording as a virtual one-man band—a role he would continue for another quarter century until his death.

▣ "Let the Good Times Roll" (Leonard Lee)

Leonard and Shirley Lee, single (1956); *Let the Good Times Roll* (2000)

Helen Humes, *'Deed I Do* (1976)

Lester Bowie, *Works* (1980)

Roy Orbison, *Legendary Roy Orbison* (1988)

Sometimes confused with any of the many similarly titled party songs (somebody should write a book about the family of interrelated songs sharing the title), Leonard Lee's "Let the Good Times Roll" was composed in 1956 when Lee and his wife, Shirley, scored a No. 1 R&B hit with it. For Dylan, Lee's "Let the Good Times Roll" was a short-lived encore cover during the 1986 tour with Tom Petty and the Heartbreakers.

In addition to "Let the Good Times Roll," Leonard Lee (born June 29, 1935, New Orleans; died October 26, 1976, New Orleans) was famous for his part in Shirley and Lee, a teenage duo featuring himself and his wife, Shirley Goodman Lee (born June 19, 1936, New Orleans). Her shrill vocals and his bluesy retorts added up to R&B gold during the fifties. "I'm Gone," their debut single on Aladdin, was a major R&B hit in 1952. Then, in 1955 and '56, they caught fire with a string of rockin' smashes all written by Lee, including "Let the Good Times Roll," which they redid in 1959 after moving to the Warwick label from Aladdin. Dubbed "The Sweethearts of the Blues," the act, but not the marriage, broke up in 1963 after a few singles for Imperial. They returned in 1974 under the name Shirley and Company with a disco version of one of their hits, "Shame, Shame, Shame."

▣ Jacques Levy
Born July 29, 1935, New York City

Jacques Levy is a New York clinical psychologist turned theater rat who became involved with musical theater in the 1960s. He directed the New York production of *Oh! Calcutta!* Levy is probably best known, though, as Dylan's collaborator on the lyrics for the *Desire* album—he's the bearded guy on the back of the album sleeve with Dylan at the microphone. Levy also played a major role in directing Dylan's 1975 Rolling Thunder Revue. The songs he cowrote with Dylan include "Black Diamond Bay," "Catfish," "Hurricane," "Isis," "Joey," "Money Blues," "Mozambique," "Oh, Sister," "Rita May," and "Romance in Durango."

Levy grew up in New York City and was educated at Michigan State University and trained as a clinical psychologist. Upon earning his Ph.D. he worked at the noted Menninger Foundation Clinic in Topeka, Kansas, where he casually drifted to directing amateur dramatics at a local community theater as a hobby. He found his extracurricular activities so exhilarating that he turned his back on psychology and returned to New York in 1965 to pursue his theater muse.

New York City's alternative theater scene (known as off-off Broadway) was beginning to find wider audiences at the time and Levy became involved with the loose-knit community, lending his skills to some of the city's most respected downtown outfits, including the Open Theater, the New Dramatists Committee, the Judson Poets Theater, and the La Mama Experimental Theater. Within a couple of years, Levy moved into the more rarefied ranks of off-Broadway when he directed *Scuba Duba* and *America Hurrah*. He shared the 1965–66 off-Broadway Obie award for his work with the Open Theater in the production of *America Hurrah,* which he directed in collaboration with Joseph Chaikin. *America Hurrah* also caught the eye of British critic Kenneth Tynan, who conceived *Oh! Calcutta!* in his last years of life, imagining it as an evening of esoteric pornography with a Victorian edge. Levy adapted the critic's ideas and commissioned a variety of high-profile writers (Samuel Beckett, John Lennon, and Sam Shepard among them) to contribute. When the stage show opened in the summer of 1969, it became something of a cause célèbre as a thinking-man's *Hair,* partially because it included some nudity.

In 1969 Levy and Roger McGuinn of the Byrds cowrote the lyrics for the songs and book for the musical *Gene Tryp,* a country-rock adaptation of *Peer Gynt,* Henrik Ibsen's important 1867 play. *Gene Tryp* was to feature several of McGuinn's best latter-day Byrds songs, among them "Chestnut Mare" and "Just a Season." Bob Dylan was, along with the likes of Jon Voight and Tim Buckley, one of those discussed as possible candidates for the lead role. Yet although producers David Merrick and Don Kirshner both expressed interest, *Gene Tryp* never made it to the stage. Levy again worked with McGuinn on the latter's first solo LP, *Roger McGuinn,* in 1973.

It was during this period that Levy began crossing paths with Dylan. In the summer of 1975, Dylan (with *Blood on the Tracks* and his 1974 tour with the Band behind him) bumped into Levy on Bleecker Street in Greenwich Village. Levy invited Dylan up to his loft on La Guardia Place and the two casually began discussing a collaboration. According to Levy, Dylan "had no specific plans at that time to do anything, and he said something like, 'I really like the stuff you do with Roger, how about if you and I do something together?' Which was really strange, right? Because he knew *I* did

lyrics and I knew *he* did lyrics. But I said, 'Sure, let's give it a shot.'" (From "Apathy for the Devil—Jacques Levy, Joseph Conrad and 'Black Diamond Bay'" by Derek Barker, in *Isis: A Bob Dylan Anthology*, edited by Derek Barker. London: Helter Skelter Publishing, 2001.)

Dylan's recollections (quoted from the *Biograph* liner notes) of the genesis of *Desire* correspond rather neatly with Levy's and elaborate on that momentous evening: "I was just in town, you know, and saw Jacques on the street. We ran into each other and we had seen each other off and on throughout the years, so we wound up just over at his place sitting around, and I had a few songs. I certainly wasn't thinking of making a record album, but I had bits and pieces of some songs I was working on and I played them for him on the piano, and asked him if they meant anything to him, and he took it someplace else and then I took it someplace else, then he went further, then I went further and it wound up that we had this song."

The two worked on it through the night, and when the cock crowed at dawn a new composition, "Isis," and a collaboration were born. Unable to really focus over the next week due the distractions of life in New York, Dylan and Levy ventured to East Hampton on Long Island to commune, and, in one of Dylan's most fruitful periods of lickety-split woodshedding, the two harvested an unprecedented number of songs—fourteen by some accounts.

As Barker further relates in "Apathy for the Devil," describing the East Hampton chapter, Levy recounted, "We went out a couple of nights. One night we went to a bar and Bob sang a couple of the songs and we hung out with some people that night just to get away from things. The pressure was tremendous and intense on both of us, and we'd stop in the middle of a song and go shoot a game of eight-ball."

In the end, Dylan and Levy wrote seven of the nine songs that appear on Dylan's 1975 album *Desire*. Another of their collaborations, an outtake from *Desire* called "Catfish," a composition about baseball pitcher Jim "Catfish" Hunter, showed up on *The Bootleg Series, Volumes 1–3*. "Rita Mae," another cowritten outtake, was performed by the Rolling Thunder Revue and released on Dylan's *Masterpieces* collection. A final outtake, "Money Blues," has never been released.

Levy's career was hardly limited to his association with Dylan or *Oh! Calcutta!* His credits also include the Broadway musical *Doonesbury*. Outside New York he has directed productions in regional theaters across the United States, as well as in London, Berlin, Moscow, and Venice. Levy is also the lyricist of *Fame, the Musical*, based on the highly successful 1977 theatrical production that began a late-nineties run in the major cities of Europe, including a year in London, and in 2000 started touring North America.

In 1992 Levy went to work at Colgate University in Hamilton, New York, as a professor of English and head of the theater program, bringing with him teaching experience from Yale, Columbia, Hunter College, the New School, and the Actors Studio. At Colgate he teaches advanced acting, an advanced directing seminar, and playwriting, and was responsible for instituting and overseeing the school's annual spring festival in which Colgate students act, direct, and design all of the productions. In addition, Professor Levy directs a major theater production at the college every year.

[S] "License to Kill" (Bob Dylan)

Bob Dylan, *Infidels* (1983); *Real Live* (1984)
Bob Dylan/Various Artists (performed by Tom Petty and the Heartbreakers), *Bob Dylan: The 30th Anniversary Concert Celebration* (1993)
Polly Bolton, *No Going Back* (1989)
Richie Havens, *Sings Beatles and Dylan* (1990)
Big Brass Bed, *A Few Dylan Songs* (2003)

"License to Kill" is a brooding meditation with apocalyptic undertones that takes on corruption and technology run amok. It became a wonderfully reckless performance vehicle during its many live outings in 1984, when Dylan kept it in heavy rotation, in comparison to its relatively restrained reading on *Infidels*. "All he believes are his eyes/And his eyes they just tell him lies," sings Dylan: what an extraordinary and frightening way to declare the doom of man.

A song that tends to get lost in the shuffle when discussion of Dylan's better compositions arises, "License to Kill" has, not surprisingly, garnered little critical attention. It seems to pick up where "Jokerman," the big song on *Infidels*, leaves off. Like some kind of dire, end-time sermon spoken in a burning temple, "License to Kill" draws on the Old Testament prophets Isaiah and Jeremiah in pointing to the many reasons man is permanently fallen. Is it because he lords over the animal kingdom and thinks he can treat Mother Earth however he likes? Or maybe it's that stagnant pool where he worships? It's only there, when he sees his reflection in it, that he feels fulfilled—an echo of both Ecclesiastes 1:2 ("Vanity of vanities, saith the Preacher, vanity of vanities; all is vanity") and the ancient but always relevant Greek myth of Narcissus, who drowned when reaching for his image in the water. And Dylan reminds us in the first verse of the song that reaching too far can bring unexpected consequences: "Man has invented his doom/First step was touching the moon."

Dylan raises the stakes with a pile-driving chorus that leaves no stone unturned in its condemnation of the havoc man wreaks upon himself and his environment as if he were a mere "actor in a plot," as the song goes, perhaps referencing the then-current occupant of the White House: former thespian Ronald Reagan.

Flitting about the fringes of this whole scene and asking the song's question ("who gonna take away his license to kill?") is a woman. Dylan never mentions her age or nationality, but her character feels wizened and old, her implicit disgust and apparent helplessness close to the surface.

On a completely different tack, *From There to Here*, a 2000 album by Beck wannabe John Oszajca, contains a track entitled "Where's Bob Dylan When You Need Him" that uses a reverbed hip-hop sampling of Dylan's *Infidels* version of "License to Kill." And close observers will notice its brief implementation during a scene in the 2002 film *Monster's Ball*.

"License to Kill" made some rare appearances during Dylan's Tom Petty phase and just one early display in the Never Ending Tour after the 1984 European outing that produced *Real Live*. Dylan's performance of the song in his 1983 appearance on television's *Late Night with David Letterman* is must-see video.

Bob Dylan performing with an electric guitar at the 1965 Newport Folk Festival.
(Photo: Diana Davies. Courtesy of the Center for Folklife and Cultural Heritage, Smithsonian Institution)

🅂 "Like a Rolling Stone" (Bob Dylan)

Bob Dylan, single (1965); *Highway 61 Revisited* (1965); *Bob Dylan's Greatest Hits* (1967); *Self Portrait* (1970); *Eat the Document* (film)/'66 (1971); *Masterpieces* (1978); *Bob Dylan at Budokan* (1979); *Biograph*/'65 (1985); *Hard to Handle* (video) (1986); *The Bootleg Series, Volumes 1–3 Rare and Unreleased, 1961–1991*/'65 (1991); *MTV Unplugged* (1995); *The Bootleg Series, Volume 4: Bob Dylan Live 1966—The "Royal Albert Hall" Concert* (1998)

Bob Dylan/The Band, *Before the Flood* (1974)

The Band (performed with Bob Dylan), *Rock of Ages (Deluxe Edition)*/'71 (2001)

Bob Dylan/Various Artists (performed by John Mellencamp), *Bob Dylan: The 30th Anniversary Concert Celebration* (1993); (performed by Articolo 31), *Masked and Anonymous* (2003)

The Turtles, *It Ain't Me, Babe* (1965)

Dino, Desi and Billy, *I'm a Fool* (1965)

The Four Seasons, *Sing Big Hits of Bacharach, David & Dylan* (1965); *Four Seasons Sing Big Hits* (1988)

Gene Norman Group, *Dylan Jazz* (1965)

Jerry Murad, *What's Happening Harmonicats* (1965)

Serfs, *The Early Bird Café* (1965)

The Surfaris, *It Ain't Me Babe* (1965)

Billy Strange, *Folk Rock Hits* (1965)

The Young Rascals, *The Young Rascals* (1966)

The Wailers, single (1966); *The Wailing Wailers at Studio One, Volume 2* (1994)

Billy Lee Riley, *Funk Harmonica* (1966)

Cher, *Sonny Side of Cher* (1967); *Bang Bang and Other Hits* (1992)

Sebastian Cabot, *Sebastian Cabot, Actor—Bob Dylan, Poet* (1967)

Calliope, *Steamed* (1968)

The Rotary Connection, *Rotary Connection* (1968)

The Arbors, *I Can't Quit Her* (1969)

Hugo Montenegro, *Dawn of Dylan* (1970)

The Undisputed Truth, *The Undisputed Truth* (1971)

Paper Lace, *First Edition* (1972)

Jimi Hendrix, *Soundtrack Recordings* (1973); *Jimi Plays Monterey* (1986)

Bettina Jonic, *The Bitter Mirror* (1975)

Spirit, *Spirit of '76* (1975); *Live at La Paloma* (1995)

Brakes, *For Why You Kicka My Donkey* (1979)

Johnny Winter, *Raisin' Cain* (1980)

Creation, *How Does It Feel to Feel?* (1982)

Bad News Reunion, *Last Orders Please* (1982)

Invictas, *Au Go Go* (1983)

Wolfgang Ambros and Fendrich, *Open Air* (1983)

Rich Lerner, *Performs Songs by Bob Dylan* (1990); *Napoleon in Rags* (2001)

Judy Collins, *Judy Sings Dylan . . . Just Like a Woman* (1993)

Mystery Tramps, single (1993)

The Outcasts, *Live!/Standing Room Only* (1993)

Mick Ronson, *Heaven and Hull* (1994)

The Rolling Stones, *Stripped* (1995)

Hugues Aufray, *Aufray Trans Dylan* (1995)

Lester Flatt and Earl Scruggs, *1964–1969, Plus* (1996)

The Paragons, *Sing the Beatles and Bob Dylan* (1998)

Insol, *Insol* (1998)

Nancy Sinatra, *How Does It Feel* (1999)

Black 47, *Live in New York City* (1999)

Gerard Quintana and Jordi Batiste, *Els Miralls de Dylan* (1999)

Various Artists (performed by David West), *Pickin' on Dylan* (1999)

Michel Montecrossa, *Born in Time* (2000)

Tiny Tim, *Live! At the Royal Albert Hall* (2000)

Patricia O'Callaghan, *Real Emotional Girl* (2001)

Various Artists (performed by Peter Himmelman), *Alive at Twenty-five: The Telluride Bluegrass Festival's Silver Anniversary* (2002)

Robyn Hitchcock, *Robyn Sings* (2002)

Todd Rubenstein, *The String Quartet Tribute to Bob Dylan* (2003)

Barb Jungr, *Waterloo Sunset* (2003)

Bob Dylan's greatest song? While that debate could go on forever (and has already raged long past the point of tedium), there is no dispute that upon its release in 1965 "Like a Rolling Stone" elevated rock 'n' roll to high poetic art once and for all.

With power, brilliance, and dynamism, Dylan's sneer at a woman who has fallen from grace and reduced to fending for herself in a hostile, unfamiliar world carries an air of faded majesty. While some have suggested the song is autobiographical, "Like a Rolling Stone" reads more like a revenge song—the angry rantings of a twenty-four-year-old middle-class kid thrust into stardom and lashing out at the privileged sycophants slumming in his wake and feeding off his aura.

With crisp brevity, Dylan takes the language of the streets and fuses it with a cascading effect that heightens Miss Lonely's descent. Dylan's use of the internal rhyme and phrasing is at its best in "Like a Rolling Stone" as he cuts her down to size with verse after pounding verse of gleefully unforgiving, "I told ya so" vitriol. She's been to the finest schools, she's made every scene there was to make with all her fancy, high-placed friends, but now, on the other side of the looking glass, things don't seem quite so easy, do they? By taking the easy way out, Miss Lonely has, like a rolling stone, gathered no moss—no useful, meaningful experience to use as a foundation for building her character.

"Like a Rolling Stone" also broke the mold of the two-minute single. Refusing to shorten the recording to fit radio's strict format, Dylan delivered a six-minute epic that would become his first number-one single and the then-longest song to ever hit the Top 40. If nothing else, the popularity of "Like a Rolling Stone" forced radio stations all over the world to reconsider their format, shattering a restricting paradigm and setting the stage for the development of free-form FM radio and rock 'n' roll.

In the *Biograph* liner notes, Dylan briefly described the creative process that produced "Like a Rolling Stone": "My wife and I lived in a little cabin in Woodstock, which we rented from Peter Yarrow's mother. I wrote the song there, in this cabin. We had come up from New York, and I had about three days off up there to get some stuff together (for the next album). It just came, you know. It started off with that 'La Bamba' riff."

Some insight into how the song was shaped into being in the studio may be gleaned both from the piano-based, waltz-time version released on *The Bootleg Series, Volumes 1–3* and those available on Dylan's CD-ROM, *Highway 61 Interactive*.

Recalling the cathartic process of writing the song, Dylan told biographer Robert Shelton for his 1986 book *No Direction Home*: "'Like a Rolling Stone,' man, was very vomitific in its structure. . . . It seemed like twenty pages, but it was really six. I wrote it in six pages. You know how you get sometimes." Dylan continued:

> And I did it on a piano. And when I made the record, I called the people who made the record with me, and I told them how to play on it. . . . When I wrote "all you got to do is find a school and learn to get juiced in it," I wasn't making this song about school. That's their idea. Their definition of school is much different than mine. My language is different than theirs. I mean REALLY TOTALLY DIFFERENT! The finest school, I mean, might just be out in the swamps. "School" here can be anything. This song is definitely not about school.

Shelton picks up on Dylan's thought and develops it. According to Shelton,

> [Dylan] was probably using "school" as a symbol of a way of life. He sees horror enveloping anyone who suddenly makes a break after being closely attracted to any form of life. For some, the experience is liberating; to others, it brings panic and helplessness. The "schoolgirl" he seems to be chastising here is probably anyone afraid to step out of his or her cocoon and into life's mainstream

without guidance, parents, structure, or crutches. The words seem crueler on the page than they sound in performance. A song that seems to hail the dropout life for those who can take it segues into compassion for those who have dropped out of bourgeois surroundings. "Rolling Stone" is about the loss of innocence and the harshness of experience. Myths, props, and old beliefs fall away to reveal a very taxing reality.

Since its concert debut at the monumental Newport and Forest Hills shows in the summer of 1965, "Like a Rolling Stone" has been a constant in Dylan's repertoire, though he has continually futzed with its arrangement and his delivery. It was the icing on the cake, in-your-face knockout-punch finale during the historic 1966 electric tour; transformed into a country bellow for the 1969 Isle of Wight show; revamped with a blustery swagger for the whirlwind '74 tour with the Band (utilized to great dramatic effect by Martin Scorsese in his segment of the 1989 film *New York Stories*); lazily delivered during the Rolling Thunder Revue; glitzed up for the 1978 big-band world tour; and molded into various balladic shapes in the 1980s and 1990s. By the time the hot 2002 incarnation of the Never Ending Tour band hit town, Dylan and company tangled in a triple guitar showdown that raised many a roof. And it continues to do so; it's a song that he never ceases blowing new life into even after version gazillion and one.

Bobcats point to a couple of other songs, in addition to the aforementioned "La Bamba" (the big 1959 Ritchie Valens hit), as possible roots of "Like a Rolling Stone": Muddy Waters's "Rolling Stone," and Leon Payne's "Lost Highway," which begins with "I'm a rolling stone." Dylan can be seen singing "Lost Highway" in the 1967 documentary *Don't Look*

Back only a month before writing "Like a Rolling Stone." Listen to these three cuts back to back to back, and you may be able to hear where and how the seeds to a masterwork were sown.

🅂 **"Lily of the West"** (Traditional; arrangement by E. Davis and J. Peterson)
Bob Dylan, single (1974); *Dylan* (1973)
Joan Baez, *Joan Baez, Volume 2* (1961)
Bascom Lamar Lunsford, *Music from South Turkey Creek* (1976)
The Chieftains, *Long Black Veil* (1995)
Dan Milner, *Irish Ballads and Songs of the Sea* (1998)

An ancient murder ballad kept alive for centuries by both print and the oral tradition, "Lily of the West" was originally an English broadside. The song gained particular popularity in the United States among parlor singers and ballad printers, and by the nineteenth century it was known throughout the land, becoming an integral part of the folk heritage upon its emergence in North America. It was so popular in Kansas in the mid- to late nineteenth century that local versifiers used the song for pioneer parody.

"Lily of the West" is the song of an unfaithful lover and shares a tune similar to "Lakes of Pontchartrain," which Dylan covered far more effectively. Though it is now primarily identified with the American West, British folklorists have collected versions of it in Devonshire, Yorkshire, and elsewhere in the United Kingdom. Some think the ballad is of Irish origin and traced it back to at least 1839, though the song they cite may not have been sung to a similar tune. The lyrics for "Lily of the West" in *Sam Henry's Songs of the People* (Athens: University of Georgia Press, 1990) are an Irish version that begin "When first I came to Ireland . . ." Another theory of its origin traces it back to the west of Ireland during the time of Cromwell.

A fingerpicked version of "Lily of the West" complete with a dreadful chorus was included on *Dylan*, an album of rehearsal outtakes released by Columbia without Dylan's sanction.

[S] "Lily, Rosemary and the Jack of Hearts"

(Bob Dylan)
aka "Jack of Hearts"
Bob Dylan, *Blood on the Tracks* (1975)
Joan Baez, *From Every Stage* (1976); *The Essential Joan Baez/From the Heart: Live* (2001)
7 Lvvas, *Nu* (1998)
Rolling Thunder, *The Never Ending Rehearsal* (2000)
Mary Lee's Corvette, *Blood on the Tracks* (2002)
Tom Russell, *Indians Cowboys Horses Dogs* (2004)

John Ford meets Lord Buckley meets *The Manchurian Candidate* by way of Robert Service in this fascinating honky-tonk morality fable from just about everybody's favorite desert-island Dylan disc, *Blood on the Tracks*. Indeed, Dylan's deft reworking of Service's "The Shooting of Dan McGrew" owes more to Buckley's hip-semantic translation, "The Ballad of Dan McGroo" (aka "Swingin' Danny McGroo," found on His Lordship's posthumously released 1960 recording *The Bad-Rapping of the Marquis de Sade*) than it does to the poet laureate of the Yukon. It should not be forgotten, however, that one of Service's books of poetry is titled *Rhymes of a Rolling Stone*. W. H. Auden's poem "Victor" has also been suggested as the source for the main structure and phrasing of "Lily, Rosemary and the Jack of Hearts." And "Big Jim," a black murder ballad collected by the Lomaxes, probably figures in here too.

Regardless of its sources, "Jack of Hearts" includes and co-opts every cliché Wild West character and situation as found, most famously, in Ford's still-untouchable 1939 film *Stagecoach*: the cardsharp, the heart-of-gold prostitute, the "good wife," the outlaw, the cunning bank-robbing desperadoes, the drunken hanging judge, and the contemptible businessman—all well-worn Dylan archetypes.

A long, lively, ambiguous yarn propelled by a crack studio band's driving rhythm and Dylan's nimble storytelling, which climaxes with the inevitable murder, "Jack of Hearts" plays out like a poker game and is vaguely reminiscent of Dylan's "The Ballad of Frankie Lee and Judas Priest," another narrative song of the Western tradition. This fifteen-verse playlet is filled with dark, enigmatic whimsy and just enough sly obscurity to keep the listener guessing.

In his *Hard Rain: A Dylan Commentary* (New York: Alfred A. Knopf, 1992), Tim Riley looks closely at "Lily, Rosemary and the Jack of Hearts" and sees a grave comment:

> Tragedy gets a bad rap, especially from pulp-culture stereotypes, where sensibilities tend toward the bite-sized. Dylan's farewell to the sixties wouldn't ring true if he didn't capture the sense of fun and danger that defined it, and he always puts his satirical instincts to work best through farcical heroics that are as impressive for their sustained length as for anything else. "Lily, Rosemary and the Jack of Hearts" is an intricately evasive allegory about romantic façades that hide criminal motives, and the way one character's business triggers a series of recriminations from people he doesn't even know. Jack is the quintessential mysterious stranger who barely has to lift a finger to set the town on its ear—he works as a dandy simile for Dylan. The Jack of Hearts is more than just a pretty face—he's such a ladies' man that his gang puts him to work as a decoy while they perform their heist. This buck is so distracting that nobody suspects his pals are in the next room dismantling the safe. And the music trots along at

L

such a steady clip that you can lose the story's thread and still get off on the pace of events.

Lily the showgirl carries on with Rosemary's husband, Big Jim, and this public triangle is the town's yardstick of Jim's wealth and prestige. But a young stud like Jack trumps Jim's opulence with a knowing smirk. Jack buys the house drinks, upstages the town's two-timing swell, narrowly escapes calamity with Lily on his lap, and blows out of town with the loot before anybody has a chance to figure out who he is. One night he simply appears—the next day he's a legend.

Jack takes the room with the same sweep with which Lily takes the stage, but Dylan insinuates a deft maneuver of action between the time the lights go down and when Jack visits Lily in her dressing room after the show. She has spotted him from the stage, perhaps even flirted with him in front of Big Jim, and she welcomes her ex-lover with the line "Has your luck run out? . . . Well, I guess you must have known it would someday." What the listener knows (but the characters don't) is the way Jack is exploiting his own good looks (and luck) to distract the audience from the heist: a public visitation to the well-known mistress of the local diamond-mine owner is bound to cause a stir. Sure enough, after a verse that Dylan leaves unsung (reprinted in *Lyrics: 1962–1985*), just as Jack embraces Lily, Big Jim and Rosemary storm the room: Jim with an unexpectedly unloaded gun (it clicks instead of fires), Rosemary with a knife in the back of her cheating husband. Rosemary's motive is apparently to kill her husband in the act of defending his mistress's "honor," but her eyes give up her feelings for Jack. The next day, Big Jim is laid into the ground, and Rosemary is up on the gallows platform. In the final verse, Lily, the showgirl with one too many agendas, rinses the dye from her hair and wonders if Jack will ever pull another job at her expense. . . .

Rosemary was ripe for revenge; the Jack of Hearts was only an appearance of opportunity. And the Jack of Hearts is enigmatic largely because we get to know him through how the others respond to his presence: Lily's feigned cool, Big Jim's insecurity, Rosemary's self-hate and jealousy (she's weary of being Big Jim's wife, but as Big Jim's revolver clicks, she understands all of a sudden why Lily would cheat on Jim).

Unlike a lot of Dylan's anti-narratives ("Stuck Inside of Mobile with the Memphis Blues Again," "Sad-Eyed Lady of the Lowlands"), "Lily, Rosemary and the Jack of Hearts" stacks up in a conventional manner that manages to mock linear concerns. You don't have to wade through the plot twists in order to take pleasure from the thoughts passing through these characters' minds. As is his specialty, Dylan delivers the song with a poker face, and everything moves at a good clip. Only after you sort out all the mixed motives and dangling expectations do you realize that Dylan has been tipping his hand the whole time: Rosemary, "lookin' to do just one good deed before she died," sets up a larger irony: she kills for love as a way of killing herself (she'd even tried suicide—she wants to take Big Jim along with her.) Lily is one of those showgirls who . . . have a little too much experience, and the Jack of Hearts neatly nixes her offstage dilemma. And in what could have been a shaggy-dog anticlimax—the scene where Big Jim's revolver clicks instead of fires—Dylan juices the tension by understatement. "You couldn't say surprised" is too sly a phrase for someone who gets stabbed by his wife the moment his gun goes shy.

The success of what Dylan sometimes throws away as elaborate emptiness is the way this farce turns out to be an apt mirror of sixties veneers. Everyone is so engaged with the romantic intrigue Jack sets in motion that they pay no attention to the drilling in the wall.

"Jack of Hearts" received some radio play upon its release, and there was even some buzz around Hollywood about turning it into a screenplay, with speculation that Dylan would play the Jack—as if he wasn't doing just that already. Interestingly, Dylan omitted a verse from the song on *Blood on the Tracks*. A version of the song recorded in September 1974 included that verse as did the album's songbook and the later *Lyrics, 1962–1985*.

Dylan allegedly performed "Lily, Rosemary and the Jack of Hearts" but once—at the last Rolling Thunder Revue show in Salt Lake City on his 35th birthday in 1976—a performance hard-core Dylanists regard as more mythology than fact, as no tape has ever surfaced.

"Little Maggie" (Traditional)
Bob Dylan, *Good as I Been to You* (1992)
Various Artists (performed by Obray Ramsey), *Banjo Songs of the Southern Mountains/'30s* (1980)
Hamish Imlach, *Ballads of Booze* (1969)
David Grisman, *Early Dawg* (1980)
The Stanley Brothers, *Starday Sessions* (1984)
Bill Monroe, *Bluegrass 1959–1969* (1991)
Red Allen, *Bluegrass Reunion* (1991)
Mike Seeger, *Way Down in North Carolina* (1996)
Doc Watson, *Home Sweet Home* (1998)

"Little Maggie" is the gun-toting first cousin in song to "Darlin' Corey" and many another wild mountain woman. Her story was a favorite among the traditional singers in the Southern hills. Bluegrass singers, especially, have been particularly fond of the hard-living damsel, considering her song the virtual national

anthem of bluegrass. Dylan's high lonesome version is a clear nod to that oeuvre.

Quintessential bluegrass, "Little Maggie" has remained pretty well constant in form over the years even as it moves from performer to performer. Typically, Dylan's version on *Good as I Been to You* seems to emerge from the many he's heard plus his own interpretation—forever unique unto itself but for perhaps an echo of Obray Ramsey's 1930s version as heard on *Banjo Songs of the Southern Mountains*.

Around the time of his release of "Little Maggie" on 1992's *Good as I Been to You*, his sepia-visioned collection of folk and blues covers, Dylan snuck a semiacoustic version of "Little Maggie" into a Perth, Australia, concert. The arrangement on that occasion sounded like the New Riders of the Purple Sage on a very good night, complete with some hot pedal-steel guitar licks courtesy of Bucky Baxter.

"Little Moses" (Traditional/A. P. Carter [sometimes credited to Bert A. Williams/Earle C. Jones])
Various Artists (performed by the Carter Family), *Anthology of American Folk Music* (1952, 1997)
Joan Baez, *Joan Baez* (1960)
The New Lost City Ramblers, *Old-Time String Band Songbook* (1964)
Various Artists (performed by Neil Morris), *Sounds of the South* (1993)
Rich Lerner, *Trails and Bridges* (1996)
Various Artists (performed by E. C. & Orna Ball), *Land of Yahoe* (1996)
John McCutcheon, *Barefoot Boy with Boots On* (1998)

"Little Moses" is essential white country-folk and a plainly beautiful recasting of the Old Testament marquee hero Moses. According to Alan Lomax in the liner notes to *White Spirituals* (Atlantic, 1960), the song "belongs to the category of the religious ballad. Such songs were common in the Middle Ages." The Carter Fam-

The Carter Family, ca. 1930s.

(From the John Edwards Memorial Collection #30003, Southern Folklife Collection, Wilson Library, University of North Carolina at Chapel Hill)

ily's autoharp and vocal-heavy recording of "Little Moses" (made at RCA's Camden, New Jersey, studio on February 14, 1929, and later included on the Harry Smith *Anthology of American Folk Music* on Folkways) was probably Dylan's primary source for this folk-song retelling of Exodus in miniature. Everything from Pharaoh's daughter's discovery of the baby Moses floating in the reeds in the straw basket to the parting of the Red Sea and the Jews' delivery to the land of milk and honey gets covered here.

"Little Moses" is fairly typical of the Carter Family, whose imprint on contemporary music can still be dimly heard on your local country music radio station. The Carters, who can rightly be heralded as the First Family of country music, came from the Great Smoky Mountains in western Virginia, where the old English ballad tradition meshed with the black folk idiom and produced the best of today's so-called hillbilly music.

Alonzo Pleasant (A. P.) Carter (born April 15, 1891, Maces Springs, Virginia; died November 7, 1960, Maces Springs) grew up in the

sticks when the sticks were the sticks. After his marriage to Sara Dougherty and the subsequent birth of their daughters, A. P. led his progeny to his greatest love, music. Over the course of a recording career that spanned the 1920s through A. P.'s death, the Carter Family band (which at its most famous included A. P., Sara, and sister-in-law Maybelle Carter) was one of the main catalysts for a change in country music's emphasis on instrumental hillbilly standards to a vocally oriented style, as evidenced by the scores of their songs that are forever embedded in its canon.

But they elevated instrumental technique and approach to the guitar as well. "Carter-picking" became and has remained a dominant nonclassical approach to the instrument since Maybelle Carter first popularly introduced it via their recordings in the late 1920s. Maybelle's stylistic innovation, characterized by playing the melody notes on the bass strings and rhythmic fills on the treble strings, cannot be underestimated, as it allowed the guitar to simultaneously perform as both a lead and rhythm instrument.

Behind autoharp chords played by Sara (who usually leads the singing) and Maybelle's Carter-picked guitar and A. P.'s fiddle licks and warbling vocals, their highly recognizable songs influenced every folk and country musician whether they know it or not. How many thousands of young string players have muddled their way through the Carters' "Wildwood Flower" as the first song they learned to play?

After years of informal and semiprofessional local appearances, the Carters were discovered by Ralph Peer, a key figure in the production and distribution of country music. Perhaps not so coincidentally, their first recording session took place in August 1927 in Bristol, Tennessee, with the other preeminent country musician of the era, Jimmie Rodgers.

Over the next seven years, the Carters gained coast-to-coast renown through their performances and recordings of literally hundreds of songs drawn from a relatively small, wholesome oeuvre: lyric folk songs, back-country ballads, and, most notably, sacred songs. "Wildwood Flower," "Bury Me Under the Weeping Willow," "I'm Thinking Tonight of My Blue Eyes," "Will the Circle Be Unbroken," "Worried Man Blues," and their theme song, "Keep on the Sunny Side," are still performed wherever bluegrass musicians gather.

Their foursquare approach to music making and virtuous messages can sound, at least in contrast with the cosmopolitan, often ribald Rodgers, numbingly dull or, depending on the beholder, as beautiful as a forest dandelion never seen by human eyes. But their down-home, folks-next-door accessibility spurred hundreds of family bands and took country music from the boondocks to the family parlor and beyond.

A. P. Carter is also celebrated as being among the first American songcatchers and music historians, even if he claimed some of his discoveries as his own work. In his travels down the region's back roads, he collected and preserved countless Anglo-American folk songs from the Appalachians.

But the quixotic A. P. was also a remote individual, prompting Sara to divorce him in 1936 in what, until recently, was a tightly guarded, embarrassing family secret revealed in respectful detail in *Will You Miss Me When I'm Gone?: The Carter Family and Their Legacy in American Music* by Mark Zwonitzer with Charles Hirshberg (Simon and Schuster, 2002). Take a look at just about any photograph of the trio snapped in the 1930s to glimpse the unhappiness emanating from their dour faces. Despite this schism, the original Carter Family did continue to record and perform together until they finally disbanded in

1943. Their family tradition has carried on in various configurations and into succeeding generations by their progeny (including June Carter, Carlene Carter, and Roseanne Cash) in a family tree too tightly embroidered to fully untangle here.

The coattribution of "Little Moses" to Bert Williams, America's first nationally beloved black entertainer, and Earle Jones presents an intriguing though probably misguided path to the song's roots. This country composition, drawn from the Old Testament epic, seems never to have appeared in any Williams or Jones discography or been touched by any black artists. Which is not to say that it couldn't have seeped from the plantations into minstrelsy into vaudeville and Williams's repertoire. Or, for that matter, from the plantation into the church into A. P. Carter's clutches.

Bert Williams (born March 11, 1875, New Providence, Antigua; died March 4, 1922, New York City) was America's premier black performing artist. Combining dry, revelatory humor with a downtrodden pre-Chaplinesque "Tramp"-like persona (an act well utilized by Dylan in his first months in New York City circa 1961), Williams was *the* major turn-of-the-century star; his career sprang from the waning days of minstrelsy into mass popularity and landed him on Broadway's vaudeville stages in the early Roaring Twenties. Songwriter, actor, director, and producer, Williams can be considered the Jackie Robinson of show business in helping to break down the racial barriers that had defined (and, some contend, continue to do so) American entertainment.

Dylan recorded "Little Moses" during the March 5, 1970, *Self Portrait* sessions, and a fragment of his playing the song on piano probably dating from November 1975 can be heard on the *Renaldo & Clara* soundtrack from the Rolling Thunder Revue tour. He performed the song in Never Ending Tour concerts of 1992 and 1993.

[S] "Little Sadie" (Traditional)

aka "Transfusion Blues"
See also "In Search of Little Sadie"
Bob Dylan, *Self Portrait* (1970)
Johnny Cash, *Now There Was a Song* (1960)
Doc Watson and Clarence Ashley, *The Original Recordings of 1960–1962* (1995)
Tony Rice, *Manzanita* (1979)
David Grisman, *Early Dawg* (1980)
Charlie Poole and the North Carolina Ramblers, *Charlie Poole and the North Carolina Ramblers* (1993)
Jerry Garcia/David Grisman/Tony Rice, *The Pizza Tapes* (2000)

"Little Sadie," Dylan's vastly improved reworking of his dismal rendition of the old Appalachian murder ballad "In Search of Little Sadie" (also from *Self Portrait*), is upbeat and well sung. One of *Self Portrait*'s real standouts, "Little Sadie" is a lovely little ditty telling the story of homicide, escape, arrest, trial, and jailing.

Dylan could have picked up either of his "Sadie" songs from any one of several sources. The 1960 Johnny Cash version from his album *Now, There Was a Song* is usually cited. But the Clarence (Tom) Ashley and Doc Watson record has been pointed to as well. A 1940 Cisco Houston variant of the same song family, "Bad Lee Brown," might have also come across Dylan's turntable at some point.

[A] *Live 1961–2000—Thirty-nine Years of Great Concert Performances*

SME Records (Sony Music Entertainment) CD SRCS 2438. Released March 2001.
"Somebody Touched Me,"* "Wade in the Water,"* "Handsome Molly,"* "To Ramona,"* "I Don't Believe You," "Grand Coulee Dam,"* "Knockin' on Heaven's Door," "It Ain't Me, Babe"* "Shelter from the Storm," "Dead Man, Dead Man,"* "Slow Train," "Dignity," "Cold Irons Bound,"* "Born in Time,"* "Country Pie,"* "Things Have Changed"*
* = Rare or previously unreleased.

One day, this officially released, limited-edition collector's item (released by Sony Japan to coincide with Dylan's spring 2001 Far East tour) may see wider distribution. Until then, the manna contained on this encoded disc will remain obscure even though it is among the best and most unusual collections of Dylanalia yet available. The old, new, borrowed, and blue are all in evidence here. The collection features a half dozen songs that were never released, five rarities that appeared on non-Dylan albums, a promo-only item, a cassette-only B-side, and a grab bag of other excellent choices.

Opening with a 2000 bluegrass version of "Somebody Touched Me," a traditional gospel number, the set jumps back to a 1961 Minneapolis recording of "Wade in the Water," another gospel chestnut. From there, we follow the arc of Dylan's stage career with stops at most of the major intersections as the young waif moves from folk music ("Handsome Molly") to his own mid-1960s originals ("To Ramona" and "I Don't Believe You"). From there we visit his post-motor-bike-crash work with the Hawks in 1968 ("Grand Coulee Dam," from the Woody Guthrie tribute concert) and the comeback tour with the Band in 1974. The collection includes a couple of songs from both incarnations of 1975 and 1976 Rolling Thunder Revue ("It Ain't Me, Babe" and "Shelter from the Storm"), a selection from the post-evangelical Dylan from 1981 ("Dead Man, Dead Man"), a half-baked 1987 cut from *Dylan & the Dead* ("Slow Train"), and his 1994 visit to *MTV Unplugged* ("Dignity"). Along with the early material, the best reason to locate a copy of this super rarity would be the quartet of performances from the latter stages of the Never Ending Tour ("Cold Irons Bound," "Born in Time,"

"Country Pie," and "Things Have Changed"). Yes, the collection could have used samples from the 1978 big-band tour, the 1979 gospel concerts, the Tom Petty and the Heartbreakers era, and perhaps some different song selections from the Never Ending Tour. But when record company guys get it mostly right, why complain?

The only major complaint with the collection is the thirty-two-page Japanese-language-only liner note brochure, chock-full of cool, rare pics of Dylan throughout his career.

[S] "Living the Blues" (Bob Dylan)

Bob Dylan, *Self Portrait* (1970)
Leon Redbone, *Red to Blue* (1987)
The Nashville Bluegrass Band, *American Beauty* (1998)

To paraphrase Duke Ellington, "to sing the blues, you gotta live the blues"; with "Living the Blues," a familiar-sounding yet original Jerry Lee Lewis–style song of romantic pining, Dylan does both. It came off pretty well on *Self Portrait* and somewhat better than that when he gave it its only public performance on television's *Johnny Cash Show* in 1969. "Living the Blues" was probably composed during the period that produced Dylan's harvest of *Nashville Skyline* songs. When it was released on *Self Portrait*, it was, along with "Minstrel Boy," the only new Dylan lyric included in that project. Dylan allegedly drew on Lewis's 1957 Sun Records recording of "I'm Feeling Sorry" for the tune of "Living the Blues." Others point out a resemblance to Guy Mitchell's "Singing the Blues."

[S] "Lo and Behold!" (Bob Dylan)

Bob Dylan/The Band, *The Basement Tapes*/'67 (1975)
Coulson, Dean, McGuinness, Flint, *Lo & Behold* (1972)
Marjoe Gortner, *Bad but Not Evil* (1972)
The Crust Brothers, *Marquee Mark* (1998)

Filled with lascivious humor and a murky plot characteristic of much of the material from *The Basement Tapes*, "Lo and Behold!" is a half-sung, half-spoken postmodern trucker's song. It combines a quiet search for revelation (never found, of course) and absolute nonsense through allusions as concrete and ridiculously strange as Moby Dick's trip to Chicken Town. Guess you had to be there—in the basement of Big Pink, that is.

In "Lo and Behold!" the disgraced narrator splits San Anton' for an unspecified misdeed, ventures to Pittsburgh, where he overhears some fellow travelers (Moby Dick and Molly) discussing the former's trip to Chicken Town (perhaps the city's red-light district), purchases a herd of flying moose for his girl, and considers a journey to Tennessee. Dylan wryly delivers the whole tall tale with the swagger of a Bourbon Street pimp egged on by the Hawks' rousing harmonies.

[S] "London Waltz" (Dick Fariña/Eric von Schmidt)

Dick Fariña and Eric von Schmidt (with Dylan pseudonymously credited as "Blind Boy Grunt"), *Dick Fariña & Eric von Schmidt* (1963)

According to the liner notes of this rare recording (a remembrance of constant slogging from party to pub and back again through calf-deep snow in the London streets), this song features Dylan contributing backing harmonica and a bit of chiming vocals under his Blind Boy Grunt alias. The liner notes also state that "London Waltz" is "a blues in 3/4 time, music by Fariña, words spontaneous."

[S] "Lone Pilgrim" (Traditional/Elder John Ellis or B. F. White and Adger M. Pace)

aka "White Pilgrim"
Bob Dylan, *World Gone Wrong* (1993)
Doc Watson, *The Doc Watson Family* (1963)
Coulson, Dean, McGuinness, Flint, *Lo & Behold* (1972)

L

Aunt Molly Jackson, *Aunt Molly Jackson* (1982)
Peter Rowan, *The Walls of Time* (1982)

"Lone Pilgrim" stands out from the balance of the 1993 *World Gone Wrong* batch as a kind of gospel-folk lullaby, and Dylan's poignant and mesmerizing treatment makes it a keeper. The song is about a believer who visits the grave of a mentor and is delivered into the arms of God. Dylan mentions his source for the song in the liner notes of *World Gone Wrong,* saying that he heard it on an "old Doc Watson record"—presumably *The Doc Watson Family* from 1963.

While the tune that "Lone Pilgrim" is sung to has been around for eons, the liner notes on the Watson album trace the song itself to the nineteenth century. That makes "Lone Pilgrim" among the oldest songs on *World Gone Wrong.* It was first published in the second edition of William (Singin' Billy) Walker's *Southern Harmony* in 1847, an extremely popular hymn collection as evidenced by the 600,000 copies that its various editions sold in the Southern states between 1835 (when the first edition was published) and the Civil War. Though "Lone Pilgrim" was first credited to Walker himself, some suggest that it is actually a variant of "The White Pilgrim," the text of which was written in 1838 by a preacher named John Ellis in response, some researchers think, to the death of Joseph Thomas, an evangelist. Known as the "White Pilgrim" (or less kindly, as "Crazy Thomas"), Thomas preached his way through the South and East dressed in white and traveling on foot. According to folklorist D. K. Wilgus in his 1950 article "'The White Pilgrim: Song, Legend, and Fact,'" published in volume 4, #3 of the *Southern Folklore Quarterly,* Thomas was inspired by an 1815 encounter with "a believing Jew" who had no name, used no money, and dressed in a plain robe. Thomas died from smallpox in Johnsonburg, New Jersey, in 1835, and John Ellis visited, according to Dilgus, "the fresh made grave of Joseph Thomas (White Pilgrim)" three years later. The song Ellis wrote about Thomas, "The White Pilgrim," became such a popular folk hymn that, in time, even Ellis himself said he came across people who claimed other sources of authorship.

As the song passed into the domain of the church it underwent various refinements and accreditation in its passage below the Mason-Dixon Line. The most notable of these are the ones that stuck, specifically to B. F. (Benjamin Franklin) White (born October 13, 1805, Union County, South Carolina; died September 2, 1878, Atlanta, Georgia), an influential composer, arranger, singing-school master, folk collector, and one-time mayor of Hamilton, Georgia, who edited various editions of hymnals closely associated with the Sacred Harp realm of the Baptist Church. And there is gravesite legend associated with White's recasting of the song as well, coming when White visited the burial plot of a Georgia friend whose final resting place lay on the lone Texas prairie.

Accreditation to Adger M. Pace (born August 13, 1882, Pelzer, South Carolina; died 1959, Lawrenceburg, Tennessee), an important figure in the Southern gospel music landscape, appears somewhat tangential and is due more for his probable popularization and rearrangement of "Lone Pilgrim."

The tune to "Lone Pilgrim" is, in some arrangements, nearly identical with "The Braes O' Balquhidder," a Scottish melody that may have even earlier roots in an old Gaelic air, "Brochan Buirn."

Dylan's recording of "Lone Pilgrim" on *World Gone Wrong*—he's never performed it live—is perfectly gauged and stylistically linked with his brilliant interpretation of "The Lakes of Pontchartrain." His lightly strummed opening builds with bell-like clarity and emphasizes the solitary, spiritual nature of the hymn.

§ **"Lonesome Bedroom"** (Curtis Jones/Champion Jack Dupree/Ernest "Buddy" Lewis)
aka "Lonesome Bedroom Blues"
See also "Highway 51"
Curtis Jones, *Trouble Blues* (1960)
Pete Franklin, *Guitar Pete's Blues* (1961)
Jimmie Gordon, *Mississippi Mudder: Jimmie Gordon, Volume 1* (1994)
Champion Jack Dupree, *Blues of Champion Jack Dupree, Volume 2* (1995)
Clarence Edwards, *Swamps the Word* (1998)

Dylan jump-started his 1978 big-band tour with this old blues song of disputed authorship. True to its title, the song deals with romantic longing in the extreme.

§ **"Lonesome Day Blues"** (Bob Dylan)
Bob Dylan, *"Love and Theft"* (2001)

Growling like a bear that hasn't eaten in years, Dylan is still straining even after all these years to decipher the wind's whispers on this tough-as-nails *Blonde on Blonde*–style blues stomp, which includes a nice five-note bridge between choruses.

Andy Gill, in his review of *"Love and Theft"* in the October 2001 edition of *Mojo*, noted that "Lonesome Day Blues" is "a great slow boogie in the vein of 'Rainy Day Women,' to whose loping riff Augie Meyers adds a little reggae afterbeat, creating a groove akin to Rosco Gordon's seminal 'No More Doggin'. Lyrically, it's packed with devastating zingers, from the sinister promise, 'I'm gonna teach peace to be conquered/I'm gonna tame the proud,' to the damning broadside, 'Well, my captain he's decorated, he's well schooled and he's skilled/He's not sentimental, don't bother him at all how many of his pals that he kills.'"

For six minutes Dylan and his band dig deep into this fairly standard twelve-bar blues as the author verbally riffs on stories about some family members, "Maggie's Farm"–style: "My Pa, he died and left me, my brother got killed in the war, my sister ran off and got married, never was heard of anymore."

Dylan called *"Love and Theft"* his most autobiographical album, and while this is hard to fathom in lieu of albums like, say, *Blood on the Tracks*, he does sing "I wish my mother was still alive" in "Lonesome Day Blues," seemingly in reference to the January 2001 passing of his mom, the beloved Beattie Zimmerman. When asked whether the line was inspired by this personal milepost, Dylan responded (in the widely distributed July 2001 "Rome Interview" with a pool of European journalists), "Probably. I don't see another motive. My lyrics develop in a stream of consciousness. I don't linger long on every word that comes to my mind."

But true to the generally very humorous tone of *"Love and Theft,"* Dylan manages to slip in the following Groucho Marxism: "You're going to need help sweetheart/You can't make love by yourself . . ."

By the end of the song, the narrator has regained the fire in his belly and, in true old black bluesman fashion, declares with prophetic belligerence, "I'm going to teach peace to the conquered/I'm going to tame the proud."

Poking deeper for reference, fans of Dr. Junichi Saga's *Confessions of a Yakuza* might recognize how the original's "Just because she was in the same house didn't mean we were living together as man and wife. . . . I don't know how it looked to other people, but I never slept with her—not once" becomes, in Dylan's song, "Samantha Brown lived in my house for about four or five months/Don't know how it looked to other people, I never slept with her even once."

Another *Yakuza* line ("There was nothing sentimental about him—it didn't bother him at all that some of his pals had been killed") is also reinvented in "Lonesome Day Blues" when Dylan sings "My captain he's decorated, he's well-schooled and he's skilled/He's not sentimental, it doesn't bother him at all how many of his pals have been killed."

Singing with a rough grumble and sounding like a cocksure alpha male, Dylan began performing "Lonesome Day Blues" in the fall 2001 Never Ending Tour, in which he showcased his new *Love and Theft* songs. There, the song sounded just as authentic and raw as Dylan and company became the kind of frothy roadhouse act you dream of stumbling across at a Mississippi fish fry.

"The Lonesome Death of Hattie Carroll"
(Bob Dylan)
Bob Dylan, *The Times They Are A-Changin'* (1964); *Don't Look Back* (film) (1967); *Biograph/'64* (1985); *The Bootleg Series, Volume 5: Live 1975—The Rolling Thunder Revue* (2002); *The Bootleg Series, Volume 6: Live 1964—Concert at Philharmonic Hall* (2004)
Judy Collins, *The Judy Collins Concert* (1964)
Hugues Aufray, *Chante Dylan* (1965); *Au Casino de Paris* (1996)
Paul Jones, *Love Me, Love My Friends* (1967)
Joe McDonald, *The Early Years* (1980)
Phranc, *Folksinger* (1985)
The 13th-Floor Elevators, *Through the Rhythm* (1998)
Martin Carthy, *Signs of Life* (1999); *Carthy Chronicle* (2001); *Carthy: Contemporaries* (2001)
Steve Howe, *Portraits of Bob Dylan* (1999)
Rory Erikson, *Hide Behind the Sun* (2000)

One of Dylan's most impassioned and enduring invectives, "The Lonesome Death of Hattie Carroll" is a heartrendingly poetic yet faithful report of the events surrounding a dark yet (except for this song) forgotten, ever more obscure incident in American racial history— perhaps the finest example of Dylan's ability to mix commentary with deft lyric acumen.

Inspired by François Villon and Bertolt Brecht's *The Ship, The Black Freighter*, Dylan wrote his modern ballad in a small notebook in a restaurant on Seventh Avenue in New York City after, as legend is told, reading an article about it on his way home from the August 1963 pro-civil rights march on Washington, D.C., at which Martin Luther King made his hallowed "I have a dream" address.

Alex Ross commented on some of general critique the song has garnered in a May 10, 1999, *New Yorker* article, writing that Dylan's phrasing "produces a feeling of helplessness, the way each line ends in a weak beat, and this seems to be the point: cry all you want, the gentle suffer. The dominant emotion is not political rage but a quavering sympathy for Hattie Carroll, whose race is never mentioned. This song certainly doesn't raise hopes for judicial reform, and it has not gone out of date, like the cardboard protest anthems of its era."

The tale behind "The Lonesome Death of Hattie Carroll" is well known among Dylan's following. William Devereux Zantzinger, twenty-four, attacked poor Hattie Carroll at 1:40 A.M. on February 8, 1963, at the Spinsters' Ball—an annual charity event sponsored by postdebutantes—at the Emerson Hotel in Baltimore. The attack led directly to Hattie Carroll's death.

Zantzinger, the scion of a prominent Washington, D.C., real estate magnate with more than a little political tug, attended the function with his twenty-four-year-old wife. A high-spirited, hard-partying young man, Zantzinger showed up at the ball drunk, proceeded to get drunker, and made an absolute spectacle of himself as the witching hour came and went. A large man, he was dressed to the nines and sported a cane that he would later wield with tragic results.

As Zantzinger's mood darkened through the night, his behavior degenerated. After uneasy, progressively disturbing confrontations with some of the other guests, the hotel staff, and even his own wife, he decided he needed yet another drink as the hour of 2:00 A.M. approached.

Making his way to the bar, he encountered Hattie Carroll, a fifty-one-year-old black "maid of the kitchen," as described in the song, who had worked at the Emerson Hotel for six years as an extra employee for special functions and ballroom events. The mother of eleven (not ten, as Dylan sings) children, she was an active, socially involved member of the Gillis Memorial Church. But she also suffered from an enlarged heart and had a history of hypertension.

Zantzinger barked out his order for a bourbon and ginger ale but Carroll was busy and replied, "Just a minute, sir." As she fumbled with the glass, Zantzinger shouted at her, "When I order a drink, I want it now, you black bitch!" Hattie tried to calm him, saying that she was hurrying as best she could. Zantzinger quickly lost control, striking her across the shoulders and head with his cane, breaking it in three places.

Within minutes, the dazed woman collapsed. An ambulance was called and took the unconscious Hattie Carroll to Baltimore Mercy Hospital.

The police were also called, and when they arrived Zantzinger and his wife fought with them. He was arrested, charged with assault, and held overnight for a morning court appearance. Still wearing tails and a carnation, he pleaded not guilty to the charges and was released on $600 bail.

But Hattie Carroll's condition worsened, and at 9:15 that same morning, while the hearing was in progress, she died, never having regained consciousness. The suspected cause of death was a brain hemorrhage caused by a blow to the head. Zantzinger was already on his way home when the court was notified of her passing, and a warrant for his rearrest was

issued, this time on homicide charges. Incredibly, it was the first time in the history of the state of Maryland that a white man had been accused of murdering a black woman.

By the time Dylan read about the case, feelings of righteousness and indignation were running high in the civil rights movement. On trial in Maryland were 350 years' worth of history and tradition. It was a case of white against black, rich against poor, master against servant.

This seems not to have impressed the three judges charged with deciding the case that June. Yes, Zantzinger was guilty, they concluded. But it was not first-degree or even second-degree murder they found him guilty of. Manslaughter was their verdict and a deferred six-month visit to the big house their sentence. With three months off for good behavior, he was home in time for Christmas and settled back into Charles County's high society.

Dylan wrings out every ounce of pathos and irony in his tragic song, never limited by the rhyme scheme. And, like a veteran beat reporter who just wants the facts, he commences with two of the most basic: the name of the accused and the murder weapon. His use of the detail that the cane was "twirled around his diamond ring finger" says much about the alleged perpetrator as any mug shot or prosecutor ever could.

Moving on to the second verse, Dylan continues his subtle attack on Zantzinger and the entire local aristocracy by calling our attention to Zantzinger's connections with "high office relations in the politics of Maryland" who "reacted to his deed with a shrug of his shoulders." By deftly downplaying the sinister, he avoids tainting his storytelling with a harsh point of the finger, even if that is exactly what he is doing.

It isn't until the third verse that he even gets around to describing Hattie Carroll. And he never mentions that she is black, yet the listener is somehow aware of this and her dignity even though, as Dylan sings, "she never sat once at the head of the table."

Dylan's description of the attack is also pretty soft. Yet when he sings that the cane "sailed through the air and came down through the room,/Doomed and determined to destroy all the gentle./And she never done nothing to William Zantzinger," we know that he is not shooting from the hip.

Dylan's sleight-of-hand technique is in prime form for the fourth and final verse. When he sings of how "the judge pounded his gavel/To show that all's equal and that the courts are on the level," that "even the nobles get properly handled," that "the strings in the books ain't pulled and persuaded," and that "the ladder of the law has no top and no bottom," we know that he means exactly the opposite.

That Dylan has never ceased performing "The Lonesome Death of Hattie Carroll" is a testament to his admiration for the song. Mostly it has been rendered as an acoustic offering in his shows, but during the Rolling Thunder Revue, at least, he worked up a fine, halting electric arrangement that is still haunting the backstreets and wharves of Baltimore. For a fine, early version of "Hattie Carroll," check out *Don't Look Back*, D. A. Pennebaker's film of Dylan's 1965 tour of Great Britain. And yes, now is the time for your tears.

🔲 **"The Lonesome River"** (Ralph and Carter Stanley)
Ralph Stanley and Friends (performed with Bob Dylan), *Clinch Mountain Country* (1998)
The Stanley Brothers, *Complete Columbia Recordings* (1996)
Ralph Stanley, *Bound to Ride* (1991)
David Grisman, *Here Today* (1982)
Joe Val, *Live in Holland* (1996)

Dylan joined Ralph Stanley on a doleful version of this Stanley Brothers classic released on *Clinch Mountain Country*, a well-received all-star 1998 collection. The narrator, true to the song's title, watches the river flow (a subject close to Dylan's heart) as he mourns the loss of his gal, who left him for another man.

🔲 **"Lonesome Town"** (Thomas Baker Knight Jr.)
Rick Nelson, *Lonesome Town* (1992)
Johnny Crawford, *Rumors* (1963)
The Venturas, *Here They Are* (1964)
Cornerstone, *Lonesome Town* (1995)
Paul McCartney, *Run Devil Run* (1999)

"Ricky Nelson, he did a lot of my songs, I'm gonna do one of his. This is called 'Lonesome Town.'"

With that, spoken at a July 15, 1986, appearance at New York's Madison Square Garden, Dylan enjoyed introducing his versions of "Lonesome Town," which he performed as a tribute to Nelson shortly after the death of the former teen-idol-turned-rocker on New Year's Eve 1985. The song concerns a place where the brokenhearted go to mend and contains musical and lyrical themes Dylan employed for his "Where Teardrops Fall" a few years later on his *Oh Mercy* album (1989). Nelson had originally hit the Top 10 with "Lonesome Town" in 1958. First performing the song with Tom Petty and the Heartbreakers, Dylan delivered some sharp versions of the song in 1986. He was aided immeasurably by his wonderful backup singers' tight, strong backing and extemporaneously scatted and played with perspectives, thus doing much with a song that would at first glance seem like a throwaway. He returned to "Lonesome Town" a few more times during the early stages of the Never Ending Tour.

The author of "Lonesome Town," Thomas Baker Knight Jr. (born July 4, 1933, Birmingham, Alabama) is one of those behind-the-scenes song laureates whose name industry heavies and in-the-know fans like to drop as a badge of honor.

Baker Knight grew up in Birmingham, served in the U.S. Air Force, and became a technical illustrator and draftsman. He had learned to play a little guitar along the way, so when Elvis Presley began wiggling and jiggling his pelvis, Baker Knight saw the light and decided that perhaps a life spent hunched over a drafting table was not for him. He formed Baker Knight and the Knightmares, a rock 'n' roll band, that gained a big Birmingham following and some quick luck when a Hollywood agent happened on their act and signed them. Their first and only hit, "Bring My Cadillac Back," sold a quick 40,000 units and was shooting up the charts when it was stricken from radio playlists because the radio honchos felt they were giving the automobile company a free plug.

The Knightmares' allotted fifteen minutes of fame quickly ran out, but Baker Knight was undaunted. He went to Los Angeles with a minuscule nest egg that evaporated as he unsuccessfully tried hawking his songs with nothing but a cliché hard-luck story to show for himself. But as necessity is often the mother of invention, Baker Knight drew on his situation and wrote "Lonesome Town," his signature song so eloquently describing the feeling of being cast adrift in the City of Angels.

Lady Luck decided to smile on Baker Knight once more. Down to literally his last thirty-six cents, he was introduced to teen idol Ricky Nelson by a mutual friend, and after playing several songs to him for his consideration, he was offered a $2,000 advance.

Nelson's recordings of "Lonesome Town" and "I Got a Feeling" both scored big time, pleasing Nelson so much that he went on to record some twenty more Baker Knight songs. Over the last forty years, a parade of popular music luminaries have recorded and performed a Baker Knight special, among them Frank Sinatra, Elvis Presley, Dean Martin, Sammy Davis Jr., Mickey Gilley, Jerry Lee Lewis, Hank Snow, Emmylou Harris, and Leif Garrett. Most recently, Sir Paul McCartney performed "Lonesome Knight" as a tribute in song to his late wife Linda, proving once and for all that, with a little looking, Elvis's "Heartbreak Hotel" can be found inside the boundaries of Baker Knight's "Lonesome Town."

"Long Ago, Far Away" (Bob Dylan)
The Brothers Four, *Sing of Our Times* (1963)
Odetta, *Odetta Sings Dylan* (1965)
Various Artists (performed by Black Country Tree), *It Ain't Me, Babe—Zimmerman Framed: The Songs of Bob Dylan* (2001)

Dylan recorded and sang with appealing Guthriesque energy (and caustic sarcasm) his only known version of "Long Ago, Far Away"—a song with Messianic references cataloguing a litany of injustices and warning that those who promote brotherhood better watch their backs or risk swinging from a tree—on an informal home tape in the summer of 1962. That cut was included on a now extremely scarce Warner Bros. demo LP.

"Long Black Veil" (Danny Dill/Marijohn Wilkin)
aka "The Long Black Veil"
See also "Detroit City"
The Country Gentlemen, *On the Road* (1963)
Johnny Cash, *Orange Blossom Special* (1965)
The Band, *Music from Big Pink* (1968)
Joan Baez, *Golden Hour* (1972)
Lefty Frizzell, *Best of Lefty Frizzell* (1991)
Burl Ives, *A Litty Bitty Tear* (1994)
Jerry Garcia/David Grisman/Tony Rice, *The Pizza Tapes* (2000)

Even well into the year 2000, Dylan continued to pull the well-known chestnut out of his folkster's chapeau. It was at this late date that he began treating his audiences with fair regularity to artfully nuanced acoustic-band renderings of "Long Black Veil," a more recent song with an old folk flavor.

The story unfolded in "Long Black Veil" is the stuff of high dramatic tragic irony as the narrator recounts (apparently from the grave) the circumstances that sealed his fate: while his best friend was murdered "by a man who looked a lot like me," the singer lay in the arms of the dead man's wife. With an unusable alibi, he must walk up the gallows steps, leaving the woman to forever roam the hills in the titular garment.

Danny Dill (born September 19, 1924, Clarksburg, Tennessee), one of the song's authors and a venerated Nashville legend, wanted to write a contemporary folk song that had that taste of danger and ancient mystery. An admirer of the repertoire and interpretive powers of songsters like Burl Ives, in writing "Long Black Veil" he drew on a couple of incidents he'd read about. One involved the murder of a Catholic priest in New Jersey, killed under the proverbial town hall light as dozens of witnesses stood by. And his love for the story of the unnamed woman dressed in the titular garment who faithfully visited the grave of the actor Rudolph Valentino also fed his inspiration. Finally, his admiration for Red Foley's "God Walks These Hills with Me" gave him a chance to lace the title of that song into his lyric.

He brought the song-in-progress to Marijohn Wilkin and together they hammered out a final draft. With their new song—sounding like an old Appalachian ballad—complete, they took it to country star Lefty Frizell, whose near-instant recording revived his faltering career when it broke nationwide.

An alive and still-kicking Nashville legend, Dill took a well-worn path to the upper strata of country music that included stops at all the major proving grounds for a career in twentieth-century American showbiz: the church choir, radio, vaudeville, the Grand Ole Opry, recording studio, and touring shows with other luminaries of his genre. Dill also wrote "Detroit City" with Mel Tillis, another song performed by Dylan.

Marijohn Wilkin (born Marijohn Melson, July 14, 1920, Kemp, Texas) is one of country music's finest songwriters; she is respected for her work, business acumen, and ability to nurture younger songwriters, a calling that earned her the sobriquet the "Den Mother of Nashville." Her road to Nashville was a bumpy one full of detours and lengthy pit stops. By the time she made it to Music City at the age of forty, she had suffered the loss of one husband in World War II, endured a divorce, and struggled as a working single mother. All of it proved great fodder for songwriting, and when eventually she was discovered singing her hard-luck songs in a Nashville bar in 1958, she was rather quickly absorbed into Nashville's coterie of songwriters.

Within a year, "Long Black Veil" and Stonewall Jackson's success with her song "Waterloo" put her on the map. The year 1962 proved to be a watershed when Jimmy Dean scored with "P.T. 109," her patriotic story song celebrating the World War II exploits of President John F. Kennedy. The money she made from that hit allowed her to start Buckwood, Nashville's first female-owned music publishing house. It was as Buckwood CEO that she scouted out the likes of Kris Kristofferson and other young turks not interested in plowing and harvesting the same-old same-old tears-on-the-pillow country song. Kristofferson proved to be a valuable friend as well. When Wilkin lapsed into alcoholism in the 1970s, he helped pull her out of it by coaxing her into writing "One Day at a Time" with him, a song that was eventually recorded by more than two hundred artists. Wilkin was able to pull herself together, and leads a quiet, religious life back home in Texas.

◧ "Long Distance Operator" (Bob Dylan)
Bob Dylan/The Band, *The Basement Tapes/'67* (1975)
The Band, *Music from Big Pink* [remastered edition] (2000)
James Cotton, *Taking Care of Business* (1971)
Various Artists (performed by James Cotton), *Chicago Blues Masters, Volume 3* (1997)

"Long Distance Operator" is Dylan and company's contribution to that critically neglected oeuvre of songs about some lonely guy plunking his last dime into a pay phone trying to make contact with his faraway gal. Here, Richard Manuel sings this bluesy tune, written, recorded, and performed early in the Dylan-Hawks relationship. The version on *The Basement Tapes* features some excellent Robbie Robertson guitar licks. "Long Distance Operator," however, appears to predate the *Basement* sessions by a good two years—Dylan performed it at least once with the Hawks (at California's Berkeley Community Theater in December 1965), just as he was unveiling his electric muse.

◧ "Long John" (Traditional)
aka "Lost John," "Long Gone"
Ella Jenkins, *Adventures in Rhythm* (1959)
Sam Hinton, *Sam Hinton Sings the Songs of Men* (1961)
Dave Van Ronk, *Inside Dave Van Ronk* (1969)
Rev. Gary Davis, *New Blues and Gospel* (1971)
Doc Watson, *Doc Watson on Stage* (1971)

While some singers, such as Sonny Terry, may have made a distinction between the songs "Long John" and "Lost John," Dylan's harmonica solo on this black prison work song from the so-called Minneapolis Hotel Tape, recorded at the home of his friend Bonnie Beecher on December 22, 1961, intermingles both versions of the ballad.

John A. and Alan Lomax provided some background information on "Long John," sung primarily during the felling of trees, complete

with accents for each chop, in their 1934 book *American Ballads and Folk Songs*:

> In the introduction to W. C. Handy's *Blues* [1926] there is a story about the escape of a Negro prisoner, one Long John Green. It seems that the county had recently acquired a pack of bloodhounds and the sheriff wanted to try them out. Long John Green, in jail at the time, was chosen to make trail, since he was famous for the way he could get over the ground. They gave John halfway round the courthouse for a start and then unleashed the pack. On his first lap John crawled through a barrel, got the hounds off the scent and then he was "long gone." Whether or not Lightnin' [an Angola Penitentiary prisoner], who sang us the following song, knew the above story, it is hard to say: his own evidence would be worth very little.

Derivations of Handy's version of the song, often titled "Long Gone (From the Bowling Green)," abound—the most famous by jazz trumpet deity Louis Armstrong.

◧ "Long Time Gone" (Traditional/arranged by Bob Dylan)
aka "Long Time Comin'"
Hamilton Camp, *Paths of Victory* (1964)
Odetta, *Odetta Sings of Many Things* (1965); *Odetta Sings Dylan* (1965)
Kinsfolk, *Up on the Mountain* (1969)
Rich Lerner, *Trails and Bridges* (1996)

Dylan cut a Witmark demo of "Long Time Gone" in 1963 and played it for friends around that time, no doubt trying to get them to buy the life story of the mythical wanderer he was pretending to be in his interviews of the era. While he cribbed elements of his melody from the venerable folk classic "The Girl I Left Behind," the sense of the song is pure Guthrie, as Dylan suggests the desperation of the human condition will always necessitate a troubadour such as himself to cast a light on its foibles. At the same time, he must have begun feeling the pressure of his role with lines like "But I ain't no prophet/An' I ain't no prophet's son."

[S] "Lord Protect My Child" (Bob Dylan)

Bob Dylan, *The Bootleg Series, Volumes 1–3: Rare and Unreleased, 1961–1991*/'83 (1991)
Lost Dogs, *Scenic Routes* (1991)

"Lord Protect My Child," a father's emotional prayer expressing a selfless plea for his child's future in an uncertain world, harks back to the sentiments found in lines from Dylan's "Masters of War" of 1963 ("fear to bring children into the world") with perhaps a nod to Bill Monroe's "Lord Protect My Soul." Unlike his own older song, however, this spiritual and bluesy *Infidels* outtake—though voicing age-old anxiety about progeny's future in the face of global and local crisis—is ultimately hopeful in its faith that, as he sings, "all will be well." In this, Dylan allows a rare glimpse into his sense of parental responsibility and, even more nakedly, his affection for his children.

Which child in particular might be the subject of question. As the song bears a 1983 copyright, some think that it was written with future teen heartthrob Jakob in mind. But it was another Dylan son, Sam, who was photographed that year with his father at his bar mitzvah at Jerusalem's Western Wall. Others point out that since the boy in the song has "got his mother's eyes" and inspection of Jakob's clearly reveals that he, in fact, has blue like his dad, Dylan may mean that Jakob observes the world through eyes similar to Sara's. Regardless of its object, while there might be a tendency to think of the song as written to a younger child, "Lord Protect My Child" does contain a few lyrical hints ("As his youth now unfolds," "For his age he's wise," etc.) that may indicate that it is directed to a boy on the threshold of manhood.

[A] *"Love and Theft"*

Columbia CD CK 85975, LP 85975. Sony Music Entertainment, Inc., SACD 90340. Recorded May 2001 in New York City. Released September 11, 2001. Produced by Jack Frost. Photography by David Gahr.
Bob Dylan—vocals, guitar, piano. Larry Campbell—guitar, violin, banjo, mandolin. Charlie Sexton—guitar. Tony Garnier—bass. David Kemper—drums. Augie Meyers—Vox organ, Hammond B3 organ, accordion. Clay Meyers—bongos on "Tweedle Dee & Tweedle Dum" and "Honest with Me"
"Tweedle Dee & Tweedle Dum," "Mississippi," "Summer Days," "Bye and Bye," "Lonesome Day Blues," "Floater (Too Much to Ask)," "High Water (for Charley Patton)," "Moonlight," "Honest with Me," "Po' Boy," "Cry a While," "Sugar Baby"

September 11, 2001, was supposed to be a day of music and joy, of anticipation relieved—the day a new Bob Dylan album was to hit the racks of music retailing outlets across the U.S. That the day will remembered for events other than the release of *"Love and Theft"* is fairly certain, but Dylan's finely crafted, stylistic paean to American music might be regarded as loosely prophetic of that terrible date as well.

Though the international turmoil coinciding with the album's early months in stores probably kept *"Love and Theft"* in the far periphery of the public's traumatized eyes, the contemporary roots album rose as high as No. 5 on the *Billboard* charts. And Dylan watchers everywhere were frankly relieved that he was able to follow one strong album with another of equal power. Dylan had a mixed history on that score. Over the years his one-two punches have either been knockouts (think *Highway 61 Revisited* and *Blonde on Blonde*; *Blood on the Tracks* and *Desire*; or *Good as I Been to You*

Dylan performing at the 44th Annual Grammy Awards, Staples Center, Los Angeles, February 2002.

(Photo: Kevin Winter/Getty Images)

and *World Gone Wrong*) or duds (think *Slow Train Coming* and *Saved*, or *Oh Mercy* and *Under the Red Sky*).

In this *Nashville Skyline* for the third millennium, a relaxed Dylan roams from Lewis Carroll–flavored rockabilly ("Tweedle Dee & Tweedle Dum"), upbeat Western swing ("Summer Days"), the hymnlike ("Sugar Baby"), twangy picaresque ("Floater"), hard-rocking confrontation ("Honest with Me"), and upper-register testing ("Moonlight") to moody Appalachian apocalypse ("High Water"), tempo-shifting experiments ("Cry a While," "Lonesome Day Blues"), country soul ("Po' Boy"), and misguided romance ("Mississippi," originally written and recorded for *Time out of Mind* and rerecorded here).

Dylan's forty-third (and thirtieth studio) album features a dozen songs and was recorded with his touring band, along with legendary

Texas keyboard player Augie Meyers and son Clay on percussion for a couple of tracks.

Allegedly written on the spot at the May 2001 New York City sessions in the same manner that produced *Blonde on Blonde* some thirty-five years before, *"Love and Theft"* reveals yet another mask of the folkie protest singer turned drug-addled electric guitar seer turned born-again has-been and back again: a Bible-drunk minstrel staring into the void and giving the end-time a come-hither wink. *"Love and Theft"* may not wind up being as legendary as the magical *Blonde on Blonde*, but it is no less provocative, steeped with enough allusion and style to keep both suburban teenagers and college professors up all night entranced by a gumbo that mixes the Bible, the blues, Shakespeare, parlor ballads, Virgil, nursery rhymes, Charles Darwin, traditional folk songs, F. Scott Fitzgerald, piano scroll music, Ernest Hemingway, rockabilly, Mark Twain, country and western, cocktail-lounge corn, Groucho Marx, rock 'n' roll, Robert Johnson, rhythm & blues, Charley Patton, jazz, Sonny Boy Williamson, Appalachia, Big Joe Turner, supper-club music, and at least one Japanese pop novel.

There may be no "hits" on *"Love and Theft,"* but unlike the generally dark *Time out of Mind,* the overall effect left by the collection is uplifting, as it slides from one musical style to another in a stroll through classic American music in all its burlesque splendor, every song an evocative period piece.

The great irony of *"Love and Theft"* is that while Dylan was being eulogized almost obituary-style as the globe marked his sixtieth birthday only months before, he was busy putting together his spunkiest, most life-affirming offering in years, as if to make sure that when he spit, he hit those pundits square in the eye—or right between them, anyway. He exudes the assured confidence of an old pro

and the unbridled energy of a rookie center fielder as he defies the expectation brought on by his previous effort and recent public victories: the lauded and awarded *Time out of Mind* and "Things Have Changed," the jaded lament he wrote for the 2000 film *Wonderboys* that netted its author both an Oscar and a Golden Globe.

Dylanists pondered the meaning of the title. The consensus seemed to be that Dylan was paying homage to the music he loved and stole from his entire life. Other conjecture focuses on Eric Lott's 1993 book of the same title, which focuses on a subject near and dear to Dylan's heart: blackface minstrelsy and the American working class.

Still deeper than the connection with Lott's book, the July 8, 2003, *Wall Street Journal* reported that *"Love and Theft"* includes about a dozen passages from Japanese writer Dr. Junichi Saga's cult book, *Confessions of a Yakuza* (Kodansha International, 1991). When informed of the alleged appropriation, Saga told the *Journal*, "Please say hello to Bob Dylan for me because I am very flattered and very happy to hear this news."

The outcry following the *Yakuza* revelation was enormous, considering that this methodology was old hat for Dylan. The cooler head of *New York Times* writer Jon Pareles prevailed when he wrote an article defending Dylan in the July 12, 2003, edition of the paper. As Pareles put it:

> He was simply doing what he has always done: writing songs that are information collages. Allusions and memories, fragments of dialogue and nuggets of tradition have always been part of Mr. Dylan's songs, all stitched together like crazy quilts.
>
> Sometimes Mr. Dylan cites his sources, as he did in "High Water (for Charley Patton)"

from the "*Love and Theft*" album. But more often he does not. While die-hard fans happily footnote the songs, more casual listeners pick up the atmosphere, sensing that an archaic turn of phrase or a vaguely familiar line may well come from somewhere else. His lyrics are like magpies' nests, full of shiny fragments from parts unknown.

Mr. Dylan's music does the same thing, drawing on the blues, Appalachian songs, Tin Pan Alley, rockabilly, gospel, ragtime and more. "Blowin' in the Wind," his breakthrough song, took its melody from an antislavery spiritual, "No More Auction Block," just as Woody Guthrie had drawn on tunes recorded by the Carter Family. They thought of themselves as part of a folk process, dipping into a shared cultural heritage in ways that speak to the moment.

Nominated for several Grammy categories, "*Love and Theft*" garnered the award for best contemporary folk album in 2002.

⬛ "Love Henry" (Traditional)

aka "Earl Richard," "Henry Lee," "Lady Margot and Love Henry," "Little Scotch-ee," "Loving Henry," "Lowe Bonnie," "My Love Heneree," "Song of a Lost Hunter," "Young Hunting," "Young Redin"
See also "Pretty Polly"
Bob Dylan, *World Gone Wrong* (1993)
Various Artists (performed by Dick Justice), *Anthology of American Folk Music*/'32 (1952/1997)
Logan English, *Kentucky Ballads* (1957)
Frank Proffitt, *Frank Proffitt of Reese, North Carolina* (1962)
Peggy Seeger, *Folk Songs with the Seegers* (1965)
Nick Cave and the Bad Seeds, *Murder Ballads* (1996)
Jimmy Tarlton, *Steel Guitar Rag* (1998)

A most durable warhorse from the "murder song" folk idiom, "Love Henry" is white balladry at its best, telling a familiar hell-hath-no-

wrath story of a woman scorned. The nameless woman in the song stabs her lover to death with a "penny knife" after he cruelly tells her that he loves another woman "far better than thee." (Dylan updates and sizes up this punk in his *World Gone Wrong* liner notes as "career minded, limousine double parked.") The crime, however, is witnessed by the murderess's parrot. She tries to buy the bird's silence, promising that its "cage shall be decked in gold/And hung on a willow tree." But the song ends ambiguously, with the bird wisely keeping his distance: "A girl who would murder her own true love/would kill a little bird like me."

In his idiosyncratic manner, Harry Smith, in the liner notes to his landmark *Anthology of American Folk Music*, described the song thusly: "Scorning Offer of Costly Trapping, Bird Refuses Aid to Knight Thrown in Well by Lady—Child (68) gives eleven versions of this song under the title 'Young Hunting.' All of his texts are from Scotland and he also mentions several similar Scandinavian ballads. His 'F' (from Motherwell's ms. p. 61) is most like the present recording. This ballad is current in many parts of the United States, but has probably not been found for 100 years in the British Isles."

In his book *The Traditional Tunes of the Child Ballads, Volume 2*, Bertrand Harris Bronson offered an additional forty variants, the nineteenth of which Dylan sings almost word-for-word on *World Gone Wrong*.

Though its parrot is a recurrent theme in numerous ballads of greater antiquity (notably "The Outlandish Knight"), one way or another, in just about every known version and variant of "Love Henry," the heartless gallant's corpse finds its way into a well where the flesh will rot off his bones.

In 1959, the musician and collector Frank Proffitt told folklorists Anne and Frank Warner about a related but different version of the mysterious "My Love Heneree," as reported in Anne Warner's book *Traditional American Folk Songs from the Anne & Frank Warner Collection* (Syracuse, N.Y.: Syracuse University Press, 1984). In Proffitt's words:

> I wonder if this should be a ballad that would be known anywhere. In trying to recall the way the song went, it is possible I use a rhyming word of my own here and there. It was sung to me at an early age. As with many other ballads a tale went with it, but only as I grew up I learned the tale, which gave me more insight into its meaning. It seems the hunter, Heneree, was lost and he came upon this evil woman's castle. She had had the paths filled up to make young hunters lose their way except for the path leading to her lands. She was not a beauty—therefore her demands for bed sharing. As I remember, she had a hole dug where each time she would dispose of her unwilling lovers. However gruesome it may sound, she took Heneree to her bed to make love after stabbing him. This part may have been in the song too, but it was not of the kind to be sung to me in my early years. Only in the tale did these facts come out. I seem to remember there was a part of the song where she too was put in the deep hole, but this part I do not have words for.

Warner points out that in "some variants the parrot stanzas from 'Lady Isabel and the Elf King' (aka 'Pretty Polly') have attached themselves to this ballad and have been found both here and in Great Britain—even in Child, version 'I.'"

Dylan has never performed "Love Henry" live in concert, but his *World Gone Wrong* recording of the song has a deep, ancient fairy tale mystique about it.

[S] "Love Her with a Feeling" (Tampa Red)

aka "Love Her with a Feelin'"
See also "It Hurts Me Too," "She's Love Crazy"
Tampa Red, *Complete Recorded Works, Volume 9* (1994)
Paul Butterfield, *Original Lost Elektra Sessions* (1964)
Muddy Waters, *Muddy Waters Live* (1977)
Johnny Jones, *Live in Chicago with Billy Boy Arnold* (1979)
Buddy Guy, *Slippin' In* (1994)
Junior Wells, *Live at Buddy Guy's Legends* (1997)
Johnny Copeland, *Live in Australia 1990* (1997)

Dylan jump-started a slew of his 1978 shows with take-no-prisoners versions of Tampa Red's "Love Her with a Feeling." He sang this song with gusto, reminding us in the salacious vernacular of the sage bluesman that you had better love your gal from the depths of your being or, as the song suggests, "don't love her at all."

As one of the handful of blues slide guitarists—Elmore James, Muddy Waters, and Robert Johnson among them—who made a lasting mark on the tradition, Tampa Red created an immediately recognizable, and widely imitated, instrumental style. One of Chicago's earliest blues stars, he was billed as "the Guitar Wizard" during his heyday in the 1920s and 1930s; his stunning slide work on his National steel guitar shows why he earned his title.

Red (born Hudson Whitaker or Woodbridge, January 8, 1903 or 1904, Smithville, Georgia; died March 19, 1981, Chicago) came into his nickname by way of his red hair and family's eventual move to Tampa, Florida. He developed his slide-guitar technique while playing on street corners for spare change and in small clubs before he moved to Chicago, sometime in the mid-1920s. There he formed a partnership with pianist Georgia Tom Dorsey in 1928 and his career took shape with "It's Tight Like That," a double-entendre blues. The song sold thousands of copies and initiated what became known as the "hokum sound," which featured light, airy melodies and sentimental or humor-ous lyrics. Capitalizing on the hit, Georgia Tom and Tampa Red performed extensively over the next couple of years as the Hokum Boys, all the while continuing to record. Dorsey, however, ended the partnership around 1930 when he became disillusioned with the blues, embraced religion, and turned exclusively to gospel music, becoming perhaps its premier practi-tioner. (Dylan has covered Dorsey's famous "Peace in the Valley.")

Tampa Red's thirty-year career produced hundreds of sides that spanned styles from hokum to pop to jive to, quite naturally, the blues. During his prime, Red could be seen in a

American blues singer and slide guitarist Hudson Whittaker (aka "Tampa Red"), early 1930s.

(Frank Driggs Collection/Getty Images)

wide variety of venues: down-home juke joints, the streets, the burlesque and vaudeville theater circuit, and the Chicago club scene. Meanwhile, his South Side apartment became something of a salon for bluesmen during the 1930s. His clas-sic compositions ("Anna Lou Blues," "Black Angel Blues," "Crying Won't Help You," "It Hurts Me Too," and "Love Her with a Feeling") are mainstays of the Chicago blues repertoire.

After World War II and as the bigger-sound-ing electric blues bands began to overshadow Tampa Red's quainter style, the ravages of his long-standing drinking problem began to take their toll and he slowly faded from the spotlight, eventually going into permanent retirement in 1962. His death coincided with his induction into the Blues Foundation's Hall of Fame.

▣ "Love Is Just a Four-Letter Word" (Bob Dylan)

Joan Baez, *Any Day Now* (1968); *Carry It On* (1971); *Van-guard Sessions: Baez Sings Dylan* (1998); *The Essential Joan Baez/From the Heart: Live* (2001)
The Sound Symposium, *Bob Dylan Interpreted* (1969)
Earl Scruggs, *Earl Scruggs: His Family and Friends* (1971)

Dylan has provided popular culture with almost countless pithy, quotable lines. Just two—"To live outside law you must be honest" and "Everybody must get stoned"—can attest to the range of human experience, from moral-ity to debauchery, to which they apply. Simi-larly, the very title of "Love Is Just a Four-Letter Word" sounds like a Dylan aphorism, even if you didn't know it was one of his songs. In it, Dylan harnesses one of his giddy poetic jags for a relationship-ending folk blues. The title is thought to be drawn from a line in the 1958 film of Tennessee Williams's play *Cat on a Hot Tin Roof*, when Paul Newman says to Burl "Big Daddy" Ives, "You don't know what love is. To you it's just another four-letter word."

But the Chordettes, a once famous but long gone and far away '50s girl group best remembered for songs like "Charlie Brown," had a minor 1955 hit with a song a teenage Bob Dylan may have heard crackling over his transistor radio under the covers late one Hibbing, Minnesota, night: "Love Is Just a Four-Letter Word."

"Love Is Just a Four-Letter Word," incidentally, is the song that Joan Baez asks Dylan to finish in D. A. Pennebaker's *Don't Look Back*—a request Dylan rudely (and ironically) ignores. Baez's own version of the song on her album *Any Day Now* contains an extra, never-published verse. Dylan appears never to have recorded (or even really finished) the song himself.

"Love Minus Zero/No Limit" (Bob Dylan)

Bob Dylan, *Bringing It All Back Home* (1965); *Don't Look Back* (film)/'65 (1967); *Masterpieces* (1978); *Bob Dylan at Budokan* (1979); *The Bootleg Series, Volume 5: Live 1975—The Rolling Thunder Revue* (2002)
Bob Dylan/Various Artists (performed by Eric Clapton), *Bob Dylan: The 30th Anniversary Concert Celebration* (1993)
Duane Eddy, *Duane Does Dylan* (1965)
The Turtles, *It Ain't Me, Babe* (1965)
Silkie, *You've Got to Hide Your Love Away* (1965)
The Spokesmen, *The Dawn of Correction* (1965)
Noel Harrison, *Noel Harrison* (1966)
The Leaves, *The Leaves* (1966)
P. J. Orion, *P. J. Orion* (1966)
Fabulous Four, *After All* (1967)
Joan Baez, *Any Day Now* (1968); *Vanguard Sessions: Baez Sings Dylan* (1998)
Julie Felix, *This Is* (1970)
Turley Richards, *Turley Richards* (1970)
Leon Russell, *Leon Russell and the Shelter People* (1971)
Rick Nelson, *Rudy the Fifth* (1971)
Buck Owens, *Bridge over Troubled Water* (1971)
Mike Batt Orchestra, *Portrait of Bob Dylan* (1972)
The Flying Burrito Brothers, *Southern Tracks* (1990)

The Janglers, *The Janglers Play Dylan* (1992)
Judy Collins, *Judy Sings Dylan . . . Just Like a Woman* (1993)
Various Artists, *Tribute to Bob Dylan, Volume 1* (1994)
Various Artists (performed by Rod Stewart), *Diana Princess of Wales Tribute* (1997)
Rich Lerner and the Groove, *Cover Down* (1999)
Doug Sahm, *The Return of Wayne Douglas* (2000)
Various Artists (performed by Eliza Gilkyson), *A Nod to Bob* (2001)
2 of Us, *From Zimmermann to Genghis Khan* (2001)
Michel Montecrossa, *Eternal Circle* (2001)
Fleetwood Mac, *Say You Will* (2003)

A song of dark ceremony that can be viewed as a companion to "She Belongs to Me" (an arguably better composition about a much different kind of woman, also from *Bringing It All Back Home*), "Love Minus Zero/No Limit" flows liltingly as it presents bleak, shimmering, Goya-esque images. These loom over the song, which contrasts the purity and strength ("true like ice, like fire") of its narrator's beloved with the brevity of William Blake's poem "The Sick Rose." "In the dime stores and bus stations," Dylan sings, "People talk of situations,/Read books, repeat quotations,/Draw conclusions on the wall"; meanwhile, "My love winks, she does not bother,/She knows too much to argue or to judge."

Andy Gill summarized "Love Minus Zero" quite nicely in his 1998 book *Don't Think Twice, It's All Right:*

> The first verse is as close as Dylan gets to amorous infatuation, marveling at a lover of elemental constancy and rocklike imperturbability, one whose emotional strength is not dependent on overt displays of emotion, but on some deeper, inner fortitude. The three remaining verses then offer a parade of the inauthentic chaos which routinely assaults the narrator's sensibilities, from which his lover's devotion provides him with necessary refuge:

critics dissect, rich girls presume, bridges tremble, statues crumble—but through it all, she remains untouched, unaffected, smiling with the knowing, Zen-like calm of the Mona Lisa. By the song's conclusion, she occupies his thoughts as completely as the eponymous bird obsesses the hapless protagonist of Poe's "The Raven"—although the closing image of the bird with the broken wing tapping at the narrator's window could simply be an expression of her essential vulnerability, despite that inner strength he so admires.

The title of "Love Minus Zero" is said to be drawn from gambling parlance and suggests all love is a risk. Dylan is remembered introducing the song in concert back in 1965 by saying "the title of this song is like math, you know, a fraction." Indeed, it appeared on some *Bringing It All Back Home* LP labels in just such a manner:

Love Minus Zero
No Limit

The idea would be to divide what is on the top by what is on the bottom, rendering an answer close to "absolutely unlimited love."

"Love Minus Zero" has long been an overlooked performance gem. Though it did receive modest attention during Dylan's 1965 and 1966 tours, it wasn't until the Band and Rolling Thunder Revue tours of 1974 through 1976 that Dylan began seriously displaying "Love Minus Zero" in concert. By 1978, he had improved the song by picking up the tempo and injecting some nimble harmonica runs in his big-band arrangement, which also included flute and violin solos. After brief outings in the post-born-again tours of 1980 and 1981, Dylan returned to the song in 1988 with the commencement of the Never Ending Tour and performed it almost yearly, if uncommonly, as a semiacoustic offering.

[S] "Love Rescue Me" (Bob Dylan/Bono Vox)

U2, *Rattle and Hum* (1988)

Dylan penned this minor song with U2's frontman/heartthrob, Bono, and probably contributed some uncredited backing vocals in the studio for its album release. Lyrically secular but religiously phrased, "Love Rescue Me" feels of a piece with the material on *Oh Mercy*, the album Dylan was beginning to conceive at the time he wrote this song; its melancholic, questioning tones are perhaps in the same vein as a song like "Ring Them Bells." Here, instead of summoning God to help raise him up above the fray of human turmoil, the singer asks for love to break the chains that prevent him from becoming a better man.

[S] "Love Sick" (Bob Dylan)

Bob Dylan, *Time out of Mind* (1997)
Duke Robillard, *New Blues for the Modern Age* (1999)
Various Artists (performed by David West), *Pickin' on Dylan* (1999)
Rolling Thunder, *The Never Ending Rehearsal* (2000)
Maroon, *Migratory* (2002)
Various Artists (performed by Tankelaus Tid), *May Your Song Always Be Sung: The Songs of Bob Dylan, Volume 3* (2003)

Time out of Mind commences with the spooky skank of "Love Sick," which aptly synopsizes what is to come on this collection. A wave of electric piano and organ washes over the song, gradually drawing the listener into an ocean of despair. As guitar, bass, and drums join the swirling currents, Dylan croons, "I'm walking through streets that are dead . . ."

Somehow this song from Dylan's latter period, great as it is, never could ring true. Bob Dylan sick of love? Forget about it. Maybe it's one of those Rimbaudian "I is another" changes of persona he's fondly mentioned as a songwriting tool. Or perhaps he was merely

L

engaging in a wound-licking session after a bad first date while listening to Hank Williams's "Love Sick Blues," which comes to mind as a possible inspiration here. Perhaps Dylan is writing and singing from the woman's perspective when he asks, "Could you ever be true?" as if to mean "real." Or is this someone (with seriously conflicting emotions) singing through jaundiced eyes with a mocking "I'd give anything to be with you." And when the narrator mentions "this kind of love," it seems to be of a brand where there are no limits, the kind of enabling vicious circle where the woman continues loving the man no matter what abuse he heaps on her.

Like "Blood in My Eyes," "Love Sick" is filled with the type of dangerous swagger and frightening imagery permeating some of those old country murder songs—the kind steeped in lust, hostility, and envy—that Dylan covered in the early 1990s.

The marketing execs at Victoria's Secret, the randy lingerie company famous for its steamy mail-order catalogues, probably didn't have that type of analysis in mind when they used an elongated snatch of "Love Sick" in a 2003 television ad featuring some lovely, come-hither models frolicking around a palazzo in Venice.

Dylan performed "Love Sick" almost nightly after its release on *Time out of Mind*. It was the song he chose to display at his 1998 Grammy appearance and has continued as on-again, off-again Never Ending Tour fodder.

🅂 **"Love You Too Much"** (Bob Dylan, Greg Lake, and Helena Springs)
aka "I Must Love You Too Much"
See also "If I Don't Be There by Morning"
Greg Lake, *Greg Lake* (1981)
The Band, *High on the Hog* (1996)

By altering lyrics and adding verses to Dylan

and backup singer Helena Springs's throwaway "I Must Love You Too Much," Greg Lake (yes, he of the '70s British pop group Emerson, Lake, and Palmer) copped a cocomposer credit for this song, which was released on his eponymous album. Lake was a member of Dylan's band at the time the song was briefly performed in 1978.

M

🅂 **"Maggie's Farm"** (Bob Dylan)
Bob Dylan, single (1965); *Bringing It All Back Home* (1965); *Bob Dylan's Greatest Hits, Volume II*/'65 (1971); *Hard Rain* (1976); *Bob Dylan at Budokan* (1979); *Real Live* (1984)
Solomon Burke, single (1965); *Cry to Me* (1984)
The Defiants, single (1966)
Ray Brown & Whispers, *Hits & Brass* (1967)
Richie Havens, *Somethin' Else* (1968); *Classics* (1995)
Sam Lay, *Sam Lay in Bluesland* (1968)
Flatt & Scruggs, *Final Fling* (1970)
Nannie Porres, *I Thought About You* (1971)
Booker T. Jones, *Home Grown* (1972)
Victor Scott, *I Want You Beside Me* (1973)
The Blues Band, *Ready* (1980)
The Specials, *The Singles Collection*/'75 (1991)
Hot Tuna, *Live at Sweetwater* (1992)
Barbara Dickson, *Don't Think Twice, It's Alright* (1992)
The Checkered Past, *Two Tone Compilation: Checkered Past* (1993)
Tim O'Brien, *Red on Blonde* (1996)
The Walkabouts, *Death Valley Days* (1996)
Alternative Biography, *Alternative Biography* (1997)
David Grisman/John Hartford/Mike Seeger, *Retrograss* (2000)
Rage Against the Machine, *Renegades* (2000)
The Grateful Dead, *Postcards of the Hanging: Grateful Dead Perform the Songs of Bob Dylan* (2002)
Various Artists (performed by Solomon Burke), *Blues & Soul Power* (2003)

When Bob Dylan shocked the pop-culture universe by plugging in his black Fender Strat at the 1965 Newport Folk Festival, he began his cosmos-altering set with "Maggie's Farm." As a result of that single event, "Maggie's Farm" might be considered his most personal protest song, one to which he has returned and reinvented many times. The song even works as folk-rock stand-up—Dylan disses Maggie and everybody in her family with a funny punchline in every woebegotten verse.

"Maggie's Farm" is seen, at least partly, as a reworking of "Penny's Farm," an old country song. "Haven't old George Penny got a flatterin' mouth?/Move you to the country in a little log house/Got no windows but the cracks in the wall," goes "Penny's Farm"; "I ain't gonna work for Maggie's pa no more/. . ./His bedroom window/It is made out of bricks," sings Dylan.

Additionally, others have linked "Tanner's Farm," a similar 1934 song recorded by Gid Tanner and Riley Puckett, to this constellation of works from which Dylan drew in composing "Maggie's Farm." It has also been suggested that Silas Magee, the owner of the Greenwood, Mississippi, farm that hosted a July 6, 1963, civil rights rally at which Dylan appeared and was seen briefly in *Don't Look Back*, provided some sort of inspiration, though "Maggie's Farm" was composed a year and a half later. Perhaps Dylan was responding in song to the many hoops he was being pressured to jump though as the "voice" of the folk/protest movement.

Yet this is a protest song of the highest order, as Dylan, in a series of cartoonish vignettes and with a bitingly sardonic delivery as heard on *Bringing It All Back Home*, manages to have his babka and eat it too with a critique of both capitalism and communism, thus avoiding any charges of red-baiting or red-diapering. In "Maggie's Farm" any system (and those that run them) that reduces its laborers to the alienated, time-clock-punching, assembly-line droids must be condemned.

Dylan did not see himself as exempt from the threat of such toil. In 1965 he wasn't going to continue being simply a gifted folkie playing for a select, sanctimoniously purist circle. He was growing as an artist, pushing boundaries. He wasn't going to work on Maggie's farm: he would follow his own muse, even—perhaps especially—if it meant confounding the expectations of his audience, his management, or the corporate interests behind him. "Got a head full of ideas/that are drivin' me insane," he sings.

In "Maggie's Farm," as in the darkly humorous "Subterranean Homesick Blues" from the same transitional *Bringing It All Back Home* album, Dylan showed us that a protest song could dole out harsh social critique and be lighthearted at the same time. Here he sneers at any kind of meaningless labor ("It's a shame the way she makes me scrub the floor") and sounds a trumpet against conformity ("everybody wants you/to be just like them)." He gets us to snicker at the narrator's plight, but the message couldn't be clearer: we all work on somebody's farm.

"Maggie's Farm" has never left Dylan's set lists throughout the twists and right angles of his career. In 1965, it was hard-driving—an energetic, wry statement of self. It was similar, but with a harder edge, on both the 1974 reunion tour with the Band and the barnstorming Rolling Thunder Revue tour of 1976. Then, in 1978, when Dylan transformed his road show into a glitzfest complete with Vegas-influenced arrangements and an Elvis Presley–inspired big band behind him, "Maggie's Farm" was still front and center, confounding even the most die-hard Dylan fans as a virtually tuneless minor-key rant. It was that same year that "Maggie's Farm" also enjoyed a renewed popularity among Great Britain's leftists as a protest against Margaret Thatcher's Conservative gov-

M

ernment. In 1984 the song was again recast as the smirking rock boogie it has remained through the 1990s and early '00s. In 2003, Dylan even began using it as a show opener. From the front lines of the class wars to the rear guard of the pop cultural zeitgeist, Bert Parks (who made a name for himself during the 1970s as host of the Miss America Pageant) performed a mind-bendingly bizarre version of "Maggie's Farm" in *The Freshman*, the 1990 black comedy mobster flick starring Matthew Broderick as a young film student and Marlon Brando doing a perfect send-up of his Don Corleone *Godfather* character.

[S] "Main Title Theme (Billy)" (Bob Dylan)

Bob Dylan, *Pat Garrett and Billy the Kid* (1973)

With its acoustic guitars, maracas, and Spanish flourishes, Dylan's mellow instrumental sets the tone for *Pat Garrett and Billy the Kid*, the Sam Peckinpah western it embellished.

M

[S] "Make Me a Pallet on Your Floor" (Traditional)

aka "Atlanta Blues," "Make Me a Bed on Your Floor"
Louis Armstrong, *Louis Armstrong Plays W. C. Handy* (1954)
Kid Ory, *Legendary Kid* (1955)
Gus Cannon, *Walk Right In* (1962)
Odetta, *Odetta and the Blues* (1962)
Archie Shepp, *Trouble in Mind* (1980)
Mississippi John Hurt, *The Best of Mississippi John Hurt/'65* (1982)
The Leake County Revelers, *Complete Recorded Works, Volume 1* (1998)
Horace Parlan, *Voyage of Discovery* (1999)

Countless artists from across the musical spectrum have had a go at this piece of ancient blues—even the jazz cipher and coronetist Buddy Bolden is remembered as having performed a vocal version of "Make Me a Pallet" in early twentieth-century New Orleans. Dylan could have picked up the tune from any number of sources, though Gus Cannon, Odetta, and Mississippi John Hurt are very likely candidates.

The song is, basically, about illicit sex. As Son Simms, an old fiddle-playing Delta bluesman who accompanied Charley Patton on some of his early Paramount recordings, is quoted in Alan Lomax's *The Land Where the Blues Began* (New York: Pantheon Books, 1993), "That's how these women will do you, when you're off from home. They don't want to get the bed nasty with them and their kid man, so they put some old quilt down on the floor so they can do their business."

Dylan's only known performance of the song dates to October 1962 on Billy Faier's radio show on New York City's WBAI-FM.

[S] "Make You Feel My Love" (Bob Dylan)

aka "To Make You Feel My Love"
Bob Dylan, *Time out of Mind* (1997)
Billy Joel, *Greatest Hits, Volume 3* (1997)
Garth Brooks, *Limited Series* (1998); *Double Live* (1998)
Various Artists (performed by Garth Brooks), *Hope Floats* (soundtrack) (1998)
The London West End Singers, *Going to the Movies: The Best of '98* (1998)
Heartland, *Heartland Plays Dylan: Your Mind Is Your Temple* (1998)
Various Artists (performed by Half Penny Marvel), *Tribute to Garth Brooks* (1999)
The Countdown Singers, *Sweet Love* (1999); *Mega Movie Hits* (1999)
Joan Osborne, *Righteous Love* (2000)
Carolyn Maier, *Sessions* (2000)
Luka Bloom, *Keeper of the Flame* (2000); *Amsterdam* (2003)
Timothy B. Schmit, *Feed the Fire* (2001)
Paul Evans, *Roses Are Red, My Love* (2003)

One of the little shocks of Dylan's *Time out of Mind* was the success of this song, which comes off like the last-ditch plea of a rejected suitor. It was covered by pop icons Billy Joel and Garth Brooks, with Brooks's version included on the soundtrack of *Hope Floats*, a Forest Whitaker–directed romance set in Texas starring Sandra Bullock and Harry Connick Jr. Dylan began performing "Make You Feel My Love" in concert shortly after its release, spitting out the lyrics like a tongue-tied lover, a practice that has continued through 2004.

Like just about every *Time out of Mind* song (perhaps with the exception of "Highlands"), "Make You Feel My Love" is at best a lament for, or at worst a creepy plea to, an unattainable woman from a man getting more desperate by the minute. Whether that guy is Bob Dylan or not would hardly seem to matter. But it is interesting that this flavor of Dylan song dealing with the theme of a guy ripped apart by his inability to forget about a woman he can't have can be traced back to some of those found on *Freewheelin' Bob Dylan*. But, unlike most of the other *Time out of Mind* material, "Make You Feel My Love" comes from the lips of a narrator in greater control of his situation than, say, the rounder on the lam singing in "Cold Irons Bound" or the grifter disappearing over the hills in "Dirt Road Blues." The smooth singer in the treacly and maudlin "Make You Feel My Love" sits smack dab in the middle of the album as if to say that all roads of desperation lead to and from its (by comparison) calm, Hallmark-card-toned core.

Or, as some contend, is "Make You Feel My Love" a theologically rich song disguised as a light love song? Perhaps, as during Dylan's gospel period, when some of his songs to God sounded as if they could have been written to a woman, "Make You Feel My Love" is a reflection of the primary relationship between God and His beloved (the human race). Or maybe Dylan is trying to kill two birds with one stone.

Taken as indulgent hyperbole, it is merely about a man trying to make contact with a woman. But if one takes it literally, one realizes that only Christ could legitimately say, "I could hold you for a million years," or even "I'd go hungry, I'd go black and blue/I'd go crawling down the avenue/There's nothing that I wouldn't do/To make you feel my love." And lines like "I could make you happy, make your dreams come true/Nothing that I wouldn't do/Go to the ends of the earth for you" could just as easily portray a man dropping every seduction cliché in the book as describe God's incarnation as a man who went the way he came: suffering and dying for humanity.

"Making Believe" (Jimmy Work/Roscoe Reid/Joe Hobson)
aka "Makin' Believe"
Jimmy Work, *Making Believe* (1998)
Emmylou Harris, *Luxury Liner* (1977)
Hank Snow, *Thesaurus Transcriptions* (1991)
Kitty Wells, *Queen of Country Music* (1994)
Merle Haggard, *Vintage Collection Series* (1996)
Ray Charles, *Complete Country and Western Recordings* (1998)

Dylan's first concert in Turkey in June 1989 was an intimate one, staged at a 3,000-seat arena in Istanbul. Perhaps it was the exotic locale that inspired his choice of Jimmy Work's country standard as the second song for that night's affair—Dylan's only known performance of the tune. Work's name is not a familiar one to most country-music freaks, but his most famous songs are easy to recognize: "Tennessee Border," "That's What Makes the Jukebox Play," and "Making Believe."

Work (born March 29, 1924, Akron, Ohio) grew up on a farm in Dukedom, Tennessee, playing guitar and violin and absorbing the music of Jimmie Rodgers et al. on the family Victrola.

A teenage songwriter, he eventually joined a touring country band that caught on with displaced white and black Southerners working in the defense and auto plants in Pontiac, Michigan. Glad to hear songs reminding them of home, these transplanted country-music fans kept Work in guitar strings. This led to appearances on local radio and the recording, for the small Trophy label, of a couple of singles that were highly derivative of Jimmie Rodgers and, accordingly, featured Work yodeling in true Singing Brakeman fashion.

"Tennessee Border," his third single, was eventually popularized via recordings by the likes of Red Foley, Tennessee Ernie Ford, and Hank Williams. It was with the Dot label that he cut his last two popular songs: "Making Believe" and "That's What Makes the Jukebox Play." Issued in 1955, "Making Believe" eventually hit No. 11 for Work while Kitty Wells's rival cover rose to No. 2.

When the rockabilly craze took off, Work's stock began to decline. He eventually returned to the farm near the border. He did, however, keep a hand in songwriting as a contracted member of the Acuff-Rose organization.

[S] **"Mama, You Been on My Mind"** (Bob Dylan)

Bob Dylan, *The Bootleg Series, Volumes 1–3: Rare and Unreleased, 1961–1991/'64* (1991); *The Bootleg Series, Volume 5: Live 1975—The Rolling Thunder Revue* (2002); *The Bootleg Series, Volume 6: Live 1964—Concert at Philharmonic Hall* (2004)
Joan Baez (as "Daddy, You Been on My Mind"), *Farewell Angelina* (1965); (performed with Bob Dylan) *Rare Live and Classic* (1993)
Johnny Cash, *Orange Blossom Special* (1965)
Judy Collins (as "Daddy, You've Been on My Mind"), *Fifth Album* (1965); *Recollections* (1969)
Dion and the Belmonts, *Together Again* (1967)
The Kingston Trio, *Once Upon a Time* (1968)
Linda Ronstadt, *Hand Sown . . . Home Grown* (1969)
Mylon Lefevre, *Over the Influence* (1972)
Rod Stewart, *Never a Dull Moment* (1972); *The Songs of Bob Dylan/'72* (1989); *Handbags and Gladrags* (1996)
Mabel Joy, *Mabel Joy* (1975)
The Original Marauders, *Now Your Mouth Cries Wolf: A Tribute to Bob Dylan* (1977)
Southwind, *Southwind* (1980)
Various Artists (performed by Judy Collins), *Bleecker and MacDougal: The Folk Scene of the 1960s* (1984)
Lee Renaldo, *Outlaw Blues* (1992)
Lester Flatt and Earl Scruggs, *1964–1969, Plus* (1996)
Rick Nelson, *Stay Young—Epic Recordings* (1998)
Steve Howe, *Portraits of Bob Dylan* (1999)
Andy Hill, *It Takes a Lot to Laugh* (2000)
Peter Mulvey, *Ten Thousand Mornings* (2002)

With its gorgeous melody and cascading, almost incantatory lyrics of romance and inevitable separation, "Mama, You Been on My Mind" is simply a great love song. Yet for a pretty straightforward love song of separation and yearning, "Mama, You Been on My Mind" is not without its surreal touch. How can the sun, for instance, be cut flat?

"Mama, You Been on My Mind" has remained a surprisingly durable performance piece for Dylan since its earliest displays in 1964, when he occasionally sang it as a wistful duet with Joan Baez at her concerts as well as at his own (as heard on *The Bootleg Series, Volume 6: Live 1964—Concert at Philharmonic Hall*). Baez, in fact, was the first to officially release the song, as "Daddy, You've Been on My Mind," on her *Farewell Angelina* album in 1965. Dylan and Baez reprised their duets on "Mama" during the Rolling Thunder Revue of 1975 and '76, when Dylan rearranged the song in jaunty bluegrass style, complete with pedal-steel licks from multi-instrumentalist wunderkind David Mansfield.

In addition to the mid-1960s and Rolling Thunder duets with Baez, Dylan performed

"Mama, You Been on My Mind" at his 1970 session with George Harrison and at one show on Tour '74 with the Band. Since the Never Ending Tour hit its stride in the early 1990s, as part of his nightly acoustic segment, Dylan has often and effectively presented the song with his trademark wheezy, reedy voice, his regret-masked delivery and feigned detachment giving the composition its emotional impact.

"Man Gave Names to All the Animals"

(Bob Dylan)

Bob Dylan, single (1979); *Slow Train Coming* (1979)
Julie Felix, *Colors in the Rain* (1980)
Townes Van Zandt, *Roadsongs* (1992)
Hugues Aufray, *Aufray Trans Dylan* (1995); *Au Casino de Paris* (1996)
Tim O'Brien, *Red on Blonde* (1996)
Rich Lerner, *Napoleon in Rags* (2001)

While Dylan called this goofy piece of Genesis-inspired reggae a "children's song," others called it the worst song he ever wrote. Either way, "Man Gave Names to All the Animals" was, like Jerry Lewis and for reasons that will never be fully explained, a *huge* hit in France. Dylan made sure to perform the song there for years afterward whenever he returned, whether as a set part of his current performance repertoire or not. Here Dylan tells some of the Garden of Eden tale, but seems to pin the blame for the Fall squarely on the serpent as he omits any mention of either Eve or Adam in this song.

In time, "Man Gave Names to All the Animals" actually became genuinely endearing in concert, thanks to Dylan's playful readings. On the *Slow Train* version of the song, Dylan sets up each animal's name with an obvious, and sometimes painful, rhyme: the animal that wasn't "too short and he wasn't too big" becomes a pig; an animal disappearing by a tree near a lake becomes a snake, etc. In concert he played

with this latter line, to his audience's obvious delight, by either misrhyming it with a different animal—a giraffe, say—or by simply leaving the snake unidentified, as if to emphasize its symbolically diabolical import. Best of all on these versions were the backup singers, who would fill the lyrical void with the snake's sound: "Sssssssssssssss . . ."

Whether or not Dylan wrote it as such, "Man Gave Names to All the Animals" does work as a children's song: a children's book of the same title with Dylan's lyrics and illustrations by Scott Menchin was published in the fall of 1999 (New York: Harcourt). Further evidence comes from Regina Havis Brown, one of Dylan's backup singers at the time, who told Scott Marshall in an interview for *On the Tracks* #18 (April 30, 2000):

> My personal favorite [on *Slow Train Coming*] was "Man Gave Names to All the Animals," because I remember being in Muscle Shoals, Alabama, and Bob Dylan and Jerry Wexler weren't sure if they were even going to put that song on the record. I remember Bob coming in and letting us hear the cut of "Man Gave Names to All the Animals."
>
> At that time my son, Tony, was three years old and he was with me. When Bob played "Man Gave Names to All the Animals" and it started talking about "Ooh, I think I'll call it a cow," my son was falling over on the floor, laughing. Then he heard "Ooh, I think I'll call it a pig," and my son was just cracking up!
>
> Dylan looked over saw how my son was laughing, and he said, "I'm going to put that on the record."

After premiering the song during the gospel tours of 1979 and 1980, Dylan pretty much laid it off after 1981. In deference to the song's status in France and among children everywhere, how-

M

ever, Dylan was known trot it out now and again in the early stages of the Never Ending Tour.

"The Man in Me" (Bob Dylan)

Bob Dylan, *New Morning* (1970)
Various Artists (performed by Bob Dylan), *The Big Lebowski* (soundtrack) (1998)
Lonnie Mack, *Hills of Indiana* (1971)
Al Kooper, *A Possible Projection of the Future* (1972)
The Persuasions, *Street Corner Symphony* (1972)
McKendree Spring, *Tracks* (1973); *God Bless the Conspiracy* (1996)
Joe Cocker, *Stingray* (1976)
Nick Kamen, *Nick Kamen* (1987)
Various Artists (performed by Emry Arthur), *The Music of Kentucky: Early American Rural Classics 1927–1937, Volume 2* (1995)
Heartland, *Heartland Plays Dylan: Your Mind Is Your Temple* (1998)
Various Artists (performed by Matumbi), *Reggae: I Am King Classic from the Rock Era* (2002)

With focus and conviction if not melody, Dylan, there is little doubt, wrote this very personal song to his then-wife, Sara, telling her that she's the only one who could have gotten "through to the man in me." Such hollow lines and sentiments never made the song popular among feminists. And if he hints that he reveals his true self only to his true love, "The Man in Me" is a song without much commitment—a feeling heightened by its shameless cribbing of the melody from "On the Street Where You Live," the Alan J. Lerner/Frederick Loewe song from *My Fair Lady* long popular among the jazz set.

"The Man in Me" was generally ignored by his critics and admirers. Dylan didn't start performing a slightly altered lyric version of the song until his glitzy 1978 big-band tour, when it received a fair amount of attention. He pulled it out of mothballs in the late 1980s and early 1990s in the early phase of the Never Ending Tour. Then, perhaps because of its newfound popularity following the 1998 release of *The Big Lebowski*, a typically off-kilter film from Joel and Ethan Coen that starred Jeff Bridges and John Goodman, Dylan began casually including the song in his set lists that year; it remained an on-again, off-again inclusion through the summer of 2002.

"Man in the Long Black Coat" (Bob Dylan)

Bob Dylan, *Oh Mercy* (1989)
Emerson, Lake & Palmer, *In the Hot Seat* (1994)
Joan Osborne, *Relish* (1995)
Michel Montecrossa, *Born in Time* (2000)
Rolling Thunder, *The Never Ending Rehearsal* (2000)
Various Artists (performed by Joan Osborne), *Doin' Dylan 2* (2002)

Dense and ambiguous, this strange, sinister, and richly evocative fairy tale of a song tells a story that lives up to its vaguely menacing title. Dylan has often shown a fondness for silent, mercurial, and faceless characters—the drifter, the mystery tramp, Señor, the Jack of Hearts, Blackjack Davey, the Daemon Lover—who would be as comfortable in a Clint Eastwood or Akira Kurosawa flick as they are in one of his songs. These strangers, some evil, others voices of wisdom, stealthily appear and suddenly disappear (often with a woman on one arm and the Grim Reaper on the other) and leave everything a little altered in their wake. They're in the eye of the songs' storms, and indeed, a hurricane is the central metaphor used in "Man in the Long Black Coat." In a musical arrangement that is downright spooky—its use of crickets make it sound as if it was recorded on the porch of an antebellum shotgun shack at the edge of a Louisiana swamp—Dylan warns of those who will twist the truths of religion in his tale of implied philandering and faithlessness.

A chilling narrative ballad suffused with a gothic sense of sin, death, illicit sex, and dark power, "Man in the Long Black Coat" is the haunting center of *Oh Mercy*. Singing the song in a husky, tormented whisper, Dylan tells of a woman who leaves her life behind for the mysterious title character (the preacher mentioned in the lyrics or maybe the Devil or even Death himself), provoking a series of reflections on the nature of conscience, religious faith, and emotional commitment perhaps best expressed with the apathetic observation that "people don't live or die, people just float." The spare musical background enhances the atmosphere and emphasizes the lack of absolutes.

Rumor has it that "Man in the Long Black Coat" (as well as its album's title) may have been inspired by a 1986 movie called *No Mercy*, starring Richard Gere and Kim Basinger, in which Basinger plays an illiterate woman from New Orleans, the Crescent City where Dylan recorded his album. The movie connection perhaps explains why in the song "there was nothing she wrote" and why she left "not even a note." And, as in the song, crickets provide a constant background sound in the movie. *The Man in the Gray Flannel Suit*, the 1956 film starring Gregory Peck as a political speechwriter who must decide between his family or career, has been suggested as another title Dylan may have been referencing here.

Burnishing the song with sinister menace, Dylan has faithfully performed "Man in the Long Black Coat" in concert since *Oh Mercy*'s release in 1989. Allegedly, Dylan once introduced the song in concert by saying, "This is a true story. Like all stories that are true, this one also has a moral." The only theory that has been floated as to what "true story" Dylan alludes to is the now almost forgotten history of the founder of the Jehovah's Witnesses, one Charles Taze Russell, whose reputation was tarnished with accusations of child molestation in 1906. Surviving photographs of Russell do indicate a fondness for the titular garment.

[S] "Man of Constant Sorrow" (Traditional)

aka "Farewell Song," "I'm a Girl of Constant Sorrow," "I'm a Man of Constant Sorrow," "In Old Virginny"
Bob Dylan, *Bob Dylan* (1962)
Mike Seeger, *Oldtime Country Music* (1962)
Rod Stewart, *Rod Stewart Album* (1969)
Almeda Riddle, *Ballads and Hymns from the Ozarks* (1972)
The Country Gentlemen, *Yesterday and Today* (1976)
The Stanley Brothers, *Complete Columbia Recordings* (1996)
Garcia/Grisman/Rice, *The Pizza Tapes* (2000)
Various Artists (performed by the Soggy Bottom Boys and Dan Tyminski), *O Brother, Where Art Thou?* (soundtrack) (2001)

Simmering with rue, this traditional Southern mountain song, which Mike Seeger (Pete's half brother) called "a mountain equivalent of the blues," has been a folksinger's favorite at least since the early country-music pioneer and popularizer Emry Arthur (born 1899 or 1900, Elk Spring Valley, Wayne County, Kentucky; died August 1966, Indianapolis), who claimed the composition as his own and made the probable first recording of it in the 1920s. In Dylan's hands, "Man of Constant Sorrow" became a story of a sucker unable to get the girl he loves after riding the rails "through ice and snow, sleet and rain," uncaring of whether he might die on the return trip home.

Arthur-penned or not, there is no doubt "Man of Constant Sorrow" is an old song and has gone through constant change, especially with regard to the narrator's home.

Archie Green untangled some of the layered history of "Man of Constant Sorrow" in the liner notes for the 1967 album *Sarah Ogan Gunning—A Girl of Constant Sorrow*, when he wrote: "In recent years, the Appalachian lament 'I Am a Man of Constant Sorrow' has become popular in urban folksong circles, in part through the performance of the Stanley Brothers and of Mike Seeger. No study of this haunting piece is available; the earliest text I have found was printed about 1913 in a pocket songster hawked by Dick Burnett, a blind singer from Monticello, Kentucky. During 1918, Cecil Sharp collected the song and published it as 'In Old Virginny' (Sharp II, 233). Sarah's recomposition of the traditional 'Man' into a more personal 'Girl' took place about 1936 in New York, where her first husband, Andrew Ogan, was fatally ill. The text was descriptive of loneliness away from home and anticipated her bereavement; the melody she remembered from a 78 rpm hillbilly record (Emry Arthur) she had heard some years before in the mountains."

Dylan's version is a rewrite of the version that was being sung in the early 1960s by the New Lost City Ramblers (Mike Seeger's ensemble), Joan Baez, and the other usual suspects. Dylan performed his "Man of Constant Sorrow" pretty consistently in 1961 and '62, as it appears on tapes from gigs and informal recordings from that period. He may have been reflecting on his problems with the mother of his then-girlfriend Suze Rotolo when he rewrote "Your friends may think I'm a stranger" to read "Your mother says I'm a stranger." In 1988 "Man of Constant Sorrow" reappeared in Dylan's Never Ending Tour acoustic set, where it was given a burning, though intermittent, airing through 1990. And again, in April 2002, as the Israeli-Palestinian cycle of violence and retribution escalated, Dylan, in true wandering Jew fashion, unleashed "Man of Constant Sorrow" on his European tour. Always, it emerged as a chillingly lonesome personal statement.

But the truly amazing surprise in the song's history is the explosive popularity it garnered through its spirited appearance in *O Brother, Where Art Thou?*, Joel and Ethan Coen's recast-ing of Homer's *Odyssey* as a Preston Sturges–style escaped-convict film set in 1930s southern Appalachia.

"Man of Peace" (Bob Dylan)

Bob Dylan, *Infidels* (1983)
The Grateful Dead (performed with Bob Dylan), *Postcards of the Hanging: Grateful Dead Perform the Songs of Bob Dylan* (2002)
Zimmermen, *After the Ambulances Go* (1998)
Holmes Brothers, *Speaking in Tongues* (2001)

With a trio of mostly gospel-infused albums behind him, Dylan included only one song on *Infidels* that found him still in high stump-preacher mode, spewing fire, brimstone, apocalyptic warning, and maybe a touch of cock 'n' bull (as well as rock 'n' roll) with the bluesy "Man of Peace." In "Man of Peace," Dylan warns of Satan's many masks, from thief, joker, and local priest to the chief of police and the Führer himself.

Dylan began performing "Man of Peace" in 1984 not long after its release, and it has remained on the fringes of his stage show since. The version of the song released on the Grateful Dead compilation CD *Postcards of the Hanging* listed above was drawn from the spring 1987 rehearsal preceding their concerts together later that summer. Dylan performed the song again that fall during his last swing with Tom Petty and the Heartbreakers. He gave it medium treatment during the early phase of the Never Ending Tour and paid intermittent visits to it in the following years.

"Man on the Street" (Bob Dylan)

aka "The Old Man," "There Was an Old Man"
See also "Only a Hobo"
Bob Dylan, *The Bootleg Series, Volumes 1–3: Rare and Unreleased, 1961–1991/'62* (1991)
Dave Van Ronk, *No Dirty Names* (1966)

In his early days as a songwriter Bob Dylan relied heavily on the folk and blues tradition for material and for basic song structures. "Man on the Street," from late August 1961, is an example, as it draws its tune from "The Young Man Who Wouldn't Hoe Corn" (a song sung by Mike Seeger) and its sensibility from Hank Williams's "Tramp in the Street." It is one of several Guthriesque tunes in which Dylan expresses compassion for society's desperate and destitute rejects, this time describing an old man who apparently manages to attract more attention in death than he did in life, whose indignities stop not even with his demise.

At the time he was writing his early songs, Dylan was reading extensively and already beginning to sneak literary and biblical references into his compositions. The most provocative image in "Man on the Street" strongly recalls snatches of Bertolt Brecht's "Litany of Breath." "There came an inspector down the street/He had a rubber club loaded with lead," runs a portion of Brecht's verse, which continues: "He smashed in the back of that man's head/And not another word he said." Dylan, in turn, sings the following: "Well, the p'liceman come and he looked around,/'Get up, old man, or I'm a-takin' you down.'/He jabbed him once with his billy club/And the old man then rolled off the curb."

In his liner notes to Dylan's eponymous debut album, for which "Man on the Street" was recorded but left off, Robert Shelton states that the song was "an original based on an episode on West Fourth Street in the Village [in which] Bob had seen a policeman jab a dead man with his club to stir him." That is entirely plausible, but even so, the Brecht connection is unmistakable, especially considering that Dylan's girlfriend of the time, Suze Rotolo, was working as a theater hand on a production of *Brecht on Brecht* and Dylan was a frequent visitor to the

set, and that "Man on the Street" also mimics the verse structure of "Litany of Breath." Perhaps Dylan found in Brecht the inspiration to describe a scene that he himself had witnessed.

Sketchy evidence indicates that "Man on the Street" was at least a sometime inclusion in Dylan's coffeehouse sets from the era; it may be found on at least one 1962 tape from the Gaslight Café in New York City. Within a few months, however, Dylan had reworked "Man on the Street" into "Only a Hobo," a much more effective song that demonstrates Dylan's startlingly rapid development as a songwriter.

▣ "Margarita" (Traveling Wilburys)
Traveling Wilburys, single (1988); *Traveling Wilburys, Volume 1* (1988)

Dylan's involvement with "Margarita," a minor Wilburys track, appears minimal. Until he chimes in with a backing vocal behind Tom Petty's lead midway through the song, one might have forgotten he was around at all.

▣ "Marine's Hymn (From the Halls of Montezuma)" (Traditional)
aka "From the Halls of Montezuma"
Various Artists (performed by the Mormon Tabernacle Choir), *God Bless America and Other Patriotic Songs* (1992)
Various Artists (performed by Fred Waring & His Pennsylvanians), *Songs That Won the War* (1995)
Various Artists, *Stars and Stripes* (1998)
John McDermott, *Remembrance* (1999)

Dylan kicked off some 1990 shows with an instrumental arrangement of the "Marine's Hymn," including a memorable rendition for the cadets at West Point as the Persian Gulf crisis boiled in the fall. Folks in the Hudson Valley are still scratching their heads, wondering if Dylan was serious or merely having some ironic fun at his audience's expense.

Surprisingly, the song's history is connected not only with military conquest but with comic opera as well. In 1805, during protracted conflict between the U.S. and the ruthless pirates of North Africa's Barbary States—one of which was Tripoli—Lieutenant P. N. O'Bannon and a tiny band of Marines assisted in the capture of Derna, a Tripolitan port. They became the first Americans to hoist the Stars and Stripes above an Old World fortress, and subsequently the Marine Corps flag was inscribed with the legend "To the Shores of Tripoli." In 1847, during the Mexican War, the Marines helped in the capture and occupation of Mexico City and the fortified hill and castle of Chapultepec (also called the Halls of Montezuma); in 1848 motto on the flag was changed to read "From the Halls of the Montezumas to the Shores of Tripoli." As part of tradition, every campaign the Marines have taken part in gives birth to an unofficial verse added to the song.

M

Musicologists trace the source of the tune of the "Marine's Hymn" to an aria from Jacques Offenbach's farcical late nineteenth-century French opera *Geneviève de Brabant.* No less an authority than marching-band composer John Philip Sousa vouched for the link. As he wrote in a 1919 letter to U.S. Marine Corps Major Harold F. Wingman: "The melody of the 'Halls of Montezuma' is taken from Offenbach's comic opera, *Geneviève de Brabant*." (For more detailed information, see the U.S. Marine Corps Web site, especially its section devoted to historical issues.)

Jacques Offenbach composed *Geneviève de Brabant*, which debuted at Paris's Théâtre de Bouffes Parisiens on November 19, 1859. The son of a Jewish cantor, Offenbach (born Jakob Weiner, June 20, 1819, Cologne, Germany; died October 5, 1880, Paris, France) was an accomplished violoncellist who later became conductor of the Théâtre Français in 1847. He is best known as a composer of many still highly regarded light operas.

The U.S. Marine Corps formerly held the copyright to "Marine's Hymn," but the song is now in the public domain.

[S] **"Mary Ann"** (Traditional)

Bob Dylan, *Dylan* (1973)
Various Artists, *Steel Bands of the Caribbean* (1992)
Cockspur Steelband, *Greatest* (1996)
Thomas Stewart, *Songs of Gambling and the Sea* (1996)

Dylan performed this song of farewell about a man sailing away from his own true love at the outset of his career—it appears on the very early May 1960 "St. Paul Tape." He returned to "Mary Ann" more than a decade later in a studio recording that Columbia released on the misbegotten *Dylan*, an album not authorized by the titular artist. The album version is an unessential item that features difficult-to-tolerate vocals by Dylan that compete with even more nauseating backup from his studio choir.

[S] **"Mary of the Wild Moor"** (Traditional)

aka "Baby on the Doorstep," "The Forsaken Mother and Child," "Mary from the Moor," "Mary from the Wild Moor," "Mary of the Moor," "Mary on the Wild Moor," "Mary of the Wilde Moore," "When Mary Came Wandering Home," "Winds Blew Across the Wild Moor"
The Louvin Brothers, *Tragic Song of Life* (1956)
Charlie Moore, *Charlie Moore Sings Good Bluegrass* (1963)
Blue Sky Boys, *Bluegrass Mountain Music* (1974)
Phyllis Marks, *Folksongs and Ballads, Volume 2* (1991)
Dolly Parton, *Heartsongs: Live from Home* (1994)
Rich Lerner, *Trails and Bridges* (1996)
Bill Harrell & the Virginians, *Blue Virginia Blue* (1997)

"This is a real old song. I used to sing this song before I wrote any songs. One of those songs you used to sing, you know, with a guitar on your back going from town to town." Thus

Dylan introduced this old chestnut in true wandering-minstrel style at a 1980 show at the Fox Warfield Theater in San Francisco.

A tragic ballad in the British-American Southern mountain music lineage, "Mary of the Wild Moor" tells the story of a mother and baby who die after being shut out in the cold of a winter's night by the woman's cruel father. Whether sung in the music halls of Victorian England as a melodramatic tearjerker or performed in an impersonal, nondramatic fashion by traditional singers, the song has an inescapable melancholy.

According to www.contemplator.com, folklorist William Barrett collected the song from a tavern in Slinfold, England, noting its popularity throughout eighteenth-century England before it traveled to America.

In their liner notes for *Getting Folk Out of the Country*, released in the early 1970s, Hedy West and Bill Clifton mention that "Mary of the Wild Moor" was credited in 1845 to a British writer named Joseph W. Turner. "Whether he was the author or reviser is unclear," they wrote. "The song has shown up all the way from Yorkshire through central and southern England, and from Nova Scotia down the entire east coast of the U.S. throughout the Mid-West and in parts of the Far West. Its widespread acceptance by traditional singers, and its lack of variation, may be explained by the frequency with which it was printed in British and American broadsides and songsters."

According to Clancy Brother Tommy Makem, his mother, Sarah, learned "The Forsaken Mother and Child" at a dance near Derrynoose in County Armagh, Northern Ireland. Given Dylan's relationship with the Clancy clan, going back to the very early 1960s, it is not improbable that the song filtered to him through them.

One of the more effective and memorable of Dylan's covers of traditional folk songs, "Mary of the Wild Moor" is noteworthy for its spare acoustic arrangement, led by Fred Tackett's mandolin. During its midset performances in 1980 and 1981, the song was presented in a sensitive duet with backup vocalist Regina McCrary, who accompanied herself on autoharp.

Masked and Anonymous
Directed by Larry Charles. Starring Bob Dylan, Jeff Bridges, Penélope Cruz, John Goodman, Jessica Lange, Luke Wilson, Angela Bassett, Ed Harris, Cheech Marin, Val Kilmer, Mickey Rourke, Bruce Dern, Giovanni Ribisi. Released 2003.

Renaldo & Clara redux, *The Times They Are Surreal,* or merely *Positively 4th Rate*? Whatever side of the critical fence one comes down on, Dylan's latest celluloid foray was at least a return to the confounding mind-tripster style of 1967's *Don't Look Back*. And it stands like *Citizen Kane* in comparison to the 1987 *Hearts of Fire* tripe in which Dylan starred.

Approached as one of Dylan's surreal, shaggy-dog songs like "The Ballad of Frankie Lee and Judas Priest," *Masked and Anonymous* comes off as something more than an unholy, incoherent mess. As A. O. Scott pointed out in his July 24, 2003, review in the *New York Times*: "As a Bob Dylan artifact, though, it is endlessly, perhaps morbidly, fascinating. If not for a handful of first-rate performances, including some of his [Dylan's] own songs and a stunning rendition of 'Dixie,' the movie would belong on the cultist's curio shelf along with Mr. Dylan's 1966 'novel' *Tarantula* and his 1978 film, *Renaldo & Clara*."

What sort of passes for a plot, an allegory of the decline and fall of the American empire set against a background of civil war that takes place sometime in the nearish middle future, is as follows: the uniformed likeness of the reigning, aging despot, Uncle Sweetheart, is pasted on every wall. Sweetheart, a bloodsuck-

A store window display featuring an array of masks of celebrities and politicians for Mardi Gras, France, 1935.

(Hulton Archive/Getty Images)

ing showbiz hustler, is played by John Goodman, attired in a horrid pale-blue tux. His character, with at least one gun pointed at his head when the cinematic curtain rises, is organizing a benefit concert—but to whose benefit is never clear. With Bruce Springsteen, Paul McCartney, Billy Joel, and Sting otherwise unavailable, Sweetheart decides that Jack Fate (played by Dylan), a faded icon just being sprung from jail for undetermined crimes, would be the perfect candidate to headline.

Holding his guitar case in one hand and a garment bag full of Nudie suits in the other, Fate emerges from the poky and makes his way to the concert, encountering the first of many characters with a bug-eyed rant—in this instance a confused revolutionary turned counterrevolutionary turned revolutionary (played by Giovanni Ribisi). Within time, Fate will encounter others with similar apocalyptic beefs, including a deranged animal wrangler (Val Kilmer spewing forth about all creatures great and small), an embittered music journal-

ist with a mega megachip on his shoulder (Jeff Bridges haranguing about Jimi Hendrix, Frank Zappa, and the evaporated dream of the 1960s), and his religiously obsessed, hair-twisting gal pal (Penélope Cruz fretting about hair-splitting Bible issues).

Other side characters and subplots involve a blowzy concert promoter, Nina Veronica (played by Jessica Lange), who runs flak against the gun-toting television network executives; Bobby Cupid (Luke Wilson in a role reminiscent of the one Bobby Neuwirth played for Dylan in the days of *Don't Look Back*)— Fate's intrepid roadie and trusty sidekick— appearing from the gloaming with Blind Lemon Jefferson's guitar; and Mickey Rourke rising to political power as the adopted son of the dying *el presidente*. The tyrant's true son? Well, let's not spoil the big surprise.

Through it all, Fate (weathered and gaunt under a cowboy hat and behind an enigmatic half smile) flits around the outskirts of the scene flipping inverted, vaguely profound one-liners with a combination of humor and suspicion. For all its impenetrability, *Masked and Anonymous* is funny in a self-referential, in-joke manner that would probably best amuse Dylan's harder-core fans.

One bottom line is not funny: Dylan can't act. Not that this was the point in the first place, but something other than a stagy, wooden, seemingly unrehearsed delivery on practically every line might have been an improvement. Yet paradoxically, the John Cassavetes–style, made-up-on-the-spot home movie exploring themes of love and identity is one of the refreshing strengths of *Masked and Anonymous*—a sharp contrast to the current era of big-budget, mass-programmed Hollywood smarm. And despite all the sometimes irritating narrative culs-de-sac, the film, in the end, can be read as uncomfortably consequential and, who knows, maybe even prophetic.

Who couldn't love a film with lines like these: "To be on my side, you've got to be born on my side"; "He's a legend. Does Jesus have to walk on water twice to make a point?"; "The secret is in the ordinary"; "I've got a lot of respect for a gun"; "All his songs are recognizable. Even when they're not recognizable, they're recognizable"; "You gave it all away, didn't you?" Yeah, word is that Dylan and director Larry Charles supposedly wrote the screenplay, but sometimes it comes off as if Casey Stengel, Satchel Paige, and Yogi Berra were banging away at the keyboard.

The music throughout, however, is stellar as Dylan leads his stripped-down band du jour through some very relaxed but focused versions of songs (diverse, acclaimed, obscure, etc.) from every period and style of his career: "Down in the Flood," "Diamond Joe," "Dixie," "I'll Remember You," "Cold Irons Bound," and more. And, as in *Renaldo & Clara*, the placement of the songs (by Dylan and others ranging from the Grateful Dead, Los Lobos, and the Dixie Hummingbirds to lesser-knowns like Sertab and Articolo 31) often dovetails with the tone of the narrative moment; also, the funky little stage and backdrop curtain in front of which Dylan and crew appear is remarkably similar to the neo-medicine-show aesthetic of the Rolling Thunder stage set.

Ⓐ *Masked and Anonymous* (soundtrack)

Sony CD 90536. Sony Music Soundtrax Bonus CD 90618. Released July 15, 2003. Produced by Jeff Rosen.
"My Back Pages" (performed by the Magokoro Brothers), "Gotta Serve Somebody" (performed by Shirley Caesar), "Down in the Flood" (performed by Bob Dylan), "It's All Over Now, Baby Blue" (performed by the Grateful Dead), "Most of the Time" (performed by Sophie Zelmani), "On a Night Like This" (performed by Los Lobos), "Diamond Joe" (performed by Bob Dylan), "Come una pietra scalciata (Like a Rolling Stone)" (performed by Articolo 31), "One More Cup of Coffee" (performed by Sertab), "Non dirle che non è così (If You See Her, Say Hello)" (performed by Francesco De Gregori), "Dixie" (performed by Bob Dylan), "Señor (Tales of Yankee Power)" (performed by Jerry Garcia), "Cold Irons Bound" (performed by Bob Dylan), "City of Gold" (performed by the Dixie Hummingbirds)
Bonus disc cuts performed by Dylan: "All I Really Want to Do," "Love Minus Zero/No Limit," "Stuck Inside of Mobile (With the Memphis Blues Again)," "Tangled Up in Blue," "Gotta Serve Somebody," "Moonlight," "Cold Irons Bound"

I suffered through a year of *Masked and Anonymous* anticipatory hype and all I got was a confusing film and this messy soundtrack! Okay, maybe that's a bit harsh. After all, the *Masked and Anonymous* souvenir CD is marked by new Dylan versions of several songs, the best officially released example of the Charlie Sexton/Larry Campbell Never Ending Tour band, and some fresh, quite international interpretations of his songs by some almost complete unknowns, and pretty good unknowns at that.

M

If it's coherence you want, don't bother looking here. But if it's a handful of decent up-to-the-decade readings of kind of live Dylan and crew easing into a quirky batch of songs, a few predictable cover versions of his tunes by the usual suspects, and/or some pretty far-out, radicalized readings of the familiar and not so familiar, then the *Masked and Anonymous* curio may be the ticket to a not-so-lonely night.

As if matters weren't already confusing enough, there is material in the film that does not—repeat, does not—appear on the CD, and vice versa. And a second version of the bonus disc does not include the above-listed tracks but a sampling of "The Reissue Series"—SACD digitally tweaked versions of material from the sweep of Dylan's catalogue.

The general excellence of Dylan's performances aside, some of the standout tracks include Sertab's Saharan arrangement of "One More Cup of Coffee," the Magokoro Brothers' ethereal "My Back Pages" in Japanese, Los Lobos's rollicking bilingual "On a Night Like This," and Articolo 31's Italian "Like a Rolling Stone" scratched out in hip-hop style.

As a trying-too-hard-to-be-novel semitribute mélange, the *Masked and Anonymous* soundtrack, though at times *interesting*, feels forced. Like the film, it never gains momentum and cannibalizes its own best moments, making for a gnarly listen.

[A] *Masterpieces*

CBS/Sony Music LP 57AP-875/6/7 released March 1978. CD 462448 released July 14, 1998.

"Knockin' on Heaven's Door," "Mr. Tambourine Man," "Just Like a Woman," "I Shall Be Released," "Tears of Rage," "All Along the Watchtower," "One More Cup of Coffee," "Like a Rolling Stone," "The Mighty Quinn (Quinn the Eskimo)," "Tomorrow Is a Long Time," "Lay, Lady, Lay," "Idiot Wind," "Mixed Up Confusion," "Positively Fourth Street," "Can You Please Crawl Out Your Window?," "Just Like Tom Thumb's Blues," "Spanish Is the Loving Tongue," "George Jackson" (big-band version), "Rita May," "Blowin' in the Wind," "A Hard Rain's A-Gonna Fall," "The Times They Are A-Changin'," "Masters of War," "Hurricane," "Maggie's Farm," "Subterranean Homesick Blues," "Ballad of a Thin Man," "Mozambique," "This Wheel's on Fire," "I Want You," "Rainy Day Women #12 and 35," "Don't Think Twice, It's All Right," "Song to Woody," "It Ain't Me Babe," "Love Minus Zero/No Limit," "I'll Be Your Baby Tonight," "If Not for You," "If You See Her, Say Hello," "Sara"

A Japanese-only import at the time of its issue in 1978, *Masterpieces* was the best-organized Dylan retrospective seen yet upon its original pressing. Its three discs thoroughly presented Dylan's best work from 1962 to 1976, include several rare singles or outtakes ("Mixed Up Confusion," "Can You Please Crawl Out Your Window?," "Spanish Is the Loving Tongue," "George Jackson," and "Rita May") and at least one great live track ("Just Like Tom Thumb's Blues")—none ever before released on an album. Eventually released outside the Far East, *Masterpieces* has enjoyed North American distribution of one kind or another over the years and was remastered and reissued on CD in the United States in 1998.

[S] "Masters of War" (Bob Dylan)

Bob Dylan, *The Freewheelin' Bob Dylan* (1963); *Real Live* (1984); *Biograph*/'63 (1985)
Bob Dylan/Various Artists (performed by Eddie Vedder and Mike McCready), *Bob Dylan: The 30th Anniversary Concert Celebration* (1993)
The Staple Singers, *Great Day* (1963); *This Little Light* (1964)
Judy Collins, *Judy Collins #3* (1964); *Forever: An Anthology* (1997)
Julie Felix, *Julie Felix* (1964)
Linda Mason, *How Many Seas Must a White Dove Sail* (1964)
Odetta, *Odetta Sings Dylan* (1965)
The Gene Norman Group, *Dylan Jazz* (1965)
De Maskers, *Dank U* (1966)

M

Various Artists (performed by Barbara Dane), *Save the Children: Songs from the Heart* (1967)
Cher, *Backstage* (1968)
José Feliciano, *A Bag Full of Soul* (1966); *Che Sara: Greatest Hits* (1998)
Leon Russell, *Leon Russell* (1970)
Pete Seeger, *World of Pete Seeger* (1974)
Bettina Jonic, *The Bitter Mirror* (1975)
Don McLean, *Solo . . . Live* (1976)
Valerie LaGrange, *Chez Moi* (1981)
Martin Simpson, *Grinning in Your Face* (1983); *Collection* (1994)
The Flying Pickets, *Lost Boys* (1984)
Roger Taylor, *Strange Frontier* (1984)
The Long Ryders, *Metallic B.O.* (1989); *The Long Ryders Anthology* (1999)
Jimmy Page, *Session Man, Volume 2* (1991)
Kevin Kinney, *The Times They Are A-Changin'* (1992)
Tim O'Brien, *Red on Blonde* (1996)
Gerard Quintana and Jordi Batiste, *Els Miralls de Dylan* (1999)
Bob Weir, *Weir Here: Best of Bob Weir* (2004)

An angry, stark, and vengeful piece of righteous and poetic vitriol, "Masters of War" has remained a fairly constant and (sadly) always salient Dylan perennial. His delivery of it has ranged from the lone, whining acoustic versions of the early 1960s to the raucously electric rave-ups of the late 1970s and 1980s and back to the lean, threatening acoustic renditions of the 1990s and forward, sung with a trademark husky death rattle that made it as foreboding as ever. While some have suggested that "Masters of War" was a farewell kiss to protest music, Dylan's musings in the 1985 *Biograph* liner notes suggest otherwise. "I never felt it ['Masters of War'] was a goodbye or hello (to protest)," he wrote.

More than two decades earlier, Dylan is quoted in Nat Hentoff's liner notes to *The Freewheelin' Bob Dylan* as saying that he surprised himself with the song's composition: "'I've never really written anything like that before. I don't sing songs that hope people will die, but I couldn't help it in this one. The song is sort of striking out, a reaction to the last straw, a feeling of what *can* you do?'"

Yet while Dylan acknowledges that "Masters of War" is a protest song, and a "pretty

Allied Supreme Command, 1944. Sitting, from left: Arthur Tedder, Gen. Dwight D. Eisenhower, Field Marshall Bernard Montgomery. Standing, from left: Gen. Omar Bradley, Admiral Bertram Ramsey, Trafford Leigh-Mallory, Walter Smith.
(Photo: Horace Abrahams/Keystone Features/Getty Images)

self-explanatory" one at that, he has denied, rather vehemently, that it is political.

"Political" or not, "Masters of War" bubbles with visceral energy no matter how it is performed, which Hentoff saw and remarked upon in his *Freewheelin'* liner notes: "The rage (which is as much anguish as it is anger) is a way of catharsis, a way of getting temporary relief from the heavy feeling of impotence that affects many who cannot understand a civilization which juggles its own means for oblivion and calls that performance an act toward peace."

Whatever peace Dylan may have had in mind seems as far away as when he debuted "Masters of War" in January 1963 at Gerde's Folk City in New York's Greenwich Village. With his diatribe, Dylan at least seemed to have remembered President (and former General) Dwight D. Eisenhower's 1961 advice to the incoming president, John F. Kennedy: "Beware of the military-industrial complex." With blunt plainspeak, Dylan effectively, if not particularly poetically, put that warning into a song musically based on a traditional tune from the British Isles, "Nottamun Town." He sees through the war masters' eyes and brains the way he sees "through the water that runs down my drain." Their reckless, mongering ways have caused him "the worst fear that could ever be hurled/The fear to bring children into the world."

And, as if to underscore his commitment to the sentiments infusing "Masters of War," Dylan performed the song at the absolute peak of the Persian Gulf "war" as part of his Lifetime Grammy Award acceptance segment in 1991. A gutsy move to say the least, even in less hysterical times.

A final note: Leon Russell's version of "Masters of War" reset Dylan's lyrics to the music of "The Star Spangled Banner." It's worth tracking down for novelty purposes alone.

"Matchbox" (Carl Perkins)
See also "Blue Suede Shoes," "Champaign, Illinois"
Carl Perkins, *Go Cat Go* (1996)
The Beatles, *Something New* (1964)
Jerry Lee Lewis, *Live at the Star Club, Hamburg* (1964)
Ronnie Hawkins, *Ronnie Hawkins* (1970)
Duane Allman, *Anthology, Volume 2* (1974)
Charlie Feathers, *Good Rockin' Tonight* (1979)
Johnny Cash, *Survivors* (1982)
The Deighton Family, *Acoustic Music to Suit Most Occasions* (1988)

"He really stood for freedom. That whole sound stood for all the degrees of freedom. It would just jump right off the turntable. We wanted to go where it was happening." Those Bob Dylan words, in a note read at Perkins's funeral, about the contribution that Carl Perkins and his contemporaries made to American music, could not have been more apt.

Carl Perkins (born April 9, 1932, Tiptonville, Tennessee; died January 19, 1998, Jackson, Tennessee) was a pioneering rockabilly singer, songwriter, and guitarist who first became a household name in 1958 with "Blue Suede Shoes." The son of a sharecropper, he began working the fields, where he heard the odd gospel song being sung by the other laborers. With that as inspiration, he began playing and singing country songs with the syncopated attack of the blues.

Eventually Perkins put together a band with his brothers. After their day jobs at a dairy, the Perkins Brothers would perform at honky-tonks in Jackson, Tennessee. As Perkins recalled in *Go, Cat, Go!*, his 1996 autobiography (with coauthor David McGee; New York: Hyperion): "I heard this clicking over here, and there was my two brothers. I knew we had a different sound."

His first break came in 1954 when Elvis Presley released a rockabilly version of a song that the Perkins Brothers had been playing, Bill Monroe's "Blue Moon of Kentucky." Carl made a beeline for Memphis, wangled an audition with Sam Phillips (the owner of Presley's label, Sun Records), and scored a regional hit with "Turn Around."

After landing a spot as Elvis's opening act, he made his next splash when Johnny Cash, then just another young Sun Records recording artist, suggested that Perkins write a song about a new item in the teenage wardrobe: blue suede shoes.

The success of "Blue Suede Shoes" landed Perkins invitations to appear on *The Ed Sullivan Show* as well as *The Perry Como Show* in New York City, both of which would guarantee national exposure. But on March 22, 1956, as Perkins and his band were driving to the Big Apple for these engagements, their Chrysler rear-ended a truck. Perkins broke his collarbone, but his brother Jay suffered a broken neck. (Jay died of a brain tumor two years later.)

Still, by summer, "Blue Suede Shoes" had sold a million copies. Perkins had recovered, resumed touring, and was writing and recording more songs that would become standards of rockabilly: "Boppin' the Blues," "Everybody's Trying to Be My Baby," "Dixie Fried," and "Matchbox," the last of which featured Jerry Lee Lewis on piano. Some sources suggest that "Matchbox" was originally a traditional blues number that Perkins recomposed with his lyrics and a new arrangement. Blind Lemon Jefferson, for instance, recorded a somewhat similar blues song as early as 1927, and there is little doubt that Perkins's interest in it can be traced to Jefferson.

On the day "Matchbox" was recorded, Elvis visited the studio and spent more than an hour singing gospel, country, and R&B songs with Perkins, Lewis, and Cash while the tape rolled. Dubbed "The Million Dollar Quartet" by a local newspaper the next day, the casual session was eventually released under that title in 1990.

Perkins earned a new crop of eager young fans and connected with older ones in 1964 during a tour of England. This latter group included the Beatles, who invited him to Abbey Road Studios for a recording session during which the Fab Four waxed a number of his songs.

From 1965 to 1975, Perkins played in Johnny Cash's band and sometimes performed as Cash's opening act. During this time, in 1969, he first met Dylan, and the two cowrote "Champaign, Illinois."

Major accolades and laurels finally began to shower upon Perkins in the 1980s. Meanwhile, he continued to shower the planet with his red-hot licks right up until his death from complications related to a series of strokes. Survived by his wife, five children, and ten grandchildren, Carl Perkins was, in the end, a satisfied man.

Though he toyed with "Matchbox" during his 1969 Nashville sessions with Johnny Cash, Dylan first performed the song at the Palomino Club in North Hollywood, California, in February 1987 with George Harrison, John Fogerty, Taj Mahal, and others during a ninety-minute public jam session of eclectic material. During the Never Ending Tour "Matchbox" popped up again as a special encore presentation, with Perkins playing alongside Dylan at a concert in the composer's hometown of Jackson, Tennessee, in 1994. Four years later, the song struck once again during a visit Down Under.

[S] **"Maybe Someday"** (Bob Dylan)

Bob Dylan, *Knocked Out Loaded* (1986)

A not fully realized yet nevertheless underrated Chuck Berryesque rave from the *Empire Burlesque* sessions—a bit of which finally landed on the by and large terrible *Knocked Out Loaded*—

M

"Maybe Someday" shows some real promise of standing beside Dylan's better work of the mid-1980s. He spits out a score of words in every phrase with a fiery vocal as his studio band kicks it into high gear. Who knows what the song is about, but if Dylan had spent the time and really worked on it—polished the lyrics and recorded another take or two—we might have had another "Foot of Pride" to ponder.

As with several of the *Empire Burlesque* songs, "Maybe Someday" draws at least one phrase from a Humphrey Bogart film—in this case *Sabrina*, the 1954 Cinderella-style dramedy of high society manners directed and cowritten by Billy Wilder and also starring Audrey Hepburn. The film's line "No gentleman makes love to a servant in his mother's house" becomes the song's "No gentleman like makin' love to his servant/Specially when he's in his father's house."

Not many critics have shown much interest in "Maybe Someday," but Nigel Hinton's comments on this passage in his article "You Are Right from Your Side I'm Right from Mine: A Viewpoint on *Knocked Out Loaded*" from *The Telegraph* #25 (autumn/winter 1986) are worth a look: "Put a capital letter on 'Father,' of course, and there are all kinds of other resonances here.... He makes his lines ring with mysterious possibilities: where one level works perfectly but where, if you care to switch contexts, the whole thing works on another level too. Thus 'Maybe Someday' is a warning farewell to a girl but it is so artfully written that it needs only a slight sideways step to see that each line carries a moral/spiritual implication. No sledgehammers, no breaking down of bedroom doors, and no moralising here: 'The love that I had for you was never my own' he tells her, and us."

Additionally, Dylan may draw on a line from T. S. Eliot's "Journey of the Magi"—"And the cities hostile and the towns unfriendly"—for a couple of his own here: "Through hostile cities and unfriendly towns/Thirty pieces of silver, no money down." The "thirty pieces of silver," incidentally, is biblical in origin, and though it's a bit difficult to pin down Dylan's direct canonical source, such prices are related to a betrayal of some sort as found in both the Old Testament (Joseph's sale to Egyptian slavery by his brothers as told in Genesis 37:28 and Delilah's two-timing of Samson as revealed in Judges 16:5) and the New Testament (the balance of Judas Iscariot's asking price for dropping a dime on his rabbi according to Matthew 26:14–16). The same lyric takes a journey from the Bible to Chuck Berry—"No Money Down" being the title of a Berry song that Dylan covered live in 1981.

If the worst that can be said about "Maybe Someday" is that it's not every rock song that can fuse Eliot, the Bible, Bogart, and Berry, then that's not so shabby.

"Mean Old Railroad" (Danny Kalb)
aka "Mean Old Southern," "Mean Old Southern Railroad"
See also *The Blues Project*
Blues Project, *Live at Town Hall/'62* (1994); *Anthology* (1997)

Danny Kalb shared vocals with Dylan on this hobo railroad song during Dylan's short five-song set on a twelve-hour radio hootenanny broadcast in the summer of 1961 from New York City's Riverside Church on the long-gone but dearly remembered WRVR. "I was at college but it was summer vacation," Kalb recalled to Mitch Blank in *The Telegraph* #47 (winter 1993). "It was at a folk festival. And I played with Bob. But I'll tell you the truth, I can't remember if we rehearsed or if that was just a spontaneous thing."

◫ "Meet Me in the Morning" (Bob Dylan)

Bob Dylan, *Blood on the Tracks* (1975)

Freddie King, *Larger Than Life* (1975); *Live at the Texas Opry House* (1992); *Boogie on Down* (1997); *Texas Flyer* (1998); *Live in Concert* (1999); *Your Move* (2000)

Merl Saunders, *You Can Leave Your Hat On* (1976); *Struggling Man* (2000)

Living Earth, *Living Earth* (1978)

Jason Becker, *Perspective* (1996)

Thomas Ealey, *Raw* (1998)

John Shain, *Brand New Lifetime* (1999)

Rolling Thunder, *The Never Ending Rehearsal* (2000)

Mary Lee's Corvette, *Blood on the Tracks* (2002)

Various Artists (performed by Steve Elliot), *May Your Song Always Be Sung: The Songs of Bob Dylan, Volume 3* (2003)

No Dylan album would be complete without a terse-versed, twelve-bar blues in D, and "Meet Me in the Morning" is a classic—one of Bob's best vocal performances in the idiom. He may throw in the modern, cubist touch or two, but his yearning is never far from the surface. And there can be little doubt that he will stand alone on Fifty-sixth and Wabasha when the cock crows.

Dylan developed the song from an earlier draft entitled "Call Letter Blues," itself later released on *The Bootleg Series, Volumes 1–3*. Never performed live, the *Blood on the Tracks* rendition is embellished by Buddy Cage's atmospheric pedal-steel guitar flourishes. Interestingly, it lacks a verse that was included in the *Blood on the Tracks* songbook.

The song is deceptively simple; even so, like much of Dylan's work, it has layers full of tangled metaphors and imagery that can spin in any interpretive direction.

◪ *The Midnight Special*/Harry Belafonte

RCA Victor Records, LP LMP/LSP 2449. Released March 1962.

In the first in a long line of sideman appearances, Dylan probably played harmonica on the title cut on this early, excellent Belafonte release, which should be sought on its own merits and not merely because it includes some riffs from a scruffy wannabe Okie folkie.

Fed up with the multiple takes required at the session, Dylan went out for a smoke and never came back. Another dispute involves the date of the session, with speculation ranging from the summer to the late fall of 1961. Either way, Dylan biographer Robert Shelton reported in *No Direction Home* (New York: Beech Tree Books/William Morrow, 1986) that "Belafonte and others at the sessions had some laughs at Dylan's expense: To keep rhythm, Bob tapped out the time with his booted right foot, but the vibrations kept registering on the tape. An engineer slipped a pillow under Bob's thudding foot."

Though the album is well known to rock collectors as the first commercial release on which Dylan appears, it is debated whether he appears on it at all, though the harmonica does bear a resemblance to his mouth-harp style at the time. *Midnight Special* is worth tracking down, as it best exemplifies Harry Belafonte's gifts as a genius recording artist. His unique interpretations of traditional material combine blues, big band, gospel, and soul as he transforms the folk warhorse "On Top of Old Smokey" into a hot blues epic.

◫ "Midnight Special" (Traditional/Leadbelly)

aka "The Midnight Special"

Harry Belafonte (performed with Bob Dylan), *The Midnight Special* (1962)

Leadbelly, *Absolutely the Best* (2000)

Big Bill Broonzy, *The Essential* (2001)

Woody Guthrie, *The Woody Guthrie Story* (2000)

Jesse Fuller, *Favorites* (1965)

The Kingston Trio, *The Kingston Trio* (1965)

Creedence Clearwater Revival, *Creedence Gold* (1972)

M

Buckwheat Zydeco, *On the Track* (1992)
Andy Griffith, *American Originals* (1993)

Dylan's only formal involvement with this piece of American folk-blues ubiquity appears to be from the Harry Belafonte session listed above.

Even if Huddie (Leadbelly) Leadbetter's claim to sole authorship of "Midnight Special" is a dubious one, the song is a classic. The earliest known commercial recordings date from as early as 1925 by the obscure Sodarisa Miller and in 1927 by the somewhat less obscure Sam Collins. Leadbelly set the mold with his musical and lyrical arrangement, so distinct that virtually every other treatment of the song bears his mark. "Midnight Special" is second only to "Goodnight Irene" as his most popular contribution to the American lexicon.

John and Alan Lomax, Leadbelly's benefactors, were the first to catch his version of the song on a summer 1934 visit to the Louisiana State Angola Penitentiary in Angola, where Leadbelly was doing hard time. The Lomaxes were floored by the stout man's distinctive style on the twelve-string guitar and his overpowering voice, recording the song directly onto vinyl with their crude mobile setup as they traveled through the South in search of the real thing.

Leadbelly begins his "Midnight Special" with a brief run on his guitar, which flows over a jouncing rhythm and into a fantasy of escape in an expressive, high-plaintive quiver. His love has come in person to ask the warden to set her man free: "Yonder comes Miss Rosie/How in the world do you know?/Well, I know her by the apron/And the dress she wore/Umbrella on her shoulder/Piece of paper in her hand/Well, I heard her tell the captain/Turn a-loose my man." Leadbelly fills each measure between the lyrics with a percolating guitar riff and, in the chorus, sings/dreams of the passing train, the Midnight Special, taking him to freedom: "Let the Mid-

night Special shine her light on me/Oh, let the Midnight Special/Shine her ever-lovin' light on me." And he leaves a fingerprint on the song by dropping a reference to his first stint at the notoriously harsh Sugarland Prison in Texas: "If you ever go to Houston/Boys, you better walk straight/And you better not squabble/And you better not fight/Benson Crocker will arrest you,/Jimmie Boone will take you down./You can bet your bottom dollar/That you're Sugarland bound." Leadbelly ends "Midnight Special" with a brutal verse, an icy slap of reality, as "jumping little Judy" brings bad news from home: "Well, she brought me the news that my wife was dead/That started me to grieving/Whooping, hollering, and crying/And I began to worry/About my great long time."

For more on the amazing story behind *The Midnight Special*, a must-read is *The Life and Legend of Leadbelly* (New York: HarperCollins, 1992), by Charles Wolfe and Kip Lornell.

"The Mighty Quinn"
See "Quinn the Eskimo (The Mighty Quinn)"

"Million Dollar Bash" (Bob Dylan)
Bob Dylan/The Band, *The Basement Tapes*/'67 (1975); *Biograph*/'67 (1985)
Fairport Convention, *Unhalfbricking* (1969)
Jonathan King, *Greatest Hits* (1970)
Music Asylum, *Commit Thyself* (1970)
The Crust Brothers, *Marquee Mark* (1998)
Various Artists (performed by Tokyo Bob), *May Your Song Always Be Sung: The Songs of Bob Dylan, Volume 3* (2003)

A playful highlight from the famous 1967 Woodstock sessions with the Band, "Million Dollar Bash" has to rank as one of Dylan's most insane compositions thanks to a campy delivery of delightfully incomprehensible lyrics.

A couple of very different takes of the song exist: the one released on *The Basement Tapes* is notable for Dylan's use of the harmonica—a relative rarity from those hallowed upstate New York sessions. Dylan has claimed that "Million Dollar Bash" was included in *The Basement Tapes* to attract other performers, but if this is so, one must wonder who exactly they had in mind.

With a lunacy straight out of Lewis Carroll's *Through the Looking-Glass*, Shakespeare's *A Midsummer Night's Dream*, George Orwell's *Animal Farm*, or one of William Browning's poems, "Million Dollar Bash" might be Dylan's "Mad Hatter" tea party recast in the Catskills; it has an alliterative kookiness that can still spin a head: "Well that big dumb blonde/With her wheel in the gorge/And Turtle, that friend of theirs/With his checks all forged/And his cheeks in a chunk/With his cheese in the cash/They're all gonna be there/At that million dollar bash."

Andy Gill sees in this goofiness some important implications for Dylan, and he describes them in his book, *Don't Think Twice, It's All Right* (New York: Thunder's Mouth Press, 1998): "Of all the *Basement Tapes* songs, 'Million Dollar Bash' most gracefully pivots on the urban/rural divide which marks Dylan's shift in attitude following his bike crash. In its ludicrous lyrical style, it's clearly in a straight line of descent from such earlier absurdist narratives as 'Tombstone Blues' and 'Stuck Inside of Mobile (With the Memphis Blues Again),' but this time Dylan's left the city for the country; instead of the cast of urbanites and outcasts that peopled previous songs, the populace of 'Million Dollar Bash' consists of hicks like Silly Nelly and Turtle, and instead of the streetwise scenarios of the preceding three albums, the action here has a rustic, barnyard setting."

"Million Miles" (Bob Dylan)
Bob Dylan, *Time out of Mind* (1997)
Indigenous, *Blues This Morning* (1999)
Various Artists (performed by Alvin Youngblood Hart), *Tangled Up in Blues: The Songs of Bob Dylan* (1999)

Back in 1963, Dylan sang of being "a thousand miles behind" in "One Too Many Mornings." Thirty-something years later, he seemed to have lost more than a little ground when he observed, "I'm still trying to get closer but I'm still a million miles from you" in this song of romantic acrimony and longing. Set to a funky, laid-back Jimmy Smith–style jazzy organ groove and sung with a lounge-lizard cool that would make Buddy Greco proud, Dylan's jaded, late-century, person-to-person confession of alienation couldn't be more plain. "Million Miles" was a concert regular in 1998, after which Dylan eased off performing it by 2002.

"Minglewood Blues" (Noah Lewis)
aka "All New Minglewood Blues," "New Minglewood Blues," "New, New Minglewood Blues"
Cannon's Jug Stompers, *Cannon's Jug Stompers—The Complete Works 1927–1930* (1990)
The Grateful Dead, *Grateful Dead* (1967)
Doc and Merle Watson, *Lonesome Road* (1977)
Guy Davis, *Call Down the Thunder* (1996)
Ruckus Juice & Chitlins, *Ruckus Juice & Chitlins, Volume 1* (1998)

"Minglewood" is the brash boast of a take-no-prisoners scoundrel on the prowl. Singing that he was "born in the desert, raised in a lion's den," this roguish woman stealer will leave only mayhem in his wake. The song's history is obscure and its geographic reference even more so. Minglewood (some say "Mengelwood") was the name of a sawmill and box factory in Ashport, Tennessee, just north of Memphis. The area, with its concomitant hardscrabble townsfolk, eventually became known as Minglewood.

M

Noah Lewis (born September 3, 1895, Henning, Tennessee; died February 7, 1961, Ripley, Tennessee), a driving force behind the 1920s jug band movement and the song's credited author, is said to have worked at the factory. He is also responsible for "Viola Lee Blues," another jug band classic covered by Dylan in the late 1990s.

Lewis's original "Minglewood Blues" is thought to be a variant of another song from the era recorded by Sleepy John Estes as "The Girl I Love, She's Got Long Curly Hair," by Charley Patton as "It Won't Be Long," and by Furry Lewis as "I'm Going to Brownsville." Lewis first recorded "Minglewood" on January 30, 1928, in Memphis as a member of Cannon's Jug Stompers, with himself on harmonica and vocals, Gus Cannon on banjo, and Ashley Thomson on guitar and vocals. The Noah Lewis Jug Band recorded the song on November 26, 1930, in Memphis in a rendering that includes Yank Rachel on mandolin and an unknown jug player. The former Jug Stompers' version of "Minglewood" (which appeared on Harry Smith's signpost *Anthology of American Folk Music*) bears a greater similarity to the version Dylan performed.

Lewis, a singer and virtuoso mouth-harp master, was the star of Cannon's Jug Stompers, one of jug band music's most influential units, which entertained at dances in and around Memphis. Lewis's harmonica riffs and wistful vocals created a signature sound and homemade approach to music making that engendered the jug band revival of the early 1960s. That revival gave rise to the Jim Kweskin Jug Band and Mother McCree's Uptown Jug Champions, the earliest configuration of the Grateful Dead. Special mention must be made of Lewis's phenomenal abilities on the harmonica. As if his innate sense of tone, timing, and technique weren't enough, his superhuman breath control allowed him to blow two harps at once, create embroidered solos, and mimic trains, birds, and the human voice. But as the Depression loomed and new musical fads arrived, jug music fell off the musical map. Lewis lived his last decades in obscurity and impoverishment, dying pathetically of gangrene incurred by frostbite.

"Minstrel Boy" (Bob Dylan)

Bob Dylan, *Self Portrait* (1970)
Wendy Erdman, *Erdman* (1970)
Jake & the Family Jewels, *The Big Moose Calls His Sweet Baby Lorraine* (1972)

Dylan and the Band worked up a version of this unusual song for their 1969 Isle of Wight concert, a performance included as one of the *Self Portrait* "bonuses." Here, even with its rural surrealism informed by the same sensibility that infuses *The Basement Tapes*, Dylan gets to play the holy fool in his very own harlequinade—a truck-driving troubadour coming back down from the mountain with a little truth for the impatient masses—and a little something else for the ladies-in-waiting. Unfortunately, like much of the Isle of Wight material, this sole performance of "Minstrel Boy" is shouted rather than sung. Perhaps the song was chosen for that gig (remembered for its impatient masses) because of its thematic similarity to an old traditional Irish song also called "The Minstrel Boy." Sometimes known as "Morean," the original was later revamped in the Tennessee hills and became very popular during the Civil War period.

"Mississippi" (Bob Dylan)

Bob Dylan, *"Love and Theft"* (2001)
Sheryl Crow, *The Globe Sessions* (1998)
Michel Montecrossa, *Jet Pilot* (2000)

Various Artists (performed by Sheryl Crow), *Doin' Dylan 2* (2002)

Big Brass Bed, *A Few Dylan Songs* (2003)

The connective tissue between Dylan's 1997 album *Time out of Mind* and his 2001 release, *"Love and Theft,"* "Mississippi" is a song about mortality, settled fates, and romantic obsession cast in a somber light of loss. The narrator, after unspecified woman troubles, has stayed in the titled state a day too long and is tipping his bowler as he exits stage north.

"Mississippi" is Dylan's great song of regret on *"Love and Theft"*. "So many things we never will undo," Dylan sighs. "I know you're sorry, I'm sorry too." But there's hope as well. "Stick with me baby, stick with me anyhow," he pleads, "things should start to get interesting right about now."

Dylan first wrote and recorded "Mississippi" for *Time out of Mind* but the song was left off that collection apparently because Dylan and the album's producer, Daniel Lanois, differed on how to treat it. So Dylan recut the song on his own for *"Love and Theft."*

As if to further reward his fans for a long wait, Dylan began performing "Mississippi" in the fall 2001 Never Ending Tour in support of *"Love and Theft"*—a practice that continued through 2002.

▣ "Mixed Up Confusion" (Bob Dylan)

Bob Dylan, single (1962); *Masterpieces* (1978); *Biograph*/'62 (1985)

Michel Montecrossa, *Eternal Circle* (1999)

Recorded in four takes on November 14, 1962, Dylan's first single was allegedly written on the cab ride to New York's Columbia Studios. It's his first electric band session and an early, *early* example of folk-rock. An attempt by Dylan to merge his Greenwich Village sensibility with a Sun Records sound, "Mixed Up Confusion" is regarded as an experiment that failed at worst and as a song before its time at best. With its "Mystery Train" beat, the single was shelved and so were any of Dylan's immediate attempts at rock 'n' roll.

Typically, Dylan distanced himself from the whole thing. "I'm not sure what I based this one on," he recalled in the *Biograph* liner notes. "It didn't do anything, whatever it was supposed to do. I didn't arrange the session. It wasn't my idea."

Still, it's amazing to consider that Dylan recorded this song as he was penning "Blowin' in the Wind," "A Hard Rain's A-Gonna Fall," and the like.

▣ "Money Honey" (Jesse Stone)

Clyde McPhatter, *Forgotten Angel*/'53 (1998)

Scotty Moore, *Guitar That Changed the World* (1964)

Ry Cooder, *Into the Purple Valley* (1971)

Jerry Garcia and Merl Saunders, *Keystone Encores, Volume 1*/'73 (1989)

The Drifters, *Live at Harvard University, December 2, 1972* (1986)

Elvis Presley, *Elvis Aron Presley* (1989)

Dylan's only performance of this piece of R&B, delivered like an old vaudeville stand-up comedy bit warning gold-digging women everywhere to keep their distance, came as 1999 drew to a close and just months after the passing of its composer. In "Money Honey" the title works as a punchline to every double entendre–steeped verse.

Jesse Stone (born November 16, 1901, Atchison, Kansas; died April 1, 1999, Altamonte Springs, Florida) wrote "Money Honey" in 1953 and it was a hit record for Clyde McPhatter's Drifters in the same year. The Drifters' release made it to *Billboard*'s No. 1 slot and stayed there for an amazing eleven weeks. Elvis Presley, however, who recorded "Money Honey" in 1956, was the song's great popularizer. Rumor has it that Elvis learned it from Buddy Holly when they shared a bill in Texas in 1955. Elvis's rendition of "Money Honey" spent five weeks on the *Billboard* Top 100 chart in 1956, at least partly on the strength of its appearance on the *Heartbreak Hotel* album.

Stone's career, one of the most influential and still criminally unheralded in the history of twentieth-century popular music, covered virtually every realm of the American entertainment experience as he moved from minstrelsy to the Swing Era to jazz to vaudeville to R&B to rock 'n' roll. Stone, the grandson of Tennessee slaves who had been freed and given land to settle, was a performing member of his family's minstrel show by the age of five. Not merely a singing and dancing curio, Stone would go on to learn to play eight instruments. In the 1920s he led a Kansas City–based "territory" jazz band, Jesse Stone and His Blue Serenaders, featuring the man for whom Adolph Sax invented the horn, Coleman Hawkins, yet to make his name as one of the deities of the tenor sax. On Duke Ellington's recommendation, Harlem's storied Cotton Club hired Stone as a performer in 1936, and he also became a staple at the Apollo Theater down the street, where he was an entertainment jack-of-all-trades—writing jokes and sketches as well as composing and arranging.

In the late 1940s and early '50s, Stone was a force in building Atlantic Records into a top R&B label. An always-at-the-ready session musician, he can be heard playing the piano on Chuck Willis's "C. C. Rider" (which he orchestrated and arranged) and on the Drifters' "Shake, Rattle and Roll," for which he took composer's credit under the pseudonym Charles Calhoun. "Good Golly Miss Molly" is another Stone perennial; it was first recorded by Big Joe Turner in 1948 and was

popularized by Bill Haley and the Comets in 1954, when it crashed through the racial barrier into acceptance by white audiences and radio stations. Within a year, Elvis was all over Stone's material and went on to record more than a few of his songs. Ironically, Stone had enjoyed similar crossover success a decade earlier when his tune "Idaho" was covered and recorded by Benny Goodman, Jimmy Dorsey, and Guy Lombardo; the latter's recording of the song sold three million copies. "Don't Let Go" was a huge hit as a straight-ahead rocker for both Roy Hamilton in 1958 and as a resplendent string- and horn-laced disco arrangement by Isaac Hayes twenty years later. And Jerry Garcia led his solo band (which also performed "Money Honey") to the perimeter of the psychedelicsphere and back with transcendent versions of "Don't Let Go" in the 1980s and 1990s. Face it, hundreds of songs fell from the quill of this very coolest (and most humble) of cats. His wife reported that just four days before his death at the age of ninety-seven, Stone had just completed a new song, entitled, appositely, "That's It."

"Moondance" (Van Morrison)

Van Morrison, *Moondance* (1970)
Grady Tate, *Movin' Day* (1975)
Bobby McFerrin, *Bobby McFerrin* (1982)
Michael Feinstein, *Forever* (1993)
Foxfire, *Where the Heart Is* (1995)
Kathie Lee Gifford, *Born for You* (2000)

Dylan performed Van Morrison's ode to nocturnal lunacy at but one November 1991 Never Ending Tour show in Erie, Pennsylvania. He gave it a half-baked arrangement and rote vocal treatment that all but ignored Morrison's jazz samba approach and famous Mose Allison–style scat vocal improv.

Morrison biographer Brian Hinton may have gotten to the heart of "Moondance" when he described it in his book *Celtic Crossroads: The Art of Van Morrison* (London: Sanctuary, 1997) as "perfect music for and about fucking. His lady's blush is not from embarrassment."

[S] "Moonlight" (Bob Dylan)

Bob Dylan, *"Love and Theft"* (2001)

"Moonlight" is another *"Love and Theft"* showcase for Dylan's upper vocal registers as he sings like a Hoagy Carmichael–style pop crooner. The song, also the album's gentlest, is an easygoing romantic ballad with a rhyme scheme and structure worthy of a Depression-era Cole Porter classic, combined with the lazy lope of Texas swing and sounding as if it had been recorded in a Parisian dance hall in the 1930s. The likely source for the chorus of "Moonlight" is thought to be "The Prisoner's Song," a 1924 composition written by Guy Massey and made popular by Vernon Dalhart and, later, Red Allen. Compare the chorus of the '24 song ("Meet me tonight, love, meet me/Meet me out in the moonlight alone/For I have a sad story to tell you/Must be told in that moonlight alone") with the last line of each of Dylan's verses ("Won't you meet me out in the moonlight alone?"), and the love and theft is plain enough.

Longing for the return of romance and intimacy, the singer woos a new flame under the darkening sky to meet him for a tryst. But while the images are very clear and beautiful ("The dusky light the day is losing/Orchids, poppies, black-eyed Susan/The earth and sky that melts with flesh and bone/Won't you meet me out in the moonlight alone?"), there is melancholy here. Yes, nature's beauty can still be perceived as the end of day (an awareness and acknowledgment of mortality) sweeps across the land. But veiled beneath the guise of this suitor may be the heart of a predator ("Well, I'm preachin' peace and harmony/The blessings of tranquility/Yet I know when the time is right to strike/I'll take you 'cross the river, dear/You've no need to linger here/I know the kinds of things you like"). One wonders whether this is a romance or a murder ballad in the making. Think "Pretty Polly" meets the noirish tone of Alfred Hitchcock's *Strangers on a Train* and some notion of the drama laid out in "Moonlight" can be glimpsed.

Dylan debuted "Moonlight" just after its release in the fall of 2001 and kept it in rotation in the Never Ending Tours through 2004.

[S] "Moon River" (Johnny Mercer/Henry Mancini)

Johnny Mercer, *My Huckleberry Friend* (1996)
Henry Mancini, *Moon River* (1993)
Lena Horne, *Lena in Hollywood* (1966)
Andy Williams, *Essence of Andy Williams* (1993)
Judy Garland, *Come Rain or Come Shine* (1995)
Jackie Gleason, *Romantic Moods of Jackie Gleason* (1996)

Dylan, in what will definitely be up there with the all-time, off-the-wall, who'd-a-thunk-it-possible cover song choices, pulled "Moon River" out of the hat for a trio of concert performances in 1990. With words by Johnny Mercer and music by Henry Mancini, "Moon River" was debuted by Audrey Hepburn in the motion picture version of Truman Capote's *Breakfast at Tiffany's* and won both a Grammy and an Oscar. It is among the most covered compositions in the American songbook.

As a singer as well as a songwriter, Johnny Mercer (born November 18, 1909, Savannah; died June 25, 1976, Los Angeles) was above all else extraordinarily hip—he boasted innately perfect phrasing, a cool drawl, and a mastery of jive.

Mercer's godlike status in twentieth-century popular music is ensured by the sheer number of compositions—roughly 1,500—credited to him. With their air of Cole Porter–like sophistication, whimsical sentiment, and deft mastery of language, rhythm, and rhymes, Mercer's songs have been jazz standards for eons. His lyrics are unfailingly upbeat and optimistic—hopelessly romantic by the standards of any era. He was also a great singer who won particularly wide notice in the 1940s with his easygoing, Southern-accented phrasing.

Mercer showed great promise as a musical talent in his youth. After his father's real estate ventures collapsed during the Great Depression, he came to New York in 1930 by stowing away on a boat. He tried to land a part in the 1930 edition of the Garrick Gaieties—a popular stage show that was essentially a lower-rent version of the Ziegfeld Follies. The show's producers didn't need any more actors but they did need a song, prompting Mercer to dash off his first professional number, "Out of Breath and Scared to Death of You."

Mercer soon fell into the acquaintance of lyricist E. Y. "Yip" Harburg and composer Harold Arlen (themselves the minds behind the *Wizard of Oz* music, including "Over the Rainbow"), and the trio went on to write hits like "Whistling for a Kiss" and "Satan's Little Lamb." The collaboration with Arlen proved to be one of the most fruitful of Mercer's career, as it produced such classics as "That Old Black Magic," "Blues in the Night," "One for My Baby (and One More for the Road)," and "Ac-cent-tchu-ate the Positive"—purportedly the first song a very young Bobby Zimmerman ever performed for his mother's mah-jongg circle way back in Hibbing, Minnesota, circa 1945.

When Ted Lewis scored a hit with Mercer's "Lazybones" in 1933, Mercer was on the path to pop glory that included gigs and collaborations with Bing Crosby, Benny Goodman, Duke Ellington, Hoagy Carmichael, and Jerome Kern. A music-biz mover and shaker and a cofounder of Capitol Records, he was instrumental in the discovery of Nat King Cole, Stan Kenton, Peggy Lee, and countless others.

Mercer contributed lyrics to the scores of seven Broadway shows, and probably made his biggest mark on the Great White Way for his work on *Li'l Abner*, the musical based on Al Capp's comic strip. Starring Stubby Kaye and including such Mercer songs as "Namely You," "Jubilation T. Cornpone," and "The Country's in the Very Best of Hands," it ran on Broadway for nearly 700 performances and was made into a movie in 1959.

Mercer was part of the great migration of songwriters and composers to Hollywood in the 1940s, and he met with great success in the movies. He wrote dozens of memorable works, including several for which he was honored with the Academy Award for best song. Most notable among these are "Moon River" and "Days of Wine and Roses," both 1960s collaborations with composer Henry Mancini.

Mercer's career slowed down in the early 1960s following an album with Bobby Darin as the onslaught of rock 'n' roll took its toll on pop music's Old Masters. Finally, after decades of providing artistic enjoyment of a rare kind, Mercer died of complications arising from brain surgery. His status as an American popular music giant has only grown with time.

Mercer's collaborator on "Moon River," Henry Mancini, was another pop music giant who, for more than thirty years, wrote dozens of film scores covering the genre's entire spectrum.

Mancini (born April 16, 1924, Cleveland; died June 14, 1994, Los Angeles) grew up as the music-loving son of Italian immigrants in the steel town of Aliquippa, Pennsylvania. He enrolled at New York's Juilliard School of Music in 1942 and began his professional music career as an arranger and pianist with the Glenn Miller Orchestra.

Gravitating toward composing, he moved to Hollywood, where his first film-scoring gig was Abbott and Costello's *Lost in Alaska!* in

1952. But his real education in the art of film scoring came during a 1952 to 1958 apprenticeship at Universal Pictures. It was during this period that Mancini developed his craft while arranging and composing for such diverse films as *The Creature from the Black Lagoon* (1954), *The Glenn Miller Story* (1954) and Orson Welles's sinister late noir classic, *Touch of Evil* (1958).

By 1960, Manicini was one of the most in-demand film composers, and he wrote his ticket for the next thirty-three years. For Blake Edwards (with whom he enjoyed one of the lengthiest and most productive composer-director relationships in American film history) his credits include *Breakfast at Tiffany's* (1961), *Days of Wine and Roses* (1962), *The Pink Panther* (1964), *Victor/Victoria* (1982), and *Switch* (1991).

Mancini worked for many other well-known directors, such as Howard Hawks (*Hatari!*, 1962), Stanley Donen (*Two for the Road*, 1967), Terence Young (*Wait Until Dark*, 1967), Vittorio De Sica (*Sunflower*, 1970), and Stanley Kramer (*Oklahoma Crude*, 1973). At the same time he continued to work in television, writing, among others, the theme for the popular series *Newhart* and the thoughtful score for ABC's ten-hour miniseries *The Thorn Birds* (1983).

Although Mancini was best known for his composition and arranging, his contributions to the science of film music may actually be his greatest legacy. For instance, he labored to improve the sound quality of film music. His use of multiple mikes was regarded with suspicion at first, but Mancini's invention irrefutably improved the musical detail in sound recordings.

Despite his enormous success in all aspects of the film-scoring profession, the soft-spoken but articulate Mancini was quick to point out that film composers are not miracle workers. "Good music can improve a bad film," he would say, "but it can never make a bad film good."

"Moonshiner" (Traditional)

aka "Kentucky Moonshiner," "Moonshine Blues," "Moonshine Dance," "Over the Waves," "Rye Whiskey"
Bob Dylan, *The Bootleg Series, Volumes 1–3: Rare and Unreleased, 1961–1991/'63* (1991)
Various Artists (performed by Frank Cloutier & the Victorian Café Orchestra), *The Anthology of American Folk Music/'28* (1952/'97)
Gerard Campbell, *Wandering Minstrel* (1959)
The New Lost City Ramblers, *Moonshine and Prohibition* (1962)
Roscoe Holcomb, *The High Lonesome Sound* (1965)
Dave Van Ronk, *Inside Dave Van Ronk* (1969)
The Clancy Brothers with Tommy Makem, *Show Me the Way* (1972)
Rich Lerner, *Trails and Bridges* (1996)

Why Dylan should have included a version of this famous edge-of-the-grave Southern mountain ballad in his Witmark demo recordings—which, with the exception of "Moonshiner," were all originals put on tape with the specific intent of copyrighting them—has always been something of a mystery. Some have suggested that his gritty masterpiece of a cover song is there mistakenly: the Witmark tapes were compiled from various Columbia sessions, and "Moonshiner" just happened to slip through. But whatever the reason for its presence there, all seem to agree that "Moonshiner" represents one of Dylan's finest early 1960s performances. Unfortunately, only one live version (from New York City's Gaslight Café in the fall of 1962) has been preserved.

Like many songs from Dylan's early repertoire, "Moonshiner" has deep roots in American folkdom. The protagonist's profession has a venerable history, as discussed by Alan Lomax in *The Folk Songs of North America*: "The age-old Celtic conflict with the excise-men flared up . . . in the American hills, for the American backwoods farmer, like his ancestors in Scotland and Ireland, was willing to fight for his right to still his own whisky. In 1780, western Pennsylvania rose in the Whisky Rebellion which President George Washington had to put down by force of arms. All during the nineteenth century, the southern backwoodsman fought a guerrilla war with government 'revenooers'—a conflict that still raises the annual tolls of shooting scrapes and court cases throughout the South. For the poor farmer, the freedom to make his own liquor is not only a point of honour and a source of pleasure, but a matter of economics. His scanty grain crop brings more cash if he markets it in liquid form."

"More and More" (Webb Pierce/Merle Kilgore)
Webb Pierce, *Wondering Boy (1951–1958)* (1990)
Mickey Gilley, *Greatest Hits, Volume 1* (1976)
Crowe and McLaughlin, *Going Back* (1993)
Carl Smith, *Satisfaction Guaranteed* (1996)
U-Turn, *U-Turn* (1997)

A million-selling No. 1 country hit made famous long ago (well, in 1954) by Webb Pierce, "More and More" got the Dylan treatment but twice: at a 1989 Never Ending Tour show in the Gulf of Mexico town of Houston, and as an encore with Van Morrison nearly a decade later.

Pierce (born August 8, 1921, West Monroe, Louisiana; died February 24, 1991, Nashville) may rank among the 1950s' great honky-tonk vocalists, but no doubt he will be remembered more for his garish attire and famous guitar-shaped swimming pool. While riding the top of the country charts for years, his flamboyant persona, onstage presence, and "if ya got it, flaunt it" approach to living gave Nashville that rhinestone cowboy veneer.

An early love of Gene Autry's cowboy movies films and hillbilly music led Pierce to the guitar, and after an army stint during World War II, he began hoeing that long row to the top one Saturday night dance and radio appearance at a time. His big break came in

1949 when he became an inaugural member of the *Louisiana Hayride*, the famed Shreveport, Louisiana, radio program that would launch many a career over the course of its history.

Signing with Decca in 1951, Pierce scored phenomenal success when his song "Wondering" hit No. 1 and opened Nashville's front door. Moving to Nashville in 1952, he made his mark with "In the Jailhouse Now" and "More and More," a song of excess that could well stand as his credo. Perhaps more significantly, he joined the cast of the Grand Ole Opry, replacing Hank Williams.

Pierce hit the charts with some consistency in the 1950s with his barroom classics. After a brief stab at changing with the times—he covered a few Everly Brothers songs and recorded some tepid rockabilly numbers—he returned to honky-tonk and stayed put.

Nashville's new country-pop sound pushed honky-tonk and Pierce to the fringes in the mid-1960s, and though Pierce could still turn them out, the hits grew fewer and farther between. But by then it mattered little: his involvement in the publishing wing of country music and wise investing had made him a wealthy man. He paraded what celebrity he maintained by indulging in a materially excessive lifestyle, marked by that guitar-shaped swimming pool he had built in the backyard of his Nashville home, still a popular tourist destination and postcard image. And the memory of his Cadillac encrusted with silver dollars has yet to recede from the frontal lobes of those who saw it cruising the byways of Music City.

Though never quite as over the top as Pierce, Merle Kilgore (born Wyatt Merle Kilgore, August 9, 1934, Chickasha, Oklahoma) is another talented extrovert who scaled Nashville's Olympian peaks. A guitar player from his youth, Kilgore found work as both a musician and DJ while still a teenager and parlayed those experiences and skills to win himself a gig as the house guitarist on the *Louisiana Hayride* radio program in 1952, where he crossed paths with Pierce.

Stints on the Grand Ole Opry and other high-profile country music venues led to record deals, and he became a reliable hit maker. In 1959 Kilgore's "Johnny Reb" was a monster hit for Johnny Horton, and not long after, Kilgore began to enjoy success as a recording artist himself, starting in early 1960 with his song "Dear Mama." He also cowrote "Ring of Fire" in 1962 with June Carter, which Carter's future husband, Johnny Cash, took to the masses. But Kilgore's most famous song is "Wolverton Mountain," cowritten with Claude King, in whose hands it reached worldwide notice.

Kilgore branched into film in the 1960s, singing the title song for and playing a bit part in *Nevada Smith* (1966), a Steve McQueen revenge western. He did some more onscreen acting in Robert Altman's *Nashville* (1975) and Michael Apted's *Coal Miner's Daughter* (1980).

Still an active recording artist into the 1980s, Kilgore today manages Hank Williams Jr.

"Most Likely You Go Your Way (and I'll Go Mine)" (Bob Dylan)

Bob Dylan, single (1966, 1974); *Blonde on Blonde* (1966); *Biograph*/'74 (1985)
Bob Dylan/The Band, *Before the Flood* (1974)
Hard Meat, *Hard Meat* (1969)
Rita Coolidge, *Nice Feelin'* (1972)
Todd Rundgren, *Faithful* (1976)
Patti Labelle, *Patti Labelle* (1977)
Jimmy Page, *Session Man: Volume 1* (1989)
The Yardbirds, *BBC Sessions* (1997)
Various Artists (performed by Vidalias), *A Tribute to Bob Dylan, Volume 3: The Times They Are A-Changin'* (2000)
Michel Montecrossa, *4th Time Around* (2001)
Various Artists (performed by Patti Labelle), *Doin' Dylan 2* (2002)

Various Artists (performed by Sue Foley), *Blues on Blonde on Blonde* (2003)

A fractured, surrealist kiss-off song set to a demented marching polka beat on its original *Blonde on Blonde* pressing, "Most Likely You Go Your Way," Dylan stated in the *Biograph* liner notes, was "probably written after some disappointing relationship where, you know, I was lucky to have escaped without a broken nose."

The tune, built around a driving, burnished blues riff and including a wacky, intrusive middle eight (the "you say my kisses are not like his" section) that somehow works, is one of Dylan's most infectious stompers and most severe antilove rants, its lyrics concocted from half of the dialogue of parting lovers.

"Most Likely You Go Your Way" served as a bookend to most of Dylan and the Band's 1974 concerts. Opening *and* closing the shows, their in-your-face version, in Dylan's words, "completed a circle in some way." Dylan revived it briefly as a sleepy lament for the 1976 leg of the Rolling Thunder Revue but then put it aside, not touching it until the 1989 edition of the Never Ending Tour. Since 1989 it has become a somewhat rare but generally perennial midset electric, rawhide-tinged offering, which Dylan renders with brooding resignation while still managing to vent with an air of remote indifference.

"Most of the Time" (Bob Dylan)

Bob Dylan, *Oh Mercy* (1989)
Bob Dylan/Various Artists (performed by Sophie Zelmani), *Masked and Anonymous* (soundtrack) (2003)
Michel Montecrossa, *Born in Time* (2000)

Relaxed and ethereal yet still familiar sounding, "Most of the Time" is a love song of haunting regret masked by feigned detachment. Rather than mourn the loss of his woman, the narrator stoically accepts their separation while cataloguing a series of reminiscences and feelings with a wry, aloof humor tinged with more than a little bitterness. The song is sung with great dignity in its expression of independence, but one wonders whether the old dog is really as tough as he tries to seem. Even if he's only attempting to convince himself, he does, however, manage to twist the knife with lines such as "Don't even remember what her lips felt like on mine/Most of the time."

One can't escape feeling that there is more of a tinge of autobiography here—somehow the memory of an ex-wife seems to gnaw at the fringes of "Most of the Time," giving the song the deep poignancy of one man's consideration of time's relentless winnowing. For a guy who once sneered at Miss Lonely in "Like a Rolling Stone," he seems pretty bereft. The strange, sirenlike music gives his words an extra push toward the void—as if he was staggering down the nameless streets of some nameless city, the rush of street traffic careening past him, a chill winter's wind blowing at his heels.

Dylan featured "Most of the Time" heavily in concert as a first encore during the 1989 Never Ending Tour, the year of its release. Thereafter, though its appearance in his set lists diminished significantly, it gained substantial power in the maestro's hands.

"Motherless Children" (Traditional/Blind Willie Johnson)
aka "Motherless Children Have a Hard Time," "Mother's Children Have a Hard Time"
See also "In My Time of Dyin'"
Blind Willie Johnson, *Complete Recordings of Blind Willie Johnson/'27* (1993)
Josh White, *Volume 5—In Chronological Order/'44* (1998)
Rev. Gary Davis, *Rev. Gary Davis* (1954)
Odetta, *My Eyes Have Seen* (1959)
Mance Lipscomb, *Texas Sharecropper and Songster* (1960)

Robert Pete Williams, *Angola Prisoner's Blues* (1961)
Dave Van Ronk, *Hesitation Blues* (1963)
Jesse Fuller, *Frisco Bound* (1968)
Eric Clapton, *461 Ocean Boulevard* (1974)
Sam Mitchell, *Art of Bottleneck/Slide Guitar* (1991)
Son House, *Father of the Delta Blues: The Complete 1965 Sessions* (1992)

Promotional advertisement for blues singer, musician, and Baptist preacher Blind Willie Johnson, ca. 1927.
(Frank Driggs Collection/Getty Images)

An early Dylan cover, this old spiritual made anew can be found in the repertoires of dozens of Southern folk and blues singers, black and white. Though "Motherless Children" (about the grim prospects facing orphaned children in the impoverished Deep South) was originally formalized and popularized by Blind Willie Johnson, Dylan's rendition more closely resembles Mance Lipscomb's widely circulated version.

Like Robert Johnson, Blind Willie Johnson was an intriguingly mysterious and mercurial Texas street singer who left a minuscule recorded legacy—only thirty songs are known to exist—in proportion to his influence and reputation.

Blind Willie Johnson (born between 1890 and 1902, Marlin, Texas; died 1947, Beaumont, Texas) used his forceful, rawhide voice and Deep South slide guitar stylings to spread the Lord's "good news" via the blues idiom.

Blinded with lye during a fight between his father and stepmother at a young age, he learned to play guitar and, with a tin cup hanging around his neck, took to the streets of small-town Texas to earn his living as a busker. Using a pocketknife (instead of the customary neck of a bottle), Johnson created spot-on accompaniments to his histrionic "I have seen the Devil and he looked back at me and smiled" voice.

That voice suited him well after he was ordained as a Baptist preacher. He married in 1927 and relocated to Dallas, where he and his wife testified using the blues as a foundation for their sermons. It was there that Johnson recorded the classic Baptist blues spirituals for Columbia that are his great legacy: "Motherless Children Have a Hard Time," "Let Your Light Shine on Me," "Jesus Make Up My Dying Bed," "Dark Was the Night, Cold Was the Ground," and, most searchingly, "The Soul of a Man." He was, in all of his songs, able to make the blues sound holy, and vice versa.

The bizarre circumstances of Johnson's death would ring of blues myth if the story wasn't true: after his house burned down, he slept on some damp bedding, contracted pneumonia, and died.

▣ "Motorpsycho Nitemare" (Bob Dylan)
aka "Motorpsycho Nightmare"
Bob Dylan, *Another Side of Bob Dylan* (1964)
Hugues Aufray, *Aufray Chante Dylan* (1965)
Various Artists (performed by Strangelove), *Outlaw Blues, Volume 2* (1995)

Dylan, with his twisted wit and laconic delivery of this song, combines Alfred Hitchcock's *Psycho* with a not-so-standard recasting of every farmer's daughter joke in the world. "Motorpsycho Nitemare" is a noirish experiment in humor that can be viewed as anticipating "Bob Dylan's 115th Dream" and "Subterranean Homesick Blues," which would be released a year later. Here, Dylan (or a narrator who looks and sounds something like him), in a broad satire on the discord between urban cool and rural conservatism, visits a Middle American hamlet of the early 1960s that's so uptight it panics at the thought of Fidel Castro and his beard. Steeped with sly lampoonery, the song tells the story of a charming hipster confronting a reactionary whose first and only weapon appears to be *Reader's Digest*. "Motorpsycho Nitemare" is little more than lighthearted filler, its composer's injection of some more offhand surrealism into *Another Side of Bob Dylan*.

▣ "Mountains of the Mourne" (William Percy French/Dr. W. Houston Collisson)
aka "Mountains of Mourne," "Mountains o' Mourne"
Will Holt, *Will Holt Concert* (1963)
Martha Schlamme, *Martha Schlamme at the Gate of Horn* (1963)
Kendall Morse, *Lights Along the Shore* (1976)

M

Dylan led his band through one instrumental version of this old ballad to kick off a 1991 show in its region of origin, Northern Ireland. "Mountains of Mourne" is a British music-hall number set to the tune of "Bendemeer's Stream," a classic Irish folk song.

The lyrics of "Mountains of the Mourne" were written in 1896 by William Percy French and the tune by his friend and collaborative partner, Dr. W. Houston Collisson. French wrote the words one day when the mountains were visible from the nearby Hill of Howth and sent the lyrics to Collisson on the back of a postcard.

French (born on May 1, 1854, Cloonyquin, County Roscommon, Ireland; died January 24, 1920, Formby, Lancashire) was one of the great entertainers of his day. He graduated from Trinity College in Dublin college with a degree in engineering and worked for seven years in Cavan, Ireland, as the chief drain inspector. But he nurtured his talents as a musician, songwriter, and painter.

In 1891 French found himself alone—his wife had died in childbirth that year—and jobless. After a stab at journalism as editor of the comic weekly newspaper *Jarvey*, he hopped on his bicycle and toured Ireland, painting and developing a one-man show in which sang the songs he composed. Later that year, he began a partnership with Collisson (born 1865; died 1920). Thereafter, Collisson wrote much of the music for the comic operas they produced, including *The Irish Girl*. French became a widely popular stage performer and he toured not only England, but the U.S. and Canada as well. French was also a skilled and admired painter who traded his works in exchange for lodging as he performed about the territories. He died while on tour near Glasgow, Scotland.

"Mountains of the Mourne" is French's most famous song and, true to his style, is a light-hearted mixture of the romantic and the bawdy.

"Mozambique" (Bob Dylan/Jacques Levy)
Bob Dylan, single (1975); *Desire* (1976); *Hard Rain* (video) (1976)

Both on record (*Desire*) and onstage with the Rolling Thunder Revue during their 1976 spring swing across the lower forty-eight, Scarlet Rivera really got to strut her stuff on the violin on "Mozambique," a light love song with lighter political overtones. Ultimately inconsequential, the song nonetheless is a romp with a great melody and an infectiousness that does not seem to age. Released as a single, "Mozambique" charted at No. 54.

At the time of the song's composition in the summer of 1975, Mozambique—a country on the southeast coast of Africa—was in the midst of a political revolution that resulted in its gaining independence from Portugal. While some on the U.S. political left attempted to read some veiled subtext into Dylan's song, it is difficult to hear in "Mozambique" little more than a sensual, fun-in-the-sun romantic lyric.

"Mr. Bojangles" (Jerry Jeff Walker)
Bob Dylan, *Dylan* (1973)
Jerry Jeff Walker, *Mr. Bojangles* (1968)
Nitty Gritty Dirt Band, *Nitty Gritty Dirt Band* (1967)
Nina Simone, *Essential Nina Simone* (1967)
Neil Diamond, *Touching Me Touching You* (1969)
King Curtis, *Live at the Fillmore* (1971)
Sonny Stitt, *Mr. Bojangles* (1973)
Harry Belafonte, *All-Time Greatest Hits, Volume 2* (1988)
Sammy Davis Jr, *Greatest Hits Live* (1995)

Dylan's passable version of "Mr. Bojangles," a classic neotroubadour song and one of the saving graces of *Dylan* (an otherwise forgettable album released by Columbia without its namesake's permission), includes a light moment near the end of the performance when he calls out to listeners to dance. Recorded by an array of talent, "Mr. Bojangles" was a hit for the Nitty Gritty Dirt Band in 1970. Nina Simone's smoky cover of the song, though, is (along with the composer's) the hands-down best of the lot.

Jerry Jeff Walker (born Ronald Clyde Crosby, March 16, 1942, Oneonta, New York) initially pursued a career as a folksinger in New York's Greenwich Village, playing gigs at the famous Café Wha? and the Night Owl. But he simultaneously moved in other directions as well, forging his eclectic reputation as a member of Circus Maximus and the Lost Sea Dreamers, a couple of long-gone but fondly recalled psychedelic rock bands that performed at the Electric Circus on St. Marks Place. One memorable occasion typical of the musical gumbo that fed Walker's roots was the night Circus Maximus performed their brand of acid rock at Carnegie Hall alongside New York Pro Musica Antiqua, which played Baroque music on period instruments.

In the late 1960s he moved to Key West, Florida, and resumed work as a solo artist with the release of *Drifting Way of Life* on the Vanguard label. "Mr. Bojangles," a tale of a spindly, down-on-his-luck street dancer Walker crafted from his experiences in the New Orleans drunk tank, was his biggest hit. Commonly, but incorrectly, the song is regarded as a paean to Bill "Bojangles" Robinson, one of the greatest tap dancers of all time.

Walker moved to Austin, Texas, in the early 1970s and assembled one of the region's most accomplished backing groups, the Lost Gonzo Band, while also becoming a kindred spirit to the city's "outlaw" country music posse, which included Willie Nelson and Waylon Jennings. As the country-rocker movement reached its peak in the 1970s, Walker's life became crowded with cocaine and whiskey, followed by a well-deserved reputation for unreliability. Seeing that promoters were losing the courage to book

Jerry Jeff Walker, composer of "Mr. Bojangles," ca. 1971.
(Frank Driggs Collection/Getty Images)

him, Walker steered himself off the low road and back onto the folk circuit, which still includes a communion with his fans at an annual birthday bash in Austin. His low-key approach to his career may have prevented him from attaining the same type of commercial success enjoyed by Nelson and Jennings, but he is held in high esteem by his colleagues and has earned a committed cult following.

In his autobiography, *Gypsy Songman* (Emeryville, Calif.: Woodford Press, 1999), Walker recalled writing "Mr. Bojangles." "At the time I was reading a lot of Dylan Thomas and I was really into the concept of internal rhyme," he explained. "One night, all alone with my guitar and a big yellow tablet, I started to write." During this process Walker recalled events from the near and distant past, of late nights, lonely walks, women, trouble, women trouble, more trouble, and all the characters he had met in jail cells and drunk tanks. Eventually the song came to him, "just sort of tumbling out, one straight shot down the length of that yellow pad. On a night when the rest of the country was listening to the Beatles, I was writing a six-eight waltz about an old man and hope."

The rise of "Mr. Bojangles" to popular notice is attributed to a 1967 late-night visit Walker paid to *Radio Unnameable*, Bob Fass's groundbreaking "free-form" WBAI-FM New York City radio show that can still be heard on the 99.5 bandwidth in the wee small hours of any Friday morning. Walker performed the then-newly penned song on the air, and Fass, according to Walker, "kept playing that song a couple of times a night, forever."

▣ "Mr. Tambourine Man" (Bob Dylan)

Bob Dylan, *Bringing It All Back Home* (1965); *Bob Dylan's Greatest Hits* (1967); *Bob Dylan at Budokan* (1979); *Biograph/'64* (1985); *The Bootleg Series, Volume 5: Live 1975—The Rolling Thunder Revue* (2002); *The Bootleg Series, Volume 6: Live 1964—Concert at Philharmonic Hall* (2004)

Bob Dylan/Various Artists (performed by Roger McGuinn and Tom Petty), *Bob Dylan: The 30th Anniversary Concert Celebration* (1993)

Various Artists (performed by Bob Dylan), *The Concert for Bangladesh* (1972); *More American Graffiti* (soundtrack) (1979)

The Byrds, *Mr. Tambourine Man* (1965); *The Byrds' Greatest Hits* (1967); *Untitled* (1970); *Original Singles, Volume 1 (1965–1967)* (1980); *The Byrds* (1990); *Definitive Collection* (1995); *Super Hits* (1998)

Odetta, *Odetta Sings Dylan* (1965)

Judy Collins, *5th Album* (1965); *Recollections: The Best of Judy Collins* (1969)

The Barbarians, *Are You a Boy or Are You a Girl* (1965)

Dino, Desi and Billy, *I'm a Fool* (1965)

Silkie, *You've Got to Hide Your Love Away* (1965)

Hugues Aufray, *À l'Olympia* (1965); *Au Casino de Paris* (1965)

The Brothers Four, *The Honey Wind Blows* (1965)

Four Seasons, *Sing Big Hits of Bacharach, David & Dylan* (1965)

Chad & Jeremy, *I Don't Want to Lose You, Baby* (1965)

Gerry Mulligan, *If You Can't Beat 'Em, Join 'Em* (1965)

The Chipmunks, *Chipmunks à Go-Go* (1965)

Hullabaloo Singers, *The Hullabaloo Show* (1965)

The Lettermen, *And I Love Her* (1965)

David Rose, *The Velvet Beat* (1965)

Saxons, *Saxons (Love Minus Zero)* (1966)

Duane Eddy, *Duane Does Dylan* (1966)

The Beau Brummels, *Beau Brummels* (1966)

Noel Harrison, *Noel Harrison* (1966)

Billy Lee Riley, *Funk Harmonica* (1966)

Stevie Wonder, *Down to Earth* (1967)

Kenny Rankin, *Mind Dusters* (1967)

Lester Flatt and Earl Scruggs, *Changin' Times* (1968)

Johnny Rivers, *Johnny Rivers Rocks the Folk* (1968)

William Shatner, *The Transformed Man* (1968)

Johnny Harris, *Love Is Blue* (1969)

The Brothers & Sisters of Los Angeles, *Dylan's Gospel* (1969)

Marmalade, *There's a Lot to Talk About* (1969)

Jonathan King, *Bubblerock Is Here to Stay* (1971)

Melanie, *Born to Be* (1969); *Four Sides of Melanie* (1972)

The Tribes, *Bangladesh* (1972)

Mike Batt Orchestra, *Portrait of Bob Dylan* (1972)

John Denver, *Beginnings with the Mitchell Trio* (1974)

The King's Singers, *Tempus Fugit* (1978)

Julie Felix, *Blowin' in the Wind* (1982)

Gene Clark, *Firebyrd* (1984); *Flying High* (1998)

The Beat Street Band, *Psychedelic Songs of the '60s* (1989)

Crowded House, *I Feel Possessed* (1989); *Unplugged in the Byrdhouse* (1995)

The Cliffs of Doneen, *The Dog Went East and God Went West* (1991)

Lester Flatt and Earl Scruggs, *1964–1969, Plus* (1996)

Phil Carmen, *Bob Dylan's Dream* (1996)

Roger McGuinn, *Live from Mars* (1996)

Abbey Lincoln, *We Used to Dance* (1997)

M

Bob Dylan performing with an acoustic guitar at the 1965 Newport Folk Festival.
(Photo by Diana Davies, courtesy of the Center for Folklife and Cultural Heritage, Smithsonian Institution)

The Daytrippers, *Daytrippers* (1997)

Two Approaching Riders, *One More Cup of Coffee* (1997)

Alison Ate, *Cake* (1998)

Disraeli Years, *Disraeli Years* (1998)

Raphael Cruz, *A Mano* (1999)

The Mamas and the Papas, *Before They Were the Mamas and the Papas* (1999)

Various Artists (performed by David West), *Pickin' on Dylan* (1999)

Various Artists (performed by Chris Hillman), *The Folkscene Collection, Volume II* (2000)

Gerry Murphy, *Gerry Murphy Sings Bob Dylan* (2002)

Various Artists (performed by Fourth Street Sisters), *Blowin' in the Wind: A Reggae Tribute to Bob Dylan* (2003)

A rightly celebrated and enduring artistic statement that suggests an otherworldliness beckoning from just beyond the veil of reality, "Mr. Tambourine Man" is one of Dylan's most profound monumental lyric poems. His quest for transcendence through a seductive, almost messianic, Pied Piper–like sprite promising escape finally delivers both the poet and listener to a place "far from the twisted reach of crazy sorrow."

Is this the only Bob Dylan song that begins with the chorus? At any rate, Dylan immediately begins invoking this mythic fairy from the get-go by asking him/it to "play a song for me" and promises to come following him in the "jingle jangle morning." It does appear to be dawn. After all, "evening's empire has returned to sand" and our singer, despite his amazed weariness, has no place to go except wherever the Tambourine Man might lead him. Over four verses, Dylan explains his plight through densely embroidered imagery laced with refracting rhymes, both enjoying the dance with the agony, ecstasy, and the muse while at the same desperately trying to escape. Or is he enacting in song the longing he felt from his adherents, becoming, in effect, the very tambourine man who repels and excites him?

In the first verse, the writer stares at the blank page, amazed at his weariness but unable or unwilling to sleep, invoking the muse. By verse two, he claims he's "ready to go anywhere" the Tambourine Man might lead if only he would cast his "dancing spell my way" but, by the third verse, he suspects that he has become a "ragged clown" left behind—fruitlessly chasing a slippery cipher of artistic and/or spiritual deliverance cast by the Tambourine Man's "vague traces of skipping reels of rhyme." In the song's last verse, the singer makes a final appeal, beckoning his muse to provide an inspirational experience beyond "all memory and fate" so he can "forget about today until tomorrow."

With its references to taking trips through smoke rings, swirling ships, and the like, "Mr. Tambourine Man" was attacked early and often for being a "drug song," which, naturally, angered Dylan. Less hysterical reaction more insightfully evaluated the song as an invocation to the singer-songwriter's muse for inspiration and the freedom that it brings. "Drugs never played a part in that song," Dylan later remarked in the *Biograph* liner notes; "'*disappearing in the smoke rings in my mind,*' that's not drugs, drugs were never that big a thing with me."

Perhaps so, but with its exultant visions and drive for transcendence, "Mr. Tambourine Man" seems to reflect a psychedelic experience—an impulse underlined by the Byrds'

euphoric version, which first popularized the song.

Academics have pointed to all kinds of source material for Dylan's inspiration. Dylan biographer Robert Shelton alone cites theories suggesting everything from black gospel music's "joyful noise" and the tambourine held by any Salvation Army troupe worth its salt to W. B. Yeats's epic poem "Byzantium."

Along with Frederico Fellini's 1954 film *La Strada* (his paean to a traveling circus starring the mighty Anthony Quinn), Dylan has cited session guitarist and bassist Bruce Langhorne (who showed up at a recording session with a gigantic tambourine) as a direct inspiration for the primary image of "Mr. Tambourine Man."

Dylan has also mentioned that the song was written upon leaving New Orleans in mid-February 1964 after experiencing Mardi Gras festivities to the fullest. But writer Al Aronowitz claims the song was penned during an all-night typing session at his house in Berkeley Heights, New Jersey. Most probably, it was a work in progress over the course of the first half of 1964.

With its bright, expansive melody, "Mr. Tambourine Man" stands among Dylan's most iridescent and meditative compositions. His haunted delivery helps keep the desired transcendence always just out of reach, and his riveting performance is burnished with melancholy and a mesmerizing harmonica solo that conjures a solitary internal reverie.

As if drawn by the song's promise of inspiration and renewal, Dylan has consistently performed "Mr. Tambourine Man" in concert since its debut in May 1964 at a concert in London. At the 1965 Newport Folk Festival he used the song to make a statement when he returned to play acoustic versions of it and "It's All Over Now, Baby Blue" after being booed for unveiling his electrified rock 'n' roll persona. Far from being a concession to those who wished to see him remain some sort of folkier bard, Dylan seems to have chosen "Tambourine Man" and "Baby Blue" that night as pronouncements of artistic purpose—that the Greenwich Village folk renaissance was over and that he was going to follow his muse dancing "neath the diamond sky" in the face of the audience's Bronx cheers. It's seldom been static—note the ghostly, harmonica-heavy acoustic renderings of 1966, the up-tempo 1974 outings with the Band, and the 1978 big-band versions replete with a flute accompaniment that made things downright happy. Over the years "Tambourine Man" has kept improving, never sounding better than it did in Dylan's bittersweet mid-1990s staccato-style renditions, stealing many a Never Ending Tour acoustic set. In 1965 Dylan sang to Mr. Tambourine Man as if he were an impatient, apprentice bodhisattva. By the early twenty-first century, his wry, shambolic delivery suggested he was on to the old trickster's game but was still captivated by the allure of the "dancing spell."

In his description of Dylan's May 15, 1966, version of "Mr. Tambourine Man" from Leicester, England, Greil Marcus touched upon some of the song's magic in his book *Invisible Republic* (New York: Henry Holt and Company, 1997):

> In Leicester Dylan began "Mr. Tambourine Man," and it would take him nine perfect minutes to find an ending in the song he could accept. As he sings, his words are clipped, his diction almost effete, as if each word can and must be presented as if it means exactly what it says. But very quickly this odd speech becomes its own kind of rhythm, and paradoxically it releases the burden Dylan has seemingly placed on each word, and each word along with every other, and the song becomes a dream of peace of mind. You cease to hear the words. For nine minutes what you

hear are two long harmonica solos, each pressing well past two minutes—solos that sway, back and forth, back and forth, a cradle rocking in their rhythm, until without warning the sound rises up like a water spout, hundreds of feet in the air, the cradle now rocking at its top, then down again, safe in the arms of the melody.

A version of "Mr. Tambourine Man" from that exact period and featuring Dylan's harmonica solo is captured in *Eat the Document* (1972), Dylan's interesting mess of a cinematic pastiche. Judging from this, Marcus knows of what he writes: this may stand as the greatest-ever moment of Dylan making music on film.

A final note: Hunter S. Thompson dedicated *Fear and Loathing in Las Vegas* to Dylan for writing "Mr. Tambourine Man."

◪ *MTV Unplugged*

Columbia-Sony CD 670001995 (Columbia); CD 472674 21995 (Sony); CS 67000 (Sony); LP 501131995 (Sony); 67000 (Sony). Recorded November 17 and 18, 1994, at Sony Studios, New York. Released April 25, 1995. Executive producer: Jeff Rosen.
Bob Dylan—vocals, guitar, harmonica. John Jackson—guitar. Bucky Baxter—pedal steel guitar, Dobro. Brendan O'Brien—Hammond organ. Tony Garnier—bass. Winston Watson—drums.
"Tombstone Blues," "Shooting Star," "All Along the Watchtower," "The Times They Are A-Changin'," "John Brown," "Rainy Day Women #12 & 35," "Desolation Row," "Dignity," "Knockin' on Heaven's Door," "Like a Rolling Stone," "With God on Our Side"

Dylan joined the army of performers to appear on MTV's popular *Unplugged* series when, in early 1995, he and his band settled into New York's Sony Studios for a couple of nights' taping before a live audience. The shows were edited down to an hour for showing on MTV

Dylan performing on *MTV Unplugged*, Sony Music Studio, New York City, November 18, 1994.

(Photo: Frank Micelotta/Getty Images)

and the songs culled for that program were released on this album. Even though eight of the eleven songs date from the 1963 to 1967 period, the freshness with which Dylan performs them is enough to remind casual fans and purists alike why those years are considered a high-water mark—and why the songs endure today. "The Times They Are A-Changin'" sounded as consequential in the Newt Gingrich "Contract with America" era as it did back in the days when Governor Orville Faubus of Arkansas tried to stop school integration in Lit-

tle Rock. Rejiggered much the way Eric Clapton did with "Layla" for his MTV appearance, "Like a Rolling Stone" here receives its only known acoustic outing. And the powerful antiwar song "John Brown" is a surprise selection, acting as a timeless totem of tragedy lurking just around the corner. Though "Knockin' on Heaven's Door" represents the 1970s in predictable fashion, "Shooting Star" and "Dignity" (the latter a previously unperformed song) showed that Dylan was still more than willing to take chances with his audiences' expectations.

Right from the opening of "Tombstone Blues"—which trades in its original double-time fervor for a confident country jaunt as Dylan spit-whispers his stream-of-consciousness verses—Dylan and his peak Never Ending Tour band approach the material in a kind and gentle manner. They give some of the old warhorses like "With God on Our Side" a sad and muted, yet still defiant, tone: the sound of the Bard playing in the planet's last gin joint on the path to country-folk-blues paradise.

The fashion conscious will note that just as Dylan wore a polka-dotted shirt when he plugged in three decades before during his soundcheck at the 1965 Newport Folk Festival, he wore a similarly styled garment when he unplugged in New York.

Dylan's *MTV Unplugged* was nominated for (but did not win) three 1996 Grammy awards: for best contemporary folk album, "Knockin' on Heaven's Door" for best male rock vocal performance, and "Dignity" for best rock song.

🖭 **"Muleskinner Blues"** (Traditional/Jimmie
Rodgers/George Vaughn)
aka "Blue Yodel No. 8," "Muleskinner," "Mule Skinner,"
"Mule Skinner Blues"
Jimmie Rodgers, *Singing Brakeman* (1996)
Bill Monroe, *Music of Bill Monroe* (1994)
Merle Haggard, *Same Train, Different Time* (1994)
José Feliciano, *Selection of José Feliciano* (1997)
Old and in the Way, *Breakdown: Live Recordings 1973* (1997)
Various Artists (performed by Van Morrison), *The Songs of Jim-
mie Rodgers: A Tribute* (1997)
Woody Guthrie, *Woody Guthrie—Muleskinner Blues: The Asch
Recordings, Volume 2* (1999)

On some of the earliest recordings capturing him on tape, Dylan performs this folk and blue-grass classic about a guy so down on his luck he's willing to carve his initials in a mule's hide, carry water for a work crew, or build a road

under the broiling Southern sun for three squares and a flop. And it's readily apparent that back in 1960 and 1962, he had not practiced his deep-breath yodeling. Because of this, it is thought that Dylan probably learned "Mule-skinner Blues" from Odetta or Woody Guthrie recordings rather than the Singing Brakeman's original. There are two known versions of Dylan performing "Muleskinner Blues," and because they are separated by nearly two years, it is a good bet that it was showing up regularly during his early coffeehouse gigs. Keen listeners and collectors will note that Dylan's jangly guitar strum introducing his 1962 rendition of "Muleskinner" at Montreal's Finjan Club will be echoed by a similar strum in "Subterranean Homesick Blues" just two years later.

In his biography *Jimmie Rodgers: The Life and Times of America's Blues Yodeler* (Urbana: University of Illinois Press, 1979), Nolan Porterfield discussed "Muleskinner Blues" under its more familiar title, "Blue Yodel No. 8": "The brash, exuberant 'Blue Yodel No. 8' is especially fine, featuring yet another variation on the form, in which the bass line is not repeated. Heard also is one of Jimmie's more protracted and—for him—complicated guitar runs, the sort of sharp, solid fret work and booming bass notes that, although rarely performed on his records, became identified as his trademark and were widely copied. The lyrics of 'Muleskinner Blues' are themselves superb, and the song has attracted a number of country singers over the years. Unfortunately, it is rarely performed as Rodgers originally did it."

🖭 **"Mutineer"** (Warren Zevon)
See also *Sentimental Hygiene*
Warren Zevon, *Mutineer* (1995)

Dylan started his fall 2002 tour in unusual fashion, performing mostly on piano and displaying a bevy of songs by others. He included three from the quill of Warren Zevon—a sweet sign of affection and respect from Dylan for the acclaimed, if underrated, singer-songwriter, who had recently announced that he was dying. "Mutineer," the most recent of the Zevon songs performed on the tour, had just the right mix of trademark dark Zevon humor and rebellious anarchy to appeal to Dylan. With lyrics like "I was born to rock the boat," "Mutineer" is a song Dylan could quickly personalize. Yet even without Zevon's looming demise, "Mutineer" became a wistful reflection on the brevity of life.

[S] "My Back Pages" (Bob Dylan)

Bob Dylan, *Another Side of Bob Dylan* (1964); *Bob Dylan's Greatest Hits, Volume II/'64* (1971)
Bob Dylan/Various Artists (performed by Tom Petty and the Heartbreakers), *Bob Dylan: The 30th Anniversary Concert Celebration* (1993); (performed by Magakoro Brothers), *Masked and Anonymous* (2003)
The Byrds, *Younger than Yesterday* (1967); *The Byrds' Greatest Hits* (1967); *History of the Byrds* (1973); *The Byrds Play Dylan* (1980); *Original Singles, Volume 2* (1982); *Definitive Collection* (1995); *Greatest Hits* (1999)
Keith Jarrett, *Somewhere Before* (1968)
The Brothers & Sisters of Los Angeles, *Dylan's Gospel* (1969)
The Hollies, *Hollies Sing Dylan* (1969)
The Nice, *Keith Emerson with the Nice* (1971); *Elegy* (1971)
Dick Gaughan, *Parallel Lines* (1988)
Greg Harris, *Things Change* (1990)
The Ramones, *Acid Eaters* (1993)
Carl Verheyen, *Garage Sale* (1994)
Phil Carmen, *Bob Dylan's Dream* (1996)
Two Approaching Riders, *One More Cup of Coffee* (1997)
Insol, *Insol* (1998)
John Stewart, *John Stewart and Darwin's Army* (1999)
Various Artists (performed by Marshall Crenshaw), *Bleecker Street: Greenwich Village in the '60s* (1999)
Various Artists (performed by Joan Osborne and Jackson Browne), *Steal This Movie* (soundtrack) (2000)
Spinatras, *@Midnight.com* (2000)
2 of Us, *From Zimmermann to Genghis Khan* (2001)
Second Floor, *Plays Dylan* (2001)
Steve Earle, *Sidetracks* (2002)

If any artist had earned the luxury of appraising his or her full life and already prodigious artistic output at the ripe old age of twenty-three, Bob Dylan probably would have to be near the top of the heap. In "My Back Pages," a fascinating and important piece of self-analysis, Dylan chides himself for having thought he'd had the answers to life's questions. In its acknowledgment of how his protest songs and the movement they were part of fell short of their lofty aims, "My Back Pages" is a compelling statement of Dylan's maturing self-awareness and an apology for the intensity of his earlier political preaching, and contains one of his most quoted lines: "I was so much older then, I'm younger than that now."

Robert Shelton points out some classical poetic elements in "My Back Pages" in his 1986 book *No Direction Home: The Life and Music of Bob Dylan*: "From Blakean 'Experience,' Dylan has moved back toward 'Innocence,' which will keep him forever young. This song of self-discovery returns to a child's openness."

Shelton goes on to quote from "It Takes a Train to Cry," an unpublished dissertation by scholar Jack McDonough, who wrote of "My Back Pages": "One of Dylan's most important poetic achievements has been this transportation of the worlds of Wordsworth and Blake into postwar America."

Shelton summarizes by saying that "My Back Pages" encapsulates Dylan's entire canon, as "Two themes dominating Dylan's whole work are the struggle of life versus death and the possibility of renewal through adoption of a younger viewpoint."

Dylan only began performing "My Back Pages" as an instrumental kickoff to his 1978 concerts, shelving it shortly thereafter. He did not pick it up until the mid-1990s, when he began singing the song again, including it as both an acoustic and electric offering during the Never Ending Tours. Here, Dylan handled the song with confessional aplomb and included a triumphant mouth-harp solo that battled his band for attention as the tune raved to closure. From 1997 onward, Dylan band multi-instrumentalist Larry Campbell was coloring the song with lush swaths of musical ambrosia courtesy of his magic fiddle as Dylan and company continued to display "My Back Pages" as a midset or encore acoustic treasure.

"My Blue Eyed Jane" (Jimmie Rodgers/Lulu Belle White)
aka "Blue Eyed Jane," "Blue-Eyed Jane," "My Blue-Eyed Jane"
Various Artists (performed by Bob Dylan), *The Songs of Jimmie Rodgers: A Tribute* (1997)
Jimmie Rodgers, *Riding High 1929–30* (1991)
Hank Snow, *Singing Ranger* (1959)
Doc Watson, *Portrait* (1988)

Dylan performed a few acoustic versions of Jimmie Rodgers's "My Blue Eyed Jane" in 1998. Perhaps not so coincidentally, Dylan's own fledgling Egyptian Records label in late 1997 released a Rodgers tribute album that Dylan shepherded through production and to which he contributed a cover of this same tune.

It's not a strong song on its own merits, according to Nolan Porterfield, who in his 1979 bio *Jimmie Rodgers: The Life and Times of America's Blues Yodeler* credits Rodgers with giving it its power. He writes that it "transcends the mediocrity of its love/turtledove lyrics as a result of Rodgers's lilting delivery and the driving, buoyant energy of the jazz accompaniment. One of the least 'country' of all Rodgers's songs, 'My Blue-Eyed Jane' has nevertheless found a place over the years in the

repertoire of many country artists—Hank Snow's version is especially fine—and it rightly deserves to be ranked among Rodgers's most memorable recordings."

"My Head's in Mississippi" (Dusty Hill/Billy Gibbons/Frank Beard)
ZZ Top, Recycler (1990)

Dylan's only performances of this ZZ Top special (sung with an evil blue funk) transpired when he used it to kick off a trio of fall 1990 shows, one in the titled state. "My Head's in Mississippi" is a fine rocker, synthesizing the gritty virtues of ZZ Top's early, grunge-boogie sound with the high-tech gloss of their later work.

With its frontmen's trademark dueling beards, ZZ Top is one of the phenomenal success stories to emerge from the Southern boogie-rock movement. The threesome—guitarist Billy Gibbons (born December 16, 1949, Houston, Texas), bassist Dusty Hill (born Joe Hill, May 19, 1949, Dallas), and beardless drummer Frank Beard (born June 11, 1949, Houston)—formed in 1970 from rival Houston-area bands. If their albums and shows are thick with the Lone Star State's big bluesy sound and rowdy Texas humor, their patented grungy groove and look may have obscured their considerable gifts as genuine roots musicians: Gibbons is one of the hottest blues guitarists on wheels and Hill and Beard in the rhythm section match him lick for fireballing lick. Their commitment to their blues roots was immortalized when they were presented a wooden plank from the Clarksdale, Mississippi, shack in which Muddy Waters grew up. They had the wood fashioned into a guitar—dubbed the "Muddywood"—which they take out on tour to raise money for the Delta Blues Museum. And whether it was by plan or chance, they are doomed to end every music encyclopedia . . . except this one.

N

ⓢ **"Nadine"** (Chuck Berry)
aka "Is It You?"
Chuck Berry, single (1964); *Chess Box/'64* (1988)
High Mountain Hoedown, *High Mountain Hoedown* (1970)
Sandy Denny, *Bunch* (1972)
George Thorogood, *Better Than the Rest* (1974)
New Riders of the Purple Sage, *Live on Stage* (1975)

"Nadine" was Chuck Berry's first postprison song, making it to the charts in 1964 and staying there for two months. A rousing first cousin to "Maybellene" (released in 1955), a more popular song in the "big bad mama" tradition, "Nadine" shares the same peppy beat and similarly witty lyrics about a woman with a car. Maybellene's Coupe de Ville became Nadine's coffee-colored Cadillac.

Dylan's supremely raggedy one-off performance of this song, for which he spit out the lyrics like a veteran Harlem stoop singer playing the dozens with a bunch of greenhorns, came as an encore at one of the earliest Never Ending Tour shows, a June 1988 presentation in Berry's hometown of St. Louis. The version was so endearingly slapdash that it sounded as if it was performed with one of Berry's notorious picked-up-on-the-fly bands. The song may have been fresh in Dylan's mind, as he had performed "Nadine" at a surprise appearance with Levon Helm and a few others at New York City's now long-gone Lone Star Café in late May 1988.

ⓐ *Nashville Skyline*
Columbia Records LP KCS-9826, CD CK-9825, CS PCT 9825; Sony Music Entertainment, Inc., SACD 90319. Recorded February 13, 14, and 17, 1969. Released April 9, 1969. Produced by Bob Johnston. Liner notes, "Of Bob Dylan," by Johnny Cash.

Bob Dylan—guitar, harmonica, keyboards, vocals. Norman Blake—vocals. Johnny Cash—vocals. Pete Drake—guitar. Kenny Buttrey—drums. Charlie Daniels—bass, guitar. Charlie McCoy—guitar, harmonica.
"Girl from the North Country" (performed with Johnny Cash), "Nashville Skyline Rag," "To Be Alone with You," "I Threw It All Away," "Peggy Day," "Lay, Lady, Lay," "One More Night," "Tell Me That It Isn't True," "Country Pie," "Tonight I'll Be Staying Here with You"

Clocking in at a mere twenty-seven minutes, *Nashville Skyline* is Dylan's shortest album but hardly his skimpiest. This collection of simple country songs marked a sales high (at the time) for Dylan, stayed on the charts for thirty-one weeks, peaked at No. 3, went platinum, and yielded the hit "Lay, Lady, Lay." And the half-baked poem that Johnny Cash provided as liner notes won a Grammy.

Despite following the all-acoustic *John Wesley Harding*, on its release *Nashville Skyline* caught many off guard. It had none of its predecessor's obtuse riddles or fables; for a Bob Dylan album, it seemed almost flat. Even the album cover, featuring what one writer described as a photo of a smiling "Ragtime Country Bob" holding a steel-string guitar (with its country-style inlaid pick guard) while tipping his hat, was somewhat unsettling to the many who considered Dylan a prophet of the urban underground. To these folks, *Nashville Skyline* was kind of like bumping into a previously aggressive friend who had suddenly mellowed. Images aside, however, the seemingly inconsequential nature of the music is what really stunned Dylan's audience. Many in that camp began suggesting that the peaches-and-cream album was proof that the muse had abandoned the once doom-saying electric seer of just a few years earlier. All the same, *Nashville Skyline*—thanks especially, no doubt, to Dylan's duet with Johnny Cash on "Girl from the North Country"—was quite influential in turning peoples' eyes toward Nashville and contributed to a late '60s reappraisal and renewed interest in country music.

All of which is not to say that *Nashville Skyline* is Velveeta Dylan. On the contrary, as with many of his best albums, the range of his concern and presentation is fairly wide. Along with his excavation of "Girl from the North Country," he gave his audience a song of seduction ("Tonight I'll Be Staying Here with You"), a fed-up blues ("One More Night"), a jealous waltz ("Tell Me That It Isn't True"), a spirited bluegrass instrumental ("Nashville Skyline Rag"), a romantic romp ("To Be Alone with You"), a self-critical dirge ("I Threw It All Away"), and at least one evergreen ("Lay, Lady, Lay").

If the presentation of the material on *Nashville Skyline* was static, many of the songs have endured, ironically enough, as Dylan performance staples. "Lay, Lady, Lay" has been a perennial since its concert debut with the Band in 1974. But over the years, "Tonight I'll Be Staying Here with You," "I Threw It All Away," "To Be Alone with You," "Country Pie," and "Tell Me That It Isn't True" have all had their live displays.

Dylan had always toyed with country music, but *Nashville Skyline* was the genuine, full-fledged article. With its steel guitars and straightforward songs, the album exudes a friendly warmth marked by Dylan's until-then-unheard gentle croon (supposedly the result of his having temporarily quit smoking) suiting the songs like a comfortable old sweater.

These sentiments are remarkable when one considers now how profoundly unhip country music was in 1969—the alcohol-saturated, pickup-truck-driving Vietnam War yang to the druggy, hippie, peace-and-love yin. Even the folks at Columbia Records, Dylan's own label, were so dismayed at his newest incarnation (which they must have regarded as some lunatic retrogression) that they supposedly begged him to remove the word "Nashville" from the album's title. However, Dylan was once again prescient: his foray into country music helped establish country-rock as a vital force in pop music. His lead was followed by the Byrds, the Flying Burrito Brothers, and even the Grateful Dead, among many others.

[S] **"Nashville Skyline Rag"** (Bob Dylan)

Bob Dylan, *Nashville Skyline* (1969)
Earl Scruggs (performed with Bob Dylan), *Earl Scruggs Performs with His Family and Friends* (1971); *The Essential Earl Scruggs* (2004)
Lester Flatt and Earl Scruggs, *Final Fling* (1970)
Mike Blatt Orchestra, *Portrait of Bob Dylan* (1972)
Dixie Flyers, *Just Pickin'* (1979)

This spirited tune is one of the few instrumentals that Dylan would ever compose, much less include on an album. Some critics suggested that its appearance on *Nashville Skyline* was a cheery piece of filler—not so far-fetched, considering that the album is only twenty-seven minutes long.

[A] ***Natural Born Killers*** (soundtrack)/Various Artists

Interscope CD 924601995, CS 9246. Released 1994.

A fragment of Dylan's "You Belong to Me" (written by Pee Wee King and Redd Stewart) appeared on this unusual soundtrack album assembled by Trent Reznor of Nine Inch Nails. The music accompanies director Oliver Stone's brutal, controversial serial-killer film; starring Woody Harrelson and Juliette Lewis, it is a heavy-handed update of Terrence Malick's brilliant *Badlands* of 1973.

[S] **"Need a Woman"** (Bob Dylan)

aka "I Need a Woman"
Bob Dylan, *The Bootleg Series, Volumes 1–3: Rare and Unre-*

N

leased, 1961–1991/'81 (1991)
Ry Cooder, *The Slide Area* (1982)

The fair-weather Dylan watcher may have been surprised by the power of some of his late '70s and '80s output when released on *The Bootleg Series, Volumes 1–3.* "Need a Woman" is as good a place as any to start the listening and the debate when the subject of Dylan's sustained viability as a singer, songwriter, and performer arises.

Recorded for *Shot of Love,* "Need a Woman" was radically rewritten during the sessions, but Dylan was never satisfied with the final wash. Amid the rewrites (which resulted in a simplified statement of physical and emotional yearning when finally published in *Lyrics 1962–1985*), Dylan seemed to wrestle most over the theme of "Need a Woman." This is not surprising in context, for *Shot of Love* owes much of its edge to a tension between religious devotion and spiritual uncertainty. And though this is assuredly the work of a man in the early stages of middle age striving to reconcile his beginning-to-dwindle libido and dusky spirituality, it's also great to hear Dylan carry on like a younger man hungering for the woman he sings to.

▣ "Neighborhood Bully" (Bob Dylan)
Bob Dylan, *Infidels* (1983)

A strident screed about Israel that really does try to rock, "Neighborhood Bully" won Dylan no small amount of criticism for the perceived pro-Zionist slant of its lyrics. A photo on the inner sleeve of *Infidels,* the album on which "Neighborhood Bully" was released, depicted Dylan touching soil while crouching near Jerusalem's Old City; concurrent rumors of Dylan's interest in the Hasidic Lubavitcher brand of extreme Orthodox Judaism fueled further speculation regarding the significance and intent of the composition.

Indeed, there are lines in "Neighborhood Bully" that appear to defend Israel's 1982 invasion of Lebanon and 1981 bombing of an Iraqi nuclear facility, justifying these actions with the notion that "the bombs [being made there] were meant for him."

Cooler heads suggested that "Neighborhood Bully" was *about* Israel, not necessarily a wholehearted defense of its politics. Many sects of Hasidic Judaism, it should be noted, believe the state of Israel as it now exists is a blasphemy: that no Jewish state should exist until the appearance of a Jewish Messiah. But Dylan appears to castigate those who question Israel's existence, and this from a guy who was reembracing his Jewish heritage after a long period of at least perceived agnosticism followed by a short, though intense, fling with born-again Christianity. It is with the real pride of a man whose tradition has survived six millennia that he sings, "Every empire that's enslaved him is gone,/Egypt and Rome, even the great Babylon./He's made a garden of paradise in the desert sand,/In bed with nobody, under no one's command./He's the neighborhood bully."

Part of determining how seriously to take Dylan in a song like "Neighborhood Bully" is that *Infidels* is stocked with songs seemingly sung by different characters with their predictably different attitudes and points of view. Where Dylan's allegiance to the rhetoric espoused in the songs begins and ends is very gray territory.

That Dylan never performed "Neighborhood Bully" in concert should be some sort of hint that even he came to think that it was the insufferable harangue nearly every critic (and fan) thought it was.

▣ "Never Gonna Be the Same Again" (Bob Dylan)
Bob Dylan, *Empire Burlesque* (1985)

A fairly forgettable morning-after song, "Never Gonna Be the Same Again" would be an acceptable (and maybe even a hit) ballad if recorded by, say, Tina Turner. But out of the mouth of Bob Dylan it rang pretty hollow as released in an extremely schmaltzy and overproduced form on *Empire Burlesque*. It was performed just once by Dylan with Tom Petty and the Heartbreakers in 1986 before being hidden away for nearly a decade. When it surprisingly popped up again during the spring 1995 Never Ending Tour, Dylan provided a delicate, halting interpretation highlighted by Bucky Baxter's pedal steel licks. "Never Gonna Be the Same Again" appeared again as a concert surprise as late as 1999 and then again in the summer of 2002.

Empire Burlesque is an album known for its utilization of lines from films, particularly Humphrey Bogart's noirs of the 1940s. In "Never Gonna Be the Same Again" Dylan sets his sights on *Shane*, the 1953 classic western starring Alan Ladd in the title role. In the film, Shane says, "I don't mind leaving, I'd just like it to be my idea." In the song, Dylan sings, "Don't worry baby, I don't mind leaving,/I'd just like it to be my idea."

▣ "Never Let Me Go" (Joseph C. Scott)
Bob Dylan, *4 Songs from Renaldo & Clara* (EP) (1978)
Leon Thomas, *Full Circle* (1973)
Johnny Ace, *Johnny Ace Memorial Album* (1974)
Curtis Mayfield, *Something to Believe In* (1980)
Bobby Bland, *Blues & Ballads* (1999)
Ruth Brown, *Good Day for the Blues* (1999)

A highlight of the acoustic sets Dylan and Joan Baez shared on the fall 1975 portion of the Rolling Thunder Revue, "Never Let Me Go" saw very limited release on a Columbia Records promo EP pushing Dylan's film *Renaldo & Clara*.

Biographical info on the song's composer, Joe Scott, is sketchy at best. He has apparently worked with Curtis Mayfield and Natalie Cole in both musical and production capacities. Dylan probably got hip to this very beautiful ballad pledging eternal fidelity via the Johnny Ace cover.

▣ "Never Say Goodbye" (Bob Dylan)
Bob Dylan, *Planet Waves* (1974)
Steve Keene, *No Alternative* (1994)
Various Artists (performed by Steve Keene), *May Your Song Always Be Sung* (1996)

Gloriously nostalgic and never performed in concert, "Never Say Goodbye" nevertheless sounds hastily written and recorded. Its yearning, wintry lyrics of proposal will never match its strange melody (reminiscent of "Something There Is About You," also from *Planet Waves*) propelled by Robbie Robertson's watery guitar work. Here Dylan mixes tenderness and realism and builds a song of strength and sensitivity, with an uncanny ability to evoke a scene with a few affecting strokes: "Twilight on the frozen lake/North wind about to break/On footsteps in the snow/Silence down below." Dylan not only gets away with quoting himself when he sings "Oh, baby, baby, baby blue," referencing his 1965 classic "It's All Over Now, Baby Blue," but also explores that secret place beyond the chaos of everyday life when he reveals that "My dreams are made of iron and steel/With a big bouquet/of roses hanging down/From the heavens to the ground."

▣ "New Blue Moon" (Traveling Wilburys)
Traveling Wilburys, *Traveling Wilburys, Volume 3* (1990)

Drawing on their evident admiration for 1950s-flavored pop, the Wilburys harmonize behind Jeff Lynne, who takes his turn as frontman.

[S] "New Danville Girl" *See* "Brownsville Girl"

[A] *New Morning*

Columbia Records LP KC-30290, CD CK-30290, CS PCT-30290. Recorded May–August 1970. Released October 21, 1970. Produced by Bob Johnston.

Bob Dylan—vocals, guitar, organ, piano. David Bromberg—guitar, Dobro. Buzzy Feiten, Ron Cornelius—guitars. Al Kooper—organ, piano, guitar, French horn. Harvey Brooks, Charlie Daniels—bass. Russ Kunkel, Billy Mundi—drums. Hilda Harris, Albertine Robinson, Maeretha Stewart—background vocals.

"If Not for You," "Day of the Locusts," "Times Passes Slowly," "Went to See the Gypsy," "Winterlude," "If Dogs Run Free," "New Morning," "Sign on the Window," "One More Weekend," "The Man in Me," "Three Angels," "Father of Night"

Retaining the bucolic vibes of his then-recent work (*Nashville Skyline*, *Self Portrait*), Dylan unpacked a grittier rock sound and returned to the layered, poetic lyrics of his mid-1960s songs with *New Morning*. Maybe he felt ashamed at having foisted *Self Portrait* on an unsuspecting public earlier in the year, or perhaps he had a sudden surge of inspiration. Whatever the reason, *New Morning* came out just four months after *Self Portrait*—Dylan's fastest follow-up to date—and may be viewed at once as an Emersonian statement of self-reliance and as a kind of sheepish apology for the slapdash character of *Self Portrait*. It stayed on the charts for three months, rising to No. 7 as Dylan snared his seventh gold album.

Recorded in New York City with a studio band led by keyboardist Al Kooper, *New Morning* was simply packaged with a sepia-tone photo portrait of Dylan (looking every bit the young rabbi) on the front cover and a charming snapshot of a very young, waiflike Bobby Dylan at a 1961 recording session with singer Victoria Spivey.

Even three decades down the pike, *New Morning* chimes as a celebration of married life and country living as Dylan sings about everything from a parable on Elvis Presley ("Went to See the Gypsy") to the introspective soul ("Sign on the Window"). The classic "If Not for You" (later covered by George Harrison) is the album's best-known song, but there are other gems here too: the slide blues guitar-driven "One More Weekend," the eloquently meditative "Time Passes Slowly," and the lilting "Winterlude" waltz all shine. And Dylan really seems to enjoy himself on "If Dogs Run Free," with its hazy hepcat improv scat that finds him uttering comical Beat-style jazz rhymes. The album ends with "Father of Night," which, along with the title cut, foreshadows the religious themes that Dylan would vehemently explore by decade's end. The last batch of originals Dylan would release for nearly three years, *New Morning* is extra unusual in that he plays piano on seven of the album's twelve songs.

Dylan has mentioned that several of the songs (though it is unclear exactly which ones) were written for Archibald MacLeish's play *The Devil and Daniel Webster*. When the playwright balked on "Father of Night," Dylan withdrew from the project.

[S] "New Morning" (Bob Dylan)

Bob Dylan, *New Morning* (1970)
Michael Henry Martin, *Real & Funky* (1971)
Grease Band, *Amazing Grease* (1975)
Lisa Loeb/Elizabeth Mitchell, *Catch the Moon* (2003)

Al Kooper lent some great organ riffs to this shining affirmation of love, music, and the muse—the vibrant title cut of Dylan's *New Morning* album. Perhaps Dylan is singing about morning in the metaphorical sense—as a rebirth—celebrating his escape from the prison of celebrity and a return to the fellowship and

N

community he was enjoying in upstate New York at the time.

When Dylan begins singing "Can't you hear that rooster crowin'/Rabbit runnin' down across the road" it is charming and sublime—as if Walt Whitman suddenly found himself leading a light country band.

Dylan reduced the song to a shambles when he started performing a fairly melody-free and virtually rewritten "New Morning" upon hitting the road with the Never Ending Tour in 1991 and 1992, when he trotted it out as an "I'm turning over a new leaf" statement to open some sixty-plus shows.

s "New Pony" (Bob Dylan)
Bob Dylan, *Street Legal* (1978)

Using that time-tested formula of mixing the blues, the Bible, and sex, Dylan comes up with "New Pony," a brooding piece of twelve-bar double entendre that, with twenty-twenty hindsight, might seem to presage his gospel period as a last-gasp bawdy foray before getting straight with God. Dylan's demonic blues comes off as a fond adieu to sensual delights and was no doubt inspired by Arthur Crudup's "Black Pony Blues" and the even more famous "Pony Blues" recorded by Charley Patton and Son House. Dylan's composition bears a strong resemblance to House's, which itself was based on Patton's, and Patton's version is surely one of the greatest country blues performances on record.

Son House and Charley Patton exemplify the sin/salvation, party Saturday night/go to church Sunday morning yin/yang tension running through much of the blues. Convinced that they were playing the "Devil's music," each at one time or another gave up the blues to become a lay preacher—only to backslide and return to the blues and its associated unpreacherly late night activities. Son House,

in his later performances, was always careful to include at least one gospel number in his sets to "sanctify" the proceedings.

Dylan's "New Pony" (a filly conveniently named Lucifer) explores these ambiguous relationships, contrasting the deep blues of the song with the gospel chant of "How much longer?," begging salvation and portraying spiritual struggle in the lyrics. That Dylan found religion soon after recording the song makes the drama between the attractions of the flesh and the spirit tangibly real.

n *Newport Broadside*/Various Artists
Vanguard Recording Society LP VRS-9144/VSD-79144.
  Released 1964.

Recorded at the 1963 Newport Folk Festival in Rhode Island, *Newport Broadside* features Dylan teamed up with Pete Seeger on "Playboys and Playgirls" and Joan Baez on "With God on Our Side." Regarded as the rarest of the various discs spawned by the Newport concerts of the early 1960s, *Newport Broadside* also lives up to its name as a musical sandwich board for the folk protest movement, with a collection of then-hot topical songs always worth considering.

This uppity document of a fleeting era (also released under the title *Newport Folk Festival 1963: Newport Broadside-Newport Folk*) includes highlights from Tom Paxton ("Rambling Boy" and "The Willing Conscript"), Sam Hinton ("Talking Atomic Blues"), and Ewan MacColl ("Come All Ye Giant Drivers"), and offerings from the Freedom Singers, Phil Ochs, and Peter La Farge.

s "Night After Night" (Bob Dylan)
Various Artists (performed by Bob Dylan), *Hearts of Fire* (soundtrack) (1987)
Michel Montecrossa, *4th Time Around* (2001)

While the film *Hearts of Fire* contained only a snippet of this song about a man obsessed with a self-destructive woman, the soundtrack album was "graced" with the entire cut—which sounds as if it was penned during teatime at the studio commissary.

[S] "900 Miles" (Traditional/Woody Guthrie)

aka "I'm 900 Miles from Home," "I Was Young When I Left Home," "900 Miles from Home," "Nine Hundred Miles"
Fiddlin' John Carson, *Complete Recorded Works, Volume 2, 1924–25* (1998)
Woody Guthrie, *Greatest Songs of Woody Guthrie* (1972)
Bert Jansch, *It Don't Bother Me* (1965)
Cisco Houston, *Folkways Years 1944–1961* (1994)
Mike Seeger, *Third Annual Farewell Reunion* (1994)
Dion, *The Road I'm On: A Retrospective* (1997)

Along with every other folkie on Bleecker Street, Dylan was singing "900 Miles" in 1960 and 1961. He later reprised it with the Band at Big Pink, as evidenced by a horribly recorded fragment present on the miles of tape that eventually resulted in *The Basement Tapes* in 1967.

Sung to one of the most beautiful and haunting melodies in all American folk music, "900 Miles" is believed to have its origins among African-American railroad workers in the South. It may even be a slave song, with the title indicating the distance to freedom. It has long been sung by black and white workers and farmers, who, as the song is goes, "hate to hear that lonesome whistle blow."

N

[S] "1913 Massacre" (Woody Guthrie)

Woody Guthrie, *Woody Guthrie—Hard Travelin': The Asch Recordings, Volume 3* (1998)
Jack Elliott, *Essential Ramblin' Jack Elliott* (1970)
Arlo Guthrie, *Hobo's Lullaby* (1972)

"First came here . . . I spent a lot of time with Woody Guthrie that February . . . last February . . . This is one of Woody's songs . . . I sing a couple more . . . This is one . . . it's one from a group of two . . ."

With that, Dylan introduced Woody Guthrie's still-resonant topical song at his poorly attended Carnegie Chapter Hall gig in 1961. It's the only Dylan performance of the song to be captured on tape. More saliently, Dylan cribbed the tune for "1913 Massacre" for his own "Song to Woody."

The event that inspired the song is described in the liner notes, penned by Guy Logsdon and Jeff Place, to *Woody Guthrie: Hard Travelin'—The Asch Recordings, Volume 3*:

> With the growing popularity and demand for cheap electricity in the late nineteenth century, the dynamo became a major industrial machine and required large quantities of copper; thus, copper mining became commercially rewarding for mine owners. At that time, Michigan was a major producing state for "pure" copper, and the rank and file laborers were confronted with joining the ever-growing union movements. Most of the copper miners joined the Western Federation of Miners that was, for a short time, affiliated with the Industrial Workers of the World. Believing that the IWW was too political, the WFM withdrew to maintain its own membership. They struck the Michigan mines in 1913, seeking safer conditions.
>
> On Christmas Eve, 1913, in Calumet, Michigan, the miners held a Christmas party at the "Italian Hall." Company strike breakers barred the doors and yelled "fire." In the ensuing panic 73 children were smothered or trampled to death; some reports place the number as high as 89. This tragic example of anti-union violence has been ignored in most histories of the United States, but Woody has immortalized it in this ballad.

◘ "Ninety Miles an Hour (Down a Dead End Street)" (Hal Blair/Don Robertson)

Bob Dylan, *Down in the Groove* (1988)
Katy Moffatt, *Katy Moffatt* (1976)
Hank Snow, *Snow Country* (1992)
John Berry, *Saddle the Wind* (1994)
Ashley Hutchings, *Guv'nor, Volume 2* (1996)

Dylan sings this stately piece of country music, a harmonizer's special, with dignified care on *Down in the Groove*, thereby delivering one of the more tolerable and interesting tracks on the album—even if it does sound like a studio warm-up. Despite its courtly qualities and tone, the song speaks of emotional, physical, and spiritual emptiness, suggesting that we are all about to hit a proverbial brick wall at ninety miles per.

The song's primary composer was Donald Irwin Robertson (born December 5, 1922, Beijing, China). His father was the head of the department of medicine at the city's Union Medical college. Upon moving back to the U.S. in the late 1920s, the Robertsons eventually settled in Chicago. They summered in Michigan, where they befriended Carl Sandburg, at whose knee Don learned many folk and western ballads, receiving instruction in basic guitar chording along the way. Don also developed a keen interest in big-band Swing Era jazz, performing in the dance bands of the late 1930s while still a teen.

By the time Robertson moved to Los Angeles in 1945, he had eschewed following his father's footsteps into medicine in favor of following his bliss. In L.A. he played the nightclubs and, by day, earned his living making demo records of new songs for publishers and songwriters, which eventually led to a job as a session pianist with Capitol Records. His repertoire as a composer had until then focused primarily on jazz and classical symphonic, but soon his original material began to reflect his earlier association with Sandburg.

Robertson's own songs did not find much success until 1953, when a trio of compositions were recorded by Rosemary Clooney, Eddy Arnold, and Frankie Laine. Robertson's "I Really Don't Want to Know" became a major hit when released by Arnold and was eventually covered by others in more than fifty recorded versions; collectively these topped five million in units sold through 1970. That started Robertson on a roll: in the 1950s and 1960s, everybody from Elvis to Nat King Cole to Les Paul to Lorne Greene to Skeeter Davis had major hits with Robertson songs. But it was country music giant Hank Snow who put "Ninety Miles an Hour" on the map and who was probably Dylan's source as well.

Though Robertson was a prolific songwriter who appealed to a variety of performers, his main claim to fame was his association with Elvis Presley, for whom he penned nine songs, including "Love Me Tonight." And his skills as an instrumentalist were of equal importance in the creation of "country style" piano as popularized by Floyd Cramer.

◘ "Nobody 'Cept You" (Bob Dylan)

Bob Dylan, *The Bootleg Series, Volumes 1–3: Rare and Unreleased/'73* (1991)

A powerful declaration of love, "Nobody 'Cept You" made quite an impression on those concertgoers who caught Dylan's earliest 1974 gigs with the Band when the returning hero performed the song as part of his solo acoustic set. Recorded for but left off *Planet Waves* in favor of "Wedding Song," "Nobody 'Cept You," some argue, is the stronger composition. The outtake, eventually released on *The Bootleg Series*, opens cautiously before Robbie Robertson's signature guitar kicks it into groove.

N

ⓐ *Nobody's Child: Romanian Angel Appeal*/Various Artists
Warner Bros. Records CD 9 26280-2, CS 9 26280-4. Released 1990.

When Olivia Arias and Barbara Bach (the wives, respectively, of George Harrison and Ringo Starr) needed some talent for this benefit album to aid Romanian orphans, they didn't have to look all that far. Harrison and the other Traveling Wilburys, including Dylan, contributed the album's title track to the effort—"Nobody's Child," Cy Coben and Mel Foree's golden oldie. The title phrase itself appeared, coincidentally or not, many years before the release of *Nobody's Child* in Dylan's antilove song, "She Belongs to Me."

ⓢ "No Money Down" (Chuck Berry)
Chuck Berry, *Chess Box* (1988)
John Hammond, *Big City Blues* (1964)
Humble Pie, *Thunderbox* (1974)
Duane Allman, *Anthology, Volume 2* (1974)

One of the quirkiest entries in Dylan's performance career, Chuck Berry's "No Money Down" provided a tour-de-force encore for a couple of consecutive concerts in the fall of 1981 with Dylan playing, of all things, tenor saxophone while his wheelchair-bound friend Larry Kegan took the vocals. The song (about a guy buying his dream car, a Cadillac) was a Top 10 R&B hit for Berry in 1956 and, with its rat-a-tat streetwise patter, a worthy contender as a hip-hop stepping-stone.

ⓢ "No More Auction Block" (Traditional)
aka "Many Thousands Gone," "Many T'ousand Go," "No More Auction Block for Me"
Bob Dylan, *The Bootleg Series, Volumes 1–3: Rare and Unreleased, 1961–1991/'62* (1991)
Odetta, *Odetta at Carnegie Hall* (1960)

Various Artists (performed by Pete Seeger), *American Favorite Ballads, Volume 4: Tunes & Songs* (1963)
Bobby Hutcherson, *Head On* (1971)
Paul Robeson, *The Peace Arch Concerts/'52* (1998)
Ella Jenkins, *African-American Folk Rhythms* (1992)

One of the first emancipation songs to be printed in the United States, this spiritual was first published in the June 1867 issue of *The Atlantic Monthly*. It is older than that, however, as there is evidence of its having been sung originally by the slaves who were taken by General P. G. T. Beauregard of the Confederate States Army to build the fortifications at Hilton Head and Bay Point in South Carolina. When these slaves escaped, many joined the Union forces, and as they marched, they sang the thrilling lines of "No More Auction Block for Me."

Musicologists have traced the melody for "No More Auction Block" to the Ashanti tribe of West Africa. Alan Lomax, in his book *The Folk Songs of North America* (Garden City, New York: Doubleday, 1960), suggests that the words originated in Canada, where it was sung by the many blacks who had fled north of the border after Britain (of which Canada was still a colony) abolished slavery in 1833—more than thirty years ahead of the United States. The "pint of salt" and "peck of corn" mentioned in the song were slave rations.

Dylan may have learned the song from Odetta's *Carnegie Hall* LP, as he has often mentioned her influence on his nascent aesthetic. And in addition to providing him with another piece in his repertoire, "No More Auction Block" gave Dylan the inspiration for one of his greatest efforts. Pete Seeger first pointed out Dylan's adaptation of the melody of "Auction Block" for "Blowin' in the Wind," a debt Dylan himself freely acknowledged in a 1978 interview with music writer Marc Rowland, reprinted in the liner notes to *The Bootleg*

A slave auction in the South, 1861.

(Illustration: Theodore R. Davis/Harper's Weekly, July 18, 1861/Library of Congress)

Series, Voumes 1–3: "'Blowin' in the Wind' has always been a spiritual. I took it off a song called 'No More Auction Block'—that's a spiritual, and 'Blowin' in the Wind' sorta follows the same feeling."

Dylan's only known performance of "No More Auction Block" took place in the autumn of 1962 at the Gaslight Café in Greenwich Village ("a heat-pipe poundin' subterranean coffeehouse . . . buried beneath the middle of Mac-Dougal Street," as described in Dylan's liner note poem for the 1963 Peter, Paul & Mary LP *In the Wind*), appearing nearly three decades later on *The Bootleg Series, Volumes 1–3*. It came amid a set consisting primarily of cover songs—even though Dylan had been writing

bushels of original material at the time—and he inhabits the narrator's newly liberated being with convincing power and dignity.

"No More One More Time" (Troy Seals/Dave Kirby)
Eddy Raven, *Cookin' Cajun* (1996)

Dylan performed this line-in-the-sand classic by Troy Seals and Dave Kirby (some attribute the song's authorship to Cajun accordionist Joel Sonnier) at a trio of 1990 Never Ending Tour shows. Seals (born November 16, 1938, Big Hill, Kentucky) plays guitar and released a couple of solo albums in the 1970s, but he is best known as a songwriter, penning hits for the likes of

Randy Travis ("Don't Take It Away"), Conway Twitty and Loretta Lynn ("From Seven Till Ten"), Hank Williams Jr. ("Two Old Cats Like Us"), Jerry Lee Lewis ("Boogie Woogie Country Man"), and, most significantly, Elvis Presley ("Piece of My Life"). He has appeared on albums by Johnny Cash (*Essential Johnny Cash 1955–1983*), Crystal Gayle (*When I Dream*), and Merle Haggard (*That's the Way Love Goes*).

Ⓐ **No Reason to Cry**/Eric Clapton
RSO Records, LP RS1-3004. Released 1976.

"Sign Language," a Dylan/Clapton collaboration, appeared on this collection, which sometimes veers from Clapton's customary blues-based rock to pop-rock. Clapton was an admitted fan of the Band, and his duet with Rick Danko on Danko's "All Our Past Times" is a high point. Ron Wood, Robbie Robertson, Richard Manuel, Jesse Ed Davis, and Dylan are just some of the top-shelf talent appearing on the album, Clapton's own recorded version of the Rolling Thunder Revue.

Ⓢ **"North Country Blues"** (Bob Dylan)
Bob Dylan, *The Times They Are A-Changin'* (1964)
Joan Baez, *Any Day Now* (1968); *Vanguard Sessions: Baez Sings Dylan* (1998)
Bettina Jonic, *The Bitter Mirror* (1975)
Frank Tovey, *Tyranny and the Hired Hand* (1989)
Various Artists (performed by Richard Meyer), *The Times They Are A-Changin'* (1994)

Sung in the persona of a woman, "North Country Blues" tells the sorry story of a single mother of three in a ghost town after its exploitation was complete. It's as if Dylan's "Girl from the North Country" woke up one day on the other side of the tracks with cardboard windows protecting her shotgun shack from the winter winds. In temperament and concept,

"North Country Blues" can be viewed both as an updating of the traditional "Dink's Song" (which Dylan performed very briefly in the early and middle parts of his career) and as a nineteenth-century western-style autobiographical ballad in which he remembers the days when he witnessed poverty firsthand as he meekly collected unpaid debts from Hibbing's needy for his father's appliance store. And at ten stanzas, the song leads one to believe that Dylan invested some time and energy into conjuring this gritty vision of hard times.

On his recording of "North Country Blues," Dylan employed some bluesy vocal filigrees straight out of the Skip James grab bag of tricks and an actor's sense of presence to embellish the emotional impact of this forbidding song, which more than hints at anticapitalism. No such musical sensitivity was employed for his only concert performance of "North Country Blues," which came amid his wine-fueled and hampered appearance at the New York City "Friends of Chile" benefit concert organized by Phil Ochs in January 1974.

Ⓢ **"Not Alone Any More"** (Traveling Wilburys)
Traveling Wilburys, *Traveling Wilburys, Volume 1* (1988)

Filled with the unabashed gratitude of a man who has finally found true love, this song, a showcase for Roy Orbison on his one and only Traveling Wilburys album appearance, was written with no one in mind but him, working as effectively as anything in his vast catalogue.

Ⓢ **"Not Dark Yet"** (Bob Dylan)
Bob Dylan, *Time out of Mind* (1997)
Various Artists (performed by Bob Dylan), *Wonder Boys* (soundtrack) (2000); *Songs Inspired by* The Passion of the Christ (2004)
Michel Montecrossa, *4th Time Around* (2001)

Barb Jungr, *Every Grain of Sand: Barb Jungr Sings Bob Dylan* (2002)
Robyn Hitchcock, *Robyn Sings* (2002)
Various Artists (performed by Zimmermen), *May Your Song Always Be Sung: The Songs of Bob Dylan, Volume 3* (2003)

Dylan acknowledges his mortality with "Not Dark Yet," a clear-eyed vision full of weary resignation from a man pushing sixty staring squarely into the dark face of the abyss. Critic Christopher Ricks has read this elegiac and sobering self-appraisal as a modern recasting of English poet John Keats's "Ode to a Nightingale." It is as if Dylan is admitting that while he once ventured on epic journeys of the mind and soul and returned with visions that he smelted into song, he is now forever escaping on the run, or, as he sings here, "I can't even remember what it was I came here to get away from."

But where is he and whom is he singing to? Evidently the narrator's sense of despair is heightened by a "Dear John" letter he's recently received. He certainly comes off like a guy trying to coax one last drop of booze out of a bone-dry shot glass as he gives the barkeep yet another "woe is me" hard-luck story. That tale goes something like this: shadows have fallen, night is here, death is just around the corner, and all I have to show for it is another hangover and this lousy T-shirt that reads, "I Survived the Twentieth Century!"

Alex Ross eloquently discussed the song in the context of Dylan's latter-day work in his May 10, 1999, *New Yorker* article titled "The Wanderer," seeing "wicked glee" in this bleak composition. Ross also notes evidence of the artist's master hand, writing that "all the flourishes of his songwriting art come together: slow, stately chords, swinging like a pendulum between major and minor; creative tweakings of the past ('there's room enough in the heavens' becomes 'there's not even room enough to

be *anywhere*'), prickly aphorisms ('I can't even remember what it was I came here to get away from'); and glints of biblical revelation. . . . Like Skip James, the cracked genius among Delta-blues singers, Dylan gives a circular form a dire sense of direction."

Dylan performed "Not Dark Yet" as a relative Never Ending Tour rarity from its release through 2002.

"Not Fade Away" (Buddy Holly/Norman Petty)
Buddy Holly, *From the Original Master Tapes* (1985)
The Rolling Stones, *The Rolling Stones—England's Newest Hit Makers* (1964)
Phil Ochs, *Gunfight at Carnegie Hall* (1970)
The Grateful Dead, *Grateful Dead* (1971)
Stephen Stills, *Thoroughfare Gap* (1977)

Buddy Holly's infectious catalogue, short life, and tragic death remain the stuff of American myth. Mixing humility, grace, and passion, this bespectacled Texan, rock 'n' roll's nerdy antidote to Elvis Presley, was a maverick at heart, spinning new popular music forms in his one-of-a-kind synthesis of country with R&B.

"Not Fade Away" was a never a big hit in its day but was notable for its syncopated, Latin-flavored "shave-and-a-haircut-two-bits" clavé rhythm and clichéd imagery mixing cars and sexuality. It was released on producer Norman Petty's Coral label in 1957 as the B side to the Crickets' "Oh Boy." Over time and through covers by the Rolling Stones and the Grateful Dead (in whose hands it became a vortical psychedelic tribal stomp), "Not Fade Away" has acquired status as a bona fide classic.

Holly (born Charles Hardin Holly, September 7, 1936, Lubbock, Texas; died February 3, 1959, Clear Lake, Iowa) grew up listening to Jimmie Rodgers, the Carter Family, and the Grand Ole Opry. He was putting little country combos together as a teenager, but when Elvis emerged he traded in his acoustic guitar for a Fender Stratocaster. Still, even after opening for Presley and cutting D.O.A. rockabilly singles for small labels, he had yet to find firm musical footing.

A few key factors merged in Holly's quick rise. He was signed by Decca Records, which steered him to the Crickets, a budding rock 'n' roll trio that included guitarist Niki Sullivan, bassist Joe Mauldin, and drummer Jerry Allison. The turning point came when they drove to Clovis, New Mexico, in 1957 and recorded at the studio there of innovative producer Norman Petty.

Petty was not a fan of the new music, but he was a Merlin whose technical experiments, using close-miking, echo effects, and double-tracking, tenderized the Crickets' sound. The result emerging from the high desert studio was "That'll Be the Day," which became the hit song of summer 1957. The popularity of "Peggy Sue" and "Words of Love" soon followed as the Crickets began to bust out.

The year that would mark the Crickets' legacy was 1958, when the band registered the hits "Early in the Morning," "Rave On," "Maybe Baby," and "Oh Boy!" Buddy Holly was in the fast lane now, performing whistle-stop style with the Crickets or in bands picked up along the way. He married, moved to New York City, and was showcased on television's *American Bandstand* and *The Ed Sullivan Show*.

But as an in-demand wunderkind, Holly had the kind of hectic schedule on those cavalcade-of-stars, one-night-only package tours featuring several bands that forced the headliners to travel by chartered light aircraft. After a gig in Fargo, North Dakota, in 1959, Holly boarded such a plane with Ritchie Valens and the Big Bopper (J. P. Richardson), two other rising stars, for an overnight midwinter trip to the next engagement. That the plane never made it to its next appointed stop has long been embedded in the lore of rock 'n' roll.

Just three days before, on January 31, a young Bob Zimmerman had sat wide-eyed in the Duluth, Minnesota, Armory witnessing one of Holly's last gigs.

Waxing mystical, Dylan specifically mentioned his debt to Buddy Holly when accepting his 1998 Best Album Grammy award for *Time out of Mind*: "When I was sixteen or seventeen years old, I went to see Buddy Holly play at the Duluth National Guard Armory and I was three feet away from him . . . and he LOOKED at me. And I just have some sort of feeling that he was—I don't know how or why—but I know he was with us all the time we were making this record in some kinda way."

Dylan first performed "Not Fade Away" at a Grateful Dead show in Los Angeles in February 1989, sitting in with the band on the first set. Later, Dylan used "Not Fade Away" as the jaw-dropping opener that kicked off an April 1997 Never Ending Tour concert in Hartford, Connecticut. Even more surprisingly, he pulled it out with some regularity in the fall and winter of 1998–99, when it was used as a show-ending rave, complete with a hot mini-jam. The commitment to "Not Fade Away" may have been partly inspired by the large number of Deadheads at his concerts, now set adrift after Jerry Garcia's death in 1995 and following Dylan more closely in the wake of the Dead's demise. Augmenting "Rainy Day Women" as the final communal celebration of an evening with Dylan, "Not Fade Away" was much more than a nostalgia trip. Rather, it was sung with showstopping, barn-burning energy, achieving what every show closer should: leave the audience hungering for more. Dylan dusted it off for a nifty encore to some of his early third millennium shows, including his return to the Newport Folk Festival, which made one wonder if he wasn't singing about his own long career.

[A] *Not for Beginners*/Ron Wood

Import/SPV Records CD 7226. Released 2002.

Dylan shows up on "King of Kings," a track on a late-career offering by his old buddy Ron Wood. *Not for Beginners* also includes contributions from guitarist Scotty Moore and two of Wood's kids, son Jesse and daughter Leah.

[S] "Nothin' but You" (Steve Earle)

Steve Earle, *Early Tracks* (1987)

Dylan included a rollicking version of this Steve Earle hit—which gives a lyrical and musical nod to Buddy Holly's "Peggy Sue" and Chuck Berry's "Sweet Little Sixteen"—at a couple of 1989 shows during a tour in which Earle performed as an opening act.

Earle (born January 17, 1955, Fort Monroe, Virginia) is at the vanguard of the second generation of outlaw country musicians—one of those reformed hard-living guys who can suggest a life story, bemoan an injustice, and snap your heartstrings in a few dozen economical, evocative words. His gritty compositions, full of ornery drifters and hopeless situations, firmly place him in the Woody Guthrie school of hard knocks songwriters.

Drawn from life experience—his peripatetic childhood in Texas, his days as a young picaresque troubadour following in the footsteps of Townes Van Zandt, and a stormy life riddled with busted marriages, drug abuse, prison, personal redemption, and artistic reclamation—Earle's songs address the insecurity and restlessness of blue-collar America.

Earle's best albums include *Guitar Town* (1986), which plugged into country culture's CB-radio zeitgeist, *Copperhead Road* (1988), which explored characters existing on society's fringes, and *Train a Comin'* (1995), his successful comeback effort in which he continued to mine literary themes.

His ability to create novelistic characters in song did not, however, sustain his attempt to do so in short-story form: *Doghouse Roses* (Boston: Houghton Mifflin, 2001), his story collection, won praise for good effort but lousy reviews.

As turmoil in the Middle East and at home in the U.S. reached new peaks of pique in the early part of the twenty-first century, Earle cast himself as a strong antiwar proponent, as heard on his 2002 album *Jerusalem*, a chaotic vision of the United States and its place in the post-9/11 world. The collection was not without controversy, however; it included "John Walker's Blues," a song that sympathetically tells the tale of John Walker Lindh, the "American Taliban" arrested in Afghanistan and later convicted to life without parole.

Earle opened for Dylan's Never Ending Tour in the summer of 1989.

[S] "Nothing Was Delivered" (Bob Dylan)

Bob Dylan/The Band, *The Basement Tapes*/'67 (1975)
The Byrds, *Sweetheart of the Rodeo* (1968)
Buddy Emmons, *Steel Guitar* (1975)
The Original Marauders, *Now Your Mouth Cries Wolf* (1977)

A moody, serious composition that fits nicely into the themes of emptiness pervading much of *The Basement Tapes* material, "Nothing Was Delivered" features moaning chorus work from the Band and the cryptic lyrics du jour from Mr. D.

"Nothing Was Delivered" uses the monologue style that marks at least a couple of the more noteworthy selections from *The Basement Tapes* ("Clothes Line Saga" and the unreleased "Sign on the Cross"); the song highlights a lively middle section featuring Dylan in confessional stump-preacher mode trying to persuade a congregation to acknowledge but forgive a murky betrayal of some vague origin—Judas's, perhaps.

In discussions taking place from church pews to the local bar, others imagine a completely different setting for "Nothing Was Delivered." Still, in *Invisible Republic*, his 1997 book about *The Basement Tapes*, Greil Marcus wrote: "I've never heard more than one story in this number, a few honest customers holding a dealer who took their money and failed to come up with the goods. With its slow, deliberate tempo, Dylan's cool cowboy vocal, and the lift of the piano, it's also the best rewrite of Fats Domino's 'Blueberry Hill' anybody's ever heard."

"No Time to Think" (Bob Dylan)
Bob Dylan, *Street Legal* (1978)

In "No Time to Think," one of a couple of *Street Legal* songs never performed in concert, Dylan sings from a place of isolated superstardom. Maybe he was describing the turmoil roiling his life at the time, as he was in the midst of divorcing his first wife, Sara, when he penned the composition. He said of this period in the *Biograph* liner notes, "I almost didn't have a friend in the world. I was being thrown out of my house. I was under a lot of pressure."

With its relentless, mariachi-heavy arrangement, hypnotic waltz rhythm, and lengthy lyrics, "No Time to Think" may be easy for listeners to dismiss as an unfocused Dylan harangue. Those who do so, however, are missing a monumental plaint that, with its complicated musical and lyrical patterns, has been compared favorably with the internal rhyme and dark tone of Edgar Allan Poe's classic, "The Raven." And as a clue to Dylan's odyssey from a broken marriage to an acceptance of Christ as his savior, "No Time to Think" certainly depicts a man teetering over an abyss of some sort. Dylan's divided self can be seen in his disillusionment ("You can't find no salvation, you have no expectations/Any-

time, anyplace, anywhere") and a hint of coming change ("Starlight in the East, and you're finally released/You're stranded, but with nothing to share").

"Nowhere Man" (John Lennon/Paul McCartney)
The Beatles, *Rubber Soul* (1966)
L.A. Workshop, *Norwegian Woods, Volume 1* (1988)
Hot Rize, *Shades of the Past* (1989)
John Bayless, *Beatlesbaylessbach* (1993)
Ofra Harnoy, *Imagine* (1996)
Tiny Tim, *Live! At the Royal Albert Hall* (2000)

In his distinctive and personal song "Nowhere Man," John Lennon describes the boredom of sitting at home in his Tudor mansion trying to coax some inspiration out of thin air. "I'd spent five hours that morning trying to write a song that was meaningful and good," he told *Playboy* in September 1980, "and I finally gave up and lay down. Then 'Nowhere Man' came, words and music, the whole damn thing, as I lay down."

But Lennon also indicated that he was disappointed with the lyrics, thinking them trite.

The Beatles recorded "Nowhere Man" in October 1965 and did not change it during the recording process—a rare thing for the Fab Four. They included it as part of their live repertoire in 1965 and '66 and released it as a single in the United States in February 1966. Entering the Top 40 in March, "Nowhere Man" hit No. 3 and spent nine weeks on the charts. The Nowhere Man came to animated life in the Beatles' *Yellow Submarine* film in the cartoon personification of Dr. Hillaru Boob, Ph.D.

Dylan's only wistful, short, breezy performance of "Nowhere Man" took place in the early phase of the Never Ending Tour in Edmonton, Alberta. What inspired his choice on that night is anybody's guess, but perhaps it was the faraway locale of the gig, the weather, or something like that.

O

"Obviously Five Believers" (Bob Dylan)

aka "Obviously 5 Believers"
Bob Dylan, single (1966); *Blonde on Blonde* (1966)
Janglers, *Janglers Play Dylan* (1992)
Toni Price, *Hey* (1995)
Chester Bigfoot, *The Devil in Me* (1996)
Various Artists (performed by Sean Costello), *Blues on Blonde on Blonde* (2003)

A fine if forgettable combination of Dylan's surreal imagery and impure roadhouse blues punctuated by Robbie Robertson's molten guitar licks and Charlie McCoy's swamp harmonica runs, "Obviously Five Believers" features a confident Dylan spunkily delivering a cockeyed lyric that sounds as if it was written in some cosmic café on the outskirts of Nashville circa 2066, not 1966. Despite a cameo appearance by Dylan's stock carnival troupe (*see* "the fifteen jugglers"), which gives the song a flash of Fellini-like imagery, "Obviously Five Believers" is a basic love moan drawing more casually on typical lines and situations from the blues: the early morning setting, the black dog barking, the hard-working mother, sexual overture and tension, the flighty gal, etc.

Some bluesologists point to Memphis Minnie's 1941 recording of the risqué "Me and My Chauffeur Blues" (a song with a complicated history involving a 1933 singing contest between Minnie and Big Bill Broonzy) as Dylan's source for the melody and structure of "Obviously Five Believers." Bo Diddley's 1956 recording of "She's Fine, She's Mine" is also suggested as a possible spark for Dylan's arrangement.

Despite composing "Obviously Five Believers" fairly early on in his career, Dylan didn't perform the song in concert until the Never Ending Tours of 1995 through 1997, when he kept it faithful to the original and pulled it off with no small bit of verve.

"Odds and Ends" (Bob Dylan)

Bob Dylan/The Band, *The Basement Tapes*/'67 (1975)
Coulson, Dean, McGuinness, Flint, *Lo & Behold* (1972)
Weather Prophets, *Gigantic* (1989)

Seeming as though it was made up on the spot, this goofy bit of Lightning Hopkins-meets-Buddy Holly–flavored rockabilly gets *The Basement Tapes* off on just the right ramshackle, nonsensical, and welcoming foot. By using the song to open the set, it was as if Dylan and the Band were saying the songs themselves were made up of the little odds and ends of weird Americana that they copied and then twisted into grotesquely beautiful shapes. If there is a story here, it would seem to randomly involve amorous betrayal, comeuppance, and spilled juice. The arrangement allows Robbie Robertson to take a glistening little guitar stroll after each chorus. Incidentally, the published lyrics in *Lyrics: 1962–1985* seem to contain the first line of an alternate, unreleased version of the song. Also, Dylan may have been aware of two other songs titled "Odds and Ends": the 1957 Jimmy Reed single and the 1960 Warren Smith release. Finally, Richard Manuel—not Levon Helm—plays drums on the track.

"Oh Babe, It Ain't No Lie" (Elizabeth Cotten)

See also "Shake Sugaree"
Elizabeth Cotten, *Negro Folk Songs and Tunes* (1958); *Live!* (1984)
The Grateful Dead, *Reckoning* (1981)
Jerry Garcia Acoustic Band, *Almost Acoustic* (1989)
Lightnin' Wells, *Ragtime Millionaire* (1999)

The little story behind "Oh Babe, It Ain't No

Elizabeth Cotten, American folk original, ca. 1980s (cover of CD brochure for her 1984 album *Elizabeth Cotten—Live!).*
(Courtesy of Arhoolie Records—www.Arhoolie.com)

Lie" is as charming as the song itself. When Elizabeth "Libba" Cotten was still a young girl living in Chapel Hill, North Carolina, she was falsely accused of doing something wrong by a woman who lived across the street named Miss Mary, who watched after the Cotten kids when their mother went to work. Her mother believed Miss Mary's story and punished Libba. Crying in her bed over the injustice of it all, Libba first had a pretty little verse come to her, and then a pretty little tune. When she had the song done in her head, she began singing it on the porch, much to enjoyment of everyone who listened, including the same Miss Mary— who evidently never did find out that the song was about her.

Elizabeth Cotten (born Elizabeth Neavills, January 5, 1895, Chapel Hill, North Carolina; died June 29, 1987, Syracuse, New York) is best remembered for her dulcet, homey folk songs of rare sentiment spanning a mélange of East Coast country blues, gospel, ragtime, and old-time Appalachian mountain music.

Cotten taught herself how to play music by plucking the family's instruments and making up songs for decades before ever even considering a career at it. But you could say that she did make up for lost time: she performed into her nineties. Paradoxically, her most famous song, "Freight Train," came to life when she was but twelve and became both a beloved staple in the folk-song repertoire and a spark plug of the British skiffle music fad that gave rise to the Beatles.

Cotten's approach to the guitar was unique. Probably because she was left-handed and unable to purchase a guitar of her own, strung to suit her handedness, she began playing the standard right-hand instrument holding it upside down—that is, with the order of the strings inverted—and using her right hand on the fretboard and her left for strumming (Jimi Hendrix was sometimes known to play the guitar this way.) This approach helped Cotten develop a unique two-finger picking style that influenced the folk revival of the 1950s. According to the liner notes to *Elizabeth Cotten, Volume 3: When I'm Gone,* penned by Mike Seeger and Alice Gerrard, "Elizabeth Cotten plays in basically five styles, first being the ragtime or two-finger style for which she is best known. She plays the three bass strings with her first finger and the three treble melody strings with her thumb, picking one string at time, alternating between treble and bass (although in her church songs she often plays treble and bass simulation). Her unique sound quality comes in part from the reversal of thumb and finger roles."

When she married in 1910 at the age of fifteen, Cotten barely touched her guitar except for occasional displays in the church. After divorcing and moving to Washington, D.C., with her daughter, Lillie, and five grandchildren, she took a job at a local department store during the late 1940s. It was there that a chance encounter eventually changed the course of her life. One day during the Christmas rush, Cotten helped a lost girl find her mother. The girl turned out to be Peggy Seeger of the famous folksinging family. And, as in all good fairy tales, she was invited to work for the Seegers as a domestic.

Spending so much time in such a musical home made playing hard to resist. Cotten

slowly edged back into music making and, at the family's urging, began recording for Folkways Records. *Folksongs and Instrumentals with Guitar* was the first, sterling result, and its acclaim gained Cotten immediate and lasting entrée into the circuit of folk and blues festivals. And she lived long enough to win a Grammy in 1985 for her last album, *Elizabeth Cotten—Live!*

Dylan first performed "Oh Babe, It Ain't No Lie" in 1990 at the famous surprise New Haven, Connecticut, warm-up gig at a joint known as Toad's Place. He offered it again in 1996 and broke it out several times a year for a period thereafter, often placing it in the acoustic opening slot at some shows in the spring of 1999 and summer of 2001.

▣ *Oh Mercy*

Columbia Records LP OC-45281, CD CK-45281, CS OCT-45281; Sony Music Entertainment, Inc., SACD 90316. Recorded March–April 1989 in New Orleans. Released September 12, 1989. Produced by Daniel Lanois. Artwork by Trotsky. Photography by Ken Regan.

Bob Dylan—vocals, six- and twelve-string guitars, harmonica, piano, organ. Mason Ruffner, Brian Stoltz, Paul Synegal—guitars. Daniel Lanois—guitar, lap steel guitar, Dobro, omnichord. Rockin' Dopsie—accordion. John Hart—saxophone. Malcolm Burn—keyboards, tambourine. Tony Hall, Larry Jolivet—bass. Willie Green, Alton Rubin Jr.—drums. David Rubin Jr.—scrub board. Cyril Neville, Daryl Johnson—percussion.

"Political World," "Where Teardrops Fall," "Everything Is Broken," "Ring Them Bells," "Man in the Long Black Coat," "Most of the Time," "What Good Am I?," "Disease of Conceit," "What Was It You Wanted," "Shooting Star"

Signaling yet another phoenixlike rise from the artistic and commercial ashes, the stunning *Oh Mercy* demonstrated that Dylan, after more than twenty-five years, could still write songs of topical concern ("Political World"), sublime spir-

O

ituality ("Ring Them Bells"), cryptic romance ("Shooting Star"), unflinching self-examination ("What Good Am I?"), jaded stardom ("What Was It You Wanted"), social diagnosis ("Disease of Conceit"), and mysterious postmodern folk ("Man in the Long Black Coat") to match any of his best work of the 1960s and '70s. And that he performed all of these songs during the Never Ending Tour is at least a testament to his notions of their durability.

Dylan had been written off many times before. But here, as always, he pulled himself off the canvas and back to his feet for at least one more flurry. And although it clocked in at a short thirty-nine minutes, *Oh Mercy* came as quite a comfort to Dylan's audience members, many of whom had begun to entertain some serious doubts as to whether the old man still had it.

Yet despite the general excellence of the material and Daniel Lanois's sympathetic, atmospheric production, *Oh Mercy* did not immediately strike gold, though it hit No. 30 during its six-week chart stint. And it gained critical acclaim: *Oh Mercy* was ranked No. 44 on *Rolling Stone*'s "100 Best Albums of the 1980s" survey, and the magazine gave it four out of five stars in its November 1989 review.

Lanois was fresh off a gig producing the Neville Brothers' *Yellow Moon*, an album that included slightly rewritten, moving versions of a couple of Dylan songs, "Hollis Brown" and "With God on Our Side." Impressed, Dylan sought out Lanois and soon set off to New Orleans, where the album was recorded at the producer's home studio in a building near the city's beautiful Garden District. With Dylan removed from the hubbub of New York or Los Angeles, Lanois was able to get him to focus on his craft and to sing with his stage voice rather than the high-register model, which tended to sound on record like a drone.

For those who are curious, the album's cover features a photo of a colorful wall painting depicting a couple embracing on one side while a bespectacled man in a gray suit looks away; the work was created in New York City's Hell's Kitchen neighborhood by a local street artist and activist who called himself Trotsky.

"Oh, Sister" (Bob Dylan/Jacques Levy)
aka "Oh Sister"
Bob Dylan, single (1975); *Desire* (1976); *Hard Rain* (1976); *Bob Dylan at Budokan* (1979); *The Bootleg Series, Volume 5: Live 1975—The Rolling Thunder Revue* (2002)
Blues & Soda, *Happy Birthday Mr. Dylan* (1992)
Caitlin Wants Pudding, *The Times They Are A-Changin', Volume 2* (1994)
Insol, *Insol* (1998)
Jimmy LaFave, *Trail* (1999)
Charlie Major, *444* (2000)
2 of Us, *From Zimmermann to Genghis Khan* (2001)
Lynn Conover, *Belle of the Ball* (2001)
Todd Rubenstein, *The String Quartet Tribute to Bob Dylan* (2003)

Whether it's Emmylou Harris (on *Desire*), Joan Baez (on the Rolling Thunder Revue), or his backup singers (on *Bob Dylan at Budokan*) providing the harmonies, "Oh, Sister" is an ambiguous hymn of love's fragility that can be interpreted as either the straightforward declaration to a sibling that its title implies (despite the fact that Dylan doesn't have a blood sister) or as a testament to a female soul mate. On a political level, perhaps Dylan was making a conciliatory overture, however off the mark, to the women's liberation movement, which was peaking at time. Lines like "And is our purpose not the same on this earth,/to love and follow his direction?" and "Our Father would not like the way that you act" would seem to suggest that his feminist studies were lacking and point instead to his religious conversion in the coming years. If it is a romantic overture, then never before had Dylan used God to court a woman. Whatever his intentions, it is said that Baez believes the song to be about her.

Dylan performed "Oh, Sister" on both phases of the Rolling Thunder Revue in 1975 and 1976. On the 1978 big-band tour, he used syncopation and tribal moaning (provided by his backup singers) to transform it from its original dirgelike arrangement into a voodoo chant full of pensive, dire warning.

▣ "Old MacDonald Had a Farm" (Traditional)
aka "Old McDonald Had a Farm," "Ol' MacDonald"
Lester Flatt and Earl Scruggs, *Flatt and Scruggs at Carnegie Hall* (1962)
Ella Fitzgerald, *Ella in Hamburg* (1965)
Rufus Thomas, *Funky Chicken* (1968)
Ronald McDonald, *Silly Sing-Along* (1996)
Barney, *Barney's Big Surprise* (1997)
Spike Jones, *People Are Funnier Than Anybody* (1998)

In the heart of the heartland (Dallas and Oklahoma City), Dylan kicked off a couple of September 1990 shows with an instrumental version of this most American of children's favorites, which, ironically, has its roots overseas.

The lyrics that Dylan did not sing are based on words that might have been penned as early as 1706 by the English humorist Thomas D'Urfey (1653–1723) for his comic play *Wonders in the Sun*. The American music dates from perhaps the 1850s; it appears to have been published originally with the title "Litoria! Litoria!" The union of words and music were first known as "The Gobble Family" and were later titled "Ohio" when published in 1917. Also, the owner of the farm in the original lyrics was named MacDougal.

▣ "Old Man" (Neil Young)
Neil Young, *Harvest* (1972)
Tim Rose, *Musician* (1975)
N'dea Davenport, *N'dea Davenport* (1998)
Captain Howdy, *Money Feeds My Music Machine* (1998)
Space Cowboys, *Space Cowboys* (2000)

As Dylan rolled down the Pacific Coast Highway with his Never Ending Tour highwaymen in early October 2002, it seemed he pulled a new kick out of his bag every night, and his unveiling of a hard-edged arrangement of Neil Young's meditation on aging wasn't even one of the more surprising of these offerings.

Before the release of *Harvest*, Young had established himself as a rock guitarist to be reckoned with, having punched the clock with both the Buffalo Springfield and Crosby, Stills, Nash & Young. But *Harvest* was a turn toward a rural persona, perhaps evidenced best on that album with "Old Man."

Young was never shy about discussing the song's inspiration: an aging ranch hand and caretaker of a northern California spread he bought in the early 1970s. "Old Man" poignantly captures the hopes, desires, and fears of every new generation standing on its own two feet and looking collectively to the future.

▣ "Old Rock 'n' Roller" (Charlie Daniels/Jack Gavin/Charlie Hayward/Taz DiGregorio)
Charlie Daniels Band, *Simple Man* (1989)
Various Artists (performed by John Wesley Harding), *Live at the Iron Horse* (1997)

Dylan performed this paean to one-hit wonders the planet over but once—at a Never Ending Tour show in Hamburg, Germany, at which he introduced it as a tongue-in-cheek autobiographical song. Portraying a has-been who touts hits of yesteryear as he plies his trade in a smoky, end-of-the-line bar with yet another edition of his tired revue, "Old Rock 'n' Roller" was written by Charlie Daniels and members of his band for their *Simple Man* album, released in 1989. Daniels, in his days as a Nashville session man, played guitar and bass on Dylan's *Nashville Skyline, Self Portrait, New Morning,* and *Dylan* albums. Later, as a ubiquitous Nashville presence, he had a hand in albums by just about the gamut of traditional country and popular music artists, including Ramblin' Jack Elliott, Lester Flatt and Earl Scruggs, the Marshall Tucker Band, Leonard Cohen, Lynyrd Skynyrd, Molly Hatchett, the Allman Brothers, Emmylou Harris, Papa John Creach, Al Kooper, George Jones, Carl Perkins, Ringo Starr, Billy Joe Shaver, Ernest Tubb, Hank Williams Jr., and Elvin Bishop.

Charlie Daniels (born October 28, 1937, Wilmington, North Carolina) is the son of a lumberjack who raised his boy with a love for bluegrass music. Daniels taught himself how to play guitar, mandolin, and fiddle as a teenager on borrowed instruments, modifying his playing when he lost the tip of his ring finger in an accident in 1955. With the Misty Mountain Boys, the first band he organized, Daniels cut the instrumental "Jaguar," a 1959 single.

Renaming themselves the Jaguars, the band wandered the South's honky-tonk netherworld as Daniels mastered the region's music. With his supple chops honed by years on the road, he settled in as a solid Nashville session man and occasional songwriter, scoring some national notice with "It Hurts Me," a tender ballad he wrote in 1964 and Elvis Presley recorded as a B-side single. Later, as a member of the band that backed Dylan on television's *Johnny Cash Show* in 1969, he more than secured a place for himself as the answer to some kind of answer in a Dylan trivia contest.

It was a year later that Daniels took the first step toward establishing a more substantial legacy when he formed the Charlie Daniels Band, a remarkable musical aggregate that continues to leaves its mark. No doubt his widest exposure came in 1979 when he reworked Stephen Vincent Benét's 1920s poem "The Mountain Whippoorwill" into "The Devil Went Down to Georgia," a story song in which the Devil and a Young Turk fiddler lock horns in a musical duel to claim the prize of a gold fiddle or the loss of the young-un's soul. The recording, which includes seven Daniels fiddle overdubs, reached No. 3 on the charts and led to the band's appearance in the 1980 John Travolta movie *Urban Cowboy*, in which the song was featured. Daniels and band stayed in the public eye over the next few years, most notably with their 1980 recording of the song "In America," written as a patriotic response to the Iran hostage crisis. But he exhibited a more personal, folksy side with the publication of *The Devil Went Down to Georgia* (Atlanta: Peachtree Publications, 1985), a collection of tall tales populated with types of creepy characters and situations found in the hit song.

No amount of record sales, however, could ever turn Charlie Daniels into a marquee attraction or heartthrob even in his prime. At 6 foot 4 inches tall, his craggy face hidden under a cowboy hat, he has always been more content to strut his brand of Southern boogie and play the role of the unreconstructed redneck. Speak politely if he sidles up to you at a saloon.

[S] "Ommie Wise" (Traditional)

aka "Deep Water," "Little Omie," "Little Omie Wise," "Oma Wise," "The Oxford Girl," "Naomi Wise," "Poor Naomi Wise," "Poor Oma Wise"

Various Artists (performed by G. B. Grayson), *Anthology of American Folk Music*/'27 (1952/1997)

Clarence Ashley, *Old Time Music at Clarence Ashley's, Volume 2* (1963)

Doc Watson, *Essential Doc Watson* (1986)
Dock Boggs, *His Folkways Recordings* (1998)
The Hammons Family, *Traditions of a West Virginia Family & Friends* (1998)

Some scholars trace the earliest antecedents of the classic murder ballad "Ommie Wise" back to England, where it was sometimes known as "The Oxford Girl." But it can also be found under many other titles and with numerous other British towns in its name. The well-known American folk song, however, apparently commemorates an actual early nineteenth-century incident: the 1808 murder of Naomi Wise by Jonathan Lewis in Randolph County, North Carolina. Wise, a cook and field hand for a local family, fell in love with Lewis—by all accounts a low-life wastrel. By the time she informed her lover that she was pregnant, he had become involved with Hattie Elliott, a lady of station and wealth who was, incidentally, the sister of Lewis's employer. With Naomi's "situation" threatening to put a crimp in his plans, Lewis lured Naomi to nearby Deep River and drowned her. Though Lewis was arrested and charged with the crime, he managed to escape from the county's ramshackle jail with the help of, perhaps not so coincidentally, Hattie Elliott's brother. When Lewis was captured and brought to trial years later, so many witnesses had died or left the county that no substantial case could be made against him and he was acquitted. Lewis supposedly confessed to the murder on his deathbed. Thus was the odd tale of Naomi Wise's murder revived and spread throughout the South, where it soon became entrenched in the region's folklore.

Though only a couple of early recordings of Dylan's rendering of "Ommie Wise" have survived, it is a good bet that he was performing the song at least semiregularly, as the recordings are from several months apart in 1961.

◱ **"On a Night Like This"** (Bob Dylan)
Bob Dylan, single (1974); *Planet Waves* (1974); *Biograph/'74* (1985)
Buckwheat Zydeco, *On a Night Like This* (1987)
Janglers, *Janglers Play Dylan* (1992)
Richard LeBouef & Two Step, *Again for the First Time* (1997)
Bob Dylan/Various Artists (performed by Los Lobos), *Masked and Anonymous* (2003)

First released as a single—which rose to No. 44 on the *Billboard* charts—the sensual "On a Night Like This" was the *Planet Waves* groove to herald both the tone of that warm-sounding LP and Dylan's imminent tour with the Band. The twangy, loose musicianship lends a rustic feel to the tune, while Dylan propels the reel with some spirited backroom harmonica work and Garth Hudson's accordion licks push things along.

In the *Biograph* liner notes, Dylan claimed to be working against type when he composed "On a Night Like This," saying, "You know, I think this [song] comes off as sort of like a drunk man who's temporarily sober. This is not my type of song. I think I just did it to do it."

Maybe so, but you can practically touch the frost on the windows and smell the wood-burning stove on this song fit for a North Country square dance.

◱ **"On the Road Again"** (Bob Dylan)
Bob Dylan, single (1965); *Bringing It All Back Home* (1965)
Deverons, single (1965)
Missing Links, single (1967)
Michel Montecrossa, *Eternal Circle* (1999)

An ironic yarn describing with urban slickness the horrors of his girlfriend's dysfunctional family, "On the Road Again" exemplifies the humorous side of Dylan's emerging surrealist streak. With its title referencing Jack Kerouac's famous Beat Generation–defining pica-

O

resque novel and the equally picaresque blues shuffle of the same name recorded by the Memphis Jug Band in 1928 (not be confused with the Willie Nelson tune written some years later), Dylan's oblique song is a taste of things to come. It depicts the grotesque in a series of then and still off-the-wall images delivered as if they were just elements of another quiet day at the Cirque Dalí: Daddy in a Napoleon mask, a pet monkey, the milkman in a derby, contentious mailmen and butlers, frogs inside socks, etc.

"On the Road Again" is set to a bright, simple blues-rock structure with a steam-shovel beat, against which Dylan gets to show off some flashy and effective harmonica. As with much early rock, the track is untidy as its thrusting beat and opposing riffs override one another in holy cacophony.

[S] "One Irish Rover" (Van Morrison)

Van Morrison, *No Guru, No Method, No Teacher* (1986)

Van the Man's heart-on-the-sleeve ballad of faded grandeur (it can be heard as a prayer to God or a song to a woman trapped in her ivory tower) had been released just a few years before Dylan started performing it as a brooding, funereal torch song with a fair degree of regularity in 1989, when he displayed it at fourteen Never Ending Tour shows. Thereafter, "One Irish Rover" was brought out of the shed only very intermittently, sometimes with Van himself, in 1991 and 1993. Dylan's first performance of the song occurred just a few days after he made a video with Morrison in Greece, so perhaps he learned the song then.

[S] "One More Cup of Coffee (Valley Below)" (Bob Dylan)

Bob Dylan, *Desire* (1976); *Masterpieces* (1978); *Bob Dylan at Budokan* (1979); *The Bootleg Series, Volume 5: Live 1975—The Rolling Thunder Revue* (2002)
Bob Dylan/Various Artists (performed by Sertab), *Masked and Anonymous* (2003)
Nutz, *Hard Nutz* (1976)
Various Artists (performed by Big Fish Ensemble), *The Times They Are A-Changin', Volume 2* (1994)
Two Approaching Riders, *One More Cup of Coffee* (1997)
Carl Edwards, *Coffeehouse Cowboy* (1998)
Gerard Quintana and Jordi Batiste, *Els Miralls de Dylan* (1998)
Various Artists (performed by N'dea Davenport), *Another Day in Paradise* (soundtrack) (1999)
Druha Trava, *Czechmate* (1999)
The White Stripes, *The White Stripes* (1999)
Andy Hill, *It Takes a Lot to Laugh* (2000)
Rolling Thunder, *The Never Ending Rehearsal* (2000)
Robert Plant, *Dreamland* (2002)
Chris Duarte, *Romp* (2003)
Big Runga with the Christchurch Symphony, *Live in Concert* (2003)
Various Artists, *John Wesley Harding, John Brown and Some Wicked Messengers Play Bob Dylan* (2004)

Evoking the Old West and all its dusty boots, rancid whiskey, stale cigar smoke, cheap life, and easy death, "One More Cup of Coffee" is a Spanish-tinged narrative ballad depicting a melodrama in miniature that sounds like a *Pat Garrett and Billy the Kid* track—yet works as an integral part of *Desire*'s song cycle. The *Desire* recording features Dylan's harmonizing with Emmylou Harris and adds a texture of Orientalism to this most exotic song. Throughout, the menace of a looming journey to the "valley below" lingers over the proceedings as if to suggest the narrator's time is running short, so he best have his say about his woman's peasant father before he skedaddles.

Reportedly inspired by an encounter with a gypsy king Dylan met while traveling in France in the spring of 1974, "One More Cup of

Happy Romanies,
ca. 1902.

(Photo: J. Ellsworth
Gross/Library of Congress)

Coffee" was first performed during the Rolling Thunder Revue in 1975 and 1976, when it was shaped by Scarlet Rivera's signature violin sound. Dylan dramatically transformed it in 1978 with an endearingly campy, herky-jerky arrangement that included a sensual conga riff, a sax solo by Steve Douglas, and some fine vocals. Dylan laid off the song until the first Never Ending Tour in 1988, but even so it has seen little exposure since then and has become one of the extreme rarities throughout the Never Ending Tours—the only other *Desire* song save "Joey" to stand the test of time as a concert choice.

Dylan spoke of "One More Cup of Coffee" and the gypsy story in his 1991 interview with Paul Zollo in the latter's book *Songwriters on Songwriting, Expanded Fourth Edition* (New York: Da Capo Press, 1997): "Was that for a coffee commercial? No . . . it's a gypsy song. That

song was written during a gypsy festival in the south of France one summer. Somebody took me there to the gypsy high holy days which coincide with my own particular birthday. So somebody took me to a birthday party there once, and hanging out there for a week probably influenced the writing of that song. . . . But the 'valley below' probably came from someplace else. My feeling about the song was that the verses came from someplace else. It wasn't about anything, so this 'valley below' thing became the fixture to hang it on. But 'valley below' could mean anything."

As reported in Clinton Heylin's *Bob Dylan: Behind the Shades—A Biography* (New York: Summit Books, 1991), Dylan recounted in 1977 that he "went to see the king of the gypsies in southern France. This guy had twelve wives and a hundred children. He was in the antique business and had a junkyard, but he'd had a heart attack before I'd come to see him. All his wives and children had left. . . . After he dies they'll all come back. They smell death and they leave."

[S] "One More Night" (Bob Dylan)

Bob Dylan, *Nashville Skyline* (1969)
Ronnie Hawkins, *Ronnie Hawkins* (1970)
New Deal String Band, *Blue Grass* (1970)
Lester Flatt and Earl Scruggs, *Final Fling* (1970); *1964–1969, Plus* (1996)
Tony Rice, *Church Street Blues* (1983)
The Rarely Herd, *Coming of Age* (1999)
2 of Us, *From Zimmermann to Genghis Khan* (2001)
Second Floor, *Plays Dylan* (2001)
Big Brass Bed, *A Few Dylan Songs* (2003)

Lost love has never been an unfamiliar theme for composers (what would they do without it?), and Dylan has been no exception. In addition to loss, "One More Night" hints at the other old staple of romance and song stuff: infidelity. The *Nashville Skyline* release of this song, an overlooked morning-afterthought, featured Dylan in perhaps his jauntiest Hank Williams mode, cribbing lines from such favorites as Elvis Presley's recording of "Blue Moon of Kentucky" and the cowboy traditional "Lonesome Prairie," and also included some nifty Dobro work by the great Norman Blake. As Dylan sings lines like "I'm as lonesome as can be," hiding his hurt under the "dark and roiling sky," there is a real sense that he knows he can't live up to his lover's expectations—not unlike the sentiments he was expressing much earlier in his career in songs like "It Ain't Me, Babe." Here, at least, he acknowledges that he has lost a friend as well as a lover—quite an admission from a guy whose work has sometimes come perilously close to being labeled chauvinistic.

Dylan's live performances of the charming "One More Night" occurred but twice, both times memorably, during the Never Ending Tour at a summer 1990 show in Toronto, where he was joined by Ronnie Hawkins, and the fall 1995 gig in Sunrise, Florida, when he was joined by the sensational bluegrass fiddler Alison Krauss.

[S] "One More Weekend" (Bob Dylan)

Bob Dylan, *New Morning* (1970)

A stomping, "Leopard-Skin Pill-box Hat"–style vamp of unfulfilled promise with a taste of the good old alienated *Blonde on Blonde* Dylan, the bluesy and ribald "One More Weekend" was the only hint on the otherwise bucolic *New Morning* collection that family life up in the Woodstock sticks was giving Dylan a bona fide case of cabin fever. Lyrics like "We'll go some place unknown/Leave all the children home/Honey why not go alone/Just you and me" would seem to indicate that he longed for the rock 'n' roll days of yore.

[S] "One of Us Must Know (Sooner or Later)" (Bob Dylan)

Bob Dylan, single (1966); *Blonde on Blonde* (1966)
The Boo Radleys, *Outlaw Blues* (1992)
Zimmermen, *After the Ambulances Go* (1998)
Michel Montecrossa, *Jet Pilot* (2000)
Various Artists (performed by Clarence Bucaro), *Blues on Blonde on Blonde* (2003)

That thin, wild, mercury sound of *Blonde on Blonde* is probably captured no more perfectly than on this majestic, piano-and-organ-propelled song about coming to terms with a relationship's crash landing. The first song recorded for *Blonde on Blonde* (in January of 1966 in New York, not Nashville like the rest of the album), "One of Us Must Know" flies out of the hi-fi speakers like an audio snapshot of a one-sided conversation between a man and woman—the man complaining of the difficulties of intimacy. Released as a single before the release of *Blonde on Blonde*, "One of Us Must Know" never made an impact on the charts, though its minor splash on the radio in the spring of 1966 gave a taste of things to come.

An alienated update of "Boots of Spanish Leather," "One of Us Must Know" closed out side one of the album with urgency—as if the lovers were trying to get their words in before a looming thunderstorm blows them away down the lonely city streets. "She's Your Lover Now," a slightly earlier Dylan work in progress, appears to have been the musical and thematic basis (or at least a catalyst) of the more fully realized "One of Us Must Know," and indeed, the line "you were just there, that's all" can be heard in both songs. Further, "One of Us Must Know" is sometimes linked to "Can You Please Crawl Out Your Window," another acidic harangue flowing from Dylan's lips. But whereas "Window" can be viewed as a skewed invitation to elope, "One of Us Must Know" is surely an autopsy of a romance stuck with a fork, with the narrator now in the postmortem forensic stage of determining exactly how, when, why, and/or where things turned permanently fatal.

With his defensive attitude, it isn't difficult to determine that the narrator in "One of Us Must Know" has no one to blame but himself. Anybody who starts his argument with "I didn't mean to treat you so bad" implies that he must have been doing at least a little bad treating and knows it. And anybody who continues his argument by claiming not to comprehend that he didn't know she'd take his behavior "so personal" obviously has little knowledge (or experience) in the give-and-take involved in being a twosome. Finishing with the hand-washing, Pilate-like excuse that "You just happened to be there, that's all" suggests that this destructive personality has no intention or ability of limiting his continued abuse.

Dylan has not often performed "One of Us Must Know" on the concert stage. It showed up at one show in Wichita, Kansas, during the second phase of the Rolling Thunder Revue in 1976, but then appeared regularly two years later when Dylan retooled it for his 1978 big-band World Tour. After rehearsing but not performing "One of Us Must Know" in the early 1990s, Dylan dusted off the song for a couple of polished and impressive Never Ending Tour displays in the summer of 1997.

🅂 **"One Too Many Mornings"** (Bob Dylan)
Bob Dylan, *The Times They Are A-Changin'* (1964); *Eat the Document/'66* (film) (1971); (performed with Johnny Cash) *The Other Side of Nashville* (1969) (film); *Hard Rain* (1976); *Hard Rain* (film) (1976); *Renaldo & Clara* (film) (1978); *The Bootleg Series, Volume 4: Bob Dylan Live 1966—The "Royal Albert Hall" Concert* (1998)
Linda Mason, *How Many Seas Must a White Dove Sail?* (1964)
Noel Harrison, *Noel Harrison* (1965)
Julie Felix, single (1966)
Joan Baez, *Any Day Now* (1968); *Baez Sings Dylan* (1998)
Burl Ives, *Times They Are A-Changin'* (1968)
Bobby Sherman, *Bobby Sherman* (1969)
Kingston Trio, *Once Upon a Time* (1969)
Jamie Brockett, *Remember the Wind & the Rain* (1969)
Lester Flatt and Earl Scruggs, *Final Fling* (1970); *1964–1969, Plus* (1996)
Turley Richards, *Turley Richards* (1970)
The Association, *Association Live* (1970)
Ian Anderson, *A Vulture Is Not a Bird You Can . . .* (1972)
Didier, *Hommage à Bob Dylan* (1974)
Jerry Jeff Walker, *A Man Must Carry On* (1977)
Johnny Cash, *Johnny & June* (1978); *Heroes* (1986); *Man in Black: 1963–1969* (1996)
Doug Sahm, *Together After Five* (1980)
Beau Brummels, *Best of the Beau Brummels: Golden Archives* (1987)
The Dillards, *Let It Fly* (1991)

Radio Flyer, *Old Strings New Strings* (1991)
Peter Keane, *Goodnight Blues* (1992)
Dion, *Dream on Fire* (1992)
Rory Erikson, *1966–1967 Unreleased Masters Collection* (1994)
Novas, *Sump'n Else Tapes* (1996)
Jimmy LaFave, *Trail* (1999)
Various Artists (performed by the Band), *Tangled Up in Blues: The Songs of Bob Dylan* (1999)
Steve Howe, *Portraits of Bob Dylan* (1999)
Sir Douglas Quintet, *Prime of Sir Douglas Quintet* (1999)
Rich Lerner & the Groove, *Cover Down* (2000)
Andy Hill, *It Takes a Lot to Laugh* (2000)
Alice Stuart, *Crazy with the Blues* (2000)
Second Floor, *Plays Dylan* (2001)
Various Artists (performed by Jamie Ness), *Duluth Does Dylan* (2001)
Robyn Hitchcock, *Robyn Sings* (2002)
Various Artists (performed by La Gran Esperanza Blanca), *May Your Song Always Be Sung: The Songs of Bob Dylan, Volume 3* (2003)

Deftly summing up a faded romance in a wistful, three-verse smoke signal in song to a departed lover who isn't coming back, the ruminative "One Too Many Mornings" captures that pureness of a lonely dusk—an example of deeply personal feelings converted into accessible, plainspoken poetry.

Along with "Boots of Spanish Leather," another heartbreaking ballad of love gone bad, "One Too Many Mornings" was one of two songs on *The Times They Are A-Changin'* linked to Dylan's breakup with Suze Rotolo, his girlfriend during his early years in New York City. By the time Dylan wrote the song, Suze had left the West Fourth Street apartment they shared and moved in with her sister Carla across town, to a neighborhood on the Lower East Side of Manhattan that today is known as the East Village. In the song, he describes a dreary Manhattan dusk as he wanders back home from his woman's flat, reflecting on what was but is never

to be again. Barking dogs pierce the moment and create a rural feeling that belies the song's urban setting. His heart might be breaking and his relationship splintered beyond repair, yet he seems to take it in stride as he replays the past and declares in the song, "You're right from your side,/I'm right from mine."

The silence that creeps across the city on little cat's feet is betrayed and crushed by "the sounds inside my mind" as he keeps coming back to the taunting refrain: "And I'm one too many mornings/And a thousand miles behind."

Here Dylan echoes the blues tradition of songs like Robert Johnson's "Crossroad Blues," placing his narrator at a pivotal life moment: a lover at the crossroads of a relationship and the precipice of departure. And if it's merely the "crossroads of my doorstep" on the Lower East Side and not some dusty outback of Delta blues legend, the mythic proportions of the moment are barely diminished. Despite his pain, the singer is still able to peek back over his shoulder and glimpse the room they shared, the street, "the sidewalk and the sign," taking a final mental snapshot before fading away.

Summing up his reasons for splitting, the singer casually chalks it up to the "restless hungry feeling" that sprang from their final, self-canceling blowup: "When everything I'm a-sayin'/You can say it just as good./You're right from your side,/I'm right from mine." His pluralization of the subject in the refrain ("We're both just one too many mornings/An' a thousand miles behind") not only makes him appear eager to spread the blame but anticipates a similar tack taken a decade later in "Idiot Wind," a song the narrator finishes by singing "We're idiots, babe."

"One Too Many Mornings" appears to be one of Dylan's personal concert favorites, though at first glance it seems an unlikely candidate for a song that has seen so many transformations— all of them good—in his catalogue. He worked up the stately, harmonically modified electrified arrangement with the Hawks (with bassist Rick Danko harmonizing on the refrain) in a version that barely conceals an ocean of tightly wound rage, as heard on *Volume 4: Bob Dylan Live 1966—The "Royal Albert Hall" Concert*. In this rendition it's as if he was telling all his folk-music fans to fuck off, performance-art style. Since revising the song—and rewriting its coda—as a juiced-up torch ballad with the Rolling Thunder Revue a decade later (as heard on *Hard Rain*), Dylan has rarely left it off of any tour's song list. It has endured as a solid acoustic selection up to the present day.

[S] "Only a Hobo" (Bob Dylan)

Bob Dylan (as "Blind Boy Grunt"), *Broadside Ballads, Volume 1* (1963); *The Bootleg Series, Volumes 1–3: Rare and Unreleased, 1961–1991*/'63 (1991)
Various Artists (performed by Bob Dylan), *The World of Folk Music: Starring Oscar Brand* (1963)
Hamilton Camp, *Paths of Victory* (1964)
Rod Stewart, *Gasoline Alley* (1970); *Mercury Anthology* (1992); *Vintage* (1993); *Handbags and Gladrags* (1996)
Augie Meyers, *Augie's Western Head Music Co.* (1973)
Jonathan Edwards (with the Seldom Scene), *Blue Ridge* (1985)
Lucky Seven, *Lucky Seven* (1986)
Hazel Dickens, *It's Hard to Tell the Singer from the Song* (1987)
Heron, *The Best of Heron* (1989)
Various Artists (performed by Rod Stewart), *I Shall Be Unreleased: The Songs of Bob Dylan* (1991)
The Johnson Mountain Boys, *Blue Diamond* (1993)
Phil Carmen, *Bob Dylan's Dream* (1996)
Carl Edwards, *Coffeehouse Cowboy* (1998)

Dylan's early fascination with the down-and-out outsider continued with "Only a Hobo," a more accomplished recasting of "Man on the Street." That earlier account of an anonymous derelict's destitution and death conveys a proud melancholy similar to that expressed in the sparse tale told in "Only a Hobo"; each song's tone is perfectly suited to convey the subtle point of the tragedy present in the passing of even the least of society.

Broadside magazine first published "Only a Hobo" in March 1963, a month after Dylan recorded it in the magazine's offices. The version was included on *Broadside Ballads, Volume 1* later that year under Dylan's most famous nom de guerre, "Blind Boy Grunt"—a consequence of his being under contract with Columbia Records at the time.

Dylan recorded the song for Witmark, *Broadside*, and Columbia (it was a *Times They Are A-Changin'* outtake), but the closest thing we have to an actual live performance of "Only a Hobo" comes from an informal April 1963 home tape. Additionally, a version of the song performed on Oscar Brand's New York City radio show saw exceptionally limited exposure through a series of extremely rare fifteen-minute releases distributed by the U.S. Department of Health, Education and Welfare in 1963.

Rootsologists point to two different songs from the past that Dylan may well have plundered in constructing his composition's melodic and lyric format: Aunt Molly Jackson's "Poor Miner's Farewell" (a folk reprisal of older songs dealing with dead sailors, dead cowboys, and the like) and Woody Guthrie's "The Great Divide" (which Dylan performed at least once in 1961).

A final note: Rod Stewart's excellent rendition of "Only a Hobo" is almost enough to make one forget "If Ya Think I'm Sexy."

[S] "Only a Pawn in Their Game" (Bob Dylan)

aka "He's Only a Pawn in Their Game," "The Ballad of Medgar Evers"
See also "Oxford Town"
Bob Dylan, *The Times They Are A-Changin'* (1964); *Don't Look Back*/'63 (film) (1967)
Various Artists (performed by Bob Dylan), *We Shall Over-*

O

come/'63 (1964); Freedom Is a Constant: Songs of the Mississippi Civil Rights Movement/'63 (1994)
Insol, *Insol* (1998)

When civil rights leader Medgar Evers was assassinated in Mississippi in the late spring of 1963, the circle of songwriters around *Broadside* magazine—Gil Turner, Phil Ochs, and Dylan, among others—quickly responded with songs about the tragedy. Dylan's "Only a Pawn in Their Game" was the strongest of the pieces to emerge. Though it is largely a snatch of reportage as sincerely PC as it is musically dull, "Only a Pawn in Their Game" has a twist that sets it apart: Dylan uses the killing of Evers to probe the root causes and political manipulations in the racist divide-and-conquer politics of the Jim Crow South. Rather than simply demonize Evers's killer outright, Dylan looks deeper to reveal that the poor Southern white is a victim of sorts, too, living under an oppression perhaps more subtle but no less insidious than that circumscribing the lives of Southern blacks.

Dylan performed the song for a spell in 1963 and 1964. The version captured in D. A. Pennebaker's 1967 documentary *Don't Look Back* was filmed at a voter registration rally at Silas Magee's Farm in Greenwood, Mississippi, on July 6, 1963. Later that month Dylan sang "Only a Pawn" on *Songs of Freedom*, a New York City television program. In August, he took it to a national stage, performing it in front of hundreds of thousands of people at the March on Washington, when Dr. Martin Luther King Jr. gave his "I Have a Dream" speech.

Medgar Wiley Evers (born July 2, 1925, Decatur, Mississippi; died June 12, 1963, Jackson, Mississippi) was one of the most important figures and early martyrs of the modern civil rights movement. His conversion to realpolitik can probably be traced to what he experienced upon coming home to the U.S. after serving in the army during World War II. Like many other African-American soldiers who had just helped return Europe to freedom, he was looking for a little taste of the same. But when he was rejected from the University of Mississippi in Oxford because of the color of his skin, he saw red. He enrolled at Mississippi's Alcorn College and became a scholar-athlete role model, graduating in 1952.

Evers's travels through Mississippi as an insurance salesman after college put him face-to-face with the miserable living conditions, poverty, educational travesties, and hopelessness that impoverished blacks *and* whites endured every day. He became an advocate of school

Medgar Evers, 1963.

(Photo: New York World-Telegram and Sun Collection/Library of Congress)

desegregation through his support of the monumental 1954 Supreme Court decision of *Brown v. Board of Education of Topeka*, took on the voting-rights laws that hindered blacks' access to the polls, organized boycotts against racially discriminating establishments, and attempted to integrate the University of Mississippi by applying to (but being rejected by) its law school. And when he was appointed Mississippi's first field secretary for the NAACP in 1954 he fought even harder, rolling up his sleeves and fighting the fight wherever it needed to be fought, even at the risk of his own hide. He investigated violence against blacks, challenged the antiquated Jim Crow statutes that forced blacks to drink from separate water fountains and the like, and pushed to get James Meredith admitted to the University of Mississippi in 1962. But if his courage helped focus national attention on the stink emanating from Mississippi, it was not exactly winning him new friends.

Evers's refusal to be daunted came at the price of his life: he was shot in the back in front of his own home. His remains were interred at Arlington National Cemetery.

After a twenty-five-year series of unsatisfactory accusations, indictments, arrests, and trials, white supremacist Byron de la Beckwith was convicted of murdering Evers and sentenced to life in prison in 1994. He died in a Jackson, Mississippi, prison hospital in January 2001.

Evers's murder upped the ante in America's civil rights battle, consecrated by President Lyndon Johnson's signing into law the Civil Rights Act of 1964 and the Voting Rights Act of 1965.

Evers's in-the-trenches legacy lives on. In a world of lies, damn lies and statistics, one set of numbers can't be denied: in 1963, only 28,000 blacks in Mississippi were registered voters. Forty years later there were more than 750,000.

⬛ "Open the Door, Homer" (Bob Dylan)

aka "Open the Door, Richard"
Bob Dylan/The Band, *The Basement Tapes*/'67 (1975)
The Floor, single (1968)
Thunderclap Newman, *Hollywood Dream* (1969)
Jake & the Family Jewels, *Jake & the Family Jewels* (1970)
Trials and Tribulations, *Trials & Tribulations* (1970)
Coulson, Dean, McGuinness, Flint, *Lo & Behold* (1972)
Marc Ellington, *A Question of Roads* (1972)
Fairport Convention, *Red & Gold* (1989)

Dylan and the Hawks recorded several versions of this song during their time at Big Pink in Saugerties, New York—some with the name Richard in the title instead of Homer. As with many of the songs from this brief but very special period, one is left scratching one's head. Maybe the best person to ask would be Homer—or was that Richard?

Some have connected "Open the Door, Homer" to "Open the Door, Richard!," a 1940s pop novelty song, though there is no similarity between the music, lyrics, or sentiment expressed in either.

In *Invisible Republic*, his 1997 book about *The Basement Tapes*, Greil Marcus suggested that "Open the Door, Homer" deals with the difficulties of maintaining friendships, and to some extent the song anticipates the tenuous bond (and the Holy Fool's loopy logic) expressed in something Dylan may already have been writing: "The Ballad of Frankie Lee and Judas Priest."

⬛ "Outlaw Blues" (Bob Dylan)

Bob Dylan, *Bringing It All Back Home* (1965)
Great Society, *Conspicuous Only in Its Absence* (1968); *Live at the Matrix* (1989)
Thin White Rope, *Outlaw Blues* (1992); *One That Got Away . . .* (1993); *Spoor* (1995)
Radiators, *Snafu 10-31-91* (1992)

Hugues Aufray, *Aufray Trans Dylan* (1995); *Au Casino de Paris* (1996)

Dream Syndicate, *Day Before Wine and Roses: Live at KPFK* (1995)

Jad Fair, *Greater Expectations* (1996)

Dave Edmunds, *The Early Edmunds* (1991); *Rockpile* (1999); *Collection* (2000)

Michel Montecrossa, *Jet Pilot* (2000)

A whacked-out Dylan rocker with nearly impossible-to-deconstruct-so-why-bother-splitting-hairs cartoon lyrics, "Outlaw Blues" should probably stand as just plain fun. With a primitive R&B beat, Dylan satirizes and reshapes blues writing as he draws on bad-man mythology in briefly recasting the Jesse James legend and standard hoodoo symbolism. At the same time, he also manages to take a cryptic swipe at the press, his audience, or anyone else who might be listening, singing "Don't ask me nothin' about nothin'/I just might tell you the truth."

▣ "Overseas Stomp" (Traditional)

aka "Lindberg Hop," "Lindy," "Lindy, Lindy"

Dick Fariña and Eric von Schmidt (performed with Dylan), *Dick Fariña and Eric von Schmidt* (1963)

Memphis Jug Band, *Memphis Jug Band—Double Album/'28* (1990)

Jim Kweskin and the Jug Band, *Jim Kweskin and the Jug Band* (1963)

Mother McCree's Uptown Jug Champions, *Mother McCree's Uptown Jug Champions/'64* (1999)

The Grateful Dead, *Historic Dead/'66* (1973)

Hotmud Family, *Stone Mountain Wobble* (1974)

Adapting and playing with the Memphis Jug Band's "Lindberg Hop," a folk celebration of Charles Lindberg's monumental transatlantic flight, Dylan and his chums Fariña and von Schmidt recorded this piece of blues madness during a wine-soaked recording session in the early 1960s on Dylan's first visit to England.

▣ "Oxford Town" (Bob Dylan)

See also "Only a Pawn in Their Game"

Bob Dylan, *The Freewheelin' Bob Dylan* (1963)

Richie Havens, *Electric Havens* (1966)

Barbara Dickson, *Don't Think Twice, It's All Right* (1992)

Tim O'Brien, *Red on Blonde* (1996)

Phil Carmen, *Bob Dylan's Dream* (1996)

Michel Montecrossa, *Jet Pilot* (2000)

A topical statement set to a jaunty country-blues melody and tempo that counters its dire subject matter, Dylan's "Oxford Town" was prompted by James Meredith's enrollment as the first black man at the University of Mississippi in Oxford. To this extent, "Oxford Town" is, at the very least, a keen reportage of the civil strife transpiring in Mississippi in the fall of 1962.

Dylan wrote "Oxford Town" in October or November 1962, recorded it on December 6 of that year, and had it published in *Broadside* #17 that same month. It's one of many songs from the folk world inspired by the civil rights movement of the early 1960s, and Dylan is said to have performed it occasionally in the fall and winter of 1962 and '63. Although Dylan biographer Robert Shelton specifically remembered Dylan performing "Oxford Town" at the October 26, 1963, Carnegie Hall concert, until Dylan's October 1990 display of the song in Oxford, Mississippi, no live versions of "Oxford Town" had been in circulation.

In *The Freewheelin' Bob Dylan* liner notes, Dylan wrote with a laugh that "Oxford Town" was "a banjo tune I play on the guitar." And yes, its country-folk musicality sets the landscape like a movie set.

Meredith's role in the integration of the University of Mississippi (whose main campus is located in the city of Oxford) was a crucial turning point in the civil rights movement. Ole Miss, as the university is still referred to, was a

O

stronghold of white Southern aristocracy, whose members aimed to keep it that way.

After a federal district court ordered the university to admit James Meredith as a senior transfer student in September 1962, the case became a monumental national flash point led, on one side, by Mississippi's virulently segregationist governor, Ross Barnett, and on the other, by a burgeoning opposition whose members felt that it was high time Mississippi grow up and enter the twentieth century by welcoming James Meredith to the university. The federal government was intent on having its authority preserved in the case and making sure that its orders were followed, even though opposition from the student body was growing ever more intense. In one instance that borders on the bizarre, Governor Barnett rallied the crowd with a speech during halftime at a football game, prompting an anti-Meredith cry from the throng that echoed his own divisive rhetoric, "Never, never, never, never, no, never!"

President John F. Kennedy took a stand on September 30, 1962, ordering the university to let Meredith register. And the government backed up that order with a strong show of force: more than 120 deputy marshals, three hundred-plus border patrolmen, and nearly a hundred federal prison guards were gathered on campus to make sure there was no trouble. And if trouble should simmer to a boiling point, federal troops and the Mississippi National Guard were at the ready.

Meredith arrived in Oxford that evening guarded by two dozen federal agents and was secreted away to a safe locale just as the threatening chants of "two-four-six-eight, we ain't gonna integrate!" were rising.

As darkness settled over the campus, a long night of violence began. The mob threw rocks and bottles, overturned cars, smashed windows, fired shots, and chased the highway patrolmen away, forcing the federal marshals to fire tear gas at the mob.

As chaos reigned, President Kennedy addressed the nation: "Americans are free to disagree with the law, but not to disobey it," he said. "Show that you are men of patriotism and integrity."

When order was restored, 160 marshals had been injured, twenty-eight of them shot. Two men were dead and two hundred had been arrested.

James Meredith finally registered as a student the next morning. Within an hour he was attending his first class—Colonial American history. By summer Meredith was holding a bachelor's degree in political science. When he stepped up to receive his diploma, some noticed a button pinned to his gown bearing the word "Never." He wore the button upside down.

"Paid the Price" (Moon Martin)
Moon Martin, *Mystery Ticket* (1982)
Michelle Phillips, *Victim of Romance* (1977)
Nick Lowe, *Abominable Showman* (1983)

Dylan performed Moon Martin's ode to dues settling at only one performance: the famous surprise show at Toad's Place in New Haven, Connecticut, in 1990. The song sounds like a 1950s love ballad in the "Earth Angel" mode.

Moon Martin (born October 31, 1950, Altus, Oklahoma) grew up with a most usual first name: John. His 1979 emergence as a player in the world of 1970s and '80s power-pop music came with a style mixing new wave and nouveau 1950s rock 'n' roll. He acquired his tag because he frequently employed lunar imagery in his songs.

Martin's rather picaresque rise through the ranks of post–Dust Bowl Oklahoma roadhouse rock began in 1968, when he graduated from high school, hooked up with members of a local band called the Disciples, and drove to L.A. There the group adopted the name Southwind, landed a recording contract, cut at least a couple of unrecognized LPs on the Blue Thumb label, and developed as a hot live act. But by 1971, just as possible stardom loomed, in typical showbiz fashion the band crashed and burned.

Martin, the band's lead guitar player, who had yet to really distinguish himself as a songwriter, lingered in Southern California as a studio musician working with the likes of Linda Ronstadt (with whom he was for a time romantically linked), Gram Parsons, Jesse Ed Davis (an old friend from Oklahoma), Del Shannon, Jackie DeShannon, and the newly forming Eagles. Slowing moving out of the studio and into a solo career, Martin took day jobs like cab driving and working in a flower shop while he developed his songwriting chops. His break finally came in 1977 when Mink DeVille recorded his song "Cadillac Walk." Recognition for that tune led him to write and sell more songs to be recorded by other artists and eventually gained him his own record deal.

But the records (showing the influence of the Beatles, Chuck Berry, Big Joe Turner, John Lee Hooker, and Freddie King)—filled with clever lyrics and the meanest rockin' this side of Springsteen—came and went. And though Martin was often compared in look, style, and substance with such contemporary new-wave hit makers as Elvis Costello and Nick Lowe (some might say he was the bastard child of Buddy Holly, Warren Zevon, and John Denver), he never rose to that level of talent or accomplishment despite four albums in as many years and a well-regarded live show backed by his band, the Ravens. Yeah, Robert Palmer had a hit with "Bad Case of Loving You" in 1978, and Martin himself hit the charts with his own "Rolene" a year later. But the last two of his albums issued on the Capitol label, *Street Fever* (1980) and *Mystery Ticket* (1982), failed to click, and Martin drifted to the periphery of the music scene for more than a decade before resurfacing in 1995 with a pair of releases, *Cement Monkey* and *Lunar Samples*.

[S] **"Pancho and Lefty"** (Townes Van Zandt)

aka "Poncho and Lefty"
Townes Van Zandt, *Live at the Old Quarter* (1977)
Hoyt Axton, *Snowbird Friend* (1977)
Emmylou Harris, *Luxury Liner* (1977)
Willie Nelson, *Pancho and Lefty* (1982)
Merle Haggard, *Pancho and Lefty* (1983)
Dick Gaughan, *Redwood Cathedral* (1998)

Dylan probably picked up on Townes Van Zandt's salutary ballad (a wonderful tale reminiscent of *Butch Cassidy and the Sundance Kid* of righteous desperadoes on the scam and lam) from Willie Nelson. Nelson and Merle Haggard topped the country charts in 1983 with "Pancho and Lefty."

"I was in Dallas. In a hotel room," Van Zandt recalled about the process of writing "Pancho and Lefty" in a conversation with Paul Zollo, published in the latter's book *Songwriters on Songwriting, Expanded Fourth Edition.* Van Zandt continued: "That one came from not having anything to do and sitting down with the express purpose of writing a song. It took one day and then I played what I had that night at a gig. And a songwriter told me, 'Man, that's a great song. But I don't think it's done yet.' So I went back to my hotel the next day and wrote the last verse. The only thing I remember thinking about while I was writing it was consciously thinking that this was not about Pancho Villa. Also a friend of mine who is an artist pointed out one time that there's nothing in that song that says Pancho and Lefty ever knew each other. I had never thought of that."

Van Zandt (born March 7, 1944, Fort Worth, Texas; died January 1, Mount Joliet, Tennessee) could have been a character in just about any one of his songs. These dark and tragic country-folk ballads serve as an eerie looking glass into his own, very troubled life. They can slap you sober or raise your soul, open the tear ducts or tickle the funny bone, bring you to the edge of the abyss or a yellow-brick road. And many are more than just a little bit creepy. He may be the most admired but still relatively unknown artist of his generation, held in such high regard that someone, somewhere, is lighting a candle in his memory.

But unlike the rogue's gallery of characters populating his songs, Townes Van Zandt grew up in a Texas oil family so rich and established that a whole county east of Dallas is named after his ancestors. However, that didn't mean he was spending any time on Easy Street. With a childhood marked by transience, Van Zandt grew up rootless. His teenage years are part of the lore: stints in military academies to straighten him up, and stays in mental institutions when he fell apart.

As he discovered himself through music and began haltingly pursuing something resembling a career, Van Zandt made his way to Houston, Texas, in the early 1960s to pursue his beatnik musician muse. He came under the sway of the city's up-and-coming cadre of singer-songwriters, including Guy Clark, Jerry Jeff Walker, and Mickey Newbury. He also ran headlong into local hero Sam "Lightnin'" Hopkins, whose downer-than-home slide guitar runs and sinewy picking had an immediate and lasting impact.

But toeing the line as a bohemian troubadour didn't turn out to be the romantic pursuit the music-industry PR promised; nor did the family oil business. Nonetheless, Van Zandt persevered. However, if one's standard of hit-ting rock bottom is eating dog food and sleeping on concert stages, then it can be fairly said that Van Zandt passed the test. It was during this period at dives like Houston's Jester Lounge that he slowly transformed his act from a set of cover tunes and bawdy barroom fare to finely crafted, revelatory originals sung like a ghost who could wake the dead in any century.

Through Mickey Newbury, Van Zandt snared a chance to record for Poppy Records in Nashville, and he made the most of it with *For the Sake of the Song*, his 1968 debut. The album featured the type of song cycle that would mark just about every subsequent Van Zandt release. Here you could find life's desperate, on-the-edge and on-the-lam losers with hearts of gold and/or stone. Despite his songs' often harrowing subject matter and ornery characters, Van Zandt offered a mix of humor and bleakness that was always seductive.

Over the next few years Van Zandt was at the height of his powers. He released four more albums for Poppy, spawning the songs for which he is most revered: "Waiting Around to Die," "Tecumseh Valley," "To Live's to Fly," and "Pancho and Lefty."

If the songs felt and sounded true, that was probably because they were. Van Zandt lived these tales of drinking, rambling, and gambling in a way few could or would ever want to. He bounced to several other labels over the years, recording a series of mostly live albums on Tomato Records, Flying Fish, and Sugar Hill. But his last years are remembered for his relentless touring as he stayed just a half step ahead of the inner demons that always seemed to be nipping at his boot heels.

Van Zandt's death at the age of fifty-two of a heart attack came a week after a hip fracture and surgery. In a final, ironic twist of fate, his death came thirty-four years to the day after his idol Hank Williams died.

P

Dylan first performed "Pancho and Lefty" in 1989 at a couple of gigs that summer. Two years later he pulled it out for a trio of concerts. When introducing the song during a 1991 bash in Cleveland, Dylan informed his audience that "Pancho and Lefty" was the only song in his repertoire that mentions Cleveland. Finally, Dylan performed the song with Willie Nelson on the latter's sixtieth-birthday CBS television special in 1993.

[S] "Pass Me Not, O Gentle Savior" (Frances J. Crosby/William H. Doane)

aka "Pass Me Not, Oh Gentle Savior," "Pass Me Not"
Bill Harwell and the Virginians, *Ballads and Bluegrass* (1986)
Al Green, *One in a Million* (1990)
Bill Monroe, *Bluegrass 1959–1969* (1991)
Stanley Brothers, *Early Years 1958–61* (1994)
Pat Boone, *Inspirational Collection* (1998)

Dylan began performing this old Puritan-flavored hymn when passing through the New England region in 1999, using an arrangement eerily reminiscent of the version sung by Robert Mitchum's homicidal Preacher in the brilliant and suspenseful 1955 film *Night of the Hunter*—Charles Laughton's only directorial turn. Mitchum's Preacher is best remembered by the words "love" and "hate" tattooed on the fingers of each hand as he pursues two children across the South in search of stolen money.

With a title drawn from Genesis 18:3 ("Do not pass your servant by") and a story drawn from the New Testament, "Pass Me Not, O Gentle Savior" was written by two of the better-known American hymn composers of the nineteenth century, Frances Jane (Fanny) Crosby (who wrote the words in 1868) and William Howard Doane (who wrote the music in 1870). "Pass Me Not, O Gentle Savior" first appeared in Doane's *Songs of Devotion*, published in 1870.

Fanny Crosby (born March 24, 1820, Putnam County, New York; died February 12, 1915, Bridgeport, Connecticut) is among history's most prolific hymnists, with literally thousands of compositions credited to her name. Accidentally blinded by a doctor when she was but six weeks old, she became famous not only for her hymns and poetry, but for her humanitarian work as well. Her involvement with the New York Institution for the Blind, first as a student and then as an English teacher, ranged at least a couple of decades and set her on a path as a person who, above all, selflessly cared for the needy.

Her missionary work with society's dregs, widely distributed hymns, and poetry made the disabled Crosby something of a celebrity and led to invitations to meet with and entertain society's intelligentsia, capped by her appearance at the funeral of former President Ulysses S. Grant in 1885.

Along with her hymns, for which she supposedly never charged more than $2, Crosby had three books of poetry and writings published during her lifetime: *The Blind Girl and Other Poems* (1844), *A Wreath of Columbia's Flowers* (1858), and *Memories of Eighty Years* (1906).

William Howard Doane (born February 3, 1832, Preston, Connecticut; died December 24, 1915, South Orange, New Jersey) made his mark on American music with more than two thousand compositions. While not nearly as well known as his close friend Fanny Crosby, he wrote the tunes to many of her lyrics. Doane was a Baptist whose day job as an executive at the J. A. Fay Company, a manufacturer of woodworking machinery, supported his love of music. In addition to his collaborations with Crosby, his major contributions to the country's musical heritage are the dozens of hymnbook collections he edited for use in the church.

P

Doane did eventually receive his Doctor of Music degree from Denison University in Cincinnati, and his memory was kept alive by the Doane Memorial Music Building in Chicago, constructed with funds distributed from his substantial estate.

Dylan's gorgeous, intimate rendition of this old gospel tune (later turned bluegrass favorite), briefly introduced during the acoustic sets of 1999 and 2000, plays off the idea of being present in a crowd when Christ returns and pleading to him, "Savior, Savior/Please hear my humble cry/When you return for the faithful/Don't pass me by." Dylan's arrangement was aided immensely by the backup harmony on the chorus by guitarists Larry Campbell and Bucky Baxter, which helped Dylan convey the mood of mortal confrontation he captured on *Time out of Mind*.

◪ Pat Garrett and Billy the Kid

MGM Films, 1973. Produced by Gordon Carroll. Directed by Sam Peckinpah. Written by Rudy Wurlitzer. Starring James Coburn, Kris Kristofferson, Richard Jaeckel, Katy Jurado, Chill Wills, Jason Robards, Bob Dylan.

With its classical themes of betrayal and redemption, *Pat Garrett and Billy the Kid* is Sam Peckinpah's elegy to the Old West with a few modernist twists. Garrett (James Coburn) and William H. Bonney—Billy the Kid (Kris Kristofferson)—used to run together, but all that changed when Garrett was pinned with a shiny sheriff's star on his breast and pressured by Governor Lew Wallace (Jason Robards) of New Mexico and a powerful cattle baron, John Chisum (Barry Sullivan), to clear the territory of riffraff, commencing with Billy. Garrett attempts to warn the Kid off, but when Billy ignores his advice to relocate somewhere south of the border, Garrett captures his old friend and throws him in the pokey. Billy escapes in

predictably dramatic and cinematically appropriate fashion and rejoins his gang with a new, enigmatic acquaintance by the name of Alias (Dylan) in tow. Naturally, Garrett forms a posse and the manhunt is on, culminating in a Faustian confrontation with destiny as corporate progress and outlaw culture go mano a mano, with a bloody result that can only be described as prophetic. In other words, the bad guys win.

Rudy Wurlitzer originally wrote *Pat Garrett and Billy the Kid* with Monte Hellman in mind as director, but MGM shied away from that uncommercial combination. Instead Sam Peckinpah, hot from the success of *The Wild Bunch* (1969), was hired to direct. With Kristofferson, Coburn, Dylan, Robards, and bit players like Harry Dean Stanton, the film was billed as the counterculture's western—an underground take on outlaw culture.

Still, Peckinpah changed the script to suit Hollywood expectations, and Wurlitzer, who had fancied himself the direct reincarnation of Billy the Kid when he was younger, felt betrayed by the changes.

For his part, Dylan seems to have regarded the experience of working on the film with mixed feelings. Discussing the project in the *Biograph* liner notes, he wrote:

> Actually, I was just one of Peckinpah's pawns. There wasn't a part for me and Sam just liked me around. I moved with my family to Durango for about three months. Rudy Wurlitzer, who was writing this thing, invented a part for me but there wasn't any dimension to it. And I was very uncomfortable in this non-role. But then time started to slip away and there I was trapped deep in the heart of Mexico with some madman, ordering people around like a little king. You had to play the dummy all day. I used to think to myself, "Well, now, how would Dustin Hoffman play this?" That's why I wore

P

Dylan in a still
from the film *Pat
Garrett and Billy
the Kid*, 1973.

(Photo: MGM Studios/
Courtesy of Getty Images)

P

glasses in that reading part. I saw him do it in *Papillon*. It was crazy, all these generals making you jump into hot ants, setting up turkey shoots and whatever and drinking tequila 'til they passed out. Sam was a wonderful guy though. He was an outlaw. A real hombre. Somebody from the old school. Men like him they don't make anymore. I could see why actors would do anything for him. At night when it was quiet, I would listen to the bells. It was a strange feeling, watching how this movie was made and I know it was wide and big and breathless, at least what was in Sam's mind, but it didn't come out that way. Sam himself just didn't have final control and that was the problem. I saw it in a movie house one cut away from his and I could tell that it had been chopped to pieces. Someone other than Sam had taken a knife to some valuable scenes that were in it. The music seemed to be scattered and used in every other place but the scenes in which we did it for. Except for "Heaven's Door," I can't say as though I recognized anything I'd done for being in the place that I'd done it for. Why did I do it, I guess I had a fondness for Billy the Kid. In no way can I say I did it for the money. Anyway, I was too beat to take it personal. I mean, it didn't hurt but I was sleep walking most of the time and had no real reason to be there. I'd gotten my family out of New York, that was the important thing, there was a lot of pressure back there. But even so, my wife got fed up almost immediately. She'd say to me, "What the hell are we doing here?" It was not an easy question to answer.

Peckinpah's aesthetic can be summed up by the opening line to *The Wild Bunch*, his cinematic eulogy to the mythologized Old West and his most controversial film (released during the height of the Vietnam War and its staggering body count): "If they move, kill 'em."

"Pouring new wine into the bottle of the western, Peckinpah explodes the bottle," observed film critic Pauline Kael at the time. That exploding bottle also christened the director with the nickname that would forever define his films and reputation: "Bloody Sam."

◭ *Pat Garrett and Billy the Kid–Original Soundtrack Recording*

Columbia Records LP 324600; CD CK-324600; CS PCT-324600. Produced by Gordon Carroll. Recorded January 20–February 4, 1973. Released May 1, 1973.

Bob Dylan—vocals, guitar, harmonica. Donna Weiss, Priscilla Jones, Brenda Patterson—vocals. Roger McGuinn, Bruce Langhorn—guitar. Carol Hunter—guitar, vocals. Byron Berline—fiddle, vocals. Jolly Roger—banjo. Fred Katz, Ted Michel—cello. Gary Foster—flute, recorder. Carl Fortina—harmonium. Terry Paul—bass, vocals. Booker T.—bass. Jim Keltner—drums. Russ Kunkel—bongos, tambourine.

"Main Title Theme," "Cantina Theme," "Billy 1," "Bunkhouse Theme," "River Theme," "Turkey Chase," "Knockin' on Heaven's Door," "Final Theme," "Billy 4," "Billy 7"

Dylan recorded the soundtrack for the film *Pat Garrett and Billy the Kid*, which consisted of some folkish instrumentals, several takes of a ballad called "Billy," and the famous "Knockin' on Heaven's Door"—a simple song that became one of his most cherished compositions. The album is, at the very least, a footnote to Sam Peckinpah's neosurrealist western.

Bolstered by the success of "Knockin' on Heaven's Door," the album hit No. 16 and stayed on the charts for fourteen weeks but remains one of Dylan's least known.

James Coburn, costar of the film, told Garner Simmons, author of *Peckinpah: A Portrait in Montage* (Austin: University of Texas Press, 1982): "When Dylan came down to Mexico, Sam didn't know who the fuck Dylan was. But when he heard Dylan sing, Sam was the first to

P

admit that he was taken with Dylan's singing. He heard Dylan's 'Ballad of Billy the Kid' and immediately had it put on tape so that he could have it with him to play."

[S] "Paths of Victory" (Bob Dylan)

Bob Dylan, *The Bootleg Series, Volumes 1–3: Rare and Unreleased, 1961–1991*/'63 (1991)
Odetta, *Odetta Sings of Many Things* (1964); *Odetta Sings Dylan* (1965)
Hamilton Camp, *Paths of Victory* (1964)
Pete Seeger, *Pete Seeger Sings Little Boxes and Other Broadsides* (1966)
Anne Murray, *What About Me* (1982); *Both Sides Now* (1997)
The Byrds, *Byrds* (1990); *20 Essential Tracks from the Boxed Set* (1991); *The Byrds Play Dylan* (2002)
Two Approaching Riders, *One More Cup of Coffee* (1997)
Various Artists (performed by the Broadside Singers), *The Best of Broadside 1962–1988*/'64 (2000)
Cat Power, *Covers Record* (2000)
Michel Montecrossa, *Born in Time* (2000)

In his liner notes to *The Bootleg Series, Volumes 1–3,* John Bauldie calls "Paths of Victory" "possibly the most Guthrieesque song that Woody never wrote."

And who could argue? With lyrics like "I walked out to the valley, I turned my head up high/I seen that silver lining that was hangin' in the sky," "Paths of Victory" does seem to tumble out of the Dust Bowl. Indeed, Dylan's forward-looking piece of civil rights agitprop, set against a pleasant, singable tune, seems almost a response to Woody's "This Land Is Your Land" by way of "Palms of Victory," a nineteenth-century song originating out of the white gospel tradition. Dylan began writing "Paths of Victory" in the summer of 1962 and worked up a couple of renditions for *Broadside* magazine and Witmark, for whom he produced a demo. A definitive version of the song was not released until *The Bootleg Series.* That take, recorded at CBS Studios in August 1963, provides one of the earliest examples of Dylan tickling the ivories.

[S] "Peace in the Valley" (Rev. Thomas A. Dorsey)

aka "(There'll Be) Peace in the Valley (for Me)"
Sister Rosetta Tharpe, *Live in 1960* (1960)
George Jones, *Sings the Hits of His Country Cousins* (1962)
Elvis Presley, *How Great Thou Art* (1967)
Johnny Cash, *A Boy Named Sue* (1979)
B. J. Thomas, *Peace in the Valley* (1982)
Charlie McCoy, *Beam Me Up, Charlie* (1989)
Patsy Cline, *Just a Closer Walk with Thee* (1995)
Tennessee Ernie Ford, *His Greatest Hymns* (1995)
Loretta Lynn, *All Time Gospel Favorites* (1998)
Original Five Blind Boys of Mississippi, *Talking to Jesus* (1999)

With "Peace in the Valley"—a grand 1989 entry in the long list of old-time one-off treats

American clergyman, pianist, and composer Thomas Andrew Dorsey with his female gospel quartet. Standing, from left: B. Armstrong, D. Gay, M. Wilson, S. Martin. Chicago, 1934.
(Photo: Frank Driggs Collection/Getty Images)

P

peppering the Never Ending Tour sets with joyous intensity—Dylan turned to the father of gospel music, Rev. Thomas Andrew Dorsey (born July 1, 1899, Villa Rica, Georgia; died January 23, 1993, Chicago). An important and influential composer and multi-instrumentalist who made a major impact on both the blues and gospel, Dorsey was raised in a religiously minded family. Not only was his father a revivalist Baptist minister, but also his mother was the church organist. A child prodigy, he taught himself a wide range of instruments, including piano and guitar, and was playing blues and ragtime while still in his teens.

Dorsey, also a singer and songwriter, studied music formally before and after moving to Chicago around 1916. "If I Don't Get There," his first composition, was probably written during his stint as "Barrelhouse Tommy" in Atlanta. In addition to accompanying Ma Rainey on tour, he made a living demonstrating music in shops and working as an arranger for Vocalion Records. He also began recording under a variety of aliases; the most famous was Georgia Tom, a name he used during his 1928–32 record dates with the Hokum Boys, a band that included Tampa Red. A prolific composer, Dorsey authored witty, suggestively racy blues songs such as the underground hit "It's Tight Like That."

Dorsey, however, eschewed the blues life in favor of religion in the 1930s and went on to become arguably the most important composer and publisher in gospel music history. To create his gospel compositions, he merged religious music with blues forms, in so doing producing some thousand gospel songs, including "If You See My Savior, Tell Him That You Saw Me" and "Take My Hand, Precious Lord." In part because his light, airy voice, which had served him well as a singer of ribald blues, did not convincingly translate to gospel music, he stopped recording in 1934. And though he toured widely into the 1940s, he concentrated on writing and lecturing about music while tending to administrative duties in his role as proprietor of the National Convention of Gospel Choirs and Choruses, Inc.

"Peace in the Valley" has quaint, pastoral origins with overtones of global cataclysm. Rev. Dorsey recalled many years later that while he was traveling by train from Indiana to Cincinnati, before World War II, the train passed through a valley. He noticed how peaceful the animals seemed to be with one another and wondered why mankind was unable to do the same. His musings on the tranquil scene inspired the song.

Although it was originally written for Mahalia Jackson, "Peace in the Valley" found its greatest success with white singers—both Elvis Presley and Red Foley, among others, scored major hits with the song. After Elvis performed it on *The Ed Sullivan Show* in January 1957, for example, his EP recording hit No. 39 on the *Billboard* charts.

Dorsey's death came after a lengthy battle with Alzheimer's disease. For more about him, read Michael W. Harris's book *The Rise of Gospel Blues: The Music of Thomas Andrew Dorsey in the Urban Church* (New York: Oxford University Press, 1992), or see the 1982 documentary *Say Amen, Somebody*, directed by George T. Nierenberg.

"Peggy Day" (Bob Dylan)
Bob Dylan, single (1969); *Nashville Skyline* (1969)
Steve Gibbons, *The Dylan Project* (1998)

A country-flavored jingle celebrating the delights of a particular amour du jour that includes a crooning Elvis Presley–like rave at the song's conclusion, "Peggy Day" was first released as the B side of the "Lay, Lady, Lay" single. The combination rose to No. 7 on the charts, where it spent fourteen weeks—Dylan's biggest hit to that point. The *Nashville Skyline* recording of the song is notable for Pete Drake's pedal steel guitar ringlets.

"I kinda had the Mills Brothers in mind when I did that one," Dylan has said of "Peggy Day."

Writing in the April 4, 1969, issue of *Newsweek*, Hubert Saal pointed out that the song "is almost a pastiche of the '30s; its rhythms recall 'swing,' and Dylan sings with the kind of lighthearted showmanship that used to come from college bandstands. And if in the song the words are plain and direct, they do not lack for cunning: 'Love to spend the night with Peggy Day,' and later, 'Love to spend the day with Peggy Night.'"

Maybe it is cunning, but "Peggy Day," never performed in concert, is doomed forever to come off like a casual throwaway, something Dylan scribbled on the back cover of a Gideon's Bible in a Holiday Inn an hour or two before the recording session was to begin.

P

[S] "People Get Ready" (Curtis Mayfield)

Bob Dylan, *4 Songs from Renaldo & Clara* (EP) (1978)
Various Artists (performed by Bob Dylan), *Flashback* (soundtrack) (1990)
Curtis Mayfield, *People Get Ready: The Curtis Mayfield Story* (1996)
The Impressions, *People Get Ready* (1966)
Aretha Franklin, *Lady Soul* (1968)
Petula Clark, *In Memphis* (1970)
Glenn Campbell, *Oh Happy Day* (1970)
Trinidad Tripoli Steelband, *Caribbean Collection, Volume 2* (1996)
Ziggy Marley, *Fallen Is Babylon* (1997)

The August 1963 March on Washington advocating equal rights at which Dr. Martin Luther King made his famous "I Have a Dream" speech had a tremendous rippling effect across the landscape of American society, politics, and culture. Dylan, as has been noted in these pages and elsewhere, was most certainly affected, as was another local hero, soulster Curtis Mayfield, who penned his classic song of unity, "People Get Ready," in honor of that fateful day and the optimistic vision it provided.

After decades of intimidation, humiliation, and trauma marked by unpunished lynchings, the Emmett Till murder, the martyrdom of leaders like Medgar Evers, cross burnings, church burnings, voting rights mischief, and the JFK assassination, the March on Washington appeared to herald a new day. And Mayfield tapped into the moment in the spirit of Joe Hill, Woody Guthrie, Johnny Cash, Dylan, or even Dr. King himself by producing one of modern gospel soul's first crossover hits, which continues to find life four decades down the pike.

"People Get Ready" has it all: the power of tradition, deep spirituality, progressive politics, hope, and a prayer that faith and respect will transcend divisions as silly as race.

When recorded by Mayfield and his group the Impressions, "People Get Ready" sounded a clarion call from its opening words: "People get ready, there's a train a-comin'/You don't need no baggage, you just get on board/All you need is faith to hear the diesels hummin'/Don't need no ticket, you just thank the Lord."

Dylan, of course, performed at the March on Washington, and his interest in the Impressions' 1965 gospel hit was instant and lasting. Not only did he record "People Get Ready" with the Hawks during the 1967 Big Pink *Basement Tapes* period shortly after the song's commercial peak, he also cut the song for his film *Renaldo & Clara* in 1975 and for the soundtrack to the 1990 screwball political comedy *Flashback*, starring Dennis Hopper and Kiefer Sutherland. In 1991, Dylan gave "People

Get Ready" its one and only concert outing, perhaps as a tribute to the song's author, who had suffered a debilitating accident about a year before.

"People Get Ready" is a moving testament to human faith, a kind of soulster rewrite of "This Train Is Bound for Glory," with a similar melodic feel and millennialist sentiment. Alan Lomax's comments about the latter song from his 1960 book *The Folk Songs of North America* could easily apply (with a politically corrected edit or two) to Mayfield's famous hymn:

> In his visions the Negro has seen many roads leading to Heaven. Sometimes he mounts a golden chariot or rides a prancing white horse. He climbs Jacob's ladder rung by rung, runs down the King's highway with the hell-hounds snapping their jaws at his heels, or inches along like a poor inch worm. Modern singers have him talking to angels through the royal telephone, with a line running "to the church-house and the receiver in my heart." Ever since the first locomotive whistle split the quiet air of the South and the black engine thundered down the rails, snorting steam and fire like the horses of the Apocalypse, the righteous have been "buying tickets on the snow-white heavenly express for glory." For the gambler, the back-biter, the crap-shooter, and other back-sliding sinners, the Black Diamond Express, manned by Satan, was booked and bound for the lower regions.

As someone who brought themes from the civil rights movement to the pop charts, as a songwriter and as a vocalist with the Impressions, Curtis Mayfield was the perfect candidate to catch Dylan's eyes and ears. After all, he was to soul what Dylan was to folk-rock: a deliverer of sermons in song that could educate as well as entertain.

Mayfield (born June 3, 1942, Chicago; died December 26, 1999, Roswell, Georgia) never reached the superstar status of many of his peers, but he certainly captured the spirit of his era in songs that will endure as classics beyond the context of the strife of the 1960s and 1970s. Mayfield wasn't just a singer with a distinctive falsetto, but an original composer and lyricist as well. This put him at the vanguard of those who were addressing both the gritty struggles and intense pride of black Americans. Whether one considers the inspirational anthem "People Get Ready," the urban lament "Freddie's Dead," or "Superfly"—his beloved low-down, badder-than-bad funk classic from the titular blaxploitation flick—Mayfield still checks out as *with it*, imbuing his songs with messages of love, optimism, unity, faith, and self-awareness. By delving into racial and political issues with courage, intelligence, and passion in powerful and prophetic songs like "We People Who Are Darker Than Blue" and "Mighty Mighty (Spade and Whitey)," he stood out from most of his contemporaries with no-punches-pulled treatises describing the most troubling aspects of inner-city life.

Mayfield may have started out as a traditionalist, but it was the fusion of his background in gospel and doo-wop that shaped the bulk of his work in the 1960s as he and the Impressions crafted a call-and-response style in songs that heralded their message of community. In the process, they trademarked Chicago soul with bold arrangements incorporating big-band horn sections and seductive Latin rhythms, all spearheaded by Mayfield's singing and phenomenal guitar work.

Mayfield broke off from the Impressions to pursue a career as a solo act in 1971. The following years found him on a peak of creativity, leading his groups with gritty guitar playing and synthesizing both funk and acid rock into

P

his potent musical stew. *Superfly* may have cemented his legacy when it topped the charts for a month in 1972, but on albums like 1975's *There's No Place Like America Today*, his songs penetrated the minds of the urban hopeless, telling them to remain strong in times of poverty, unemployment, and racial violence. And he was a highly regarded producer too, shepherding releases by soul music's A-list: Aretha Franklin, the Staple Singers, and Gladys Knight and the Pips.

Along with Stevie Wonder and Marvin Gaye, Mayfield was one of the era's soul auteurs. But despite the messages of philosophical and physical strength under adversity found in much of Mayfield's music, his career began to falter in the age of disco.

In 1990 Mayfield was paralyzed from the neck down in a freak accident when a lighting fixture fell on him during a Brooklyn, New York, concert. While he heroically continued to compose and record, his health deteriorated. He developed diabetes as a result of the injury, and his battle with the disease led to the amputation of his right leg.

Before his death, Mayfield was able to enjoy a mild renaissance. Superstar-studded tribute albums (including work by the likes of Eric Clapton and Springsteen) spread his gospel far and wide, and he was inducted into the Rock and Roll Hall of Fame in 1991 as a member of the Impressions, and in 1999 as a solo act.

"Percy's Song" (Bob Dylan)
Bob Dylan, *Biograph*/'63 (1985)
Fairport Convention, *Unhalfbricking* (1969); *Heyday* (1987)
Arlo Guthrie, *Washington County* (1970)
Michael Moore, *Jewels & Binoculars: The Songs of Bob Dylan* (2000)

A widely bootlegged song and early Dylan concert rarity, "Percy's Song" was recorded for *The Times They Are A-Changin'* but didn't find a place on a Dylan album until the release of the *Biograph* retrospective in 1985. Dylan's narrator comes off like a country lawyer on this one, making a case that the ninety-nine-year sentence given to his friend for manslaughter "in the highest degree" is too severe. (Interestingly, in the song it follows on *Biograph*, "The Lonesome Death of Hattie Carroll," he makes just the opposite case, that a manslaughter sentence is far too lenient.) Yes, "Percy's Song" is probably a bit too long and legally muddled for the situation it describes, but Dylan's elegiac mantra woven into each verse ("Turn, turn, turn again. . . . Turn, turn to the rain and the wind") casts a compelling spell over the listener.

This moving tale of backcountry injustice might seem more disturbing if it had actually taken place in the backcountry—not Joliet, Illinois—or some indignation could be mustered from the sketchy situation it tries to describe and condemn. As it is, the case seems to involve a car accident with the driver (the narrator's friend) being pinned with a highly suspicious ninety-nine-year rap for manslaughter. Ninety-nine years (a standard punishment found in countless songs from the blues and folk canon) is a pretty harsh manslaughter edict by any standard, whether handed down in the inner city, backcountry, or outback.

The song's beautiful melody line was cribbed from Paul Clayton, one of Dylan's fellow Greenwich Village folkies. Dylan remembered Clayton and the elements that contributed to "Percy's Song" and a few others written around that time in the *Biograph* liner notes: "Paul was just an incredible songwriter and singer. He must have known a thousand songs . . . We played on the same circuit and I traveled with him part of the time. When you're listening to songs night after night, some of them kind of rub off on you. 'Don't Think

Twice' was a riff that Paul had. And so was 'Percy's Song' ... A song like that would come to me because people were talking about the incident ... A song like 'Percy's Song,' you'd just assume another character's point of view ..."

The "incident" to which Dylan refers is a mildly debated topic among Dylanists. Some have suggested that it was sparked by the arrest of a Gaslight Café worker who was busted with a little grass and had the book thrown at him. Others point to the proliferation of eighteenth-century English ballads and broadsides dealing with a character named Percy as a possible reference and/or inspiration.

Dylan didn't mention that he picked up elements of the lyrics and melody to "Percy's Song" from a piece he sang even earlier in his career: "The Two Sisters" (Child Ballad No. 10, aka "The Twa Sisters" or "Oh, the Wind and Rain"), an amazing and eerie old folk chestnut of British lineage about a murdered woman who comes back to life as a fiddle to identify her murderer in a tune played on the instrument. Dylan also utilized themes from "The Two Sisters" in crafting the dour "Ballad in Plain D."

Very little has been written about the mysterious "Twa Sisters." According to the liner notes by Alan Lomax and Peter Kennedy for volume 1 of *Classic Ballads of Britain and Ireland: Folk Songs of England, Ireland, Scotland & Wales*:

> Once again, this is an old story, whose origins seem lost in the mists of the past, of a jealous girl who murders her younger sister. In Scotland and on the continent, the body of the murdered sister is found by a harper who makes strings for his harp from her hair. When he plays this instrument at the court of her father, the human harp accuses the wicked sister, and she is brought to justice.

Child prints 27 texts of this ballad. In one of these, a broadside that appeared in 1656, the miller makes a viol of the drowned girl's body. In some other versions it is a fiddle or a harp, but this musical instrument motif is absent in most of the English and American copies. The story is widely distributed in Slavic folklore, and may have originated there. Archer Taylor (*Journal of American Folklore*, Vol. 17, page 238 ff.) argues that the ballad form may have come into Great Britain from Scandinavia before 1600 ...

Hard-core fans will also note that Joan Baez sings "Percy's Song" in the infamous hotel scene in *Don't Look Back*, D. A. Pennebaker's film about Dylan's 1965 tour of Britain. A live October 1963 version of "Percy's Song" recorded at New York City's Carnegie Hall was to be included on the never-released *Bob Dylan in Concert*, and there is a still-unreleased Witmark demo of the song floating about.

◪ *Planet Waves*

Asylum Records LP S-7E-1003. Reissue: Columbia Records LP PC-37637, CD CK-37637, CS PCT-37637; Sony Music Entertainment, Inc., SACD 90339. Recorded November 2–10, 1973. Released January 17, 1974. Produced by Rob Fraboni. Liner notes by Bob Dylan. Art by Bob Dylan.

Bob Dylan—vocals, guitar, harmonica. Robbie Robertson—guitar. Garth Hudson—organ. Rick Danko—bass. Richard Manuel—drums, piano. Levon Helm—drums.

"On a Night Like This," "Going, Going, Gone," "Tough Mama," "Hazel," "Something There Is About You," "Forever Young," "Forever Young," "Dirge," "You Angel You," "Never Say Goodbye," "Wedding Song"

Planet Waves is one of Dylan's great, underappreciated albums. It contains some pretty good music from Dylan and the Band but, more importantly, is a natural bridge between its predecessor, *New Morning*, and its successor,

Dylan performing in concert with the Band, featuring guitarist Robbie Robertson
at left and drummer Levon Helm at right, 1974.

(Photo: Joseph Sia/Getty Images)

Blood on the Tracks, mixing the declarations of marital and familial contentment with severe criticisms of the singer himself and others. Ultimately, Dylan creates a palpable tension between his private life and his public muse on *Planet Waves*.

The first Dylan-Band collaboration ever to be released officially, *Planet Waves* was put together on the extreme fly in the autumn of 1973 as Dylan and his old mates prepared for the epochal Tour '74. In the studio Dylan returned to the modus operandi that had served him best since early in his career—

spontaneity—and it worked well with this group that already knew (and therefore could anticipate and complement) him so well.

Down-to-earth to a fault and at times annoyingly simplistic, the collection—Dylan's first of all-new material in three years—finds the recording artist at his most open and accessible. From basement rock ("Tough Mama"), from ballads ("Hazel") and romantic devotionals ("Wedding Song") to an instant fan favorite ("Forever Young"), from the lower depths ("Dirge" and "Going, Going, Gone") to backwoods jubilation ("On a Night Like This") and back again to the

North Country ("You Angel You" and "Something There Is About You"), Dylan proudly wears his heart on his sleeve as he has on few other albums. And though it may not have been the "instant classic" that (in his *Rolling Stone* review) noted critic Ralph J. Gleason proclaimed for it upon release, *Planet Waves* remains as listenable (and sing-alongable) as anything from Dylan's '70s catalogue.

Not necessarily based on its merits but certainly bolstered by Tour '74, *Planet Waves* shot to No. 1 (a first in Dylan's then thirteen-year-old career), stayed there for a month, and remained on the charts for another two. Dylan and the Band did feature some of the material from *Planet Waves* on their tour, but other than the occasional outing of "Going, Going, Gone" in 1976 and 1978 and "Tough Mama" during the Never Ending Tour, only "Forever Young" has lasted as a concert perennial. Dylan included two versions of "Forever Young" on the album. The first, better-known rendition is somewhat mournful and ends side one. A more sprightly take opens side two.

Dylan contributed the cover art as well as liner notes for the release. The notes are a bit rough-and-ready, but they do convey his enthusiasm about returning to the studio and road. The cover art depicts muddy portraits of grotesque figures and contains the words "Cast-Iron Songs and Torch Ballads." That's as apt a description as any that can be found of the music on *Planet Waves*, suggesting that Dylan was, at least on this occasion, a skilled assessor of his own work.

[S] **"Playboys and Playgirls"** (Bob Dylan)

aka "Ye Playboys and Playgirls"
Various Artists (performed by Bob Dylan with Pete Seeger), *Newport Broadside/'63* (1964); *Folk Duets/'63* (1998)
Carolyn Hester, single (1965)

Dylan performed this rarely heard original with Pete Seeger at the July 1963 Newport Folk Festival some months after it had been published in *Broadside* #20. Though this take with Seeger is the only version of the song officially available, Dylan had also recorded "Playboys and Playgirls" for *Broadside* with some unidentified musicians the previous November. "Playboys and Playgirls" is a by-rote finger pointer that takes on the usual suspects (fallout shelter–selling war profiteers, laughing lynch mobs, red baiters, and phony propagandists, etc.) in fairly unoriginal fashion.

[A] ***The Player***/David Bromberg

See also *David Bromberg*
Columbia/Legacy Records CD 65263. Released 1998.

David Bromberg's fifteen-song, career-spanning retrospective includes cameo performances by Dylan (on "Sammy's Song"), George Harrison, David Amram, Andy Statman, Tracy Nelson, Emmylou Harris, and members of the Grateful Dead.

[S] **"Please, Mrs. Henry"** (Bob Dylan)

Bob Dylan/The Band, *The Basement Tapes/'67* (1975)
Chris Spedding, *Backwoods Progression* (1971)
Manfred Mann, *Earth Band* (1972)
Trials and Tribulations, *Trials and Tribulations* (1975)
Cheap Trick, *Sex, America, Cheap Trick* (1996)
The Crust Brothers, *Marquee Mark* (1998)
Various Artists (performed by Cheap Trick), *Doin' Dylan 2* (2002)

The ribald plea of a guy trying to at least get his shot glass filled just one more time, "Please, Mrs. Henry" is another one of those postmodern "Face on the Barroom Floor"–type tunes in the vein of poems by Robert Service (1874–1958) that Dylan and the Hawks seemed to be making up as they went along during their jams at Big Pink in the summer and fall of 1967. Dylan can clearly be heard cracking up on the version released on *The Basement Tapes*.

"A drinking song of authentic tipsiness, 'Please, Mrs. Henry' features a drunkard's confused invocations to a barmaid, moving with intemperate randomness through an alcoholic fog of desires," writes Andy Gill in *Don't Think Twice, It's All Right*, his 1998 book about Dylan's early compositions. "First he thinks he's had enough to drink and wants to be taken to his room; then as he wavers in the hallway, lustfulness overtakes him and he propositions her with a fanciful string of animal metaphors; rejected, he becomes sullen and truculent, waving her away; finally, poised for a piss, he's trying to catch her eye for another round of drinks, his penniless state notwithstanding. Rolling along on the back of bar-room piano and giddy organ, it's one of the more good-natured songs in Dylan's entire canon, buoyed with a light-heartedness that finds the singer corpsing into a chuckle as the final chorus begins."

"Pledge My Head to Heaven" (Keith Green)
See also *So You Wanna Go Back to Egypt* . . .
Keith Green, *So You Wanna Go Back to Egypt* . . . (1980)

So you wanna talk obscure? Here's obscure: Dylan took a sideman turn on harmonica on "Pledge My Head to Heaven," a piece of gospel-rock recorded during Dylan's evangelical phase for Green's nearly impossible-to-find outing.

"Pledging My Time" (Bob Dylan)
Bob Dylan, single (1966); *Blonde on Blonde* (1966)
Blues & Soda, *Happy Birthday Mr. Dylan* (1992)
Various Artists (performed by Luther Johnson), *Tangled Up in Blues: The Songs of Bob Dylan* (1999)

Various Artists (performed by Greg Brown), *A Nod to Bob* (2001)
Various Artists (performed by Duke Robillard), *Blues on Blonde on Blonde* (2003)

The singer sounds reluctant, fatigued, and maybe even a little stoned, but the atmospheric "Pledging My Time" expressed a straightforward commitment to both matrimony and music. The strong performance captured on *Blonde on Blonde* includes some great mouth harp, too.

Dylan's slow, pulsing, and seemingly improvised blues is heavy with that thick electric Chicago sound made famous by Muddy Waters and Chess Studios. Dylan swipes at his harp, punctuating the tune with extended solos.

Perhaps partly based on Robert Johnson's sultry "Come On in My Kitchen," "Pledging My Time" shares with that song a similar and interesting turn of phrase: "Some joker got lucky, stole her back again," sings Johnson; Dylan turns that into "Somebody got lucky, but it was an accident."

Dylan only began performing "Pledging My Time" in concert in 1987, when he played it thrice (and very convincingly) on his final tour with Tom Petty and the Heartbreakers. In 1989 and 1990 Dylan trotted out "Pledging My Time" a total of five times, and it made some rare, usually once-a-year appearances in the mid- and late 1990s as well.

"Po' Boy" (Bob Dylan)
Bob Dylan, *"Love and Theft"* (2001)

With its sweet sway, breezy melody, and romantic expressions masking underlying tensions, the rarely performed "Po' Boy" displays borscht-belt humor in heroically absurd extremes as Dylan's lived-in voice jumps over a light acoustic jingle to become a Groucho Marx for the third millennium: "Poor boy, in the hotel called the Palace of Gloom/Calls down to room service, says, 'Send up a room.'" And that's even before he gets to the knock-knock joke ("Freddy or not, here I come"; oy gevalt!). Dylan is hilarious here, but it's no parody: he digs into an antique style and milks it for all the romance and sepia-toned mystery he hears in it. As Greg Tate wrote in "Intelligence Data," his October 2, 2001, *Village Voice* assessment of *"Love and Theft,"* the song "is what hip-hop would be if it told the tale of all those players doomed to lives of quiet desperation—*Po' boy 'neath the stars that shine, washing them dishes, feeding them swine.*"

As with a surprising number of his songs, Dylan may have cribbed the title for "Po' Boy" from an identically titled song collected by folklorists John A. and Alan Lomax and reported by them to be a fragment of "The Cryderville Jail," a widely known prison song from the Old West said to be composed by Sam Houston, the infamous late ` ` nine-teenth-century desperado.

And, as with a few of the *"Love and Theft"* songs, lines from Dr. Junichi Saga's *Confessions of a Yakuza* (Tokyo and New York: Kodansha International, 1991; translated by John Bester) found their way into "Po' Boy." *Yakuza*'s "My mother . . . was the daughter of a wealthy farmer . . . (she) died when I was eleven . . . my father was a traveling salesman . . . I never met him. (My uncle) was a nice man, I won't forget him . . . After my mother died, I decided it'd be best to go and try my luck there" became "My mother was a daughter of a wealthy farmer/My father was a travelin' salesman, I never met him/When my mother died, my uncle took me and he ran a funeral parlor/He did a lot of nice things for me and I won't forget him" in the Dylan song.

[S] "Political World" (Bob Dylan)

Bob Dylan, *Oh Mercy* (1989)
Michel Montecrossa, *Born in Time* (2000)

The opening track of Dylan's superb *Oh Mercy* album is a churning rocker stricken full of anxiety and despair that immediately throws the listener into the peculiarly dislocated world that has marked some of the artist's work since at least "Ballad of a Thin Man"—a strangely cold and incomprehensible place where "icicles hang down" and "death walks up the stairs to the nearest bank." The worldview here is dangerous and suspicious, as Dylan warns of a spiritual death wrought by the familiar masters of war. The video produced for the song, directed by John Mellencamp, underscores these themes, as it features Dylan performing the piece to a gathering of movers and shakers from the military-industrial complex who meanwhile party the night away with a harem of young and willing females; it's a grotesque portrait of unrepentant gluttony. Maybe it was shot at one of those private corporate gigs Dylan takes now and then?

But Dylan, the master at covering his own tracks, was typically oblique and evasive when discussing "Political World." As related by Derek Barker in issue #28 of *Isis* magazine (December 1989), Dylan commented: "Just because it's called 'Political World' doesn't necessarily mean it's a political song. You can extract any line from any song you know and make it into what you want it to be. You could do that with 'White Christmas,' you know, 'sleigh bells will ring,' you could make a political statement out of that if you cared to, or a revolutionary statement."

On *Oh Mercy*, "Political World" is fueled by swirling guitars, a pulsating bass line, and ominous congas. When Dylan played it on the 1990 Never Ending Tour (virtually the only stretch

P

during which he did so), "Political World" took on a harder edge.

[S] "Poor Lazarus" (Traditional)

aka "Cornbread, Meat and Molasses," "Every Mail Day," "Muley on the Mountain," "Po' Lazarus," "Po' Laz'us," "The Poor Man Was Lazarus"

Various Artists (performed by Woody Guthrie), *American Folksay Ballads and Dances, Volumes 5 & 6* (1995)
Dave Van Ronk, *Inside Dave Van Ronk* (1969)
The Vipers Skiffle Group, *10,000 Years Ago* (1996)
Various Artists (performed by Bright Light Orchestra), *Southern Journey, Volume 1: Voices from the American South* (1997)
Various Artists (performed by Henry Morrison, James Carter, and other prisoners), *Southern Journey, Volume 5: Bad Man Ballads*/'59 (1997)
Various Artists (performed by James Carter), *O Brother, Where Art Thou* (soundtrack)/'59 (2001)
Various Artists (performed by Booker T. Sapps), *The Blues Roots of Bob Dylan* (2000)

Dylan adapted Woody Guthrie's take on this traditional African-American bad man's ballad and made it all his own when he was performing it in the very early 1960s. Woody's version was a far cry from the original; he changed the perspective from third to first person and introduced elements of his own wry humor into it. Unchanged, however, was the indomitable spirit of a desperate man driven by adversity to desperate measures.

The song tells the biblical story of Lazarus—not the Lazarus Jesus raises from the dead who appears in John, chapters 11 and 12, but the Lazarus of Luke 16, a sick beggar in one of Christ's parables. (This parable, incidentally, is the only one in which a character is named.)

"Poor Lazarus" isn't the only title the song is found under. "'Po' Laz'us' was also known locally as 'Muley on the Mountain,'" points out folklorist and writer Bruce Bastin (as quoted by Görgen Antonsson in "Stealin', Stealin': Bob Dylan & the Blues, 1960–1963" in *The Telegraph* #54 [spring 1996]), "and was a widespread work song, collected in penitentiaries from Virginia to Mississippi. It became popularized by Woody Guthrie as 'Cornbread, Meat and Molasses.'"

Alan Lomax was among the first to collect "Poor Lazarus" on a September 1959 visit to Parchman Farm (aka the Mississippi State Penitentiary) during which a man named James Carter led some other prisoners through a melancholy version of the piece. "The ballad of 'Po' Lazarus' is always sung as a work song, by a gang of men swinging picks, axes, or hammers and joining their leader after he gives the first phrase," explained Lomax in his 1960 book *The Folk Songs of North America.* Lomax continues:

> As with most Negro ballads, every performance produces a fresh version, the stanzas occurring in the same order only by chance. This is ballad in its primal stage, communally recreated with each performance, the song being merely one member of an extended family of work songs including "This Old Hammer," "Ham and Eggs," "East Colorado Blues," etc. I have never been able to find out anything definite about the origin of the ballad or the identity of its hero; Negroes in the Deep South do not gossip freely with white men about such matters.
>
> Known to convicted and gang workers from Virginia to Mississippi, "Po' Lazarus" concerns the doomed attempt of an exploited and underpaid black laborer to even up the score by stealing the payroll from his bosses. The ballad sets forth in stark and unforgettable language the essential tragedy of the black man as his condition used to be in the South. If he resisted, he was killed, and his family suffered.

"Po' Laz" had its greatest success as part of the soundtrack to *O Brother, Where Art Thou?*, the 2000 film by the Coen Brothers retelling Homer's *Odyssey* in the South during the 1930s. The soundtrack for the film and accompanying album were crafted by ex-Dylan Rolling Thunder Revue bandmate T-Bone Burnett, who came across the recording of James Carter and his fellow prisoners singing the song during a listening session at the Lomax Archives in New York City. "'It just made a deep impression,' he [Burnett] said. 'It was such a beautiful version, a soulful version of a great song,'" as related by Bernard Weinraub in his March 3, 2002, *New York Times* article "An Ex-Convict, a Hit Album, an Ending Fit for Hollywood."

The *O Brother* soundtrack album sold millions of copies and won Album of the Year honors at the Grammy Awards ceremony in 2002 and four other Grammys to boot. One of the recipients of those awards was James Carter, who was tracked down with no small effort by Burnett, the Lomax Archives, and Chris Grier, a *Sarasota (Florida) Herald-Tribune* reporter, following the album and song's surprising rise to popularity.

One of Dylan's first performances of the song was as a duet with Danny Kalb at a marathon half-day-long hootenanny broadcast on radio station WRVR in Riverside Church in New York in the summer of 1961. "I'd got my version of 'Poor Lazarus' from Dave Van Ronk and I shared it with Dylan in the kitchen of Fred Underhill's house in Madison [Wisconsin]," Kalb told Mitch Blank in an interview for *The Telegraph* #47 (winter 1993). "He learned that from me, although my version was really based on Dave Van Ronk's."

Dylan was probably performing "Poor Lazarus" often in this early era, but other than the Riverside Church gig, only a version from the December 22, 1961, "Minnesota Hotel Tape"

has been preserved. Six years later, he and the Band worked up an adaptation, telling the story of a black man who is murdered for refusing to back down, during the ad hoc sessions that eventually produced *The Basement Tapes* at Big Pink in upstate New York.

"Positively 4th Street" (Bob Dylan)
aka "Positively Fourth Street"
Bob Dylan, single (1965); *Bob Dylan's Greatest Hits/'65* (1967); *Masterpieces* (1978); *Biograph/'65* (1985)
Jerry Murad, *What's New Harmonicats* (1965)
Johnny Rivers, *Realization* (1968)
The Byrds, *Untitled* (1970); *The Byrds Play Dylan* (1980)
Jerry Garcia and Merl Saunders (with David Grisman), *Live at Keystone* (1973)
John "Speedy" Keen, *Previous Convictions* (1973)
Terry Melcher, *Terry Melcher* (1974)
Björn Afzelius, *Innan Tystnaden* (1982)
Antiseen, *Noise for the Sake of Noise* (1989)
Janglers, *Janglers Play Dylan* (1992)
Casandra Lange, *15 Forever* (1995)
Beat Farmers, *Manifold* (1995)
Various Artists (performed by Moose), *Outlaw Blues, Volume 2* (1995)
New Folk Generation, *New Folk Generation* (1996)
Jimmy LaFave, *Trail* (1999)
The Stereophonics, *I Wouldn't Believe Your Radio* (1999)
Sue Foley, *Back to the Blues* (2000)
Jerry Garcia Band, *Shining Star* (2001)
Simply Red, *Home* (2003); *Home: Live in Sicily* (DVD) (2004)

Perhaps Dylan's most bitter put-down song, "Positively 4th Street" flows with an acidic spite that has barely diminished over the past three and a half decades since it was first released.

Dylan recorded "Positively 4th Street" a mere four days after his controversial electric appearance at the 1965 Newport Folk Festival, which provoked a firestorm of criticism from those accusing him of "going commercial" (betraying folk music and all that some believed it represented culturally and politically). Though probably a work in progress before that infamous appearance, the song, not surprisingly, was often interpreted as Dylan's vitriolic reaction to those critics.

But "Positively 4th Street" is something more than a brush-off to critical response, something Dylan himself confessed in specific regard to the song in the *Biograph* liner notes, where he commented, "I don't write songs to critics."

Every line in "Positively 4th Street" is loaded with acrimony. It was as if Dylan, in twelve short verses, were going out of his way to burn each and every bridge behind (or in front of) him, determined to leave everyone on the other side with the thought that the song could be about them. Indeed, as Dylan had lived on West 4th Street in Greenwich Village, it was an easy song for those who knew him in the general Village milieu to get paranoid about. Some must have felt, perhaps correctly, that Dylan had caught them picking at the crumbs left at the table of his movable creative feast, fingering them for crimes of usurpation, opportunism, and—gasp!—unoriginality.

This would appear to jibe somewhat with assessments of Dylan at the time he wrote "4th Street," during a stretch when he would hold court in New York's niteries with a coterie that included Bob Neuwirth, Victor Maimudes, David Blue, and (until he was banished) Phil Ochs. Anyone stupid enough to approach, much less intrude upon, this contingent would be subject to a verbal skewering from Dylan that would make Mr. Jones from "Ballad of a Thin Man" feel as though he had gotten off easy.

And just to confuse everybody, Dylan once introduced "4th Street" as "one of my songs about friendship." On another occasion he is said to have remarked: "'Positively 4th Street' is extremely one dimensional, which I like."

But there is a tenderness hidden in the folds of "Positively 4th Street." In the lines "I do not feel so good when I see the heartbreaks you embrace/If I were a master thief perhaps I'd rob them," one can glimpse a guy who, despite being angry, still feels for the person he's singing to. But don't get too comfortable; Dylan ends the song with one of his most fearsome brush-offs: "I wish that for just one time you could stand inside my shoes, you'd know what a drag it is to see you."

Released as an A-side single in 1965, "Positively 4th Street" hit No. 7 on the *Billboard* chart, and its appearance on *Bob Dylan's Greatest Hits* in 1967 was one of the great incentives for consumers to buy that compilation. After performing at least a few versions during the fall 1965 and spring 1966 tours, Dylan put the song away for a decade. Then he brought it out once in 1976, at the infamous Night of the Hurricane 2 concert in Houston's Astrodome—and promptly ignored it for another ten years. "Positively 4th Street" began to appear on a more regular basis during his 1986 tour with Tom Petty and the Heartbreakers. It has remained in somewhat irregular rotation since, and even through 2002 its tone is every bit as wounded as it must have been in 1965. In these later, quietly venomous versions (including the one he performed upon his much-heralded return to the Newport Folk Festival in 2002), the song sounded more like a recollection of pain or a sarcastic whine, rather than a venting of anger, as though he had washed his hands of the whole affair.

▲ *Postcards of the Hanging—Grateful Dead Perform the Songs of Bob Dylan*/Grateful Dead
Arista CD 14069. Released 2002.

The Grateful Dead toyed with the songs of Bob Dylan throughout their three decades as the world's premier psychedelic road band. From the mid-1980s on, they delved deeper than ever into Dylan's earliest catalogue and performed one of his songs at nearly every show from that point on. By extension, this eleven-song collection, compiled by David Gans (a musician, writer, and host of radio's nationally syndicated *Grateful Dead Hour*), features material culled from that last, sometimes tepid epoch of Grateful Deaddom. More than just a tribute highlighting the Dead's mostly magic touch (especially lead guitarist Jerry Garcia's) on many of Dylan's most famous songs, the disc includes a bonus track of "Man of Peace" from the still-unreleased 1987 Dead/Dylan rehearsals held in preparation for their short concert tour that summer.

[S] "Precious Angel" (Bob Dylan)

Bob Dylan, *Slow Train Coming* (1979)
World Wide Message Tribe, *Heatseeker* (1998)

In January 1980, soon after inaugurating his gospel tour, Dylan introduced this song to his muse with the following rap, as recorded on a concert tape from January 14, 1980, at the Paramount Northwest Theater, Seattle: "I was stopped by somebody last night who travels around, and she said she was riding in a cab once in a big city and the cab driver turned round in the cab and said, 'Did you hear Bob Dylan's a Christian now?' And this woman said, 'Yeah, I think I have heard that. How does that make you feel? Are you a Christian?' And the driver said, 'No, I'm not but I've been following Bob for a long time.' And the lady said, 'Well, what do you think of his new things?' He said, 'I think they're real good, but if I could meet that person that brought Bob Dylan to the Lord, I think I might become a Christian too.' This here is a song—this is all about that certain person."

A love song to his delivering angel—or maybe, with its reggae lilt, just a love song—"Precious Angel" mixes the sacred and the profane with such lyrics as "You're the queen of my flesh" and "You're the lamp of my soul." The composition is chock-full of enough Bible references to keep a divinity student divine and enough hot Mark Knopfler guitar licks to make any luthier proud. And the song is not without the vengeful, paranoid streak consistent with some of Dylan's gospel-period material when he sings, "My so-called friends have fallen under a spell/They look me squarely in the eye and they say, 'All is well'/Can they imagine the darkness that will fall from on high/When men will beg God to kill them and they won't be able to die." Simple scriptural musing, perhaps. Another "Positively 4th Street," most definitely not.

Performed only during Dylan's gospel shows of 1979 and 1980, "Precious Angel" was a fairly constant midset and always intensely passionate selection during that controversial era.

[S] "Precious Memories" (J. B. F. Wright/arrangement by Bob Dylan)

Bob Dylan, *Knocked Out Loaded* (1986)
Aretha Franklin (performed with Rev. James Cleveland), *Amazing Grace* (1972)
Jim Reeves, *Gentleman Jim 1955–1959* (1989)
Andy Griffith, *Somebody Bigger Than You and I* (1996)
Edwin Hawkins, *Very Best of the Edwin Hawkins Singers* (1998)
Tammy Wynette, *Inspirational Favorites* (1998)

Only Dylan could take an old country gospel song that looks fondly at the past, record it with a halfhearted reggae twist and steel-drum track, mix a female chorus into the background, bury it on a forgettable record, and practically walk away from it forever. He pulled it out a couple of times at Never Ending Tour

P

shows in the fall of 1989 and then once more as an encore on the memorable night he closed Toad's Place in New Haven, Connecticut, in 1990.

The version of "Precious Memories" released on *Knocked Out Loaded* in 1986 was originally recorded by Dylan at Delta Sound in New York City in late July 1984 and over-dubbed substantially afterward.

According to Ray Maxwell Stone in *Our Hymns and Gospel Songs* (1972): "J. B. F. Wright, author-composer of 'Precious Memories' (originally copyrighted in 1925), was born in Tennessee, February 21, 1877. In contrast to the majority of modern-day writers and composers, Mr. Wright has never taught nor does he claim a great amount of music education. He writes from inspiration, and in his own words, '. . . when words come spontaneously, flowing into place when I feel the divine urge.' Mr. Wright is a member of the Church of God, and his writing, as did his church work, began at a very early age."

▣ "Pressing On" (Bob Dylan)

Bob Dylan, *Saved* (1980)
Various Artists (performed by Chicago Mass Choir), *Gotta Serve Somebody: The Gospel Songs of Bob Dylan* (2003)

Perhaps Dylan's most uplifting gospel song, "Pressing On" was a smart encore choice when it was performed during the 1979–80 born-again tour, as its catchy refrain sent the flock home feeling good inside. Modest but genuine, the muted album release of this song (on *Saved*) featured some gorgeous piano playing by Dylan.

Paul Williams provided some dramatic first-hand reportage of Dylan's initial 1979 San Francisco performances of "Pressing On" in his book *Bob Dylan: Performing Artist—The Middle Years, 1974–1986* (Novato, Calif.:

Underwood-Miller, 1992), writing that Dylan presented the song as a second encore, "playing piano on the first verse, then walking to the front of the stage and clapping his hands, singing the second verse and chorus into a microphone with no guitar between him and the audience." Later in the book Williams elaborates, describing the encore performance as "a simple but very special gift from Dylan to his live audience. He plays the piano (a moment of conscious intimacy, like the harmonica solos but even rarer); he sings out in a stirring, full-hearted voice; and finally he stands before us and (rare moment indeed) acknowledges and accepts our love, communicating by his presence how much he does in fact appreciate it. . . . And then he disappears into the night."

▣ "Pretty Boy Floyd" (Woody Guthrie)

aka "The Ballad of Pretty Boy Floyd"
Various Artists (performed by Bob Dylan), *Folkways: A Vision Shared—A Tribute to Woody Guthrie and Leadbelly* (1988)
Woody Guthrie, *Woody Guthrie—Buffalo Skinners: The Asch Recordings, Volume 4* (1999)
Joan Baez, *Joan Baez in Concert, Part 1* (1962)
Cisco Houston, *Cisco Houston Sings Woody Guthrie* (1963)
Country Joe McDonald, *Thinking of Woody Guthrie* (1969)
Christy Moore, *Live in Dublin* (1978)
Arlo Guthrie and Pete Seeger, *Precious Friend* (1982)
Ramblin' Jack Elliott, *Hard Travelin'* (1989)
Pete Seeger, *Link in the Chain* (1996)

A great song about an infamous (yet beloved by some) American outlaw, "Pretty Boy Floyd" was in Dylan's repertoire very shortly after the singer hit New York City in 1961; his first known performance includes neo–jug band maestro Jim Kweskin on shared vocal and guitar. In 1975, "Pretty Boy Floyd" was part of a quirky three-song jam session that Dylan shared with Jack Elliott at the Other End in

Greenwich Village. It turned up again during a spirited duet with G. E. Smith at Neil Young's December 1988 Bay Area concert for the Bridge School. Earlier in 1988, Dylan contributed a heartfelt "Pretty Boy Floyd" to *A Vision Shared*, Folkways Records' Guthrie/Leadbelly tribute album. The recording came as a breath of fresh air—a new "old" song and a then-rare acoustic foray to boot, presaging Dylan's cover-song albums of the early 1990s. It was also something from his past that he was arranging for the here and now, baring his heart and practically inhabiting the very being of ol' Charlie Floyd while making a subtle point or two. In so doing, Dylan showed what a skillful interpreter of the American folk canon he could be; his "Pretty Boy Floyd" bristles with counter-rhythms as he dances over the narrative.

Some background on the song may be found in Guy Logsdon and Jeff Place's liner notes for *Woody Guthrie: Buffalo Skinners—The Asch Recordings, Volume 4*:

> This is one of Woody's best-known ballads; he made an American Robin Hood out of an Oklahoma murderer. Of course, the reason Floyd, Robin Hood, and other thieves did not steal from the poor is that the poor had nothing to steal, but Pretty Boy Floyd did have many friends who helped him elude the law for a few years. Charles Arthur Floyd was born on 3 February 1904 in Georgia to parents who were basically hard-working, honest, illiterate rural laborers. Not long after his birth the family moved to eastern Oklahoma near the small town of Akins in the Cookson Hills, where numerous outlaws had hidden during the late nineteenth century. At the age of eighteen he married, but did not want to farm as a living to support his wife and son. In 1925 he joined migrant harvesters working northward, and along the way robbed a

Bank robber Charles Arthur "Pretty Boy" Floyd with Beulah Ash, ca. 1930.

(Photo: American Stock/Getty Images)

> $12,000 payroll in St. Louis, Missouri. He was arrested and sentenced to five years in a Missouri penitentiary, and was paroled in 1929.
>
> The name "Pretty Boy" was given to him by a gangster madam in Kansas City, and his robberies and killings ranged from Oklahoma to Ohio. Indeed, he shared some of his loot with relatives and friends and Cookson Hills farmers who during the early Depression days hated banks and bankers, but his

> killings negated any generosity. By 1934, Floyd was listed as "Public Enemy #1," and on 22 October 1934 near East Liverpool, Ohio, he was killed by FBI agents led by Melvin Purvis. It continues to be believed that twenty thousand people attended his funeral. Not all Oklahomans considered Floyd to be a Robin Hood.

In *Woody Guthrie: A Life*, Joe Klein asserts that Woody wrote "Pretty Boy Floyd" in March 1939. Klein goes on to discuss the song thusly: "If the police considered Pretty Boy Floyd a criminal, he was a hero to the poor farmers who gave him food and shelter and, in return for their hospitality, often found their mortgage had been paid off or a thousand dollar bill left at the dinner table. As the song progressed, Woody's claims for his hero became more extravagant: Pretty Boy even sent a truckload of groceries to provide Christmas dinner for all the families on relief in Oklahoma City."

In his book *The Folk Songs of North America*, Alan Lomax presents Guthrie's own description of the colorful outlaw:

> "[Pretty Boy Floyd] was born and raised right down in there where I was. I talked to lots of people that knowed him personal. Said he wasn't much of a bad feller. Fact, some of them respected him lots more than they did the sheriff and his deputies. Anyhow, something went wrong and Pretty Boy went to packing shooting irons, blowing his way into the banks where the people's money was. Grabbed up big sacks of it and took it out and scattered it everywhere, give it to the poor folks up and down the country.
>
> ". . . Pretty Boy had the right idea, but the wrong system. The outlaw is in his grave today. Jesse James, Billy the Kid, Cole Younger and Belle Star, all of them in their graves, but we still sing about them. You hear songs about those fellers, springing up everywhere like flowers in the right early spring. That's the way it was with my piece. It tells tales I heard concerning his life and what kind of man he was. We never had a governor that was half as popular as Pretty Boy. Back in them times, you couldn't come down in my part of Oklahoma and say nothing against him. If you did, something was liable to hit you, son, and it wouldn't be no train . . ."

For a wonderfully cheesy portrait of the outlaw hero, check out *Pretty Boy Floyd*, a 1960 film starring an energetic John Ericson in the title role, supported by Peter Falk and "Grampa" Al Lewis. For the more literal-minded, *Pretty Boy: The Life and Times of Charles Arthur Floyd* (New York: St. Martin's Press, 1992) by Michael Wallis is recommended.

[S] "Pretty Peggy-O" (Traditional)

aka "Bonnie Lass O Fyvie," "The Bonnie Lass Fyvie-O," "Fennario," "The Maid of Fife-E-O," "Peggy-O," "Pretty Peggy of Derby"

Bob Dylan, *Bob Dylan* (1962)
Various Artists (performed by John Strachan), *World Library of Folk and Primitive Music, Volume III: Scotland/'51* (1998)
Ewan MacColl, *Scots Folk Songs* (1956)
Clancy Brothers, *The Clancy Brothers & Tommy Makem* (1961)
Joan Baez, *Joan Baez in Concert, Volume 2* (1962)
Walter Forbes, *Ballads and Bluegrass* (1962)
Judy Collins, *Golden Apples of the Sun* (1963)
The Corrie Folk Trio, *Corrie Folk Trio* (1964)
Simon and Garfunkel, *Wednesday Morning 3 A.M.* (1966)
John Stewart, *American Journey* (1996)
Jock Duncan, *Ye Shine Whar Ye Stan!* (1997)
The Grateful Dead, *Dick's Picks Volume 15/'77* (1999)

Soldiers marching off to war and leaving their

P

gals behind is ancient folk-song fodder, and "Pretty Peggy-O," which tells the tragic story of a young woman who loses her beloved captain when he dies in battle, is among the most famous. Perhaps because of its implicit anti-war sentiment, "Peggy-O" attracted the likes of Dylan, Joan Baez, Judy Collins, Simon and Garfunkel, and the Grateful Dead, all of whom recorded it or included it in set lists at one time or another. Predictably, Dylan's snarling early version had a harder, angrier edge than most of the others, whose arrangements stuck closer to the sweeter melodies of the Baez and Collins takes. It is in that dichotomy, however, that the power of the song lies: the incredibly sad tale is juxtaposed with an equally tender melody, both of which can be effectively interpreted a number of ways.

Considered together, all of the versions suggest the story of a love affair between a traveling enemy soldier and a local girl that is thwarted by the girl's ambitious mother, who wants a son-in-law with more money and a higher social status. Thus, his declarations of love transform into threats against the locals' lives when he returns from his next march. But he dies brokenhearted.

"Only in ballads do soldiers die of broken hearts," says *Reprints from* Sing Out!, *The Folk Song Magazine*, volume 6 (1964). "Captain Willie, refused by pretty Peggy-O because his 'fortune is too low,' appears in English, Scottish and American versions of this song. Originally an English broadside ballad, 'Pretty Peggy of Derby,' the song became popular in Scotland where it is known as 'the Bonnie Lass of Fyvie-O.' Many versions have been collected in America and, as in this one, poor Willie is laid to rest in Louisiana."

The liner notes to Jock Duncan's 1997 album *Ye Shine Whar Ye Stan!* examine some of the history informing "The Bonnie Lass o Fyvie":

This song telling of the dragoon captain who died for the love of the bonnie lass o Fyvie has been widely popular. There are over 20 versions in the Greig-Duncan Collection with considerable variation in text and tune. The song was collected by Cecil Sharp in the Appalachians under the title "Pretty Peggy-O" and Ford's *Vagabond Songs* has a song "Bonnie Barbara O" localised in Derby. But the song seems certainly to belong to Fyvie.

There may or may not have been a barracks in or near Fyvie but it is clear from the song and local tradition that Fyvie was a staging post on the military route from Aberdeen to Fort George on the Moray Firth.

The literary minded should be steered to Sharyn McCrumb's novel *If Ever I Return, Pretty Peggy-O* (New York: Simon & Schuster, 1990), the first of the author's series of mountain mysteries loosely based on songs from the folk canon.

"I been around this whole country, but I never yet found Fennario," said a mischievous Dylan on his debut-album cut of "Pretty Peggy-O," and indeed, the location of Fennario, the song's setting, has long been a curiosity among folklorists. The general consensus is that it is a fictitious place derived from the words "fen" and "area," poeticized as "ario" in the song. Appearing in any number of ancient and relatively modern folk pieces, the term denotes, according to the *Oxford English Dictionary*, "low land covered wholly or partially with shallow water, or subject to frequent inundations; a tract of such land, a marsh ... esp. the fens: certain low-lying districts in Cambridgeshire, Lincolnshire, and some adjoining counties."

"Pretty Peggy-O" appeared on Dylan's debut album, where it lost its Scottish burr and acquired a Texas accent. Dylan performed the song very early in his career and returned to it mostly as an acoustic number through the 1990s. He arranged it in electric garb mid-decade, giving it an almost funereal air, the ghosts of bagpipes bleating in the mournful shadows of the tragic song.

▪ "Pretty Polly" (Traditional)

See also "Love Henry"
Paul Clayton, *Bloody Ballads* (1956)
Pete Steele, *Anglo-American Ballads* (1958)
Various Artists (performed by Estil C. Ball), *Southern Journey, Volume 5: Bad Man Ballads/'59* (1997)
Walter Forbes, *Ballads and Bluegrass* (1962)
Bert Jansch, *Jack Orion* (1966)
Sandy Denny, *Sandy Denny* (1979)
Davey Graham, *Home Is Where the Heart Is* (1988); *Fire in the Soul* (1999)
Jean Ritchie and Doc Watson, *Jean Ritchie and Doc Watson at Folk City* (1990)
The Stanley Brothers, *Complete Columbia Recordings* (1996)
Dock Boggs, *His Folkways Years (1963–1968)* (1998)

Traditionally, when unmarried couples violated sexual taboos, the woman paid a higher price than the man. "Pretty Polly" tells the story of one man's doomed effort to protect himself and his family from the stigma associated with an out-of-wedlock pregnancy and the attendant shotgun wedding, only to bring about a greater tragedy. Scholars believe that "Pretty Polly" has antecedents in the British broadside ballad known as "The Cruel Ship's Carpenter" or "The Gosport Tragedy."

According to folklorist Alan Lomax in his book *The Folk Songs of North America*, this murder ballad was "America's favorite crime story, the same tale that Dreiser used as the theme of *An American Tragedy*. Pretty Polly is pregnant and Willie puts her out of the way."

"If this bloody Southern mountain ballad was originally inspired by an actual event, the tragedy took place a long way from the hills of Tennessee and Kentucky," according to *Reprints from* Sing Out!, *The Folk Song Magazine*, volume 6 (1964). "The English Channel town of Gosport, near Portsmouth, Southampton, and the Isle of Wight provided the setting for the grisly murder sung in this ballad. The first appearance of the song is around 1750 in broadside form in England. A 27-stanza ballad was still current almost 100 years later, appearing in print in early American songsters. As the old ballad entered oral tradition, the folk chipped away at the almost interminable story, boiling the original down to bare essentials. In many cases, the motive for the murder (Willie had gotten unsuspecting Polly pregnant) has been eliminated or only woven into the song subtly. In a great variety of forms, the song has taken a fast hold on the folk consciousness. Collectors have found the tragic ballad in many versions throughout the South and Southeast."

Folklorist and Lomax colleague Anne Warner's research of "Pretty Polly" took the song's roots back even further, revealing the many permutations and stories that fall under the general title. And inspection of the lyrics she presents in her book *Traditional American Folk Songs from the Anne & Frank Warner Collection* (Syracuse, N.Y.: Syracuse University Press), "Pretty Polly" reads more like "Love Henry," a song of romantic murder recorded by Dylan for *World Gone Wrong* in the early 1990s. According to Warner, "This ballad is a version of Child No. 4, 'Lady Isabel and the Elf King,' which some scholars trace back to a ballad of the twelfth century in the Lower Rhine region. As is usually the case in American versions, the supernatural nature of the lover has been forgotten or is not mentioned. This element of the supernatural, present in so many ancient ballads, did not travel over the water. We do not really know why."

P

A couple of early (circa 1961) versions of Dylan performing this antique have been in circulation for years—one from the famed "Minnesota Party Tape" in May, the other from his first known appearance at New York City's Gaslight Café in September. And he made a return of sorts to the song when he recorded "Love Henry," a cousin to "Pretty Polly," on his second album of mostly archaic covers, *World Gone Wrong*.

▣ "Property of Jesus" (Bob Dylan)
Bob Dylan, *Shot of Love* (1981)

Helped by Cliff Pickhardt's swift piano, Dylan's little side trip back to Bibleland is not only tolerable but inviting: more proof that Dylan's best gospel works were the ones with a touch of his old snarly attitude, not necessarily the ones that called listeners to "get on board." His exuberant vocal on this tune is a joy. Never performed in concert, "Property of Jesus" is said by some to be a song Dylan wrote in response to some snide comments Mick Jagger made regarding Dylan's conversion. Either way, "Property of Jesus" was, along with the album on which it appeared, a return to form after *Saved*—even if some of the song's clever lyrics mask elements of self-pity and resentment.

Q

▣ "Queen Jane Approximately" (Bob Dylan)
Bob Dylan, *Highway 61 Revisited* (1965); single (1966)
Bob Dylan/The Grateful Dead, *Dylan & The Dead* (1989)
The Four Seasons, *Sing Big Hits of Bacharach, David & Dylan* (1965)
John Schroder, *Dylan Vibrations* (1971)
Lilac Angels, *I'm Not Afraid to Say Yes* (1973)
Steven Keene, *Keene on Dylan* (1990)

The Grateful Dead, *Postcards of the Hanging: Grateful Dead Perform the Songs of Bob Dylan* (2002)

This impish put-down song has been taken to be everything from a snub of Joan Baez (Baez was, at the time of the song's release, "the Queen of Folk" and Dylan the abdicated king) to a reimagining of the early-sixteenth-century English-Scottish ballad called "The Death of Queen Jane" (Child ballad No. 170). Other imaginations have claimed it to be a veiled reference to a marijuana score or a solicitation to a drag queen. (After all, Dylan did tell Nora Ephron and Susan Edmiston in a 1965 interview in the New York office of his manager, Albert Grossman, that "Queen Jane is a man.") An underappreciated song from Dylan's most prolific period, "Queen Jane" is—both lyrically and musically—full of weariness, compassion, condescension, self-righteousness, and (though he might be loath to admit it) regret, as the singer expresses romantic aloofness while also aiming an attack at stilted and stifling domestic ritual.

Baez would seem the likely target here as Dylan appears to be coolly warning that a long fall from grace is imminent, as if he has the scars from such a catastrophe to validate his opinion—or that he was merely too cool to fall for the kind of snare that could lead to such a plunge. But whether it is Baez or some other anointed female, the narrator clearly sees himself as the one who will put her back together, unlike all the queen's horses and men of Humpty-Dumpty infamy, after her advisers are finished heaving "their plastic at your feet to convince you of your pain" and she finally stops fooling herself.

Even those familiar with the Dylan song may be unaware of the history evoked by its rather witty title. History's Queen Jane did not enjoy her high royal position for long—she lasted a mere nine days! If Dylan was aware of this, the implication would be that the subject of his song would tumble from her (or his) elevated position sooner rather than later. In any case, calling the character a queen indicates that she is an accomplished woman, or at least one of high station. Her life, though, is not all that it might seem: she is manipulated by family who have filled her with notions of grandeur from a very young age, and she is only dimly aware of just how bleak her future really will be. And if she isn't, Dylan is not only sticking that reality in her face but suggesting he may be there for her when she falls. Or maybe not.

Dylan didn't start performing "Queen Jane Approximately" in concert until he hooked up with the Grateful Dead in 1987. While the renditions from that partnership may have been a little lackluster, "Queen Jane" has improved in its semiregular airings on the Never Ending Tour over the 1990s and early 2000s, perhaps most notably at his 1993 Supper Club shows in New York City.

A final note: "Queen Jane Approximately" got the dramatic visuals it always deserved in Bernardo Bertolucci's 2004 film, *The Dreamers*.

Q

[S] "Quinn the Eskimo (The Mighty Quinn)"

(Bob Dylan)

aka "The Mighty Quinn"

Bob Dylan, *Self Portrait* (1970); *Bob Dylan's Greatest Hits, Volume II* (1971); *Biograph/'67* (1985)

Manfred Mann, single (1967); *The Mighty Quinn* (1969); *Watch* (1978); *Semi-Detached Suburban* (1979); *Budapest Live* (1984); *20 Years of Manfred Mann's Earth Band 1971–1991* (1991); *Chapter Two: The Best of the Fontana Years* (1994)

Ian and Sylvia, *Nashville* (1968); *Greatest Hits!* (1987); *Best of the Vanguard Years* (1998)

Ramsey Lewis, *Maiden Voyage* (1968)

Gary Puckett and the Union Gap, *Young Girl* (1968)

1910 Fruitgum Company, *1, 2, 3, Red Light* (1968)

Kettels, *Overflight* (1968)

James Last, *Non Stop Dancing* (1968)

Uncle Bill, *Socks It to Ya* (1968)

The Ventures, *Flight of Fantasy* (1968)

Family Frog, single (1968)

The Hollies, *Hollies Sing Dylan* (1969); *Words and Music by Bob Dylan* (1969); *Long Cool Woman* (1971)

The Brothers & Sisters of Los Angeles, *Dylan Gospel* (1969)

Julie London, *Yummy Yummy* (1969)

Carmen, *Carmen* (1969)

Peter Schickele, *Good-Time Ticket* (1969)

Lulu, *It's Lulu* (1970)

Mike Batt Orchestra, *Portrait of Bob Dylan* (1972)

Leon Russell, *Leon Live* (1973)

Meissberg & Walters, *Love's an Easy Song* (1977)

Ducks Deluxe, *Last Night of a Pub Rock Band* (1981)

Various Artists (performed by Sheryl Lee Ralph with Cedella Marley and Sharon Marley Prendergast), *The Mighty Quinn* (soundtrack) (1989)

Blues & Soda, *Happy Birthday Mr. Dylan* (1992)

The Little Angels, single (1993)

Brewer and Shipley, *Archive Alive* (1997)

The Grateful Dead, *Dick's Picks, Volume 17* (2000); *Postcards of the Hanging: Grateful Dead Perform the Songs of Bob Dylan* (2002)

Michel Montecrossa, *Born in Time* (2000)

Various Artists (performed by Reggae Rockers), *Blowin' in the Wind: A Reggae Tribute to Bob Dylan* (2003)

The English pop group Manfred Mann's Earth Band caused a minor stir in the summer of 1969 with their release of "The Mighty Quinn" from Dylan's then hush-hush (but already widely bootlegged in the music industry) *Basement Tapes* recorded with the Hawks in 1967. The song's success was, apparently, a bit of a surprise to Dylan, who once commented on its odd qualities. "I don't know what it was about," he declared in the *Biograph* liner notes. "I guess it was some kind of a nursery rhyme."

The *Basement* version was eventually released on *Biograph*, but a later rendition of

"Quinn the Eskimo" by Dylan and the Band, performed at the Isle of Wight concert in 1969, was released before that. This was a wild, howling, slippery version and a good reason to actually buy *Self Portrait* in 1970 and/or *Bob Dylan's Greatest Hits, Volume II*, on which the same live recording was also released a year later. Although "Quinn" was one of Dylan's most popular and oft-covered songs, he appears not to have performed it again until almost exactly thirty-three years later during the summer 2002 Never Ending Tour, which hit points east and at high altitude: at a Harley-Davidson motorcycle celebration at Baltimore's Pimlico Race Track, a Hamptons All for the Sea

Actor Anthony Quinn (carrying spear) in a still from the film *The Savage Innocents*, 1959.

(Photo: Paramount Pictures/Courtesy of Getty Images)

benefit show on Long Island the very next night, in Fargo, North Dakota, and at a final display in Aspen. In 2003, Dylan brought it out for a rapturous performance at London's Shepherd's Bush Hall.

Some Dylan scholars point to the maestro's interest in film as a source for "Quinn," citing an obscure 1959 flick called *The Savage Innocents*. In that film, Anthony Quinn plays an Aleut leading the fight for, in critic Leonard Maltin's words, the "simple ways of Eskimo people vs. Civilization." Peter O'Toole, who later makes a cameo in Dylan's song "Clean Cut Kid," also appears in *The Savage Innocents*.

There is debate among Dylanists as to the song's significance; some insist that it's trivial, while others point to a messianic subtext. Greil Marcus, in *Invisible Republic: Bob Dylan's Basement Tapes* (New York: Henry Holt and Company, 1997), may merge the two views when he calls "Quinn" "a famous song about deliverance from nothingness, about a hero's conquest of boredom."

Nobody, by the way, can seem to agree on the exact title of the song: is it "Quinn the Eskimo" or "Quinn, the Eskimo"? Or maybe "Quinn the Eskimo (The Mighty Quinn)"? Or did somebody say "The Mighty Quinn"? It has been published under these titles and a few other permutations on official releases and songbooks. Columbia Records' Dylan Web site, www.bobdylan.com, lists it as "Quinn the Eskimo (The Mighty Quinn)," so let's just go with that.

Finally, the screwball Denzel Washington political comedy flick *The Mighty Quinn* (1989), set on a Caribbean island, is worth a look.

"Quit Your Low Down Ways" (Bob Dylan)
aka "Quit Your Lowdown Ways," "You Better Quit Your Low Down Ways"

Bob Dylan, *The Bootleg Series, Volumes 1–3: Rare and Unreleased, 1961–1991/'62* (1991)
Peter, Paul & Mary, *In the Wind* (1963)
George Edwards, *Early Chi* (1965)
The Hollies, *Hollies Play Dylan* (1969); *Words and Music by Bob Dylan* (1969)
Sebastian Cabot, *Sebastian Cabot, Actor—Bob Dylan, Poet* (1967)
Manfred Mann's Earth Band, *Nightingales and Bombers* (1975)
Various Artists (performed by the Hollies), *I Shall Be Unreleased/'69* (1991)
Various Artists (performed by Giljunko), *Duluth Does Dylan* (2001)

Regarded as a crude but nevertheless effective country-blues pastiche and sung by Dylan in the voice of an old, grizzled black man, "Quit Your Low Down Ways" was recorded in July 1962 for, but did not appear on, *The Freewheelin' Bob Dylan*. Some sources suggest that it was recorded earlier and was a *Bob Dylan* outtake. It was preserved also as a Witmark demo for copyright purposes that December. "Quit Your Low Down Ways" first gained public recognition from the version Peter, Paul & Mary included on *In the Wind*, their 1963 collection for which Dylan penned an extensive liner-note poem ("In the Wind") and on which they presented their famous version of "Blowin' in the Wind," which put Dylan on the radar screen of popular culture.

Dylanists point to "Milk Cow Blues" as a source for "Quit Your Low Down Ways"; the first two verses of "Quit" are basically lifted from Kokomo Arnold's 1934 version of that older song. Dylan's interest in and enjoyment of the folk blues during this period is unmistakable. And the song was a common performance choice for Dylan in 1962 as he toyed with varying arrangements and vocal deliveries before finally shelving it forever.

R

[S] "Ragged and Dirty" (Traditional/Willie Brown)

aka "Broke and Hungry," "Broken Hearted, Ragged and Dirty Too," "I'm Broke an' I'm Hungry"
Bob Dylan, *World Gone Wrong* (1993)
Blind Lemon Jefferson, *Matchbox Blues/'26* (1998)
Various Artists (performed by Willie Brown), *Negro Blues & Hollers/'42* (1962)
Sleepy John Estes, *Broke and Hungry* (1963)
Larry Johnson, *Fast & Funky* (1974)
Sam Mitchell, *Falling Down* (1978)
Cedell Davis, *Cedell Davis* (1994)

Dylan jump-started his great November 1993 Supper Club shows in New York City with incendiary readings of this dusty, footloose, come-on blues, which had also appeared on his *World Gone Wrong* album earlier in the year. Dylan sang "Ragged and Dirty" with a real edge—as if he'd just hopped off a freight train and was begging for a plate of grits and a cup of cold coffee from a sultry waitress at a local greasy spoon somewhere in deep Ozark country.

According to Dylan in his *World Gone Wrong* liner notes, "one of the Willie Browns did this." The Willie Brown in question is not the Mississippi Delta bluesman who followed in the footsteps of Charley Patton and Robert Johnson. Rather, he was an Arkansas plantation worker who recorded "Ragged and Dirty" for the Library of Congress in 1942. Despite his sourcing, Dylan's version of the song owes more to the 1929 Sleepy John Estes rendition.

Brown is often given credit for "Ragged and Dirty," but the song is much older than his version, of course. Its floating verses in the many renditions recorded suggest that it is scarcely an individual blues song, but it should never be confused with Peg Leg Howell's 1929 "Broke and Hungry Blues."

[S] "Ragtime Annie" (Traditional)

Chet Atkins, *A Man and His Guitar* (1961)
Clark Kessinger, *Legend of Clark Kessinger* (1964)
Asleep at the Wheel, *Wheel* (1977)
Eric Thompson, *Bluegrass Guitar* (1978)
Dick Solberg, *Riding High* (1981)
Dakota Dave Hull, *Hull's Victory* (1988)
Charlie Poole, *Old Time Tunes, Volume 2* (1996)

This sawdust-on-the-floor instrumental is associated with Bluegrass Appalachia but has roots in Irish music (and its close choreographic relative, line dancing). The song mysteriously appeared as a late-career concert inclusion performed just once—at a Chicago show with surprise guest David Bromberg on guitar during Dylan's club date tour in the waning days of 1997.

[S] "Railroad Boy" (Traditional)

aka "The Butcher Boy," "The Butcher's Boy," "The Fatal Courtship," "Go Dig My Grave," "In London City Where I Did Dwell," "The Railroad Lover," "She Died in Vain"
Bob Dylan, *Hard Rain*/video (1976)
Various Artists (performed by Buell Kazee), *Anthology of American Folk Music/'28* (1952/1997)
Peggy Seeger, *Songs of Courting and Complaint* (1955)
Tommy Makem, *Songs of Tommy Makem* (1961)
Joan Baez, *Joan Baez, Volume 2* (1961)
Sam Hinton, *The Wandering Folk Songs* (1967)
Almeda Riddle, *Ballads and Hymns* (1972)
Jean Ritchie and Doc Watson, *Jean Ritchie and Doc Watson at Folk City* (1990)
Judy Canova, *Judy Canova* (1998)
Lilly Brothers, *Have a Feast Here Tonight* (1999)
Damian Jurado, *Holding His Breath* (EP) (2003)

An incredibly dark and vivid portrayal of a brokenhearted young girl driven to hang herself, "Railroad Boy" was one of the best duets Dylan pulled off with Joan Baez during the 1976 leg of the Rolling Thunder Revue. The singers became the young woman reading from her own suicide note: "Over my coffin place a snow-white dove/To warn this world I died for love." No doubt cribbed from the 1928 Buell Kazee version as heard on the *Anthology of American Folk Music*, Dylan was also performing this song in 1961, and it is included on the so-called Minneapolis Party Tape recorded at Bonnie Beecher's apartment in May of that year.

Early musicologists considered "Railroad Boy," a distant cousin of "Barbara Allen," to be an amalgamation of several eighteenth-century British products, including "The Cruel Father," "London City," "Go Bring Me Back My Blue-Eyed Boy," and "There Is an Alehouse in Yonder Town," though their merger apparently occurred in the U.S., one version even using Jersey City as its locale.

Carl Sandburg wrote about the "London City" variant as early as 1927 in his book *The American Songbag*: "Here too is a 'sad-like' tune . . . And the words match the tune . . . The seventh verse is an addition by someone wanting a dash of horse sense to finish off the fatal childish romance."

For a decidedly postmodern spin on the song and yarn, check out Neil Jordan's 1997 film *The Butcher Boy*.

R

S "Rainy Day Women #12 & 35" (Bob Dylan)
aka "Everybody Must Get Stoned"
Bob Dylan, single (1966); *Blonde on Blonde* (1966); *Bob Dylan's Greatest Hits* (1967); *MTV Unplugged* (1995)
Bob Dylan/The Band, *Before the Flood* (1974)
Bob Dylan/Various Artists (performed by Tom Petty and the Heartbreakers), *Bob Dylan: The 30th Anniversary Concert Celebration* (1993)
Earl Scruggs, *Nashville Airplane* (1970)
Rude Awakening, *Rude Awakening* (1989)
A Subtle Plague, *Marijuana's Greatest Hits* (1992)
David Harris, *The Times They Are A-Changin'* (1992)
Various Artists (performed by the Black Crowes), *Hempilation:*

Freedom Is Normal (1995)
Various Artists (performed by Dodgy), *Outlaw Blues, Volume 2* (1995)
Little Mike and the Tornadoes, *Flynn's Place* (1995)
Lester Flatt and Earl Scruggs, *1964–1969, Plus* (1996)
Come Lily, *Come Lily* (1999)
Various Artists (performed by Black Labels), *Duluth Does Dylan* (2001)
Various Artists (performed by Brian Soltz), *Blues on Blonde on Blonde* (2003)

An anarchist novelty song if ever there was one, "Rainy Day Women #12 and 35" is both one of Bob Dylan's loopier compositions and among his most commercially successful. Just like "Like a Rolling Stone" had the year before, it rode to No. 2 on the *Billboard* charts in 1966. Considering that it came from the quill of one of his generation's most accomplished lyricists, it is a darling stroke of lunacy—invigoratingly funny and a refreshing lark for Dylan and his studio musicians (who all sound as if they were spiking their coffee with bourbon) during the *Blonde on Blonde* recording session.

"Rainy Day Women," despite its memorable refrain/war cry "Everbody must get stoned," would, with a touch of irony probably intended by its author, appear to parody the '60s drug culture as much as it lauds it. Even through decades of performances of "Rainy Day Women," it is difficult to determine whether Dylan was making an unrepentant statement of hipsterism or merely having some fun at his audiences' (often oblivious) expense.

Not to say that in the heat of the 1960s there wasn't a huge outcry accompanying the song's release. The controversy was so strong that it prompted Dylan to announce: "I never have and never will write a 'drug song.'"

On another occasion Dylan remarked, in typically cryptic fashion, that "'Rainy Day Women' happens to deal with a minority of cripples and

Orientals and the world in which they live." This quote and the preceding one are recorded by Robert Shelton in *No Direction Home: The Life and Music of Bob Dylan* (New York: Beech Tree Books/William Morrow, 1986).

Despite Dylan's claim and flip observations, "Rainy Day Women" was banned by American and British radio stations, and *Time* magazine, in response to the release of the song, reported in its July 1, 1966, issue, as cited by Shelton, that "In the shifting, multilevel jargon of teenagers, to 'get stoned' does not mean to get drunk, but to get high on drugs . . . a 'rainy-day woman,' as any junkie knows, is a marijuana cigarette."

While the song is about persecution and criticism, the meaning of its title is still being hashed out. Is it about marijuana, alcohol, or even—gulp—sex? Along with the *Time* magazine definition, the title is also said to reference, as does the Waylon Jennings song "Rainy Day Woman" of a few years later, an alternate girlfriend for days when the regularly scheduled, fair-weather woman is just too annoying to deal with. Another story purports that during the recording of the song, two females (ages twelve and thirty-five) showed up at the studio in the midst of a cloudburst. Here's another doozy: multiplying the two numbers equals four twenty—stoner's code for prime time to fire up a joint. Then there are the logomaniacs who connect the numbers to Christ and God. A more likely theory: it is a nonsense title conceived on the spur of the moment, like "Alcatraz to the 9th Power."

Indeed, the *Blonde on Blonde* version conveys a hungover New Orleans funeral street procession, complete with a trombone, tambourines, and an "oompah" bass drum adding to the song's sensory abandon. An outburst of sheer joy, "Rainy Day Women" finds Dylan at his most truculent as he toys with the title, the exaggerated instrumentation, the ragtag ensemble singing, the giggling, and the implied games about liquor or dope.

Speaking of the trombone on the *Blonde on Blonde* track, keyboardist Al Kooper swears, in his book written with Ben Edmonds, *Backstage Passes: Rock 'n' Roll Life in the Sixties* (New York: Stein and Day, 1977), that when they were recording the song at Columbia's Nashville studio and were in dire need of that particular sound, fellow sideman Charlie McCoy made a 4:30 A.M. phone call and trombonist Wayne Butler marched in, ax in hand, a half hour later.

The inspiration of the song had, according to legend, serendipitous roots. Phil Spector told Dylan biographer Robert Shelton that he was hanging out with Dylan at the Fred C. Dobbs Coffee Shop in L.A. when Ray Charles's "Stoned" started playing on a jukebox. According to Spector, they "were surprised to hear a song that free, that explicit."

Maybe it's just the unrepentant rebel in him, but Dylan has never stopped performing "Rainy Day Women" right from its debut as a virtual call to arms with the Band in 1974 (replete with fine soloing by organist Garth Hudson and guitarist Robbie Robertson, which turned the *Blonde on Blonde* Salvation Army–style version on its ear) until its concert-ending raves twenty-five years later. Some of the 1978 renditions were performed as instrumentals. During its early twenty-first-century Never Ending Tour incarnation, the song had been remodeled into a roadhouse blues, taking on so much racy swagger that a mass striptease sometimes seemed imminent.

"Ramblin' Down Thru the World" (Bob Dylan)
aka "Ramblin' Down Through the World"

Dylan's only preserved live performances of this clichéd road song (adapted from at least a couple of Woody Guthrie tunes—"Sally Don't

You Grieve" and "Ramblin' Round") were staged: a late 1962 version recorded at an unknown New York location (probably a Gerde's Folk City hootenanny) and at the Town Hall show a few months later at which the ill-fated, never released *Bob Dylan in Concert* LP was recorded.

[S] "Rambling Gambling Willie" (Bob Dylan)

aka "Ramblin' Gamblin' Willie"

Bob Dylan, *The Bootleg Series, Volumes 1–3: Rare and Unreleased, 1961–1991/'62* (1991)

Clancy Brothers, *Older but No Wiser* (1995); *Irish Pub Songs* (2000)

Michel Montecrossa, *Bob Dylan & Michel Fest 2000* (2003)

Dylan is thought to have first performed this funny and accomplished original about a roving gambler for a January 1962 demo recording made to establish copyright for the Duchess Music Corporation, an affiliate of Leeds Music, on the recommendation of John Hammond (who had signed Dylan to Columbia Records). That Dylan maintained an enthusiasm for the song is evidenced by his rerecording of it for *The Freewheelin' Bob Dylan* sessions that April.

Inhabiting the same legendary turf as Paul Bunyan, the Cincinnati Kid, or Minnesota Fats, Will O'Conley, the "Willie" of this song's title, is depicted by Dylan in a picaresque tall tale that is pure Americana. No place, or woman, is safe whenever this roving gambler shows his face. Be it the White House, a Mississippi riverboat, or a saloon in the Rocky Mountains, Willie is sure to hold the winning hand as he eyes the prettiest gal in the joint. With twenty-seven children left in his wake and not a wife to show for it, Willie somehow manages to keep them all fed.

Dylan was inspired to pen his romp by hearing the Clancy Brothers perform "Brennan on the Moor," their rousing song about the highwayman Willie Brennan, an Irish Robin Hood folk-hero figure who was hanged in Cork in 1804.

Dylan's love of the subject matter is evident in all his preserved recordings of it. As reported in the liner notes to *The Bootleg Series, Volumes 1–3*, he told film director Derek Bailey in 1984, "I'd never heard those kind of songs before . . . all the legendary people they used to sing about—Brennan on the Moor or Roddy Macaulay . . . I would think of Brennan on the Moor the same way as I would think of Jesse James or something. You know, I wrote some of my own songs to some of the melodies that I heard them do."

Included in early, now extremely rare, withdrawn test pressings of *Freewheelin'*, "Rambling Gambling Willie" was, along with three other songs, dropped for the final cut of the album after Dylan had written several new major songs that he and/or Columbia were eager to put out.

[S] "Ramblin' Man" (Dickie Betts)

The Allman Brothers Band, *Brothers and Sisters* (1973)

Dylan's only performance of this Allman Brothers signature song came with its composer at a down-home 1995 gig in Florida.

Dickie Betts wrote "Ramblin' Man" at about 4:00 A.M. in the kitchen of a home in Macon, Georgia, shared by members of the band in 1973. His initial inspiration came from Hank Williams's 1951 song of the same title. Because it was so country, Betts didn't originally think it fit the Allmans, and he all but apologized to his bandmates when he played it to them for the first time. They looked at him like he was nuts because they recognized it for the great song that it was, telling him that if the Allman Brothers couldn't do it, then nobody could.

[S] "Ramblin' on My Mind" (Robert Johnson)

Robert Johnson, *The Complete Columbia Recordings* (1990)
Otis Spann, *Complete Candid Recordings* (1960)
John Mayall, *Bluesbreakers with Eric Clapton* (1966)
Eric Clapton, *Just One Night* (1980)
Robert Jr. Lockwood, *Plays Robert and Robert* (1982)
Savoy Brown, *Slow Train* (1986)

This Robert Johnson classic—the only one in which he combined both shuffle and slide guitar techniques—describes in poetic terms a consciously considered nomadic life (the "mean things" on his mind are inspiring him to catch the first mail train he sees and leave the devil-minded Miss So-and-So), with the music specifically echoing the theme. Dylan's performance of the song, a raw, half-remembered rendition, has been preserved from just one early engagement, the July 1962 show at Montreal's storied Finjan Club.

[S] "Ramblin' Round" (Woody Guthrie)

aka "(As I Go) Ramblin' 'Round," "Ramblin' Around," "Ramblin' Blues," "Ramblin' 'Round Your City"
Woody Guthrie, *Woody Guthrie—This Land Is Your Land: The Asch Recordings, Volume 1* (1998)
Various Artists (performed by Odetta), *Tribute to Woody Guthrie* (1972)
Arlo Guthrie, *Last of the Brooklyn Cowboys* (1973)
Ramblin' Jack Elliott, *Ramblin' Jack* (1996)
Martin Simpson, *Cool & Unusual* (1997)

A feature of his earliest surviving tapes, the picaresque "Ramblin' Round" fit Dylan's scruffy, Guthriesque image to a tee when he was absorbing Woody's canon in 1960–61.

According to *Reprints from* Sing Out!, *The Folk Song Magazine*, volume 8 (1965): "If 'Hard Traveling' has become the anthem of a real American type, the hard-working, hard-living laborer, and has elevated the figure to the stature of a genuine folk-hero in the eyes of the generation that has grown up with Woody Guthrie's songs, 'Ramblin' Blues' is surely a more lyric interpretation of the condition of this wandering, dusty-footed worker-hero. In 'Ramblin' Blues,' Woody emphasizes the spark of sentimentality and nostalgia that often gleams behind the rough-and-ready exterior mask of the hard-bitten hobo. Lesser men have written entire novels in search of lines like these: 'My mother prayed that I would be a man of some renown/But I am just a refugee as I go ramblin' around.'"

In their liner notes to *Woody Guthrie: This Land Is Your Land—The Asch Recordings, Volume 1*, Guy Logsdon and Jeff Place mention that "a dated manuscript does not exist to indicate when Woody wrote these lyrics, but it is thought to be one of his Bonneville Power Administration songs that expresses a migrant worker's nostalgic thoughts."

[S] "Ranger's Command" (Traditional/Woody Guthrie)

Woody Guthrie, *Woody Guthrie: Buffalo Skinners—The Asch Recordings, Volume 4* (1999)
Cisco Houston, *Cisco Houston Sings Woody Guthrie* (1963)
Joan Baez, *Farewell, Angelina* (1965)
Chris Hillman, *Hillmen* (1971)
Jim Kweskin, *Lives Again* (1977)

An old song reworked and updated by Woody Guthrie, "Ranger's Command" was performed by Dylan very early on—a version from Gerde's Folk City in 1961 is believed to be his only preserved recording of this rarity in circulation.

Joan Baez was one of the first to offer some history behind "Ranger's Command." As she wrote in *The Joan Baez Songbook* (New York: Ryerson Music Publishers, 1964), "This is Woody Guthrie's version of a cowboy song about which very little is known. One of Vance Rudolph's Ozark singers told him it was already 'an old song in 1893.' The story of the pioneer

R

woman who fought beside her menfolk is as much real history as romance. In other versions the woman is killed by Indians, after which the cowboys ride out to avenge her death."

As reported in the liner notes to *Woody Guthrie: Buffalo Skinners—The Asch Recordings, Volume 4*, Ramblin' Jack Elliott claimed that Guthrie wrote "Ranger's Command" to encourage women to become involved in the war against Hitler, thus making the song a cowboy girl allegory, if you will.

"Rank Strangers to Me" (Albert E. Brumley)
aka "Rank Strangers," "Rank Stranger"
See also "I'll Fly Away"
Bob Dylan, *Down in the Groove* (1988)
Stanley Brothers, *For the Good People* (1960)
Ralph Stanley, *1971–1973* (1995)
Carl Story, *Best of Carl Story* (1975)
Osborne Brothers, *Bluegrass Collection* (1978)
Country Gentlemen, *Early Rebel Recordings 1962–1971* (1998)
Albert E. Brumley Jr., *I'll Fly Away* (2004)

Dylan began performing this bit of gospel-inflected country melancholia (recorded and popularized by the Stanley Brothers) as a somber acoustic encore around the time he released it on his weak *Down in the Groove* collection in 1988. In 1997 "Rank Strangers" was soundchecked for his audience with Pope John Paul II and reintroduced as an acoustic set choice within a fortnight. By the following summer Dylan and his Never Ending Tour band were performing this otherworldly bluegrass in an arrangement that perfectly mimicked the Stanley Brothers' version, complete with background call-and-response chorus parts. Dylan always brought a profound sense of isolation to his renditions of this sad song about a man who discovers that you can't go home again.

According to *Reprints from* Sing Out!, *The Folk Song Magazine*, volume 8 (1965), "Rank Stranger" is the "best-known of the Stanley Brothers' gospel songs. Ralph [Stanley] says it is based on a traditional sacred tune he remembers hearing in his youth. The plaintive lead is set off by close-knit harmonica, shadows of the old-time church-style hymn singing that has been the Stanleys' greatest contribution to bluegrass vocal style."

Rattle and Hum/U2
Island Records. Released 1988.

After penning "Love Rescue Me" with U2's frontman heartthrob, Bono, Dylan contributed backing vocals in the studio for the song's album release. Dylan also played organ on another tune on the album, "Hawkmoon 269."

Rattle and Hum was the audio companion to U2's eponymous documentary, in which they attempted to distance themselves from the anthemic material that had made them famous in the 1980s.

"Rattled" (Traveling Wilburys)
Traveling Wilburys, *Traveling Wilburys, Volume 1* (1988)

Dylan's contribution to Jeff Lynne's Sun Studio–style rockabilly number on the Wilburys' debut album seems limited to backing vocals and guitar. Lynne does a nice vocal interpretation of a rattlesnake on the recording.

Real Live
Columbia Records LP FC 39944; CD CK-39944; CS FCT-39944. Recorded live in Europe, summer 1984. Released December 3, 1984. Produced by Glyn Johns.
Bob Dylan—guitar, harmonica, vocals. Carlos Santana, Mick Taylor—guitar. Ian McLagen—keyboards. Greg Sutton—bass. Colin Allen—drums.

Dylan performing in Europe, 1984.

(Photo: Express Newspapers/Getty Images)

R

"Highway 61 Revisited," "Maggie's Farm," "I and I," "License to Kill," "It Ain't Me, Babe," "Tangled Up in Blue," "Masters of War," "Ballad of a Thin Man," "Girl from the North Country," "Tombstone Blues"

Long before the Never Ending Tour, Dylan had been fulfilling his role of troubadour with extended tours in the U.S. and abroad. Though he hit Europe only in 1984, Dylan was an old hand at reinventing his songs and himself, and

Real Live exhibits an artist attacking his classic catalogue with fearless, if flawed, fervor.

Dylan's fourth live release in a decade wasn't easy to figure, coming off as an exploitative souvenir of his uneven though well-received 1984 European tour. Live performances of "Highway 61 Revisited," "Maggie's Farm," and "Ballad of a Thin Man" had already been released, and these shrill, stripped-down versions didn't exactly lend nuance to the familiar warhorses. "Tombstone Blues," "Masters of War," and "Girl from the North Country," on the other hand, were legitimate live-release rarities, and the rewrite of "Tangled Up in Blue" worth the ticket price alone. The newer material from the then-recent *Infidels* ("I and I" and "License to Kill") stands up against the older offerings pretty well, too.

The album's cover shows, in a yellowish, grainy photo, a leather-jacketed Dylan strumming his acoustic guitar and blowing into his harmonica. No liner notes were included. *Real Live* was the first Dylan album that failed to chart since *The Times They Are A-Changin'* two decades before.

▣ "Real Real Gone" (Van Morrison)
Van Morrison, *Enlightenment* (1990)
Campus Tramps, *Stay Dumb!* (1995)
Emerald Rock, *Emerald Rock* (1995)

Dylan only performed "Real Real Gone" (a Van the Man Morrison meditation on something more than the surface romance suggested by a guy shot by Cupid's arrow) four times in the mid-1990s, and two of those were as duets with the composer.

The opening song on *Enlightenment*, "Real Real Gone" is a cry of need in the grand tradition of soul music's great poets. Yet Morrison, fronting a big brass section on the song's debut release, seems to sing it with a smile on his face.

▣ "Red Cadillac and a Black Moustache"
(William May/Lillian Bea Thompson)
See also "Uranium Rock"
Various Artists (performed by Bob Dylan), *Good Rockin' Tonight: The Legacy of Sun Records* (2001)
Warren Smith, single (1957); *Warren Smith/'57* (1977)

Nomads, *Showdown* (1994)
Danny Gatton, *Humbler: Live* (1996)
Radio Sweethearts, *New Memories* (1997)
Robert Gordon, *Fresh Fish Specials (with Link Wray)* (1997)

Dylan's three subtle renditions of this classic piece of rockabilly *j'accuse!* made famous by Sun Records hero Warren Smith in 1957 transpired during the summer phase of his 1986 tour with Tom Petty and the Heartbreakers.

Here, a scorned lover has heard it through the grapevine that his lady love has been out burning the midnight oil with the mustachioed, Caddy-driving scoundrel of the song's title. So it was with no small measure of surprise that Dylan returned to the piece some fifteen years later, contributing a new, even better recording with his Never Ending Tour band to *Good Rockin' Tonight*, a Sun Records tribute album, wringing every ounce of profoundly sad emotion out of the lyrics like a Hank Williams for the new millennium. If you liked the way Dylan sang "Delia," you'll love this.

In some ways "Red Cadillac" bears a resemblance to Dylan's own "Man in the Long Black Coat," as evidenced by the following excerpt: "Somebody saw you at the break of day/Dining and a-dancing in the cabaret/He was long and tall, he had plenty of cash/He had a red Cadillac and a black moustache."

▣ "Red Hot" (Billy "The Kid" Emerson/Billy Lee Riley)
See also "Repossession Blues" and "Rock with Me Baby"
Billy Lee Riley, *Red Hot—The Best of Billy Lee Riley* (1995)
Willie and the Poor Boys, *Tear It Up Live* (1994)
Robert Gordon, *Too Young to Die* (1982)
Danny Gatton, *Humbler: Live* (1996)
Sleepy LaBeef, *Rockin' Decade* (1997)

Dylan's only performance of "Red Hot" (a song that became a favorite in strip joints across the globe) was offered at a 1992 show when its composer, the old rock 'n' roller Billy Lee Riley, joined him onstage for a unique one-off.

Billy Lee Riley (born October 5, 1933, Pocahantas, Arkansas) heads the list of the Sun Records faithful who coulda, shoulda, and woulda been national headliners had the fates blown a break or two their way. He had the looks, talent, and adaptability to make it to the top and stay there.

Through a career that has lasted nearly half a century, Riley has remained a vital performer who refuses to hang it up.

But his roots are as humble as humble gets. As one of seven children of a painter forced into sharecropping during the Great Depression of the 1930s, Riley had a childhood that was marked by the kind of callused-hand experience that either breaks or makes a human being but almost always inspires great art. These were Arkies who didn't pack up the old jalopy and head for California like Woody Guthrie or Tom Joad. Billy Lee was a kid who was up at dawn, working a twenty-five-acre plot with his pappy when he was but seven years old. Things were so tough, in fact, that the Rileys didn't even always have a roof over their heads, living for a good long spell under a huge army surplus tent. But Billy Lee had a harmonica, then a guitar, and always a love for the music he heard being sung by singers on the street and tumbling from jukeboxes in the black sections of the towns near where his family lived. Befriending kids both white and black, Riley began picking up the blues. One older, black bluesman in particular, Jericho "Lightnin' Leon" Carter, took the young Riley under his wing and proceeded to impart some serious schooling.

Though his family continued to survive in hardscrabble, pillar-to-post fashion, Riley stuck with his music through his teenage years and began merging hillybilly forms with the blues into that great sound of freedom: rockabilly.

Piggybacking on the success of Elvis Presley, Riley caught the ear of Memphis's Sun Records poobah Sam Phillips, who signed him to a record deal in 1956. Phillips locked horns with everybody, Riley included, but the commercial vs. creative tension between the two produced some of rockabilly's greatest sides over the next few years. Along with "Red Hot," a few of Riley's big Sun hits recorded between '56 and 1960 were "Trouble Bound," "Rock with Me Baby," "Flyin' Saucers Rock and Roll," "I Want You Baby," "Down by the Riverside," and "One More Time." And Riley's sound was something a bit more raucous that the usual Sun fare, marked for a time by Jerry Lee Lewis's pumping piano rhythms.

The Little Green Men, Riley's backing band during his Sun heyday, remains a Memphis legend. With guitar whiz Roland James and drummer James Eaton, the group played backup to virtually every rockabilly side Sun released.

As part of the Sun team, Riley was on package tours with the likes of Johnny Cash, Roy Orbison, Carl Perkins, and Warren Smith, traveling the various circuits in cars packed with musicians and instruments. High school proms, auto shows, drive-in theaters—any kind of gig one can imagine, these young guys played. And, with his fire-eyed, hell-raising stage act that would have been the envy of any Pentecostal preacher, Riley could steal just about anyone's thunder *and* lightning.

As the popularity and novelty of rockabilly ceded to other fads and ultimately the British invasion, Riley's star power faded and he moved to Los Angeles, where he became a prized studio musician ready to lend his harmonica blowing and guitar picking to just about any style you can name. He appeared on records by everybody from Herb Alpert to the

R

Beach Boys to Sammy Davis Jr., and he was able to cut records for both Mercury and the smaller GNP and Crown labels, which at least kept his name in circulation.

Riley bounced around the South for the balance of the 1960s and early 1970s, working in a variety of capacities in the music biz before easing out nearly entirely by 1975. But he was coaxed back to the stage when Europe's appetite for rockabilly and Riley's '50s act refused to die. Along with nearly semiannual visits to the Continent, Riley developed a following in the States and can still be found performing the blues and a toned-down version of lobster-eyed rockabilly in shows that find him strutting his stuff like an ageless daddy-o always ready to remind you, as he sings in "Red Hot," exactly whose girl is doodly-squat.

Dylan, a longtime Billy Lee Riley fan, apparently went to great lengths to track the man down in 1992 so that he could invite one of his heroes to open a show for him in Little Rock, Arkansas.

⒠ *Renaldo & Clara*

Released 1978. 232 minutes. Directed by Bob Dylan. Produced by Circuit Films/Lombard Street Films. Written by Bob Dylan and Sam Shepard.

Starring Bob Dylan, Sara Dylan, Joan Baez, Ronnie Hawkins, Ronee Blakely. Also featuring Jack Elliott, Harry Dean Stanton, Bob Neuwirth, Allen Ginsberg, David Blue, Roger McGuinn, Sam Shepard, Roberta Flack, Joni Mitchell, Helena Kallianiotes.

Renaldo & Clara is Bob Dylan's impressionistic art film chronicling the 1975 leg of the Rolling Thunder Revue. The film combines concert footage with thematically related segments that featured himself, Sara Dylan, Joan Baez, Allen Ginsberg, and a host of other subterraneans improvising from philosophically based notions of persona, marriage, loyalty,

life, death, God, sex, etc. Are you still with us? Good, because *Annie Hall* this is not.

Dylan spent way too much of mostly his own money and time on the film and was liberally roasted by the press for what, on the face of it, is a very messy affair. Dylan plays the ambiguous Renaldo, Sara plays Clara, Baez is the mysterious woman in white, while Ronnie Hawkins and Ronee Blakely play Dylan and his wife, respectively. If you love Dylan, the film is an endlessly fascinating, highly watchable tableau, as songs like "When I Paint My Masterpiece," "Isis," "It Ain't Me Babe," "Knockin' on Heaven's Door," "Hurricane," "Romance in Durango," "One Too Many Mornings," "One More Cup of Coffee," "Sara," "Just Like a Woman," and "A Hard Rain's A-Gonna Fall" resonate with Dylan's wandering mystic cinéaste vision. If one approaches it from the standpoint of its being a *really* long, updated version of *Don't Look Back* or *Eat the Document* (earlier attempts by Dylan and company to plumb celluloid gold and toy with iconographic concepts), then the film is easier to take. But if one is on the fence about this guy at all, *Renaldo & Clara* comes off as the pretentious morass it was accused of being upon its original release.

How to adequately, and fairly, explain this gargantuan four-hour home movie? With a plot line that can be charitably defined as loose, editing that is very hard on the eye, characters that fuzz into and out of the sometimes documentary/sometimes quasifictional narrative, staged scenarios that can often come off as watered-down John Cassavetes at best, horrible sound, and jagged camera work, *Renaldo & Clara* would be an impossible film to sit through if not for Dylan's hovering, almost always fascinating presence.

That said, many scenes do remain fixed in the subconscious mind like the memory of some weird dream of many years before. Who can shake the image of Allen Ginsberg giving a poetry reading to a gathering of mah-jongg-playing grandmothers, Dylan trading his woman for a horse, the visit to an elderly woman named Mama, or the symbolic deflowering of David Mansfield by a cadre of nubile temptresses? And what of Dylan's secret-agent-style chase scene through the snowy streets of Montreal, the Hurricane Carter sequences, the man-on-the-street-interviews outside Harlem's Apollo Theater, the ugly domestic squabble between Ronee Blakely and Bob Neuwirth, Ronnie Hawkins disguised as Bob Dylan, the backstage mischief, or the diner scenes with a clueless Harry Dean Stanton? Dylan's ever-shifting notions of persona and perspective are, to say the least, dizzying. And in what may be the most stable narrative foundation is the musician David Blue, who appears intermittently through the film as some kind pinball wizard–cum–Greek chorus recalling the days of early 1960s Greenwich Village lore and yore. Well, nobody said any of this was actually supposed to make sense.

Even Dylan came off as confused in his interviews plugging the film, with comments like "It's about the essence of man" to *Playboy*'s Ron Rosenbaum in 1978.

Yet in some oblique way, the set pieces can be seen as resonating with the tone of the songs they accompany. For example, Dylan's scene with a horse in a frigid rural setting feels as if it could be sung as a verse straight out of "Isis," which is more or less performed near this part of the film. If one looks at *Renaldo & Clara* as tapestry of music and related atmospheric imagery, then some kind of method to Dylan's madness can be grasped.

Whether you love it, hate it, or can't figure it out, *Renaldo & Clara* remains Dylan's great cinematic "messterpiece."

Poster for the film *Renaldo & Clara*, covering Dylan's Rolling Thunder Revue concert tour, 1978.

(Photo: Blank Archives/Getty Images)

"Repossession Blues" (Billy Lee Riley)
See also "Red Hot" and "Rock with Me Baby"
Billy Lee Riley, *Classic Recordings, 1956–1960* (1990)

Dylan covered this plaint about a repo man at the start of a couple of shows during his 1978 big-band tour. Some think he may have been singing from the heart (and the pocketbook) on this one, as his performances of "Repossession Blues" came on the heels of his public (and expensive) divorce from his wife Sara.

"Restless Farewell" (Bob Dylan)
Bob Dylan, *The Times They Are A-Changin'* (1964)
Joan Baez, *Any Day Now* (1968); *Vanguard Session: Baez Sings Dylan* (1998)
De Danann, *1/2 Set in Harlem* (1991)
Clancy, O'Connell and Clancy, *Clancy, O'Connell and Clancy* (1998)
Various Artists (performed by Norman Blake and Peter Ostroushko), *A Nod to Bob* (2001)

Nicely adapting "The Parting Glass," an old Irish drinking ditty, Dylan closed *The Times They Are A-Changin'* with this song of remorse and introspection.

In the midst of an alcoholic reverie, the singer replays the past as if he knows every scene by heart: the money blown, the friends blown off, the bars he closed, the women he's wooed and woed, the battles won and lost, and the tortured thoughts that have led him to this moment. As the narrator sings his song about lost love, he reveals a toughness that suggests he will survive. "Restless Farewell" was also, like several of Dylan's songs from the era, interpreted as an adieu to the folk-music community and its parochial demands.

According to J. R. Goddard, in his May 1964 notice in *HiFi Review*, "'Restless Farewell' is an unremitting 'apologia pro vita sua' consisting of Dylan's oblique answers to the 'dust of rumors'

that he claims have been visited on him by those who do not understand his message. But his message, rather than being transformed into art, is turned into sulky mannerism."

Only a couple of Dylan's performances of "Restless Farewell" have survived from 1964: his February 1 television appearance in Toronto on the Canadian Broadcast Company's series *Quest* and his May 17 concert in London at the Royal Festival Hall. However, it's the rendition Dylan delivered in 1996 as a guest on Frank Sinatra's eightieth-birthday tribute show on national U.S. television that is regarded as the one for the ages: he treated the song with an all-the-stops-pulled-out reverence, producing a simply stunning moment. Typically, U.S. TV's networks edited the song down to three verses for reasons known only to them and their sponsors. Dylan trotted out "Restless Farewell" one last time, to commemorate Sinatra's passing in 1998.

"Return to Me" (Danny DiMinno/Carmen Lombardo)
aka "Ritorna a Me"
Various Artists (performed by Bob Dylan), *The Sopranos: Peppers & Eggs (Music from the HBO Original Series)* (2001)
Hank Snow, *Singing Ranger, Volume 3* (1994)
Marty Robbins, *Super Hits* (1995)
Chris Isaak, *Baja Sessions* (1996)
Dean Martin, *Return to Me* (1998)
The Gaylords, *All-Time Greatest Hits* (1999)

Just like a Mafia lifer who keeps on getting pulled back in for one more job, Dylan got dragged into the *Sopranos* phenomenon, contributing a fetchingly cornball version of "Return to Me"—a famous piece of B-grade Sicilian cheese—to the soundtrack that ran over the closing credits for an episode of the HBO television show about the comic/tragic travails of a New Jersey gangland family. At a mere two minutes and twenty-two seconds, the track is among the shortest Dylan has ever released; like Dean Martin, who had a 1958 hit with the tune, Dylan offers up a verse in Italian. Dylan's shambling, jazzy approach to the song is reminiscent of his late Never Ending Tour arrangements of "If Dogs Run Free" and "Tryin' to Get to Heaven," featuring snippets of melodies and chord progressions overlaying one another to create a blurry aural effect evoking the kind of drunken stupor that pervades closing time at the Bada-Bing Club.

"Return to Me," cowritten by Guy Lombardo's brother Carmen with Las Vegas lounge lizard Danny DiMinno in the 1950s, quickly became a Rat Pack standard. Carmen Lombardo (born July 16, 1903, London, Ontario; died April 17, 1971, Miami, Florida) was a key member of his brother's famous band, the Royal Canadians, best known for their nationally broadcast New Year's Eve performances of "Auld Lang Syne" long before the dropping of the ball in Times Square became such a ritualized to-do. In addition to popularizing the instrumental medley, the Royal Canadians held sway as an endearing, technically proficient but schmaltzy North American institution from the late 1920s to Guy Lombardo's death in 1977.

At the time of Carmen's death, in 1971, the Royal Canadians were still very popular, making, as was their credo, "The Sweetest Music This Side of Heaven."

"Riding on the Train" (Bob Dylan)

Little is known about this song, which Dylan performed just twice as a show opener on his first tour with Tom Petty and the Heartbreakers during a swing through Australia in February 1986. The first night it was performed as an instrumental, the second with a few very rough lyrics.

"Ring of Fire" (June Carter Cash/Merle Kilgore)
aka "(Love's a) Ring of Fire"
See also Johnny Cash, "More and More"
Various Artists (performed by Bob Dylan), *Feeling Minnesota* (soundtrack) (1996)
Johnny Cash, *Complete Live at San Quentin* (2000)
Tom Jones, *Green, Green Grass of Home* (1967)
Animals, *Love Is* (1968)
Dwight Yoakam, *Guitars, Cadillacs, Etc. Etc.* (1986)
Frank Zappa, *The Best Band You Never Heard Of* (1991)
Dick Dale, *Unknown Territory* (1994)

A wonderful equation of passion and its consequences for the heart and soul that the author of the *Inferno* may have been proud to call his own, "Ring of Fire" is one of those songs that, once heard, is nearly impossible to stop singing. And who would want to?

"A song like that goes on forever," Johnny Cash told Nashville's *Tennessean* in 2002. In the liner notes to her 1999 *Press On* album, Mrs. Cash described the inception of "Ring of Fire": "I felt like I had fallen into a pit of fire and I was literally burning alive."

"Ring of Fire" was written by June Carter and Merle Kilgore in 1962 when the two lived in the same Nashville suburb and regularly met to write songs. Inspired by a line in a book of Elizabethan poetry that had belonged to her uncle, Carter Family and country music patriarch A. P. Carter, "Ring of Fire" began its rise to its status as an American classic first through a recording by June's sister Anita, and then by her future husband, Johnny Cash, when he recorded it with a Mexican-style horn section punctuating the arrangement. That arrangement, Cash claimed, came to him in a dream.

Valerie June Carter Cash (born June 23, 1929, Maces Springs, Virginia; died May 15, 2003, Nashville) grew up as country music royalty as a member of the extended Carter Family. Even as a young girl, June was, along with her sis-

R

ters, touring and recording with an expanded version of the family group. Accompanying herself on autoharp and singing in a full-throated warble, June took center stage at least once a night. And she dabbled in comedy, developing vaudeville-style, deep-country characters—like her beloved "Aunt Polly"—that became an integral part of the Carter Family act. That shtick led to a 1949 session with Homer and Jethro, country music's answer to Abbott and Costello, and a hit with "Baby, It's Cold Outside."

Through the 1950s, June continued to grow as an artist and personality while the Carter Family reigned as Grand Ole Opry regulars. Her life and career kicked into higher gear with her marriage to singer Carl Smith, with whom she toured as part of Elvis Presley's revue. The couple had two daughters, one of whom, Carlene, went on to enjoy acclaim in country music circles. Though June's union with Smith was not to last, it led to her first meetings with the man who would ultimately share her life, Johnny Cash.

In the mid-1950s June branched into acting after film director Elia Kazan (*On the Waterfront, A Streetcar Named Desire, A Face in the Crowd*) saw her perform and persuaded her that a visit to New York City and classes with Lee Strasberg and Sanford Meisner at the city's famed Neighborhood Playhouse might expand her range and opportunities. Throughout her career, June could be seen on everything from television's *Gunsmoke* and *Little House on the Prairie* to edgier fare, such as Robert Duvall's 1997 film *The Apostle*.

The Carter Family joined Johnny Cash's touring show in the early 1960s and, sticking to the old-fashioned, wholesome image they had cultivated for nearly forty years, were quite the counterbalance to Cash, who was descending into his darkest period of drug abuse. June

became one of Cash's inner circle, a close confidant who began hiding and throwing away the barbiturates and amphetamines that were driving him to ruin. Eventually she was able to persuade him to find counseling. Cash often claimed, quite truthfully, that she saved his life. Neither of them ever made any secret that "Ring of Fire" described this early, enormously difficult phase of their relationship.

Johnny and June married in 1968 and she became a fixture at her husband's concerts as well as a collaborator, business partner, muse, and mother to their son John Jr. Who could ever forget the sight of Johnny and June striding to the center of the stage and tearing into "Jackson," "I Walk the Line," or "Ring of Fire" to commence one of the thousands of shows they played together over the years.

June Carter Cash's death in the spring of 2003 of complications following heart surgery left a huge chasm in the no-bull community of country music and its family of fans. Her Nashville funeral and burial were attended by thousands, who sang "Will the Circle Be Unbroken" at her gravesite. And it was with little surprise that Johnny Cash joined her on the other side of this life before the year was out.

Dylan's mid-1990s studio recording of "Ring of Fire" appeared on the soundtrack to the eminently forgettable lame-brain black comedy *Feeling Minnesota* (1996), starring Keanu Reeves and Cameron Diaz. Dylan's involvement in the flick was just about the only thing Minnesotan about it. Even better is the unreleased version Dylan sang with Cash at the February 1969 *Nashville Skyline* recording sessions.

"Ring Them Bells" (Bob Dylan)
Bob Dylan, *Oh Mercy* (1989); *Bob Dylan's Greatest Hits, Volume 3* (1994)
Joan Baez, *Rare, Live and Classic* (1993)

Rinde Eckert, *Do the Day Over* (1996)
Steve Gibbons, *The Dylan Project* (1998)
Jubilant Sykes, *Wait for Me* (2001)
Barb Jungr, *Every Grain of Sand: Barb Jungr Sings Bob Dylan*
 (2002)

A deeply spiritual song that would have felt right at home in one of Dylan's gospel shows, "Ring Them Bells" shares its title with numerous, similarly themed gospel songs and represents the jubilant and celebratory heartland of his *Oh Mercy* album. With his voice like the breath of life, Dylan sings the song as if enhanced by true vision and blessed by grace. Listen to the way he enunciates simple phrases like "the shepherd is asleep, where the willow weeps" and feel the spine tingle. Dylan invokes Saints Peter, Catherine, and Martha to remind "those of us who are left" that we are not alone or forgotten. Aching with compassion, "Ring Them Bells" is as positive as Dylan has sounded since the mid-1970s.

Dylan sang "Ring Them Bells" with the calm conviction of a true believer in his Never Ending Tours of the 1990s and early '00s.

"Rise Again" (Dallas Holm)
Dallas Holm, *Early Works: The Best of Dallas Holm* (1991)
Acapella, *Acappella Resurrection* (1994)
Bill Gaither, *Revival* (1995)
Bill Young, *Visiting Hours* (1997)

Dylan's Christian devotion was still hanging tough when he covered "Rise Again"—Dallas Holm's invocation of the Second Coming—at a handful of shows in 1980 and 1981. Dylan's versions of the song were arranged as an effectively intimate piano duet with backup singer Clydie King.

"Rise Again," Holm's signature song, is written in the first person from The Man himself. That's right, Jesus Christ steps forward

Dallas Holm, American gospel composer and musician, ca. 1990s.

(Photo by Robert Langham)

through Holm's muse to warn all those who do not heed His Word.

Holm (born November 5, 1948, St. Paul, Minnesota) is not a person to be taken lightly. Go ahead, dismiss his very religious music if you dare. But remember that this is a man whose life and music have figured profoundly in the lives of thousands of people who have been spiritually "saved" and set on the path toward Jesus Christ during one of his revivals.

His songs focus on the Crucifixion, but they are hardly one-note exercises in mindless worship. Rather, Holm uses the blues, bluegrass, reggae, country, and folk arrangements of classic hymns as well as his multitude of originals to testify to the Word. After committing himself to Christ's teaching as a sixteen-year-old, Holm trained for a life as a minister at Minnesota's North Central Bible College and recorded his first album, *I Saw the Light,* with a group known as the Tri-Tones in 1968 while still a student. In so doing, he took a lead in the contemporary Christian music movement before it was ever even termed as such.

Over the next decade he continued to release albums that, while leaving little to the imagination, had an enormous evangelical impact. And he was as hard-core a road warrior as any folkie troubadour, touring with the youth crusades of the charismatic preacher David Wilkerson. With his own group, Praise Ministries, Holm led the Jesus Movement to any church or auditorium that would have them, a practice that continues to this day. In the very large world of Christian music, his well-known songs include "I Saw the Lord," "Here We Are," "Before Your Throne," and his signature composition, "Rise Again."

S "Rising Sun" (Steve Hufsteter/Tito Larriva/Tony Marsico/Charlie Quintana)
aka "Rising Son"
The Cruzados, *The Cruzados* (1984); *Unreleased Early Recordings* (performed with Bob Dylan on harmonica) (2000)
Various Artists (performed by the Cruzados with Bob Dylan on harmonica), *May Your Song Always Be Sung: The Songs of Bob Dylan, Volume 3/'84* (2003)

The Cruzados (formerly the Plugz) were a Los Angeles–based rock band with a Latin twist that were ever so briefly but most famously associated with Dylan when they backed him up for his mercurial appearance on *Late Night with David Letterman* in March 1984. Some-

where in there they managed to coax Bob into the studio to contribute harmonica licks to "Rising Sun," a minor rocker that seems to be playing off both Dylan's flirtation with the sacred (born-again Christianity) and the profane (as in "House of the Rising Sun"—a song about the perils of the brothel). While not a bootleg, this collection of songs was privately produced by the Cruzados and obtainable through their official home page on the Web when released in 2000. "Rising Sun" became more widely available when released on a "various artists" tribute album, *May Your Song Always Be Sung: The Songs of Bob Dylan, Volume 3,* in 2003.

S "Rita May" (Bob Dylan/Jacques Levy)
aka "Rita Mae"
Bob Dylan, single (1977); *Masterpieces* (1978)

Recorded at the July 1975 sessions in New York City, this outtake from *Desire* (a raggedy plaint to a departing lover the narrator has been warned against) did see glorious life as a rompin', stompin' barn burner at one New Orleans concert during the 1976 Rolling Thunder tour. Reminiscent of the old novelty hit "Yakety Yak" and maybe even the Beatles' "Lovely Rita" from *Sgt. Pepper's Lonely Hearts Club Band,* this rockabilly-style hoedown song about a bookish woman and a suitor's inability to impress her is said to be Dylan's tribute to writer Rita Mae Brown (author of 1973's *Rubyfruit Jungle*), though the connection seems tangential at best.

S "River Theme" (Bob Dylan)
Bob Dylan, *Pat Garrett and Billy the Kid* (soundtrack) (1973)

A lilting if short chorale of Southwestern atmospheric filler, this *Pat Garrett* track features a chorus singing nonlyrics.

[S] **"Rock of Ages"** (Traditional/Augustus Montague Toplady/Thomas Hastings)
Ray Price, *Faith* (1960)
Mahalia Jackson, *The Power and the Glory* (1960)
Patti Page, *Patti Page Sings America's Favorite Hymns* (1966)
Johnny Cash, *Johnny Cash Sings Precious Memories* (1975)
Al Green, *Precious Lord* (1982)
Stanley Brothers, *Early Years 1958–1961* (1994)
Osborne Brothers, *Our Favorite Hymns* (1995)

Dylan's performances of one of gospel's most venerable songs (it is no doubt being sung at a wake, funeral, or religious meeting as your eyes pass over these words) came as a Never Ending Tour acoustic offering as the millennia switched.

The title of this famous hymn is drawn from Isaiah 26:4—"The Lord is the Rock eternal" (New International Version).

The lyrics are sometimes attributed to Augustus Montague Toplady, who is said to have written them on a playing card after taking refuge in the cleft of a rock near Cheddar Gorge in England's southeast. Toplady (born November 4, 1740, Farnham, Surrey, England; died August 11, 1778, Kensington, Middlesex, England) was one of England's most preeminent seventeenth-century theologians and religious figures. After studying at London's Westminster School and Dublin's Trinity College, he was ordained an Anglican priest in 1762, served as curate at Blagdon and Farleigh, and in 1766 became the vicar of Broadhembury, Devonshire. But he seems to have caused a bit of a stir near the end of his life when he left the Anglican church in 1775, moved to London, and took an active role in the French Calvinist church.

The music to "Rock of Ages" is more usually attributed to Thomas Hastings (born October 15, 1784, Washington, Connecticut; died May 15, 1872, New York City), one of the more important hymn composers of the nineteenth century. A doctor's son, Hastings was reared as an archetypal farm boy who walked the proverbial six miles to school in the winter. Starting out as a music teacher, he moved to Utica, New York, where he assumed a post as editor of a local newspaper, the *Recorder*. In 1832 he began training choirs and developing religious music, and from then until practically the day of his death, penned nearly one thousand hymn tunes and six hundred hymn texts.

There is some more lore attached to "Rock of Ages": it was sung at the 1898 funeral of British prime minister William Gladstone in London's Westminster Abbey. Later, Prince Albert requested that it be sung at his deathbed. Perhaps the most dramatic story is one related by W. T. Stead in *Hymns That Have Helped*, as quoted by www.cyberhymnal.org: when the steamship *The London* foundered in the Bay of Biscay, January 11, 1866, on her journey to Australia, drowning some 220 souls, "the last thing which the last man who left the ship heard as the boat pushed off from the doomed vessel was the voices of the passengers singing 'Rock of Ages.'"

[S] **"Rocks and Gravel"** (Traditional/Bob Dylan)
aka "Solid Road"
Peg Leg Howell, *Rocks and Gravel Blues* (1928)
Mance Lipscomb, *Trouble in Mind* (1961/2000)
Big Joe Williams, *Stavin' Chain Blues* (1966)
Steve James, *Two Track Mind* (1993)
Ian and Sylvia, *Ian and Sylvia* (1995)

"Rocks and Gravel," which Dylan enjoyed performing, was an outtake from *The Freewheelin' Bob Dylan* sessions. Some have suggested that the song is adapted from Lenny Carr's "Alabama Woman Blues" and/or Brownie McGhee's "Solid Road." Others call it an arrangement of a traditional song. Whatever the case, Dylan sang it with real drama—as if he had spent a year or two choking on dust on a Deep South chain gang and learning to fingerpick from some forgotten blues sage next to a levee.

"Rocks and Gravel" was technically released on some now extremely rare versions of *Freewheelin'* test pressings; it was later replaced by "Girl from the North Country." On that album and on the sheet music published by M. Witmark & Sons, Dylan is credited with full authorship. Of this song Dylan once told journalist Nat Hentoff, who recorded his words in an unpublished portion of the *Freewheelin' Bob Dylan* liner notes, "I learned one verse from Big Joe Williams, and the rest I put together out of lines that seemed to go with this story."

Though that could be true, there are numerous other possibilities: Alan Lomax's 1947 recordings of Parchman Farm convicts singing work songs such as "Early in the Morning" (which includes the title verse of "Rocks and Gravel"), Ian and Sylvia, Mance Lipscomb, or Horace Sprott's now unfindable 1954 "Take Rocks and Gravel (to) Make a Solid Road."

[S] "Rock with Me Baby" (Billy Lee Riley)

See also "Red Hot"
Billy Lee Riley, *Red Hot: The Best of Billy Lee Riley* (1999)

Dylan performed Billy Lee Riley's "Rock with Me Baby" as a penultimate concert selection at about five shows during his 1986 summer tour with Tom Petty and the Heartbreakers.

[A] *Roger McGuinn*

Columbia Records LP KC-31-946. Released 1972.

Dylan's harmonica can be heard on "I'm So Restless," a McGuinn–Jacques Levy track from Jolly Roger's titular solo debut. The album was an outgrowth of the Byrds' reunion album and still sounds good. The effort marked the first formal Dylan/McGuinn collaboration; McGuinn subsequently appeared on the *Pat Garrett and Billy the Kid* soundtrack album, joined Dylan's 1976 Rolling Thunder Revues, and appeared with Dylan onstage in various functions in the 1980s and 1990s.

[P] Jimmie Rodgers

Born September 8, 1897, Meridian, Mississippi; died May 26, 1933, New York City.

Some call him "The Singin' Brakeman," others "Mississippi's Blue Yodeler." But no matter what you call Jimmie Rodgers, his meteoric rise and legacy left a mark on the American musical landscape so powerful, it can still be heard and seen each time Garth Brooks (whether he knows it or not) struts his stuff on a stage near

Jimmie Rodgers, country music icon, ca. 1930s.

(From the John Edwards Memorial Collection #30003, Southern Folklife Collection, Wilson Library, University of North Carolina at Chapel Hill)

you. The great lineage of male country music stars that has produced Brooks stretches back through the great supernovas of the genre—Willie Nelson, Merle Haggard, Hank Williams, Hank Snow, Lefty Frizzell, Gene Autry, and some might say Bob Dylan—to the great Jimmie Rodgers.

Rodgers's songs are full of the rounders and gamblers, bounders and ramblers he knew from his years working on the railroad and as a medicine-show-circuit troubadour. While his contemporaries sang exclusively mountain and mountain/folk music, he threw hillbilly country, gospel, jazz, blues, pop, cowboy, and folk into a home brew that resulted in his classic material: "TB Blues," "Waiting for a Train," "Travelin' Blues," "Train Whistle Blues," and his monumental song cycle of thirteen "blue" yodels.

No, Jimmie Rodgers was not the first to yodel on record, but his style set him apart from the others. He didn't yodel merely to sugarcoat a song, but rather used the technique as an emotional embellishment as important as a lyric: mournful and plaintive or happy and carefree.

Jimmie was the youngest of three sons. His childhood was marked by his mother's early death and resulted in his being passed from relative to relative in southeast Mississippi and southwest Alabama before he eventually returned home to live with his father in Meridian. Despite the hardships, music was never far away even for a rascal growing up in rural Mississippi. Field hollers, good-times music, and the sacred sounds of blacks and whites were as natural to the local population as the seasonal floods. Music and singing in particular were, along with the grueling agrarian life, one of the few pleasures shared by both races in post–*Plessy v. Ferguson*, divided but "equal" Mississippi. This intermingling undoubtedly

had a massive effect on Rodgers's approach to performing, for he can and often does sound on surviving recordings as black as coal.

Jimmie's love for entertaining came at an early age. When he was thirteen, he twice organized and set off on his own traveling show, only to be brought home by his father, who tried to quell the boy's wanderlust by getting Jimmie his first job: working on the railroad as water boy on his father's work gang. A few years later he became a brakeman on the New Orleans and Northeastern Railroad.

The great paradoxical moment of Rodgers's life occurred in 1924 when he contracted tuberculosis—a disease that, while temporarily ending his rugged railroad life, gave him the chance to get back to his first love: entertainment. By that time, Rodgers had begun to regularly play in legitimate traveling shows. Though these years were difficult, they were important in the development of Jimmie's musical style as he began to develop his distinctive blue yodel, work on his guitar skills, and perform in blackface comedy skits across the Southeast.

In 1927, now married and with a daughter, Rodgers visited Asheville, North Carolina, and was so taken with the local music scene there that he vowed never to work on the rails again.

In short order Rodgers began performing on WWNC, Asheville's first radio station. He recruited a group from Tennessee called the Tenneva Ramblers and secured a weekly slot on the station as the Jimmie Rodgers Entertainers. An audition with Ralph Peer of Victor Records in the summer of 1927 led to a recording session that yielded a $100 paycheck and a couple of songs: "Sleep, Baby, Sleep" and "The Soldier's Sweetheart."

The 78-rpm release enjoyed only modest success but inspired Rodgers. He journeyed to New York City and talked his way into the recording

R

session that made him a legend in his own time, even though but four songs emerged from the date: "Ben Dewberry's Final Run," "Mother Was a Lady," "Away out on the Mountain," and "T for Texas." In the next two years, the acetate that contained his signature song "T for Texas" (released as "Blue Yodel") and "Away out on the Mountain" sold nearly half a million copies, impressive enough to rocket Rodgers into stardom. This flush of success propelled him into the position as country music's first bona fide superstar. Throngs fought to hear, touch, or just catch a brief glimpse of him as he toured, primarily in the South and Southwest.

The last few years of Rodgers's life were a whirlwind. He appeared in a movie short, or "soundie," as the genre was known, *The Singing Brakeman*, which spread his gospel in a way MTV would for other, lesser lights more than a half century later; toured with humorist Will Rogers as part of a Red Cross Midwest swing; and, perhaps most significantly, made some of the first notable crossover bids—a recording of "Blue Yodel #9" with a young jazz trumpeter by the name of Louis Armstrong.

His song cycle of blue yodels may well enshrine him on a Mount Rushmore in musical Valhalla, but his entire oeuvre cast a pretty wide net over American music. It can be argued that he was the guy to first attempt to coalesce all the myriad streams of sound (country, old-time, jazz, Tin Pan Alley, blues, ragtime, etc.) into a unified, popular whole. And if his urbane look seemed modern (most photographs show him with a straw hat perched jauntily on the back of his head, his bony frame cloaked in a natty suit and polka-dot tie), one could always hear the backwoods sound expressing the yearnings of country folk longing for better days in his songs.

But as his TB began to get the better of him, Rodgers's role as a recording and touring artist

began to diminish. The Depression did not help either: concert bookings and record sales stalled. And, even though he was ill, he had to perform anywhere he could—be it vaudeville shows or nickelodeons—to feed his family.

It was clear to Rodgers that he was running out of track. He persuaded Victor to schedule a final recording session in New York City to provide needed financial support for his family. In a final act of strength and courage he soldiered his way through the sessions. Like some character from the pages of Homer, Rodgers almost literally sang his heart out: within a day or so of completing the sessions, "The Father of Country Music" was dead from a lung hemorrhage in his hotel room.

His final train ride to Meridian is the stuff of country music legend: the body riding in a converted baggage car, the train blowing its whistle as it passed through cities and small towns—a Stygian journey if ever there was one. Back in Mississippi, his body lay in state as thousands of people came to pay their last respects to the departed minstrel.

Dylan's celebration of Rodgers's music has been an ongoing project from his days as a pimply kid in Hibbing. Along with performing songs written by or associated with Rodgers ("My Blue Eyed Jane," "Diamond Joe," "Frankie and Albert," "Muleskinner," and "Southern Cannonball"), Dylan released *The Songs of Jimmie Rodgers*, a wonderful, star-studded tribute album.

The inscription on the Jimmie Rodgers statue in Meridian should still sound a clarion call of sorts: "His is the music of America. He sang the songs of the people he loved, of a young nation growing strong. His was an America of glistening rails, thundering boxcars, and rain-swept nights, of lonesome prairies, great mountains and a high blue sky. He sang of the bayous and the cornfields, the wheated plains, of the little towns, the cities, and of the winding rivers of America."

[S] "Roll On, John" (Traditional)

Various Artists (performed by Bob Dylan), *There Is No Eye: Music for Photographs* (2001)
Buell Kazee, *Buell Kazee* (1978)
Mike Seeger, *Southern Banjo Sounds* (1998)
Middle Spunk Creek Boys, *Table for One* (2000)
John Herald, *Roll On John* (2001)

Twenty-year-old Bob Dylan ambled into the funky studios of New York City's WBAI radio station on January 13, 1962, to appear on Cynthia Gooding's program, *Folksinger's Choice.* Nearly four decades later, one of the works he sang for Gooding and greater New York was a somber yet highly ornamented folk song called "Roll On, John"—not officially released until its unusual appearance on *There Is No Eye: Music for Photographs,* a Smithsonian Folkways collection that also included cuts from the kind of company Dylan had been dying to keep since that cold winter's day: Woody Guthrie, Bill Monroe, Roscoe Holcomb, and Doc Watson. Dylan told Gooding that he collected the work song "Roll On, John" from folklorist and musician Ralph Rinzler.

[S] "Romance in Durango" (Bob Dylan/Jacques Levy)

Bob Dylan, *Desire* (1976); *Biograph/'75* (1985); *The Bootleg Series, Volume 5: Live 1975—The Rolling Thunder Revue* (2002)
Fagner, *Focus* (2002)

With its dramatic tempo shifts, a story that could have been directed by Sam Peckinpah, and following a Tex-Mex tradition set forth by Marty Robbins's "El Paso," "Romance in Durango" was a blistering stage natural for the Rolling Thunder Revue in 1975 and 1976. Propelled by Scarlet Rivera's transcendent, molten violin sawing, the live versions from 1975 can be found on *Biograph* and *The Bootleg Series, Volume 5,* and contrast with the sleepier, studio-recorded, mariachi-arranged rendition on *Desire.* Mariachi, it should be noted, is a kind of guitar- and brass-heavy genre generated by street musicians; it originated in the state of Jalisco in northern Mexico (where Dylan spent some time filming *Pat Garrett and Billy the Kid*) and is most often associated with marriage and the marriage ceremony—a theme and subject that permeates *Desire.* And notice that the lyrics include references to the fandango (a dance featured in Mexican weddings) and castanets (those trilling percussion instruments worn on fingers often heard in music the fandango is danced to). If nothing else, Dylan had made himself a true authority on the subject—musically, poetically, and (like it or not) personally.

Written with theater rat Jacques Levy during their famous July 1975 two-week woodshedding session in East Hampton, New York, "Romance in Durango" began with a wordless Mexican-type tune Dylan had been carrying around for a while. Their inspiration for the song's opening lines ("hot chili peppers in the blistering sun") came from a postcard Levy received from playwright Jack Gelber with a picture of a bunch of chili peppers strung in front of a Mexican shack.

The song certainly jibes with one of the main themes running through *Desire*: the neo-American outlaw etched into a cinema song. Dylan and Levy explored this character in just about all the songs on the album with the exception of "Mozambique" and "Sara." The south-of-the-border, itchy-fingered hombre with a price on his head haunting the luminescent landscape of "Romance in Durango" is every bit the outsider looking in as Hurricane, Joey, the grave-robbing narrator of "Isis," the visitor to the Gypsy clan in "One More Cup of

Coffee," or the triple dealers inhabiting "Black Diamond Bay."

Just about the only critic to explore the deceptively layered "Romance in Durango" with any depth was John Herdman, who, in his 1982 book *Voice Without Restraint: A Study of Bob Dylan's Lyrics and Their Background*, addressed the outlaw character and other issues relating to the song:

> It exhibits in a remarkable degree Dylan's ability to project himself into an alien cultural experience and extract essence: and he does this through an instinctive understanding of the nature and power of stereotypes. "Joey" enters thus into the world of the hoodlum, *Nashville Skyline* epitomizes the country mood, and I suspect that something not essentially dissimilar happens in relation to fundamentalist Christianity in *Slow Train Coming*. "Romance in Durango" makes use of the stereotypes—including the *musical* stereotypes—of Mexican mythology, in order to reach the feelings and the colors of the real communal experience to which they point. Simply by taking them seriously, by refusing to adopt towards them the attitude of the enlightened metropolitan who can see in them nothing but cliché, he rediscovers their meaning and avails himself of their continued resilience. Dylan can sometimes sneer but he never patronizes.

The song bases its structure on a device which we saw used briefly in "Isis"—the use of a journey to tell a story retrospectively. In this case the narrator looks forward as well as back, creating a kind of phantom continuation of the story which is destined never to become reality. The only directly narrated action is the catastrophe of the last verse, and that is told dramatically and continuously, in the moment that it occurs. This technique makes for

admirable narrative tightness. The first four lines give us both the essentials of the situation from which the story is to be told—a man and his girl fleeing on horseback from the law—and the pervading atmosphere: "Hot chili peppers in the blistering sun/Dust on my face and my cape/Me and Magdalena on the run/I think this time we shall escape."

Mood and narrative elements are balanced so unobtrusively that we do not think of distinguishing between them. The journey itself summons up the history and culture of the Mexican people and this helps to invest the particular incident with the depth and the heroism which it might otherwise lack: "Past the Aztec ruins and the ghosts of our people/Hoofbeats like castanets on stone." This leads naturally into the narrator's "dream of bells in the village steeple," a dream in which he sees "the bloody face of Ramon." The background to the flight is then narrated through a swift and typically cinematic flashback: "Was it me that shot him down in the cantina?/ Was it my hand that held the gun?/Come, let us fly, my Magdalena/The dogs are barking and what's done is done."

The cultural setting has been established with such tact and sincerity (both lyrical and musical) that we do not feel inclined to smile at the stereotypes of the fight in the cantina, the tracker dogs, and others to come; and Dylan can execute a typical Mexican quaver on the *i*-sound of 'cantina' without lapsing into parody. Our sympathy for the escaping couple is subtly built up and consolidated, not least by the chorus with its haunting Spanish lines, which looks forward to the end of the long journey through the desert.

As the first verse presents the immediate situation, and the second looks back at the cause of the flight, so the third directs our attention forward towards the happy outcome which the narrator envisages. They will sit in the shade and watch the bullfight, "drink tequila where our grandfathers stayed/When they rode with Villa into Torreon." With all the ceremony traditional to their people, the couple are to be married in the little church. Then there comes, in four lines additional to the verse structure as it holds in the other stanzas, one of those strange flashes which impact a further dimension, a kind of numinous depth into the sense of a ballad: "The way is long but the end is near/Already the fiesta has begun./The face of God will appear/With His serpent eyes of obsidian."

The reference, presumably, is to a mask or image of the serpent god that will be carried in the fiesta procession. But into the little idyll that has been evoked, the words introduce a discordant and sinister element; the God of the "serpent eyes" appears like a cruel and avenging spirit, the face of the evil destiny which hangs over the heads of the fated pair. The sense of foreboding which the image carries with it lends a new irony to the "Dios nos vigila" of the chorus which follows.

The fourth verse recalls us swiftly to the present, and in only eight brief lines relates for us the final events of this tragic romance through the direct speech of the narrator. We are not witness to the last act, which occurs only after the song has ended, though it is implied in the poignancy and longing of the final chorus; but we are in no doubt of the outcome. "Aim well, my little one," sings the hero, "We may not make it through the night." The song remains forever poised between our foreknowledge of the end and its enactment.

"Romance" is just about the only Dylan original (save "Black Diamond Bay" and its quick snatches of mangled French) that immediately springs to mind that includes some lines in a foreign language, Spanish. At the end of each verse, Dylan sings, "No llores, mi querida/Dios nos vigila/Soon the horse will take us to Durango/Agarrame, mi vida/Soon the desert will be gone/Soon you will be dancing the fandango," which loosely translated means "Don't cry, my love/God is watching us ... Hold me tight, my dear (my life) ..."

Dylan revived "Romance" in a dramatic and very moving, *Desire*-style arrangement at one of the already famous London concerts at the end of his 2003 European shows.

"The Roving Blade" (Traditional)
aka "The Flash Lad," "I Am a Rolling Blade," "The Irish Robber," "Newlyn Town," "Newry Highwayman," "Newry Town," "The Rambling Blade," "The Rambling Boy," "The Rich and Rambling Boy," "The Robber," "The Wild and Wicked Youth"
Peggy Seeger, *Three Sisters* (1958)
Martin Carthy, *Second Album* (1966)
The Johnstons, *The Barley Corn* (1969)
Bob Scarce, *Folk Songs of Britain, Volume 7: Fair Game and Fowl* (1972)
Roger Nicholson, *Nonesuch for Dulcimer* (1975)
John Faulkner, *Kind Providence* (1986)
Tom Dahill, *Ragged Hank of Yarn* (1988)
Tommy Makem/Liam Clancy, *Two for the Early Dew* (1992)
Boiled in Lead, *Antler Dance* (1994)
Rich Lerner, *Trails and Bridges* (1996)

Though he was probably long familiar with "The Roving Blade," Dylan may have paid attention to the song only recently. But how remains a mystery.

The composition belongs to a class of traditional ballads about the life and deeds of a man about to be hanged; the "hero" in this example is a dashing chap who marries young, becomes a highwayman to pay the bills, and commits one too many daring robberies along the King's road. Eventually he is caught and sentenced to death, though he seems not to regret his misfortune, as he concludes with instructions for his funeral.

Folk-song collectors Frank and Anne Warner did some fine work in uncovering the North Carolina roots of "The Roving Blade" (which they call "The Rambling Boy"); their information was published in the book *Traditional American Folk Songs from the Anne & Frank Warner Collection* (1984): "We were excited when we heard it, for it sounded to us like a forerunner of 'The Unfortunate Rake,' and indeed it may be. It is certainly Irish, and the funeral directions are similar, and the story in both instances is about a young man brought down in his prime—one to an untimely death that stemmed from his riotous living, and one, in this case, brought to the gallows by his career of robbing on the king's highway."

Dylan first trotted out "Roving Blade" in performance during a summer 1992 acoustic set in France, where it was the show's highlight. Almost exactly six years later, he dusted it off for an even better rendition at a concert in Ireland. It popped up a last time in 2000 at a spring display in Reno, Nevada. Dylan's best performances of the song have included inspired vocal touches that made it sound as if he were channeling the eighteenth-century highwayman-narrator as he rots away in a dank cell awaiting his moment at the gallows.

"Rovin' Gambler" (Traditional)
aka "I Am a Roving Gambler," "I'm a Rovin' Gambler," "I'm a Gambler," "Mary Phagin," "Roving Gambler," "Roving Moonshiner"
New Lost City Ramblers, *New Lost City Ramblers, Volume 1* (1958)
The Everly Brothers, *Songs Our Daddy Taught Us* (1958)
The Brothers Four, *The Brothers Four Greatest Hits* (1962)
Hobart Delp, *Ballads and Songs of the Blue Ridge Mountains* (1968)

John Jacob Niles, *Best of John Jacob Niles* (1968)
Senator Robert Byrd, *Mountain Fiddler* (1978)
Tennessee Ernie Ford, *Greatest Hits* (1993)
Peter Case, *Sings Like Hell* (1994)
Sons of the Pioneers, *Songs of the Prairie* (1998)

Freely admitting an addiction to gambling and eye for the ladies, the hero of "Rovin' Gambler" narrates an unrepentant, exuberant travelogue exploring some shady characters inhabiting society's underbelly. One of the song's more interesting aspects is the sheer number of characters who get speaking roles. Along with the gambling picaro himself, a weak-kneed pretty little miss, her mother, another cardsharp, and a prison warden all play at least minor roles in this yarn about nefarious doings. The hero ends up with a number for a name after shooting a cheater dead. But even though the warden tells him he's gambled his last game as the cell door slams shut, one can easily imagine that this cad will be playing croupier in the prison yard before too long.

In *The American Songbag*, his 1927 book surveying the landscape of the nation's musical legacy, Carl Sandburg discusses "Rovin' Gambler" as part of a family of songs in which a footloose girl falls in love with a dapper stranger who arrives in town with a thick wallet and a shiny gold chain hanging from his vest. "There is a swing and self-assurance to the tune and words," Sandburg writes, "the swagger of the old-time minstrel troupe going down Main Street and around the public square, led by the high-hat drum-major holding aloft a long baton with a golden ball gleaming on the end." Sandburg and others agree that these songs have their origins in English popular songs of centuries past that worked their way across the ocean and into the repertoire of minstrelsy.

Dylan was singing "Rovin' Gambler" in 1960 but did not return to it until a single

A DEN IN BAXTER STREET.

Illustration of a gambling den in Baxter Street, New York City, ca. 1867.

(*Frank Leslie's Illustrated Newspaper*/Library of Congress)

November 1991 Never Ending Tour show in South Bend, Indiana. He dusted it off again in 1997 and included it as a centerpiece of his acoustic sets through 2000 in a version that featured a four-part harmony very similar to the well-known 1960 rendition by the Brothers Four. But Dylan could also have learned the song from any one of a number of sources.

"Ruben Remus" (Richard Manuel/Robbie Robertson)
Bob Dylan/The Band, *The Basement Tapes*/'67 (1975)

This rare, original, and truly enigmatic novelty song with a hint of looming violence from the Band sung by Richard Manuel may include Dylan as an accompanist on its sole *Basement Tapes* recording.

R

S

[S] "Sad-Eyed Lady of the Lowlands" (Bob Dylan)

Bob Dylan, *Blonde on Blonde* (1966)
Joan Baez, *Any Day Now* (1968)
Richie Havens, *Mixed Bag II* (1974)
Bad News Reunion, *The Easiest Way* (1980)
Steve Howe, *Portraits of Bob Dylan* (1999)

A private soul song from a private individual, "Sad-Eyed Lady of the Lowlands" poses a series of questions in rhyme that sound as if they are being spoken at the Delphic Oracle.

The first and only title to which Dylan devoted an entire album side (back when there were such things), "Sad-Eyed Lady of the Lowlands" is an epic and ambitious, if murky, song-poem. Widely regarded as having been written to his then-newly betrothed, the song is filled with fractured hallucinations of a woman who has captured him heart and soul.

Though Bob Neuwirth, a Dylan crony in the mid-'60s, once told Robert Shelton that "Bob never wrote a song about any one person. They are about a lot of people, and sometimes not about any people at all," this song is almost assuredly a wedding song for Sara H. Lownds, whom Dylan married on November 22, 1965—two years to the day after the assassination of President John F. Kennedy. And Dylan all but admitted that Sara was the sole subject and focus of the song when, as he sang on *Desire*'s "Sara" ten years later: "I stayed up for days in the Chelsea Hotel/Writing 'Sad-Eyed Lady of the Lowlands' for you." And let us not forget the Dylan kabbalists who make the alliterative connection between the words "lowlands" and "Lownds" as some sort of additional proof that this is Sara's song.

A long, languid surrealist love ode in the tradition of the epic folk ballad with a slow-as-molasses Nashville twist, the eleven-plus minute "Sad-Eyed Lady of the Lowlands" posits the heroine as surrounded by men all too ready to undermine her while positioning the narrator as her valiant paladin. He alone prizes her abundance of saintly charms: "With your mercury mouth in the missionary times/And your eyes like smoke and your prayers like rhymes/And your silver cross and your voice like chimes." But he is also smart (and together) enough not to build an altar and canonize her just yet: "With your sheets like metal and your belt like lace/And your deck of cards missing the jack and the ace/And your basement clothes and your hollow face."

For those sifting the ever-shifting sands of Dylanism for some granules of autobiographical revelation in "Sad-Eyed Lady," perhaps a good start would be the lyric "With your sheet-metal memory of Cannery Row/And your magazine-husband who one day just had to go/And your gentleness now, which you just can't help but show/Who among them do you think would employ you?" All of this and more probably points to Sara's brief job as a Playboy bunny some years before meeting Dylan, her busted marriage to magazine photographer Hans Lownds, the daughter born of that union, and her intimate relationship with Dylan while he was still involved with Joan Baez, herself a product of John Steinbeck's Monterey, California, Cannery Row country.

But the heavy influence the poetic school of Symbolism (as embodied in the lives and work of Rimbaud and Baudelaire) was having on Dylan at the time should scatter the gossip-mongers. Like so many of Dylan's songs in general but particularly those from his *Blonde on Blonde* period, "Sad-Eyed Lady of the Lowlands" is about evoking a pure, emotional response in the listener, not getting stymied by the interpreta-

S

tion of each specific image for some revelatory "meaning." Yes, it is a lot of fun to try cracking Dylan's nightingale codes: the cross (think Christ), the streetcar visions (think desire, Brando), or the sad-eyed prophet (Dylan himself?) who seems unsure of his own worthiness to present his beloved with his gifts of "Arabian drums" (think Magi). But traveling down that road would seem to be a trap set by the sly artist as a young man—a trap, one might add, that can still ensnare even after all these years.

Several have attempted to plumb the depths of "Sad-Eyed Lady." Among them was Robert Shelton, who wrote in his 1986 Dylan biography, *No Direction Home: The Life and Music of Bob Dylan*:

> Before taping this, Dylan told me he regarded this as "the best song I ever wrote." In the last side of *Blonde*, folk tradition meets modern poetry. The title line, echoed in the five verses, has an antique flavor, since Scots-English balladry often refers to lowlands. Paul Nelson called this haunting portrait of a woman: "celebration of woman as work of art, religious figure, and object of eternal majesty and wonder."
>
> The otherworldly woman suffers from the incursions of the material world. She is spiritual, yet corporeal; mystic, yet human; noble, yet pathetic. Her travails seem beyond endurance, yet she radiates an inner strength, an ability to be reborn. This is Dylan at his most romantic.

Richard Goldstein was one of the first to attempt to tackle "Sad-Eyed Lady of the Lowlands." "'Sad-Eyed Lady' is one of Dylan's least self-conscious songs . . . the most moving love song in rock," he wrote in his book *The Poetry of Rock* (New York: Bantam Books, 1969). "Even its foibles conspire to convey the paradoxical reality of its heroine; this sad-eyed lady who can be so nonchalantly strong, and so pre-

dictably weak; so innocent, yet so corrupted . . . His sad-eyed lady is everyone's girl, and everyone's girl is what the love song is all about. . . ."

And Patrick Humphries threw in his two cents' worth in his book *The Complete Guide to the Music of Bob Dylan* (London: Omnibus Books, 1995): "Of all Dylan's atmospheric songs of the period, 'Sad-Eyed Lady' . . . weaves its own world around Dylan . . . There is a lot of puff here (What, please, is a 'geranium kiss'? Describe a 'cowboy mouth') but there is also a rolling hymn of devotion with some extraordinarily intense commitments and pledges contained therein."

Dylan never performed the song in concert, but a rehearsal tape recorded during the Rolling Thunder Revue in October 1975 has preserved at least one other version of this haunting wedding vow in song.

🅂 "Sally Gal" (Woody Guthrie)
aka "I'm Gonna Get You, Sally Gal," "Sally, Don't You Grieve"
Woody Guthrie, *Woody Guthrie: The Asch Recordings Volume 3— Hard Travelin'* (1998)
Woody Guthrie/Cisco Houston, *Woody Guthrie/Cisco Houston* (1969)
Lonnie Donegan, *Best of Lonnie Donegan* (1989)
Lester Flatt and Earl Scruggs, *1964–1969, Plus* (1996)

Dylan apparently adapted this holler about a fellow on the prowl from "Sally, Don't You Grieve," a Woody Guthrie tune. He performed "Sally Gal" at his better-known early sets and recorded it for but did not include it on *The Freewheelin' Bob Dylan*.

According to the liner notes for *Woody Guthrie: The Asch Recordings Volume 3— Hard Travelin'*, written by Guy Logsdon and Jeff Place, Guthrie

> . . . claimed this ["Sally, Don't You Grieve"] as his song, but on a manuscript dated 1942 in

the Asch/Folkways Collection, Woody typed "and the Almanac Singers." However, that was the time when the Almanacs often claimed "communal" composition: subsequent manuscripts list Woody as the only author, and according to Pete Seeger it was, indeed, entirely Woody's composition. On a manuscript dated 10 April 1938 and with different verses (the choruses are basically the same) in a private collection, Woody wrote "Original Song."

On another manuscript typed after his 1944 recording session, Woody wrote: "We bought two big guitars for which we are still in debit. This was one of the first songs we knocked off on the new guitars. Cisco [Houston] sung sort of a rooftop tenor and knocked off a deep bass on his guitar while I led off of the tune and jumped around on my high strings."

[S] **"Sally Sue Brown"** (Arthur Alexander, E. Montgomery, T. Stafford)
Bob Dylan, *Down in the Groove* (1988)
Arthur Alexander, *Shot of Rhythm and Soul* (1982)
Sugar Ray and the Bluetones, *Knockout* (1989)
C. C. Adcock, *C. C. Adcock* (1994)
Various Artists (performed by Elvis Costello), *Adios Amigo—Tribute to Arthur Alexander* (1994)

Dylan has some fun—at his fans' expense—on this up-tempo rocker, which was released on his forgettable album *Down in the Groove*.

"Sally Sue Brown" was cowritten and first recorded by the brilliant Arthur Alexander (born May 10, 1940, Florence, Alabama; died June 9, 1993, Nashville). Alexander's best work evoked the same type of inspirational qualities most closely associated with gospel music, while at the same time invoked the darker elements of the blues—stark, distressed vocals, heavily echoed piano, and layered lyrics—that could lay a hoodoo whammy on even the casual listener. And, in a prime example of less is more, Alexander's single-track version of "Sally Sue Brown" is as present and focused on his release as Dylan's is lost on the multitrack *Down in the Groove* rendition.

Alexander's link in the chain of popular music as a premier singing, songwriting progenitor of country soul (a genre that united Southern black R&B singers and directly led to the whole Muscle Shoals scene) cannot be overestimated. Elvis Presley memorably covered "Burning Love," the Beatles had a Top 10 hit with Alexander's "Anna (Go to Him)," the Stones covered "You Better Move On" (which became an anthem of the subculture), and "A Shot of Rhythm and Blues" became a staple of the British Beat scene. This has made him the answer to the trivia question: "Whose songs were covered by Dylan, Elvis, the Beatles, and the Rolling Stones?" Critics suggest that his fragile personality was particularly susceptible to the pressure of Nashville's production modus operandi, and he was forced to take jobs (like driving a bus) outside the music business for years.

After a few unsuccessful stabs at getting back into the biz with recordings for Dot Records and the like, Alexander reemerged in 1972 with *Arthur Alexander*, which included "Rainbow Road," Dan Penn's fictionalized biography of the singer in song. He soldiered on despite an illness that kept him on the fringes of the music scene, though he did write, record (including at least one session with Carl Perkins), and enjoy the odd release.

Alexander suffered a fatal heart attack only a month after signing a new record deal and just after recording a new album (the gentle *Lonely Like Me*, released shortly after his passing). His death also occurred just as he was returning to the concert stage amid renewed interest in his modest but vital catalogue—a cruel, ironic fate for such an important voice.

Dylan unveiled "Sally Sue Brown" at a pair of 1992 Never Ending Tour shows.

[S] "Sammy's Song" (David Bromberg)

David Bromberg, *David Bromberg* (1971); *The Player/'71* (1998)

Dylan plays background mouth harp on "Sammy's Song," a graphic and chilling Bromberg original that Dylan recorded with its composer.

[S] "San Francisco Bay Blues" (Jesse Fuller)

Jesse Fuller, *San Francisco Bay Blues* (1963)
The Weavers, *Wasn't That a Time* (1993)
Peter, Paul and Mary, *Song Will Rise* (1965)
Richie Havens, *Mixed Bag* (1967)
Ramblin' Jack Elliott, *Essential Ramblin' Jack Elliott* (1970)

"San Francisco Bay Blues" was Jesse "The Lone Cat" Fuller's endearing and enduring glad-to-be-unhappy theme song, influencing many white folk-blues artists of the early 1960s. While not really a blues in the classic tradition, Fuller's song has enjoyed fame, comparable to that of Woody Guthrie's "This Land Is Your Land," among the more knowledgeable city folksingers.

Jesse Fuller (born March 12, 1896, Jonesboro, Georgia; died January 29, 1976, Oakland, California) was a folk-blues singer par excellence for sure and even more of an oddity—a Bizarro World combination of Reverend Gary Davis and Moondog. There really hasn't been anything or anybody else like this unique one-man band and idiosyncratic songwriter. Picking the twelve-string guitar Piedmont-style, blowing his mouth harp (or kazoo) attached with a necklace, and summoning the lower register notes from his renowned "fotdella"—a homemade bass constructed with piano strings and played with a foot pedal—combined with the swish of his cymbals and the rhythmic scrape of his washboard, Fuller could become a surrealistic, postmodern avant-garde jug band all by his lonesome—a theme that runs through his otherwise joyful music.

Fuller's brand of country folk-blues with a smile hints at his quintessentially American experience: a childhood spent in extreme poverty followed by a circuitous, seemingly random series of events that brought him to a pinnacle of one-of-a-kind creations. He never really knew his natural parents and was raised by a couple who treated him "worse than a dog," starving and beating the young lad. He escaped that predicament when he was nine and went to live with a family named Wilson near Macedonia, Georgia. There, he had what passed for a normal rural life, working the family's fields and going to school.

Somewhere during his difficult youth, his keen abilities as an instrument maker emerged when he constructed himself a mouth bow. "I made a bow like the Indians used to use and put some wax on the string," he explained to Barbara Dane for an article that appeared in an issue of *Sing Out!* magazine (volume 13, #5, December 1963–January 1964). "I put the bow in my mouth and pick the string and it sounded like a jew's-harp. I don't know how the idea ever came into my head." By the age of ten, he had also built a crude guitar and was learning to play songs from various musicians he met at Saturday night dances that he managed to sneak into. These were no swing-your-partner affairs, for as Fuller told Dane, "They was really rough. People got killed sometimes."

True to his "Lone Cat" moniker, Fuller finished third grade, ran away from the Wilsons, and proved himself to be a true survivor. He worked on farms and in factories, cleaned

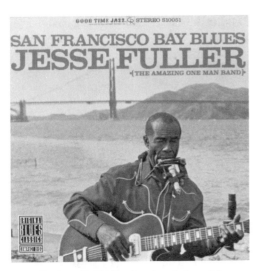

Jesse "The Lone Cat" Fuller, American folk musician, ca. 1960s (cover of CD brochure for his 1963 album *San Francisco Bay Blues*).

(Courtesy of Fantasy, Inc.)

houses and delivered groceries, laid down railroad track and chopped wood—whatever it took to make ends meet.

But it wasn't all work: he was no stranger to the itinerant minstrel shows that crisscrossed the region, and it was from them that he picked up many traditional folk and blues songs, which he learned to play on guitar or harmonica.

He moved to Cincinnati in the early '20s, taking a job first on a streetcar and then as a roustabout for the Hagenbeck Wallace Circus. While touring with the circus he discovered he could make even more money playing his guitar on the streets for the entertainment of soldiers returning home from World War I.

Heeding the advice of the times ("Go West, young man"), Fuller hopped freight trains to

California, landing in Los Angeles, where he shined shoes outside the gates of the United Artists Studio. It was there that he befriended Douglas Fairbanks and Raoul Walsh—the respective Tom Cruise and James Cameron of their day—who got him bit roles in several films, including *The Thief of Baghdad, East of Suez, Hearts of Dixie,* and *End of the World,* and eventually set him up with a hot dog stand outside the studio lot.

But Fuller was not one to be satisfied with a lifetime of flipping franks. In the following decades he worked as a farm laborer, shipbuilder, and Southern Pacific Railroad man— an itinerant, footloose life that can be heard in the imagery of wanderlust informing his songs.

After marrying and starting a family in Oakland, California, he slowly began a transition to the life of an artist. Though he continued to eke out a living working odd jobs, he began performing at parties, street corners, clubs, and local events. He opened another shoeshine spot on College Avenue near the University of California, Berkeley, in the 1950s that drew the avant-garde folk-music bohemian set, who dug both the traditional stuff and his own originals, too.

It was during this period that Fuller began devising his aforementioned "fotdella," the big six-string bass viol that he played via a system of pedals and levers. Looking like something out of a Rube Goldberg cartoon, Fuller used his right foot to play the fotdella, his left foot to run a high-hat cymbal, and a harness to hold both a harmonica and kazoo while he sat amid his one-man-band rig with a twelve-string guitar sitting on his lap.

The idea of starting his one-man band came out of necessity, but the name of the fotdella came from his wife. "I got hearin' about fellers

S

who were making lots of money on records," Fuller told Dane of *Sing Out!* "I tried to get some fellers to play with me but they were always busy—drinking wine and gamblin'. So I said, 'I'm goin' to make me a one-man band' and I did. My wife she call it a fotdella—that's like 'foot diller,' cause I play it with my foot. And that's its name."

Committing himself more wholeheartedly to his music, he wrote his trademark tune, "San Francisco Bay Blues," in 1954. His one-man-band routine drew attention and he was "discovered" in a local bar a year later. He began his recording career in 1955 with the release of the album *Folk Blues: Working on the Railroad with Jesse Fuller*, which included "San Francisco Bay Blues."

As his reputation grew, recording sessions for other labels followed as well as an extensive and fruitful touring regime that included the college coffeehouse circuit, the famous 1964 Newport Folk Festival, and Europe. It was during this phase that he shared an April 20–22, 1962, bill with Bob Dylan at Goddard College in Ann Arbor, Michigan. And Dylan included Fuller's "You're No Good" on *Dylan*, his debut LP. Seasoning his set lists with folk and religious numbers, rags, and country blues, Fuller was an expansive musician who grounded his performance on a rhythmic style that brimmed with good humor while barely concealing a life of hard work and harder times.

Dylan was performing the winsome "San Francisco Bay Blues" very early in his career and returned to it twice in 1988, appropriately during visits to the Bay Area. These late performances—aided by the guitar work of premier Never Ending Tour sideman G. E. Smith—are full of jaunty, smiling-through-tears jubilation.

▣ "Santa-Fe" (Bob Dylan)
aka "Sante Fe"
Bob Dylan, *The Bootleg Series, Volumes 1–3: Rare and Unreleased, 1961–1991/'67* (1991)

Standard-issue nonsense Dylan shared and the Hawks recorded during the fomentation of *The Basement Tapes* in 1967, "Santa-Fe" would have sounded just right on the *Pat Garrett and Billy the Kid* soundtrack. It is among the more traditional-sounding songs to have emerged from those legendary upstate New York sessions.

▣ "Sara" (Bob Dylan)
Bob Dylan, *Desire* (1976); *The Bootleg Series, Volume 5: Live 1975—The Rolling Thunder Revue* (2002)
Rich Lerner & the Groove, *Cover Down* (2000)

One of the true departures in Dylan's vast catalogue, "Sara" is a rarity: simple, sentimental, soul-baring, and autobiographical. It is at once a last-ditch plea and ballad in faded Polaroid to his estranged wife and another entry in his Woman vs. God as Salvation discourses, a theme that runs through his entire oeuvre.

Dylan's release of "Sara" on *Desire* was, for an artist and public figure who has always worked pretty hard at obscuring analysis of his work, a true eye-opener. Yet, steeped in pan-cultural mythological allusion ("sweet virgin angel," "Scorpio Sphinx," "glamorous nymph with an arrow and bow"), the mystical heroine of his song remains as tantalizingly out of reach ("So easy to look at, so hard to define") to the listener as she did for the singer.

"Sara" begins and ends with a scene on the beach. In the beginning, the narrator portrays a summer idyll as he watches his children play in the sand. He slowly moves into flashback mode as he replays the past in impressionistic snapshots recalling scenes of courtship, marriage, and emotional fracture. At the song's

S

end, we are again shown the beach, empty now except for some kelp and a piece of an old ship—symbolic images of weeds and shipwreck that leave the listener marooned.

"Sara" also includes the famous revelation about how Dylan stayed up "for days in the Chelsea Hotel,/Writing 'Sad-Eyed Lady of the Lowlands'" for her—a claim that was savaged by the critic Lester Bangs in "Bob Dylan's Dalliance with Mafia Chic," his infamous dismissal of *Desire* in the April 1976 edition of *Creem*: "If he really *did* spend days on end sitting up in the Chelsea sweating over lines like 'your streetcar visions which you place on the grass' [from "Sad-Eyed Lady"], then he is stupider than we gave him credit for."

Sara was born Shirley Noznisky on either October 31 or November 1, 1940. When or why she changed her name to Sara is unclear, but when she married magazine photographer Hans Lownds (not Victor Lownes, as some sources cite), she took his last name. Dylan first met her through their mutual friend Sally Grossman in 1964 and they were married on November 22, 1965. Though divorced in July 1977 in (for Dylan) a fairly public split, they have reportedly remained in regular contact since, no doubt due to the three sons (Jakob, Jesse, and Samuel) and daughter (Anna) they brought into the world. At some point Dylan adopted Maria, the daughter Sara had with Hans Lownds. Retreating from the public eye, she has allegedly cut an extremely remote, somewhat tragic figure on the fringes of the Dylan mythoscape.

Dylan performed "Sara" as a nightly feature during the first phase of the Rolling Thunder Revue in the fall of 1975. But the most legendary performance of the song took place in semiprivate during *Desire* recording sessions. According to Howard Sounes's 2001 biography of the man, *Down the Highway: The Life of Bob Dylan* (New York: Grove Press):

> Sara Dylan arrived unexpectedly on the night of the second session, July 31 [1975]. "She came to New York, I guess, to see if there would be some kind of a getting back together. I guess that was in her mind. I know it was in his mind," says [theater director and lyricist Jacques] Levy, who had not seen Sara the whole summer (she had been on vacation in Mexico). Bob went back into the studio with his band and picked up a guitar. He sang "Sara" to his wife as she watched from the other side of the glass. The song began by recalling holidays on the beach when the children were small, and mentioned the long-ago holiday in Portugal when they were first together. He asked her forgiveness for his recent transgressions, and sang at the end: "Don't ever leave me, don't ever go." "It was extraordinary. You could have heard a pin drop," says Levy. "She was absolutely stunned by it. And I think it was a turning point. It did work. The two of them really did get back together." This remarkable first take of "Sara" became the last track on *Desire*.

[S] "Sarah Jane" (Traditional/Bob Dylan)

aka "Rockabout My Saro Jane," "Rock About My Sarah Jane," "Saro Jane"
Bob Dylan, *Dylan* (1973)
Kingston Trio, *Kingston Trio* (1958)
Odetta, *My Eyes Have Seen* (1959)
Uncle Dave Macon, *Early Recordings* (1971)
Various Artists, *Old Virginia Fiddlers* (1977)
Matokie Slaughter & the Black Creek Buddies, *Marimac* (1990)
Jazz Gillum, *Key to the Highway 1935–1942* (1996)

After performing this song at the outset of his career (it appears on the very early, debated May 1960 "St. Paul Tape"), Dylan returned to

S

"Saro Jane" during the winter 1970 *New Morning* sessions, where he rearranged it as a folksy doo-wop replete with a cringe-inducing chorus for reasons unknown. It wound up being released on the unessential, personally unauthorized *Dylan* album.

According to volume 6 of *Reprints from Sing Out! The Folk Song Magazine* (New York: Oak Publications, 1964):

> This is a rousing traditional roustabout song from the days of Mississippi River steamboating. The last verse was apparently added during Civil War days, by some rebel sharpshooter. Lee Haring points out that, as befits a song of hard-working men, the piece is loaded with secondary sexual meanings. (No more clues. You have to figure out the rest for yourself.) One of the earliest recordings of the song was by Uncle Dave Macon and his Fruit Jar Drinkers back in 1927. Uncle Dave recalled hearing it sung by "a steamboat's colored crew singing on Front Street in Nashville, Tennessee, in 1887."

One can only imagine what lyrics like "Engine gave a crack and the whistle gave a squall/The engineer gone to the hole in the wall/O Saro Jane!" actually mean, but the lascivious mind shouldn't have such a hard time coming up with a corresponding image. Whether the song has hidden meaning or is just nonsense, "Saro Jane" feels as if it was cut out of the same cloth that produced the musical tapestry that is *The Basement Tapes*.

▣ "A Satisfied Mind" (J. H. "Red" Hayes/Jack Rhodes)
aka "Satisfied Mind"
Bob Dylan, single (1980); *Saved* (1980)
Red Foley, *Red Foley Story* (1964)
The Byrds, *Turn! Turn! Turn!* (1965)

Joan Baez, *Farewell, Angelina* (1965)
Bryan Bowers, *View from Home* (1977)
Porter Wagoner, *Thin Man from West Plains* (1989)
Mahalia Jackson, *Gospels, Spirituals and Hymns* (1991)

A classic C&W gospel standard covered by many folk artists over the past four decades, "A Satisfied Mind" was the first nonoriginal song Dylan had released since some of the material on *Self Portrait*. Dylan was studying this song as early as the summer of 1961 and included a seemingly improvised version as an introduction to *Saved* (which leads directly into the title track on the album). Still, he never performed "Satisfied Mind" during the 1979–80 gospel tour, or on any other tour, for that matter, until he pulled it out for a surprise 1999 demonstration.

According to J. H. "Red" Hayes, as quoted in the 1973 book *Country Music People*:

> The song came from my mother. Everything in the song are things I heard her say over the years. I put a lot of thought into the song before I came up with the title. One day my father-in-law asked me who I thought the richest man in the world was, and I mentioned some names. He said, "You're wrong, it is the man with a satisfied mind." It has been done a lot in churches. I came out of the Opry one night and a church service was going on nearby. The first thing I hear was the congregation singing "Satisfied Mind." I got down on my knees.

Porter Wagoner had the biggest hit with the song and used the title for his autobiography.

Information on the song's two composers is sketchy—a surprise, considering that one of them, Jack Rhodes (born Andrew Jackson Rhodes, Mineola, Texas), is a member of Nashville's Songwriters Hall of Fame and wrote or cowrote some of country music's most memorable songs, including "Beautiful Lies,"

S

"Conscience Guilty," "Too Young to Settle Down," "Hangin' On to What I've Got," and "Silver Threads and Golden Needles."

◪ *Saved*

Columbia Records LP PC-36553; CD CK-36553; CS PCT-36553. Recorded February 15–19, 1980, at Muscle Shoals Studios, Sheffield, Alabama. Released June 20, 1980. Produced by Jerry Wexler and Barry Beckett. Photography by Arthur Rosato. Artwork by Tony Wright.
Bob Dylan—guitar, vocals, harmonica. Tim Drummond—bass. Jim Keltner—drums. Fred Tackett—guitar. Spooner Oldham—keyboards. Terry Young— keyboards, vocals. Clydie King, Regina Havis, Mona Lisa Young—vocals. Special guest artist—Barry Beckett.
"A Satisfied Mind," "Saved," "Covenant Woman," "What Can I Do for You?," "Solid Rock," "Pressing On," "In the Garden," "Saving Grace," "Are You Ready?"

One listen to *Saved* and it is immediately apparent that Dylan's born-again Christian fervency had not yet let up from *Slow Train Coming*. His songwriting and performance is muted on this sophomore gospel album, and his preachifying is overbearing, to say the least. But the power of Dylan's commitment is undeniable.

One of the few Dylan albums to fail to achieve gold-record status, *Saved* made it only as high as No. 24 during its five weeks on the charts. The release commenced a nearly ten-year commercial drought for the recording artist, which would end with 1989's *Oh Mercy*.

Columbia released the album with two different covers. First was a garish painting of God's hand touching one of five outstretched hands in a graphic that could have come from the front page of the lamest-looking religious tract lying in a Times Square gutter. The second, somewhat more acceptable, image was of a watery, wannabe cubist portrait of Dylan and band in performance. Both pictures featured a

shot of Dylan and his ensemble on the back cover in a disturbingly out-of-focus photograph and a quote from the Old Testament's Book of Jeremiah (chapter 31, verse 31), rendered in that same bogus religious pamphlet typeface: "Behold, the days come, saith the Lord, that I will make a new covenant with the house of Israel, and with the house of Judah."

An indication that even Dylan eventually tired of the material on *Saved* may be that only three of the songs, "In the Garden," "Saving Grace," and "Solid Rock," have seen any life beyond the initial performances of these compositions in 1979 and 1980. There are a few other worthy works here, too. The album opens with an a cappella version of "Satisfied Mind," a country gospel favorite made famous by Porter Wagoner. "Covenant Woman" celebrates Dylan's declaration of faith by describing a lady who has a "contract with God"; "Pressing On" ranks as Dylan's most inspirational song; and the title track is worthy of a Wednesday night prayer meeting in the basement of a parish church in Anytown, U.S.A.

Discussing fundamentalism with Eduardo Bueno in June 1991 (as published in the Brazilian magazine *Caderno 2* later that month), Dylan said: "I've never been a Fundamentalist. I've never been Born Again. Those are just labels that people hang on you. They mean just about as much as 'folk singer,' 'protest singer,' 'rock star.' That's to say that they don't mean anything at all."

⬛ **"Saved"** (Bob Dylan/Tim Drummond)
Bob Dylan, single (1980); *Saved* (1980)
Sandra Payne, *Sandra Payne* (1997)
Various Artists (performed by Mighty Clouds of Joy), *Gotta Serve Somebody: The Gospel Songs of Bob Dylan* (2003)

Among Dylan's most die-hard gospel tunes, "Saved" was cowritten with Tim Drummond, his bassist during the gospel era and, ironically, one of the few non-Christians in the group. Certainly "Saved" does its best to jump-start the titular album on which it appears—a fiery damnation and hellfire rant, preachin' and testifyin' salvation through Jesus Christ in the charismatic tradition of Elmer Gantry. But on its album release, the song falls a little flat.

However, live and in person was another matter. Describing an early Dylan performance of "Saved" in November 1979 in his book *Dylan—What Happened?* (Glen Ellen, California: Entwhistle Books, 1979), Paul Williams wrote:

> [It] is a moving, effective production number, fun to watch and sing along with. Terry Young gets to really rock out on the piano on this one, and the last night we went I was also quite impressed by the guitar solos. Fred Tackett, lead guitar for the concerts, is technically excellent but seemed to be cowed by Dylan—his playing got more self-confident and louder as the nights passed, but it still lacked the bite that such passionate music deserves.
>
> "Saved" starts with a fine "Jumping Jack Flash" opening: "I was blinded by the devil" (he [Dylan] sure uses the word "blinded" a lot)/"Born already ruined/Stone cold dead as I stepped forth from the womb." Mostly he's telling us he's so glad (to have been saved) and he just wants to "thank you Lord." This "thank you" is a lot more casual than "Saving Grace" or "What Can I Do for You?," but it's a fun song, at least in concert. One rather revealing line: "No one tried to rescue me/Nobody dared." It fits in with my theory that Dylan needed Christ because only a full-blown religion with all the trimmings could offer the discipline necessary to keep him faithful, to restrain his mighty ego from running off on its own trip again. Other situations might also have offered awakening, but only Christ offered Dylan the chance to really surrender himself—which, since it was his ego (sense of his own power) that was torturing him, was the one thing he needed most. Says me.

"Saved" never charted when released as a single and was liberally but exclusively performed from 1979 through 1981 during Dylan's gospel revue, sometimes as a show-opening rave.

Bassist and "Saved" cowriter Tim Drummond (born April 20, 1940, Bloomington, Indiana) first played with Dylan at the March 23, 1975, SNACK (Students Need Athletic and Cultural Kicks) benefit concert in San Francisco, and was a fixture in Dylan's touring band from 1979 through to 1981. He appears on *Slow Train Coming*, *Saved*, and *Shot of Love*. Drummond is one of those journeymen performers and studio musicians who have never stopped working, yet go largely unrecognized for their contributions. A short list of those he has worked with: James Brown, Neil Young, Graham Nash, J. J. Cale, David Crosby, David Lindley, Charlie Daniels, Ronnie Hawkins, Rick Danko, Hoyt Axton, Ry Cooder, Paula Abdul, Eric Clapton, and Roy Buchanan.

[S] "Saving Grace" (Bob Dylan)

aka "Saving Grace That's Over Me"
Bob Dylan, *Saved* (1980)
Various Artists (performed by Aaron Neville), *Gotta Serve Somebody: The Gospel Songs of Bob Dylan* (2003)

By the time listeners got to "Saving Grace" on *Saved* they probably felt as if they had been there and done that. When practically every tune on an album is thanking God for something, it gets a wee bit redundant to hear it again . . . and again. The fact that it's performed out of tune on the *Saved* release doesn't exactly help matters.

Though "Saving Grace" commences with a sweet, melodic roll, it is in fact a song of a man—once blinded by the Devil's light—who found his way from a sinful world gone terribly wrong.

Still, "Saving Grace" is not without its nuanced virtues. With the startling brutal observation that "to search for love, that ain't no more than vanity," Dylan raises the kinds of gray-area concepts and paradoxes that make his nonsecular work so compelling. Paul Williams explores this a bit further in his 1992 book *Bob Dylan: Performing Artist—The Middle Years, 1974–1986*:

> Dylan is writing his own spirituals. As "Solid Rock" reaches back to "Rock of Ages," "Saving Grace" is (lyrically) a cousin to "Amazing Grace." The singer describes the joy of living in a state of trust and vulnerability, living by God's will, as opposed to the hell of living in a state of cynicism where one follows nothing except the voice of one's ego (he identifies the "search for love" as vanity, narcissism; in this sense the philosophy expressed here is opposite to—and arises naturally from—the state of mind that expressed itself on *Street Legal*). "Trouble in Mind" from the *Slow Train Coming* session described the problem; "Saving Grace," which touches on many of the same issues, describes the solution, not theoretically or as taught but as experienced. Dylan is bearing witness. The song's delicacy and sweetness derive in part at least from the fact that the despair, fear of death, and sense of hopelessness he speaks of are not in the past but still in his present; God's love has not rescued the singer from his pit, but rather allows him to live in the midst of it. "Thy rod and thy staff they comfort me." In "Saving Grace" Dylan gives this comfort a name and a location, and allows us to feel (ah those rippling guitar lines) how sweet its presence can be.

Dylan's performances of "Saving Grace"—displayed during the 1979–80 gospel tour and then again out of the blue in 2003–04, as the world was thrown into global crises—were an improvement over its *Saved* release when, nestled firmly in the middle of the show, it was unleashed with a fire missing from *Saved*.

[S] **"Searching for a Soldier's Grave"** (Jim Anglin)

See also "Humming Bird," "This World Can't Stand Long"
The Bailes Brothers, single (1945)
Blue Sky Boys, *Blue Sky Boys* (1963)
Ralph Stanley, *Pray for the Boys* (1990)
Louvin Brothers, *Close Harmony* (1992)
Kitty Wells, *Queen of Country* (1999)

Hank Williams once called this song of mourning—sung by a woman traveling across the sea to find her true love's cross-mark on a foreign shore—"one of the purdyest songs I reckon anybody ever wrote," and he may well have been Dylan's source for "Searching for a Soldier's Grave," even if he apparently never performed it himself.

No doubt inspired by World War II, the song was written by Jim Anglin, who sold "Searching for a Soldier's Grave" to Roy Acuff (who is often cited as its composer). Anglin also sold Acuff "This World Can't Stand Alone," another song Dylan started performing very late in the game. In Dylan's hands, "Searching for a Soldier's Grave" became a high-lonesome homage to all of the bands of brothers that he has admired through the decades, be they the Clancys, the Stanleys, the Louvins, the Everlys, or, of course, the Anglins.

Dylan began sprinkling in performances of

S

"Searching for a Soldier's Grave" starting with the summer 2000 edition of the Never Ending Tour, and returned to it with some degree of frequency (and the nerve of a caballero) in the fall of 2001 as the bombs fell over Kabul.

[S] "Seeing the Real You at Last" (Bob Dylan)

Bob Dylan, *Empire Burlesque* (1985)
The Zimmermen, *The Dungeon Tapes* (1996)

A song about reckoning, "Seeing the Real You at Last" gives a blow-by-blow description of a relationship on the rocks and a sharp portrayal of the woman with whom Dylan had reached a critical moment of truth. An all-too-infrequent, always welcome, and still occasionally performed concert inclusion since Dylan's first tour with Tom Petty and the Heartbreakers, "Real You" works as a contemporary, hard-edged gestalt.

Not a put-down song in the classic sense, "Real You" sometimes gives one the feeling that Dylan is holding a mirror to his own face when he cranks it out on stage. While the official release of this stinging rebuke can be described as "rock lite," Dylan's live presentations of "Seeing the Real You at Last" remain incendiary, sounding like a song a modern-day Odysseus may have sung upon returning from his Poseidon-cursed voyage only to discover that Penelope had finally given up the ghost and shacked up with one of those obnoxious suitors lingering around the estate in craggy Ithaca.

History buffs will note that Dylan incorrectly utilizes Annie Oakley and Belle Starr as metaphors in the song: it was Belle Starr who was known for her riding abilities and Annie Oakley for her sharpshooting skills—not the other way around. And Dylan cribbed that line ("You could ride like Annie Oakley/You could shoot like Belle Starr") from Clint Eastwood's *Bronco Billy*.

Film buffs will further note that Dylan's lines "Well, I have had some rotten nights/Didn't think that they would pass" are drawn, as are lyrics to a few other songs on *Empire Burlesque*, from a Humphrey Bogart reel. In *The Maltese Falcon*, the fabulous 1941 John Huston–directed noir set in San Francisco and based on the Dashiell Hammett novel, Bogey (playing Sam Spade) sends Mary Astor (his murderess lover) up the river and leaves her with the admission that "I'll have some rotten nights after I've sent you over—but that'll pass."

Dylan also drew on *The Big Sleep* (1946), another top-notch (if totally baffling) Bogart noir, directed by Howard Hawks and based on Raymond Chandler's detective epic. The film features many a precoital joust between Bogey's Philip Marlowe character and bad little rich girl Lauren Bacall, including the closing slice of dialogue (Bogey: "What's wrong with you?" Lauren: "Nothing you can't fix."). Dylan took this exchange and shaped it into his own: "At one time there was nothing wrong with me/That you could not fix."

Dylan pillaged two other Bogart-Bacall films in "Seeing the Real You at Last." The song's opening phrase ("Well, I thought that the rain would cool things down/But it looks like it don't") virtually falls from the lips of Edward G. Robinson's bad-guy character Johnny Rocco in Huston's 1948 *Key Largo* ("Think this rain would cool things off, but it don't"). And the song's "baby talk" reference appears to have been drawn from *To Have and Have Not* (1944), yet another Hawks-directed Bogart-Bacall tropical (and then topical) romantic drama in the *Casablanca* mode, based on the Ernest Hemingway novel with a screenplay cowritten by William Faulkner.

Perhaps Dylan should have titled the song "Seeing the *Reel* You at Last."

[S] **"See That My Grave Is Kept Clean"** (Blind Lemon Jefferson)
aka "One Kind Favor," "See That My Grave Is Kept Green," "Six White Horses," "Two White Horses in a Line"
Bob Dylan, *Bob Dylan* (1962)
Blind Lemon Jefferson, *King of the Country Blues* (1985)
Lightnin' Hopkins, *Lightnin' Hopkins* (1959)
Bill Monroe, *Father of Bluegrass Music* (1962)
Mississippi Fred McDowell, *My Home Is in the Delta* (1964)
Merl Saunders, Jerry Garcia, Greg Kahn, Bill Vitt, *Keystone Encores/'73* (1989)

With the chill and portent of an Old Testament seer, the harrowing "See That My Grave Is Kept Clean" is Blind Lemon Jefferson's most famous recording. Transforming his guitar into a tolling bell, Jefferson renders the old song as an ominous blues spiritual that looks death squarely in the face and shrugs.

Despite its ingrained association with Jefferson, "See That My Grave Is Kept Clean" has its origins in "Two White Horses in a Line," a song from the British folk tradition adapted to the blues by blacks in the nineteenth century. Blues scholars of a literary bent have traced the song's silver spade/golden chain imagery all the way back through a nineteenth-century sea chantey to "Who Killed Cock Robin," another older British song. And Bible hounds will find shades of many of the lyrics and motifs in this very influential plea in Negro spirituals, themselves drawn from Old and New Testament sources.

Dylan performed "See That My Grave Is Kept Clean" at his very early coffeehouse gigs as if he was the octogenarian son of a slave singing in a Mississippi Delta shotgun shack. He used the song to close his eponymous debut album in 1962 on a dark note and toyed with a still not officially released Delta/Nashville-style arrangement on *The Basement Tapes*.

Greil Marcus surveyed the song's history and its particular relevance to Dylan and the Hawks' unreleased *Basement Tapes*–era recording, oeuvre, and related configurations in his 1997 book *Invisible Republic*:

> It seemed impossible that a twenty-year-old folkie could find his way through this profound song, learned from a 1928 Jefferson recording collected on the *Anthology of American Folk Music*, but on his self-titled first album Dylan pulled it off. He did more than that: the intensity he brought to the piece all but broke it down, until Jefferson's challenge to Death became a kind of invitation, an almost hysterical date.
>
> The song went back a long way, to the year just after the Civil War, when it emerged as a composed piece meant to comfort a land now covered with hundreds of thousands of new graves—mass graves, unmarked graves. The song was called "See That My Grave Is Kept Green," and it was sentimental, a sing-along, a reach to heaven for the blessing of dignity in death. As recorded in 1927 by Bela Lam and His Greene County Singers, led by banjoist Zandervon Obeliah Lam, the plea remained as it had been generations before: abstract, impersonal, a joyous prayer for all, and the singers know it will be answered. If somehow your loved ones cannot water the grass around your place of rest, God will send the rain.
>
> When the song migrated into the repertoires of itinerant black singers, it was not only new words and new imagery that changed it (the six white horses, the tolling bell) but a new tone. It turned harsh and cold, and the community was no longer present in the music. Now it was a solitary's protest against death, which is to say against life. There is no polite request for a sylvan grave: just keep it clean, Jefferson says. Death has

taken God's place in the song; Jefferson might be giving over his body as long as Death is willing to sweep up. Death apparently agrees; not halfway through Jefferson's performance, you can feel that it is Death, not Jefferson, that is singing. The voice is that sure.

Jefferson (born September 1893, Couchman, Texas; died December 1929, Chicago) still ranks among America's first famous and influential country bluesmen. Not only did his popularity eventually run from coast to coast during the 1920s, but also his 78s breached the racial divide.

Like so many figures in the blues, Jefferson is shrouded in great mystery. Not even his real name survives. And the facts of his early life are particularly sketchy, though it is believed that he was born blind and was one of seven children. Music was one of the few alternatives for a poor blind man of color in Texas during the early twentieth century, and Jefferson learned enough guitar to scrape out a living as a busker in Dallas's rowdy Deep Elem.

Jefferson was the complete package: mesmerizing singer, miraculous guitar player, and compelling lyricist. His voice—more of an elastic, thinly veneered whine drawn from the singing of cotton workers—transformed his grab-bag repertoire of religious hymns, spirituals, work songs, and folk tunes into a sound that could have a patent number. He played the guitar as few ever have, using it as a second voice, full of halting rhythms that seemed to magically materialize at the end of a lyric and then swirl into elaborate solo flourishes before vaporizing back into a rhythm part. And his blue-ribbon songwriting, crafted with the ear of a poet, is ripe with vivid images that immediately bring early 1900s Southern black culture to life.

Blind Lemon Jefferson's death in December 1929, at the end of the first great blues era, was as fitting as the legend of his demise: it is said that he became lost on the streets of Chicago during a severe blizzard and froze to death. Nearly forty years after his passing, after discovering where his remains were interred, a cult of Jefferson's admirers erected a gravestone in the Worthman Black Cemetery in Worthman, Texas, with the predictable epitaph inscribed on the marble: "See That My Grave Is Kept Clean."

Self Portrait

Columbia Records LP C2X-30050; CD C2X-30050; CS C2X-30050. Recorded May and August 1969; February and March 1970. Released June 8, 1970. Produced by Bob Johnston.

Bob Dylan—guitar, harmonica, keyboards, vocals. Norman Blake—guitar. Doug Kershaw—violin. David Bromberg—guitar. Al Kooper—guitar, horn, keyboards. Robbie Robertson—guitar, vocals. Frank Smith—bass. Rick Danko—bass. Pete Drake—guitar. Fred Carter—guitar. Bill Pursell—vocals. Martin Katahn—vocals. Ron Cornelius—guitar. Byron Bach—violin. Brenton Banks—synthesizer, violin. George Binkley III—violin. Albert Wynn Butler—horn. Kenny Buttery—drums. Marvin Chantry—viola. Charlie Daniels—bass, guitar. Dorothy Dillard—vocals. Delores Edgin—guitar. Anthony Ferron—guitar. Bubba Foller—guitar. Fred Foster—guitar. Solie Fott—trombone. Dennis Goode—trombone. Emanuel Green—violin. Hilda Harris—vocals. Levon Helm—mandolin. Freddie Hill—trumpet. Karl Himmel—drums. Garth Hudson—keyboards, saxophone. Mildred Kirkham—violin. Sheldon Kurland—violin. Richard Manuel—drums, keyboards, vocals. Martha McCrory—cello. Barry McDonald—trumpet. Ollie Mitchell—trumpet. Carol Montgomery—bass. Bob Moore—bass. Gene A. Mullins—vocals. June Page—vocals. Rex Peer—vocals. Albertine Robinson—vocals. Al Rogers—drums. Maretha Stewart—vocals. Gary Van Osdale—viola. Bob Wilson—bass. Stu Woods—bass. Charlie McCoy—guitar, harmonica.

"All the Tired Horses," "Alberta #1," "I Forgot More Than

You'll Ever Know," "Days of '49," "Early Morning Rain," "In Search of Little Sadie," "Let It Be Me," "Little Sadie," "Woogie Boogie," "Belle Isle," "Living the Blues," "Like a Rolling Stone," "Copper Kettle," "Gotta Travel On," "Blue Moon," "The Boxer," "The Mighty Quinn (Quinn the Eskimo)," "Take Me as I Am (Or Let Me Go)," "Take a Message to Mary," "It Hurts Me Too," "Minstrel Boy," "Wigwam," "Alberta #2"

Self Portrait surprised Dylan's following on its release, as it was mostly devoted to covers of traditional material, classic blues, country chestnuts, modern folk-pop, and a few ragged tracks drawn from his August 1969 Isle of Wight concert. After his classic albums of the 1960s, this padded two-record set was tough to swallow in one sitting.

Although most critics often point to *Self Portrait* as proof positive that Dylan was suffering from writer's block as the 1960s turned into the 1970s, there are others who have reevaluated it as both the ultimate put-on and the ultimate self-realization.

The collection is at times so meandering that it is difficult to determine what Dylan had in mind when he began recording *Self Portrait* about a month after the light but generally focused *Nashville Skyline* was released. Did he think that he'd stumbled on a formula for commercial success that he was anxious to repeat? Was he looking to join the realm of schmaltzy mainstreamers like Perry Como or Johnny Mathis? Was this the first step in an on-again, off-again campaign to demythologize himself?

Dylan has done a pretty good job of distancing himself from the project over the years. As early as 1974, he was telling Ben Fong-Torres of *Rolling Stone*: "I didn't live with those songs too long. They were just kind of scraped together."

Dylan's own gaudy cover art, a raw, Picassoesque self-portrait, may be the most memorable element of the album.

Amazingly, on Dylan's reputation alone, *Self Portrait* hit No. 4 during a three-month stint on the charts and earned gold record status.

With the passage of time, the album seems almost willfully eccentric and stands among the least understood in Dylan's catalogue—an odd moment in a career even then chock-full of left turns. Dylan doesn't even appear on the opening tune, "All the Tired Horses"; his presence is replaced by a female chorus repeating the gospel-folk refrain over strings and organ. Some of the album picks up where *Nashville Skyline* left off, with Dylan crooning in country melodrama: "Alberta," "I Forgot More Than You'll Ever Know," and "Little Sadie." And the cover material he chose to tackle was not exactly standard fare: Gordon Lightfoot's "Early Morning Rain," Simon and Garfunkel's "The Boxer," and the Everly Brothers' "Take a Message to Mary." Dylan's homespun approach to the traditional material is symbolic of his approach to the entire album, as he keeps himself at arm's length from the anthemic hook that the Woodstock generation would have loved to hang their preconceptions on.

Perhaps Greil Marcus summed up *Self Portrait* best when he wrote in *Rolling Stone*, "What is this shit?"

▧ "Señor (Tales of Yankee Power)" (Bob Dylan)

Bob Dylan, single (1978); *Street Legal* (1978); *Biograph*/'78 (1985)

Bob Dylan/Various Artists (performed by Jerry Garcia), *Masked and Anonymous* (soundtrack) (2003)

Jerry Garcia Band, *Jerry Garcia Band* (1991)

Tim O'Brien, *Red on Blonde* (1996)

Two Approaching Riders, *One More Cup of Coffee* (1997)

Pix Lax, *Stilve* (1998)

Rolling Thunder, *The Never Ending Rehearsal* (2000)

Various Artists (performed by Backyard Swings), *A Tribute to Bob Dylan, Volume 3: The Times They Are A-Changin'* (2000)

Rich Lerner, *Napoleon in Rags* (2001)
Marc Carroll, *Mrs. Lullaby* (2003)

A song of murky portent, "Señor" finds the narrator setting off as Sancho Panza on a dark and desolate Quixote-like journey into a nefarious borderland world that appears to involve anarchy at the very least—not unlike the mysterious (and equally dangerous) quest described in "Isis." Further coloring a landscape of disillusion with stark, Goyaesque flourishes, the singer asks his comrade early on whether they are traveling someplace benign (Lincoln County Road) or malignant (Armageddon) as they consider moving on. One can only imagine why he follows.

Some place "Señor" as an anticolonialist meditation—a dark vision of where America may have been heading when he wrote the song, and is surely closer to now. Others may spot religious symbolism and literary reference (Graham Greene's novel *The Power and the Glory*, about a dance with the Devil, has been suggested as a source or model) informing the cloudy action.

Like songs as diverse as "Blowin' in the Wind" and "What Was It You Wanted?," "Señor" asks many questions, none of which are answered. "Do you know where we're headin'?" "How long are we gonna be ridin'?" "Do you know where she's hidin?" The song revolves with such questions directed at the titular (but never actually seen) character. Even if there were an answer forthcoming, this tale takes place in a burgh where no words should be taken at face value and trust is just a word.

Another question: when and where does this song take place? The curtain appears to rise in a bottom-of-the-barrel cantina of some sort (note the references to "door," "floor," and "tables"), as our narrator queries his guide in a setting with the distinct feeling of the turn-of-

the-century Old West. After all, wasn't Lincoln County (mentioned in the first stanza) the locale where Pat Garrett and Billy the Kid had it out back in 1881? If so, either road (one headed to Lincoln County, the other to Armageddon) would appear to lead to doom.

As the storyteller recounts his journey by ship ("There's a wicked wind still blowin' on that upper deck"), train (loaded with fools), and horseback (the "hard as leather" line suggests some rough riding in a saddle), it is evident that he is in search of a woman wearing an iron cross with whom he may have had only the most fleeting and not particularly promising encounter in a vacant lot ("where she held me in her arms one time and said, 'Forget me not'") in what sounds like the distant past. Yet he has, for reasons that are never explained, embarked on an apparently illusory, globe-trotting hunt for this person, a person he suspects will not provide the salvation he so desperately desires. Perhaps a key to understanding the song lies in allegory, that the woman is actually America and the narrator is on a quest to rein her in before she is destroyed by her own excess.

As he continues to brood, his thoughts darken as he comes to terms with the futile truth of his situation. The "tail of the dragon" he smells hints of incendiary ruin, the stripping and kneeling he suffered suggests a forced humiliation, the "trainload of fools bogged down in a magnetic field" references the Ship of Fools—the floating asylum of medieval times—symbolic of the entire society's being in free fall. The gypsy with the broken flag not only underlines the sense of anarchy pervading the background scenery of the song, but has a speaking part, bringing the narrator down to earth with some crushing news, that what he sees is what he's got: "'Son, this ain't a dream no more, it's the real thing.'"

S

With this, the mood and attitude of the narrator appears to shift from deer-in-the-headlights passivity to irate rebellion when he sings, "Well, give me a minute, let me get it together" and begins to pick himself up off the floor for another go at things: "I'm ready when you are, señor."

The song ends with more than an inkling of violence to come, with the singer and his compadre ready to "disconnect these cables" (a reference to the then scandalously topical ITT involvement with the CIA-backed 1973 coup in Chile that toppled the democratically elected Socialist government of President Salvador Allende—or merely to a strategic first strike to eliminate the enemy's power source) and "Overturn these tables" of polite decorum (a final gesture challenging "Yankee Power" or a nod to Jesus's confrontation with the money-changers, take your pick) and take matters into their own hands. Like the final gunfight at the end of *Butch Cassidy and the Sundance Kid*, when the two antiheroes scamper into a hail of hot lead, one senses that self-preservation is less important to the singer and his señor than making a climactic statement, even if at the price of their lives.

And what of the cipherlike señor? Is he really there as an unseen, unspeaking corporeal presence in the song, or some phantom figment of the singer's imagination? That Dylan's religious conversion was quickly approaching when he wrote "Señor" makes things even more interesting. He may be the Devil or the Lord.

Forgotten in the discussion of this dream-figure archetype was Dylan's own testimony regarding the song's inspiration, as heard in the unusual introductory raps with which he prefaced performances of his songs in concert during a brief spell in the very late 1970s. At a November 1978 show, for example, he extemporaneously riffed on the roots of "Señor" (as heard on a concert tape):

I was riding on a train one time through Mexico, traveling up north to San Diego, and I must have fell asleep on this train and I woke up and it was about midnight... and the train had stopped at a place called Monterrey... This bunch of children were getting off the train, this family—there must have been about seventeen children and a mother and father and they were getting off the train. And at that time, I was watching it all through the glass; it was dark outside so the whole side of the train was like a mirror. So I was watching it all happen and I saw this old man stumble up onto the train and he gets onto the car, and he was walking down and he took a seat right across the car from me. I felt a vibration in the air... I turned to look at him and I could see he wasn't dressed in anything but a blanket; he was just wearing a blanket. He must have been a hundred fifty years old. I turned around to look at him and I could see both his eyes were burning out— they were on fire and there was smoke coming out of his nostrils. I said, "Well, this is the man I want to talk to."

"Señor" is the only item from *Street Legal* to stand the test of time in concert, and Dylan has generously kept it as a dramatic performance choice since its 1978 unveiling, including a revamped acoustic arrangement debuted on the spring 2002 Never Ending Tour.

▣ *Sentimental Hygiene*/Warren Zevon
Virgin America Records LP SC-40870. Released 1987.

In 1987 Warren Zevon returned with his first new album in half a decade. Not only did its feature of R.E.M. as musical support help Zevon's music take on a tough yet melodic edge, but Dylan's harmonica part on "The Factory" may have helped it travel a little farther too. *Sentimental Hygiene* was easily Zevon's best release since *Excitable Boy* nearly ten years before, which contained probably his most famous song: "Werewolves of London."

"September on Jessore Road" (Allen Ginsberg)
Allen Ginsberg, *Holy Soul Jelly Roll*/'71 (1995)

Probably the greatest (and easily the most exotic) piece to emerge from Dylan's work with Allen Ginsberg, "September on Jessore Road" is a poignantly sympathetic vision of humanity as the narrator travels on a byway in India.

Before its release on *Holy Soul Jelly Roll*, the definitive Allen Ginsberg boxed set, "September on Jessore Road" was one of those talismanic Ginsberg/Dylan collaborations that you were more likely to hear on some oddball radio station at 3:00 A.M. than find in the "Spoken Word" section of your local used-record store. Its original release, if you can call it that, was as a flexidisc in *Sing Out!* magazine in 1971.

According to Ginsberg in his *Holy Soul Jelly Roll* liner notes:

> In between Record Plant sessions I wanted to write something worthy of Dylan's attention, a poem long and beautiful like "Sad-Eyed Lady of the Lowlands," but W. C. Williams–like natural reportage, and spiritual—something to astonish Dylan to tears. I wrote an account of exactly what I'd seen on a recent trip to India, words and music simultaneous on my Indian harmonium. I'd based the music on the chords of Varja Guru Mantra, and the rhyme form echoed Blake's "On Another's Sorrow." Dylan took the pages home, and when he came back next day said he'd wept. But he couldn't get his guitar in accord with my harmonium, which was a half-step off Western tuning. Also I misdirected him calling this song a blues—a form

he'd tried teaching me weeks before. He restrung or retuned his guitar but it never quite got in pitch. He took two or three rounds till his hand ached while I did vocals simultaneously. Then he went over and put in another guitar and organ part and then started dropping piano bombs, percussive punctuations underlining different phrases. That was the high point of the recording—Dylan coming down with all ten genius fingers intermittently at the right places. . . .

> . . . I'd been disappointed that my magnum opus, which I thought as good as anything I'd written since "Kaddish," though in a more classic rhymed form, hadn't resulted in fame, fortune, beauty, sublimity, and public proclamation. But I was over ambitious, actually, and vain. Dylan had said, "Well, save the songs to sing to your friends."

"Series of Dreams" (Bob Dylan)
Bob Dylan, *The Bootleg Series, Volumes 1–3: Rare and Unreleased, 1961–1991*/'89 (1991); *Bob Dylan's Greatest Hits Volume 3* (1994)
Various Artists (performed by the Zimmermen), *May Your Song Always Be Sung* (1996)
The Zimmermen, *After the Ambulances Go* (1998)
Michel Montecrossa, *Born in Time* (1998)

An outtake from Dylan's 1989 *Oh, Mercy* album, "Series of Dreams" can be viewed as a metaphor for Dylan's entire career, catalogue, and guises. In his liner notes to *The Bootleg Series, Volumes 1–3: Rare and Unreleased, 1961–1991*, John Bauldie summed up the song with a series of dreamy observations: "From the opening, insistent thrumming of the bass and drums . . . the song is on fire, and there's no letup as it continues to build in intensity and drama as the dreams are recounted. The images are vaguely perceived or half-remembered, incoherent, disconnected, somehow fleet-

S

ingly significant, undoubtedly but enigmatically symbolic, occasionally disturbing, often moving, yet ultimately steadfastly refusing to allow their wonderful mystery to be translated into any kind of literal sense."

The video of the song is one of the better ones associated with Dylan, consisting of very short clips of black-and-white film, edited together into dreamlike sequences with some lyrics from this and other Dylan songs superimposed. Clips from *Don't Look Back*, the "Most of the Time" video, and *Renaldo & Clara* make visual cameos, and images of Dylan's parents, Allen Ginsberg, Dylan Thomas, Jack Kerouac, Arthur Rimbaud, Lenny Bruce, and others are all brilliantly interwoven with the text of the song and contribute to make a provocative, respectful, funny, perceptive, intelligent, and occasionally breathtaking work.

Dylan's only and very unexpected performances of "Series of Dreams" came about during the 1993 and 1994 legs of the Never Ending Tour.

[S] **"Seven Curses"** (Bob Dylan)

Bob Dylan, *The Bootleg Series, Volumes 1–3: Rare and Unreleased, 1961–1991/'63* (1991)
Sebastian Cabot, *Sebastian Cabot, Actor—Bob Dylan, Poet* (1967)
Albion Band, *Saturday Rolling Around* (1989)
Larry Barrett, *Porch Song Ginger* (1995)
The Zimmermen, *After the Ambulances Go* (1998)
Andy Hill, *It Takes a Lot to Laugh* (2000)
Various Artists (performed by Chris Wilson and Andrew Pendlebury), *The Woodstock Sessions: Songs of Bob Dylan* (2000)
Various Artists (performed by Andy Hill), *May Your Song Always Be Sung: The Songs of Bob Dylan, Volume 3* (2003)

Dylan's deft reworking of a venerable tale about a young woman trying to save her father's life was not only used by Shakespeare in *Measure for Measure*, it's been handed down through the centuries with such titles as "The Prickly Bush," "The Briery Bush," and "The Prickle Holly Bush." But though Child Ballad No. 95, "The Maid Freed from the Gallows," may be the earliest version, "Anathea," a song often performed by Judy Collins, is pointed to as the most likely direct source for the story.

The story is usually a dire one. A fellow named Reilly steals a stallion, and is caught and thrown in jail with a chain around his neck. When his daughter gets the news, she rides all night to the town to plead for mercy for her father. But when the patronizing, lecherous judge lays his corrupt old eyes on Reilly's daughter, he names his price for her father's life: her virtue. Despite Reilly's plea that he's as good as dead and that she'd do best to get right back on her horse and ride away, she agrees to the judge's deal. Slowly, the inevitable and ultimate betrayal begins to reveal itself, portrayed ever more chillingly by Dylan's deadpan vocal delivery. When she awakes to see the "hangin' branch a-bendin'" with her father's broken body, she damns the judge with seven curses that will doom him for eternity. With no anger, he sings plainly about the way things are when it comes to justice's dealing with common folk, employing a technique he would refine shortly after with "The Lonesome Death of Hattie Carroll."

"Seven Curses" was first recorded for Witmark in May 1963 and again in the studio for Columbia's *The Times They Are A-Changin'* session (the version eventually released on *The Bootleg Series, Volumes 1–3*). But there is only one known rendition of Dylan performing the song from that or any other era—an October 26, 1963, concert at New York's plush Carnegie Hall.

☒ "Seven Days" (Bob Dylan)

Bob Dylan, *The Bootleg Series, Volumes 1–3: Rare and Unreleased, 1961–1991/'76* (1991)
Bob Dylan/Various Artists (performed by Ron Wood), *Bob Dylan: The 30th Anniversary Concert Celebration* (1993)
Ron Wood, *Gimme Some Neck* (1979)
Various Artists (performed by Ron Wood), *I Shall Be Unreleased/'79* (1991)
Rob Stoner, *Patriotic Duty* (1980)
Joe Cocker, *Sheffield Steel* (1982)
Jimmy Barnes, *Freight Train Blues* (1988); *Barnestorming* (1995)
Loup Garou, *Dobbs Ferry* (2003)

A dynamic rockin' propulsion with more than a small hint of pining romance, mystery, and intrigue, "Seven Days" was first performed by Dylan and the Rolling Thunder Revue a few times in late April 1976 and is notable for some tricky singing by its composer. The song is well known through Ron Wood's faithful cover version. The lyrics, imbued with a taste of symbolism from Genesis, share enough facts of a story to hold us but never quite reveal much about the narrator's "beautiful comrade from the north." And as he promises that he's been good while waiting for his true love to return, one has to surmise that Dylan was not speaking from personal experience in matters of long-distance love affairs.

Dylan wrote the song in March 1976 while Eric Clapton was recording *No Reason to Cry* at Shangri-La Studios in Malibu, California. Clapton recalled that Dylan "was just hanging out. He was actually living in a tent in the bottom of the garden. He would keep sneaking into the studio to find out what was going on, trying to catch me in there."

Also around and recording was Ron Wood, who told John Bauldie, as quoted in *The Telegraph* #33 (summer 1989), "That's where I got 'Seven Days' from. He played it to me and Eric

in the studio, and he said to Eric, 'You can have this song if you want it.' And I took him up on it and Eric didn't."

After performing "Seven Days" with great drama during the second leg of the Rolling Thunder Revue in 1976, Dylan returned to the piece exactly twenty years later during a brief phase of the Never Ending Tour.

☒ "Seven Deadly Sins" (Traveling Wilburys)
Traveling Wilburys, *Traveling Wilburys, Volume 3* (1990)

Dylan handles the lead vocals of this languid C&W-style children's doo-wop for adults. The song would have fit comfortably on his *Under the Red Sky* album or on the B-side of a '50s single, or could have been crooned by a quartet of Bronx harmonizers on a street corner off the Grand Concourse.

☒ "Shake a Hand" (Joe Morris)
Faye Adams, *Shake a Hand/'53* (1961)
Little Richard, *Fabulous Little Richard* (1959)
Elvis Presley, *Elvis Aron Presley* (1961)
Jackie Wilson, *Reet Petite* (1985)
Ike and Tina Turner, *The Seductive Provocative Tina Turner & Ike* (1997)

Another oldie but goodie liberally played during Dylan's 1986 tour with Tom Petty and the Heartbreakers, "Shake a Hand" was written by Joe Morris and originally recorded by Faye Adams, who had a million-seller with the song way back in 1953. Dylan, Petty, and friends were probably aware of "Shake a Hand" through Elvis's popular recording. Morris (born 1922, Montgomery, Alabama; died November 21, 1958, Phoenix) was a jazz trumpeter probably best known for his work with Lionel Hampton and Buddy Rich in the 1940s. Later, he led his own band that included tenor saxophonist Johnny Griffin, alto saxophonist Jimmy Heath, pianist Elmo Hope,

S

and drummer Philly Joe Jones. Morris also backed up singer Dinah Washington on a series of memorable recordings.

[S] "Shake Sugaree" (Elizabeth Cotten)

aka "I've Got a Secret"
See also "Oh Babe, It Ain't No Lie"
Elizabeth Cotten, *Live!* (1984)
Fred Neil, *Everybody's Talkin'* (1966)
Pat Boone, *Departure* (1969)
Taj Mahal, *Shake Sugaree* (1990)
Stefan Grossman, *Northern Skies, Southern Blues* (1997)

Dylan opened some 1996 Never Ending Tour shows with Libba Cotten's lively, poignant, and whimsical piece of folk poetry as a semi-acoustic offering with beautiful lines artfully describing a person who has rid himself of all earthly goods and is as ready as he'll ever be "to go to heaven in a split pea shell."

According to Mike Seeger in the April/May 1966 issue (volume 16, #2) of *Sing Out!*:

> One evening a couple of years ago as Elizabeth Cotten was putting her great-grandchildren to bed, the oldest, Johnny, made the first verse of this song. Elizabeth gave it a tune, a verse or two and (according to the next eldest, Brenda) the chorus. The remainder of the song evolved gradually during the following weeks. "Now, that 'Shake Sugaree,' that's more my (four great) grandchildren's song. They made the verses and I played the music. The first verse my oldest (great) grandson, he made that himself, and from that each child would say a word and add to it. To tell the truth, I don't know what got it started . . . but it must've been something said or something done. That's practically how I pick up all my songs. There's somebody'll say something or do something and this . . . something will come into your mind . . ."

When asked what she meant by the "split pea shell" mentioned in the lyrics, Cotten once explained that when peanut pods ripen, they "fall" and twirl themselves into the ground, actually planting themselves for the next year. To harvest peanuts, one must wait until they "fall" and dig them out (which is why they are also called ground peas). Cotten was saying that like the peanut that buries itself in the soil, she hoped to reach Heaven through interment six feet under the ground.

Robert Hunter and Jerry Garcia's "Sugaree" is regarded as a direct tip of the hat to Cotten, and the Grateful Dead later recorded her "Oh Babe, It Ain't No Lie" with the specific intention of making sure she received royalty checks.

[S] "She Belongs to Me" (Bob Dylan)

Bob Dylan, single (1965); *Bringing It All Back Home* (1965); *Don't Look Back* (film) (1967); *Bob Dylan's Greatest Hits Volume II* (1971); *The Bootleg Series, Volume 4: Bob Dylan Live 1966 (The "Royal Albert Hall" Concert)* (1998)
Barry McGuire, *Eve of Destruction* (1965); *Anthology* (1994)
Sir Henry and His Butlers, *Sir Henry and His Butlers* (1965)
Duane Eddy, *Duane Eddy Does Bob Dylan* (1965)
West Coast Pop Art Experimental Band, *The Legendary Unreleased Album* (1966); *Volume One* (1997)
The Phantoms, *The Phantoms* (1966)
Tina Turner, *Tina Turns the Country On* (1967)
Rose Garden, *Rose Garden* (1968)
Jimmy Gilmer, *Firewater* (1968); *Sugar Shack: The Best of Jimmy Gilmer* (1996)
The Nice, *The Nice* (1969)
Rick Nelson, single (1969); *Rick Nelson in Concert* (1970); *Decca Years* (1982); *Best of 1964–1975* (1990); *Best of the Later Years (1963–1975)* (1997)
Billy Preston, *That's the Way God Planned It* (1969)
Lester Flatt, *Flatt Out* (1970); *Flatt on Victor and More* (1999)
Leon Russell, *Leon Russell and the Shelter People* (1970);

S

Gimme Shelter: The Best of Leon Russell (1996)

Hugo Montenegro, *Dawn of Dylan* (1970)

Ray Stevens, *Everything Is Beautiful* (1970); *Country Hits Collection* (1998); *Misty: The Very Best of Ray Stevens*
(1999)

Bell & Arc, *Bell & Arc* (1971)

The Mystic Moods Orchestra, *Country Lovin' Folk* (1971)

Dr. Marigold, *Hello Girl* (1973)

Wolfgang Ambros, *Live LP* (1979)

Flying Burrito Brothers, *Cabin Fever* (1985)

Tom Tom Club, *Boom Boom Chi Boom Boom* (1988)

Birdland, *Birdland* (1991)

Harry Connick Jr., *Blue Light, Red Light* (1991)

Little Women, *Pretty Wiped Out* (1992)

The Grateful Dead, *Backstage Pass* (video) (1992); *Postcards
of the Hanging: Grateful Dead Perform the Songs of Bob
Dylan* (2002)

Pete Anderson, *Working Class* (1994)

Naked Babies, *Tarnished* (1996)

Trish Murphy, *Crooked Mile* (1998); *Captured* (2001)

Various Artists (performed by Kante), *Spielkreis 03* (1998)

Blue Dogs, *For the Record* (1999)

Various Artists (performed by David West), *Pickin' on Dylan*
(1999)

Jimmy Page, *Hip Young Guitar Slinger & His Heavy
Friends/'65* (2000)

The Robins, *The Robins Sing Dylan* (2000)

Wallflower Complextion, *Wallflower Complextion* (2000)

Various Artists (performed by #1 Family Mover), *A Tribute to
Bob Dylan, Volume 3: The Times They Are A-Changin'*
(2000)

Various Artists (performed by Ross Wilson), *The Woodstock
Sessions: Songs of Bob Dylan* (2000)

Dylanesque, *Basement Fakes* (2001)

Family Tree, *Family Tree* (2001)

Gerry Murphy, *Gerry Murphy Sings Bob Dylan* (2001)

Second Floor, *Plays Dylan* (2001)

Hank Shizzoe & Loose Gravel, *In Concert* (2003)

Big Brass Bed, *A Few Dylan Songs* (2003)

"She Belongs to Me," Dylan's ironically titled, oft-quoted antilove ballad to a diabolically mys-terious woman, finds a manipulated singer spending the entire song trying to convince the listener that the object of his worship doesn't belong to him, even when it would seem just the opposite. Adding to the paradox is Dylan's precious reading of the song both on its official release and in his many concert performances of it: the balmy melody contrasted with the bit-ter poetry and pathetic, ensnared situation.

"She Belongs to Me" is one of the earliest and best examples of Dylan maturing the love song, a genre that in popular music had, up to then, dealt mainly with the most superficial aspects of romance. With symmetry and preci-sion, Dylan creates a camouflaged blues-waltz of pedestaled devotion that may at least be partly about Joan Baez and at least one other woman who wears an Egyptian ring and "can take the dark out of the nighttime and paint the daytime black." His first verse ("She's got every-thing she needs/She's an artist, she don't look back") was echoed in the title of his film *Don't Look Back* (1967), itself the title of a John Lee Hooker blues. That motto, however, was first popularized by baseball pitcher Satchel Paige, a heroic/comic/tragic figure of the fabled Negro Leagues, who once famously said, "Don't look back, something may be gaining on you." By the song's second verse, Dylan describes how this vamp can cut any man down to size ("You will start off standing/Proud to steal her any-thing she sees/But you'll wind up peeking though her keyhole/Down upon your knees") with the clarity of a man trapped in her boudoir. By the end we get to the heart of the song's irony and its title. In telling us that "She never stumbles, she's got no place to fall/She's nobody's child, the law can't touch her at all," he seems to imply that this free spirit belongs to no one, including him.

Dylan began performing "She Belongs to Me" right after cutting it for *Bringing It All*

Back Home, and it has endured (albeit with the occasional hiatus) as an acoustic concert presentation since then—as if to remind himself of just how bad things can get. The version released on *Self Portrait* is a live recording from the 1969 Isle of Wight concert. Some of the song's roots may lie in "I'm a Stranger Here," a traditional folk blues that includes lines in its third verse that bear a striking resemblance to Dylan's lines "She never stumbles/She's got no place to fall."

Rick Nelson had a Top 40 hit with his single in 1969, and Elvis reportedly sang "She Belongs to Me" in his 1970 concerts.

◨ "Shelter from the Storm" (Bob Dylan)

Bob Dylan, *Blood on the Tracks* (1974); *Hard Rain* (1976); *Bob Dylan at Budokan* (1979); *Live 1961–2000—Thirty-nine Years of Great Concert Performances/'76* (2001)

Various Artists (performed by Bob Dylan), *Jerry Maguire* (soundtrack)/'74 (1996)

Mission, single (1987)

Steven Keene, *Keene on Dylan* (1990)

Jimmy LaFave, *Austin Skyline* (1996)

The Zimmermen, *The Dungeon Tapes* (1996)

Manfred Mann, *Mann Alive* (1997)

Two Approaching Riders, *One More Cup of Coffee* (1997)

Mary Lee's Corvette, *Blood on the Tracks* (2002)

Cassandra Wilson, *Belly of the Sun* (2002)

Gerry Murphy, *Gerry Murphy Sings Bob Dylan* (2002)

Big Brass Bed, *A Few Dylan Songs* (2003)

Describing a tempest-tossed state of being with elemental symbolism and only three chords, "Shelter from the Storm" finds a man taking stock of himself, the dangerous world around him, and his lost love. The poet once found shelter but now "it's doom alone that counts." With its Yeatsian "horsemen pass by" overtones of finality, "Shelter from the Storm" seems to transpire in a flat, primeval setting—

as if the listener were transported into the Botticelli painting *The Birth of Venus* (circa 1485).

That fantastic landscape is front and center as the curtain rises, the singer even using archaic, almost biblical language to set the tone: "'Twas in another lifetime, one of toil and blood/Blackness was a virtue, the road was full of mud/I came in from the wilderness, a creature void of form/'Come in,' she said, 'I'll give you shelter from the storm.'" The Christian symbolism continues throughout the song and in the next verse is utilized as a way of deflating his own ego when the highly idealized woman ("try imagining a place where it's always safe and warm") is shown removing his crown of thorns. She also provides a "salvation" that the "ravaged" narrator, much to his regret, took for granted. That flip attitude toward unconditional love and support appears to be his unraveling: his signals get crossed and he takes a long fall that results in his very soul being bargained for. But the song does end on an optimistic note as Dylan sings, "Beauty walks a razor's edge/Someday I'll make it mine," as if the possibility of redemption still exists. The way he sings it, you can bet it does.

Contrary to the song's spare, vivid reading on its album debut (in which his vocal, guitar, and harmonica parts are accompanied only by Tony Brown's bass), Dylan created some bombastic arrangements of "Shelter from the Storm" with hit-and-miss results. Its live debut during the second leg of the '76 Rolling Thunder Revue (in which Dylan colored the tune with some choice licks on slide guitar) had a blustery, metallic edge complete with screeching electric guitar crescendos—one of Dylan's great officially released recordings as heard on *Hard Rain*. A couple of years later—during his 1978 big-band tour—Dylan approached it as a torch song with a staccato vocal that was not helped by a strident backing chorus overlaying a stylized arrangement complete with an emotionless lead vocal and sax solo. He shelved "Shelter" until 1984, when it returned with a rockier, if forgetful, flair. Since then it has surfaced on virtually every tour, usually as an effective, slinky rock 'n' reggae, which allowed for some of Dylan's all-time great performances in the mid-1990s (though he did tinker with an acoustic bluegrass variation in 1994).

The version of "Shelter from the Storm" released on the *Jerry Maguire* soundtrack album was a previously unknown and unreleased one that had been recorded during the *Blood on the Tracks* sessions.

Finally, in 2001, the *Blood on the Tracks* version of "Shelter from the Storm" was used with Dylan's blessing on a World Wildlife Fund public service radio announcement. It was, amazingly enough, believed to be the first time that he had allowed one of his songs to be used in such a manner. "It's nice to know something I did a long time ago can help save animals today," he said. "WWF is a good cause, I support them, and am proud to lend my music to this effort. Early on, animals were the only ones who liked my music. Now it's payback time."

"Shenandoah" (Traditional)
aka "The Wild Miz-Zou-Ree"
Bob Dylan, *Down in the Groove* (1988)
Alan Mills and Gilbert Lacombe, *Songs of the Sea* (1957)
James Galway, *Wayward Wind* (1982)
Harry Belafonte, *Harry Belafonte Collection* (1984)
Paul Robeson, *Essential Paul Robeson* (1987)
Paul Clayton, *Sailing & Whaling Songs of 19th Century* (1994)
Pete Seeger, *Kisses Sweeter Than Wine* (1996)

Dylan's inclusion of a Bo Diddley–style arrangement of this true American chestnut was one of the highlights of his otherwise slip-shod album *Down in the Groove*. He went on to open three 1990 Never Ending Tour shows with an instrumental variation of "Shenandoah."

Don't try looking for this "Shenandoah" in an atlas, as the song references the name of an Indian chief residing near the Missouri River, not the Shenandoah Valley in the Appalachian Mountains.

Originating with French Canadian voyageurs and/or Missouri River boatmen, "Shenandoah" was quickly claimed by high-seas sailors and became a well-known and frequently used capstan chantey. The earliest versions of the song tell the story of how a white trader courted Shenandoah's daughter and bore her away in his canoe. Naturally, the sailors added their own words and a verse about "Sally," leaving us with a version that makes little sense.

Pete Seeger's annotation in *American Favorite Ballads* (1961) briefly questioned the popularity of "Shenandoah" when he wrote, "Why should this favorite sea chantey concern an Indian chief, and a Midwestern river? And why does everyone love it so and refuse to change it?"

In a letter to folklorists John A. and Alan Lomax (published in the latter's 1960 book *The Folk Songs of North America*), Major Isaac Spalding from the Office of the Chief of Staff in Washington, D.C., offered this lineage of "Shenandoah":

> The history of this well-known and widely sung song, like that of so many others, is an illusive and tantalizing will-o'-the-wisp. One follows a promising clue only to find the end of one trail is but the beginning of another. The song has been sung in different forms as a soldier song and as a sea chantey. Captain W. B. Whall, in his *Ships, Songs, and Shanties*, concludes that it was originally a

S

song, not a sea chantey, and ascribes its probable origin to American and Canadian voyageurs. He gives a version of the song in which a white trader courts the daughter of Chief Shenandoah and carries her away across the "wide Missouri." Joanna C. Colcord, in *Roll and Go*, has a version called "Shenandoah," which was used on ships after the Civil War . . . The cavalry jealously claims this song for its very own, having acquired it, no doubt, during the frontier days.

[S] **"She's About a Mover"** (Doug Sahm)

See also *Doug Sahm and Band*
Doug Sahm, *Live* (1988)
Sir Douglas Quintet, *The Best of Doug Sahm: She's About a Mover (The Crazy Cajun Recordings)* (1999)
Ringo Starr, *Old Wave* (1983); *Starr Struck* (1989)
Steve Earle, *Shut Up and Die Like an Aviator* (1991); *Ain't Never Satisfied* (1996)

Dylan's only performance of this Sir Douglas Quintet Tex-Mex, sexually charged, classic male fantasy came about in 1988 with the song's author, Doug Sahm, sharing the stage for an encore presentation at a Never Ending Tour show in Edmonton, Alberta. Dylan performed the song again in June 2000—presumably in tribute to Sahm's passing in 1999—in a sharp, authoritative study punctuated by sideman Charlie Sexton's funky electric guitar lead.

[S] **"She's Love Crazy"** (Tampa Red)

See also "Love Her with a Feeling"
Various Artists (performed by Tampa Red), *Boogie Woogie, Volume 2: The Small Groups* (1996)

Dylan ignited four dozen of his 1978 big-band-tour shows with this favorite from the pen of Tampa Red. Regardless of the fact that "She's Love Crazy" is hard to come by in anyone's discography, Dylan was on a Tampa Red kick in '78 and began performing the song in lieu of another memorable Red romance rant, "Love Her with a Feeling."

[S] **"She's My Baby"** (Traveling Wilburys)

Traveling Wilburys, *Traveling Wilburys, Volume 3* (1990)

All four surviving Wilburys take a vocal turn on this funny throwaway song, which has more than one ironic twist or two. It rivals "Groom's Still Waiting at the Altar" as the hardest rock song ever sung by Dylan, who gets all the best one-liners. A promotional MTV-style video was made of "She's My Baby" in 1990.

[S] **"She's Your Lover Now"** (Bob Dylan)

aka "Just a Little Glass of Water"
Bob Dylan, *The Bootleg Series, Volumes 1–3: Rare and Unreleased, 1961–1991/'66* (1991)
The Original Marauders, *Now Your Mouth Cries Wolf* (1977)
Rich Lerner and the Groove, *Cover Down* (2000)

A complex and brilliant composition dramatizing a scenario for three players but only one narrator, "She's Your Lover Now" has that late-night Manhattan miasma that marks so much of the album from which it was excised, *Blonde on Blonde*. The whole scene here could be played out on a SoHo street corner at four in the morning as the traffic hurtles by.

In his liner notes to *The Bootleg Series, Volumes 1–3*, John Bauldie begins and ends his analysis of the song with its narrator, "who's attempting to unravel a tangled web of complicated emotions: anger, resentment, recrimination, dismay, disgust, love, loss, and responsibility in the presence of his ex-lover and her new boyfriend. The feelings he has within himself are just as confused, and they make themselves variously felt, ever more grotesquely, either towards her or towards him or towards himself, as the song progresses. It's just about

S

impossible to do justice to its achievement, without writing an entire dissertation on the many simultaneous levels on which this song works."

Two very different versions of "She's Your Lover Now" were recorded in Nashville during the January/February 1966 *Blonde on Blonde* sessions: the driving, near-perfect ensemble version as released on *The Bootleg Series, Volumes 1–3,* and a slow piano and vocal take that remains underheard. "She's Your Lover Now" was left off *Blonde on Blonde* perhaps because of its similarity in construction and sentiment to "(One of Us Must Know) Sooner or Later," or maybe because Dylan slipped on the lyrics near the song's ending. The last verse was not included in either of Dylan's books of lyrics (1973's *Writings and Drawings*, or 1985's updated, second edition of *Lyrics, 1962–1985*). Bauldie, however, made sure that they were included in the booklet accompanying *The Bootleg Series* album released in 1991.

Excessively vitriolic—even by Dylan's standards at the time—"She's Your Lover Now" remains one of his best mixes of surrealistic imagery, anger, jealousy, and humor, all cushioned by the pleasant roll of fairly standard but still weird-sounding blues progressions marked by the clash of his piano and Garth Hudson's organ. The narrator comes off like a bit of a jerk, but his pointed use of language can't be denied. And while we all wish we could come up with some of the put-downs he uses here in the heat of battle ("Now you stand here expectin' me to remember somethin' you forgot to say"), very few of us could have come up with this final hallucinatory salvo: "She'll be standin' on the bar soon/With a fish head an' a harpoon/An' a fake beard plastered on her brow/You'd better do somethin' quick/She's your lover now."

[S] "Shooting Star" (Bob Dylan)

Bob Dylan, *Oh Mercy* (1989); *MTV Unplugged* (1995)
Various Artists (performed by Bob Dylan), *Wonder Boys* (soundtrack) (2000)
David Gog, *Bare Bones* (1999)
Andy Hill, *It Takes a Lot to Laugh* (2000)

Signing off *Oh Mercy* with this wistful, dreamy number, Dylan gestures at time slipping away, a dark regret that all experience is wasted—chances lost are lost for good, lost time not found again. Reminiscent of "Restless Farewell," "Shooting Star" is a quiet and sober adieu with three simply crafted verses and as mismatched a break in the middle of the song as anything in Dylan's catalogue. Like its subject, the song is decorously fleeting as it flares and vanishes, leaving only an illusory luminescence. And, like the songs on the rest of *Oh Mercy*, hope is at a premium. Perhaps most remarkable is Dylan's ability to take one of the most clichéd and overdone symbols and invest it with new shades.

Like all of the *Oh Mercy* material, "Shooting Star" got its days in the performance sun, especially when Dylan showcased it heavily in 1990, the year after its release. Though its appearance diminished in his sets over the next few years, Dylan is still known to give it an airing now and then.

In the realm of popular culture, "Shooting Star" was played at the conclusion of television's series *Crossing Jordan* in April 2002.

[A] *Shot of Love*

Columbia Records LP TC-37496; CD CK-37496; CS PCT-37496. Recorded April 7–May 11, 1981. Released August 12, 1981. Produced by Bob Dylan, Chuck Plotkin, and Bumps Blackwell.

Bob Dylan—guitar, vocals, piano, harmonica, percussion. Clydie King—vocals. Ron Wood, Fred Tackett, Steve Ripley, Danny Kortchmar—guitar. Steve Douglas—alto saxo-

S

phone. Carl Pickhardt, Benmont Tench—piano, keyboards. William "Smitty" Smith—organ. Donald "Duck" Dunn, Tim Drummond—bass. Jim Keltner, Chuck Plotkin, Ringo Starr—drums. Regina McCrary, Carolyn Dennis, Madelyn Quebec—background vocals.

"Shot of Love," "Heart of Mine," "Property of Jesus," "Lenny Bruce," "Watered Down Love," "The Groom's Still Waiting at the Altar," "Dead Man, Dead Man," "In the Summertime," "Trouble," "Every Grain of Sand"

Dylan's muse returned in force for *Shot of Love*, one of his best records of the 1980s and among the most overlooked collections of his career. Certainly "Every Grain of Sand" and "The Groom's Still Waiting at the Altar" rate as among his great songs from the decade. ("Groom," by the way, was not included on the original release but, because it got a nice response as a single, was eventually added in 1985.)

Some call *Shot of Love* the last in the trilogy of Dylan's religious records, which began with *Slow Train Coming* in 1979, followed by *Saved* a year later. While this is accurate to a certain extent, it would probably be a bit more on the money to suggest that it was a rock album with religious overtones. It was as if Dylan was gamely holding on to the flash of his conversion, but all that was flowing out were great secular songs.

Dylan gave the album high marks, telling Cameron Crowe for the *Biograph* liner notes: "People didn't listen to that album in a realistic way . . . The record had something that, I don't know, could have been made in the '40s or maybe the '50s. There was a cross element of songs on it . . . The critics, I hate to keep talking about them, wouldn't let people make up their minds."

Despite Dylan's love of the collection and its genuine excellence, *Shot of Love* was (by Dylan's standards) a box-office bust, making it to just No. 33 on the charts during its short, three-week stay there—the first Dylan album to fail to crack the Top 30 since *Another Side of Bob Dylan* in 1964.

The album's cover was notable for its imitation Roy Lichtenstein art depicting a comic book–style explosion with the words "Shot of Love" bursting out of the middle. The back cover was a grainy black-and-white photograph of Dylan admiring a rose. No liner notes accompanied the release, only another dogged, unsubtle quote from the New Testament's Matthew 11:25: "I thank thee, O Father, Lord of heaven and earth, because thou hast hid these things from the wise and prudent, and hast revealed them unto babes."

With its raw, garage-band sound, *Shot of Love* captures Dylan at his most immediate, before he let the pop meisters gloss his better songs into a forgettable state later in the decade. These simple compositions capture some primal Dylan work, from the heroic ballad "Lenny Bruce" to the self-revealing love song "Heart of Mine," the gritty and pridefully religious "Property of Jesus," the reggae dirge "Dead Man, Dead Man," the Gershwinesque bit of nostalgia "In the Summertime," and at least one deeply profound and moving masterwork, "Every Grain of Sand."

▤ **"Shot of Love"** (Bob Dylan)

Bob Dylan, *Shot of Love* (1981)
Michel Montecrossa, *Michel's Bob Dylan Fest* (2001)
Various Artists (performed by Develish Doubledylans), *May Your Song Always Be Sung: The Songs of Bob Dylan, Volume 3* (2003)

Rock 'n' roll infused with the gospel-blues underscored by a vague reggae beat, "Shot of Love," in Dylan's fervent performance of the song on the album by the same name, is matched by Clydie King's astounding vocal backing. As the song's narrator says, he doesn't need heroin, turpentine, codeine, or whiskey—just a shot of love. It's the only thing capable of bringing this sinner to his knees in supplication of the Lord: "I seen the kingdoms of the world and it's makin' me feel afraid./What I got ain't painful, it's just bound to kill me dead/Like the men that followed Jesus when they put a price upon His head."

In an interview published in the January 2, 1984, issue of *Us* magazine, Dylan told Martin Keller: "The purpose of music is to elevate and inspire the spirit. To those who care where Bob Dylan is at, they should listen to 'Shot of Love.' It's my most perfect song. It defines where I am at spiritually, musically, romantically, and whatever else. It shows where my sympathies lie. It's all there in that one song."

Conversely, writers Michael Roos and Don O'Meara detected no small measure of bitterness in "Shot of Love" when discussing the song in their article "Is Your Love in Vain—Dialectical Dilemmas in Bob Dylan's Recent Love-Songs," published in a 1987 edition of *Popular Music* magazine (and included in a 1990 anthology titled *The Dylan Companion*, edited by Elizabeth Thomson and David Gutman). "Shot of Love," they suggest, "is as bleak a piece of paranoia as has ever been put on record. Never has he seemed so angry at his public. The implication seems to be that his life is in ruins, and the public is at fault. The tone of cynicism makes much of his writing during the past ten years difficult to take, but he *has* been able to provide us with some powerful studies of his struggle for the public artist to find true love in intimate relationships. And some of these songs must rank artistically among his best work."

Shortly after the song's 1981 release, Dylan debuted "Shot of Love" with a fiery passion aided by both his backup singers and his crack band of the era. He returned to "Shot of Love" in 1986 during his tour with Tom Petty and the Heartbreakers in a rendition aided by the Dylanettes. But even without the help of backing vocalists, Dylan could still make the song burn, as he did when he performed "Shot of Love" during the early phase of the 1989 Never Ending Tour.

"Sign Language" (Eric Clapton/Bob Dylan)
Eric Clapton, *No Reason to Cry* (1976); *Crossroads* (1988)

According to an interview published in *The Telegraph* #29 (spring 1988), Clapton said that he cowrote "Sign Language" with Dylan. Clapton apparently "put the chords" in as Dylan "came up with lyrics." The song sounds pretty much as if it had been made up on the spot: the alienated narrator plays mind games with his amour while he eats a sandwich and listens to Link Wray on the jukebox. Not exactly the stuff of deep contemplation.

Dylan shared the vocals and played guitar on Clapton's *No Reason to Cry* release, which was recorded at Shangri-La Studios in Malibu, California, in the spring of 1976 with the Band's Robbie Robertson and Rick Danko.

"Sign on the Cross" (Bob Dylan)
Coulson, Dean, McGuinness, Flint, *Lo & Behold* (1972)
Michael Moore, *Jewels and Binoculars* (2000)

The longest recording from Big Pink's legendary basement is, as Greil Marcus suggests in his 1997 book *Invisible Republic*, a strange pilgrim's quest that merges a fire-and-brimstone sermon with the jeers of an unbeliever, transforming both into a character who, like Hank Williams's Luke the Drifter persona, "sends his money to a radio preacher so he can hear his prayer read on the air."

While some critics have pointed to "Sign on the Cross" as an early sign of Dylan's conversion to Christianity more than ten years hence, others have suggested that it is a mock spiritual and the key song from the Basement Tapes sessions, with its tongue-in-cheek amalgamations of tradition and oddball fantasy.

Paul Williams interpreted it as a musical breakthrough, as reported in his 1992 book *Bob Dylan: Performing Artist—The Middle Years, 1974–1986*:

> "Sign on the Cross" is built like a symphony, with four separate movements. The first is deliberate and elegant, Dylan singing with sublime slowness while Robbie Robertson plays gorgeous grace notes all around him.
>
> The second movement starts with an inspired bridge (could be the chorus, but we never hear it again), rousing and passionate, transitioning into a restatement of the musical theme from the first movement.
>
> The third movement is spoken/sung monologue—Dylan's vocal performance on this is nothing short of genius, and the improvised music is dazzling in its complexity and accuracy.
>
> Another great segue takes us to the concluding movement, which starts with echoes of the bridge but immediately moves onto new structural ground, the music just as fresh and surprising now as when the song started, while successfully incorporating everything that's happened so far.

This is one of those songs that Dylanists seem to take far more seriously than its composer does. Sure, "Sign on the Cross" begins like an offbeat spiritual and carries on in that vein for a few verses. However, by the song's end you can hear Dylan barely containing his laughter, as if straining not to blow the joke.

▫ "Sign on the Window" (Bob Dylan)

Bob Dylan, *New Morning* (1970)
Melanie, *Good Book* (1971)
Jennifer Warnes, *Shot Through the Heart* (1979)
Steven Keene, *No Alternative* (1994)

Dylan, playing piano, sings this gentle, blatantly nostalgic testament to the joys of family life as if he was a member of the Sacred Harp choir, admitting that after years of questing, parenthood "must be what it's all about." Yet this is a composition sung by someone who's plainly been ditched by a flighty "Brighton girl"; she, like the moon and its many phases, has changed faces and scampered off to California with her new boyfriend. No matter where the singer turns, he can read the sign on the window—and the writing on the wall.

Refusing to dismiss "Sign on the Window" as mere filler, Tim Riley was one of the few to explore at length the layers of this deceptive song in his 1992 book *Hard Rain: A Dylan Commentary*; as he wrote, "The key episodic tableau here is 'Sign on the Window,' which achieves in microcosm what *New Morning* skirts in broad strokes: the dissolution of the counterculture, and the transient sweep of post-adolescence. Like *Blood on the Tracks*, his tour-de-force treatment of this theme (decaying romance as a symbol of a fading epoch), 'Sign on the Window' works as a precarious fable of the mood swings this record's liaisons summon up."

A pop-culture note: "Sign on the Window" was played in the final scene of the 2002 season finale of the television show *Friends*.

▫ "Silver Dagger" (Traditional)

Bob Dylan, *The Bootleg Series, Volume 6: Live 1964—Concert at Philharmonic Hall* (2004)
Joan Baez, *Joan Baez* (1960)
Dave Van Ronk, *Inside Dave Van Ronk* (1969)
Sarag Ogan Gunning, *Silver Dagger* (1976)

Dolly Parton, *The Grass Is Blue* (1999)

Dylan played some back-up harmonica for Joan Baez on "Silver Dagger" during her brief appearance at his famed 1964 New York City Halloween concert.

Passed from mother to daughter for generations, "Silver Dagger" is representative of why ballads and traditional songs provide fascinating insights into the lives of ordinary women in centuries past. In the hands of a sensitive performer, it can be heard as part of the great song cycles about love, childbirth, marriage, and adventure, revealing what daily life was like for women in Europe and America from about 1600 to 1900.

According to *The Joan Baez Songbook* (1964): "Family opposition to the marriage of lovers takes many forms in traditional ballads, almost all of which end either with the lovers committing suicide or one of them being done away with by the recalcitrant parents. In this version of 'The Silver Dagger,' however, the ballad ends inconclusively, for we are not told what will be taken by the rejected lover."

[S] **"Silvio"** (Bob Dylan/Robert Hunter)

See also Robert Hunter
Bob Dylan, single (1988); *Down in the Groove* (1988); *Bob Dylan's Greatest Hits Volume 3* (1994)
Shane Howard, *Time Will Tell* (1993)
Various Artists (performed by Mello), *Blowin' in the Wind: A Reggae Tribute to Bob Dylan* (2003)

A snappy, if undistinguished, four-chord riff with boastful, if tongue-in-cheek, come-on lyrics laced with Messianic filigrees written by Grateful Dead lyricist Robert Hunter, "Silvio" represents another semi-collaborative entry in the Dylan canon.

Remembering how Dylan came to his songs, Hunter told journalist and musician David Gans in 1988:

> You couldn't be easier to work with than Dylan. I brought the book—I think it had fifteen to seventeen songs—in to the Dead before we made *In the Dark*, of which "When Push Come to Shove" and "Black Muddy River" were selected. I took about three of them for the *Liberty* album, and Dylan took two of them for his album, set 'em, and sent me a tape. That's what I call easy to work with! He just flipped through the songbook that was sitting there at Front Street [the Dead's office in San Raphael, California], liked these tunes ["Silvio" and "Ugliest Girl in the World"], put 'em in his pocket, went off, set 'em to music, recorded 'em, and . . . First time I met him he said [Dylan voice] "Eh, I just recorded two of your tunes!" And I said, "Neat!"
>
> Bob Dylan doesn't have to ask a lyricist if he can do his tunes! Come *on*, man!
>
> I gotta just say this for the record: you got your Grammies, you got your Bammies, you got your Rock and Roll Hall of Fame—as far as I'm concerned, Bob Dylan has done two of my songs, and those other things sound far away, distant, and not very interesting.

For the recording session, Dylan included Jerry Garcia, Bob Weir, and the Dead's keyboard player, Brent Mydland, on backup vocals, but they are all but indistinguishable in the final wash, if they are there at all.

Dylan seems to have enjoyed performing "Silvio," as it has remained a fairly constant inclusion in his set lists since its Never Ending Tour introduction in 1988. After Jerry Garcia's death in 1995, "Silvio" was one of several tunes associated with the Grateful Dead that Dylan performed practically every night. "Silvio," in particular, was transformed into a jamfest that took the song to some very dynamic and Dead-like spaces.

[S] "Simple Twist of Fate" (Bob Dylan)

Bob Dylan, *Blood on the Tracks* (1974); *Bob Dylan at Budokan* (1979); *The Bootleg Series, Volume 5: Live 1975—The Rolling Thunder Revue* (2002)
Joan Baez, *Diamonds and Rust* (1975)
Jerry Garcia, *Jerry Garcia Band* (1991)
Judy Collins, *Judy Sings Dylan . . . Just Like a Woman* (1993)
Concrete Blonde, *Still in Hollywood* (1994)
Steve Gibbons, *The Dylan Project* (1998)
Jimmy LaFave, *Trail* (1999)
Gerard Quintana and Jordi Batiste, *Els Miralls de Dylan* (1999)
Andy Hill, *It Takes a Lot to Laugh* (2000)
Rich Lerner and the Groove, *Cover Down* (2000)
The Robins, *The Robins Sing Dylan* (2000)
Gene Murphy, *Gene Murphy Sings Bob Dylan* (2001)
Mary Lee's Corvette, *Blood on the Tracks* (2002)
Gerry Murphy, *Gerry Murphy Sings Bob Dylan* (2002)

"Simple Twist of Fate," Dylan's sad, two-ships-passing-in-the-night tale of abandoned love, finds the poet at his most vulnerable. His delivery of the song on record is whispered, resigned, understated, and frustrated as he recounts his unsuccessful and obviously painful search for his departed lover in this oil painting of a song.

The guy singing "Simple Twist of Fate" may keep telling himself he doesn't care, but his actions speak volumes as he scours the city's nether fringes for his woman. He gives in to his remorse by the song's end, but then puts blame on the simple twist of fate that brought them together in the first place. Is it the same twisted fate, he wonders, that eventually tore them apart?

Perhaps, as on "Tangled Up In Blue," Dylan is singing about several intertwined characters and situations in "Simple Twist." But it appears obvious enough that there are but two players on this stage. The first verse finds the couple in a crepuscular setting worthy of a film's opening shot: sitting in the park as sunset turns into night. But even though she takes his hand and he "feels a spark tingle to his bones" it was also "then he felt alone." Slipping in and out of the third person, Dylan toys with the song's point of view, shifting from the detached narrator to a probable participant and back again. It's as if he'd betrayed some blood pact with himself: "They walked along by the old canal/A little confused, I remember well/And stopped into a strange hotel with a neon burnin' bright/He felt the heat of the night hit him like a freight train." He manages to keep the third-person mask attached over the course of the following three wrenching verses, but sheds it completely for the song's climactic final scene: a monologue that seems to take place as the camera comes in for a close-up of our tragic narrator: "People tell me it's a sin/To know and feel too much within/I still believe she was my twin, but I lost the ring/She was born in spring, but I was born too late/Blame it on a simple twist of fate." It is as if in running away from his situation he ran full speed into himself.

Enhancing the emotional, narrative effectiveness of "Simple Twist of Fate" is its heart-tugging melody—a descending chord progression that Dylan mostly suspends through the first three lines of each verse until the tranquil resignation is shattered by a mournful howl as the fourth line is sung. The pain that has been carefully withheld finally comes bursting out like a crash on the levee.

Dylan first performed "Simple Twist" on the television PBS special *The World of John Hammond*, broadcast September 10, 1975, just before he made it a Rolling Thunder Revue staple. Since then, this bittersweet rumination has never been far from his mind, though it has never sounded better than it did during Dylan's tentative return to secular music in late 1981. The 1978 version was, most agree, dreadful, as he sped up the tempo, which made him appear to trip over the words and thus taint one of the best songs from *Blood on the Tracks*. Once calling it his "invasion of privacy song," Dylan stretched his performances of the song to an astounding eight minutes when it was an acoustic set highlight of the 1992 leg of the Never Ending Tour. Thereafter, it has been an irregular but annual inclusion in his acoustic sets.

"Sitting on a Barbed-Wire Fence" (Bob Dylan)

aka "Killing Me Alive"
Bob Dylan, *The Bootleg Series, Volumes 1–3: Rare and Unreleased, 1961–1991/'65* (1991)
Kim Thurston and Epic, *Outlaw Blues* (1992)
Michel Montecrossa, *Eternal Circle* (1999)

Dylan's improvisational approach to writing and recording is clearly evident in this tough, electric 1965 up-tempo blues shuffle—a *Highway 61 Revisited* outtake similar in hard rock sound and tone to the more realized "From a Buick 6" from the same album. With a gnarly guitar riff and chiming piano (played by Dylan) dominating the recording (and its unreleased alternate), the song is full of sneeringly humorous lines, obtuse punch lines ("She's making me into an old man, and, man, I'm not even twenty-five!"), and characters who resemble Thin Men-in-waiting, ready to be plucked into the folds of more pointed fare.

"(Sittin' on) The Dock of the Bay" (Steve Cropper/Otis Redding)

aka "(Sittin' on the) Dock of the Bay," "The Dock of the Bay"
Otis Redding, *The Dock of the Bay* (1968)
T. Rex, *Bolan's Zip Gun* (1975)
Booker T. and the MGs, *Time Is Tight* (1979)
World Saxophone Quartet, *Rhythm & Blues* (1988)
Al Jarreau, *All Fly Home* (1995)
Ted Hawkins, *Love You Most of All* (1998)

The late, great Otis Redding cowrote and recorded "Dock of the Bay," a meditative classic of twentieth-century soul. The gently affecting song was his last, posthumous hit and pointed away from the histrionic, take-no-prisoners ballads with which he'd gained international acclaim . . . and r-e-s-p-e-c-t.

The genesis of "Dock of the Bay" came in the summer of 1967 while Redding, visiting the Bay Area for a gig at San Francisco's Fillmore West, was staying on a rented houseboat in Sausalito. In this idyllic and reflective setting, Otis took to sitting on the deck of the boat with his acoustic guitar, writing a song that offered the first tangible sign of a modern rock influence on his own music. He didn't have much more than a melody, the first couple of lines, and a title. It wasn't much, but it was enough for him to know that it was a completely different song, unlike anything he had ever written before. It couldn't even be described as R&B. In fact, it was even closer to folk than rock 'n' roll.

The son of a minister, Redding (born September 9, 1941, Dawson, Georgia; died December 10, 1967, near Madison, Wisconsin) grew up on a farm in the rural South, hearing both white country music and black gospel, and did his first singing in church. Though painfully shy as a child, Fortune smiled on this young lover of the music of Sam Cooke, Little Richard, and Hank Williams. In one of show biz's odder breaks, Redding's chance to audition for a Stax Records big shot arose when another band he had driven to Memphis (Johnny Jenkins and the Pinetoppers) came up short. Summoned to save the day, he sang "These Arms of Mine," a ballad of his own composition. Stax signed him and waxed the song; it hit the R&B Top 20, and Redding became a local star. Following that up with "Pain in My Heart," a slow ballad showcasing his dramatic approach, Redding joined other popular groups on the so-called chitlin' circuit that toured the South.

Producer Phil Walden (a white Southerner who would go on to shepherd the Allman Brothers Band to rock stardom) took Redding under his wing. Walden engendered a series of recordings in 1964 and 1965 that displayed a tight call-and-response interplay of voice and horns with a raving ending that became Redding's signature approach to handling a song. Redding's first Top 30 pop hit, "I've Been Loving You Too Long," cowritten by Redding with Jerry Butler, remains a moving and complex love song by any measure.

"Respect" was another self-penned Redding hit in 1965, even though Aretha Franklin put a lock on the song a couple of years later, prompting Redding to jokingly lament, "That girl just stole my song."

He really began hitting his stride, however, with a string of raucous, up-tempo songs using a unique stuttering technique to convey overwhelming emotion. Redding also had the uncanny ability to transform minor ballads like "Try a Little Tenderness" into heartrending and rocking testaments in which the tempo accelerates with every verse, a dramatic device that he exploited with a passion worthy of a fire-and-brimstone–spewing stump preacher overwhelmed with intense spirit and emotions.

Redding already had a large black following and he gained a big-time crossover audience with his covers of the Rolling Stones' "Satisfaction," the Beatles' "Day Tripper"—and, most famously, through his volcanic, take-no-prisoners performance at the Monterey Pop Festival in 1967.

The trip to Monterey and the nearby San Francisco Bay Area evidently inspired "Dock of the Bay" and, after recording it complete with the sounds of surf mixed in, Redding was poised to assume the mantle of Ray Charles. But fate intervened. En route to a Midwestern gig, Redding

and all but one other aboard a private twin-engine Beechcraft were drowned in an icy lake near Madison, Wisconsin, after the plane encountered trouble in heavy fog and crashed. Ironically and inevitably, the elegiac "Dock of the Bay" reached No. 1 on the pop charts a month after his death, won a Grammy Award for best R&B song, and will always serve as Otis Redding's epitaph.

Dylan's only performance of "The Dock of the Bay" came as a jaw-dropping shock at an August 1990 Never Ending Tour show in George, Washington.

▣ "Sittin' on Top of the World" (Traditional/Walter Jacobs, Lonnie "Bo" Chatmon)
aka "Sitting on Top of the World"
Bob Dylan, *Good as I Been to You* (1992)
Victoria Spivey (with Bob Dylan and Big Joe Williams), *Three Kings and a Queen*/'61 (1964)
The Mississippi Sheiks, *Complete Recorded Works*/'30 (1991)
Lonnie Smith and Band, *Sounds of the South*/'40s (1995)
Ray Charles, single (1949); *Brother Ray* (1980)
Howlin' Wolf, single (1957); *The Real Folk Blues* (1963)
Doc Watson, *Old Timey Concert* (1967)
The Grateful Dead, *Grateful Dead* (1967)
Cream, *Wheels of Fire* (1968)
Various Artists (performed by Othar Turner, R. L. Boyd, Reid Jones), *Traveling Through the Jungle: Negro Fife and Drum Band Music of the Deep South*/'69 (1995)
Taj Mahal, *Dancing the Blues* (1993)
Memphis Slim, *Alone with My Friends* (1996)

There are almost as many versions of "Sittin' on Top of the World" as there are musicians who adapted, rewrote, and reconceived this ancient country blues. Bob Wills, Ray Charles, Carl Perkins, Ralph Stanley, Clarence Williams, and Cream are just a few of the dozens of artists who have taken a whack at this all-too-confident boast of a song sung by a guy who you know just won't be able to stand prosperity. Tomorrow or the day after tomorrow at the very latest, events will have conspired to pull a one-eighty on him and he'll be making like Sisyphus once again: pushin' that mother boulder up the hill of eternity.

Though he never performed "Sittin' on Top of the World," Dylan contributed harmonica and backing vocals on a version of the song on a Victoria Spivey/Big Joe Williams session in late 1961/early 1962, warmed up a *Desire* recording date with a run-through in 1975, and released his own roguish version in 1992 on *Good as I Been to You*, his solo acoustic collection of old blues and folk songs.

John Way detailed both the song's history and its relation to Dylan in *The Telegraph* #44:

> This influential song was written by two members of one of the most adaptable and enjoyable of the early blues bands, the Mississippi Sheiks. They recorded it during their first-ever studio session in Shreveport, Louisiana, on February 17, 1930. It was immediately so popular that within a year several other blues artists had covered the song on record. This popularity continued to spread right up the post-war electric blues.
>
> By a curious twist of fate, the Sheiks' recordings appeared in the "old time" (white) record listings, which may help to explain a similar popularity among "hillbilly" artists, or through the Western Swing bands of the '30 and '40s to such post-war rural singers as Doc Watson. All this before Cream picked up on Howlin' Wolf's 1957 recording of the song and included it on their double album, *Wheels of Fire*, in 1968.
>
> Some readers will be familiar with the popular song "I'm Sitting on Top of the World (Just Rolling Along)" (written by Lew Browne, Ray Henderson, and Sam Lewis in 1925). It's quite likely that the Sheiks performed this song for white audiences before they first recorded, and were inspired to write a "reply." (They had performed at least one other song by the same writers.) Their own song, with its deep mixture of pathos and irony (which calls to mind Dylan's own "Most of the Time," or even the earlier "Guess I'm Doin' Fine") seems rather to be directly inspired by the Depression blues "Things About Comin' My Way" (from 1929), which even uses the same musical form and melody.
>
> It's interesting to recall that Dylan actually helped Big Joe Williams out on a recording of the song in the early 1960s, and his own version has elements of Williams treatment, though I don't think it owes a great deal to any particular earlier singer, white or black.

[S] "Slow Train" (Bob Dylan)

Bob Dylan, single (1979); *Slow Train Coming* (1979); *Live 1961–2000—Thirty-nine Years of Great Concert Performances*/'87 (2001)
Bob Dylan/Grateful Dead, *Dylan & The Dead* (1989)

Dylan has never been big on introducing his songs in concert but his gospel tour of 1979/1980 was an exception when he took to the bully pulpit *every* night. He saved one of his best introductory raps for "Slow Train Coming" in November 1979: "You know we read every day what a horrible situation this world is in. Now God chooses to do these things in this world to confound the wise. Anyway, we know this world's gonna be destroyed; we know what. Christ will set up His Kingdom in Jerusalem for a thousand years, where the lion will lie down with the lamb. Have you heard that before? Have you heard that before? I'm just curious to know, how many believe that? [enthusiastic response] Alright. This is called 'Slow Train Coming.' It's been coming for a long time, and it's picking up speed."

Unlike the balance of his gospel songs,

"Slow Train" gestures at something of a narrative. The song is bookended by a reference to a relationship with a backwoods girl from Alabama who sounds like she's been around the block a few times at the very least. Her warning that he better fly right or "be just another accident statistic" creates a mood of imminent catastrophe that laces the song. That she dumps his sorry little white ass for a guy oozing with danger by the song's end comes as no surprise. Yet "Slow Train" feels more like one of Dylan's finger-pointing protest songs than it does a diagnosis of Babylon with its walls about to fall as he casts a klieg light on his usual suspects: injustice, hypocrisy, and greed.

Dylan first used the symbol of a slow train in the *Highway 61 Revisited* liner notes and he returned to it in the title track of one of his most controversial albums, recasting it as a fire-and-brimstone invective of the spiritual state of the Union. Some of the imagery in the song sounded like misguided jingoism when it was released and so does it still. Yet, the apocalyptic portent imbedded in the man's preaching make the song a keeper. The train as a symbol of salvation was used by Woody Guthrie for the title of his autobiography, *Bound for Glory*, and was drawn from the song "This Train," which declares "This train is bound for glory, this train." "People Get Ready," Curtis Mayfield's famous pop spiritual, also explores this theme, and it was expressed in numerous other American songs that Dylan was no doubt familiar with by the time he wrote "Slow Train."

Dylan unveiled "Slow Train" on television's *Saturday Night Live* on October 20, 1979, and, when he commenced his first all-gospel shows ten days later, it remained as kind of centerpiece for the tour, complete with Dylan's man-from-Hades vocals and white-hot band augmenting the delivery with revivalist intensity. Along with the release of the song on the *Slow Train Com-*

ing album in August 1979, it was also released as a single at the time but failed to chart.

Dylan has never stopped riding this slow train and his reinterpretation of the song was one of the surprise treats of his 1987 concerts with the Grateful Dead.

Hardly one to disavow his work, when asked by Florida journalist John Dolen in 1995 if he still saw a "slow train coming," Dylan had this to say: "When I look ahead now, it's picked up quite a bit of speed. In fact, it's going like a freight train now."

Slow Train Coming

Columbia Records LP FC-36120; CD CK-36120; CS PCT-36120; Sony Music Entertainment, Inc., SACD 9032. Recorded May 1–11, 1979, at Muscle Shoals, Alabama. Released August 18, 1979. Produced by Jerry Wexler and Barry Beckett. Artwork by Catherine Kramer.

Bob Dylan—guitar, harmonica, keyboards, vocals. Muscle Shoals Horns—horns. Barry Beckett—percussion, keyboards. Mickey Buckins—percussion. Carolyn Dennis, Regina Havis, Helena Springs—vocals. Tim Drummond—bass. Mark Knopfler—guitar. Pick Withers—drums.

"Gotta Serve Somebody," "Precious Angel," "I Believe in You," "Slow Train," "Gonna Change My Way of Thinking," "Do Right to Me Baby (Do Unto Others)," "When You Gonna Wake Up," "Man Gave Names to All the Animals," "When He Returns"

> The songs that I wrote for the *Slow Train* album frightened me . . . I didn't plan to write them, but I wrote them anyway. I didn't like writing them, I didn't want to write them . . .
> —BOB DYLAN, 1984

Groundbreaking. Shocking. Inspiring. One of Dylan's best-performed, best-recorded and best-produced albums, *Slow Train Coming* reflects one man's profound religious awakening. But while "Gotta Serve Somebody" and "When You Gonna Wake Up?" present the type of prophetic invective long associated with Dylan, the album's "you're either with me or against me" attitude toward Dylan's religious choice of the time can still be daunting to the faint of heart. Yet why should it be? Fans of jazz giant John Coltrane certainly recall no such hubbub when the maestro released his religious suite *A Love Supreme* in 1965.

Bob Dylan was at a crossroads at the end of the 1970s. After returning to the spotlight in the middle of the decade with a series of highly praised albums and tours, the center was no longer holding. His film *Renaldo & Clara* was widely condemned as a confusing, self-indulgent morass, his 1978 World Tour took the starch out of him, and his new *Street Legal* material was not exactly setting the world on fire. Hanging over all of this were his failed marriage, public divorce, custody battles, and a whopping alimony tab.

It was while on the road with his big band and under the weight of all this that Dylan claims he experienced a profound spontaneous conversion in a Phoenix hotel room, becoming a born-again Christian late in 1978.

Whatever the spark, Dylan's public conversion was stupefying. The man whose art seemed to refute dogma had succumbed to the Western world's most obvious form of it.

With record-biz legend Jerry Wexler behind the console and Dire Straits guitarist Mark Knopfler acting as bandleader, *Slow Train Coming* was made at Alabama's famed Muscle Shoals studio over the course of ten days in the summer of 1979. And even though its notoriety spurred it to commercial heights, the fallout continues to this day. It is still not uncommon to meet people who think that Dylan remains in the thrall of religion even though he edged away from strict observation and proclamation of born-again precepts in the following few years.

At the time it seemed as though Dylan drew a line in the sand that his fans never thought they would ever be challenged to cross. Either you were a believer or you weren't—there was no middle ground. It was a major shift in philosophy for an artist who had always encouraged his audience to think for themselves.

Lost in the shock of the moment was the fact that this harvest of Dylan songs was particularly strong. Whatever one's spiritual orientation, it is hard to deny the power of "Gotta Serve Somebody," "I Believe in You," "Slow Train," "Gonna Change My Way of Thinking," and "When You Gonna Wake Up?" And if these screeds came on a little strong, Dylan was wise enough to balance his proclamations with songs of solace ("Covenant Woman"), advice ("Do Right to Me Baby"), warning ("When He Returns"), and even levity ("Man Gave Names to All the Animals").

Despite, or maybe because of, the controversy simmering around the content of the album, *Slow Train Coming* was immensely successful, hitting No. 3 during its half-year stint on the charts en route to going platinum. The album had no liner notes, but its front cover image, a brown-hued, pen-and-ink drawing on a brown background depicting men lying down on tracks as a train approaches was a memorable one. Less affecting was the back-cover photograph of a man looking more than a little like Dylan in silhouette standing by a cross as the sun sets across the ocean behind him.

The exact specifics of Dylan's conversion are typically murky. The story plays out something like this: when his big band passed through San Diego in mid-November 1978, he was a man on the ropes. When he visited town a year later he told the audience: "I came (here) just about a year ago, I think . . . just about towards the end of the show . . . someone out

S

Dylan performing shortly before his religious awakening, 1978.

(Photo: Joseph Sia/Getty Images)

there in the crowd, they knew I wasn't feeling too well. I think they could see that. And they threw a silver cross on the stage. Now usually I don't pick things up in front of the stage. Once in a while I do. Sometimes I don't. But I looked down at that cross. I said, 'I gotta pick that up.' So I picked up the cross and put it in my pocket. A little silver cross, I'd say maybe so high. And I brought it backstage and I brought it with me to the next town, which was in Arizona—I think it was Phoenix. Anyway, I got back there. I was feeling even worse than I'd felt when I was in San Diego. I said, 'Well I need something tonight.' I didn't know what it was. I was used to all kinds of things. I said, 'I need something tonight that I didn't have before.' And I looked in my pocket and I had this cross. So if that person is here tonight, I just wanna say thank you for that cross."

Perhaps a bit more earnestly, he told journalist Karen Hughes in May 1980 that "Jesus put his hand on me. It was a physical thing. I felt it. I felt it all over me. I felt my whole body tremble. The glory of the Lord knocked me down and picked me up."

By the end of the 1978 tour in mid-December, he could be seen wearing a large metal cross on stage, had transformed the lyrics in "Tangled Up in Blue" to reference the New Testament (rather than "a book of poems"), and was soundchecking new compositions that would become "Slow Train" and "Do Right to Me Baby."

Retreating to his Malibu home to sort out his experiences, Dylan was, in relatively short order, introduced to pastors from the Vineyard Fellowship in West Los Angeles by a girlfriend, Mary Alice Artes, a black actress who is often acknowledged to have inspired his songs "Precious Angel," "Covenant Woman," and maybe the secular "Caribbean Wind." After he told the Vineyard Fellowship's pastors Larry Myers and Paul Emond that he wanted Christ in his life, they prayed and he received the Lord. Dylan's baptism, contrary to myth, did not transpire in Pat Boone's swimming pool but at some other, still debated location.

The style of born-again Christianity embraced by the Vineyard Church appears to have been quintessentially Californian. Journalist Ron Rosenbaum described the church's logo as making Christ "look like a Marin County coke dealer, a late-70s smoothy."

Despite the iconography, Dylan was soon ensconced in an intensive course at the Vineyard School of Discipleship from 8:30 A.M. to noon, four days a week, for three and a half months. The course focused on the life of Jesus, principles of discipleship, the Sermon on the Mount, and what it means to be a believer while at the same time providing a solid overview of the Bible. According to witnesses, Dylan's attendance record was impeccable.

By all accounts, Dylan began writing the balance of songs that would later find their way onto *Slow Train Coming* during his tutelage with the Vineyard Fellowship, using Myers as a backboard for the lyrics. Reportedly, Myers eventually joined Dylan's gospel band on the road as a kind of pastor roadie, leading them in prayer and Bible study while ministering to Dylan personally.

Even more unclear is the role Hal Lindsey's millenarian tract, *The Late Great Planet Earth*, figured in Dylan's conversion and subsequent worldview. Lindsey was an influential member in the Vineyard Fellowship at the time of Dylan's heavy involvement. Dylan is said to have attended Lindsey's Bible study classes, which presumably focused on the Bible's more apocalyptic traditions—specifically the Book of Revelation—on which much of Lindsey's speculative approach to deconstructing the New Testament relied.

Lindsey's philosophy boiled down to the notion that the end of the world was imminent, with then-current world events and figures (the Soviet Union, the Middle East Crisis, etc.) involved in disputes leading to the Battle of Armageddon, at which, according to Lindsey, "Christ will return to prevent the annihilation of all mankind."

While the link between Lindsey's personal vision and Dylan's developing gospel is cloudy (Lindsey's influences on political figures such as future president Ronald Reagan are better documented), the premillennial raps—referencing Revelation and Lindsey—with which Dylan introduced his material during the "born-again" shows of 1979–1980 are filled with the type of passionate fire-and-brimstone rhetoric any stump preacher would love. This was easily Dylan's most voluble phase as an artist/showman, as his testifying would often stretch on for minutes between songs.

Dylan supposedly wondered if releasing the *Slow Train* material under his own name was a wise move, even considering Carolyn Dennis (one of his backup singers) as the conduit to spread the music and the gospel.

Dylan's all-gospel shows would be a thing of the past by the fall of 1980, but they are among his most compelling. The dynamite band (Dylan's most racially and sexually integrated), complete with backup singers, was tight and even "looked" the part for this short-lived but intense period of his career.

"Solid Rock" (Bob Dylan)
aka "Hanging on to a Solid Rock," "Hanging on to a Solid Rock Made Before the Foundation of the World"
Bob Dylan, single (1980); *Saved* (1980); *Biograph*/'80 (1985)
Heart of Gold Band, *Heart of Gold Band* (1989)
Various Artists (performed by Sounds of Blackness), *Gotta Serve Somebody: The Gospel Songs of Bob Dylan* (2003)

Just as he was commencing his one-off gospel tour in November 1979, Dylan introduced his recently penned "Solid Rock" with the following rap: "We all know we're living in the end times, near the last of the end times. The end times are perilous times, in the last days perilous times indeed. You're gonna need something strong to hold onto. 'Hanging on to a Solid Rock Made Before the Foundation of the World.' You need something that strong."

Dylan's continued commitment to fervent gospel material was evidenced in his composition of a batch of new songs to support his extended evangelical tour of 1979–1980. The "solid rock" described in the song is the church and when he sings "won't let go till it lets go" you better believe it and hang onto something as well. Even after he got off the stump, Dylan continued performing "Solid Rock" through 1981 with a slowed-down arrangement. In early April 2002, as the world anxiously and helplessly watched Israeli-Palestinian violence spiral out of control, "Solid Rock" reemerged as a surprise mid-concert choice on Dylan's European tour. As he sang the lines "Nations are angry, cursed are some/People are expecting a false peace to come" with his leathery bray, it was not hard to consider that he was throwing in his two cents regarding the apparent hopelessness of not only that situation, but the post-9/11 world crisis as well.

One of the better cuts on *Saved*, his second, stiffer offering of religious music, "Solid Rock" is an up-tempo piece with sharp vocals and focused lyrics. When released as a single, however, "Solid Rock" failed to chart. If *Saved* had more songs like "Solid Rock," the album could have been a classic.

[S] "So Long, Good Luck and Goodbye" (Weldon Rogers)

Weldon Rogers, *Tryin' to Get to You*/'57 (1998)

A swaggering piece of 1957 rockabilly used by Dylan and the Heartbreakers to inversely open a string of shows on the second leg of their 1986 tour, "So Long, Good Luck and Goodbye" was also given one 1990 Never Ending Tour airing. With a title like "So Long, Good Luck and Goodbye," Dylan should have considered closing his shows with the song. Additionally, Dylan is said to have lifted the bass line off the original 1957 Weldon Rogers recording of the song for his own 1989 effort, "Everything Is Broken."

The little-known Rogers (born 1927 near Marietta, Oklahoma) was among the last of the great honky-tonk singers—a songwriter with a great ear that could be both emotionally honest and commercial. His rise to prominence in the mid- to late 1950s coincided with the country's transition from a largely regional to a more national focus in country music—a seismic shift that Rogers's recordings (many self-produced) alternately reflected and defied.

[A] *Somebody Else's Troubles*/Steve Goodman

See also *The Essential Steve Goodman*

Buddah Records LP BDS-5121. Released 1972.

Crediting himself with the literary moniker Robert Milkwood Thomas (Dylan Thomas wrote a play entitled *Under Milkwood*), Dylan played piano and sang backup on the title track of Goodman's small label outing. The LP also includes a fine mixture of ballads ("The Dutchman") and good-time songs ("The Auctioneer") from one of Chicago's late, great troubadours.

[S] "Somebody Touched Me" (Traditional)

Bob Dylan, *Live 1961–2000—Thirty-nine Years of Great Concert Performances*/'00 (2001)

Bill Monroe, *Bluegrass 1959–1969* (1991)

The Sullivan Family, *The Sullivan Family Alive* (1971)

Ralph Stanley, *1971–73* (1995)
Doc Watson, *Songs from the Southern Mountains* (1994)

Dylan led off a series of summer and fall of 1999 Never Ending Tour shows with an acoustic version of this nugget of gospel bluegrass recounting a spiritual encounter best known from the versions recorded by the Stanley Brothers, Doc Watson, and Bill Monroe. He continued to trot out the song as an occasional show opener through 2002. A spirited piece of salvation in the hands of Bob Dylan and his band, "Somebody Touched Me" treads the same ground as Dylan's "Saved" (in which he sang "By this hand I've been delivered"). Even though he can't quite seem to pinpoint the exact moment the revelation occurred (it could have been in church on Sunday), there is no doubt in his mind that his Savior has tapped him on the shoulder and whispered, "Behold!"

[S] **"Someone's Got a Hold of My Heart"** (Bob Dylan)

See also "Tight Connection to My Heart"
Bob Dylan, *The Bootleg Series, Volumes 1–3: Rare and Unreleased, 1961–1991*/'83 (1991)

A song that began life during the *Infidels* period, "Someone's Got a Hold of My Heart" was rewritten and appeared on *Empire Burlesque* as "Tight Connection to My Heart;" it was subsequently released in its original rough form under the above title on *The Bootleg Series, Volumes 1–3.*

[S] **"Something"** (George Harrison)

The Beatles, single (1969); *Abbey Road* (1969)
George Harrison, *Live in Japan* (1969)
Joe Cocker, *Joe Cocker!* (1969)
Chet Atkins, *Me & Jerry* (1970)
Count Basie, *Basie on the Beatles* (1970)
Shirley Bassey, *Live at Carnegie Hall* (1973)
Frank Sinatra, *Trilogy* (1979)
Tony Bennett, *Tony Bennett's Something* (1995)

"The greatest love song of the past fifty years." Those words from the lips of Frank Sinatra (who knew a thing or two about a good love song) should come as the greatest endorsement for any song. And the song he was talking about? Why, George Harrison's "Something," naturally.

Dylan's lone performance of Harrison's most commercially successful composition came about in November 2002 in New York City a few weeks before a gala London concert celebrating George's life and music a year after his passing. Dylan was originally slated to appear at the show, but begged off around the time he surprised a Madison Square Garden throng with an encore display of the beloved Harrison classic.

George wrote "Something" on piano during a break in the making of *The Beatles* (better known as the *White Album*) in 1968. Paul was busy with laying down some overdubs so George strolled into an empty studio and composed it too late to be included on the *White Album.*

"When I wrote it," George said of conjuring "Something," "in my mind I heard Ray Charles singing it, and he did do it some years later."

George gave it to Joe Cocker, the apoplectic British songster who enjoyed his first flush of success with a frenzied cover of "With a Little Help from My Friends" the year before. While he didn't repeat that success, Cocker's version on *Joe Cocker!* was the premier of "Something."

Harrison rerecorded "Something," adding a dozen violas, a quartet of violins, another four cellos, and a string bass. Featured on *Abbey Road*, it also (at the insistence of Allen Klein, the Beatles' U.S. manager/publisher) became a single, giving George his first-ever Beatles Aside and, issued with "Come Together," reached No. 3 on the U.S. pop charts.

Easily Harrison's most popular song, "Something" has been covered by more than 150 recording artists, with James Brown's and Smokey Robinson's renditions apparently favored by George.

[S] "Something's Burning, Baby" (Bob Dylan)
Bob Dylan, *Empire Burlesque* (1985)

A stately, lone wolf on-the-prowl torch song for his woman that references beat novelist Jack Kerouac's *Mexico City Blues*, "Something's Burning, Baby" is set to a somber, funereal drumbeat that underscores the dying romance (or was that an invocation of the Last Days?) depicted in the song. The singer has tracked down his gal after she has apparently been avoiding him. Her aloofness is tangibly felt as he attempts to understand and coax her into a reunion of sorts. But even though she is sung to with majesty and drama, her lack of presence on the other end of the intercom seems to say it all: "nothing doing."

Madelyn Quebec shares the vocal with Dylan on the never-performed *Empire Burlesque* track.

S

[S] "Something There Is About You" (Bob Dylan)
Bob Dylan, single (1974); *Planet Waves* (1974)

Dylan looks back. A strange, cloudy love song of reminiscence uniting the phantoms of his youth in old Duluth and a mysterious woman of the present, "Something There Is About You" was effectively performed by Dylan and the Band during their 1974 tour even if the song proved a difficult one to sing. The track was released as a single but, despite the enormous publicity both the '74 tour and the album garnered at the time, it did not chart.

Despite being one of the more memorable *Planet Waves* songs, few critics have really considered "Something There Is About You" with any degree of serious contemplation. In his 1982 book *Voice Without Restraint: A Study of Bob Dylan's Lyrics and Their Background*, John Herdman wrote that "Something There Is About You" is

> . . . another song of restlessness, and seems to be about Dylan's effort to get back to a true view of himself and his aims. It is addressed to someone who evokes something, "I can't quite put my finger on," but which is associated with his roots and the values they symbolize. There is a livingness and fluidity about the music that endows the words with a sense more poignant than nostalgic . . . It is a sense of the validity of this felt but undefined truth and of commitment to it, which determines the seriousness of his attitude towards the lover who is "the soul of many things."
>
> *I could say that I'd be faithful*
> *I could say it in one sweet easy breath.*
> *But to you that would be cruelty*
> *And to me it surely would be death.*
>
> This is in effect a repudiation of his most cherished stances of the previous six years, which he had devoted mainly to saying just such things "in one sweet easy breath"—a phrase which, as Dylan sings it, beautifully gives form to the idea it expresses. He now clearly announces his intention to opt for full creative life instead of the easy half-life which he has been singing about since giving up the inner struggle undertaken in *John Wesley Harding* . . .

[A] *Songs for the New Depression*/Bette Midler
Atlantic Records LP SD-18155. Released 1976.

Dylan's fans know this record for his duet with

Bette Midler on a lilting "Buckets of Rain" but her cover of Tom Waits's "Shiver Me Timbers" also makes the disc worth seeking out.

ⓐ *The Songs of Jimmie Rodgers: A Tribute*/Various Artists

See also Jimmie Rodgers

Egyptian-Columbia Records CD CK 67676. Released 1998. Executive Producers: Jeff Kramer and Jeff Rosen. Liner notes by Bob Dylan.

"Dreaming With Tears In My Eyes" (Bono), "Any Old Time" (Alison Krauss and Union Station), "Waiting for a Train" (Dickie Betts), "Somewhere Down Below the Mason Dixon Line" (Mary Chapin Carpenter), "Miss the Mississippi and You" (David Ball), "My Blue-Eyed Jane" (Bob Dylan), "Peach Pickin' Time Down in Georgia" (Willie Nelson), "In The Jailhouse Now" (Steve Earle and the V-Roys), "Blue Yodel #9" (Jerry Garcia, David Grisman, and John Kahn), "Hobo's Last Ride" (Iris DeMent), "Gambling Bar Room Blues" (John Mellencamp), "Mule Skinner Blues" (Van Morrison), "Why Should I Be Lonely" (Aaron Neville), "T for Texas" (Dwight Yoakam)

"Jimmie Rodgers is one of the guiding lights of the 20th century." Dylan's declaration, printed in the liner notes to this audio homage to "The Singing Brakeman," was as fine an introduction as any to this all-star celebration honoring the legendary "Father of Country Music" and commemorating the centennial of his birth.

The Songs of Jimmie Rodgers: A Tribute may not be the perfect album paying homage to a musical legend, but it is handled with a class missing from similar audio memorials. Dylan was wise enough to assemble a quirky who's who of popular, mostly Americana for this (the first and so far the only) release on his fledgling Egyptian record label. Between Dylan, Van Morrison, Mary Chapin Carpenter, Bono, John Mellencamp, Willie Nelson, Steve Earle, Alison Krauss, Dwight Yoakam, and Jerry Garcia (in his last recorded studio per-

formance), the material is treated with affection for Rodgers even if some of it comes off as a bit studied. Earle's rock-up of "In the Jailhouse Now," Nelson's "Peach Pickin' Time Down in Georgia," Garcia's familiar "Blue Yodel #9," and Dylan's "Blue-Eyed Jane" (which he briefly performed around the time of the album's release) achieve everything they should, delivering on their own terms while inspiring the listener to seek out the real deal.

ⓢ "Song to Woody" (Bob Dylan)

Bob Dylan, *Bob Dylan* (1962); *Masterpieces* (1978)
Christy Moore, *Prosperous* (1972)
Earl Scruggs, *Anniversary Special Volume 1* (1975)
Wizz Jones, *Magical Flight* (1977)
Dave Van Ronk, *Somebody Else, Not Me* (1978) [different sources give 1979 and 1980]
Rex Foster, *Artist* (1991)
Singin' Mike Seeger, *Singin' Mike Seeger Sings Good Ol' Folk Songs* (1997)
Michel Montecrossa, *Jet Pilot* (2000)
Various Artists (performed by Rex Foster), *May Your Song Always Be Sung: The Songs of Bob Dylan, Volume 3* (2003)

A tribute, benediction and song of farewell all rolled into one, "Song to Woody" is easily the greatest of Dylan's very first compositions. Tucked in near the conclusion of his debut eponymous LP, Dylan casts himself as the worthy heir to Woody Guthrie's mantle. He walks down Woody's same dusty road, raises a toast to Guthrie's peers, laces some in-the-know references into his own song, assesses the ill health of humanity, and humbly implies that its salvation lies in the hands of those who can effectively cast a mirror on its diseased soul before rolling up their sleeves and getting to work.

By nearly all accounts, Dylan wrote his elegy at the Mills Hotel bar in Greenwich Village on February 14, 1961, after a sad meeting with the severely disabled Guthrie at the Gleason's—

Woody's friends who hosted little musical get-togethers at their East Orange, New Jersey, home. A variant on a traditional tune Guthrie used in his "1913 Massacre," the folkish melody sways with an easy delicacy, creating an intimate portrait of the two men side by side. Dylan also does a nice little rewrite of a lyric from Guthrie's "Pastures of Plenty" and is sure to mention his own credentials as a "hard travelin'" man.

An uncommon and generally neglected performance choice, "Song to Woody" has essentially appeared in most of Dylan's main eras: the early folk days, the comeback tour with the Band in '74, the stadium shows with Tom Petty and the Heartbreakers, the Never Ending Tour, and the special outing at the thirtieth-anniversary concert in 1992.

[A] ***The Sopranos: Peppers & Eggs (Music from the HBO Original Series)***/Various Artists

Sony CD 85463. Released 2001.

Any true lover of *The Sopranos*—the wildly popular black dramedy about a never-ready-for-network-primetime New Jersey mob family—always waited for the cable television show's closing credits. That was when a different song—not the show's theme or a song necessarily played during the episode—was aired. Some of the songs were familiar (like Otis Redding's "My Love's Prayer") but many were not. Some, like Dylan's remake of "Return to Me," were cut specifically for the broadcast. *The Sopranos: Peppers & Eggs* collects all of these and more from the show's second season. Along with the Dylan, highlights include Frank Sinatra's "Baubles, Bangles and Beads," Cecilia Bartoli performing a Vivaldi aria, and one of the more incredible medleys this side of Jersey City: the Police's "Every Breath You Take" and Henry Mancini's "Theme from *Peter Gunn*."

[S] **"The Sounds of Silence"** (Paul Simon)

aka "The Sound of Silence"
Simon and Garfunkel, *Wednesday Morning 3 A.M.* (1966)
Chet Atkins, *Solid Gold '68* (1968)
Paul Simon, *Live Rhymin'* (1974)
Stanley Jordan, *Standards, Volume 1* (1986)
Art Garfunkel, *Up 'til Now* (1993)

Dylan's only performances of Paul Simon's No. 1 hit were with its composer during the duet encore sets of their joint 1999 tour.

The song first appeared on Simon and Garfunkel's debut album *Wednesday Morning 3 A.M.* When the album tanked, producer Tom Wilson took a track off the album, overdubbed a complete rock orchestration, and remixed it as a single. The song, "The Sounds of Silence," soared to the No. 1 position for two weeks and boosted *Wednesday Morning 3 A.M.* to No. 30. When the dust cleared, Paul Simon's writing was being mentioned in the same breath as Dylan and Lennon/McCartney, but much of his best writing was yet to come.

Along with "Mrs. Robinson," "The Sounds of Silence" is probably the best-known Simon and Garfunkel song. And though much has been written about its inspiration (reportedly the November 1963 assassination of President John F. Kennedy), impact, commercial success, and enduring appeal, Art Garfunkel perhaps best articulated the essence of the song in the *Wednesday Morning 3 A.M.* liner notes when he wrote, "The 'Sounds of Silence' is a major work. We were looking for a song on a larger scale, but this was more than either of us expected. Paul had the theme and the melody set in November, but three months of frustrating attempts were necessary before the song 'burst forth.' On February 19, 1964, the song practically wrote itself.

"Its theme is man's inability to communicate with man. The author sees the extent of com-

S

munication as it is on only its most superficial and 'commercial' level (of which the 'neon sign' is representative). There is no serious understanding because there is no communication— 'people talking without speaking—hearing without listening.' No one dares take the risk of reaching out ('take my arms that I might reach you') to disturb the sound of silence. The poet's attempts are equally futile ('. . . but my words like silent raindrops fell/And echoed in the wells of silence'). The ending is an enigma. I find my own meaning in it, but like most good works, it is best interpreted by each person individually. The words tell us that when meaningful communication fails, the only sound is silence."

ⓐ *So You Wanna Go Back to Egypt . . .* (Keith Green)
Pretty Good Records LP PGR-1. Released 1980.

Keith Green (born October 21, 1953, Brooklyn, New York; died July 28, 1982) was raised in a religious and musical family. A natural singer, Green started to sing and play the ukulele at the age of three, graduated to piano by the age of six, and was writing songs as an eight-year-old. His songwriting matured so rapidly that, by the time he was eleven, he had become the youngest-ever member of the American Society Of Composers, Authors And Publishers (ASCAP) after cutting a deal with Decca Records.

He became a born-again Christian in the early 1970s, appeared on television's evangelical program *Barry McGuire's Anyone but Jesus*, and spread the word at church congregations throughout the Golden State. With his wife Melody, he wrote for numerous Christian and secular recording artists and founded the Last Days Ministries, which urged the Christian community to "purge itself" of biblical

impurity. He began his own solo recording career in the mid-'70s with *For Him Who Has Ears to Hear* for Sparrow Records.

Green's later albums mixed contemporary Christian protest songs with historical church tracts drawing on the literature of nineteenth-century evangelism. Sadly, at the height of his success he died in an east Texas plane crash.

Green's brand of musical evangelism was *way* over the top. He turned down lucrative offers from labels for fear they were satanic temptations and even mortgaged his house to make *So You Wanna Go Back to Egypt . . .*, saying God wanted him to give his albums away to anyone who couldn't afford the sticker price. While his controversial zeal was often more interesting than his not particularly inventive mellow '70s piano-heavy gospel rock, the passionate intensity of his religious conviction lights a spark in his performances. And though he would never be confused with Bill Cosby, he infused his biblical storytelling with doses of Southern Cal hippie humor.

Dylan, a fan of Green's debut *For Him Who Has Ears to Hear* album, befriended Green during his own period of fascination with Christianity and played harmonica on *So You Wanna Go Back to Egypt. . . .*

ⓢ "Spanish Harlem Incident" (Bob Dylan)
aka "Gypsy Gal"
Bob Dylan, *Another Side of Bob Dylan* (1964); *The Bootleg Series, Volume 6: Live 1964—Concert at Philharmonic Hall/'64* (2004)
Byrds, *Mr. Tambourine Man* (1965); *Byrds Play Dylan* (1980); *Byrds* (1990)
Dino, Desi and Billy, *Memories Are Made of This* (1966)
The Pozo Seco Singers, *Shades of Time* (1968)
Dion, *Wonder Where I'm Bound* (1969)
Zimmermen, *The Dungeon Tapes* (1996)
Chris Whitley, *Perfect Day* (2000)

Various Artists (performed by Chris Whitley), *May Your Song Always Be Sung: The Songs of Bob Dylan, Volume 3* (2003)

A vital little testament to a pearly-eyed Gypsy gal comes forth with street-scene immediacy. This fortune-telling street urchin from the other side of the tracks (or East 96th Street) is an early entry in Dylan's list of female muse figures. Her lack of education and exotic manner is a definite turn-on for a guy looking for solace, and obviously happy to have a break from the bookish middle-class women he'd been hanging out with in the Village. Think of "One More Cup of Coffee," "Slow Train," and "Highlands" as later songs dealing with a similar character. With its breathy, sensual froth of language dappling New York's mean streets, the exuberant "Spanish Harlem Incident" marks one of Dylan's first impressionistic breakthroughs that would yield his harvest of mid-'60s classics.

Dylan's only known performance of this intoxicating, three-verse gem came at the famous New York City All Hallow's Eve Philharmonic Hall concert in 1964 (as heard on *The Bootleg Series, Volume 6*).

▣ "Spanish Is the Loving Tongue" (Charles Badger Clark Jr./J. Williams)
aka "A Border Affair," "Spanish Is a Loving Tongue"
Bob Dylan, single (1971); *Dylan* (1973); *Masterpieces* (1978)
Ronnie Gilbert, *Folk Songs and Minstrelsy* (1962)
Ian and Sylvia, *Four Strong Winds* (1964)
Liam Clancy, *Dutchman* (1993)
Richard Dyer-Bennet, *Volumes 1–7* (2001)

Dylan made all other versions of "Spanish Is the Loving Tongue" look good when he cut a version of it that showed up as the B-side single of "Watching the River Flow" in 1971 and

on *Dylan*, the 1973 embarrassment released without his permission. Dylan must have seen something here: perhaps some noir border town detective story worthy of Orson Welles's attention.

"Spanish Is the Loving Tongue" is one of the most bittersweet poems anywhere, and is often sung under the title "A Border Affair." In the days of the Old West, gringo cowboys looking for a little more excitement and variety (or to hide from the lawmen north of the border) would ride into towns like Sonora, Mexico, and sometimes settle in for a spell. If a cowpoke committed an extremely serious crime on one side of the border and then fled to the other, he couldn't "cross the Line" again without risking capture and execution.

Dakota cowboy poet Charles Badger Clark Jr. (born January 1, 1883, Albia, Iowa; died September 26, 1957, Custer State Park, South Dakota) cleverly imbued his lyric with not only the prevalent attitude of many Americanos in the Old West toward Mexican people, but with the implied and unspoken realization by the cowboy narrator that the arrogant prejudices of gringos are wrong and dishonorable. Somewhere along the line, in the wondrous, subtle alchemic way folk songs are created, a shortened version of the poem was wedded to this lovely melody. Richard Dyer-Bennet heard the song from a friend and made it popular through his recordings of it.

According to Earl Robinson's notes in Irwin Silber's *Songs of the American West*: "Of all the cowboy love songs which sang of sweethearts true and false, this touching literary ballad by the well-known western poet Charles Badger Clark Jr., has enjoyed the most sustained popularity. Written under the title, 'A Border Affair,' the poem struck a responsive note in a sentimental age. Its story of true love thwarted by the barrier of 'racial' differences ... had wide appeal in a romantic age. And long after many another cowboy ballad had been consigned to the printed page, 'A Border Affair' was sung and declaimed by cowboys out on the range. For there is a sentiment which appeals to us all in this bittersweet ballad of the rough-hewn cowpuncher who doesn't 'look much like a lover' and the señorita who whispered, 'Adios, mi corazon.'"

Clark did for cowboy poetry what Zane Gray did for the cowboy novel: painting word pictures of a way of life, with all its vanishing values, and singing of the beauty of the Black Hills. After growing up in the South Dakota towns of Plankinton, Mitchell, Huron, and Deadwood, he spent four years as a ranch hand near Tombstone, Arizona, where he started writing poems about his life and work among the cowboys. After his stepmother sent one to *Pacific Monthly*, Clark's new career began. By 1910, when he was writing full time, Clark returned to South Dakota and settled in the Black Hills where he wrote several books of poetry, including the 1915 *Sun and Saddle Leather* (in which "Spanish Is the Loving Tongue" was published) and *Spike*, a collection of short stories. Along with "Spanish Is the Loving Tongue," Clark's most famous poems are "The Job" and "A Cowboy's Prayer." In 1938, South Dakota governor Leslie Jensen appointed Clark South Dakota's first Poet Laureate (aka the "Poet Lariat") of the West—a title retained for the rest of his life while living in the "Badger Hole," a popular destination in Custer Park.

In this nostalgic love song, a girl from the Southwest remembers her Mexican lover and the dreams she once had. Between 1967 and 1976, Dylan explored this song in a variety of contexts. At what was perhaps the first *Basement Tapes* session at Big Pink (the West Saugerties, New York home of the Hawks), "Spanish Is a Loving Tongue" was one of a cou-

ple of traditional songs recorded in the summer of 1967. In 1969 and 1970, Dylan toyed with the song extensively in the studio during the sessions that eventually produced *Self Portrait* and an intricate arrangement from this period appeared on the aforementioned sub-mediocre 1973 disc, *Dylan*. A fabulous solo version of Dylan performing the song on piano in the studio from the *Self Portrait* sessions was released on the greatest hits–style pseudo-import *Masterpieces*. Dylan sang the song (with Arlo Guthrie, Dave Van Ronk, Pete Seeger, Phil Ochs, and others) at the ill-fated "Friends of Chile" benefit concert at New York's Felt Forum in 1974, and with Eric Clapton at a March 1976 birthday party for Clapton in L.A., finally performing it later that year as the Rolling Thunder Revue began winding down in the Southwest. That the song's action transpires in that region was probably not lost on Dylan.

There is some confusion on authorship. Clark and composer J. Williams are usually given credit, but Dylan has, at times, been listed as an arranger. Elsewhere, the song has been noted being in the public domain.

▧ "Stack A Lee" (Traditional)

aka "Billy Lyons and Stack O'Lee," "Stackalee," "Stack-A-Lee," "Stack O' Lee," "Stagger Lee," "Staggerlee," "Stagolee"

Bob Dylan, *World Gone Wrong* (1993)

Various Artists (performed by Frank Hutchison), *Anthology of American Folk Music/'27* (1952, 1997)

Ma Rainey, *Madame Gertrude "Ma" Rainey Master's Collection 1923–38* (1994)

Mississippi John Hurt, *1928 Sessions* (1990)

Furry Lewis, *Furry Lewis 1927–1929* (1986)

Cab Calloway, *Cab Calloway and His Orchestra 1931–1935* (1991)

Sidney Bechet, *The Best of Sidney Bechet/'30s* (1994)

Woody Guthrie, *Muleskinner Blues/'44* (1999)

S

Jesse Fuller, *Jazz, Folk Songs, Spirituals and Blues* (1958)
Lloyd Price, single (1959); *Greatest Hits* (1982, 1994)
Paul Clayton, *Bloody Ballads* (1960)
Dave Van Ronk, *Inside Dave Van Ronk* (1961)
Tim Hardin, *This Is Tim Hardin/'62* (1966)
Julius Lester, *Julius Lester* (1965)
Merle Travis, *Rough, Rowdy and Blue/'60s* (1986)
The McCoys, *(You Make Me Feel) So Good* (1966)
Wilson Pickett, single (1967), *I'm in Love* (1968)
The Grateful Dead, single, *Shakedown Street* (1978)
Nick Cave, *Murder Ballads* (1996)
Taj Mahal, *Hanapepe Dream* (2003)

An enigma wrapped inside a mystery wrapped inside a myth wrapped inside a legend that just happens to be true, "Stack A Lee" is arguably the most enduring and archetypal song in the American music lexicon—be it ragtime, folk, blues, jazz, rock, rap, or name your style. The venerable relic dates to the late nineteenth century, when songs functioned not only as entertainment but as oral history and a brand of moral teaching and catharsis in both black and white society.

The hundreds of different recorded versions of "Stack A Lee" sung by so many people include so many different story lines that its actual history has nearly been forgotten (but not lost) forever. Blacks and whites were singing it decades before recording equipment was even a gleam in anyone's eyes so, not surprisingly, its origins are steeped in the gloam of Midwest Americana from more than a century ago when folk music was deeply imbedded into the oral historical fabric and psyche of society and culture—when memory and creativity were relied upon to pass the song on. But, like some of the all-time great folk songs, the yarn seems to have more than a little germ of historical truth . . . just not the one that has often been recounted. Forget the stories about the bastard mulatto child of a prosperous Mem-

phis, Tennessee, family who came back to haunt his parsimonious clan with his murderous ways in the levee gin joints or any of the other alleged sources of this Passion Play in song . . . they are all wrong.

No, the real Stagger Lee story begins on December 25, 1895, in St. Louis, Missouri, when a black man named Lee Shelton shot an acquaintance named Billy Lyons over a hat (and much more) in the Bill Curtis Saloon at the very hub of the city's notorious "Deep Morgan" or "Chestnut Valley" red-light district, where a colorful sporting crowd had established an intricate sociopolitical culture in the decades after the Civil War. What went wrong between the two men is open to some speculation, but most of the evidence would make it appear as if both local politics and a longstanding grudge were the primary contributing factors . . . and, yes, a Stetson hat.

Whatever the actual details, elements of the story soon became a song—which traveled downstream on the riverboats, across the Great Plains on wagon trains, to other points on the compass by other means of transportation. They were often grafted upon already existing melodies and stories as it began to filter into what passed for the American mainstream at the turn of the century.

Lee Shelton was something of a hero among the hardened East St. Louis rounders, best known as a member of a group of exotic, well-groomed pimps called "macks" who presented themselves with all the pomp and signifyin' flair of a Parisian china shop window. Lyons had come to the Bill Curtis Saloon expecting trouble, packing iron and a knife loaned to him by a friend as a precaution. According to witnesses (and a little legend), Shelton, a cross-eyed thirty-year-old mulatto who stood five feet, seven inches (not the gargantuan ogre sometimes graphically depicted in the song)

S

walked into Bill Curtis's and asked, "Who's treating?" After someone gestured to Lyons, Shelton approached him and began drinking and laughing with his acquaintance for quite a while. But when the subject of politics arose, they began exchanging blows by striking each other's hats. Shelton damaged Lyons's derby and Lyons demanded "six bits" for its replacement. When Shelton refused, Lyons snatched Shelton's Stetson hat and refused to hand it back, ignoring Shelton's demand for its return. Shelton then threatened to blow Lyon's brains out if the hat was not immediately handed back. Lyons refused again; Shelton pulled a .44 Smith and Wesson revolver from his coat and smacked Lyons on the head with it. Lyons still refused to relinquish the Stetson. Shelton continued his demand, again threatening to kill him if he didn't get the hat back here and now.

When Lyons brandished his knife and approached Shelton, saying, "You cock-eyed son of a bitch, I'm going to *make* you kill me," most of the two-dozen patrons were already rushing the front door so that only a few, including the bartenders, remained to witness the final moments of the gutter drama play itself out to the inevitable finale: Shelton shooting Lyons.

As Lyons hung on the bar with his last dying breaths, Shelton snatched his hat back, put it back on his head, and strode out of the saloon saying, "Nigger, I told you give me my hat!"

The next part of the tale reads in fairly predictable fashion: the police arrest Shelton and an ensuing inquest (complete with the witnesses, a girlfriend, an angry mob of three hundred blacks outside the Dickensian courthouse demanding Shelton's neck as police held them back with weapons drawn, and even Lyons's cold dead body lying on a marble slab) results in an indictment, then a trial (complete with a

brilliant but dissipated lawyer and a shady judge), and, eventually, a murder conviction with a twenty-five-year sentence in the Missouri State Penitentiary at Jefferson City.

By the time Shelton was paroled on Thanksgiving 1909, his exploits had been long transformed into song. He may have even heard one or two of them himself as he began employment as a yard worker at St. Louis' Benevolent Order of Peerless Knights, Othello Lodge No. 1. But he couldn't stay straight. Less than two years later, he was back in the joint for having robbed and beaten a man. This last stay, however, was destined to be a short one. Shelton, ailing with tuberculosis, was quickly wasting away, and he died in the prison hospital on March 11, 1912.

Much of the key to understanding and grasping the importance of "Stack A Lee" can also be gleaned from knowledge of Billy Lyons, the alleged "victim" celebrated in the song. Born in Missouri in 1864, Lyons came from a respectable, well-to-do family and was employed as either a levee hand or watchman by the time the 1895 holiday season rolled around. But while many versions of the "Stack A Lee" ballad contain a verse at least referencing his wife (often depicted begging "mean ol'" Stag to have mercy and spare poor Billy's life) and two children, Lyons was unmarried with three children the night he stepped into the Curtis saloon.

And Lyons had some history with Shelton, too: a relative of Lyons had killed a friend of Lee's in another Deep Morgan bucket-of-blood some years before; the idea that this slaying played into the men's emotions that fateful Christmas night cannot be discounted. Of greater significance were the men's political affiliation. Lyons and his family were connected with the area Republicans who were in the middle stages of reforming the red-light district and weeding the rougher, undesirable elements from its environs. Shelton, not merely a pimp but a club owner and fairly major player in the local human misery racket, could not have been too pleased with the prospect of having his livelihood and lifestyle taken away from him. Indeed, he may have seen red when he saw Lyons at the bar.

Interestingly, it was William Lyons, not Lee Shelton, who was known to the area's constables as "Billy the Bully"—a rowdy from a good family who had once terrorized the patrons of the Curtis saloon with a long, double-edged blade. That the roles have been altered as the song evolved is one of the more curious attributes not only of the folk process, but in the societal roles played by both men as perceived in the popular culture.

What of the name "Stack A Lee" and its myriad variations? Confusion reigned from the outset: the December 29, 1895, edition of the *St. Louis Star-Sayings* refers to Lee Shelton as "Stag" Lee; the coroner's report calls him "Stack" Lee. Most of the early research on the subject traces the source to a Mississippi River steamer called the "Stack Lee" owned by the aforementioned Memphis family named Lee or to a beloved black steamboat captain named Stack Lee as popular choices. But the word "stack" also has its gambling connotations as in arranging the sequence of a deck of cards before dealing for the purposes of cheating and, perhaps more saliently, in "Stag Craps"—a style of craps games that may have figured in the creation of the ballad as the dice game appears in so many of the versions as the contest in which Lee wagered and lost his beloved chapeau.

Songcatcher Alan Lomax was among the first to disseminate the "Stack A Lee" myth and, incorrect or not, his writings on the subject in his book *Folk Songs of North America* are worth a look: "The men who ran the river were hard guys. Memphis was their capital city, and the murder rate in Memphis has been one of the highest in the world as long as there have been comparative statistics in this field. No one can be quite certain who the original Stagolee was, whether black or white, whether a Memphis gambler or a hard-headed river runner." Folklorist, collector, and writer Shields McIlwaine in *Memphis Down in Dixie* (New York: EP Dutton, 1948) tells of Stack Lee, a dashing Confederate cavalryman, son of a Mississippi river captain, a skull-cracking steamboat officer, and the father of many mulatto babies; one of his Negro sons, Jim Stack Lee, was, according to McIlwaine, the bad-eyed killer about whom the rousters sang . . .

> Stack-o-Lee's in the bend,
> Ain't doin' nothin' but killin' good men . . .

Others say that the bad man was a rouster named after the famous steamboat 'Stack-o-Lee'—others that he was a tough Memphis sport, who had sold his soul to the Devil in return for a magic Stetson hat. However, the facts are less important than the legend of the Negro bully and the killer, who proves the virility of the group by defying all the conventions of the society which imprisons him. To a dying man who begs for mercy, Stagolee responds, 'Die, damn it and prove it!' There was only one destination for such a hero . . .

> Stagolee went down to Hell, lookin' might curious,
> The Devil says, 'Here's that sport from East St. Loui-ous.'

But Stagolee felt right at home in Hell. After all, he had lived there all his life. He passed out ice-water to everybody in the place and turned the dampers down to make it more comfortable for all his ex-Memphis pals. Then he romped to West Hell, where it was

S

hot enough to suit him, snatched up the Devil's pitchfork and hollered . . .

> 'Listen, Tom Devil, you an' me's gonna have some fun,
> You play on your cornet, and Black Betty, you beat the drum.'

The riverboats were known as dens of prostitution and other vices—a natural place for a cad like Lee Shelton to conduct a little business. Either way, the epithet "Stack Lee" would have suited him admirably. And adopting a stylish, aggressive moniker was and remains a common signifying practice among African-Americans—more than a bit similar to the modern hip-hop artists who adopt stage names like Fifty Cent instead of using their own. Or maybe even to a twenty-year-old (circa 1961) Jewish Minnesotan cribbing a name from a romantic Welsh poet.

But the variations of "Stagger Lee" with a "g" are also quite prevalent in the song's titular journey. The word Stag has connections to the era's Democratic party, with which Lee was, as mentioned, at least tangentially (if not deeply) associated. But the word "Stag," with its associations to both the black community ("Buck Town" or "Stagg Town"—as in first a young male deer and later young black men—were common nineteenth- and early twentieth-century terms referring to American "Negro" settlements) and notions of male sexual potency (as in "stag parties" or "stag films") are likely sources for the nickname. And that pictures and heads of stags or their antlers adorned many an elegant late 1800s bordello connects the word not only to Lee Shelton's primary occupation but to his haberdashery as well—adventures that may well have come to symbolize his potency and power.

Yes, the infamous Stetson hat, like Charlie Kane's lost sleigh "Rosebud" or Queequeg's prophetic coffin in *Moby Dick*, emerges as the central symbol in every permutation of the Stack A Lee mytho/legend. Lee Shelton's hat was a vital aspect of his personal projection in the rough-and-ready crowd that visited the mixed-race "black and tan" joints he frequented. Dress among the St. Louis sports was unique and their high-stakes style wars were the stuff of controversy decades before the first zoot suiters strutted their stuff on L.A.'s Central Avenue and nearly a century before a hip-hopper turned his Oakland Raiders cap backward for the first time. Copying their perceptions of fashions from Paris' West Bank and combining it with specifically American accouterments like a colored Stetson hat with a high felt crown—brim slightly rolled—would have been perfectly natural for a St. Louis mack.

In *Stagolee Shot Billy* (Cambridge, Mass.: Harvard University Press, 2003), a monumental and absolutely *essential* 2003 book deconstructing "Stack A Lee" from every conceivable viewpoint (historical, social, political, cultural, racial, musical, etc.), author Cecil Brown brings a novelist's touch to his subject. He even devotes a whole chapter to Dylan's rendition. Regarding the importance of the hat in the culture of the era and the fabric of the song, Brown wrote, "Although there is no mention in the eyewitness reports of the kind of hat being fought over, the first singer of the ballad may well have assumed that it was a Stetson, since it was typical of Chestnut Valley. The Stetson was the archetypal western hat; in the 1890s its inventor had christened it 'Boss of the Plains.' In that era it was a mark of highest status for blacks, coming to represent black St. Louis itself."

Going on to connect the hat as both a Jungian-style archetype and a Freudian symbol of male genitalia, Brown summarizes his discussion of the hat by writing, "Thus knocking off someone's hat also symbolizes his castration.

Black male culture adds a fatal measure of determinism to such symbolism, such that a black man must kill anyone who challenges his masculinity. This is why in most versions the refrain says that Stagolee was '*bound* to take Billy's life,' conveying a sense of inevitability."

Dylan's use of the hat is worth a mention here. Certainly it is a visual prop that he has used from his ragamuffin days as a Dinkytown folkie in 1960 as depicted on the front and back cover of his first album, the back cover *Bringing It All Back Home* photos with him under a gray top hat, tipping his hat on the cover of *Nashville Skyline*, the flower-bedecked ten-gallon Rolling Thunder model circa 1975, the gypsy head scarf of Rolling Thunder '76, the famous black top hat under which he performed at the 1978 Blackbushe concert, the Guthriesque straw version during tour '84, the yarmulkes and tefillin of Jewish orthodoxy adopted and shed, right through his on-and-off use of hats of many descriptions during the long and winding Never Ending Tour (including high-profile media attention–getters like the Lifetime Achievement Grammy Award, the Papal concert, and the Oscar appearance via satellite). Finally, a glance at the front and back covers of *World Gone Wrong*, the Dylan tableaux of mostly traditional and sometimes archaic folk songs on which his sole recording of "Stack A Lee" appears, brings the connection all the way back to Bill Curtis's. The front cover shows Dylan, top hat teetering perilously on his head, looking a bit like a deer in the headlights as he sits in what could pass for a postmodern, surreal version of Billy Lyons waiting to meet his maker in the back of the Curtis tavern. The back cover sports a more vicious-appearing, blood-in-his-eyes Dylan playing the role of mean ol' Stag peering ahead and surveying his prey from under the wide-brimmed shadow of a tan Stetson.

Given that St. Louis was the hub for ragtime (the era's musical rage), it is possible, if not probable, that the Stagger Lee ballad was originally a ragtime tune. St. Louis native Tom Turpin (1873–1922), a friend of ragtime deity Scott Joplin and an important ragtime pianist and composer in his own right ("Harlem Rag" being his first and still most famous piece), signed a petition supporting the commutation of Lee Shelton's sentence, so he was most certainly familiar with the case if not also having a hand in the creation of its first musical expression. But the story also mingled with and then supplanted what was known as "The Bully Song," a popular bordello toast (a spoken, chanted or sung barb meant to alternately praise and insult) that covered some of the same theatrical ground as "Stack A Lee" before merging first with work songs and then the country blues. The Lomaxes thought that the earliest known version of "Stagger Lee" dated back to the early twentieth century when it was "sung by Negroes on the Memphis levee while they were loading and unloading the river freighters," the words being "composed by the singers," according to a letter they received from a Texas woman.

In this way, "Stack A Lee" can be seen as a kind of not-so-missing link between the call-and-response slave chants that can be traced directly to Africa's storytelling or "griot" tradition and its evolution in Anglo-influenced musical forms like ragtime, blues and, eventually, jazz.

While the early versions of "Stagger Lee" find justice being duly meted, the tale was embellished over time to empower Stag with superhuman powers and/or portray him as the owner of a soul darker than even Beelzebub's. The Stetson hat (some versions imbue it with the most powerful mojo), the particular game being gambled (cards or craps), the number of children Billy's death left fatherless (two through five), and the police's willingness or unwillingness to pursue the accused are all variables in the song which transmogrify in the most delightfully outlandish ways. The only constant would seem to be the awe and dread in which Stagger Lee is held and, of course, the fabled hat. The legendary figure is said by some renditions to be so evil that the devil won't let him in Hell.

Gertrude "Ma" Rainey, Furry Lewis, and Mississippi John Hurt recorded very different but equally influential takes on the legend in the mid-1920s. Hurt's "Stagolee" had the biggest impact on the succeeding generation of Southern bluesmen and was a virtual counterpart for Dylan's 1992 recording even though he claimed Frank Hutchinson's 1927 version from Harry Smith's *Anthology of American Folk Music*—the Rosetta Stone (or was that Odetta Stone?) of modern folk music—as his source. Woody Guthrie recorded the song in a 1940s version that appears to have inspired the Grateful Dead's poet-at-large Robert Hunter, who extended the yarn in 1978 so that Billy's wife wreaks revenge by wading through the dead man's blood to enforce the code of Hamurabi tooth-for-a-tooth, eye-for-an-eye style. As fodder for the popular culture, New Orleans maestro Lloyd Price took a horn-heavy raging rock-and-roll rendition of "Stagger Lee" to No. 1 on both the R&B and pop charts in 1958 but had to rewrite the storyline to tone down the violence for that year's appearance on television's *American Bandstand*. The Wilson Pickett and Tommy Roe soul revivals in 1967 and 1971 respectively were the last time "Stagger Lee" has overtly impacted the popular consciousness, but it continues to be recorded, ensuring and confirming that its murky impulses still color the American psyche. This has manifested itself in everything from James Bald-

win's introspective poem "Stagger Lee Wonders" to a tame Broadway musical, to Stagger Lee's being, in Cecil Brown's words, "an invisible hero" of hip-hop. From Jack Johnson to Muhammad Ali and Hurricane Carter, from West Indian Archie to Nicky Barnes, from Sojourner Truth to Marcus Garvey to Martin Luther King Jr. to Malcolm X to Al Sharpton, from Sidney Bechet and Paul Robeson to Tupac Shakur, from John Henry to O.J., the specter of Stag Lee and his necessary defiance looming in the back alley shadows never seems too far away.

In his 1996 article "Stagger Lee," published in *Mojo* No. 25, Greil Marcus (who had already written extensively and quite admirably on the subject in his book *Mystery Train*) boiled down the song and legend thusly: "In the blues, Stack changed names, but little else. He was the Crawling Kingsnake; Tommy Johnson pouring Sterno down his throat, singing 'Canned heat, canned heat is killing me'; Muddy Waters's cool and elemental Rollin' Stone; Chuck Berry's Brown-Eyed Handsome Man; Bo Diddley with a tombstone hand and a graveyard mind; Wilson Pickett's Midnight Mover; Mick Jagger's Midnight Rambler. . . . When the civil rights movement got tough, [Staggerlee] took over. And Staggerlee would come roaring back to the screen in the '70s as Slaughter, Sweet Sweetback, Superfly."

But why not let Bob Dylan have the last words on "Stack A Lee." As he wrote in his *World Gone Wrong* liner notes, "what does the song say exactly? it says no man gains immortality thru public acclaim. truth is shadowy. in the pre-postindustrial age, victims of violence were allowed (in fact it was their duty) to be judges over their offenders—parents were punished for their children's crimes (we've come a long way since then) the song says that a man's hat is his crown."

S "Stand by Me" (Charles Albert Tindley)
aka "Oh Lord, Stand by Me"
Elvis Presley, *Elvis Gospel 1957–71* (1989)
Original Five Blind Boys of Alabama, *Oh Lord, Stand by Me* (1991)
Ernest Tubbs, *Let's Say Goodbye Like We Said Hello* (1991)
Various Artists (performed by Lou Bell Johnson), *Wade in the Water, Volume II—African American Congregational Singing: Nineteenth-Century Roots* (1994)
Mavis Staples, *Spirituals and Gospel: Dedicated to Mahalia Jackson* (1996)

Dylan only performed this gospel song (*not* the same tune popularized by Ben E. King and by the effective 1989 adolescent buddy flick starring the late River Phoenix) at one 1990 concert—a sleepy, tentative rendition of a song taken to great spiritual heights by the Original Five Blind Boys of Alabama. Copyrighted in 1905, Dr. C. A. Tindley's "Stand by Me" is second only to Thomas Andrew Dorsey's "Precious Lord" in gospel music popularity. Tindley was founder of the Tindley Methodist Church in Philadelphia, where blues singer Bessie Smith was buried in 1937. Dorsey (*see* "Peace in the Valley") was inspired by Tindley to pursue gospel music as a calling.

Widely regarded as one of the founding fathers of American gospel music, Tindley (born July 7, 1851, Berlin, Maryland; died July 26, 1933, Philadelphia, Pennsylvania) represents so much of this country's best kind of history. Born a slave, he taught himself how to read as a teenager when the Civil War was anything but a distant memory in the national psyche. His family moved to Philadelphia, where he worked as janitor at the Calvary Methodist Episcopal Church while attending night school, eventually earning his divinity degree through a correspondence course with the Boston Theological Seminary. In an amazing irony he became the pastor of the very same church at

which he had been a janitor. Over the next three decades he built up the church's membership to more than 10,000 and made frequent nationwide tours. Ever popular, Tindley was awarded the degree of Doctor of Divinity by Bennett College in North Carolina. Tindley wrote nearly forty hymns in his lifetime, which, at their best, draw on the call-and-response tradition of black spirituals and are characterized by memorable lyrics couched in simple melodies. His "I'll Overcome Some Day" was a basis for the American civil rights anthem "We Shall Overcome," popularized in the 1960s.

S "Standing in the Doorway" (Bob Dylan)
Bob Dylan, *Time out of Mind* (1997)

One of those cliché-steeped, on-the-prowl country ballads that manage to ring true *and* sound fresh, Dylan only started performing "Standing in the Doorway" in the summer of 2000—nearly three years after its release on *Time out of Mind.*

Another latter-day Dylan mélange, "Standing in the Doorway" may draw on a Jessie Mae Hemphill 1980 gut-bucket blues lament ("Standing in My Doorway Crying") for its title, and perhaps its got-done-wrong-down-on-my-luck lover narrative tone. Dylan may also crib his lyric "the stars have turned cherry red" from Big Joe Turner's 1939 and 1956 recordings of a song titled "Cherry Red," and the image of the narrator "Smokin' a cheap cigar" could be from any one of a number of variants of Jimmie Rodgers's "Waiting for a Train." "Cherry Red" was also used by the Rolling Stones as a symbol of blood and sexuality in "You Can't Always Get What You Want" and the title of this Dylan song is vaguely reminiscent of the Stones' "Have You Seen Your Mother, Baby, Standing in the Shadows?" Dylan's line "Buddy, you'll roll no more" recalls both the Ramblin'

S

Jack Elliott/Derroll Adams 1956 LP "Roll On, Buddy" and "Buddy Won't You Roll Down the Line," a seminal Uncle Dave Macon 1928 track appearing on *The Anthology of American Folk Music*. And the mention of the "midnight train" is, at the very least, a reminder of Jim Weatherly's "Midnight Train to Georgia" as made famous by Gladys Knight and the Pips. Finally, Dylan's "Blues wrapped around my head" is an edited allusion to the ubiquitous blues phrase "blues around my head."

All allusion and its resonant metaphor aside, "Standing in the Doorway" can be placed in the mini "Dylan in Nighttown" oeuvre that goes back at least as far as "One Too Many Mornings" in 1964, continued with "Where Are You Tonight?" in 1978 and "Something is Burning" in 1985. These are songs in which the narrator, in some pitch of love-soured fever, wanders the city's streets in search of romantic/spiritual deliverance that will, in the end, be denied. Here, the camera begins rolling on a man aimlessly strolling in the midst of a thick summer nocturne—a time and place recalling at least a couple of other *Time out of Mind* songs, "Not Dark Yet" and the opening lines of "Love Sick"—that gives the whole affair a sense of unity. Music filters from the jukebox in a diner or café he passes, singing to a woman who is evidently not present ("Don't know if I saw you/If I would kiss you or kill you"). He's not making any bones about his evidently homeless situation: since his woman left him standing' in the doorway cryin', his mind has been clearly out of time.

As the song progresses, the action appears to move inside, where, in the cheap cigar haze of some juke joint, our po' boy is seeing cherry-red stars while strumming his gay guitar—an image that recalls Picasso's absinthe-haunted painting, "Man with a Blue Guitar." But whether he is performing on stage or noodling in the corner, he can't shake the "ghost of our old love." The singer continues but vows not to tell tales on his ex-lover even as he addresses her in a manner reminiscent of Dylan's old "Eternal Circle," in which he unsuccessfully woos a potential amour from the stage. This small ray of humor and hope and the hollow boasts ("Got ice water in my vein/It would be crazy if I took you back/It would go up against every rule") help "Standing in the Doorway" stand apart from most of the rest of *Time out of Mind*, which is so mired in the muck and stench of permanent decay.

A bit later he hears the sound of church bells and wonders for whom they toll, suggesting that he has put another anxious all-nighter under his belt. He seems to be coming to terms with the end of all things, be they relationships or life itself. Even though he danced with a stranger, he vows to live his life right and move on with dignity and grace.

▣ "Stealin'" (Traditional)
aka "Stealin' Stealin'"
Memphis Jug Band, *Memphis Jug Band—Double Album*/'28 (1990)
Dave Van Ronk, *Dave Van Ronk & Ragtime Jug Stompers* (1960)
Jesse Fuller, *San Francisco Bay Blues* (1963)
The Grateful Dead, *The Golden Road (1965–1973)*/'66 (2002)
Arlo Guthrie, *Running Down the Road* (1969)
Jim Kweskin, *Jim Kweskin's America* (1971)
Taj Mahal, *Happy to Be Just Like I Am* (1971)
Dr. John, *Destively Bonaroo* (1974)
Jerry Garcia/David Grisman, *Shady Grove* (1996)

Forty years before he admitted to love and theft, Dylan was performing "Stealin'"—a randy jug band relic that probably dates back to the nineteenth century. The song was first released as a so-called "race" record in 1928 when it was cut by the Memphis Jug Band, one of the most popular and influential black jug bands spawned in the middle South in the pre-Depression. Led by Will Shade (born February 5, 1898, Memphis, Tennessee; died September 18, 1966, Memphis, Tennessee) on a bass made from a garbage can, a broom handle, and a string—and comprised at various times and in various configurations of premier Hawaiian-style guitarist/vocalist Will Weldon, "Shakey Walter" Horton on harmonica, vocalist Hattie Hart, jug-blowers Hambone Lewis, Charlie Polk, and Jab Jones, Vol Stephens on banjo and mandolin, kazoo player Ben Ramey, and others—the Memphis Jug Band possessed a light, often sweet musical sensibility that was the reverse of the deep country blues gurgling out of the Mississippi Delta at the time, belying the dark nature of some of their most famous songs: "Cocaine Habit Blues," "He's in the Jailhouse Now," "Insane Crazy Blues," and "I Whipped My Woman with a Single Tree." By giving the blues a softer touch, the Memphis Jug Band ensured that traditional blues didn't drown in its own melancholia and desperation.

Shade (aka Son or Sun Brimmer for his ubiquitous wide-brimmed chapeau) was the group's guiding force and played in a spin-off of the original unit right up to his death. Like the bands led by Noah Lewis and Gus Cannon—other popular jug gurus who also recorded in the late 1920s and early 1930s—Shade provided his band with a hodgepodge of a repertoire that easily mingled blues, jazz, folk, rag, novelty, and pop songs, enhancing them with the sleight-of-hand flair of the minstrel and tent shows at which they undoubtedly appeared. They assuredly performed at local events and were a popular attraction at Church Park (now W. C. Handy Park) in Memphis. Under the guidance of Howard Yancey's Beale Street management outfit, the Memphis Jug Band found themselves booked at some of the city's more tony events and venues, like the Chickasaw Country Club, the Hunt Polo Club, and conventions at the Peabody Hotel. Edward H. Crump, the onetime Memphis mayor, local political boss, and proverbial man in the smoky back rooms, hired them for private parties and fundraisers. Later they were also hired by food stands and restaurants as a promotional attraction, even playing on the back of flatbed trucks advertising Colonial Bread and Schlitz Beer.

Despite heavy competition from rival jug bands (some of whose members included the likes of Furry Lewis and Sleepy John Estes) picking up on the craze, the Memphis Jug Band was the most recorded of the local combos, recording over sixty playful, eye-rolling, infectiously sly sides for Victory between 1927 and 1930. By the time of their last recordings for Okeh/Vocalion in Chicago in 1934, the final Memphis Jug Band sides displayed a jazzier sound. The Great Depression hit Memphis hard. It had long been a hub for murder, prostitution, and gambling; and when the gin joints and brothels were finally rousted out of existence by police crackdowns, the jug band era was at an end. This did not stop Shade, who, along with guitarist Charlie Burse, continued to put together jug bands through at least part of the 1940s before the instrument's eventual rediscovery by bluesologist Samuel Charters.

The title of "Stealin'" may appear misleading at first. One listen, however, is all one needs to discover that the stolen item is not exactly of material value. Rather, it is the virtue of a woman, most often already betrothed. The song is also chock full of those famous stock folk blues words and phrases like "easy rider" and "put your arms around me like a circle 'round the sun."

The rerelease of the Memphis Jug Band's "Stealin'" in the early 1960s inspired an appreciation for their funky, accessible sound. Discovering that jug band music was as much fun to perform as it was to listen to, urban practitioners soon sprang up, including New York's Even Dozen Jug Band, the Jim Kweskin Jug Band from Boston, and the San Francisco area's Mother McCree's Uptown Jug Champions—the proto–jug band version of the Grateful Dead.

"Stealin'" was a frequent Dylan vehicle in his earliest gigs and was rehearsed with the Grateful Dead in the spring of 1987.

[S] **"Steel Bars"** (Bob Dylan/Michael Bolton)

Michael Bolton, *Time, Love and Tenderness* (1991)
Various Artists (performed by Michael Bolton), *Doin' Dylan 2* (2002)

"Steel Bars" was cowritten by Dylan and—get this—pop schlockmeister Michael Bolton. Anyway, that's what it said on the CD jacket even if the song, a very watered-down lonely-heart croon following the theme of the metaphorically caged victim of "She Belongs to Me," wasn't one of the best associated with Bob. Those steel bars, in case you haven't figured it out already, are wrapped around the singer/prisoner's heart. It did, for better or worse, indicate that Bolton might have possibilities, thus far unnoticed, for Dylan's continued (if on-again, off-again) interest in doing the Tin Pan Alley strut.

Still, no matter how you slice it, "Steel Bars" is one of Dylan's more unlikely collaborations. But, like many of these type of creations, it came about rather casually.

[S] **"Stepchild"** (Bob Dylan/Helena Springs)

aka "Am I Your Stepchild?," "(You Treat Me Like a) Stepchild"
See also "If I Don't Be There by Morning"
Solomon Burke, *Don't Give Up on Me* (2002)

Written with Helena Springs (one of his backup singers for a couple of years), "Stepchild" is a slithering, Howlin' Wolf–styled blues with a intimate club feel in the familiar accusation-lament pattern that recalls (but pales against) everything from the B. B. King vehicle "How Blue Can You Get" to Blind Willie McTell's "Death Cell Blues" (and similarly mordant blues from the Mississippi flood lands). Marked by Steve Douglas's accompaniment on saxophone, Dylan performed "Stepchild" extensively and exclusively during the last leg of his 1978 Vegas-style tour.

Speaking of his use of "Stepchild" and other covers on his above-listed comeback album, Solomon Burke addressed the song's personal nature, saying, "I have twenty-one children and sixty-three grandchildren, and I believe that when you marry into a family, that's your family. That song is tapping into me, that's what's so phenomenal and how freaked out I am that these people knew something about me mentally and spiritually that they could write these songs."

As if to prove the adage that the cream always rises to the top, Burke's rendition of "Stepchild" was nominated for a W. C. Handy Blues award for 2002's best blues song of the year.

S

[S] **"Step It Up and Go"** (Traditional/Blind Boy Fuller)

See also "Weeping Willow"
aka "Oil It Up and Go," "Touch It Up and Go"
Bob Dylan, *World Gone Wrong* (1992)
Blind Boy Fuller, *Complete Recorded Works, Volume 5 (1938–1941)* (1992)
Black Cats and The Kitten, *Roots N' Blues: The Retrospective 1925–1950/'40* (1992)
John Hammond, *John Hammond* (1963)
Brownie McGhee, *Complete Brownie McGhee* (1994)

Dylan had great, if unambitious, fun on *World*

Gone Wrong when he transformed this old gut-bucket dance song probably derived from the more common "Bottle It Up and Go," a favorite dating back to the jug band heyday, into an acoustic rocker. Think "The Groom's Still Waiting at the Altar" with a country blues twist. There is some history to the song. Blind Boy Fuller historians believe that Fuller's manager, J. B. Long, heard a version of "Step It Up and Go" in Memphis in the late 1930s and rewrote it for Fuller and Sonny Terry; their recording of it became a huge country blues hit at the time. The Black Cats and the Kitten also presented an early example of "Step It Up and Go" in an arrangement that would shortly come to be called rhythm and blues in 1940—the kind of music other cats like Willie Dixon would butter their bread with.

S "Stone Walls and Steel Bars" (Ray Marcum/Ray Pennington)
Stanley Brothers, *Hills of Roan County* (1998)
Ralph Stanley and Friends, *Clinch Mountain Country* (1998)

Dylan first performed this bluegrass ode to the Big House (and indeed all prisons of the body and soul) at the May 22, 1997, Simon Wiesenthal Center dinner benefiting Holocaust issues and began including it in his concerts semi-regularly for the next few years. After a hiatus in 2001, Dylan brought "Stone Walls" back for his 2002 summer tour for a show in Baltimore on the fringes of the bluegrass country in which the song was planted, grown, and sown.

Though the Stanley Brothers are most closely associated with "Stone Walls and Steel Bars," it was written by a couple of lesser-known country music lights. The better known, Ray Pennington (born 1933, Clay County, Kentucky), began his career as a sixteen-year-old guitar player on Cincinnati television before joining the band Bluestone with Jerry McBee

and the Mid-West Rhythm Boys—his own Bob Wills–styled western swing band. When popularity in bluegrass waned in the late 1950s, they became an R&B outfit.

But it was as a songwriter and A&R man that he made his biggest mark. "Three Hearts in a Tangle," "Walking on New Grass," and "Ramblin' Man" are, along with "Stone Walls and Steel Bars," his more famous compositions. And as a Nashville A&R man he worked with Hank Thompson, Faron Young, and Waylon Jennings. Most recently, he has been at the helm of Step One Records, a well-respected independent label where his work with steel guitar master Buddy Emmons on a series of country swing albums has been widely noted.

S "The Story of East Orange, New Jersey"
(Bob Dylan)

Recounting his trip to the East Coast via this piece of autobiographical talking folk, the *young* Bobby Dylan must have gotten a lot of mileage out of the tale when he played it for friends during a brief visit back in his home state (as one December 1961 recording attests) and on the Greenwich Village folkie circuit on which he also must have showcased it at the time.

Street Legal
Columbia Records LP JC-35453; CD CK-35453; CS PCT-35453; Sony Music Entertainment, Inc., SACD 90338. Recorded at Rundown Studios, Los Angeles, California, April 1978. Released June 15, 1978. Produced by Don Devito. Photography by Howard Alk. Liner notes by Bob Dylan.

Bob Dylan—guitar, harmonica, keyboards, vocals. Steve Douglas—saxophones. Les Cooper—engineer, keyboards, vocals. Bob Hall—percussion. Bobbye Hall—percussion. Steven Soles—guitar, background vocals. Billy Cross—guitar. Biff Dawes—engineer. Carolyn Dennis—vocals. Jo Ann Harris—vocals. Steve Madaio—trumpet. David Mansfield—guitar, mandolin, violin. Alan Pasqua—keyboards. Jerry Scheff—bass, guitar. Helena Springs—vocals. Ian Wallace—drums.

"Changing of the Guards," "New Pony," "No Time to Think," "Baby Stop Crying," "Is Your Love in Vain," "Señor (Tales of Yankee Power)," "True Love Tends to Forget," "We Better Talk This Over," "Where Are You Tonight? (Journey Through Dark Heat)"

Ready to hit the road for a world tour in 1978 after spending months in the editing room with his film *Renaldo & Clara*, Dylan rehearsed and put together a large eight-piece band (plus three backup singers) he could perform and record with. They were perfect to tackle both the richly textured new songs he began writing and the exotic, if sometimes hit-and-miss, rearrangements of his older material. After a series of concerts in Japan and Australia, Dylan and crew spent two weeks recording *Street Legal* before resuming their globetrot.

Here Dylan presents a group of songs as impressionistic and acidic as his material from the mid-1960s. The tone poem "Changing of the Guards," the apocalyptically desperate "Señor," and the Beat-style lone wolf prowl "Where Are You Tonight?" are among the notable songs here but all of the material hangs together well, if not memorably.

Despite some medium-cool success (*Street Legal* made it to No. 11 during its two-month stay on the charts en route to earning Dylan his thirteenth gold album), the release commenced Dylan's five-year descent into the commercial depths and came on the heels of the misunderstood film *Renaldo & Clara*, as well as a messy, public divorce, and just before the fervent "born-again Christian" phase which lost him critical and popular support.

It was as if critics were waiting in the alley, knives sharpened.

The album has actually aged quite well (especially after a remix in 1999), and his performances of the material during the best parts of his 1978 world tour truly shined.

A final note: the album is dedicated to Emmett Grogan, an elusive '60s character who has achieved near-mythic status in the radical underground. Poet, radical, and novelist (he lays it *all* out in *Ringolivio*, his devastatingly dark, must-read semi-autobiographical phantasm of a novel), Grogan was a force behind San Francisco's Diggers, whose Robin Hood–style approach to local social politics ignited the hippie migration to that city in the mid- to late 1960s. Dylan swung past Grogan's Montreal pad during the Rolling Thunder tour in 1975, and Grogan was one of the MCs at the Band's *The Last Waltz* in 1976. He died somewhat mysteriously on a New York City subway train in 1978.

[S] "Stuck Inside of Mobile (with the Memphis Blues Again)" (Bob Dylan)

Bob Dylan, single (1975); *Blonde on Blonde* (1966); *Bob Dylan's Greatest Hits Volume II* (1971); *Hard Rain* (1976)
The Candymen, *The Candymen Bring You Candypower* (1968)
Steve Colt, *Paradox* (1970)
Thomas Helmig, *Thomas Helmig* (1992)
Catbird Seat, *The Times They Are A-Changin'* (1992)
The Zimmermen, *The Dungeon Tapes* (1995)
Moon Martin, *Lunar Samples* (1995)
Steve Gibbons, *The Dylan Project* (1998)
The Grateful Dead, *Nightfall of Diamonds* (2001); *Postcards of the Hanging: The Grateful Dead Perform the Songs of Bob Dylan* (2002)
Various Artists (performed by Joe Louis Walker), *Blues on Blonde on Blonde* (2003)

"Stuck Inside of Mobile (with the Memphis Blues Again)," a lucid, Looney Toon epic of rock 'n' roll hipster impressionism starring Dylan's kooky stock characters, remains an uproarious tableau etched in midnight blue

S

Dylan performing at the Blackbushe Pop Festival, Hampshire, England, July 17, 1978.

(Photo: Express Newspapers/Getty Images)

satin of a world gone terribly wrong. Dylan's exuberant musical score counters the cyclone of his Beat-style poetry as he mixes elation and despair in the martini shaker of his soul.

The narrator travels in obtuse territory here. Whether crossing paths with Shakespeare in an alley, a double-dealing senator with some dangerous connections, a strangely attired preacher, or a girl named Ruthie who tries to woo him to her honky-tonk lagoon, the chances of surviving any encounter unscathed are iffy at best. More than likely, he will down a lethal dose of Texas medicine, have his cigarette punched, or be clobbered with a brick by one of those neon madmen roaming Grand Street. And let's not forget to mention Mona, the circle-sketching ragman, mama and grandpa, the preacher, the railroad men, or the rainman . . . this is one Dylan song where you practically need a scorecard to keep up with the quickly shifting sands of lyrical surrealisms. But buried deep beneath the waves of his gallows humor are the themes consistent with his

work of the period: suspicion of authority figures, solicitous females, and a confused, persecuted, and possibly intoxicated narrator. In other words, if he was lucky enough to pass through the Gates of Eden and/or make it down Desolation Row and back in one piece, he better abandon all hope as he enters Mobile humming his fateful blues.

In seven incandescent minutes Dylan stuffs nine antic verses with enough action to make Joe Friday feel like he's dropped a hit of LSD and taken a wrong turn on Rue Morgue Avenue. Each verse recounts a preposterous microvignette portraying modern dislocation. In the first stanza, our narrator is rendered mute by the aforementioned mute ragman while falling under the spell of some women who feel like they've emerged like the nine muses of ancient Greek lore from the shadows of another century. Next he encounters Shakespeare in the alley dressed like a foppish 1960s pop star deep in conversation with a French girl (perhaps a reference to the romantic song made famous not too long before by Ian and Sylvia) whose claims of acquaintance with the narrator spike his paranoia quotient—a feeling reinforced by the news that the post office has been stolen and mailbox locked. Mona (recalling Bo Diddley's swamp vixen) takes center stage in verse three, warning our little boy lost to beware of the railroad men who drink blood like wine for mere sport. Foolishly brazen, the singer comes back with the absurd boast of his only experience with one such gentleman: "he just smoked my eyelids/An' punched my cigarette."

But things only get more crazed: Grandpa's pyromania and subsequent death are coolly recounted; the corrupt, ingratiating senator displays his weapons fetishism and nepotism while freezing out the narrator with ill intent; the clueless, dogmatic preacher oblivious to the twenty pounds of headlines stapled to his chest; the rain man who lures our guy into overdoing it with doses of Texas medicine and railroad gin that appear to permanently warp his already whacked-out perspective and grip on things; down in the honky-tonk lagoon, Ruthie tries to take advantage of his intoxicated state by coaxing him into some earthy relief from his rich gal pal: "Your debutante knows what you need/But I know what you want." Symmetry of some kind seems to return by the song's conclusion on Grand Street. The singer attempts to sort out the hallucinations, reality, experiences, allusions, and delusions that have swamped him in a tidal wave of absurdity, and figure out a way to avoid enduring the whole mess again.

Old-time music enthusiasts should check out the Nite Owls' 1938 "Memphis Blues" for investigation of the song's titular roots.

Since he first performed "Stuck Inside of Mobile" with the Rolling Thunder Revue in 1976, Dylan has never stopped returning to his "Memphis Blues" for renewed and vigorous

interpretation without really matching the smooth accuracy evidenced on *Blonde on Blonde*. Still, his virtuoso performances mix gloom and rapture, each clever phrase acting as a bumper sticker for the chronically cool. Man, he made it seem easy.

"Subterranean Homesick Blues" (Bob Dylan)
Bob Dylan, single (1965); *Bringing It All Back Home* (1965); *Bob Dylan's Greatest Hits* (1967); *Don't Look Back* (film) (1967); *The Bootleg Series, Volumes 1–3: Rare and Unreleased, 1961–1991/'91* (1965)
Chas McDevitt, *16 Big Folk Hits* (1965)
Doug Kershaw, *Louisiana Man* (1971)
Michael Stanley, *Michael Stanley* (1973), *Michael Stanley Band* (1987)
Harry Nilsson, *Pussy Cats* (1974)
Mitch Ryder, *Live Talkies* (1982)
Red Hot Chili Peppers, *The Uplift Mofo Party Plan* (1987); *Under The Covers* (1998)
Fair & Gillette, *Roll Out the Barrel* (1988)
Dave Stewart and Barbara Gaskin, *Big Idea* (1989)
Janglers, *Janglers Play Dylan* (1992)
Greg Kihn, *Mutiny* (1994)
Dave Van Ronk, *To All My Friends in Far-Flung Places* (1994)
Tim O'Brien, *Red on Blonde* (1996)
Reckless Kelly, *Reckless Kelly: Live at Stubbs* (1999)
Gerard Quintana and Jordi Batiste, *Els Miralls de Dylan* (1999)
Michel Montecrossa, *Jet Pilot* (2000)
Big Brass Bed, *A Few Dylan Songs* (2003)

Who knows what people thought when they first heard "Subterranean Homesick Blues" blaring from the AM band of their transistor radios in the spring of 1965. This wasn't exactly a song made for twisting the night away. With his biting rat-a-tat-tat word burst, Dylan has a hip koan for just about every occasion somewhere in the back pocket of his chinos—just be careful not to ask.

An early, acoustic version released on *The Bootleg Series* is worth checking out and comparing with the thumping original. But it is that lead-off track to *Bringing It All Back Home* that sent a message to the folkies and anyone else who cared to listen: Bob Dylan was going electric!

Written in the apartment of John Court (an associate of Dylan's then-manager, Albert Grossman), "Subterranean Homesick Blues" will, for better or worse, forever be associated with the classic, Charlie Chaplin–esque cue card scene that opens *Don't Look Back*, D. A. Pennebaker's film verité documenting Dylan's 1965 visit to England. There, a baby-faced Dylan stands in a grim London alley holding up the big cards with words from the song, which he discards one by one.

In "Subterranean Homesick Blues," with its biting, hypnotically incanted hopscotch lyrics exploding against a sledgehammer of rock 'n' roll, Dylan declared a new musical direction with a vehemence that was taking no prisoners. Making the song the lead-off track to *Bringing It All Back Home* further underscored Dylan's commitment to conjuring the surrealistic electric muse no matter the cost. And what great, cascading lyrics this song has, with lines etched in the national lexicon as sage aphorisms cynically commenting on the politically/ religiously self-serving ("Don't follow leaders"), the rat race and higher learning ("Twenty years of schooling and they put you on the day shift"), and the media ("You don't need a weatherman to know which way the wind blows"). The latter line, of course, was later infamously and unfortunately adopted by the politically radical Weather Underground as opposition to the Vietnam War crested in the late 1960s and early 1970s. That's just how seriously some people were taking Dylan at the time.

While Dylan has a blast with the tongue-twisting word play in "Subterranean," it is one of his darkest rants against the system whose "users, cheaters, six-time losers" will twist and threaten an honest man. Like some jump-cut Keystone Kop flick played sideways at breakneck speed, Dylan's shady cast of characters includes everybody from the DA to a cough syrup–peddling dealer in a trench coat—all of them seeking to undermine our hero in a landscape of brittle paranoia Dylan soon took to even darker and more surreal extremes in such songs as "Desolation Row." The phone is tapped, women play him for a fool, and he's always just a dollar short. The song's only lyrical anchor ("Look out, kid"), repeated in the second part of every verse, is the only place of cold, No-Doze comfort for Dylan's persecuted Kafkaesque martyr.

The oddly stimulating "Subterranean Homesick Blues," which eventually rose to No. 39 on the charts, drew from two modern sources with both Chuck Berry's "Too Much Monkey Business" and the Woody Guthrie/Pete Seeger plaint "Taking It Easy" pointed to as the likely suspects in song, as Dylan created new skipping reels of rhyme and dozens shooting that would have impressed Redd Foxx ("shooting the dozens" is a form of verbal one-upmanship popularized by African Americans).

Dylan didn't touch "Subterranean" in performance until he kicked off his inaugural Never Ending Tour concerts of 1988 with the song, delivered with the maniac intensity of a fifteen-year-old punk rocker who had just picked up a Telecaster for the first time. He kept it as part of his stage show through 1991. In 2002, the song was reintroduced as urgent rockabilly—an electrified hoedown with a very different treatment with half-time rhythm and odd vocal syncopation that created a powerful and dynamic performance. And in 2003, "Subterranean" was revived for a more straightforward reading during the summer tour with the Dead.

A final note: "Subterranean Homesick Blues" would appear to be one of several Dylan songs referencing a Jack Kerouac novel in its title, in this instance *The Subterraneans*—the Beat bard's interracial love-triangle tragedy.

▣ "Sugar Baby" (Bob Dylan)
Bob Dylan, *"Love and Theft"* (2001)
Barb Jungr, *Every Grain of Sand: Barb Jungr Sings Bob Dylan* (2002)

"Sugar Baby" is a languorous lament infused with the deepest and most enveloping expression of romantic despair and, as the closing track on *"Love and Theft,"* ends an otherwise life-affirming collection on a dark tone. Here we hear the narrator carrying the torch for a woman who still provokes conflicting emotions as he admits, "Some of these memories you can learn to live with/And some of them you can't." But Dylan, singing with a ragged whisper, plays with this message to an estranged lover somewhere between a tired, final goodbye and a sardonic put-down—a common (and old) Dylan device.

"Sugar Baby" can also be heard as the triumphant dirge that forms the emotional core of *"Love and Theft."* Here, Dylan gets to play prophet yet one more time: "I got my back to the sun 'cause the light is too intense," he sings softly. "I can see what everybody in the world is up against." But he's a prophet without a plan— a poignant reality in the age of anthrax and hijacked airplanes. "Any minute of the day the bubble can burst," he warns, "You always got to be prepared, but you never know for what."

But he also sounds like a Taoist sage dressed in a gold lamé glittersuit going for the jugular with sleepy, gloomy glee: "Every moment of existence seems like some dirty trick/Happiness can come suddenly and leave just as quick. . . . Trying to make things better for someone/

Sometimes you just end up making it a thousand times worse . . . Your charms have broken many a heart and mine is surely one."

Taking a page from his breakup songs of yore like "Don't Think Twice" and "It Ain't Me, Babe," Dylan comes off at once angry and proud as he tries to say goodbye one last time: "Sugar Baby get on down the road, you ain't got no brains no how/You went years without me, might as well keep goin' now." With lines like these that can crush the listener's heart as profoundly as any from *Blood on the Tracks*, one begins to question and wonder if Dylan (or the narrator) is even singing about a woman here. Perhaps this is the song of man singing to (and cursing) the very personification of Aphrodite.

When Dylan hit the road in support of *"Love and Theft"* in the fall of 2001, "Sugar Baby" was one several songs from that album that debuted and has stayed in the set list.

▣ "Sukiyaki" (Rohusuke Ei/Hachidai Nakamura)
Kyu Sakamoto, *Sukiyaki and Other Japanese Hits* (1963)
Kenny Ball & His Jazzmen, *Midnight in Moscow* (1963)
King Curtis, *Blow Man, Blow!* (1963)
Ventures, *Surfing* (1963)
Kai Winding, *Soul Surfin'* (1963)
A Taste of Honey, *Anthology* (1995)
Cover Girls, *I Need Your Lovin'* (1997)
Little Singers of Tokyo, *Little Singers of Tokyo* (1998)

"Sukiyaki" is a surf music classic which Dylan performed at a trio of Japanese concerts with the Heartbreakers in 1986 when he hummed— rather than sang—the lyrics as a site-specific homage and goof. The song was written in 1963 by Rokusuke Ei under the Japanese title "Ue O Muite Aruko" ("Walk with Your Chin Up") and became the first U.S. No. 1 hit performed entirely in Japanese, no small feat some twenty-two years after Pearl Harbor. It is said

S

that Ei wrote the song after his heart was broken by a Japanese actress.

The song's amazing history really began when Pye Records' president, Louis Benjamin, heard Sakamoto's original "I Look Up When I Walk" recording while on a business trip to Japan and promptly had Pye artist Kenny Ball recut the song, renaming it after his favorite Japanese cuisine (and something familiar to the Western ear)—a type of broiled meat. After Kyu Sakamoto's Japanese recording of "Sukiyaki" was released in the U.S., it enjoyed enormous popularity, reaching No. 1 on the *Billboard* charts and eventually getting covered by a quirky variety of talent. Its popularity has been retained through various "techno" remixes for the rave crowd. Kyu (pronounced "cue") was one of the 520 people who died in the crash of a Japan Airlines 747 near Tokyo on August 12, 1985. He was forty-three.

"Summer Days" (Bob Dylan)
Bob Dylan, *"Love and Theft"* (2001)

A romping, rockabilly ripple with echoes of Carl Perkins and/or Chuck Berry with a smidgen of "Jumpin' Jack Flash," this merry twelve-bar blues is jubilant, jowls-full-of-words Dylan at his late best as he encourages, "Everybody get ready, lift up your glasses and sing/Well, I'm standing on the table, proposing a toast to the King."

If humor is what you're looking for, "Summer Days" has more than just about any recent Dylan song, save "Highlands," in years. His previous disc, *Time out of Mind*, found Dylan staring into the abyss, but on tracks from *"Love and Theft"* such as this, it appears as if he's concluded that, when faced with the travails of late middle age, humor is the oil of the soul.

But don't be fooled into thinking Dylan's mechanisms for the literary allusion were in need of a squirt of WD-40. The lines "She said, Ya can't repeat the past/I said, Ya can't? Whaddya mean ya can't—of course ya can!," as any Dylanologist worth his obsessive mustard can tell you, are, like "When I Paint My Masterpiece," drawn and reworked from F. Scott Fitzgerald's 1929 novel *The Great Gatsby*.

And, looking to the East, "Summer Days" was one of a few *"Love and Theft"* songs to appropriate lines from Dr. Junichi Saga's book *Confessions of a Yakuza*. Where Saga wrote, "'Break the roof in!' . . . splashed kerosene over the roof and led a fuse from it outside," Dylan sings, "I'm leavin' in the mornin' just as soon as the dark clouds lift/Gonna break the roof in—set fire to the place as a parting gift." More clearly, *Yakuza*'s "D'you think I could call myself a yakuza if I couldn't stand up to some old businessman?" is rephrased by Dylan into "What good are you anyway if you can't stand up to some old businessman?"

The primary text which Dylan appears to have reshaped, however, is the last chapter of Ecclesiastes when the preacher is speaking metaphorically about his aging body falling apart.

As has been his custom with new material, Dylan incorporated several songs from *"Love and Theft"* into his performances soon after its release, and "Summer Days" was among those he chose for live display in the fall of 2001. Within a year, it had matured to the point where the Charlie Sexton–Larry Campbell jaw-dropping double-guitar attack could make you swear a horn section had invaded the stage.

Sun City: Artists United Against Apartheid/Various Artists
Manhattan Records, ST-53019. Released 1985.

Compared with the likes of "We Are the World" (in which Dylan also participated), *Sun City* was, by definition, the most edgy and political of all of the star-studded, high-profile, consciousness-raising charity rock albums of the 1980s. Sun City, itself, is the name of a controversial resort in South Africa at which a number of A-list performing artists worked despite the country's then-unabashed segregationist Apartheid policies. Little Steven Van Zandt said, "Enough!" and wrote the justifiably angry title song, then produced this line-in-the-sand album enlisting heavyweights including Dylan, Miles Davis, Peter Gabriel, Jimmy Cliff, Bruce Springsteen, Jackson Browne, Run-D.M.C., and Lou Reed. The extremely listenable result may not have had much to do with Nelson Mandela's eventual release from prison and rise to South Africa's presidency, but it surely gained sympathy and support for the cause.

[S] "Suze (The Cough Song)" (Bob Dylan)

Bob Dylan, *The Bootleg Series, Volumes 1–3: Rare and Unreleased, 1961–1991/'63* (1991)

Though Dylan has never executed an all-instrumental album, his recorded legacy is sprinkled with non-vocal oddities such as "Turkey Chase," "Woogie-Boogie," "Wigwam," and "The Cough Song."

Presumably referencing his early '60s New York City girlfriend, Suze Rotolo, "Suze" gets its phlegmy subtitle from the extant recording wherein Dylan begins coughing at the end of the finger-picking run before claiming that the song was supposed to have ended before he began his bronchial convulsions as heard on the recording.

[S] "Sweetheart Like You" (Bob Dylan)

Bob Dylan, single (1983); *Infidels* (1983)
Tony Rice, *Me & My Guitar* (1986)
Judy Collins, *Judy Sings Dylan . . . Just Like a Woman* (1993)
Various Artists (performed by Andrew Hyra), *Tribute to Bob Dylan, Volume 1* (1994)
Jimmy LaFave, *Buffalo Return to the Plains* (1995)
Rod Stewart, *A Spanner in the Works* (1995)
The Zimmermen, *Dungeon Tapes* (1996)
Mary Cutrufello, *Songs from the 6* (2001)
Various Artists (performed by Guy Davis), *A Nod to Bob* (2001)
Various Artists (performed by Judy Collins), *Doin' Dylan 2* (2002)

Dylan caught some flak for sexism with "Sweetheart Like You," a song that can be interpreted as delivered by a condescending, if not creepy, pick-up artist on the make. He tells the woman that she should be at home where she belongs and asks her what she's "doing in a dump like this?," as if he has a better idea and no better cliché for an opening line. Others have suggested that the song be interpreted as social commentary or another, different kind of "self-portrait." And still others have commended Dylan for suggesting that *everybody* should have "somebody nice who don't know how to do you wrong." Any way you slice it, it is incredible that Dylan (or whoever) chose not only to release "Sweetheart Like You" as an A-side single (it hit No. 55 on the *Billboard* chart) but to make a video out of the song as well, his first such endeavor. And to think that the masterpiece "Blind Willie McTell" was left off *Infidels* in favor of rich but nonetheless far lesser fare like this has led many to wonder exactly who was in the driver's seat when the final *Infidels* mix was delivered post-paid to Columbia's front door.

Yet a peek at the many levels on which "Sweetheart Like You" can operate may enhance its sub-par reputation. Perhaps the first thing to note is that the dive ("the dump like this") at which the action transpires is not just your run-of-the-mill gin joint. Rather, it is the most desperate kind of bucket-of-blood, where life's cheapness can be measured by the number of goons packing iron in the backroom game of high-and-low. The allusion to a game of cards is metaphorically explored later in the song's bridge with sport's illusory qualities and possibilities as the narrator warns the naïf to whom he sings: "In order to deal in this game, got to make a queen disappear/It's done with a flick of the wrist." Indeed, a game of some kind is playing itself out through "Sweetheart Like You" but who is being played for the fool is never clear.

Early on, the singer casually tells the woman, "You know, I once knew a woman who looked like you/She wanted a whole man, not just a half/She used to call me sweet daddy when I was only a child/You kind of remind of her when you laugh." Was this the woman with whom he lost his virginity, who turned him from half a man into a whole one? Is the narrator suggesting a kind of role reversal for the scene playing out in the song? And is the woman to whom he sings an innocent or a femme fatale luring *him* into some dark, undisclosed scheme of her own? All along, Dylan inhabits this character that could have stepped out of an old Bogart film or a new David Mamet play, singing like a vintage soul balladeer disguised as a Rolling Stone.

And true to his tried-and-true methodology of cut-and-paste pop culture/high culture dada, Dylan also manages to twist a Samuel Johnson aphorism and a Eugene O'Neill line into new forms that resonate with the song's dire ambience. Johnson's "Patriotism is the last refuge of a scoundrel" becomes "They say that patriotism is the last refuge to which a scoundrel clings," while "Steal a little and they throw you in jail/Steal a lot and they make you king/There's only one step down from here, baby/It's called the land of permanent bliss" is a variation on a line from *The Emperor Jones*, O'Neill's parable of a play about a man who bites off way more than he can chew, and pays the price with his life.

On a still deeper level, perhaps "Sweetheart Like You" is taking place in the afterlife, and "the dump" is, in actuality, Hell. After all, the narrator (maybe the Devil himself) seems to know at least a little something about the woman in the very one-sided conversation taking place in the song. He does tell her that one has "Got to be an important person to be in here, honey/Got to have done some evil deed" and in an inversion of the angels playing their string harps in Heaven, he invokes the blues and his harmonica when he informs her that in order to remain she's "Got to play your harp until your lips bleed." Or maybe the narrator is God, and the woman who called him "daddy" when he was a child was the Virgin Mary. The mention of her father's house having "many mansions" is a clear reference to the New Testament's God and concept of Heaven.

[S] "Swing and Turn Jubilee" (Traditional)

Carolyn Hester (performed with Dylan), *Carolyn Hester* (1962)
Guy Carawan, *This Little Light of Mine* (1959)
Jean Ritchie and Doc Watson, *Jean Ritchie and Doc Watson at Folk City* (1991)

Dylan played harmonica as a sideman on this old square-dancing number during the 1961 Carolyn Hester studio session at which he met John Hammond Sr. "Swing and Turn Jubilee" is a tidy mix of work and play, labor and romance, sin and salvation exemplified in couplets like: "Hardest work I ever done/Workin' on the farm/Easiest work I ever done/Swingin' my true love's arm" and "Some will come on a Sat'day night/Some will come on Sunday/If you give 'em half a chance/They'll be back on Monday."

S

T

"Take a Message to Mary" (Felice Bryant/Boudleaux Bryant)

See also "Take Me As I Am"
Bob Dylan, *Self Portrait* (1970)
Everly Brothers, *Fabulous Style of the Everly Brothers* (1960)
Flying Burrito Brothers, *Back to the Sweethearts* (1996)
Don Cherry, *Cherry Picked* (1997)

Felice and Boudleaux Bryant, the landmark Nashville husband-wife team, wrote this dark song evoking the Code of the West for the Everly Brothers. The "message" to Mary is actually a lie, intended to make her think that her beloved is somewhere other than where he really is, in prison for murder. The Everlys originally cut "Take a Message to Mary" in a spare arrangement (with percussion effects provided by Boudleaux Bryant) suggestive of the folk genre the brothers were exploring at the time. The track is notable for being one of their first stereo recordings, a sign that technology was finally catching up to Don and Phil Everly.

The Bryants wrote nearly all of the Everlys' early material. Boudleaux (born February 13, 1921, Shellman, Georgia; died June 25, 1987, Knoxville, Tennessee) was a violin prodigy who was playing for the Atlanta Philharmonic by the age of seventeen. He fell into country music and then jazz as a lark and as a way to make money in music, playing in touring dance bands. Boudleaux began writing songs, some recorded by the Pine Ridge Boys, in 1939. When his own band performed at a Milwaukee hotel in 1945, he met Felice, who was employed as an elevator operator, and in three days' time they were married.

Felice (born Matilda Genevieve Scaduto, August 7, 1925, Milwaukee; died April 22, 2003, Gatlinburg, Tennessee) had also been deeply involved with music since she was a youngster, both as a performer and writer, so writing songs with her husband came easily. Like a couple of lovebirds, they initially wrote merely to amuse themselves. As Chet Flippo reported in the April 24, 2003, *Country Music Times*, "Her life with Boudleaux is a great love story.... 'Felice' came later from a nickname Boudleaux gave her. Felice told me that when she saw Boudleaux walking toward her through the hotel lobby, 'I had dreamed of Boudleaux when I was eight years old. When this man was walking toward me, I recognized him right away. The only thing that was wrong was that he didn't have a beard, although he grew one for me later. In the dream we were dancing to our song. Only it was our song.' Their life together became one song, in many ways."

At the urging of a friend, the couple sent some songs to Fred Rose, the honcho at Nashville's premier music publisher, Acuff-Rose. In short order, Little Jimmy Dickens had a hit with one of them, "Country Boy," in 1949. Over the next forty years, the two wrote 3,000 songs, which eventually sold 300 million copies worldwide. They provided hits for Frankie Laine ("Hey Joe"), Eddy Arnold ("I've Been Thinking"), Roy Orbison ("Sweet Deceiver"), Buddy Holly ("Raining in My Heart"), Jim Reeves ("Blue Boy"), Charley Pride ("We Could"), and, most famously, the Everly Brothers, whose renditions of "Wake Up Little Susie," "Bye Bye Love," "All You Have to Do Is Dream," and "Take a Message to Mary" brought them stardom.

The importance of the twenty-nine songs the Bryants penned for the Everlys cannot be underestimated, forming, along with the songs for Elvis and Buddy Holly, the very bedrock of rock 'n' roll. Not only did their productivity and success lend credence to the role of the

T

Nashville songwriter, Felice's emergence as a major female talent in a testosterone-driven town did as much if not more to break down gender-based barriers than any Gloria Steinem screed could. Some Nashville insiders confess that without Felice Bryant there may never have been a Loretta Lynn, Tammy Wynette, Dolly Parton, or Faith Hill.

Flippo expanded on Felice's contribution in his *Country Music Times* article, writing, "As the first woman to move to Nashville to write songs and as the lyricist of the Bryant songwriting team, she was instrumental in building country music, in launching rock music, and in turning Nashville into the publishing and recording center it has become. She and Boudleaux were also ahead of their time in protecting their copyrights and getting them eventually returned to them, resulting in their forming the House of Bryant for their thousands of copyrighted songs. Their musical output is literally staggering."

The Bryants' golden touch was probably best summarized by Barry McCloud, who wrote in his book, *Definitive Country* (New York: The Berkeley Publishing Group, 1995), "They wrote simple songs that made the foolish say 'I could have written that' but of course they couldn't. It takes genius to write like that. Ask any of the songwriters who look for a hit on 16th Avenue."

If you can suffer through the female chorus that opens Dylan's rendition on a trite note, his "Take a Message to Mary" ain't bad.

▪ "Take Me as I Am" (Boudleaux Bryant)
aka "Take Me as I Am (Or Let Me Go)"
See also "Take a Message to Mary"
Bob Dylan, *Self Portrait* (1970)
George Jones, *George Jones Sings Like the Dickens!* (1964)
Osborne Brothers, *From Rocky Top to Muddy Bottom* (1977)

Don Gibson, *Singer, the Songwriter (1949–1960)* (1991)
Little Jimmie Dickens, *Country Giant* (1995)

A syrupy but beautifully sung slice of pure, unadulterated, 100 percent country from Dylan's uneven *Self Portrait* album, "Take Me as I Am" sounds as if it would have fared better on *Nashville Skyline*. Ray Price had a Top 10 country chart hit with the song.

▪ "Talkin' Bear Mountain Picnic Massacre Blues" (Bob Dylan)
Bob Dylan, *The Bootleg Series, Volumes 1–3: Rare and Unreleased, 1961–1991/'62* (1991)

Bob Dylan often took inspiration for his songs from articles he clipped from newspapers, and "Talkin' Bear Mountain" may be the first. Noel Stookey (later the "Paul" of Peter, Paul & Mary) cut the article that inspired this song out of the June 19, 1961, edition of the *New York Herald Tribune* and showed it to Dylan. The article concerned a story (both horrific and amusing) of the *Hudson Belle*, a boat that a Harlem social club chartered for a Father's Day picnic excursion to upstate New York. When rumors—which later turned out to be true—that hundreds of counterfeit tickets had been hawked, a mob clambered to board the boat when it arrived two hours late. Some two dozen people sustained injuries in the frenzy. Needless to say, the *Hudson Belle* never did make it to Bear Mountain that day. According to legend, Dylan took one day to turn the article into a song.

Dylan regularly performed "Talkin' Bear Mountain" and recorded it for his debut album, though it didn't make the final cut. The song is a seasoned Dylan foray into the talking blues, a form he had been experimenting with for a while. First he had copied Woody Guthrie songs, such as "Talking Columbia" and "Talking Merchant Marines," but he probably also studied earlier Southern practitioners of the idiom—those forgotten hill people who took the wry, deadpan deliveries to even greater heights. Chris Bouchillon, a South Carolina singer, is often credited with developing the idiom in the 1920s, with such features as verses that end with a bitingly sardonic comment. The genre is ready-made for satire. "Talkin' Bear Mountain Picnic Massacre Blues" not only lampoons avarice, but also paints an uproarious portrait of the debacle.

Among Dylan's first so-called topical songs, "Talkin' Bear Mountain" draws on the folk roots traditional while siphoning its content from the present. "Talkin' Bear Mountain" was soon popular in the Greenwich Village folk clubs, where Dylan performed it regularly in 1961 and 1962. Its appeal probably came less from its humor or its traditional roots than from the example it provided for many folkies: within short order "topical songs" would trumpet the renaissance of the protest songs that would soon dominate the 1960s.

Actor Sir Henry Irving dressed in a devil's costume as Mephistopheles in *Faust*, ca. 1885.

(Illustration: Abbe/Hulton Archive/Getty Images)

"Talkin' Devil" (Bob Dylan)
aka "Talking Devil"
Various Artists (performed by Bob Dylan), *Broadside Ballads, Volume 1* (1963)

Dylan recorded this little one-off of a rap at the *Broadside* magazine office in New York City in the winter of 1963 and it appeared on the *Broadside Ballads, Volume 1* album under his famous early pseudonym, "Blind Boy Grunt." There are but two verses of "Talkin' Devil," which seems more like a work in progress than a song—a germinal idea about the earth's hidden devil, a theme Dylan has never tired of exploring. Here, he is probably talking about the Ku Klux Klan.

"Talkin' Hava Negeilah Blues" (Bob Dylan)
Bob Dylan, *The Bootleg Series, Volumes 1–3: Rare and Unreleased, 1961–1991/'62* (1991)

Dylan originally directed this goofy little jape at those who called out requests for songs way out of his oeuvre. He began including "Talkin' Hava Negeilah Blues" in his set in the late summer of 1961 and it was one of the songs mentioned in what was perhaps the most important concert review in his entire career. Robert Shelton's September 29, 1961, piece in the *New York Times* pointed out that "Mr. Dylan is both comedian and tragedian. Like a vaudeville

T

actor on the rural circuit, he offers a variety of droll musical monologs. . . . 'Talkin' Hava Negeilah Blues' burlesques the folk music craze and the singer himself."

As released on *The Bootleg Series, Volumes 1–3*, "Talkin' Hava Negeilah" is notable for Dylan's studio quips about having learned this "foreign song" in Utah.

"Talkin' John Birch Paranoid Blues" (Bob Dylan)

aka "Talkin' John Birch," "Talkin' John Birch Society Blues"
Bob Dylan, *The Bootleg Series, Volumes 1–3: Rare and Unreleased, 1961–1991/'63* (1991); *The Bootleg Series, Volume 6: Live 1964—Concert at Philharmonic Hall* (2004)

"This is called 'Talkin' John Birch Blues' and there ain't nothing wrong with this song."

With this introduction at his October 26, 1963, show at New York's Carnegie Hall, Dylan fired a salvo in response to the first high-profile controversy in his emerging, almost always-to-be-controversial career.

For those who may not remember what all the fuss was about, the John Birch Society is a right-wing U.S. organization founded to combat communism. It's named after an American Baptist missionary (some say an American intelligence officer) who Robert Welch, founder of the society, viewed as the first casualty of the cold war. John Birch was in China before World War II, escaped capture by the Japanese when the war began, and, while hiding out, stumbled across Captain James Doolittle and some of his men (the "Flying Tigers"). He led them to safety and then signed up with Claire Chennault (U.S. commander of the American Volunteer Forces in China) to provide intelligence against the Japanese. This he did quite effectively for the next few years. On a mission to free American prisoners in August 1945, he

ran across communist Chinese guerrillas. He refused to surrender his gun and got into an argument with the guerrilla leader, who had him shot and bayoneted to death a few days after V-J Day.

"Talkin' John Birch Paranoid Blues" initially appeared in print in the premier edition of *Broadside* in February 1962, nine months before Dylan recorded the song during his *Freewheelin' Bob Dylan* sessions—a version later released on the *Bootleg Series, Volumes 1–3*.

Broadside began life as a mimeographed magazine as part of the burgeoning New York City folk music scene to provide a forum for new songwriters to publish their newest compositions and disseminate them to would-be performers. Writing more songs in a week than most people write in a lifetime, Dylan was a

U.S. Army Captain John Birch, missionary and O.S.S. officer.

(Photo: New York World-Telegram and Sun Collection/Library of Congress)

T

natural contributor, and for a time (in *Broadside* #48 though #58) he was listed on the publication's masthead as a contributing editor.

With more than a passing nod to the Greenwich Village old guard, Dylan's sardonic, sharp lampoon of the arch-conservative "better dead than Red" John Birch Society was sure to catch *Broadside*'s notice, yet no one could have predicted the brouhaha "Talkin' John Birch" would stir in the coming months. First, the song was one of four scrapped from *The Freewheelin' Bob Dylan*, allegedly because Columbia Records' lawyers hit the panic button, fearing that the John Birch Society might sue over an overt suggestion in the lyrics that its members shared "Hitler's views." But even when Dylan replaced the song on the LP with "Talkin' World War III Blues" (another satirical yarn dealing with the then, and still, contemporary zeitgeist), his problems with "Talkin' John Birch" were far from over. Ironically, when finally released on *The Bootleg Series* some thirty years later, the song did not contain the Hitler lyric. Well, history sometimes does repeat itself.

Dylan was booked for the May 12, 1963, broadcast of *The Ed Sullivan Show*, after Sullivan and the show's producer had heard Dylan perform "Talkin' John Birch" earlier in the week during an informal audition at their studio. Albert Grossman, Dylan's manager, was thrilled at the prospect of the media exposure the appearance afforded. But when Stowe Phelps, editor of CBS TV's department of program practices, heard Dylan perform "Talkin' John Birch" at the show's dress rehearsal, he put the kibosh on the song choice, suggesting that Dylan perform a Clancy Brothers song instead. Justifiably flabbergasted, Dylan walked out—a ballsy move in any era.

While the "Talkin' John Birch" flap continued for some days in the press, Grossman could not have been more delighted with the upshot of the controversy. His boy had not been granted a showcase on Sullivan's cathode cathedral, but he was being defended far and wide, and, best of all, he was receiving ample free publicity to boot. Undeterred, Dylan continued to perform the song in concert for another year and a half, often introducing it as the "song they wouldn't let me sing on TV."

In fact, TV censorship shows up in the song itself, in Dylan's reference to "*Hootenanny* television" in the lyrics. *Hootenanny* was a network folk music program on which Dylan and several other socially conscious artists had refused to appear, because the likes of Pete Seeger and the Weavers were not allowed to perform on the show. They were banned because networks were then still subject to the McCarthy-era blacklists preventing entertainers with alleged communist ties from appearing on American television or in films.

A final note: Dylan had first auditioned for the Sullivan show in the spring of 1962. After performing some of his debut album material ("Pretty Peggy-O," "Man of Constant Sorrow," and "Song to Woody") for talent bookers who barely responded, a baffled Dylan wandered over to a Times Square flea circus to "see the man from Borneo again."

[S] "Talkin' New York" (Bob Dylan)

Bob Dylan, *Bob Dylan* (1962)
Judy Collins, *An Audio Discography* (1979)

"Talkin' New York" (which Dylan supposedly wrote on the road in May 1961 while traveling home to Minnesota for a visit and drew partially from a still unreleased bit, "Talkin' Folk Lore Center") was the first original Dylan song to appear on record. The song works both as a rube's travelogue and stealthy critique of life in the big city. Dylan's dry wit allows him to adopt

T

Bob Dylan with Sam Gilford, guitar, and Joe Gilford, banjo, Washington Square Park, Greenwich Village, New York, ca. 1966.

(Photo: Jack Gilford/Courtesy of Madeleine Gilford)

an aloof stance when he confuses (and needles) the urban yokels with "hillbilly" pronunciations of "GreenRICH Village" while wending his way downtown to sing at a folkie coffeehouse. Woody Guthrie had already tilled this plot, and Dylan must have been aware of Woody's "Talkin' Subway," "New York Town," and "Pretty Boy Floyd" when writing "Talkin' New York."

Dissing the coffeehouse scene, Dylan complained to Robert Shelton in the *Bob Dylan* liner notes, "They wanted satin shirts and gut strings, while I played all steel strings, and you know I don't wear satin shirts."

Other than the recording for Columbia, only one other rendition of "Talkin' New York" has been preserved; this is from a spring 1962 club date at New York City's Gerde's Folk City, in, where else, GreenRICH Village.

"Talkin' World War III Blues" (Bob Dylan)
Bob Dylan, *The Freewheelin' Bob Dylan* (1963); *Don't Look Back* (film) (1967); *The Bootleg Series, Volume 6: Live 1964—Concert at Philharmonic Hall* (2004)

"Talkin' World War III Blues" is an utterly charming Dylan talking blues at its very best—a wry phantasm assessing the planet the morning after nuclear annihilation. Though he begins the Guthriesque shaggy-dog story song by saying that he had a dream about being the only person still alive after the war, he immediately describes encountering a man who runs away, a woman who tells him he's crazy for wanting to follow Adam and Eve's example, and, eventually, a psychiatrist who attempts to comfort him by suggesting that his dreams "are only in your head."

As an antidote for a few of the heavier songs on *The Freewheelin' Bob Dylan* ("Blowin' in the Wind," "Hard Rain," "Oxford Town," and "Masters of War"), "Talkin' World War III Blues" affords a glimpse of Dylan's acerbic sense of humor. Nat Hentoff, in his *Freewheelin'* liner notes, says that the song "was about half formulated beforehand and half improvised at the recording session itself. . . . In this piece, for example, he has singularly distilled the way we all wish away our end, thermonuclear or 'natural.' Or at least, the way we try to."

Dylan began performing "Talkin' World War III Blues" almost immediately after composing and recording it in 1963, using the song as part of his live presentations for the next two years. A fragment of Dylan performing the song for the last time can be glimpsed in D. A. Pennebaker's film vérité, *Don't Look Back.*

[S] "Tangled Up in Blue" (Bob Dylan)

Bob Dylan, single (1975); *Blood on the Tracks* (1975); *Renaldo & Clara* (film) (1978); *Real Live* (1984); *Biograph*/'75 (1985); *The Bootleg Series, Volumes 1–3: Rare and Unreleased, 1961–1991*/'74 (1991); *Bob Dylan's Greatest Hits, Volume 3* (1994); *The Bootleg Series, Volume 5: Live 1975—The Rolling Thunder Revue* (2002); *Masked and Anonymous* [bonus edition] (2003)
Half Japanese, *1/2 Gentlemen Not Beasts* (1979)
Hoodoo Rhythm Devil, *Safe in Their Homes* (1976)
Kim Larsen, *Sitting on a Time Bomb* (1982)
Jerry Garcia, *Jerry Garcia Band* (1991)
The Phantoms, *The Phantoms* (1992)
Indigo Girls, *The Times They Are A-Changin'* (1992); *1200 Curfews* (1995)
Janglers, *Janglers Play Dylan* (1992)
St. Christopher, *Lioness* (1996)
Whitlams, *Eternal Nightcap* (1998)
Carl Edwards, *Coffeehouse Cowboy* (1998)
The Zimmermen, *After the Ambulances Go* (1998)
Various Artists (performed by David West), *Pickin' on Dylan—Tribute* (1999)
Gerry Murphy, *Gerry Murphy Sings Bob Dylan* (2001)
Mary Lee's Corvette, *Blood on the Tracks* (2002)
Barb Jungr, *Every Grain of Sand: Barb Jungr Sings Bob Dylan* (2002)
Robyn Hitchcock, *Robyn Sings* (2002)
Gerry Murphy, *Gerry Murphy Sings Bob Dylan* (2002)
Dan Emmitt, *Freedom Ride* (2002)
Various Artists (performed by the Indigo Girls), *Doin' Dylan 2* (2002)
Todd Rubenstein, *The String Quartet Tribute to Bob Dylan* (2003)

A Dylan masterpiece of ecstatic agony, "Tangled Up in Blue" uses the allegory of a busted romance to capture a sense of personal and political loss as the creatively revolutionary spirit of 1960s ebbs into the spiritual void of 1970s America. Intensely bittersweet, "Tangled Up in Blue" is one of Dylan's most recognizable and admired songs—a masterful, seven-verse synthesis introduction to *Blood on the Tracks,* whose grand subject is the rapacious waters of mature romantic relationships.

John Nogowski offered this wonderful description of the song in his book *Bob Dylan: A Descriptive, Critical Discography and Filmography, 1961–1993* (North Carolina, 1995): "Rarely has Bob Dylan matched music and words so aptly as he has on this song. The tale of interrupted love is perfectly matched by the melody, built around a two-chord riff. As the riff

T

builds, the song begins to gather momentum as the chorus approaches—like the buildup of the relationship. Then comes a succession of quick chord changes—symbolizing the sudden, abrupt shifts in his life—and he delivers the title line, a perfect metaphor for his situation. He then returns to the opening riff, back to the beginning—the same old problems all over again. And on the song goes. His closing harmonica solo, trying to dance in the face of these heartaches, is almost heroic."

On all of his officially released versions of "Tangled Up in Blue" and through three decades of performance display, Dylan has experimented with changing the pronouns in the lyrics. This unorthodox approach was reportedly inspired by Norman Raeben, a painting-cum-philosophy teacher with whom Dylan studied in 1974.

Dylan commented in the *Biograph* liner notes, "I guess I was just trying to make it like a painting where you can see the different parts, but then you also see the whole of it. With that particular song, that's what I was trying to do ... with the concept of time, and the way the characters change from the first person to the third person, and you're never quite sure if the third person is talking or the first person is talking. But as you look at the whole thing, it really doesn't matter."

Again commenting in the *Biograph* liner notes, Dylan wrote: "On *Real Live* it's more like it should have been. I was never really happy with it. On *Real Live*, the imagery is better and more the way I would have liked it than on the original recording."

What Dylan did in the *Real Live* version was to depersonalize the song by changing the "I" to "he" in the first verse. Eventually the sober, autobiographical account Dylan had offered in *Blood on the Tracks* became someone else's fractured fairy tale—a someone whom it is harder to care about. Surely, in the yet-to-be-written doctoral thesis on Dylan's use of pronouns, "Tangled Up in Blue" would be a logical starting point.

Dylan has reinterpreted and even rewritten "Tangled Up in Blue" over the years. In fact, the *Blood on the Tracks* version, with which even the most casual Dylan watcher is familiar, was reworked from an earlier draft.

Dylan first recorded the songs for *Blood on the Tracks* in September 1974 while living in New York City. Employing spare instrumentation, the result was ten songs pressed on a promo disc, which was distributed in very limited quantities to select radio stations later that autumn.

But, after reviewing the album over the Christmas holidays in Minnesota, Dylan quickly grew dissatisfied with the results and rerecorded several of the tracks with a group of local musicians rounded up by his brother David Zimmerman. "Tangled Up in Blue" was one of the songs he rerecorded. When "Tangled Up" was released as an A-side single, the song peaked at No. 31 on the *Billboard* chart.

One of the Minnesota musicians who rerecorded the track with Dylan, guitarist Keith Odegard, has said the wonderful signature sound that opens "Tangled Up in Blue" was drawn from an album by Joy of Cooking, a band out of Oakland, California. In the same 2001 interview, conducted by Tom Mischke with Paul Metsa and published in *On the Tracks*, #21, Odegard also relates a great story about the production of the song. At one point during the session, Dylan asked Odegard what he thought of the arrangement. When Odegard responded "Passable," Dylan was incredulous. "*Passable*?," he asked. "What do you mean 'passable'? What does that *mean*, 'passable'?"

Cooler heads soon prevailed. As Odegard said, "... basically the song was just *laying* there. It wasn't doing much, in that key, for him. So I think he said in his mind, 'Well, what the hell, let's try it, let's move it up, let's go to A on it.'

"So we all capoed up to A and tried it. He *reached* for the note, he strained a little bit in his voice, he gave it the urgency it needed, it gave it the immediacy and the excitement that you hear. . . . We got half way through the song on rehearsal, and he said, 'Stop. Roll it.' And that was the tape. We had no more rehearsal on that, that was it."

The primary narrative change to arise during the Minnesota recording session occurs in the sixth verse. For the first time a third character is mentioned, and the narrator sings, "I lived with them on Montague Street," hinting that he may have joined an existing relationship.

This last relationship appears to have held a great deal of sway over the singer. By the song's end he has left them and everyone else in the dust and we find him where we first encountered him: "still on the road, headed for another joint," determined to find the woman he first mentioned in the beginning of the song.

Interpreting this song is a rather slippery slope. Is Dylan describing the arc of a single, obsessive relationship? Several couples' itinerant meetings and breakups? Or one man's relationship with many women? A close inspection would seem to err primarily on the side of the latter.

With a deceptively deft pen and a well-placed phrase or two in each stanza, Dylan leads the listener into assuming that he is chronicling the lives of two star-crossed lovers who coincidentally keep bumping into each other along the American byway, only to be torn asunder once more.

As the curtain rises "early one mornin'," the singer is lying in bed (itself a clichéd subversion of "woke up this mornin'," the old lyric that opens a multitude of "Walkin' Blues"–like blues songs) ruminating on a woman and her red hair—the last time such a physical characteristic is mentioned. He goes on to blame their split on "her folks," who "never did like Mama's home-made dress/Papa's bank book wasn't big enough" and finds himself cast aside, the rain pouring out his shoes (a stand-in for the tracks of his tears) as he hitches a ride east.

The woman of verse two would appear, however, to be quite a different creature. She was, after all, "married when we first met/soon to be divorced"—not the type who would be too concerned if her folks started to quibble over the style of dresses or the girth of bank accounts when the time came to choose another man. The verse ends with a vague on-the-lam scene in which the narrator and his new lover drive a car as far they can, abandon it (and their romance?), parting with the even vaguer suggestion that they will "meet again some day/On the avenue."

Verse three finds the singer flying solo—working as a cook in "the great north woods," getting the axe, then drifting for a job on a fishing boat. Even as the narrator admits that he has "seen a lot of women" (hinting that the song may be about a few of them), he can't shake the vision of a woman (most probably the redhead from verse one) from his head. At the same time, though, he reinforces the charade that the imagined composite couple are about to cross paths again.

When we see the singer stopping in for a beer at the topless place in verse four we are led to believe that he recognizes the profile of his true love in the spotlight. The woman, for her part, "studies the lines" on his face. Her "bending down to tie the laces" of his shoes seems a very bold come-on for a character who has sunk pretty low indeed, and his implied acceptance of her pass depicts the corruption of a guy who finds himself in even lower depths.

This gesture extends naturally into verse five, a further scene of seduction at her (or some other woman's?) place, where she lights the literal (and sexually figurative?) stove, offers him a pipe (filled with what?), and hands him the book of poems written by that unnamed thirteenth-century Italian poet (Dante and his verses to Beatrice, the unrequited object of his desire, are an excellent bet).

Things appear to hit rock bottom in verse six with a tawdry ménage-a-trois on Montague Street (Brooklyn Heights, as a point of information, has such a street, known back in the early to mid-twentieth century as a hotbed of radical and bohemian activity). When that nefarious scene implodes, the singer comes to his senses and perseveres ("to keep on keeping on"), realizing that he has to attempt to bring his personal narrative full circle and return to the one he can't shake from his being, "like a bird that flew."

Back on the road in the eighth and final verse, the singer considers his and his true love's intertwined but fractured pasts. Only one thing matters now: return.

Dylan performed "Tangled Up in Blue" as an intense solo acoustic vehicle with the Rolling Thunder Revue in 1975 and 1976 and managed to wring ever more passion out of it with his dirgelike arrangement in 1978 during the short-lived big-band phase (and an even shorter-lived series of performances in which he replaced the song's mention of the "book of poems" with a reference to the New Testament, perhaps the effect of his emerging Christianity). Dylan's secular, rewritten, pronoun-altered version returned "Tangled Up in Blue" to a solo acoustic rendering in 1984, and he performed a semidisastrous one-off with the Grateful Dead in the summer of 1987 (though the rehearsal tapes from earlier in the year suggest it could have been otherwise). During the Never Ending Tour, Dylan recast the song a few times, ranging from a white-hot electric version through the mid-1990s to a smoldering semiacoustic, minor-key bluegrass-style arrangement that presented the song with casual, though passionate, aplomb marked by excellent musicianship that reached some truly sublime peaks.

◻ *Tarantula*
New York: Macmillan, 1971.

In this collection of urban prose poems, Dylan echoes the wordplay and street-savvy rhythms of his mid-1960s songs and liner notes. *Tarantula* found Dylan at a point in his artistic evolution when word games and spontaneously combusting ideas were coming as naturally to him as breathing.

Written mostly in 1966, this rather disjointed but personal work is full of snapshots of people and places, and seems to have been written in an amphetamine daze. (Watch *Eat the Document* and read *Tarantula* to get some idea of the insanity surrounding Dylan at this time.)

Critic Dave Marsh may have been pretty close to hitting the mark when he described *Tarantula* as a "versified novel without a plot or point." Dylan may have come closer when he said, "The book don't begin or end," and described the book as a "fragmentary novel."

However one wishes to characterize *Tarantula*, few could argue that the novel isn't "novel."

Tarantula was originally scheduled to be published in September 1966, but the project was shelved after Dylan's motorcycle accident and retreat to seclusion that summer. Unauthorized versions of the book began appearing and circulating and became something of a hush-hush talisman for the card-carrying hipnoscente. But when Macmillan finally pub-

T

lished the rather slender tome in 1971, it was met with a thick girth of negative criticism from just about everyone, still not an uncommon response.

Actually, the long-winded mind-breath exhale of surrealisms that is *Tarantula* has aged quite well, especially if one reads it aloud, beatnik style, and approaches the text as an epic Dylan liner note—like the kind he wrote for *Bringing It All Back Home* or *Highway 61 Revisited* back in the days.

Some of Dylan's greatest put-on lines came in fending off reporters asking what the book was all about. As he told the paparazzi gathered for a May 3, 1966, interview at London's Mayfair Hotel, "It's called *Tarantula*, it's about spiders. It's an insect book. Took about a week to write, off and on. There are three hundred and sixty pages. My next book is a collection of epitaphs." (*New Musical Express*, 1966.)

[S] "Tears of Rage" (Bob Dylan/Richard Manuel)

Bob Dylan/The Band, single (1975); *The Basement Tapes/'67* (1975)
The Band, *Music from Big Pink* (1968); *Best of the Band* (1976); *Across the Great Divide* (1994)
Joan Baez, *Any Day Now* (1968); *Vanguard Sessions: Baez Sings Dylan* (1998)
Ian and Sylvia, *Full Circle* (1968); *Long Long Time* (1994)
Marc Ellington, *Marc Ellington* (1969)
Gene Clark, *White Light* (1971)
Albert Lee, *Black Claw & Country Fever* (1991)
Barbara Dickson, single (1992)
Dish, *Boneyard Beach* (1995)
Jerry Garcia Band, *How Sweet It Is* (1997)
Primal Fear, *Primal Fear* (1998)
Marty Ehrlich, *Malinke's Dance* (2000)

Dylan and the Hawks recorded three very different versions of this song about the finality of loss during the *Basement Tapes* era. A rare, no-nonsense song from that 1967 epoch, "Tears of Rage" is among the first-documented collaborations between Dylan and another artist, in this case Richard Manuel—the singer, pianist, songwriter, and occasional drummer with the Band.

Manuel once described the quick manner in which "Tears of Rage" came together. "He [Dylan] came down to the basement with a piece of typewritten paper . . . it was typed out—in line form—and he just said, 'Have you got any music for this? I had a couple of musical movements that fit . . . so I just elaborated a bit, because I wasn't sure what the lyrics meant." (*Mojo*, May 1999.)

Dylan suggested in the *Biograph* liner notes that, along with "Too Much of Nothing," "Tears of Rage" (with allusions to familial schism) was influenced by William Shakespeare's *King Lear*. What he didn't point out was that he probably wrote "Tears of Rage" from the point of view of Cordelia (Lear's daughter), who saw the manipulative trap her father set for his children. But that description barely scratches the surface of this complex song.

In his book *Hard Rain: A Dylan Commentary*, Tim Riley sees the song as a "soldier's curse upon his commander." Riley continues:

> It's the voice of a man who followed his leader into battle, saw his friends slaughtered for a cause he may never have fully believed in, only to return to find his superior running for political office, turning his back on the values that were so easily sacrificed. "We carried you in our arms/On Independence Day" is the kind of battle-scar allusion that Robbie Robertson will flesh out in songs like "The Night They Drove Old Dixie Down," on the Band's second album. "Tears of Rage" doesn't depend on the same associations, but it pursues the same memories, and voices a disbelief in and cynicism about authority so charged with resentment it can barely work

T

up the steam to get pissed off. (On *Any Day Now*, Joan Baez turns this song into a robust a cappella spiritual, as though it had been written for Odetta.) Who knows how many Vietnam protesters—and veterans—might have called this song their own had it been released before the fall of Saigon?

This leader who was carried in the arms of his troops, who scratched his name in the sand, must now hear the bitter voice of his dissenters. The song can be read as an allegory for the Vietnam experience from the side of the dispirited soldier instead of the peaceniks, the usual heroes of the antiwar songs written in this period (Neil Young's "Ohio," John Lennon's "Revolution").

"Tears of Rage" closes with a summary of how earthly riches (gold) corrupt spiritual values, and make love and honor go from bad to worse. This is betrayal of the most profound kind: having sacrificed everything for a cause, only to find that the leader of the cause never believed in the battle's purpose to begin with.

Describing Manuel's vocal approach on *The Basement Tapes* versions of "Tears of Rage," Thomas Friedrich wrote in the May 1999 *Mojo*: "Richard's range of sincerity, anguish and resentment grabs the listener and doesn't let go. The pain of a father's broken relationship with his child was the defining statement of the huge generation gap of the late 1960s, and Manuel's delivery is unmatched."

Though Jerry Garcia had been performing "Tears of Rage" with his own bar band since the mid-1970s, Dylan did not begin singing the song in public until 1989, when it began seeing limited action as a turbulent confessional every bit as wounded as its *Basement Tapes* predecessor. Over the course of the next decade Dylan occasionally sang "Tears of Rage" at his

Never Ending Tour concerts. During Dylan's summer 2003 tour with the retooled Dead, he was joined by Joan Osborne for a couple of stunning performances of the song, featuring alternating turns on the lyric.

🅂 "Tell Me" (Bob Dylan)
Bob Dylan, *The Bootleg Series, Volumes 1–3: Rare and Unreleased, 1961–1991/'83* (1991)

An *Infidels* outtake that could have slid off the bandwidth of an AM radio, "Tell Me" is a long, open-minded song that sounds like it is being sung to a newfound amour on a first date. The narrator is just dying to know everything about this blank slate on his arm but he just won't let her get a word in edgewise. In so doing, he may be telling her more about himself than he realizes.

🅂 "Tell Me, Momma" (Bob Dylan)
aka "Tell Me, Mama," "Tell Me Mama"
Bob Dylan, *Eat the Document/'66* (film) (1971); *The Bootleg Series, Volume 4: Bob Dylan Live 1966 (The "Royal Albert Hall" Concert)* (1998)
The Original Marauders, *Now Your Mouth Cries Wolf* (1977)
Michel Montecrossa, *Jet Pilot* (2000)
Robyn Hitchcock, *Robyn Sings* (2002)

"Tell Me, Momma," a deranged and bluesy rock song, emerged on Dylan's 1966 tour with the Hawks and opened nearly every electric set on that *very* bumpy road. Never booed, it came out of the gate like greased lightning, Dylan and company riding the roar of the instant momentum like surfers who have caught the Big Kahuna and must absorb every ounce of energy in the geometry of the moment if they are to make it safely to the cool, groovy sands of serenity. Snide, funny, baffling, and empathetic, the lyrics dance around what seem like yet another romantic freeze-out.

[S] "Tell Me That It Isn't True" (Bob Dylan)

Bob Dylan, *Nashville Skyline* (1969)

Dylan's moving but standard piece of country fare about infidelity (and sounding like it was written expressly for Elvis Presley) is unusual only because it follows "One More Night," another song dealing with the same subject on *Nashville Skyline*. Some have wondered whether this was a veiled admission on Dylan's part or merely a piece of the album's thematic fabric.

The song collected dust for more than three decades, but Dylan began performing "Tell Me That It Isn't True" (reworked Lefty Frizzell/Hank Williams-style) in early 2000 and has kept it in light rotation through 2004, as if to drop a reminder that it's never too late to fret about betrayal of any kind.

[S] "Temporary Like Achilles" (Bob Dylan)

Bob Dylan, *Blonde on Blonde* (1966)
Various Artists (performed by Deborah Coleman), *Blues on Blonde on Blonde* (2003)

Perhaps Dylan was crossing a Greenwich Village street on a sultry summer afternoon or praying before the porcelain altar in the commode of a dank Bourbon Street dive when his muse whispered this puzzling song into his ear.

Dylan rescued the chorus and part of the tune from "Medicine Sunday"—a stab at a song he fooled around with in 1965—and created this hazy, dawdling blues in which he vaguely observes a woman with whom he is breaking up and her new (evidently disposable) boyfriend du jour. The narrator hardly seems flustered, and Dylan's wheezing harmonica perfectly fits the song's mood of detachment and restrained disgust. Perhaps he senses that this hunk named after Achilles (an almost invulnerable Greek hero) will be discarded as quickly as he was.

A final note: in 1987, Dylan's original folio, a neatly handwritten sheet of the lyrics of "Temporary Like Achilles," was offered by Christie's auctioneers and sold for $4,000 to an anonymous buyer.

[S] "10,000 Men" (Bob Dylan)

Bob Dylan, *Under the Red Sky* (1990)

An enigmatic yet humorous song about men, women, and sexuality, with some sharp imagery straight out of an Ingmar Bergman film like *The Seventh Seal*, "10,000 Men" comes off like an Old Testament children's story that Dylan might have dashed off on a coffee break during a recording session.

In "10,000 Men" Dylan casts a cold eye on heroes and heels. In a pastiche of mindless conformity and uniformity, the clean-shaven men in question all appear in Oxford blue duds and march to the beat of the same drum, whether they are digging for silver and gold, on the move, or playing it straight ("None of them doing nothin' that your mama wouldn't disapprove"), even as they face death.

On the other side of the song's stage are 10,000 women all dressed in white, who not only seem to be aware of the singer but to approve of him as well ("Standing at my window wishing me goodnight").

By the song's end, the men seem not only to be wasting away, but to be at the narrator's beck and call—the tables are turned on those wine-drinking businessmen and earth-digging plowmen who reared their heads in "All Along the Watchtower" all those many moons ago.

Dylan's sole live display of "10,000 Men" seems pointed enough, coming as it did in the midst of the frenzy of the 2000 presidential election ballot counting and jockeying, when the world's television screens were full of well-dressed men and women looking at hanging chads in Florida.

Ⓐ *Texas Tornado*/Doug Sahm
Atlantic Records LP SD-7287. Released 1973.

Culled from the same October 1972 New York City recording session that produced *Doug Sahm and Band*, *Texas Tornado* includes Dylan harmonica, guitar, and organ contributions to three more songs on this release: "Tennessee Blues," "Ain't That Loving You," and "I'll Be There."

ⓈT"That'll Be the Day" (Jerry Allison/Buddy Holly/Norman Petty)
Buddy Holly, *Chirping Crickets* (1957)
Everly Brothers, *Rock N' Soul* (1965)
Linda Ronstadt, *Hasten Down the Wind* (1976)
Bobby Vee, *Early Rockin' Years* (1995)

Dylan's only performances of this Buddy Holly classic came as part of an encore medley paired with "The Wanderer" and sung with Paul Simon during their 1999 summer tour. The lively "That'll Be the Day" has particular significance in the rise of Buddy Holly. It was among a handful of songs he recorded with his band the Crickets at the now-famous 1957 Clovis, New Mexico, recording sessions that caught the ear of a major record company, Decca. When released as a single on Decca's subsidiary Brunswick label not long afterward, "That'll Be the Day" was the first hit and million-seller by Buddy Holly and the Crickets. Jerry Allison and Norman Petty (the two who share the composer credit with Holly on the song) were the Crickets' drummer and producer, respectively.

Ⓢ "That Lucky Old Sun" (Haven Gillespie/Beasley Smith)
aka "Lucky Old Sun," "That Lucky Old Sun (Just Rolls Around Heaven All Day)"
Frankie Laine, single (1949); *The Essence of Frankie Laine* (1993)
Ray Charles, *Standards* (1959)
Willie Nelson, *One for the Road* (1980)
Jerry Garcia Band, *Jerry Garcia Band* (1991)
Louis Armstrong, *Essential Satchmo* (1998)
Aretha Franklin, *Sings Standards* (1998)

Written in 1949, "That Lucky Old Sun" hit No. 1 on all the charts and was sung by a high-class range of talent. This classic describes the narrator's jealously for that lucky old sun, who gets to roll around Heaven all day while we mere mortals have to fuss and fight down here on planet earth. Dylan is rumored to have first recorded an unreleased version of the song during the 1971 New York City recording session with Leon Russell that produced the initial versions of "Watching the River Flow" and "When I Paint My Masterpiece." He sang "That Lucky Old Sun" during the Tom Petty and the Heartbreakers era in 1985 (he debuted it at the first Farm Aid benefit concert in Champaign, Illinois) and in 1986. Full of sleepy, hard-fought gospel soul, "Lucky Old Sun" became truly memorable when Dylan and Petty brightened it with swooping harmonies from Dylan's backup singers at the time: Queen Esther Morrow, Madelyn Quebec, Carolyn Dennis, and Louise Mathoon. Dylan brought the song out only four times over the next decade, during Never Ending Tour shows (some of these were unique acoustic renditions).

The better remembered and more highly regarded of the two composers of "That Lucky Old Sun" is lyricist James Lamont Haven Gillespie (born Haven Gillespie, February 6, 1888, Covington, Kentucky; died March 14, 1975, probably Las Vegas). Along with J. Fred Coots, he was the coauthor of "Santa Claus Is Coming to Town," undoubtedly his greatest claim to songwriting immortality. (He wrote the classic on the back of an envelope during a short spin on the New York City subway, allegedly recalling his mother's warnings about behaving well so Santa wouldn't forget him on Christmas Eve.) But even without that success, Gillespie's story is an inspirational one. One of ten children, he left school in sixth grade, though he was an excellent student, and moved to Chicago with an older sister. There he began working at a printing press, eventually joining the International Typographic Union—a membership he kept for life. Finding extra work as a song plugger (one who made the rounds of the Tin Pan Alley music publishers promoting his own songs and those of others by performing them on the office piano in hopes of collecting a commission on their sale), Gillespie moved to New York City and actively pursued his career as a lyricist. The results were phenomenal. "You Go to My Head" (written after closing a Prohibition-era speakeasy and made famous by Billie Holiday), "Breezing Along with the Breeze" (written with frequent collaborator Dick Whiting), "Drifting and Dreaming," "God's Country," "Lucky Old Sun," and the indestructible "Santa Claus Is Coming to Town" all earned him a place in the Songwriters Hall of Fame. Written in 1934, "Santa Claus Is Coming to Town" debuted, ironically enough, on Jewish singer Eddie Cantor's Thanksgiving radio program at the insistence of Cantor's wife and was soon selling 25,000 copies of sheet music a day.

But despite the success, Gillespie's life was marred by alcoholism—a problem he heroically faced at the age of sixty-nine by joining (and sticking with) Alcoholics Anonymous. Accounts of his death are unclear. Las Vegas is the preferred site but California and Kentucky are also mentioned as points of his planetary departure.

John Beasley Smith (born September 23, 1901, McEwen, Tennessee; died May 14, 1968, Nashville) is best remembered as a band leader and music biz figure in a career that stretched from the early 1920s, when he formed his first orchestra, through his presidency of Randy-Smith Music Corporation in the 1950s and as a Dot Records arranger and A&R man in the 1960s.

There Is No Eye: Music for Photographs/Various Artists

Smithsonian Folkways 4001. Released November 2001.

In *There Is No Eye: Music for Photographs*, photographer, filmmaker, folklorist, and musician John Cohen (of the New Lost City Ramblers) presents some of the finest American roots recordings ever made. On their own, these songs are authentic and captivating. Yet they are only one half of a conceptual whole—Cohen has also released a thirty-two-page booklet of photographs, *There Is No Eye*, showcasing the musicians featured on the recording as well as many others, shown in a range of visual urban, rural, and exotic environments in America and abroad (most noteworthy Peru) during the 1960s and 1970s. Experienced together, the music and the photographs create new dimensions of possibility in our collective drive to understand and appreciate people's music. Included on the CD are previously unreleased, rare, and/or super obscure music from Dylan (the somber "Roll On John" from a 1962 New York City radio appearance), Rev. Gary Davis ("If I Had My Way"), Woody Guthrie ("Ramblin' Round"), Roscoe Holcomb ("Man of Constant Sorrow"), Bill Monroe ("John Henry"), Carter Stanley ("Come All You Tenderhearted"), Muddy Waters ("I Can't Be Satisfied"), and many more. This collection should be stored in a satin vault.

The title for the collection comes from a line from Dylan's own liner notes for *Highway 61 Revisited*, in which he references Cohen: "you are right john cohen ... I cannot say the word eye anymore ... there is no eye."

▣ "They Killed Him" (Kris Kristofferson)
Bob Dylan, *Knocked Out Loaded* (1986)
Kris Kristofferson/Various Artists (performed by Kris Kristofferson and Bob Dylan), *Singer/Songwriter* (1991)

Kris Kristofferson's sanctimonious bit of historical commentary, including a children's chorus, has to rate as one of the most laughably lame tracks on any Dylan album (some may argue any album, *period*). Kristofferson actually had the cojones to sing this poor man's "Abraham, Martin and John" on the Johnny Carson–hosted *Tonight Show* in the mid-1980s. Despite the song's silliness, the sentiment behind "They Killed Him" is a good one, and it conveys the kind of succinct directness that powered Dylan's earliest work. Dylan's version also appears on the Kristofferson disc listed above—a unique concept album that features both the singer/songwriter's version of seventeen of Kristofferson's songs and cover versions of those same songs done up by the likes of Janis Joplin, Ray Price, Johnny Cash, and others.

Kris Kristofferson (born June 22, 1936, Brownsville, Texas) has cut a large swath in show business and politics as a Rhodes Scholar, groundbreaking country music legend, film star, and political activist.

It was Janis Joplin's version of Kristofferson's "Me and Bobby McGee," recorded just before her death in 1971, that helped catapult the songwriter, singer, and actor into stardom. With his five-year marriage to folk-pop warbler Rita Coolidge, Kristofferson took on the trappings of a leftist folk hero, campaigning elo-

quently for progressive causes. He became increasingly absorbed with a film career that kept him on location (*Pat Garrett and Billy the Kid* in 1974, the notorious bomb *Heaven's Gate* in 1981, and John Sayles's highly acclaimed *Lonestar* in 1996 are three of his more notable efforts), but Kristofferson returned to recording in the mid-1980s with releases that included superior collections of bitter songs about contemporary America, such as *Repossessed* and *Third World Warrior*.

▣ "Thief on the Cross" (Bob Dylan)

A late inclusion into Dylan's gospel repertoire, "Thief on the Cross" was performed only once, at a New Orleans show in late 1981, and then somewhat indecipherably (if passionately). The song is written from the point of view of a witness gathered at the Crucifixion (maybe one of the robbers nailed to a cross beside Christ); he looks into Christ's eyes and wants to reach out to him. "Thief on the Cross" sounds like another discarded, tail-end gospel era song, "Cover Down Break Through." Maybe Dylan only needed to perform it once.

▣ "Things Have Changed" (Bob Dylan)
Bob Dylan, *Live 1961–2000—Thirty-nine Years of Great Concert Performances/'00* (2001)
Various Artists (performed by Bob Dylan), *Wonder Boys* (soundtrack) (2000); *Paramount Pictures' 90th Anniversary: Memorable Songs* (2002)
Michel Montecrossa, *Jet Pilot* (2000); *4th Time Around* (2001)
Barb Jungr, *Every Grain of Sand: Barb Jungr Sings Bob Dylan* (2002)
Pat Nevins, *Shakey Zimmerman* (2003)

Dylan's first new song since *Time out of Mind* in 1997 was "Things Have Changed," a cynical shuffle in which he, true to his latter form,

T

sings: "I used to care, but things have changed." Clearly the times weren't the only thing changing.

Unsettling and daunting, the narrator can barely mask his condescending contempt for the world around him and his excruciating self-revulsion bristles at the surface of "Things Have Changed." With an almost mocking air, he sings as if he can hardly be bothered to explain what's on his mind, yet he manages to spit out words that appear to describe a man who has ceased caring and is only able to view a weary world with detached, bemused irony, waiting with a woman sitting on his lap, drinking champagne until the "last train" pulls out of the station.

"Things Have Changed" is, of course, notable in the Dylan canon in that it won him the 2001 Oscar for best song for a motion picture, *Wonder Boys*, directed by Curtis Hanson (*L.A. Confidential*) and based on a book by Michael Chabon. The film, released in 2000, stars Michael Douglas as a troubled novelist/professor with writer's block mentoring a young prodigy played by Tobey Maguire.

Dylan submitted the song after viewing about 90 minutes of rough footage at Hanson's Santa Monica editing room.

Dylan and his band performed the song (sans a lyric involving Hollywood superficiality) live via satellite from Australia at the awards ceremony (they were there on tour) in what has to rank as one of his best television displays—even if those close-ups of Dylan sporting his new Chaplinesque mustache were a little tight. And his short acceptance speech (sure to inspire a thesis or two) was one for the ages. After thanking the usual suspects (director Hanson, Paramount Pictures, various and sundry record weasels, and Columbia Records, etc.), Dylan cut right to the chase when he said, "And I want to thank members of the Acad-emy, who were bold enough to give me this award for this song, which obviously is a song that doesn't pussyfoot around nor turn a blind eye to human nature."

Indeed. Writing in "Beauty Walks a Razor's Edge," his article published in *On the Tracks*, #21, Tom Noonan compared "Things Have Changed" with "Abandoned Love," "Angelina," "Series of Dreams," and "Dignity" as another important song, despite its media laurels, that has generally gone unheard. "The song appears over Curtis Hanson's closing credits in *Wonder Boys*," Noonan notes. "Unfortunately, today most moviegoers head toward the exits the second a film's final shot fades out.

"'Things Have Changed' hauntingly depicts the less-than-glamorous qualities of human nature: hopeless isolation frozen in the present ('no one in front of me and no one behind'); confronting finality ('waiting on the last train . . . standing on the gallows with my head in a noose'); sexual betrayal ('woman on my lap . . . got assassins eyes'); seeking the ultimate escapism ('I'm in the wrong town, I should be in Hollywood . . . trying to get as far way from myself as I can'); coming to grips with unpleasant reality ('you can't win with a losing hand'); and seeking comfort for all the wrong reasons ('I'm in love with a woman who doesn't even appeal to me'). Such a desperate state of mind consequently leads one to tempt his fate with the antithesis of Lady Luck ('Mr. Jinx'). The song cautiously averts this tragic leap with the singer assuring us 'he's not that eager to make a mistake.' Not exactly *Sound of Music* material for the Oscar-viewing crowd to digest with their carrots and dip."

As if to prove his fancy with "Things Have Changed" was not merely to cash in on a Hollywood opportunity, Dylan began performing it upon the release of *Wonder Boys* in early 2000. He also won the Golden Globe award for the

T

song. And, as if to prove how genuinely honored he was to have received the Academy Award, Dylan saw to it that Oscar himself was duct-taped to one of his amps in concerts following the ceremony for a couple of years.

As pop culture fodder, the phrase "Things Have Changed" replaced "The Times They Are A-Changin'" as a popular newspaper headline on everything from the sports pages to the financial pages, from analysis of Los Angeles a decade after the 1992 riots to the sex-abuse scandals in the Catholic church to reportage of Enron and its related fallout.

[S] **"This Land Is Your Land"** (Woody Guthrie)

Woody Guthrie, *Woody Guthrie—This Land Is Your Land: Asch Recordings, Volume 1* (1999)
Jack Elliott, *Talking Dust Bowl Blues* (1986)
Bruce Springsteen, *Live 1975–1985* (1986)
The Weavers, *Wasn't That a Time* (1993)
Pete Seeger, *A Link in the Chain* (1996)
Peter, Paul & Mary, *Around the Campfire* (1998)

Dylan performed "This Land Is Your Land," Woody Guthrie's great American anthem with more than a dash of cloaked anarchy, very early on in his career. He returned to the song during the 1975 leg of the Rolling Thunder Revue, when he displayed it as a show-closing rave with Revue members spontaneously contributing verses, hoedown style.

Woody Guthrie couldn't have picked a worse time to hitchhike from California to New York. January and February are always pretty dicey months for any ribbon of highway north of the equator, and the early months of 1940 were no exception. Caught in one terrible blizzard after another, Guthrie, then twenty-seven, nearly froze to death while on a bridge in Pennsylvania. Everywhere he roamed and rambled, Irving Berlin's "God Bless America" was playing on the radio. All the while, a different kind of anthem was piecing itself together in his fevered head. Woody was never a big fan of popular music, which he considered insincere at best, and by the time he hit New York City, he was primed to write his own song of America. On February 23, 1940, at the Hanover House (a fleabag hotel on Sixth Avenue and Forty-third Street) he let vent his passions. Angry, frustrated, and feeling sorry for himself, having hit on hard times in New York City, he took it out on Irving Berlin, writing a response to "God Bless America" with melodic touches from the Carter Family's "Little Darlin', Pal of Mine."

After composing the song, Guthrie completely forgot about it and didn't touch it until four years later, when he recorded "This Land Is Your Land" for Moe Asch's Folkways label.

"This Land Is Your Land" is sometimes suggested as a possible replacement for the "Star Spangled Banner" as the national anthem, but it has also been used (with unintended, sacrilegious irony) as an advertising jingle by United Airlines and the Ford Motor Company, as well as (more forgivably) by George McGovern for his 1972 presidential campaign. Even as recently as 2002, a variation of the song was used as part of an Air Jamaica tourist advertising campaign. In 1975 millions of U.S. schoolchildren sang it simultaneously one morning to open the first annual Music in Our Schools Day. What started out as a sardonic reply to a popular song has become a celebration. Even without the "purple mountain's majesty" of a song like "America, the Beautiful," Guthrie's song still conveys the beauty of the United States.

As recently as the 2004 U.S. presidential campaign, the tune of the song was used as a parody of both candidates, Bush and Kerry, in a popular animation freely swapped on the Internet.

This type of use of "This Land Is Your Land" and other Guthrie compositions made

Woody's old associates fearful that his legacy was being usurped—native radicalism toned down for public consumption—and that his anger and bitter humor were being replaced by a devil-may-care vapidity. For instance, when the U.S. Department of the Interior commended Woody for his Pacific Northwest songs and the Bonneville Power Administration named a substation after him in 1966, his old friend Irwin Silber raged, "They're taking a revolutionary, and turning him into a conservationist."

In the mid-1960s, when Guthrie's health began to seriously fail, he still had enough strength to take his son, Arlo, out to the backyard of their home in Queens, New York, and have him memorize the old radical verses that he'd written for "This Land Is Your Land"—the ones that no one sings anymore now that it has become a patriotic anthem. He was afraid that if Arlo didn't learn them, the words would be forgotten. But Arlo hasn't forgotten his dad's words—he always makes sure to include the verse about the sign that reads "No Trespassing."

"This Old Man" (Traditional/arranged by Malcolm Arnold)
aka "Children's Marching Song," "Knick-Knack Paddy Whack"
Various Artists (performed by Bob Dylan), *For Our Children* (1991)
Joanie Bartels, *Sillytime Magic* (1980)
Ella Jenkins, *Early Childhood Songs* (1990)
Barney, *Run, Jump, Skip & Sing* (1997)
Jim Campilongo, *Table for One* (1998)

Knick-knack Paddy-whack, give the dog a bone!

Adapted by Malcolm Arnold (born October 21, 1921, Northampton, England) in 1958 from an English children's counting song, "This Old Man" was performed by Ingrid Bergman in the film *The Inn of the Sixth Happiness*—and since then by just about any parent who's tried to get

a child to sleep. Arnold is best known as a classical composer whose work in film has brought him the greatest renown (his music for *Bridge on the River Kwai* in 1957 won him an Oscar).

Bob contributed this famous old children's song to *For Our Children*, a collection recorded in support of the Pediatric AIDS Foundation and released on Walt Disney Records. He joined the likes of Paul McCartney, Sting, Elton John, Brian Wilson, Bruce Springsteen, and many others on this tame but well-meaning release. The well-recorded collector's item includes Dylan on guitar and harmonica, and there's an organ floating around there in the mix, too. Dylan's recording of "This Old Man" came on the heels of his album *Under the Red Sky*, a collection that drew heavily on the traditions and importance of the nursery rhyme—another sign of Dylan's interest in children's songs at this time.

"This Wheel's on Fire" (Bob Dylan/Rick Danko)
aka "Wheel's on Fire"
Bob Dylan/The Band, *The Basement Tapes/'67* (1975)
Julie Felix, *This World Goes Round & Round* (1967)
The Band, *Music from Big Pink* (1968); *Rock of Ages* (1974); *The Night They Drove Old Dixie Down* (1992); *Across the Great Divide* (1994)
Ian and Sylvia, *Greatest Hits!* (1987); *Nashville* (1968); *Best of the Vanguard Years* (1998); *Ian & Sylvia: The Complete Vanguard Studio Recordings* (2001)
The Byrds, *Dr. Byrds and Mr. Hyde* (1969); *Play Dylan* (1980); *Byrds* (1990)
Leslie West, *Mountain* (1969)
The Hollies, *Hollies Sing Dylan* (1969)
Paul Jones, *Come into My Music Box* (1969)
Brian Auger, *Best of Brian Auger and the Trinity* (1970)
Brenda Patterson, *Keep On Keepin' On* (1970)
Mike Batt Orchestra, *Portrait of Bob Dylan* (1972)
Julie Driscoll, *Julie Driscoll* (1982)
Siouxsie and the Banshees, *Through the Looking Glass* (1987); *Twice Upon a Time: The Singles* (1992)

The Cuckoos, *Outlaw Blues* (1992)
The Golden Earring, *Love Sweat* (1995)
Rick Danko, *Times Like These* (2000)
Second Floor, *Plays Dylan* (2001)
Various Artists (performed by Rick Danko), *May Your Song Always Be Sung: The Songs of Bob Dylan, Volume 3* (2003)

With its mood of warning, reckoning, fear, and delight, "This Wheel's on Fire" captures a relish for destruction as clearly as anything else from *The Basement Tapes* does. Dylan sings great on the early version, and the Band dug the song so much they included a rendition on their debut record. Cinematically dramatic, "This Wheel's on Fire" may be the most immediately striking of the basement performances, reaching peak after peak of excruciating intensity, highlighted by the impressive eschatological image of a gigantic fiery wheel of apocalyptic power rolling down the road and destroying everything in its path. The narrator is a mysterious, shady Messiah figure (the very hot wheel itself) prophetically returning to settle an old (and final?) score with humanity.

The song could also be autobiographical. "Wheel's on Fire" was written, after all, on the heels of Dylan's motorcycle accident, in which his wheels did explode.

Along with "Tears of Rage," which Dylan cowrote with Richard Manuel, "This Wheel's on Fire" was one of two collaborations spawned from the *Basement Tapes*. As reported in Clinton Heylin's Dylan bio *Behind the Shades*, Hawks bassist Rick Danko recalled the genesis of this famous song: "We would come together every day and work and Dylan would come over. He gave me the typewritten lyrics to 'Wheel's on Fire.' At that time I was teaching myself to play piano. Some music I had written on the piano the day before just seemed to fit with Dylan's lyrics. I worked on the phrasing and melody. Then Dylan and I wrote the chorus together."

Dylan is said to have had an open Bible lying around his house in Woodstock, New York, at the time he was working on the *Basement* songs. Perhaps he saw this passage from the Book of Daniel 7:9 and 10 and was inspired to write "This Wheel's on Fire": "I beheld till the thrones were cast down, and the Ancient of days did sit, Whose garment was white as snow, and the hair of His head like the pure wool; His throne was like the fiery flame, and His wheels as burning fire. A fiery stream issued and came forth from before Him: thousand thousands ministered unto Him, and ten thousand times ten thousand stood before Him: the judgment was set, and the books were opened."

Dylan began performing "Wheel's on Fire" during the spring leg of the 1996 Never Ending Tour, and through 1998, the song popped up pretty frequently at his shows. From 1999 to 2004, however, Dylan rarely performed it.

A final note: the British comedy show *Absolutely Fabulous* not only uses "Wheel's on Fire" as the theme song, but it also shows up in a memorable karaoke scene involving the two main characters.

[S] **"This World Can't Stand Long"** (Jim Anglin)

aka "This World Can't Stand," "This World Can't Stand Too Long"
See also "Humming Bird," "Searching for a Soldier's Grave"
Johnnie and Jack, *Johnnie and the Tennessee Mountain Boys* (1992)
Roy Acuff, *Essential Roy Acuff (1936–1949)* (1992)
Allan McHale, *New River Train* (1992)
Benton Flippen, *Old Time, New Times* (1994)
Mac Martin, *Best of Mac Martin: 24 Favorites* (1998)

Dylan began performing this portentous bit of country gospel prophecy (written by Jim Anglin and popularized by Roy Acuff) in 1999

T

as an acoustic centerpiece at his shows. He adorned the song with Larry Campbell's warm mandolin, the Never Ending tour band's shimmering harmonies, and, most chillingly, his own funeral harmonica clarion call punctuation. The premise of the song (and its vision of the world) is essentially the same as the one Dylan described in "Down in the Flood," in which he sings, "if you go down in the flood it's gonna be your fault." That is, the Maker won't let the human race carry on in a depraved fashion much longer. Along with "Searching for a Soldier's Grave," another Jim Anglin song dealing with some big issues, Dylan retained "This World Can't Stand Long" as a concert number through 2002.

⬛ "Three Angels" (Bob Dylan)
Bob Dylan, *New Morning* (1970)
Persuasions, *Spread the Word* (1972)

An affecting if corny hymn delivered like a prayer, "Three Angels" hints at Dylan's religious period (both born-again Christian and Jew) to come a decade hence.

The narrator sings from a desolate big-city street and wonders why no one is able to hear the music of the angels—the still, small voice within. He wonders if they can't or refuse to hear the cosmic symphony and, standing there on the curb, he muses with sadness on mankind's blind, inhumane ignorance.

In his article "Dylan's New Morning," published in the August 25, 1971, issue of *Christian Century* magazine, Robert Cantwell placed the song in the context of Dylan's shift from the macro to micro in his worldview. "'Three Angels' is one of the songs that shows the broad change of emphasis that has taken place in Dylan's work," he wrote. "In the early years his songs spoke of war, poverty, race relations. Now the poet's concern has shifted to the individual's

denial (or acceptance) of his own spirituality. The lyrics focus on three angels—Christmas decorations placed on poles over a city street. The representatives of mankind pass by during the day, all of them too wrapped up in the concerns of their everyday life to see the divine nature of existence: 'The angels play on their horns all day/The whole earth in progression seems to pass by/But does anyone hear the music they play/Does anyone even try?'"

The liturgically minded will note that the image of three angels appears in at least two key junctures in the Bible, coincidentally or not in its first and last book. The first visitation would be in the Old Testament's Genesis (chapter 18) when Abraham is visited by three angels before his until-then-barren wife, Sarah, became pregnant. Christian commentators understood the story of Abraham's encounter with the three angels as an Old Testament prefiguration of the Christian Trinity. The second crucial tri-angelic visitation would then be found in the Book of Revelation (14:6–12) where each angel brings a different, preapocalyptic warning to mankind.

Old denizens of Woodstock, New York, remember a café called Three Angels, which may have inspired the song's title—or vice versa.

⬛ *Three Kings and the Queen*/Victoria Spivey
Spivey Records LP-1004. Released 1964.

At the October 1961 recording session (some sources cite March 2, 1962) for this song, the waiflike Dylan was photographed with the aging, sassy-looking Victoria Spivey, who has her arm around him; the image adorned the back cover of *New Morning*. Dylan plays harmonica and adds some backing vocals to a couple of tracks here: "Sitting on Top of the World" and "Wichita." Big Joe Williams, the

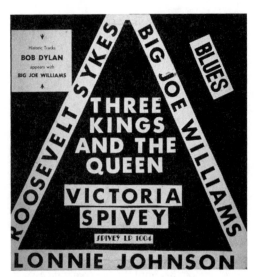

Cover of *Three Kings and the Queen*, 1962.

(Photo: Blank Archives/Getty Images)

hallowed (and extremely cantankerous) blues belter, is also a featured performer on this rarity, which includes pianist Roosevelt Sykes on the closing track, "Thirteen Hours."

A few things to keep in mind here: twenty-year-old white kids didn't just stroll into sessions like this one. They have to be invited. Clearly, Dylan's early genius at the blues must have been evident to the likes of Spivey and Williams, neither of whom appear to have been types to suffer pretenders easily. Even more remarkable is Dylan's ballsy and soulful harp work on this outing. Talk about chutzpah!

Dylan probably met Spivey during her two-week residency at Gerde's Folk City in mid-September 1961. Speculation is that Spivey listed the earlier recording date, which predates Dylan's signing with Columbia, so she wouldn't have to request formal permission to use him in her session.

According to "Big Joe Williams—Memory of the Road," an article published in the

March/April 1995 issue of *Blues Revue* magazine: "A very young Bob Dylan had been similarly impressed with Williams's performances and began a kind of musical partnership with Williams when Big Joe was booked in the fall of 1961 by [Delmark Records founder Bob] Koester at Gerde's Folk City in New York City. Joe performed regularly during a two week period with Dylan frequently sitting in. They were billed as Big Joe and Little Joe, or Joe Junior. Len Kunstadt was subsequently talked into letting Dylan play for some of Williams's studio sessions by his wife, Victoria Spivey."

Spivey (born October 15, 1906, Houston, Texas; died October 3, 1976, New York City) got her musical education by the side of Blind Lemon Jefferson in the brothels of east Texas and was recording at the age of nineteen. She had a couple of early hits with "Black Snake Blues" and "T.B. Blues"—songs marked by her unmistakable nasal singing and barely-appropriate-for-any-age lyrics. She can be seen in the 1929 early black film musical *Hallelujah*, directed by King Vidor. She toured with Louis Armstrong in the 1930s, stopped recording until 1937, and joined the vaudeville circuit until hanging it up in the early 1950s. After singing only in church for years, a comeback in 1960 found her still able to sing and write a great blues tune. She established the Spivey Records label in 1962, issued a few valuable recordings, and coaxed old friends like Lucille Hegamin and Alberta Hunter back into the studio. Spivey, who dubbed herself "The Queen" and showed a hyperenergetic style, was propelled by total self-belief and her songs are marked by themes of drugs, violence, and sexuality.

🅰 ***Three Kings and the Queen, Volume II***/Victoria Spivey
Spivey Records LP-1014. Released 1972.

Blues chanteuse Victoria Spivey scraped the very bottom of her archive when she released "It's Dangerous," a track featuring Dylan on harmonica in this obscure potpourri recorded in the fall of 1961.

[S] "Tight Connection to My Heart (Has Anybody Seen My Love)" (Bob Dylan)

See also "Someone's Got a Hold of My Heart"
Bob Dylan, single (1985); *Empire Burlesque* (1985)
John Martyn, *Piece by Piece* (1986)

An on-the-run apology (or was that confession?) from a man unable to commit to matters of the heart or soul but desperately wants to, "Tight Connection to My Heart" started life out as an *Infidels* composition. The song then spent some time on the backburner, was rewritten (though not necessarily improved), rearranged to include raving back-up singers, and released as the lead-off track to the uneven if generally underrated *Empire Burlesque* album a couple of years later. Because Dylan dropped his back-up singers (who had sung the title of the song as part of the chorus), by the time he began performing "Tight Connection" (oft times with stellar mouth-harp surges), he adopted a semi-official title for the song, "Has Anybody Seen My Love"—a line from the chorus that remained intact.

"Tight Connection" unfolds with great, if convoluted, cinematic drama—like *The Maltese Falcon*, the Bogart film that supposedly inspired the song's tone and some lyrics—with an intangible yet captivating movement and mystery. Released as a single, "Tight Connection" rose to a not-so-mighty No. 103 on the *Billboard* chart—this at the peak of Madonna mania.

Taken as a romantic murmur, "Tight Connection" comes off as a song about a wanted man who's all too eager to go it alone and shed the entanglements and dead weight that encumber his progress through the underbelly of the post-industrial American night—full of danger, violence, rough trade, and neon—in search of experiential, spiritual, and artistic ore. Taken as a song to Christ, the song seems to make even more sense. Maybe that someone around the narrator's neck is actually a something: a crucifix. Maybe when he sings "I'd send for you and I did/What did you expect?" he's dropping the "charade" of organized religion. Just like Bogey when pressed into a corner, he's the one calling the shots from now on.

Noting the song's celluloid qualities, Dylan once commented that "'Tight Connection to My Heart' is a very visual song. I want to make a movie of it. Of all the songs I've ever written, that's the one that's got characters that can be identified with . . . I can see people in it." (*Spin*, Vol. 1, No. 8, 12/85) Paul Schrader (*American Gigolo*, *Affliction*, *Auto Focus*) directed a video of "Tight Connection," but both he and Dylan distanced themselves from the final results.

As for the *Maltese Falcon* connection, Dylan draws on an exchange in the film between Bogart's Sam Spade character and an acquaintance in the San Francisco police force. The cop says, "We wanna talk to you, Spade," and Spade responds, "Well, go ahead and talk." Dylan extracts the opening lines for the second stanza of "Tight Connection": "You want to talk to me/Go ahead and talk."

But Dylan didn't stop there, drawing on a couple of other Bogey films (*Sirocco* and *Tokyo Joe*) for the song's lyrical inspiration. From 1951's *Sirocco* (essentially *Maltese Falcon* meets *Casablanca* in this unfulfilling knockoff set in the Sahara Desert), Dylan pulled "Well I had to move fast/And I couldn't with you around my neck" and "But I can't figure out if I'm too good for you/Or if you're too good for me" straight from Bogart's lips. *Tokyo Joe* (a mediocre post-war, pro-Japanese reconstruction propaganda flick told through Bogey's angry eyes) provided Dylan with the lines "I'll go along with the charade/Until I can think my way out."

But there's more Bogey. The lyric "While they're beatin' the devil out of a guy/Who's wearin' a powder-blue wig" is a clear nod to *Beat the Devil*, a John Huston–directed, Truman Capote–penned 1953 spoof about rogue-adventurers searching for uranium in East Africa. This least-known and most-underrated of the five-film Huston-Bogart collaborations also stars Peter Lorre, Robert Morley, Jennifer Jones, and Gina Lollobrigida.

And for the lines "In a town without pity/Where the water runs deep," Dylan was probably aware of *Town Without Pity*, the 1961 courtroom drama starring Kirk Douglas and rocker Gene Pitney (who sings the title song) about the victimization of a young German woman at the hands of four American soldiers that bears no relation to the plot, murky though it is, in the song. But Dylan, ever the cross-genre splicer, may also have been, as Bert Cartwright pointed out in his article "The Bible in the Lyrics of Bob Dylan: 1985–1990" published in *The Telegraph*, #38, Spring, 1991, "mindful of Jeremiah 20:16 which speaks of 'the cities which the Lord overthrew without pity. . . .' and Lamentations 2:17 tells of the cities the Lord 'has demolished without pity.'"

Cartwright goes on to suggest that Dylan's lyric "I can still hear his voice crying/In the wilderness" may "allude to John the Baptist, who cried in the wilderness (Mathew 3:3) but more likely is still thinking of the Song of Solomon (8:5): 'Who is that coming up from the wilderness, leaning upon her beloved? Under the apple tree I awakened you. There your mother was in travail with you, there she who bore you was in travail.'"

And the lines "What looks large from a distance/Close up ain't never that big," Cartwright believes, may be drawn from Dylan's notion of the Israelites who discovered giants inhabiting the Promised Land, which they were to inherit. Advance word indicated that the invasion appeared hopeless (Numbers 13:26–35), but the task was surmountable "up close" as dramatized in the story of David the giant-killing hero of 1 Samuel 17.

Cartwright wraps up his deconstruction by focusing on the first two lines of the last verse, "Never could drink that blood/And call it wine/Never could learn to love you, love/And call you mine" and argues that the song is Dylan's refusal to fully and finally commit to a Christian life and ideology.

Dylan debuted "Tight Connection" at the famous January 1990 Toad's Club show in New Haven, Connecticut, and played it another eleven times that year. In a stroke of brilliance, he dusted off the song for a couple of downright jazzy acoustic band performances complete with a smoky harmonica run at the special New York City Supper Club shows in November 1993, the second of which stands one of his greatest moments on stage—a teetering, on-the-high wire tour de force that brought out every ounce of drama the song has to offer. Dylan must have realized he would never top himself on that one: He has never performed the song again.

"'Til I Fell in Love with You" (Bob Dylan)
Bob Dylan, *Time out of Mind* (1997)

A loping prowl of a song with raw guitar jabs and opiated organ licks that could have oozed from the grooves of a Jimmy Smith LP or the backdoor of the Brill Building, "'Til I Fell in Love with You" is not exactly the kind of undying devotional testament a girlfriend is pining to hear over a beer and a smoke at the local pub. Dylan might as well just be saying, "Hey girl, things were cool before we became involved." Yet he sounds perfectly at home in the chaos of the relationship.

Like just about all the songs on *Time out of Mind*, Dylan began featuring this plaint ravaged by doubt and need almost immediately after its release in 1997 and it remained a Never Ending Tour staple through the following year when Dylan performed "'Til I Fell in Love with You" nearly seventy times. After laying off the tune for a couple of years, he returned to it in 2001 with some regularity and once again in 2002.

[S] "'Til I Get It Right" (Red Lane/Larry Henley)

Tammy Wynette, *Tammy* (1976)
George Jones, *Together Apart* (1997)
George Jones and Tammy Wynette, *Together Again: Jones and Wynette* (1997)
Engelbert Humperdink, *Don't You Love Me Anymore* (1981)
Millie Jackson, *Just a Li'l Bit Country* (1981)

Dylan's concerts of 1980 and 1981 were notable for the rare, oddball cover songs he performed and "'Til I Get It Right"—a Sisyphean country plaint about a guy who keeps making the same mistakes in matters of the heart—was among them. He performed the song once in 1980 and at a thirty-plus string of 1981 shows.

Songwriter Red Lane (born Hollis Rudolph DeLaughter, February 9, 1939, Bogalusa, Louisiana; some sources say Zona, Louisiana) is a legendary Nashville songsmith and session man who has recorded with a *who's who* in country music, the blues, and pop: Clarence "Gatemouth" Brown, Willie Nelson, Merle Haggard, Dennis Wilson, Johnny Cash, Elvis Costello, Engelbert Humperdinck, Waylon Jennings, Grandpa Jones, Loretta Lynn, Reba McEntire, Jack Palance, George Strait, Conway Twitty, and Tammy Wynette, in whose hands "'Til I Get It Right" became a hit a 1973.

Lane's memorable songs ("Raggedy Ann," "Three Six Packs, Two Arms and a Juke," "Throw a Rope Around the Wind," "Miss Emily's Picture," and "'Til I Get It Right," to name just a few penned over a forty-year Nashville career) have endured as something more than pop-cult dross full of stock clichés and undistinguished melodies. Perhaps that's because Lane's early, itinerant life was full of hard knocks and no luck as his impoverished, sharecropping family wandered the lower forty-eight in a caravan of cars always on the prowl for a field to harvest. In one year alone, Red attended four different schools. Along the way, his guitar-playing father taught him some licks on the lap steel guitar and the two began jamming after a hard day on the farm.

The military was the next, natural stop for Lane, who joined the Air Force in the late 1950s, where he worked as an aircraft and engine mechanic. While stationed in Hawaii he picked up guitar and absorbed the styles of Chet Atkins and Merle Travis, competing in the Air Force talent shows on a borrowed instrument (he finished second after a night of heavy drinking) and appearing on "Hawaii Calling," a local radio show.

Upon his discharge, Lane slowly began trying to get his music career off the ground with a series of failed bands. But his luck changed when he caught a 1964 Justin Tubb (son of country music icon Ernest Tubb) gig and, according to legend, played him some of his own songs backstage. When Tubb encouraged Lane to send Tree Publishing honcho Buddy Villon a tape, things began to fall into place: Tree signed him to an exclusive songwriting deal after just one listen. Tubb also invited Lane to join his band and the two hit the road, commencing with a show at Nashville's Grand

Ole Opry in 1964. Within a few years Faron Young had a hit with Lane's "My Friend on the Right."

Lane continued performing with Tubb and then Dottie West's band the Heartaches, for whom he penned "Country Girl" in 1968. That same year, Waylon Jennings had a hit with Lane's "Walk On Out of My Mind," followed by Eddy Arnold's score with "They Don't Make Love Like They Used To." "'Til I Get It Right" revived Lane's profile as a cutting-edge Nashville songwriter in 1973. He did record the occasional song, and the title track (written with Larry Henley and Johnny Slate) from his debut album, *The Word Needs a Melody*, reached the Top 40 in 1971. The road also beckoned, and he toured as a guitarist in Merle Haggard's early 1980s band; Lane wrote "My Own Kind of Hat" with Haggard. B. J. Thomas's version of "New Looks from an Old Lover" (cowritten with Henley and Johnny Slate) was Lane's last major success.

Larry Henley (born June 30, 1941, Arp, Texas) has credentials of an almost equally impressive stature, even if his biography is a little sketchier: He has recorded with an unlikely cadre that has included Hamiet Bluiett, Sheena Easton, Bobby Goldsboro, Levon Helm, George Jones, Patti Labelle, Delbert McClinton, Bette Midler, and Tammy Wynette.

ⓐ *Till the Night Is Gone: A Tribute to Doc Pomus*/Various Artists

Rhino CD 71878. Released 1995.

One of the best tribute albums ever conceived, recorded, and released, *Till the Night Is Gone* is an audio kowtow for the ages. The legendary Doc Pomus and his dipped-in-sterling songs helped create the soundscape of mid-twentieth-century pop, as evidenced by the performers who sang them: Elvis, the Coast-ers, Bobby Darin, Ray Charles, Dion, and the Drifters, among many others. There's a lot of ground covered on *Till the Night Is Gone*, and between Dylan ("Boogie Woogie Country Girl"), Los Lobos ("Lonely Avenue"), Shawn Colvin ("Viva Las Vegas"), The Band ("Youngblood"), and B. B. King ("Blinded By Love"), the album confirms Jerry Wexler's prophetic words: "If the music industry had a heart, it would be Doc Pomus." Indeed, Pomus's best efforts, like "This Magic Moment" or "Save the Last Dance For Me," are so ingrained in the rock 'n' roll mytho canon they seem as ever-present as folk songs.

Pomus (born Jerome Felder, June 27, 1925, Brooklyn, New York; died March 4, 1991, New York City) fell in love with the blues as a teenager when he heard a Big Joe Turner record. Crippled by polio in his childhood, Pomus never let his disability get in the way of his career. Recognized as one of the top white blues singers of the late 1940s and early 1950s, he sang in a thousand-and-one blues clubs. Realizing there was no way he could raise a family singing blues, he decided to write them. He didn't have to look far when it came time to choose a collaborator: his piano-playing partner for dozens of years, Mort Shuman.

Riding the wave of Tin Pan Alley's last gasp, the two cranked out hit after hit. Their songs helped secure Presley's place in the pantheon and made stars out of Fabian and the like, while Doc's behind the scenes work boosted Lou Reed and resurrected Big Joe Turner. Doc was a ubiquitous presence on New York City's club scene, a hulking force hanging out in the fringes of joints like the Bottom Line and the Lone Star Café, always with his sharp ear attuned for a new voice or a good story. Lung cancer claimed his life.

A final biographical note: divorce attorney Raoul Felder is Doc's brother.

⚠ *Timeless: Hank Williams Tribute*/Various Artists
Uptown/Universal CD 170239. Released 2001.

Considering Hank Williams's stature as one of American music's genius icons, it is extraordinary that it took so long for the now-customary all-star tribute album to be produced in his honor. Dylan had signed on for projects like this in the past (his "Boogie Woogie Country Girl" can be found on the Doc Pomus tribute collection *Till the Night Is Gone*) and he had produced (and contributed to) the potpourri homage, *The Songs of Jimmie Rodgers: A Tribute*. The fact that Dylan has included the odd Williams tune in his performance grab bag through the years surely made him an easy sell when the subject of cutting a track for *Timeless* arose. Along with his version of "I Can't Get You off of My Mind" (a somewhat obscure Williams song Dylan briefly took to the concert stage in 2001), *Timeless* includes some dusky jewels from artists across the pop and age spectrum: Sheryl Crow's faithful re-creation of "Long Gone Lonesome Blues," Beck's barebones "Your Cheatin' Heart," Keith Richards's intimately boozy "You Win Again," Lucinda Williams's Spartan "Cold, Cold Heart," and Johnny Cash's reading of "I Dreamed About Mama Last Night" all contribute to a passionate kowtow to an American giant.

⚠ *Time out of Mind*
Columbia CD CK 68556, CS 68556, LP 68556. Recorded
    1997 at Criteria Recording Studios, Miami, Florida.
    Released September 30, 1997. Produced by Daniel Lanois.
Bob Dylan—vocals, acoustic guitar, electric guitar, harmonica,
    piano. Robert Britt—acoustic, electric guitars. Daniel
    Lanois—acoustic guitar, electric guitar, mando-guitar. Bucky
    Baxter—acoustic, pedal steel guitars. Duke Robillard—guitar. Cindy Cashdollar—slide guitar. Jim Dickinson—Wurlitzer piano, pump organ, keyboards. Augie Meyers—organ,
    accordion. Tony Garnier—acoustic, electric bass. Winston

Watson, Jim Keltner, David Kemper, Brian Blade—drums.
Tony Mangurian—percussion.
"Love Sick," "Dirt Road Blues," "Standing in the Doorway,"
    "Tryin' to Get to Heaven," "'Til I Fell in Love with You,"
    "Not Dark Yet," "Cold Irons Bound," "Make You Feel My
    Love," "Can't Wait," "Highlands"

Dylan's extreme generosity as a performing artist in the early and mid-1990s was countered by his stinginess as a recording artist—the decade saw only two collections of traditional songs (*Good as I Been to You* and *World Gone Wrong*) and the imminently forgettable *Under the Red Sky* in 1990. As the years rolled past, the wish for some current cosmic weather report from the postmodern bard became more tangible. So news of a Dylan album created considerable stir in the summer of 1997.

With producer Daniel Lanois at the helm, *Time out of Mind* was atmospherically reminiscent to *Oh Mercy*—the album Dylan recorded with Lanois nearly a decade before. But while that first effort is dipped in sepia, *Time out of Mind*, narrated by an older man eyeballing life with the Grim Reaper at his side, is ominous and gritty. The album came out only months after Dylan's near fatal bout with a coronary infection, underlining the flimsiness of all things mortal. Deftly mixing the bitter and the sweet, Dylan gives his songs resigned and anguished readings. And if some of the emotional impact of the material may be a bit blunted, Dylan's attachment to this harvest was underscored by a commitment to nearly all the songs as performance tools in the years that followed.

Time out of Mind entered the pop charts at No. 10 and swiftly hit gold—Dylan's first gold studio collection since *Infidels* in 1983. As for the album's title, no popular theories abound. However, the titular phrase does appear on the first page of J. R. R. Tolkien's premier novel,

T

The Hobbit, so perhaps Dylan had some postindustrial, blues-drenched Middle Earth in mind as a setting for these songs. The phrase is an old one and can be found referenced in several other well known and arcane sources, including the W. B. Yeats poem "He Thinks of His Past Greatness When a Part of the Constellations of Heaven," a collection of poems by Rachel Field, a novel by Pierre Boulle (*Planet of the Apes* and *Bridge on the River Kwai*), Edna St. Vincent Millay's "Dirge Without Music," and, most famously, Shakespeare's *Measure for Measure* and *Romeo and Juliet*, to name just a few.

Crammed with the temporary freedom of train-song rhythms ("Cold Irons Bound"), swampy, organ-studded soul ("'Til I Fell in Love with You"), personal crisis disguised as epic humorous ballad ("Highlands"), failed romance ("Love Sick"), worn-out, on-the-lam blues ("Dirt Road Blues"), and mortal personal assessments ("Not Dark Yet"), *Time out of Mind* might be Dylan's ultimate loner's road trip—the scattered thoughts of a progressed pilgrim headed to the grave.

Like the best of his early songs, *Time out of Mind* uses simple plain speak while portraying the conceptual thread of a restless, middle-aged man still walking down that long, lonesome road with the rain pouring out of his shoes. But, unlike the kid from "Don't Think Twice" or the searcher from "Tangled Up in Blue," our narrator doesn't seem too excited about what might be lurking over the hill as he views the scraps of his life in a series of flashbacks. Yet, through all the doom and gloom, there are moments of profound humor, gallows though it may be.

It was gratifying (but not very surprising) when *Time out of Mind* won the 1998 Grammy Award for album of the year. What was surprising was that Dylan never won the prize before.

T

[S] "Time Passes Slowly" (Bob Dylan)

Bob Dylan, *New Morning* (1970); *Biograph/'70* (1985)
Judy Collins, *Whales & Nightingales* (1970)
Rachel Faro, *Refugees* (1970)

The PR rap on Dylan during the *New Morning* period was that he was content to be a homebody dad, rearing a family in upstate New York and casually writing/releasing material. The frustrations of the life, however, may seep through in the otherwise pastoral "Time Passes Slowly," a piano song suggesting that he senses he has fallen out of step with his muse and the scene.

Coming across an old salt sitting by a stream in the Catskills reminiscing about the fine and good-looking sweetheart he once had back in Hibbing, Minnesota, Dylan sounds a little sad—as if the search for love is an illusion, a social formality that brings the prison bars clanging down.

[A] *The Times They Are A-Changin'*

Columbia Records. LP CL-2105; CD CK-8905; CS CS-8905. Recorded in New York City, August 6, 7, 12; October 23, 24, 31, 1963. Released January 13, 1964. Produced by Tom Wilson. Liner notes ("11 Outlined Epitaphs") by Bob Dylan. Cover photograph by Barry Feinstein.

"The Times They Are-Changin'," "Ballad of Hollis Brown," "With God On Our Side," "One Too Many Mornings," "North Country Blues," "Only a Pawn in Their Game," "Boots of Spanish Leather," "When the Ship Comes In," "The Lonesome Death of Hattie Carroll," "Restless Farewell"

From its unadorned, faded black-and-white cover of a weathered Bob Dylan doing his best to look seriously Guthriesque to its let's-get-down-to-business collection of mostly topical songs, *The Times They Are A-Changin'* has its place on the shelf as a sometimes inspired, well-intentioned outing. At least half the songs on this third Dylan album are classics and staples in his performance repertoire. But the recording is flat and was never much fun to begin with . . . not that it was supposed to be. Apparently the rest of the world agreed. Though the album hit No. 20 on the *Billboard* charts, it stayed there for a mere five weeks.

Perhaps the album's meager reception had something to do with the trials and tribulations the country had endured between the release of this LP and *The Freewheelin' Bob Dylan* a year before. With John Kennedy and his assassin dead, the Vietnam War and civil rights movement beginning to tear the United States apart, and the mood throughout the land muted and withdrawn, Dylan's songs, almost by necessity, cry out to a lost innocence.

Commencing with the anthemic title track, Dylan mixes indignation ("The Lonesome Death of Hattie Carroll"), social diagnosis ("Ballad of Hollis Brown"), political deconstruction ("Only a Pawn in Their Game"), radical historical revisionism ("With God on Our Side"), and our-time-will-come optimism ("When the Ship Comes In"), while managing to sneak in a couple of his great romantic statements ("Boots of Spanish Leather" and "One Too Many Mornings").

The liner notes are worthy of note here: Dylan's famed free verse "11 Outlined Epitaphs" were included on the back cover and on both sides of an insert accompanying the disc.

A final note: this was the first of six Dylan albums named for a song on the record.

🅂 **"The Times They Are A-Changin'"** (Bob Dylan)
Bob Dylan, single (1964); *The Times They Are A-Changin'* (1964); *Bob Dylan's Greatest Hits* (1967); *Bob Dylan at Budokan* (1979); *Biograph/'*64 (1985); *The Bootleg Series, Volumes 1–3: Rare and Unreleased, 1961–1991/'*64 (1991); *MTV Unplugged* (1995);

"Love and Theft" [Deluxe Edition]/'64 (2001); *The Bootleg Series, Volume 6: Live 1964—Concert at Philharmonic Hall* (2004)

Bob Dylan/Various Artists (performed by Tracy Chapman), *Bob Dylan: The 30th Anniversary Concert Celebration* (1993)

Various Artists (performed by Bob Dylan), *Freedom: Songs From the Hearts of America* (2002)

Peter, Paul & Mary, *In Concert* (1964)

Linda Mason, *How Many Seas Must a White Dove Sail?* (1964)

Odetta, *Odetta Sings Dylan* (1965)

The Seekers, *A World of Our Own* (1965)

The Silkie, *You've Got to Hide Your Love Away* (1965)

Hugues Aufray, *Chante Dylan* (1965); *Au Casino de Paris* (1996)

The Byrds, *Turn! Turn! Turn!* (1966); *The Preflyte Sessions* (2002)

Simon and Garfunkel, *Wednesday Morning 3 A.M.* (1966)

Beach Boys, *Beach Boys' Party!* (1966)

Sebastian Cabot, *Sebastian Cabot, Actor—Bob Dylan, Poet* (1967)

Hounds, *The Lion Sleeps Tonight* (1967)

Cher, *With Love* (1968)

Burl Ives, *Times They Are A-Changing* (1968)

Human Beings, *Nobody but Me* (1968)

Bob Lind, *The Elusive Bob Lind* (1968)

Yankee Dollar, *Yankee Dollar* (1968)

Nina Simone, *To Love Somebody* (1969)

The Hollies, *Hollies Sing Dylan* (1969)

Lester Flatt and Earl Scruggs, *Nashville Airplane* (1969); *1964–1969, Plus* (1996)

The Brothers & Sisters of Los Angeles, *Dylan's Gospel* (1969)

Mike Batt Orchestra, *Portrait of Bob Dylan* (1972)

Spirit, *Spirit of '76* (1975)

Various Artists (performed by James Taylor), *No Nukes* (1980)

The Wanderers, *The Only Lovers Left Alive* (1981)

Pete Kennedy, *Bound for Glory* (1986)

Nervous Eaters, *Hot Steel and Acid* (1986)

Richie Havens, *Sings Beatles & Dylan* (1987); *Cuts to the Chase* (1994)

Billy Joel, *In Concert—"Kohept"* (1987)

Veil of Ashes, *Pain* (1989)

T

Dylan performing at the 1964 Newport Folk Festival;
Pete Seeger is seated behind him at left.

(Photo: Bill Eppridge/Time Life Pictures/Getty Images)

Billy Bragg, *Goes to Moscow & Northern Virginia* (1991)
Eddie Owen, *The Times They Are A-Changin'* (1992)
Youth Gone Mad, *West/East* (1991)
Dead Moon, *Crack in the System* (1994)
Phil Collins, *Dance into the Light* (1996)
Manfred Mann, *Mann Alive* (1997)
Judy Collins, *Both Sides Now* (1998)
Joshua Redman, *Timeless Tales (For Changing Times)* (1998)
Various Artists (performed by David West), *Pickin' on Dylan* (1999)
Gerard Quintana and Jordi Batiste, *Els Miralls de Dylan* (1999)
Various Artists (performed by Billy Joel), *Doin' Dylan 2* (2002)
Various Artists (performed by Mankind), *Blowin' in the Wind: A Reggae Tribute to Bob Dylan* (2003)

With its Old Testament tone of dire prophetic warning, "The Times They Are A-Changin'" still sounds an alarm that's hard to ignore.

Dylan's timing with composing and releasing "The Times They Are A-Changin'" was uncanny, coinciding with the assassination of President John F. Kennedy in the fall of 1963 and the cresting of both the Vietnam War and the civil rights movement. Along with "Blowin' in the Wind," "The Times They Are A-Changin'" became a virtual clarion call to left-wing political activism throughout the 1960s.

In the *Biograph* liner notes, Dylan pointed to the song's roots in the Irish and Scots traditions that produced such ballads as "Come All Ye Tender Hearted Maidens."

As much as any of Dylan's other songs, "The Times They Are-Changin'" (suffused with prophetic Biblical imagery of imminent and irrevocable cataclysm and revolution) gave a generation its voice. Tapping perfectly into the mood of the era, Dylan eloquently and simply stated the obvious. Although the song can viewed as temporally clichéd, Dylan's later performances—sung with more than a bit of cynicism—kept it fresh as the world around him became even darker.

In his Dylan biography *No Direction Home*, Robert Shelton impressionistically discussed "The Times They Are A-Changin'" when he wrote that the song was a:

> ... summation of the sixties mood. No cautious questioning now, but a prophetic voice trumpeting a changing order. The song was widely recorded and translated into Serbian, French, Hebrew, and other languages. The imagery is primal, homespun: a flood tide, fate's spinning, a blocked doorway, the storm of battle, a changing road. While this could be played over the film clips of Prague, Paris, Chicago, and Berkeley, it is also a timeless dialogue between those restrained by old ways and those daring something new.
>
> At first the lyrics' biblical roll seems to reflect black gospel song. The title line suggests the warning in Revelation 1:3: "... for the time is near." There is an echo from Mark 10:31: "But many that are first will be last, and the last first."
>
> As biblical flood waters rise and Armageddon approaches: "There's a battle outside/And it is ragin'," does not criticize the old as much as entrenched, rigid thinking, "to separate aliveness from deadness," as he later said. In the midst of a stern challenge, Dylan offers parents, writers, critics, and even politicians a chance to join the changing tide: "Please get out of the new [road]/If you can't lend your hand." The hortatory performance, seemingly sung through clenched teeth, matches the lyrics' bold cadences and messianic tone.

Considering its venerable place in Dylan's performance slate, "The Times They Are A-Changin'" has been relatively untouched over the decades. The song has the unique quality of reflecting any era in which it is performed. As Dylan told French interviewer Philippe Adler in a 1978 interview, "Each time I sing it, I feel like I wrote it the day before."

[S] "The Times We Have Known" (Charles Aznavour)

aka "Les Bons Moments," "The Times We've Known"
Charles Aznavour, *You and Me* (1995)

"I usually play these songs all by myself. But I feel all by myself now," announced Dylan before his acoustic one-off of this English-language version of Frenchman Charles Aznavour's ballad—a surprise hit at an autumn 1998 show in the Big Apple's Madison Square Garden.

Aznavour (born Shanaur Varenagh Aznavourain, May 22, 1924, Paris, France) is a diminutive, raspy-voiced songster of primarily self-composed chansons as well as a sad-eyed thespian who came to personify "Frenchness" for Anglo-Saxon audiences. Of Armenian extraction, Aznavour first studied acting but turned to songwriting as a means of support in 1942, when he wrote "J'ai bu" with Pierre Roche for George Ulmer. Encouraged by Maurice Chevalier and Edith Piaf (who became his mentor), Aznavour gained a reputation as a singer at the Paris Olympia Theatre and appeared in *Paris Music Hall*, a 1957 documentary. George Franju's *La Tête Contre les Murs* in 1958 and François Truffaut's *Shoot the Piano Player* in 1960, in which he plays a café entertainer, are regarded as his most memorable film roles, highlighting the melancholy aspect of his personality. Those roles opened doors in both France and Hollywood and he has appeared in many films in the past four decades.

"Sur Ma Vie" in 1955, "Il Faut Savoir" and "Je Voyais Déjà" in 1958, "Je t'Attends" in 1961, and "La Mama" written with Robert Gall in 1963 were his big music hits. "La Mama" (rewritten with English words and retitled "For Mama") provided Matt Monro with a minor British hit in 1964. After *Monsieur Carnival*, an operetta he

T

French singer, songwriter, and actor Charles Aznavour, 1965.

(Photo: Reg Lancaster/Express/Getty Images)

T

wrote in 1965, Aznavour has focused on his cinematic career, writing songs or even entire scores for the films in which he appears. His last major musical success came in 1974 with "She" and "The Old-Fashioned Way," but he still frequently appears in films—most recently in *Ararat*, a meditative 2002 Atom Egoyan–directed dramatization of the plight of Armenia that also stars Eric Bogosian.

Dylan holds Aznavour in high regard and, as he told *Rolling Stone* in a 1987 interview, he believes that Aznavour is among the greatest live performers he's ever seen. And in 1998, Dylan told *Mojo*, "I became aware of him in 1962. I actually saw him perform in New York because I'd seen a movie he was in called *Shoot the Piano Player*. I saw that movie a bunch of times because the snow part of it reminded me of back where I came from. . . . Well, everything about that movie I identified with. Everything. So Charles Aznavour came to New York to play—and I was the first one in line for a ticket."

[S] "Tiny Montgomery" (Bob Dylan)

Bob Dylan/The Band, *The Basement Tapes/'67* (1975)
Coulson, Dean, McGuinness, Flint, *Lo & Behold* (1996)

Bob plays the part of Father Time on this nugget that seems to be about sending an enigmatic message to a friend. This is a fractured, melody shy nursery-rhyme of the type Dylan would reexplore with some of his *Under the Red Sky* songs a quarter of a century later. Like "Million Dollar Bash," another song from the *Basement Tapes* featuring Dylan's sideshow freaks, "Tiny Montgomery" is full of characters with names like Skinny Moo, Half-Track Frank, Lester, and Lou, some or all of whom may be doing the bizarre calisthenics suggested in the song: scratching your dad and doing the bird. If the song could be translated into a screenplay, think *High Plains Drifter* meets *Alice in Wonderland.*

Greil Marcus reported that "Tiny Montgomery" was rumored to be named for a stockcar racer but there was also a famed abalone diver who made that name for himself in Morro Bay, California (just down the road from "ol' Frisco," mentioned in the song). Regardless, the stranger who blows into town and leaves behind a greeting for everyone has always been the stuff of storytelling fodder.

Andy Gill's assessment of "Tiny Montgomery" was considerably more down to earth when he wrote in his book *Don't Think Twice, It's All Right*: "Another trifle with more character than meaning, 'Tiny Montgomery' has an engaging boozy bonhomie. . . . Tricked out in short, imponderable phrases—'Honk that stink/Take it down/And watch it grow'—chosen more for sound than sense, it has the weird hermetic logic of a private language, the kind of thing that members of cults or secret organizations use to communicate with each other."

Bassist Rick Danko told Marcus: "We played some of the basement songs for friends. I remember we played 'Tiny Montgomery.' People laughed at us."

[S] "To Be Alone with You" (Bob Dylan)

Bob Dylan, *Nashville Skyline* (1969)
Catherine Howe, *Harry* (1975)
Marshall Chapman, *Take It On Home* (1982)
Steve Gibbons, *On The Loose* (1992)
Sue Foley, *Big City Blues* (1995)
Michel Montecrossa, *4th Time Around* (2001)

Dylan commenced many of 1991 and 1992 shows with this agreeable, country-tinged love song as a kind of open, if muddled, invitation to his audience and performance muse. A decade later, Dylan reintroduced the song as a show opener, remaking it into a rousing rock 'n' roll revival that quickly had everyone on their feet.

Typical of the type of over-analysis a Dylanist might devote to a single song or even a phrase, John Herdman's assessment of "To Be Alone with You" and *Nashville Skyline* in his book *Voice Without Restraint: A Study of Bob Dylan's Lyrics and Their Background* is worth a look. "Dylan has said in an interview that 'on *Nashville Skyline* you had to read between the lines,'" Herdman begins. "Taking up that hint we might start at the beginning of the first song: 'To be alone with you/Just you and me/Now won't you tell me true/Ain't that the way it oughta be?' That question-mark can be taken as being eloquent. It seems to represent an acknowledgment that Dylan is here *willing* himself to take up a position which he does not really *feel* . . . authenticity of feeling forms the stated basis of his art, without which nothing serious is possible."

[S] "Tombstone Blues" (Bob Dylan)

See also "Jet Pilot"
Bob Dylan, *Highway 61 Revisited* (1965); *Biograph/'65* (1985); *Real Live* (1984); *MTV Unplugged* (1995)
Anastasia Screamed, *Outlaw Blues* (1992)
Various Artists (two different versions performed by Henry Kaiser's Obsequious Cheeselog and Dogmeat), *Outlaw Blues, Volume 2* (1995)
Tim O'Brien, *Red on Blonde* (1996)
The Rockridge Synthesizer Orchestra, *Plays Bob Dylan Classic Trax* (1997)
Sheryl Crow, *Sheryl Crow and Friends: Live in Central Park* (1999)
Various Artists (performed by Black Eyed Snakes), *Duluth Does Dylan* (2001)

Painting a dark landscape of a mad, mad, mad, mad world, Dylan invites a memorable cast of characters (Ma Rainey, Beethoven, Paul Revere's horse, Galileo, Belle Starr, and Jack the Ripper) to make cameos is this episodic piece of beat-thumping, twelve-bar surrealism.

Fresh from his turbulent appearance at the Newport Folk Festival and primed with his new electric band, Dylan was hitting his stride in his alchemy of Chicago blues, rock 'n' roll and freestyle poetic rantics when he entered Columbia Records Studio A in July 1965 to resume work on *Highway 61 Revisited*. With Michael Bloomfield playing his trademark (if out of time) stinging electric guitar riffs, the manic "Tombstone Blues" defines the sound of that landmark release as much any other song on the album does.

It was as if Dylan were imagining what kind of song Marcel Duchamp and Luis Buñuel might have come up with had they joined Little Richard's band: "Tombstone Blues" is steeped with the type of non sequiturs and absurdist, though pointed humor, with which they all might have felt quite comfortable. Dylan combines topsy-turvy, through-the-looking-glass poetic and vocal wordplay with political, historical, and mythological iconography to breathlessly portray his vision of a world going wrong. Check out the lines "The Commander-in-Chief answers him while chasing a fly/Saying, 'Death to all those who would wimper and cry'/And dropping a barbell he points to the sky/Saying, 'The sun's not yellow, it's chicken'" or "The ghost of Belle Starr she hands down her wits/To Jezebel the nun she violently knits/A bald wig for Jack the Ripper who sits/At the head of the chamber of commerce."

Yes, maybe "Tombstone Blues" can come off like some kid's stream-of-consciousness rantings that take cliché potshots at the establishment's sacred cows. Or maybe Dylan was merging the form and function of both the surrealists and symbolists. Wasn't it Buñuel who was once quoted as saying, "All of us were supporters of a certain concept of revolution, and although the surrealists didn't consider themselves terrorists, they were constantly fighting a society they despised. The principle weapon was not guns, of course, it was scandal. Scandal was a potent agent of revelation, capable of exposing social crimes as exploitation of man by another, colonialist imperialism, religious tyranny—in sum, all the secrets and odious underpinnings of a system that had to be destroyed." And wasn't it symbolist poets such as Rimbaud, Baudelaire, and Ver-

laine who held that as long as a poem sounded great and moved the listener into some heightened reverie of Blakean awareness, any need for explanation is moot? Considering that Dylan was deeply involved with these two schools of thought and practice at the time he wrote "Tombstone Blues," then its form, content, and intent appears wholly and totally natural and comprehensible.

Dylan's comments in the *Biograph* liner notes trace the impetus of "Tombstone Blues" to an unlikely locale: a bar frequented by off-duty New York cops where he overheard conversations describing the most desperate situations.

Some have suggested that Dylan drew on Leroy Carr's "Papa's on the Housetop," a jump blues with many variants, as the musical and lyrical root source for the chorus of "Tombstone Blues" (the "Mama's in the fac'try/She ain't got no shoes" refrain). This would explain lines like "Baby's in the cradle, made a lot of time/Sister's in the parlor trying on a gown/Mama's in the kitchen messing around/And Papa's on the housetop, won't come down." But some of Chuck Berry's songs, particularly "Promised Land" or "Hail, Hail Rock 'n' Roll," with their loping rat-a-tat scansion, also come to mind.

Though only a couple of Dylan performances of "Tombstone" survive from the time of its composition, Dylan did return to the song briefly for some shrill outings for the 1984 European tour, in an *MTV Unplugged* appearance in 1994, and on the Never Ending Tours thereafter.

▣ "Tomorrow Is a Long Time" (Bob Dylan)
aka "Tomorrow's a Long Time"
Bob Dylan, *Bob Dylan's Greatest Hits, Volume II/'63* (1971); *Masterpieces* (1978)
Joan Baez, *Joan Baez in Concert, Part 2* (1963)
Ian and Sylvia, *Four Strong Winds* (1964); *Greatest Hits* (1987); *Ian & Sylvia: The Complete Vanguard Studio*

Recordings (2001)
Hamilton Camp, *Paths of Victory* (1964)
Linda Mason, *How Many Seas Must A White Dove Sail?* (1964)
The Brothers Four, *The Brothers Four Sing Of Our Times* (1964)
Silkie, *You've Got to Hide Your Love Away* (1965)
Judy Collins, *5th Album* (1965); *Recollections: The Best of Judy Collins* (1969)
The Empty Set, *Early Morning Rain* (1965)
Odetta, *Odetta Sings Dylan* (1965)
Esther & Abi Ofarim, *Sing* (1965)
Elvis Presley, *Spinout* (1966); *In Demand* (1977); *Elvis: A Legendary Performer, Volume 4* (1980); *Valentine Gift for You* (1985); *From Nashville to Memphis* (1993); *Ballads* (1999); *Tomorrow Is A Long Time* (1999)
Sebastian Cabot, *Sebastian Cabot, Actor—Bob Dylan, Poet* (1967)
Glen Yarborough, *For Emily Wherever I May Find Her* (1967)
Street, *Street* (1968)
Dion, *Dion* (1968); *Abraham, Martin & John* (1990)
Kingston Trio, *Once Upon a Time* (1969)
We Five, *Catch the Wind* (1970)
Rod Stewart, *Every Picture Tells a Story* (1971); *Vintage* (1993); *Ballad Album* (1998)
Sandy Denny, *Sandy* (1972); *Who Knows Where the Time Goes* (1986); *Gold Dust: Live at the Royalty—The Final Concert* (1998); *Ballad Album* (1998)
Carol Hedin, *Devil Take Me with You* (1971)
Heaven & Earth, *Refuge* (1973)
Shirl Milete, *Shirl Milete* (1974)
Magna Charta, *Pulling It Back Together* (1976)
Earl Scruggs, *Family Portrait* (1976)
Nana Mouskouri, *Roses & Sunshine* (1979)
Chris Hillman, *Morning Sky* (1982)
Hugh Moffatt, *Loving You* (1987)
Passion Fodder, *Fat Tuesday* (1988)
Steve Keene, *Keene On Dylan* (1990)
Various Artists (performed by Ian and Sylvia), *Troubadours of the Folk Era, Volume 1* (1992)
Insol, *Insol* (1998)
Dream City Film Club, *Stranger Blues* (1999)
Michel Montecrossa, *Eternal Circle* (2000)
Aui & Alex, *Aui & Alex Sing Dylan* (2000)

Gail Davies, *Gail Davies & Friends Live and Unplugged at the Station Inn* (2001)
Various Artists (performed by Rosalie Sorrels), *A Nod to Bob* (2001)
Nick Drake, *Time Is Told Me* (2002)

A precious song describing the poet's early vision of beauty in all things—but most especially his memory of his true love once laying beside him, "Tomorrow Is a Long Time" was composed in the midst of Dylan's remorse of seeing his first true New York City love, Suze Rotolo, sail away to Italy. Presley's 1966 recording of the song shows that the song is closer to the King than to the likes of Woodie Guthrie.

Part of the beautifully poetic chorus of the eloquently wrought "Tomorrow Is a Long Time" ("...and I lay in my bed once again") was evidently inspired by "O Western Wind" and "The Lover in Winter Plaineth for the Spring," two anonymous poems, circa 1530, of which only these words survive: "Westron winde, when will thou blow/The smalle raine downe can raine/Christ, if my love were in my armes/And I in my bed againe." One of the most famous early English verses, the poem is widely anthologized, so it is not surprising that Dylan may have run across it. The "western wind" referenced in the old song probably refers to Zephyrus, the spring wind, and was used by Dylan at a particularly dramatic moment in "Boots of Spanish Leather," another song spun from Rotolo's absence.

"Tomorrow Is a Long Time" has a complicated history in the Dylan recording canon. Dylan wrote and first performed the song in mid-1962, but the song didn't make it to vinyl until 1971, when a live 1963 version appeared on *Bob Dylan's Greatest Hits, Volume II* as a buyer's incentive. This officially released version of "Tomorrow Is a Long Time" was originally to be included in *Bob Dylan in Concert,*

T

which was never released. The album was to combine songs from two 1963 concerts at New York's Town Hall and Carnegie Hall, but some Dylanists contend that the album was canned because the material, which was not exactly Dylan's strongest to begin with, would no longer have been representative of Dylan's songs by the time the album came out.

As performance fodder, the impressionistic, lyrically simple "Tomorrow Is a Long Time" has come and gone and come again throughout Dylan's performance career. After the exquisitely light and tender performances of the early 1960s, the song didn't pop up again until Dylan's 1978 big band tour, when he gave it a considerably lush treatment. The song exhibited Nashville-style during the Dylan–Grateful Dead shows in 1987 and became notable for Jerry Garcia's rare turn on pedal steel guitar. "Tomorrow Is a Long Time" showed up during the Never Ending Tour from the get-go in 1988, and Dylan has used it alternately as both an acoustic and electric offering since then.

"Tomorrow Night" (Sam Coslow/Will Grosz)
Bob Dylan, *Good as I Been to You* (1992)
Big Joe Turner, *Very Best of Big Joe Turner* (1951)
Count Basie, *Just the Blues* (1960)
Elvis Presley, *Reconsider Baby* (1985)
Lonnie Johnson, *Blues Masters* (1991)
Charles Brown, *Boss of the Blues* (1963)
Pat Boone, *Fifties: Complete* (1997)
Etta James, *These Foolish Things* (1995)

Dylan sings the sleepy "Tomorrow Night" as a crooning lament, the missing link in the Elvis Presley–Dylan lineage or the Al Jolson–Dylan pedigree, or just a great song choice by someone who knows how to pick 'em. A promise in song that all things of the body, spirit, and heart will soon be consummated, "Tomorrow Night" was popularized by 1930s big-band leader and talent sniffer Horace Heidt and revived by Lonnie Johnson, who made a hit record out of it when he was pushing sixty.

Sam Coslow (born December 27, 1902, New York City; died April 2, 1982, New York City) was the best known of the two composers of "Tomorrow Night." Coslow came up through the same Tin Pan Alley ranks that produced the likes of Irving Berlin, Richard Rodgers, and Sammy Cahn. While Coslow never had much success on Broadway, a move to Hollywood in 1929 ignited a successful run in the film biz. With composer Arthur Johnston, his main collaborator, Coslow produced hit songs for Bing Crosby's first cinematic vehicles (*College Humor* and *Too Much Harmony*) and a string of films that reached into the 1950s: *Murder at the Vanities* (1934), *Turn Off the Moon* (1937), *Thrill of a Lifetime* (1938), *Copacabana* (1947), and *Affair with a Stranger* (1953). His most famous songs ("Sing You Sinners," "Just One More Chance," "Thanks," "Moon Song," and "Cocktails for Two") date from the 1930s and he shared an Oscar for his work on *Heavenly Music*, a 1943 short. A successful venture into "Soundies," coin-operated machines showing song-movie shorts, led to a small career as a movie producer in the 1940s. Later he became a successful publisher.

The song was always effective in its 1993 and 1994 concert displays (and its one subsequent performance, in 1998), and Dylan could mold himself into an avant-garde Mel Torme from Purgatory when he sang "Tomorrow Night."

"Tonight I'll Be Staying Here with You"
(Bob Dylan)
Bob Dylan, single (1969); *Nashville Skyline* (1969); *Bob Dylan's Greatest Hits, Volume II/'69* (1971); *The Bootleg Series, Volume 5: Live 1975—The Rolling Thunder Revue* (2002)

Tina Turner, *Tina Turns the Country On* (1967)
Cher, *3614 Jackson Highway* (1969)
Dave Kelly, *Willing* (1969)
Orange Bicycle, *Last Cloud Home* (1969)
Ben E. King, *Rough Edges* (1970)
Jeff Beck, *Jeff Beck Group* (1972)
Pat McLaughlin, *Wind It On Up* (1981)
Nappy Brown, *Tore Up* (1984)
Albert Lee, *Black Claw and Country Fever* (1991)
Eddie Adcock, *Dixie Fried* (1991)
Larry Barrett, *Porch Song Ginger* (1995)
Pat McLaughlin, *Wind It on Up* (1996)
Esther Phillips, *Best of Esther Phillips (1962–1970)* (1997)
Jimmy LaFave, *Trail* (1999)
Various Artists (performed by Charlie Chesterman), *A Tribute to Bob Dylan, Volume 3: The Times They Are A-Changin'* (2000)
Second Floor, *Plays Dylan* (2001)
Pat Nevins, *Shakey Zimmerman* (2003)

This seductive *Nashville Skyline* ballad drops the curtain on Dylan's first formalized foray into country music. He didn't perform "Tonight I'll Be Staying Here with You" until the Rolling Thunder Revues of 1975–76 and didn't revive it again until the 1990s, when he sometimes gave it an early concert airing during the Never Ending Tour. In whatever era it was performed, "Tonight I'll Be Staying Here with You" served as a kind of pledge of intimacy from artist to audience assuring them that, for the next few hours at least, they had Dylan's undivided attention.

The sort of song a Grand Ol' Opry chanteuse (or Tenderloin stripper) would still enjoy belting out, "Tonight I'll Be Staying Here with You" hit No. 50 on the *Billboard* chart when released as an A-side single. Dylan also recorded a nice, unreleased version with Johnny Cash in 1970.

Graceful and sincere, Dylan croons "Tonight I'll Be Staying Here with You" on *Nashville Sky-*

line like he'd been singing country music since he was in diapers—not merely creating a Nashville caricature just for the sake of doing it. Here Dylan sings of a devotion that compels him, after years of writing songs about escaping on the run, to squelch his innate wanderlust, tear up his ticket for the next train out of Dodge, and knock on his true love's door.

High Times reviewer Michael Simmons nailed the spirit of Dylan's souped-up 1975 Rolling Thunder version of the song when he wrote in the December 2002 issue of the magazine, "For a nutshell understanding of how astounding this collection is, one need look no further than the opener, 'Tonight I'll Be Staying Here with You.' What was a sweet and sexy country song from *Nashville Skyline* becomes a hormonal call to fuck, a knock-the-door-down-honey-I'm-here-to-make-you-scream-with-pleasure anthemic rocker."

A final note: Dylan supposedly wrote "Tonight I'll Be Staying Here with You" on a Ramada Inn notepad in a Nashville hotel room while in town recording *Nashville Skyline*.

"Too Much of Nothing" (Bob Dylan)

Bob Dylan/The Band, *The Basement Tapes/'67* (1975)
Peter, Paul & Mary, single (1967); *Late Again* (1968); *Ten Years Together* (1970)
Spooky Tooth, *It's All About Spooky Tooth* (1968); *Spooky Tooth* (1987)
The Original Marauders, *Now Your Mouth Cries Wolf* (1977)
Fotheringay, *Fotheringay* (1970)
Albert Lee, *Black Claw and Country Fever* (1991)

A courtly tune with a bizarre melody that seems to continually ascend, "Too Much of Nothing" is dour Basementalia at its most quintessential.

Dylan once suggested that "Too Much of Nothing" and "Tears of Rage" were influenced by William Shakespeare's *King Lear*. Since the song contains pointed references to a king and the same kind of hostile, desperate landscape of the soul found in *Lear* ("when there's too much of nothing, it just makes a fella mean"), that idea may not be so farfetched. And, with references to "the day of confession," "Too Much of Nothing" hints at the heavy biblical influence seeping into Dylan's songs and which would loom large in *John Wesley Harding*, his next album. Rarely has Dylan sounded as wise or messianic as he does while singing these timeless truths and half-formed fantasies, even as he manages to rhyme "Valerie" and "Vivian" with "salary" and "oblivion."

Hard to believe, but Peter, Paul & Mary had a Top 40 hit with "Too Much of Nothing" in 1967, the first song from the *Basement Tapes* sessions to be commercially released. Even harder to believe is that Dylan is said to have written the song expressly for them.

■ **"To Ramona"** (Bob Dylan)

Bob Dylan, *Another Side of Bob Dylan* (1964); *Biograph/'64* (1985); *Live 1961–2000—Thirty-nine Years of Great Concert Performances/'65* (2001); *The Bootleg Series, Volume 6: Live 1964—Concert at Philharmonic Hall* (2004)
Noel Harrison, *Noel Harrison* (1966)
Alan Price, *Price on His Head* (1967); *Profile* (1980); *Anthology* (1997)
Flying Burrito Brothers, *Flying Burrito Brothers* (1971)
Lee Hazelwood, *20th Century Lee* (1976)
Texas Tornados, *Hangin' On By a Thread* (1992)
Various Artists (performed by Sinéad Lohan), *Loving Time* (1997)
Rich Lerner & The Groove, *Cover Down* (2000)
Various Artists (performed by Flying Burrito Brothers), *Doin' Dylan 2* (2002)

Dylan's open letter to a wounded woman whose fate disturbs him, "To Ramona" works as both instruction and tribute to a relationship that can only find closure with this song. Set to a beautiful but strangely tense melody that hints at the sexual longing lurking within the song, "To Ramona" finds Dylan working with marvelous, elliptically sensuous verses filled with vivid imagery ("cracked country lips") and the type of angular yet wise aphorisms admirers had already begun to expect from him ("Everything passes/Everything changes/Just do what you think you should do"). Fluid and rich, intimate and affecting, "To Ramona" is a lurid tapestry depicting a relationship sprung from desperation and desire as it withers like the flower in the city Dylan sings of in the song.

Part of the same conflicted, often internal, repartee that produced songs like "Don't Think Twice, It's All Right," "Boots of Spanish Leather," "It Ain't Me, Babe," "I Don't Believe You," and a few others from this early 1960s Dylan period that combine separation and flashing gestalt to kindle a moment of narrative insight, "To Ramona" is a breakup song in which the singer pulls himself away from a superficial woman misguided by the "worthless foam" spewing from "fixtures, forces and friends."

But though Dylan was beginning to write songs in which, like Woody Allen, he was placing his women characters under a pedestal, "To Ramona" is no "Ballad in Plain D"—another song from the same album that rails spitefully at love gone really bad. Rather, a deep sense of sympathy and sentiment ease the sense that *Another Side of Bob Dylan* is a battleground in the war between the sexes.

"To Ramona" is another song dealing with the nuts and bolts behind Dylan's breakup with Suze Rotolo. Eased by the yearning sway of the melody and the lyrics' mature acceptance of the inevitability of change or any possibility of reconciliation, "To Ramona" remains one of Dylan's most elegant songs.

T

As Dylan wrote of "To Ramona" in the *Biograph* liner notes, "Well, that's pretty literal. That was just somebody I knew."

"To Ramona" has popped up during most of Dylan's tours since 1964—a surprisingly resilient evergreen, even if he sometimes slurs the lyrics like a drunken pub crawler and deconstructs and transforms the melody into a barely recognizable cipher of the original. Since the mid-1990s Never Ending Tours, Dylan has presented the song cloaked in a south-of-the-border ranchero arrangement and he sounds like a paramour strumming his guitar under a moonlit balcony.

"Tough Mama" (Bob Dylan)
Bob Dylan, single (1974); *Planet Waves* (1974)
Sandoz, *Unfamiliar Territory* (1989)
Jerry Garcia Band, *How Sweet It Is* (1997)

Debatably the best song on *Planet Waves*, "Tough Mama" is a metallic country stomp evoking hard times on the other side of the tracks while vaguely recalling another song from this Dylan oeuvre, "Tombstone Blues." Dylan's voice and Garth Hudson's organ do a Vulcan mind-meld to bring out the earthy timbres and essence of "Tough Mama"—whoever and wherever she is.

This one among several songs on *Planet Waves* that deal with the tensions and possibilities of spiritual and sexual fidelity amid life as a touring artist is often forgotten when discussion of Dylan's great songs arises. It is hard not to interpret this song as Dylan's declaration to his wife and audience that he is returning to the fray after years of holing up in his rural idyll. Here, Dylan presents himself at a crossroads reflecting on his past while invoking his muse to give him the power to move on. But even though he senses what is ahead for him, he knows full well that it is his wife who will be feeling the brunt of

his decision. So when he sings "I'm gonna go down to the river and get some stones," he's trying to sell her on the idea that his return to public life as a performing artist is as real as staying home and raising the kids. Again and again he praises her with physical and spiritual platitudes, as if calling her "dark beauty," "sweet goddess," or "silver angel" is his way of buttering her up. Despite the drama and excitement with which he sings "Tough Mama," he still manages to come off like a guy who just can't wait to hit the road. Yet his song to his soul mate rings true. He knows that she is a survivor able to make it with or without him. She has, after all, already outlasted the other characters mentioned in the song (Sister, Papa, Jack the Cowboy, and Lone Wolf) and he seems pretty sure that she will accept his golden ring and meet him at the border at the appointed hour.

Dylan and the Band featured rather blustery but no less effective renditions of "Tough Mama" for three shows on their 1974 tour. Dylan did not dust the song off again for another couple of decades, when it made appearances during the latest phases of the Never Ending Tour, through 2003. Jerry Garcia performed a *great*, jam-packed version of "Tough Mama" with his band Legion of Mary in the mid-1970s and was even known to air it out for the odd performance late in his life with the Jerry Garcia Band.

"The Trail of the Buffalo" (Traditional/Woody Guthrie)
aka "Buffalo Skinners," "Range of the Buffalo"
Woody Guthrie, *Woody Guthrie—Buffalo Skinners: The Asch Recordings, Volume 4/'44* (1999)
Cisco Houston, *Cisco Houston Sings Woody Guthrie* (1963)
Ramblin' Jack Elliott, *Essential Ramblin' Jack Elliott* (1970)
John Renbourn, *Faro Annie* (1972)
Arlo Guthrie, *One Night* (1976)

T

Just about every roughneck vocation that includes the lurking threat of death has a song like "The Trail of the Buffalo," a close cousin in song to the lumberjack version of "Canadee-I-O" and "The Hills of Mexico." Dylan performed his version of "The Trail of the Buffalo" early and late in his career and stayed pretty close to the version he learned off a Guthrie disc. During Never Ending Tour concerts of 1988–92, he presented the song in both acoustic and electric formats. The story here (a model that Dylan loosely utilized for his own "Isis") concerns a young man enlisted by a famous cattle-buster to join a drive in the spring of 1883. Naturally, he gets in *way* over his head. Soaked to the bone by torrential storms, injured by cactus, and unable to control the cattle, he ends up in debt to his boss by the song's end. The phrase "our trip was not a pleasant one" from "The Trail of the Buffalo" made its way into Dylan's own song of frontier injustice deferred, "Drifter's Escape."

"The Trail of the Buffalo" most likely came Dylan's way through Woody Guthrie's 1945 Folkways release. In the liner notes of *Woody Guthrie—Buffalo Skinners: The Asch Recordings, Volume 4,* rereleased in 1999 as part of a massive Guthrie retrospective, Smithsonian archivists Jeff Place and Guy Logsdon wrote "Unlike those in many other occupations, cowboys sang very few cowboy songs. Mild complaints about working in adverse conditions, bad horses, or wild cattle occasionally were expressed, but usually through humor. Since cowboying was an occupation of choice, the men knew, as they know today, that not much money could be earned and that bad weather, cropped off fingers, broken bones, a few bad horses, crazy cattle, and possibly death were just part of the job.

"Woody Guthrie took these lyrics from a song called 'Boggy Creek' in John A. and Alan Lomax's book *Cowboy Songs* (1938) and set them to music. It is a cowboy version of 'Buffalo Skinners'; yet in the Lomax version no mention is made of buffalo skinners. Woody's version tells about an unemployed cowboy who agrees to work on a cattle drive into New Mexico, and after successfully combating the drive problems and delivering the herd, he and the rest of the cowboys kill the drover when he tries to cheat them out of their pay. Woody left out one verse and changed 'out in New Mexico' to 'on the trail of the buffalo.' It's a genuine cowboy protest song."

John A. Lomax bring the lifestyle of the men on the range into full, life-is-cheap focus in his 1947 book *Adventures of a Ballad Hunter.*

One day out in Abilene, Texas, I met an old-time buffalo hunter and asked him to tell me some of his adventures. Back in the days just after the Civil War, these hunters used to go out on the plains in wagon trains and kill buffalo for their hides. The stark naked, ghastly looking bodies were left lying on the plains and down along the ravines to rot and to furnish food for wolves and buzzards. (My Uncle Charlie Cooper killed as many as seventy-five a day with his famous Needle gun.) The hides were hauled to the nearest railroad and from there shipped East where the skin side was tanned and softened, while the "warm side, fur side, outside," was left untouched. The fur was long, soft, shiny, of all shades from light brown to deep black. Big buffalo bull fur was often jet black at certain seasons of the year. The first hunters were glad to get a dollar for one undressed hide. Years later, a fine, dressed buffalo hide sold for one hundred dollars, buffalo overcoats up to 250 dollars. Buffalo hides, properly tanned, made beautiful rugs and were also often cut and fashioned into cloaks for fair ladies. The Indians likewise wore

Roughnecks on a cattle drive, ca. late 1800s.
(Library of Congress)

them thrown over their shoulders, and also sometimes used them as floor covering for their teepees.

The old man had been a sharpshooter in his younger days. He carried a Needle gun and killed the buffalo for the entire hunting party. The gun carried so far that the bullet "never landed till next day." While some of the gang skinned the dead animals and spread the skins out to dry, the others packed the hides and loaded them into the wagons. "Two to shoot, four to skin, one to cook," says

an old chronicle. The old hunter went on to tell the story of a group of buffalo hunters that he had led from Jacksboro, Texas, to that region of Texas far beyond the Pease River. The hunt lasted for several months. The plains were dry and parched. The party drank alkali water, 'salty as hell-fire,' so thick it had to be chewed; fought sandstorms, flies, mosquitoes, bed-bugs, and wolves. The Indians watched to pick them off from near-by Mexico. At the close of the season the manager of the outfit, who had been hauling the hides to the nearest market, announced to the men as they broke camp for the trip home that he had lost money on the enterprise and could not pay them any wages. The men argued the question with the manager.

"So," the old man told me, "we shot down old Crego, the manager, and left his damn ol' bones to bleach where he had left many hundreds of stinking buffalo. It took us many days to get back to Jacksboro. As we sat around the campfire at night, some one of the boys started up a song about our hunt and the hard times and old Crego. And we all set in to help him. Before we got to Jacksboro we shaped it up and our whole crowd would sing it together.

And he sang to me in nasal, monotonous tones, "The Buffalo Skinners." Professor Kittredge called it his favourite American ballad. From twenty-one separate versions from all over the West, I put together the five stanzas quoted here and six others.

[S] "Train A-Travelin'" (Bob Dylan)

Various Artists (performed by Bob Dylan as "Blind Boy Grunt"), *Broadside Reunion/'62* (1972)
Bettina Jonic, *The Bitter Mirror* (1975)

Dylan recorded this affable if unremarkable rarity—his only known rendition—in late 1962 at the offices of *Broadside* magazine in New York City and it was released under his famous "Blind Boy Grunt" pseudonym on one of the Broadside compilation discs a decade later. The lyrics were published around the time of the recording in *Broadside* number 23, and they bore the Dylan copyright.

[S] "Train of Love" (Johnny Cash)

Johnny Cash, *Songs That Made Him Famous* (1958)
Various Artists (performed by Bob Dylan), *Kindred Spirits: A Tribute to Johnny Cash* (2002)
Doc Watson, *Docabilly* (1995)
Boxcar Willie, *Achy Breaky Heart* (1996)
Robert Gordon, *Robert Gordon* (1997)

"Hey, Johnny, I wanna say 'Hi!' and sorry we can't be there, but that's just the way it is. I wanna sing you one of your songs about trains. I used to sing this song before I ever wrote a song, and I also want to thank you for standing up to me, way back when."

With those words, Dylan introduced "Train of Love," an early Sun Records era Johnny Cash song about a pining suitor abandoned at the station. The song fit Dylan's passion for roots music to a tee, and at the April 1999 "Man in Black" tribute concert at New York City's Hammerstein Ballroom he performed via prerecorded video. Even across the video chasm Dylan shined, hitting the notes high and low—even dancing a little jig during the guitar solo.

[A] *Traveling Wilburys, Volume 1*

Wilburys Records (Warner Bros. Records) LP 9 25796-1; CD 9 25796-2; CS 9 25796-2. Released October 1988. Produced by Otis and Nelson Wilbury (Jeff Lynne and George Harrison)

"Handle With Care," "Dirty World," "Rattled," "Last Night," "Not Alone Anymore," "Congratulations," "Heading for the Light," "Margarita," "Tweeter and the Monkey Man," "End of the Line"

> "...outside of writing with the Traveling Wilburys, my shared experience writing a song with other songwriters is not that great."
> —Bob Dylan, 1991.

The unlikely matching of Dylan, George Harrison, Roy Orbison, Tom Petty, Jeff Lynne, and session drummer Jim Keltner created music that was novel, at times profound, and always fun. The Traveling Wilburys wisely eschewed creating a grand-scale epic all-star ego-driven

T

album that would surely have gone down in pop annals as a bizarre flop. Instead, they astutely realized that less-was-more in crafting a down-to-earth, everyman collection even your stodgy great aunt might find herself tapping her toes to. While "Handle with Care" and "End of the Line" were the big single hits, each song on the disc works to the group's (and its featured singer's) strengths.

Traveling Wilburys, Volume 1 began as a serendipitous goof but wound up a sensation and went platinum, Dylan's first since *Desire*. The story goes something like this: Warner Brothers needed one last song from George Harrison to fill out a twelve-inch single. Problem was, George didn't have one. He told Jeff Lynne over dinner that he was just going to have to hunker down and write one and record it. When he asked Lynne, who was producing Roy Orbison at the time, if he could recommend a studio, Lynne mentioned Dylan's little garage set-up in Malibu. They called Dylan, who invited them over. On the way, Harrison had to stop over at Tom Petty's digs to pick up a guitar he had left there. When Petty heard where they were going he invited himself to tag along. Somewhere along the way, someone remembered to call Orbison, and the Wilburys were born.

After working up "Handle with Care," the remaining cast members refused to allow Harrison to put it on the Warner Brothers platter, vowing like blood brothers to pull together enough material for an album.

◪ Traveling Wilburys, Volume 3

Wilburys Records (Warner Bros. Records) LP 9 26324-1; CD 9 26324-2; CS 9 26324-3. Released October 19, 1990. Produced by Spike and Clayton Wilbury (George Harrison and Jeff Lynne)

"She's My Baby," "Inside Out," "If You Belonged to Me," "The Devil's Been Busy," "Seven Deadly Sins," "Poor House,"

"Where Were You Last Night?" "Cool, Dry Place," "New Blue Moon," "You Took My Breath Away," "Wilbury Twist"

Ignoring a *Volume 2* album (the omission was probably both a tribute to fallen brother Roy Orbison and a confirmation of their quirky place on the American entertainment landscape) but acceding to popular demand, the Wilburys came up with a *Volume 3* album that rocked harder than their debut effort, unified their vision and talents, and retained the fun, easy-going seat-of-the-pants sensibility that endeared them in the first place. It was as if the Wilbury mask allowed Dylan, Harrison, Petty, and Lynne to ditch their living legend status and rediscover themselves with good humor and good music.

◪ A Tribute to Woody Guthrie, Part Two/Various Artists

Warner Bros. K46144. Released 1972.

Dylan's first public stage appearance after his motorcycle accident in 1966 was at the Woody Guthrie memorial concert held at New York's Carnegie Hall in January 1968. Backed by the Hawks (soon and always to be the Band), Dylan showed the world that he was back in action as he displayed his still-edgy Guthrie chops on a trio of Woody's best: "Grand Coulee Dam," "Dear Mrs. Roosevelt," and "I Ain't Got No Home."

But while Dylan's inclusion here was undoubtedly the album's main selling point, *A Tribute to Woody Guthrie* has numerous qualities to make it a classic. Most noteworthy are appearances by Odetta ("Rambling Round Your City"), Ramblin' Jack Elliott ("1913 Massacre"), Tom Paxton ("Pastures of Plenty"), and, of course, Woody's son, Arlo ("Oklahoma Hills").

Note: *A Tribute to Woody Guthrie, Part One* (Columbia KC-31171) includes a twenty-four-second clip of Woody's arrangement of Big Bill

T

Broonzy's "This Train Is Bound for Glory," featuring Dylan on harmonica backing Arlo Guthrie, Pete Seeger, Judy Collins, and Odetta.

§"Trouble" (Bob Dylan)
Bob Dylan, *Shot of Love* (1981)

Though a mite predictable, Dylan lets it all hang out with this raunchy and ragged swampy blues. Like most of the blues, the song's cliché message (inane lyrics and all) is a simple one: Life is Hell. Wherever you roam, trouble is the one thing you'll be sure to find.

Dylan performed "Trouble" at seven concerts during the summer leg of the 1989 Never Ending Tour.

§"Troubled and I Don't Know Why" (Bob Dylan)
aka "I'm Troubled and I Don't Know Why"
Joan Baez (performed with Bob Dylan), *Rare, Live & Classic*/'63 (1993)
Various Artists (performed by Bob Dylan and Joan Baez), *Songs from* Sing Out! (limited edition)/'63 (2002)

While some sources have suggested that Dylan cowrote "Troubled and I Don't Know Why" with Joan Baez, with whom he performed the song as a duet in the summer of 1963, most agree that Dylan probably composed it alone with such a duet in mind.

§"Trouble in Mind" (Bob Dylan)
Bob Dylan, single (1979)

A *Slow Train Coming* outtake that shoulda, woulda, and coulda been included on that powerful, first collection of "Gospel Bob," this murky blues tells of a man in spiritual pain. It was released as the B side to the "Gotta Serve Somebody" single with an extra verse edited out. Regardless of the omission, this edgy little nugget of evangelical Dylan blues references the Old Testament story of Lot seeing his wife turn to stone upon leaving Sodom and Gomorra and further confirms that the euphoric rush accompanying Dylan's salvation did not dull his creative flame.

This is one of those songs in which Dylan describes warfare with the Devil as if he were on the front lines. Within the bounds of this world there is no escaping the power of the Devil's powerful grip and here the singer appeals to the Lord to deliver the imagination from its bondage to Satan.

§"True Love Tends to Forget" (Bob Dylan)
Bob Dylan, *Street Legal* (1978)

This expertly crafted pop song, which would have felt quite at home on a Neil Diamond record, was performed exclusively on Dylan's 1978 big-band tour.

The theme of betrayal—both personal and spiritual—is strong in "True Love Tends to Forget," as Dylan attempts to bid adieu to failed love. Likening a relationship to playing Russian roulette and suggesting (in a double reference to Exodus) that he had been left in the reeds to suffocate while his woman roamed the wilderness among other men, reveals more than a tad of bitterness.

§"Trust Yourself" (Bob Dylan)
Bob Dylan, *Empire Burlesque* (1985)
Carlene Carter (performed with Dylan), *Hindsight 20/20* (1996)

This simple song of age-old advice with an obvious message evident in the title sounded alternately stilted and humorous as released on *Empire Burlesque*—especially as backup singer Madelyn Quebec struggles to guess what lyrics Dylan is going to sing next. Hidden in the song's message to look inward is the singer's plea not to look to him for advice.

As a performance vehicle, "Trust Yourself" *rocked* when displayed during the tours with Tom Petty and the Heartbreakers in 1986—it was one of several *Empire Burlesque* songs to really shine on stage.

[S] "Tryin' to Get to Heaven" (Bob Dylan)

Bob Dylan, *Time out of Mind* (1997)
Druha Trava and Peter Rowan, *New Freedom Bell* (1999)
Michel Montecrossa, *4th Time Around* (2001)

Still attempting to crash through the Pearly Gates of Paradise like a leather-jacketed hood muscling in on an East Hampton garden party, in "Trying to Get to Heaven" Dylan directly quotes as many as a dozen old songs from various genres: country gospel ("I've been walkin' that lonesome valley"), mainstream American folk music ("I was ridin' in a buggy with Miss Mary Jane"), even bluegrass ("I'm just goin' down that road feelin' bad"). And then, of course, there's Dylan's self-citation, the echo in the song's refrain ("I'm just tryin' to get to Heaven before they close the door") of a secular hymn that has already entered the pantheon: "Knockin' on Heaven's Door."

With his trusty band beside him, Dylan performed "Tryin' to Get to Heaven" with some frequency between 1999 and 2004.

[S] "Tupelo Honey" (Van Morrison)

Van Morrison, *Tupelo Honey* (1971)
Wayne Toups, *Blast from Bayou* (1988)
Cassandra Wilson, *Blue Light Til Dawn* (1993)
Dusty Springfield, *Anthology* (1997)

Dylan got together with Van the Man in 1984 and 1991 for a couple of encore performances of "Tupelo Honey," a transporting ballad and one of the last and sweetest expressions of what we think of as "the 60s." Recorded in San Francisco, Morrison's album *Tupelo Honey* and its title track still evoke images of "Old Old Woodstock," articulating a translucent vision of peaceful, back-to-the-earth domesticity with Morrison casting himself as a country homebody.

Notoriously cantankerous, Morrison was an unlikely candidate to envision the hippie dream in its waning days. However, he was at least temporarily able to enjoy the fruits of what, until then, had been a tumultuous career. With Them, the raw Irish R&B band he helped form in the mid-60s, he already had written the immortal "Gloria," one of the great anthems of rock. While the record company battles he then endured have left him cynical at best, he released two musical and commercial haymakers before *Tupelo Honey*: *Astral Weeks* in 1968 and *Moondance* in 1970.

Melodically reminiscent of Curtis Mayfield's "People Get Ready," "Tupelo Honey" and the album on which it appeared picked up where Morrison's earlier releases left off, reflecting the country-shaded idyll he enjoyed with his wife, Janet Planet, and their children in Woodstock, New York, and Marin County, California. Planet also contributed background vocals and was the clear inspiration for some of the album's notable songs: "You're My Woman," "I Wanna Roo You (Scottish Derivative)," and "Tupelo Honey." Though Van and Janet divorced in 1973, "Tupelo Honey" remains an eloquent testament to a fleeting era.

[S] "Turkey Chase" (Bob Dylan)

Bob Dylan, single (1973); *Pat Garrett and Billy the Kid Soundtrack* (1973)

This very upbeat piece of instrumental western bluegrass (aided by Bonnie Berline's fiddle and Roger McGuinn's banjo) was composed for and used in Sam Peckinpah's *Pat Garrett and*

Billy the Kid. It is also remembered for being perhaps the first Dylan recording to be used in a television commercial—for a brand of Greek beer in 1979.

[S] "T.V. Talkin' Song" (Bob Dylan)

Bob Dylan, *Under the Red Sky* (1990)
Heartland, *Heartland Plays Dylan: Your Mind Is Your Temple* (1998)

Reexploring and updating a song form he left years before (the "talking song"), Dylan delivers a "Subterranean Homesick Blues"–style rant about a subject he probably could have railed against in his days of yore: television. The gist of the message here is that once the boob tube is turned on it will likely remote control your soul. Springsteen's "57 Channels (And Nothin' On)" (1992) was a more era-appropriate diagnostic. Still, as Dylan skips between reason and insanity, pathos and absurdity with the vigor of the Mad Hatter in *Through the Looking-Glass*, "T.V. Talkin' Song" captures much of the exuberance he displays on a good day—even if he might have been aiming for something a little more profound.

With "T.V. Talkin' Song," Dylan recalls the mass-hysteria found in songs like "Drifter's Escape," the topsy-turvy landscape of "I Shall Be Free," and the cynical voyeurism in "Talking John Birch Society Blues" while playing with the perspective-shifting story-telling device he employed in "Black Diamond Bay."

For the uninitiated, the action of "T.V. Talkin' Song" takes place in Hyde Park, where the famed "Speakers' Corner" has for generations provided an open forum for anyone to speak his or her mind about anything. Chicago's Bughouse Square has served a similar function in the U.S.

Performed about twenty times during the 1990 Never Ending Tour in support of that year's *Under the Red Sky* album, Dylan's display of "T.V. Talkin' Song" showed that he was capable of transforming raw matter into gold.

[S] "Tweedle Dee & Tweedle Dum" (Bob Dylan)

Bob Dylan, *"Love and Theft"* (2001)

For those who have ventured to the other side of the looking glass while listening to a Dylan song, "Tweedle Dee & Tweedle Dum" may be just the right track to bring them back over here. This driving, bleakly menacing "From a Buick 6"–style rocker which opened Dylan's *"Love and Theft"* collection in *Highway 61 Revisited* fashion also sounds as if it fell between the cracks of Harry Smith's *Anthology of American Folk Music*, took a ride on Elvis's "Mystery Train," and landed in Dylan's lap. Like "The Ballad of Frankie Lee and Judas Priest" or "Tweeter and the Monkey Man," this tousled, hard-hoodoo shuffle is a dense fable that uses nursery-rhyme structures to relate its morally vague tale of violence and betrayal. And it's chock-full of the type of crazy Zen wisdom and mayhem that made Dylan songs like this famous long ago—Dee and Dum dominate center stage with their "two big bags of dead man's bones" and "brains in a pot, beginning to boil."

Writing in *Guitar World Acoustic* magazine, Isaiah Trost observed, "The song recounts a long—very long—yet fast-moving and very odd conversation between the title protagonists made famous in Lewis Carroll's *Alice in Wonderland*. While the lyrics, a barrage of vivid images, old aphorisms and non-sequiturs, are Dylanesquely obscure, the song is expressively sung and carried along by the crunchy acoustic rhythm playing and booming bass and drums."

Dylan shed only a bit of oblique light on his intentions with "Tweedle Dee & Tweedle Dum" when he told Edna Gunderson of *U.S.A. Today* that "evil might not be coming your way as a monstrous brute or the gun-toting devilish ghetto gangster. It's the bookish-looking guy in the wire-rimmed glasses who might not be entirely harmless." Perhaps that's why he chose to use the song with its unsavory duo conveying the modern face of wickedness, in his first-ever TV ad.

In *Bandits*, a 2001 film starring Bruce Willis and Billy Bob Thornton, "Tweedle Dee & Tweedle Dum" was used in the opening sequence and also in a later scene.

Dylan began performing "Tweedle Dee & Tweedle Dum" at his fall 2001 concerts in support of *"Love and Theft."* He kept the song in fairly heavy rotation and, for a period immediately following Election Night 2002, established it as a set-opening warning, signaling, perhaps, his feelings about how the two-party political system had handled affairs. A year later, its appearance as his show-openers continued, suggesting and begging comparison to the two-headed hydra dominating the media at that moment: George W. Bush and Saddam Hussein.

"Tweeter and the Monkey Man" (Traveling Wilburys)
Traveling Wilburys, *Traveling Wilburys, Volume 1* (1988)
Headstones, *Picture of Health* (1993)

A song that boasts one of Dylan's weirdest titles ever, "Tweeter and the Monkey Man" is also up there with the best examples of Dylan's talents in the long narrative song. It is cut out of the same desperado filmlike cloth as "Lily, Rosemary and the Jack of Hearts" and "Hurricane." While a great Dylan song is often greater than the sum of its parts (and this is no exception), the slick production from the Traveling Wilburys (complete with slide guitar nuancing the chorus) further enhances Dylan's

archetypal tale of love, betrayal, and death.

Don't be fooled: "Tweeter and the Monkey Man" is a complex song with several interweaving characters and plot lines. The Monkey Man (the cocaine and hash-selling anti-hero of the song), Tweeter (the Monkey Man's sidekick who may be a woman), Jan (the song's approximation of a heroine), an Undercover Cop (bad guy, Jan's brother, Monkey Man's *bête noire*), Bill (Jan's racketeering husband), and the narrator (who enters the fray at the song's finale) enact a noir passion play in the New Jersey outback that unfurls like a cagey Nicholas Ray flick. Whether it is sarcasm, homage, or a little of both, Dylan, in a clever and humorous twist, acknowledges Bruce Springsteen by lacing several of the Boss's song titles into this composition: "Thunder Road," "State Trooper," "Mansion on the Hill," "Stolen Car," and, natch, "Jersey Girl."

Dylan's movie song, which begins with a drug deal and ends with a scene out of *Miami Vice* (with more than a genderbending twist or two on the bumpy road), creates a streetwise and shady atmosphere on the darker side of the Jersey underbelly.

As if there were any doubt, the Traveling Wilburys' songbook cites Special Rider Music (Dylan's music publishing company) as the copyright holder, indicating that he was, at least, the song's chief (if not only) creator and contributor.

"20/20 Vision" (Joe Allison/Milton Estes)
Gillis Brothers, *Ice Stone Cold* (1992)
Jimmy Martin, *One Woman Man* (1995)

Dylan only performed "20/20 Vision" at but a single 1991 concert in Austin, Texas, as a probable tip of the hat to singin' cowboys everywhere. With its resigned mood of what should have been, "20/20 Vision" is sung from the point of view of a guy who has played Monday morning quarterback one too many times.

Nashville insiders knows Joe Allison (born October 3, 1924, McKinney, Texas; died August 2, 2002, Nashville, Tennessee) through the songs he penned for the likes of Jim Reeves, Tex Ritter, and Faron Young. With his sophisticated and modern approach to the idiom, Allison's contribution to country music's emergence in the cities of America in the 1950s and '60s was huge. A jack-of-all-trades, Allison went on to become one of country music's behind-the-scene talents, who climbed the ladder in fairly unusual fashion—as a musician, radio deejay, TV personality, producer, record executive, scriptwriter—spreading country music through every medium imaginable.

Like many stars, Milton Estes (born May 9, 1914, Arthur, Tennessee; died August 23, 1963, Oklahoma City, Oklahoma) learned music from singing in churches but it was in the prohibition-era speakeasies that he polished his talent as a teenager, graduating to vaudeville stages in Cincinnati, Chicago, and New York. Like Allison, Estes wore many hats during his career. He toured the circuit with Pee Wee King's Gold West Cowboys in the late 1930s, wrote and plugged songs in the early 1940s, and performed at the Grand Ol' Opry later in the decade. He recorded for Bullet, Decca, Coral, and MGM, but alcoholism led to a quick fade into the showbiz woodwork and an early death.

ⓢ "2 x 2" (Bob Dylan)
aka "Two by Two"
Bob Dylan, *Under the Red Sky* (1990)
7 Lwas, *Pirata* (1995)

Dylan's goofiest song since "Man Gave Names to All the Animals," "2 x 2" comes off as a retelling of the story of Noah's ark that lacks the panache given to it by Bill Cosby (who did wonders with the Great Flood tale in his 1960s

comedy act). A couple of other simple counting songs—the standard "This Old Man" and Dylan's own "I Shall Be Free No. 10"—come to mind as Dylan adds another nugget to *Under the Red Sky*, his grab bag of post-modern nursery rhymes.

Two problematic aspects of this vaguely Beatlesque foray are the thin melody and the performer's lethargic singing. Dylan sounds pretty bored. And the benign lyrics (e.g., "Two by two, to their lovers they flew"/ "Two by two, into the foggy dew") lack momentum, floating along with rhyme—but seemingly no reason—to engage the listener.

Elton John and David Crosby add accompaniment to the sublimely ridiculous "2 x 2" and Dylan opened some 1992 Never Ending Tour shows with fairly unintelligible, blues-rock treatments of it.

ⓢ "Two Soldiers" (Traditional)
aka "The Battle of Fredricksburg," "The Battle of Gettysburg," "Blue-Eyed Boston Boy," "Boston Boy," "Civil War Ballad," "Custer's Last Charge," "The Last Fierce Charge," "The Two Brothers," "The Two Soldiers"
Bob Dylan, *World Gone Wrong* (1993)
Mike Seeger, *Mike Seeger* (1964)
Hazel and Alice, *Hazel & Alice* (1973)
Jerry Garcia and David Grisman, *Jerry Garcia/David Grisman* (1991)
David Grisman/Daniel Kobialka, *Common Chord* (1995)
Various Artists (performed by Monroe Gevedon), *Music of Kentucky: Early American Rural Classics, 1927–1937, Volume 2* (1995)
Michael Moore, *Jewels and Binoculars* (2000)

A Civil War song much collected in the Southern Appalachians and in the Ozark Mountains of Arkansas, "Two Soldiers" only seems to have come to Dylan's attention late in his career. Still, he wrings every mournful piece of horror from this massacre in melody which

Two dead soldiers, Battle of Fredericksburg, Virginia, 1862.
(Library of Congress)

tells the story of two doomed innocents and the void their slaughter leaves behind.

According to Dylan, writing in the *World Gone Wrong* sleeve notes: "Jerry Garcia showed me 'Two Soldiers' (Hazel & Alice do it pretty similar) a battle extraordinaire, some dragoon officer's epaulettes laying liquid in the mud, physical plunge into Limitationville, war dominated by finance (lending money for interest being a nauseating and revolting thing) love is not collateral."

The song tells a simple story: Two soldiers await to enter battle. They mutually promise that should one of them survive, the other will contact the loved ones of the deceased. In ironic, bitterly poignant fashion, neither rises from the killing ground to fulfill the blood pact; they leave only their bleak silence behind with "no one to write" to the women left bereft far away.

According to the July 1964 *Sing Out!*: "Vance Randolph reports two texts of this song collected in Missouri, where it is often known as 'The Battle of Fredricksburg,' although the narrative has also served to dramatize Custer's Last Stand as well as the more conventional Civil War vignette included here. Mike Seeger's version of the song ... comes from the Gevedon family of Kentucky minus the usual introductory stanza describing the eleventh hour pact between the youth and his 'tall, dark' partner-in-arms: the survivor of the battle is to send the last letter of the fallen comrade home to mother or sweetheart. The rather Victorian stage irony of the ending relies on one of the most lovely lyric airs in American folk music for its dramatic validity."

Dylan first performed "Two Soldiers" in the traditional acoustic slot during the first Never Ending Tour of 1988. He continued to sporadically and rarely display the tragic ballad through 1994 in renditions as dignified as the one he recorded.

T

▣ "Two Trains Runnin'" (Muddy Waters)

aka "Still a Fool," "Two Trains Running"
Muddy Waters, *Best of Muddy Waters* (1957)
John Hammond Jr., *John Hammond* (1962)
Johnny Shines, *Master of the Modern Blues* (1966)
The Paul Butterfield Blues Band, *East-West* (1966)
The Blues Project, *Projections* (1997)
James Cotton, *Deep in the Blues* (1996)

The blues of a treacherous man ready to ride the rails out of town on the midnight train (and if that don't come or he's busy getting one last taste of the forbidden jelly roll, the one that leaves at the break of day) and find a woman who will "ride like a Cadillac car," "Two Trains Runnin'" appears on one of the earliest Dylan tapes in circulation (the May 1961 so-called "Minnesota Party Tape") and is included on a surviving performance tape—from the deservedly ballyhooed July 2, 1962, Fin Jan Club appearance in Montreal. The song had appeared on the eponymous album of Dylan's friend John Hammond, Jr., that same year, so perhaps that was a source. Or maybe Dylan picked it up at the feet of Waters himself who was a familiar sight on the stages of clubs, festivals, and concert halls at the time. A final Dylan instrumental rendition of "Two Trains Runnin'" recorded at the New York City home of friends Eve and Mac McKenzie in April 1963 also survives.

Waters is thought to have based "Still a Fool" (the song's proper, copyrighted title) on Tommy Johnson's 1928 "Bye Bye Blues," which shares a similar line ("Well, two train runnin', runnin' side by side") and a virtually identical tune. Dylan uses two of Muddy's three verses and adds a couple of his own that show an early grasp of the stock blues lyrical liturgy. All Dylan's spot-on renditions feature a funky guitar line and singing that gets ever more vehement as the song rolls along—definitely not a paint-by-numbers, fill-in-the-blanks approach here.

U

▣ "Ugliest Girl in the World" (Bob Dylan/Robert Hunter)

See also Robert Hunter
Bob Dylan, *Down in the Groove* (1988)

Dylan picked "Ugliest Girl in the World" for his slapdash album *Down in the Groove* out of a group of songs Robert Hunter (Grateful Dead lyricist and poet-at-large) wrote in the mid-1980s. The song is alternately outrageous, lighthearted, extremely lightweight, and highly suspicious, and Dylan reveled in singing it. But "Ugliest Girl in the World" is not for the humorless, PC-rabid listeners in your house. A song that would have suited Fats Waller just fine, it may be loosely modeled on a whole litany of songs, from country bluesman Sleepy John Estes's 1941 "Little Laura Blues" to Preston Young's piece of '30s hokum "Darn Good Girl" and the funny put-down songs (both male- and female-directed) emanating from hillbilly America.

▣ "Unbelievable" (Bob Dylan)

Bob Dylan, *Under the Red Sky* (1990)

This rocking bit of cynicism retreads Dylan's theme of distaste for a corrupt world and its corrupting influences. His zealous singing of "Unbelievable," recorded with session god guitarist Waddy Wachtel and old keyboard buddy Al Kooper, didn't disguise another wordy (and pretty mediocre) doomsday-culture head-banger in the spirit of "When the Night Comes Falling from the Sky." Dylan performed the song with somewhat greater success more than two dozen times several years after its release, and then again for a couple of 1995 outings.

Like just about all of the *Under the Red Sky* songs, "Unbelievable" pillages the literature of

U

nursery rhymes, specifically the riddles "There Was a Man Who Had No Eyes" and "Lady, Lady in the Land," which first appeared in print in the mid-sixteenth century. Dylan's references to the blind man standing beneath "the silver skies" and the listener that "must be living in the shadow of some kind of evil star" recalls the plight of Shakespeare's King Lear; the character caught his imagination at least as early as *The Basement Tapes* era in 1967, in songs like "Tears of Rage" and "Too Much of Nothing."

In the video for "Unbelievable," Dylan plays a chauffeur who escorts a pig with a ring in its nose. Sally Kirkland and Molly Ringwald costar.

[S] "Unchain My Heart" (Teddy Powell/Bobby Sharp)

David "Fathead" Newman, *It's Mister Fathead* (1958)
Herbie Mann, *Glory of Love* (1968)
Ray Charles, *Berlin 1962* (1996)
Joe Cocker, *Unchain My Heart* (1987)
Nancy Wilson, *Best of Nancy Wilson: Jazz & Blues Sessions* (1996)
Jesus's Son, *Jesus's Son* (2000)

Both Ray Charles and Joe Cocker had hits with this gyrating gospel rock testimonial begging for the chains of love to be permanently unlocked—as if the power of the heart were something to be shunned forever. Dylan covered the song with a kind of evil zeal and (with the spirited help of his backup singers) sang it as a snappy show opener briefly during his 1986 tour with Tom Petty and the Heartbreakers.

Teddy Powell (born March 1, 1905, or 1906, Oakland, California), the better known of the song's two composers, led one of the top big bands in jazz during the heyday of the Swing Era. He took up the violin as an eight-year-old and was playing the banjo as a teen. In 1927 he began playing guitar and banjo with Abe Lyman's band, and stayed with them until 1935 when he became a radio producer for an advertising agency. He also branched out as a songwriter with hits such as "Take Me Back to My Boots and Saddle," "All I Need Is You, Snake Charmer," and "March Winds and April Showers." Royalties from these and other songs helped him finance a big band in 1939, for which he used some key personnel from the Tommy Dorsey and Benny Goodman bands and arrangements contributed by Ray Conniff. After some early success, the Teddy Powell Orchestra only scraped by as a second-tier band for several years, even with some of the better known Swing musicians passing through its ranks, including tenor-saxophonist Charlie Ventura and trumpeter Pete Candoli. When the band dissolved in the late 1940s (after the musicians lost their instruments in a fire at a New Jersey gig), Powell reinvented himself as a composer and arranger. He wrote several hit songs in addition to "Unchain My Heart"—including "Bewildered," Ridin' the Subway," and "If My Heart Could Only Talk"—and filmed a version of the novelty "Joltin' Joe Dimaggio" as a "soundie" for use in rear-projection jukeboxes that were installed in bars, nightclubs, and other entertainment spots. Powell went on to make a third career for himself as head of his own music publishing house.

[A] *Under the Red Sky*

Columbia Records LP C-46794; CD CK-46794; CS CT-46794. Recorded: January–March, 1990. Released September 17, 1990. Produced by Don Was, David Was, and Jack Frost.

Bob Dylan—guitar, piano, accordion, harmonica, vocals. George Harrison—slide guitar. Bruce Hornsby—piano. Elton John—piano. Al Kooper—organ, keyboards. David Lindley—bouzouki, guitar, slide guitar. Robben Ford—guitar. Sweet Pea Atkinson—vocals. Kenny Aronoff—drums. Rayse Biggs—trumpet. Sir Harry Bowens—vocals. Paulinho Da Costa—percussion. David Crosby—vocals.

U

David McMurray—saxophone. Donald Ray Mitchell—vocals. Jamie Muhoberac—organ. Slash—guitar. Jimmie Vaughan—guitar. Stevie Ray Vaughan—guitar. David Was—vocals. Don Was—bass. Waddy Wachtel—guitar. Randy Jackson—bass.

"Wiggle, Wiggle," "Under the Red Sky," "Unbelievable," "Born in Time," "TV Talking Song," "10,000 Men," "2x2," "God Knows," "Handy Dandy," "Cat's in the Well"

Coming as it did on the heels of the solid *Oh Mercy* in 1989, and after a few years of even more solid stage work, hopes were high for Dylan's next record. So it was something of a letdown that, despite an all-star cast that included everybody from Stevie Ray Vaughan, George Harrison, and Slash from Guns N' Roses to Bruce Hornsby, David Crosby, and Elton John, *Under the Red Sky* landed with a resounding thud. The album never rose above a No. 76 standing during its two-month stay on the charts. Actually, it has aged pretty well and Dylan has, for his part, continued to perform and sharpen some of what happens to be stealthily strong material well into the late 1990s and beyond.

Overstocking of talent on the other side of the studio glass may have been a contributing factor in the diluted final result. Three producers (the Was brothers and Dylan disguised as Jack Frost) are a bit too many for one album, even if they were some of the top guns in the biz. The inability to merge modern recording technology with Dylan's spare needs also contributed to creating a wooden release.

Critics delighted in savaging *Under the Red Sky*, but they may have been misguided in their ire: Dylan had often mentioned recording an album for children and they were probably unaware that what was spinning in their CD players was as close as they were likely to come to hearing one. Naturally, Dylan never explicitly copped to this, but at least half the record comprises little fables that feel as though they came tumbling off the pages of a dusty (and frightening) Brothers Grimm collection.

No liner notes came with the album but song lyrics were included. The album cover, which depicts Dylan dressed in a suit and wearing white alligator shoes while squatting over and contemplating the desert, suggests a man on the edge of a physical, cultural, and spiritual wasteland, devoid of life or meaning. It also evokes memories of a famed photograph of actor Noel Coward in a similar setting.

But the material, at least at its official release, came off as among Dylan's most inane. Maybe he was attempting a return to the immediacy of a direct, blues-based form of songwriting or to the pure simplicity of the folk idiom. Whatever his intentions, nearly every song on the album falls flat. Don Was gave the record a professional veneer and it is listenable; but the songs seem to drift into the air. If *Under the Red Sky* was Dylan's attempt to jump-start his songwriting juices, it failed miserably: Dylan didn't release an album of new, original material for a full seven years.

Some suggest that *Under the Red Sky* ended Dylan's post-Christian 1980s phase, a period in which he grafted his voice over stompin' gospel and blues, raucous R&B, and ballads. Here he goes garage, content just to get his ya-yas out, although with Don and David Was producing, *Under the Red Sky* carries a sheen that disguises his approach.

▨ "Under the Red Sky" (Bob Dylan)
Bob Dylan, *Under the Red Sky* (1990); *Bob Dylan's Greatest Hits Volume 3* (1994)
The Robins, *The Robins Sing Dylan* (2000)

Whether he was inspired by the unfolding Persian Gulf crisis or just plain spooked, Dylan titled his album after this piece of strange, symbolic, apocalyptic angst.

Dylan once cryptically mentioned that "Under the Red Sky" was "about my hometown." *Under the Red Sky* album coproducer Don Was also commented on this eerie fairy tale of horror that recalls the Brothers Grimm and "Hansel and Gretel," saying, "It's such a great little fable. These people have all the opportunity and everything and they choose to be led around by a blind horse and they squander it. It's beautiful and it was so simple and he just sang it one time through and it was perfect."

Much has been made regarding Dylan's use of nursery rhyme in *Under the Red Sky*. The "man in the moon," the little boy and girl, the old woman who lives in a shoe, various prince and princess tales, "Sing a Song of Sixpence" (in which four-and-twenty blackbirds are baked into a pie), and forbidden romance all figure into Dylan's vision of a threatening and dangerous world where children, and by extension innocence or trust, have little, if any, place. It is as if Dylan were doing with the nursery rhyme what he did with country folk and blues in his mid-'60s electric surrealisms: twisting the old traditions into a new structure to tell old stories but make new points. The album's title song may be most successful in its incorporation and gothic implementation of this archaic literary form.

Dylan performed "Under the Red Sky" throughout the 1990s and early '00s on his Never Ending Tour with semiregularity.

∎ "Under Your Spell" (Bob Dylan/Carole Bayer Sager)
Bob Dylan, *Knocked Out Loaded* (1986)

This unconvincing love song closes out a terrible album in odd fashion. And in mysterious fashion, too, as the circumstances behind Dylan's one-off collaboration with one of America's best-known latter-day Tin Pan Alley–style composers remains a shrouded oddity. The results certainly sound as if

"Under Your Spell" was put together at the piano bar of the Beverly Hills Hilton.

Carole Bayer Sager (born on March 8, 1946, New York City) has been one of the great, consistent hitmakers of the past four decades, the late-20th century's answer to Dorothy Fields (see "I'm in the Mood for Love"). She was discovered in the early 1960s by producer Don Kirschner when she was still a student at New York's Music and Art High School. Submitting her lyrics to the last vestiges of Tin Pan Alley located in the city's hallowed Brill Building, Sager went on to enmesh herself in the country's pop zeitgeist. Following her first hit with the Mindbenders' version of her "A Groovy Kind of Love" in 1966, she went on to help shape the repertoire of the Monkees, write the lyrics for the 1970 off-Broadway show *Georgy*, and collaborate with Melissa Manchester on songs such as "Midnight Blue" in the mid-1970s before moving to Hollywood.

It was there during the 1970s and 1980s that she enjoyed her heyday, most notably with "Nobody Does It Better," the Oscar-nominated theme to the James Bond movie, *The Spy Who Loved Me*, written with her then-husband, celebrated pop composer Marvin Hamlisch. The song, sung for the film by Carly Simon, became a No. 2 hit. And it was with Hamlisch that she wrote *They're Playing Our Song*, a Broadway musical about the trials and tribulations of a hit songwriting team. It was during this period that she released several solo albums, the third of which (*Sometimes Late at Night* in 1981) produced a big hit single title "Stronger Than Before."

When her marriage to Hamlisch ended, she teamed with future husband Burt Bacharach and won a songwriting Oscar for 1981's "Arthur's Theme (Best That You Can Do)" for *Arthur*, the 1981 Dudley Moore–Liza Minnelli *Pygmalion*-style romp. Their most notable collaboration was undoubtedly "That's What Friends Are For," her most famous and consequential song. It was written for the 1982 black comedy *Night Shift*. Later, in the hands of Dionne Warwick, it became a huge hit and was used to raise funds for AIDS research.

Other films to which she contributed songs include *Ice Castles* ("Through the Eyes of Love"), *Beethoven's 2nd* ("Look What Love Has Done"), *Junior* ("Look What Love Has Done"), and *Quest for Camelot* ("The Prayer").

Since her divorce from Bacharach in 1991, she has continued her career most recently as the musical consultant on the hit Broadway show *The Boy From Oz*.

◼ "Union Sundown" (Bob Dylan)
Bob Dylan, single (1983); *Infidels* (1983)
Rich Lerner, *Napoleon in Rags* (2001)

This well-intentioned if ultimately shallow rant defends organized labor while condemning union exploitation and corruption. "Union Sundown" is helped only a little by some decent guitar work and not at all by Dylan's vocal track, which sounds like it was recorded in a cave. Still, Dylan deserves credit for writing a sympathetic song that ultimately defends the labor movement at a low ebb in its history. Some, however, have suggested that "Union Sundown" conveys a conservative message that might have been cut-and-pasted from a Ronald Reagan stump speech. Either way, the political intent behind the song appears muddled at best.

Dylan performed "Union Sundown" with Tom Petty and the Heartbreakers at a half-dozen shows during their 1986 tour. He returned to this piece of post-Guthrie unionism for two dozen performances with his Never Ending Tour band in the presidential election year of 1992.

◼ "Up to Me" (Bob Dylan)
Bob Dylan, *Biograph*/'74 (1985)
Roger McGuinn, *Cardiff Rose* (1976); *Born to Rock & Roll* (1992)
Zimmermen, *After the Ambulances Go*
Various Artists (performed by Joseph Arthur), *A Tribute to Bob Dylan, Volume 3: The Times They Are A-Changin'* (2000)

A subdued companion piece to "Buckets of Rain," the reconciliatory "Up to Me" was recorded at the late September 1974 New York City *Blood on the Tracks* sessions. Dylan comes across as vulnerable and honest in this song about artistic and personal commitment. It is another in the rare (and always welcome) line of nonnarrative confessional troubadour songs sung to his wife Sara or to one of those mystery women fluttering around his muse like a moth around a flame. Playing with his own inscrutable persona, Dylan commented on "Up to Me" in the *Biograph* liner notes, "I don't think of myself as Bob Dylan. It's like Rimbaud said, 'I is another.'"

Perhaps inspired by Joni Mitchell's "Down to You," from her 1973 album *Court and Spark*, "Up to Me" is a blueprint for the major themes found on *Blood on the Tracks*—obsession, denial, and melancholy humor. Dylan's scene of urban loneliness, time's relentless dominion, and opposites momentarily united is hung with one-liners ("Oh, the only decent thing I did when I worked as a postal clerk/Was to haul your picture down off the wall near the cage where I used to work"). Aimless characters tread water in shady situations in places where only the downtrodden can find themselves, such as the Thunderbird Café. The song acts as Dylan's song to himself with such lines as "How my lone guitar played sweet for you that old-time melody/And the harmonica around my neck, I blew it for you, free. . . ./You know it was up to me."

[S] "Uranium Rock" (Warren Smith)

Warren Smith, *Warren Smith* (1977)
Cramps, *Bad Music for Bad People* (1984)
Catfish and Crawdaddies, *Blues from Another Delta* (1998)
Mike Henderson, *Thicker than Water* (1999)

Dylan performed "Uranium Rock" as an alternate penultimate rockabilly encore number at about a dozen shows during his 1986 performances with Tom Petty and his Heartbreakin' posse.

Warren Smith (born February 7, 1932, Louise, Mississippi; died January 31, 1981, Longview, Texas) was an immensely talented if little remembered Elvis-styled Sun Studio alumnus who was equally adept at fiery rockabilly and the three-hanky country ballad. With a voice that was pure country and a edgy attitude to boot, Smith regarded his hits (few that they were) as his birthright. Yet despite his Hollywood good looks and drive, he managed but one short-lived hit for Sun and enjoyed only a short-lived flash of celebrity.

[S] "The Usual" (John Hiatt)

Bob Dylan, *Hearts of Fire* (soundtrack) (1987)
John Hiatt, *Warming Up to the Ice Age* (1985)
George Thorogood, *Rockin' My Life Away* (1997)

Dylan handles John Hiatt's ode to hard livin' with more interest than he showed his own songs in the *Hearts of Fire* travesty. Exhibiting his skill as a fine interpretive artist, he makes "The Usual" all his own, sounding as if he'd been dropping by the same roadside dive for years for his nightly highball.

John Hiatt (born August 20, 1952, Indianapolis) is one of those archetypal "musician's musicians" whose bank account isn't what it should be considering the high quality of his work. As a singer and guitarist using just the right amount of midwestern twang, his talents would not have gone unnoticed even in a deaf, dumb, and blind world. But it is his stellar songwriting for which he has gained acclaim, and not just from the wide range of talent who have recorded his songs, including Dr. Feelgood, the Searchers, Iggy Pop, Three Dog Night, Desert Rose Band, Bonnie Raitt, Nick Lowe, Rick Nelson, and the Neville Brothers.

A fan of both Dylan and the Rolling Stones, Hiatt cut his teeth in Indiana R&B bands during the late 1960s. He moved to Nashville in 1970 where he got a job as staff songwriter for Tree Publishing for twenty-five dollars a week.

After signing with Epic Records, Hiatt recorded the southern-fried *Hanging Around the Observatory* (1974) and *Overcoats* (1975). He moved to MCA for his next two albums, *Slug Line* (1979) and *Two-Bit Monsters* (1980), before signing with Geffen Records and moving to California.

His interest in punk rock resulted in songs with an angrier edge; however his albums of the early to mid-1980s (*All of a Sudden* in 1982, *Riding with the King* in 1983, and *Warming Up to the Ice Age* in 1985), although critically lauded, failed to produce a hit and Geffen unceremoniously dropped him from their label.

Following this reversal of fortune, Hiatt's professional and personal life hit the skids. He sunk into alcoholism and his wife committed suicide. He began pulling it back together when he cofounded Little Village, a groovy unit consisting of Hiatt, Ry Cooder, Nick Lowe, and Jim Keltner that propelled Hiatt's compositions and profile into a higher orbit. Little Village's *Bring the Family* (1987) included the song "Thing Called Love," which Bonnie Raitt turned into a huge hit. This raised Hiatt's stock and provided a momentum that he carried over to his next two releases, 1988's *Slow Turning* and 1990's *Stolen Moments*. However, his 1992 release, *Little Village*, did not live up to expectations and, despite some fine musical moments, headed straight for the cutout bins.

Hiatt tapped into his own "grunge" roots during the height of the alternative rock movement with his rocking 1994 release, *Perfectly Good Guitar*. Mandolins, acoustic guitars, and a return to the country-rock sound earned Hiatt his first Grammy nomination for *Walk On* (1995). Hiatt's sharp wit and bluesy side are evident on *Little Head* (1997) and *The Tiki Bar Is Open* (2001), an electric mélange hailed as a return to his eclectic roots. In the 1990s, Hiatt could also be seen hosting PBS television's music program *Sessions on West 57th Street*.

V

▣ "V.D. Blues" (Woody Guthrie)
aka "V.D. City," "V.D. Waltz"

The only recording of Dylan performing Woody's impossible-to-find pre-AIDS song cycle is from December 1961, and it sounds as if Dylan might be singing from personal experience.

All of the songs in the V.D. cycle can be summarized by Paul Cable's observation of "V.D. City" in his book *Bob Dylan: His Unreleased Recordings*: "a simple, pleasant melody with highly evocative, if slightly over-romantic lyrics about people lying around in gutters and doorways rotting to death. This, the song tells us, is what you get for 'an hour of passion and vice.' Not particularly enlightened philosophy, but it is only a song."

Ramblin' Jack Elliott once claimed himself as Dylan's source for the songs, saying, "I suppose I taught Bobby a few of my songs. Those old V.D. songs by Woody that nobody wanted the young kids to know, he picked them up from me."

▣ "V.D. Gunner's Blues (Landlady)" (Leadbelly)

During his one-off recorded performance of Woody Guthrie's venereal disease song cycle in December 1961, Dylan threw in this similar song for good measure. It is attributed to Leadbelly, but Dylan discographers may be confusing Leadbelly's "T.B. Blues" as the song Dylan casually recorded.

▣ "V.D. Seaman's Last Letter" (Bob Dylan)

Dylan wrote a number of songs in the summer of 1961 while staying at the New York City home of his friends, the McKenzies; one of those is "V.D. Seaman's Last Letter" (evidently inspired by the Guthrie V.D. song cycle), for which no recording is known to exist. Dylan's interest in songs of illness is not limited to this original or to his covers of Woody Guthrie's or Leadbelly's social disease songs in the early 1960s. In the mid-1970s he wrote "Legionnaires' Disease," a song that addressed the deadly outbreak of a mysterious killer virus at a convention of the American Legion. And, of course, his later "Disease of Conceit" deals with illness of the soul; but, then again, that could be said about many of his diagnoses in song.

▣ "Vincent van Gogh" (Robert Friemark)
aka "The Ballad of Vincent van Gogh," "Most Definitely NOT van Gogh," "The Painting by van Gogh"

Dylan and Bob Neuwirth (his old '60s pal) took to performing very ragged, bawdy house, vaudeville-style versions of this obscure, comic country folk song based on the legend of the genius painter during the 1976 leg of the Rolling Thunder Revue. Postings on the Internet point to Neuwirth's claim that the author of the song was his art teacher, Robert Friemark. Neuwirth has also mentioned that he, Dylan, and Kris Kristofferson threw in a line here and there in reshaping the song for the concert stage. This song is not to be confused with a half-written, similarly titled song about van Gogh performed by Dylan and Robbie Robertson in a Denver hotel room in 1966 and recorded by Robert Shelton, which has circulated via pirate albums through the years.

"Viola Lee Blues" (Traditional/Noah Lewis)
See also "Minglewood Blues"
aka "99 Year Blues," "Some Get Six Months"
Various Artists (performed by Julius Daniels), *Anthology of American Folk Music*/'27 (1952/'97)
Cannon's Jug Stompers, *The Complete Recordings*/'30 (1995)
Gus Cannon, *Complete Recorded Works, Volume 1 (1927–29)* (1995)
The Jim Kweskin Jug Band, *See Reverse Side for Title* (1966)
Grateful Dead, *Grateful Dead* (1967)
Solar Circus, *Twilight Dance* (1992)

Dylan could have copped this classic prison blues song by Noah Lewis of Cannon's Jug Stompers from the Julius Daniels version on *Anthology of American Folk Music*, or from any one of a number of different sources; but the Jim Kweskin Jug Band (who recorded it on their 1966 album, *See Reverse Side for Title*) is also a strong possibility. Cannon's Jug Stompers recorded "Viola Lee Blues" a couple of different times in the late 1920s; Geoff Muldaur (guitarist with the Kweskin band) found the tune on an old, Victor label 78, and it was he who introduced his leader to it. Confusion, however, arises because the Jug Stompers recorded the song twice. According to the liner notes of a 1990 release of their material, the second take of the song was never released. But the takes differ significantly in that a key verse performed by Kweskin ("I wrote a letter/mailed it in the air") was only sung on the second, unreleased take. All this begs the question: Where

did Kweskin learn the unreleased take? Finally, who or what is Viola Lee? The words appear nowhere in the lyrics. Could it be the name of the prison from which the song is sung or the woman who led our letter writer into its lonely cells? Either way, this is a song about someone being sent up the river for a loooong time.

Bluesologists hear the strains of "Viola Lee Blues" in earlier, related songs; they suggest the song stretches back to before even Gus Cannon's group gained acclaim with it, as "Some Got Six Months" and/or "99 Year Blues," a plaint from Louisiana's notorious Angola state prison farm. Perhaps that's a key to the title.

Dylan only performed "Viola Lee Blues" once, as an acoustic surprise during a 1997 concert.

"Visions of Johanna" (Bob Dylan)
aka "Freeze-Out," "Mother Revisited," "Seems Like a Freeze-Out"
Bob Dylan, *Blonde on Blonde* (1966); *Biograph*/'66 (1985); *The Bootleg Series, Volume 4: Bob Dylan Live 1966 (The "Royal Albert Hall" Concert)* (1998)
Quinaimes Band, *Quinaimes Band* (1971)
Marianne Faithful, *Rich Kid Blues* (1988)
Austine Delone, *Delone at Last* (1991)
Peter Laughner, *Take the Guitar Player for a Ride* (1994)
Various Artists (performed by Lee Renaldo), *Outlaw Blues, Volume 2* (1995)
The Zimmermen, *The Dungeon Tapes* (1996)
The Grateful Dead, *Fallout from the Phil Zone*/'95 (1997)
Michael Moore, *Jewels and Binoculars* (2000)
Robyn Hitchcock, *Robyn Sings* (2002)
Gerry Murphy, *Gerry Murphy Sings Bob Dylan* (2002)
Various Artists (performed by Anders Osborne), *Blues on Blonde on Blonde* (2003)

A song from deep inside Dylan's netherworld, "Visions of Johanna" is an undisputed masterwork. At the time of its composition, Dylan had been writing longer songs for some time, lacing images and characters for surreal verse heaped

V

upon surreal verse, beguiling listeners with intangible intricacies and dusky beauty. And yes, if that mercurial, blurry photo of a scowling Dylan that graces the wraparound cover of *Blonde on Blonde* (the album on which the song first appeared) could sing a song, it would probably sound a lot like "Visions of Johanna."

The narrator of "Visions of Johanna" is trapped in a seven-and-a-half-minute epic of claustrophobic longing with a woman named Louise and her boy toy, but his mind chases the unattainable Johanna through nocturnal Manhattan's lofts, subways, empty lots, and a secret museum where "infinity goes up on trial." Throughout his vision quest, he picks up on flashes of overheard conversation and encounters one "little boy lost" (who may or may not be his mirror image); he is threatened by the all-night girls on the D train, discovered by a flashlight-shining night watchman, and pursued by the ghost of electricity. His grip on reality slowly loosens so that by the song's hallucinatory end, his "visions of Johanna are all that remain." About the only thing that keeps "Visions of Johanna" anchored is its simple folk melody, against which Dylan's descent into a lyrical and psychic vortex can be grasped.

"Visions of Johanna," according to Andy Gill in his book *Don't Think Twice, It's All Right*, "remains one of the high points of Dylan's canon, particularly favored among hard-core Dylanophiles, possibly because it so perfectly sustains its position on the cusp of poetic semantics, forever teetering on the brink of lucidity, yet remaining impervious to strict decipherment."

According to biographer Robert Shelton in *No Direction Home: The Life and Music of Bob Dylan*, "Visions of Johanna" is a "major work in which five long verses and a coda structure nightmares, hallucinations, trances. The instrumental introduction draws us into a seven-and-a-half-minute work. The mournful mouth harp plaintively breaks the silence; chugging drums and stealthy organ insinuate themselves. The organ maintains the haunting feeling. The singing is superb, so purposefully phrased, so weary with rhythmic emphases as portentous as heartbeats. Electric guitar fills in, underlining and deepening. The skittering images hurl off like fragmentary chips from a mind floating downstream, neither time nor structure holding forces in check. The nonsequential visions are like a swiveling camera recording a fractured consciousness. The atmosphere is almost unbearably fetid and sad until verse four, where the rapidly piled-up rhymes of 'freeze,' 'sneeze,' 'Jeez,' and 'knees' lighten the mood. We are back again among the grotesques: peddlers, countesses, all-night girls, lost little boy, Mona Lisa."

The *Blonde on Blonde* version of "Visions of Johanna" is nothing short of amazing, as is an oft-circulated studio outtake complete with an extra line squeezed in at the end. But the ghostly solo acoustic versions performed on the 1966 tour—available on *Biograph* and *The Bootleg Series, Volume 4: Bob Dylan Live 1966 (The "Royal Albert Hall" Concert)*—with their exhausted, bittersweet vulnerability, stand as a rarely paralleled moment in Dylan's career as a performing artist.

And for those who suspect that "Visions of Johanna" owes its surreal fluidity to the ingestion of psychedelic agents, check out how Dylan introduced the song at the actual 1966 Royal Albert Hall concert (*not* the Manchester show released on *The Bootleg Series, Volume 4*): "This is a typical example of probably one song that your English music newspapers here would call a 'drug song.' I don't write 'drug songs.' You know, like I never have. I wouldn't know how to go about it. But this is not a drug song. I'm not saying it for any kind of defensive reason or anything like *that*, it's just not a drug song . . . it's just vulgar to think so."

Those looking for autobiography informing "Visions of Johanna" will be similarly bamboozled. All available evidence suggests that "Visions of Johanna" was written and initially performed some six months after Bob and Joan Baez split up and almost exactly at the time of Bob's marriage to Sara; but what does this add to the song? Some think it more interesting to hear in the name the echo of the name "Gehenna," the Hebrew word for hell, prison, or torture. Others suggest that the key to the song is figuring out the relationship between Johanna and Louise (the available female character depicted in the lyrics), a situation not unlike the triangle alluded to in "Fourth Time Around"—another *Blonde on Blonde* curio.

With its first 1966 performances, "Visions of Johanna" became something of a musical/poetic/spiritual talisman for fans attending Dylan's shows—always hoped for and very rarely delivered. Dylan performed it once with acoustic guitar in 1974 during his tour with the Band and again during the spring 1976 Rolling Thunder Revue tour. Its special reemergence during the middle and latter stages of the Never Ending Tour have not disappointed either; Dylan's performances of the song have contained all the frail power and world-weariness of his previous ones.

[S] "A Voice from on High" (Bill Monroe/Bessie Lee Mauldin)

aka "I Hear a Voice Calling"
See also "Blue Moon of Kentucky"
Bill Monroe, *A Voice from on High* (1969)
Stanley Brothers, *Stanley Series, Volume 2* (1989)
Joe Val, *Diamond Joe* (1995)
Ricky Skaggs, *Solider of the Cross* (1999)

Dylan first trotted out this high, lonesome, show-opening piece of gospel bluegrass—courtesy of the genre's patriarch, Bill Monroe, and his lover, tumultuous muse, and bass player, Bessie Lee Mauldin—in the 2002 Never Ending summer tour.

Monroe first recorded "A Voice from on High" on January 25, 1954, and it was released as a single with "Working on a Building" on the flip side. The song is laced with biblical references to, for example, Matthew 7, Romans 5, and Philippians 3. In an undated interview, Monroe discussed not only the song's composition, but also its inspiration, saying, "I sure want to be ready on that day. And I speak in my writing of a song the way I really feel about it. I really want to hear that voice calling me. . . . I believe a person should try to live the best life he can and enjoy it and live a decent life.

"I was trying to do something with the tenor you know and tie some words together with the tune. So I wrote the chorus to that song and I meant it for the tenor to have the high part there, and it was about as high as I could sing. Bessie Lee Mauldin helped on the verses to that song."

Bessie Lee Mauldin (born December 28, 1920, Norwood, North Carolina; died February 8, 1983, North Carolina), nicknamed the "Carolina Songbird," was one of the early female pioneers of bluegrass music. She recorded and toured extensively with Bill Monroe and the Blue Grass Boys from 1954 to 1964. As the stand-up bass player in that famous band, she cut a striking pose with her platinum blonde hair and robust figure. Along with Hazel Dickens, Alice Gerrard, Rose Maddox, Kitty Wells, and Sara Carter, Mauldin was one of the first female role models in country music who stepped from the sidelines to command the stage as a peer—an icon to spotlight rather than part of the music itself.

Monroe is often cast as a no-cussin', drinkin', or carousin' type—a no-nonsense, austere fellow. But he did love women and none so seriously as Mauldin, the one true love of Monroe's life. Although they never married, they had a daughter together who they gave up for adoption. In his 2001 biography, *Can't You Hear Me Callin': The Life of Bill Monroe*, Richard Smith brings out the tragic elements of their lengthy, stormy relationship, and, indeed, succeeds in inspiring great sympathy for the woman who became Monroe's muse. Her sad, lonely death erased whatever input we could have had from the only person on the planet who ever understood Monroe.

[S] "Vomit Express" (Allen Ginsberg/arrangement by Bob Dylan)

Allen Ginsberg, *First Blues*/'71 (1983); *Holy Soul Jelly Roll*/'71 (1995)

Dylan joined poet Allen Ginsberg and a crack cast of cool cats in a 1971 session at the Record Plant in New York City for a long visit into the poetic and musical unknown. Some of the cuts recorded eventually surfaced on the fabulous Ginsberg retrospective *Holy Soul Jelly Roll*, which was released in 1995.

Ginsberg claimed the recording came about after Dylan heard a poetry reading at New York University's Loeb Auditorium with composer and musician David Amram. Moved by the spontaneity of the event, Dylan called Ginsberg late that night, and the wheels for a recording session were set in motion.

According to Ginsberg in the liner notes to his CD compilation *Holy Soul Jelly Roll*, "'Vomit Express' was a phrase I got from my friend Lucien Carr, who talked about going to Puerto Rico, went often, and we were planning to take an overnight plane a couple of weeks later, my first there. He spoke of it as the 'vomit express'—poor people flying at night for cheap fares, not used to airplanes, throwing up airsick."

W

[S] "Wade in the Water" (Traditional)

Bob Dylan, *Live 1961–2000—Thirty-nine Years of Great Concert Performances*/'61 (2001)
Odetta, *Tin Angel* (1954)
Bill McAdoo and Pete Seeger, *McAdoo Sings with Guitar* (1960)
Big Mama Thornton, *Way It Is* (1970)
Sweet Honey in the Rock, *Live at Carnegie Hall* (1988)
Charlie Haden, *Steal Away* (1994)
Mavis Staples, *Spirituals and Gospel: Dedicated to Mahalia Jackson* (1996)

This traditional gospel song is one of America's oldest. Dylan may have been hip to Odetta's 1954 rendition; it is lyrically similar to his own harrowing, spine-tingling, Robert Johnson–style version, which was captured on but one December 1961 recording and released on the Sony import *Live 1961–2000—Thirty-nine Years of Great Concert Performances.*

Gospelologists cite "Wade in the Water" as an example of a song composed for one purpose and used secretly for another. Slaves created it to accompany the rite of baptism, but it was used by Underground Railroad conductor Harriet Tubman (dubbed "a woman named Moses") to communicate to fugitive slaves escaping to the North that they should "wade in the water" to throw bloodhounds off their scent. Tubman's and others' improvisations on the spiritual were employed clandestinely in the struggle for freedom at many stops along the Underground Railroad. The way Dylan sings this, he could well be one of the Railroad's tormented passengers.

[S] "The Wagoner's Lad" (Traditional)

aka "The Waggoner's Lad," "Loving Nancy," "My Horses Ain't Hungry"

Various Artists (performed by Buell Kazee), *Anthology of American Folk Music Volume 1/'28* (1952/1997)
Peggy Seeger, *Songs of Courting and Complaint* (1955)
Dock Boggs, *His Folkways Years, 1963–68* (1998)
Joan Baez, *Joan Baez* (1970)
Rich Lerner, *Trails and Bridges* (1996)
Roger McGuinn (performed with Joan Baez & Eliza Carthy), *Treasures from the Folk Den* (2001)

The extensively recorded "The Wagoner's Lad" and "On Top of Old Smoky" are first cousins in that complex Anglo-American family of "kiss-and-run lover" folk songs that also includes, among others, "East Virginia," "The Cuckoo," "Sugar Baby," and "Pretty Polly." Originally a nineteenth-century British broadside ballad, the transformation of "The Wagoner's Lad" into an American lyric folk song involved, against the sage advice of Polonius, a free borrowing and lending of verses to and from a score of songs.

According to Alan Lomax in his book *The Folk Songs of North America*, "Prominent among the roaring blades of the frontier were the wagoners who, before the days of railroads, transported a great part of the freight of the growing country. Davy Crockett, when he ran away from home, cruised round the country for several years, working on the wagons that plied between his native Tennessee and Eastern cities. As free-lance entrepreneurs, sophisticated travellers and men with the smell of money and far places about them, the wagoners cut a wide swathe among the ladies. The song of the girl seduced and deserted by a dashing wagoner comes from England but became a universal favourite in the mountains of the South, turning up in all sorts of combinations. A slow banjo piece, it seems to be the ancestor of the 'Jack of Diamonds' or 'Rye Whiskey.'"

The version Dylan sings stands pretty close to Peggy Seeger's recording and concerns the

unsuccessful seduction and abandonment of a poor, unfortunate girl by the wagoner's lad—already on his way to the next town with a new notch on his belt. With the whole band sounding like God's great Autoharp in the sky, Dylan included "The Wagoner's Lad" as part of his Never Ending Tour, performing it regularly in his 1988 acoustic sets and trotting it out for one-offs in 1989 and 1990.

"Wait for the Light to Shine" (Fred Rose)
Don Gibson, *No One Stands Alone* (1959)
Mac Wiseman, *Grassroots to Bluegrass* (1990)
Louvin Brothers, *Close Harmony* (1992)
Roy Acuff, *King of Country Music (1936–1947)* (1998)
Hank Williams, *Complete Hank Williams* (1998)
Pat Boone, *Golden Treasure of Hymns* (1999)

In his fall 2001 U.S. arena tour in support of *Love and Theft* (and for a country still reeling from the events of September 11), Dylan opened his shows with Fred Rose's "Wait for the Light to Shine." This Hank Williams–era bluegrass spiritual marked by fine picking and strong harmonies pleads for enlightenment and encourages all listeners to "pull yourself together, keep lookin' for the sun." Dylan may have remembered the song from his childhood in Hibbing, Minnesota, when it served as the theme for the country-western TV show *Town Hall Party*.

Rose (born August 24, 1897, Evansville, Indiana; died December 1, 1954, Nashville, Tennessee) was one of the grand pooh-bahs of country music. With his publishing and composer partner, Roy Acuff, Rose not only left some of the most enduring songs in popular music but helped propel the careers of many a superstar, Hank Williams foremost among them.

Rose was no son of the South. He grew up playing piano in Indiana and was a professional musician by the age of ten. At fifteen he ventured to Chicago to pursue a singing career. He landed nightclub gigs, recorded player-piano rolls alongside Fats Waller (the future Holy Fool of jazz), and even performed briefly with one of the first great popularizers of jazz, Paul Whiteman and his Orchestra. Rose's associations with Chicago's version of Tin Pan Alley led to some early songwriting success ("Deed I Do," "Honest and Truly," and "Doo Dah Blues") and got him a job as host of a daily radio show.

When his second marriage failed in 1933, Rose, now thirty-six, moved to Nashville where he hosted "Fred Rose's Song Show" on WSM. The show became something of a local hit, but Rose did not stay put in Music City for long. He bounced to New York and back again to Chicago, then pitched his tent in Hollywood and began writing songs for Gene Autry. He garnered an Oscar nomination for "Be Honest with Me," from Autry's 1941 film *Ridin' on a Rainbow*. His return to Nashville's WSM shortly thereafter resulted in the partnership with Grand Ole Opry star Roy Acuff that made both their fortunes. Acuff-Rose Publishing became not only Nashville's premier music publishing concern but the first to represent only country songs. Because he saw himself as an artist first, Rose turned over the day-to-day operations of the firm to his son Wesley in 1945 in order to devote more time to songwriting. Country music certainly benefited from the songs Rose contributed to its canon, among them, "Pins and Needles," "No One Will Ever Know," "Blue Eyes Crying in the Rain," "Roly Poly" (made famous by Bob Wills and the Texas Playboys), "It's a Sin" (written for and popularized by Eddy Arnold), "Texarkana Baby," "Waltz of the Wind," "We Live in Two Different Worlds," and "Afraid."

Without a doubt, the turning point for Acuff-Rose Publishing occurred in 1946 when Hank Williams came a knockin' on their door and gave a brief audition. With the likes of Pee Wee King and Redd Stewart already in his stable, Rose immediately signed the lanky bard of country and western music. Rose set about masterminding Williams's career, landing him an MGM contract in 1947 and cowriting (or at least taking credit and royalties for) some of the classic Hank songs: "A Mansion on the Hill," "Kaw-Liga," "Crazy Heart," "Settin' the Woods on Fire," "I'll Never Get Out of This World Alive," and "Take These Chains from My Heart."

Perhaps Rose's greatest talent as a businessman was his uncanny ability for placing Acuff-Rose songs with pop stars whose recordings not only spread their gospel but filled their coffers as well.

Sadly, the strain of keeping all of those spinning plates aloft was too much for Rose: He died of a heart attack in 1954. "Name me a song that everybody knows/And I'll bet you it belongs to Acuff-Rose," a line from the Jeff Tweedy song "Acuff-Rose," could easily be his epitaph.

■ "Waitin' for You" (Bob Dylan)
Various Artists (performed by Bob Dylan), *The Divine Secrets of the Ya-Ya Sisterhood* (2002)

Who could blame Dylan if his Oscar win in 2001 (for "Things Have Changed," from *Wonder Boys*) went to his head a little bit? "Waitin' for You," his contribution to the 2002 film *Divine Secrets of the Ya-Ya Sisterhood* (a feel-good chick flick starring Sandra Bullock, Ellyn Burstyn, James Garner, et al.), didn't exactly bring it all back home. Even so, his vocals on this swirly amble with as many banal lines as good ones ("Happiness is but a state of mind/Anytime you want, you can cross the state line") evoke Slim Harpo's slippery growl.

Dylan, the grand master of the postmodern folk pastiche, spreads himself far and wide for his phraseology in "Waitin' for You." Like some minstrel show version of T. S. Eliot, the words are cut-and-pasted from wherever in this creation. The line "I lost my gal at the boatman's ball" is inspired by "De Boatman Dance," by Dan Emmett (*see also* "High Water" and "Dixie"). The words "Among the good and true" appear in "The Faded Coat of Blue," an American Civil War ballad written by J. H. McNaughton circa 1865. "St. Anne's Reel," an old Irish tune, may have been the source for the "fiddler's arm" reference. "The night has a thousand hearts and eyes" seems an obvious nod to "The Night Has a Thousand Eyes," the famous 1962 song by Ben Weisman, Dottie Wayne, and Marilyn Garrett that was recorded by Bobby Vee and John Coltrane, among many others. "It's Been So Long" is the title of a 1950s Webb Pierce song (*see* "More and More"). And "Hope may vanish, but it never dies" is plucked from "Hellas" Percy Bysshe Shelley's 1822 poem.

Regarding Dylan's involvement in the project, *Ya-Ya* soundtrack-meister T-Bone Burnett told Gary Graff of the *Cleveland Plain Dealer*, "We just sent him the movie and asked him. The movie had become a waltz, really; it seemed like, somehow, the rhythm of the thing fit a waltz. So we asked Bob what he would think about writing a waltz for the end of it, and he did. He hadn't written a waltz for years, and he came up with this mad, really beautiful waltz for us."

[S] "Walk a Mile in My Shoes" (Joe South)

Joe South, single (1969); *Best of Joe South* (1990)
Willie Hightower, single (1969)
Bryan Ferry, *Another Time, Another Place* (1974)
Elvis Presley, *Walk a Mile in My Shoes*/'70 (1995)
Freddie Notes and the Rudies, *Montego Bay* (1995)

Dylan's only known performance of "Walk a Mile in My Shoes," Joe South's hard-luck credo in song, led off the famous 1990 show at Toad's Place (a venue in New Haven, Connecticut) in experiential fashion.

When South (born February 28, 1948, Atlanta, Georgia) hit as a solo artist in his very early twenties, he had already just about done it all, having worked as a country music DJ, seasoned session man, and producer. His studio sessions included the electric guitar parts for Simon and Garfunkel's "Sounds of Silence," and he wrote and produced a quartet of medium hits for Billy Joe Royal. Most saliently, he can be heard playing guitar on Dylan's *Blonde on Blonde* version of "Stuck Inside of Mobile (with the Memphis Blues Again)."

"Games People Play" was South's first big solo hit; it reached No. 12 in 1968 and won the Grammy Award for song of the year in 1969, establishing him as a preachy, straight-talking southern artist. South wrote "Walk a Mile in My Shoes" in 1969, and his recording of it later that year also hit No. 12. Elvis began covering the song while South's version was still riding high.

South has kept a pretty low profile since the 1970s, for a time living in the jungles of Maui, Hawaii, to *really* get away from it all. More recently he has resumed performing and songwriting.

[S] "Walkin' Down the Line" (Bob Dylan)

Bob Dylan, *The Bootleg Series, Volumes 1–3: Rare and Unreleased, 1961–1991*/'63 (1991)
Glen Campbell, *The Astounding 12-String Guitar of Glen Campbell* (1964)
Hamilton Camp, *Paths of Victory* (1964)
Odetta, *Odetta Sings Dylan* (1965)
Jackie DeShannon, *In the Wind* (1965)
The Baytown Singers, single (1965)
Joe & Eddie, *Walkin' Down the Line* (1965)
The Gene Norman Group, *Dylan Jazz* (1965)
Rick Nelson, *Bright Lights & Country Music* (1966); *Country*

W

Fever (1967)
Joan Baez, *Any Day Now* (1968); *Vanguard Sessions: Baez Sings Dylan* (1998)
Evergreen Blueshoes, *The Ballad of Evergreen Blueshoes* (1969)
Orange Blossom Sound, *Blue Grass & Orange Blossoms* (1970)
The Country Gentlemen, *The Award Winning Country Gentlemen* (1972)
The Dillards, *There Is a Time (1963–70)* (1972)
Arlo Guthrie and Pete Seeger, *Together in Concert* (1975)
Rising Sons Featuring Taj Mahal & Ry Cooder, *Rising Sons*/'66 (1992)
Steven Keene, *No Alternative* (1994)
Michel Montecrossa, *4th Time Around* (2001)

Dylan first recorded "Walkin' Down the Line"—a dusty, footloose piece of folk blues that deals with clichéd subjects (women, money, and hedonism) in a fresh way—in November 1962 at the offices of *Broadside* magazine. This was in the early phases of his manager Albert Grossman's master plan to use his client's songs to create a cover-a-Bob Dylan song cottage industry. As such, "Walkin' Down the Line" was one of dozens of songs Dylan wrote for copyright purposes but never seriously considered for performance or official release. Grossman's strategy would seem to have paid off: For a song that remains under the radar of most Dylan fans, it has been recorded often.

Dylan seems not to have taken the lively "Walkin' Down the Line" to the concert stage. He did toy with an endearing if rough arrangement decades later during his rehearsals with the Grateful Dead in the spring of 1987. A version of Dylan handling the song with Ric von Schmidt has surfaced, possibly from the spring of 1964 although there is some debate concerning the location, circumstances, and authenticity of its recording.

W

[S] **"Walk Out in the Rain"** (Bob Dylan/Helena Springs)

See also "If I Don't Be There by Morning"

Eric Clapton, *Backless* (1978)
Various Artists (performed by Eric Clapton), *I Shall Be Unreleased: The Songs of Bob Dylan* (1991)
Robbie and Ron McCoury, *Robbie and Ron McCoury* (1995)
Various Artists (performed by Ann Christy), *May Your Song Always Be Sung Again* (2001)

Dylan cowrote "Walk Out in the Rain," a straightforward tale of a breakup told with the simplicity of a '50s heartbreaker, with backup singer and confidante Helena Springs in 1978, during the *Street Legal/At Budokan* era. If that was the case (and no Dylan recording of the song has ever surfaced), Eric Clapton probably decided to record the song based on the demo tape of that session. Clapton's bittersweet performance—aided by subtle organ surges and steady rhythm guitar that insinuates itself rather than blows you away—is a collectible must.

A final note: The McCoury brothers' version of "Walk Out in the Rain" reached No. 12 on the bluegrass charts in 1997.

[S] **"Wallflower"** (Bob Dylan)

Bob Dylan, *The Bootleg Series, Volumes 1–3: Rare and Unreleased, 1961–1991*/'71 (1991)
Doug Sahm (performed with Bob Dylan), *Doug Sahm and Band* (1972)
David Bromberg, *Wanted Dead or Alive* (1974); *The Player* (1998)
The Clancy Brothers, *Irish Folk Songs & Airs* (1997)
Various Artists (performed by the Holmes Brothers), *Tangled Up in Blues: The Songs of Bob Dylan* (1999)
The Robins, *The Robins Sing Dylan* (2000)
Buddie and Julie Miller, *Buddie and Julie Miller* (2001)
Various Artists (performed by Doug Sahm), *Doin' Dylan 2* (2002)

"Wallflower" is a charming, if lightweight, country waltz recorded in November 1971 as part of the New York City session that produced "George Jackson." Leon Russell (using the pseudonym Russell Bridges for contractual reasons) played bass on the cut. This was a period when Dylan was resettling in the city after an extended stretch in Woodstock, New York, some hundred miles to the north; it was a time he was later to describe in *The Bootleg Series, Vol. 1–3* liner notes as "the worst time of my life, when I tried to search for the past, when I went back to New York for the second time. I didn't know what to do. Everything had changed. I tried to write and sing at the same time and sometimes that drove me crazy."

That would make certain lyrics in "Wallflower" ("Just like you I'm wonderin' what I'm doin' here/Just like you I'm wonderin' what's goin' on") ring particularly true.

Despite the personal and musical turmoil Dylan may have been experiencing when he composed "Wallflower," the song made a big impression on Patti Smith, who once recalled: "I always wanted to dance with boys and nobody ever asked me to dance, I had to wait for ladies' choice. . . . I was so pathetic. But Bob understands that 'cos he wrote the song 'Wallflower.'"

Finally, look no further when determining the source of the name of Jakob Dylan's (Bob's son) popular band.

[S] **"Walls of Red Wing"** (Bob Dylan)

aka "The Walls of Red Wing"

Bob Dylan, *The Bootleg Series, Volumes 1–3: Rare and Unreleased, 1961–1991*/'63 (1991)

Joan Baez, *Any Day Now* (1968); *Vanguard Sessions: Baez Sings Dylan* (1998)

Ramblin' Jack Elliott (with John Prine), *Friends of Mine* (1998)

If *The 400 Blows*, François Truffaut's 1959 film about adolescent turmoil, had a corollary in American song, it might be "Walls of Red Wing."

The notorious Minnesota State Reform School (now called the Minnesota Correction Facility at Red Wing), located in an otherwise gorgeous area of southeastern Minnesota, was opened in 1891 to "counteract the results of idleness and evil companionship by moral and intellectual instruction." Though Dylan never spent a night in the joint, he sings his song with the authority of someone who might have known someone who had—or at least of someone threatened with the place if he didn't turn off that damn rock 'n' roll music, straighten up, and fly right.

In reality, Red Wing is not quite the grim, troubled teen gulag he depicts, though for stretches in its storied history it was a pretty depressing place. There are, in fact, no walls surrounding the institution. But the wrought iron gates and gloomy original buildings do create an imposing and humbling ambiance, and Dylan's imagination conjured the horrors that might befall one incarcerated in such a Dickensian dungeon.

Regarded as mediocre fare, "Walls of Red Wing" seems not have been a popular recording choice among Dylan's songster contemporaries. The song is, however, one of several compositions that heralded his entree into the realm of the protest song.

There is some indication that, as a teenager in the very late 1950s, Dylan spent a semester or so at an all-boys boarding school in Pennsylvania that dealt with difficult adolescents. If so, he might have drawn on the isolation of that experience in composing "Walls of Red Wing."

"The Road and the Miles to Dundee," an old Scottish folk song, is deemed to be the source for the melody of "Walls of Red Wing." Dylan may have come across the song when he visited London in early 1963 and soaked up archaic material from singers such as Martin Carthy and Nigel Davenport.

Dylan first recorded "Walls of Red Wing" at an informal New York City studio session in early 1963. Only three concert field recordings, captured between the springs of 1963 and 1964, have survived.

[S] "The Wanderer" (Ernest Maresca)

Dion, *Runaround Sue* (1961)
The Beach Boys, *Beach Boys Concert* (1964)
Leif Garrett, *Leif Garrett* (1977)
Arthur Alexander, *Story of Rock N Roll* (1977)
Delbert McClinton, *Delbert McClinton* (1993)

Dylan's only performances of this famous picaresque, James Dean–style bit of teenage existential angst occurred with Paul Simon during the encore duet sets of their 1999 tour. "The Wanderer" was written in 1961 by Ernest Maresca and was a hit for Dion. Leif Garrett revived the song in the late 1970s.

Maresca (born April 21, 1939, Bronx, New York) was a minor songwriter and an even more minor doo-wop recording artist. Along with "The Wanderer," his style of boastful Bronx hoodlum pap reached its peak with "Runaround," a hit for the Regents in the early 1960s.

[S] "The Wandering Kind" (Bob Dylan/Helena Springs)

See also "If I Don't Be There by Morning"
Paul Butterfield, *The Legendary Paul Butterfield Rides Again* (1986)

"The Wandering Kind" is one of a passel of songs Dylan wrote, recorded, and copyrighted with soul mate *du jour* Helena Springs in 1979. (The title is perhaps a semi-titular nod to the 1959 film *The Fugitive Kind*, a recasting of the Tennessee Williams's play *Orpheus Descending* in a xenophobic Mississippi town. The film was written by Williams and directed by Sidney Lumet and stars Marlon Brando.) The song comes off as a dusty border-town drama dealing with a footloose (and loose) woman who betrays the singer. But she is double-crossed herself and left in "that dark adobe cell" as the singer rides off singing in "take that!" style that he's also one of the wandering kind. Dylan apparently never recorded the song, but a Springs demo probably filtered to Paul Butterfield who made it one of his last recordings. Part of what makes "The Wandering Kind" and the other half dozen or so songs Dylan completed with Springs notable is that their creation seemed to come in the frothy middle of his religious conversion, even though they themselves are secular compositions—an underconsidered paradox in Dylanology, if ever there was one.

[S] "Wanted Man" (Bob Dylan/Johnny Cash)

aka "The Fugitive"
Johnny Cash, *At Folsom Prison and San Quentin* (1969); *Mystery of Life* (1990); *Essential Johnny Cash (1955–1983)* (1992); *Wanted Man* (1994); *Complete Live at San Quentin* (2000)
Various Artists (performed by Johnny Cash), *Little Fauss and Big Halsy* (soundtrack) (1970)
Lester Flatt and Earl Scruggs, *Final Fling* (1970); *1964–1969, Plus* (1996)
John Schroder, *Dylan Vibrations* (1971)
Graham Bell, *Graham Bell* (1972)
Seatrain, *Watch* (1973)
Earl Scruggs Revue, *Family Portrait* (1976)
Joe Cocker, *Luxury You Can Afford* (1978)
George Thorogood and the Destroyers, *Bad to the Bone* (1982)
Thore Holm Hansen, *Wanted Man* (1982)
Nick Cave, *The Firstborn Is Dead* (1985)
Kevin Kasub, *Wanted Man* (1986)
Various Artists (performed by George Thorogood), *The Songs of Bob Dylan/'82* (1989)
Dump, *I Can Hear Music* (1995)
Various Artists (performed by Section One), *Americana: Tribute to Johnny Cash* (2000)

W

Dylan had Johnny Cash (one of his admitted heroes) specifically in mind when he wrote "Wanted Man," about a lovable on-the-lam rogue desperado who leaves empty banks and brokenhearted lovers in his wake. The song perfectly captures the bemused weariness of both men (but especially Cash) with lines like, "Went to sleep in Shreveport, woke up in Abilene/Wonderin' why the hell I'm wanted at some town halfway between."

Because Cash rewrote a few of the lyrics and arranged the song to better suit his style, and because "Wanted Man" is so closely associated with him, he has come to share, at least informally, composer credit. Yet a Chuck Berry ability to cram an itinerary fit for a runaway con and the breezy road-trip sensibility of a Jack Kerouac picaresque novel is uniquely Dylan. What other Dylan or Cash song for that matter mentions California, Buffalo, Kansas City, Ohio, Mississippi, Cheyenne, Colorado, Georgia, El Paso, Juarez, Shreveport, Abilene, Albuquerque, Syracuse, Tallahassee, *and* Baton Rouge?

Film freaks are already hip to where "Wanted Man" first appeared: *Little Fauss and Big Halsy*, the neglected 1970 buddy road flick starring Robert Redford and Michael J. Pollard as a couple of always-on-the-make motorcycle-racing losers.

[S] "Watching the River Flow" (Bob Dylan)

Bob Dylan, single (1971); *Bob Dylan's Greatest Hits, Volume II* (1971)
Various Artists (performed by Bob Dylan), *Where We Live* (2003)
Seatrain, *Watch* (1973)
Joe Cocker, *Luxury You Can Afford* (1978)
Ole "Fesser" Lindgreen, *Best of Fesser's City Band* (1986)
Heart of Gold Band, *Double Dose* (1989)
Gadd Gang, *Gadd Gang* (1991)
Candy Kane, *Knockout* (1995)
Dan Papaila, *Full Circle* (1997)
Various Artists (performed by Chris Farlowe), *Wine, Women and Song* (1998)
Various Artists (performed by Leon Russell), *Tangled Up in Blues: The Songs of Bob Dylan* (1999)
Steve Forbert, *The I-10 Chronicles, Volume 2: One More for the Road* (2001)

Its nonchalant melody perfectly suits this song about a man chiding himself for his lack of public involvement as he ambivalently considers changing from an observer to a participant. "Watching the River Flow" recalls Huck Finn floating aimlessly down the Mississippi River or a guy hanging a "Gone fishin'" sign on the locked door of his closed-for-the-afternoon country store. When released as a single it hit No. 41 on the *Billboard* chart.

Dylan originally recorded the blues-structured "Watching the River Flow" at Blue Rock Studios in New York in March 1971; the session, supervised by keyboard player and producer Leon Russell, also spawned "When I Paint My Masterpiece." In both songs Dylan confronted his continuing artistic stagnation. This initial roller-coaster version of "Watching the River Flow" is a festive honky-tonk affair that finds a man at a crossroads (or, in this case, a riverbank), musing on whether or not to remain in his rural idyll or return to the city where only "with the one I love close at hand" can he resummon his muse. These tunes were recorded near the bottom of that relatively fallow period in the early 1970s when Dylan's lack of activity, momentum, enthusiasm, or direction became subject matter in and of itself. He even begins this song by complaining "what's the matter with me?," an interesting subversion of a whole school of blues songs that commence with or are even titled "what's the matter with you?"

Dylan didn't perform "Watching the River Flow" until his 1978 World Tour; he didn't touch it again for another decade, when he trotted it out for two of the West Coast Dylan/Grateful Dead shows as a semi-successful surprise. Later, he began performing it, sometimes frequently, as a Never Ending Tour grunge band–style standby. Perhaps by 2002 the mood and outlook expressed in the song had changed somewhat, with Dylan not only urging his audience to take a psychic step back, keep cool, and consider all options and possibilities before running headlong into war or peace, but to respect the power of that rapacious river from higher ground.

"Watered Down Love" (Bob Dylan)
Bob Dylan, *Shot of Love* (1981)

A deft R&B, Smokey Robinson–style Zen recasting of 1 Corinthians 13, "Watered Down Love" is an eminently singable *Shot of Love* appeal to the heart disguised as lightweight fluff.

Compare Dylan's catalogue of love's attributions (which begins, "Love that's pure hopes all things, believes all things") with the passage from 1 Corinthians 13:4–7: "Love is patient and kind; love is not jealous or boastful; it is not arrogant or rude. Love does not insist on its own way; it is not irritable or resentful; it does not rejoice at wrong, but rejoices in the right. Love bears all things, believes all things, hopes all things, endures all things."

Dylan's only performances of "Watered Down Love" transpired during his 1981 tour, in which he not only jumbled the order of the lyrics but incorporated some phrases from another *Shot of Love* song, "Groom's Still Waiting at the Altar." He apparently also worked up an arrangement of the song in 1996 but did not perform it. The album release edited out an extra verse that is included in the published text.

"The Water Is Wide" (Traditional)
aka "O Waly, Waly," "Waly, Waly"
Bob Dylan, *The Bootleg Series, Volume 5: Live 1975—The Rolling Thunder Revue* (2002)
Roger McGuinn, *Roger McGuinn* (1973)
Joan Baez, *Very Early Joan Baez* (1983)
Jim Hendricks, *Appalachian Memories: Front Porch Favor* (1993)
Rich Lerner, *Trails and Bridges* (1996)
Pete Seeger, *Pete* (1996)

Originally called "Waly, Waly" and sharing the same melody as the later hymn "The Gift of Love," "The Water Is Wide" appears in folklorist Cecil Sharp's fine collection, *One Hundred English Folksongs*, first published in 1916, and published again as *One Hundred English Folksongs: For Medium Voice* in 1975 (New York: Dover Publications, 1975, c. 1916). With little change in the basic idea, it became known as "The Water Is Wide" sometime in the nineteenth century. It is an excellent example of the British lyric song. The unfortunate heroine of "Waly, Waly" is thought to be the daughter of the ninth Earl of Mar, Lady Barbara Erskine, who was deserted by her husband, James, Marquis of Douglas in the reign of King Charles II. First published in 1724, "O Waly, Waly" is a stock from which many branches have grown, the most familiar being the burlesque "There Is a Tavern in the Town."

A nightly, double magic highlight of the Rolling Thunder Revue was the Dylan/Joan Baez acoustic duet slot, and "The Water Is Wide" was among the best of their collaborations. The lyric, as Dylan and Baez sang it, suggests that the heart is not necessarily always to be trusted and laments the withering effects time and space can have on romance: "Oh, love is handsome and love is fine/Gay as a jewel when first it is new/But love grows old, and waxes cold/And fades away like summer dew."

W

And for those who revel in finding the symbolism to keep a Freudian shrink in clover for years, try this stanza on for size: "I put my hand into one soft bush/Thinking the sweetest flow'r to find/I prick'd my finger to the bone/And left the sweetest flow'r alone." Given their stormy (and once steamy) history, Dylan and Baez could almost have been singing about themselves . . . and probably were. Dylan briefly returned to the song during the early phase of the Never Ending Tour in 1989.

A *We Are the World*/Various Artists
Columbia Records LP CL-40043. Released 1985.

The famously schlocky title song of this well-intentioned album was recorded by an all-star chorus, including Dylan, to raise money for famine relief in Africa. Commenting on the project, Dylan said: "It's a worthwhile idea, but I wasn't so convinced about the message of the song. To tell you the truth, I don't think people can save themselves."

S "We Are the World" (Michael Jackson/Lionel Richie)
USA for Africa, single (1985); *We Are the World* (1985)

More of the same from the who's-who cast of music biz celebrities who turned out in force to contribute vocals for what is unfortunately still a necessary cause. Maybe they should think about doing it again.

Supposedly, Stevie Wonder had to teach Dylan to sound more like Dylan when he was recording his part.

S "Weary Blues" (Hank Williams)
See also Hank Williams
aka "Weary Blues from Waiting," "Weary Blues from Waitin'"
Hank Williams, *Complete Hank Williams* (1998)
Ray Price, single (1951)

Del Shannon, *Del Shannon Sings Hank Williams* (1965)
Steve Goodman, *Say It in Private* (1977)
Hans Theesink, *Titanic* (1983)
Don Walser, *Texas Top Hand* (1996)

> To me, Hank Williams is still the best songwriter.
> —BOB DYLAN, 1991

An oddity done up acoustic-style with shared Dylan/Bobby Neuwirth vocals, the 1976 Rolling Thunder Revue cover of this Hank Williams rarity was only performed at a small handful of shows. There is also reportedly an early May 1965 version of Dylan performing "Weary Blues" in his Savoy Hotel room in London on some uncirculated footage from *Don't Look Back*.

Williams recorded "Weary Blues" in the fall of 1951 in Nashville, shortly before his death. In anybody's hands it is the sob story of a brokenhearted man watching the frost gather on his windowpane as young lovers stroll by and ruing what could have been.

S "We Better Talk This Over" (Bob Dylan)
Bob Dylan, *Street Legal* (1978); single/'78 (1985)
Julie Felix, *Colors in the Rain* (1980)

With this sober look at a marriage in self-destruct, Dylan may have been trying to mend things with his wife—or simply convincing himself that the jig was up. Certainly "We Better Talk Things Over" comes across like a well-rehearsed "Dear Jane, let's break up" speech, with just enough spontaneity to make it appear as if he's a man on the brink impulsively speaking with his heart and soul.

Wilfrid Mellers deconstructed "We Better Talk This Over" musically and lyrically in his article "God, Mode and Meaning in Some Recent Songs of Bob Dylan," published in *Popular Music*, #1, in 1981. In a discussion of the paradox of human love, always imperfect

W

when contrasted with the purity of God's, he wrote, "This kind of paradox is more overt in 'We Better Talk This Over,' in which jazzy elements further compromise hymnic solemnity. It might be a song of loss in that its ambiguous thirds are very blue and its rhythms both broken and irregular, the four pulse alternating with uneasy fives. Yet although Dylan says he is 'displaced, I got a low-down feeling,' because his woman has been double-dealing, and although he will have to leave tomorrow because there is nothing left of their love except 'the sound of one hand clappin',' the song's *general* statement is far from being a negation."

Dylan thought highly of this semi-confessional, and it does have an undeniable intimacy despite its sometimes strained musical arrangement. He performed "We Better Talk This Over" as a 1978 world tour exclusive, and brought it back as a short-lived Never Ending Tour performance experiment in the late winter of 2000.

[S] **"Wedding Song"** (Bob Dylan)

Bob Dylan, *Planet Waves* (1974)
Dave Browning, *Forever Young* (1982)

Among his most heartfelt, desperate, and rare public gestures of love to his then-wife Sara, "Wedding Song" finds the stripped-down Dylan bearing his soul with just his guitar, mouth harp, and voice. Some believe Dylan is explaining why he's stayed out of the limelight for so long (and why he wishes to reembrace it) when he sings that he's sacrificed the world for his betrothed.

Upon its release, "Wedding Song" was heavily scrutinized by those obsessed with unearthing some connections between Dylan's life and art. Like a few songs on *Planet Waves*, the "Wedding Song" comes off as a weak renewal of his marriage vows, circling around the narrator's assessment of their life together with hints that he may need to sprout some wings and fly the coop, at least for awhile. That Dylan began touring with this and the rest of his batch of *Planet Waves* songs shortly after recording certainly adds credence to the notion that he was ready to reemerge as a performing artist even though he sings that he loves her "more than life itself." If Bob and Sara Dylan were trying to reinvent themselves as some kind of mid-20th century transcendentalists in the tradition of Thoureau and Emerson in upstate New York, then this song seems to dismiss that idea as a grand but noble failure. Now, with thirty years of rough road in the rear view mirror, lines like "I love you more than ever now that the past is gone" sound like a mere ploy to get her to accept his decision.

Dylan's only performances of "Wedding Song" took place during his 1974 tour with the Band, a time that, ironically, is said to have been the beginning of his marital woes.

[S] **"Weeping Willow"** (Blind Boy Fuller)

See also "Step It Up and Go"
Blind Boy Fuller, *Complete Recorded Works, Volume 3* (1937) (1992)
Bert Jansch, *Nicola* (1967)
Stefan Grossman, *Country Blues Guitar* (1977)
Cephas and Wiggins, *Guitar Man* (1987)

This fine Dylan one-off was pulled off with some aid from sideman Bucky Baxter's pedal steel at the famed November 1993 Supper Club in New York City. Blind Boy Fuller's "Weeping Willow" is the slow, prowling moan of a man on the edge crying under the trees for his woman as she strolls down the dirt road on a lazy summer evening. At one point he even threatens to buy a bulldog to watch his straying lover. By the song's end, our boy is still empty-handed, baying at the moon. Dylan handled the song like he'd been singing it for years, adding a perfectly placed "aw shucks" into his delivery as if to emphasize his character's frustration.

Fuller (born Fulton Allen, July 10, 1907 [or '08 or '09], Wadesboro, North Carolina; died February 13, 1941, Durham, North Carolina) was among the most prolific and influential bluesmen of his age, despite the fact that he didn't take up music with any seriousness until he was grown. An expert in and amalgamator of styles, Fuller merged ragtime, pop, blues, slide, and Piedmont, picking into a singular musical palette. All that is known about his youth is that he was born with sight and did not come from a musical family. His schooling is not believed to have progressed beyond the fourth grade. After his mother died in the mid-1920s, his family moved to Rockingham, North Carolina. The move proved to be a good one for Allen as it was there that he met Cora Mae Martin, whom he married in 1926 despite the fact that she was only fourteen.

Soon after his marriage Allen's eyes began giving him problems. The couple bounced around North Carolina seeking help and employment. He toiled in a coal yard for a spell, but his failing sight soon stopped even that. No doctor or family member could prevent his inevitable blindness. Allen's luck began to change when he moved to Durham, North Carolina, perhaps to gain better access to federal aid for the blind, and met the Reverend Gary Davis. Perhaps the greatest of all Piedmont bluesmen, and blind himself, Davis taught Allen some basic guitar licks and a few songs to boot. Allen eventually settled in Durham and began making a decent living busking on the streets. It was on Durham's curbs in the winter of 1935 that he caught the ear of J. B. Long. Long had already found a measure of success at uncovering country and gospel talent for the American Record Company. That summer, he

drove Allen (whom he dubbed "Blind Boy Fuller"), Davis, and Bull City Red (a nearly forgotten washboard player whose real name was George Washington) to New York City to record with Art Satherley. (Contrary to his British upbringing, Satherley went on to become one of the secret heroes of recorded American black and white roots music.) The session went well and Blind Boy Fuller was brought back to record the following spring as a solo act. Despite contractual confusion and double-dealing, over the next few years Fuller continued to record and improve as a musician; his synthesis of styles and techniques, enhanced by his National steel guitar, was reminiscent of Robert Johnson. Like his revered peer, Fuller was a frighteningly expressive vocalist and a guitar master with a knack for the catchy, up-tempo ragtime hits he recorded during this period. These included "Rag Mama Rag," "Trucking My Blues Away" and "Step It Up and Go"—the latter a song Dylan recorded for his 1992 *Good as I Been to You* album of acoustic cover songs from the blues and Anglo-American canon. Fuller could get down with deeper material, too. "Lost Lover Blues" or "Mamie" can stand proudly next to any Delta blues moan from the strings and lips of a Robert Johnson or Blind Willie McTell.

Fuller's last great phase came when he met, performed, and eventually recorded with the harmonica genius Sonny Terry. Terry was being groomed as a star himself, and in addition to accompanying Fuller, he had begun recording on his own. In fact, when John Hammond was looking for Fuller for his 1938 "From Spirituals to Swing" Carnegie Hall concert and found Fuller in jail, he used Terry as a replacement.

Fuller's fast and hard living took its toll on his health. In 1938 he was diagnosed with arrested syphilis and chronic kidney and bladder ailments. His slow, painful decline was at

W

least peppered by numerous recording sessions that have kept his legacy alive. He wrote and recorded "Weeping Willow" near the end of his short life of trouble; its lines "mourning like a dove" could stand as a kind of epitaph.

[S] "We Had It All" (Donnie Fritts/Troy Seals)

aka "You and Me (We Had It All)"
See also "No More One More Time"
Donnie Fritts, *Everybody's Got a Song* (1997)
Waylon Jennings, *Honky Tonk Heroes* (1973)
Bob Neuwirth, *Bob Neuwirth* (1974)
Willie Nelson, *Take It to the Limit* (1983)
Dolly Parton, *Love Album, Volume 2* (1990)
Ray Charles, *Complete Country and Western Recordings 1* (1998)
Tina Turner, *Good Hearted Woman* (1998)

This oft and widely covered piece of country has found its way into the catalogues of a motley cross section of recording artists. Dylan's exclusive performances of "We Had It All" came about during his 1986 tour with Tom Petty and the Heartbreakers and will be remembered as a primal showcase for his backup singers.

"We Had It All" is the product of two bright lights of country music: Donnie Fritts and Troy Seals. Dylan could have gotten hip to the song in any number of ways: His buddy Bobby Neuwirth recorded it shortly after Waylon Jennings's recording rose to No. 28 on the charts; Dolly Parton charted a version in 1986; and Willie Nelson's "We Had It All" is also well known.

Fritts (born November 8, 1942, Florence, Alabama) is a bedrock of the Muscle Shoals sound that fused southern soul, pop, country, and R&B into a musical putty that acted as an earthy antidote for the sheen of Nashville. He started out as a drummer with local bands before hooking up with cats like Arthur Alexander, Dan Penn, and Spooner Oldham. His early songs were recorded by some pretty diverse talent: Percy Sledge, Dusty Springfield, the Box Tops, and Tommy Roe.

Fritts made the move to Nashville in the late 1960s. While employed as a staff writer, he wrote songs recorded by Charlie Rich and Jerry Lee Lewis and began collaborating with another newcomer named Kris Kristofferson. When Kristofferson took his act on the road around 1970, Fritts was along for the twenty-year ride as the keyboardist in the band; he even had a walk-on in the Kristofferson film vehicles *Pat Garrett and Billy the Kid, Bring Me the Head of Alfredo Garcia,* and *A Star Is Born.*

Prone to Lean, his debut 1974 solo LP produced by Kristofferson and Jerry Wexler, came and went and is now a collector's item. Almost a quarter of a century would pass before his follow-up, *Everybody's Got a Song,* which included new versions of Fritts classics ("We Had It All" and "A Damn Good Country Song") recorded with some inner-circle friends made along the way: Waylon Jennings, Willie Nelson, John Prine, Lucinda Williams, and Delbert McClinton.

Seals (born November 16, 1938, Big Hill, Kentucky) got his start playing guitar in his teens. In 1960, while in an Ohio club with Lonnie Mack, he befriended visiting performer Conway Twitty, who introduced him to Jo Ann Campbell, a pop singer with a couple of hits in her back pocket. Seals and Campbell fell in love, married, and began working as a duo. In 1964 they made the U.S. R&B charts with "I Found a Love, Oh What a Love." After working in construction for a time, Seals moved to Nashville to sell his songs. "There's a Honky Tonk Angel (Who'll Take Me Back In)," written by Seals and Denny Rice, became a No. 1 hit for Twitty (Cliff Richard's version for the UK market was withdrawn when he discovered what a honky-tonk angel is).

Though, like Fritts, Seals took a stab at a solo career with two albums in the 1970s, he is best known as a writer of country songs. His big hits were "Rattle the Windows" (Shenandoah), "I Won't Need You Anymore (Always & Forever)" (Randy Travis), "Don't Take It Away" (Conway Twitty), "From Seven till Ten" (Twitty and Loretta Lynn), "Two Old Cats like Us" (Hank Williams Jr.), "Pieces of My Life" (Elvis Presley), "Seven Spanish Angels" (Willie Nelson), and "Boogie Woogie Country Man" (Jerry Lee Lewis). He also wrote the score for the 1976 film *The Commitment*.

An ace session man, Seals's guitar can be heard on dozens of sessions by a pretty wide swath of talent, including Eric Anderson, James Brown, Doug Kershaw, Randy Travis, and Conway Twitty.

[S] "We Just Disagree" (Jim Krueger)

Jim Krueger, *Sweet Salvation* (1978)
Dave Mason, *Let It Flow* (1977)
Billy Dean, *Fire in the Dark* (1993)
After the Love, *After the Love* (1995)

A concert rarity performed at a handful of shows in 1980 and 1981, Dylan's version of "We Just Disagree" fit right into his ongoing interest in neo-American classico. This sober impasse of the sexes in song ("There ain't no good guys, there ain't no bad guys/There's only you and me and we just disagree") was made famous in 1977 by British rocker Dave Mason when his version hit No. 12 on the *Billboard* chart. Guitarist Jim Krueger, who wrote "We Just Disagree," put out one album with Columbia in 1978 entitled *Sweet Salvation*. A colleague of Mason's, Krueger (born Manitowoc, Wisconsin; died March 29, 1993, Manitowoc) appeared on many of his albums and toured with him in the 1970s, '80s, and '90s. Mason helped to popularize Dylan's "All Along the Watchtower," so perhaps performing "We Just Disagree" was Dylan's way of thanking him.

[S] "Well, Well, Well" (Bob Dylan/Danny O'Keefe)

Danny O'Keefe, *Runnin' from the Devil* (2000)
Maria Muldaur, *Fanning the Flames* (1996)
David Lindley, *Twango Bango Deluxe* (1998)
Steve Howe, *Portraits of Bob Dylan* (1999)

An environmentally savvy song about the politics of water, "Well, Well, Well" is another mysterious collaborative anomaly in the Dylan catalogue, particularly, until recently, in regard to how it came into being. Cowriter Danny O'Keefe's comments to the author via email cleared this up: "In the early Nineties (not sure of exact date) Bob sent a tape that had the basis for 'Well, Well, Well' to Tina Snow who was running his publishing company, Special Rider Music at the time, with the suggestion that I might want to write lyrics to it. As the only words on the tape were Bob saying 'Well, well . . .' I simply added another 'well' and made it a song about ground water and the preciousness of the Earth. I believe I was the only writer working for Special Rider Music at the time, other than Bob. It was a pleasure and an honor to be associated with him and his company."

Danny O'Keefe (born May 20, 1943, Spokane, Washington) cut his teeth as a performer on the Minnesota coffeehouse circuit of the mid- to late 1960s, and perhaps that's why Dylan took a shine to him. A chance meeting with folk-rock's Buffalo Springfield led to a telephone audition for Atlantic Records' prexy Ahmet Ertegun and landed O'Keefe a deal with that renowned label and a trio of releases. His 1972 album *O'Keefe* featured the melancholy but catchy hit "Good Time Charlie's Got the Blues"—a song that, since its initial thrust onto the airwaves, has been waxed by Elvis Presley, Waylon Jennings, Willie Nelson, Leon Russell, Charlie Rich, Jerry Lee Lewis, Charlie McCoy, Cab Calloway, Earl Klugh, and Chet Atkins, among others (Mel Tormé even sang it on the hit television series *Night Court*). *Breezy Stories* followed in 1973; like its predecessor, it showcased O'Keefe's classic story songs and caught the attention of the biggest names in the music biz. The album led to even greater success, with O'Keefe supplying songs for Presley, Judy Collins, and Jackson Browne. A final Atlantic Records release, *So Long Harry Truman* (1975), was followed by two albums for Warner Brothers: *American Roulette* (1977) and *The Global Blues* (1979). O'Keefe founded his own Coldwater Records in 1984, and in 1985 released *The Day to Day* (re-released in 1989 as *Redux*) from which a couple of songs, "Along for the Ride" and "Someday," received wide, positive notice, helped by a VH1 video of "Along for the Ride."

A dependable opening act, O'Keefe lived out of his suitcase for much of the 1970s and early '80s, touring with Jackson Browne, Bonnie Raitt, Jimmy Buffet, Jessie Colin Young, Maria Muldaur, Linda Ronstadt, Loggins and Messina, and the Hollies.

Many have spread the words of O'Keefe via their recordings, including Jackson Browne ("The Road"), John Denver ("Along for the Ride," cowritten with Bill Braun), Judy Collins ("Angel Spread Your Wings"), Sheena Easton ("Next to You," cowritten with George Merrill), David Lindley ("The Jimmy Hoffa Memorial Bldg. Blues," "More than Eva Braun," and "Well, Well, Well"), Jesse Colin Young ("On the Edge" and "Catfish"), and Alison Krauss ("Never Got Off the Ground").

More recently, O'Keefe released *Runnin' from the Devil* (2000), the title of which may or may not refer to his absence from the limelight.

This multitiered album covers themes of love, loss, temptation, and social responsibility. It is the best of what audiences have come to expect from O'Keefe, complete with heartfelt messages wrapped in soulful troubadour stylings.

O'Keefe is also a force in environmental circles. A lover of songbirds, which have inspired both his music and his activism, O'Keefe founded the Songbird Foundation (www.songbird.org), which seeks to protect songbirds' habitats by halting the deforestation caused by aggressive sun-grown coffee practices in Latin America. The Foundation educates and encourages coffee drinkers to drink coffee grown in a way that has the least environmental impact. In other words, no chain saws felling trees through large swaths of rain forests in Latin America, please.

"Went to See the Gypsy" (Bob Dylan)
Bob Dylan, *New Morning* (1970)
Al Kooper (performed with Bob Dylan), *Rare and Well Done/'70* (2001)
Pat Nevins, *Shakey Zimmerman* (2003)

This never-performed song could have been titled "The King and I," as Dylan allegedly wrote it about his meeting with Elvis Presley. At the very least, Dylan is fessing up to his special feelings about Elvis and his music with the admiring lyric, "He can move you from the rear/Drive you from your fear/Bring you through the mirror/He did it in Las Vegas and he can do it here." If the song is to be taken as accurate reportage, their introduction was uncomfortable: "He smiled when he saw me coming/And he said 'Well, well, well!'/His room was dark and crowded/Lights were low and dim/'How are you?' he said to me/I said it back to him!" In the last line, as he watches the dawn in a small Minnesota town (like Hibbing), the twenty-nine-year-old Dylan may be pondering his future in lieu of Presley's rapacious route to celebrity and the mass hysteria of his cult following.

ⓐ *We Shall Overcome: Documentary of the March on Washington*/Various Artists

Council for the United Civil Rights Leadership LP UCR-1. Released 1964. Folkways Records LP FH-5592. Released 1964.

Dylan's performance of "Only a Pawn in Their Game" (incorrectly listed as "The Ballad of Medgar Evers" on this obscure release) occurred at the famous August 28, 1963, March on Washington, which also produced the Reverend Martin Luther King's even more famous speech, "I Have a Dream." Dylan's rendition is cut in half on this politically correct (before P.C. was PC) sampler mixed with speeches by Floyd McKissick and John Lewis. The LP was first released by the Council for the United Civil Rights Leadership, a student group, before being absorbed by the Folkways label.

ⓢ "We Shall Overcome" (Traditional/Zilphia Horton)

aka "I Shall Overcome," "We Will Overcome"
Various Artists (performed by Bob Dylan and others), *Evening Concerts at Newport, Volume 1*/'63 (1964)
Various Artists (performed by Bob Dylan and others), *We Shall Overcome: Documentary on the March on Washington*/'63 (1964)
Pete Seeger, *World of Pete Seeger* (1973)
Joan Baez, *Joan Baez in Concert, Part 2* (1963)
Louis Armstrong, *What a Wonderful World* (1970)
Mahalia Jackson, *Great Mahalia Jackson* (1991)
Toots and the Maytals, *Bla. Bla. Bla.* (1993)

The line from the church to the union hall is, at least musically speaking, often a short and direct one, as evidenced by the fact that some of the great labor organizing songs and rallying cries have been adopted from hymns, gospel songs, and spirituals. "We Shall Overcome" is probably the most famous and enduring example of this musical lineage. Here a folk work song became a hymn and then was used politically, for the first time on the picket lines of the tobacco workers' strike in South Carolina in 1945.

According to the reprints from *Sing Out!* (vol. 6, 1964), "This song, which has become almost an unofficial theme song of the integration movement in the South, is an adaptation of an old hymn. At the height of the successful Montgomery (Alabama) bus boycott led by Rev. Martin Luther King, a few years back, it was sung by Negroes in the face of a hostile mob—and television cameras caught the simple, moving dignity of the song and the people who sang it for the entire nation to see and hear."

Dylan's only documented performance of "We Shall Overcome" wrapped up the 1963 Newport Folk Festival during an ensemble finale with Joan Baez, Pete Seeger, Peter, Paul and Mary, Odetta, and others. "Blowin' in the Wind" was also performed as a group sing-along at the festival.

ⓢ "West L.A. Fadeaway" (Jerry Garcia/Robert Hunter)

See also Robert Hunter
The Grateful Dead, *In the Dark* (1987)

"West L.A. Fadeaway" is a bluesy shuffle portraying America's underbelly. Biographer/publicist Dennis McNally's snap impression of the song in his monumental *Long Strange Trip: The Inside History of the Grateful Dead* (2002) certainly rings true: "a musically simplistic take on the traditional San Francisco disdain for Los Angeles." Life on the run, nefarious dealings with dangerous people, and no clear path of safe escape are the themes here.

Dylan covered some very atypical Dead songs in the early and middle phases of the

W

Never Ending Tour and his acoustic and electric performances of "West L.A. Fadeaway" were among the more curious. During the summers of 1986 and 1987, the Dead performed the song at most of the concerts at which they shared the bill or stage with Dylan, and perhaps it was then that Dylan became impressed by it. Fairly edgy by Grateful Dead standards, Dylan gave "West L.A." even more of a bite when he performed it thrice in both acoustic and electric guises in 1992. He repeated the act six times in the fall of 1995, shortly after, and presumably in honor of, Garcia's passing.

"West Texas" (Traditional/Bob Dylan)
aka "Going Down to West Texas"

Only one field recording of Dylan performing this feral piece of a dusty road song at Greenwich Village's Gaslight Café from the waning days of 1962 has survived the test of time. Two things are notable about the song: Dylan's interminably lengthy guitar and its tangled, murky lineage. Most Dylanologists agree that it is a semi-original pastiche mingling lyrics from several probable sources including Mance Lipscomb and Sleepy John Estes. Snatches of lyrics from "West Texas" can be found in songs from the late 1920s and early 1930s by really obscure Texas bluesmen Willie Reed's "Texas Blues" (1928), Texas Alexander's "Work Ox Blues," and Marshall Owens's "Texas Blues," but it is doubtful that Dylan was aware of them at the time he worked up his arrangement.

"We Three (My Echo, My Shadow and Me)" (Dick Robertson/Nelson Cogane/Sammy Mysels)
Brenda Lee, *Brenda Lee Story (Her Greatest Hits)* (1974)
Frank Sinatra, *I'll Be Seeing You* (1994)
Platters, *From the Golden Vaults* (1995)
Ink Spots, *We Four: The Best of the Ink Spots* (1998)

Dylan performed this loner's lullaby (made famous by the Ink Spots and Frank Sinatra in the 1940s) during his 1986 stint with Tom Petty, and again as a 1988 acoustic Never Ending Tour one-off, in a rendition that sounded like an old Hoagy Carmichael groove. There is also evidence that Dylan rehearsed the song for his 1984 tour (in which he included a forlorn, woe-is-me spoken section) and recorded it during the 1985 *Empire Burlesque* sessions, probably as a warm-up. The Ink Spots, the groundbreaking black a cappella foursome that paved the way for doo-wop, took "We Three" to the top of the *Billboard* charts for three weeks in 1940–41.

Dick Robertson (born 1903, New York City) the song's best-known composer, was a singing Swing Band orchestra leader from the late 1920s through the early 1940s. He did cross paths with the likes of Duke Ellington, Fletcher Henderson, Benny Goodman, Bix Beiderbecke, Tommy Dorsey, and Red Allen but is largely forgotten by even the most dedicated jazz mavens.

Nelson Cogane (born December 25, 1902; died July 1985) was also known as Jack Miller when he was writing theme songs for shows in the early days of television.

Biographical info on Sammy Mysels is almost as sketchy. He wrote a few other songs with Cogane and collaborated with a fellow named Dick Sanford on a song titled "The Singing Hills," featured in *Gaucho Serenade*, a 1940 film starring Gene Autry.

"What Can I Do for You?" (Bob Dylan)
Bob Dylan, *Saved* (1980)
Various Artists (performed by Helen Baylor), *Gotta Serve Somebody: The Gospel Songs of Bob Dylan* (2003)

Clichéd, overbearing, downright dull—any one of these brief descriptions have been applied to this love letter to the Holy Spirit in which the narrator humbly asks God in what ways He would like to be served. God, by the way, does not answer.

"What Can I Do for You?" suffers from its stale beseeching style, as if Dylan is desperately propositioning, rather than communing with, God. The whole feeling of the song comes off as Christian-lite with very little, if any, playfulness. But then, who ever said religion was supposed to be fun? Threats of hellfire are way more interesting bully pulpit fare than thanks to God for salvation.

As might be imagined, Dylan draws on the Good Book for several of his lyrical allusions in "What Can I Do For You?" For example, Ephesians 6:11–16 ("Put on the whole armour of God. . . . Above all, taking the shield of faith, wherewith ye shall be able to quench all the fiery darts of the wicked") finds itself reshaped into "I know all about poison, I know all about fiery darts." And much of the song's questioning tone appears drawn from the Passover psalm 116, which asks, "What shall I render unto the Lord for all his benefits toward me?" (116:12).

Dylan ignored all such criticisms and poetic hairsplitting, con and pro, of "What Can I Do For You?" when he performed it, complete with some mesmerizing harmonica work (some of his best since the stoned concerts of '66), exclusively during the gospel tours of 1979 and 1980.

◼ "What Good Am I?" (Bob Dylan)

Bob Dylan, *Oh Mercy* (1989)
Barb Jungr, *Every Grain of Sand: Barb Jungr Sings Bob Dylan* (2002)

Asking the hardest questions about man's responsibility to himself and to God and/or his muse, this sweet, delicate song of Christian humility points out that knowledge and self-criticism are only valid if acted upon—as if saying that, rather than judge, we should attempt to invoke our higher selves and to speak the truth. The song is an unflinching look into the most revealing of mirrors. Dylan recorded "What Good Am I?" as a piano-based song, with tinkling ivories worthy of one of those mature Sam Cooke ballads.

He performed "What Good Am I?" in abundance—more than one hundred times—from 1989 to 1994, oft-times on piano. He began laying off the song in the mid-1990s, performing only a few versions a year through 1999, the last year it was displayed.

◼ "What Was It You Wanted?" (Bob Dylan)

Bob Dylan, *Oh Mercy* (1989)
Bob Dylan/Various Artists (performed by Willie Nelson), *Bob Dylan: The 30th Anniversary Concert Celebration* (1993)
Steven Keene, *Keene on Dylan* (1990)
Willie Nelson, *Across the Borderline* (1993)
Chris Smither, *Up on the Lowdown* (1995)
Various Artists (performed by Willie Nelson), *Doin' Dylan 2* (2002)

Maybe Dylan's most potent comment on not only his fans but the entire, dangerous game of celebrity and its parasitical, phony core, "What Was It You Wanted?" presents a Dylan eye view of the world and its sycophants (a term that perhaps applies to the reader *and* writer of these words), and it is not a very pretty picture. Like an '80s "Positively 4th Street," he seems to be asking someone (everyone?) to back off, or at least to question the kind of obsession that can make his life at best a drag and at worst downright frighteningly paranoid (in light of John Lennon's fate). At one point he goes so far as to suggest a Judas-like connection with the one he's addressing, singing, "What was it you wanted/When you were kissin' my cheek?" The song's aloof, jaded delivery and edgy humor

W

belie a deeper hurt. In many ways, Dylan asks the same kinds of questions here that he's been asking since at least as far back as "It Ain't Me Babe" in 1964—chiding questions about expectations, expectations that the singer has failed to meet, implicitly because of their unreasonable nature.

Dylan performed "What Was It You Wanted?" twenty times in 1990 and once in 1991.

[S] **"When Did You Leave Heaven?"** (Walter Bullock/Richard A. Whiting)

Bob Dylan, *Down in the Groove* (1988)
Bunny Berigan, *Sing! Sing! Sing!, Volume 1: 1936–1938* (1986)
Hank Crawford, *After Hours* (1965)
Big Bill Broozny, *Lonesome Road Blues* (1986)

When Dylan gets cornball, lock the door and bury the key! While the *Down in the Groove* version of this song should be avoided like anthrax, a more acceptable rendition is found in Dylan's acoustic duet with G. E. Smith during the first leg of the 1989 Never Ending Tour. A decent electric ensemble arrangement was also staged from 1989 to 1991.

"When Did You Leave Heaven?" (with words by Walter Bullock and music by Richard A. Whiting) was introduced by Tony Martin and Alice Faye in the 1936 comedy-of-manners musical *Sing, Baby, Sing*, for which it won an Academy Award.

Bullock (born May 6, 1907, Shelburn, Indiana; died August 19, 1953, Los Angeles, California) was among the first big composers and lyricists of Hollywood when the studios ruled the day. Just like the actors of the time, he was under contract to Twentieth Century-Fox for his entire career, save a loan-out here and there, all the while contributing to jaunty but light fare like *The Three Musketeers* and Shirley Temple's *Just Around the Corner* and *Little Miss Broadway*. As a screenwriter, he was responsible for the memorable "Gift of the Magi" sequence in the experimental 1952 film *O. Henry's Full House*.

Whiting (born November 11, 1891, Peoria, Illinois; died February 10, 1938, Beverly Hills, California) collaborated on dozens of songs that found their way to the silver screen. Some of them—"Anything Goes," "Till We Meet Again," "Hooray for Hollywood," "Too Marvelous for Words," and "Breezin' Along in a Breeze"—are still sung today.

[S] **"When He Returns"** (Bob Dylan)

Bob Dylan, *Slow Train Coming* (1979)
Various Artists (performed by Rance Allen), *Gotta Serve Somebody: The Gospel Songs of Bob Dylan* (2003)

With the somber assurance of a man who has seen and knows "the Truth," Dylan sang "When He Returns," drawn from the Book of Revelations, as an impassioned yet serene piece of prophesy and spiritual resolve. For those who like to snicker at Dylan's singing, the *Slow Train Coming* release shows why the Great White Wonder could make a believer out of just about anyone. With Barry Beckett laying down some exquisite piano licks, Dylan's newfound religious belief brought his vocals to new heights of expressiveness.

"When He Returns" is a song absolutely steeped in biblical reference. "For like a thief in the nights/He'll replace wrong with right" is drawn from Matthew 24:42–44 and repeated in Luke 12:39–40, 1 Thessalonians 5:2, and, perhaps most famously, 2 Peter 3:10, when Christ tells his disciples, "But the day of the Lord will come as a thief in the night." This oxymoronic match emphasizes the strange contradiction at the core of Christ's analogy while correctly summarizing the profundity of his message.

W

But Dylan hardly stops there. The reference to the "iron rod" and the "iron hand" in the first verse of "When He Returns" connects with both the rod Moses employed to assist the Israelites' escape from the Egyptians and Isaiah's prophesy foretelling the coming of Christ in Isaiah 11:1–4 ("there shall come forth a rod out of the stem of Jesse, and a Branch shall grow out of his roots: And the spirit of the Lord shall rest upon him, . . . the spirit of the knowledge and of the fear of the Lord; . . . with righteousness shall he judge the poor, and reprove with equity for the meek of the earth: and he shall smite the earth: with the rod of his mouth, and the breath of his lips shall he slay the wicked"). When Dylan sings, also in the first verse, "For all those who have eyes and all those who have ears," he uses a common rhetorical hook found throughout the New Testament (see Matthew 13:43, Mark 4:9, 4:23, 7:16, and 8:18, and Revelation 2:7, 2:11, 2:29, 3:6, 3:13, and 3:22) that originally appeared in Ezekiel 12:1–2 ("The word of the Lord also came unto me, saying, Son of man, thou dwellest in the midst of a rebellious house, which have eyes to see, and see not; they have ears to hear, and hear not"). It is a hook he used in songs as early as "Blowin' in the Wind": "Yes'n how many ears must one man have" and "Yes'n how many times must a man turn his head/Pretending he just doesn't see?"

The balance of "When He Returns" is similarly steeped with cagey biblical rewrites. At the start of the second verse, Matthew 7:14 ("Because strait is the gate, and narrow is the way, which leadeth unto life, and few there be that find it") becomes another rhythmic, half-rhyming repetition in Dylan's hands: "Truth is an arrow, and the gate is narrow, that it passes through." And ideas from Revelation and Genesis 4:10 are patched into Dylan's line "Surrender your crown, on this blood-stained ground, take off your mask." But the biblical themes

Dylan picks up are anything but tangential. Rather, he cuts right to the core of the Bible's biggest issues: the Fall, Cain and Abel, the Sermon on the Mount, and, most obviously and importantly, Judgment Day.

After its 1979 release, "When He Returns" was displayed as a 1979–80 gospel tour exclusive; Dylan's brooding arrangement, a stump preacher–style tour de force, featured his vocal supplication at an empathetic peak.

"When First Unto This Country" (Traditional)
aka "When First Unto This Country a Stranger I Came"
Peggy Seeger, *Songs of Courting and Complaint* (1955)
Ian & Sylvia, *Ian & Sylvia* (1963)
New Lost City Ramblers, *Early Years (1958–1962)* (1991)
Casse Culver, *3 Gypsies* (1976)
Jerry Garcia/David Grisman, *Not for Kids Only* (1993)
Spider John Koerner, *Stargeezer* (1996)
Bray Brothers, *Prairie Bluegrass* (2000)

"When First Unto This Country" is a folk relic describing the hardships encountered by newly arrived immigrants to America's shores. Musician and folklorist Peggy Seeger felt the song was a fragmentary ballad and believed her version to be "the shortening of a longer song or the telescoping of two versions." The song is not to be confused with Oscar Brand's "When I First Came to This Land," a children's song written in the 1940s, or with the old song sung by whalers, "When First into This Country."

Dylan based his own obscure 1963 composition "Liverpool Gal" on "When First Unto This Country" and went on to perform it just twice nearly three decades later: in Virginia as a perfunctory 1989 electric send-up and in Yugoslavia as a remarkable 1991 acoustic duet with John Jackson, his guitarist *du jour*. Once introducing it as "my foreign language song," Dylan always sang it like a man who had suffered every indignity life could possibly serve up, and yet had managed to stay on his feet to take some more abuse.

"When First Unto This Country" recounts the singer's courtship of Nancy, who turns him down. For reasons that are not exactly explained, he steals a horse and is imprisoned. He complains of his ill-treatment, then adds, "With my hands in my pockets and my cap put on so bold/With my coat of many colors, like Jacob of old." This last reference to the prisoner's "coat of many colors," is an example of what Seeger sees as the song's connection to some other song. The person of legend who wore the "coat of many colors" (modernized for dramatic consumption as the "technicolor dream coat") was Jacob's son Joseph from the book of Genesis (37:1–36). It is worth noting that Joseph's possession of the robe caused his brothers to resent him and led to his eventual enslavement in Egypt.

▣ "When I Paint My Masterpiece" (Bob Dylan)

Bob Dylan, *Bob Dylan's Greatest Hits, Volume II* (1971); *Renaldo & Clara* (film) (1978)

Bob Dylan/Various Artists (performed by the Band), *Bob Dylan: The 30th Anniversary Concert Celebration* (1993)

The Band, *Cahoots* (1971); *Anthology* (1978); *Across the Great Divide* (1994)

John Betmead, *A Vision of Heaven* (1977)

Barbara Dickson, *Don't Think Twice, It's Alright* (1992)

Dead Ringers, *Dead Ringers* (1993)

Tim O'Brien and The O'Boys, *Oh Boy! O'Boy* (1993)

Emmylou Harris, *Portraits* (1996)

The Grateful Dead, *Dozin' at the Knick/'90* (1996); *Postcards of the Hanging: Grateful Dead Perform the Songs of Bob Dylan* (2002)

Dave Swarbrick with Fairport Convention, *SwarbAid* (2000)

Various Artists (performed by Ballyhoo), *Duluth Does Dylan* (2001)

Various Artists (performed by Julian Dawson), *May Your Song Always Be Sung: The Songs of Bob Dylan, Volume 3* (2003)

High literature meets the funny pages in "When I Paint My Masterpiece"; it is one of a couple of tunes Dylan cut with Leon Russell in March 1971 that wound up on *Bob Dylan's Greatest Hits, Volume II* in a not-too-veiled marketing decision to move product. Like "Watching the River Flow," "When I Paint My Masterpiece" comes off as a clear admission by Dylan that his songwriting pockets were bare during the fallow and muted *New Morning* period and at the same time serves as an attempt to resummon his abandoned muse. The narrator sings from Rome—its dilapidated streets thick with the air created by two millennia of decaying history. But wherever he wanders, even in an escape to Brussels, he is unable to escape the shadow of his own personal history.

While some Dylan scholars have connected the song with fragmentary elements found in *Tender Is the Night*, by F. Scott Fitzgerald (a fellow Minnesotan who himself was no stranger to the concept of America's lack of second acts), "When I Paint My Masterpiece" still reads as an obtuse yet poignant travelogue that would have fit in just fine on *The Basement Tapes*. It is as if Dylan (already a man with "Visions of Johanna," "Like a Rolling Stone," and "Hard Rain" under his belt) knew that he could still top himself, create something that would last longer than the long gone but still historically resounding Roman Empire he alludes to in the lyrics. Yet the idea that "when" might mean "never" looms over "Masterpiece" like a fickle sprite.

Dylan first recorded "Masterpiece" in mid-March 1971, when Leon Russell invited him to a three-day session at New York's Blue Rock Studios. He publicly unveiled the song later that year in a surprise New Year's Eve concert with the Band at New York's Academy of Music. Dylan performed it almost nightly during the Rolling Thunder Revue in 1975 and 1976. (*Renaldo & Clara*, Dylan's beautiful mess of a home movie aspiring for something higher, opens with a '75 version of the song, complete with the performers wearing weird, clear masks.) He has revived it only sporadically for the Never Ending Tours—most recently in 2002 in an arrangement that essentially mirrored the 1971 studio version.

[S] "When the Night Comes Falling from the Sky" (Bob Dylan)

Bob Dylan, single (1985); *Empire Burlesque* (1985); *Hard to Handle* (video) (1986); *The Bootleg Series, Volumes 1–3: Rare and Unreleased, 1961–1991/'85* (1991)
Jeff Healy Band, *See the Light: Live from London* (1989)
Various Artists (performed by Jeff Healy), *Roadhouse* (soundtrack) (1989)
Rich Lerner, *Performs Songs by Bob Dylan* (1990); *Napoleon in Rags* (2001)
Willie Hona, *Keep an Open Heart* (1991)
The Zimmermen, *After the Ambulances Go* (1998)
The Black Crowes, single (1999); *By Your Side* (1999)

Relatively tame (by Dylan standards) but nonetheless compelling and perhaps even important, this person-to-person S.O.S. in song finds a brooding Dylan contemplating both a fragile relationship and the apocalypse. One can easily imagine that the number was intended as the big "Like a Rolling Stone" song of *Empire Burlesque*; in this regard it falls a bit flat, its semilifeless, overproduced album pressing helped only by Madelyn Quebec's husky background vocals. But Dylan (or his people) showed some real smarts when they released a roaring and raunchy roadhouse outtake with Roy Brittan and Miami Steve Van Zandt of Bruce Springsteen's E Street Band on *The Bootleg Series, Volumes 1–3*. Chalk up another one on the "woulda, coulda, shoulda" list in the "length is no guarantee of substance" ledger: An "All Along the Watchtower" for the 1980s this song is not quite.

Those hip to the *Empire Burlesque–Maltese Falcon* connection (Dylan drew lines from this and a few other Humphrey Bogart films in composing the songs for *Empire Burlesque*) will find a scant reference in "When the Night Comes Falling from the Sky." In the film, Miles Archer (Sam Spade's [Bogart's] slimy partner) flirts with Mary Astor's murderous femme fatale, saying, "You don't have to look for me. I'll see you." Dylan compresses this into, "Don't look for me, I'll see you."

The whole spirit of "When the Night Comes Falling from the Sky," in fact, sounds like a long Bogart "I'm through playing the sucker" riff—just like the kind he gives Astor at the end of *The Maltese Falcon* when he sends her down the elevator, up the river, and to a probable noose around her "pretty little neck."

The film references continue: Dylan lifted his "for the love of a lousy buck" quip from the lips of Karl Malden's tough priest character in *On the Waterfront* and turns a Henry Fonda line from *Twelve Angry Men* ("You thought you would gamble for support") into his own, "But you were gambling for support."

And let's not overlook the Bible. The song's opening lines ("Look out across the fields, see me returning") echo John 4:35, in which Christ is reported to have said, "behold, I say unto you, Lift up your eyes, and look on the fields; for they are white already to harvest."

Whatever its deficiencies as a fully satisfying Dylan composition, "When the Night Comes Falling from the Sky" was a concert powerhouse when Dylan performed it with Tom Petty and the Heartbreakers in 1986 and 1987—commencing as a smoldering a cappella doo-wop with his backup singers that acted as a kind of musical fuse that detonated after the first verse when the rest of the band kicked in. A rarely screened video of the song directed by Markus Innocenti and Eddie Arno was made and aired in 1985, and Dylan performs a snatch of "When the Night Comes Falling from the Sky" in *Hearts of Fire*, the lousy *Star Is Born* 1987 retread film in which he appeared.

[S] "When the Ship Comes In" (Bob Dylan)

Bob Dylan, *The Times They Are A-Changin'* (1964); *The Bootleg Series, Volumes 1–3: Rare and Unreleased, 1961–1991/'63* (1991)
Bob Dylan/Various Artists (performed by the Clancy Brothers), *Bob Dylan: The 30th Anniversary Concert Celebration* (1993)
Gaslight Singers, *Turning It On* (1964)
Hugues Aufray, *Chante Dylan* (1965)
Peter, Paul & Mary, *A Song Will Rise* (1965)
The Hollies, *Hollies Sing Dylan* (1969)
Chris Hillman, *The Hillmen* (1971)
Julie Felix, *The Second Album* (1975)
David Franklin, *The Times They Are A-Changin'* (1992)
Barbara Dickson, *Don't Think Twice, It's Alright* (1992)
Arlo Guthrie, *Hobo's Lullaby* (1972); *More Together Again, Volume 1* (1994)
The Clancy Brothers, *Older but No Wiser* (1995)
The Pogues, *Pogue Mahone* (1995)
The Zimmermen, *The Dungeon Tapes* (1996)
Steve Gibbons, *The Dylan Project* (1998)
Thirteenth Floor Elevators, *Through the Rhythm* (1998)
The Byrds, *Byrd Parts* (1998)
Andy Hill, *It Takes a Lot to Laugh* (2000)
Michel Montecrossa, *Jet Pilot* (2000)

Like a jaunty folkster's Sermon on the Mount, "When the Ship Comes In" is an upbeat, inspiring number predicting a day when justice will be meted and the victory of good over evil will be achieved. In addition to the version released on *The Times They Are A-Changin'*, Dylan recorded the song three more times: a live version on October 26, 1963, at New York's Carnegie Hall, for inclusion on *Bob Dylan in Concert* (the completed, ready-to-be-shipped but never released live LP); for a 1963 Witmark demo; and at the infamous, botched 1985 Live Aid outing with Keith Richards and Ron Wood, when the whole world was watching.

With "When the Ship Comes In," Dylan merges the Old Testament (the respective upset victories of Moses and David over the Pharaoh's tribe and the Goliath), the New Testament (Revelation's description of the stopping of the winds on Judgment Day), modern theater (Pirate Jenny's revenge fantasy, as sung in "The Black Freighter" from the Brecht/Weill *Three Penny Opera*), and contemporary poetry (the last lines from Dylan Thomas's "Fern Hill") with a real life experience, meting his own revenge in words and music.

The song was inspired by an incident when Dylan was on the road with Joan Baez. Embarrassed by the staff at a hotel who refused to believe that this ragamuffin was traveling with the Queen of Folk, Dylan sat down and wrote the song in a single evening as a type of catharsis.

Taken on face value, the story behind the song is further evidence of Dylan's extraordinary ability to transform an ordinary experience into an emotional, prophetic ballad suggesting a complete overthrow of the social order.

In his 1991 interview with Paul Zollo, which appeared in *Songwriters on Songwriting, Expanded Fourth Edition*, Dylan offered another inspiration for "When the Ship Comes In." "You know, there again, that comes from hanging out at a lot of poetry gatherings," he said. "Those kind of images are very romantic. They're very gothic and romantic at the same time. And they have a sweetness to it, also. So it's a combination of a lot of different elements at the time.... That's not sitting down and writing a song. Those kind of songs, they just come out. They're in you so they've got to come out."

The most famous line in "When the Ship Comes In"—"the whole world is watching"—

W

became a common protest chant during the Vietnam War.

[S] "When You Gonna Wake Up?" (Bob Dylan)

aka "Strengthen the Things that Remain"
Bob Dylan, single (1979); *Slow Train Coming* (1979)
Rich Lerner, *Performs Songs by Bob Dylan* (1990); *Napoleon in Rags* (2001)
Various Artists (performed by Lee Williams & the Spiritual QC's), *Gotta Serve Somebody: The Gospel Songs of Bob Dylan* (2003)

In its high, menacing, evangelical, you-all-been-asleep, see-the-light, repent-ye-sinners-the-end-is-nigh mode, Dylan's belligerent born-again rallying cry stands among his best and most confrontational gospel creations. One has to give Dylan credit for composing a piece infused with the kind of political finger-pointing invective that marks his earliest material. By daring to condemn Henry Kissinger *and* Karl Marx in a single breath, while extolling the higher calling of the Lord, Dylan reclaimed that rarefied moral territory with an anger not heard since his early twenties. Still, the song was at first a little tough to swallow, coming as it did from a guy who declared just over a decade earlier, "People that march with slogans and things tend to make themselves a little too holy. It would be a drag if they, too, started using God as a weapon."

How had he turned from someone who could write and lovingly sing lines about a woman who "knows too much to argue or to judge," as he had in "Love Minus Zero/No Limit" fifteen years before, into a moral commentator complaining about "adulterers in churches/And pornography in the schools"? Did that pornography include any Bob Dylan songbooks or merely *The Catcher in the Rye*?

In his debut gospel gigs, Dylan set the tone for performances of "When You Gonna Wake Up?" with introductions such as the following one from his November 19, 1979, concert: "I don't know what kind of God you believe in, but I believe in the God that can raise the dead. So look around. So many people are conditioned to bad news they don't know good news when they see it. So we're watching one thing: God don't make promises He don't keep. Let he who thinketh, stand and take heed lest he fall."

Dylan performed "When You Gonna Wake Up?" with fire-and-brimstone vehemence in 1979 and 1980, when he was in the grip of The Word. He rewrote "When You Gonna Wake Up?" and gave it a metallic edge when he toured Europe in support of *Infidels* in 1984. Five years later, he asked the question in concert one last time at a show in Poughkeepsie, New York, a couple of hours north of the city that never sleeps.

[S] "Where Are You Tonight? (Journey Through Dark Heat)" (Bob Dylan)

Bob Dylan, *Street Legal* (1978)
Rolling Thunder, *The Never Ending Rehearsal* (2000)

A forgotten, dusky jewel, "Where Are You Tonight?" plays out like a Beat writer's psychedelic rewrite of the "Night Town" chapter from James Joyce's *Ulysses*. Here the tormented narrator wanders lower Manhattan's valley of death streets (years before that became a reality) in a fruitless search for his soul mate and his soul. Flashing with after-hours neon and brimming with hopeless desperation, the song finds a pub-crawling man at the end of his rope. It is no small wonder that the next stop for the writer of "Where Are You Tonight?" was church.

Jonathan Cott was one of the few critics who paid much attention to "Where Are You Tonight?" In his book *Dylan* (New York: Delphin/Doubleday, 1985), Cott wrote that the song reminded him of "the last work Van Gogh painted before his suicide . . . a work unstable and charged with tempestuous excitement. . . . The artist's will is confused, the world moves toward him, he cannot move toward the world. It is as if he felt himself completely blocked, but also saw an ominous fate approaching."

Dylan's immaculate performances of "Where Are You Tonight?" transpired only during his 1978 big-band tour, when he was showcasing some of the *Street Legal* material.

"Where Were You Last Night" (Traveling Wilburys)

Traveling Wilburys, *Traveling Wilburys, Volume 3* (1990)

Acrimony, suspicion, and accusation are at the heart of this falling-out-of-love Wilburys song that Dylan sings with some aid from George Harrison.

"Where Teardrops Fall" (Bob Dylan)

Bob Dylan, *Oh Mercy* (1989)

A song of intense sorrow, "Where Teardrops Fall" exposes the truth of most lives where tears are shed in secret. But this is no "Tears of a Clown." Seeing beauty shot through with remorse, Dylan quotes "The Unfortunate Rake," "The Streets of Laredo," and other traditional songs from the folk idiom in which, after a futile death in battle, a funeral band "beats the drum slowly, and sounds the fife lowly" in reflection of the loss and inhumanity of war both romantic and military. Using obtuse couplets, Dylan comments on the lack of real sentiment in the secular concept of love.

Dylan's only performances of "Where Teardrops Fall" transpired during half a dozen 1990 Never Ending Tour shows, where it was featured as a mid-concert lament.

"The White Dove" (Carter Stanley)

aka "White Dove"
See also *Clinch Mountain Country*
Stanley Brothers, *Early Years 1958–61* (1994)
Ralph Stanley, *Clinch Mountain Country* (1998)
Old & In the Way, *Old & In the Way* (1973)
Jim and Jesse, *Music Among Friends* (1991)

Dylan may have heard the Stanley Brothers perform "The White Dove" at the Newport Folk Festival in the summer of 1964; but he only began performing this somber, biblically tinged bluegrass song in late 1997 as a mid-concert homage to his country and bluegrass passions. After half a dozen performances, in both electric and semi-acoustic arrangements, Dylan brought the song back for a single 2000 performance. Like "Rank Strangers," another mournful Stanley Brothers favorite of Dylan's, "The White Dove" deals with the introspection accompanying the death of parents and the winnowing of time. On stage, Dylan's straightforward country reading of "The White Dove" came perilously close to sounding like parody, yet always came off in terrific fashion.

"Who Killed Davey Moore?" (Bob Dylan)

Bob Dylan, *The Bootleg Series, Volumes 1–3: Rare and Unreleased, 1961–1991/'63* (1991); *The Bootleg Series, Volume 6: Live 1964—Concert at Philharmonic Hall* (2004)
Various Artists (performed by Pete Seeger), *Broadside Ballads, Volume 2: Songs from* Broadside *Magazine* (1963); *We Shall Overcome: The Complete Carnegie Hall Concert* (1989)
Hamilton Camp, *Paths of Victory* (1964)
The New Wine Singers, *The New Wave* (1964)
Linda Mason, *How Many Seas Must a White Dove Sail?* (1964)
Sebastion Cabot, *Sebastion Cabot, Actor—Bob Dylan, Poet* (1967)
Phil Ochs, *The Early Years* (2000)

W

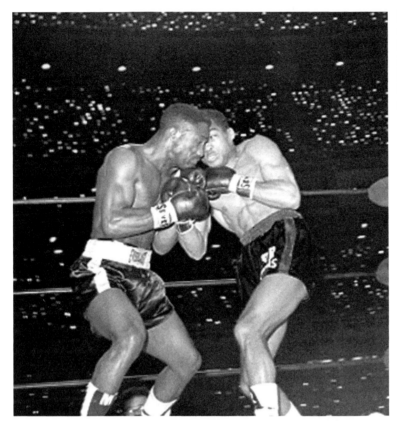

Defending featherweight champ Davey Moore, left, trading punches with Sugar Ramos at Dodger Stadium, Los Angeles, March 21, 1963.

(AP/Wide World Photos)

"If you want to know about the abolishment of boxing I would ask Miss Benny Kid Parent or Mrs. Davey Moore before I asked Cassius Clay. Just a personal tendency there."

That's how Dylan introduced "Who Killed Davey Moore?" at his April 12, 1963, concert at New York City's Town Hall. It is, despite his claim, a song about a boxer, boxing, and much more.

Boxer Davey Moore died four days after Ultiminio "Sugar" Ramos knocked him out on March 21, 1963, at Dodger Stadium in Los Angeles. It was the stuff of newspaper headlines and spurred renewed demands for the abolition of the sweet science.

Moore, twenty-nine, of Columbus, Ohio, had come into the fight as boxing's world featherweight champion; but he lost the crown and his life to Ramos, twenty-one, of Cuba, on what was ruled a technical knockout. Although he had taken a savage beating from the sixth round on, Moore was not knocked down until the tenth round. He finished that round draped on the ropes, and then reeled to his corner, at which point his manager, Willie Ketchum, ordered the fight stopped. Moore collapsed in his dressing room after he left the ring. He was taken to a hospital, where he remained unconscious until his death. Neurosurgeons reported on March 25 that Moore probably had sustained his fatal brain injury, which had caused the brain stem to swell, when the back of his head hit the lower stand of the ropes in the tenth round.

On March 22, California governor Edmund G. Brown called for the abolition of boxing in California and vowed he would immediately seek a bill authorizing a public referendum to outlaw the sport in 1964. Brown said that the California Athletic Commission had conducted the fight properly, but that, "Boxing, even under ideal conditions is a brutal sport, if it can be called a sport. There is only [one] way to prevent death and serious injury in the ring. That is to outlaw the so-called sport completely."

Pope John XXIII said on March 24 that professional boxing was "barbarous" and "contrary to natural principles." On March 25 the Vatican radio announced that prizefighting was "immoral" and urged a revision of the rules to bring boxing "within the tolerable limits of civilization."

The story was hard to avoid in the last week of March 1963; it must have caught Dylan's eye, because at his New York Town Hall concert of April 12, just two-and-a-half weeks later, he debuted his invective against prizefighting. "Who Killed Davey Moore?" became a hard-edged concert regular for the next year and a half; it was included on *Bob Dylan in Concert*, an album never released on the grounds that its compositions had become dated, as Dylan was coming up with so much new, superior material. The song appeared in *Broadside* #29 (July 1963) under the title "The Ballad of Davey Moore."

Like "Blowin' in the Wind," "Who Killed Davey Moore?" asks pointed, socially conscious questions but receives predictable answers. Dylan would return to the boxing song genre with much greater success in 1975 with "Hurri-

cane." And in "I Shall Be Free No. 10," he mentions Cassius Clay (later Muhammad Ali): "I figured I was ready for Cassius Clay/I said 'Fee, fie, fo, fum, Cassius Clay, here I come/Five, four, three, two, one, Cassius Clay you'd better run.'" Dylan was photographed with Ali during the Rolling Thunder tour in which "Hurricane" was featured. Still later, Dylan befriended Canadian light heavyweight fighter, Donny Lalonde. Lalonde, a fan of Dylan, was fond of playing "Hurricane" in his dressing room before entering the pugilistic ring. That seems not to have helped him when, in Las Vegas on ·November 7, 1988, with Dylan at ringside, he was knocked cold by Sugar Ray Leonard in the eighth round. As recently as May 2001, Dylan was caught ringside at Madison Square Garden watching Felix Trinidad successfully defend his middleweight title against William Joppy.

Dylan based "Who Killed Davey Moore?" on the traditional "Who Killed Cock Robin?" a nightmarish children's song that can be found in many variations stretching back to antiquity.

"Why Do I Have to Choose?" (Willie Nelson)
See also Across the Borderline, "Heartland"
Willie Nelson, *Take It to the Limit* (1983)
Merle Haggard, *Seashores of Old Mexico* (1987)
Jimmy Sturr, *Live at Gilley's* (1992)

Dylan trotted out Nelson's no-win, lose-lose piece of country quietude (in making a choice between two women, he risks losing them both) at a string of shows during the 1984 tour of Europe that produced *Real Live*, turning it into a majestic encore marked by Mick Taylor's guitar solo.

"Wichita" (Big Joe Williams)
See also "Big Joe, Dylan and Victoria"
Victoria Spivey, *Three Kings and a Queen/'62* (1964)

W

Dylan blows some mouth harp and sings backup vocals on "Wichita," a rare track from a rare recording with Victoria Spivey and Big Joe Williams in March 1962. The recording found its way onto the first of two Spivey albums including Dylan. Over the years some confusion has arisen over a different song Dylan was developing at the time—the semitraditional "Wichita (Going to Louisiana)"—that was left on *The Freewheelin' Bob Dylan* outtake scrap heap.

▣ "The Wicked Messenger" (Bob Dylan)
Bob Dylan, *John Wesley Harding* (1968)
Small Faces, *First Step* (1970)
Marion Williams, *Standing Here Wondering* (1971)
Mitch Ryder, *Live Talkies* (1982)
Tim O'Brien, *Red on Blonde* (1996)
Patti Smith, *Gone Again* (1996)

The Old Testament mentions him in Proverbs (13:17)—"a wicked messenger falleth into mischief: but a faithful ambassador is health." Sophocles noted his karma in *Antigone*—"None love the messenger who brings bad news." Shakespeare describes his paradoxical job in *King Henry IV, Part 2* (act 1, scene 1)—"The first bringer of unwelcome news/Hath but a losing office." Dylan drew on these ideas and then some in creating his own archetype in "The Wicked Messenger," a song speaking of the poet's uncomfortable (and sometimes unfortunate) role throughout history as a teller of truth.

Dylan's "Messenger" is a scathing portrait of a mute stranger with strange powers who mysteriously appears in town. The song is suffused with archaic diction fitting its ancient subject matter and is musically noteworthy for its brusque descending contours, which draw equally on the blues and the dirge.

As Robin Witting summarized "Wicked Messenger" in his book, *Isaiah for Guitar: A Guide to John Wesley Harding*: "Here, however, we have a wicked, false messenger—false ransom, using the message for his own ends. Who can you trust? It is never quite divulged just what his message is. Though the answer is clear-cut in the last line. No tidings of 'good news,' the 'good news' of the Messiah. This is the punch line to the song."

The performances of "The Wicked Messenger" in the Dylan/Grateful Dead shows of 1987 were one of the tour's biggest surprises, as were its subsequent performances during Dylan's tour with Tom Petty and the Heartbreakers later that year. Given the large venues both tours swung through, the song may have been somewhat ill-chosen. Jerry Garcia included it as an on-again, off-again number in his own band's repertoire, and Patti Smith included it in her set lists when she opened for Dylan in their short fall tour in 1995. As the Never Ending Tour entered the third millennium, Dylan gave "The Wicked Messenger" new wings with an arrangement marked by a relentless, pyrotechnically climactic guitar riff that made the song sound like it was born under a bad sign—transforming it from a stark, biblical ballad into a declamatory howl of rage set against a vehement blues stomp.

▣ "Wiggle, Wiggle" (Bob Dylan)
Bob Dylan, *Under the Red Sky* (1990)

A slinky little ditty about a modern day Salome with some R-rated imagery thrown in just make sure the point gets across, "Wiggle, Wiggle" opens Dylan's *Under the Red Sky* album. Dylan was still performing this song in the very early 1990s as a jump rocker any New Age Shaker would enjoy gyrating to; it was showcased in concert through 1992. Dylan drew on lines from Blind Willie McTell's "Southern Can Is Mine" ("You might wiggle like a tadpole") and Sam Cooke's "Shake" ("Shake it like a bowl

W

of soup/Make your body loop-de-loop") in constructing this minor, though funny and very danceable, pastiche. Like the balance of his *Under the Red Sky* collection, Dylan laces "Wiggle, Wiggle" with allusions to and appropriations of children's nursery rhymes; "Little Robin Redbreast," for example, includes the following, somewhat familiar, stanza: "Little Robin Redbreast/Sat upon a rail/Niddle noodle went his head/Wiggle waggle went his tail."

"Wigwam" (Bob Dylan)
Bob Dylan, single (1970); *Self Portrait* (1970)
Various Artists (performed by Bob Dylan), *The Royal Tenenbaums* (soundtrack) (2001)

An unmemorable caricature, this country folk–style acoustic instrumental was released as a single (backed with "Copper Kettle") and rose all the way to No. 41 on the *Billboard* charts. Bob might as well have spit in his audience's collective face. Still, "Wigwam," along with "Woogie Boogie" from the same *Self Portrait* album, does represent an anomaly in the Dylan recording and performing catalogue: the instrumental.

"Wilbury Twist" (Traveling Wilburys)
Traveling Wilburys, *Traveling Wilburys, Volume 3* (1990)

All four surviving Wilbury "brothers" take a turn singing on "Wilbury Twist," a joyous piece of danceable rock. The Traveling Wilburys' most lighthearted song, it was made into an even fluffier video, filmed in a L.A. mansion in the summer of 1991; in the video, a host of celebs (John Candy, Whoopie Goldberg, Fred Savage, and Eric Idle included) make cameos dancing the Wilbury Twist as Dylan and the other Wilburys "perform" the song and morph through several costume changes.

"Wild Mountain Thyme" (Traditional/Frank McPeake)
aka "The Braes of Balquhidder," "The Flowers of Peace," "Will You Go Lassie, Go?"
Joan Baez, *Farewell, Angelina* (1965)
Marianne Faithfull, *Go Away from My World* (1965)
The Byrds, *Fifth Dimension* (1966)
Bert Jansch, *Heartbreak* (1982)
Tannahill Weavers, *Dancing Feet* (1987)
Daniel Kobialka, *Going Home Again* (1992)
Various Artists (performed by the McPeake Family Trio), *Traditional Songs of Ireland* (1995)
Roger McGuinn, *Live from Mars* (1996)
Clancy Brothers, *Irish Folk Songs* (1996)
Rich Lerner, *Trails and Bridges* (1996)

Dylan performed the excruciatingly gorgeous, lilting love song "Wild Mountain Thyme" as early as 1961. He also played it as a duet with Joan Baez in 1965 during their short spring tour; at the 1969 Isle of Wight concert with the Band; as a duet revival with Baez during the 1976 leg of the Rolling Thunder tour; and as a brilliant one-off acoustic display at a June 1988 Cincinnati Never Ending Tour show. Dylan always seemed to sing this song with a sense of tremendous urgency, as if the future of mankind rested on the answer to the only question really worth asking: "Will you go, lassie, go?"

Some scholars of music from the British Isles suggest that "Wild Mountain Thyme" has its roots in "The Queen Among the Heather," a folk song from Northern Ireland. They credit Frank McPeake of the famed musical McPeake family of Belfast, Ireland, with refashioning that song into "Wild Mountain Thyme." Other folkologists firmly place its origins in the Scottish tradition, as a direct descendant of "The Braes of Balquhidder," proving their theory by pointing to words and phrases such as "lassie" and "bloomin' heather." The sleeve notes to the Tannahill Weavers' *Dancing Feet* album contains this observation: "If Scottish folk song has an anthem then this ('Wild Mountain Thyme') is it—everybody, but everybody, knows it. So much so, in fact, that it received the ultimate accolade for a song, becoming so popular that it became taboo to sing it. Just a strange example of the things that happen in the music business."

The Scots brought this song to America, where it became one of the most popular ballads, especially in Tennessee and North Carolina. The song remains popular at folk festivals, Renaissance Faires, and the like, still with the power to immediately sweep the listener into the Scottish Highlands.

Hank Williams

Born Hiram King Williams, September 17, 1923, Mount Olive, Alabama; died December 31, 1952 [or January 1, 1953], Oak Hill, West Virginia

Shakespeare may have been in the alley when Dylan sang of him in "Stuck Inside of Mobile (with the Memphis Blues Again)," but he could also have been spotted blazing a trail through the southern United States smack dab in the middle of the twentieth century in the name of Hank Williams. Williams's career lasted a mere decade, but the Hank Williams songbook bursts forth with one American classic after another: Tales of misery and joy, love lost and won, Saturday night dancing and Sunday morning devotion, fish fries and jambalaya, full wallets transformed into empty bottles, all crafted with grace and wisdom. The Williams legacy remains white hot.

Williams's importance to America's heritage can't be exaggerated. His message is truer today than it was at the peak of his fame a full half-century and change down the long lonesome highways he immortalized. Composer, recording artist, performer extraordinaire, Hank left a legacy that may well age as well as

Hank Williams, American country music legend, ca. 1950.

(Photo: New York World-Telegram and Sun Collection/Library of Congress)

any sonnet from the Bard's quill—his songs all models of simple soulful expression.

When an old World War I injury forced his father into long-term care at the V.A. hospital in Biloxi, Mississippi, Williams was raised by his formidable mother, Lillie Williams, in a rural, dirt-poor community. Like Woody Guthrie's experiences in Oklahoma and points west, Williams's hand-to-mouth childhood in the Depression-era South forged his character, filling him with a spirit of independence and compassion for society's left-behinds.

W

If more than a little trace of the blues can be sniffed in the music of Hank Williams, it can probably be traced to his family's relocation to Greenville, Alabama. There he encountered Rufe Payne (aka "Tee-Tot"), a black street singer and guitar player who gave him, as he was to later say, "all the musical training I ever had."

Hank made his first public appearance when the family moved to Montgomery in 1937. Billed as "the Singing Kid" at a local amateur night, he performed a topical blues number about the Works Progress Administration (the New Deal agency). WSFA gave him a regular slot and soon he tried his hand at songwriting. His first known song is "Six More Miles (to the Graveyard)," a bluesy Roy Acuff knockoff that even at that early date showed off Hank's gallows humor. Performing a combination of Acuff tunes and other popular songs of the day with his band, the Drifting Cowboys (a name he would use for backup bands throughout his career), Williams became a familiar face at southern Alabama venues.

Though not yet a full-time musician, Williams stayed in action during the early 1940s. Things began getting serious in 1943 when he met Audrey Mae Sheppard at a medicine show. They married and Audrey took over the very full-time job of managing her husband: she learned how to play stand-up bass in the band, collected admission fees at the doors of schoolhouses and roadside honky-tonks where the band played, and made sure Hank arrived at his gigs—juiced or not.

Hank's talent and Audrey's drive led to Nashville and a deal with country music's power broker Fred Rose, who shepherded Williams's meteoric rise. Rose, initially struck by Williams's songwriting, was quickly wowed by his potential as a performer. After a couple of impressive sessions for Sterling Records, Rose led Hank to an MGM contract and his first hit, the bluesy and ballsy "Move It On Over," which hit No. 5 on the country charts in 1947. Acting as both artistic and professional mentor as well as father figure, Rose quickly became a major force in Hank's life. What exactly he contributed to Hank's songs remains a matter of debate amongst Williamsologists, though the common conclusion is, as one of Hank's biographers put it, "Williams produced the gems and Rose polished them." Two of these gems were "Honky-Tonkin'," an anthem to the lowlife, and "I Saw the Light," a recasting of a sacred song that became one of his best-known compositions.

An invitation to perform on the prestigious *Louisiana Hayride* radio program in 1948 gave Hank a powerful, heavy-kilowatt stump from which to spread his gospel throughout the land. When his cover of an old 1922 Tin Pan Alley novelty number, "Lovesick Blues," hit No. 1 in the country charts a year later (enjoying, ironically enough, a type of success that none of his self-penned and arguably much better songs would ever touch), Williams became a cinch for the *Grand Ole Opry* radio show, even though his already problematic alcoholism was well known.

Initially, Hank was able to rebound from the problems his addictions caused him. He got an all-too-fleeting grip on his life when his son, Randall Hank (aka Hank Williams, Jr.), was born in the spring of 1949. The young family moved to Nashville, where Hank put together the classic edition of the Drifting Cowboys.

Whether it was some cosmic alignment, a present from God, or just something in the firewater, the Muse began singing on the shoulder of Hank Williams big-time. The floodgates of country music–making Nirvana

W

opened and he churned out songs at a breakneck pace, almost as if he knew his time on the planet was bound to be shorter than most people's. He synthesized just about every form of American popular music into perfect emotional nodules, drawing on blues, bluegrass, standard pop, backwoods hillbilly, honky-tonk, Cajun, the blue yodel, and even jazz. All the while, Rose shrewdly peddled his songs to artists as varied as Tony Bennett, Frankie Laine, Tennessee Ernie Ford, Teresa Brewer, and Ray Charles, all of whom scored with Williams's material. Naturally, virtually every noteworthy country artist eventually recorded an album of Hank songs and standards. "Kaw-Liga," "Your Cheatin' Heart," "Jambalaya," "I'm So Lonesome I Could Cry," "Cold, Cold Heart," "Hey, Good Lookin'," and "You Win Again" can still be heard on jukeboxes from Bangor to San Diego.

In a recording career that lasted a mere six years, Hank Williams left about one hundred titles. In addition to writing songs, Williams, in an appeal to those lost souls of the world, recorded a series of spiritual/philosophic recitations in 1950, pseudonymously released under "Luke the Drifter," though it was an open secret who the speaker was.

Williams's final years were easily his most prolific, but they were also his most tortured. Just when his opportunities for happiness were at their strongest, everything fell apart for him. His drinking took on a life of its own, exacerbated by his dangerous mixing of alcohol and painkillers (which were originally prescribed to alleviate the constant aggravation he experienced from spina bifida). His spiraling addictions led to the dissolution of his already tempestuous marriage and a pomp-filled quickie wedding to another woman, Billie Jean Jones. Expelled from the Opry for showing up drunk

once too often, Hank fell into a downward spiral from which he was never able to escape. There is much evidence suggesting that he probably never drew a sober breath during the last year of his life, which ended in the back of his new powder-blue Cadillac on the way to a New Year's Day gig in 1953. Ironically, Williams's last recording, "I'll Never Get Out of This World Alive," peaked at No. 1 just after his passing from alcoholism at age twenty-nine left a irreplaceable void in America's musical tapestry.

Dylan had often acknowledged Hank Williams as his first hero, telling television's Les Crane in February 1965, "I started writing songs after I heard Hank Williams." Dylan has even been known to adopt Williams's lush country whine, with perhaps *Nashville Skyline* and some of his early informal recordings the best examples of this vocal morphing. Dylan performed and/or recorded many songs from the Williams songbook: "Hey, Good Lookin'," "Honky Tonk Blues," "A House of Gold," "I Can't Get You off of My Mind," "(I Heard That) Lonesome Whistle," "Kaw-Liga," "Weary Blues," and "You Win Again."

The Williams legacy refuses to die. He is the subject of a bad biopic starring George Hamilton, a good biography by Colin Escot, and a fabulous play, *Lost Highway*, that is enjoying a Broadway run even as these words are being written. And let's not forget Hank Williams, Jr., who, though brandishing a very different approach to country music, has probably done more than anyone to sustain a keen interest in his dad's work.

Listen to Hank Williams late some night and experience the harrowing emotional intensity of this man and his music. So real, so sincere, so stuck with all the joys and sorrows of everyday life, the vision of Hank Williams feels as legit as a page from Genesis.

W

[S] **"Willin'"** (Lowell George)
Little Feat, *Little Feat* (1971); *Sailin' Shoes* (1972)
The Byrds, *Untitled* (1970)
Linda Ronstadt, *Heart Like a Wheel* (1974)

Dylan gracefully and tenderly performed Lowell George's "Willin'" (a vintage 1970s country rocker not unlike his own "Wanted Man") at half a dozen 1990 Never Ending Tour shows, and he revisited it annually over the following two years. In Dylan's hands, one could still hear the ghost of George flying over the white lines of the midnight interstate singing about a guy who has been over every mile of life's rough road but can still claim a true heart.

The sadly forgotten Lowell George (born April 13, 1945, Hollywood, California; died June 29, 1979, Arlington, Virginia) completed "Willin'" in 1969 and the Byrds immediately picked up the song in 1970. Inspired by a job pumping gas after he left art school in the mid-1960s, George kicked "Willin'" around in his head for quite awhile before finally setting it down. "Willin'," according to John Tobler's liner notes for *As Times Goes By: The Very Best of Little Feat*, "quickly became a favorite among America's truckdrivers, many of whom continue to regard it as the anthem of their profession . . . although absurdly it never has been a hit."

George recorded the song three times during his short lifetime. He used his own raspy voice and Ry Cooder's spare steel guitar accompaniment for a release on Little Feat's titular debut LP in 1970. Two years later, he was joined by the entire band on *Sailin' Shoes* in a version that includes four vocal harmonies and a nifty Bill Payne piano solo. And in 1978, Little Feat released the hymnic and perhaps best version of "Willin'" on their live album *Waiting for Columbus*.

In his book *Rock and Roll Doctor—Lowell George: Guitarist, Songwriter, and Founder of Little Feat*, author Mark Brend takes special note of "Willin'," writing, "The alliterative place name poetry of the lyrics 'Tucson to Tucumcari—Tehachapi to Tonapah' and there is enough happening to make the song distinctly memorable. There is hit-single potential here. Until, that is, George gets to the 'weed, whites and wine' line—dope, pills and booze in one hit—ensuring that widespread airplay would be denied if the song were to be released as a single.

"That particular act of commercial suicide apart, it's easy to see why 'Willin'' has proved to be such an enduring song. A simple structure, a mournful yet uplifting melody and a rousing chorus make for a good start. Then the lyrics combine traditional country subject matter with more obvious rock 'n' roll references, summoning the sort of romanticized blue-collar myth of truck-driving 'rigs' all night might not immediately make sense to a European audience—or even middle-class Americans—but it has romantic appeal nonetheless. The whole package amounts to a country rock classic."

George was the founder and catalyst of Little Feat, that compact jazzy rock 'n' funk band that hit its peak in the late 1970s. The band combined elements of country, folk, blues, soul, boogie, and loads of humor into a sound that was not only theirs and theirs alone, but one that has never really been approached, much less replicated or bettered. However, there was nothing slick about Little Feat, and George's idiosyncratic songs could never do more than earn them a cult following. When the band broke up in 1979, George set out on his own musical path but was downed by a fatal heart attack, no doubt spurred by his excessive lifestyle.

[S] **"Will the Circle Be Unbroken"** (Traditional/A. P. Carter) or (Ada Ruth Habershon/Charles Hutchinson Gabriel)

aka "Let the Circle Be Unbroken," "Will the Circle Be Unbroken?"

Ramblin' Jack Elliott (with Bob Dylan as "Tedham Porterhouse"), *Jack Elliott* (1964); *The Essential Jack Elliott* (1970)
Carter Family, *In the Shadow of Clinch Mountain*/'35 (2000)
Pat Boone, *Hymns We Love* (1957)
Stanley Brothers, *Hymns of the Cross* (1964)
Staple Singers, *Freedom Highway* (1965)
Nitty Gritty Dirt Band, *Will the Circle Be Unbroken* (1972)
John Lee Hooker, *This Is Hip* (1980)
Jerry Lee Lewis, *Ferriday Fireball* (1986)

Dylan visited "Will the Circle Be Unbroken," a venerable song of eternal faith, during his earliest days as a ragamuffin Minnesota minstrel boy. It was the encore to his freelance appearance with Neil Young and others at the March 1975 SNACK benefit concert at San Francisco's Kezar Stadium; a finale to an ad hoc performance with Patti Smith, Bobby Neuwirth, and others at the First Annual Village Folk Festival at the Other End in Greenwich Village on July 5, 1975; and an encore with the Rolling Thunder Revue at the May 8, 1976, Houston, Texas, show, where the band was joined by Willie Nelson. In between (under the pseudonym Tedham Porterhouse), Dylan contributed harmonica backing on a 1964 Ramblin' Jack Elliott recording of the song.

William Ferris did a fine job of connecting "Will the Circle Be Unbroken" to the most important Sacred Harp rituals of the American South when he wrote in the Smithsonian's *River of Song* project, "The Southern family reunion stresses the importance of ancestors and kinship. My grandmother was fond of saying that 'blood is thicker than water,' a proverb with which every Southerner can identify. As the hymn 'Will the Circle Be Unbroken?' suggests, many Southerners believe their family celebrations will continue even in the afterlife. They believe family reunions will continue after death as deceased kinfolk reunite in an unbroken circle."

Credit for authorship of the song is often attributed to A. P. Carter, but, as is often the case, attribution of many American chestnuts is nothing but an exercise in semantics. After all, putting one's name on traditional tunes is nothing new. Take Carter as an example. Through the early part of the twentieth century he and his kin scoured Appalachia, copyrighting dozens of centuries-old tunes that had their origins in the British Isles. To this day an ancient song like "Will the Circle Be Unbroken" is credited to A. P. Carter. Those in the know just chuckle and say, "Well, A. P. had the smarts to put his name on it before anybody else."

Some sources cite Charles Hutchinson Gabriel and Ada Ruth Habershon as the song's true composers, although the details of their formation of the song are unclear.

Born and raised on a farm, Gabriel (born August 18, 1856, Wilton, Iowa; died September 15, 1932, Los Angeles) was reared in a religious and musical household. He taught himself how to play the family organ and was writing songs as a youngster. After teaching singing in local schools, he moved to San Francisco, where he became the music director of the Methodist church in San Francisco. But his days as one of the world's most prolific hymn composers didn't come until after a move to Chicago in 1895. His hymns (some estimates put the number at eight thousand) became popular at Billy Sunday's evangelistic campaigns between 1910 and 1920. Gabriel had a respectable day job as well—from 1912 until his death in 1932, he was an editor for the Homer Rodeheaver Publishing Company, where he was involved in the production of more than 160 songbooks for choruses and religious schools.

Habershon (born January 8, 1861, London, England; died February 1, 1918) was the youngest daughter of a British doctor. Brought up in a Christian home, her whole life was, it appears, devoted to God's service. In 1901 she began writing poetry while ill and came up with what is still one of her better known hymns, "Apart with Him." She visited the United States not long afterward, and it was then that she encountered Gabriel and that "Will the Circle Be Unbroken" allegedly emerged into being. Along with writing hymns, Habershon was a noted and published lecturer on the Old Testament.

The original "Will the Circle Be Unbroken" was written by Gabriel and Habershon in 1907 and is now in the public domain; but the better-known Carter Family version, "Can the Circle Be Unbroken," first cut in 1935 and using the original refrain, is still under copyright. The Carters changed the verses so that they refer to the death not of various family members but of the mother.

Some country gospelologists suggest that "Will the Circle Be Unbroken" is related to "Glory Glory," a black traditional gospel better known as "When I Let My Burden Down."

[S] "Winterlude" (Bob Dylan)

Bob Dylan, *New Morning* (1970)
Steve Gibbons, *The Dylan Project* (1998)

This comedic, unabashedly romantic waltz, like some precious keepsake in an Edith Wharton novel, shows that Dylan didn't always have to play the prophet. Sounding like the music made by an old Wurlitzer organ at an ice-skating rink, "Winterlude" has, despite its Victorian musical trappings, a refreshing sexuality and innocence expressing a sense of being seriously out of place in the Dylan catalogue.

[S] "With God on Our Side" (Bob Dylan)

Bob Dylan, *The Times They Are A-Changin'* (1964); *MTV Unplugged* (1995); *The Bootleg Series, Volume 6: Live 1964—Concert at Philharmonic Hall* (2004)
Joan Baez, *Joan Baez in Concert, Part 2* (1963); *The First Ten Years* (1970)
Linda Mason, *How Many Seas Must a White Dove Sail* (1964)
Odetta, *Odetta Sings Dylan* (1965)
Chad Mitchell Trio, *Typical American Boys* (1965)
Ramblin' Jack Elliott, *Bull Durham Sacks and Railroad Tracks* (1970)
Manfred Mann, *Semi Detached Suburban* (1978)
Wire Train, *Between Two Worlds* (1985)
The Neville Brothers, *Yellow Moon* (1989)
Barbara Dickson, *Don't Think Twice, It's Alright* (1992)
Judy Collins, *Judy Sings Dylan . . . Just Like a Woman* (1993)
Gerry Murphy, *Gerry Murphy Sings Bob Dylan* (2001)
Various Artists (performed by Hart Rouge), *A Nod to Bob* (2001)
Various Artists (performed by Onelinedrawing), *May Your Song Always Be Sung: The Songs of Bob Dylan, Volume 3* (2003)
Michael Moore, *Jewels and Binoculars* (2000)

Sarcastically observing that winners of war usually control the manner in which history is written, Dylan dryly makes the still-salient, revisionist point that no matter what conflict it finds itself in, the good old U.S. of A. always manages to claim that its actions are just because it has "God on our side."

Here, in nine succinct eight-line verses, our singer takes us through cowboys and Indians, the Civil and Spanish-American wars to World Wars I and II, the cold war, and beyond, questioning the school-taught versions of their histories. The reason for fighting World War I he "never did get," and he observes that if an enemy gets God on its side and pledges allegiance to the United States, then the atrocities of a Holocaust are quite forgivable. Dylan even turns theologian in the penultimate verse, wondering whether Judas Iscariot had God on his side when he gave up Jesus. Following this logic, the song ends by suggesting that God's existence can only be proven by God preventing a nuclear war in the future.

Dylan performed the song consistently from early 1963 through his last all-acoustic concerts in 1965. He revisited the tune for one-off performances during the first phase of the Rolling Thunder Revue in 1975 and his hard-rock tour of Europe in 1984. Dylan began including a new verse about Vietnam in his 1988 Never Ending Tour performances of "With God on Our Side"; the verse was apparently written by the Neville Brothers, as they included it in their recording of the song. Dylan kept the song in moderate circulation but rarely retained it during the later phases of the Never Ending Tour.

Ⓐ *Wonder Boys (soundtrack)*/Various Artists
Sony CD 63849; CS 63849. Released 2000.

Dylan wrote "Things Have Changed" for Curtis Hanson's 2000 film, starring Michael Douglas, about the curse and blessing of early success as seen through the eyes of a writer in deep midlife crisis and his blossoming prodigy. With four tracks ("Things Have Changed," "Shooting Star," "Not Dark Yet," and "Buckets of Rain"), Dylan dominates the *Wonder Boys* soundtrack, which also includes music by Van Morrison, Neil Young, John Lennon, and Leonard Cohen.

An opponent of hodgepodge soundtracks of unrelated radio-aimed songs, Hanson integrated the entire soundtrack into the film, even playing some tunes for actors on the set to convey a scene's aural texture.

"Things Have Changed" was Dylan's first contribution of original material to a soundtrack since *Hearts of Fire* in 1987.

Ⓑ *Wood on Canvas: Every Picture Tells a Story*
Ronnie Wood and Catherine Roylance. Guildford, Surrey, England: Genesis Publications, 1998.

A man of many talents, Rolling Stoner Ron Wood is (like Dylan, Jerry Garcia, Tony Bennett, and Anthony Quinn, to name a few) one of those celebrity painters whose work critics love savaging (often out of jealousy and spite) even though it is sometimes pretty good. This very expensive, high-quality, limited-edition, and hard-to-find book was packaged with a four-song CD that included "Interfere," an instrumental (later overdubbed and released on Wood's *Not for Beginners* CD in 2001), recorded with Dylan at Woody's castle in Ireland.

Ⓢ "Woogie-Boogie" (Bob Dylan)
Bob Dylan, *Self Portrait* (1970)

With nary a touch of the auteur, Dylan closed his willfully confused *Self Portrait* collection with "Woogie-Boogie," a tight piece of instrumental fodder that could have been performed by any able Merle Travis–style picker. The song's title was apparently lifted from the lips of none other than Chico Marx, who (playing a piano teacher in the 1941 Marx Brothers film *The Big Store*) can be heard imparting this piece of wisdom to his students: "Keep practicing while I'm away—but remember: NO woogie boogie!"

Ⓐ *World Gone Wrong*
Columbia Records CD 57590; CS Sony 57590. Produced by Bob Dylan. Production supervised by Debbie Gold. Recorded summer 1993. Released October 26, 1993. Liner notes by Bob Dylan. Photography by Ana Maria Velez, Randee Saint Nicholas.

W

Bob Dylan—guitar, harmonica, vocals, arranger.
"World Gone Wrong," "Love Henry," "Ragged and Dirty,"
"Blood in My Eyes," "Broke Down Engine," "Delia,"
"Stack A Lee," "Two Soldiers," "Jack-A-Roe," "Lone
Pilgrim"

Following the same formula as *Good as I Been to You* (a similar collection of chestnuts released a year previously), but cutting even deeper, *World Gone Wrong* is another choice rummage through the basement of American song. This journey into folk and blues obscura is a genuinely moving document and one of Dylan's best albums of any era.

Saying more with other people's songs than most do with their own, Dylan creates a scathing, concerned commentary about modern society with this collection of traditional songs. On *World Gone Wrong*, the ciphers of early twentieth-century American music are invoked by the Dylan hoodoo. With both *Good as I Been to You* and *World Gone Wrong*, Dylan tips his hat to the musical lineages that informed his aesthetic while giving a hint at the road he would travel. The Mississippi Sheiks' "Blood in My Eyes" could well have been a source for "Corrina, Corrina," and the archetypal, covered-by-everyone "Stack A Lee" is a model for the narrative murder song "Lily, Rosemary and the Jack of Hearts."

But there are a wealth of other great performances of important songs to be found on *World Gone Wrong*. The eerie murder ballad "Love Henry" comes complete with a talking bird; "Ragged and Dirty" sounds about as footloose and dangerous as its title; Blind Willie McTell's "Broke Down Engine" is full of unleashed sexuality and unvarnished emotion; the devastatingly somber "Delia" (another McTell song) tells the tragic tale of murder and its consequences; the ironic "Two Soldiers" stands as a powerful antiwar statement; "Jack-A-Roe" is a gender-bending yarn of heroism and romance; "Lone Pilgrim" is about the narrator's religious faith in the face of death; and the title track expresses personal regret disguised as a social-cultural-political diagnosis. All the compositions on this album add up to a powerful vision of the contemporary human experience.

Dylan also saw fit to include a quirky eight-page liner-note essay (his first such contribution since *Desire* nearly two decades prior), worth the sticker price alone, in which he rambles in whacked-out but always strangely to-the-point free verse about the songs and himself with lines like "Give me a thousand acres of tractable land & all the gang members that exist & you'll see the Authentic alternative lifestyle, the Agrarian one," and "no man gains immortality thru public acclaim. Truth is a shadow."

Albums like this don't normally chart well, if at all. But being that it was a Bob Dylan record, it entered the charts at No. 70 and stayed on the list for a month, no small victory for traditionally based music. In keeping with the album's theme of an older sensibility, the ghostly, angular cover photograph of a top-hatted Dylan seated at a table in a café could have come off the paintbrushes of van Gogh or an absinthe-induced nightmare from Picasso's blue period.

A typically strange, unconfirmed story involving the album's delivery to Columbia sewed another thread into the tapestry of Dylan's mythos. Strolling into the company's Los Angeles office one day, Dylan sauntered up to the receptionist, plunked a cassette into her palm, and announced, "This is my new album." Apparently unaware of this character's identity, she politely replied, "Oh. Thank you."

Anonymity at last.

W

[S] **"World Gone Wrong"** (Traditional/Lonnie Chatmon)
aka "The World Is Going Wrong," "World Gone Wrong"
See also "Blood in My Eyes"
Bob Dylan, *World Gone Wrong* (1993)
Mississippi Sheiks, *Complete Recorded Works, Volume 2 (1930–31)* (1991); *Stop and Listen*/'31 (1999)

With this personal moment of truth and regret disguised as social diagnosis and rendered as country blues, Dr. Dylan pays homage to the Mississippi Sheiks in a dire though resigned rendition of a song they cut for an October 24, 1931, field recording by Columbia as "The World Is Going Wrong." Perhaps not so coincidentally, Blind Willie McTell made his first recording of "Broke Down Engine Blues" (also to be found on *World Gone Wrong*) at the same studio in Atlanta the day before the Sheiks made their recording.

Is it any wonder Dylan changed the title of the song, taking it from a moment of transition (the world *is* going wrong) to a past tense stick-a-fork-in-it done deal?

[S] **"Worried Blues"** (Traditional/Hally Wood)
Bob Dylan, *The Bootleg Series, Volumes 1–3: Rare and Unreleased, 1961–1991*/'62 (1991)
Sonny Terry, *Sonny's Story* (1960)
Mississippi John Hurt, *Worried Blues* (1963)
Skip James, *She Lyin'* (1964)
Doc Watson, *Elementary Doctor Watson!* (1993)
Frank Hutchison, *Complete Recorded Works, Volume 1* (1997)

When Dylan recorded "Worried Blues" in late April 1962 at a session for *The Freewheelin' Bob Dylan*, the song had been a sporadic inclusion in his set list for about half a year and featured the kind of crafty guitar picking Dylan wouldn't really revisit until *Good as I Been to You* and *World Gone Wrong*, his two albums of cover songs released in the early 1990s. But the roots of this plaint are as vague as any in his songbook.

Biographical info on Hally Wood is extremely sketchy. Some say that she was a black folk singer. Other, somewhat more reliable, research suggests that she was a white Texas songster who was recorded by the Lomaxes and married to blackballed writer/historian/humorist John Henry Faulk. Dylan appeared on *Folk Songs and More Folk Songs*, a Faulk-hosted television program in 1963.

British musicologist John Way has suggested that Dylan's fingerpicking style here—a style he seems to have abandoned by the end of 1964—is similar to that on earlier folk renditions of "Barbara Allen," "Kentucky Moonshiner," or his own "Don't Think Twice, It's Alright," and may owe something to Elizabeth Cotten.

According to Görgen Antonsson in *The Telegraph* #54 (Spring 1996), "Worried Blues" is "probably from the white tradition and Dylan found it in *Folk Blues: 110 American Folk Blues*, where the only reference to a recording is to a Stinson LP by folksinger Hally Wood.... The 'chilly winds' verse... is a refrain in black banjoist Papa Charlie Jackson's c. December 1925 recording 'Where the Chilly Winds Don't Blow' as well as in Ida Cox's 'Southern Woman Blues.'... Neither of these are Dylan's source, of course, and are cited only as an indication of how far back the tradition goes."

X

[S] **"Xmas Island"** (Dick Fariña and Eric von Schmidt)
Dick Fariña and Eric von Schmidt (with Dylan as "Blind Boy Grunt"), *Dick Fariña & Eric von Schmidt* (1963)

Dylan's contribution to this obscure "Big Rock Candy Mountain"–style original folk song was his background harmonica stylings.

Y

☐ "Yazoo Street Scandal" (Robbie Robertson)
Bob Dylan/The Band, *The Basement Tapes/*'67 (1975)
The Crust Brothers, *Marquee Mark* (1998)

Robbie Robertson's autobiographical rocker recalling the roots of the Band was included on *The Basement Tapes* release. However, it does not seem to include Dylan as a background performer.

☐ "Ye Shall Be Changed" (Bob Dylan)
Bob Dylan, *The Bootleg Series, Volumes 1–3 (Rare and Unreleased) 1961–1991/*'79 (1991)

One of three known *Slow Train Coming* outtakes, "Ye Shall Be Changed" is a spirited sermonette on a hill combining gospel-like syncopations with troubling apocalyptic lyrics. Some Dylanists insist this song is a condensed version of Chapter 11 of *The Late Great Planet Earth*— a millennialist tract written by Hal Lindsey, who was associated with the Vineyard Fellowship, Dylan's church during the period. But Dylan was also clearly cribbing from Paul's First Epistle to the Corinthians 15:51–52, from which he took "we shall all be changed,/In a moment, in the twinkling of an eye, at the last trump: for the trumpet shall sound, and the dead shall be raised incorruptible, and we shall be changed" and changed it to "Ye shall be changed, ye shall be changed/In a twinkling of an eye, when the last trumpet blows/The dead will arise and burst out of your clothes/And ye shall be changed."

☐ "Yea! Heavy and a Bottle of Bread" (Bob Dylan)
Bob Dylan/The Band, *The Basement Tapes/*'67 (1975)
Midnight Dread, *Deep Word Dub: Bonus Singles* (2003)

Dylan and the Hawks recorded a couple of versions of this great piece of rollicking whimsy, which seemed to materialize spontaneous-combustion-style out of the thick basement air with some degree of regularity. Nothing quite makes sense or comes together as Dylan does his Buster Keatonesque deadpan, stand-up rap about a bus trip with a comic book. The song includes one of the standout mantras from *The Basement Tapes*: "Take me down to California, baby."

In his book about Dylan's early songs, *Don't Think Twice, It's All Right*, Andy Gill became just about the only writer to pay any attention to "Yea! Heavy and a Bottle of Bread," writing:

> Dylan's delivery is deceptively conversational, adding to the illusion of common sense, and though there's something tentative and spontaneous about the recurrent little piano phrase that adds a soupçon of character to the song, the other musicians join lustily enough on the choruses to dispel suspicions about its ultimate destination (though not, perhaps, in the case of the baritone harmony on the final "bread," which fluctuates drunkenly before settling on its proper note). Ticking along blithely as if he knows exactly where it's going, "Yea! Heavy and a Bottle of Bread" winds up as one of the most engaging of the album's songs, its appeal accentuated, if anything, by the fact that its meaning is unfathomable.

Speaking of the realm of spontaneous combustion, in one of the more incredible examples of dusting off old gems decades after they'd been stashed away and more or less forgotten, Dylan and his Never Ending Tour band's gleaming two-time-only reggae/calypso–arranged Madison Square Garden display of "Yea! Heavy" at the tail end of his immaculately hip 2002 tour (he performed it again in late '03) reminded all that the master songster remained a master trickster.

[S] **"You Ain't Goin' Nowhere"** (Bob Dylan)

Bob Dylan (with Happy Traum), *Bob Dylan's Greatest Hits, Vol. II* (1971)
Bob Dylan/The Band, *The Basement Tapes/'67* (1975)
Bob Dylan/Various Artists (performed by Mary Chapin Carpenter, Roseanne Cash, Shawn Colvin), *Bob Dylan: The 30th Anniversary Concert Celebration* (1993)
Joan Baez, *Any Day Now* (1968); *Vanguard Sessions: Baez Sings Dylan* (1998)
The Byrds, *Sweetheart of the Rodeo* (1968)
Earl Scruggs, *His Family & Friends* (1972)
Flying Burrito Brothers, *Live from Amsterdam 1985* (1985)
The Rave-Ups, *Town & Country* (1985)
Texas Instruments, *Sun Tunnels* (1988)
The Nitty Gritty Dirt Band, *Will the Circle Be Unbroken, Volume 2* (1989)
Phil Carmen, *Bob Dylan's Dream* (1996)
The Crust Brothers, *Marquee Mark* (1998)
Cracker, *Garage d'Or* (2000)
Dumptruck, *Lemmings Travel to the Sea* (2001)

Dylan and the Hawks' stumbling, charming, half-spoken versions of "You Ain't Goin' Nowhere," recorded in 1967, contrast sharply with each other and with the bonus track laid down by Dylan and Happy Traum for *Bob Dylan's Greatest Hits, Vol. II* a few years later. Dylan's joyous delivery on the latter sounds like it's coming from a man with places to go. On the less familiar version recorded during the *Basement* era, Dylan sings the song in a talking drawl similar to that found on some of the other material cooked up at the time, like "Lo and Behold" and "Yea! Heavy and a Bottle of Bread."

But just go and try to figure out what "You Ain't Goin' Nowhere" is all about. Whether taken as a final revel before the arrival of a mail-order bride, a little jape about ducking work, or deadpan mountain-music nonsense, the song remains just about the most singable from *The Basement Tapes*.

In his book *Don't Think Twice, It's All Right*, Andy Gill summarized "You Ain't Goin' Nowhere" thusly: "[W]hile the brisk meteorological details—the frozen railings, rain and clouds—lend the first verse a stark rural cohesion, subsequent stanzas drift further away from logic until the final verse twists off into a *non sequitur* concerning Genghis Khan's inability to keep his kings supplied with sleep."

Greil Marcus's notes in his book *Invisible Republic* on the two *Basement Tapes* versions of the song cut a little deeper into the sense of "You Ain't Goin' Nowhere." Of the first take, Marcus writes, "Given that the verses here are a shambling improvisation on the necessity of finding someone to feed the cat—the aching choruses, perhaps the most appealing air of the basement compositions, are the same as in the finished version of the song—it's hard to see how the number ever *got* finished. Unless it was already finished, merely not yet recorded, and the cat was making a nuisance of itself."

Of the second take, Marcus opines, "It's so sweet, this melody; when Dylan sings, 'Ooo-wee, ride me high,' he might be singing to his own music. None of the many who have covered this number has ever come close to recapturing its glorious sense of anticipation, its promise that you must learn life's most valuable lessons before you can expect your life to change—not even Dylan himself, redoing the piece with Happy Traum in 1971, for his *Greatest Hits, Volume II*."

Another song Dylan rediscovered late in his career, "You Ain't Goin' Nowhere" was first performed in 1999 as a surprise early concert offering. It was a slicked-up countrified feature (à la the Byrds' *Sweetheart of the Rodeo* arrangement) at his return to the Newport Folk Festival in 2002 (and at points beyond), complete with wonderful background harmonies and loping pedal steel guitar licks provided by multi-instrumentalist Larry Campbell.

▣ "You Angel You" (Bob Dylan)

Bob Dylan, single (1974); *Planet Waves* (1974); *Biograph*/'74 (1985)

Alpha Band, *Spark in the Dark* (1977); *Interviews* (1988)

New Riders of the Purple Sage, *Best of the New Riders of the Purple Sage* (1976)

Manfred Mann's Earth Band, *Angel Station* (1979); *Best of Manfred Mann's Earth Band* (1996)

Not quite as lightweight as it is often dismissed as being, "You Angel You" is sung by Dylan with the passion of a man who really is overjoyed to be with his gal again. Still, Greil Marcus's words upon the song's 1985 *Biograph* rerelease sting; he called the song "a bouncy piece of junk; an affirmation of nothing."

Dylan's recollections of the song's genesis, as expressed in the *Biograph* liner notes, are vague: "I might have written this at one of the sessions probably, you know, on the spot, standing in front of the mike . . . it sounds to me like dummy lyrics."

Dylan only twice visited "You Angel You" as a performance vehicle, during the 1990 edition of the Never Ending Tour.

▣ "You Belong to Me" (Pee Wee King/Redd Stewart/Chilton Price)

Various Artists (performed by Bob Dylan), *Natural Born Killers* (soundtrack) (1994)

Jo Stafford, *You Belong to Me*/'52 (1989)

Bing Crosby, *Radio Years, Volume 1*/'50s (1987)

The Duprees, *Best of the Duprees*/'62 (1990)

Vonda Shepard, *Songs from Ally McBeal* (1998)

A leftover from the *Good as I Been to You* sessions recorded at his Malibu home, the acoustic "You Belong to Me" wound up in the harsh Oliver Stone–directed road-kill flick starring Woody Harrelson and Juliette Lewis. Full of exotic North African locales (the Pyramids, Algiers, etc.), the quintessential 1950s love

song has a creepy, disturbing edge—as if the singer were a stalker reminding his prey that escape is impossible.

The better-known composer of "You Belong to Me" is Pee Wee King (born Julius Frank Anthony Kuczynski, February 18, 1914, Abrams, Wisconsin; died March 7, 2000, Louisville, Kentucky), an eclectic and innovative country music entertainer best remembered as the lyric writer of the pop classic "Tennessee Waltz." Starting out as a master accordion and concertina player in his father's band on the 1920s Midwestern polka circuit, he met and performed with Gene Autry before the latter starred in Hollywood westerns. He changed his name to Pee Wee King ("Pee Wee" because he was short, and "King" in homage to Wayne King, another Polish bandleader) after that and settled in Louisville. There he formed the Golden West Cowboys (some say from the remnants of Autry's band) and signed on with the *Grand Ole Opry* in 1937. They are said to be the first band to use electric guitars, trumpets, and drums at the hallowed hub of country music. (Okay, so maybe it wasn't quite as jaw-dropping as Dylan's electric set at Newport in 1965, but it did mark a significant turning point for the Opry and like venues.)

King's dual reputations as an innovator and an entertainer continued hand in hand. Eschewing the hillbilly motif, he and his bandmates dressed in some of the first flamboyant get-ups designed by Nudie the Rodeo Tailor. Never shy about experimenting with a nontraditional approach to country music, King successfully merged the polka and the waltz into his (by Nashville standards) off-the-grid sound.

As a member of the Camel Caravan in World War II, he entertained at army bases. King was also an early cohort of Hank Williams, even buying Hank's earliest songs. His biggest success came with "Tennessee

Waltz," which he penned with vocalist Redd Stewart (born Henry Ellis Stewart, Ashland City, Tennessee, May 27, 1923; died August 2, 2003, Louisville Kentucky). Stewart, a longtime associate of Pee Wee's, started his career in music as a commercial songwriter for a car dealer while in his mid-teens.

Until he hooked up with King, Stewart was a somewhat successful vocalist and bandleader in and around 1930s Louisville. It was only when he joined forces with the brash King that he achieved stardom, mainly after WWII, when King's band hit full stride and Stewart began writing. His first hit actually came through Ernest Tubb, whose recording of a song inspired by Stewart's military service, "A Soldier's Last Letter," was a smash.

Though King had already written a few songs celebrating Tennessee ("Tennessee Polka," "Tennessee Tears" with Ernie Lee, and "Tennessee Tango" with Stewart), King and Stewart, inspired in part by Bill Monroe's "Tennessee Waltz," hunkered down and wrote their own "Tennessee Waltz" in 1946. They recorded it for RCA Victor a couple of years later, but the song languished until Patti Page's 1950s recording for Mercury sold more than three million copies, making it among the most successful singles of the day. Its popularity was of such renown that, some fifteen years later, "Tennessee Waltz" was named an official song of the Volunteer State.

The plot thickened in 1951 when King's recording of "Slow Poke," a novelty song credited to him, Stewart, and a woman named Chilton Price (born Chilton Searcy, 1917, Fern Creek, Kentucky), became his only No. 1 hit. With more than a million copies sold, the trio also sold "You Belong to Me" in 1952, which, when recorded by Jo Stafford in 1952, became a monster hit, selling two-million-plus copies. Its popularity was such that it would be covered by scores of recording artists as varied as Pat Boone, Benny Carter, Patti Page, Oscar Aleman, Rosemary Clooney, Mose Allison, Anita Baker, Floyd Cramer, Paul Anka, Petula Clark, Dean Martin, Carly Simon, Bing Crosby, and the odd punk band or two.

Recent revelations, however, suggest that King and Stewart had little or nothing to do with the actual composition of "You Belong to Be"—that their involvement with the song's success was from their connections and PR. (As reported by Nick Clooney in his article "To Chiton Goes All the Credit," available at http://www.cincypost.com/2002/sep/27/cloon 092702.html.)

Price, still alive, kicking, and writing songs, recently discussed the history of both "You Belong to Me" and "Slow Poke." She started writing songs as a hobby. Coincidentally, she worked in the same radio station where King had a show and she became friendly with him. She came up with "Slow Poke," which included lyrics she felt aptly and affectionately described him. She gave him the song (melody included) and he loved it so much that he recorded it with Stewart handling the vocals. Without a hint of rancor, Price maintains that King and Stewart did not write a word or note of either "Slow Poke" or "You Belong to Me." And she appears never to have been upset that the two claimed co-authorship and shared the songs' substantial financial success. "I didn't know anything about the music business," she said. "If they hadn't pushed it, there probably would have been no record at all. I'm grateful to them."

So the pattern was set: King-Stewart-Price. She would write a song. They would promote it and share on the credit and the profits. While some might legitimately cry foul, Price took a big-picture view of the situation when discussing her career: "People praised my work. I even wrote a song for Doris Day that she sang

Y

in a movie. The way I see it, none of that would have happened without Pee Wee King and Redd Stewart. I'm grateful to them."

Along with Dylan's rendition of "You Belong to Me" in *Natural Born Killers*, the song has made at least two other film appearances—*Forbidden* (a 1953 noir starring Tony Curtis) and *Shrek* (the beloved 2001 computer-animated comedy about a monster who finds true love)—and is central to the plot of *You Belong to Me*, Mary Higgins Clark's best-selling 1998 murder mystery.

[S] "You Can Always Tell" (Dick Fariña/Eric von Schmidt)

Dick Fariña and Eric von Schmidt (with Dylan as "Blind Boy Grunt"), *Dick Fariña & Eric von Schmidt* (1963)

Recording under the infamous alias "Blind Boy Grunt," Dylan contributed to this and five other tracks at a mid-January 1963 London session by Richard Fariña and Ric von Schmidt, which was eventually released by Folklore Records.

According to the album liner notes, the song was from "a tune based on Furry Lewis's 'Dry Land Blues,' with additional verses."

[S] "You Changed My Life" (Bob Dylan)

Bob Dylan, *The Bootleg Series, Volumes 1–3 (Rare and Unreleased) 1961–1991*/'81 (1991)

A late entry in Dylan's gospel catalogue and a *Shot of Love* outtake, "You Changed My Life" is a powerful and compelling (if a little by-rote) percussion-driven religious song thanking the Lord for having transformed the singer's life. *The Bootleg Series, Volumes 1–3* finds Dylan performing the song with vigorous commitment and confidence despite a faltering backup band.

Cut out of the same fabric as "Property of Jesus," "You Changed My Life" alternately deals with the reaction of others to the singer's conversion and his embrace of his Savior. He's surrounded by corrupt, unrepentant vipers whose gluttony both blinds them and tempts him. But he can still see the light at the end of the tunnel most clearly, and therein lies his salvation. There's at least one notable Biblical reference as Dylan transforms Exodus 22:21 ("Thou shalt neither vex a stranger, nor oppress him: for ye were strangers in the land of Egypt") into "Making me feel like a stranger in a strange land," a motif most famously appropriated by sci-fi scribe Robert Heinlein in his allegorical novel *Stranger in a Strange Land*.

[S] "You Don't Know Me" (Eddy Arnold/Cindy Walker)

Eddy Arnold, *Best of Eddy Arnold* (1967)
Ray Charles, *Modern Sounds in Country and Western Music* (1962)
Elvis Presley, *Clambake* (1967)
Emmylou Harris, *Cowgirl's Prayer* (1993)
Van Morrison, *Days Like This* (1995)
Ray Charles, *Ultimate Hits Collection* (1999)

Dylan's only known performances of "You Don't Know Me" are a half-dozen 1989 curiosities that sounded like a cross between the slow dance at the prom and the ultimate tribute to Ray Charles.

"You Don't Know Me" was written by Eddy Arnold and Cindy Walker in 1955. Jerry Vale's 1956 single release hit No. 14 and paved the way for Arnold's later release, which hit No. 10. Ray Charles's 1962 release of the song became the first recording of "You Don't Know Me" to become a million-seller. Elvis sang the song in *Clambake*, his 1967 movie.

If there was one cat who could rightly claim that he urbanized hillbilly music, it was Eddy Arnold (born May 15, 1918, Madisonville, Tennessee). Arnold's smooth vocals complemented his velvety voice and his layered orchestrations made him something of country music's reply to Nelson Riddle. Certainly, his commercial success rivaled just about all comers: he wound up with twenty-eight No. 1 singles and charted more than any other recording artist. But that popularity is also a measure of just how good he was at spreading country music to the masses. It wouldn't be unusual to find an Eddy Arnold record in the collections of people who didn't particularly like or know much about the genre. Arnold came out of the whole Gene Autry school of cowboy crooners popular in the 1930s and 1940s. And because he eschewed the hillbilly style and persona, he was more easily accepted into the high strata of showbiz and stayed there in a career that ran from World War II to well into the 1990s with hit recordings and sold-out concerts.

"The dean of Texas songwriters," "the greatest living songwriter of country music," or just plain "fine," Cindy Walker's half century as a grande dame of American music has left an indelible mark. Of the hundreds of songs she wrote, several became hits for country stars and non-country stars alike. And her catalogue ran the gamut: cowboy songs, beer-drinking songs, rockabilly tunes, bluegrass songs, and country-pop numbers. Gene Autry, Bob Wills, Hank Snow, Ernest Tubb, Roy Orbison, and, of course, Eddy Arnold are just a few of the more notable artists who enjoyed a fruitful association with Walker.

Walker (born July 20, 1918, Mart, Texas) grew up in a small town about fifty miles south of Dallas, the granddaughter of the famed hymnist Professor F.L. Eiland and the daughter of a music-loving mom who nurtured Walker's songwriting, which began in early childhood. She broke into show business very early, too, when she landed a job as a dancer at Fort Worth's Casa Mañana, run by famed impresario Billy Rose. Walker got her first big break when she penned a theme song ("Casa de Mañana") for the joint that was played on a nationwide radio broadcast by Paul Whiteman, the bandleader who was an early and important popularizer of jazz.

A visit to Hollywood around this time resulted in deals with both Bing Crosby and Gene Autry. Crosby recorded Walker's "Lone Star Trail" and Autry hired her to write songs for a string of C-grade cowflicks beginning with *Ride, Tenderfoot, Ride* in 1940. And she began to record, with immediate success; "When My Blue Moon Turns to Gold Again" hit the country charts in 1944 and eventually became a bluegrass standard. She tracked down Bob Wills when the "King of Western Swing" made a stop in Tinseltown. Within a week, Wills had recorded five of her songs, thereby commencing a musical relationship that would last a quarter century. Wills's music (an amazingly infectious blend of country & western, bluegrass, jazz, and novelty) was marked by brilliant musicianship, but his band, the Texas Playboys, lacked good original material until he met Walker. In all, she wrote more than fifty songs for and with Wills, including "Can It Be Wrong," "Sugar Moon," "Bubbles in My Beer," "New Playboy Rag," "It's the Bottle Talkin'," "Born to Love You," and "It's a Good World."

From the mid-1940s through the early 1960s, Walker enjoyed a great ride as the giants of country, bluegrass, and pop covered her songs. She was not much for recording herself, but a fine representation of Walker in her prime can be found on *Words and Songs*, an album released in 1964. And following in her grandfather's footsteps, she published a hymnbook entitled *Of Thee I Sing* in the late 1980s. An extremely private person, Walker's success allowed her to move back to Mexia, Texas, in the 1960s and it is from there that she has danced with her muse—at a safe remove from Nashville.

Y

▪ "(You Give Me) Fever" (Otis Blackwell/Eddie Cooley)

Otis Blackwell, *All Shook Up* (1976)

Little Willie John, single (1956); *Fever: The Best of Little Willie John* (1993)

James Brown, *Cold Sweat* (1967)

Elvis Presley, *Aloha from Hawaii* (1973)

Toots and the Maytals, *In the Dark* (1976)

Peggy Lee, single (1958); *Fever & Other Hits* (1992)

Written by Otis Blackwell and Eddie Cooley in 1956, "Fever" was a million-seller for both Little Willie John and Peggy Lee as well as a hit for the rock group the McCoys in 1965.

Otis Blackwell (born February 16, 1931 or 1932, Brooklyn, New York; died May 6, 2002, Nashville) was one of the great unsung heroes of mid- to late-twentieth-century American music. He performed, it is true, but it was his songwriting that has secured him a spot in the pantheon. The author of more than one thousand songs, he scored dozens of hits when they were recorded by performers as diverse as the Who ("Daddy Rollin' Stone"); James Taylor ("Handy Man"); Otis Redding; Peggy Lee ("Fever"); Jerry Lee Lewis ("Great Balls of Fire"); and, most famously, Elvis Presley, with his recordings of "Don't Be Cruel" and "All Shook Up," to name just a couple. At last count, sales of Blackwell songs have topped 185 million copies, and all have that Blackwell touch (an amalgam of pop sentimentality, country twang, and R&B propulsion—as identifiable as that of Willie Dixon, Leiber and Stoller, Cole Porter, or Hank Williams. Along the way, Blackwell helped devise the syntax of rock 'n' roll when the genre was taking its first baby steps.

A kid from Brooklyn, Blackwell grew up wanting to be a singer. While recording songs for a small company in New York City, he was asked to write songs as well. Blackwell's demos later not only supplied Presley with songs, but also with a way of performing them. This style was once described by song scribe Doc Pomus as a "strange little tense passion."

Blackwell's own influences were a bit unusual for a black kid growing up in the Big Apple. A huge fan of the B westerns that screened at the local movie house every Saturday afternoon, Blackwell worshipped the likes of Tex Ritter, who not only always saved the day, but sang in his films, too. Of his love for country music, Blackwell once said, "Like the blues, it told a story. But it didn't have the same restrictive construction. A cowboy song could be anything."

This early interest in crossover genres, combined with his family's regular gatherings around the piano to sing gospel songs, no doubt planted the seeds for Blackwell's later musical breakthroughs. Chuck Willis (*see* "It's Too Late"), the exotic R&B performer, was an early musical hero, and it was his style that Blackwell emulated when he parlayed a 1952 "Amateur Night" win at Harlem's Apollo Theater into a record deal—first with RCA and then with Jay-Dee. Enjoying some early recording and performing success (most notably with the throbbing "Daddy Rollin' Stone"), he found his first love was songwriting and by 1955 had settled into the groove that he would ride for decades.

"Don't Be Cruel" was one of the first songs Blackwell ever sold. It turned out to be not only a major hit, but also a pop milestone, after a young man by the name of Elvis Presley recorded it on July 2, 1956. The 45 rpm released a couple of weeks later, which also included "Hound Dog" by Jerry Leiber and Mike Stoller, became among the first releases where both sides of a single became No. 1 in every category. "Don't Be Cruel" remained on the pop charts for eleven weeks, and—on its way to selling more than 3 million copies—it simultaneously crested in the top plateau on both the country and R&B charts as well.

That breakthrough led to a long partnership in hit-making, though, amazingly enough, Blackwell and Presley never met. As Peter Guralnick, Presley's most respected biographer, said, "Otis wrote in a style that came to define a new synthesis that Elvis was groping for. From the first moment Elvis heard 'Don't Be Cruel,' he just snapped on it. It was a perfect song for him."

Blackwell's relationship with Presley is one reason his songwriting legacy is so complex. As part of his arrangement with Elvis, he shared songwriting credit (but also a significant portion of the royalties) with The King on the songs he provided, even though Presley's contribution was at best minor. As reported in his *New York Times* obituary, Blackwell said, "I was told that I would have to make a deal." But with songs that sold in the millions, he hardly sounded bitter: "I wrote my songs, I got my money and I boogied."

The Presley arrangement was not Blackwell's only arrangement; he shared authorship on numerous titles with other writers and often used pseudonyms. Cowritten with Eddie Cooley under the name John Davenport for contractual reasons (Blackwell was technically obligated to Jay-Dee when the song was penned), "Fever" was his first bona fide megahit and reputedly opened the pearly gates to Graceland.

Blackwell's songs were smelted into gold by Elvis and the lesser lights of rock 'n' roll's early heyday, including Clyde McPhatter, Dee Clark, Ben E. King, the Drifters, Bobby Darin, and Gene Vincent. And if the British Invasion left the Brill Building dormant, Blackwell revived himself in the mid-1970s with an album of his most famous songs. He suffered a paralyzing stroke in 1991, but his influence has endured, as proclaimed by *Brace Yourself!*, a 1994 all-star tribute album that showcased his most memorable songs.

Dylan only performed a trio of versions of "Fever" in late 1980 and early 1981 as he was emerging from the peak (or was that pique?) of his gospel period.

"Young But Daily Growing" (Traditional)

aka "A-Growing" "A Long Time A-Growing," "Father Oh Father," "Lang A-Growin'," "Trees They Do Grow High," "The Trees They Do Grow Tall," "The Trees They Grow So High"

Joan Baez, *Joan Baez, Volume 2* (1961)
Martin Carthy, *Martin Carthy* (1965)
Pentangle, *Sweet Child* (1968)
John Renbourn, *John Renbourn Sampler* (1971)
Various Artists (performed by Robin and Barry Dransfield), *Troubadours of British Folk, Volume 1: Unearthing the Tradition* (1995)
Liam Clancy, *Irish Troubadour* (1999)

An early Dylan performance vehicle (he let it shine on the May 1961 "Minnesota Party Tape" and at the ill-fated Carnegie Chapter Hall show later that year) that he later brought to the 1967 *Basement Tapes* sessions with the Hawks, "Young But Daily Growing" could stand next to just about any ballad collected by Francis Child. It is a very old folk song originating in the British Isles (Somerset, Surrey, Devon, Essex, Yorkshire, Dorset, Hertford, Lancashire) but found less frequently on this side of the pond (Nova Scotia, Kentucky, Connecticut, Vermont). According to *The Penguin Book of English Folk Songs*, edited by R. Vaughn Williams and A.L. Lloyd, "It is sometimes said that the ballad is based on the actual marriage of the juvenile laird of Craighton to a girl several years his senior, the laird dying three years later, in 1634. But in fact the ballad may be older; indeed, there is no evidence that it is Scottish in origin. Child marriages for the consolidation of family fortunes were not unusual in the Middle Ages and in some parts the custom persisted far into the seventeenth century."

Greil Marcus was just about the only contemporary writer to assess "Young But Daily Growing." As he wrote in *Invisible Republic*, his

Y

book about the *Basement Tapes* and points beyond:

> [T]his ancient song (often described as "one of the only Child ballads Francis Child missed") is told in the voice of a young woman who discovers that her father has married her to a rich man's son: a child. There's an oddness that can barely be spoken when she hears schoolboys playing—among them her husband. And yet what she never wanted she soon can hardly bear to live without: "At the age of sixteen years, he was a/Married man/At the age of seventeen/He was the father, of a son/At the age of eighteen years/Round his grave the grass grew long." As the song ends, the woman walks through the fields, savoring the springtime, thinking of summer and her young son; it's unsurpassably sentimental, and you can feel sunlight bursting over yourself as you listen.
>
> That's how it is when Dylan sings the song. Whenever he sang it—in May 1961 in Minneapolis, taping the tune in a friend's apartment (along with, that same night, "Pretty Polly," Rabbit Brown's "James Alley Blues," and "Henry Thomas' 'Fishing Blues"); in November that same year at his first concert, in New York at the Carnegie Recital Hall; or on the basement tapes—he brought everything he had to the story. His approach never changed. Alone, as in 1961, or surrounded by Danko's deep bass, Manuel's lap Hawaiian guitar, with his own acoustic guitar barely leading the music—it's so slow, it barely can be led; the melody pulls back against the singer—he gives himself up to the song, disappears into it, becoming all of its actors, with as much sympathy for the father as for the daughter as for the husband as for the son."

[S] "You're a Big Girl Now" (Bob Dylan)

Bob Dylan, *Blood on the Tracks* (1975); *Hard Rain* (1976); *Biograph/'75* (1985)
Ian Moore, *Ian Moore's Got the Green Grass* (1999)
Gerard Quintana and Jordi Batiste, *Els Miralls de Dylan* (1998)
Travis, single (2001)
Mary Lee's Corvette, *Blood on the Tracks* (2002)
Various Artists (performed by Sugar Black), *Blowin' in the Wind: A Reggae Tribute to Bob Dylan* (2002)
Various Artists (performed by Elin Sigvardsson), *May Your Song Always Be Sung: The Songs of Bob Dylan, Vol. 3* (2003)

One of six songs Dylan recorded in New York in September 1974 which he re-recorded later in the year for *Blood on the Tracks*, "You're a Big Girl Now" is a return to a theme common to Dylan's work in the '60s, and which ran, subtly, even through his brighter work of the early 1970s: abandonment. And while each of Dylan's releases of the song is different—as if he can't make his mind up on the whole messy subject—the portrait of a man romantically, spiritually, and physically bereft is always clear enough.

Perhaps taking its cue from Hank Williams's "I Can't Help It (If I'm Still in Love with You," another song in which the narrator observes from afar his former gal moving on to new romantic vistas, Dylan's leading man in "You're a Big Girl Now" is haunted by the realization that her instincts were correct. The songs share some lyrical qualities as well. Compare Hank's "Today I passed you on the street/And my heart fell at your feet/I can't help it if I'm still in love with you" with lyrics from "Big Girl," "Our conversation was short and sweet/It nearly swept me off-a my feet./And I'm back in the rain, oh, oh,/And you are on dry land./You made it there somehow/You're a big girl now."

"You're a Big Girl Now" is one of many songs from *Blood on the Tracks* in which Dylan pulled down the masks that had previously obscured the line between his song's narrators and their

Y

author. Pete Hamill, in his *Blood on the Tracks* liner notes, quotes Irish poet W.B. Yeats ("We make out of the quarrel with others rhetoric, but of the quarrel with ourselves, poetry") in portraying the songs on Dylan's masterful collection as the confessional product of a man searching for the emotional truth at the core of human interaction. It is a quarrel that can be heard in lines like "I can change, I swear, oh, oh,/See what you can do./I can make through,/You can make it too." And it is a quarrel that can be observed on every great work—be it a panel on the Parthenon frieze or *In the Wee Small Hours*, Frank Sinatra's assemblage of introspective, brokenhearted ballads. Ol' Blue Eyes didn't even ink any of those songs, yet it is obvious that he chose them for the same reasons that Dylan settled on the final track list for *Blood on the Tracks*: they are songs that cut to the marrow.

Dylan always denied that the tortured, agonizingly vulnerable songs on *Blood on the Tracks* were autobiographical, but somehow the denials could never ring true. When speaking of "You're a Big Girl Now" in the liner notes to *Biograph*, he observed, "I read that this was supposed to be about my wife. I wish somebody would ask me first before they go ahead and print stuff like that. I mean, it couldn't be about anybody else but my wife, right? Stupid and misleading jerks sometimes these interpreters are. Fools, they limit you to their own unimaginative mentality. They never stop to think that somebody has been exposed to experiences that they haven't been . . . anyway, it's not the experience that counts, it's the attitude towards the experience."

Okay, so call us stupid.

A song overflowing with remorse, "You're a Big Girl Now" was first performed with the 1976 version of the Rolling Thunder Revue as Dylan sang it as though he was both chiding his soon-to-be ex-wife Sara and still pining for her big-time—an odd but strangely effective

contradiction. Dylan kept the song close by for some shows during the globe-trotting 1978 tour but did not return to it until one 1987 concert with Tom Petty. A frequent Never Ending Tour inclusion, "You're A Big Girl" was performed in the late 1980s and throughout the 1990s, but rarely in the early '00s.

▣ "You're Gonna Make Me Lonesome When You Go" (Bob Dylan)

Bob Dylan, *Blood on the Tracks* (1975)
Shawn Colvin, *Cover Girl* (1994)
Starland Vocal Band, *Afternoon Delight* (1995)
Various Artists (performed by Christine Collister), *Outlaw Blues, Vol. 2* (1995)
Mary Lou Lord, *Live City Sounds* (2001)
Mary Lee's Corvette, *Blood on the Tracks* (2002)
Pat Nevins, *Shakey Zimmerman* (2003)

With bittersweet resignation, the singer bids adieu to a lover in "You're Gonna Make Me Lonesome When You Go." He convinces himself that they'll meet again, that he'll see her face in the blue sky, that'll he'll carry the best of what they shared with him forever . . . but his pain is never far from the surface as he tries his best to deal with a hopeless situation: "You could make me cry if you don't know./Can't remember what I was thinkin' of/You might be spoilin' me too much, love,/Yer gonna make me lonesome when you go." This is never more evident than when he compares their affair to Verlaine and Rimbaud, the French poets who were drawn into an unrequited, and ultimately violent, relationship. Still, Dylan sings this song with a wry smile on his face and it is, paradoxically, the *Blood on the Tracks* tune with the warmest heart. At times Dylan even sounds downright giddy, as when he sings, "Crickets talkin' back and forth in rhyme,/Blue river runnin' slow and lazy,/I could stay with you forever/And never realize the time." But even he knows that it was too good to

Y

last: "I'll look for you in old Honolulu, San Francisco, Ashtabula/Yer gonna have to leave me now, I know." Dylan's juicy, country-flavored harmonica work and light guitar strumming accompanied only by Tony Brown's bass on its official release contributes to the wistful aura coloring this bright song and make that breaking heart hurt even worse.

Dylan's only (and very few) Nashville-style performances of "You're Gonna Make Me Lonesome When You Go" came during the second phase of the Rolling Thunder Revue in 1976.

"You're Gonna Quit Me" (Traditional/Blind Blake)
aka "You're Goin' to Quit Me, Baby" "You Gonna Quit Me Blues"
Bob Dylan, *Good as I Been to You* (1992)
Blind Blake, *Complete Recorded Works, Volume 2 (1927–1928)* (1991)
Rev. Gary Davis, *Demons and Angels: The Ultimate Collection* (2001)

A neat country blues that nods at "Corrina Corrina," "Baby, Let Me Follow You Down," or any one of a number of different Piedmont blues songs from Dylan's debut album and early repertoire, "You're Gonna Quit Me" fits wonderfully into the dusty tapestry of archaic music found on *Good as I Been to You*, Dylan's first album of all cover material since *Dylan* and *Self Portrait* twenty years earlier. Though Dylan gives the song an ethereal reading here, its simple structure and refreshingly unhurried pace lack some of the haunting qualities that mark the balance of the songs Dylan explored in his roots experiment, rendering "You're Gonna Quit Me" more forgettable. Still, he sounds like some late-nineteenth-century stag man holding court in the backroom of an East St. Louis sporting house in this easygoing honky-tonk arrangement.

Dylan's lazy rendition of "You're Gonna Quit Me" is a clear homage to Blind Blake's 1927 recording, but his interest in the song may also

lead to Rev. Gary Davis, another blind bluesman whose own "You're Goin' Quit Me, Baby" bares more than a passing resemblance to Blake's.

After recording "You're Gonna Quit Me" for *Good as I Been To You*, Dylan performed the song nearly thirty times in 1993 before returning to it in 1999 when he led off a trio of European shows with an acoustic band rendering.

"You're No Good" (Jesse Fuller)
aka "Crazy About a Woman"
See also "San Francisco Bay Blues"
Bob Dylan, *Bob Dylan* (1962)
Jesse Fuller, *Brother Lowdown* (1959)

"You're No Good" was the very first song that listeners heard when they plunked their turntable needles (remember those?) on the A-side of Dylan's debut disc. His frenetic rendition of Fuller's chestnut is addressed to a woman the singer claims he loves but doesn't know why. But other than the officially released version on *Bob Dylan*, the only other preserved Dylan rendition of "You're No Good" comes from a recording made at the home of some early New York City friends (the McKenzies) around the same time he cut that first album.

According to Robert Shelton's liner notes from *Bob Dylan*: "The number that opens this album, 'You're No Good,' was learned from Jesse Fuller, the West Coast singer. Its vaudeville flair and exaggeration are used to heighten the mock anger of the lyrics."

"You're Too Late" (Lefty Frizzell/Herman P. Willis)
Lefty Frizzell, *Life's Like Poetry* (1992)

Dylan's one and only performance of "You're Too Late" came in 1999, amid a period during the Never Ending Tour when he and his band were also covering material by Hank Williams and Buddy Holly. The song was first released as a single in 1954 and is not considered one of Lefty Frizzell's most memorable. It was cowritten with the elusive Herman P. Willis, with whom Frizzell wrote at least four other songs: "I've Been Away Too Long," "Tragic Letter," "Two Hearts Broken Now," and "You Can Always Count on Me."

A hero of honky-tonk, Lefty Frizzell (born William Orville Frizzell, March 31, 1928, Corsicana, Texas; died July 19, 1975, Nashville) defined the genre's vocal style for generations to come—smoothing out the rough edges by singing longer, flowing phrases and taking it into the mainstream while retaining its gnarly, roadhouse roots.

Maybe if he had died young and tragically with but a slim catalogue to his name, Frizzell's name would be whispered in the same hushed reverence as "Jimmie Rodgers" or "Robert Johnson." But he was an innovator in every way, who not only influenced the way a song can be sung (everybody from George Jones to George Strait owes him a tip o' the hat on that score), but was a stylistic original. His fringed-sleeved, rhinestone-studded Nudie suits and decorated guitars added a zesty, urban touch to country music.

Frizzell grew up in El Dorado, Arkansas, after his father, a footloose roughneck, moved the family from one oil-drilling job to another when Lefty was a baby. One of eight children, he copped his moniker as the result of a schoolyard fight—not, as is usually reported, during a career as a teenage Golden Glove boxer.

Frizzell slowly made a name for himself as a regional barroom and radio performer, both in the Dallas-Waco honky-tonk/barn dance circuit playing in others' bands covering Rodgers and Ernest Tubbs hits and as a country troubadour whose travels took him as far west as Las Vegas and as far down as a jail cell, where he did a short term for statutory rape. Settling in as a regular at the Ace of Clubs in Big Springs, Texas, upon his release, he knocked the lobes off Columbia A&R man Don Law, who chanced upon his act in 1950.

In astoundingly short order, Frizzell recorded "If You've Got the Money (I've Got the Time)," a single that, due to his upfront lyrics and eccentric vocalisms (accentuated by a streamlined ensemble that introduced a fiddle, subtracted a steel guitar, and anticipated the classic Nashville sound by some years), won immediate acclaim and shot to No. 1 on the charts.

Frizzell's halcyon year was 1951, when he had four songs riding in the country Top Ten at the same time—a feat never achieved by any artist in any category on any chart any time since. With popularity like that, Lefty and his band, the Western Cherokees, were in high gear, recording hundreds of singles, making the scene at both the *Grand Ole Opry* and the *Louisiana Hayride* radio shows, and touring constantly over the next several years performing his new bag of songs, often with gimmicky, parenthetical titles.

Riding high as he might, Frizzell's drinking was beginning to take its toll. He became known for his volatile unpredictability as much as for his ability to produce a song on demand. In 1952, he fired his manager and his band, quit the *Opry*, and headed to Los Angeles, where he landed a job on *Town Hall Party* (the displaced Southerner's version of the *Opry*), turning out a few hits over the next couple of years.

But Frizzell's career stalled through the end of the 1950s. Whether it was Columbia's waning interest in his material, his alcoholism, or the fact that the creative well had run dry is a bit hard to definitively confirm. Suffice it to say that it wasn't until he recorded "Long Black Veil" in 1959 that he was temporarily able to resuscitate himself by abandoning the beer-soaked honky-tonk sound and riding Nashville's story-song craze, which peaked with his last hurrah in 1964, a song called "Saginaw, Michigan."

The last decade of Frizzell's life was not a pretty picture, for while he did perform until

Y

his death, the ravages of firewater, record company squabbles, and life on the endless ribbon of highway took their inevitable toll.

Maybe Frizzell had to die to be rediscovered; a new generation of artists hailed him as an influence and an idol. It was one thing for older guys like Merle Haggard, Willie Nelson, and George Jones to sing his praises, but when the younger guys George Strait and Randy Travis began kowtowing in homage of Saint Lefty, the reissue beast had to be loosed, and there is no shortage of comprehensive Frizzell collections available. His posthumous 1982 induction into the Country Music Hall of Fame sealed the deal, and a listen to any hard country music will reveal more than an echo of his voice.

[S] "You Took My Breath Away" (Traveling Wilburys)

Traveling Wilburys, *Traveling Wilburys, Vol. 3* (1990)

Dylan is a virtual nonentity in this Wilburys homage to Roy Orbison featuring Tom Petty's lead vocals and George Harrison's nifty slide guitar work.

[S] "You Wanna Ramble" (Herman Parker, Jr./Bob Dylan, additional lyrics)

(AKA "I Wanna Ramble")
Junior Parker, single (1954); *Junior's Blues: The Duke Recordings, Vol. 1*
Bob Dylan, *Knocked Out Loaded* (1986)

Dylan gets down with this minor gutbucket blues on *Knocked Out Loaded*, relishing the chance to let go in the studio in a manner that suggests "You Wanna Ramble" would have been a choice concert inclusion. Dylan added some lyrics (specifically the line "What happens tomorrow/Is on your head, not mine," itself drawn from a snatch of Burl Ives's dialogue in the film *The Big Country*) when he recorded "Ramble" and apparently copyrighted it that year as well. The *Knocked Out Loaded* music book, however, does not list Dylan's Special Rider Music as the song's co-publisher.

The honey-voiced Herman Parker (born March 3, 1927 or March 27, 1932, Clarksdale, Mississippi; died November 18, 1971, Blue Island, Illinois) practically grew up on Beale Street and is known as both "Little" and "Junior" (or both). As a child, Junior Parker sang in local gospel choirs around Clarksdale, Mississippi. In his early twenties, he learned how to play the harmonica from Sonny Boy Williamson II (Rice Miller). It was Williamson who eventually let Parker lead his local band when he went on the road.

Parker also played with Howlin' Wolf and B.B. King. He began recording for the Sun label around 1953. Although in later years he was never as big as he was in the 1950s, he never stopped performing and recording. His greatest success came when Elvis Presley recorded "Mystery Train" for Sun Records in 1953. He died after surgery for a brain tumor.

[S] "You Win Again" (Hank Williams)

See also Hank Williams
Hank Williams, *40 Greatest Hits* (1978)
Fats Domino, *Let the Four Winds Blow* (1961)
Ray Charles, *Modern Sounds in Country & Western Music* (1962)
Jerry Lee Lewis, *The Greatest Live Show on Earth* (1964)
Gerry & the Pacemakers, *I'll Be There* (1965)
Del Shannon, *Del Shannon Sings Hank Williams* (1965)
The Grateful Dead, *Europe '72* (1972)

If ever there was an autobiographical song, Hank Williams's "You Win Again" may have to be it. Is it any coincidence that the song was recorded only a day after his divorce from his wife Audrey became official on July 10, 1952? This is a song that could have been transcribed from his diary. With lines like "You have no heart, you have no shame/You take true love and give the blame," Williams sang the song like a guy who was going to be licking his wounds for a long time to come. But like all of his best songs, he is able to take well-worn subjects like betrayal and invest in them an immediacy that never gets old.

Dylan was no doubt familiar with the song decades before his summer 2003 one-off performance of "You Win Again" with the retooled Dead. The oddity of *Europe '72*, Jerry Garcia's cover of this Hank Williams special was only performed by the Grateful Dead at a score of shows between November 1971 and September 1972 before its revival with Dylan.

Z

William Zantzinger

See "The Lonesome Death of Hattie Carroll"

Warren Zevon

Born January 24, 1947, Chicago; died September 7, 2003, Los Angeles

With a pulp-fiction imagination; gallows humor; literary bent; and a colorful, picaresque past, Warren Zevon cut a paradoxical swath through the fields of popular Americana—like a psychedelic Grim Reaper mixing hard-boiled, cinematic stories with tender, romantic confessions. Songs like "Werewolves of London," "Poor, Poor Pitiful Me," "Lawyers, Guns and Money," and "I'll Sleep When I'm Dead" were terse, action-packed tales siphoning a screenplay's worth of narrative, character development, and dramatic irony into a four-minute yarn that often starred Death in the closing scene.

Discussing the macabre element in his music, Warren Zevon once said, "I can't disagree that there's a violent quality in my work, and it may not be something that familiar in

pop songs. But in any other art form, it's the artist's prerogative to inject the adrenaline. Restraint has never been one of my virtues."

Yet he was capable of exhibiting muted qualities of vulnerability and longing in ballads like "Mutineer," "Accidentally Like a Martyr," and "Hasten Down the Wind."

Zevon's odd upbringing may have contributed to his creative development. Raised mostly in Arizona and Los Angeles, he had a Russian-Jewish father who was a professional gambler—a career choice that kept the family on the move—and a mother, a sickly woman, who was a Mormon.

A classically-trained pianist, Zevon admired composers like Igor Stravinsky and Aaron Copland. But he also loved rock 'n' roll and folk music, picking up a guitar as a teen. After his parents divorced, he drove to New York City in a sports car his father won in a card game with hopes of cracking the folk circuit.

Zevon's wickedly black sense of humor and love for tough rock 'n' roll fared better in L.A., where he formed Lyme and Cybelle, a duo act with Violet Santangelo, and began to get his songs heard. One of the groups who came upon his work was the Turtles, who recorded one of his early, brighter songs, "Like the Seasons." This version received wide exposure when pressed on the B-side of the hit single "Happy Together," and the royalty checks from that score not only helped pay the rent for years, but allowed Zevon to expand his horizons.

Though a 1969 debut LP, *Wanted Dead or Alive*, was ignored, Zevon entrenched himself in the city's music scene, doing everything from writing commercial jingles to fronting the Everly Brothers backup band. And his emergence into the coterie of new, younger local songwriters like Jackson Browne and J.D. Souther helped bring depth to California's pallid mid-1970s soft rock. By then he had become a popular songwriting pro by tempering his dark streak with some evocative and personal ballads surveying the lifestyle trappings found in the City of Lost Angels.

In short order, Zevon graduated to a higher echelon of notice when Linda Ronstadt picked his "Hasten Down the Wind" as the title song of her 1976 album; Browne produced *Warren Zevon* that same year; and a 1978 follow-up, *Excitable Boy*, made the Top Ten in 1978. A single from that album, "Werewolves of London," reached No. 21 on the charts.

Bad Luck Streak in Dancing School, Zevon's 1980 album, was followed by the live *Stand in the Fire* collection, which showed him to be a ferocious performer, far edgier than his L.A. songwriting peers. *The Envoy*, released in 1982, included a mysterious elegy to Elvis Presley while evoking the sound of the 1960s girl groups. In all his work, Zevon's word and sound pictures captured a gamut of moods and feelings, boisterously offering a precise grasp of human nature always colored with the bizarre, violent, rowdy, and comic.

But Zevon fell fast and hard, succumbing to the pressures of success and temptation. Abusing alcohol and drugs, he began packing heat and, unable to maintain control onstage or off, was soon in the revolving door of rehab and relapse. No Zevon albums were released between 1982 and 1987. Realizing, as he said years later, that alcoholism is "a real coward's death," he reemerged clean and stayed that way, developing a steady, respected career as both a touring and recording artist.

Sentimental Hygiene, his 1987 return effort, featured backing by members of R.E.M. and appearances by Dylan, Neil Young, and David Lindley. His work with R.E.M. continued with a release under the name Hindu Love Gods in 1990. And a move to theme-song and score writing for television's *Tales from the Crypt*, *Route 66*, and

Tekwar spread his round-peg-in-a-square-hole sensibility deeper into the mainstream.

Album releases continued with *Transverse City* in 1989, *Mr. Bad Example* in 1991, *Learning to Flinch* in 1993, *Mutineer* in 1995, *Life'll Kill Ya* in 2000, and *My Ride's Here* in 2002, the year Zevon was diagnosed with untreatable lung cancer. The title song of the latter album was, ironically, about a hearse, and it was one of several songs that became self-fulfilling prophecies. On the dark twists in his life and art, Zevon commented in 2002, "I keep asking myself how I suddenly was thrust into the position of travel agent for death. But then, of course, the whole point of why it's so strange is that I had already assigned myself that role so many years ago of writing ago."

In an unprecedented act of public homage, Dylan showcased several Zevon songs during his fall 2002 Never Ending Tour: "Accidentally Like a Martyr," "Boom Boom Mancini," "Lawyers, Guns and Money," and "Mutineer."

In a brazen act of winking back at the Grim Reaper, Zevon's slide into the abyss was one of the most public in recent memory. After announcing his terminal condition on *Late Show with David Letterman*, a show on which he had been a frequent guest musician, he invited a camera crew from VH1 into the recording sessions to make a documentary about what was sure to be his final album.

To be sure, that album, *The Wind* (2003), was full of death-haunted songs like "Prison Grove," "Keep Me in Your Heart," and a cover of Dylan's "Knockin' on Heaven's Door." But Zevon's devilish, sardonic humor was also in irrepressible evidence. As he sings in the opening line of the first track, "Dirty Life and Times": "Some days I feel like my shadow's casting me."

During the recording of *The Wind*, Zevon said he wanted to make one final point to his friends and admirers: "This was a nice deal: life."

BIBLIOGRAPHY

Ashley, Al, ed. *Golden Encyclopedia of Folk Music.* Hasbrouck Heights, NJ: Lewis Music Publishing, 1985; distributed by Hal Leonard Publishing.

Baez, Joan. *The Joan Baez Songbook.* New York: Ryerson Music Publishers, 1964.

Bauldie, John. *Wanted Man: In Search of Bob Dylan.* London: Black Spring, 1990.

Berry, Chuck. *Chuck Berry: The Autobiography.* New York: Harmony Books, 1987.

Blanton, DeAnne, and Lauren M. Cook. *They Fought Like Demons: Women Soldiers in the American Civil War.* Baton Rouge: Louisiana State University Press, 2002.

Brend, Mark. *Rock and Roll Doctor—Lowell George: Guitarist, Songwriter, and Founder of Little Feat.* London: Backbeat Books, 2002.

Bronson, Bertrand Harris, ed. *The Traditional Tunes of the Child Ballads.* 4 vols. Princeton, NJ: Princeton University Press, 1959–72.

Broonzy, William. *Big Bill Blues.* With Yannick Bruynoghe. London: Cassell, 1955.

Burns, Peter. *Curtis Mayfield: People Never Give Up.* London: Sanctuary Publishing, 2003.

Cable, Paul. *Bob Dylan: His Unreleased Recordings.* New York: Schirmer Books, 1980.

Canfield, Michael, and Alan J. Weberman. *Coup d'État in America: The CIA and the Assassination of John F. Kennedy.* New York: Third Press, 1975.

Carlin, Richard. *English and American Folk Music.* New York: Facts on File, 1987.

Carter, Rubin "Hurricane." *The Sixteenth Round: From Number 1 Contender to #45472.* New York: Viking Press, 1974.

Cash, Johnny. *Man in Black: His Own Story in His Own Words.* Grand Rapids, MI: Zondervan, 1975.

Child, Francis James. *The English and Scottish Popular Ballads.* 5 vols. New York: Dover Publications, 1965. Reprint of first edition, 1882–1898.

Clayson, Alan, and Spencer Leigh. *The Walrus Was Ringo: 101 Beatles Myths Debunked.* New Malden, UK: Chrome Dreams, 2003.

Cohn, Lawrence, ed. *Nothing but the Blues: The Music and the Musicians.* New York: Abbeville Press, 1993.

Cole, William. *Folk Songs of England, Ireland, Scotland, and Wales.* Garden City, NY: Doubleday, 1961.

Collins, Ronald K. L., and David M. Skover. *The Trials of Lenny Bruce: The Fall and Rise of an American Icon.* Naperville, IL: Sourcebooks MediaFusion, 2002.

Cott, Jonathan. *Dylan.* Garden City, NY: Doubleday, 1984.

Daniels, Charlie. *The Devil Went Down to Georgia.* Atlanta: Peachtree Publications, 1985.

Davis, Francis. *The History of the Blues: The Roots, the Music, the People from Charley Patton to Robert Cray.* New York: Hyperion, 1995.

Davis, Stephen. *Old Gods Almost Dead: The 40-Year Odyssey of the Rolling Stones.* New York: Broadway Books, 2001.

Day, Aidan. *Jokerman: Reading the Lyrics of Bob Dylan.* Oxford, UK, and New York: Basil Blackwell, 1988.

Dixon, Willie. *I Am the Blues: The Willie Dixon Story.* With Don Snowden. New York: Da Capo Press, 1989.

Dundas, Glen. *Tangled Up in Tapes.* 3rd ed. Thunder Bay, ON: SMA Services, 1994.

Dylan, Bob. *Drawn Blank.* New York: Random House, 1994.

———. *Lyrics, 1962–1985.* 2nd ed. New York: Alfred A. Knopf, 1985.

———. *The Original.* New York: Warner Brothers, 1968.

———. *Tarantula.* New York: Macmillan, 1971.

———. *Writings and Drawings.* New York: Alfred A. Knopf, 1973.

Earle, Steve. *Doghouse Roses.* Boston: Houghton Mifflin, 2001.

Escott, Colin. *Hank Williams: The Biography.* With George Merritt and William MacEwen. Boston: Little, Brown, 1994.

———, and Martin Hawkins. *Good Rockin' Tonight: Sun Records and the Birth of Rock 'n' Roll. New York: St. Martin's Press, 1991.*

Evers, Myrlie. *For Us, the Living.* With William Peters. Garden City, NY: Doubleday, 1967.

Flanagan, Bill. *Written in My Soul: Rock's Great Songwriters Talk About Creating Their Music.* Chicago: Contemporary Books, 1986.

Fowke, Edith. *The Penguin Book of Canadian Folk Songs.* London: Penguin Books, 1973.

Gans, David. *Conversations with the Dead: The Grateful Dead Interview Book.* New York: Citadel Underground, 1991.

Gill, Andy. *Don't Think Twice, It's All Right: Bob Dylan, the Early Years.* New York: Thunder's Mouth Press, 1998.

———, and Keith Odegard. *A Simple Twist of Fate: Bob Dylan and the Making of* Blood on the Tracks. New York: Da Capo Press, 2004.

Goddard, Donald. *Joey.* New York: Harper & Row, 1974.

Goldstein, Richard, ed. *The Poetry of Rock.* New York: Bantam Books, 1969.

Gray, Michael. *Song & Dance Man III: The Art of Bob Dylan.* London and New York: Continuum International Publishing Group, 2000.

———, and John Bauldie, eds. *All Across the Telegraph: A Bob Dylan Handbook.* London: Sidgwick & Jackson, 1987.

Grover, Carrie B., ed. *A Heritage of Songs.* Reprint ed. Norwood, PA: Norwood Editions, 1973.

Guralnick, Peter. *Lost Highway: Journeys & Arrivals of American Musicians.* Boston: D. R. Godine, 1979.

Guthrie, Woody. *Bound for Glory.* New York: E. P. Dutton, 1943.

Hajdu, David. *Positively 4th Street: The Lives and Times of Joan Baez, Bob Dylan, Mimi Baez Fariña, and Richard Fariña.* New York: Farrar, Straus & Giroux, 2001.

Hardy, Phil, and Dave Laing. *The Faber Companion to 20th-Century Popular Music.* London and Boston: Faber & Faber, 1990.

Harris, Michael W. *The Rise of Gospel Blues: The Music of Thomas Andrew Dorsey in the Urban Church.* New York: Oxford University Press, 1992.

Harrison, George. *I, Me, Mine.* New York: Simon and Schuster, 1980.

Herdman, John. *Voice Without Restraint: A Study of Bob Dylan's Lyrics and Their Background.* New York: Delilah Books, 1982.

Herzhaft, Gerhard. *Encyclopedia of the Blues.* Fayetteville: University of Arkansas Press, 1992.

Heylin, Clinton. *Bob Dylan: Behind the Shades—A Biography.* New York: Summit Books, 1991.

———. *Bob Dylan: A Life in Stolen Moments: Day by Day, 1941–1995.* New York: Schirmer Books, 1996.

———. *Bootleg: The Secret History of the Other Recording Industry.* New York: St. Martin's Press, 1995.

———. *Can You Feel the Silence? Van Morrison: A New Biography.* London and New York: Viking Penguin, 2002.

———. *Dylan's Daemon Lover: The Tangled Tale of a 450-Year-Old Pop Ballad.* London: Helter Skelter Publishing, 1999.

Hinton, Brian. *Celtic Crossroads: The Art of Van Morrison.* London: Sanctuary Publishing, 1997.

Hitchcock, H. Wiley, and Stanley Sadie, eds. *The New Grove Dictionary of American Music.* 4 vols. New York: Macmillan, 1986.

Horstman, Dorothy, comp. *Sing Your Heart Out, Country Boy.* New York: E. P. Dutton, 1975.

Humphries, Patrick. *The Complete Guide to the Music of Bob Dylan.* London: Omnibus Books, 1995.

———, and John Bauldie. *Oh No! Not Another Bob Dylan Book.* Brentwood, UK: Square One Books, 1991.

Huntington, Gale, and Lani Herrmann, eds. *Sam Henry's Songs of the People.* Athens: University of Georgia Press, 1990.

Jackson, Blair. *Goin' Down the Road: A Grateful Dead Traveling Companion.* New York: Harmony Books, 1992.

Kallmann, Helmut, Gilles Potvin, and Kenneth Winters, eds. *Encyclopedia of Music in Canada.* Toronto: University of Toronto Press, 1981.

Kennedy, Peter, ed. *Folksongs of Britain and Ireland.* London: Cassell, 1975.

King, Bill. "The Artist in the Marketplace." PhD diss., University of North Carolina at Chapel Hill, 1975.

Kingston, Victoria. *Simon and Garfunkel: The Definitive Biography.* London: Sidgwick & Jackson, 1996.

Klein, Joe. *Woody Guthrie: A Life.* New York: Alfred A. Knopf, 1980.

Kooper, Al. *Backstage Passes: Rock 'n' Roll Life in the Sixties.* With Ben Edmonds. New York: Stein and Day, 1977.

Krogsgaard, Michael. *Positively Bob Dylan: A Thirty-Year Discography, Concert & Recording Session Guide, 1960–1991.* Ann Arbor, MI: Popular Culture, 1991.

———. *Twenty Years of Recording: The Bob Dylan Reference Book.* Copenhagen: Scandinavian Institute for Rock Research, 1981.

Lair, John. *Songs Lincoln Loved.* New York: Duell, Sloan, and Pearce, 1954.

Lee, C. P. *Like the Night: Bob Dylan and the Road to the Manchester Free Trade Hall.* London: Helter Skelter Publishing, 1998.

Leisy, James. *The Folk Song Abecedary.* New York: Hawthorn Books, 1966.

Lisle, Tim de, ed. *Lives of the Great Songs.* London: Penguin Books, 1995.

Lisseur, Robert. *Lisseur's Encyclopedia of Popular Music in America: 1888 to the Present.* New York: Facts on File, 1996.

The Little Red Song Book. Chicago: International Workers of the World, 1913.

Lloyd, A. L. *Folk Song in England.* London: Lawrence & Wishart, 1967.

Lomax, Alan. *The Folk Songs of North America.* Garden City, NY: Doubleday, 1960.

———. *Hard Hitting Songs for Hard-Hit People.* New York: Oak Publications, 1967.

———. *The Land Where the Blues Began.* London: Methuen, 1993.

Lomax, John A. *Adventures of a Ballad Hunter.* New York: Macmillan, 1947.

———. *Songs of the Cattle Trail and Cow Camp.* New York: Macmillan, 1919.

———, and Alan Lomax. *American Ballads and Folk Songs.* New York: Macmillan, 1934.

Longhi, Jim. *Woody, Cisco, & Me.* Urbana: University of Illinois Press, 1997.

McGregor, Craig, ed. *Bob Dylan, The Early Years: A Retrospective.* New York: Da Capo Press, 1990.

McKeen, William. *Bob Dylan: A Bio-Bibliography.* Westport, CT: Greenwood Press, 1993.

McNally, Dennis. *Long Strange Trip: The Inside History of the Grateful Dead.* New York: Broadway Books, 2002.

Malone, Bill C. *Country Music U.S.A.: A Fifty-Year History.* Austin: Published for the American Folklore Society by the University of Texas Press, 1968.

Marcus, Greil. *Invisible Republic: Bob Dylan's Basement Tapes.* New York: Henry Holt and Company, 1997. (Later retitled and published as *The Old, Weird America: The World of Bob Dylan's Basement Tapes.* New York: Picador, 2001.)

Marshall, Scott. *Restless Pilgrim: The Spiritual Journey of Bob Dylan.* With Marcia Ford. Lake Mary, FL: Relevant Books, 2002.

Mellers, Wilfrid *A Darker Shade of Pale: A Backdrop to Bob Dylan.* London: Faber & Faber, 1984.

Michel, Steve. *The Bob Dylan Concordance.* Grand Junction, CO: Rolling Tomes, 1992.

Nogowski, John. *Bob Dylan: A Descriptive, Critical Discography and Filmography, 1961–1993.* Jefferson, NC: McFarland, 1995.

Norman, Phillip. *Shout! The Beatles and Their Generation.* New York: Fireside/Simon & Schuster, 1981.

Oliver, Paul. *The Meaning of the Blues.* New York: Collier, 1963. (Originally published as *Blues Fell This Morning: The Meaning of the Blues.* London: Cassell, 1960.)

———. *Screening the Blues: Aspects of the Blues Tradition.* London: Cassell, 1968.

———. *Songsters and Saints: Vocal Traditions on Race Records.* Cambridge, UK, and New York: Cambridge University Press, 1984.

Perkins, Carl, and David McGee. *Go, Cat, Go! The Life and Times of Carl Perkins, the King of Rockabilly.* New York: Hyperion, 1996.

Pickering, Stephen. *Bob Dylan Approximately: A Portrait of the Jewish Poet in Search of God.* New York: McKay, 1975.

Porterfield, Nolan. *Jimmie Rodgers: The Life and Times of America's Blue Yodeler.* Urbana: University of Illinois Press, 1979.

Pruett, Barbara S. *Marty Robbins: Fast Cars and Country Music.* Metuchen, NJ: Scarecrow Press, 1990.

Riley, Tim. *Hard Rain: A Dylan Commentary.* New York: Alfred A. Knopf, 1992.

Rimbaud: Complete Works, Selected Letters. Translated by Wallace Fowlie. Chicago: University of Chicago Press, 1966.

Ritchie, Jean. *Singing Family of the Cumberlands.* New York: Oak Publications, 1963.

Saga, Junichi. *Confessions of a Yakuza: A Life in Japan's Underworld.* Translated by John Bester. Tokyo and New York: Kodansha International, 1991.

Sandburg, Carl, comp. *The American Songbag.* New York: Harcourt, Brace, 1927.

Santelli, Robert. *The Big Book of Blues: A Biographical Encyclopedia.* New York: Penguin Books, 1993.

Scaduto, Anthony. *Bob Dylan: An Intimate Biography.* New York: Grosset & Dunlap, 1971.

Scobie, Stephen. *Alias Bob Dylan.* Red Deer, AB: Red Deer College Press, 1991.

Secrest, Meryle. *Somewhere for Me: A Biography of Richard Rodgers.* New York: Alfred A. Knopf, 2001.

Shelton, Robert. *No Direction Home: The Life and Music of Bob Dylan.* New York: Beech Tree Books/William Morrow, 1986.

Shepard, Sam. *Rolling Thunder Logbook.* New York: Viking Press, 1977.

Silber, Irwin, ed. *Reprints from* Sing Out!, *The Folk Song Magazine.* 11 vols. New York: Oak Publications. Vol. 8, 1965; vol. 9, 1966.

———, and Ethel Raim, eds. *American Favorite Ballads: Tunes and Songs as Sung by Pete Seeger.* New York: Oak Publications, 1961.

Simmons, Garner. *Peckinpah: A Portrait in Montage.* Austin: University of Texas Press, 1982.

Sloman, Larry. *On the Road with Bob Dylan: Rolling with the Thunder.* New York: Bantam Books, 1978.

Snow, Hank. *The Hank Snow Story.* With Jack Ownbey and Bob Burris. Urbana: University of Illinois Press, in association with the Canadian Country Music Hall of Fame, 1994.

Sounes, Howard. *Down the Highway: The Life of Bob Dylan.* New York: Grove Press, 2001.

Spitz, Bob. *Dylan: A Biography.* New York: McGraw-Hill, 1989.

Stambler, Irwin. *Encyclopedia of Pop, Rock & Soul. New York: St. Martin's Press, 1974.*

———, and Grelun Landon. *Encyclopedia of Folk, Country and Western Music.* New York: St. Martin's Press, 1969.

Stein, Jean. *Edie: An American Biography.* Edited with George Plimpton. New York: Alfred A. Knopf, 1982.

Thomson, Elizabeth, and David Gutman, eds. *The Dylan Companion.* New York: Delta Books, 1990.

Von Schmidt, Eric, and Jim Rooney. *Baby, Let Me Follow You Down.* Garden City, NY: Anchor Books 1979.

Walker, Jerry Jeff. *Gypsy Songman.* Emeryville, CA: Woodford Press, 1999.

Wallis, Michael. *Pretty Boy: The Life and Times of Charles Arthur Floyd.* New York: St. Martin's Press, 1992.

Warner, Anne. *Traditional American Folk Songs from the Anne & Frank Warner Collection.* Syracuse, NY: Syracuse University Press, 1984.

Waterman, Christopher A. "Race Music: Bo Chatmon, 'Corrine Corrina,' and the Excluded Middle." In *Music and the Racial Imagination,* edited by Ronald M. Padano and Philip V. Bohlman. Chicago: University of Chicago Press, 2000.

Weberman, Alan J. *My Life in Garbology.* New York: Stonehill, 1980.

Whitfield, Stephen J. *A Death in the Delta: The Story of Emmett Till.* New York: Free Press, 1988.

Williams, Juan. *Eyes on the Prize: America's Civil Rights Years, 1954–1965.* New York: Viking Press, 1987.

Williams, Paul. *Performing Artist: The Music of Bob Dylan.* Vol. 1, *1960—1973.* Novato, CA: Underwood-Miller, 1990.

———. *Bob Dylan: Performing Artist. Vol. 2, The Middle Years, 1974–1986. Novato, CA: Underwood-Miller, 1992.*

———. *Dylan—What Happened?* Glen Ellen, CA: Entwhistle Books, 1979.

———. *Watching the River Flow: Observations on Bob Dylan's Art-in-Progress, 1966–1995.* London: Omnibus Press, 1996

Witting, Robin. *Isaiah for Guitar: A Guide to John Wesley Harding.* North Lincolnshire, UK: Exploding Rooster Books, 1997.

Wolfe, Charles, and Kip Lornell. *The Life and Legend of Leadbelly.* New York: HarperCollins, 1992.

Worth, Fred L., and Steve D. Tamerius. *Elvis: His Life from A to Z.* Chicago: Contemporary Books, 1988.

Yorke, Ritchie. *Van Morrison: Into the Music.* London: Charisma Books, 1975.

Zollo, Paul. *Songwriters on Songwriting, Expanded Fourth Edition.* New York: Da Capo Press, 1997.

Zwonitzer, Mark. *Will You Miss Me When I'm Gone?: The Carter Family and Their Legacy in American Music.* With Charles Hirshberg. New York: Simon and Schuster, 2002.

■ Various Web Sites Consulted

http://www.allmusic.com

http://www.bjorner.com/Chronologies.htm

http://www.bobdylan.com

http://www.bobdylanroots.com

http://www.contemplator.com/folk.html

http://dylancoveralbums.com/songsa.htm

http://www.cyberhymnal.org

http://db.dylantree.com

http://www.dylanchords.com/

http://www.expectingrain.com

http://www.expectingrain.com/dok/div/influences.html

http://www.folkinfo.org/songs/default.asp

http://www.halloffame.org

http://www.interferenza.com/bcs/interv.htm

http://www.rockabillyhall.com

http://www.songwritershalloffame.org

CREDITS

Bob Dylan Lyrics

"City of Gold"
Copyright © 1980 Special Rider Music

"Coming from the Heart (the Road Is Long)"
by Bob Dylan and Helena Springs
Copyright © 1979 Special Rider Music

"Covenant Woman"
Copyright © 1980 Special Rider Music

"Cry a While"
Copyright © 2001 Special Rider Music

"Dark Eyes"
Copyright © 1985 Special Rider Music

"Dead Man, Dead Man"
Copyright © 1981 Special Rider Music

"Dear Landlord"
Copyright © 1968; renewed 1996 Dwarf Music

"The Death of Emmett Till"
Copyright © 1963; renewed 1991 Special Rider Music

"Desolation Row"
Copyright © 1965; renewed 1993 Special Rider Music

"Dignity"
Copyright © 1991 Special Rider Music

"Dirge"
Copyright © 1973 Ram's Horn Music

"Down in the Flood (Crash on the Levee)"
Copyright © 1967; renewed 1995 Dwarf Music

"Driftin' Too Far from Shore"
Copyright © 1986 Special Rider Music

"Eternal Circle"
Copyright © 1963; renewed 1991 Special Rider Music

"Every Grain of Sand"
Copyright © 1981 Special Rider Music

"Farewell, Angelina"
Copyright © 1965; renewed 1993 Special Rider Music

"Floater (Too Much to Ask)"
Copyright © 2001 Special Rider Music

"It's All Over Now, Baby Blue"
Copyright © 1965; renewed 1993 Special Rider
Music

It's Alright Ma (I'm Only Bleeding)"
Copyright © 1965; renewed 1993 Special Rider
Music

"It Takes a Lot to Laugh, It Takes a Train to
Cry"
Copyright © 1965; renewed 1993 Special Rider
Music

"Joey"
Copyright © 1975 Ram's Horn Music

"John Brown"
Copyright © 1963; renewed 1991 Special Rider
Music

"Jokerman"
Copyright © 1983 Special Rider Music

"Just Like a Woman"
Copyright © 1966; renewed 1994 Dwarf Music

"Just Like Tom Thumb's Blues"
Copyright © 1965; renewed 1993 Special Rider
Music

"Leopard-Skin Pill-Box Hat"
Copyright © 1966; renewed 1994 Dwarf Music

"Let Me Die in My Footsteps"
Copyright © 1963; renewed 1991 Special Rider
Music

"License to Kill"
Copyright © 1983 Special Rider Music

"Lonesome Day Blues"
Copyright © 2001 Special Rider Music

"Lord Protect My Child"
Copyright © 1983 Special Rider Music

"Love Minus Zero/No Limit"
Copyright © 1965; renewed 1993 Special Rider
Music

"Love Sick"
Copyright © 1997 Special Rider Music

"Maggie's Farm"
Copyright © 1965; renewed 1993 Special Rider
Music

"Make You Feel My Love"
Copyright © 1997 Special Rider Music
All rights reserved. International copyright
secured. Reprinted by permission.

"Man in the Long Black Coat"
Copyright © 1989 Special Rider Music
All rights reserved. International copyright
secured. Reprinted by permission.

"Man on the Street"
Copyright © 1962; renewed 1990 MCA
All rights reserved. International copyright
secured. Reprinted by permission.

"Maybe Someday"
Copyright © 1986 Special Rider Music
All rights reserved. International copyright
secured. Reprinted by permission.

"Million Dollar Bash"
Copyright © 1967; renewed 1995 Dwarf Music
All rights reserved. International copyright
secured. Reprinted by permission.

"Moonlight"
Copyright © 2001 Special Rider Music
All rights reserved. International copyright
secured. Reprinted by permission.

"Most of the Time"
Copyright © 1989 Special Rider Music
All rights reserved. International copyright
secured. Reprinted by permission.

"Mr. Tambourine Man"
Copyright © 1964; renewed 1992 Special Rider
Music
All rights reserved. International copyright
secured. Reprinted by permission.

"Neighborhood Bully"
Copyright © 1983 Special Rider Music
All rights reserved. International copyright
secured. Reprinted by permission.

"Never Say Goodbye"
Copyright © 1973 Ram's Horn Music
All rights reserved. International copyright
secured. Reprinted by permission.

"New Morning"
Copyright © 1970 Big Sky Music
All rights reserved. International copyright
secured. Reprinted by permission.

"Not Dark Yet"
Copyright © 1997 Special Rider Music
All rights reserved. International copyright
secured. Reprinted by permission.

"No Time to Think"
Copyright © 1978 Special Rider Music
All rights reserved. International copyright
secured. Reprinted by permission.

"One More Weekend"
Copyright © 1970 Big Sky Music
All rights reserved. International copyright
secured. Reprinted by permission.

"One of Us Must Know (Sooner or Later)"
Copyright © 1966; renewed 1994 Dwarf Music
All rights reserved. International copyright
secured. Reprinted by permission.

"One Too Many Mornings"
Copyright © 1964; renewed 1992 Special Rider
Music
All rights reserved. International copyright
secured. Reprinted by permission.

"Outlaw Blues"
Copyright © 1965; renewed 1993 Special Rider
Music
All rights reserved. International copyright
secured. Reprinted by permission.

"Paths of Victory"
Copyright © 1964; renewed 1992 Special Rider
Music
All rights reserved. International copyright
secured. Reprinted by permission.

"Standing in the Doorway"
Copyright © 1997 Special Rider Music

"Subterranean Homesick Blues"
Copyright © 1965; renewed 1993 Special Rider Music

"Sugar Baby"
Copyright © 2001 Special Rider Music

"Summer Days"
Copyright © 2001 Special Rider Music

"Sweetheart Like You"
Copyright © 2001 Special Rider Music

"Tangled Up in Blue"
Copyright © 1974 Ram's Horn Music

"Things Have Changed"
Copyright © 1999 Special Rider Music

"Three Angels"
Copyright © 1970 Big Sky Music

"Tight Connection to My Heart (Has Anybody Seen My Love)"
Copyright © 1985 Special Rider Music

"The Times They Are A-Changin'"
Copyright © 1963; renewed 1991 Special Rider Music

"Tiny Montgomery"
Copyright © 1967; renewed 1995 Dwarf Music

"To Be Alone with You"
Copyright © 1969; renewed 1997 Dwarf Music

"Tombstone Blues"
Copyright © 1965; renewed 1993 Special Rider Music

"Too Much of Nothing"
Copyright © 1967; renewed 1995 Dwarf Music

"To Ramona"
Copyright © 1964; renewed 1992 Special Rider Music

"Tough Mama"
Copyright © 1973 Ram's Horn Music

"Trouble in Mind"
Copyright © 1979 Special Rider Music

"Tryin' to Get to Heaven"
Copyright © 1997 Special Rider Music

"Tweedle Dee & Tweedle Dum"
Copyright © 2001 Special Rider Music
All rights reserved. International copyright
secured. Reprinted by permission.

"Up to Me"
Copyright © 2001 Special Rider Music
All rights reserved. International copyright
secured. Reprinted by permission.

"Visions of Johanna"
Copyright © 1966; renewed 1994 Dwarf Music
All rights reserved. International copyright
secured. Reprinted by permission.

"Wanted Man"
Copyright © 1969; renewed 1997 Big Sky
Music
All rights reserved. International copyright
secured. Reprinted by permission.

"Watered Down Love"
Copyright © 1981 Special Rider Music
All rights reserved. International copyright
secured. Reprinted by permission.

"We Better Talk This Over"
Copyright © 1981 Special Rider Music
All rights reserved. International copyright
secured. Reprinted by permission.

"Wedding Song"
Copyright © 1981 Special Rider Music
All rights reserved. International copyright
secured. Reprinted by permission.

"Went to See the Gypsy"
Copyright © 1970 Big Sky Music
All rights reserved. International copyright
secured. Reprinted by permission.

"What Can I Do for You?"
Copyright © 1980 Special Rider Music
All rights reserved. International copyright
secured. Reprinted by permission.

"What Was It You Wanted?"
Copyright © 1989 Special Rider Music
All rights reserved. International copyright
secured. Reprinted by permission.

"When He Returns"
Copyright © 1979 Special Rider Music
All rights reserved. International copyright
secured. Reprinted by permission.

"When the Night Comes Falling from the Sky"
Copyright © 1985 Special Rider Music
All rights reserved. International copyright
secured. Reprinted by permission.

"When You Gonna Wake Up?"
Copyright © 1979 Special Rider Music
All rights reserved. International copyright
secured. Reprinted by permission.

"Ye Shall Be Changed"
Copyright © 1979 Special Rider Music
All rights reserved. International copyright
secured. Reprinted by permission.

"You Changed My Life"
Copyright © 1982 Special Rider Music
All rights reserved. International copyright
secured. Reprinted by permission.

"You're a Big Girl"
Copyright © 1974 Ram's Horn Music
All rights reserved. International copyright
secured. Reprinted by permission.

"You're Gonna Make Me Lonesome When You
Go"
Copyright © 1974 Ram's Horn Music
All rights reserved. International copyright
secured. Reprinted by permission.

Dylan Album Liner Notes

Liner-note excerpts from *Biograph*, *Bob Dylan*, *Bootleg Series* records, *World Gone Wrong*, and *The Freewheelin' Bob Dylan* reprinted with the permission of Bob Dylan Music Co.

Other Lyric and Text Quotations

"Little Black Train" adapted by Woody Guthrie © Copyright 1965 (renewed) by Woody Guthrie Publications, Inc. All rights reserved. Used by permission.

"I Hate a Song" excerpt from WNEW by Woody Guthrie © Copyright 1965 (renewed) by Woody Guthrie Publications, Inc. All rights reserved. Used by permission.

"Pretty Boy Floyd" by Woody Guthrie Copyright © 1958 (renewed) by Sanga Music, Inc. All rights reserved. Used by permission.

Other quotes by Woody Guthrie © Copyright by Woody Guthrie Publications, Inc. All rights reserved. Used by permission.

Woody Guthrie quotes from Smithsonian Folkways releases used courtesy of Smithsonian Folkways Recordings.

Excerpts from *Traditional American Folk Songs from the Anne & Frank Warner Collection* by Anne Warner (Syracuse, NY: Syracuse University Press, 1984) used with the permission of Syracuse University Press.

Excerpts from *Woody Guthrie: A Life* by Joe Klein, copyright © 1980 by Joe Klein. Used by permission of Alfred A. Knopf, a division of Random House, Inc.

Excerpts from *Hard Rain* by Tim Riley, copyright © 1992 by Tim Riley. Used by permission of Alfred A. Knopf, a division of Random House, Inc.

Excerpts from *The New York Times* reprinted with permission by the New York Times Company.

Excerpts from *No Direction Home: The Life and Music of Bob Dylan* by Robert Shelton. Copyright © 1986 by Robert Shelton.

Reprinted by permission of HarperCollins Publishers Inc.

Excerpts from *Invisible Republic: Bob Dylan's Basement Tapes* by Greil Marcus copyright © 1997 by Greil Marcus. Reprinted by permission of Henry Holt and Company, LLC.

Excerpts from *Songwriters on Songwriting, Expanded 4th Edition* by Paul Zollo used by permission of Paul Zollo.

Excerpts from "The Wanderer," copyright © 1999 by Alex Ross, originally published in the May 10, 1999, issue of *The New Yorker*, used by permission of Alex Ross.

Excerpts from *Song & Dance Man III: The Art of Bob Dylan* by Michael Gray copyright © 2000 reprinted by permission of The Continuum International Publishing Group.

Excerpts from *Voice Without Restraint: Bob Dylan's Lyrics and Their Background* by John Herdman, copyright © 1982, used by permission of John Herdman.

Excerpts from *Like the Night—Bob Dylan and the Road to the Manchester Free Trade Hall* by C. P. Lee, copyright © 2002, used by permission of C. P. Lee.

Excerpts from Paul Williams's books *Performing Artist: The Music of Bob Dylan. Vol. 1, 1960–1973; Bob Dylan: Performing Artist. Vol. 2, The Middle Years, 1974–1986; Dylan—What Happened?*; and *Watching the River Flow: Observations on Bob Dylan's Art-in-Progress, 1966–1995* used by permission of Paul Williams.

Excerpts from *On the Tracks* magazine used by permission of Rolling Tomes, Inc.

Excerpts from *Sing Out!* magazine © *Sing Out!*. Used by permission. All rights reserved.

Comments to the author from Max Dyer about the song "I Will Sing" were received by e-mail and used by permission of Max Dyer.

Text from *American Ballads and Folk Songs* by John A.. Lomax and Alan Lomax, *Adventures of a Ballad Hunter* by John A.. Lomax, *Folk Songs of North America* by Alan Lomax, and liner notes from *Classical Ballads of England and Ireland, Volumes 1 and 2* by Alan Lomax and Peter Kennedy courtesy of the Alan Lomax Archive, all rights reserved.

Comments to the author about the song "Well, Well, Well," written by Danny O'Keefe and Bob Dylan (© 1996 Bicameral Songs [BMI]/Wild Rider Music [BMI]), were received from Danny O'Keefe by e-mail and used by permission of Danny O'Keefe.

Excerpts from "The Fire Within: Johnny Cash, a Flame to Consume His Demons" by David Segal are from the September 13, 2003, issue of *The Washington Post.* © 2003, *The Washington Post.* Reprinted with permission.